The editors

JONATHAN LORIE is Editor of *Traveller*, Britain's most distinguished
travel magazine, and Director of Travellers' Tales, the travel writing
and photography training agency. He is a Fellow of the Royal
Geographical Society, and has traveled in Africa, Asia and Europe.

AMY SOHANPAUL was brought up in Kenya and now lives in
London, where she is Deputy Editor of *Traveller* magazine and
specializes in travel and food journalism.

JAMES INNES WILLIAMS has traveled extensively in Africa,
America and Europe, and just launched a career as a travel
journalist. He is a contributor to *Traveller* magazine.

THE TRAVELER'S HANDBOOK

The insider's guide to world travel

THE TRAVELER'S HANDBOOK

Editors Jonathan Lorie & Amy Sohanpaul
Assistant Editor James Innes Williams

This U.S. edition published in 2006 by The Globe Pequot Press.

Library of Congress Cataloging-in-Publication Data is available.

ISBN 0-7627-4090-6

Every effort has been made to ensure that the facts in this Handbook are accurate. However, travelers should still obtain advice from consulates, airlines, etc., about current travel and visa requirements and conditions before traveling. The editors and publishers cannot accept responsibility for any loss, injury or inconvenience, however caused.

Type design by typo⁶, London. Cover design by Wylie Design, London. Printed and bound by Nutech, Delhi, India.

Additional research by Timothy Hunter and Duncan Mills.

COVER PICTURES *Main picture by World Pictures; right to left: Andrew Gunners/Digital Vision/Getty Images, Jeff Hunter/ Photographer's Choice/Getty Images, Panoramic Images/Getty Images; spine picture by Steve Bloom; picture of Michael Palin by Basil Pau.*

Contents ❧

AFTERWORD: FROM OUR ARCHIVE

Foreword

The art of real travel
by John Simpson

TRAVEL BROADENS ALL SORTS OF THINGS, but I'm not sure the mind is always among them. People throughout the world are travelling more than they have ever done, and yet so often they simply take their own little worlds with them. That precious couple of weeks in some place where the sunshine and a full, all-day English breakfast are guaranteed have become rooted in our culture, but some centripetal force operates on the majority of travellers, so that they scarcely ever leave the poolside or the beach. The same strange force tends to operate on business travellers: the office, the bar, the restaurant, the interior of the taxi, the hotel bedroom, and a quick visit to the duty free at the airport to prove they've been away.

It seems safe to assume that you have not bought this *Handbook* because you are planning to do that kind of travelling. What you will encounter in the pages that follow is of a different order altogether: real travelling, which usually involves difficult and strange places, awkward moments, uncertainties, problems of communication. For if you just want to stick to your certainties, whatever is the point of leaving home?

Those who know the pleasures of striking out into the unknown find themselves changed utterly. They tend to find themselves staring out of the window more when they are at work, looking off into the distance, going quiet when other people talk about their plans for the future; and the business of gathering together their gear and heading off assumes a particular significance for them. They have become wanderers – explorers, perhaps, even if they never go anywhere that plenty of others haven't been before. Real travelling is as much a state of mind as taking a package holiday.

You have to work a great deal harder nowadays at real travelling, because the world has shrunk before our eyes. Yet the possibility of doing it still exists perfectly well. The world may be smaller, but it still isn't entirely uniform, and certainly isn't altogether safe and ordered and boring.

I have taken this *Handbook* with me to many places, precisely because the unexpected always comes up when you penetrate the zone of uncertainty and unpredictability. You will find it, I think, a great help. I certainly have. 🙶🙶

Section 1: **Inspirations** ❧

The travelling life

Departures and arrivals
by Eric Newby

WHATEVER ELSE WE REMEMBER OF OUR TRAVELS, we remember our departures and arrivals. Often they are the most enduring of all our memories of them. In 1963, together with Wanda, my wife, I embarked on the Ganges in an open boat to row from the foothills of the Himalayas to the Indian Ocean. Some 200 metres from our starting point, from which we had been seen off by an old man who dropped sacred sweets on us as provisions for the journey, and some 1,900 kilometres short of our destination in the Bay of Bengal, the boat grounded in some 40 centimetres of water which proved to be the uniform depth of the Ganges at this season at this point, and it took five-and-a-half days to cover the next 56 kilometres, mostly by pushing it.

Nothing in the course of the entire trip, which took three months to accomplish, left such an indelible imprint on our minds as the moment when we discovered that the Ganges was only 40 centimetres deep and that our boat drew 46 centimetres when loaded.

To depart is often more satisfying than to arrive unless you are the first on the scene. Nothing was more deflationary to Scott and his companions than to find that they were the second party to reach the South Pole. Would I have set off at all if I had known what the journey would be like or what I was going to find at my destination are questions I have often asked myself, reminded of the wartime poster which read 'Don't waste food! Why did you take it if you weren't going to eat it?' To which some wit added a codicil: 'I didn't know it was going to taste like this!'

For years explorers attempted to reach Timbuktu, the mysterious city on the edge of the Sahara that, ever since the twelfth century, had been the hub of the North African world, and in which salt had been traded for the seemingly inexhaustible gold of Guinea, a city in which, according to the Muslim traveller Leo Africanus, who visited it in 1526, there were plates and sceptres of solid gold 'some whereof weigh 1,300 pounds'.

The first-known European to reach Timbuktu and return in one piece was Réné Caillieé, a penniless young Frenchman who had been inspired to become an explorer by reading *Robinson Crusoe*. Too late to see it in its heyday – the trade in gold had more or less come to an end – he reached the fabled city after a terrifyingly dangerous journey on 20 April 1828. 'I looked around,' he wrote, 'and found the sight before me did not answer my expectations of Timbuktu. The city presented, at first view, nothing but a mass of ill-looking houses, built of earth. Nothing was to be seen in all directions, but immense plains of quicksand of a yellowish-white colour.'

No one really enjoys arriving anywhere by train. (Nor does anyone in their right mind enjoy departing or arriving by plane, with the possible exception of the pilot whose toy it is.) Will there be any porters? Will there be any trolleys for the luggage if there aren't? Will there be any taxis? Will they be fitted with meters? These and similar questions that even the most hardened travellers ask themselves as the train comes into the platform all help to contribute to the particular form of angst, the generally non-specific but nonetheless acute form of anxiety described by Cyril Connolly (disguised under the *nom de plume* Palinurus) in *The Unquiet Grave* as the *Angoisse des Gares*, the Agony of the Stations: 'Bad when we meet someone at the station, much worse when we are seeing them off; not present when departing oneself, but unbearable when arriving....'

The best arrivals are by sea, that is unless your engine has broken down and the Cliffs of Moher are a lee shore. The first sight of a great city from the sea is big medicine, powerful magic, unforgettable, however much of a let-down it may prove to be on closer acquaintance. New York seen from the Hudson in the early morning with the sun

My passion for travel cools when I consider that it consists entirely of departures and arrivals.
– MARQUIS DE CUSTINE

roaring up over the East River turning the tall buildings into gigantic Roman candles; Venice as your vessel runs in through the Porto di Lido into St Mark's Basin with the domes and campaniles liquefying and reconstituting themselves in the mirage; Istanbul as your ship comes up the Marmara and sweeps round Seraglio Point towards the Golden Horn and you see silhouetted against the evening sky the fantastic, improbable, incomparable skyline of Old Stamboul.

It is not only the great cities that have this effect on the arriving traveller. This is how TE Lawrence described his first sight of Jidda, the then little port of Mecca, seen from the deck of a passenger ship in the Red Sea while he was on his way to meet the leaders of the Arab revolt in 1917: 'When at last we anchored in the outer harbour off the white town, between the blazing sky and its reflection in the mirage which swept and rolled over the wide lagoon, then the heat of Arabia came out like a drawn sword and struck us speechless.... There were only lights and shadows, the white and black gaps of streets: in front, the pallid lustre of the haze shimmering upon the inner harbour; behind, the dazzle of league after league of featureless sand running up to an edge of low hills, faintly suggested in the far away mist and heat.'

It is these and similar vistas, whether wild or civilised, that make one want to shout 'How beautiful the world is!', that made an elderly lady of my acquaintance, when taken on an outing from her native village in the Po Valley which she had never previously left, cry on arriving on the watershed of the Apennines from which there was an extensive view, 'Com'è grande il mondo!'... 'How big the world is!'... and insist on being taken home. ❧

ERIC NEWBY is one of Britain's most distinguished travel writers.
He was made CBE in 1994. This extract is taken from 'Departures and Arrivals',
published by HarperCollins.

The independent traveller
by Dervla Murphy

QUESTION: WHEN IS A FREAK NOT A FREAK? Answer: When she feels normal. I was in my late forties before the realisation came, very, very slowly, starting as a ridiculous-seeming suspicion that gradually crystallised into an exasperated certainty. Many people think of me as a freak.

By middle age one should be well aware of one's public image, given a way of life that makes such an accessory unavoidable. But if what an individual does feels normal, and if people are decently reticent about analysing you to your face, it's quite understandable that for decades you see only your self-image, vastly as it may differ from the false public image meanwhile gaining credibility.

The freakish thing is, of course, not me, but the modern world – from which I, like millions of other normal folk, need to escape at intervals. Those of us born with the wandering instinct, and not caught in a job trap, can practise the most effective form of escapism: a move back in time, to one of the few regions where it is still possible to live simply, at our ancestors' pace. To describe this as returning to reality would be absurd; for us the modern world is reality. However, escapist travelling does allow a return to what we are genetically fitted to cope with, as we are not fitted to cope with the freakishly hectic, technological present.

Hence the notorious 'pressures', paralleling our marvellous conveniences. We have reduced physical effort to the minimum; everything is 'labour-saving' – transport, communications, entertainment, heating, cooking, cleaning, dressing, marketing, even writing (they tell me) if one uses a repulsive-sounding thing called a 'word processor'. Yet the effort of coming to terms with this effortless world is too much for many of us. So we get ulcers, have nervous breakdowns, take to uppers and/or downers, gamble on the stock exchange – or travel, seriously, for several months at a stretch.

Today's serious travellers are often frustrated explorers who would like to have been born at least 150 years earlier. Now there is nowhere left for individuals to explore, though there may be a few untouched corners (in Amazonia?) accessible only to expeditions. But the modern hi-tech expedition, with its two-way radios and helicopters on call for emergencies, naturally has no appeal for escapist travellers. Among themselves, these lament that their traditional, simple journeys have come to seem – by a cruel twist of the technological spiral – paradoxically artificial. A century ago, travellers who took off into the unknown had to be completely isolated from their own world for months or years on end. Now such isolation is a deliberately chosen luxury and, to that extent, phoney. Had I died of gangrene in the Himalayas or Simiens or Andes, that would have been my own fault (no two-way radio) rather than a sad misfortune.

So the escapist traveller is, in one sense, playing a game. But only in one sense, because the actual journey is for real in a way that the modern expedition, with its carefully prearranged links to home and safety, is not. Whatever happens, you can't chicken out: you are where you've chosen to be and must take the consequences.

Here some confusion arises about courage. There is a temperamental aspect to this issue: optimism versus pessimism – is a bottle half empty or half full? Why should your appendix burst or your bones break abroad rather than at home? Optimists don't believe in disasters until they happen. Therefore they are not fearful and have no occasion to display courage. Nothing puts my hackles up faster than being told I'm brave. This is nonsense – albeit significant nonsense. Where is our effortless civilisation at when physical exertion, enjoyed in remote places, is repeatedly mistaken for bravery?

Genuine travellers, far from being brave, are ultra cautious. That is an essential component of their survival mechanism and one of the dividing lines between them and foolhardy limelight seekers. Before they start they suss out all foreseeable hazards and either change their route, should *He travels the fastest who* these hazards seem excessive and the risk silly, or pre- *travels alone.* pare themselves to cope with reasonable hazards. *– RUDYARD KIPLING* Thus what looks to outsiders like a daring journey is in fact a safe toddle – unless you have bad luck, which you could have at home. Six times I've broken my ribs; the last time was at home, falling off a ladder. The other times were in Afghanistan, Nepal, Ethiopia, Peru and Madagascar. You could say I have an unhappy karmic relationship with my ribs.

Recently I was asked, "Why is independent travel seen as so much more of an intellectual challenge? And what does it take to cope with it?" That flummoxed me. I have been an escapist traveller for more than 40 years without it ever occurring to me that I was meeting an intellectual challenge. A stamina challenge, usually; an emotional challenge, sometimes; a spiritual challenge, occasionally. But an intellectual challenge? I don't see it. Unless by intellectual one means that slight exertion of the grey cells required to equip oneself more or less suitably for the country in view. Yet surely that is a matter of common sense, rather than intellect?

Granted, equipping oneself includes a certain amount of reading; but this, in a literate society, scarcely amounts to an intellectual challenge. I refer only to reading history, not to any sort of heavy sociological or political research – unless of course you happen to fancy that sort of thing, in which case it will obviously add an extra dimension to your journey. Otherwise, for the average traveller, enough of current politics will be revealed *en route*, should politics be important to the locals; and in those few happy regions where domestic politics don't matter, you can forget about them. But to travel through any country in ignorance of its history seems to me a waste of time. You can't then understand the why of anything or anyone. With this view some travellers violently disagree, arguing that all preliminary reading should be avoided, that each new country should be visited in a state of innocence and experienced purely subjectively. The mind on arrival should be a blank page, awaiting one's own vivid personal impressions, to be cherished ever after as authentic and unique. Why burden yourself in advance with loads of irrelevancies about the past and piles of other people's prejudiced interpretations of the present? On that last point I concur; travellers rarely read travel books – unless they have to review them.

Reverting to this odd concept of an intellectual challenge: is the adaptability required of travellers sometimes mistaken for an intellectual feat? That seems unlikely because we're back to temperament: some people slot in easily everywhere. If travellers saw the need to adapt as an intellectual challenge they probably wouldn't slot in anywhere, except perhaps on some pretentious radio show.

Maybe the overcoming of language barriers is seen as an intellectual challenge? Yet there could scarcely be anything less intellectual than urgently saying "P-sssss!" when you must get fast to the nearest earth closet – or at least out of the *tukul*, which has been locked up for the night. The basic needs of human beings – sleeping, eating, drinking, peeing – are so basic that they can easily be understood; all our bladders function in exactly the same way. The language barrier unnecessarily inhibits many who otherwise would seek out and relish remote regions. On the practical level, it is of no consequence. I can state this with total assurance, having travelled on four continents using only English and those courtesy phrases of Tibetan, Amharic, Quechua or whatever that you happen to pick up as you go along. Even on the emotional level, it is not as formidable as it may seem; the human features – especially the eyes – are wonderfully eloquent. In our own society, the extent to which we wordlessly communicate goes unnoticed. In Far Flungery, where nobody within 200 miles speaks a syllable of any European language, one becomes very aware of the range of moods and subtle feelings that may be conveyed visually rather than aurally. However, on the exchange-of-ideas level the barrier is, quite simply, insuperable. Therefore scholar-travellers – people like Freya Stark, Patrick Leigh Fermor, Colin Thubron – consider the learning of Arabic or Albanian or Russian or Mandarin to be as essential as buying a map. And there you have what seems to me (linguistically inept as I am) a bona fide intellectual challenge.

As a label, 'the independent traveller' puzzles me. It verges on tautology; travellers, being inherently independent, don't need the adjective to distinguish them from those unfortunate victims of the tourist industry who, because of sun-starvation on our islands, are happy to be herded annually towards a hot spot where tea and chips are guaranteed and there is no danger of meeting the natives.

I can, however, see that holiday-makers (the category in between travellers and tourists) may validly be divided into 'dependent' and 'independent'. The former, though liking to make their own plans, contentedly follow beaten tracks and book their guesthouses in advance. The latter are often travellers manqué for whom unpredictability gives savour to their journey: setting off at dawn with no idea of where one will be by dusk, or who with or what eating. Only a lack of time or money prevents them from reaching travellers' territory and usually time is their problem. Travelling can be done on quite a short shoestring, and often must be so done for the excellent reason that the traveller's theatre of operations offers few consumer goods.

Independent holiday-makers are in general much more tolerant and sociable than travellers, whose escapist compulsion causes them to feel their day has been ruined if they glimpse just one other solitary trekker in the far distance, and who break out in spots if they come upon even a vestigial trace of tourism. But that last nightmare contingency is unlikely; the paths of travellers rarely converge, unless one finds oneself within a few miles of somewhere like Machu Picchu and it seems 'stupid not to see it'. Incidentally, Machu Picchu provided me with my most grisly travel memory – an American helicopter landing amid the ruins and spewing forth a squeal of excited women whose paunchy menfolk were intent only on photographing them beside the mournful resident llamas. My timing was wrong; you have to get to Machu Picchu at dawn, as I did later.

The past decade or so has seen the emergence of another, hybrid category: youngsters who spend a year or more wandering around the world in a holiday-making spirit, occasionally taking temporary jobs. Some gain enormously from this experience, but many seem to cover too much ground too quickly, sampling everywhere and becoming familiar with nowhere. They have been from Alaska to Adelaide, Berlin to Bali, Calcutta to Cusco, Lhasa to London. They tend to wander in couples or small packs, swapping yarns about the benefits – or otherwise – of staying here, doing that, buying this. They make a considerable impact on wherever they happen to perch for a week or so, often bringing with them standards (sometimes too low) and expectations (sometimes too high) that unsettle their local contemporaries.

Of course one rejoices that the young are free to roam as never before, yet such rapid 'round-the-worlding' is, for many, more confusing than enlightening. It would be good if this fashion soon changed, if the young became more discriminating, allowing themselves time to travel seriously in a limited area that they had chosen because of its particular appeal to them, as individuals. ❧

DERVLA MURPHY has been an intrepid traveller and distinguished travel writer since the 1950s. Lately she has turned to more political subjects, with books on her experiences in post-conflict nations such as Rwanda, Albania and former Yugoslavia.

How travel shaped my life
by Esther Freud

A S A CHILD GROWING UP IN RURAL SUSSEX, travelling by bus between East Grinstead and Tunbridge Wells, gazing out at the tiny, sleepy villages, the misty green fields, the cricket pitch, I was always aware that there were other worlds out there. Wilder, hotter, stranger worlds. Countries with mules and camels, horse-drawn taxis, kaftans and hennaed hair. This knowledge had a huge effect on me.

I was four when I went off travelling with my mother and elder sister, and six when we came back. For almost two years we wandered through Morocco. We rented small rooms in Medina hotels, hitchhiked, bartered, attended festivals and *hammams*, spoke Arabic and French. We ate the food they cooked in cauldrons in the square of Marrakech, played with the beggar children, befriended the women who sold drums. My sister went to a Moroccan school and learnt about the pillars of Islam, the laws by which the people lived their lives. She also learnt the names for all the animals and how to count to ten. My mother became interested in Sufism and started praying towards Mecca on a rug.

Sussex by comparison was quiet and still. I remember, age six or seven, sitting in my classroom listening to the teacher ask if anyone had 'news'. 'News' was an opportunity for children with pressing things on their minds to reveal them then at the beginning of the class, and hopefully remain quiet until break. "Yes," my hand shot up, "I've got some news." And I darted to the front of the class and told them how I'd once ridden in the saddlebag of a donkey, my sister on the other side, and how terrified I was as the donkey clipped down the mountain path, how every second I was sure its hooves were going to slip. I wanted my school friends to see the mountain, the procession of bright people scrambling down, and to know that at the top, a camel decked in flowers had had its head chopped off.

"I think that's enough for today," the teacher quietened me with a restraining hand, and reluctantly I went back to my desk.

For the next ten years I hardly left Sussex. The world outside became fixed in my mind as impenetrable and very far away. I had no idea that people went on package tours, arriving at their destinations within hours, or took weekend breaks that involved no life-threatening illness or

Travel is more than the seeing of sights; it is a change that goes on, deep and permanent, in the ideas of living.
– MIRIAM BEARD

delays. But the further away my own travels became the more determined I was not to forget them. My class at school received regular bulletins about orange groves and oases, the taste of cumin in *bissara* soup, and once when I had the floor all to myself I told them a long story about how my sister and I once saw a mirage. We were in the desert, riding on camels, half dead from thirst, when there in the distance we saw an island of palm trees and green grass. We trotted thankfully towards it only to find that it had disappeared. It's from this point that I can trace my future as a fiction writer. Of course I'd never ridden into the desert on a camel, never seen a mirage, although to this day I wish I had, instead I'd simply read about one in a Tintin book and exchanged the characters of Thompson and Thompson for my sister and myself. But by now I'd told my class so many unlikely stories it meant nothing to them to accept one more, and from then on I was free to elaborate and embroider, and the more I did it, the more natural it became.

But then something happened that stopped me in my tracks. A new boy arrived at our school and at 'news' he told us about Thailand. He'd seen a jellyfish, all wobbly and white, and he told us how it had floated up to him and brushed against his arm. The class shivered and gasped. "Did it sting you?" the teacher asked, and I thought I saw him hesitate before he launched into a detailed description of his rash. Thailand was fascinating and new, and no one wanted to listen to Moroccan adventures any more. My role had been usurped. Occasionally I did still tell the stories, but only to myself. I practiced them, honed them down, elaborated on them. If I was going to share them with anyone again I was going to make sure they were as good as they could get. And then slowly, slowly, my own life took over. I started living in the present, I made real friends, and Morocco faded into the past.

Years later, in my early twenties, I started going to a creative writing class, and after a series of assorted exercises we were set a task. Simply to write a longer piece. A five- or six-page piece about anything at all. What could I write about? I had no idea, and then as soon as I sat down, alone in a quiet room, my stories all came back to me. Of course I'd write about the camel festival and the cumin, the beggar girls, the drummer women in the square, and although when I closed my eyes I could remember, almost cinematically, my life as it was then, I realised I did have a head start. I'd practiced these stories before.

But sometimes, especially if my book was going well, I'd stop and gaze off into space. What if I could never write about anything else? What if I did think up another story, would I have to practice and embellish it for the next 20 years of my life? By now I'd fallen in love with the whole process of writing and I couldn't bear to think I'd ever have to do anything else. But as soon as I'd finished *Hideous Kinky*, (as my first novel became), I found there was a reservoir of stories waiting to be told. In fact Morocco had been so vivid and so colourful that it had almost submerged the importance of everything else.

I've since discovered that one of the most wonderful things about being a novelist is that, in your own mind at least, you can travel anywhere you want. I've just spent the last two years back in Sussex, conjuring up those mist-green fields, remembering the quiet of the country lanes where foxgloves and snapdragons grow tall. Once I set my mind to it, it was easy to find enough drama and suspense to fill a book, even on the Ashdown Forest golf course. Any number of things could happen in those leaded phone boxes, or even at the plank-board bus stops where as a teenager I'd been so overwhelmingly bored. Sitting in a London study with the sounds of the city never far away, I took great pleasure in sending my characters rustling through bracken, scooping up great armfuls of white hay or hacking down a gorse bush with an axe. But what I'll never know is how long it would have taken me to find my courage and become a writer if I hadn't had that first, pressingly urgent travellers' tale handed to me on a plate. ❧

Esther Freud is the author of 'Hideous Kinky' (made into a feature film starring Kate Winslet), 'Peerless Flats', 'The Wild' and most recently 'The Sea House'. She was one of 'Granta' magazine's Best of Young British Novelists in 1993.

The global suburb
by John Simpson

IN AUGUST 1939, A MATTER OF DAYS before the Second World War broke out, an elderly relative of mine, who was then a boy of 12, left England to rejoin his parents in Hong Kong. Rather daringly, they sent him by Imperial Airways. That meant that he took off in a flying-boat from Southampton, flew to Marseille, then across the Mediterranean to Alexandria, on to Aden, then Singapore. He got out at every stage, was given dinner at a decent restaurant and spent the night in a decent hotel bed, and finally arrived off Hong Kong Island on the fifth day.

Having just made the flight direct from Heathrow to Hong Kong in a little over twelve hours, I don't feel particularly favoured by the comparison. I had two indifferent meals, watched a film so stupid I am ashamed to recall its title, half-sat and half-lay with my head at an awkward angle in a seat designed for someone much shorter and narrower, and woke up a few hours later aching and bad-tempered. Someone seemed to have borrowed my tongue during the night and used it to give a thorough cleaning to the carpet in economy class. It took me a couple of days to get over it all: not the jet-lag, but the discomfort of the flight.

In other words, we can travel a great deal faster now, but in spite of the impression the airline advertisements would like to leave with you, the experience is scarcely one you would choose to remember. It's just about getting you somewhere else quickly, that's all.

For a short while, back in the 1960s, that was a novel and rather useful idea. When I first went to New York, aged 18, I sailed steerage on the already elderly Queen Mary; returning a few months later, I flew in an early Boeing 707. Being in a hurry to get back, I rather preferred the Boeing. But very quickly speed alone ceased to have much attraction: it was the sensation of real travelling I missed, the sense of being transported in a way that was entertaining and anecdote-rich. In our brave new millennium, the act of travelling has become dangerously anecdote-poor; and the very notion of travel as a mild but definite form of exploration is disappearing fast.

The number of countries where you can be fairly certain you will not run up against Westerners is now tiny. China, which until the early 1980s was one of them, certainly isn't now. Walking down recently Wang Fu Lin, the famous shopping street in Beijing, I was stopped by three different Westerners, one of whom I actually knew. Back in the 1980s, when I was reporting on China for the BBC, I went to a village near Beijing where my government minder said they had never seen a foreigner. I asked the local Party functionary about this; not true, he said, there had been plenty of foreigners here. I looked reproachfully at the minder, then asked, "When was that?"

"Oh, about the year 1250," said the Party functionary offhandedly. "It was the Mongols."

Now, though, the only places where you don't find Westerners are the dangerous ones: Iraq, Saudi Arabia, Somalia, Afghanistan, Chechnya. And, speaking as someone who goes to places like these for professional reasons, it's actually quite a relief when you do occasionally find a few Westerners there.

Our world has been mapped with complete accuracy, and there can be scarcely any peoples or species left uncatalogued. In 1999 a surprisingly large new species of tree rat was discovered in Peru. The previous year two separate bands of unknown wandering tribesmen were discovered in Papua New Guinea. They possessed no spoken language, and conversed solely in signs. In the dense forest in the far west of Brazil I came across a man who had found the arrows of various different groups of Indians unknown to ethnography. Groups in the Congolese jungle or the Kalahari Desert have probably not made contact with the outside world. But that is just about all. There are more people alive now than in the whole of mankind's past, which creates problems for those who believe in reincarnation. Yet for the first time we all know one another.

Worse, the differences between us are disappearing as fast as the animal, bird and insect species we share our planet with. In the 1960s you could still work out where you were when you drove across the United States by the accents and the food; not any longer. In the 1970s French was still an important second language in countries as divergent as Iran, Yugoslavia and Romania; alas, for those of us who have laboured to improve it over the years, not any more. An inalienable sameness has settled over the globe. The spirit of place is evaporating fast.

The earth belongs to anyone who stops for a moment, gazes and goes on his way.
- COLETTE

We are losing our distinctiveness, our human biodiversity, with appalling speed. As Gertrude Stein wrote of Oakland, California, 'There's no *there* there.' We tend to think of the process as being American-inspired, but it is merely American-led; the United States has gone farther and faster down this particular road then the rest of us, that's all.

Europe is doing its utmost to catch up. The powerful sense of regional identity that used to exist throughout Europe has faded very quickly. The first time I stayed in Venice in the early 1970s I remarked to the old lady who was showing me to my room in the Pensione Seguso that there were a lot of tourists about.

"Ah well, you see, it's Easter in Venice," she told me.

It was as if this was something special to the city, which those of us who lived elsewhere wouldn't necessarily appreciate.

Not long afterwards I spent a weekend on the charming Ile St Louis in Paris, and needed to buy a bottle of ink to write some letters.

"I'm sorry, *M'sieu*," said the elderly lady in the general store on the corner, "we don't sell ink. I doubt if you'll get it anywhere on the island."

The Ile St Louis is about 50 metres equidistant from the Left and Right banks of the Seine. Nowadays it is full of twee shops selling *crêpes* and glove puppets and paintings by Bernard Buffet, and English buskers queue up on the bridge, waiting for their half-hour turn in front of the tourists. Then it was a separate place with its own clearly established sense of identity.

"It is," said General de Gaulle in the late 1950s, "impossible to hold together a country which has 265 specialities of cheese."

All but two or three of those specialities can still be found in France, though European Union regulations make it illegal to sell even Brie and Camembert if it is produced in the strictly traditional method. France, once the most idiosyncratic, regionally diverse and uncontrollable country in Europe, is settling into the same uniformity as the rest of us. There are Body Shops and Holiday Inns in large numbers there too, and more McDonald's in Paris than in London. Obesity, the defining disease of Western man and woman, distinctly hamburger- and Coke-related, is beginning to affect France as it has long affected Britain. As for America, airlines are beginning to introduce wider seats to accommodate the growth in American arse sizes, and lavatories are being manufactured two inches wider.

In other ways, too, the choices are lessening. Until about 1980, furniture shops in Wales sold what was known as 'the Welsh bed', wider and shorter than the types available in the rest of the United Kingdom. Officially, we are all the same size now.

And we are all equal in the face of technology. There was a time when, travelling abroad, I could go for days without contacting my office. Now I am fortunate if more than a couple of hours pass without a call from London; even during the night, if they forget about time difference – the one major element of distinction between one place and another that no one has yet suggested ironing out.

When the local telecommunications system doesn't run to the use of mobile phones – and I have used one to call my office from the Khyber Pass, the Great Wall of China and the flat of a drugs baron in Medellin – then I can always take a satellite phone the size of a small briefcase with me. In the 1970s my foreign desk used to communicate with me by telex. The technology was untrustworthy and the language strange:

"All well w u? ga"

"Yeah, tho cash a prob ga"

"So what new, eh? ga."

("Ga" stood for "go ahead.")

By the late 1980s the office sent me faxes, though they were on a shiny paper which curled up, and the words faded fast. If you went into the hotel business centre, another Eighties concept, and asked to use a desktop computer, you would never know which of a dozen or so types of software it might use. Now, from Damascus to Lahore to Xian, everyone uses Microsoft. Sometimes you have to work out how to get out of Chinese or Arabic characters and into Roman ones, but that's all. It probably won't be long before that little nuisance to the manufacturers is ironed out too, and everyone will speak and write a kind of English.

Convenience has driven out variety; and not merely in the hotel business centre. Which American mall doesn't have its JC Penney, its Radio Shack, its Häagen Dazs? Which British high street doesn't have its Marks and Spencer, its WH Smith, its Principles? And when you come across these shops abroad, your first response is not a pleasant flash of recognition but a dull sense that you haven't really reached anywhere different after all.

In the Yemeni capital, Sana'a, there are almost as many mobile phones per capita as there are in New York City. In Bokhara and Samarkand you can buy hamburgers and hot dogs on the street corner. In the remotest reaches of the Amazon the children who play in the dust wear T-shirts with the Nike or Coca-Cola logos. In Iran, I have seen posters advertising a Sylvester Stallone film on the walls of the holy city of Qom.

The feeling is growing, especially in the United States, that there is no need to travel abroad, since abroad is travelling to you. In Washington DC I have been driven by a taxi driver who had been the leader of an Afghan *mujaheddin* group, and in Paris by another who had been an Iranian air force general. In Denver I once found a taxi driven by a North Korean who spoke not a single recognisable word of English, and in New York City a taxi driver from, I think, Equatorial Guinea, who had no idea where or what Wall Street was.

In London there are colonies tens of thousands strong of Colombians, Thais and Ethiopians – people without the remotest colonial links to Britain. There are Japanese restaurants in Kinshasa, Beijing and Geneva, and Italian restaurants in Amman, Minsk and Pretoria. You find the best Thai food in the world in Australia, the best *balti* in northern England, and the best Persian *fesanjun* in Los Angeles. *Tandoori* has become the quintessential British dish, while curry has supplanted fish and chips as the most popular take-away food. Hamburgers are far more popular among the 13 to 18 age group in France than *steak-frites* or *magret de canard*.

"I recognised him because he was dressed like a foreigner," says a character in a pre-war Graham Greene novel, and as late as the 1970s you could still recognise Frenchmen by the cut of their jackets, Englishmen by their checks and brogues, Italians by the narrowness of their trousers, Americans by the shortness of theirs and the thickness of the welts on their shoes. Nowadays large parts of the entire world's population, from Kuwait to Sydney and from Galway to Dalian, buy the same kinds of clothes, often made in Indonesia or Guatemala.

Once, caught unexpectedly in St Petersburg, I had to kit myself out at short notice from head to toe from the local Hugo Boss shop (the original Hugo Boss, incidentally, prospered in the 1930s and '40s as a tailor to Himmler's ss, and still seems to favour black). I then found that half the members of my audience of Russian literati and local politicians were also wearing Hugo Boss clothes.

The only big international corporations which like to give the impression they think there is any worthwhile difference between one culture and another are hotel groups and (occasionally) banks. The rest understand they will make more money if we can all be persuaded to eat the same food, wear the same clothes and running shoes, listen to the same music and use the same software.

In a world where discarded wrappers for American chocolate bars blow along the paths to Mount Everest, and the little rings from old Coca-cola tins litter all the main abyssal depths of the world's oceans, there are just a handful of places left on earth where you can avoid this rising tide of sameness. If you really want to get away from the English football results, *USA Today*, the McDonalds golden arches, Microsoft, and Kate Moss's face, then you must take your courage in both hands and seek out the very few really difficult, unpredictable places which remain.

Yet, sooner or later, even these last sand-castles of independence will be washed away. One day the Habana Libre Hotel will turn back into the Havana Hilton, Libya will have Haagen-Dazs ice-cream parlours, Afghanistan will watch *Desperate Housewives*, North Korea will take American Express, and earnest guides from the Holiday Inn or the Sheraton will lead you in total safety on themed 'Warlord' walking tours of Mogadishu, holding flags with the Nike symbol on them over their heads.

How wonderful. I can't wait. ❧

John Simpson is the BBC's World Affairs Editor and one of Britain's most distinguished broadcasters. The third volume of his autobiography, 'A Mad World My Masters', is published by Macmillan.

Coming home
by John Blashford-Snell

Until Rula Lenska joined us on a quest in Nepal I had no idea that actors and expeditioners suffer from the same problem at the end of the show. Both tend to get 'post-project depression' (PPD) or 'after-expedition blues'.

When a play ends or the filming of a series finishes, Rula explained, the cast is suddenly split up, left to find new jobs or return home for a well-earned rest. The friendships and working relationships break up, the team disappears and a different lifestyle starts overnight. So it is with expeditioners.

Dr John Davies, one of Britain's leading exploration medics, once started a lecture at the Scientific Exploration Society with the statement: "Expeditions may endanger your health." He went on to point out that, for the novice, the experience can be an introduction to the negative aspects of one's personality that are easily suppressed in normal daily life. However, with appropriate counselling and support, this can be a journey of self-discovery leading to increased confidence and a more enlightened attitude to others.

Seasoned adventurers, like experienced actors, recognise post-expedition blues, the symptoms of which are similar to bereavement. This is triggered by the loss of one's new-found 'family' of expedition friends in a widely different culture and suddenly being cut off from the excitement on return home.

"I just can't face going back to nine to five in the Tax Office," groaned an Inland Revenue Officer who had spent three months in the Gobi. A routine and mundane lifestyle aggravates the condition and, for many, it is cured only by involvement in another challenge. Returning explorers also face isolation from family and colleagues, who have no concept of their recent intense experience. They are often perplexed by the indifferent response to their stories and may end up silent and withdrawn. The envy and resentment of the uninitiated, who imagine that one has been on a jolly picnic or at best some self-inflicted masochism, is also common.

"Don't know what you've done to my mother," complained a son after his mum had returned from one of the Discovery Expeditions in South America. "She's awfully quiet." But meeting the lady in question at a reunion a few months later I found her in great spirits, reliving the experience with her old pals.

John Davies, with whom I have been on many trips, advises 'returnees', especially the older ones, to spend several days enquiring about the day-to-day problems that have occurred in their absence before slowly beginning to recount their experiences. So, on being met by my wife as I stepped off a comfortable British Airways flight from Delhi recently, I asked: "How are those new trees in the garden coming on?"

"Have you gone mad?" replied Judith, well used to a dozen tales of high adventure before we reached the car park. But perhaps I'm beyond hope!

However, there may be medical problems, as I discovered a year after a Sandhurst expedition in Ethiopia, when my right leg started shaking uncontrollably while I was lecturing. 'How strange,' I thought, trying not to notice the offending limb. Two weeks later, lying racked with a fever in hospital, it was found that I had malaria, by which time I also had blurred vision and had lost nine kilos. But, once diagnosed, malaria is usually fairly easily cured.

Sadly not all ailments are so quickly dealt with, as I realised after 12 months of visits to the St Pancras Hospital for Tropical Diseases. Strange hot flushes, violent stabbing pains in my stomach, aches and itches in awkward places were making life extremely uncomfortable. "There's nothing wrong with you," boomed one of the world's leading specialists in tropical diseases after exhaustive tests proved negative. "You young fellows imagine you've caught everything under the sun if you spend six weeks in the jungle. When I was in Burma…" he droned on. My morale at was rock bottom and it took great courage to return to the hospital a few weeks later, after the symptoms had become almost unbearable.

As luck would have it, a charming and much more sympathetic Asian doctor was on duty and, in no time, he had me face-down on a trolley with a flexible viewing device inserted up my rear end and my shirt over my head. "Keep him still," he beseeched as two strapping Fijian nurses pinned me down. "Oh, my goodness," he exclaimed. "What a fine example. Excuse me, sir, but you have a splendid parasite. It is quite unusual to see one so well developed. Would you mind if we allowed a class of medical students to see it?" Before I could protest, I was wheeled into a theatre full of students, many of whom, I noted, looking between my legs, were attractive young women. One by one they came forward, without even a titter, to peer intently up my bottom. At last I was taken away and the awful tube removed. "What now?" I asked.

Once you have travelled, the voyage never ends, but is played out over and over again in the quietest chambers… the mind can never break off from the journey.
– Pat Conroy

"Oh – just swallow these pills and you'll be as right as rain," smiled the doctor.

So it is my advice that if you feel ill after an overseas visit, go straight to your GP and say where you have been. Mark you, they might diagnose jet lag, which can affect one more than most care to admit.

This handbook contains useful tips on surviving the onslaught and reducing its effects to the minimum, so I'll not dwell on it. Suffice to say that when I get home I keep going until nightfall, doing simple, uncomplicated things such as unpacking or weeding, then I take a very mild sleeping pill and totter off to bed. With luck I can usually sleep for six hours. The important thing is to avoid stressful situations and don't make any important decisions until after your body has readjusted. In my case this usually takes 24 hours. Indeed, even weeding may not be a good idea. Having stepped off a long flight from Mongolia, I pulled up all my wife's carefully planted ground cover instead of the weeds.

If I am still feeling low, I concentrate on writing my thank-you letters (if not done on the plane!) and amending my packing list while memory of all the things I forgot to take and all unnecessary items that went with me is still fresh. Then it's down to sorting out photos, slides, videos and writing reports and articles. Next come repairs to kit, getting cameras serviced and preparing lectures.

If you start to feel sorry for yourself, you are not really bringing the benefits of your experiences to your life at home. Indeed I expect you will find that you have changed but the world has not.

The whole point is to keep active and look forward to the next challenge, and, if you can't afford another trip, why not use your energy to help others in your area, sick children, old people or anyone who could use some voluntary assistance?

For the adventurous there is the opportunity of supporting organisations such as the Duke of Edinburgh's Award or Riding for the Disabled and there are dozens of environmental groups needing help.

The great cry is, if you want to avoid PPD, keep busy. ❧

COLONEL JOHN BLASHFORD-SNELL *is one of the world's foremost explorers. He is a founder of Operation Drake and Operation Raleigh, and President of the Scientific Exploration Society.*

What kind of traveller are you?

The first-time traveller
by Jonathan Lorie

JUNE 27: LOMÉ BEACH, TOGO. *My first night in Africa. Lying on a long beach, counting the shooting stars. Deep black sky. Sand between my toes as white as icing sugar, stars so close you could lick them. Coconut palms dancing in the sea breeze. Moonlight bright enough to write this.*

Last night I was in a tapas bar in London, saying goodbye to friends. Sports cars

whizzed past with their roofs rolled down, drivers in shades, jazz-funk blasting. I had
a glass of wine and an ironed shirt, and people asked me what I'd miss in Africa. I said
friends and books and clean sheets. Also toilets.

This morning I walked from the airport into Lomé. A capital city built from sheets
of tin. The central market was a madhouse of stalls selling gaudy cottons, dead fish,
bicycle tyres, voodoo skulls. Noise, people, heat, sunlight. Hands coming at me from
the crowd, saying "Patron, patron." Boys frying bowls of rice and plantain on fires in
the gutter. Old men in kaftans squatting outside the central bank, waving handfuls of
filthy notes for exchange. Inside the bank a clerk took my English pounds, put them in
his jacket pocket, produced an envelope of local currency at a generous exchange rate
and said "Sans papiers."

Next door was a supermarché where white people were buying a little bit of home –
ice buckets, saucissons, perfume, wine. It had air-conditioning. Outside there was a
beggar on crutches with one leg stopped at the knee. Inside there were deep-frozen
croissants.

Tonight the town's electricity failed but the street stalls were lit with candles and
my taxi drove slowly between hundreds of soft flames in the hot velvet darkness.

THAT WAS A DIARY EXTRACT FROM MY FIRST VISIT TO AFRICA. And if you're contemplating your first big trip abroad – wherever it is – you might recognise
some of these emotions. As a first-time traveller, perhaps the biggest hazard you'll
encounter is your own state of mind. The trick is knowing how to handle yourself.

First there's the anticipation before you go, the sense of not quite knowing what
you're getting into: the heady mix of fear and excitement. Don't be put off by this.
Seasoned travellers will tell you that they still get this buzz – and still relish it – but
like any addict, they have to go further and further to feel it. On the other hand,
good pre-departure preparation can do wonders for your confidence.

So use this book (and perhaps a regional guidebook) to prepare yourself: there
are lots of chapters here that would help you. And talk to people who've been
there. Do some background reading to get your bearings, and pack carefully.

Then, when you arrive, there's the shock of being out there for the first time, in
a strange place with different ways and values. You may have no way of understanding what's going on or being said. As many people say of India, it may challenge your entire view of the world. At the least, you won't know how to order a
decent meal.

Again, don't despair. Many travellers find that the shock of the new is actually
liberating: it allows them to leave behind the person they were at home, their inhi-
bitions or preconceptions. Others never quite adjust. But if you don't want to be
the kind of tourist who spends all day sheltering in the hotel compound or arguing
with the locals, I suggest you try the adjustment option.

This may take a little time. It depends on how much difference you're adjusting
to. For my first three weeks in India, I hated the place: the poverty, the dirt, the
crowds. Travellers on short trips often get no further than this stage, because they
don't have the time; it's important to allow yourself the right amount of time for
the place you're visiting. India takes longer than most places, but slowly I began to

enjoy things: a family who invited me home for rose-scented tea, pilgrims bathing in a river, even the hurly-burly of the trains.

The third and best emotion, if all goes well, is wonder. I don't need to tell you about that. You'll know it when it hits you and you ask yourself why you never did anything like this before.

So now we've sorted out your head, let's look at handling the outside world.

Rules of the road

1. **Talk to people.** Whether it's fellow travellers or locals, the people you meet are one of the great pleasures of any trip. They're also the best source of inside information on what's really good to see or to avoid locally.
2. **Don't plan too much.** You'll find that local information or simple serendipity open opportunities which you could never anticipate – a side trip you hadn't planned, a festival you didn't know about, a place you want to savour for longer than expected. So be flexible: leave unscheduled gaps in your trip and try not to buy tickets you can't change.
3. **Be patient:** Especially in developing countries. Where the infrastructure is poor, getting things done can take ages. You stand more chance of achieving your goal by persisting very patiently and politely, than by demanding Western standards where they could not exist.
4. **Never lose your temper.** It goes down much worse than it might at home, and can escalate situations rather dramatically.
5. **Trust your instincts.** If a situation seems unnerving in any way, duck out of it. Always take your security precautions seriously. Learn to judge people and situations quickly and act accordingly. Equally, if something seems unexpectedly appealing, go for it.
6. **Enjoy.** Don't take everything too seriously. Allow yourself to appreciate the strangeness of foreign cultures, and exercise your sense of humour regularly.

And finally

Let me leave you with a portrait of another first-time traveller: my friend Marius. He's a game warden in South Africa, six foot six and built like a rhino. Out in the bush he's a bit of a daredevil, known to chase lions on foot and to fly his microlight above wild game. I drove with Marius right across the deserts of Namibia and none of our adventures scared him.

But Marius had never been outside southern Africa, until the day he visited London. I suggested we meet in Covent Garden, a trendy part of town. And there he was, an unmistakable figure among the glittering designer-shoppers and black-clad *cappuccino*-drinkers, dressed just as I had last seen him in the Transvaal: khaki shorts, dusty T-shirts, 'feltie' boots. On his belt he carried an enormous bush knife (until I said he'd better hide it, because in England it would be confiscated as an offensive weapon).

He stood on the kerb and we talked a long time, until I realised that he was rooted to the spot. "Pretty glad to see you, Jon," he said in his Afrikaans accent. "Man, I can take anything back home, but your traffic here scares me stiff."

And it was true. The cars down Long Acre had him running for cover. He'd rather walk round the block than cross the street. And the crowds of shoppers just baffled him. He stood there like a bull elephant sniffing the wind. How he managed the underground trains I cannot imagine.

Then I took him to see the Changing of the Guard outside Buckingham Palace, and he wept at the pageantry of it all. Later he explained that he'd never seen snow before, so I put him on a train for the Scottish Highlands – after buying him his first pair of jeans, just to keep him warm up there. And he still talks about that trip with fondness.

Which just goes to show that, however great our experience, we're all first-time travellers at heart. ⁊⬥

The woman traveller
by Isabella Tree

THE ART OF TRAVELLING IS LEARNING TO BEHAVE LIKE A CHAMELEON. So said a woman friend of mine on her second year around the world and I don't believe a truer word was ever spoken. Blending into the background is not only a prerequisite to understanding and observing a different culture, it also keeps you out of trouble.

Indecent exposure

For women in particular, how you behave and especially how you dress can be construed as camouflage or an open invitation; it can make you one of the crowd or a moving target. This may be an unfair state of affairs but it's a fact of life and in someone else's country one is in no position to rail against it.

Call it ignorance or misdirected feminism, but many women make the mistake of travelling in a 'no compromise' frame of mind. They wear shorts and bra tops in Marrakech and Istanbul, G-strings in Goa and Phuket, and nothing at all in the Mediterranean. I know and you know that this does not mean they are 'loose women', but it does show a distinct lack of respect for local custom and the sensitivities of the men, and women, of the country.

Dress is the first line of defence and the most immediate symbol of respect. If you get that wrong you are starting your travels with a glaring disadvantage. Codes of dress differ wildly from country to country. In southern Africa and part of the Indian subcontinent, short sleeves and hemlines not far below the knee are fully respectable. In Iran and strict Muslim countries, the body must be totally covered, usually by a black *chador* which drapes you completely from head to foot. A woman not wearing a veil risks flogging or imprisonment, although as a foreigner you are likely to be let off with a caution and forced to cover up.

There are legally enforced dress codes at home as well, though they're so familiar we may take them for granted. But it serves to show that though conventions may differ, they are universal. In London, or Paris or New York, you would be a fool for walking the street topless, let alone racing across a cricket pitch, and not expecting to be arrested. In rainforest tribal communities from Sumatra to the Amazon, on the other hand, bare breasts are *de rigeur*.

A culture's standard of dress has a lot to do with what parts of the body are considered sensuous or provocative. In China the feet are still thought erotic, while in many countries direct eye contact can be as promiscuous as the offer of a spare key to your hotel room. In Papua New Guinea you can bare your breast to the world, but your thighs must be covered at all times. Not only that, but the space between your legs is so sexually suggestive that trousers can be as much of a turn-on as wearing nothing at all.

It pays to be prepared for the dress sense of your destination before you head off for a pre-holiday splurge in the high street, but clearly this is not always possible. As a general rule it can be said that tight and skimpy clothes are inappropriate for most countries outside Europe and the United States, and that generous, loose-fitting clothes are not only more comfortable to travel in, but less controversial.

If you don't want to wear dresses and skirts, you can't do better for propriety's sake, especially in tropical heat, than the kind of cool, cotton pyjamas worn by Chinese or Kashmiri women, or a Moroccan *jalaba*. However, in places like Burma, Thailand and Vietnam, particularly in the cities, this may be too casual. Asian women take a great deal of trouble with their appearance however poor their background, and while torn jeans and a tattered T-shirt may seem relaxed and inoffensive to the Westerner, it can seem dirty and disrespectful in Bangkok.

If conventions are strict on the street they are doubly so in places of worship. I once met a French woman who had been stoned in Turkey – one of the most relaxed of the Muslim countries, for being dressed inappropriately in a mosque. In Greece you may be provided with frumpy, elasticated skirts to hide your trousers or miniskirt when entering an Orthodox Church. You may even be asked to cover your head. Never enter even a remote chapel on a beach in anything else than full daily dress. You may get away with it, but the distress you will cause a worshipper who stumbles on you wearing a bikini in the crypt is indefensible. In all these cases, a simple length of wrap-around cotton, like an Indian *lungi* or a sarong, or an African *kanga* or *kikoi*, is a handy extra to have.

The hands-off approach

Perhaps the most persistent and aggravating problem a woman has to deal with, particularly if she is travelling alone, is male harassment. Satellite TV and black market videos have a lot to answer for. In Third World countries Victoria Beckham and Britney Spears are seen as the archetypal western woman; while the steamier side of Swedish exports, now providing a boom business for the black market in Asia, gives the impression that American or European women have an indiscriminate and insatiable appetite for sex. Black western women fare even worse than blondes because they are considered 'exotic'.

Safety tips for women travellers

1. Trust your instincts. If you have any doubts about getting into a car with someone or meeting them for a drink, don't do it. And don't feel bad about not turning up to a prearranged meeting if you've had second thoughts.

2. Dress to respect local customs, which in most cases is conservatively. It may seem archaic, but pick your principles or pick preservation. Long skirts instead of short, trousers not shorts, long sleeved not short. As a consolation prize, think of the comfort – and the protection against sun damage.

3. You may find it useful to wear a wedding ring, even if you're not married. Or carry photos of a scary-looking 'boyfriend'.

4. Walk confidently, and avoid direct eye contact with strangers. Wearing sunglasses should do the trick. Take a book or magazine into bars and restaurants with you to avoid eye contact with all those men staring at you. (Yes they do.)

5. Try and plan your arrivals into big towns before it gets dark. Plan any journey in terms of daylight hours.

6. Be aware of your surroundings (people, cars, doorways) so you know which way to head if you get into trouble. If you're being followed, walk into a tourist hotel or a shop and ask the staff for help.

7. Be careful about disclosing where you are staying. Lock your room when you are in it. Better still, take your own padlock (a common travellers' precaution). When staying in a hotel, check with reception staff before answering the door to visitors.

8. If groped on public transport, you may wish to draw attention to the fact – loudly.

9. Don't cut yourself off from the excitement of meeting new people. Befriend local women or families. You'll be surrounded by hospitality, so you can learn about their different culture – and they often have valuable advice about the area for the solo female traveller.

10. And just in case you do embark on a holiday romance, do carry your own supply of Western-manufactured condoms.

The sad truth is that you can be dressed modestly and impeccably on a bus in Lima or Tangiers and still feel a hand on your bum. Ironically it is often in Catholic or Muslim countries, where impropriety is most despised, that local men feel they can take liberties with foreigners. Most self-defence experts advise: 'Never create a 1:1 confrontation'. "Get your hands off my bum, you filthy expletive," can exacerbate the situation or even incite a violent response. The best solution is to make a scene and enlist the support of other passengers. "Did you see what that man did to me?" creates a sense of moral outrage and people, when directly appealed to, will be more eager to leap to your defence. The same attitude that implies that Western women are 'loose', can work as an effective antidote to harassment when the groper, having been sprung, is hounded out of the bus and given a going-over by the other male passengers.

In general, the first rule of self-defence is awareness. Be alert, listen to the advice of locals and fellow travellers, develop a street sense and try not to be in the wrong place at the wrong time. Good judgement is every traveller's personal responsibility and the chances are, if you find yourself alone, late at night and being pursued up a dark alley, you could have avoided being there in the first place.

It is politically incorrect nowadays to suggest that women should ever play a 'passive' role, or – heaven forbid – that they could court disaster. But avoidance and weak-minded submissiveness are two completely different things, and the distinction is one that is crucial to survival, especially in foreign countries where the threat is an unknown quantity.

A woman is rarely a physical match for a man. And even if she is a black-belt in the martial arts, it would be unwise to launch into front kicks and elbow strikes if the man confronting her is just after money. Hand over the wallet and have done with it. Your pursuer may be armed, crazy or drunk and there is no need ever to find out if it can be avoided.

Most confrontational scenarios must be played by ear to a great extent, but there are a few universal rules. Don't turn a scary situation into a dangerous one if you can help it. Don't panic, don't show fear and don't allow the person accosting you to get the upper hand. Try to gain the psychological advantage by throwing him of his balance. In most cases a man who is attempting to intimidate a woman believes himself invulnerable and a strong show of resistance will unnerve him enough to make him back down. Never be persuaded to try and resolve the situation by moving to another place, like a car, a hotel room or someone else's house.

If you do find yourself in a dangerous, enclosed situation, try to anticipate the aggressor's next move and plan ahead for it. You may only get one chance to defend yourself – the earlier the better – and you won't want to miss it. As the innocent one in confrontation you have the advantage of surprise, but if you are forced to strike back physically, make sure it is a crippling blow that gives you a chance to escape. The last thing you want is to provoke a more serious physical attack. As one London-based martial arts master recommends: "There is only one thing better than a kick in the balls – and that's two kicks in the balls."

If you are worried about your ability to gauge dangerous situations and to defend yourself if they get out of hand, a few classes in the basic strategies of awareness and self-defence before you travel can boost your confidence immeasurably.

Warm receptions

Stay alert and these 'worse case scenarios' should never arise. I've travelled most of my life, some of it on my own, and though I'm certainly no Kate Adie, I've been caught up in anti-British demonstrations in Peru, tear-gassed in Czechoslovakia and Papua New Guinea, been ambushed by tribal warriors in Indonesia, and never had a hand laid on me in earnest.

Appreciation of the dangers should never stop you from sharing in the action, or making friends. One of the great advantages of being a woman is that men and women find you more approachable. Sometimes the offers of hospitality and kindness can be overwhelming. And any woman who has travelled with a child or a baby can regale you with stories of such warmth and tenderness that it melts the heart and restores all your faith in human nature. These are the moments one travels for and that stay with you for ever.

Contraception and feminine hygiene

Contraception is often difficult to come by abroad and should be acquired before you leave home. Time changes should be taken into consideration if you take a low dosage contraceptive pill. Stomach upsets and diarrhoea may also reduce or neutralise the effectiveness of oral contraception.

Condoms are not as freely available, especially to women, as they should be, and packets that you do find in clinics or chemists in areas off the beaten track may be past their sell-by-date and the rubber may break or corrode. Always take condoms with you, however remote the possibility of sex. AIDS and other sexually-transmitted diseases are a universal threat.

Women should be aware that the physical stress of travel, jet-lag and time difference can upset the biological clock and throw even the most regular period out of kilter. Sanitary towels and tampons are often difficult to buy abroad, especially in the Third World. A form of Tampax, with plastic or cardboard applicator, is the most hygienic and convenient to take with you, as on some occasions you may find it difficult to find clean water and soap to wash your hands. If you do prefer to take the more discreet-sized tampons without applicators, carry a sachet of disinfectant wipes to clean your hands which will guard against the transmission of germs.

Be sensitive about cultural attitudes to menstruation. In some places, especially tribal areas, men are really frightened of the powers a woman has when she is menstruating. Some cultures believe it is contaminating, and will not allow you to touch or even walk near their food. Of course, they need never know, but be careful how you dispose of sanitary towels and tampons in this situation.

In brief conclusion, don't be a loud tourist, keep an open mind, stay cool and be wise, and travelling, especially if you are a woman, will be a fulfilling and exciting adventure. ❧

ISABELLA TREE is a travel journalist and author of four travel books.

The family traveller
by Matthew Collins

WE RETURNED TO OUR CAMPGROUND OUTSIDE ORLANDO to find several gleaming, giant customised Harley Davidsons parked in the space next to ours. "Get off!" I bawled to my kids, who were clambering onto them, "or the owners will be really angry." The owners *were* angry. A group of greasy, dangerous-looking Hell's Angels approached, menace in their eyes.

"Why have you got tattoos?" asked Charlie, four.

"Be quiet," I muttered. "And get off those bikes now…."

"They're cool," said the ugliest one. "You wanna know why we got tattoos? 'Cos we're just a bunch o' dumb guys. You won't get tattoos when you're older, will you son?"

"Yes, I will," said Charlie. "I'm going to get a Postman Pat tattoo."

Oh the relief… Who would have thought that several hours later I would be discussing British and American children's TV with die-hard US bikers?

But that incident illustrates one benefit of travelling with kids: they are fantastic ice-breakers.

They also lend a fresh pair of eyes. A couple of days later we were at Seaworld, waiting for the *Shamu, The Killer Whale* show to start. Suddenly a 40-ton, aquatic mammal shot out of the massive swimming pool. "That's not a penguin, *is* it?" three-year-old Nicolai confirmed.

Our American journey (three months in a motorhome, two kids, no wife) was the most ambitious trip I've ever made. My wife, Khelga, was busy with work exams, so I proposed the idea of a drive across the States. I would fulfil a Kerouac dream. The boys and I would have a father-and-sons' adventure. She would have calm space in which to study.

Khelga took a while to buy the idea, but as soon as she was persuaded I remortgaged the house. For three months I had zero income, substantial expenses and 24 hours a day with two pre-school kids.

But that was a benefit. How many children and parents (especially dads) spend 24 hours a day together outside the annual summer holiday? The boys and I got to know each other extremely well and shared a unique experience.

"Wasn't it hard work?" people always ask. The answer is: no. At least, less hard than normal life in London. At home nearly everything has to be organised, outdoor activities are weather-dependent and the city often makes the kids feel claustrophobic.

Driving through the southern states in a motorhome in summer, stopping off at beautiful parks and campgrounds, they had space, sunshine and freedom.

"But how do you keep them entertained?" Americans asked constantly. "You don't even have an on-board VCR."

"We talk," I informed them. And we did, about anything – Elvis Presley, Bill Clinton, Fireman Sam, Mickey Mouse….

North America is one of the easiest countries to travel in with children, but the boys and I have ventured into other places too: Egypt, Israel, Iceland, Kenya, Europe, the Caribbean, Russia. We've driven, we've flown, we've taken trains and ferries, we've cycled, we've even hitchhiked together.

To progress from being a traveller to being a globetrotting parent is a fear-inducing, lifestyle-jolting, jump. But even the most jaded palate will find new sensations in a world suddenly filled with little people. There's no set formula for travelling with children and, as with any trip, there is always a risk. To help things go smoothly here are some tips I've acquired from my own experiences, both good and bad.

When to start

"Do as much as possible while he's still being breastfed," friends advised when Charlie arrived. "You're much more self-sufficient and don't need so much junk." (I did need the wife though, which wasn't a problem).

The first trip was two weeks in Puerto Rico, followed by a winter stay in Canada. Charlie was two months old.

First disaster was the loss of our luggage when we flew to Montreal from San Juan. It had been plus 30°C when we took off. It was 30° below in Montreal. "Not to worry," I said cheerily, as we walked to our car in a blizzard, snow and ice strafing our arms and legs. My wife and I were dressed in shorts and T-shirts, Charlie was swathed in borrowed airline blankets.

Lesson one in travelling with children: always keep a spare supply of clothes as hand luggage. You never know when you might need them. And as for travelling while the baby's still breastfeeding – nothing can be taken for granted. The following week my wife's milk dried up.

As kids reach toddler stage they sleep less, and demand more attention and equipment. (It's only when you can chuck the buggy away that you finally begin to feel liberated.) Kids aren't really going to appreciate their travels until they begin to communicate. Of all the animals on safari in Kenya, two-year-old Nicolai loved the local sparrows best.

Preparation

Make sure that you've had all the required injections well in advance.

Prepare lists of everything you need. As well as practical stuff, don't forget favourite teddies, toys or books. But don't go mad. Limit what you take – travellers accumulate stuff. And if you're going to North America, take very little (and buy over there – nearly everything is cheaper than it is in Europe). In hot and cold climates, remember that hats are extremely important.

As children get older, prepare them psychologically for travelling. If you're having an adventure (rather than a holiday) they should know life will be different.

Flights

Flying with children isn't *always* a nightmare. Letting the kids go to bed late the night before is a high-risk strategy but it *can* work. My boys were so excited the night before one long-haul trip that they didn't settle until midnight. Such was their exhaustion, they fell asleep shortly after take-off and I spent most of the flight undisturbed. But you can't rely on that. You often have to think on your feet. One tip here: sick bags fascinate *all* children and, with some decoration, make good glove puppets, too.

Airlines vary in their attitude to kids. Virgin Atlantic are deservedly famous in that department. They give out lots of goodies and staff are very tolerant. But some charter airlines can be hell – even exhausted children can have problems sleeping in cattle truck conditions. If you're making a long-haul flight consider the advantages of scheduled over charter.

Manage expectations. If you're flying to South-East Asia and your children want to know if you've arrived just as you pass over Hounslow Heath, *be honest*.... Tell them they are going to be on the plane *a very long time*.

Food

No matter how well airlines cater for children their idea of a child-friendly meal is usually revolting fast-food junk. Sugar and additives aren't the most child-calming ingredients for a flight. So don't feel obliged to order a kids' meal. As a precaution, pack your own in-flight snacks – with whatever healthy things your children like.

When it comes to food, I must confess to being totalitarian with my boys. So they're used to a varied diet and generally eat everything on their plate. This has been useful on our travels as they're happy trying out new things. Prepare children for a different diet by producing new dishes at home before travelling (and warn them that they won't be able to have burgers for every meal.) If your kids are fussy eaters, stock up on supplies they'll probably like – dried mince or noodles usually go down well. And use different tricks to lure them into trying new things: e.g. Superman eats *tom yum* when he's in Thailand; Mickey Mouse eats *pork fat* when he's in Costa Rica; Batman eats *turtle blubber* when he visits the San Blas Islands.

On the road

The most important requirement when travelling with children is flexibility. It's all very well making itineraries, but one tired toddler ruins everything. Never push kids. Go with the flow. If they seem tired, err on the side of caution.

Be prepared to do or see half the things you want to do or see. Be prepared for days of doing nothing – catching up on sleep (you *and* the kids); lounging by a pool, chilling out....

If you've crossed a time zone, give the children time to adapt. On the third day of our American trip I was woken at four in the morning by two naked boys cycling *inside* the motorhome.

Compromise. If you're a culture vulture don't expect your children always to share your interest. If you have to visit a museum, check whether it has a children's section. If it doesn't, take into account the kids' tolerance threshold and reward them for their patience with a treat – a visit to a waterpark, swimming pool or zoo, anything they're bound to enjoy.

Don't lose the children. But if you do (and you probably will) make sure they have some information – their own name, your name, where you're from. I had a frightening experience when Nicolai vanished on a campground outside Nashville. After 15 minutes he was delivered by a fellow camper. "Sir," said the man. "Are you Mr Collins?"

"Yes, I am," I said, hugely relieved.

"I thought you were," said the man. "Your son told me his dad was bald, not very tall and had huge, size-12 feet. So I guessed it had to be you...."

Illness

If you're away for more than a fortnight, it's likely your child will be ill. First tip:

make sure you have good insurance. Second tip: choose the contents of your medical bag carefully – preferably in consultation with your family doctor (and keep it with you at all times). Third tip: (again) don't push your children. If they get over-tired they're more likely to get ill.

Our worst experience was when Nicolai suffered febrile convulsions on a ferry from Santander to Plymouth. We had to watch helplessly while a nervous French doctor calculated the appropriate dose of sedative. Oh, the guilt… we'd travelled all the way from Seville that day.

Take the usual culinary precautions – peel fruit and veg, avoid buffet food (which has been left standing out), and avoid ice in drinks. Watch your child's fluid intake. Children dehydrate more quickly than adults. If they develop a fever or any illness involving diarrhoea or vomiting, get them to take water mixed with sugar and a little salt. The juice of an orange makes it palatable. Pack camomile tea. You can use it for everything from upset tummies (drink it) to heat rash (apply it).

If your child develops a temperature over 39°C, find a doctor, fast.

Final tip

Warn your child when he or she goes back to school that, just because he/she has spent the summer trekking up the Himalayas or sailing down the Amazon, he/she mustn't expect every other child in the class to have done the same. After my Charlie had recounted his tales of bear spotting, trout fishing and glacier crossing in Canada, his friend William informed the class he'd spent the summer in Clacton with his granny. But at least William was more interested in Charlie than a boy called Thomas, who hadn't been away at all. "Oh, be quiet," he said. "We're not interested in Charlie's boring travel stories." ❧

MATTHEW COLLINS was a reporter for the BBC's 'Travel Show' for ten years, before going freelance . He is the author of 'Across Canada With The Boys And A Granny'.

The older traveller
by Cathy Braithwaite

A ROUGH ORANGE DIRT TRACK IN THE SCORCHING MASAI MARA. In a small van, five travel journalists – the young and intrepid type – clutch their seats, knuckles white, jaws set, staring straight ahead, hating every minute of the bouncy, five-hour journey. "These roads are just too bumpy, too uncomfortable. This is ridiculous – you can't possibly call this a holiday," complains one, just as another van carrying two elderly but beaming tourists bounces by.

Lesson one: journalists have tender bottoms and mature travellers can be a darn sight more adventurous. In fact, these days senior citizens think nothing of tackling the most demanding challenges, and relish new experiences at an age

A reader writes...

I would strongly urge your older readers not to give up the enlivening and rejuvenating habit of travel. My travelling companion is in his early nineties, and by no means robust, but I guess if you have been adaptable, you stay that way.

On one of our four trips last year, we stopped over in Tromso for three days before the departure of our boat for Spitzbergen. There wasn't a room to be had. To compound the problem, my 91-year-old succumbed to an alarmingly bad head-cold plus bronchitis. But he insisted that the disappointment of cancelling the trip would be far more dangerous for his health than three nights on an airport bench followed by the temperatures of the Arctic.

In the end we were rescued by a kindly hotel porter. My friend retired to a camp-bed in an empty room, and by our first storm-tossed night en route to Spitzbergen he was on his way to recovery. It was one of our best trips ever – beautiful scenery and wildlife (polar bear and cub, walruses, whales, birds, seals…) and cosmopolitan company.

Here are my tips for elderly travellers:

1. Always carry a 'scissor seat' so you can sit down anywhere while waiting (airport check-ins, for instance). You can also use it instead of your usual walking-stick. The lightest one (2.5 lb) is the Quatro from Linden Leisure (telephone 01242 604545).

2. Don't be too proud to ask for a wheelchair at airports. Save your energy for more thrilling things than airport corridors – and get vip treatment boarding the plane.

3. Always take a fairly laid-back younger friend with you.

4. Do keep rolling, fellow-wrinklies!

Mary Alexander, London

---

when they have the time and money. And this is the essence of the growing market for older travellers: time and money.

The retired can travel when and for as long as they choose. No jobs to groaningly return to; no children to force through school gates. You can break the journey up into manageable sections, pausing for periods of rest when necessary. This is good news for any travel operator or airline. Though it's hardly a problem to sell travel in the high season, it's a different story off-peak, which is when the buying power of older travellers really comes into its own.

The benefits of off-peak travel are many and varied: temperatures are kinder, there are fewer crowds and lower prices, and travel industry staff are delighted by your off-peak business. All you, the traveller, have to do is decide is where, how and when to go. There need not even by a 'why'. Your horizons are impressive, and while your age may prove a restriction with some operators and car hire companies (usually for travellers aged over 65), you will doubtless be spoilt for choice.

Whether you are a fit older person who can happily cope with a two-week camp-and-trek holiday in the Himalayas, or you feel a lack of stamina precludes a two-month tour of Australia's outback or a six-month journey around the world, if you recognise your limitations and are realistic about your expectations it is possible to make travel in retirement safe and exhilarating.

Destinations

Today even the most remote corners of the world are accessible, and it is tempting to embark on the most unusual and exciting journey you can find. First establish what you want from your holiday. Then weigh up your own ability to cope. Don't fool yourself: there is no shame in admitting that a whirlwind tour of six South American countries in 30 days would be too much for you. It is far worse to arrive at the start of what would be the experience of a lifetime, only to realise your holiday has turned into a test of endurance. The maxim 'different strokes for different folks' is never more apposite than in the context of older people and travel. What to one person is tame and unadventurous to another is the most daring project they've ever contemplated. But whether you are the type who would take out a mortgage to buy the latest walking boots or you follow the 'have timetable, will travel' school of travelling, building your own itinerary maximises your choice. You can choose how to travel, when and where to overnight and whether or not to spend a couple of days at a stopover, and you can make the whole experience as demanding or relaxed as you wish.

Preparation

While it is romantic and inspiring to think of intrepid 85-year-olds throwing more knickers than shirts into a bag and wandering wherever their fancy leads, life is so much easier if you take a few basic precautions.

Explore visa requirements and apply as much in advance as possible. Passport regulations can also differ. If you suffer from a medical condition, make sure the destination you visit easily meets your needs. Invest in insurance which will cover all eventualities including the cost of repatriation (not all insurance policies include this, so do check). You may need to shop around for a policy that will cover a traveller of advancing years, but they do exist.

See your doctor well before you embark on your trip. He or she will be able to advise and arrange vaccinations and will prescribe any regular medicinal needs during your time overseas. Doctors can normally only prescribe a limited quantity under the NHS, but your GP may be able to make an exception or advise you of what is available at your intended destination/s. The countries you visit may also impose restrictions on certain medicinal drugs. It is always a good idea to carry notification of any significant medical condition you suffer from.

Health

The older you are, the longer it takes to recover from an illness or broken bone. So it is common sense to preclude predicaments such as being stuck in a Nepalese hospital with a leg in plaster because you were convinced you could imitate that mountain goat – and failed. Assess your fitness before deciding where to travel.

Up-to-date information on health problems in any country you plan to visit is available from clinics across the UK. Contact British Airways Travel Clinics for your nearest clinic, or try the Medical Advisory Service for Travellers Abroad (www.masta.org). It is sensible to have a full medical check-up before you leave.

For a free copy of the Department of Health leaflet *The Traveller's Guide to Health* (ref. T6), see your doctor, travel agent, local post office or call 0207 210 4850. Remember, you will not enjoy your holiday if you are constantly tired. And if you feel tired, rest. Pushing yourself to the limit all day every day will only cause the excitement of being in a new place and witnessing a different culture to pall.

Services for older people

There are now a number of travel companies that provide holidays specifically for older travellers. Most offer packages, but there is an increasing demand for holidays which combine the advantages of package deals (easy travel arrangements and the support of large organisations should you need help) with independence once you reach your destination.

A number of specialist operators now cater for older travellers. Forty years ago, Saga pioneered holidays exclusively for the over-60s, long before anyone else realised the market potential. The company has since moved on a continent or two from UK seaside hotel holidays. It also includes travel insurance in the cost of all overseas travel and offers a free visa service. Numerous other companies such as Thomsons and Cosmos have followed the trend, offering package holidays tailored to the needs of older people, making it worth your while to shop around.

Practicalities

No matter how dauntless you are, nothing makes for a grouchier traveller than the lack of life's little comforts. So take small inflatable cushions to rest that weary head, and cartons of drink to quench that thirst when you are nowhere near civilisation. Use luggage with wheels or spread the load over a couple of soft-pack bags.

And if you are the type who would consider the ultimate travel experience ruined by a lack of milk, let alone tea, check that in the destination of your choice they also appreciate such basics. ❧

*CATHY BRAITHWAITE has worked for the Saga Group,
which specialises in travel for the elderly.*

The honeymoon traveller
by Lucy Hone

A HONEYMOON IS THAT ULTIMATE OF HOLIDAYS, one which we all hope to take at some stage in our lives. It will probably be the most expensive trip you've ever been on, so it should be your perfect holiday, one that provides you with memories to cherish for years to come. What a dreadful shame then that so many couples get it so horribly wrong. In my research for *The Good Honeymoon Guide*, I have come across scores of honeymoon couples with disappointing tales to tell:

couples lured by discount deals to the Caribbean in August only to find themselves caught in a hurricane; couples promised wonderful ocean views but given a room overlooking an adjacent building site; and the surprise sailing honeymoon booked by a groom who didn't know that his spouse was prone to seasickness. Any seasoned traveller will tell you that the obstacles encountered while travelling are all part of the adventure, but for honeymooners such problems are nothing short of an intergalactic disaster.

The honeymoon traveller is unlike any other kind of traveller: the trip is billed as the holiday of a lifetime, and the pressure is on to enjoy every minute. As a result, couples regard their honeymoon in a totally different light than they would any 'normal' trip. Many couples have travelled extensively before their marriage, seeking out imaginative and far-flung destinations for in-depth exploration, but the moment the ring slips upon the finger all that changes: independent travellers who have, for years, lived and slept by their *Lonely Planet* bibles suddenly find themselves looking through brochures full of what they would normally refer to as 'boring beach holidays'.

Oh, the earth was made for lovers
– EMILY DICKINSON

When it comes to booking a honeymoon, couples always seem to play it safe, which usually translates into them all trooping off to the same old trusted haunts. They flock in droves towards the reliable and idyllic islands of the Indian Ocean and the Caribbean: Mauritius, the Maldives, the Seychelles, St Lucia, Antigua and Barbados – all appear regularly in the honeymoon Top Ten. If you are the one who is booking a honeymoon, you'll know that this is largely because newlyweds want to be assured of that essential honeymoon ingredient: a romantic hotel with a bedroom to die for.

For many couples this is their first opportunity to stay in a luxurious hotel with all the trimmings, allowing them to revel in the glorious excesses of the hotel's room service, swim-up bars and jacuzzis. However, an all too common mistake is made by couples who dream of simply lazing around on the beach for two weeks on their honeymoon, and actually end up feeling bored and frustrated if there's nothing to do. Check with the hotel or travel agent and find out exactly what leisure facilities and cultural diversions are available should you get bored of the bedroom or the beach lounger!

Similarly, those planning an active honeymoon, with plenty of touring, sightseeing, and adventure activities, should take care to build in plenty of time for rest and relaxation: spend a few days lying on the beach or holed up in a mountain hideaway before you hit the trail. If you *do* decide on a really alternative destination, remember that you don't have to dash around and see every single highlight of that country in your two weeks. Many tour operators, particularly the specialist ones who are so enthusiastic about their countries, tend to push people into doing too much. Don't feel afraid to say no to some sightseeing and spend the day relaxing on your own instead.

Flights are also a big consideration when booking a honeymoon, as couples tend to be pretty exhausted after the wedding and may not necessarily feel like spending hours cooped up on an aeroplane. Don't think that romantic necessarily has to mean distant. It doesn't. Having said that, if you've absolutely set your heart on a country and a hotel that is thousands of miles away, why not take the plunge – there are always sleeping pills to fall back on.

Alternative honeymoon destinations

If you want to avoid the crowd, there are a comforting number of alternative destinations that offer culture, eco-tourism or adventure, as well as some really wonderful hotels where you can recharge your batteries and get into some serious honeymoon indulgence along the way. There's hardly a corner of the world now that doesn't boast some kind of superb hotel, making less-traditional honeymoon destinations such as Costa Rica, Indonesia, Morocco, Borneo, Chile, Tanzania, India, Thailand, Brazil and Egypt all realistic contenders for your dream trip.

Keep an open mind when selecting your destination. Many couples have looked aghast at the suggestion of India or Costa Rica, but have been readily convinced by the discovery that they would be staying in luxurious palace hotels if they chose India or exotic lodges set deep in the heart of the rainforest in Costa Rica.

The one golden rule of honeymoons is not to go somewhere that one of you has been to before – especially not with an ex, as there's nothing more tedious than being given a blow-by-blow account of a holiday they enjoyed, or even didn't enjoy, with someone else.

Who should book the honeymoon?

The first thing to do once you get engaged is to decide who is going to book the honeymoon. Although most couples now choose to plan this important holiday together, there are those who still believe in the tradition that it's a man's job. As one husband-to-be recently said to me: "Melissa is sorting out everything else, I just want to have something that I can say is totally and utterly all mine. She hasn't got a clue where we're going, but as soon as I saw it in a brochure I knew it was just perfect for the two of us, and I'm having such a great time planning it all in secret."

Surprise honeymoons are great. They are romantic, dreamy, exciting and thrilling, as long as you both feel that way. So before you take the ball off into your own court, do check that your other half is genuinely happy to go ahead with the plan. And check that they are still happy to hang in there until the departure lounge a week or two before the wedding, and once more a day or two before the big day. Bear in mind that many people also find it difficult to get excited about a holiday they cannot visualise.

If you are booking a surprise, the key is to really think about your other half and decide, honestly, what you think they would want. Don't book a trekking holiday in northern Thailand if all your fiancée wants to do is lie on the beach. If your opinions differ markedly on what constitutes the perfect holiday, the best trick is to plan a two-centre honeymoon with something for you both, say a few days on the beach at either end of the trip and a few days in the middle for your trekking, white-water rafting, canoeing, diving, temple tours, safari or whatever. Talk to her about the fundamentals – hot or cold – and the things that she wants to avoid – injections, spiders or a long flight.

Before you go

Some countries require proof of citizenship or visas, so make sure you check with your travel agent or the tourist commission that you've got everything you both need as soon as you book, as it can take months to get through the bureaucracy. If your plane tickets and your passport are under different names, take your wedding certificate to the airport with you or, better still, arrange to send your passport off about three months prior to the trip to have it changed into your married name.

Consult your doctor about inoculations and anti-malaria pills: some countries require certificates of vaccinations and will not permit you to enter without them.

Lastly, whatever you decide, it's essential to get straight on with your booking as the best rooms, the best views and the best deals always go first. Also, don't forget to stock up on all necessary prescriptions (including contraceptives!) Try to leave these in their original bottles and keep a copy of the prescription to satisfy curious customs officials. ❧

Lucy Hone is a freelance travel writer and author of 'The Good Honeymoon Guide'.

The solitary traveller
by Nicholas Barnard

THE NOISE AND MOVEMENT OF AN ELDERLY LAND ROVER negotiating a footpath within dense bush was no foil to the impact of the tales of swamp life I was being subjected to. "Of course, you realise that the crocodiles are the least of your worries," the great white pot-bellied hunter paused, wrenched the wheel this way and that, before continuing with great deliberation, "No, the crocodiles will have what is left of you after the hippo have chewed up your dug-out."

The 'Hip-po', previously a happy word of the nursery and cartoon, was instantly dismembered by his accent to create a clear onomatopoeic vision of a wobbly dug-out snapping in the jaws of the snarling monster. Turning to look at me in the moonlight, my host shared with me a calabash-full of pertinent information. "As for the snakes for which this part of Africa is famous – don't worry, there may be a snake bite kit in the back, but if there is, what use will it be to you? Moments after most snake bites you will be completely paralysed and the polers will be standing around watching you die, for none speak or read a word of English."

By the time we reached our fishing camp near the Angolan border at dawn, I believed that I had come to terms with the prospect of travelling alone for at least eight days in such taciturn company; but dying alone in their presence was an untenable thought. To endure that journey down the Okavango to the Kalahari was an early and rigorous introduction to the art of travelling alone, to the condition of being able to survive alone.

Between the concept of travelling alone and the reality of the journey, there exists a gulf that will be bridged by painful as well as pleasing experience. From country to country and culture to culture, the act of travelling alone exposes the myths and expectations of a singular path. No manner of preparation and solitariness will disguise the fact that, by leaving a homeland, one becomes inescapably foreign and obtrusive. How the citizens of each culture will react to this small-time intrusion will make or break the experience of travelling alone. The solitary habit may help the desire to achieve inconspicuousness or it may increase the attention received: within one land one may know just how lonely a journey may be in the close company of others and, yet again, how intrusive a train compartment of strangers may prove. Dependent upon the age and sex of the would-be loner, the choice of destination certainly needs careful thought.

Travelling alone enjoys a different status within the varied regions of the world. Successful solitude may be found in the most unlikely destinations or modes of transport. Without exception, it is very difficult to travel alone outside Europe and North America. Consider how easy it is to take a railway or a bus journey across Europe in delicious isolation from the friendliness of the companions of the carriage. To ignore a possible foreigner is acceptable in those parts – in southern Asia it is unthinkable. If you want isolation from the land and its people when travelling the subcontinent, take the first class air-conditioned wagon or the Air India flight. There you will be forced to endure the foppish company of the politician, the government official or the corporation executive. I take the clamour of second-class reserved and share the ever-proffered tiffin with the broad-beamed smiles of the families in my compartment – and even answer all the questions I am able concerning the greatness of Manchester United, the Spice Girls and Tony Blair. Indeed, I have come to relish, to look forward to these casteless ceremonies of intimate hospitality so alien to my first desire to be alone – despite seeking to be that sentinel of isolation with my open and over-thumbed leaden volume of social history I never fail to pack, never finish and always discard at a faraway hotel for a more appreciative reader.

The obtrusiveness of being foreign has, seemingly, considerable demerits. Escaping to the Omayid mosque from the demographic froth of the most wonderful Damascene bazaar, I passed through a gate to behold for the first time that temple of temples to monotheism. Bewitched, I entered the cathedral-lofty prayer hall and sat near the tomb of John the Baptist (for reassurance, I suppose) and observed the interplay of women and children, men and boys, at prayer and at play. The all-pervading sense of tranquillity was an unparalleled experience and it was wise to have drunk so deeply, so rapidly, for my peace was to be cast aside by the introduction of a student of agriculture eager to exercise his World-Service English. It was not the interruption that was so galling, but the fact that he was so charming, so genial and good – characteristics that precluded any beastly dismissiveness on my part. As ever, so gentle a meeting converted solitude to a shared and unforgettable experience of being led with gusto to the hidden tombs, chapels and by-ways of ancient Damascus.

Being foreign and a woman alone in certain cultures is an unenviable circumstance. Certain countries are simply not enjoyable to visit for the single woman, whether for the mismatch of the religious, cultural or social mores with our own. Chittagong, like so many conurbations of Muslims the world over, is not a forum for the proselytising of worthy feminine liberal sentiments. The paucity of any kind of foreigners draws undesirable companionship, as mosquitoes to the ear. Boarding a bus, I was approached by an English girl and her train of admirers. After so long in the company of well-wrapped women I was as shocked and confused by the state of her lack of clothing as the gathered young Bangladeshis. The crowd was divided in sentiment – from the full-scale stoning party to lascivious indulgence – and I was delighted when the bus pulled out of the station. I had to ask about her dress, but I should have known that I was wasting my time. Fixing me with a stare that took my eyes permanently away from her partly dressed torso, she stated her view with a certain clarity: "Of course I realise what I should wear. These people simply will have to learn." I forfeited my 45p all-night bus ride and got off before the perimeter of the city.

The personal qualities needed for successful solitary travel are multifarious. Sitting at this desk to map out the requisite facets of character, I wrote: 'foresight, diligence, flexibility and humour'. With a smile I scribbled over these worthy notions and thought of my most memorable expeditions. Many of my journeys were undertaken in a parlous mental condition for, from the experience of travel, I was seeking solutions. It is this balance of being able to allow the outside world to influence one's inward-beseeching world that makes a solitary expedition worthwhile. Take a reserve of worthy notions and a good health insurance policy, for there is nothing more miserable and frightening than to be ill or damaged while on the road alone.

> To awaken quite alone in a strange town is one of the pleasantest sensations in the world.
> – FREYA STARK

What I appreciate about travelling alone are the extremes of experience so often encountered. The sense of solitude in a tropical land will be acutely felt in the early evening after eating – when the darkness falls like a shutter and the hours before sleep are many. A bright-beamed small torch is essential, for the lighting in inexpensive hotels is never unfailingly diabolical. The slim volumes of my favourite poets are dog-eared from browsing and memorising, and a capacious hip flask of fine whisky is always a soothing companion. By contrast, one may be transported without warning from a cycle of long evenings of quiet thoughtfulness to a night of wayward indulgence. The invasion of my private oceanside guest-house in Cochin by a group of exuberant and friendly New Zealanders resulted in days of parties that became nights with new-found companions, complete with the exhausting surfeit of conversation.

Without companions the pace and direction of travel may vary to one's will. About to depart for the Amazon, I sat in a Quito hotel eating a silent breakfast, seeking not to overhear the siren conversations in English amid the guttural clutter of the local Spanish. From such precocious eavesdropping, I gleaned an introduction to a Galapagos ornithological enthusiast. His vision was an inspiration: "You haff walked a jungle before?" He swung the questions with the directness of a large Swedish wood axe, "Well, you haff seen enough. Go to the Galapagos. If you like wildlife and, most important, the birds, then there is no decision!" So inspired, I ditched an elaborate and painstakingly calculated schedule of buses and aeroplanes and flew west to the Pacific. He was right, there is no decision.

If you had no notion of writing a journal, the action of travel in would-be solitude is the finest inspiration. Not only is there much more time and space for the quiet dissemination and recording of days, but the act of mute concentration over a pen and paper will deter all but the most callous interloper of personal privacy.

Whereas the lack of company may be a boon for privacy and quietude, the security of companionship is often sorely missed. That the urban centres of the world are hotbeds of energetic and endemic crime is obvious. The need for vigilance when alone is a source of debilitating fear for many, and so it is best to avoid taking a visible array of baggage that may create so much desire. I feel safest travelling light and take less and less each journey, looking to pack what is worthless to both parties or (as necessary with a camera, travellers' cheques and cash) securely covered by a reliable traveller's insurance policy.

No manner of personal privations, however, will dampen my enthusiasm for the act of travelling alone. The diverse memories I carry from such journeys are legion. From anguish to exhilaration, fulfilment to the most intense and destructive frustration that only alien bureaucracy will create, I may recall the extremes of experience with a shudder or a smile. It is ironic that what makes this practice of attempted solitude so consuming and addictive is the participation of others. Leaving home without a companion is an excellent beginning, for without a partner or friends one may be a susceptible witness to the openness of the human condition that is simple friendship. Of the greatest pleasures of travel, the new-found and often sweetly ephemeral companionship of others is my source of guiding inspiration and steadfast joy. ❧

Nicholas Barnard specialises in writing on the tribal and folk arts.

The escorted traveller
by Hilary Bradt

THEY USED TO BE CALLED PACKAGED TOURS, which conjured up an image of coach-loads of tourists thinking: 'If it's Tuesday this must be Belgium'. Rebranded as escorted journeys, these off-the-peg and tailor-made holidays cover almost every country on the planet, and certainly all those for which a tourist visa is obtainable. Not only are there hundreds of places to choose from, but dozens of ways to enjoy them, from museum tours to pottery workshops or, for the energetic, from kayaking to trekking or mountain biking. There is something for everyone, whatever their age, whatever their interests and whatever – let's be honest – their suitability for adventure travel. But the moment of truth comes at the airport check-in counter or departure lounge, where passengers cast covert glances at the luggage tags of their fellow travellers, with hearts lifting or sinking as they recognise those who are on the same tour.

It is no exaggeration to say that a trip can be made or destroyed by the people on it and, on a fixed-departure trip, there is nothing you can do about it. There is always the risk of encountering a nutter seeking a soul mate. And the more exotic the destination, the more likely it is to attract 'trophy hunters' who are more interested in bagging another country than they are in discovering the enjoyment it has to offer. It is not surprising, therefore, that more and more people are opting for the more expensive but less risky tailor-made tour, which is put together just for them, whether 'they' are a couple or a group of friends.

Although there are fewer risks inherent in a tailor-made trip there are still ways of ensuring that it goes smoothly. Couples will be fine – the problems arise when a group of friends and acquaintances get together for exotic travels. Bear in mind that people with whom you get on well at home may be disastrous travel companions and, since you are friends, you cannot simply ignore them. Remember, too, that many people who have only travelled in Europe and the Western world will be unprepared for the developing countries. They may take it in their stride or they may spoil the enjoyment of the rest of the group. They will need someone to complain to, so one member of the group must take on the role of leader.

Apart from being willing to listen to grumbles, he/she should be an experienced traveller who will know what questions to ask the travel agent or tour operator before departure – such as, is there a danger of being combined with another group for certain tours? The risk here is that you could be put with a larger, non-English-speaking party. The leader should also consider the problems of smokers versus anti-smokers and decide on rules that suit both parties.

A compromise between a tailor-made tour and a fixed-departure trip is to get your own group together, decide on your preferred travel dates, and negotiate with a tour operator for a discount on one of their standard itineraries. With your agreement he can add some more clients to make up the numbers.

Whether tailor-made or fixed-departure, how do you choose the perfect holiday? First take a long hard look at… not the holiday brochures, but yourself. One of the paradoxes of travel in the developing world – and I am assuming that most readers of the *Traveller's Handbook* will be venturing to the more unusual destinations – is that the type of person who can afford the trip is often the type least suited to cope with a very different culture. In the West a strong sense of right and wrong, assertiveness and organisational skills are the personality traits that lead to success in business, and thus the income to finance exotic travel. But these 'A-type' personalities often find the developing world unbearably 'inefficient' and frustrating. By having control over their itinerary through a tailor-made tour, such people are more likely to get the most out of their trip with the minimum of frustration. A group tour, where they must 'go with the flow', may be the least successful option. Conversely, the happiest group travellers are often those who can adopt the attitude of one elderly woman, who announced to her leader: "I'm going to give up thinking; it doesn't work in Madagascar". It doesn't, and she had a great time!

If asked to pick out the two main reasons to choose an escorted tour over a tailor-made itinerary, I would say friendship and knowledge. When a group really jells the holiday will be remembered for all time, and reunions will take place each year because these new friends can't bear to let go after a fortnight of shared laughter and awe, when the lows become highs because of the feeling of camaraderie. Several of my close friends are people I met on group trips up to 20 years ago. Fixed-departure tours are an excellent choice for single people, who should be advised that the inevitable singles supplement is usually preferable to the risks of sharing with a stranger.

The knowledge part of the equation comes with the expert leaders provided by the best tour operators. A truly great leader is able to share his or her knowledge of the country in an enthralling way, so that no one is bored and no one feels diminished because their level of knowledge or interest is less than that of the others. Your leader should be an extrovert and a raconteur, as well as a smoother of ruffled feathers and a diplomat able to deal calmly with the trickiest situation. Such paragons are hard to find but do exist: personal recommendations are invaluable.

After that long, hard look at yourself you need to take a long, hard look at your bank statement and promise yourself you'll spend as much as you can afford. If you are planning to go somewhere genuinely exotic, try not to be influenced by price or name. What matters is not saving the odd £100, but the itinerary and the leader, particularly in special-interest groups. Be wise to the false glamour of a posh name – once you arrive at your destination your holiday arrangements are likely to be in the hands of a ground operator who provides the same service to all their overseas partners, big and small.

Before you even start looking at brochures, buy a good guidebook and get a feeling for the country of your choice and the places you would most like to see. Then send for AITO's *Holiday Directory*. The Association of Independent Tour Operators (www.aito.co.uk) has around 160 members, who are all very knowledgeable in their own area. With the directory it is easy to see which operators cover the region you are interested in, and the activity that you find most appealing.

Magazines are the best source of information on tour operators offering special-interest trips. If you are looking for a riding holiday buy a horse magazine, if it's painting you are after look in an art magazine, and so on.

Travel shows such as the Daily Telegraph Adventure Travel Show and Destinations in London and the Independent Travellers' World in other parts of the UK give you the chance to meet and talk to tour operators as well as find inspiration. By the time you are ready to make a choice you will be well informed enough to pick out the tour operators who do not know the country they are selling (yes, it happens!). If place names are wrongly spelled or animal species incorrectly named you should be wary of travelling with that company. Much better to choose a specialist with a proven track record.

Don't hesitate to ask for the contact details of people who have been on the trip you are interested in. A successful tour operator will have no qualms about putting you in touch with former clients. If you enjoy your trip you can volunteer to be a referee for that company afterwards. It is also helpful to talk to the trip leader beforehand and to some of the other people who have signed up.

If you have an independent travel agent whom you trust and have worked with before, let them do the leg work – it will cost you no more. They will save you lots of time and can help sort out any serious problems that arise while you are away.

Here's a little story to close this section. Once upon a time in Bolivia a group of Americans assembled to enjoy a trek over the Andes and into the jungle. The first obstacle to holiday bliss was evident immediately: the party was made up of 11 women and one man. The next obstacle emerged a few hours later: the women were divided into two groups, one of which had signed up because they were ardent feminists and would only consider a trip that had a woman leader; the others were hoping to meet the man of their dreams. The one man was oblivious to both – he was a cocaine addict who was fully occupied by his quest for coca leaves. None of the 12 travellers was particularly interested in trekking.

The guide, Jean-Paul, was a Frenchman who looked like Rudolf Nureyev. He was a poet and a mountaineer, had romantically flared nostrils and a temper to match. One of his first comments was that he hated women and Americans.

Highlights, or rather lowlights, of the next six days included the news, on a village radio, of an attempted coup in La Paz ("Tanks and dead bodies all over the place," said Jean-Paul dramatically, but not entirely accurately), food-free days because the muleteers had sold our provisions to villagers along the way to make up for their lack of wages, part of the group becoming separated from the others and sleeping on the floor of a village school, and one of the feminists threatening to castrate Jean-Paul with her Swiss Army knife. The group divided into two factions, with one lot refusing to speak to, or sit with, the others. It rained incessantly.

The last night should have been spent in a luxury hotel recovering from the ardours of trekking. Instead it was spent with the group split between two whorehouses. One had no bathroom of any kind and the most prudish of the women was reprimanded by the village policeman for squatting in the street, while the other had an outhouse that was occupied by a monkey chained to the toilet seat.

Sometimes you need a truly dreadful trip to fully appreciate the good ones! ❧

HILARY BRADT is the founder and Managing Director of the Bradt travel guide series. She is also a tour leader and travel writer.

The extreme sports traveller
by Steve Watkins

THE REALISATION, OVER THE LAST DECADE OR SO, that a refreshing holiday doesn't have to mean lounging on a beach with a good book has led to an explosion of operators offering extreme sports trips to satisfy almost anyone's desire for an invigorating adventure. While the vast majority of trips are based around activities where the perceived danger is far greater than the real danger, it is important to remember that there are some risks involved. It is worth putting extra effort into ascertaining the level of competency of any operator you intend using. Check their guides' qualifications and experience levels, ask about the safety equipment they use and how often it is maintained and replaced and inquire as to the guide/client ratio to ensure that you will receive a reasonable amount of personal tuition and contact. Once you are satisfied, hold onto your hat and prepare to be thrilled. Below are just some of the sports that can lift your adrenaline levels to new highs.

Canyoning

One of the new kids on the adventure sport block, canyoning has rapidly become one of the most popular of such activities in Europe, with its accessibility and high fun factor playing a significant part in its rise. It involves scrambling through rocky gorges, abseiling down waterfalls and leaping carefree into deep river pools while wearing a special, reinforced wetsuit and helmet to help protect against bumps and scrapes. If you like getting wet then canyoning could be your thing. A two-day introductory course would leave you confident of the simple ropework and scrambling skills needed, then it is just down to practice. Although it is possible to canyon independently, this should only be attempted by more experienced canyoners. It is far better and easier to link up with a local operator, who will have qualified guides who know the best areas and the possible problems associated with regional weather conditions. Canyons are constricted waterways and heavy rain can cause devastating flash floods. Canyoning was born in Europe and the Alps is still the Mecca, though there are usually operators in any suitable mountain area. In the UK, there are no real canyons, but gorge walking is a close parallel and takes place in Wales and Scotland.

Coasteering

This is the latest addition to the adventure sports' world and is suitable for anyone who is a reasonably strong swimmer and has a head (and heart) for leaping from rocks. It originated on the coastline of southwest Wales and the name was derived from the similar, inland, sport of canyoning. Clad in a wetsuit and buoyancy aid, topped off with a protective helmet, you get to scramble, swim and leap your way around spectacular and otherwise unreachable sections of rugged coastline. Being tumbled around in the ebb and flow of the tidal surge is an exhilarating experience, but nothing can match leaping from rocks into the ocean for adrenaline-rush value. Most courses are based around half-day excursions, with instruction on how to negotiate the obstacles safely. Although the coasteering word is spreading rapidly, it is still predominantly a UK-based activity, with west Wales at the forefront. Courses are also available in north Wales, Scotland and Cornwall.

Hang-gliding

You may have dreamed of having wings and soaring high over the hills, but hang-gliding is as close as you can get at present. With a delta-shaped wing over you and your own prone position, your similarity to a bird lies in more than your ability to get airborne. If you correctly read and pick the thermal currents that rise from the Earth's surface, it is possible to stay in the air almost indefinitely. Beginners' courses start out on gentle slopes and tether the hang-glider to the ground to stop you from getting too high until you have mastered the feel of flying. Short-hop flights follow, and eventually you can take off alone and soar along a ridge. Taster courses are available if you just want to try it, as full pilot qualification training takes money and a reasonable amount of time. If you invest in your own hang-glider, then the costs are reduced. It is possible to fly anywhere you can find a hill and steady wind conditions, so the world becomes your potential playground.

Hydrospeeding

Think of white-water rafting and then personalise it with a one-person raft – that is the gist of hydrospeeding. There is no better way of getting up close to the frothing torrents of a river. The hydrospeed raft is like the front half of a small bobsleigh and allows you to protect your arms and head from impact while your finned legs dangle off the back to provide the power and steering. Extra-thick wetsuits are specially designed to protect any exposed parts of your body. The hydrospeeds are incredibly manoeuvrable and you can swoop through pounding rapids with ease. You need to be a competent swimmer and then a straightforward instruction session will teach you the basic skills for steering and reading the water flow. It has become very popular and courses are offered on most rivers where rafting takes place throughout Europe.

Ice climbing

Human interaction with the environment rarely comes in a more spectacular form than it does when you go ice climbing. The stark beauty of towering walls of ice, or even frozen waterfalls, contrasts sharply with the seemingly gravity-defying ascent of a person using only two axes and a pair of crampons, special pointed attachments to climbing boots. It is wonderful to feel the sprinkling shards of freezing ice shower your face each time you place an axe. Ice climbing is a highly skilled activity and involves the ropework aspects of rock climbing, so it is essential to get full and proper instruction. Although weekend courses are available, it is far better to dedicate a week to learning the fundamentals. Most course prices include the hire of all the specialist equipment needed, but you will have to supply your own suitable outdoor clothing. There are many places around the world where you can practice ice climbing, including the Rocky Mountains in Canada and the USA, the European Alps and Scotland. It is always advisable to check on weather conditions before booking as ice routes vary considerably throughout the winter months.

Kite surfing

This is the new cool wave sport where surf board riders use big, powerful kites to power themselves across the ocean, leaping from waves and pulling tricks while gaining massive amounts of air time. Some of the worldwide kite surfing hotspots are the same as those for the longer in the tooth sport of windsurfing, such as Tenerife and there are even long distance races, including one across the Straits of Gibraltar. The rectangular kites with air tubes are similar to those used for skydiving and are big enough to lift you off the ground even standing on a beach - the place to start learning this exciting new sport. Mastering kite control is essential as 'wet launching' the kite if it goes down in the sea is an advanced skill, so it is worth spending time practising to keep it flying. The best part is that flying the kites on a beach is great fun too - it's like having two sports for the price of one, which is useful as the equipment is quite expensive to buy. Once you have mastered the basics of kite flying, you can just step into your surfboard's foot straps and literally take off on the ride of a lifetime.

Paragliding

For those who find having their feet on the ground slightly mundane, paragliding is the ultimate way to fly. With only a thin seat between you and a plummet to Earth, you get to soar on thermal air ridges using a rectangular canopy that allows you to control both direction and speed. After a weekend starter course, you can be up and flying solo, though it is very advisable to take as much qualified instruction as possible to learn about the fine nuances that will eventually enable you to stay in the air longer and more safely. If you get hooked then it will be a relief to know that paragliding is one of the cheapest ways to get airborne, though it still doesn't cost peanuts. Some of the most inspiring places to paraglide are in the Alps, with Chamonix in France, the Jungfrau region of Switzerland and the mountains around Lake Constance being among the best. There are plenty of places to try your hand at flying in the UK, with the south coast area being a popular choice.

Rock climbing

Few activities require the level of concentration and ability necessary to subdue the body's natural reaction to danger as rock climbing does. Even when you are securely tied to a rope that will stop you from falling far, a tricky move has fear welling up inside you. By controlling those fears and directing that energy into your fingers and feet, it is possible to scale rock faces that, from the ground, seem to have no holds. It is essential to receive proper training in the techniques and ropework required, as the consequences can be dire if mistakes are made. A weekend course should be enough to get you started and then the world is your oyster. There are almost limitless places to climb, with some of the most renowned being in the USA, such as the huge granite walls at Yosemite, though Wadi Rum in Jordan and Arapiles, near Melbourne, may appeal too. Europe is awash with great rock routes, too, with the Alps and Spain being particularly good locations. Getting yourself fully kitted out can be expensive, but as you need at least two people to climb the costs can be split.

Scuba diving

Many people are unaware of the incredible world that exists beneath the sea, yet donning a mask and snorkel and glimpsing this other world for the first time is one of the most exciting and life-changing experiences around. While snorkelling is a great and easy way to see the bright colours of coral reefs and the plethora of rainbow-coloured fish that live on them, it is frustrating to have to surface for air continually. Scuba diving not only solves that problem, it adds a completely different dimension to the experience. To move around effortlessly for up to an hour or so, swimming among shoals of exotic fish and maybe even seeing dolphins, turtles, manta rays or sharks, is possibly the most refreshing and thrilling adventure sport you can do. It is essential to take a recognised instruction course, such as those offered by PADI, BSAC or NAUI, that shows you how to use the equipment, the standard methods of communicating underwater and how to handle emergencies. Most beginner courses can be completed in a total period of one week or so. Once you are qualified you are free to roam the world's oceans in search of the big blue.

Sea kayaking

Setting off on a voyage has always been one of the more romantic faces of adventure travel, and heading off for open oceans in a sea kayak is as challenging as voyaging becomes. The feeling of being really out there is almost tangible when waves roll through and you bob up and down, seeing the land appear and disappear behind each one. Thankfully for beginners, though, many sea kayaking trips are run in areas where the oceans are at their most placid and beautiful, and most rarely venture too far from a coastline. The paddling skills needed for kayaking can be learnt relatively quickly, a couple of days will give a grasp of the basics, but it does take time to learn enough about tides, weather, navigation and ocean currents to enable you to head off without a guide. If you think sea kayaking involves too much time spent on bland ocean, you may be surprised to hear that it is a great way to spot ocean wildlife, too. Turtles, dolphins, flying fish and even whales can be seen in some areas and the peaceful nature of paddling means the animals are less likely to be scared off. Baja California in south-western America is one of the prime areas for sea kayaking, but the more adventurous may fancy a trip to the glacial waters of Patagonia.

Ski touring/mountaineering

When winter bites, it puts paid to many adventurous opportunities, but at the same time creates others, such as ski touring and ski mountaineering, sports that may offer the most adventurous ways of getting out into wilderness areas during the coldest months. There can be few experiences more exhilarating than cresting a ridge on skis and taking in the panoramic view of a snow bowl filled with glacial ice and surrounded by craggy snow-capped peaks. Special hairy strips, known as 'skins', attach to the bottom of the skis and, together with bindings that allow your heels to lift, enable you to walk up very steep snow slopes. It is not vastly more exacting than mountain hiking, but you do need to be a competent off-piste skier to negotiate the testing terrain safely. Ski mountaineering simply involves ski touring and climbing to a summit, which may require climbing and ropework skills. While there are super opportunities to ski tour in the Alps, with the spectacular Vallée Blanche near Chamonix being one of the most accessible and do-able runs for newcomers, there are also great ski touring routes in Scotland, Scandinavia and the Rocky Mountains.

Skydiving

The thought of falling to Earth from a plane is a nightmare to some people and an exciting dream for others – the difference being that people in the latter group imagine doing it with a parachute on. If you want to have your entire body and mind overcome with a potent mixture of fear and excitement, then take yourself down to an airfield and find yourself a skydiving instructor. There are several variations available for beginners, with the simplest and cheapest being a static line jump. On this course, you are taught how to land properly, like the soldiers in those old Second World War movies. You're then launched from a plane at around 600 metres above the ground. The parachute is automatically opened on exit from the plane, so you just get to enjoy the descent. Tandem skydives involve you being lashed to the front of a skydive instructor and then launched together from a plane at around 3,500 metres. The instructor does all the work, so again you get the thrill without needing too many of the skills. If you want to fast track yourself to skydiving alone, then an accelerated freefall course can have you qualified in less than a week. Some of the best skydiving spots are in California and South Africa.

Snowboarding

With its rebellious image and street-style clothing, snowboarding is distinctly different from skiing and there has been a fair amount of tension between the two sports over the last decade or so. Things seem to have calmed now and the upstart sport of snowboarding is openly accepted at most ski resorts in the world. With only one piece of wood strapped to your feet to think about, it is easier to learn how to snowboard than it is to ski, but it requires many hours of practice to become really good. It is like surfing on snow and the techniques and body movements of the two sports are not dissimilar. There are snowboard instructors at all the major ski resorts of the world, and a day or two of learning the basics will have you whooshing down the slopes.

White-water rafting

Team spirit is the key factor in a successful rafting trip, and the exhilaration that comes with getting through a big rapid with a committed team effort puts other sports in the shade. Most rafts can seat up to six or eight people, and it is essential that everyone instantly obeys the commands of the river guide. "Forward hard", "back paddle" and "high side left" are all common commands that can make the difference between emerging safely from a rapid and the boat flipping over to send everyone swimming. There are no real courses where you can learn about rafting as it is one of the most straightforward of adventure sports. A half-hour briefing session will take you through all the commands and safety aspects and as long as you are a reasonable swimmer, you are free to go and get wet and wild. Most rafting rivers have grades between iii and vi: the latter are the domain of experts who happen to have a screw loose and the former provide a fun and challenging ride for beginners. There are endless numbers of places to raft in the world, so if there are mountains in an area then there is usually rafting, too.

STEVE WATKINS *is a photographer and writer specialising in travel, outdoor sports and culture. He is the photographer and co-author of the BBC books 'Unforgettable Things to Do Before You Die' and 'Unforgettable Journeys to Take Before You Die'.*

The mountaineer
by Sir Christian Bonington

IT DOESN'T MATTER HOW BRILLIANT THE ADVENTURE, how talented the team – if a vital piece of equipment is missing, or the food or fuel has run out, not only could the expedition fail to achieve its objective, but lives could be put at risk. Sound logistical planning ensures that you have the right supplies to achieve the objective and survive, in relative comfort and with enjoyment. The principles are the same for any type or scale of expedition or journey, though the size of the party and the nature of the objective obviously must affect the complexity of the logistics. Since my own expertise is in mountaineering, I shall use the planning of a mountaineering expedition as my model, but the principles behind this could be transposed to almost any venture.

It is important to start by deciding exactly what the objective is to be – this might sound very obvious but it is amazing how many people become confused about precisely what they are trying to achieve and end up with a set of conflicting objectives, which in turn make it difficult, if not impossible, to prepare a workable plan. There could, for instance, be a conflict between trying to introduce a group of youngsters of different nationalities to the mountains and tackling a very difficult unclimbed peak.

Having clarified the aim, the next step is to formulate an outline plan of how to achieve it. In the case of a mountain objective the first consideration is the style of climbing proposed to tackle it. There are two approaches: alpine style – packing a rucksack at the bottom of the peak and then moving in a continuous push to the top, bivouacking or camping on the way; or siege style – establishing a series of camps up the mountain, linked by fixed rope on difficult ground. The latter inevitably demands a larger team, more gear and more complex logistics. These have to be worked out in detail, from the number of camps needed, the quality of rope to be fixed if the ground looks steep, the cooking gear needed for each tent, and then the amount of food and fuel necessary to feed the climbers and/or porters while they force the route and ferry loads.

It pays to start the calculations with a summit bid of, say, two people from a top camp of one assault tent, and then work back down the mountain. As a rule of thumb, estimate a camp every 500 metres which represents a reasonable distance for a load carry. Loads of around 15 kilos can be carried comfortably up to 7,000 metres, but the higher you get the lighter the load should be. It is also important to allow adequate rest periods, so that the team doesn't burn itself out. Using a spreadsheet on a computer makes the calculations easier and the various 'what if?' scenarios can then be played out.

Planning in this detail at an early stage automatically supplies information about the size of the team needed and the kind of skills required. This will help choose a team that is not only the right size but also the right composition. This may not appear to come under the heading of logistics but it most certainly does, for without the right people to carry out the tasks in hand, the best laid plans and logistics fall apart. From this point of view, in choosing a team it is essential to have a good balance between people who are capable of taking on organisational or management roles and those with skills to attain the objective – in the case of a climbing expedition, talented climbers, or for a scientific one, people with the right scientific qualifications and knowledge. It is also important that the team is compatible, that the brilliant expert – climber, canoeist or scientist – will work effectively for the team as a whole.

The foundations of the expedition are laid in this initial planning phase and are then built into the organisational stage in the home country when everything is being assembled. If vital items of food or equipment are left out, shipping arrangements mishandled or, perhaps most important of all, there is a shortfall in the amount of money to pay for the enterprise, it could be condemned to failure before even setting out. In this organisational phase it is important for the leader to delegate responsibility

I think that maybe we do not climb a mountain because it is there. We climb it because we are here.
– JON CARROLL

effectively (in the first instance ensuring that the right person has been given the right job), give briefs of what is required and the deadlines to be reached, and finally leave them to get on with it; but maintain a reporting-back system so that if there are any critical problems, the leader can take any necessary action. This role should be one of support rather than interference.

Sound budgeting and raising sufficient funds is obviously a key task in this preparatory phase. In getting sponsorship it is also very important to be realistic over what is promised, so that not only can the promises be fulfilled but, equally important, the commitments to a sponsor do not prejudice achieving the end objective or the way the expedition is conducted.

It pays to build some slack into the schedule to allow for delays and crises. In 1970 when I went to the south face of Annapurna, we sent all the expedition gear by sea, scheduled to arrive in Bombay a fortnight before we were due to reach Nepal by air. The ship carrying it broke down off Africa and was over a month late, giving us a major crisis at the very beginning of the expedition. We got round it with the help of an army expedition going to the north side of Annapurna. They allowed us to send some gear out with their air freight and loaned us some excellent army compo rations. This kept us going until the main gear caught up with us, but we experienced a lot of unnecessary worry and delay. Even today, when most expeditions use air freight for their baggage, gear can be lost, delayed in customs or sent to the wrong place. So it pays to allow plenty of time, particularly for clearing customs.

When packing, keep in mind at which stage of the trip the different items of food or gear will be used, and also how they are going to be carried to the base of operations. Put together all the items not needed until base camp. The gear and food for use on the approach march needs to be separate and accessible. It is best carried in lockable containers and it pays to get a set of padlocks with a uniform key so that any team member can get access to communal equipment.

It saves a lot of time and hassle if containers are kept to a weight that can be carried by local porters or pack animals, and are protected robustly to withstand rough treatment and exposure to the weather. It is best to distribute similar items in different loads, so that if a single box goes missing the total supply of a vital piece of equipment is not lost – all the oxygen masks, for example, or all the matches. The other vital task is to list everything and mark all the boxes clearly with some form of identification that gives no clue of the contents to the casual observer.

Remember that certain items cannot be sent by air. It is irresponsible and dangerous to try to smuggle such items. Gas cylinders can be sent by cargo plane, but must be specially packed. The air freight agent can give advice on these matters.

Once at the roadhead, life becomes much simpler. At last everyone is together and, with luck, all the gear and food is there with you. It is just a matter of keeping the porters happy – not always easy – and keeping tabs on gear and loads. To make this easier, on some expeditions I have issued each porter with a numbered plastic disk to coincide with the number of their load, and then taken a Polaroid photo of him holding his disk and load.

An approach march can be a leisured delight or a nightmare, depending on the behaviour of the porters. Very often, problems with the porters are outside your control, since so much depends on the local situation, the attitude of the liaison officer and the conduct of the *naik* or overseer, who might have extracted a large commission from the porters in return for employment. It is very difficult to advise on any specific reaction other than to stay cool, to listen carefully and to bargain effectively.

And so to base camp. The objective – in my case, a mountain – is in sight and some might think that this is where the real challenge begins. However, the eventual success or failure will have been strongly influenced by everything that has been done in the preparatory phase and the approach. If the expedition has been planned in detail, all the essential gear that was packed in containers to go straight to base camp is now ready for use. Provided team members are fit and relaxed and happy, they certainly have a much better chance of success, or at least of having a good try at achieving the objective and enjoying themselves at the same time.

In the case of a mountain, particularly one that is unclimbed, the first priority, after making base camp comfortable, is to make a thorough recce, to check out if the actual terrain corresponds with what pictures and maps you have managed to get hold of, and to assess whether the plan of campaign needs changing or adjusting. A plan should always be flexible. It is possible to change and adapt it to circumstances, but it must be a well thought out plan in the first place. On the south-west face of Everest in 1975, we completed a detailed plan using a computer model in Britain, but made frequent changes during the actual expedition. However, without the original plan as a solid foundation, we could never have climbed the south-west face as quickly and smoothly as we did.

It is all too easy, when the weather is good, to believe it will last forever. Each fine day needs to be regarded as the last one you will get on the expedition. Equally, when the weather is bad, it is also easy to slip into lethargy. It is just as important to be poised to take advantage of a clearance.

We all want to achieve success, to reach our objective, but I believe it is important to remember that the journey is as important as the final objective. The way that journey is carried out not only determines the eventual outcome but, equally important, how you are going to feel about it in the future. If the logistics are right, if everyone works well together as a team, with each individual being prepared to sacrifice personal ambition for the good of the group as a whole, being aware of the needs of others and helping where necessary, then the venture has achieved complete success. Sound planning from the very beginning provides the foundations of that success. ❧

Sir Christian Bonington, cbe, is one of the world's greatest mountaineers. He was the first to climb the south-west face of Everest in 1975. His current project is an expedition to an unclimbed range in north-west India.

The equestrian traveller
by Robin Hanbury-Tenison

IF THE TERRAIN IS SUITABLE, THEN RIDING A HORSE is the ultimate method of travel. Of course, in extreme desert conditions, or in very mountainous country, camels, donkeys or mules may be more appropriate. The chapters on travelling by pack animal and camel, in Part 3, describe these methods clearly and give a great deal of excellent practical advice that is equally applicable to horses and which should be read by anyone planning a long-distance ride. This is especially the case if the decision is to take a pack animal or animals, since the care of these is as important as that of the animal you are riding yourself.

But for me the prime purpose of riding is the freedom that it can give to experience fully the sounds, smells and sights of the landscape through which I am passing; to divert on the spur of the moment so as to meet local people or look closer at interesting things; to break the tedium of constant travel by a short gallop or a longer canter in the open air, surely the closest man or woman can come to flying without wings.

One way to achieve this freedom is to have a back-up vehicle carrying food for both horses and riders, spare clothes, kit and all the paraphernalia of modern life, such as film, paperwork and presents. Often it may not be necessary to meet up with the support team more than once or twice a week, since it is perfectly possible to carry in saddle-bags enough equipment to survive for a few days without over-loading your horse. In this way an individual, couple or group can live simply, camping in the open or in farm buildings. If a rendezvous is pre-arranged, the worries of where to stop for the night, whether there will be grazing for the horses and what sort of accommodation and meal awaits at the end of a long day in the saddle are removed.

Fussing about this can easily spoil the whole enjoyment of the travel itself, and it is well worth considering carefully in advance whether sacrificing the ultimate vagabondage of depending solely on equestrian transport for the serenity of mechanical support is worth it. It does, however, involve a certain amount of expense, although this may be less in the long run than being at the mercy of whatever transport is available locally in an emergency, and most significantly, as with ballooning, it depends on having someone who is prepared to do the driving and make the arrangements. The alternative is to use time instead of money and resolutely to escape from a fixed itinerary and desire to cover a pre-determined distance each day. This is quite hard to do, since we all tend today to think in terms of programmes and time seems to be an increasingly scarce commodity.

Where to go

After half a lifetime spent on other types of exploratory travel through tropical rainforests and deserts, I came to long-distance riding more by accident than design. My wife and I needed some new horses for rounding up sheep and cattle on our farm on Bodmin Moor in Cornwall, and we bought two young geldings in the Camargue, where the legendary white herds run free in the marshes. Riding them home across France we discovered that the footpaths are also bridle-paths and there is an excellent and well-marked network of *sentiers de grande randonnée.* Thanks to this, we were able to avoid most roads and instead ride across country. It was an idyllic and addictive experience during which we rode some 1,600 km in seven weeks. Leaving the horses to graze each night in grassy fields, for which we were never allowed to pay, we either camped beside them or stayed in remote country inns so far off the beaten track that the prices were as small as the meals were delicious. This was an unexpected bonus of riding: the need to arrange accommodation around a daily travelling distance of no more than 45 km or so – and that, in as straight a line as possible, took us to villages that did not appear on even quite detailed maps but where the culinary standards were as high as only the French will insist on everywhere.

Later, we were to ride 1,600 km along the Great Wall of China. There we had to buy and sell three different pairs of horses, and my suspicions were confirmed that horse dealers the world over tend to be rogues. We were luckier with our mounts on similar rides in New Zealand and Spain, but with horses nothing is certain and it is essential to be constantly on guard for the unexpected. However, this only serves to sharpen the senses and when something really wonderful happens, such as reaching a wide, sandy beach on the coast, riding the horses bareback out into huge breakers and teaching them to surf, then you know it has been worthwhile.

Practicalities

This piece is meant to be full of practical advice and information, but I am hesitant to give it where horses are concerned. People are divided into those who are 'horsey' and those who are not. The former know it all already and do not need my advice. The latter (and I include myself among them, in spite of having spent much of my life around horses) have to rely on common sense and observation. It is, on the whole, far better to fit in with local conditions than to try and impose one's ideas too rapidly. For example, we learned to appreciate the superb comfort of the Camargue saddles that we acquired for our ride across France and we took them with us on all our subsequent rides. But in both China and Spain, I found that mine did not suit the local horse I was riding and, to preserve its back, I had to change to a local model, which was much less comfortable for me but much better for the horse.

And it is the horses' backs that should be the most constant concern of all on long-distance rides. Once a saddle sore develops it is very difficult to get rid of and prevention is by far the best cure. To begin with, it is wise to use a horse whose back is already hardened to saddle use. Scrupulous grooming and regular inspection of all areas where saddle or saddle-bags touch the horse is essential. Washing helps, if water is available, and a sweaty back should be allowed to dry as often as possible, even if it does mean unsaddling during a fairly brief stop when one would rather be having a drink and a rest oneself. A clean, dry saddle-cloth is essential (felt, cotton or wool), so find out what the horse is used to.

There are many local cures for incipient sores. I have found surgical spirit good, though it will sting if the skin is at all sore or sensitive. Three tablespoons of salt to half a litre of water will help harden the skin if swabbed on in the evening, but complete rest is the best treatment. The same goes for girth galls, although these should be avoided if the girths are tightened level and a hand run downwards over the skin to smooth out any wrinkles. A sheepskin girth cover is a good idea too, as it prevents pinching. If it is absolutely essential to ride a horse with a saddle sore, the only way to prevent it getting worse is to put an old felt numnah under the saddle with a piece cut out so as to avoid pressure on the affected part.

It is also vital to keep checking the feet, ideally every time you rest and dismount. Stones lodge easily between the frog and the shoe and soon cause trouble if not removed. Small cuts and grazes can be spotted and treated with ointment or antiseptic spray at the same time and a hand passed quickly up and down each leg can give early warning of heat or other incipient problems. Once again the best general cure is usually to take the pressure off horse and rider by resting, if necessary for a day or two.

While putting on a new set of shoes is a skilled business that should not be attempted by the amateur, it is invaluable to have enough basic knowledge of shoeing to be able to remove a loose shoe or tighten it by replacing missing nails from a supply of new ones, which should always be carried in the saddle-bag. I have had to do this with a Swiss Army knife and a rock, but it is much better to carry a pair of fencing pliers since these are essential in an emergency if your horse should get caught up in wire.

Your own footwear is also important on a long ride, since it is often necessary to walk leading your horse almost as much as you ride. Riding boots that protect your calves from rubbing on the saddle are useful, especially at the start and if you are using an English or cavalry saddle, but you must be able to walk in them. With a Western type of saddle and once your legs have settled down, it is better to wear comfortable walking shoes or trainers. Leather chaps, which can be found at most country shows, are also invaluable. The protection they give to legs both against rubbing and from passing through bushes easily outweighs the heat and sweat they may generate in a hot climate.

Choosing your horse

As Christina Dodwell says in *A Traveller on Horseback*, a valuable horse is more likely to be stolen and what you need is 'a good travelling horse'. Tschiffely, on the most famous of all long distance rides, from Buenos Aires to Washington in the 1920s, had two Argentinian ponies, which were already 15 and 16 years old when he acquired them. He covered 16,000 km in two-and-a-half years, covering about 30 km a day on the days he rode, but making many long stops and side trips.

Tim Severin started out on his ride to Jerusalem on a huge Ardennes heavy horse, as used on the First Crusade. In spite of suffering from heat exhaustion, it reached Turkey before being replaced with a more suitable 13-hand local pony. The ideal horse for covering long distances in comfort is one possessing one of the various 'easy' inbred gaits, which lie between a walk and a trot. We were lucky enough to use 'amblers' in New Zealand. These had been bred to have a two-beat gait in which the legs on either side move together, giving an impression a bit like the wheels of a steam engine. Once we learned to relax into the unfamiliar rhythm and roll a little from side to side with the horse, we found it wonderfully comfortable and the miles passed effortlessly and fast. However, even then we seldom averaged more than seven kmph.

Unless you are setting out to break records or prove a point, the object of a long-distance ride should be the journey itself, not the high performance of your mount. The close relationship that develops between horse and rider is one of the bonuses of such a journey, and as long as your prime concern is your horse's welfare before your own you won't go far wrong.

On a horse it is uniquely possible to let an intelligent creature do most of the thinking and all of the work, leaving you free to enjoy and absorb your surroundings. Birds are not afraid to fly near and be observed; the sounds of the countryside are not drowned by the noise of a motor or the rasping of one's own breath; and if you are lucky enough to have a congenial companion, conversation can be carried on in a relaxed and pleasant way. Notes can even be taken *en route* without the need to stop or the danger of an accident, especially if you carry a small portable tape recorder. This helps greatly in taking down instant impressions for future inclusion in books and articles which are surely the chief justification of pure travel. Photographic equipment can be readily to hand in saddle-bags, and much more can be carried.

Above all, those you meet along the way, whether they be fellow travellers, farmers or remote tribes people, are inclined to like you and respond to your needs. 🙚

ROBIN HANBURY-TENISON, OBE, is a distinguished explorer and energetic champion of indigenous peoples. He is the founder of Survival International (a charity defending tribal groups) and an author and broadcaster.

The cyclist
by Nicholas Crane

EVER SINCE JOHN FOSTER FRASER and his buddies Lun and Lowe pedalled round the world in the 1890s, the bicycle has been a popular choice of vehicle for the discerning traveller. The most efficient human-powered land vehicle, it is clean, green and healthy to boot.

The standard bicycle is also inexpensive, simple and reliable. Its basic form is similar the world over, with its fundamental parts available in Douala and downtown Manhattan alike. With the exception of remote settlements accessible only on foot, most of the world's population is acquainted with the bike. It can never be as symbolic of wealth as a motor vehicle, and neither is a bike-rider insulated from his or her surroundings by metal and glass. It's a humble vehicle. It is approachable and it is benign. Birdsong and scents are as much a constant companion as voices and faces.

Cycling is slow enough to keep you in touch with life; fast enough to bring daily changes. A fit rider ought to be able to manage an average of 80 to 100 kilometres a day. Pedalling puts you partway between pedestrians and motor cars: a bike can manage a daily distance four times that of a walker and a third that of a car.

Bikes can be carried in planes, trains, boats and cars, on bus roofs and in taxi boots. They can be parked in hotel bedrooms and left-luggage stores. They can be carried by hand and taken apart.

But isn't cycling hard work? Sometimes, but for every uphill stretch or head-wind there's a descent or tailwind that's as fun as flying. What happens when it rains? You get wet or stop in a bar. How many punctures do you get? On my last ride (5, 200 kilometres), two. How do you survive with so little luggage? It's leaving behind the clutter of everyday life that makes bike touring so fun.

Where to go

If you are doubtful about your stamina, choose somewhere docile such as East Anglia or northern France for your first trip. Beware of being tricked by the map: it's not always the places with the highest mountains that are the most tiring to ride. Scotland, where the roads often follow valley floors, is a lot easier than Devon, where the roads hurry up and down at ferocious angles. The Fens, Holland and the Ganges Delta may be as flat as pancakes, but it is this very flatness that allows the wind to blow unchecked – exhilarating if it's going your way, but not if it isn't....

You may already have a clear idea of where you would like to ride. Hilliness, prevailing winds, temperature, rainfall, whether the roads are surfaced or dirt: all these factors are worth quantifying before you leave. Then you must fit the route with places of interest and accommodation. There may be duller sections that you would like to skip; if so, you need to find out in advance whether you can have your bike transported on buses or trains.

You do not have to be an athlete to ride a bicycle, or even able to run up three flights of stairs without collapsing. It is a rhythmic, low-stress form of exercise. Riding to work or school, or regularly during evenings and weekends, will build a healthy foundation of fitness. If you have never toured before, try a day's ride from home (40 kilometres maximum), or a weekend ride.

Once you know how far you can comfortably ride in a day, you can plan your route. Always allow for a couple of 'easy' days to begin with: set yourself distances which you know you can finish comfortably, and this will allow you to adjust to the climate and the extra exercise. It will also let your bike and luggage 'settle in'.

Main roads are to be avoided. This means investing in some good maps. As a rule, a scale of 1:200,000 will show all minor roads. For safe cycling on rough tracks, you will need maps of 1:50,000 or 1:25,000. Stanfords (12-14 Long Acre, London WC2E 9LP, 020 7836 1321, www.stanfords.co.uk) is the best supplier of cycling-scale maps.

The type of accommodation you decide upon will affect the amount of luggage you carry – and the money you spend. Camping provides the greatest flexibility, but also requires the greatest weight of luggage. With (or without) a tent you can stay in all manner of places. Farmers will often let you use the corner of a field, and in some wilderness areas you can camp where you choose (leave nothing; take nothing). With two of you, you can share the weight of the tent, cooking gear and so on. If you are using youth hostels, bed-and-breakfasts or hotels, you can travel very lightly but your route is fixed by the available accommodation.

'Wild camping', where you simply unroll your sleeping bag beneath the stars on a patch of unused land, is free and allows you to carry a minimum of camping gear. Always be careful to check the ownership of the land, and bear in mind that you have no 'security' beyond your own ability to remain inconspicuous.

The best source of information on the geography of cycle travel is the CTC (Cyclists' Touring Club). To join, contact the CTC at Cotterell House, 69 Meadrow, Godalming, Surrey GU7 3HS, 0870 873 0060, www.ctc.org.uk.

The bike and clothing

Unlike a motorised expedition vehicle, a bicycle need cost no more than a good camera or backpack. Neither need it be an exotic mix of the latest aluminium alloys and hi–tech tyres. John Foster Fraser covered 19,237 miles through seventeen countries on a heavy steel roadster fitted with leather bags. And while steel bike frames may be repaired by local blacksmiths if necessary, carbon-fibre, titanium or even aluminium alloys will be beyond their skills. Destinations are reached because of the urge to make the journey, not the colour of the bike frame.

Given a determination to arrive, virtually any type of bicycle will do. The writer Christa Gausden made her first journey – from the Mediterranean to the English Channel – on a single-speed shopping bike. My early tours across Europe were made on the heavy ten-speed I had used for riding to school. Spending time and money on your bike does however increase your comfort and the bike's reliability. So does reading *Richard's 21st Century Bicycle Book* (Macmillan), the updated classic that provides the answers to almost anything velocipedal.

For road riding the most comfortable machine is a lightweight multi-speed touring bike. Gear ratios in the uk and usa are measured, somewhat quaintly, in inches – the given figure representing the size of wheel that it would have been necessary to fit to a penny farthing to achieve the same effect. *Richard's 21st Century Bicycle Book* (among others) contains detailed gear ratio tables. For normal touring, the lowest gear should be around 22 to 25 inches; the highest, 80 to 90 inches. With these ratios, a fit rider ought to be able to pedal over the Pyrenees, while the top gear is high enough to make the most of tailwinds.

Good-quality wheels and tyres are important. If you can afford it, have some wheels built by a professional wheel-builder, asking him to use top-quality prestretched spokes and the best hubs and rims. For continental touring it is handiest if the rims are of the size to take the metric 700 C-tyres. Some rims will take a variety of tyre widths, allowing your one set of wheels to be shod either with fast, light, road tyres, or with heavier tyres for rough surfaces. Buy the best tyres you can afford. Quality tyres can be expected to run for 8,000 kilometres on a loaded bike ridden over mixed road surfaces.

'Drop' handlebars are more versatile than 'uprights', providing your hands with several different positions and distributing your weight between your arms and backside. Drops also permit for riding in the 'crouch' position – useful for fast riding or pedalling into headwinds. Drop handlebars come in different widths; ideally they should match the span of your shoulders. Flat, multi-position 'hybrid' bars are a recent alternative to drops. The saddle is very much a question of personal preference: try several before deciding. (Note that you should fit a wide 'mattress' saddle if you have upright handlebars, as most of your weight will be on your backside.) Solid leather saddles need treatment with leather oils then 'breaking in' – sometimes a long and painful process but one which results in a seat moulded to your own shape. Also very comfortable are the padded suede saddles which require no breaking in. Since they never change shape, be sure this sort of saddle is a perfect fit before you buy. Steer clear of plastic-topped saddles.

It is very important that your bike frame is the correct size for you. There are several different methods of computing this, but a rough rule of thumb is to subtract 25 centimetres from your inside leg measurement. You should be able to stand, both feet flat on the ground, with at least three centimetres between the top tube and your crotch. The frame angles should be between 71 and 73 degrees. The strongest and lightest bike frames are commonly made from Reynolds tubing. An option for those with fatter purses is to have a bike frame built to your own specifications and size. Many of the top frame-builders advertise in *Cycling Weekly* magazine and in *Cycle Touring and Campaigning*, the magazine of the CTC.

Generally speaking, the more you spend on your brakes and pedals, the stronger and smoother they will be. Pedals should be as wide as your feet (note that some Italian models are designed for slim continental feet rather than the flat-footed Britisher). Toe-clips and straps increase pedalling efficiency.

Luggage should go in panniers attached to a rigid, triangulated carrier that cannot sway. Normally, rear panniers should be sufficient. If you need more, use a low-riding set of front pannier carriers (such as the Blackburn model) and/or a small handlebar bag. Lightweight items such as sleeping bags can be carried on top of the rear carrier if necessary. The golden rule is to keep weight as low down and as close to the centre of the bike as possible. Never carry anything on your back.

Clothing chosen carefully will keep you warm and dry in temperate climates, cool and comfortable in the heat. Choose items on the 'layer' principle: each piece of clothing should function on its own, or fit when worn with all the others. The top layers should be windproof, and in cold or wet lands, waterproof too. Goretex is ideal. Close-fitting clothes are more comfortable, don't flap as you ride, and can't get caught in the wheels and chainset. In bright conditions a peaked hat or beret makes life more comfortable, and cycling gloves (with padded palms) will cushion your hands from road vibration. Choose shoes with stiff soles (i.e. not tennis shoes or trainers) which will spread the pressure from the pedals and which are good for walking too. Specially designed touring shoes can be bought at the better bike shops.

Mountain bikes

If you are planning to venture off the beaten track, on rough roads and tracks, a mountain bike will provide strength and reliability. Mountain bikes evolved in California from hybrid clunkers during the Seventies, first arriving in Britain en masse in 1982. Since then, they have become lighter, swifter and stronger. For tarmac riding, a mountain bike is still heavier, harder work and slower than a lightweight touring bike. The mountain bike's fatter tyres create greater rolling resistance, and the upright riding position offers greater wind resistance. The additional weight also requires more pedalling effort on hills. But on dirt roads and trails mountain bikes are in their element: easy to control, with excellent traction and superb resistance to vibration, knocks and crashes.

Mountain bikes generally come with 18 to 27 gears, with a bottom gear of around 22 inches (though in practice five or so of these gears are always unusable because of the sharp angle the chain is forced to make when it is running on the largest front chainring and smallest rear sprocket – and vice versa). Mountain bike brakes are generally more powerful than those on road bikes, and the heavy-duty ribbed tyres are virtually puncture-proof. Lighter tyres with smoother tread patterns and higher pressures can be fitted for road-riding. For sheer toughness a mountain bike is impossible to beat, but you pay for this toughness by pedalling more weight in a less efficient riding position. 'Hybrid' bikes, which fall some-where between the pure mountain bike and conventional tourer, are extraordinar-ily versatile: well balanced and tough on road surfaces, fast and relatively light on roads. In addition touring bikes that are based around the 26-inch mountain bike wheel are now available. These bikes have the design features of touring bikes, such as racks, but offer the 'go-anywhere' capability of the stronger mountain bikes, and the wheel size can be found in most parts of the world, should the need for a replacement arise.

Buying second-hand

Buying second-hand can save a lot of money – if you know what to look for. Tour-ing bikes, 'hybrids' and mountain bikes are advertised regularly in the classified columns of the bi-monthly magazine of the CTC, the monthly cycling magazines, and in *Cycling Weekly*. Before you buy, check that the frame is straight, first by sight, and then by (carefully) riding no-hands. If the bike seems to veer repeatedly to one side, the frame or forks are bent. Spin the wheels and check they are true. Wobble all the rotating parts; if there is a lot of play the bearings may be worn. Above all, buy only from somebody you feel is honest.

On the road

The greatest hazard is other traffic. Always keep to your side of the road, watching and listening for approaching vehicles. In Asia and Africa, buses and trucks travel at breakneck speeds and expect all other vehicles to get out of their way. Look out too for carts and cows, sheep, people, pot-holes and ruts – all of which can appear without warning.

Dogs deserve a special mention. Being chased uphill by a mad dog is every cyclist's nightmare. I've always found the safest escape to be speed, and have yet to be bitten. If you are going to ride in countries known to have rabies, consider being vaccinated before departure. It goes without saying that you should check with your gp that you have the full quota of inoculations (including tetanus) suit-ed for your touring area.

Security need not be a problem if you obey certain rules. Unless you are going to live with your bike day and night, you need a strong lock. Always lock your bike to an immovable object, with the lock passing round the frame and rear wheel. For added security, the front wheel can be removed and locked also. Before buying, check that the lock of your choice is big enough for the job. Note that quick-release hubs increase the chance of the wheels being stolen. Always lock your bike in a public place, and if you are in a café or bar keep it in sight. In most Third World countries it is quite acceptable to take bicycles into hotel bedrooms; elsewhere, the management can usually be persuaded to provide a safe lock-up. The CTC sells travel insurance and bicycle insurance policies.

Expedition cycling

Bikes have been ridden, carried and dragged in some ridiculous places: across the Darien Gap, through the Sahara and up Kilimanjaro. They have been pedalled round the world, many times. And they have been used as a sympathetic means of transport into remote, little-visited corners of the globe. The step up from holiday touring in Europe to prolonged rides to the back-of-beyond requires sensible planning. The choice of bicycle and equipment will have a considerable bearing on the style of the ride. If you want to be as inconspicuous as possible, the best machine will be a local black roadster. Such a bike will probably need constant attention, but pays off handsomely in its lack of Western pretension. I once pedalled across the African Rift Valley on a bike hired from a street market in Nairobi; the bike fell apart and had to be welded and then rebuilt, but the ride was one of the most enjoyable I've ever had.

For serious journeys defined by a set goal and a time limit, you need a well-prepared, mechanically perfect machine. If much of the riding is on dirt roads, a mountain bike may well be the best bet. If you can keep your weight down, a lightweight road-bike will handle any road surface too. On the Journey to the Centre of the Earth bike ride across Asia with my cousin Richard, our road bikes weighed ten kg each, and our total luggage came to eight kg each. We carried one set of clothes, waterproofs and a sleeping bag each, picking up food and water along the way. Our route included a crossing of the Himalayas, followed by a south-to-north traverse of the Tibetan Plateau and Gobi Desert. Objectivity obliges me to note that I've seldom come across other cyclists travelling this light, most saying that they would rather carry their cooking stove, pans, food, tent and extra clothes.

Spares

Lightness gives you speed. One spare tyre, one spare inner tube and a few spokes are the basic spares. Rear tyres wear faster than front ones, so switch them round when they become partly worn. For rides of over 5,000 kilometres, in dry or gritty conditions, a replacement chain will be necessary too. In 'clean' conditions a good-quality, regularly lubricated chain will last twice that distance, although to maximise durability some experts recommend a change at every 3, 000 kilometres. The tool kit should include a puncture repair kit, appropriate Allen keys, chain-link remover, free-wheel block remover, small adjustable wrench and cone–spanners for the wheel-hubs. Oil, grease and heavy tools can be obtained from garages and truck drivers along the route.

On a bicycle I am exposed to all local experiences as no other modern traveller can hope to be. Moving quietly along at gentle speeds allows me to see, hear, and smell the country, in a way that isn't possible encapsulated in a motorcar or a bus.
– BETTINA SELBY

Saving weight saves energy. Look critically at your equipment, and have some fun cutting off all unnecessary zips, buckles, straps and labels. Discard superfluous clothing and knick-knacks. Make sure there are no unnecessary pieces of metal on the bike (such as wheel guides on the brakes).

It is useful to know the absolute maximum distance you can ride in one day, should an emergency arise. For a fully fit person riding a loaded bike on tarmac, this could be as much as 2-300 kilometres, but it will vary from person to person.

With a constant air-flow over the body and steady exertion, a cyclist loses body moisture rapidly, and in hot climates it is possible to become seriously dehydrated unless you drink sufficient liquid. You need a minimum of one litre carrying capacity on the bike; whether you double or treble this figure depends on how far from habitation you are straying. In monsoon Asia I've drunk up to thirteen litres a day.

You may have surmised (correctly) from all this that there are as many different ways of making an enjoyable bicycle journey as there are stars in the sky. I've yet to meet two cyclists who could agree on what equipment to carry. ❧

NICHOLAS CRANE is a broadcaster, author and celebrated long-distance walker and cyclist. He has walked the length of Europe and cycled in 29 countries. He has also presented the recent TV series 'Coast' on the BBC.

The charity challenger
by Mick Kidd

OKAY, IT'S HANDS UP TIME. For me the initial motivation for doing a charity challenge was neither charity nor challenge but destination – in this case Cuba, a place I'd always meant to visit but never got round to. Like everyone else, I'd noticed the increasing number of adverts for charity challenges but disregarded them on the grounds that a) I'd never be able to raise the minimum sponsorship money and b) why go all that way to do them in mainly poor countries when you can cycle from say London to Brighton at considerably less administrative cost? Obviously trekking in Ladakh/Nepal/Peru beats bypassing Haywards Heath hands down *vis-à-vis* exotic allure. But what swung it for me was a friend in Devon who had done a charity cycle ride in Cuba and was knocked out by both the place and the experience.

So now that I've done one myself, what's my opinion? The trip I went on was for the National Deaf Children's Society. It was brilliantly organised, the cycling strenuous but never so arduous as to make it unenjoyable (I'd done plenty of preparatory training). We all bonded in a common cause and the charity made heaps of money even after deducting costs. There were 55 in our group (a mixture of teachers, journalists, doctors, nurses, freelance artists and students plus the inevitable website designer) and between us we raised £140,000. About half of everyone's minimum of £2,300 sponsorship went to cover costs, although most people surpassed the minimum target so it was in effect less than half. Ours was the last of seven rides in Cuba in the winter of 1999/2000, and there are other challenge rides/treks in China, Sri Lanka, Mexico, Jordan and Iceland.

But what does Cuba get out of it? Last year the charity donated £20,000 from its aggregate net income for local projects and equipment. A similar sum is expected to be donated this year. This may seem paltry, but is still a significant amount in local terms. Nevertheless, maybe a larger sum would offset using a beleaguered country (Cuba is still severely affected by the us trade embargo) as a venue. The trip was nine days in length, five days cycling at approximately 50 miles a day, two days flying there and back and a day at either end to acclimatise and unwind. The charity had delegated the nuts and bolts of the ride – flights, bikes, accommodation, food plus mechanical and medical support – to a tour company who invoiced the charity for their services. They weren't cheap but did an excellent job, taking part in the ride themselves. They also provided an intelligent ongoing commentary on Cuban politics, economy and culture far removed from the patronising patter of the 'warmth of the people will remain with you long after your tans have faded' variety I've experienced elsewhere.

Our itinerary took us off the normal tourist routes and through agricultural landscapes (mainly sugar cane), villages and small towns where local residents, especially the children, often applauded us through. Whether this is because such sights are becoming familiar (apparently there was another charity ride going the other way not long after ours) I'm not sure. I like to think it was our being on bikes, albeit multi-gear hybrids, rather than in luxury coaches, that endeared us to Cubans for whom cycles are an integral part of getting around, as are horses and carts. One place we stayed in offered buggy rides, which in our ignorance we took to be for tourists but were in fact for residents, petrol being an expensive commodity thanks to the us embargo.

At the end of each day we'd arrive at our accommodation in state-run hotels or holiday chalets. This meant the money went back into the Cuban economy more directly than in the all-inclusive, hermetically sealed luxury hotel complexes in places like Varadero, which are funded and part-owned by international consortiums. We stayed in Varadero for two nights at the end of the ride, and I found it utterly soulless and devoid of Cubans except in ancillary roles.

Being in a large group tended to keep us separate from local life. Backpackers, for instance, can live and eat with families, whereas we were in hotels. And during the day we'd be toiling away on the bikes. Other than that, we did the usual tourist things in our free time – listening to the ubiquitous bands (music seemed to be on the wind), dancing to the salsa beats, hanging out in small bars drinking beers or *mojitos*, the rum cocktail beloved of Ernest Hemingway, or making visits to places mentioned in our guide books. My favourite was the Museum of the Revolution in Havana, with its extensive photographic record of the overthrow of Batista in 1959 and various memorabilia including Che Guevara's sock.

Tourism is a fairly recent development in Cuba – part of the adjustment following the collapse of the Soviet Union in 1991 . Tourism brings in much-needed revenue, but with it the dangers of a two-tier economy (those with and those without dollars) in a country dedicated to social equality. So our being there both helps and hinders. Still, *je ne regrette rien*. I've done my bit for charity and been somewhere I always wanted to go.

My friend down in Devon says the experience in part changed her life. I wouldn't go that far, but then I've always subscribed to the Roman poet Horace's take on travel. He wrote, 'they change their sky but not their soul who cross the sea', doubtless before setting off to do a chariot challenge in Asia Minor to raise funds for an Iron Age good cause. ❧

MICK KIDD is the acclaimed 'Guardian' cartoonist 'Biff'.

The serious walker
by Nicholas Crane

WE ARE ALL BIPEDS. WE ARE ALL EXPERTS AT WALKING. Legs require no skills to use or licence to operate. They're built in, cost us nothing to use and are greener than any other means of transport. Legs! Stick 'em in a couple of boots and they'll do thousands of miles without so much as a service. Marvellous things.

Legs have been a recent discovery for me. For years I've been travelling on bicycles, occasionally boats and, under pressure, some kind of motorised transport. Horses are fine, but are limited to particular types of terrain. Legs are versatile. You can vary your mode of transport on a whim. Rides in trains or hay-carts, buses and boats are all possible complements to a foot-journey.

At walking pace you become part of the infinitely complicated countryside. After a while, animals and birds tend not to take flight at your approach. Strangers stop to chat, flattered that you are exploring their neighbourhood at a civilised, respectful pace. On foot you pose no threat and appear to have nothing to hide.

My life as a leg-advocate began with a walk across Europe, following the mountain ranges of the continent from Cape Finisterre in Spain to the Black Sea. This 10,000-kilometre hike took me one and a half years, and was the greatest adventure of my life. I learned a lot from that walk and I hope that the notes below will be helpful to you. I must however ask you to remember that I am a newcomer to long-distance walking (my only other hikes have been a youth hostelling trip in the Peak District with my mother, a one-week hike in Wales, and another week in the Greek mountains) and so my 'tips' are based on a limited number of extremely vivid experiences rather than a lifetime's worth of muscled miles.

First, let us consider the principles.

Principles

When I began my trans-European walk I made the mistake of being so excited that I forgot to rest. I walked for eighteen days non-stop through the sierras of northern Spain. It did not occur to me to take a break until my right leg swelled up like a gourd and reduced me to an agonised hobble. After that I stopped every five to seven days for at least one day's rest. I learned that being conscious of incipient ailments will prevent them from becoming problems. Blisters, muscle strain and back-pain can be avoided by being aware of how your body is functioning.

The Romans, who were experts at thousand-mile marches, walked to a system of three days on, one day off, a routine which they found ideal for legions crossing continents. One other authority I'd like to mention is Christopher Whinney, who once walked from London to Rome and who subsequently set up the walking-holiday company Alternative Travel Group. After prolonged trial and error, Christopher found that, just like the Romans, his groups remained at their happiest and most cohesive if they took every fourth day as a rest day.

Ultimately, of course, you must find your own rhythm. There is no golden mean for everyone. If you walk one day and take two off, that's fine if it's bringing the best rewards from the journey. On several occasions on my European amble, I spent a week or so in one place, or made wide detours from my planned route, and on a couple of occasions walked *backwards* to visit places I'd missed the day before. There is no magic distance that should be covered each day; a fit walker with a medium-sized pack can cover say 20 or 30 kilometres in one day with no trouble. Sometimes I've walked over 50 kilometres in one day, but as a result have been wrecked the following day.

I'll just add that I'm not a believer in training. If you want to try a long-distance walk, just go. Take it easy and use the first days (or weeks) to get fit.

So much for the rhythm. Now, where to go? Because walking is the slowest form of travel, you do need to choose a route that brings variety on an almost hourly basis. Either you choose a landscape that is chock-a-block with physical diversity, or you learn to spot the interest in what to many would seem a dull landscape. An interest in flora and fauna, history, geomorphology, agricultural implements, mountain cultures... whatever (the list is endless) will turn a walk into a fascinating quest. Some landscapes hand the walker hourly interest on a plate. Rambling in mountains; following the courses of rivers; following coastlines: all are 'themes' which, through the natural lie of the land, will create a change of view with every hour. Also in this category is the long-distance footpath, way-marked and 'themed' to provide interest. The pilgrims' Camiño de Santiago, across northern Spain, falls into this category.

The one area of essential knowledge that is required before embarking upon a long walk in wilderness areas is navigation. This means being able to use a compass accurately and in gales and mists. It also means being able to read maps and to master 'dead-reckoning' – estimating how much time it will take to cover a certain compass-bearing. It is essential to know this before walking in mountains.

There are some terrains, and I'm thinking of mountains in particular, which are potentially dangerous for inexperienced walkers. It is important not to be lulled into a sense of false security by a belief that superior equipment is a substitute for old-fashioned savvy. Had I not spent 25 years messing about trying to climb mountains in Scottish winter white-outs, I would not have survived my trans-European wander. To walk safely in mountains, it is essential to feel confident using a map and compass in zero visibility and gale force winds on precipitous ridges. This is unlikely ever to happen, all being well, but it is a possibility and you need to be ready to cope. This kind of knowledge can be built up over time, in the company of a more experienced companion, on, say, the hills of Wales, the Pennines, the

Lake District or Scotland. The most testing ground I've ever found for navigation in mist was Dartmoor.

Saving weight has the dual benefit of making the walking less strenuous and reducing the clutter of everyday life to a minimum. I cut my comb in half, trim the edges of maps and keep my hair short, not because these minor weight reductions are noticeable individually, but because each reminds me daily not to overload my rucksack with unnecessary stores. Carrying a half-kilo of jam unopened from one town to the next is a waste of effort. And while a shortage of water is to be avoided at all costs (dehydration is lethal), it is worth remembering than one litre of liquid really does weigh one kilogram. It pays to think ahead. Ask locals where the next spring or tap can be found rather than loading up like a camel.

Practicalities

It is not worth getting obsessive about equipment, beyond the one rule of minimal weight and maximal safety. There are, however, a number of equipment items whose suitability to your needs will affect your enjoyment of the walk.

The single most important requirement is footwear. The first decision to make is between running/training shoes or boots. The former do not need wearing in, are far lighter than boots and have a 'softer' feel. Boots offer ankle support, a leather construction which breathes better than man-made fibres, a degree of waterproofness and grippy treads for steep or uneven surfaces. Again, it is down to personal preference. When my cousins Richard and Adrian made their foot-traverse of the Himalayas in 1982, they wore running shoes; when I made my European mountain hike ten years later, I wore boots. After much experimentation I settled on the British-designed 'Brasher Boot', which combines running-shoe technology with the construction of traditional leather boots. Brasher Boots are lightweight and comfortable.

Footwear, more than any other item of walking equipment, has the power to determine whether a hike is hellish or heavenly. A perfect fit is critical. My method for selecting the correct size (taught to me by Chris Brasher, the Olympic gold medallist runner and designer of the Brasher Boot) is to push my foot forward as far as possible in the unlaced boot or shoe. There should be space to fit a finger down the gap between the heel and the inside of the boot/shoe. Footwear which is slightly too tight is the most common cause of foot problems. No matter how good the footwear, extraneous factors such as wet weather or extreme heat can cause sores and blisters. On extended hikes, washing feet daily helps to prevent infection. Too-long toenails collide with the front of the boot or shoe during descents and, after a period of excruciating discomfort, will turn black then fall off. During my hike I lost a total of ten toenails, to no noticeable disadvantage. They seem fairly superfluous.

Foot problems can be largely circumvented by giving these put-upon appendages considered thought at least three times a day. At the end of a day's walk I wash my feet, even if doing so means using precious supplies of drinking water. With practice, it is possible to wash two feet in half a litre of water, tipped in a trickle from a mug. In winter, feet can be cleaned by running very fast on snow, but the subsequent pain as they thaw is dramatic. Washing feet in the evening means that they spend the night bacteria-free in the sleeping bag, thus encouraging the healing of any sores.

In the morning I inspect each toe and every point of wear on each foot. I always pierce blisters the moment they appear, using the tip of a sewing needle, sterilised in the flame of a cigarette lighter. Blisters are more likely to appear when the skin has been softened by waterlogged footwear or sweat. Morning is also the time to clip toenails which, left unattended, can wear holes in adjacent toes and abrade the ends of socks. At midday, I de-boot for lunch, giving my feet the chance to bask in ultra-violet light and my boots the opportunity to air. This pleasurable diversion has to be forsaken if lunch is being taken in a bar or restaurant.

Toe problems can be averted by using Scholl's Toe Separator. This is a small wedge of foam rubber which can be inserted into the gap between two quarrelling digits. For anyone prone to pronation (walking on the outside of your feet), a toe divider inserted between the two smallest toes on each foot will prevent the little toe being rolled under the ball of the foot and gradually eroded.

While I'm dealing with leg-matters, I'll briefly mention knees. After feet, these are the rambler's least reliable component. Aches (and damage) most frequently occur as a result of long descents or stumbles. I have no idea whether there is any physiological sense in this, but my own technique on long descents is to take exaggeratedly short steps, keeping my knees bent. Walking thus, the legs act like car shock-absorbers. The shorter strides also allow greater control and more precise placement of every footstep. It is easier to be thrown off balance while carrying a loaded rucksack, and knees are frequently the weak link which hit the ground first, or which suffer violent twisting. An accident can be caused by a minor misplacement of the foot: a boot skating on a tiny, unseen pebble, or glancing off a curl of turf, or a heel skidding on a coin-sized spot of ice.

Many walkers protect their knees by using a walking aid. There are three alternatives. A conventional walking stick is the least expensive and in most mountainous areas can be bought locally. They are usually heavy and cannot be adjusted for length. Far better is the lightweight, adjustable walking pole, such as the Hillmaster series sold by the Brasher Boot Company. These poles come with a variety of hand grips and can be adjusted to suit body weight and terrain. The carbon-fibre model weighs only 266 grams. When not in use, the sections retract, allowing the poles to be strapped to the side of the rucksack. Finally there is the combined umbrella/walking stick (see below).

After boots, the rucksack is the next most critical item of equipment. Like footwear, the rucksack should be carefully chosen to fit the wearer. A waist belt is essential, as is a chest strap. A properly-fitting rucksack divides the load between the shoulder straps and the waist-belt. Rucksacks of the same capacity can range widely in weight. In the Karrimor range, for example, the 35-litre capacity ultra-light 'Kimm 35' model weighs only 650 grams, while the high-specification 'Alpiniste 45+10' (45 litres) weighs 1,900 grams. After various experiments, I now find that it is worth carrying the extra grams to guarantee that a rucksack is comfortable. Rucksacks with non-adjustable backs are substantially lighter than the more sophisticated adjustable models. A zip compartment at the foot of the rucksack can be useful for stowing a tent, where it can be kept separate from the rest of the luggage; a sensible precaution since it will sometimes be wet.

Individual items of clothing should be chosen for their light weight, comfort and insulation properties. On my legs I usually wear poly-cotton trousers, which dry quickly and, with the 'poly' for extra strength, tend to last longer than all-cotton trousers. The most comfortable walking trousers I have ever worn were made from Ventile by Snowsled Clothing (01666 500852). Ventile is a very fine weave of cotton, which is both windproof and has an almost silk-like feel. Snowsled also make a superb range of Ventile smocks and jackets. My shirts are always 100 per cent cotton. With a rucksack semi-permanently glued to the shirt, natural fibres are easier on the skin. I favour shirts with two breast pockets for carrying my compass and money. If possible, the shirt should have double shoulders, to cope with the wear of the rucksack straps.

For summer walking I usually wear Marks and Spencer wool/nylon mix ankle socks, which are durable and which dry overnight after being washed. For extra insulation in the winter, the 'Thor-Lo' brand, with their differentially-padded panels, are comfortable and warm (and expensive). A foot-trick of which I am rather proud is my practice of carrying a spare set of 'footbeds' (the insoles which fit into the floor of the boot). When my boots get wet, I start the next day with the spare, dry pair of footbeds, thus thwarting the misery of early-morning rising damp.

I always carry an 'emergency layer' such as a second fleece jacket or a sleeping bag (which, wrapped around the torso beneath a waterproof jacket, works like a duvet). I have an 'emergency rule' which is that one set of thermal underwear is kept inside my sleeping bag, which is kept inside a plastic bag, inside the rucksack. Under no circumstances are the sleeping bag or underwear allowed to get wet. This means that in a crisis I always have a complete set of warm, dry insulation.

The item I feel most particular about is my hat, which should have a brim to keep the sun (the ultra-violet is intense at higher altitudes) from the eyes and the back of the neck. French berets are virtually indestructible but cast shade on only one part of the head at a time. More suitable is the Basque beret, with its greater diameter. Best of all is the lightweight travelling trilby, which can be rolled up like a cornet when not in use. On the head, its generous brim works well as a cranial parasol. The best trilby is made by Herbert Johnson of New Bond Street, London. It should be noted that the trilby does not perform well in high wind. I always carry supplementary headwear, in the form of a very lightweight thermal balaclava. And my waterproof jacket (whether Ventile or Goretex) has an integral hood. Reducing heat loss from the head is one of the most efficient methods of maintaining overall body temperature. The other item essential for head protection is a pair of sunglasses. In mountains some walkers prefer the glasses which have leather side-pieces fitted, which cut out lateral glare. Walking on snow with unprotected eyes can cause 'snow-blindness', both painful and damaging to the eyes.

The only item that I duplicate is my compass. Without one I am lost. I use liquid-filled, Swedish-made 'Silva' compasses. The Type 3 model tucks into my breast pocket, tied with cord to the buttonhole. The much smaller Type 23 model, which weighs only 15 grams and is supplied in a modified form for the pilots' survival packs in the seats of Tornado aircraft, is kept in reserve in my rucksack.

Without maps, long-distance walking can be erratic. Every popular mountain area in Western Europe is mapped at a scale of 1:50,000 or, even better, 1:25,000. No other series is comparable for accuracy or clarity to the Ordnance Survey, however, so Britons heading overseas must prepare for a lesser quality of cartography. The best source for walking maps in Britain is Stanfords, 12-14 Long Acre, London WC2E 9LP. For hiking in Eastern Europe, the best source is Fretytag & Berndt, Kohlmarkt 9, Vienna 1010, Austria and the Bundesamt fur Eich-und Vermessungswesen at Krotenthallergasse 3, Vienna 1080, who sell the old maps of the Austro-Hungarian Empire. The sense of history imparted by these beautifully drawn maps compensates for the fact that most users will spend 90 per cent of the time completely lost. I relied on them for walking 3,000 kilometres through the Carpathians. They were invaluable.

There is an inverse relationship between the number of days you've been hiking, and the number of tent-pegs remaining to erect your nightly home. Pegs disappear in long grass, drop down rabbit holes, or get used as a tea-stirrer then left on a tree-stump. Peg loss can be reduced by reciting BBC-man Brian Hanrahan's famous Falklands quote ('I counted them all out; I counted them all back'), when inserting pegs in the evening and retrieving them next morning.

I've often noticed how that red-handled talisman, the Swiss Army knife, is more treasured than it is used. At the top of the Victorinox range of penknives is the 'Swiss Champ', whose 29 features (among them a hacksaw, a reamer and a ballpoint pen) would be useful for hikers who think that they might be called upon to construct a biplane using nothing but driftwood and the contents of their rucksack. I carry the smallest and lightest in the range, the two-bladed Pocket Pal. I use the larger blade for cutting food and the smaller blade for less hygienic roles such as emergency chiropody.

The sun blazes overhead and hours pass, while you trudge through the fiery inferno; scintillations of heat rise from the stones and still you crawl onwards, breathless and footsore, till eyes are dazed and senses reel.
– Norman Douglas

I would not go walking without an umbrella. Furled, it can be used for parrying dog-attacks or beating back briars. Driven spike first into the ground, it is handy for drying socks. Reversing the umbrella and holding the spike converts it into a harvesting tool for out-of-reach blackberries. In the open mode, it is both rain and snow shelter, a sun shade and a handy wind-break. My favourite umbrella was obtained when I visited the 'Que Chova' ('What Rain!' in Galician) umbrella factory in Santiago de Compostela, one of the wettest places in Europe. The best mountaineering umbrellas are made by James Smith & Son (53 New Oxford Street, London): their hickory-shafted model is strong enough to serve as a walking stick, and unlike the metal-shafted models, does not act as a lightening conductor when strapped to a rucksack. A good mountaineering umbrella has 8 ribs, and it is fallacy to imagine that 10- and 16-rib umbrellas are tougher: the extra ribs create variable shrinkage in the umbrella's fabric, and thus encourage wear and tear.

After some experimentation, I have settled on the Parker 'Vector' fountain pen, which costs less than a round of beer and is available throughout Europe (on the Continent it is a favourite among French schoolchildren, an indication more of its durability than its writing quality). Such a pen is more suitable than a ballpoint, whose ink become treacly at low temperatures and leaks in the heat, while fancy fibre-tips are expensive and have to be thrown away once they have run dry – not a very green option. In sub-zero temperatures, the conventional ink in my fountain pen will thaw from frozen after a few minutes compression under an armpit. Ten spare Parker cartridges bunched in an elastic band lasted me about 1,000 kilometres of note-making and postcard writing. Uni-ball rollerball pens (by Mitsubishi Pencil Company) write well and are filled with waterproof ink.

Diet is not a facet of everyday life that many long-distance walkers are likely to be able to control to any great extent. You eat what you can find (I do not carry food from home, since part of the interest of travelling is in discovering the local food). But on extended walks, dietary deficiencies can lead to a lowering of the body's defences against bugs and a reduction of its capacity to heal wounds. During my 507-day hike across Europe I lived largely on bread and sardines, bread and pork fat, and bread and jam – the staples available in mountain villages. During the same period I ate 1,014 tablets of Vitamin B Complex, Vitamin C and zinc. I was never ill and wounds healed within 3 or 4 days, without the use of antiseptic.

I'll round off this fairly random checklist of my tips with a thought: the best way of finding out about long-distance walking is to start with a short walk and not to stop. ❧

The student traveller
by Nick Hanna, Greg Brookes and Susan Griffith

STUDENT TRAVELLERS CAN TAKE ADVANTAGE of a comprehensive range of special discounts both at home and abroad which enable them to go almost anywhere in the world on the cheap. To qualify for a range of discounts on train, plane and bus fares, on selected accommodation, admission to museums, and so on, you need an International Student Identity Card (ISIC) which is recognised all over the world. The ISIC is available to all students in full-time education. There is no age limit though some flight carriers do not apply discounts for students over 31. To obtain a card (which is valid for 15 months from September) you will need to complete the ISIC application form, provide a passport photo, proof of full-time student status (NUS card or official letter) and the fee. Take these to any students' union, local student travel office or ISIC Mail Order (OPS Hull Ltd, Unit 132, Louis Pearlman Centre, Goulten St, Hull HU3 4DL).

When issued with an ISIC, students also receive a handbook containing travel tips, details of national and international discounts and how to get in touch with the ISIC helpline, a special service for travelling students who need advice in an emergency. The ISIC website (www.isic.org) has general county-by-country travel information (provided by the guidebook publisher Lonely Planet) and links to student travel offices worldwide and forthcoming events. Also issued by the International Student Travel Confederation is the IYTC (International Youth Travel Card) which is a discount card for travellers aged under 26 but not students.

Alternative discount and identity cards are not so universally recognised but may have special features that suit your circumstances. The International Student Exchange (ISE) card is available to all students plus anyone aged 12-26. It can be ordered from ISE Cards, 11043 North St Andrew's Way, Scottsdale, AZ 85254, USA (1-800-255-8000 or 480-951-1171, www.isecard.com) at a cost of $25 or from appointed agents in the UK and elsewhere (see website). The Euro<26 card operates on a smaller scale but gives access to discounts in most European countries to members who must be under 26 (www.euro26.org). In England, the card is administered by the National Youth Agency (17-23 Albion Street, Leicester LE1 6GD, 0116 285 3781, www.nya.org.uk).

The Federation of International Youth Travel Organisations is the trade organisation of providers specialising in youth travel. Its website (www.fiyto.org) lists member organisations and companies worldwide that can be useful if looking for specialist student agencies, language courses, hostel groups, etc.

Accommodation

The international youth hostelling movement continues to thrive, despite keen competition from other hostel groups and private hostels. Hostelling International, to which the Youth Hostels Association (YHA) of England and Wales belongs, is still the first port of call for many travelling students and young people. Individual YHA membership costs £15.50 or £10 for those under 26; contact the YHA at Trevelyan House, Dimple Road, Matlock, Derbyshire DE4 3YH (0870 770 8868, www.yha.org.uk). Seasonal demand abroad can be high, so it is always preferable to book in advance if you know your itinerary. You can pre-book beds over the internet on www.hihostels.com or through individual hostels and national offices listed in the Hostelling International Guides: Volume I covers Europe and the Mediterranean, Volume II covers the rest of the world. They can be ordered by ringing Customer Services on the above number or online for £6.50 each including postage. Note that ISIC card holders over 18 can claim a discount of up to £3 on hostel stays within Britain, bringing an average overnight stay down from £11/£14 to £8/£11.

An explosion of budget accommodation for students and young people has taken place around the world and many leads can be found on the internet. For example, Hostels of Europe (www.hostelseurope.com) allows you to book at any of 3,000 hostels around Europe. Also check www.hostels.com, www.hostelworld.com or www.hostels.net for a selection worldwide. The VIP Backpacker hostel group (www.vipbackpackers.com) includes hundreds of hostels in Australia, New Zealand, South Africa and Europe; a membership card costs £16.

Three hundred hostels are listed in the pocket-sized annually revised Independent Hostel Guide Britain & Europe from the Backpackers Press, Speedwell House, Upperwood, Matlock Bath, Derbyshire DE4 3PE (tel/fax 01629 580427, sam@backpackerspress.com), at a cost of £4.95 (plus £1 postage); most are in the UK. Hostel details are now online at www.IndependentHostelGuide.co.uk.

Travel discounts

Cheap rail travel is dependent chiefly upon age and is generally open to everyone under the age of 26. Inter-Rail is available on a zonal basis – from £145 for 16 days in one zone to £285 for a month-long all-zones pass covering all 29 countries on the network as well as offering discounts on Eurostar and cross-Channel travel. Inter-Rail passes are available from youth travel agencies and from Rail Europe, 178 Piccadilly, London W1, (tel 08705 848848, www.raileurope.co.uk).

For more flexible rail travel, Euro Domino is a go-as-you-please touring pass valid for three to eight days of travel during any one month. You simply buy a coupon for each country you wish to visit. Sample under-26 prices include £23 for three days of travel in Turkey or £88 for seven days in Switzerland.

Eurolines is the name given to all the separate national coach services of Europe working together and selling various coach passes. To find out about a 15, 30 or 40-day coach pass covering 35 cities, as well as straightforward journeys from England to the Continent, check the National Express website www.nationalexpress.com. Pass prices start at £149 for a 15-day youth pass in the low season (mid-September to mid-June) and rise to £305 for 40 days in summer.

For smaller independent coach operators, check advertisements in London magazines like TNT. For example Kingscourt Express, 125 Balham High Road, London SW12 9AJ (tel 020-8673 7500, www.kce.cz) runs daily between London and Prague or Brno, with standby fares from £50.

One of the most interesting revolutions in youth travel has been the explosion of backpackers' bus services which are hop-on hop-off coach services following prescribed routes. These can be found in New Zealand, (for example Magic Bus, www.magicbus.co.nz), Australia (try www.waywardbus.com.au), South Africa (www.bazbus.com), Turkey (feztravel.com) and Europe. For example a month long European coach pass on Busabout Europe, 258 Vauxhall Bridge Road, London SW1V 1BS (tel 020-7950 1661, www.busabout.com) costs £339 for those under 26.

Hitch-hiking seems to have fallen sadly out of fashion. However ride-sharing or 'Allostop' is alive and well, whereby drivers are matched with passengers who contribute to expenses. Check notice boards in hostels or youth travel bureaux or try websites such as http://europe.bugride.com, which publicises long-distance rides offered and sought on its site. There are dozens of lift-sharing outlets across Europe, especially in Germany, which has Citynetz offices in most big cities.

In Britain, travellers with a Young Person's Rail Card (www.youngpersons-rail-card.co.uk) costing £20 are entitled to a third off most rail travel for one year (tel 08457 484950). To qualify you must be a full-time student or aged 16-25. National Express markets an NX card for young people aged 16-26. It costs only £10 for a year and gives holders a 20-30 per cent reduction on all standard fares; phone bookings can be made on 08705 808080 or www.nationalexpress.co.uk. Megabus (www.megabus.com) is increasing its network around the UK and is favoured by many students for its very low fares – starting at £1 per journey if booked in advance online.

Travel offices

Specialist youth and student travel agencies are an excellent source of information for just about every kind of discount. Staff are often themselves seasoned travellers and can be a mine of information on budget travel in foreign countries. But check out your High Street or local independent travel agent as well, in order to compare prices before making a final decision.

The leading youth and budget travel specialist is STA Travel which can organise flexible deals, domestic flights, overland transport, accommodation and tours. It is now a major international travel agency with 450 branches in 75 countries (tele-sales 0870 160 6070, www.statravel. co.uk).

Another nationwide agency that originated in Australia is Flight Centre (0870 499 0040, www.flightcentre.co.uk) with many branches in London and around the UK (1200 shops worldwide). Cheap student flights and extra services like working holiday packages are available through its specialist department Student Flights (0870 499 4004, www.studentflight.co.uk).

Working abroad

Established organisations that run working abroad programmes are invaluable for guiding students and other young people through the problems of red tape, and for providing a soft landing for first-time travellers. BUNAC (16 Bowling Green Lane, London EC1R 0QH, tel 020 7251 3472) is a student club which helps British students to work abroad. It offers a choice of programmes in the United States, Canada, Australia, New Zealand, South Africa, Ghana, Costa Rica and Peru, and in all cases assists participants in obtaining the appropriate short-term working visas. In some programmes participants have jobs arranged for them, for instance as counsellors or domestic staff at American children's summer camps; in others, individuals must find their own summer jobs once they arrive at their destination.

On behalf of the Council on International Educational Exchange in the USA, IST Plus delivers work abroad and other programmes in the USA, Canada, Australia, New Zealand, Thailand and China (Rosedale House, Rosedale Road, Richmond, Surrey TW9 2SZ, tel 020 8939 9057, www.istplus.com).

Many other youth exchange organisations and commercial agencies offer packages that help students to arrange work or volunteer positions abroad. Camp America (37a Queen's Gate, London SW7 5HR, tel 020 7581 7333, website www.campamerica.co.uk) sends thousands of young people to the US, and Camp Counselors USA (CCUSA, Devon House, 171/177 Great Portland St, London W1W 5PQ, 020 7637 0779, info@ccusa.co.uk) places camp counsellors in the US, Russia and Croatia, plus arranges work experience in the US, Australia, New Zealand and Brazil. Other agencies specialise in placing young people in families as au pairs, as voluntary English teachers or in a range of other capacities.

The best way of finding out about these mediating agencies and companies is to visit the library of a student careers office. These have key reference books and other resources, such as the useful series published by Vacation Work Publications.

According to industry sources, work experience is the fastest growing sector in youth and student travel. Established in October 2003, the Global Work Experience Association (GWEA, www.gwea.org) has about 100 member organisations actively engaged in arranging international work experience placements. The organisations include language schools providing work experience, youth exchange agencies, training organisations and student travel agencies. The GWEA website includes clear links to its members and is a good starting place for anyone interested in fixing up work experience (most of which is unpaid) in Europe.

Gap year students

Far more students have been taking a year out between school and higher education to volunteer, work and travel than used to be the case. According to the most recent statistics from UCAS (the Universities & Colleges Admissions Service), a record 28,727 students in the UK requested deferred entry, an increase of 12% over two years. This means that approximately 1 in 13 university applicants defers a place for a year. Students should apply as early as possible in their final year at school – early acceptance leaves more time for fund-raising which is usually an intrinsic part of the experience.

A plethora of organisations, both charitable and commercial, offer a wide range of packaged possibilities to gap year students, from learning to dive in the Philippines for a reef conservation project to teaching English in Nepal or Ecuador. Some placements are straightforward to arrange and require little more than phoning a UK partner agency, filling out some forms and paying a fee.

Pre-arranged placements are seldom self-financing, and most organisations charge up-front fees of £2,500-£4,000 for, say, a three-month placement in South America combining language instruction, a stint of voluntary work with a conservation or welfare project and an expedition. In a very few cases, outside funding is available; for instance the European Union's European Voluntary Service (Connect Youth, British Council, 10 Spring Gardens, London SW1A 2BN, tel 020 7389 4030, www.connectyouthinternational.com) provides training, travel, board and lodging free of charge for 6-12 month attachments on social projects in Europe.

For more information see www.gapyear.com and www.gapadvice.org or a book such as *Taking a Gap Year* (Vacation Work, £12.95) or Lonely Planet's *Gap Year Book* (£12.99). An association of placement agencies called the Year Out Group was launched in 2000. It exists to promote the benefits of well-structured gap year programmes and publishes guidelines to help students and their parents choose a responsible and appropriate scheme (Queensfield, 28 Kings Road, Easterton, Wilts. SN10 4PX, 07980 395789, www.yearoutgroup.org).

Studying abroad

To study abroad you must first be sure you can cope adequately with the local language. If possible, ask someone who has just returned for details about local conditions. The most successful way of learning a language is by speaking it with the natives. A number of British companies represent a range of language schools abroad offering in-country language courses. They are very familiar with differences between schools, qualifications, locations, etc. and what is most suitable for clients. CESA Languages Abroad (CESA House, Pennance Road, Lanner, Cornwall TR16 5TQ, 01209 211800, www.cesalanguages.com), Cactus Language (4 Clarence House, 30-31 North St, Brighton BN1 1EB, 0845 130 4775, www.cactuslanguage. com) and Caledonia Languages Abroad (The Clockhouse, 72 Newhaven Road, Edinburgh EH6 5QG, 0131-621 7721, www.caledonialanguages.co.uk), among others, have wide-ranging programmes.

For studying at a foreign university, Socrates-Erasmus grants are available to students following a course of higher education in the UK who wish to study part of their course (between 3 and 12 months) in one of 30 European countries. It is possible to study with Erasmus in every subject area from Agriculture to Nursing. The Erasmus programme is administered by the UK Socrates-Erasmus Council (Rothford, Giles Lane, Canterbury, Kent CT2 7LR, tel 01227 762712, www. erasmus.ac.uk). An Erasmus grant covers tuition fees at the host university and provides a contribution towards the extra costs which arise from studying abroad, but it does not cover all living expenses. Anyone interested in taking part should consult *Experience Erasmus*, a copy of which may be obtained from ISCO Careerscope Publications (01276 21188, www.isco.org.uk) for £15.95.

A subsidiary programme is called Lingua2 which enables students to go abroad to improve foreign language communication skills. Details are available from the Education and Training Group at the British Council, 10 Spring Gardens, London SW1A 2BN, 020 7389 4157, www.britishcouncil.org/socrates-he-language-learning.htm. The British Council also runs the Language Assistants programme whereby modern language students and recent graduates aged 20-30 spend an academic year assisting with English lessons abroad.

Ask your university, higher education department or local authority if they have any special trust funds for study abroad or student travel. Otherwise trawl through the *Directory of Grant Making Trusts* in your college or local library.

The safari traveller
by Amy Sohanpaul

YOU CAN TAKE A SO-CALLED 'SAFARI' ANYWHERE NOW, most holiday brochures to most countries offer them. After all, the Swahili word means 'journey', and not specifically 'journey in a jeep through African bush'. So strictly speaking, it can apply to tiger trekking in India, whale watching in the Atlantic, a trip down the

Amazon river or perhaps even a journey around the local supermarket.

And yet... for the purist, for the smitten, a safari is only a safari in Africa. It's a journey, yes, but one under vast skies through savannahs shimmering under the sun: savannahs softened by swirling dust, punctured by thorn trees, made surreal by upside-down baobab trees. It's stopping for still, silent afternoons that hide languorous, lethargic, simply-can't-be-bothered-to-move lions. It's the sharp, hot smell of Africa. It's the excited, rustling burst of noise from the bush as darkness falls, campfires roar reassuringly and a hundred million sparkling stars appear. Above all, it's a window to the world as it must have been at the beginning of time. At least – that's how it feels.

Catch it while you can. The winds of change blow swiftly in Africa. I spent 14 years in Kenya and even in that dot of time the decline in wildlife was astounding. Somehow, seeing it disappear in front of your eyes is more alarming than reading statistics about it. On one journey, driving on the main road from Nairobi to Mombasa, we stopped and marvelled as a herd of elephants loomed out of the bush and crossed the road – not a common experience outside a game reserve, but not an infrequent one either, in those days. A few years later we drove for days around a nearby game park, and didn't see a single elephant. That's just one example. The park, Tsavo, was

How can one convey the power of Serengeti? It is an immense, limitless lawn under a marquee of sky. The light is dazzling, the air delectable; kopjes rise out of the grass at far intervals, some wooded; the magic of the unraped prairie blends with the magic of the animals as they existed before man.
- CYRIL CONNOLLY

ravaged by drought and poaching at the time. The situation has improved; and now, like most parks in Africa where you can still see plenty of game, the animals survive mainly because of the tourist dollar.

The name of the game

Everyone has an animal that they really really want to see more than any other. Elephants, lions, buffalos, leopards and rhinos are the classic Big Five species. For some people, the gawky giraffe with its supermodel legs and eyelashes-to-die-for is top of the list, others find grunting warthogs curiously engaging, plenty want to witness the sleek speed of a cheetah.

It's best not to get too obsessed about ticking off a list, however. No matter what the brochures tell you, there are no guarantees that you will see everything on one trip. Animals have their own patterns and, while experienced guides can second-guess where they might be at any given time, this isn't fool-proof. And animals are no fools. In some reserves, cheetahs have wised up to the fact that most game drives take place in the early morning or late afternoon and have started to avoid going out at those times.

For that reason, it's best to spend a few days in one reserve. Relax, soak up the glory of the bush and of the more common creatures. If you're on constant standby for a 'big' beast, you might miss the drama of an ostrich mating dance; or the delightful 'zic-zic' sound of the delicate dik-dik; or fail to appreciate the graceful bounds and leaps which impalas insist on making out of sheer *joie de vivre*. The Big Five will probably stroll up, eventually. If you only have a week (a minimum of ten days is best, to allow for travel to the reserves), try to spend it at one place or, at most, split between two. You can cram in more reserves if you try, but will probably see less. And you will be very sore from bumpy travel.

Safari etiquette

Game reserves seem so vast that it's easy to forget that they are home to numerous animals, which were there first but may not be for much longer if their habitat and habits are not protected. The rules of the wild are essential for your enjoyment, your safety and their survival:

- Most parks have a list of rules that they give out as you enter. Stick to them. Most close at sundown: make sure you're out by then or in a game lodge or camp. If you miss this deadline and can't leave for any reason as night falls, stay in your car until found – all night, if necessary.

- Never leave your vehicle except at designated places. And never go for a walk without an experienced guide. Some parks have areas deemed 'safe' for walking – heavenly after being shaken and stirred on the road for hours. Many of these spots are chosen for their stunning views.

- Don't leave your vehicle if it breaks down, not even to change a tyre. If you're not on an organised safari, wait for the park wardens to find you on their rounds.

- Make sure that you/your driver stick to designated tracks. Off-road driving injures smaller game, particularly young animals concealed in bushes and grass. It also destroys the ecosystem: Amboseli in Kenya was reduced to a dustbowl by stampeding 4x4s. It's also illegal in many African game parks.

- Don't under any circumstances follow a predator chasing dinner. The chances of a successful kill are greatly hampered if a lioness or cheetah is accompanied by a crashing jeep. And particular care is needed with cheetahs. However thrilling it is to watch them running at full speed, they get extremely agitated if followed, can turn much faster than the average four-wheel drive in the bush and have been known to crash into them.

- Don't join the vultures circling the feast. It's better to watch animals with their kill from a distance. Some animals are so used to the presence of cars that they will carry on eating, if you don't get too close. Others find it very stressful and try to drag the kill away – don't follow them. Some will abandon their meal altogether and then have to summon up the massive energy needed to make another kill.

- Stick to the speed limit – *pole pole* (a favourite Swahili phrase meaning 'go slowly'). Your chances of spotting animals are greatly increased, and slowness gives you time to stop should an animal leap out onto the road.

- Blend into the surroundings (as much as you can in a lumbering Land Rover). Leave bright coloured clothes at home. Be very silent in the presence of animals.

Low murmurs of appreciation inspired by the beauty in front of you are probably acceptable to others sharing the vehicle. Loud cries of over-excitement, or loud cries of any sort, are just not on. They frighten the animals and ruin the spectacle. Persistent offenders are at risk from their fellow travellers, who may want to throttle them with the nearest camera strap.

■ However hot and dusty you are (and you will be) don't be tempted to take a dip with hippos, crocodiles or bilharzia. That means avoiding most rivers and lakes.

■ Don't interact with the animals in any way. This means not feeding them – people have lost fingers giving bananas to baboons. It also means not provoking them by revving the engine, making sudden movements or calling out to them. No big cat is going to obey 'hello kitty' calls from anyone.

What kind of safari?

The possibilities are as varied as the wildlife.

Once, the only way to go on safari was to go with a mobile camp. Trucks with tents, cooking equipment and staff would follow. Thankfully this is still possible, in two versions: budget, where you pitch your own tent; or luxury, where someone does it for you and feeds you with delicacies. Most people stay at permanent tented camps (which range from basic to blissful) or at game lodges (ditto).

After the accommodation decision has been made, you only need to decide if you want to safari by jeep (the usual method), on horseback, on foot or by bicycle (with experienced guides, obviously) – you can even take a canoe safari in the Okavango delta. Or you could stay in a private game reserve – the latest, most luxurious trend, and go on night-drives with spotlights to glimpse all that nocturnal activity. Then there's flying safaris – light aircraft drifting close to the game – very *Out of Africa* – or hot air balloon safaris. Take your pick.

There are hundreds of specialist safari operators to choose from, many online. If you want to leave it until you get in-country, speak to as many local operators as possible and make your choice. Be aware that some operators may swap vehicles between themselves depending on availability – make sure you know what kind you're getting, and that you will get a window seat. That usually means a maximum of four to six people, depending on the car. Another thing to bear in mind is that some parks and game-lodges don't allow children under the age of eight or 12, depending on the country: check this before you go. And don't go during the rainy season – most parks become quagmires.

You can organise a safari yourself, but by the time you've sorted out the right vehicle, equipped it, paid the park fees and found an authorised camping site, the cost will be the same as getting an expert to do it for you. In any case, breakdowns are common in the bush and it's better to have an experienced hand with you. Unless you're an experienced hand yourself, in which case you don't need to read this.

Where to go

SOUTH AFRICA: Despite a tendency for surfaced roads in some reserves, which somehow feel all wrong, South Africa takes its wildlife very seriously. It is home to

Safari survival list

Pack to be prepared – but only take essentials, particularly if you're flying between reserves – the allowance for light aircraft is minimal; and soft, 'squashable' bags are better than rigid suitcases. The basics are:

- Wide-brimmed hat or scarf for sun protection – and to keep the dust at bay.
- Long-sleeved shirts – preferably in cool but tough cotton, to protect against mosquitoes, tsetse files and sunburn.
- If you plan to walk through the bush, wear comfortable but sturdy boots and impenetrable trousers, and you should be safe from snakes and scratches.
- Clothes in neutral colours – it doesn't have to be khaki, but a sand/sludge spectrum is best.
- A fleece or jumper. Early morning and evening game drives can be cool, and temperatures plummet at night in the higher regions.
- A small torch or flashlight just in case you need to wander about at night.
- A good penknife.
- Insect repellent, mosquito coils (possibly a small portable mosquito net), anti-bacterial cream or wipes.
- Sunscreen, sunglasses
- Camera – with at least 300mm zoom, dust cover, waterproof cover and plenty of film.
- Binoculars.
- Water bottle.
- Swimming gear – plenty of lodges have swimming pools.

Africa's oldest national park, the Kruger, which is larger than Wales and slightly wilder. A long stay is best in the Kruger: it is so vast that it's easy for the animals to hide. Still, the roads do lead to popular watering-holes so you will see the local animal population popping in for a pint if you time it right. Private game reserves line the unfenced western boundary of the Kruger – Sabi Sands, Timbavati, Manyeleti and Thornybush all offer high concentrations of game. In KwaZulu Natal, the Hluhluwe-Umfolozi game reserves are the best place on the continent to see black and white rhinos in numbers. Also worth a look is the Greater St Lucia Wetland Park, which houses the highest forested dunes in the world, swamps, sandforests, a palm belt, hippos, crocodiles and outstanding bird life.

BOTSWANA: With the exception of elephants, almost every other variety of game can be found in the Central Kalahari Game Reserve – the Kalahari is the desert with the highest species diversity in the world. An organised safari is best: there are no permanent camps and facilities are minimal. The Okavango delta is Botswana's 'don't miss' attraction. The northern end is permanently etched with deep channels, placid pools and papyrus; the south is interspersed with wooded

Some things never change

(From the 1949 edition of the *South and Eastern African Yearbook and Guide*)

Please:

Don't molest or frighten the animals you see along the roads by chasing them with your motor car, or alarm them in other ways. You will make them afraid to stay near the road; and they will run off when they hear a motor car coming. Moreover, it is a most unsportsmanlike thing to do, seeing that it is very unfair towards others who might be following you by the same road. The animals are now confiding only because they have not yet learned to be afraid of cars.

Don't leave your car to take photos of animals near the roads; they will run away as soon as they see you get out of the car.

Don't bathe; there are often crocodiles in the smallest pools.

Don't become alarmed if lions stand and stare at your car. They mean no harm and in fact are looking at your car and not at you. The lion's nose tells him at once that a car is not good to eat and only smells of petrol.

Don't imagine because the lions are passive that they are therefore tame, and that you can go up and pat them. If you get out of your car in close proximity to lions you are courting trouble. Remember that a startled or frightened lion is just as dangerous as an angry one. A lioness with cubs, though she may take little notice of cars, is almost certain to attack a human being walking towards her cubs.

Don't forget that if you wound a lion or lioness you are making unnecessary trouble and creating a danger to yourself and other visitors. The animal, probably merely curious before, will become indignant and may attack you and others

Don't travel at a speed exceeding 25 mph. Remember the slower you travel the better your chances are of seeing game.

When passing through **Elephant Country** visitors are warned:

(a) To travel very slowly especially round corners, and not to pass any cow elephants with young ones, but to get away back as soon as possible, or if that is not possible to remain perfectly quiet till the elephants have gone.

(b) In the case of bull elephants which it is desired to photograph near the road, drive a little past the animal before stopping the car, and not to stop to take photographs, while he is still in front.

(c) Not to stop and photograph a herd of cows and calves, but to make haste to get away.

islands; all of which are home to masses of small mammals and birds. Venice has gondolas, the Okavango has *mokoros* – canoes that are the best way to explore this lush region. Finish off with a visit to Chobe National Park, famous for elephants, or Moremi Game Reserve, covering almost every wildlife habitat – and animal.

NAMIBIA: It's got to be Etosha. The 'place of dry water' houses elephants, giraffes, cheetahs, leopards, lions, and black rhinos – all against a stunning backdrop of desert and dunes. And although the infrastructure is improving all the time, Etosha is far from crowded – which means that the animals are relaxed. This and the clear light make for superb photo opportunities.

ZAMBIA: Smaller, more intimate lodges than in other parts of Africa, in a totally unspoilt backdrop rich in game. Lower Zambezi National Park offers fabulous views of the Zambian escarpment and a river to float down, as well as sightings of lions, elephants and buffalos; while South Luangwa is best known for its walking safaris, and Kafue for its size and incredible profusion of game.

UGANDA: Bwindi Impenetrable Forest is the place to visit. There are only about 600 mountain gorillas left on the planet. Half of them live within Bwindi. Take a trek through the dense brush and swinging vines for the exhilarating experience of coming face to face with a silverback.

KENYA: The old favourite, the best known safari destination, and therefore more crowded than other countries. As a result, the concept of staying on private ranches or houses is a growing one here. On the other hand, Kenya's variety of parks is superb, from the suburban Nairobi National Park (easily accessible for a morning or afternoon) to the lofty heights of Mount Kenya National Park. The parks are so varied and spread out that it's best to combine just one or two – or stay for a couple of months. Try an overnight at the Ark hotel in the hilly, forested Aberdares and watch animals all night long from the balcony, or spot sable antelope in tiny Shimba Hills National Reserve (just 30 miles away from the delightful marine park at Wasini on the coast), or elephants covered in red dust in Tsavo. Every animal you see in Amboseli will be against the stunning backdrop of Mount Kilamanjaro.

Then there's the northern trio – Buffalo Springs, Samburu and Shaba – all *Born Free* territory. A hot air balloon trip over the Masai Mara at dawn, watching the world and the animals awake, is like flying over an earthly Eden – but better, because you stop for a champagne breakfast. The real 'don't miss' however, is the wildebeest migration between the Mara and the Serengeti in Tanzania.

TANZANIA: As above, try and catch the wildebeest migration. Dry, dusty, endless Serengeti Plain is home to over three million animals, so despite its size – over 5,000 miles – spotting large concentrations of prides or herds is easy. Ngorongoro Crater is a self-contained paradise concentrated and protected within one crater, with exceptional game viewing. The crater is one of the best places to view a lion or hyena hunt – try and get there early in the morning. It can get busy, however. Tanzania is starting to catch up with Kenya in tourist traffic, but there are still places where you can say "I want to be alone" and mean it. One is Katavi, the remotest game park in Tanzania, a 3- or 4-day drive from Dar es Salaam; the other is the Selous Game Reserve, the largest reserve in Africa. The main attraction of Selous is the space, and a speciality is walking safaris where you are likely to encounter no other humans but plenty of game – although the elephant population is no longer what it was – great herds, some 300,000 strong once roamed the reserve. You'll still see a few, though. ❧

The clubbing traveller
by Chris Mooney

Of COURSE, 'IT WAS BETTER IN 1990'. It's the one thing that links the clubbing veteran and the seasoned traveller – an unshakeable conviction that everything was better at a vaguely defined point in the past. So if you are going around the world with the express purpose of visiting the legendary locations you've heard about, uncovering new and exciting music in its home country and meeting like-minded enthusiasts, it's something you're going to have to get used to.

It is, of course, total rubbish. Just as every traveller brings a fresh set of eyes to the world, so does the world of sweating, dancing, flirting and chatting constantly renew itself. Unfortunately, this perennial moan is the only thing that unites the concept of 'the clubbing traveller'. How, for example, do you reconcile the following experiences?

Bouncing in the perennially popular Banana Club in Cusco, Peru, to the background of head-drilling hardcore techno randomly mixed with local salsa. The floor has at least a metre of give in the centre, so even retiring wall-flowers standing meekly by the edge jig helplessly, catapulted into the air by the laws of physics.

Negotiating the sticky-floored Cocktails and Dreams in Australia's Surfer's Paradise, where every Tuesday punters claim one hour of free beer, and where ten bottles in that hour is not only common practice, but positively expected.

Laying on a straw mat on a pre-built-up Hat Rin in Thailand in 1989, taking delivery of a cold melon juice and watching a flawless purple-bruise sunrise, while in the background a squealing voice declares: 'harrrrrcore techno y'know, foo moon partaaaay' to the accompaniment of head-splitting firecrackers.

Negotiating the velvet rope outside New York's The Tunnel by peering over a bouncer's shoulder at a name on the guest list, only to find yourself at a party celebrating 'sadomasochistic art through the ages'.

No jaunt around the world is going to be the same. This guide can only give the merest hint of what is going on in every corner of the globe. The only advice you need, which is what every budding traveller wants to hear, is: get out there and define your own map of the world. But we all need a helping hand, so let's start with some familiar names.

The big three: Ibiza, Goa, Ko Pha-Ngan

Whatever your opinion of patchouli oil or The Grateful Dead, hippies do deserve our thanks for establishing three of Earth's grandest clubbing institutions.

Throughout the 1960s and 1970s, intrepid longhairs on their meandering trail round the world gradually tired of all that movement and stuck a stick in the ground. Ibiza and Goa in the 1960s, and Thailand's Ko Pha-Ngan in the early 1990s, became semi-permanent tie-died enclaves. All three offered the winning double of cheap accommodation and the opportunity to frolic naked, which may also explain their lasting appeal. These days, of course, all three are well-stomped parts of any young and excitable traveller's itinerary, but don't let that put you off.

Ibiza needs no introduction – the white isle can now claim to be the clubbing capital of the world without causing too many raised pierced eyebrows. If you've even a passing interest in the repetitive beat, you'll be familiar with the names of the main clubs – DC10, the terrace at Space and Pacha in particular are absolutely stunning, and that goes for the decor, the music and the bar staff.

Stay out of San Antonio if you don't like beer and football, although make sure you see at least one sunset from Café Del Mar or Café Mambo. Don't fall asleep on the beach. The season runs from June to September, and for a late summer break the closing weekend parties are hedonism at its most eye-popping. The website www.ibiza-voice.com/ contains unbiased updates and sensible advice for a visit.

Goa, on the south-west coast of India, is the original hippy port that is now home to backpackers looking to see if all they've heard is true. By and large, it is – Calangute is the 'party beach', but for a long stay it can become oppressive. A good plan is to stay in Baga, a bit further north – it has all the beauty of Calangute, but more opportunities to escape the crowds. Don't expect groundbreaking music – a psychedelic trance regime is strictly enforced – but the white beaches, sunsets and transcendental conversations are all beautiful. Man.

Hat Rin beach on Ko Pha-Ngan is home to the infamous 'full moon parties', held, well, every full moon. Until fairly recently you could only get here by bribing a willing local fisherman to take you from Ko Samui, but you can now catch a ferry straight from Surat Thani on Thailand's east coast, or even fly to Ko Samui's new international airport and jump on a speedboat. Hat Rin is surprisingly small, and it's well worth to get away from its increasingly concrete beach: the rest of the island, and Ko Tao to the north, both come close to the conventional descriptions of paradise. Back on the main beach, time seems to obey different rules – many people have lost whole weeks falling into the papaya shake, seafood and sun lifestyle. It's also not to everybody's taste – the scathing parody in Alex Garland's *The Beach* is transparently based on Ko Pha-Ngan, complete with travelling one-upmanship and some seriously damaged psyches.

Warning: If you come across someone at any of these three destinations who has been there since 'the very beginning' (a sliding date that will tend to vary with each storyteller), don't try and get much sense out of them. You won't.

Where else can I go?

One of the world's more timeless clubbing events is The Berlin Love Parade – the one time that the city completely throws off its somewhat drab reputation and takes to the streets in style. The two days of homespun techno, sequins and Teutonic mayhem make you wonder where on earth these people get to for the rest of the year. It tends to take place around May, but not much forward planning is needed – accommodation is cheap and plentiful.

Forward planning, however, is vital if you're going to the Rio Carnival. This needs no introduction, running from Sunday to 'Fat Tuesday', 40 days before Lent (usually February or March). You won't be alone in the crowds of tourists, but it's guaranteed to leave a smile tattooed to your mouth for the full four-day celebration. The usual caution applies when travelling in Rio – don't carry large amounts of money, keep to the main streets and don't stray too far from the town centre.

The Sydney Mardi Gras also takes place around March; it's a time when the city's gay and lesbian population celebrate as only Australians can. Last year's highlights included a float made entirely from beer cans, a mobile lesbian wedding centre and a 'tallest tranny' competition. End the evening in the clubs of Kings Cross and Pitt Street and you'll have enough tales to bore your friends for weeks.

Ayia Napa in Cyprus is now the world convention for garage and R'n'B every summer, with top DJs promising residencies. The town itself shares Ibiza's beered-up temporary clientele, but the atmosphere rarely goes beyond frisky. Seeing Mickey Finn and the Ganja Kru gleefully playing their raucous drum'n'bass to a small

Young men should travel,
if but to amuse themselves.
– LORD BYRON

crowd of bewildered Cypriots is just one lasting memory – although these days you're more likely to be rubbing shoulders with footballers and fake tans.

If you're heading to Japan, Tokyo's Shibuyaku district is unparalleled for ice-cool posing, superb homegrown techno and hip-hop and a strict 'no-dancing' policy – look cool at all costs. The clothes and styling are obsessively dapper, and you're also likely to pick up some superb outfits to mail home. Just don't expect them to be fashionable for a few years.

For the more skilled bloggers out there, try and invite yourself to Miami's Winter Music Conference (don't worry, 'winter' doesn't mean it's cold). Every DJ, record label, hack and hanger-on invades South Beach for the most complete selection of music and venues you'll find.

But just take a look at the itinerary of any big DJ for the full story of clubbing around the world. For example, at the time of writing, David Morales' last two weeks were spent spinning in London, Taipei, Athens, Vancouver, Montreal, Mexico City, and Miami. And always remember a golden rule – follow the heavens. If you're in a beautiful part of the world and there's a full moon or eclipse, someone somewhere will be hosting a party worth being at.

Dos

Like the best restaurants and the best guesthouses, the best clubs are not always listed in handy guides like these. You'll need to get out there and talk to people (locals, fellow thrill-seekers, the melon-seller, anyone). A truly unique clubbing experience is one of the only joys left in travelling that can't be exhaustively researched and printed in a book – in a year it will be gone.

Visit local record shops, whether it's DownTown Records on New York's West 25th St – a vinyl junkie's dream – or a tin shack booming out reggaeton in Caye Caulker, Belize. Buy a tape in each one and you'll have an amazing set of memories, not to mention reams of unlistenable-to tat that 'sounded good at the time'. And as at home, search out any magazines, flyers and fanzines – the quickest route to where you want to be.

The internet is obviously essential – it's more up to date than the advice you picked up two months down the road, and chat rooms are often full of like-minded people only too willing to trade stories. The website www.clubbing.com has reliable guides to the major cities around the world, and local music websites are never hard to find: google your favourites and follow your nose.

Another tip that tends to go against the grain: carry a reasonably smart, crease-free outfit in your backpack, including shoes that aren't trainers. Heavy and annoying, yes, but if you're intending to go out anywhere grander than the local pub in a major Western city, they won't let you in wearing Birkenstocks and a 'Free Tibet' t-shirt. Australia, France and the USA are particularly strict.

ID with a photo is also a must for city nightclubs – even a UK driving licence often isn't enough if it doesn't have a picture. If you're younger than 21 you may have the occasional problem, but an international student card with a slightly 'optimistic' birth-date will get you past most doormen.

Don'ts

Be careful that you're not the kind of 'clubbing traveller' who is also the 'selfish hedonist'. Don't throw your rubbish everywhere – beautiful places became popular for a reason. Respect local customs at all times – there may be a big discrepancy between acceptable behaviour at home and the country you're in. You may offend religious sensibilities and local custom by assuming the world loves to dance to loud drum'n'bass in Lycra and bikinis. Anyone who has spent time in Thailand or India, among a tolerant and religious people, will have seen their occasional dismay at behaviour they cannot condone. Be aware of your surroundings.

'A global clubbing culture is spreading sexual diseases around the world' screeched a headline in a recent issue of the *Nursing Times*. If you're going to have sex with strangers (and that's half the point, surely), always use a condom.

And, most importantly, remember that nightclubs picked up a seedy reputation for a reason. Tales of clubs in Patpong being locked until everyone pays to get out are not urban myths. Use your head – which brings us to the next subject.

Drugs

Whether you like them or not, and it's impossible to deny that many people do, drugs are part of many clubbing cultures. But before you join in, consider the following facts carefully.

You're often nowhere near the kind of medical help you may need, you're not in a controlled environment, and you're more likely to be experimenting with something you haven't tried before (and by and large, drugs in a country outside the UK tend to be stronger than the much-travelled and stepped-upon produce our national youth consume). Most importantly, drug laws are usually harsh and, contrary to rumour, often enforced.

Working as a DJ

Working in clubs abroad is not as hard as you may think, although the pay is likely to be restricted to board and expenses. Budding DJs will need their own records, something that obviously needs planning. You're unlikely to lug mountains of vinyl around on the off chance, but most people looking for work leave them in a left-luggage locker and chance their arm. Most clubs these days will tolerate CD-mixing, but not all, so don't rely on it. It doesn't look as cool, anyway.

Often the right accent, the right record names to drop and a convincing sound-ing DJ history (even if it's three nights at The Wheeltappers and Shunters, Armley) will go far in a world that often slavishly follows the West in dance music trends. Happily, though, a lot of the world has yet to discourage enterprising and talented DJs, a complaint you hear more and more in the UK. So if you know you can mix and entertain a crowd – rather than just think you can – give it a go.

The up and coming scene

If you really want to join the club of 2015 who will confidently and dismissively claim that 'it was better in 2005', then you should know that Eastern Europe is rapidly destroying its reputation for bad haircuts and worse music. A refreshing lack of cynicism and pragmatic creativity is throwing up some forward-thinking clubs. A recent trip to Talinn in Estonia revealed hidey-holes such as Privé – home to the most beautiful crowd this correspondent has ever seen. Don't dress down – as the young people throw off their communist shackles, bling is definitely king.

Canada is also emerging from America's shadow – particularly in Vancouver. The happy coincidence of a snowboarding community, beautiful scenery, and the same idealistic anti-corporate vibe that spawned such places as Goa are coming together to offer more fine venues to dance until sunrise.

Have a great time

And don't forget – if you're setting off on a trip around the world there's much, much more to travelling than music and dancing. Make the most of every place you visit, see the sights, meet the people and take time to relax. Nightlife is all very well, but the world looks better in daylight. Have a great time. ❧

CHRIS MOONEY started his career at the Ministry of Sound and is now International Editorial Director of FHM. He was Radio 4 Young Critic of the Year in 1993.

The spiritual traveller
by Rupert Isaacson

IT WAS NEVER MY INTENTION TO BECOME A 'SPIRITUAL TRAVELLER'. Nor do I know if I really qualify for the title, having never stayed in an ashram or fol-lowed a guru. It all happened in spite of myself, through a series of accidents rather than any thought-out design. It began, I think, when I was 19, on my year off be-tween school and university. I was visiting a cousin who was a born-again Christ-ian and lived in Botswana. "So Rupert," he asked me on my first night in his hot, drought-ridden country, while huge moths and other insects I didn't recognise fluttered at the candles: "At what stage in your spiritual odyssey are you?"

I had no answer. I was a teenager, concerned with girls, adventure and, well, girls. It had never occurred to me that my life might be a spiritual journey. But despite my inability to respond, and my innate resistance to my cousin's rather rigid brand of spirituality, the question resonated. And three years later, while living on my wits as an illegal immigrant in Canada, it raised its head again. I had been surviving any old how, doing various kinds of labouring jobs, when it occurred to me that I might be able to make my living by my pen – or rather, begin the long, long process of establishing such a living. I was living in Montreal at the time. While there, a story much in the Canadian newspapers concerned the intention of a government-sponsored power company called Hydro Quebec to flood an area of land equivalent to the size of France in Northern Quebec. The water and hydro power would be sold to America. Problem was, the land belonged to the Cree Indians, and they didn't want the flooding. No one was reporting on the story back in the UK. I managed to get an on-spec commission for a British magazine and headed north to do my first reportage.

What I found was a people intimately connected with the land, and who were not afraid to apply the words God and spirit to everything around them. Trees, rocks, water, animals, people, even machines – everything was seen as a manifestation of divine spirit. The woods around the Crees' canvas settlements echoed to the clack of bones and antlers tied to the trees to honour and invoke animal spirits they had taken. Medicine bundles full of prayers were fastened with strips of caribou hide to the forks of silver birch trees. They believed that to take more from the forest than was needed was to abuse God, but that to take as much as was needed was to honour God. This deliberate, focused, intimate relationship with a God of all things seemed to give the Cree a palpable strength of resolve. They won their battle against Hydro Quebec, and safeguarded the land. And I came away questioning my own world view. The Crees' belief in the interconnectedness of things had a kind of instinctive logic to it that was hard to ignore.

A few months later, back in Britain, the chance came my way to update a guidebook to – as it happened – spiritual retreats. I spent several months tramping up and down the UK, staying in Benedictine monasteries, Buddhist centres, New Age/Pagan communities such as Findhorn in Scotland, and even colleges of the pan-religious Ba'Hai faith. During that time I learned that – interested though I was – I was not yet ready for the rigour of a specific, regular spiritual practice. Yet I could see that life without such a practice was only half a life – the people in all these places were just too damn fulfilled by their own spiritual practices to dismiss. And I could see that, whether I liked it or not, my life was – as my cousin had once told me – a journey towards finding my own spirituality. But I was hung up on the idea of virtue: how could I try to follow a spiritual path when I had a young man's libido and thirst for adventure to contend with? It seemed an insoluble quandary.

The following years – the mid to late 1990s – brought a succession of contracts to write guidebooks to South Africa, Zimbabwe, Botswana and Namibia. These projects revived an old interest in the wild Kalahari area, the vast dry grassland that lies at the centre of all four countries, and which my South African mother had told me stories of when I was a child growing up in grey, unexotic London. Many of those stories had been about the svelte, golden-skinned hunter-gatherers who inhabited that vast land of singing grasses – the people known as Bushmen. I began to get more curious about these people, whose culture (it was said) dated back at least 30,000 years. Yet it wasn't easy to make contact with them. After several attempts to overcome the obstacles of vast distance, the need for an expensive 4x4, language barriers and lack of local knowledge, I finally managed to meet and make a friend among the Ju'/Hoansi Bushmen of northern Namibia. One of the last clans to live almost entirely by hunting and gathering they – like the Cree – were resisting the appropriation of their land; in this case by aggressive, cattle-owning tribes such as the Herero, Batswana and Ovambo, who wanted the Bushman hunting grounds for grazing.

Perhaps inevitably, I became quickly drawn into reporting on the Bushmen's emerging political struggle. Two communities, the Xhomani of South Africa and the Nharo of Botswana, eventually became sufficiently comfortable with me to invite me to the trance, or healing, dances for which the Bushmen are famous. These dances last all night, a chorus of women weaving a sonic web of hand-clapping rhythm and shrilling song while the men dance a slow-stamping circle between them and the fire, led a by a healer. When the healer achieves his trance, the sight is spectacular; he shrieks, sobs with the pain of it. Blood and mucus pour from his mouth and nose. Quite miraculous healings take place – I have seen, for example, a woman cured of angry red swellings on her legs, and a child's whooping cough taken away in a single night of dancing. But almost more important than the individual healings is the effect these dances have on the communities themselves. Ancestral spirits are called in to flush out any tensions and conflicts that threaten the unity of the group. The importance of this cannot be over-emphasised. As Dawid Kruiper, leader of the Xhomani Bushmen, once told me: "We are the jackals, the little ones who sit in the dunes and wait while the lions eat." A pacifist culture surrounded by warrior societies – both black and white – the Bushmen were certain that this continual renewal of spiritual strength through the trance dance had given them the strength to survive the continual assaults that it has been their lot.

A good traveller is one who does not know where he is going to, and a perfect traveller does not know where he came from.
– LIN YUTANG

They also showed me, sometimes very graphically, how leading a spiritual life does not necessarily require being a saint. All the Bushman healers I know drank (though not to achieve trance). Many of them cheated on their wives, fought sometimes, and said and did thoughtless things. And the same is true of healers I have met at home. Though not so extreme a character as the Bushman shamans, one Cornish healer I know is very much a red-blooded male. Yet his ability to heal – by channeling love, as he calls it – is extraordinary. He once healed me, long distance, of a blinding toothache (he was in Cornwall, I was in Idaho, trying to live-capture a mountain lion in a snowstorm as part of a wildlife study). Another time, when I fell from a horse in Colorado and got up coughing blood, I made a successful mental appeal to him – 9,500 kilometres away – to stop the bleeding. And these episodes pale beside what he has done for cancer patients. As he says: "God expects devotion, not perfection."

Recently, during this life of travelling to and fro between the Kalahari (where most of my work is), England (where my commissions come from) and America (where I now live), I have become more interested in the Eastern traditions. Most of this has come through my wife, whom I met in India. Neither of us were there for any spiritual purpose – she was collecting data for her psychology PhD among Indian high school students and I was in between Africa projects, writing another guidebook. But my wife, whose hippy-minded Californian parents introduced her early to the Hindu and Buddhist traditions, already had a daily meditation practice. The equanimity this brought her was evident from the start of our relationship. I felt inspired to follow. Though my practice is, as yet, much more erratic than hers, together we have been exploring yoga and the teachings of the Vietnamese Buddhist monk Thich Nhat Hanh, who preaches a philosophy of non-attachment to objects and ideas, and who was highly influential in the peace talks that brought an end to the Vietnam War. Coming soon is my first yoga retreat – which will take place on a remote ranch in northern Texas. And I am working up the courage to try, this summer, the discipline of my first meditation retreat, hopefully at Thich Nhat Hanh's Plum Village community in Southern France.

Which brings us back to where we began – travelling with a spiritual purpose. It is a cliché to say that life itself is a spiritual journey. But, like most clichés, it holds true. Although I never set out to travel as a means to a spiritual end, it happened anyway. Through the Cree and the Bushmen I learned the necessity of honouring God in all things and applying love to all situations – or at least as much as possible, given the limitations of ego and desire. Without the strength that their beliefs brought them, these two peoples might well have succumbed to the outside aggressors. And from the isolated spiritual communities of the West I have learned that a life lived in fear of the word God is a life devoid of any real meaning. Now, it seems, I am at last about to start travelling with more of a direct spiritual purpose in mind. But where this will lead, I have no idea. All one can do – in this as in all journeys – is begin. ❧

Rupert Isaacson's account of his time with the Bushmen is 'The Healing Land'.

The retreat traveller
by Stafford Whiteaker

G OING ON RETREAT IS THE ALTERNATIVE HOLIDAY that is winning new converts by the thousand every day across Europe and the United States. Here is the ultimate journey to that most mysterious place of all – your inner space. It is a way of recharging your energies and getting some peace and quiet in a hectic and demanding world. It is a chance to get away from it all, to think things through, and to reflect on your life and relationships. Travelling this way means shedding stress and rediscovering the inner person.

Who goes on retreat?

Going on retreat can be an exciting adventure for anyone. You meet people of all ages and from every kind of background – students, housewives, grandparents, business people, the rich, the famous and the unemployed. You do not have to be a Christian or Buddhist or indeed religious at all, or know anything about spiritual things, even if you stay in a monastery. People of all faiths and none go on a retreat. But a retreat is a spiritual adventure, and so the mind, body and spirit are all involved, with unity of the whole person as the goal. This process can be a lot of fun as well as a way to renew the inner person.

What is a retreat?

A retreat is simply a deliberate attempt to step outside your ordinary life and relationships and take some time to reflect, rest and be still. It is a concentrated time in which to experience yourself and think about your relations to others – and, if you are fortunate, to gain a sense of the eternal. It can give you a view of the world that surpasses the one from the highest mountain and is bigger than any ocean.

There is a wide and international choice of retreat places, from Christian, Buddhist and Hindu to Yoga and Alternative Spirituality centres. Alternative Spirituality is a collection of many ideas and practices aimed at personal growth, which may range from alternative healing practices, reincarnation, environmental concern, inner voice singing and telepathy to occultism and spiritism. Many of these ideas, techniques and approaches spring from well-established traditions of healing, self-help and self-discovery.

No matter where you go – traditional monastery or ashram, healing centre or workshop on shamanism – the result should be the same: self-discovery and a new view of life. A retreat may last from a day to many months, but for most people a long weekend or a week make the best lengths of stay.

Almost all places of retreat in Europe are Christian, Buddhist or Alternative Spirituality based and the use of a particular approach in the form of spiritual exercises is common. These incorporate various ancient and modern forms of meditation, contemplation, vocal and mental prayer, ways of looking at reality, and other techniques that clear up mental clutter, put your body in a relaxed state and serve to open up the inner person. Such activities are designed to make you fully aware of yourself and others in new and refreshing ways.

The ways in which humanity handles its spiritual dimension are innumerable, and dozens of approaches are available today. For Christians, the spirit is helped to become open to love and to the discovery of God's will. Buddhist practices develop a capacity for awareness and compassion, so that we may become more awakened to reality. Retreats based on Native American shamanistic practices may lead into the spirit world. Other spiritual traditions aim to bring consciousness of the unity of all creation and of the eternal.

These are enormous goals – but then, why not? Unlike the mind and body, your spirit goes forth with unlimited prospects. You were born fully equipped for this kind of travel.

Different kinds of retreat

Retreats divide into two major groups : private retreats to which you go alone, and group retreats, which often have a theme and cover a particular topic or approach to spirituality and inner healing. Many group retreats take the form of workshops lasting a week or a weekend. Some are designed to help you unwind. Others are highly structured around a particular system of spiritual exercises, such as those of Ignatius Loyola, or based on a well defined-form of meditation such as Vipassana.

The private retreat

Here you are strictly on your own. You decide what you will do and how you will approach your sanctuary time. You can opt for self-catering if you don't want the meals on offer. There will be time to walk, read and just rest. No radios or television or mobiles here – just your inner voices. All is simple, easy and peaceful.

The traditional retreat

Traditional weekend retreats are the most popular option, and if you are in a group are likely to run along the following lines. You arrive on Friday evening, find your room and meet the retreat leader and other guests. After supper there may be a short discussion about the programme. Then you might go for a walk in the garden or spend some time getting acquainted. Early to bed is the usual rule, but not necessarily early to rise. From the first night, you cease doing much talking except when gathered together for a group discussion. There may be prayer or meditation. If you are in a monastery there may be set times for spiritual practices such as sung prayers, which you can attend if you want to.

Theme and activity retreats

These offer courses and study that combine body and spiritual awareness. The methods used spring from alternative healing practices, group psychology, or are based on rediscovering traditional religious forms of creating spiritual awareness. You enter an activity, such as painting or dance, through which you may gather your feelings, senses and intuition together into a greater awareness of yourself, of others and of life as part of the cosmic creation. There are a great number of ways to explore this form of retreat. Some are ancient arts and others very much of our own time. Yoga retreats employ body and breathing exercises to achieve greater physical and mental stillness as an aid to meditation and contemplation. Embroidery, calligraphy, and painting retreats focus on awakening personal creativity. Nature and prayer retreats help you to see things freshly, appreciating colour, shape and texture to heighten your awareness of creation at work all around you.

Healing and renewal retreats

Ancient and modern techniques are drawn upon to help achieve this goal in a healing retreat. These may range from discovering the child within you, to flotation sessions, nutritional therapy, holistic massage or aromatherapy. The established churches have regained their awareness of this almost lost aspect of their faith. Now inner healing and healing of the physical body through prayer and the laying on of hands have become prominent features of many Christian ministries.

Renewal retreats

A renewal retreat is usually Christian and is seeking to find a new awareness of the presence of Christ, a deeper experience of the Holy Spirit, and a clearer understanding for the committed Christian of his or her mission in the Church.

Taking the family or going just for the day

For those places that have suitable facilities, a whole family may experience going on retreat together – even the dog may be welcome in some places. This needs to be well-planned and worked out so that each member of the family from the youngest to the oldest has a real chance to benefit from the experience. Buddhist centres and monasteries often have a children's Dahampasala, which is a school study session held each Sunday. Some convents offer crêche facilities for mother-and-baby day retreats. Many places have camping facilities or a family annex.

Meditation retreats

These are for the study and practice of meditation from the beginner level to the advanced practitioner. It is a way of opening yourself to an inner level of wellbeing. There are many kinds of approaches to meditation from the various Buddhist traditions to those of the Christian and Hindu faiths as well as non-religious ones.

The experience of silence

The most ancient retreat of all is the one of contemplation and solitude. Here you live for a few days in that great school of silence in which the legendary hermits and saints of old sought God and made all else unimportant. Silence and stillness are very great challenges in this age of diversion and aggression. Even after a few hours of stillness, an inner consciousness arises and those bound up in busy lives are often surprised at the feelings which surface. This kind of retreat is best done in a monastery or convent where the atmosphere is very peaceful.

Going on retreat

Once you decide to go, select a place which strikes you as interesting and in an area you want to visit. Most places have a brochure or list of activities which includes charges. Write, giving the dates you would like to stay with an alternative, and making it clear whether you are a man or a woman, for some facilities are single gender. You need not declare your faith or lack of it or your age. Enclose a stamped, self-addressed envelope.

Going on retreat for people with disabilities

The number of retreat places offering facilities for independent people with disabilities is increasing all the time, but always double-check before booking so that you know exactly what is on offer.

How much does it cost?

Room and food are usually included in the price. Costs are modest in comparison with ordinary holiday hotel rates. In France, for example, you can expect to pay from 40 to 60 euros per day for full board. In Britain the range is £25 to £35 a day, and weekends cost between £55 and £250. Expect most courses and workshops to cost about the same as programmes of similar quality at colleges or craft centres.

Alternative Spirituality places, offering healing therapies and special counselling, usually charge a commercial rate for accommodation, treatments and courses. These range from £75 a day to over £350 for a weekend, plus individual treatment fees. Many Christian and Buddhist retreat houses refuse to put a price on their hospitality and ask only for a donation. If you are a student or unwaged, a special lower rate is often possible. Some places offer camping or caravan facilities or a room with a common kitchen for DIY eating.

Food

Vegetarians and special diets are often catered for in Britain and the United States, if you give advance notice. The food in other countries is apt to reflect the national diet and include meat. Self-catering facilities often exist in retreat guesthouses and this is one way around diet problems.

A bed for the night

The hospitality traditionally offered by monasteries and convents around the world is still available today. If you have little money, knock on the door and say so – you are likely to find a meal and a bed for the night. A bit of gardening or cleaning is usually welcomed as a way of repaying such hospitality, bearing in mind that many religious communities are either poor or have too few members to fulfil their practical needs. Many monasteries still have rooms only for guests of the same gender as members of their own community, though this is changing.

Further information

The Good Retreat Guide by Stafford Whiteaker (Rider £12.99) lists over 400 places in Britain, Ireland, France and Spain; *Sanctuaries* by J & M. Kelly (Bell Tower, NY) covers the USA. In France try the *Guide des Centres Bouddhistes en France* (Editions Noésis, Paris) and the *Guide des Monastères* by Maurice Colinon (Editions Pierre Horay). For India, *From Here to Nirvana* by Anne Cushman and Jerry Jones (Rider £12.99). For other countries you will probably need to contact a religious organisation to find out what is on offer. OTHER CONTACTS: Retreats Association, 256 Bermondsey Street, London SE1 3UJ (0845 456 1429); Friends of the Western Buddhist Order, 51 Roman Road, Bethnal Green, London E2 0HU (020 8981 1225). ❧

STAFFORD WHITEAKER is author of 'The Good Retreat Guide'.

The travelling artist
by Mary-Anne Bartlett

TRAVEL INCREASES CREATIVITY. After all, travel is inspiring - it requires us to think and act creatively. A nomadic artist can take their skill anywhere in the world and, with few materials, can enjoy brilliant cross-cultural communication and follow other interests, such as social development or wildlife conservation. I view travel art as a healthy throwback to Victorian-style documentation, first-hand message-bearing in a medium packed with memory and personal informa-tion – and it allows its future viewers to travel in their imagination. There is noth-ing more intriguing to look through than a travel-log sketchbook complete with all its annotations and comments, sketches, paintings, quotes, tickets, etc.

Making art has become my reason to travel – a mad and wonderful scramble of images. I've exchanged portraits with Siberian snow sculptors, painted murals in airports, sketched camels in India, drawn colourful markets across Europe and recorded exhilarating sights in Africa. As I paint I find myself flung between adrenaline and relaxation, but I know I am taking in all the detail of what I see.

Once you've cracked the first blank page, art is addictive, you want to record everything you see - and others soon catch the creative travel bug. Recently on Art Safari we sketched alongside three game scouts who lay down their guns in their new-found addiction to drawing (never mind the elephants, boys).

As an artist you travel with an open and flexible mind - you never know when or where or what the next inspiring sight will be. You learn to observe your envi-ronment differently, with an artists eye, ready to remember the next typical, curi-ous or exotic image, the next fleeting moment or scene from the sublime. Of course, if you are determined to catch a particular subject, then go to the right place for it – nudist beaches are great for life drawing!

What kind of an artist are you?

There are three types of artists who travel: the 'painting traveller', the 'artist on holiday' and the 'travel artist'.

A 'painting traveller' travels to see the world, but takes a sketch-book, pencil and paints as an alternative to diary or camera. Filling the pages is highly enjoyable and relaxing, can fill the empty hours spent waiting for buses, creates an essential time-out space apart from fellow travellers and makes for a fascinating record.

Moonlight is sculpture, sunlight is painting.
– NATHANIEL HAWTHORNE

An 'artist on holiday' usually has a sketching or painting habit, so has planned to dedicate time to it. Over the last 20 years there has been a proliferation in enticing art holidays and courses worldwide, from luxury to trek style, for all standards and all media, often also offering gallery and museum opportunities for culture vultures. *Painting Holiday Directory* editor, Anne Hedley, advises potential bookers to read publicity material carefully and ask the right questions about

Artist's materials

For a six-month painting trip in East Africa recently I took:

- Full pan 24-colour watercolour box.
- Travellers' full pan 12-colour watercolour box.
- Watercolour brushes in a tube.
- Ten sketch-books (avoid spiral-bound books).
- Loose-leaf watercolour and drawing paper (in waterproof A1 portfolio).
- Pencils and graphite sticks.
- White gum rubber.
- Putty rubber.
- Water bottle and mug.
- Scalpel.
- Lightweight board.
- Bulldog clips.

In addition, I find that binoculars, clothing with big pockets, a hat, sun-cream, a good day-sack and A1-size plastic bags are vital equipment.

teaching, media, style, accommodation and comfort. Art magazines *Artists & Illustrators*, *The Artist and Leisure Painter* publish special holiday issues and carry many advertisements for art courses and holidays. The web is also a great place to search.

A 'travel artist' is a professional who travels to collect images, either as sketches or as source material for studio work back home, for exhibition and publication.

Expeditions occasionally take professional artists with them to document the trip. Invariably the artist is roped into doing some research work and needs to strike a balance between this and their own work. The Royal Geographical Society (www.rgs.org) should be the first port of call when you're trying to find out about expeditions, though my first expedition was with a university.

There are travel bursaries for artists to develop their own work and take influence from other cultures and craft expertise, artist-in-residence schemes abroad (where you are developing your own work in situ) and international commissions (where you have a specific subject to document creatively). Start with Google, also *AN* magazine gives details of residencies and travel grant information in each issue. *The Directory of Grant Making Trusts* in your local library and your regional Arts Council will also be valuable sources of information.

Equally, if you are brave enough to go to an unknown country and say, "I'm an artist", then you'll have incredible adventures, encounter brilliant people and be shown rare sights. Research and relevant contacts are essential, being open to opportunities is more important still, especially if your aim is to have an exhibition out there. The artist and ex-pat communities will feed you with ideas and contacts, and give you the courage to visit the embassies, NGOs, government offices, businesses and individuals who might help.

Financial assistance is unlikely, but help in kind can be overwhelmingly generous. I have found that the British Council, the French Cultural Institute, the

Contacts

Art Safari (tel 01394 382235, www.artsafari.co.uk)

Indian Romance (tel 020 7603 9616, www.indianromance.co.uk)

Indus Tours and Travel (tel 020 8901 7320, www.industours.co.uk)

Red House Studio (www.redhousestudios.com)

British Council (tel 020 7930 8466, www.britcoun.org)

Winston Churchill Memorial Trust (tel 020 7584 9315, www.wcmt.org.uk)

Publications

The Painting Holiday Directory (tel 01830 540215, www.wavenet.co.uk/users/kirkland/phd)

Writers' and Artists' Handbook (published by A&C Black)

Artists and Illustrators (www.quartomagazines.com)

Leisure Painter (www.leisurepainter.co.uk)

AN Magazine and helpline (www.anweb.co.uk)

Directory of Grantmaking Trusts (held in public libraries)

British and American embassies, and various countries' government ministries for arts or culture, are all helpful.

Audiences

Whichever kind of travelling artist you are, you will be a performance artist. A crowd will appear to watch. Enjoy it - it's rare to get immediate audiences for visual art! Adults and children can keep up an excited chatter of comment and laughter as you build the image, they block the view and challenge your concentration and patience to breaking point. I now remain unruffled and concentrate on the subject, because with a certain amount of polite and jovial view-clearing people will allow you to continue with your work. If you're lucky there might be a chorus of "ooohs" and "aaahs" – drawing is often seen as magical and treated with respect and awe in countries where images are still scarce. I always hold up the finished item for the crowd to see, however dreadful I think it is.

Preparation

Don't be rusty when you arrive. To make the most of your time painting abroad, you need to be in training, you wouldn't climb the Himalayas without already being fit first, so get your eye in by joining a painting class here or sketching at home (a great habit to have all year round). Learn all about your paint-box and your paper before you leave, and never travel with a new brand.

Materials

The equipment you need will depend on your medium and how quickly you go through materials. You will need to consider whether you want exhibition-quality materials. Don't rely on being able to find art materials in the country you're travelling to and remember you can always give away excess materials to local artists.

I take pencils and watercolour equipment when travelling, with a mass of sketch-books and loose-leaf paper of all formats. I then take the odd diversion into local crafts if I feel the whim.

The creative dimension

Creativity adds a further dimension to the riches of travel. The keen observation needed for taking down visual images gives a heightened awareness of a new environment. You take time to look at detail, recognise the differences, appreciate and gently imbibe the wonders, without judgement.

If you spend longer than a couple of days painting in a place you will soon be regarded as a regular, even as a fellow worker, and you find that you are accepted and welcomed by local people. This brings a great sense of belonging. Your images (especially portraits) can work for you as passports: even in tourist-hostile places, you can win people's hearts and laughter (their fish market, their bus stop...).

Lastly, remember that the time you spend is encapsulated in the finished artwork, meaning that in months and years to come you can look at a painting and recall that concentrated timeframe in all its magical detail. ❧

MARY-ANNE BARTLETT is a travel artist, specialising in East Africa. She also runs Art Safari, painting holidays for adventurous artists of all standards in East Africa.

The wine-loving traveller
by Andrew Barr

IN ORDER TO TASTE GOOD WINE, YOU DO NOT NEED TO LEAVE HOME. You do not even need to leave your house. One telephone call, and the finest wines in the world can be delivered to your front door. Such a wide range of wines is imported into Britain and North America nowadays that it is possible to drink wine instead of travelling, as a means of experiencing another country's culture vicariously. Nothing captures the smells and tastes of the place from which it comes better than a bottle of wine, made from grapes harvested in a single vineyard in the autumn of a single year.

The taste of the soil

Admittedly, most ordinary wines are made from a blend of grapes from different vineyards and are subjected to extensive processing, causing them to taste much like one another, but it is the purpose of fine wines to express the character of the raw material from which they have been made, to allow the flavours inherent in the grapes to express themselves. The buzz word in the wine world at the moment is 'terroir', which literally means 'soil' but actually refers to the whole environment in which the grapes are grown. This should be expressed in the taste of the wine, through a 'goût du terroir'. A Cabernet Sauvignon from California will never taste like a red Bordeaux (claret) nor a Chardonnay from Australia like a white burgundy, however hard the wine-makers may try to follow the same methods, because the warmer climates naturally express themselves in riper, fruitier flavours in the wines. In general, however, the characteristics of terroir are much less obvious than this; and are expressed through subtle differences that can only be appreciated by travelling to the place where the grapes have grown, by gaining one's own sense of the environment.

Out of the way

This environment may well be one that you would not otherwise experience, because most fine wines are produced in out-of-the-way places. Historically, in Europe, fertile farmland was too precious to waste on growing a crop intended for inebriation rather than nutrition, and vines were restricted to poor soils that could not support other forms of agriculture. Ironically, this accounts for the origin of fine wine. In poor soils, vines have to dig deep to find moisture and nutrients, and produce small crops of finely flavoured fruit. If they were to be grown on lush farmland, they would have it too easy, and produce large quantities of fat but tasteless grapes. The best vineyards are situated on the sides of hills and valleys, and sometimes half-way up mountains.

The same is true of countries in what wine connoisseurs still insist quaintly in describing as the New World – the Americas, Australasia and South Africa – but for a different reason. These countries are generally too warm for fine wines: grapes ripen too quickly, and develop coarse, 'cooked' flavours. The solution is to go up hills and mountains, where the climate is cooler, or (in the case of California) to seek out remote coastal valleys that are cooled by afternoon fogs.

As a result, vineyard scenery can be magnificent. Best of all is probably Rippon Vineyard on the South Island of New Zealand, on the shores of Lake Wanaka and overlooked by the Southern Alps. The price of their beauty is that the vineyards can be hard to find. If you contact the trade department of the relevant embassy in Britain or the United States, they should be able to put you in touch with the official representative body of the wine region you are intending to visit, which should be able to supply you with information and maps. Guides to a few vine-growing regions are also produced by Mitchell Beazley under the series titles, *Touring in Wine Country* and *Wine Atlas*, but be warned that Hugh Johnson's famous *World Atlas of Wine* is not detailed enough for this purpose.

When to go

The difficulty of finding some vineyards can be compounded if you visit them at the one time of year you can be sure the wine-maker will be able to receive you – the middle of winter. I spent several years travelling through fog, ice and snow in Burgundy in January because estates there are essentially one-man operations and I needed to see the person in charge. The underground cellars were slightly warmer than the air outside but I still kept on my overcoat. I also found it essential to wear thermal socks and boots with thick soles. If this does not appeal, then wine-makers also have some free time in the middle of summer – of which they often take advantage in order to go on holiday.

The period when wine-makers are busiest and are least able to see you is unfortunately also the best time to visit, during the harvest in the autumn. You can see the grapes being picked (still usually by hand) and the wine being made, and taste the previous year's vintage. Grapes are harvested in the northern hemisphere in September and October, and in the southern hemisphere in March and April. (It took me a long time to accept that natural events really do occur the other way round in the southern hemisphere. When Australian wine-makers first told me that their vineyards faced north, towards the sun, rather than south, as in the northern hemisphere, I was convinced they were pulling my leg.)

Catching your wine-maker

You will definitely miss out, however, if the wine-maker is unable to see you. Like dogs and cars, wines tend to reflect the character and self-image of the people responsible for them. It is very difficult to appreciate the style of a particular wine without meeting the man or woman who has made it. Contrary to what a wine-maker may claim ("the wine just makes itself"), personality does influence terroir.

In order to persuade a wine-maker to make the time to see you, it is helpful to obtain a recommendation, through a merchant who imports the wine into Britain or America, through the official representative body in the area, or through a local restaurant. The last of these is often a very good place to try a wine that you might not have encountered back home. The restaurateur will generally be flattered if you ask to try an interesting local wine, and, if you like it, will be especially keen to give you a recommendation that will ensure you are well received by the producer.

Communication

Once you have caught your wine-maker, he is likely to be friendly. People who grow grapes and make wine generally do so because they love it. If they happen to have inherited a vineyard but are not interested in wine, they will not bother to make wine themselves but will sell their grapes to someone else. Wine-makers are certainly not in the business to make money. It is often said that, in order to make a small fortune in the wine business, it is necessary to invest a large one.

Wine-makers are friendly but, in a business where the product continues to be consumed for decades after it was made, they have long memories. If, when being shown round an estate in France by an older wine-maker, he asks you whether you are German before taking you down to his cellar, please remember that the correct answer to this question is "No". In that case, he will warn you to avoid knocking your head on the stone lintel above the steps.

Because they make wines as an expression of their personality, wine-makers are generally keen to communicate. They are not necessarily comprehensible, however. Many of them use technical language or refer philosophically to the influence of *terroir*. There are also a number of ex-pot-heads in the wine business in California and Oregon who lost part of their brain to drugs a generation ago and may have some difficulty in expressing themselves in a manner that other people can readily understand. Nor do wine-makers tend to be linguists. Large commercial wineries in Europe will organise guided tours in English, but at small estates the wine-maker will almost certainly be able to speak only in his own language (and often with a heavy regional accent).

Commercial wineries

I would not generally recommend visiting large commercial wineries, where you will be forced to relinquish all hope of dialogue with a like-minded individual and abandon yourself to a well-organised publicity machine. Worst of all, you will probably be obliged to spend some time observing the workings of the company's bottling line, an experience that provides roughly the same degree of enjoyment as filling in one's annual tax return.

This said, it is well worth visiting one of the big Champagne companies in order to see the huge underground cellars where they mature their wines, and where they will demonstrate the elaborate process by which the bottles are gradually turned to bring the sediment to the cork. With the exception of the wine, however, Champagne is a pretty boring part of the world. There is Rheims cathedral, but otherwise its main virtue lies in its proximity to Paris.

Organised tours

The easy solution to the problems of travelling at the time of your choice, of arranging appointments with English-speaking wine-makers, and of avoiding the most commercial wineries, is to take an organised wine tour with a specialist company. These are package tours, it is true, but of a very civilised kind. In traditional wine regions they will enable you to see prestigious estates that would not otherwise receive you. For example, the American company France In Your Glass organises visits to top Bordeaux châteaux such as Margaux and d'Yquem and leading Burgundy estates, including those of Roumier and Dujac. The premier British wine tour company is Arblaster and Clarke. If you want to touch the cutting edge of the wine revolution, you might think of taking their tour to Chile and Argentina. There are also wine-and-walking tours, wine-and-cycling tours, wine-and-camping tours, wine-and-skiing tours, wine-and-cruise tours, wine-and-big-game tours, wine-and-classical-music tours, and so on *ad infinitum*.

Spit or swallow

Tasting with a wine-maker in his cellar may seem a bit daunting, but he knows that you are not a professional and will expect only that you show an interest in his wine. Using a pipette, he will draw a sample of his latest vintage from a tank or wooden barrel and empty it into glasses so that you and he can taste it together. You should look at the wine against the light (if any is available), swirl it in the glass and smell it before you sip. If you can, you should suck air over the wine while holding it in your mouth, which helps to bring out its flavour, but don't worry if you can't manage this at first.

Specialist wine tour operators

Allez France 27 West Street, Storrington, West Sussex RH20 4DZ (tel 01903 745044).

Arblaster and Clarke Farnham Road, West Liss, Hants GU33 6JQ (tel 01730 893344, website www.arblasterandclarke.com).

Backroads 9 Shaftesbury Street, Fordingbridge, Hants SP6 1JF (tel 01425 655022).

DER Travel Service 18 Conduit Street, London W1S 2XN (tel 0870 142 0960, website www.dertravel.co.uk).

Eurocamp Hartford Manor, Greenbank Lane, Northwich, Cheshire CW8 1HW (tel 01606 787000, website www.eurocamp.co.uk).

France In Your Glass 814 35th Avenue, Seattle, WA 98122, USA (tel 1-800-578-0903, website www.inyourglass.com).

Friendship Travel Enkalon Business Centre, Antrim, BT41 4LD (tel 0289 446 2211, website www.friendshiptravel.com).

Fugues en France 11 square Jean Cocteau, 91250 St German les Courbell, France (tel 33 1 6075 8916, website www.fugues-en-france.com).

Moswin Tours The Birds Building, Fleckney Road, Kibworth Beauchamp, Leicester LE8 OHJ (tel 08700 625040).

Page and Moy 136-40 London Road, Leicester, Leics LE2 1EN (tel 0870 833 4012).

Tanglewood Wine Tours Tanglewood House, Mayfield Avenue, New Haw, Surrey KT15 3AG (tel 01932 348720, website www.tanglewood.com).

The Parker Company 152 Lynnway, Lynn, MA 01902, USA (tel 1-800-280-2811, website www.theparkercompany.com).

Viking River Cruises 5700 Canoga Ave, Suite 200, Woodland Hills, CA 91367, USA (tel 1 818 227 1234, website www.rivercruises.com).

Winetrails Greenways, Vann Lane, Ockley, Dorking, Surrey RH5 5NT (tel 01306 712111, website www.winetrails.co.uk).

Wink Lorch Church Farm, Windmill Road, Fulmer, Bucks SL3 6HD (tel 07785 555705, website www.winklorch.com).

The decision whether to spit or swallow is purely personal. Obviously, if you are driving, it is wiser to spit, and the wine-maker will not be offended if you insist on so doing, but he will be flattered if you swallow the wine and then explain that it was too good to spit out. Professionals always spit, but then they can taste hundreds of wines a day. In many European wineries, tasters spit on the floor, although it is best to aim in the general direction of a drain; in America, spitting on the floor is illegal and the wine-maker may insist that you use a spittoon or bucket.

If you cannot already suck or spit like a professional, you may well find it helpful to practise these skills at home before attempting them in public.

Appropriate comments

The wine-maker will expect you to make some appropriate comments about his produce. You may well have a great deal to say but, if not, the key is to remember to offer an observation that appears to have been carefully considered rather than simply describing every sample he offers you as 'delicious'. References to balance, harmony and length on the palate are always appreciated. The latter applies to the length of time you can taste the wine after spitting or swallowing and is generally considered a sign of high quality.

If the wine is tasteless, I would suggest describing it as 'elegant' or 'delicate'; if bad, then there is always 'interesting'. Alternatively, take on the wine-maker at his own game and explain how, in your opinion, his product expresses true regional character in the form of a *goût du terroir*.

Bringing wine home

You should never tip a wine-maker for showing you his wares, and you are not obliged to buy them. Wines are always much cheaper bought direct from the grower, often costing only half as much as you would pay in a shop back home, but, remember, they always seem better on the spot. They are designed to suit the local weather and food – not just in Europe, but also in the New World, where the vibrantly fruity style of many wines perfectly suits currently fashionable 'fusion' or 'Pacific Rim' cuisine. Serve them with a plate of good old British stodge in damp, grey weather and they do not taste the same at all. ❧

ANDREW BARR is a wine writer and historian, and the author of 'Wine Snobbery', 'Pinot Noir' and 'Drink: a social history'. He no longer visits Burgundy in mid-winter.

The gourmet traveller
by Paul Wade

As a child I was lucky. My family roamed Europe during the holidays, spending time in what were then exotic spots: Dubrovnik in the former Yugoslavia, Rapallo in Italy and Salzburg in Austria. My memories are of scorched, rocky shores, pavement cafés, hulking castles and... food. Post-war Britain was still strictly a 'meat-and-two-veg' country, with powdered eggs and stock cubes in every pantry. Like a jangling alarm clock, the Mediterranean flavours of fresh tomatoes and giant watermelons woke up my taste buds. Slurping spaghetti splashed with purple squid sauce and munching a properly prepared schnitzel ensured they would never go back to sleep.

Ever since this awakening, food has been an integral part of any trip, whether it's a day out in the nearby English countryside or weeks in the distant pueblos of Mexico. With my wife, who shares the same enthusiasm, I pore over guidebooks, searching for the elusive tip that might send us to a restaurant where we can eat what the locals regard as traditional dishes. Our aim is to add taste and smell to the other three senses, which are sharpened by being on holiday.

Guided tours

Sadly, many guidebooks concentrate on museums and mosques, shopping and beaches, with food little more than an afterthought. How often is the list of 'best places to eat' merely a roll-call of the poshest French restaurants in town – whether you happen to be in Chicago or the Caribbean, Munich or Manchester? These are lists for business executives, keen to impress clients with the size of their tips and their knowledge of over-priced wines. But how can you say you understand Catalonia if you have not attended a *cocotada* (an onion barbecue, washed down with the local black wine) in Valls? How can you boast that you 'know' the USA if you have not put on a bib and tucked into a lobster in Maine or made a pilgrimage to the birthplace of the hamburger or the pizza?

By eating what we rate as the best rice in the world (in Iran), the best grass-fed beef (in Argentina), the most delicious oysters (straight from the squeaky-clean waters off the coast of Tasmania), my wife and I have rounded off our experience of those countries. We also have had the bonus of meeting the people. Interest in good food overcomes any language or cultural barrier. The fastest way to get into conversation with locals is to ask about their specialities.

Word play

Before I forget, let's be clear about what I mean by that much over-used word: 'gourmet'. Too often, along with 'connoisseur' and '*bon viveur*', it screams snob. It also shouts 'expensive'. But in my dictionary a gourmet is 'a judge of good fare', and in my experience, real 'gourmet travellers' don't need a gold credit card. Sure, once in a while, it is fun to splurge, but it is just as educational to seek out local produce that is prepared with care, in which freshness is rated higher than fashion and flavour is more important than fancy frills. That is why our holiday highlights include just as many simple meals as complex creations. The mountain *taberna* in Spain where we enjoyed thick pork chops, drizzled with lemon juice and grilled quickly over vine roots, is in no guidebook that I know – and never will be. The old lady near Cortina d'Ampezzo in Italy who used to open up her house for dinner on two nights a week died several years ago, but we will always remember her holding a vast copper pan and whipping up the most sensual warm zabaglione we have ever eaten. The texture and flavour of a pink-fleshed giant trout, freshly hooked and hot-smoked on the shore of New Zealand's Lake Taupo is forever etched on our gastro-memory.

Star signs

The problem is how to find these honest-to-goodness local dishes. Let's start with

France, a country where food is so important that great chefs commit suicide if they lose a Michelin star. The famous red guide, with its mind-boggling array of wingdings, may be the bible of gastronomy, but it lacks the Bible's poetry and description. Back in the 1970s, we added the more outspoken, idiosyncratic Gault Millau guide to our library. Founded by a couple of journalists who focused on new French cooking and dared to praise innovation, this big yellow guide has rarely let us down. Years later, when the trendy wave of nouvelle cuisine and its descendants threatened to eradicate France's traditional regional dishes, Gault Millau introduced its *Lauriers du Terroir* awards. This laurel wreath symbol signifies restaurants offering dishes that *gran'mère* would have been proud of, often with portions to match. These have helped us to find unusual sweet wines in the Loire Valley, black radishes in Albi and *mouclade* (mussels in cream) on the Ile de Ré. Michelin has taken up the challenge, introducing a grinning Michelin man to point out value-for-money restaurants where food rather than formality is the priority.

These renowned guides are reliable in France but less trusty beyond its borders. The Michelin guide for Britain is notorious for praising French chefs and French-style restaurants. This is no Anglophobia; other neighbours suffer from similar chauvinism. When we are asked to choose our gastronomic heaven, we usually sigh and dream of the Engadine Valley in Graubunden, in western Switzerland. Look up five of our memorable hotel–restaurants in the Michelin guide to Switzerland, however, and the symbols tell you that they are pleasant and quiet, have terraces, exceptional views and let in dogs. What they do not and cannot tell you is that this valley is a foodie enclave, with five of our favourite chefs working close to one another, conjuring up some of the best nosh in the universe.

Empire-building

A few years ago, we were in Montreal reporting on Christmas in this most Francophile of cities. Everyone we talked to recommended 'authentic' French restaurants. These turned out to be run by expatriate Frenchmen serving up food that was considered *haute cuisine* 30 years ago. It was a classic example of the emperor's new clothes. Yet, right in the city, talented young Québecois chefs were, and still are, following the French rules on techniques and use of local ingredients, yet producing totally individual results that we rated ten on the foodies' Richter scale.

It is not fair to expect such a momentous meal every night. We are just as happy with simple, clean flavours and honest dishes. Even that, however, can be difficult to find. Take the Caribbean, where the demands of the American tourist have stifled local ambition in the kitchen and swamped supermarkets with foodstuffs processed in the USA. On some small islands, it is impossible to buy locally caught fish or locally raised fruit and vegetables. Food has been replaced by T-shirts and baskets in the market, and restaurants serve American hamburgers, Italian veal *piccata* and New Orleans blackened shrimp.

When we were on the relatively unspoiled island of St John in the US Virgin Islands, we searched in vain for true Caribbean cuisine. We even tried having lunch with the taxi drivers and road builders, but heavy stews and gristly pigs' trotters defeated us in the tropical heat. The best meals we had were cooked in a tiny restaurant by an American with a Thai mother. He knew how to wheedle chickens and vegetables from the islanders' own backyards and his use of spices contributed to the sense of place that is important when in another country.

The English disease

Although the 'think local' campaign has won the hearts and minds of many chefs, another food phenomenon has swept through other kitchens. This is the 'United Nations' attitude to cooking, where ingredients from anywhere in the world are combined, with results veering between triumph and disaster. It has taken hold, in the main, in countries where English is the common language. Perhaps that's because, for example, in the USA and Australia, much of the food used to echo Britain's: plain and hearty home cooking that rarely translated successfully on to the restaurant plate.

As in the UK, chefs in these countries are now so eclectic that critics try to wedge them into pigeonholes so that readers have some idea of what to expect: 'Floribbean' for Miami chefs who draw on Florida and the Caribbean for inspiration; 'Pacific Rim' for the mixing and matching of, say, Asian spices with Peruvian purple potatoes and low-cholesterol kangaroo meat. Perhaps these novelties will eventually become classics in their own right. Perhaps not.

In trendy cities such as New York and London, 'new' has come to mean 'good', whilst 'newest' is equated with 'best'. Restaurants open every week but the star chef who stood at the stove when the first diners came through the door may have moved on to another project after a few months, leaving a deputy to maintain his and the restaurant's reputation. What was tantalising yesterday may be tired today.

Tried and tested

Consistency: that is the problem. In countries such as France and Italy, where restaurants are often family enterprises going back decades, the secret of success is to do the same thing well, day after day, year after year. Not so long ago, deep in the countryside of southern France, we ate in the same restaurant that Elizabeth David had immortalised decades before. We ordered the same chicken dish (roasted, with mushrooms stuffed under the skin) that she had enjoyed. The owners saw no reason to change a winning formula, which appealed to guests old and new.

Cultural cringe

So how do you find a 'good place to eat'? The restaurants we like least are those that advertise most. We avoid anywhere that sells its charms in an airline magazine or on a card at the airport. To avoid ending up in a culinary ghetto with other foreigners, we rarely take advice at hotels unless the concierge seems particularly in tune with our tastes. Unfortunately, tourism is such a rampant industry that standardisation in hotels and restaurants is not only commonplace, but even embraced by local people as a sign of new-found sophistication.

What Australians refer to so vividly as 'the cultural cringe' is a major handicap when it comes to food. Why should anyone have to imitate European-style restaurants to gain gastronomic credibility? Italian restaurants in Africa, Greek restaurants in South America, pseudo-French bistros in Japan may offer an alternative for the inhabitants but are sheer torture for us.

Heard it on the grapevine

The way we dig out good restaurants is by talking to people in the trade. If we like the look of a bakery or delicatessen, a butcher or fishmonger, we go inside and chat. Wine and cheese makers are usually a good bet, since they supply the better restaurants. Once two agree on their favourite spot, off we go.

We not only keep our eyes and ears open, we keep our noses sniffing. We watch where locals head when offices close. We listen for the happy hum of contented eating. We track down the source of delicious smells. Then, we order the daily special, even though we may have no idea what it is. When, in a suburb of Buenos Aires, the waiter announced that the dish of the day was *mondongo*, I chose it, only to discover that it was what I hate most: tripe. My sole consolation was that it was cheap and that I had expanded my vocabulary by one word. In Tasmania recently we came across a 'bush restaurant', part of a growing trend to utilise indigenous produce, as opposed to plants and vegetables introduced by the Europeans. Here, bunya nuts, native limes and rosella petals flavoured dishes ranging from crocodile and sweet potato spring rolls to wattle grubs. Although these may not be recipes to replicate at home, they certainly provide the raw ingredients for travellers' tales.

Of course, you don't have to go to such extremes of geography and gastronomy. Europe may seem old hat since we are all part of the EU, but familiarity need not breed contempt. After all, with barely a wave of a passport, we can order mouthwatering meals in 15 different countries, each with dozens of regional cuisines. Travel only broadens the mind when you meet and talk to people. Understanding another culture comes more easily with a glass in one hand and a fork in the other. Years ago, in a bar in Madrid, we ordered some tapas, including *pulpo*. The Spaniard next to us was incredulous: "Do you really want *pulpo*? Do you know what it is? Do you like it?" When we answered "Si" to each question, he grinned his approval and quipped, "You cannot be English if you like octopus." It was the beginning of a long and enjoyable evening. ❧

PAUL WADE is a freelance travel journalist, guidebook writer and broadcaster.

The expeditionary
by Shane Winser

FOR MANY, INDEPENDENT TRAVEL IS A DAUNTING TASK, and the prospect of joining a group with a pre-determined objective is attractive. Others may feel that they wish to make a contribution to the communities or environment through which they travel. The options open to such individuals are enormous: from adventure holidays to community work and scientific fieldwork overseas. The better-known and well-established groups can be found in specialist directories or on the internet. It may be more difficult to find out about the credentials of smaller and/or newly emerging groups. Almost all will require some sort of financial contribution. Don't be afraid to ask questions, either about the organisation itself or what your payment covers. Try and get a feel for the organisation, and if you are not happy with its overall aims or the attitudes of the people who run it, don't sign up.

Whether you want to climb Everest, walk to the South Pole or visit a remote tropical island, there is now a tour company out there to help you achieve your dream. Naturally, you pay for someone else to organise your expedition, but the preparation time and responsibilities for you are correspondingly less. For example, the WEXAS members' Discoverers brochure has many such trips; others are advertised in outdoor-interest magazines and the national press. The useful directory *Adventure Holidays* (Vacation Work Publications, 9 Park End Street, Oxford OX1 1HJ, tel 01865 241978, website www.vacationwork.co.uk) lists holidays by the type of sport or activity. Magazines such as *Traveller, Wanderlust, Global Adventure* and *Geographical*, and the travel sections of the weekend newspapers, are useful for finding out more about the unusual and exotic.

> *We climbed and climbed, and we kept on climbing; we reached about 40 summits, but there was always another one just ahead.*
> – MARK TWAIN

There is an increasing trend to combine an adventurous journey with the challenge of raising funds for a charitable cause. The initial financial contribution required to join these charity fund-raising expeditions is often low, but the effort required to meet both challenges can be immense. Be prepared to train hard. Whatever the organisers tell you, you need to be fit and acclimatised to the conditions you are going to meet. And when it is all over and your friends' hard-earned cash is on the way to the charity, satisfy yourself that it is being well spent on a cause dear to your heart.

Adventure holidays and genuine expeditions differ in many ways. A scientific expedition will be expected to add to human knowledge, to 'discover' something new. Those joining such expeditions will usually be expected to give up considerable time to help with preparations, be whole-heartedly committed to the project's overall aim and objectives, and be capable of working as a skilled member of the team. And that is to say nothing of the efforts required to raise the necessary funds for the expedition.

In Britain, the Royal Geographical Society (with The Institute of British Geographers) at 1 Kensington Gore, London SW7 2AR (website www.rgs.org) is the principal organisation concerned with helping those carrying out scientific expeditions overseas. Through the work of its Expedition Advisory Centre (tel 020 7591 3000), the RGS-IBG provides information, advice and training to 500 or so groups each year – groups that carry out scientific and adventure- and youth-oriented projects abroad. For those who have a clear idea of what they want to do and have

Expedition life
by Richard Snailham

Expeditions used to be unmitigated hell. You would go with Franklin to try to find the North-West Passage and die of lead poisoning, starvation or the bitter cold. Or with Henry Morton Stanley to rescue Emin Pasha and be flogged through Congo's impenetrable Ituri forest, stung near to death, menaced by hostile natives, only to find Emin Pasha and discover that he didn't need to be rescued at all.

Over the last 150 years expeditions, thankfully, have got safer, less large and more numerous. There are plenty of opportunities, at school, at university, in the armed services or after. And you can generally count on having a jolly good time, with perhaps a few privations to make it feel like an expedition and to talk about in the pub when you get home (or bore the family with in interminable slide shows).

Botanists, geologists – scientists of all stripes, can carry out their fieldwork on the context of an expedition and generally enjoy it. With my friend and co-author John Blashford-Snell you can become handsomely elevated in status – idle pickers-up of pottery shards find themselves appointed Archaeologists, estate agents become Surveyors. Expeditions are not exclusive. Anybody can take part. One of his expeditions was the only one, I daresay, to have two dentists practising their craft and a harpist (useful in Paraguay, a very harpy country).

Notwithstanding the sometimes baleful influence of the health and safety industry, expeditions can involve risk. And they should do so. Risk offers a whiff of challenge, it tests people, and gives a sense of subsequent achievement, however spurious.

In some 25 expeditions I have been capsized in rapids and nearly drowned, erupted on by an active volcano, shot at by bandits (twice) and bitten by a potentially rabid bat. And I have not always been in the front line, having variously been treasurer, author, camel trek group leader, second-in-command, driver, interpreter, historian, even bartender.

It is very satisfying to bring home the goods – zoological specimens to keep monograph writers at work for two decades (Blue Nile expedition, 1968), material for a book (Sangay, 1976), 65 happy, fulfilled lower-sixth students (Peter Drake's YSES or Brathway expeditions), slide photo material with which to beguile rotary clubs and women's institutes (almost all), memories of clinics built, water pipes laid, game counted (Operations Drake and Raleigh).

Do they do any good for young people? I'm sure of it. People still speak highly of Operations Drake and Raleigh: participants, their relatives and the public generally. Many of my friends, now leaders and assistants in expeditions themselves, began as junior members. *(continues right)* already formed a group of like-minded individuals, the centre has a number of useful services, including the annual seminar on planning a small expedition that takes place each November.

Many of the groups helped by the centre are based at schools and universities, as the principle of outdoor adventure and challenge is widely accepted as an important training ground both for young people and potential managers alike. As a result, a number of charitable and commercial organisations now offer expeditions to people of all ages. The Expedition Advisory Centre publishes a directory of these, entitled *Joining an Expedition*. The directory includes advice on choosing an appropriate project and ideas for raising funds to join projects. Many of the organisations listed in the directory can also be accessed via the Expedition Advisory Centre's website (www.rgs.org/eac). Individuals with special skills to offer – doctors, nurses, mechanics and scientists – are invited to become listed in the register of personnel available for expeditions that is maintained by the centre and used by expedition organisers to recruit skilled volunteers and staff.

Amongst the well-established youth-focused exploration societies, there are:
▪ Brathay Exploration Group (Brathay Hall, Ambleside, Cumbria LA22 0HP, tel 015394 33942, website www.brathayexploration.org.uk) and The Dorset Expeditionary Society (Lupins Business Centre, 1-3 Greenhill, Weymouth, Dorset DT4 7SP, tel 01305 775599, website www.dorsetexp.co.uk). Both send out several expeditions each year, both within the UK and abroad, and members tend to be between the ages of 16 and 21.
▪ The British Schools' Exploring Society, (1 Kensington Gore, London SW7 2AR, tel 020 7591 3141, website www.bses.org.uk) organises six-week-long expeditions for

Expeditions are great social levellers: two Raleigh Venturers chatting after a few weeks together discovered they came from the same south-coast town. "What did you do there?" asked one. Pause. "I done a bank, didn't I?" The first found that he kept his account at the branch robbed by the second. They remained good friends.

There is generally great camaraderie, beginning in the training and preparations phase, on the expedition itself and afterwards: reunions are well attended. And the friendships are not just between expedition members. It has become usual for expeditions to have some nationals of the host country as members, and there is probably a truer view of the country to be had as an expedition member than by studying it in many other ways. Expeditions have led to my total involvement with Ethiopia, and now Bolivia.

So go for it!

Richard Snailham has taken part in expeditions in many continents since the 1960s, and is leading member of the Scientific Expedition Society.

17- to 20-year-olds during the summer holidays and six-month-long expeditions for those in their 'gap' year between school and university. BSES Expeditions has always had a strong scientific component to its work and provides an excellent training for those hoping to go on and organise their own research expeditions.

■ Raleigh International (27 Parsons Green Lane, London sw6 4hz, tel 020 7371 8585, website www.raleigh.org.uk) regularly recruits 17- to 25-year-olds to take part in demanding community projects and conservation programmes that last up to 12 weeks.

With increasing public concern for the environment, a number of other organisations offer a chance to get involved in conservation projects overseas on a fee-paying basis. Among them are:

■ The British Trust for Conservation Volunteers (163 Balby Road, Doncaster, South Yorkshire dn4 0rh, tel 01302 572 244, website www.btcv.org), which has links with many similar organisations in Europe.

■ Greenforce (11-15 Betterton Street, Covent Garden, London wc2h 9bp, tel 020 7470 888, website www.greenforce.org) uses volunteer field assistants on ten-week research expeditions in Zambia and the Peruvian Amazon as well as on reef surveys in the South Pacific and South China Sea.

■ Trekforce Expeditions (Naldred Farm Offices, Borde Hill Lane, Haywards Heath, West Sussex rh16 1xr, tel 01444 474 123, website www.trekforce.org.uk) has been carrying out rainforest conservation work throughout the Indonesian archipelago since 1990, and is now working in Sabah, Malaysian Borneo and Belize.

■ Coral Cay Conservation Programme (The Tower, 13th Floor, 125 High Street, Collier's Wood, London sw19 2jg, tel 0870 750 0668, website www.coralcay.org) recruits qualified divers to monitor reefs in a marine reserve off the coast of Belize.

■ Earthwatch (267 Banbury Road, Oxford ox2 7ht, tel 01865 318838, website www.earthwatch.org) teams paying volunteers with scientists who need their help to study threatened habitats, save endangered species and document our changing environmental heritage. Volunteers do not need to have any special skills to join Earthwatch expeditions and anyone aged 16 to 75 may apply.

■ For budding archaeologists, Archaeology Abroad (31-34 Gordon Square, London wc1h 0py, tel 020 8537 0849, website www.britarch.ac.uk/archabroad) helps directors of overseas excavations find suitable personnel through its bulletins.

■ For those taking a gap year, a new organisation, The Year Out Group, (Queensfield, 28 Kings Road, Easterton, Wiltshire sn10 4px, tel 07980 395789, website www.yearoutgroup.org) promotes the concept and benefits of a well-structured year for young people between school and university, or between university and work. It has drafted a series of questions to help young people decide which year-out experience might be best for them. GAP Activity Projects (tel 0118 959 4914, website www.gap.org.uk) and Gap Challenge (tel 020 8728 7200, website www.world-challenge.co.uk) are specialists in this field.

For many, the experience of meeting and working alongside people in the host country is one of the great attractions of travel:

■ Wind, Sand & Stars (6 Tyndale Terrace, London n1 2at, tel 0870 757 1510, website www.windsandstars.co.uk) specialises in journeys and expeditions to the desert and mountain areas of Sinai, travelling and working with members of the local Bedouin tribes.

▓ Teaching and Projects Abroad (Aldsworth Parade, Goring, West Sussex BN12 4TX, tel 01903 708300, website www.teaching-abroad.co.uk) and I to I International (tel 0870 333 2332, website www.i-to-i.com) arrange work placements in a number of different disciplines.

▓ Quest Overseas (tel 01444 474744, website www.questoverseas.com) and VentureCo Worldwide (The Iron Yard, 64-66 The Market Place, Warwick CV34 4SD, tel 01926 411122, website www.ventureco-worldwide.com) both offer a combination of language training, community projects and an adventurous expedition.

Those wishing to work or study abroad without necessarily joining an expedition should consult the Central Bureau (10 Spring Gardens, London SW1A 2BN, tel 0207389 4004, website www.britcoun.org/cbeve), whose publications are extremely useful. The Bureau, which also has offices in Edinburgh and Belfast, holds details of jobs, study opportunities, youth organisations and holidays in some 60 countries. Vacation Work Publications (9 Park End Street, Oxford OX1 1HJ, tel 01865 241978, website www.vactionwork.co.uk) publishes many guides and directories for those seeking permanent jobs or summer jobs abroad, unusual travel opportunities, voluntary work and working travel. ❧

SHANE WINSER runs the Expedition Advisory Centre at the Royal Geographical Society, and has helped to organise scientific expeditions to Sarawak, Pakistan, Kenya and Oman.

The polar traveller
by Sir Ranulph Fiennes

THIS, FOR ME, WAS THE MOST DIFFICULT AND TESTING EXPERIENCE *in 35 years of exploration worldwide.... "After a memorably unpleasant night Mike and I followed an unnamed tributary that descended steeply into the crevasse-streaked maw of the Mill Glacier. The horizons which now opened to us in slow motion were awesome, a sprawling mass of rock and ice locked in suspended motion. This was the headwater of a moving ice-river. Constrictions caused by 15,000-foot-high mountains had formed, and were even now renewing savage whirlpools and mighty maelstroms of cascading pressure-ice. Huge open chasms leered from distant foothills and standing ice-waves reared up at the base of black truncated cliffs.*

I found this canvas full of power and wonder and thanked God for this moment of being alive. Nothing else lived here nor ever had since the dinosaurs of Gondwanaland. No birds nor beasts nor the least bacteria survived. Only the deep roar of massive avalanche, the shriek and grind of splitting rock, the groan of shifting ice, and the music, soft or fierce, of the winds from a thousand valleys, moved to and fro across the eternal silence." – SIR RANULPH FIENNES

THERE IS A DANISH WORD, *POLARHULLAR*, meaning 'a yearning for the polar regions' that grips the soul of a traveller so that nowhere else will ever again satisfy his appetite for the essence of 'over there and beyond'. A victim of *polarhullar* will forever be drawn back to the very extremities of Earth.

Antarctica is expensive and difficult to reach, which is why, blocked by the roughest seas in the world, nobody penetrated its fastness until, only 90 years ago, Scott, Amundsen and Shackleton struggled over the Ross Ice Shelf and on to the vast inland plateau; while the Arctic Ocean, peopled by Eskimos, who, for centuries, have survived along its coastlines, is infinitely more accessible to travellers. Sledgers who cross Greenland, the Canadian north and Svalbard often describe themselves as polar travellers, using the Arctic Circle as their yardstick. Thus there are a great many more veterans of the Arctic than of Antarctica.

Travel in the remote polar reaches of the Arctic Ocean itself and the high plateaux of Antarctica demands careful preparation and constant wariness due to unpredictable weather and local hazards, which can rapidly prove lethal. On the other hand, during the summer season, polar travel can be easy and almost temperate on windless days and away from problem areas. I have travelled to both poles without suffering unduly from the cold, yet I lost part of a toe from frostbite during a weekend army exercise in Norfolk. A need for wariness is not a uniquely polar prerogative.

A brief history of previous polar travellers in Antarctica would have to start in 650AD when, according to the legends of Polynesian Rarotonga, their chief Uite headed south in a war canoe until the ocean was covered with 'white powder and great white rocks rose into the sky'.

Soon after the discovery of America by Columbus and Cape Horn by Drake, Britain annexed Australia (1616). Then, in 1700, the astronomer Halley reached South Georgia, and by 1774 Captain Cook had sailed south of the Antarctic circle. He then circumnavigated Antarctica without ever sighting land. Nobody overwintered on the continent until the British–Norwegian Southern Cross expedition of 1900, which preceded the 'heroic age' of the pole racers, made famous by the deaths of all Scott's team soon after Amundsen reached the south pole in 1911. In 1914 Shackleton attempted to traverse Antarctica. He failed, but in 1958 the crossing was successfully achieved by the team led by Dr Vivian Fuchs and Sir Edmund Hillary.

A full resumé of Arctic travel that stretched over three centuries would fill many pages. Ships' captains from America and Britain vied with each other throughout the nineteenth century to find a 'north-west passage'. Entire expeditions disappeared in a mist of rumoured mutiny, murder and cannibalism.

The urge to be the first to the north pole ended early this century with mutually disputed claims by two Americans, Peary and Cook. Both were later accused of fudging their records and the first proven journey to the north pole was that of

Ralph Plaisted, an American preacher, in 1968, a year before Britain's Wally Herbert completed the first surface crossing of the Arctic Ocean via the pole.

The achievement of linking up expeditions north and south into a circumpolar journey encircling the earth was proposed by Charles de Brosses, an eighteenth-century French geographer, and finally executed by the Transglobe Expedition (1979-1982). This expedition's ice group, myself and Charles Burton, travelled from Greenwich across Antarctica and the Arctic Ocean, then back to Greenwich. We became the first people to reach both poles by surface travel and to circumnavigate Earth on its polar axis.

In 1993, with Mike Stroud, I crossed the Antarctic continent on the longest un-supported polar journey in history. This took nearly 100 days but, a year later, vari-ous types of wind-powered kites and parawings emerged that enabled Antarctica to be crossed with far less effort in a mere 50 days.

Now it is possible to traverse both Antarctica and the Arctic Ocean with no 'outside' support, by harnessing the wind with lightweight sails.

A sledger, using modern kites, can pick up and harness winds from over 180 de-grees. Until 1994, the great journeys of Shackleton and his successors utilised crude sails, which could only run before a directly following wind. Should Mike and I have described our 1993 expedition, or Shackleton's, as 'unsupported' when we harnessed the wind, albeit in a minimal way? Should I, in 1996, have used a vastly improved modern kite gadget and still have called my journey 'unsupported'? It is a question of definition, for there is, after all, no polar version of the International Olympic Committee.

In 1993 Mike Stroud and I suffered considerable physical damage crossing the Antarctic continent by manhaul and minimal use of sails that could only use fol-lowing winds. Our sledge loads, each in excess of 215 kg, required brute force to shift and 16 km a day was a fair average manhaul stint, costing a daily deficit of 8,000 calories and leading to slow starvation.

In 1996, again towing a load of nigh on 225 kg, I deployed a 4.5 kg kite and man-aged up to 190 km a day with minimal physical effort and correspondingly less calorific expenditure. My sledge load could be halved in terms of fuel and food. What had previously proved remarkably difficult was now comparatively simple.

Polar travel has been truly revolutionised by such wind devices. It is now possi-ble to cross Antarctica in under two months. Of course the element of luck can still play tricks. Broken equipment, unusually bad weather, sudden illness and well-hidden crevasses can still prevent a successful outcome, but at least the reality of polar travel is now within the grasp of the many, not just the few.

My instructions for this section of the *Handbook* are to provide practical infor-mation, and this would be difficult without lists. These are the result of a dozen polar journeys in many regions and with differing purposes. I have spent more days and nights out on the Arctic pack and Antarctic plateau than anyone alive, but my kit lists and general tips are by no means infallible. They will not prevent you falling into the sea or an ice crack. You may still become hypothermic, snow blind or lost or eaten by a polar bear, but I hope they will at least help you get start-ed as a polar traveller of reasonable competence.

First of all, read as much available literature by previous travellers in the area of your chosen trip. Study the annexes at the rear of expedition books. Lists of sponsors and manufacturers are often quoted and can save you time.

Then apply, perhaps through the Royal Geographical Society's expedition advisory office, for information on expeditions currently planning to go into your area of interest. It will help if you have a skill to offer (cook, communications, photographer, mechanic, etc.).

Go on other people's trips to Greenland, Svalbard, Iceland, Norway, anywhere with snow and ice, to gain experience before progressing to the deep south or north and to leading your own projects, eventually to and across the poles if that strikes your fancy.

Here are some guidelines. Feel free to ignore or alter them wherever you can garner more appropriate advice elsewhere.

Equipment

Clothing:

1. Fleece jacket with hood.
2. Ventile outer trousers with braces and long-length anorak (baggy).
3. Down duvet jacket with hood attached (for periods when not manhauling).
4. Wick-away underwear (long sleeves and legs).
5. Meraklon headcover.
6. Duofold balaclava with mouth hole.
7. Separate lip protector mouthpiece with elastic to hold in place.
8. Ski goggles and ski glacier glasses with nose-protecting felt pad glued in place.
9. 1 pair thick wool socks.
10. 1 pair thin Helly Hansen socks.
11. 1 pair vapour barrier socks.
12. 1 pair Dachstein mitts.
13. 1 pair Northern Outfitters heavy gauntlets.
14. 1 peaked cap, kepi-style and with under-neck strap
15. 1 pair thin working gloves.
16. 1 pair vapour barrier mitts (optional). Some folk swear by them.
17. Footwear, as advised by polar travellers of your acquaintance (or from their books!). There are too many alternatives to be specific here. Correctly fitting boots are of great importance.
18. For polar work when using snow machines, skis or dogs, shops specialising in the relevant sports gear will be able to advise you best.

NOTE: *The heavier the weight you tow when manhauling with no wind support, the more difficult the selection of clothing, as you will sweat, despite the cold, when working and various parts of your body, especially feet and crotch, will suffer if your clothing choice is not excellent.*

General items:

1. Geodesic dome tents are best (two- or three-man), but beware of the elastic

holding the poles together. When cold it loses elasticity so, if you have room on a sledge, keep as many of the pole sections permanently taped together as possible. Black tents make the most of the sun's heat and can be seen nearly as well as fluorescent colours.

2. Sledge harness and traces (solid traces are best for crevassed areas). In the Arctic Ocean pack ice, your sledge should be 'amphibious'.

3. Skis, skins, ski sticks and relevant spares. (Make sure your ski bindings mate well with your boots.)

4. With your sleeping bag and tent, use stuff sacs that don't need too much effort to squeeze in. In 2000, the best custom-made down gear in the UK comes from Peter Hutchinson Designs in Stalybridge.

5. MSR (Mountain Safety Research) cooker. Coleman fuel is best in extreme cold. (Be sure to get a secure fitting fixed to the lid of the box you carry your cook gear in.) Clip the MSR fuel bottle into it firmly before priming. You need a firm base. Take a spare MSR and bag of spares, especially a pricker. (Ensure your MSR fuel bottle tops have winterised washers if you intend to use them in extreme temperatures.)

6. Brush to clear snow (hard bristles).

7. Insulated mug and spoon. Set of cooking pots and pot holder.

8. Zippo lighter and spare flints. Use Coleman fuel.

9. Spare lighter.

10. Silva (balanced) compass and spare compass.

11. Reliable watch and spare.

12. Optional: a light rucksack.

13. Optional: windsail kit and spares in bag (unless travelling 'unsupported').

14. 2 ice screws. 1 pair jumars with loops.

15. Ice axe (very small, light model).

16. 16 m length of para cord.

17. 30 m of thinnest relevant climbing rope.

18. Optional: foldaway snow shovel.

19. Karabiners.

20. Karrimat.

21. Sleeping bag with inner (and optional outer) vapour barriers.

22. Pee bottle (Nalgene or Rubbermaid).

23. PLB (Personal Locator Beacon) and spare lithium battery.

24. GPS (Global Positioning System) and spare lithium battery (Garmin model is recommended).

25. Optional: HF radio and ancillaries (or Global Satellite mobile phone).

26. Video and still camera kit. Polythene bags to avoid misting up.

27. Steel thermos.

28. Rations (high-calorie and low-weight). Be-well Nutrition is best for extreme polar work. Pack as for a 24-hour day per tent.

29. Personal bag. This may contain: small adjustable spanner, pin-nose pliers, dental floss, needles, thin cord, Superglue, wire, diary and pencil, Velcro, charts and maps, Swiss Army knife (all necessary) and spare underwear (optional).

Medical kit:

This should include all that polar travellers advise, and may well include:

■ PAIN: Paracetamol for mild pain. For more severe pain and when inflammation is involved, use Ibuprofen. For severe pain, MST tablets or Buprenorphine or morphine (on prescription). Voltarol suppositories are a good additional painkiller. Be sure to study the instruction paper that comes with each of the above.

■ INFECTIONS/ANTIBIOTICS: Augmentin for dental and chest infections. Ciproxin is excellent for severe spreading infections of skin or gut or anything non-responsive to Augmentin. Cicatrin powder for dressing superficial cuts and rashes. Chloromycetin for eye infections. Flucloxacillin is powerful. Good for painful frostbitten toe areas.

■ WOUNDS: For deeper wounds, take threaded surgical needles. Take Lignocaine for self-injection for local anaesthetic. Use Steristrips for smaller wounds. For open blisters, burns and frost injuries, Flamazine cream is effective. Take alcohol swabs to clean wounds. Tegaderm second-skin dressings are useful. Granuflex dressings are good for open blisters and frostbite areas. Canesten powder for crotch fungal infection.

■ SICKNESS: Immodium is best for diarrhoea. If not effective, use Ciproxin. Buccastem is good for nausea (absorb in mouth, don't swallow).

■ SUNBLINDNESS: Take Amethocaine drops.

■ TEETH: Take oil of cloves. Also dental cement pack.

■ OTHER: Jelonet dressings for burns/scalds. Rolls of sticky plaster and gauze dressings. Bonjela for mouth ulcers. Neutrogena for hand sores. Anusol for haemorrhoids.

Other considerations

Remember that insurance, fully comprehensive and including possible search and rescue costs, is often mandatory and always sensible.

In Antarctica the best air charter company, Adventure Network International, will give you all the necessary advice on every side of your expedition. In the Canadian Arctic, First Air is the best (based at Resolute Bay, NWT). Remember that your cargo will cost a great deal at both ends. (In Antarctica, count on US$70 per kg above your basic allowance to get you there from Chile.)

Final advice

Don't go to the Arctic or Antarctica to do difficult journeys with folk you don't know about. They should be reliable, easy-going and experienced. You can get to both poles by paying expert guides to help you there. Some are to be avoided. Others, such as Pen Hadow, are excellent. All are expensive. Pay more and an aircraft will take you all the way to either pole and allow you an hour or two there, before whisking you back to warmer climes.

Never leave litter nor harm life in any form while you are there. The Everest climbers have polluted their grail. Keep our poles clean.

Plan with great care and never rely on gizmos working, PLBS and GPSS for instance, or count on immediate rescue, since storms can keep search planes away for days, even weeks, so play safe.

If you aim to join the weirdos' section by bicycling across Ellesmereland or 'collecting' different poles (geomagnetic, magnospheric, lesser accessibility, etc.) then plan accordingly. For example, if you intend doing the south pole on a pogo-stick, don't forget lots of low-temperature grease and your haemorrhoid cream. Have fun and stay cool. 🕏

Sir Ranulph Fiennes, bt, is one of today's greatest polar explorers.
He has been awarded the Founder's Medal of the Royal Geographical Society,
and the Polar Medal (with bar).

The motorbiker
by Ted Simon

IT SEEMS POINTLESS TO ARGUE THE MERITS OF MOTORCYCLES as against other kinds of vehicles. Everyone knows more or less what the motorbike can do, and attitudes to it generally are quite defined. Most are against it – and so much the better for those of us who recognise its advantages. Who wants to be part of a herd? Let me just say that I am writing here for people who are thinking of travelling through the broad open spaces of Africa, Latin America or Asia.

Here then are some points in favour of motorcycles for the few who care to consider them. In my view, the motorbike is the most versatile vehicle there is for moving through strange countries at a reasonable pace, for experiencing changing conditions and meeting people in remote places. It can cover immense distances and will take you where cars can hardly go. It is easily and cheaply freighted across lakes and oceans, and it can usually be trucked out of trouble without too much difficulty, while a car might anchor you to the spot for weeks.

Sit up and take notice

In return, the bike demands the highest levels of awareness from its rider. You need not be an expert, but you must be enthusiastic and keep your wits about you. It is an unforgiving vehicle that does not suffer fools. As well as the obvious hazards of potholes, maniacal truck drivers and stray animals, there are less tangible perils such as dehydration, hypothermia and mental fatigue to recognise and avoid.

The bike, then, poses a real challenge to its rider – and accepting it may seem to be almost masochistic, but my argument is that by choosing to travel in a way that demands top physical and mental performance you equip yourself to benefit a thousand times more from what comes your way.

You absolutely must sit up and take notice to survive at all. The weather and temperature are critical factors; the moods and customs of the people affect you vitally; you are vulnerable and sensitive to everything around you; and you learn fast. You build up resistances faster, too, your instincts are sharper and truer, and you adjust more readily to changes in the climate, both physical and social. Here endeth the eulogy upon the bike.

One's company

I travelled alone almost all the way around the world, but most people prefer to travel in company. As a machine, the motorcycle is obviously at its best used by one person, and it is my opinion that you learn faster and get the maximum feedback on your own, but I know that for many such loneliness would be unthinkable. Even so, you need to be very clear about your reasons for choosing to travel in company. If it is only for security, my advice is to forget it. Groups of nervous travellers chattering together in some outlandish tongue spread waves of paranoia much faster than a single weary rider struggling to make contact in the local language. A motorcycle will attract attention in most places. The problem is to turn that interest to good account. In some countries (Brazil, for example) a motorcycle is a symbol of playboy wealth, and an invitation to thieves. In parts of Africa and the Andes, it is still an unfamiliar and disturbing object. Whether the attention it attracts works for the rider or against him depends on his own awareness of others and the positive energy he can generate towards his environment.

It is very important in poor countries not to flaunt wealth and superiority. All machinery has this effect anyway, but it can be much reduced by a suitable layer of dirt and a muted exhaust system. I avoided having too much glittering chrome, and I regarded most modern leathers and motorcycle gear as a real handicap. I wore an open face helmet for four years, and when I stopped among people, I always took it off to make sure they saw me as a real person.

Don't...

Finally a few things I learned not to do. Don't ride without arms, knees and eyes covered, and watch out for bee swarms, unless you use a screen, which I did not. Don't carry a gun or any offensive weapon unless you want to invite violence. Do not allow yourself to be hustled into starting off anywhere until you're ready; something is bound to go wrong or get lost. Do not let helpful people entice you into following their cars at ridiculous speeds over dirt roads and potholes. They have no idea what bikes can do. Always set your own pace and get used to the pleasures of easy riding. Resist the habit of thinking that you must get to the next big city before nightfall. You miss everything that's good along the way and, in any case, the cities are the least interesting places. Don't expect things to go to plan, and don't worry when they don't. Perhaps the hardest truth to appreciate when starting a long journey is that the mishaps and unexpected problems always lead to the best discoveries and the most memorable experiences. And if things insist on going too smoothly, you can always try running out of petrol on purpose. ❧

TED SIMON has twice circled the globe on a Triumph 500 CC motorbike, recounted in 'Jupiter's Travels' and 'The River Stops Here'.

The hitch-hiker
by Simon Calder

WHY HITCH? HITCH-HIKING AS AN ART, OR SCIENCE, is almost as old as the motor car. Originally the concept was largely synonymous with hiking. You started walking, and if a car came along you put out your hand; mostly you ended up hiking the whole way. From this casually optimistic pursuit, hitching has evolved into a fast, comfortable form of travel in some parts of the world. Elsewhere it remains one big adventure.

Hitching has many virtues. It is the most environmentally sound form of motorised transport, since the hitcher occupies an otherwise empty space. Socially it can be rewarding, enabling you – indeed obliging you – to talk to people whom you would not normally meet. Financially it is highly advantageous: hitching allows you to travel from A to B for free or next to nothing, whether A is Aberdeen or Auckland, and B is Birmingham or Bucharest.

Yet standing for hours at a dismal road junction with the rain trickling morosely down your neck as heartless motorists stream past is guaranteed to make you question the wisdom of trying to thumb a ride. And placing yourself entirely in the hands of a complete stranger can be harrowing. Some travellers dislike the degree of dependence upon others that hitch-hiking engenders. Hitch-hiking can also be enormously lonely. Expect the elation of getting the ideal lift to be tempered with stretches of solitude and frustration and bear in mind that motorists rarely give lifts out of pure philanthropy. Your role may be to keep a truck driver awake with inane conversation, to provide a free English lesson or to act as a sounding board for a life history. But no two rides are ever the same. Techniques and conventions of hitch-hiking vary considerably around the world, most notably the divergence between fast, money-saving hitching in the West and the slower and more chaotic practices of lift-giving in less developed countries.

The West and the developed world

In Europe, North America and Australasia, hitching can be an almost mechanically precise way of travelling. The main criteria are safety and speed. To enable a motorist to decide whether or not to pick you up, he or she must be able to see you and stop safely. The driver must evaluate whether he or she can help you, and if you would enhance the journey. Make yourself as attractive as possible by looking casual but clean. Hitching in a suit raises driver's suspicions (normal dress for an average hitcher being denim). Looking as though you've been on the road for a year without a wash is equally counter-productive. So freshen up, choose a suitable stretch of road, smile and extend your arm. The actual gesture is a source of possible strife. In most parts of Europe and North America, the raised thumb is understood to be an innocent gesture indicating that a lift is needed. Elsewhere it represents one of the greatest insults imaginable. A vague wave in the general direction of the traffic is safest.

Never accept a lift with anyone who is drunk, high or otherwise gives you cause for concern (e.g. by squealing to a halt in a cloud of burning rubber after crossing six lanes of traffic to pick you up). Turning down a ride is easier said than done, especially if you have been waiting for six hours on a French *autoroute* and night is falling, but try to resist the temptation to jump into a van full of dubious characters. If you find out too late that you've accepted a dodgy ride, feign sickness and ask to be let out. It sometimes works.

Some offers should be turned down simply because they are not going far enough. Hitching through Germany from the Dutch border to the Polish frontier can be done in a day, but is best achieved by discriminating in your choice of lifts. Refuse a ride that would take you only 20 km to the next town. By hopping from one *autobahn* service area to another, you can cover ground extremely quickly.

All kinds of gimmicks can help you get rides more easily. The most effective device is a destination sign. Road systems in developed countries are often so complex that a single road may lead in several different directions. The only commonly enforced law on hitching is the one forbidding hitching on motorways, freeways or *autopistas*. By using a sign you minimise the risk that the driver who stops will want to drop you at an all-motorway junction such as those on London's M25 or the Boulevard Peripherique in Paris. Make your destination request as modest or as bold as you wish – from London you could inscribe your sign 'Dover' or 'Dar Es Salaam', but always add 'Please'.

Sophisticated hitchers concentrate their attention on specific cars. The real expert can spot a Belgian number plate at 100 metres. He or she will refuse lifts in trucks (too slow), and home in on the single male driver, who is easily the most likely provider of a lift. So good is the hitching in Germany that if you vowed to accept only lifts in Mercedes, you would still get around. Neighbouring France, in contrast, is hell for hitchers, as is much of southern Europe and Scandinavia.

Hitch-hiking is a cumulative experience, a never-ending happening of unknown factors which contribute to a memory of what real travelling is all about – the feeling that at one time, somewhere, even if only for an instant, you felt like you had become part of the land through which you travelled.
– KEN WELSH

Hitch-hikers fare well in the newly liberated nations of eastern Europe, especially Poland. It has a Social Autostop Committee – effectively a ministry for hitch-hiking – which provides incentives for motorists to pick up hitchers.

Having taken Lou Reed and Jack Kerouac's advice, and hitch-hiked across the USA, I would hesitate to recommend the experience to anyone. While the chances of being picked up by an oddball or religious fanatic in Europe are tiny, in the States almost every lift-giving motorist is weird and not necessarily friendly. New Zealand could not be more different: if you need a place to stay, just start hitching around nightfall, and a friendly Kiwi will almost certainly offer you a ride and a room. In Australia, the hitcher is the object of greater abuse than anywhere else, with insults (and worse) hurled from car windows alarmingly often.

One exception to the hitching lore of the developed world is Japan. Western hitch-hikers are picked up, usually very quickly, by one of the extremely considerate local drivers. In the absence of any other information, he or she will assume that you want to go to the nearest railway station. But upon learning that your final destination is hundreds of kilometres away in, say, Kyoto, the driver may feel duty bound to take you all the way there.

Japan is one place where women can feel comfortable hitching alone. The conventional wisdom is that women should never hitch alone. Single women hitch-hikers are all too often victims of male violence. Nevertheless, women continue to hitch alone, and get around without problem; some maintain that safety is largely a question of attitude: if you are assertive and uncompromising, you survive.

If 'real' hitching does not appeal, ride-sharing agencies exist in many countries. The idea is that travellers share expenses, and often the driving, and pay a small fee to the agency that arranges the introduction. Be warned, however, that there is no guarantee that a driver you contact in advance will not turn out to be a psychopath or a drunk as you hurtle through the Rocky Mountains or central Australia.

The concept of hitching can be extended to boats and planes. Hitching on water can involve anything from a jaunt along a canal in Europe to a two-month voyage to deliver a yacht from the Canary Islands to Florida. And in countries where private flying is popular, rides on light aircraft have been procured.

Less-developed countries

At the other extreme are the dusty highways of Nigeria or Nicaragua. In the Third World, the rules on hitching are suspended. Almost any vehicle is a possible lift-provider, and virtually every pedestrian is a potential hitch-hiker. Amid such good-natured anarchy, hitching is tremendous fun.

You have to accept any form of transport, from a horse and trap upwards. To make the most of opportunities, it helps to be adept at riding side-saddle on a tractor engine, or pillion on a moped for one.

Purists who regard paying for petrol as contrary to the ideals of hitch-hiking, and dismiss the idea of asking a driver for a ride as capitulation, can expect a miserable time in the Third World. Definitions of what constitutes a bus or a taxi, a truck or a private car, are blurred. Sometimes the only way to reach a place is by hitching, and local motorists may exploit their monopoly position accordingly.

El Salvador's transport system has been devastated. Everyone hitches, and you are expected to pay the equivalent of the fare on the (notional) bus. The same applies in large swathes of Latin America, Africa and south Asia. Unless you have insurmountable moral objections or a serious cash-flow crisis, you should always offer something for a ride. More often than you might expect, the ride will cost nothing more than a smile. In Indonesia, for example, the Western hitch-hiker is a curiosity, to be taken (temporarily) home and paraded in front of friends and relations as an exotic souvenir. You too can become an instant celebrity.

Cuba has massive transport problems, some of which are solved by an intriguing form of mass hitch-hiking. Little old ladies and large young louts join forces to persuade passing trucks to stop, or pile into a Lada saloon driven by a grumbling member of the bourgeoisie.

In such places hitching is at its simplest and most effective. Thumbing a ride enables you to see corners of the world that might otherwise remain hidden, and to meet people whom you would surely pass by. And, in the final analysis, there are worse ways to travel than being chauffeur-driven. ✍

SIMON CALDER is the Travel Editor of 'The Independent' and the author of several guidebooks, notably the 'Hitch-hiker's Manual (Britain and Europe)' and 'Panamericana'.

The luxury traveller
by Amy Sohanpaul

THE WORD LUXURY HAS BEEN USED so lavishly and slavishly by press officers and chocolate makers that we're in danger of forgetting what it really means. Not that the dictionary definition is perfect: 'something desirable for comfort or enjoyment, but not indispensable.'

Not indispensable? A little luxury is essential for real well-being. Happily, luxury doesn't always have a hefty price-tag. Stretching out in a sunny spot, finding time to stand and stare, having the papers delivered to the doorstep, a glass of wine in the bath: everyone has their own personalised version.

Luxury and travel

However, if you have a lot of time and a lot of money, or even just the latter, travel is one of those areas where you can find absolutes of luxury. A stratospheric price tag equals a whole exclusive world, far from the madding crowd. And if you're travelling first class, it starts at the airport – or if you're flying with Virgin it starts on your doorstep as they send a chauffeur to pick you up.

At the airport you're whisked through the speediest check-in to a private lounge and ushered into first class and, on some planes, tucked into bed. British Airways beds come with velvet head cushions and real cashmere blankets. If you must eat or drink, simply summon staff just desperate to serve you haute cuisine at 20,000 feet. Is the world your oyster or is the oyster your world?

The sky's the limit

What could be better than flying by first class? Travelling by private jet? TCS Expeditions will sort it out for you. Passengers travel aboard specially modified Boeing 757s. These give you access to the smaller airports in remoter places: you can hop between one exotic destination and the next as easily as a grasshopper leaps between blades of grass. The staff-to-passenger ratio is high – including chefs and professional expedition leaders and academic guides.

A few sample itineraries include Around Africa by Private Jet – Mali, Namibia and Madagascar are just a few of the stops on this trip. Or spend 21 days rediscovering History's Lost Cities from Angkor to Uzbekistan. If that isn't good enough, they can custom-make your own private jet expeditions (see www.tcs-expeditions.com). Many upmarket tour operators will organise exclusive private arrangements for you – fancy flying to the Caribbean at short notice and need a private jet, limousine transfers and a fully crewed and catered sailing ship? WEXAS and Abercrombie & Kent are just two companies who will organise it all while you pack your bikini.

Of course, you don't have to fly. Cruising is even more laid back than a reclining seat in first class, and increasingly popular. But don't let that put you off, just be aware that ships these days range from standard to sublime and choose accordingly. Those in the know have described the superliner Aurora as 'standard bucket-and-spades four star', notwithstanding the ship's penthouse suites, butler service and 30-foot cascading waterfall. The QEII still impresses, thanks to staff who endeavour to satisfy your every whim, fantastic suites with private balconies, and ever-changing views – this grandeur will probably always be a favourite for the classic transatlantic crossing, and is justifiably loved for its World Cruise – three months of non-stop glamour and luxury.

The lines that are repeatedly cited as the very best include Silversea Cruises, Crystal, Seabourn (part of Cunard), Radisson and Peter Dielmann. If you're still not convinced, then hire yourself a superyacht instead – complete with helicopter landing pads, mahogany bedrooms, jacuzzis on deck and cinemas inside (www.eliteyacht.com).

If you get sea-sick even in superliners, there's always the humble train. Such as the splendid Rovos Rail Pride of Africa trains – two restored steam trains that wind their way from Cape Town to Dar Es Salaam, or shorter routes, taking in overnight stays at selected game reserves. Still in South Africa, the Blue Train is another delight, and a spectacular way to travel between Pretoria and Cape Town. You can relax in en-suite compartments with crisp white bedding, telephones and televisions. Some even boast cd players, for playing blue savannah songs as Africa rolls past. After this hotel on wheels, try the Palace on Wheels – the only way to travel through Rajasthan. Passengers view forts and resplendent royal residences during stops and then retire to the air-conditioned elegance of their 'bed-chambers' or enjoy a pink gin in the bar as the train moves onto the next glorious place.

The world is his who has money to go over it.
– RALPH WALDO EMERSON

Or try the legendary Orient-Express; well, you don't have to try very hard. The food is splendid, the service even more so. This quality is a standard on all Orient-Express trains, which include the Great South Pacific Express between Cairns and Sydney, and the Eastern & Oriental Express between Bangkok and Singapore.

On the Venice-Simplon-Orient-Express the brass gleams, the wood shines, the original carriages are inlaid with marquetry. The view from the windows isn't too bad either, when you wake up in the Swiss Alps. And at the end of it all, there's Venice. Glorious even if staying in a sleeping bag, sublime when staying at the

Hotel Cipriani, with its elegance, sumptuous simplicity and views of the lagoon. The Gritti Palace runs it close for style and comfort, and houses Harry's Bar, the best place in the world to drink a Bellini.

That's Venice, which only leaves the rest of the globe to choose from. There simply isn't room to list all the most luxurious rooms and hotels within this chapter. Suffice to say that any member of Small Luxury Hotels of the World, of the reliable Relais & Chateaux group, or of The Leading Hotels of the World, is probably going to meet the mark.

There are some hotel groups which you just know will provide the best of the best – Four Seasons' hotels, from New York to the Maldives, hit the perfect spot every time; while the Aman hotels aren't so much hotels as experiences – of sheer indulgence.

Take their Amanwana resort in Indonesia, for example. It's as rough and ready as an Aman hideaway gets – tents on a jungle-covered island. It's a long hop, skip and jump to this remote retreat and the final leg is on a motorcruiser, when the fun begins as the taste of champagne mingles with the delicious spray of the ocean. Winding paths of sand lead to each tent – which seems as appropriate as calling Windsor Castle a wee wigwam. They come complete with living room, writing desks and state of the art bathrooms with his and hers sinks. Staff outnumber guests by at least three to one.

People do get addicted to the Aman group. In the Amanwana bar I met a couple on honeymoon who had decided to spend it visiting various Aman resorts. They had planned on a year, which seemed fair. Or unfair, if you had to get back to work sometime soon, as I did.

I want to be alone

Of course, even the most exclusive hotels can seem a little crowded at times, which is when only a villa will do. It's possible to have anything from a château to a reworked cowshed at your disposal, with or without maid service. Some villas are part of hotels so you get full-on service and privacy. For instance, the two bedroom Royal Villa, is part of the beautiful Rajvilas resort in Jaipur, comes complete with grand dining-room, private garden and its own pool.

Traditional, private villas are just as luscious. Villas of the World offer gems in fabulous settings around the globe, with air-conditioned bedrooms, stunning pools, plus a full-time staff at your disposal, including a chauffeur. Smaller companies come up with the goods too, and the better ones have personal knowledge of all the properties on their books. Tuscany Now is particularly good for anything from a one-bedroom cottage to a thousand-year-old castle in Italy.

The most scenic, most idyllic privacy belongs to island retreats. Mnemba Island off the coast of Zanzibar is a shoeless haven, serenity lapped by gentle waves. Some of the Maldives resorts are worth a retreat before the islands disappear altogether, due to rising water levels. The Four Seasons at Kuda Huraa (with wonderful water-villas built on stilts over the lagoon) and Soneva Fushi (notable for its splendid spa) are among the best resorts on these enchanted islands.

Fiji is paradise for Robinson Crusoe fans: with over 330 islands to choose from, one or two are going to make the perfection grade. Vatulele Island Resort does, with just 18 Fijian-style *bures* (thatched huts) fronting a fantasy white beach, with an extra extra-special *bure* for honeymooners which is booked up virtually all year every year. The ultimate has to be Turtle Island, with 14 *bures* (thatched huts) and 14 private beaches. The bliss of a beach each cannot be overestimated.

Dream on

The most wonderful thing about luxury travel is that the possibilities are endless. The best of the best is out there and there are numerous companies who will be delighted to put it together for you, such as WEXAS. Fancy a personalised safari with your own guides, virtually your own game reserve, as well as exquisite three course dinners in the bush? A private pool to float in between game watching? No problem, speak to Abercrombie and Kent or any number of safari specialists. A personalised shopping tour in India? Western and Oriental, or Cox and Kings, are India experts. Not sure when to go or where to go, but money no object? See any of the above, or the small but knowledgeable Nomadic Thoughts, whose offices I visited on a bleak rainy day in London. Large gin and tonics were poured as map after map of the world was unfurled and route after route was planned and plotted.

Deciding where you're going to go, whether you choose an old jalopy or a private jet is the most fun. But perhaps the simple privilege of being able to travel is the greatest luxury of them all. ❧

AMY SOHANPAUL is an Editor of 'The Traveller's Handbook' and has a predilection for the finer things in life.

The green traveller
by Matthew Brace

FIRST, A DEFINITION. 'ECOTOURISM', a buzz word for the twenty-first century, is a *portmanteau* word used to describe a wide range of approaches, from ultra-green forest lodges operating in complete harmony with their environment to hotels that trample acres of precious forest and then name their rooms after the rare birds that used to live there. ❧

A better term, and the one preferred by the pressure group Tourism Concern, is 'sustainable tourism', which is variously defined as responsible travel to natural areas that maintains care for the environment and improves the welfare of the local people. By its very nature, tourism is rarely wholly ecologically friendly. Even if you sailed on a homemade driftwood raft to a holiday island, dropped no litter, killed only time and left only footprints (to quote a wise if oft-used phrase), you would still inevitably have some impact on the environment. However, it is possible to explore this wonderful planet while at the same time dramatically reducing your impact on its ecosystems, and in some cases actively helping by contributing tourist money to conservation programmes. No self-respecting independent traveller with a passion for the environment should leave home without the will to seek out the most ecological way to travel.

What is needed is a modicum of respect. Respect for a rainforest's beauty, respect for a tribal people's beliefs and customs, respect for nature. A little more respect, say, than is currently being displayed by a company offering what they call an 'eco-safari', in which tourists are given the opportunity to shoot pellets of washable luminous-pink paint at the noble elephants of Zimbabwe. And just in case the elephant takes offence, a hunter is on hand to shoot it with a real bullet.

So when you step set out on your trip, take time to check that, along with the sun creams and guidebooks, you have also spared a thought for why the destination attracted you in the first place and what impact your visit will have.

Why should we care?

Increasing numbers of people are travelling to more and more distant destinations. One exotic spot that has gained huge popularity for its wildlife and beauty is the small Central American nation of Costa Rica. Its position – forming a bridge between North and South America – means it is blessed with some of the most diverse flora and fauna on Earth. But all is not well in the forest. In 1980, Costa Rica had just 3,000 international visitors. In 1998 943,000 came and in 2000 the figure was over 1 million. By 1992 that figure had jumped to 64,000. Tourism brought in US$700 million in 1996, which was 30 per cent of total exports and 8.5 per cent of GNP. The year 1998 heralded a $4 million government publicity campaign, and in 1999 Costa Rica welcomed over 800,000 visitors. In 2000 the revenue brought in through tourism was more than US$1,100 million. The country is now at a crossroads in terms of tourism development. Biological reserves such as the Monteverde Cloud Forest Reserve face the problem of balancing the preservation of their ecosystems with the streams of paying tourists that come to see them.

Rodrigo Carazo, former Costa Rican president, is very much aware of the problem but views the situation as a positive opportunity to reduce deforestation: "It is about selling one tree a million times through tourism, rather than once through timber logging." Throughout the 1980s, however, Costa Rica had one of the highest deforestation rates in the world, mainly as a result of the demand for land for cattle-ranching and timber production. Forests covered 72 per cent of Costa Rica in the late 1950s. Now the only remaining forest is within protected areas and represents just 14 per cent of the country.

The world's most popular tourist honeypots are also under intense threat. According to UN predictions, visitors to the Mediterranean could total 760 million by 2025, adding to a resident population of 150 million. This would put huge strain on the environment, vastly increasing the amount of sewage discharged into the sea and thus endangering the habitat of marine animals and plants.

Coral reefs are the most endangered of all the world's ecosystems (more so even than the rainforests), yet only recently have conservation projects begun in earnest. Among other measures, these aim to protect reefs against the tourist habit of breaking off coral (accidentally or intentionally) to provide ornaments for their mantelpieces back home.

Programmes for change

On paper...

Ecotourism has burgeoned to such an extent that an international agency has been set up to monitor its direction worldwide. The Washington-based International Ecotourism Society (TIES) recently reported that currently, in the US alone, the 'ecological lifestyle market', which includes ecotourism, is estimated to be worth US$81.2billion per year.

"TIES remains convinced that 'green' certification programmes and eco-labels are important tools in helping to set standards and measure consequences," said Executive Director Martha Honey. "Our vision is to launch in 2006, along with a coalition of partner organisations, the Sustainable Tourism Stewardship Council to act as a global accreditation body for 'green' certification programs."

And in action...

Major TIES projects have included visitor management schemes in the Galapagos Islands (a rapidly growing tourist destination with a fragile ecosystem); national park-user fees in Costa Rica; and guidelines and monitoring programmes for nature tour operators with sustainable planning and design recommendations. Most recently, they have also embarked on a consumer education campaign highlighting the impact of travel and how to choose responsible tour operators.

Governments the world over have formulated national ecotourism projects, and many have even signed up, via the United Nations Commission on Sustainable Tourism, to international commitments to sustainable tourism. At the same time, local communities are also taking matters into their own hands, making a success of smaller projects that bring positive results for local residents. These are the communities who know only too well that 'sustainable tourism' is an empty concept if it does not include people as well as flora and fauna.

Environmental and ecological protection tends to work best when it takes into account the benefits for local people. Tourism Concern's *Community Tourism Guide* includes community-based projects and tours all over the world.

Some simple steps for sustainable travel

Do your homework. Choose your destination with care. Read up and and inform yourself about the current issues of environmental contention. Ecotourism is the flavour of the month for travel agents and tour operators. A number of them are far from green, however, and are merely using the phenomenon of green travel as a device to sell more holidays. Tourism Concern has some useful questions to ask your travel agent before you go:

- Is any of the hotels you use owned or managed by local residents?
- Can you assure me that the hotels you use do not diminish the supply of water to local people for domestic, animal or agricultural use?

- Is adequate provision made for disposing of sewage and other waste without damaging the local environment?
- Can you assure me the hotels are not built on sacred sites or burial grounds?
- Can you assure me that the tourism developments you are offering have not deprived people of their homes or livelihoods?
- Are you working with Tourism Concern or any human rights organisations to work out how to deal with these issues?

They may not have the answers at their fingertips, but give them time to check. And Tourism Concern would like to know what they have to say.

And when in paradise?

The renowned conservationist David Bellamy believes certain rules must be adhered to if tourism is to function in harmony with the environment:

- Visitor numbers must be limited.
- At least 50 per cent of all profits should go back to the local community.
- Accommodation should be built on land that has already been altered.
- Alternative sources of energy and renewable local resources must be used where possible.
- Local travel should be by foot or boat, with the use of internal combustion engines kept to a minimum.

"If that sounds boring," adds the great professor, "then please stay away. If you demand more, many people and their resources will not stand a chance. I sincerely believe that this is both their and our last chance."

Take Bellamy at his word and add a few more sustainable travelling tips to your list. Use public transport whenever possible to save fuel. If public transport is not available, get together with other sustainable travellers you meet along the way and hire a minibus (it will save you money, too). Bicycle hire can be very cheap, and can offer you access to areas that you would not be able to reach by motor vehicle. Don't drop litter (piles of pink toilet paper are reported in the foothills of the Himalayas). And when walking through eco-sensitive areas such as national parks, keep to the trails. This will not merely help to preserve the beauty of these areas – it might also save you from a close encounter with a territorially defensive snake. ❧

MATTHEW BRACE is a journalist specialising in environmentally-aware tourism.

The gay traveller
by Caspar van Vark

I NEVER EXPECTED DUNEDIN, on New Zealand's south island, to have a vibrant gay scene. And I was right – it doesn't. But it was Saturday night, and I was in town on my own. I certainly wasn't about to spend the evening watching CNN. I popped into an internet café and logged on to Gaydar. I soon found the Dunedin chat room, and a local student messaged me. Would I like to come to the university's gay night down at the union bar? Would I ever! I went along and had a great night of beer and darts with the local students.

At times like that, especially as a solo traveller, it's quite handy being gay. Scratch the surface of any town, and you'll usually find a few queens somewhere clutching their designer beers. It's not quite like *Cheers*, where everybody knows your name, but it can still be fun to tap into local gay scenes.

Of course, typically gay holiday destinations don't require any such effort. They say that in London, you're never more than five feet from a rat. In Sitges, Mykonos and Gran Canaria, you're never more than five feet from a nipple-ring and *Kylie's Greatest Hits*. But no-one really needs any more information on these places. Even Paris Hilton goes to Mykonos now. Sydney, New York, San Francisco and Cape Town? Yes, yes, we know. Many gay men and lesbians love those cities, but a survey in California recently found that 56 per cent of gay men and lesbians take three or more holidays a year. It doesn't have to be Soho-on-Sea every time, or any time. Gay men and lesbians enjoy the Amalfi coast and trekking in Nepal as much as anyone else. Strewth, I found other gay travellers in Alice Springs, and I wasn't even looking. (No *Priscilla, Queen of the Desert* jokes, please.)

On the other hand, there are still some no-go zones. Getting off the beaten track is fun; getting beaten up isn't. So before we list some new hotspots, let's name and shame a few places where it's not so cool to be queer.

How about Egypt? Yes, the pyramids are awe-inspiring. But in 2001, 23 gay men received up to five years' hard labour for 'debauchery'. Three years before that, the Cayman Islands turned away a gay cruise ship. In Nigeria, two men recently received death sentences for sodomy, and President Mugabe has led a vigorous crackdown on gay people in Zimbabwe, calling them 'worse than dogs and pigs'. Fortnight in Harare, anyone? Or maybe you fancy Jamaica, easily the most homophobic country in the Caribbean. Oh, and three cheers for progressive Zanzibar, which in 2004 made gay sex punishable with 25 years in prison (lesbians are lucky – they only get seven years).

Gay people can and do still travel to these places and others, and everyone can choose to do so. I found Saudi Arabia fascinating to visit, even if it's a terrible place to be gay. And besides, you don't have to go far to get a hostile reception: only last year a B&B in Scotland famously refused to give a gay couple a double room.

Meanwhile, other places are growing in popularity. Puerto Vallarta in Mexico has sprung up as a gay destination in the past few years (www.gayguidevallarta.com) and now boasts over 15 gay bars and clubs and many gay-friendly hotels. It's popular with Americans but less well-known to UK travellers. Costa Rica has also become a popular choice (www.gaycostarica.com), particularly the beach town of Quepos which has a large expatriate gay population.

Buenos Aires is more low-key than Rio, but since 1996, anti-discrimination laws have helped relax the atmosphere for gay people. It has a European feel, with a lively café culture and an open-minded society. Gay tourism from the US is reportedly booming there.

Pink pink sunshine

Our World (gay/lesbian travel mag) www.ourworldmagazine.com

Out & About (newsletter) www.outandabout.com

Passport (gay/les travel mag, 8 times a year) www.passportmagazine.net

Gay Travel News (gay destination web site, updated quarterly, with links to 200 gay friendly travel agents and hotels around the world) www.gaytravelnews.com

www.outtraveler.com (by the publishers of OUT and the Advocate)

Gaydar Travel (www.gaydartravel.com) new travel site from the Gaydar dating brand

Olivia (www.olivia.com) lesbian tour operator

Purpleroofs.com (guide to gay/friendly hotels and B&Bs)

Global Gayz (www.globalgayz.com) Worldwide gay travel guide, info, photos, news

And speaking of the US, did you know that Dallas has a huge gay population of around 120,000? Pamela Ewing is alive and well on the cabaret circuit there. Dallas also has the largest gay and lesbian church in the world, with over 30,000 members. Las Vegas and Minneapolis are known for being pinker than average too.

On the other side of the world, Israel emerged in the Nineties as something of a gay oasis in the Middle East, with the most liberal laws in the region. Tel-Aviv has a Western-style bar and club scene and there are annual, if controversial, pride marches there and in Jerusalem.

In all of these places and many more, travelling lesbians are generally less well-catered for than gay men. Typical gay destinations remain male-biased, even though all generally welcome the sisterhood. Hurrah for the internet, then, because there are some good resources aimed at lesbian travellers. Starting at home, www.gingerbeer.co.uk is a hub for lesbian London. The portal www.lesbian.com has a good travel section, and www.sistertrip.com has travel messageboards too. If you're heading to New Zealand, www.womentravel.co.nz is a must. And Damron (www.damron.com) publishes a travel resource for lesbians covering North America, Europe, Mexico and the Caribbean.

There are also a number of resorts and companies aimed at lesbians, such as Olivia (www.olivia.com), a US travel company, and Pearls Rainbow (www.pearlsrainbow.com), a women-only resort in Key West, Florida. In the UK, lesbians seem limited to Walking Women (www.walkingwomen.com) which, unsurprisingly, organises walking holidays in the UK, but also operates abroad, as far away as South Africa. However, gay travel companies like Respect (www.respect-holidays.co.uk) and even Man Around (www.manaround.com) cater equally to gay men and lesbians.

The internet has also spawned a few gay home exchange schemes. These include www.gayhometrade.com and www.gayhomexchange.com. One advantage of using these over a mainstream home exchange must be that you don't have to de-gay your home for Joe and Betsy from Kansas. Heterosexuals are welcome to use these exchanges too, but don't be taken in by the myth that gay people are legally required to have fabulous homes. It really isn't true.

And finally, as if there weren't already enough good reasons to travel, we now have gay wedding tourism. Canada recently legalised gay marriages, and unlike Holland, Belgium and Spain, it does not have citizenship requirements, so anyone can get married there. The UK has civil partnerships now too, and even some US states allow marriage or civil unions. These changes mean people from less open-minded parts of the world want to go to a place where they can marry. Just Google 'gay wedding package' to find companies willing to arrange gay wedding trips.

If you own a copy of Spartacus, the weighty global gay guide, you'll know that it's easy to fill a whole book with gay travel tips. There isn't room for that here, but just to prove how diverse gay travel can be, I urge you to visit www.bear-olderman-yachting.com. This travel company specialises in yachting trips around Turkey for overweight, hairy, older gay men – known as 'bears'. If that isn't a niche market, I don't know what is. ❧

CASPAR VAN VARK grew up in South-East Asia and the Middle East. He is now a London-based freelance writer, editor and broadcaster.

The disabled traveller
by Carey Ogilvie

S O ACCESSIBLE HAS THE WORLD BECOME IN THE LAST 20 YEARS or so that no one now blinks an eyelid if you click on to www.lastminute.com on the spur of the moment and dash off to Paris for the weekend. The ease with which we are able to travel the world grows annually. With more people travelling, the industry fights for our custom; airlines negotiate new routes and tantalise us with special offers on the internet; operators offer more and more irresistible deals; and guidebooks and information abound as never before: the world, in short, is our oyster.

The same is not true for disabled travellers, however. Although numerous or-ganisations and charities have consistently offered help and advice, it is only in the last five years or so that attitudes have begun to change within the tourist industry. As with most changes in any industry, this has been market-forced: according to the us National Organisation of Disability, 54 million Americans have some sort of disability. In the UK, meanwhile, even with the 1995 Disability Discrimination Act in force, there is still a long way to go before travel becomes plain sailing for the wheelchair-bound.

But success as a disabled traveller often depends on your attitude of mind, and great things are possible even though you may not always find that the system works for you. Nevertheless, there are a number of organisations that exist in order to help you.

Independent travel

On the whole, public transport wherever you may be is not designed with the disabled in mind, but improvements are taking place and in the UK are set to continue with the implementation of the transport regulations of the Disability Discrimination Act.

Airlines have greatly improved the facilities they offer, and most now have set procedures for assisting disabled passengers. But – unlike other forms of transport – there are no discounts available, and there is a strong feeling among disabled people that airlines do not actively encourage us to travel by air.

Generally, the best advice is to give the airline as much notice as possible and to obtain detailed advice from the airline regarding exactly what they can and will provide. If you are in a wheelchair, you are more than likely to remain in your wheelchair until just before boarding. Most airlines provide an on-board wheelchair, but it all depends on the aircraft, the airline and the airport. Tales of being hoisted up through the cargo holds are not unknown.

Everybody's Airline Directory (www.everybody.co.uk) offers a listing of each airline's disabled policy, including whether they will carry guide dogs, whether the cabin staff are disability trained, whether disabled passengers must be accompanied or not, and so on. Most of the major leading airlines have some planes equipped with accessible toilets. Check with the airline concerned, but do not assume either that this will be the case or that they will not change the aircraft at the last moment.

Like your suitcase, your wheelchair runs the risk of being damaged by the time it is returned to you, but on the whole airlines do try to make an effort. A notable exception is Ryanair, which instead tries to make money: their policy is to charge passengers with disability a handling charge of £12.50 per assistance required, i.e. on boarding and disembarkation. A return fare therefore costs an extra £50, making Ryanair not quite the low-cost carrier it claims to be.

If you are travelling by ferry, the general rule again is to let the ferry company know your needs. Ask them if you can board your vehicle at the head of the queue, so that you can get out of it before another car is parked alongside it (making it almost impossible to open a door, let alone move a wheelchair).

Discounts on ferry travel are available to members of the Disabled Drivers' Motor Club, Cosy Nook, Cottingham Way, Thrapston, Northamptonshire NN14 4PL, tel 01832 734724 or the Disabled Drivers' Association, Ashwellthrope Hall, Ashwellthrope, Norwich, NR16 1EX, tel 0870 770 3333. Even if you are not a member of one of these organisations, some ferry companies still offer discounts, so do enquire.

The main challenge of travelling by rail in the UK is not so much the rolling stock but the stations, many of which have footbridges and stairs. Each rail operator is required to offer a dedicated number that disabled passengers may ring to arrange assistance. The national rail travel helpline, on 08457 484950, will be able to give you individual numbers for the required rail service. All credit to Eurostar, who have really got their act together: all their facilities are fully accessible to people in wheelchairs, those with walking difficulties, the partially sighted and people with hearing difficulties. Blind people and wheelchair users with one travelling companion are entitled to a preferential fare, moreover. The equivalent of less than the regular Standard Class price, this includes seating in First Class accommodation, which features a special wheelchair area.

Getting to most airports and railway stations – and above all getting across London – almost invariably requires a sense of humour and a great deal of patience. Although no longer banned from the London Underground, wheelchair users will find the London Underground system almost impossible (the Manchester Metrolink, by contrast, is fully accessible and has one wheelchair space in each carriage).

Too often… I would hear men boast only of the miles covered that day, rarely of what they had seen.
– LOUIS L'AMOUR

Two publications are available to help you across London. *Access to the Underground* is available from RADAR (the Royal Association for Disability and Rehabilitation, 12 City Forum, 250 City Road, London EC1V 8AF, tel 020 7250 3222), price £1. It provides a general description of each line, a guide to fixed stairs in stations with escalators, access details from station entrances to platforms and interchange information. The excellent guidebook *Access in London*, available in bookshops, includes chapters on travel in and around the capital.

And what about hotels? Unlike airlines, the hotel industry caters well for the disabled traveller. When choosing a hotel (especially abroad), check that the facilities that are important to you are accessible. They might have a room designed for the disabled, but then you may find five steps leading up to the restaurant. As always, explain your needs and wishes when you book. An excellent alternative to staying in a hotel is a home exchange. Accessible Home Exchange, run by the Swedish organisation Independent Living, has a web site (www.independentliving.org) offering a good choice of homes. Swapping homes with another person with similar needs in another part of the world is a low-cost and practical solution to accommodation problems.

Cruising is one of the easiest and most popular forms of travel for the disabled. The choice of cruise ships and destinations grows each year, as a wider choice of accessible ships becomes available. On the whole, the most recently built ships offer the most facilities for the disabled. The *2005 Guide to Cruising* (Berlitz) is a good place to start your research into different cruise lines and ships. As well as assessing all cruise ships and offering advice on selecting and booking a cruise, it also has an entire chapter dedicated to cruising for the disabled.

Organisations offering general help and advice on travelling with disabilities include not only RADAR but also Tripscope (The Vassall Centre, Gill Avenue,

Useful books

- *Smooth Ride Guides – Freewheeling Made Easy* (Smooth Ride Guides, tel 01279 777966, www.smoothrideguides.com) are a series of comprehensive guides for travellers in wheelchairs.

- Mobility International USA (PO Box 10767, Eugene, OR 97440, USA, tel 00 1 541 343 1284) publish a comprehensive two-volume guide entitled *A World Of Options*. Its 600+ pages are packed with personal travel accounts and essential information on travelling, working or being a volunteer abroad. It also offers in-depth critiques of airlines, car rental companies, hotels, cruise ships and adventure packages.

- If you are worried about the challenge of travelling, Patrick Simpson's *Wheelchair Around the World*, telling the story of how he and his wife Anne fulfilled their lifelong dream to travel around the world, is inspirational. The Simpsons' advice could stand as a resourceful guide for all, and their story exudes an addictive spirit of adventure that will inspire many to follow in their tracks.

- For the past 20 years, RADAR has published *Holidays in Britain and Ireland – A Guide for Disabled People*. The current edition includes detailed information on over 1,300 places to stay. It is available from www.radar.org.uk. RADAR also produces three excellent *Holiday Facts* packs to guide you through every stage of a holiday.

Bristol BS16 2QQ, tel 08457 585641, www.tripscope.org.uk) and the Holiday Care Service, 7th Floor, Sunley House, 4 Bedford park, Croydon, Surrey CR0 2AP, tel 0845 124 9971 www.holidaycare.org.uk). Holiday Care Service, a registered charity established in 1981, has been instrumental in changing attitudes within the industry. It now publishes UK regional guides to accommodation that is accessible for the wheelchair user, all of which can be booked through the organisation at discounted prices. The free service provided by Tripscope is perhaps the most informative of all: although they are not a travel agent and therefore cannot arrange bookings, their suggestions pave the way.

Various travel agents (often run by people with disabilities) specialise in travel for the disabled. Can Be Done (tel 020 8907 2400, www.canbedone.co.uk) arranges group and individual travel for people with all types of physical limitation.

Organised tours

Numerous companies organise tours for the disabled. Some are mixed ability tours while others are solely for the handicapped; some are charities and others work on a commercial basis. The opportunities, however, are endless.

One of the most inspiring charities is Across, who organise tours and pilgrimages for the severely disabled in their Jumblances. They started in 1972 with a transit van to Lourdes, and now offer a wide range of holidays in Europe and the Holy Land. Jumblances are fitted with adjustable tubular aluminum beds, sleeper and reclining seats, resuscitation equipment, oxygen, pressure mattresses and every other facility necessary for the comfort and safety of their passengers.

For those who want to go below the surface, the Scubatrust (tel 07985 025385) is the brainchild of a group of diving enthusiasts and instructors who were determined to give people with physical disabilities an equal opportunity to experience the pleasures of snorkelling and diving.

Neverland Adventures (3940, 7th Avenue, Suite 103, San Diego, California, USA, tel 00 1 619 291 8226, www.neverland-adventures.com) is a company owned and staffed by people with disabilities, whose specialty is adventure trips to Australia and now New Zealand. Their Outback Experience includes a hot-air balloon trip at Ayers Rock.

Another sporting holiday on offer is skiing. As they say at the Uphill Ski Club, "Why shouldn't you have a wheelchair at the top of a mountain?" Founded over 25 years ago, the club is committed to providing winter sports activities for people with a wide range of disabilities, including cerebral palsy, spina bifida, epilepsy, learning difficulties, head injuries and sensory handicaps. For further information, contact them at 6A Emson Close, Saffron Walden, Essex CB10 1HL, tel 01799 525406, or through their Northern Office at Cairngorm Mountain, Via Aviemore, Invernesshire PH22 1RB, tel 01479 861 272, or visit www. uphillskiclub.co.uk.

The most important thing for both the consumer and the travel industry to remember is that there is no such thing as a holiday that is unsuitable for people with disabilities, whatever their needs: everything depends on the degree of disability and the attitude of all concerned.

Happy freewheeling. &

CAREY OGILVIE was Assistant Editor of a previous edition of 'The Traveller's Handbook' and now works in the travel industry.

Where do you want to go?

Tomorrow's destinations
by Jonathan Lorie

WHERE'S HOT, WHERE'S HIP, WHERE'S 'HAPPENING'? The burning question for the independent traveller is how to find the next generation of destinations, the places that are 'special' but still unspoilt.

The reality, of course, is that there is almost nowhere left on the surface of this planet that is completely 'unspoilt'. Possibly on the steppes of outer Mongolia, but even there they're hooking up satellite television sets to oil-burning generators in an effort to enter the global culture. Even in the rainforests of central Africa, there are villagers clothed in T-shirts that read, bizarrely, 'Vote for Bill Clinton'. There is precious little escape from our modern world. And in the era of the internet and the mobile phone, it is almost impossible to sever the ties from home.

One solution, for those who can afford it, is to escape into the realm of luxury travel. There is a whole range of private islands, stucco hotels, grand trains and shiny yachts, in which the affluent traveller can recreate a version of how travel might once have been, in the days before cheap flights filled the globe with resorts.

Not so much a destination as a way of life, luxury travel is opening new frontiers all the time. Its big success right now is cruising, and the cruise operators are aiming for a younger, hipper customer. The appeal behind it all is the fact that the scenery comes to you, as you lie on deck enjoying the comforts of five-star service.

Lolling on a sun deck quaffing champagne is nice work if you can get it, but it's not the same as experiencing the reality and the totality of a country that is new to tourism. Such places do still exist. The ultimate example is probably Bhutan, a tiny kingdom high in the Himalayas, where only a trickle of travellers is permitted entry. This is the most 'unspoilt' Buddhist culture on earth. Next door is tiny Mustang, an even more restricted kingdom, about which almost nothing is known.

Even less well-known areas exist in the inhospitable hinterlands of the world. In Papua New Guinea, explorers do still encounter tribesmen who have not seen white skin before. The Amazon basin is opening up for tourism, especially wildlife and river safaris – and including, I am told, a jungle nudist resort. Australia has vast areas of outback that are uncharted territory: though there may be good reasons for this. Essentially, the rawest travel experiences will be found in those places that are the most unpleasant to visit – malarial swamps in the Congo, say.

Slightly more enjoyable for the ordinary traveller are those countries which are just opening the door to foreigners. Vietnam was the classic example, 15 years ago, and still offers a wonderful experience of the fragile beauty of Indochina. Next on the way is Cambodia, home to the jungle-clad ruins of Angkor. Interestingly, the isolation of both countries was a historical accident (caused by the Vietnam War), and it is such 'victims' of history that can be the most rewarding to visit.

Cuba is the outstanding example of this. Long embargoed by the United States, it has emerged from Cold War quarantine and become a massive hit with travellers of all kinds. It offers hot music, fine beaches, picturesque towns and the frisson of history. Because it was isolated for so long from the modern world, its traditions and essential character have been preserved intact – for the time being at least.

The same is true of Libya, which has some of the finest and emptiest Classical sites in the Mediterranean, and is now opening for business as the politics sort themselves out and it enters the global community.

South Africa, too, has transformed itself from a pariah state under apartheid – only a decade ago – to the tourist hub of southern Africa. Right now it is booming. But just as politics opened the doors there, politics in neighbouring Zimbabwe have closed the doors, and travellers no longer flock there. In the same region, newly opened countries like Namibia and Mozambique are attracting tourists for their 'unspoilt' and dramatic beauty.

Could this be the future for Africa's other failed states, if stability ever comes? Could it happen in Sudan, which has more ancient pyramids than Egypt? Sierra Leone, which is an achingly beautiful place? Ethiopia could go either way. In such places, politics and history are everything.

Closer to home, the time-warp effect is visible in many post-Soviet countries. Romania and Hungary offer a glimpse of a picturesque older Europe as it existed before the Second World War. The Baltic republics bristle with fairytale castles and quaint cities, in a classic northern European landscape of pine forests and lakes. Montenegro is a jewel of Ottoman imperial architecture. Georgia offers fine skiing and cheap champagne. And all the countries that have just joined the European Union are suddenly open, accessible, and eager for your visit: the eastern coast of the Adriatic, a string of pretty islands and Baroque towns, is booming.

Central Asia is another beneficiary of the Soviet Union's collapse. Samarkand, Bokhara, Tashkent – these are names dripping with myth. Now you can fly there from London. The Silk Route can be traced from start to finish, with or without an organised tour. No longer are you subject to endless red tape and incomprehensible official guides – though the crumbling infrastructure can be a real challenge.

And as Russia collapsed, so China relaxed. Foreigners have been able to travel through most of the celestial republic for 15 years now. Some areas are closed off, others are just impenetrable, but in a country this big there's plenty to discover. Catch it while you can, before it goes the way of so much of the newly-rich Far East and becomes a sprawling suburb of shopping malls and shabby skyscrapers.

But the effect of politics on tourism cuts both ways, and in our era of global tensions there are losers and winners. The Muslim world, most obviously, is losing tourists fast, as Westerners become nervous about safety and hostility.

How far those anxieties are justified is a matter of debate. One still hears many examples of the traditional hospitality and elaborate courtesy of the Middle East being extended to travellers, as before. On the other hand, clearly some countries offer greater opportunities for Islamic militants than others, and many travellers are wary of unruly places like Somalia or the wilder tribal areas of Pakistan.

However, hardier travellers may be pleased to visit certain destinations when they are so empty. This is your best chance to visit the rock-cut city of Petra or the crusader castles of Syria without the crowds. Iran has dazzling Islamic architecture and very hospitable people. Adventurers are even returning to Afghanistan – though you'd have to think hard about the safety issues there.

A less obvious result of the current 'war on terrorism' is that tourists are turning to a continent not affected: Latin America. Traditionally this has been a low priority for most Europeans, but it has a wealth of attractions, and in recent years its crime rates and political troubles have eased somewhat. Here you'll find some of the world's most dramatic mountains, jungles and ethnic cultures, vibrant modern cities and stunning beaches.

Bolivia is a case in point. A giant slumbering in the heart of Latin America, it spans the dramatic Andes, the mysterious *altiplano* and the luxuriant Amazon jungle – but no one goes there. Peru has fabulous Inca sites and the mysterious Nazca lines, Ecuador has the wildlife paradise of the Galapagos islands, Chile has the brooding statues of Easter Island, Argentina has the majestic wilderness of Patagonia, Guatemala has stunning Mayan ruins and Caribbean beaches....

Moving on from the big trends, there are other destinations which ought to be ruined by tourism, but remain surprisingly quiet. Madagascar is an island the size of Britain, blessed with the sunshine and beaches of the Indian Ocean. Its people are a beguiling mixture of African and Arabic, and its unique ecosystem ranges from rainforest to desert to mountains. It's empty of tourists.

Sri Lanka ought to be full. Imagine India without the madness, a lush and laid-back island where Buddhism sets a gentle tone and history has left resonant monuments. It's a delight.

Botswana doesn't receive many visitors, although the Okavango delta is one of the most magical places anywhere. Floating through the reeds in a dugout canoe surrounded by singing birds and flowering lilies, or walking the islands among giraffe and cheetah and zebra – there's nowhere on earth quite like it.

Not all destinations are actual places, of course. There's a whole new category of holidays that are based around activities. Never mind painting holidays or wine-tasting tours. Eco-warriors are volunteering to conserve species from South African dolphins to Indian wolves. Charity fundraisers are rafting Guatemala, trekking Nepal, cycling Jordan. Extreme sportspeople are hang-gliding the Himalayas, snow-boarding the Rockies or dog-sledding the Arctic.

And the Arctic represents a real frontier that is opening for the mainstream traveller. Opportunities now exist to walk on the ice pack, indulge in polar transport and walk with the penguins. It takes several weeks to arrive via luxury cruiser, and you'd better be a good sailor for those wild seas, but you can now experience the most extreme environment on our planet.

Which only leaves one destination 'unspoilt': outer or inner space. And guess what? The tour operators are already working on that one. It may never become part of mass-tourism, but soon you may be able to stay in a space station, view the curvature of the earth, experience total weightlessness and even feel a little vertigo.

Personally, I'll be staying on planet earth. Apart from the vertigo, I reckon there's enough down here to keep us busy for a good while yet. ❧

Through China by train
by Colin Thubron

IN MY TRAIN TO JIAYUGUAN THERE WAS SCARCELY ROOM to sit on the floor, and the cold was so intense that people's breath blinded the windows to frost-patterns inside.

For a few miles we followed the Yellow River before it looped under a bridge and was gone. Then night came. Padded and scarved, passengers slept where they were, heaped among their bundles as if in camp, their children sprawled loose over their knees. Every time the train stopped, a new influx sent a tremor of suffocation through the mass. I found a space in the bridge between two carriages, where my quilted overcoat enclosed me like an eiderdown, and tried to sleep. I was crushed amongst Hui farmers, who sang to themselves in small, toneless voices, propped against one another's backs and shoulders, or asleep on their feet like horses. Women brought their babies to urinate down the joint between the carriages beside us, holding them proudly steady. The urine froze within seconds.

I woke to morning and a changed country. The Qilian range had retreated southward behind a ravelin of snowy foothills, and to the north stretched a sandy, level plain – the southern rim of the Gobi. The mountains dropped into it with a frozen brilliance. I half expected them to sizzle. But the desert was as cold as they were. An intermittent dust of grey stones covered it, and here and there the wind had swept it into a liquid tumult of dunes. All around us, the horizon was closed by the shaped splendour of those mountains, or by nothing at all. It was the end of one wilderness and the start of another. Our engine smoke divided them with a pink streamer in the early sun.

We reached Jiayuguan at midday. It was a bungaloid steel town, built for the desert to howl in. I was the only person in my hotel. I gnawed through a near-inedible meal, my head full of the fortress I had glimpsed in the desert close by. In my restaurant the suggestions book had last been inscribed a month before by a lone Japanese: 'The service was dreadful. Nobody even spoke to me.'

I marched to the fort in cold excitement. It had been rebuilt by the Ming in 1372, and dubbed the 'Impregnable Pass under Heaven', and for two millennia, under almost all dynasties, its site had marked the western limit of the Great Wall. From here, since the early years of the Roman Empire, the Silk Road had linked China to the Mediterranean. Even now it invited a journey westward through the Muslim oases of Xinjiang, but the snows and the enormous fort – the traditional terminus of China – dissuaded me.

Massed foursquare on the desert's edge, the slope of its bastions lent it an Assyrian austerity. But as I approached, its ramparts erupted into a delicacy of coloured gate-towers, like a funfair inside a prison, and beyond them a little open-air theatre, now restored, had been painted with women and animals in an absurd, defiant sweetness of civilisation at the end of the world.

I climbed its ramparts into the wind, my eyes streaming. To the south, the pass which it defended opened between the black folds of the Mazong range and the white of the Qilian mountains. To the west, the Great Wall crossed the desert in isolated scarps and beacon-towers. For a moment, restored to its thirty-foot height, it wrapped the fortress in an outer curtain, then faltered southward a few more miles to its end.

But to the north the Gobi – the drowner of cities – spread void under the colourless sky. A mauve band dissolved its horizon. This was the feared hinterland of the Chinese mind, a chaotic barrenness racked by demons and the ever-lingering nomad. From where I stood, a flying crow, hunting for civilisation, would spread its wings a thousand miles south-west across Qinghai and Tibet before alighting hopelessly on Everest. If instead it endured a thousand miles due west, it would plummet into the wilderness of Taklimakan far short of the Afghan frontier; and northward, after crossing Mongolia, it might wander Siberia for ever.

Into any region beyond the Great Wall, disgraced Chinese were banished in despair. Jiayuguan was 'China's Mouth'. Those beyond it were 'outside the mouth', and its western gate – a vaulted tunnel opening into the unknown – used to be covered with farewell inscriptions in the refined hand of exiled officials. Local people called it the Gate of Sighs. Even if the outcasts survived among the surly Mongols, they would die beyond the reach of any heaven. Demons would torment them in their sandy graves, and Buddhists be condemned to an eternal cycle of barbarian reincarnations.

It was early evening when I started across the sand the last few miles to the Wall's end. I withdrew my head into my overcoat like a tortoise. The wind flayed every chink of exposed skin. In front of me the rampart had long since shed its gloss of tamped clay, and was blistered to earth innards. Often the desert had overwhelmed it, pulling a pelt of stones and camel thorn over the parapets until the sand slid down the far side and subsumed them. Ahead the Qilian ranges were divorced from the plain by haze – a glistening mirage. I could understand why Yu loved them.

I had been walking for two or three miles. The light was fading. The only life was a pair of Bactrian camels browsing on nothing. In the approaching mountains I saw no trace of ramparts, no sign where the Wall went.

Suddenly the land dropped sheer beneath my feet. In its canyon, two hundred feet deep, wound a concealed river – an ice-blue coldness out of nowhere. It must have started as a glacial torrent, but over millennia it had sliced the earth clean. The ground looked so unstable I was afraid to approach the edge. I found myself shivering. All colour had been struck out of it, except for mineral greys and blues. Under the Wall's last, broken tower the river moved to its end in the Gobi through the steel-grey earth under the white mountains. ❧

COLIN THUBRON is one of Britain's finest travel writers, winner of many prizes including the Thomas Cook Travel Book Award. This is an extract from his book 'Behind the Wall: A Journey Through China', published by Vintage/Random House.

The souks of Morocco
by Elias Canetti

IT IS SPICY IN THE SOUKS, AND COOL AND COLOURFUL. The smell, always pleasant, changes gradually with the nature of the merchandise. There are no names or signs; there is no glass. Everything for sale is on display. You never know what things will cost; they are neither impaled with their prices, nor are the prices themselves fixed.

All the booths and stalls selling the same thing are close together – twenty or thirty or more of them. There is a bazaar for spices and another for leather goods. The ropemakers have their place and the basketweavers have theirs. Some of the carpet dealers have large, spacious vaults; you stride past them as past a separate city and are meaningly invited inside. The jewellers are grouped round a courtyard of their own, and in many of their narrow booths you can see men at work. You find everything – but you always find it many times over.

The leather handbag you want is on display in twenty different shops, one immediately adjoining another. A man squats among his wares. There is not much room and he has them all close around him. He need hardly stretch to reach every one of his leather handbags, and it is only out of courtesy that, if he is not a very old man, he rises. But the man in the next booth, who looks quite different, sits among the same wares. And it is like that for perhaps a hundred yards, down both sides of the covered passage. It is as if you were being offered all at once everything that this largest and most famous bazaar in the city, indeed in the whole of southern Morocco, possesses in the way of leather goods. There is a great deal of pride in this exhibition. They are showing what they can produce, but they are also showing how much of it there is. The effect is as if the bags themselves knew that they were wealth and were flaunting themselves in their excellence before the eyes of the passers-by. It would come as no surprise if the bags were suddenly to begin moving rhythmically, all of them together, displaying in a gaily-coloured, orgiastic dance all the seductiveness of which they were capable.

The guild feeling of these objects, their being together in their separation from everything different, is re-created by the passer-by according to his mood on each stroll through the souks. 'Today I'd like to explore the spices,' he says to himself, and the wonderful blend of smells is already in his nostrils and the great baskets of red peppers before his eyes . 'Today I feel like some dyed wools,' and there they hang, crimson, deep blue, bright yellow, and black, all around him. 'Today I want to see the baskets and watch them being woven.'

It is astounding what dignity they achieve, these things that men have made. They are not always beautiful; more and more trash of dubious origin finds its way in here, machine-made imports from the northern countries. But they still present themselves in the old way. In addition to the booths that are only for selling there are many where you can stand and watch the things being manufactured. You are in on the process from the start, and seeing it makes you feel good. Because part of the desolation of our modern life is the fact that we get everything delivered to the door ready for consumption as if it came out of some horrid conjuring device. But here you can see the rope-maker busy at his work, and his stock of finished ropes hangs beside him. In tiny booths hordes of small boys, six or seven of them at a time, operate lathes while youths assemble the pieces the boys have turned for them into little low tables. The wool with its wonderful, glowing colours is dyed before your eyes, and there are boys sitting about everywhere knitting caps in gay, attractive patterns.

Their activity is public, *displaying* itself in the same way as the finished goods. In a society that conceals so much, that keeps the interior of its houses, the figures and faces of its women, and even its places of worship jealously hidden from foreigners, this greater openness with regard to what is manufactured and sold is doubly seductive.

What I really wanted to do was find out how bargaining worked, but whenever I entered the souks I temporarily lost sight of the bargaining for the things that were its object. To the naïve observer there seems to be no reason why a person should turn to one Morocco merchant in particular when there are twenty others beside him whose wares hardly differ from his own. You can go from one to another and back to the first. Which stall you buy from is never certain in advance. Even if, say, you have made up your mind to this or that, you have every opportunity of changing it.

Nothing, neither doors nor windows, separates the passer-by from the merchandise. The merchant, sitting amongst the latter, has no name on display and is able, as I have said, to reach everything with ease. The passer-by finds each object obligingly held out to him. He may hold it in his hands for a long time, discuss it thoroughly, ask questions, express doubts, and if he likes, tell his life story or the history of his tribe or the history of the whole world without making a purchase. The man amongst his wares has one quality above all else: he is composed. There he sits. He has little room or opportunity for expansive gestures. He belongs to his wares as much as they to him. They are not packed away somewhere; he always has his hands or eyes on them. There is an intimacy, an alluring intimacy between him and his things. He watches over them and keeps them in order as if they were his enormous family.

It neither bothers nor embarrasses him that he knows their precise value, because he keeps it a secret and you will never discover it. This lends a touch of heady mystery to the bargaining process. Only he can tell how close you come to his secret, and he is an expert at vigorously parrying every thrust so that the protective distance to that value is never threatened. It is considered honourable in the purchaser not to let himself be cheated, but this is no easy undertaking for him because he is always groping in the dark. In countries where the price ethic prevails, where fixed prices are the rule, there is nothing to going shopping. Any fool can go out and find what he needs. Any fool who can read figures can contrive not to get swindled.

In the souks, however, the price that is named first is an unfathomable riddle. No one knows in advance what it will be, not even the merchant, because in any case there are many prices. Each one relates to a different situation, a different customer, a different time of day, a different day of the week. There are prices for single objects and prices for two or more together. There are prices for foreigners visiting the city for a day and prices for foreigners who have been here for three weeks. There are prices for the poor and prices for the rich, those for the poor of course being the highest. One is tempted to think that there are more kinds of prices than there are kinds of people in the world.

Yet that is the beginning of a complicated affair regarding the outcome of which nothing is known in advance. It is said that you should get down to about a third of the original price, but this is nothing but a rough estimate and one of those vapid generalizations with which people are brushed off who are either unwilling or unable to go into the finer points of this age-old ritual.

It is desirable that the toing and froing of negotiations should last a miniature, incident-packed eternity. The merchant is delighted at the time you take over your purchase. Arguments aimed at making the other give ground should be farfetched, involved, emphatic and stimulating. You can be dignified or eloquent, but you will do best to be both. Dignity is employed by both parties to show that they do not attach too much importance to either sale or purchase. Eloquence serves to soften the opponent's resolution. Some arguments merely arouse scorn; others cut to the quick. You must try everything before you surrender. But even when the time has come to surrender it must happen suddenly and unexpectedly so that your opponent is thrown into confusion and for a moment lets you see into his heart. Some disarm you with arrogance, others with charm. Every trick is admissible, any slackening of attention inconceivable.

In the booths that are large enough to walk around in the vendor very often takes a second opinion before yielding. The man he consults, a kind of spiritual head as regards prices, stands in the background and takes no part in the proceedings; he is there, but he does not bargain himself. He is simply turned to for final decisions. He is able, as it were against the vendor's will, to sanction fantastic deviations in the price. But because it is done by *him*, who has not been involved in the bargaining, no one has lost face. ❧

ELIAS CANETTI won the Nobel Prize for Literature in 1981. This is an extract from his book 'The Voices of Marrakesh', published by Marion Boyars Publishers.

The mountains of Afghanistan
by Jason Elliot

THE ANJOMAN PASS IS NOT TRULY the head of the Panjshir valley but lies to the south of the river, which below us had narrowed to a few feet. The source of the Panjshir, I now realized, emerges from a jostling mass of snowy peaks where no path leads. From the west side where we were, the approach to the pass is slow and steady. But it is quite high – over thirteen thousand feet. If not for this pass there would be no direct route to the north; Panjshir would lead nowhere, and the route to Badakhshan would pass either through Nuristan or along the northern flank of the Hindu Kush, which the modern road follows. Both are much longer and indirect. But there is a pass; and through it the whole history of the place has been funnelled. Afghans trotted over it without fuss; Westerners like myself took cigars in their bags to celebrate reaching it.

Ali Khan talked about hunting as we thawed. There were bears, wolves, snow leopards and various great mountain goats, he said. He conjured an idyllic summer, when the flanks of the mountains were the colour of emerald and the smell of blossom lingered in the balmy air. If I came back then, he said, he would find a gun and we would go hunting for an animal he called an *ahu*. I thought this meant gazelle; he must have meant the famous Marco Polo sheep (*Ovis polii*) for which prosperous foreigners before the war paid thousands of dollars to hunt in the area. I unbent my tingling fingers and drew a curly-horned animal in my notebook; no, no, he said, it was like this – and drew a duck-like creature with flattened, spindly ears. He apologized for the quality of the drawing, saying pen and paper were not his thing. What he had drawn was an ibex.

Above us the sunlight hit the high peaks with an explosion of gold against ice, and they roared into life as if hungry for its touch. It was several hours' trek to the pass in the remorseless wind. The sun, although it gave more hope than warmth, was a gift more precious than I can describe. The lower Panjshir had dropped far below us, and looking back I saw wave after wave of mountains and the icy cap of Mir Samir just proud of the other ranges.

At the pass, the view was breathtaking. Ahead of us to the east was a great cluster of snowy peaks, vast spires of frozen rock eighteen thousand feet high. They looked close enough to touch. Beyond the pass the land fell steeply, scarred with tight switchbacks that disappeared towards a valley several thousand feet below. In the far distance about a hundred miles away towered a vast, gold-draped pyramidal beacon of ice. There was only one mountain like that, I knew. It was the magnificent Tirich Mir, the 25,000-foot monster on the Chitral side of the border.

We were three times the height of Ben Nevis, and I wanted a photograph. I fumbled at the controls of my camera with numb fingers, and took a picture of Ali Khan. At that very moment we were joined by a solitary man who had popped up from the other side of the pass. They posed together. It seemed impossible to believe that one day the film would reach home, let alone render intelligible pictures. I had hoped to catch Ali Khan smiling. But Afghans strike such stern and martial bearings at the sight of a camera it is rare to catch a smile on film, and the resulting impression – these days invariably embellished with guns and grenade launchers – is deeply misleading; no other people I know break more readily into smiles.

It was simply too cold to linger, and I was warned not to stray from the path onto the scree-covered slopes, which Ali Khan said were covered with Russian mines. Just as I had found it hard to picture tanks squeezing through the valley below us, I had trouble imagining the pass echoing with the clatter of giant helicopters, gunfire and explosions. But not far from us was a huge crater, and wondering whether it was natural or not I looked for others in line with it. Sure enough there were two other craters from what I guessed were thousand-pound bombs, and I thought of how the valley must have echoed. ❧

JASON ELLIOT won the Thomas Cook Travel Book Award with his debut novel 'An Unexpected Light: Travels In Afghanistan', from which this is an extract. It is published by Picador.

The island of Bali
by Pico Iyer

IT WAS DARK WHEN I SET FOOT ON THE ISLAND, and it felt as if the darkness was chattering. I could see oil lamps flickering at the edges of the forest. I could hear the gamelan coming from somewhere inside the trees, clangorous, jangled and hypnotic. I could see people by the side of the road as I drove in from the airport, but I couldn't tell how many there were, or what they were doing in the dark. When I woke up, jet-lagged, in the dead of the night, and walked down to the beach, figures came out of the shadows to offer me "jig-jig" or some other amenity of Paradise. There was a holy cave on the island, I had read, inhabited only by bats; there was a temple in the sea guarded by a snake.

The bush is burning only for those who are completely foreign to it, I had often thought; in the works of VS Naipaul, say, the jungle is seldom a force of magic, and if it is, it speaks for a magic that is only pushing back and down the clear daylight world of reason. Those born to nature seldom have to go back to it. Yet in Bali all these ideas are upended. Bali is a magical world for those who can see its invisible forces and read all the unseen currents in the air (that woman is a leyak witch, and that shade of green portends death). Yet for everyone else, it is simple enchantment. We stand at the gates of Eden, looking in, and choose to forget that one central inhabitant of the Garden is a snake.

I walked through the unfallen light my first day in Bali, to the beach, to watch, as foreigners do, the sun sink into the sea. Snake-armed masseuses were putting their things away for the day and boys were kicking a soccer ball into the colouring waves. As the outlines of the place began to fade, and the dark to take over, a woman came up to me and asked if I'd like to take a walk with her.

I couldn't really see her in the dark, and the name she gave me – Wayan – is the same name given to the oldest son or daughter of every family on the island. It was pitch-black as we walked along the sand, and pitch-black when we turned into what I thought was the little lane that led back to my guest house. At night in Bali, the dogs come out, and they are nothing like the serene creatures who sit outside the temples of Tibet, seeming to guard the monks. The dogs in Bali howl and curse and bite. As we walked through the forest on the path back to where I slept, I could feel the dogs very close to us, and everywhere.

We know Bali, those of us who read about it, as a magic island where there are thirty thousand temples in a space not much bigger than a major city; we have heard that it is a forest of the kind you see in *A Midsummer Night's Dream*, where people fall in love with the first Other they meet. A childhood friend of mine had had her first experience of real transport with a stranger in a thatched hut on Kuta Beach; all round, you can see what look like asses – or rude mechanicals – waiting to be picked up by Titania.

But the stranger by my side did not seem interested only in romance as she led me up into the heart of her islands' cosmology of light and dark. We walked along the buzzing lanes of Kuta after dark, dogs growling on every side. We walked along a beach on the other side of the island, where couples are supposed to walk on full-moon nights. We took a ride up into the interior, where whole villages are given over to ritual dance: small girls were fluttering their bare arms in the temple court-yards, and boys were chattering in a trance. Foreigners often awaken in the night in Bali to see ghosts standing by their beds; when a brother needs to communicate with a brother, a Balinese dancer once told me, with no drama in his voice, he finds telepathy easier than the telephone.

I walked through all these spaces with the girl from the beach, and through the scepticism I brought to them, and felt at times we were walking through parallel worlds; she could read everything around us, and I could read nothing. This was the way people were buried on the island, she said; this was why black magicians lived in that forest of monkeys. Part of the excitement of being a foreigner in a place like Bali is that you can't reduce the signs around you to an everyday language.

That is also what is unsettling about being a foreigner in a place like Bali, and after some days I slipped away from the girl, and went to the airport, to fly away. When I got there she was standing at the gate, come, she said, to say goodbye. We would not meet again, she went on, because she had dreamed the previous night that she would put on a white dress and go across what is the Balinese equivalent of the Styx. ❧

Pico Iyer is one of the best-known names in travel writing. This is an extract from his book 'Sun After Dark: Flights into the Foreign', published by Bloomsbury and Alfred A Knopf Inc.

The Italian city of Siena
by HV Morton

THERE WERE MOMENTS WHEN I THOUGHT SIENA the most beautiful town I had seen in Italy, Florence not excepted, but one should not compare them; one cannot compare the fourteenth century with the fifteenth. When I went into the country and looked back at Siena, mounted above the ridged vineyards, I saw a vision of the Middle Ages that filled me with delight. If one could return either to the fourteenth or the fifteenth century, what a difficult decision it would be: at least I thought so as I walked the narrow hilly streets lined with old palaces; and again, as I stood in the striped cathedral, and as I admired the tender, tenuous Virgins of Lorenzetti and Simone Martini as they leaned against their gold backgrounds, dreaming of Byzantium. What a problem it would be indeed: the century of S. Catherine or that of Lorenzo the Magnificent?

Curiously enough, just as the swarming crowds of Venice had lent vitality and colour to the Piazzetta, so the crowds in Siena, infected with the Palio fever, brought from the past a memory of the city's violent rivalries. These crowds, however, were content to pack the streets, to watch men putting down cart-loads of sand on the outer perimeter of the Campo, where the race would be run. They wandered about happily and bought the mediaeval sweetmeat, *Pan Forte*, or the almond cakes called *Ricciarelli*, which reminded me of the little marzipan cakes of S. Teresa, which are made at Avila, in Spain.

Apart from the cathedral, which was packed from morning until night, the crowds kept to the main roads, and I found the picture galleries to be comparatively empty. I had no idea how much I was to enjoy them. Here I seemed to find myself in a curious cul-de-sac of art; a marvellous collection of enlarged miniatures, a development, if you like, of book illustration, or illumination, which appeared to moving towards the Renaissance, yet never arriving there. What a perfect town Siena must have been for a conservative! To a Sienese of the Renaissance, how revolutionary, almost blasphemous, Florence must have seemed with its peasant Virgins! Here in Siena, as befits the Virgin's own town, the Queen of Heaven is always a lady. It is this wistful and almond-eye aristocrat, sometimes dreamy and melancholy, her Child in her arms and a halo of burnished gold behind her head, who presides over an enchanted land.

I passed from room to room marvelling at this beautiful mediaeval world, full of miracles and grace, where celestial beings hung suspended in the air with nothing to proclaim their origin save that their feet were in the clouds; a world where any goose-girl could meet a saint, or the Queen of Heaven herself, standing among the olive trees; where kings and queens wore their crowns, even in bed; a world where angels and devils mingled with the people in the narrow streets of castellated cities. At a time when Uccello and his contemporaries were wrestling with the problems of perspective, these painters of Siena, only forty miles away, were still painting uphill tables and floors, painting with their backs to Florence and their faces to Ravenna.

I enjoyed the sight of the sunlight filling the superb piazza of herring-bone brick, the Campo. It is often compared to a shell, though I think it looks more like an open fan. Its nine ribs radiate outward from the handle – the Palazzo Pubblico – and form a colossal semi-circle, each segment a marvel of brickwork. The Campo hummed with effort. Carpenters were putting the final hammer blows to the grandstands which obscured the lower storeys of the old palaces, now shops, while men were spreading six inches of sand along the crazy racecourse; and carts were arriving piled with mattresses, which were stacked up to block the entrance into the Via San Martino. This is the Beecher's Brook of the Palio. As the bareback riders come round the bend of the piazza and gallop downhill towards this street, a horse unfamiliar with the course will generally bolt into the Via San Martino. Even now, I was told, though the entrance is blocked with hoardings and padded mattresses, there are often bad falls at this place.

Here, I thought, was the memory of Italy which I should never forget: the sunlight on the red bricks of the tall Mangia Tower; the town hall with the white and black shield of Siena, the *Balzana*, above each pointed Gothic window; the tourists and country folk wandering over the immense slope of the piazza; a man selling balloons and sweets; the noise of hammering; the carts grinding over the sand with timber and mattresses; and a little girl holding a red and yellow balloon on a string as she watched the pigeons drinking at the *Fonte Gaia*. ❧

Extracted from 'A Traveller in Italy', by the late H.V. Morton, published by Methuen, copyright Marion Wasdell and Brian de Villiers.

Rio de Janeiro
by Jan Morris

ON THE STEPS OF THE TEATRO MUNICIPAL in Rio de Janeiro, a Dutch combo plays Dixieland jazz. It is an extremely white, blonde and stalwart combo, and on its flank four Dutch airline hostesses (for it is in the nature of an advertising session) oscillate to the music with a well-built air of carnival. I sit beside them on the steps, and between the lot of us, so blatantly northern European, so patently un-Dixie, we present a comically incongruous spectacle, in the heart of the great Brazilian city, at the height of the noonday rush.

But it does not matter in the least. The city effortlessly absorbs us anyway. Some thirty or forty people of all ages, all colours, are stomping, clapping and laughing with us at the foot of the steps, and very soon the occasion is more or less taken over by an elderly, half-crazed man who prances with rhythmic grace up the steps, singing the while and grinning inanely to universal applause.

The legendary fizz of Rio is not merely infectious, but actually possessive. It seizes one, sets one wriggling and jerking to the beat of things and often leaves one laughing when one should really be crying. When that band went off, still trumpeting, to its next stand, pursued by its own poor Fool, I stood up myself and found the back of my shirt splodged with some chocolaty sticky substance. The crowd examined it with interested concern. Whether it had been sprayed on me by a disgruntled street hawker, or dropped upon me by some arcane Brazilian bird, they were unable to decide, but they took me off to a small ornamental pond where I might wash it off.

I dipped my handkerchief in the scummy water and found it to be alive with tadpoles: a thousand incipient Brazilian frogs, there beside the Avenida Rio Branco, squirming indefatigably as I washed the stuff off my shirt, and the music of the Dutch sounded fainter and fainter across the effervescent city.

Wiping off the last of that muck, and a few tenacious tadpoles with it, I walked around the corner into the nineteenth century. Rio is not all travel-brochure glitz. It is an old merchant city, a seaport, and its downtown is venerable with offices, banks, warehouses, bars where the businessmen go for lunch, city alleys and squares with statues in them. In old photographs this busy commercial area *is* Rio de Janeiro, and a solid, sensible, business-like place it looks.

A surviving glory of that era is the Colombo on Rua Gonçalves Dias, one of the best cafés in the world. Clad as grandiloquently in mirrors as Versailles itself, it is a very palace of refreshment. Its ceiling is of stained glass, its floors are tiled and it gleams with glass cabinets full of bottles, cakes, cookies and neatly stacked table linen. Clusters of old-fashioned lamps illuminate it, and fans laboriously keep it cool.

The multitudinous bow-tied waiters of the Colombo look as though they have spent their whole lives in its service, and at lunchtime they are all old-school professionalism, scurrying and skirting through the tables that jam the huge floor space, bowing here, waving a response there, pushing in and out of kitchen doors or dimly to be glimpsed attending to the customers who sit, precariously it seems, at gilded tables on the high, narrow balcony above.

The noise is terrific, and the clientele ranges from the stately to the alternative, by way of many eccentric and atavistically made-up dowagers. Things have hardly changed here, I suspect, since the place opened in 1894. Rio, however, is Rio, and the atmosphere is peculiarly relaxed. When I finished my meal, I walked out past the cake cabinets, and there, leaning against a counter, brushing crumbs from his black jacket, was the waiter who had just served me, taking time off to eat a cake himself. I wished him *bon appétit*, but he could only smile and bow slightly in response, for he had his mouth full.

Youth, of course, is the thing in Rio. It is an old-young city – he was an old-young waiter – and on the beach at Copacabana, any weekend morning, the human ageing process seems mysteriously disrupted. Here I stroll along the famous beach, eating a banana, and all round me the laws of nature are defied.

It is clearly impossible, physically impossible, for that grand motherly lady to touch her toes so easily. It is positively unnatural for that group of aged gents to throw themselves about with such agility in their game of ball: their faces are wizened, their hair is white, but some weird Brazilian alchemy has kept their muscles iron-taut and their movements uncannily springy. Then what about these geriatric couples striding along the promenade? By what dispensation do they wear shoes, hats and swimsuits a couple of generations too young for them, yet get away with it so stylishly? There is an old dear on the beach who would surely be, in another society, confined if not to the back kitchen at least to the church flowers committee; here at Copacabana she is oiling herself sinuously on her sunbed, wearing a wide yellow hat and rhinestoned sunglasses, and now and then drinking from a can she has embedded in the sand like a bottle of champagne in an ice bucket.

The young too, seem younger still upon this magic shore. They plunge more frantically into the surf. They scamper more merrily round the sunshades. They build big platforms of sand on which they sit cross-legged like gurus, playing cards or squabbling. They play ever more demanding games: for example, a ferocious kind of volleyball in which the ball may be touched by any part of the body except the head, requiring such excruciating leaps and contortions that it makes me breathless just to watch them.

Out at sea a haze of spray hangs over the breakers and half obscures the islands beyond. Through it a squadron of white-sailed yachts scuds and tacks, and presently a grey warship appears around the point and disappears into the Atlantic. It looks a wild southern sea out there. The sun goes slowly, very slowly, down. The madcap rejuvenations of Copacabana continue apace. Crossing the street to one of the cafés behind, I order a Brazilian drink of great potency that instantly restores me to youth myself.

There Fagin's boys are hanging around, looking for likely victims, nice American tourists with watches to be snatched or handbags to leave lying around on the beach. They are all too obvious little rascals – like stage villains – making overacted gestures to each other, whistling conspiratorially across street corners and posing in the most perfunctory of ways as boot-blacks or sellers of trinkets.

Alas, they are not in the least loveable. There is not an Oliver among them. They look perfectly horrid, and swarming around them I fancy always the fleas and flies of the slums they come from – whose greyish shambled precincts one can see from this very beach, like spills of garbage tumbling down the hillsides. Christ himself stands high above, arms outstretched on the summit of Corcovado, but those shanty towns below, like those small thieves on the beach, look utterly beyond his benediction.

A streak of loveless abandonment runs through the life of Rio, and not least through its exhilaration – through the panache of the street crowds, through the disturbing hyperactivity of the beach, through all the luxuries of the Rio rich. The city is scrawled over with unsightly graffiti. Some proclaim political slogans, but most are senseless squiggles and scrawls, reaching to the second floor of houses sometimes, when daring nihilists have climbed up trellises or hung upside-down from balconies. This mindless mess suggests to me a message from the void, telling us always of the helplessness, amounting to a kind of communal exhaustion, that lies beneath the glitter of Rio de Janeiro.

I sit now in a motionless bus near the foot of the Sugar Loaf, at a place where a small park runs down to the sea. There are military offices nearby, and in constant twos and threes colonels and captains walk by carrying briefcases. A few children are there with their mothers, too, and tourists come and go from the funicular station, but my eye is captured by a solitary middle-aged man hanging about at the edge of the park. He bears himself elegantly, slim and erect in a well-cut grey suit, but there is something wrong with him.

It seems to be partly physical, partly mental, and partly, perhaps, too much coffee. He can never get comfortable. If he sits on a bench, after a moment he gets up again. If he takes a turn around the grass, he abruptly stops. Sometimes he looks at the hill above, but it seems only to disappoint him, as if he cannot see what he is looking for up there. He inspects the passing officers keenly (was he once a colonel or captain himself?) but he recognises none. He gazes longingly out to sea, but the sun gets in his eyes. When my bus starts, and we move away from the park, I wave at him through my window, and he waves abstractedly back – but not at me, I think, not at me. ❧

JAN MORRIS is the grande dame of travel writing. This is an extract from her collected writings in 'A Writer's World: Travels 1950-2000', published by Faber and Faber.

India in the Monsoon
by Alexander Frater

A LINE OF SPECTATORS HAD FORMED behind the Kovalam beach road. They were dressed with surprising formality, many of the men wearing ties and the women fine saris which streamed and snapped in the wind. Their excitement was shared and sharply focused, like that of a committee preparing to greet a celebrated spiritual leader, or a victorious general who would come riding up the beach on an elephant; all they lacked was welcoming garlands of marigolds. As I joined them they greeted me with smiles, a late guest arriving at their function. The sky was black, the sea was white. Foaming like champagne it surged over the road to within a few foot feet of where we stood. Blown spume stung our faces. It was not hard to imagine why medieval Arabs thought winds came from the ocean floor, surging upwards and making the surface waters boil as they burst into the atmosphere.

We stood rocking in the blast, clinging to each other amid scenes of great merriment. A tall, pale-skinned man next to me shouted, "Sir, where are you from?"

"England!" I yelled.

The information became a small diminishing chord as, snatched and abbreviated by the elements, it was passed on to his neighbours.

"And what brings you here?"

"This!"

"Sir, us also. We are holiday-makers! I myself am from Delhi. This lady beside me is from Bangalore and we too have come to see the show!" He laughed. "I have seen it many times but I always come back for more!"

The Bangalore woman cried "Yesterday there were dragonflies in our hotel garden. They are a sign. We knew monsoon was coming soon!" She beamed at me. "It gives me true sense of wonder!"

More holiday-makers were joining the line. The imbroglio of inky clouds swirling overhead contained nimbostratus, cumulonimbus, and Lord knows what else, all driven by updraughts, downdraughts, and vertical wind shear. Thunder boomed. Lightning went zapping into the sea, the leader stroke of one strike passing the ascending return stroke of the last so that the whole roaring edifice seemed supported on pillars of fire. Then, beyond the cumuliform anvils and soaring castellanus turrets, we saw a broad, ragged band of luminous indigo heading slowly inshore. Lesser clouds suspended beneath it like flapping curtains reached right down to the sea.

"The rains!" everyone sang.

The wind struck us with a force that made our line bend and waver. Everyone shrieked and grabbed at each other. The woman on my right had a plump round face and dark eyes. Her streaming pink sari left her smooth brown tummy bare. We held hands much more tightly than was necessary and, for a fleeting moment, I understood why Indians traditionally regard the monsoon as a period of torrid sexuality.

The deluge began ❧

ALEXANDER FRATER is an award-winning journalist and travel writer. This is an extract from his book 'Chasing the Monsoon', published by Picador/Macmillan.

On safari in Africa: 1
by Karen Blixen

OUT ON THE SAFARIS, I had seen a herd of Buffalo, one hundred and twenty-nine of them, come out of the morning mist under a copper sky, one by one, as the dark and massive, iron-like animals with the mighty horizontally swung horns were not approaching, but were being created before my eyes and sent out as they were finished. I had seen a herd of Elephant travelling through the dense Native forest, where the sunlight is strewn down between the thick creepers in small spots and patches, pacing along as if they had an appointment at the end of the world. It was, in giant size, the border of a very old, infinitely precious Persian carpet, in the dyes of green, yellow, and black-brown.

I had time after time watched the progression across the plain of the Giraffe, in their queer, inimitable, vegetative gracefulness, as if it were not a herd of animals but a family of rare, long-stemmed, speckled gigantic flowers slowly advancing. I had followed two Rhinos on their morning promenade, when they were sniffing and snorting in the air of the dawn, – which is so cold that it hurts in the nose, – and looked like two very big angular stones rollicking in the long valley and enjoying life together. I had seen the royal lion, before sunrise, below a waning moon, crossing the grey plain on his way home from the kill, drawing a dark wake in the silvery grass, his face still red up to the ears, or during the midday-siesta, when he reposed contentedly in the midst of his family on the short grass and in the delicate, spring-like shade of the broad Acacia trees of his park of Africa. ❧

KAREN BLIXEN was a literary journalist and author, celebrated for her memoir of farming in Kenya, 'Out Of Africa', from which this is an extract.

On safari in Africa: 2
by Ryszard Kapucinski

W E DROVE ONTO THE ENORMOUS PLAIN of the Serengeti, the largest concentration of wild animals on earth. Everywhere you look, huge herds of zebras, antelopes, buffalo, giraffes. And all of them are grazing, frisking, frolicking, galloping. Right by the side of the road, motionless lions; a bit farther, a group of elephants; and farther still, on the horizon, a leopard running in huge bounds. It's all improbable, incredible. As if one were witnessing the birth of the world, that precise moment when the earth and sky already exist, as do water, plants, and wild animals, but not yet Adam and Eve. It is this world barely born, the world without mankind and hence also without sin, that one can imagine one is seeing here. ❧

Ryszard Kapuscinski was a foreign correspondent for 'Polish News' for many years. This is an extract from his book 'The Shadow of the Sun: My African Life', published by Allen Lane/The Penguin Press/Penguin Books and Alfred A Knopf Inc.

Across America by Greyhound bus
by Irma Kurtz

E VERY COUNTRY BOILS DOWN TO ONE-THIRD LANDSCAPE and two-thirds people. Let a traveller cover a nation from coast to coast. Let him visit every monument and admire all its natural beauties. Let him live off the fat of its land, take a million photos and send home ecstatic postcards. Unless the traveller meets locals, and learns to know them on their own turf, he will remain two-thirds short of even the foggiest notion of where on earth he has been. For any free spirit possessed of real curiosity and a degree of fortitude travelling by good old proletarian bus is an unceasing revelation: a way not just to see the country – a way to befriend it. And nowhere is this wonderful intimacy more likely to occur than in the United States of America, where the general populace is innocent of shyness or awe and the average length of a bus journey easily accommodates uninhibited confidences.

During happy months spent criss-crossing America on Greyhound Buses I met students and strippers, gamblers on their uppers, Quakers, Amish and similarly thrifty sectarians, and scores of ordinary Americans who for one reason or another – decrepitude or youth, poverty, criminality, illness or genuine concern for the planet – do not use a car. As the magnificent countryside unrolled outside the windows, loquacious strangers exchanged opinions and personal history. Occasionally overcome by a longing for silence and solitude, I learned that if I faked a hacking cough or – explain it if you can! – was seen to be writing in a notebook, new boarders gave me a wide berth. American buses are democratically filled, first-come, first-serve, and it is worth arriving early at the terminal to secure a window-seat. Sometimes, when there was no pregnant or disabled passenger with priority, I was bold enough to snare the front seat. The views through the windscreen of a Greyhound Bus – dawn waking the flatlands of Kansas, great cities gathering themselves slowly out of America's rural heartland – are the most engulfing and dramatic on the open road. However, because of the front seat's proximity to the driver, whose authority on a long-haul bus is as absolute as a captain's at sea, its occupant is subtly raised and separated from his fellows. The position therefore tends to attract exhibitionists and snobs doing their best to show they wouldn't be there, except for the fact that their cars are in for servicing.

"There will be no smoking on this bus," said our driver on the road to Winnemucca, Nevada. "That includes them magic cigarettes. Anybody smokes them on my bus gonna find hisself magically turned into a hitch-hiker."

And the smug blonde in the front seat turned to smirk and nod at us lesser types.

Nice ordinary Americans choose the middle rows; by tacit agreement preferring to sit next to their own sex and race. Yea verily, as, since the first bus was launched, bad boys go straight to the back.

"Whenever there's trouble," said our driver into St. Louis, "I know it will come from them last five rows."

Often I chose my next stop – Dinosaur, Bald Knob, Sault Sainte Marie – simply because I liked the sound of it. My book of blank tickets, bought in advance from Greyhound's English agent, did not hold me to any itinerary. But 99 out of 100 of my fellow passengers were purposefully en route, some to visit family, others to job hunt, and a few to flee trouble or find a new place to make trouble, never to start it on the bus.

Though we were boarded in South Texas by armed police searching for 'illegals', and by Louisiana troopers looking (fruitlessly) for a fugitive wife who had fatally ventilated her husband with a carving knife, there was no violence on board. On the contrary, whatever the boys in the back get up to – drinking bourbon camouflaged in Coke tins and cutting some quiet deals – the Greyhound Bus must be one of the safest places in the USA. Terminals, however, though heavily policed, define the wrong side of the tracks in any town, and the surrounding areas can be threatening. Fortunately, there are taxi ranks outside every station; not once was I steered wrong by a taxi driver when I asked about a clean, cheap place to stay.

The long-distance bus traveller will probably spend at least one night out of every two or three on board. Sleeping on board entails a weird descent through skin after skin of consciousness until the constant Greyhound rock and rumble finally delivers you, its passenger, into dreams. Except on Thanksgiving and holiday weekends, when all Americans go home, the neighbouring seat is likely to be free at night, and with the help of an invaluable inflatable pillow, it could be worse. Sometimes I'd wake momentarily to see the passing ghost of a small town; once I opened my eyes on a flotilla of fairyland lights that turned out to be an oil refinery outside Corpus Christi.

"But I'm not much over five feet tall, I can't imagine how you manage," I said to a six-footer on what he figured would be a four-, maybe five-day journey to Seattle from the depths of Florida.

"No problem, ma'am," he said. "I just close my eyes and curl up like a snake."

Eating, like boozing and smoking, is forbidden on American buses. Frequent rest stops allow passengers to avail themselves of a more commodious lavatory than the one on board, which is used only in emergencies. ("What do you do about the loo?" is the question most frequently put to old bus hands by bus virgins). While smokers light up, the others rush to satisfy an apparently national addiction to junk food.

Too many of the stops are anonymous greasy-spoon burger chains. Once in a while, however, especially in the wild reaches of northern America, where the breadth of a smaller nation lies between cities, the regular stop is somewhere the driver is greeted by name and his 'usual' is already in the oven. For half an hour or so, passengers join authentic Americana in mom-and-pop places like, say, Del's Café. In the backroom of Del's, a bunch of local women setting up a jumble sale had stopped to try on hats and were howling with laughter.

"Won't you join us?" one of them in a fedora called when she saw me in the doorway. And, for an instant, I was truly tempted to stop and end my days as a matron of Melrose, Minnesota, population 2,235.

America is a road country, and in the modern era of one-man-one-car, the road uniting all its states can be a lonely, congested, irascible, scary place to be. But not on a big bus. On a Greyhound out of Fargo, I listened as two men behind me swapped recipes for venison sausage. A woman across the aisle had just told us a story about the ghost of a bear said to haunt a forest on Minnesota's Upper Peninsula. My neighbour, an 80-year-old local, bound for her son's home a few hundred miles down the road, began describing the old days, when all her neighbours were homesick immigrants from Russia who thought they had found a replica of the Steppes in the North Dakota landscape.

"Good-looking boys, those Russians," she said, with a big wink. "I speak pretty good Russian to this day."

From the close, safe warmth of the bus, I smiled out at the endless telephone poles etching a dusky sky: my neighbour called them "our local tree". Taking the bus is more than travelling in space: it is nearly travelling in time, too. Taking the Greyhound Bus is as close as any westerly romantic can ever again come to crossing America by stagecoach. ❧

Irma Kurtz is the agony aunt of 'Cosmopolitan' magazine. She is the author of several books, including 'The Great American Bus Ride'.

How travel has changed
by Ian Wilson

IT'S A HARD LIFE, LIVING IN A SHRUNKEN WORLD that once brimmed with the chance to see new faces and places. Or so people keep telling me. Everywhere is supposed to be spoiled now. Spoiled for the locals and spoiled for the visitors. It's as if you might as well stay at home and just send your money instead.

Until recently I felt this way too, regretting that the places I used to enjoy had lost their charm. I have done a lot of travelling around the world since the 1970s, and it is true that since then the travel experience has changed hugely. Once, the world was your oyster – but is it still?

There were fads 20 years ago, much as there are fads now. The Seychelles had already come and gone, so to speak. Sri Lanka was just starting to happen, only to see its budding tourist industry hit by civil war a few years later. Bali and Kenya, too, were taking off, but no one was thinking about visiting Vietnam and Laos, and even Thailand and Malaysia were not yet on most travellers' visiting lists.

The favourites of the old hippie trail of the 1960s and 1970s were still pulling in an ever-ageing tourist population of former flower children – in particular Kathmandu, Goa, Kashmir, Lake Toba in Sumatra and Jogjakarta in Java. Later there would be Koh Phangan in Thailand. But if the places were changing, so were the types who went to them. In Bali, the hippies gave way to the surfies, who also took over the town of Jaco on the Pacific coast of Costa Rica.

Where you went depended a lot on your age and income. Places that pulled in the impecunious with a good ration of cheap living, inspiring the $5 a Day books in the pre-inflationary 1960s and 1970s, included Morocco and Turkey, as well as Afghanistan and Iran – compulsory visits on the overland route to India and beyond in the days when the Magic Bus from London was part of the hippie vocabulary. After it was over, they all said the same thing: the experience was great, but, like most rites of passage, they wouldn't want to do it again.

The package holiday industry, which was limited to Europe for most travellers in the 1970s, started to move further afield after that. The mass market ventured as far as Tunisia, then Florida, Barbados, St Lucia and Cuba (for the less affluent). Going east, there was coastal Turkey, then Israel. Terrorism has made visitors think twice about Egypt, Morocco, Turkey and Bali, though each of these countries has recovered well from bombing atrocities. Chechnya, Iraq and Afghanistan will be unsafe for a long time to come, but they were never on the tourist map in the first place. For the really intrepid there were Kenya, the Maldives and the destinations pioneered by the hippies for the mainstream market that followed: Goa, Bali, Nepal and Thailand.

So what destinations are left for the seasoned traveller seeking sun and sea? The good news is that although the world may have shrunk and the cities have become polluted hellholes, there is still plenty of unspoilt coastline out there. My own favourite, in some ways, is Nicaragua. It has all that Costa Rica has to offer, at half the price and with virtually no tourists.

Much of Africa has had a pretty bad press in recent years, but a lot of it is fabulous. In particular, I like the coast of Ghana, while the southern part of Senegal, known as the Casamance, is a great place for a short winter break in the sun. But most sub-Saharan African tourism is in southern Africa today, and that means Namibia, Botswana, South Africa and Mozambique, now noted for an ever increasing tourist infrastructure on its offshore islands. But Zimbabwe is a write-off, Kenya has become dangerous, and even Tanzania has its problems. As for South Africa, here we have a paradox. The locals know how dangerous it can be – many who can afford to are getting out – yet at the same time tourist numbers are growing. Will South Africa go the way of Zimbabwe under pressure for land reform? The jury is still out.

Closer to home, the Baltic states and the former communist states of Eastern Europe are growing as tourist destinations at a hectic pace, especially Croatia. In fact, many tourists like the places they visit so much that they relocate or build a second home there. Though France and Spain have been the big winners here, new places like Croatia are fast catching up.

And what about Dubai and, to a lesser extent, the other Gulf states such as Muscat and Oman? Dubai has become, in a decade, the Middle East's answer to Miami Beach. It's closer to Europe and marginally cheaper. On the other hand, it doesn't have much to offer beyond, sun, sand, sea and a lot of duty free shopping.

The Caribbean is hardly a new destination, but most people don't realise how interesting it is if you get away from the well-known spots. My favourites there include San Salvador, Cat Island and Mayaguana in the Bahamas. Then there are the Turks and Caicos Islands, especially Grand Turk. I go back from time to time to Anegada, a coralline island in the British Virgin Islands that is hardly visited. Carriacou, north of Grenada, is a weird and interesting place to spend a few days far from the crowds. And the best thing about the Caribbean is the total lack of problems with terrorism.

But it's the Indian Ocean I like most – places such as Sainte Marie, off the coast of Madagascar, or Rodrigues, to the east of Mauritius, or Chagos in the middle of the ocean, which I've been to, although it's strictly off-limits to tourists at present.

The Pacific, by comparison, simply doesn't compare with either the Indian Ocean or the Caribbean in the league table of tropical islands. The sea can be great, but I have to admit I quickly get bored on most of the Pacific islands. They just don't grab me. I usually find only the diving is great.

You can get away from it all nearly anywhere. The secret, for me, is in following the coast away from the roads and any signs of habitation. You can do it almost any place in Europe, including England. I've walked the hundred or so miles of the Dorset coastal path, and even in summer it's possible to leave the crowds behind simply by walking a few miles.

Even when you're going somewhere less popular, the experience of flying has not got any easier in the last 20 years. Airports are still a nightmare; and if you're travelling from somewhere like London, it takes twice as long to get to the airport from the centre of town as it did two decades ago. Traffic congestion and airport security checks are the biggest crosses the modern traveller has to bear. Then there's the growing crime problem all over the world and the sad fact that travellers have increasingly become targets for terrorism, rather than innocent victims caught in the crossfire. The numbers may be small compared with deaths from road accidents, but one bomb has the potential to kill off a country's tourist trade for years to come. There are signs, though, that travellers are becoming more blasé about bombs, and places are now recovering faster than ever before – Bali being the prime example.

Latin America, as a whole, is considered a danger zone by many, thanks to a reputation for street and car crime. Particular cities – Rio de Janeiro, São Paulo, Bogotá, Caracas, Lima, Colon and Panama City, for example – feature on my list of danger spots. However, much of Latin America is relatively safe, especially away from the cities, and there are signs that tourism is doing well and growing, for no better reason than the area is seen as largely free from terrorism.

So don't go to the cities – any cities. If you do, get out of them as fast as possible. The countryside is usually a far safer place, whether you're in South America or South Africa. You should rarely feel threatened in rural areas, assuming all reasonable precautions are taken. I am sure that there are plenty of exceptions, but on the whole the further you are from a city and other foreign visitors, the more hospitable and honest the local people tend to be. And travel with small children if you can. They act as great ice-breakers.

Where would I recommend for a really interesting experience? I've already suggested Nicaragua. How about Mauritania? Or the Azores in spring? Or, for spectacular scenery not too far from home, you could try the far north-west of Scotland. Or for total safety (and they speak English too) you could join thousands of others and head for New Zealand. There, you will find Great Barrier Island, the country's best kept travel secret. Go there if you get the chance, and stay at the fabulous Mount St Paul Lodge (www.mountstpaullodge.com). You won't regret it.

If you look hard enough, the world is still your oyster. ❧

Ian Wilson is the founder and Chairman of Wexas, the traveller's club.

Section 2: **Destinations** ❧

AFGHANISTAN

WHEN TO GO

WEATHER High altitudes and landlocked terrain create a cold continental climate, with wide temperature swings between seasons and day/night. Blisteringly hot summers (June-August), freezing cold winters (December-February).

FESTIVALS One of the most important holidays in Afghanistan is Nawros (New Days), celebrated in March. Special foods - wheat for the ladies and veal for the men - are prepared, and wine drunk. Liberation Day takes place on 18 April, and probably isn't the time to flaunt any connections you might have with the West. It's followed by Revolution Day, 28 April, making the whole month a great time for flag waving. Other festivities are based around the Islamic calendar.

TRANSPORT

INTERNATIONAL AIRPORTS Kabul (sometimes closed).

INTERNAL TRAVEL Risky. Few roads remain and most require 4x4 vehicles. Otherwise donkey is safest, helicopter quickest. Some internal air services from Kabul, depending on political/military conditions.

RED TAPE

VISAS REQUIRED (UK/US) Required.

VACCINATIONS REQUIRED: See 'Vaccinations required around the world' on page 653.

DRIVING REQUIREMENTS International Driving Permit.

COUNTRY REPS IN UK/US UK: 31 Prince's Gate, London SW7 1QQ, tel (020) 7589 8891, fax (020) 7581 3452, email afghanembassy@btinternet.com. US: 360 Lexington Avenue, 11th Floor, New York, NY 10017, tel (212) 972 2277, fax (212) 972 9046, email info@consulate.net.

UK/US REPS IN COUNTRY UK: 15th Street, Roundabout Wazir Akbar Khan, PO Box 334, Kabul, tel (70) 102 000, fax (70) 102 250, email britishembassy.kabul@fco.gov.uk. US: Malak Azghar Road, Kabul, tel (20) 293 005, fax (86) 6890 9988, email contact@afghanistan-mfa.net

PEOPLE AND PLACE

CAPITAL Kabul.

LANGUAGE Officially Pashtu and Persian. Also Dari, Turkmen, Uzbek, Persian.

PEOPLES Pashtu, Tajik, Hazara, Uzbek.

RELIGION Muslim (mainly Sunni).

SIZE (SQ KM) 652,225.

POPULATION 22,930,000.

POP DENSITY/KM 35.2.

STATE OF THE NATION

SAFETY Highly volatile following the recent war. Few foreigners work here, and are targets. Women must observe strict *sharia* Islamic law and never travel alone.

LIFE EXPECTANCY M 42.71, F 43.1.

BEING THERE

ETIQUETTE Afghanistan is an intensely Muslim country. During Ramadan, from sunrise to sunset devout Muslims who can physically handle it are asked to go without food, drink, cigarettes and just about everything else. It's illegal - not to mention rude - to do any of these things in front of people observing this important holiday.

CURRENCY *Afghani* (Af) = 100 *puls.*

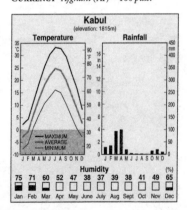

Kabul (elevation: 1815m)

HIGHLIGHTS

HERAT A seat of Persian culture. The Friday Mosque, Masjid-i-Jami, is Herat's number one attraction and among the finest Islamic buildings in the world, featuring some exquisite Timurid tilework. The covered bazaar in Charar Su is a bustling complex of shops and artisans' workshops.

KABUL Formerly a Silk Route hub and, more recently, a popular stop-off on the hippy trail to India, the Afghan capital was ruined by civil war and years of subsequent fighting. The pleasant Gardens of Babur are a cool retreat and one of the most peaceful and beautiful spots.

GHAZNI This modern town to the west of Kabul is known mainly for its fine bazaar, featuring local goods and those from neighbouring countries. There are also some fine minarets and a recently discovered ancient Buddhist stupa.

KANDAHAR The second-largest city in Afghanistan, and former Taliban base. A cloak that once belonged to the Prophet is housed in the Mosque of the Sacred Cloak. Close to the city, the Chihil Zina, or 'Forty Steps,' lead up to a niche carved in the rock by Babur, founder of the Mughal empire, which is guarded by two stone lions.

NURISTAN Meaning 'Land of Light', Nuristan is mountainous, remote, little visited and memorably described in Eric Newby's hilarious book *A Short Walk in the Hindu Kush*. Shahr-i-Zohak, The Red City, enshrines the remains of an ancient citadel which guarded Bamiyan.

FINANCE Credit cards not accepted. Traveller's cheques OK.

BUSINESS HOURS Sat-Wed 0800-1200, and 1300-1630 Thurs 0800-1330, Friday sabbath.

GMT +4.5.

VOLTAGE GUIDE 220 volts AC, 50 Hz.

COUNTRY DIALLING CODE 93.

CONSUMING PLEASURES

FOOD & DRINK Indian-style, spicy, poor ingredients. Specialities include *pilau* and *kebabs*. Kabul restaurants offer international cuisine.

SHOPPING & SOUVENIRS Turkman hats, Kandahar embroidery, glassware, nomad jewellery, handmade carpets and rugs, Nuristani woodcarvings, silkware, brass, silverwork. Craft items may require licence for export.

FIND OUT MORE

WEBSITES www.afghanembassy.co.uk, www.embassyofafghanistan.org, www.britishembassy.gov.uk/afghanistan, www.afghan-web.com.

LOCAL MEDIA *Kabul New Times* is the only English-language paper. There are three TV channels, one state owned, two independent. One state owned radio station and several independents.

TOURIST BOARDS IN UK/US n/a.

" I was smitten. Afghanistan has been my yardstick ever since for judging every country I go to - beauty of landscape, of people, of hospitality."

Elizabeth Chatwin, on her visit with husband Bruce in 1969

ALBANIA

WHEN TO GO

WEATHER June to September is warm and dry. Cool and wet from October to May. April to June and September to October are the best times to visit.

FESTIVALS The Tirana International Film Festival takes place each December as a showplace for artists and students alike. Independence and Liberation Day is celebrated on 28 November. Other celebrations follow religious calendars.

TRANSPORT

INTERNATIONAL AIRPORTS Tirana Rinas (TIA), 29km from the capital. Entry tax payable on arrival.

INTERNAL TRAVEL Limited rail network, roads in variable condition used by pedestrians, cyclists, herds of cattle, wagons, tractors and an increasing number of cars.

RED TAPE

VISAS REQUIRED (UK/US) None.

VACCINATIONS REQUIRED: See 'Vaccinations required around the world' on page 653.

DRIVING REQUIREMENTS International Driving Permit or national driving licence. Fully comprehensive insurance essential.

COUNTRY REPS IN UK/US UK: 2nd Floor, 24 Buckingham Gate, London SW1E 6LB, tel (020) 7828 8897, fax (020) 7828 8869, email amblonder@hotmail.com. US: 2100 S Street, Washington, DC 20008, tel (202) 223 4942, email albaniaemb@aol.com

UK/US REPS IN COUNTRY UK: Rruga Skenderbej 12, Tirana, Albania, tel (42) 34975-5, fax (42)47697, email visatiran@fco.gov.uk. US: Rruga Elbasanit 103, Tirana, Albania, tel (42) 47285-9, fax (42) 32222.

PEOPLE AND PLACE

CAPITAL Tirana.

LANGUAGE Albanian, Greek in the South. Some Italian and English.

PEOPLES Albanian, Greek.

RELIGION Islam, Catholicism, Eastern Orthodox Christianity.

SIZE (SQ KM) 27,398.

POPULATION 3,141,000.

POP DENSITY/KM 109.3.

STATE OF THE NATION

SAFETY Recovering from a civil war, and still fairly lawless.

LIFE EXPECTANCY M 74.6, F 80.15.

BEING THERE

ETIQUETTE Mannerisms resemble those of mainland Greece with a nod meaning 'no' and a shake of the head meaning 'yes'. Men are addressed *Zoti*, women *Zonja*, for Mr and Mrs. Gifts are usually given when a guest at someone's house, but not often flowers. Accept offers of *raki*, coffee, and sweets. Dress is informal and bikinis can be worn on the beach. Foreigners are often charged more than locals in restaurants, shops and attractions. Keep EU entry passports, foreign currency and cameras safe. Avoid remote areas. Tipping is now gratefully received in restaurants.

CURRENCY *Lek* (Lk) = 100 *qindarka*.

FINANCE MasterCard and Eurocard accepted by banks and many hotels. Traveller's cheques less so.

BUSINESS HOURS 0800-1600 Mon -Fri.

GMT +1 (+2 from last Sunday in March

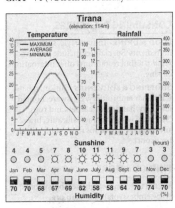

Tirana (elevation: 114m)												
Sunshine (hours)												
4	4	5	7	8	10	11	11	9	7	3	3	
Jan	Feb	Mar	Apr	May	June	July	Aug	Sept	Oct	Nov	Dec	
70	70	68	67	69	62	58	58	64	70	74	70	Humidity (%)

HIGHLIGHTS

TIRANA The small capital's architecture is influenced by Italian and Turkish designs, since it is located midway between Rome and Istanbul. Its best examples are the Ethem-Bey Mosque, built at the turn of the nineteenth century, and the clocktower. Most visitors start exploring from the heart of the city, at Skënderberg Square.

THE ANCIENT RUINS OF BUTRINT Greeks settled here in the sixth century BC, to make it a fortified trading city with an acropolis. Later a theatre, public baths, and a baptistry with mosaics of animals and birds were added.

DURRËS Founded in 627 BC by Greeks, the city's port was the largest in the Adriatic, marking the start of the Via Egnatia to Constantinople. Byzantine. Now the country's second largest city, a rich scattering of Roman and Byzantine ruins bring colour to the city.

SHKODRA One of Europe's oldest cities and the traditional centre of the Gheg cultural region. Today old meets new, as the skyline is dominated by the newly built impressive Sheik Zamil Abdullah Al-Zamil Mosque.

BERAT The 'city of a thousand windows', it is known for the number of windows in the red-roofed houses, and is a picturesque city on the slopes of a mountain.

SARANDA The southern coastline is unspoilt. Lying opposite the Greek island of Corfu, Saranda is now becoming a much visited resort for day-trippers, keen to explore the previously inaccessible.

to Saturday before last Sunday in October).

VOLTAGE GUIDE 220 volts AC, 50 Hz.

COUNTRY DIALLING CODE 355.

CONSUMING PLEASURES

FOOD & DRINK Balkan with Turkish influence s such as *kofte* and *shish* kebabs. Several private restaurants are now opening. Specialities include *tarator*, a cold yoghurt and cucumber soup, *kukurec*, stuffed sheep's intestines, *paça*, breakfast soup of animals' innards, and *oshaf*, a fig and sheep's milk pudding. *Raki*, an Albanian drink, is found in all bars and restaurants, as is Albanian cognac.

SHOPPING & SOUVENIRS Carpets, silver and copper, wooden carvings, ceramics and needlework are all available to be bartered over.

FIND OUT MORE

WEBSITES www.uk.al (British Embassy), www.usemb-tirana.rpo.at (US Embassy), www.albanian.com.

LOCAL MEDIA English-language newspapers include *Balkan News* and *Albanian Daily News*, while English pages are included in *Albania*, *Gazeta Shqiptare*, *Shekulli*, and *Ekonomia*.

TOURIST BOARDS IN UK/US UK: Regent Holidays (UK) Ltd, 15 John Street, Bristol BS1 2HR, tel (0117) 921 1711, email regent@regent-holidays.co.uk, web www.regent-holidays.co.uk.

Albanian has a total of 27 different words for moustache

ALGERIA

WHEN TO GO

WEATHER Saharan temperatures can be especially ferocious during the summer months. Sandstorms also occur, while rainfall is relatively low. However, desert temperatures drop dramatically at night. Coastal resorts are cooled by sea breezes. In general, the best times to visit are March to April, or October to November.

FESTIVALS Many of the major festivities are dictated by the religious calendar and vary accordingly. Secular events include Independence Day on 5 July and Revolutionary Readjustment on June 19. For the hardy - or the foolish - the Sahara Marathon takes place in Tindouf in February.

TRANSPORT

INTERNATIONAL AIRPORTS Algiers Houri Boumediene (ALG), 20 km from Algiers, Oran (ORN), 10 km from the city, Annaba (AAE), 12km from the city, Constantine (CZL), is 9km from the city.

INTERNAL TRAVEL Internal air flights most practical for travel to the south. Slow rail services but reasonable road surfaces. Vehicles travelling in the desert must be well equipped as breakdown facilities are virtually non-existent. Car hire can be arranged at the airport, in most towns and at many hotels.

RED TAPE

VISAS REQUIRED (UK/US) Required (no Israeli stamps in passports).

VACCINATIONS REQUIRED: See 'Vaccinations required around the world' on page 653.

DRIVING REQUIREMENTS International Driving Permit. A *carnet de passage* may be necessary if you own the vehicle.

COUNTRY REPS IN UK/US UK: 6 Hyde Park Gate, London SW7 5EW, tel (020) 7589 6885, fax (020) 7589 7725, email algerian-consulate@yahoo.co.uk US: 2137 Wyoming Avenue, NW, Washington, DC 20008, tel (202) 265 2800, fax (202) 667 2174, email ambassadoroffice@yahoo.com.

UK/US REPS IN COUNTRY UK: Hilton Hotel International, 7th Floor, Pins Maritimes, Palais des Expositions, El Mohammadia, Algiers, tel (21) 230 068, fax (21) 230 067, email visaenquiries.algiers@fco.gov.uk. US: 4 Chemin Cheikh Bachir El-Ibrahimi, Algiers, tel (21) 691 255, fax (21) 693 979, email coltoneo@state.gov.

PEOPLE AND PLACE

CAPITAL Algiers (El Djezair).

LANGUAGE Arabic and French.

PEOPLES Arabic, Berber, French.

RELIGION Sunni Muslim (99%).

SIZE (SQ KM) 2,381,741.

POPULATION 31,070,000.

POP DENSITY/KM 13.

STATE OF THE NATION

SAFETY Very high risk area due to a low-level civil conflict in which thousands have died including tourists.

LIFE EXPECTANCY M 71.45, F 74.63.

BEING THERE

ETIQUETTE Islamic religious practices and festivities should be duly respected. The Algerian observance of Ramadan has relaxed and some restaurants and business centres will be open in the day. However, in the towns and oases of the south, religious observance is more orthodox.

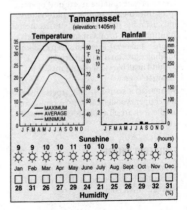

Tamanrasset (elevation: 1405m)

HIGHLIGHTS

THE SAHARA The most striking and forbidding feature of the country, the vast desert comprises more than four-fifths of Algeria's total area. It also provides a breathtaking landscape of shifting sands, dotted with pleasant oasis villages.

ALGIERS Vibrant capital, a port since Roman times. The dry climate has preserved a number of impressive Roman, Punic and Christian ruins, including those at Djemila, Timgad and Tipasa. Algiers retains a Maghreb feel, with zig-zagging alleyways, mosques and an interesting *casbah*. The Bardo Ethnographic and Local Art Museum and the National Museum of Fine Arts are among the finest in north Africa.

GHARDAIA Distinctive Saharan town inhabited by a Muslim fundamentalist sect called the Mozabites. Mozabite towns feature four-spire minarets.

TURQUOISE COAST An area of rocky coves and long beaches, within easy reach of Algiers, where visitors can enjoy watersports and cruises.

ATLAS MOUNTAINS Cool retreat from the stifling summer heat. Sights include the Grand Mosque and Mansourah Fortress located in the imperial city of Tlemcen, on the Hauts Plateaux, in the Tellian Atlas foothills.

TAMANRASSET Colourful and vibrant centre in the Hoggar Mountains, an important stopping place for trade with west Africa. Used as a base for hikers and a popular winter resort, it is also regularly visited by the camel caravans of *les hommes bleues*, the blue-robbed Touregs.

CURRENCY *Dinar* (AD) = 100 *centimes*.
FINANCE Limited acceptance of credit cards and only more expensive hotels and government-run craft shops accept traveller's cheques.
BUSINESS HOURS 0900-1530, Sunday-Thursday.
GMT +1.
VOLTAGE GUIDE 220 volts AC, 50 Hz.
COUNTRY DIALLING CODE 213.

CONSUMING PLEASURES

FOOD & DRINK Local cooking includes roast meat and *cous-cous* with vegetable sauces. French and Italian influenced dishes in hotels in Algiers and coastal resorts, but with spicier sauces. Good fish dishes. More limited range of foodstuffs in the south. Alcohol only available in expensive hotels and restaurants. The country produces good wines but they are hard to find locally.

SHOPPING & SOUVENIRS Leatherware, rugs, copper and brass, dresses, jewellery, Berber carpets, basketwork, pottery. Bargaining is customary.

FIND OUT MORE

WEBSITES www.algerianconsulate.org.uk (Algerian UK Embassy), www.algeria-us.org (Algerian US Embassy), www.britishembassy.gov.uk/algeria, www.lexicorient.com/algeria/index.htm.
LOCAL MEDIA The daily *Horizons* has an English section. There is one TV channel and four radio stations, all are state run.
TOURIST BOARDS IN UK/US n/a.

"I am never going to stand in line waiting for the first tickets to the moon. I have already seen the moon. That is, I have seen Tamanrasset in the Sahara."
John Gunther, 'Inside Africa', 1955

ANDORRA

WHEN TO GO

WEATHER Summer runs from May to September. Temperate climate with warm summers and cold winters.

FESTIVALS Between July and September most Andorran settlements will have a 'village festival', where locals come together to mark their heritage with music, dancing, wine and feasts. The capital has a three day festival, beginning on the first Saturday in August. Mare de Deu de Meritxell, the national festival of the Virgin Mary, is celebrated on 8 September with a pilgrimage to Meritxell, situated 7 km to the northeast.

TRANSPORT

INTERNATIONAL AIRPORTS Nearest internationals are Barcelona (BCN) in Spain 225 km away, or Toulouse (TLS) in France 180 km away.

INTERNAL TRAVEL One major east-west route. Buses and mini-buses between villages. Taxis are also available, and sharing is common practice.

RED TAPE

VISAS REQUIRED (UK/US) No requirements for entry into Andorra but the relevant regulations for Spain or France should be followed, depending on which country is transited to reach Andorra.

VACCINATIONS REQUIRED: See 'Vaccinations required around the world' on page 653.

DRIVING REQUIREMENTS National Driving Licence accepted.

COUNTRY REPS IN UK/US UK: 63 Westover Road, London SW18 2RF, tel (020) 8874 4806, fax \9020) 8874 4902, email andorra.embassyuk@ btopenworld.com. US: Permanent Mission of the Principality of Andorra to the United Nations, 2 United Plaza, 25th Floor, New York, NY 10017, tel (212) 750 8064, fax (212) 750 6630, email andorra@un.int.

UK/US REPS IN COUNTRY
UK: Casa Jacint Pons, 3/2 La Massana, tel/fax 893 840, email

britconand@mypic.ad. US: The American consulate in Madrid (see Spain) deals with enquiries regarding Andorra.

PEOPLE AND PLACE

CAPITAL Andorra La Vella.

LANGUAGE Officially Catalan, but French and Spanish also used.

PEOPLES Spanish, Catalan, French, Portuguese.

RELIGION Roman Catholic (94%).

SIZE (SQ KM) 467.8.

POPULATION 67,159.

POP DENSITY/KM 143.6.

STATE OF THE NATION

SAFETY Safe.

LIFE EXPECTANCY M 80.6, F 86.6.

BEING THERE

ETIQUETTE Dress is informal. Handshaking is the usual greeting. Smoking is very common. Customs are similar to those in Spain, and normal social courtesies should be used when visiting someone's home.

CURRENCY The Euro (€) = 100 *cents* is commonly used.

FINANCE Major credit cards accepted.

BUSINESS HOURS Vary considerably - lunch is after 13.30 and can extend through the afternoon.

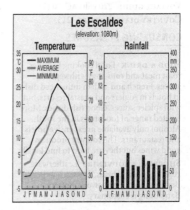

Les Escaldes (elevation: 1080m)
Temperature / Rainfall

HIGHLIGHTS

ANDORRA LA VELLA
The capital is also the country's most commercial centre, focussed on its duty-free status and winter sports. However, there are some sights including the Casa de la Vall, the ancient seat of the government.

CALDEA
Escaldes-Engordany's spa is Europe's largest spa complex. Its lagoons, hot tubs and saunas are all fed by thermal springs.

SOLDEU Most ski resorts in Andorra have good facilities. Soldeu is the main centre, and also the first town on the road after the French border at Port d'Envalira. It has nursery slopes and skiing for intermediates.

LA RABASSA Centre of cross-country skiing in Andorra.

CANILLO Summer mountainous extreme sports destination, home to canyon clambering, a *via ferrata* climbing gully and a climbing wall. It also has a year-round ice rink and pool. There are many guided walks and hikes here too.

GRANDVALIRA
Soldeu, Canillo, and El Tarter club together to form Grandvalira when the snow comes. Together they are the largest ski playground in the Pyrenees, with 192 kilometres of runs and a lift system capable of moving up to 90,000 people an hour.

ESCALDES-ENGORDANY
The spa town lies adjacent to the capital and is home to many examples of Romanesque architecture. It is these two towns that are the centre of the vivid festival of Mare de Deu de Meritxell.

GMT +1 (+2 in Summer)
VOLTAGE GUIDE 240AC, 50Hz.
COUNTRY DIALLING CODE 376.

CONSUMING PLEASURES

FOOD & DRINK Catalan, with plenty of pork and ham dishes. Restaurants quite expensive. Local dishes include *coques*, flavoured flat cakes, *trinxat*, a potato cabbage dish, and *truites de carreroles*, a mushroom omelette. Alcohol from shops is cheap as Andorra is a duty-free zone.

SHOPPING & SOUVENIRS Duty-free shopping for all goods means that petrol, alcohol, cameras, watches and electrical goods are good targets for bargain hunters.

FIND OUT MORE

WEBSITES www.andorra.ad, www.turisme.ad, www.caldea.com.

LOCAL MEDIA No English-language newspapers, one independent commercial television station and six independent commercial radio stations.

TOURIST BOARDS IN UK/US n/a.

Andorra is a 'parliamentary co-princedom', nominally ruled by the President of France and the Catholic bishop of La Seu d'Urgell (just across the Spanish border). It is the only country to have Catalan – related to both Spanish and French – as the state language

ANGOLA

WHEN TO GO

WEATHER May to October is dry and there is a slight decrease in temperature. The rest of the year is hot and wet.

FESTIVALS Christmas is the biggest celebration of the year. A feast, or *ceia*, is held on 24 December of turkey and rice. After the *ceia*, gifts are exchanged, and handmade cakes and dried fruits are eaten, including grapes with which wishes are made. They attend church on Christmas Day itself. Public holidays to mark anniversaries are held throughout the year.

TRANSPORT

INTERNATIONAL AIRPORTS Luanda (LAD), 4 km from the city.

INTERNAL TRAVEL Strictly controlled and most of the country is only accessible by air. Rail services are erratic and much of the road infrastructure has been destroyed. Local buses run in Luanda.

RED TAPE

VISAS REQUIRED (UK/US) Required.

VACCINATIONS REQUIRED: See 'Vaccinations required around the world' on page 653.

DRIVING REQUIREMENTS International Driving Permit.

COUNTRY REPS IN UK/US UK: 22 Dorset Street, London, W1U 6QY, tel (020) 7299 9850, fax (020) 7486 9397, email embassy@angola.org.uk. US: 2100-2108 16th Street, NW, Washington, DC 20009, tel (202) 785 1156, fax (202) 785 1258, email: angola@angola.org.

UK/US REPS IN COUNTRY UK: PO Box 1244, Rua Diogo 4, Luanda, tel (2) 334 582, fax (2) 333 331, email postmaster.luanda@ fco.gov.uk US: 32 Rua Houari Boumedienne, CP 6468, Luanda, tel (2) 445 481, fax (2) 446 924.

PEOPLE AND PLACE

CAPITAL Luanda.

LANGUAGE Officially Portuguese and Bantu Languages

PEOPLES Portuguese, Umbundu, Kimbundu, Kikongo.

RELIGION Mainly Roman Catholic. Other Christian minorities. Local Animist beliefs are held by a significant minority.

SIZE (SQ KM) 1,246,700.

POPULATION 13,184,000.

POP DENSITY/KM 10.6.

STATE OF THE NATION

SAFETY Just recovering from a lengthy civil war, which has left many landmines and little infrastructure.

LIFE EXPECTANCY M 36, F 37.25.

BEING THERE

ETIQUETTE Normal social courtesies should be observed. Do not photograph public places, buildings or events. Permits should be given to the British Embassy and held at all times. Tipping is not officially encouraged, but may be given in kind (e.g. cigarettes).

CURRENCY *Kwanza* (Kzr) = 100 *lwei*.

FINANCE Credit cards are not generally accepted and traveller's cheques are uncommon. US Dollars widely accepted.

BUSINESS HOURS 0830-1230, 1400-1800, Monday to Friday. Some offices open 0830-1230 Saturday.

GMT +1.

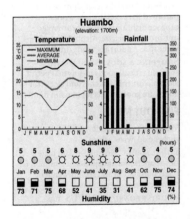

HIGHLIGHTS

LUANDA The nation's capital has a number of places for the traveller to visit including, the Museum of Armed Forces, the National Museum of Anthropology, and the Museum of Slavery (just outside the capital). Five minutes from the capital are the Ilha beaches, suitable for bathing.

KISSAMA NATIONAL PARK Once home to elephant, rhino, and buffalo, but only eland, waterbuck, manatee, marine turtles, and other small creatures have been sighted recently. An extensive game count is needed for a reliable estimate of the situation. A large variety of bird life is still in the park, however, following the 21-year war, and widespread poaching. Accommodation is available in bungalows in the middle of the park.

MUSSULO A bay formed from the sediment of the Kwanza River, with wide, white, sandy beaches covered with coconut palms and home to fishermen living in *cubatas*. Whiting and grouper are the most common fish. On the other side of the bay, weekend houses and a tourist complex and water-sports centre have now been built.

THE CALANDULA WATERFALLS Located in the Malanje area, these waterfalls provide an impressive spectacle, especially at the end of the rainy season when water levels are at their highest.

PALMEIRINHAS A long and deserted beach 45 kilometres south of Luanda. Its scenery is magnificent but bathing is hazardous. Instead, it is best enjoyed as a relaxed fishing spot.

VOLTAGE GUIDE 220 AC, 60 Hz.
COUNTRY DIALLING CODES 244.

CONSUMING PLEASURES

FOOD & DRINK Severe food and drink shortages at present. Book well ahead at the few hotels and restaurants. Make sure all food is prepared properly.

SHOPPING & SOUVENIRS Traditional handicrafts. Shopping best done in cities.

FIND OUT MORE

WEBSITES www.angola.org.uk, www.angola.org, http://luanda.usembassy.gov, www.britishembassy.gov.uk/angola.

LOCAL MEDIA There are no English-language newspapers, two TV channels (one independent, one state-controlled), and five radio stations (one state-controlled).

TOURIST BOARDS IN UK/US n/a.

This oil- and diamond-rich country has suffered almost continuous civil war since independence from Portugal in 1975. At last it is at peace

ANTIGUA & BARBUDA

WHEN TO GO

WEATHER Tropical, warm and relatively dry throughout the year. Some rainfall from September-December. Best visited during the cool and dry December to April period, the peak tourist season.

FESTIVALS Carnival, Antigua's big annual festival, starts at the end of July and culminates in a parade on the first Tuesday in August. Most Carnival activity takes place in St John's. Calypso music, steel bands, masqueraders, floats and street 'jump-ups' are all part of the celebrations. Another music event is the annual Antiguan Jazz Festival, which takes place in October. Antigua's Sailing Week is a major week-long yachting event in April, attracting about 150 boats. In addition to races, there are rum parties and a formal ball, with most activities taking place at Nelson's Dockyard and Falmouth Harbour. In June, Barbuda has a celebration of its own called Caribara.

TRANSPORT

INTERNATIONAL AIRPORTS VC Bird International (ANU), 8 km from St John's.

INTERNAL TRAVEL Light aircraft and boats between islands, good all weather roads and car hire easy to organise on arrival. Local buses are infrequent but taxis are available everywhere with standard rates.

RED TAPE

VISAS REQUIRED (UK/US) None.

VACCINATIONS REQUIRED: See 'Vaccinations required around the world' on page 653.

DRIVING REQUIREMENTS Local Driver's Permit.

COUNTRY REPS IN UK/US UK: 15 Thayer Street, London W1U 3JT, tel (020) 7486 7073, fax (020) 7486 9970. US: 3216 New Mexico Avenue, NW, Washington DC 20016, tel (202) 362 5122, fax (202) 362 5225, email embantbar@aol.com.

UK/US REPS IN COUNTRY UK: Price Waterhouse Cooper Center, 11 Old Parham Road, St John's, tel 462 0008/9, fax 562 2124,

email: britishc@candw.ag US: The embassy in Bridgetown (see Barbados) deals with enquiries .

PEOPLE AND PLACE

CAPITAL St John's.

LANGUAGE English.

PEOPLES Most of African descent, some Europeans and South Asians.

RELIGION Mainly Anglican and Protestant.

SIZE (SQ KM) Antigua: 280, Barbuda 161.

POPULATION 77,426.

POP DENSITY/KM 175.3.

STATE OF THE NATION

SAFETY Safe.

LIFE EXPECTANCY M 69.53, F 74.38.

BEING THERE

ETIQUETTE As with many islands around the world, the pace of life on Antigua and Barbuda is deliciously slow, particularly on the smaller Barbuda, which is home to just two per cent of the country's population. Best to chill out, grab a cocktail and just go with the flow. Casual wear is accepted in all bars and restaurants, however it is not acceptable to wear scanty clothing or beachwear in towns or villages.

CURRENCY Eastern Caribbean dollar (EC$) = 100 cents

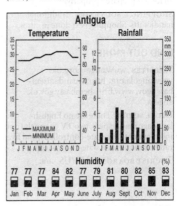

	Jan	Feb	Mar	Apr	May	June	July	Aug	Sept	Oct	Nov	Dec
Humidity (%)	77	77	77	84	82	77	79	81	80	82	85	83

HIGHLIGHTS

St John's Antigua's capital and the island's major tourist centre, but a place which retains a strong West Indian feel. Browse the shops, restaurants and galleries built in wooden huts along the harbour front complexes of Heritage Quay and Redcliffe Quay. St John's also has an interesting community-run museum, with an eclectic collection of displays depicting island life. The town's landmark is the twin-spired St John's Anglican Cathedral, which dates from 1847.

English Harbour Formerly a naval base, this popular spot has restored buildings, hilltops forts and museums, which make for an enjoyable day's roam. Nelson's dockyard is one of the safest landlocked harbours in the world, and was used by Admirals Nelson, Rodney and Hood as a base during the Napoleonic Wars.

Deep Bay Pleasant little bay with a sandy beach and protected waters. In the middle of the bay stands the coral-encrusted wreck of the *Andes*, a barque which went down 100 years ago and which

still peeks above the water, as snorkellers swim around in the shallows.

Fort James This small fort was first built in 1675, but most of the present structure dates from 1739. It still has a few original cannons, a powder magazine and a fair portion of its walls intact.

Dickinson Bay Resort with a white-sand beach, popular for swimming and watersports. Reggae music hangs in the air and stall holders sell T-shirts and jewellery. Trips to Great Bird Island can be made.

Finance Major credit cards, traveller's cheques.

Business hours 0800-12.00, 1300-1630, Monday to Friday.

GMT - 4.

Voltage guide 220/110 AC, 60Hz.

Country dialling code 1 268.

CONSUMING PLEASURES

Food & drink Superb seafood, including lobster and red snapper. Extensive choice in hotels including local curries, pilaffs, and roast suckling pig. Local drinks include coconut milk, ice-cold fruit juices and rum punches. There are no licensing restrictions.

Shopping & souvenirs Straw goods, pottery, batiks, silk-screens, jewellery (with semi-precious Antiguan stones), bone china, crystal, French perfume, watches and table linens.

FIND OUT MORE

Websites www.antigua-barbuda.com, www.antigua-barbuda.org.

Local media All are in English - the main paper is the *Daily Observer*, *The Outlet* is weekly and *Antigua Sun* is published twice a week. There is one state-owned television channel, one independent. One state-owned radio station and five independents.

Tourist boards in UK/US UK: As for country rep in UK except, fax (020) 7486 1466, email antbar@msn.com. US: 610 Fifth Avenue, Suite 311, New York, NY 10020, tel (212) 541 4117, fax (212) 541 4789, email info@antigua-barbuda.org.

Antigua's tourist office boasts that the island has 365 beaches – one for each day of the year

ARGENTINA

WHEN TO GO

WEATHER Subtropical in the north, with rain throughout the year, the far south is sub-arctic. The central mainland is temperate - visit throughout the year.

FESTIVALS Home to many festivals and celebrations including; the Snow Carnival in ski resorts in August; the Polo Argentine Open, first staged in 1893, is hosted between November and December in Palermo; the traditional Carnival at Humahuaca full of dance and folklore is held near Ash Wednesday; the Buenos Aires Tango Festival is held between February and March; and the International Video-Dance Festival is held each July in Buenos Aires.

TRANSPORT

INTERNATIONAL AIRPORTS Ezeiza Ministro Pistarini (EZE), 42km from Buenos Aires.

INTERNAL TRAVEL Air travel most efficient way to get around but the services are busy and often subject to delay. Long-haul train services have been disrupted since privatisation. Buses are a reliable form of long distance transport. Trunk roads fine, rural roads become impassable after rain.

RED TAPE

VISAS REQUIRED (UK/US) None required although business traveller's should check with the Argentinian consulate.

VACCINATIONS REQUIRED: See 'Vaccinations required around the world' on page 653.

DRIVING REQUIREMENTS International Driving Permit - must be stamped by the Automóvil Club Argentino, and carried at all times.

COUNTRY REPS IN UK/US UK: 27 Three Kings Yard, London W1Y 1FL, tel (020) 7318 1340, fax (020) 7318 1349, email fclond@mrecic.gov.ar US: 1600 New Hampshire Avenue, NW, Washington, DC 20009, tel (202) 238 6400, fax (202) 332 3171, email info@embajadaargentinaeeuu.org.

UK/US REPS IN COUNTRY UK: Dr Luis Agote 2412, C1425E0F Buenos Aires, tel (11) 4808 2200, fax (11) 4808 2274, email askconsular.baires@fco.gov.uk US: Avenida Colombia 4300, Buenos Aires, C1425 GMN, tel (11) 5777 4533, fax (11) 5777 4240, email bue-publicopinion@state.gov.

PEOPLE AND PLACE

CAPITAL Buenos Aires

LANGUAGE Officially Spanish, English widely spoken.

PEOPLES Mainly European. Remainder Mestizo, Indian.

RELIGION Roman Catholic (90%).

SIZE (SQ KM) 2,780,400.

POPULATION 37,486,938.

POP DENSITY/KM 13.

STATE OF THE NATION

SAFETY Beware petty crime (pickpockets, theft).

LIFE EXPECTANCY M 72.17, F 79.85.

BEING THERE

ETIQUETTE Greet friends by kissing cheeks, if going to someone's home bring a homemade dish or dessert. Avoid casual discussion of the Falklands/Malvinas war. Dress is informal but conservative away from the beach.

CURRENCY *Peso* (P) = 100 *centavos*.

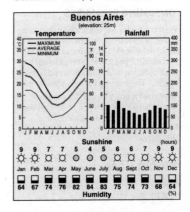

HIGHLIGHTS

BUENOS AIRES One of the world's largest metropolitan areas is an elegant shopper's paradise and cosmopolitan centre that is home to the Teatro Colón, the world's largest opera house, and the immense Catedral Metropolitana - the final resting place of San Martin, Argentina's liberator.

IGUAZÚ FALLS Two and a half miles long, 275 cascades plummet to 90 metres. Located in the UNESCO World Heritage listed Iguazú National Park whose subtropical rainforest supports 2,000 identified plant species and 400 bird species, the falls are formed by the River Paraná, split into numerous channels. The most impressive is Granta del Diablo, Devil's Throat. Take a free trip to the Isla San Martin for a crowd-free look.

PATAGONIA A vast region comprising the southernmost portion of the country, with numerous parks and nature reserves that are home to large herds of seals, sea lions, blue whales, and countless penguins.

TIERRA DEL FUEGO The gateway to the Antarctic. Ushuaia is the provincial capital, and the world's southernmost city, set among jagged glacial peaks, reaching 1,500 metres high, with their base at sea-level.

THE ANDES Near the Chilean border lies the famous Mount Aconcagua, the highest mountain in the Western hemisphere at 6,995 metres. Nearby are some of the best ski resorts: Las Leñas, the most prestigious, the Valles del Plata, and Los Penitentes. While in the area visit the Puente del Inca, a natural stone bridge over the River Mendoza.

FINANCE US dollars and major credit cards generally accepted. Often difficult to exchange traveller's cheques in small towns.

BUSINESS HOURS 0900-1900 Mon-Fri.

GMT -3.

VOLTAGE GUIDE 220 AC, 50 Hz.

COUNTRY DIALLING CODE 54.

CONSUMING PLEASURES

FOOD & DRINK Beef of very high quality and *parrilladas* (grill rooms) offer a large variety of barbecue-style dishes. Local food is largely a mixture of Basque, Spanish and Italian, including *empanadas* (minced meat, puff pastry and other ingredients) and pork and maize stew or *locro*. Local wines are very good and also inexpensive.

SHOPPING & SOUVENIRS Buenos Aires is a shopper's paradise, maybe the best in Latin America. Crafts and leather are best buys.

FIND OUT MORE

WEBSITES www.argentine-embassy-uk.org, www.embassyofargentinausa.org, http://buenosaires.usembassy.gov, www.argentour.com, www.sectur.gov.ar, www.britain.org.ar.

LOCAL MEDIA *The Buenos Aires Herald* is the leading English-language newspaper.

TOURIST BOARDS IN UK/US UK: 65 Brooke Street, London, W1K 4AH, tel (020) 7318 1340, fax (020) 7318 1301, email embar.ru@btclick.com. US: 12 West 56th Street, New York, NY 10019, tel (212) 603 0443, fax (212) 586 1786, email ifegarra@turismo.gov.ar.

"What exists here is a ludicrous form of nationalism. Our entire country is imported. Everyone here is really from somewhere else."

Jorge Luis Borges

ARMENIA

WHEN TO GO

WEATHER June to September is hot and dry (temperatures fall sharply at night). Winters are extremely cold with heavy snow. However, if you like sliding down icy slopes, then this time of year is popular with skiers. Armenian resorts are best visited in January and February.

FESTIVALS Concerts, recitals and traditional dance and music performances are held year-round, often on large outdoor stages. The town of Hrazdan hosts an annual autumn festival, called Voski Ashun, with concerts, traditional dancing and music in October. The largest holiday of the year is New Year, when people exchange gifts and houses are opened to walk-in guests. The Armenian Orthodox Church celebrates Christmas on 6 January. On 9 May, the heroes of World War II are revered for their sacrifices. Small children give them flowers and a kiss, while older children offer shots of vodka and *konyak*.

TRANSPORT

INTERNATIONAL AIRPORTS Zvartnots (EVN) 10 km from Yerevan.

INTERNAL TRAVEL May be disrupted by fuel shortages. Daily trains to most towns. Poor road surfaces and dangerous drivers. Some internal air travel.

RED TAPE

VISAS REQUIRED (UK/US) Required.

VACCINATIONS REQUIRED: See 'Vaccinations required around the world' on page 653.

DRIVING REQUIREMENTS n/a.

COUNTRY REPS IN UK/US UK: 25A Cheniston Gardens, London W8 6TG, tel (020) 7938 5435, fax (020) 7938 2595, email armembuk@onetel.net.uk. US: 2225 R Street, NW, Washington, DC 20008, tel (202) 319 2983, fax (202) 319 2982, email amembusadm@msn.com.

UK/US REPS IN COUNTRY UK: 34 Baghramian Street, Yerevan, 375019, tel (1) 264 301, fax (1) 264 318, email info.yerevan@fco.gov.uk. US: 18 Baghramyan Avenue, Yerevan 375019, tel (1) 520 791, fax (1) 520 800, email usinfo@arminco.com.

PEOPLE AND PLACE

CAPITAL Yerevan.

LANGUAGE Armenian and Russian.

PEOPLES Armenian. Small Azeri and Russian minorities.

RELIGION The world's oldest Christian nation. The Armenian Apostolic Church remains predominant. Catholic, Protestant and Russian Orthodox communities.

SIZE (SQ KM) 29,743.

POPULATION 3,330,099.

POP DENSITY/KM 111.9.

STATE OF THE NATION

SAFETY Some political and religious unrest, take great care and register with relevant embassy on arrival.

LIFE EXPECTANCY M 67.97, F 75.75.

BEING THERE

ETIQUETTE Entertaining overwhelmingly takes place in private homes. Guests may well receive great hospitality and generosity. In return, take a small gift, such as flowers, chocolates or alcohol (preferably imported), and join in wholeheartedly with the enthusiastic and endless toasts.

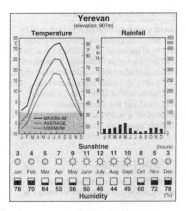

Yerevan
(elevation: 907m)

HIGHLIGHTS

YEREVAN Historic capital city and one of the oldest continuously inhabited settlements anywhere in the world, founded nearly 2,800 years ago in the time of Babylon. Its modern architecture, however, owes more to the Soviet regime than its ancient roots. The city boasts no fewer than 20 museums, the History and Art Museum being one of the best. The Vernisaj flea market, at weekends, is popular with tourists.

ECHMIADZIN Formerly the capital, from 180-340 AD, this holy city is the site of the Cathedral of St Gregory the Illuminator, which is the country's most important cathedral and a fine example of seventeenth-century Armenian ecclesiastical architecture. It is the spiritual home of the head of the Armenian Orthodox Church, and is said to house a piece of wood from Noah's Ark.

LAKE SEVAN The largest lake in the Caucasus, and much vaunted for its pure waters, stunning setting and delicious salmon trout. Ill-planned irrigation and hydroelectric projects have made it shrink and fears exist for its future.

DILIZHAN Hill resort and the source of much of the country's mineral water. Armenians say that heaven must be like Dilizhan, on account of its beautiful mountain scenery, with woods and springs. The town also offers a number of furniture and carpet factories for the keen shopper.

MOUNT ARAGATS The country's highest peak at 4,090 metres high, on which stands the ancient Amberd fort and church.

CURRENCY Armenian *dram* (AMD) = 100 *luma*.

FINANCE Credit cards and traveller's cheques generally accepted in shops and hotels. US dollars are also widely accepted.

BUSINESS HOURS n/a.

GMT +4.

VOLTAGE GUIDE 220 AC, 50 Hz.

COUNTRY DIALLING CODE 374.

CONSUMING PLEASURES

FOOD & DRINK Typically *hors d'oeuvres* of peppers, stuffed vine leaves and vegetables followed by lamb served as kebabs with flat bread or prepared as soup (*bozbash*). Armenian brandy has a good reputation. Coffee is served strong and black in small cups.

SHOPPING & SOUVENIRS The economy is largely undeveloped, although inroads are now being made. The Vernisaj flea market in Yerevan is worth a visit.

FIND OUT MORE

WEBSITES www.sunvil.co.uk, www.armeniaemb.org, www.britishembassy.am, www.usa.am, www.tourismamenia.org.

LOCAL MEDIA *Noyan Tapan* is an English-language weekly circulated among foreign missions and business.

TOURIST BOARDS IN UK/US UK: Sunvil House, 9 Upper Square, Old Isleworth, Middlesex, TW7 7BJ, tel (020) 8568 8899, fax (020) 8560 9889, email travel@sunvil.co.uk.

Winston Churchill drank Armenian brandy, in preference to French, with his ever-present cigar, after being given a bottle at the Yalta conference in 1945 by Josef Stalin

AUSTRALIA

WHEN TO GO

WEATHER If you plan to tour extensively, keep to the southern coasts in summer (December to March) and head north in winter (July to September). Travel to the dry interior during the transitional seasons between April and June or October and November.

FESTIVALS The Festival of Sydney, in January, features open air concerts, street theatre and fireworks. Sydney also hosts the famous annual Gay & Lesbian Mardi Gras, in February/March. Each March, Adelaide hosts Womadelaide, an outdoor festival of world music and dance. Melbourne holds a Comedy Festival in April, the world's biggest Writers' Festival in September and the Melbourne International Festival in October. Aboriginal arts and culture are celebrated at the Stompen Ground Festival, in Broome in October and the Barunga Wugularr Sports & Cultural Festival, near Katherine in June.

TRANSPORT

INTERNATIONAL AIRPORTS Sydney (SYD), Adelaide (ADL), Melbourne (MEL), Perth (PER), Brisbane (BNE), Darwin (DRW), Hobart (HBA), Cairns (CNS), Townsville (TSV).

INTERNAL TRAVEL Air travel is fastest due to vast distances. Well served by rail, although only one service goes from coast to coast (*The Indian Pacific*). Driving off major roads in the Outback is difficult from November to February because of summer rain. Car hire available at all major airports and hotels to those over 21.

RED TAPE

VISAS REQUIRED (UK/US) Required.

VACCINATIONS REQUIRED: See 'Vaccinations required around the world' on page 653.

DRIVING REQUIREMENTS International Driving Permits for those who's country's official language is not English. International Driving Permit only valid with a valid national licence.

COUNTRY REPS IN UK/US UK: Australia House, The Strand, London WC2B 4LA, tel (020) 7379 4334, fax (020) 7240 5333, email firstenquiries.lhlh@dfat.gov.au US: 1601 Massachusetts Avenue, NW, Washington, DC 20036, tel (202) 797 3000, fax (202) 797 3168, email public.affairs@austemb.org.

UK/US REPS IN COUNTRY UK: Commonwealth Avenue, Yarralumla, Canberra, ACT 2600, tel (2) 6270 6666, fax (2) 6273 3236, email bhc.canberra@uk.emb.gov.au. US: Moonah Place, Yarralumla, ACT 2600, tel (2) 6214 5600, fax (2) 6214 5970, email info@usembassy.gov.

PEOPLE AND PLACE

CAPITAL Canberra.

LANGUAGE English.

PEOPLES European 95%, Aboriginal, Asian and other peoples.

RELIGION Roman Catholic 26%, Protestant 24% and smaller minorities of all other major religions.

SIZE (SQ KM) 7,692,030.

POPULATION 19,546,792.

POP DENSITY/KM 2.54.

STATE OF THE NATION

SAFETY Safe (except for virulent poisonous wildlife).

LIFE EXPECTANCY M 77.52, F 83.4.

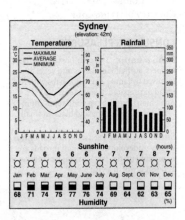

Sydney (elevation: 42m)											
Sunshine											(hours)
7	7	6	6	6	6	6	7	7	7	8	7
Jan	Feb	Mar	Apr	May	June	July	Aug	Sept	Oct	Nov	Dec
68	71	74	75	77	76	74	69	64	62	63	65
Humidity											(%)

HIGHLIGHTS

SYDNEY The country's oldest city and economic powerhouse. Cosmopolitan and blessed with sun-drenched natural attractions, dizzy skyscrapers, superb restaurants and friendly folk. Don't miss the Opera House, the Harbour Bridge and the famous breaks at Bondi.

GREAT BARRIER REEF Magnificent reef that runs along the coast of Queensland and is considered one of the world's great natural wonders. It is the biggest structure made by living organisms on earth, home to abundant underwater life and popular with divers.

KAKADU In the heart of the Northern Territory, this World Heritage reserve encompasses a variety of landscapes, swarms with wildlife and showcases some of Australia's best Aboriginal rock art.

WEST COAST Less touristy than its east coast counterpart, the west offers unspoilt Indian Ocean beaches and a vibrant and modern city in Perth, one of the most isolated cities in the world. Northerly Broome is an easy-going town and a centre for pearls.

OUTBACK It's incredibly vast, but the Outback is a true Australian experience. Popular for bushwalking and characterised by colourful towns with fair dinkum Aussie pubs. The highlight for many is Ayers Rock, or Uluru, a site of deep cultural significance to the Anangu Aboriginals. It's especially impressive at dawn and dusk when the red rock changes colour.

BEING THERE

ETIQUETTE An informal atmosphere prevails. As the locals say, 'no worries mate'.

CURRENCY Aus dollar (A$) = 100 cents.

FINANCE Major credit cards and traveller's cheques in major currencies accepted.

BUSINESS HOURS 0900-1700 Mon-Fri.

GMT North-east/south-east +10, central +9.5, West + 8.

VOLTAGE GUIDE 220/240 AC, 50 Hz.

COUNTRY DIALLING CODE 61.

CONSUMING PLEASURES

FOOD & DRINK Australia produces high quality local produce and seafood. Asian cookery has contributed to the lauded Pacific Rim cuisine. Top quality wines are produced in many areas.

SHOPPING & SOUVENIRS Local wines, wool, clothing, leather, precious stones, modern art, tribal objects, boomerangs.

FIND OUT MORE

WEBSITES Too many to list them all, but try www.australia.com, www.australia.org.uk, www.tourism.australia.com, www.about-australia.com, www.britaus.net, www.travelaustralia.com.au, www.sydneyvisitorcentre.com, www.discovertasmania.com.au.

LOCAL MEDIA The main papers are *The Australian* and the *Australian Financial Review*, while the biggest weeklies are the *Sunday Telegraph* and the Sunday Mail.

TOURIST BOARDS IN UK/US UK: Gemini House, 10-18 Putney Hill, London, SW15 6AA. tel (020) 8780 2229, fax (020) 8780 1496, email info@tourism.australia.com. USA: 2049 Century Park East, Suite 1920, Los Angeles, CA 90067, tel (310) 229 4870, fax (310) 552 1215.

" I like to think of it as the only Anglo-Saxon country with Mediterranean qualities."
John Douglas Pringle, 1958

AUSTRIA

WHEN TO GO

WEATHER Warm, pleasant summers, sunny winters with high snow levels, ideal for winter sports.

FESTIVALS The Wiener Festwochen in Vienna has a wide-ranging arts programme between mid-May and mid-June. A free rock, jazz, and folk concert is held in the city at the end of June. The Salzburg Festival stages opera, dance, and concerts in July and August with nearly 200 performances.

TRANSPORT

INTERNATIONAL AIRPORTS Vienna (VIE), Innsbruck (INN), Salzburg (SZG), Klagenfurt (KLU).

INTERNAL TRAVEL Efficient rail service, excellent road network. Vienna has a light rail and tramway service.

RED TAPE

VISAS REQUIRED (UK/US) Not required for stays of up to 3 months.

VACCINATIONS REQUIRED: See 'Vaccinations required around the world' on page 653.

DRIVING REQUIREMENTS National driving licences issued by EU countries accepted, UK licences without photo require other photo id to be carried (e.g. passport). A Green Card is compulsory.

COUNTRY REPS IN UK/US UK: 18 Belgrave Mews West, London SW1X 8HU, tel (020) 7235 3731, fax (020) 7344 0292, email embassy@austria.org.uk. US: 3524 International Court, NW, Washington, DC 20008, tel (202) 895 6700, fax (202) 895 6750, email austrianembassy@washington.nu.

UK/US REPS IN COUNTRY UK: Jaurèsgasse 12, A-1030 Vienna, tel (1) 7161 35151, fax (1) 7161 35900, email visa-consular@britishembassy.at. US: Boltzmanngasse 16, A-1090 Vienna, tel (1) 313 390, fax (1) 313 392 351, email embassy@usembassy.at.

PEOPLE AND PLACE

CAPITAL Vienna.

LANGUAGE German.

PEOPLES German (93%), Croat, Slovene, Hungarian minorities.

RELIGION Roman Catholic (78%), non-religious (9%), Muslim, Jewish and Protestant minorities

SIZE (SQ KM) 83,858.

POPULATION 8,169,929.

POP DENSITY/KM 97.4.

STATE OF THE NATION

SAFETY Safe.

LIFE EXPECTANCY M 76.03, F 81.96.

BEING THERE

ETIQUETTE Austrians are formal in business and social dealings. On first introduction first names are not used, but can be from the second meeting onward. Handshaking is the normal greeting. When entering restaurants or shops it is important to say 'Guten Tag', or 'Grüss Gott', and 'Auf Wiedersehen' when leaving. If invited to dinner, it is the usual custom to give flowers to the hostess. The Church is well respected in their society, and the traveller should keep this in mind. Dress smartly for the opera or theatre.

CURRENCY Euro (€) = 100 cents.

FINANCE Major credit cards, Eurocheque

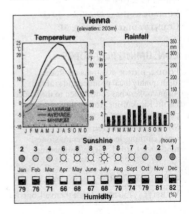

Vienna
(elevation: 203m)

	Temperature		Rainfall	

— MAXIMUM
— AVERAGE
— MINIMUM

J F M A M J J A S O N D   J F M A M J J A S O N D

Sunshine (hours)

| 2 | 3 | 4 | 6 | 8 | 9 | 8 | 7 | 4 | 2 | 1 |

Jan	Feb	Mar	Apr	May	June	July	Aug	Sept	Oct	Nov	Dec
79	76	71	66	68	67	68	70	74	79	81	82

Humidity (%)

HIGHLIGHTS

VIENNA The beautiful architecture of the capital is extremely rich. Schloss Schönbrunn, the sumptuous summer palace, rivals Versailles. The city is home to many fine art collections, and over 50 museums. The Ferris Wheel from the film *The Third Man* still stands in the Prater amusement park, and still draws crowds. The Spanish Riding School in the Hofburg is famous for the white Lipizzaner stallions that perform exquisite dressage manoeuvres to Viennese classical music.

SALZBURG Another elegant city full of Baroque architecture, set against a striking mountain backdrop. Largely pedestrianised, sights are in easy walking distance of the old city centre, now with World Heritage Status. The birthplace of Mozart, who is commemorated with an annual music festival.

CARINTHIA Home to the nation's tallest mountain, Grossglockner, famous lakes that reach 28 degrees C in summer and become skating rinks in winter, and ten ski resorts with 1,000 kilometres of runs.

STYRIA Now a popular and attractive destination, with skiing possible all year round. The southern part of the region is home to a number of vineyards and pine forests, perfect for a summer hike.

UPPER AUSTRIA Less well known to tourists, the region operates at a slower pace, ideal for restful holidays among the rolling plains, dense woodland and lush meadows. The region's capital, Linz, straddles the Danube, and any tour should visit its fifteenth-century castle and churches.

cards, traveller's cheques widely accepted.
BUSINESS HOURS 0800-1230, 1330-1730 Monday-Friday.
GMT +1.
VOLTAGE GUIDE 220 AC, 50 Hz.
COUNTRY DIALLING CODE 43.

CONSUMING PLEASURES

FOOD & DRINK Viennese cuisine is strongly influenced by southeast European cooking. Mostly meat dishes, such as *wiener schnitzel*, with potatoes or dumplings. Over 57 varieties of *torte,* often consumed with coffee at a *kaffehaus*. Excellent, cheap local wines, usually white.

SHOPPING & SOUVENIRS Handbags, glassware, china, winter sports gear.

FIND OUT MORE

WEBSITES www.bmaa.gv.at/london, www.austria.org, www. austria.info/uk, www.britishembassy.at, www.austria.info/us, www.usembassy.at, www.austria-tourism.aat, www.info.wien.at.

LOCAL MEDIA National press in German but English-language papers are widely available, especially in big cities and tourist resorts. Two state owned TV channels, one independent.

TOURIST BOARDS IN UK/US UK: 9-11 Ricmond Buildings, Dean Street, London, W1D 38F, tel (020) 7440 3830, fax (020) 7440 3848, email info@anto.co.uk. US: 120 West 45th Street, 9th Floor, New York, NY 10036, tel (212) 944 6880, fax (212) 730 4568, email travel@austria.info.

" Baroque Vienna knows that an illusion which makes you happy is better than a reality which makes you sad. "
Alan Whicker

AZERBAIJAN

WHEN TO GO

WEATHER Generally very warm. Low temperatures can occur in the mountains and valleys. Most rainfall in the west. The months of June to September are best for general travel, as it's warm and dry in much of the country - though it can be scorching in the high summer.

FESTIVALS The Islamic calendar dictates many of the country's major festivals, including Ramadan, the month of daily fasting (dates change). Public holidays include World War II victory day on 9 May, Republic Day on 28 May and Independence Day on 18 October.

TRANSPORT

INTERNATIONAL AIRPORTS Baku Bina (BAK), 25 km from Baku.

INTERNAL TRAVEL Restricted - many regions near the border require special permission. Many roads in poor condition. Car hire available from Avis in Baku. Most visitors use taxis or private cars. 4x4 vehicles recommended for travel in the mountains.

RED TAPE

VISAS REQUIRED (UK/US) Required.

VACCINATIONS REQUIRED: See 'Vaccinations required around the world' on page 653.

DRIVING REQUIREMENTS International Driving Permit required.

COUNTRY REPS IN UK/US
UK: 4 Kensington Court, London W8 5DL, tel (020) 7938 3412, fax (020) 7937 1783, email sefir@btinternet.com. US: 2741 34th Street, NW, Washington DC 20008, tel (202)337 3500, fax (202) 337 5911, email: azerbaijan@azembassy.com.

UK/US REPS IN COUNTRY
UK: 45a Khagani Street, Baku, AZ1010, tel (12) 497 5188, fax (12) 497 7434, email: office@britemb.baku.az. US: 83 Azadliq Avenue, AZ1007 Baku, tel (12) 498 0335, fax (12) 465 6671, email consularbaku@state.gov.

PEOPLE AND PLACE

CAPITAL Baku.

LANGUAGE Azerbaijani.

PEOPLES Mostly Azeri. Very small Russian, Armenian and Jewish minorities.

RELIGION Predominantly Shia Muslim.

SIZE (SQ KM) 86,600.

POPULATION 8,347,000.

POP DENSITY/KM 90.1.

STATE OF THE NATION

SAFETY A ceasefire has lasted since 1994, following a separatist conflict.

LIFE EXPECTANCY M 59.24, F 67.66.

BEING THERE

ETIQUETTE Visitors to Azerbaijan may find themselves the recipient of many gifts, so it's best to be prepared to reciprocate. Local women, especially in rural areas, tend to be extremely retiring. They will serve a meal, but will seldom eat with foreign guests. Foreign women are treated with elaborate courtesy, which can develop into excessive attention. It's advisable to dress modestly and adopt a coolness of manner. Muslim practices and festivals, such as Ramadan, should be respected.

CURRENCY *Manat* (AM).

FINANCE Generally a cash-only economy with US dollars, pounds sterling and euros preferred currencies. Credit cards accepted

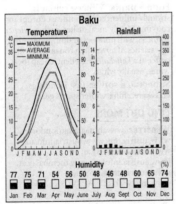

HIGHLIGHTS

BAKU The country's busy capital, the biggest metropolis in Transcaucasia, and home to about a fifth of Azerbaijan's population. The heart of the historic city is Ichari Shahar, the walled Old Town. There, archaeological digs have revealed Bronze Age burial chambers. It's a fascinating maze of alleys, dead ends and *caravanserais* (inns), sometimes called the 'Acropolis of Baku'.

ATESHGAH FIRE TEMPLE A centre of worship for thousands of years, built on the site of a natural gas vent. Flames spontaneously erupt from the ground - hence the country's other name, Odlar Yourdu, or Land of Fires. Influenced by India, the majestic temple features Sanskrit and Hindi inscriptions and an onion dome.

ASPERHON PENINSULA Stretching out to the Caspian Sea beyond Baku, this is the site of several fine medieval castles, built by the Shirvan *shahs* fearing attack from the sea. At Ramana you can also see the remains of ancient oil fields, while at Mardakyany is a botanic garden and a fifteenth-century mosque.

SHEMAKHA Formerly a major trading centre, this little town in the foothills of the Caucasus maintains a reputation for carpets and wine. Old capital of the Shirvan *shahs*, and many of the past royals are buried here.

QOBUSTAN MUSEUM An open-air museum littered with neolithic rock drawings. It has 4,000 petroglyphs that go back 12,000 years, depicting Stone Age people sporting loin cloths, hunting and dancing.

in major hotels and all banks in Baku.

BUSINESS HOURS Mon - Fri 0930-1730.

GMT +4

VOLTAGE GUIDE 220 AC, 50 Hz.

COUNTRY DIALLING CODE 994.

LOCAL MEDIA No English-language newspapers. The main daily paper is *Azerbaijan*.

TOURIST BOARDS IN UK/US n/a.

CONSUMING PLEASURES

FOOD & DRINK Combination of Turkish and central Asian dishes, kebabs, rich soups, spinach, chickpeas, rice and yoghurt. Sturgeon still available - at a price. Tea houses serve sweet black tea in tiny glasses. Local wines and brandies, Russian vodka available.

SHOPPING & SOUVENIRS Nardaran is the best place to find Azeri carpets. The Sharg Bazary in Baku sells silk, ceramics and other craftwork. Negotiate on prices.

FIND OUT MORE

WEBSITES www.britishembassy.az, www.azembassy.com, www.usembassybaku.org, www.azerb.com.

The denationalisation of the oil industry in 1872 changed Baku from a dusty backwater to a wealthy and sophisticated city attracting European investors, including the Rothschilds, and accounting for more than half of the world's oil production by the end of the nineteenth century

BAHAMAS

WHEN TO GO

WEATHER Mid-December to mid-April slightly cooler than other Caribbean island groups due to the proximity of North American cold-air systems.

FESTIVALS Nassau hosts a Junkanoo celebration each year, a city-wide carnival on Boxing Day and repeated on New Year's Day. The Goombay Summer Festival runs June to August, in Marsh Harbour and Treasure Cay in the Abacos, with concerts, food, and dancing. The Cat Island rake 'n' scrape Music Festival is held in late June in New Bight. A Pineapple Festival, featuring eating contests, music, and games takes place over three days in early June. The Plymouth Historical Weekend is held in December to celebrate the settlement's Loyalist heritage. Regattas are held throughout the year.

TRANSPORT

INTERNATIONAL AIRPORTS Nassau International (NAS), 16 km from city, Freeport International (FPO), 5 km from the city.

INTERNAL TRAVEL Charter flights between islands. A mail boat serves the Out Islands. Car hire easy, but buses, bicycles and taxis readily available.

RED TAPE

VISAS REQUIRED (UK/US) None.

VACCINATIONS REQUIRED: See 'Vaccinations required around the world' on page 653.

DRIVING REQUIREMENTS International driving licence required, be 21 or over.

COUNTRY REPS IN UK/US UK: 10 Chesterfield Street, London W1J 5JL, tel (020) 7408 4488, fax (020) 7499 9937, email information@bahamashclondont.com US: 2220 Massachussetts Avenue, NW, Washington, DC 20008, tel (202) 319 2660, fax (202) 319 2668, email bahemb@aol.com

UK/US REPS IN COUNTRY UK: The British High Commission in Kingston (see Jamaica) deals with enquiries for the Bahamas US: 42 Queen Street, Nassau, tel 322 1181, fax 328 7838, email: visanassau@state.gov

PEOPLE AND PLACE

CAPITAL Nassau.

LANGUAGE English.

PEOPLES Of African descendent, Caucassian minority.

RELIGION Christian denominations, mainly Baptist, Anglican, Roman Catholic.

SIZE (SQ KM) 13,939.

POPULATION 303,000.

POP DENSITY/KM 21.7.

STATE OF THE NATION

SAFETY Safe.

LIFE EXPECTANCY M 62.11, F 69.04.

BEING THERE

ETIQUETTE Life in The Bahamas is generally leisurely, informal wear is accepted in the resorts, but smarter clothing should be worn in the evenings especially if dancing, dining, or playing the casinos. It is not acceptable to wear beach clothing in towns.

CURRENCY Bahamian dollar = 100 cents.

FINANCE Major credit cards widely accepted. The US dollar is accepted as legal tender.

BUSINESS HOURS 0900-1700 Mon-Fri.

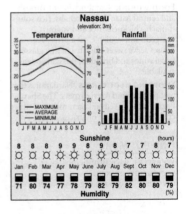

Nassau
(elevation: 3m)

	Jan	Feb	Mar	Apr	May	June	July	Aug	Sept	Oct	Nov	Dec
Sunshine (hours)	8	8	8	9	9	8	9	8	7	7	8	7
Humidity (%)	71	80	74	77	78	79	82	79	82	80	80	79

HIGHLIGHTS

NASSAU The capital of The Bahamas, on New Providence Island, has much to see. From the bustling straw market, the tropical flowers and pink flamingos of the Ardastra Gardens, to eighteenth-century Fort Charlotte on West Bay Street (complete with moat) and Fort Fincastle (built in the shape of a ship's bows). For panoramic views of the island, take the elevator to the top of the Water Tower. Finally, relax at Cable Beach, a two and a half mile stretch lined with bars.

PARADISE ISLAND Accessible via bridges from New Providence, Paradise Island lays claim to the world's largest open-air aquarium, a massive 14 acres. In the same complex is a large casino. A more relaxed time can be had on the island's beautiful beaches.

GRAND BAHAMA White sandy beaches, two casinos, and good shopping facilities are located here, but away from the tourist gridlock is Lucaya National Park, a maze of mangrove creeks ideal for sea kayaking and exploration.

ELEUTHERA A narrow island, only 3 kilometres wide, but 177 kilometres long, with great beaches. The most beautiful, Club Med Beach, is a long expanse of powdery pink sand set against a tall forest. Nor'Side Beach is backed by high dunes and has rolling surf. Good scuba opportunities on the island.

THE EXUMAS A chain of islands described by some yachtsmen as the finest cruising region in the world, with spectacular reefs in the sea and ruined and deserted plantation houses on land.

GMT -5 (-4 in summer).
VOLTAGE GUIDE 120AC, 60Hz.
COUNTRY DIALLING CODE 1 242.

CONSUMING PLEASURES

FOOD & DRINK Seafood specialities include grouper, conch, baked crab, red snapper in anchovy sauce. Local drinks are based on rum. Fresh fruit is brought from the Out Islands, including sweet pineapple, mango, breadfruit and papaya.

SHOPPING & SOUVENIRS China, cutlery, leather, fabrics, Scandinavian glass and silver, Swiss watches, French perfume, local straw products, seashell jewellery and wooden carvings.

FIND OUT MORE

WEBSITES www.bahamas.co.uk, www.un.int/bahamas, www.bahamas.com.

LOCAL MEDIA The *Tribune*, *Nassau Guardian*, *Freeport News*, and *The Bahama Journal* are printed daily. International papers are also available, including The *Daily Telegraph*, *The Times*, *USA Today* and *The Miami Herald*.

TOURIST BOARDS IN UK/US UK: Bahamas House, 10 Chesterfield Street, London W1J 5JL, tel (020) 7355 0800, fax (020) 7491 9459, email info@bahamas.co.uk. US: 150 East 52nd Street, New York, NY 10022, tel (212) 758 2777, fax (212) 753 6531, email bmotny@bahamas.com.

The name Bahamas comes from the Spanish *baja-mar*, meaning 'shallow sea'

BAHRAIN

WHEN TO GO

WEATHER Spring and late autumn are the most pleasant months to visit. June to October hot and humid, December to March quite cool.

FESTIVALS The Islamic holidays of Eid Al-Fitr (the end of Ramadan), Eid Al-Adha (the end of the pilgrimage season) and the Islamic New Year are major holidays. Dates vary according to the religious calendar. Bahrain's large Shiite community celebrates the religious festival of Ashoora, which marks the death of Emam Hussein, the grandson of the Prophet. Processions, led by men expressing sorrow through self-flagellation, take place in April and March.

TRANSPORT

INTERNATIONAL AIRPORTS Bahrain International (BAH), 6.5 km from Manama.

INTERNAL TRAVEL Excellent road system, car hire easy at the airport. Over 300 internal flights a week. Travel between the smaller islands by dhow or motorboat.

RED TAPE

VISAS REQUIRED (UK/US) Required.

VACCINATIONS REQUIRED: See 'Vaccinations required around the world' on page 653.

DRIVING REQUIREMENTS International Driving Permit. Must be endorsed by the Traffic and Licensing Directorate.

COUNTRY REPS IN UK/US
UK: 30 Belgrave Square, London SW1X 8QB, tel (020) 7201 9170, fax (020) 7201 9183, email enquiries@bahrainembassy. co.uk US: 3502 International Drive, NW, Washington, DC 20008, tel, (202) 342 1111, fax (202) 362 2192, email info@ bahrainembassy.org.

UK/US REPS IN COUNTRY
UK: 21 Government Avenue, PO Box 114, Manama 306, tel 1757 4100, fax 1757 4101, email: britemb@ batelco.com.bh
US: Building 979, Road 3119, Block 331, Manama, tel 1724 2700, fax 1727 2594, email manamaconsular@state.gov.

PEOPLE AND PLACE

CAPITAL Manama.

LANGUAGE Arabic and English.

PEOPLES Bahraini. Also other Arab, Iranian, Indian and Pakistani.

RELIGION Islam.

SIZE (SQ KM) 710.9.

POPULATION 666,442.

POP DENSITY/KM 937.5.

STATE OF THE NATION

SAFETY Safe.

LIFE EXPECTANCY M 71.76, F 76.78.

BEING THERE

ETIQUETTE Traditional beliefs and customs are strong influences and people are generally more formal than Westerners. Attitudes to women are more liberal than in most Gulf States. Homosexuality, however, is illegal. It is acceptable to sit cross-legged on cushions or sofas in people's homes but it is insulting to display the soles of the feet or shoes. It is also rude to accept food or anything else with the left hand. It is polite to drink two small cups of coffee or tea when offered. Sports clothes may be worn in the street and short dresses are acceptable, but revealing clothing should be avoided.

CURRENCY *Dinar* (BD) = 1000 *fils*.

FINANCE Major credit cards accepted in hotels, large stores and restaurants. Smaller

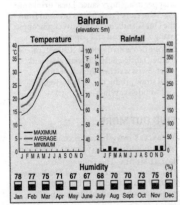

HIGHLIGHTS

MANAMA The very new capital of a very old place, dominated by a Manhattan-style skyline. Spanking new hotels and official buildings are located on areas of reclaimed land. The *souk* is enchanting, especially after dark. The National Museum, housed in a modern building, has excellent exhibits marked in both Arabic and English and covers 7,000 years of the country's history.

AL-AREEN WILDLIFE PARK A small conservation park which is home to many of Arabia's indigenous species, including the Arabian oryx. There are also zebras and other animals introduced to the island from elsewhere.

BARBAR TEMPLE An ancient complex of temples, probably dedicated to Enki, the God of Wisdom and the Sweet Waters Under the Earth. A series of walkways provides a viewpoint of the excavated buildings.

BANI JAMRAH Little village to the west of Manama famous for weavers, who sell their clothwork at shacks on the outskirts of the settlement. Visitors watch demonstrations of weaving.

BAHRAIN GRAND PRIX A new addition to the Formula 1 calendar, the Bahrain GP, early in the season, takes place at one of the most advanced tracks in the world, with ultra modern facilities and exciting oasis-to-desert racing.

BEACHES Bahrain has fine stretches of sandy beach, fringed by abundant reefs. The best is Al Jazair. From there, take a trip by traditional *dhow* to some of the nearby islands.

shops prefer cash.

BUSINESS HOURS 0800-1300, 1500-18/1900 Sat-Wed, 0800-1300 Thu. Some offices work 0800-1600 Mon-Thu with an hour's break for lunch.

GMT +3.

VOLTAGE GUIDE 230AC, 50Hz (Awali, 120AC, 60Hz)

COUNTRY DIALLING CODE 973.

CONSUMING PLEASURES

FOOD & DRINK Spicy, strongly flavoured Arabic food. Several restaurants serve international cuisine. *Arak* (aniseed-flavoured grape spirit) and beer often drunk - while the sale of alcohol is not encouraged it is available to non-Muslims at clubs, good hotels and restaurants.

SHOPPING & SOUVENIRS Modern shopping complexes offer luxury goods. Local products include pearls and famous red clay pottery from A'ali, and baskets.

FIND OUT MORE

WEBSITES www.bahrainembassy.co.uk, www.ukembassy.gov.bh. www.bahrainembassy.org, www.usembassy.gov.bh, www.bahraintourism.com.

LOCAL MEDIA *Gulf Daily News, Bahrain Tribune* are both English-language papers, business magazines are also available in English. One state-owned TV channel, one state-owned radio station, one independent.

TOURIST BOARDS IN UK/US n/a.

In Arabic the word 'Bahrain' means 'two seas' and refers to the natural phenomenon of freshwater springs from beneath the sea rising to the surface and mingling with salt seawater

BANGLADESH

WHEN TO GO

WEATHER Avoid the monsoon season from April to October when temperatures are highest. The best time to go is during the cool season, between November to March.

FESTIVALS Durga Puja, a five day festival, is held in October, ending with a parade of effigies to Sadarghat. A *mela* is held in Dhamrai in late June/early July during the full moon. Between November and mid-February fishing is ceaseless in the Sundarbans and a festival is held over three days by low-caste Hindus. Sitakunda, north of Chittagong, holds the Siva Chaturdasi Festival over ten days during February, attracting thousands of Hindu pilgrims. Buddhist festivals are held every Bengali New Year in Chitmorong in mid-April. Comilla holds Hindu and Buddhist festivals in November as part of a local trade fair. Holi, the Spring Festival is held in March.

TRANSPORT

INTERNATIONAL AIRPORTS Dhaka International (DAC), 20 km from the city.

INTERNAL TRAVEL Slow but efficient rail system, limited by geography but river ferries provide links. Road travel can also be slow, as frequent ferry services a necessity.

RED TAPE

VISAS REQUIRED (UK/US) Required.

VACCINATIONS REQUIRED: See 'Vaccinations required around the world' on page 653.

DRIVING REQUIREMENTS International Driving Permit.

COUNTRY REPS IN UK/US UK: 28 Queen's Gate, London SW7 5JA, tel (020) 7584 0081, fax (020) 7581 7477, email bdesh.lon@dial.pipex.com. US: 3510 International Drive, NW, Washington, DC 20008, tel (202) 244 0183, fax (202) 244 7830, email bdootwash@bangladoot.org.

UK/US REPS IN COUNTRY UK: United Nations Road, Baridhara, Dhaka 1212, tel (2) 882 2705-9, fax (2) 882 3437, email ppabhc@citecho.net US: Diplomatic

Enclave, Madani Avenue, Baridhara, Dhaka 1212, tel (2) 885 5500, fax (2) 882 3744.

PEOPLE AND PLACE

CAPITAL Dhaka.

LANGUAGE Bengali and English.

PEOPLES Bengali (98%).

RELIGION Islam (Sunni), Hinduism.

SIZE (SQ KM) 147,570.

POPULATION 130,200,000.

POP DENSITY/KM 882.3.

STATE OF THE NATION

SAFETY Safe if you're sensible. Observe Islamic customs carefully.

LIFE EXPECTANCY M 62.13, F 62.02.

BEING THERE

ETIQUETTE It is acceptable to sit cross-legged on cushions or on the sofa. If giving a gift, do not give money, as it can be offensive. Respect all religious customs, do not photograph women specifically unless there is no objection. Women should wear trousers or long skirts, and revealing clothing should be avoided, especially in religious places. Men's dress is generally informal.

CURRENCY Bangladeshi *taka* (Tk) =100 *poisha*.

FINANCE Limited acceptance of major credit cards. Hotel bills must be paid in a major convertible currency or with

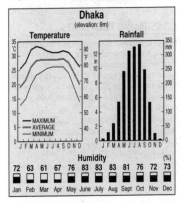

Dhaka
(elevation: 8m)

HIGHLIGHTS

DHAKA The historic city sits on Buriganga River which connects it to all the major inland ports. The old part of the city is dominated by commercial bustle. Visit the unfinished seventeenth-century Lalbagh Fort, the exquisite Ahsan Manzil palace museum, and the dilapidated Chotta Katra. Also of note are the Dhakeswari Temple, the Botanical Gardens, the Khan Mohammed Mirdha Mosque, the Mausoleum of Pari Bibi, and the collection of rare plants at the Baldha Gardens. There are dozens of mosques and bazaars but Kashaitully Mosque is arguably the most beautiful. North of the city lies Rajendrapur National Park, with varied bird species and Madhabkunda, a spot noted for beautiful panoramic views and enchanting waterfalls.

CHITTAGONG The second largest city in the country is a thriving port set amid charming natural surroundings, with coconut palms, mosques and minarets. Several mosques and the Chilla of Bada Shah, a place of meditation, are found here.

KHULNA The Sundarbans National Park is located in this marshland and jungle division. It is a supreme example of lush coastal vegetation and the variety of wildlife it supports, including tigers.

RAJSHAHI Often ignored by tourists, this area in the northwest contains many archaeological sites. Paharpur is home to the best of these: the Buddhist monastery of Somapuri Vihara and the Satyapir Vita temple are both worth visiting.

traveller's cheques.

BUSINESS HOURS 0900-1700.

GMT +6.

VOLTAGE GUIDE 220/240AC, 50Hz.

COUNTRY DIALLING CODE 880.

CONSUMING PLEASURES

FOOD & DRINK Limited availability of Western food, although served in some hotels and restaurants. Local specialities based on chicken, lamb and seafood, served with rice. Alcohol expensive and availability is limited due to strict Muslim customs.

SHOPPING & SOUVENIRS Pink pearl, handloom fabrics, silks, printed saris, coconut masks, bamboo products, mother-of-pearl items, leather goods, wood and cane craftworks, folk dolls.

FIND OUT MORE

WEBSITES www.ukinbangladesh.org, www.bangladeshhighcommission.org.uk, www.bangladoot.org, www.usembassy-dhaka.org, www.bangladeshonline.com/tourism, www.virtualbangladesh.com.

LOCAL MEDIA There are eight daily English-language papers, including *Bangladesh Observer, Daily Star, New Nation*, the *Independent* and the *Financial Express*. Weeklies include the *Bangladesh Gazette*, the *Dhaka Courier* and *Holiday*.

TOURIST BOARDS IN UK/US n/a.

"I have never seen so lovely a place to look at, nor one so loathsome to live in."
John Beames, 1878

BARBADOS

WHEN TO GO

WEATHER During the dry season from December-June, although even the 'wet' season sees an average of eight hours of sunshine per day.

FESTIVALS The island's top event is the Crop-Over Festival, which originated in colonial times as a celebration of the sugar cane harvest. Festivities stretch over a three-week period beginning in mid-July. There are spirited calypso competitions and fairs around the island. The festival culminates with a Carnival-like costume parade on Kadooment Day.
In February, the Holetown Festival celebrates the 1627 arrival of the first English settlers on Barbados. The week-long festivities include street fairs, a music festival at the historic parish church and a road race. There are also a handful of international sporting events, including the Barbados Windsurfing World Cup, held at Silver Sands in January, and the Caribbean Surfing Championship, held in early November at Bathsheba.

TRANSPORT

INTERNATIONAL AIRPORTS Barbados (BGI), 11km from Bridgetown.

INTERNAL TRAVEL Good road network. Petrol is comparatively cheap, and cars may be hired by the hour, day or week.

RED TAPE

VISAS REQUIRED (UK/US) None.

VACCINATIONS REQUIRED: See 'Vaccinations required around the world' on page 653.

DRIVING REQUIREMENTS Barbados Driving Permit required. Also a valid national or International Driving Permit.

COUNTRY REPS IN UK/US UK: 1 Great Russell Street, London WC1B 3ND, (020) 7631 4975, fax (020) 7323 6872, email london@foreign.gov.bb. US: 2144 Wyoming Avenue, NW, Washington, DC 20008, tel (202) 939 9200, fax (202) 332 7467, email washington@foreign.gov.bb.

UK/US REPS IN COUNTRY UK: Lower Collymore Rock, St Michael, Bridgetown tel 430 7800, fax 430 7860, email britishcb@ sandbeach.net. US: Canadian Imperial Bank of Commerce Building, Broad Street, Bridgetown, tel 436 4950, fax 429 5246, email consularbridge2@state.gov.

PEOPLE AND PLACE

CAPITAL Bridgetown.

LANGUAGE English.

PEOPLES African descendants, small groups of South Asians and Europeans.

RELIGION Christian, with an Anglican majority, Roman Catholic minority. Small Jewish, Hindu and Muslim communities.

SIZE (SQ KM) 430.

POPULATION 267,000.

POP DENSITY/KM 620.9.

STATE OF THE NATION

SAFETY Muggings increasing: do not carry valuables.

LIFE EXPECTANCY M 69.46, F 73.39.

BEING THERE

ETIQUETTE Social attitudes, like administration and architecture, tend to echo the British provincial market town. Bajans (as the locals call themselves) are known for their optimistic attitude, laid-back manner and sense of humour.

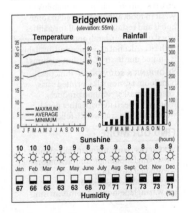

Bridgetown (elevation: 55m)

HIGHLIGHTS

BRIDGETOWN Busy commercial hub and capital, a mish-mash of modern and colonial buildings. The city has an English feel, with a miniature of London's Trafalgar Square - complete with a statue of Lord Nelson. It's small and easily walkable. Sights include the Government House, the Barbados Museum, St Michael's Cathedral and a distinctive Old Synagogue. Temple Yard has a Rastafarian street market.

HOLETOWN Founded in the 1620s, this is the oldest town in Barbados and several buildings from this early period remain. A narrow beach off Folkestone Park is a pleasant spot for picnics, swimming and surfing.

ST LAWRENCE One of a cluster of low-key towns on the southwest coast of the island, noted for powdery white sand, interesting local crafts and places to eat and drink.

BARBADOS WILDLIFE RESERVE A walk-through zoo featuring an array of green monkeys, red-footed turtles, caimans, brocket deer, iguanas and agoutis. Animals roam freely through the lush mahogany forest.

WATERSPORTS The island's splendid coral reefs offer excellent scuba diving and snorkelling. Seahorses, frogfish and hawksbill turtles can be spotted. Carlisle Bay, near Bridgetown, has 200 wrecks to explore. Windsurfing and surfing are also popular activities.

SUNBURY PLANTATION HOUSE Offers an insight into the sugar trade, which was vital to the island during colonial times.

Casual wear is acceptable in most places.

CURRENCY Barbados dollar (Bd$) = 100 cents.

FINANCE Major credit cards and traveller's cheques widely accepted.

BUSINESS HOURS 0800-1600 Mon-Friday.

GMT -4 (-5 in summer).

VOLTAGE GUIDE 110 AC, 50 Hz.

COUNTRY DIALLING CODE 1 246.

CONSUMING PLEASURES

FOOD & DRINK Bajan specialities include superb seafood, including flying fish, lobster and sea urchins. Sweet potatoes, plantain, breadfruit, yams, avocados, pears, soursops, paw paws, bananas, figs, and coconuts are produced locally. Rum based cocktails, such as rum punch, sangria, and pina coladas. British pubs are emulated.

SHOPPING & SOUVENIRS Jewellery, clothing, ceramics, rum, straw goods, coral and batiks. High quality goods, but expensive. Some items duty-free on production of passport and air ticket.

FIND OUT MORE

WEBSITES www.barbados.org/uk, www.foreign.gov.bb, www.britishhighcommission.gov.uk/barbados, www.barbados.org

LOCAL MEDIA *The Nation, The Barbados Advocate* and *East Caribbean News* are the main dailies. One state-owned TV channel.

TOURIST BOARDS IN UK/US UK: 263 Tottenham Court Road, London W1T 7LA, tel (020) 7636 9448, fax (020)7637 1496, email btauk@barbados.org. US: 800 Second Avenue, 2nd Floor, New York, NY 10017, tel (212) 986 6516, fax (212) 573 9850, email btany@barbados.org.

Barbados boasts more world-class cricket players on a per capita basis than any other nation

BELARUS

WHEN TO GO

Weather Temperate continental climate.

Festivals The National Convention of Belarusian Composers meets in Minsk in January to discuss music and host a series of concerts. The city holds an international language festival in April, Expolingua. June sees the Festival of Poetry at Lake Svityaz, where celebrations of the work of Belarusian and Russian poets are held. November sees the festivals return to Minsk for the Belarussian Musical Autumn, a festival of folk and classical music and dance.

TRANSPORT

International Airports Minsk, 43 km from the city.

Internal travel 5488 km of rail track in use, regular service from Minsk. Most roads are hard-surfaced, poor lighting.

RED TAPE

Visas required (UK/US) Required.

Vaccinations required: See 'Vaccinations required around the world' on page 653.

Driving requirements International Driving Permit.

Country reps in UK/US
UK: 6 Kensington Court, London W8 5DL, tel (020) 7937 3288, fax (020) 7361 0005, email uk@belembassy.org. US: 1619 New Hampshire Avenue, NW, Washington, DC 20009, tel (202) 986 1604, fax (202) 986 1805, email usa@belarusembassy.org.

UK/US reps in country UK: Karl Marx 37, 220030 Minsk, tel (17) 210 5920/1, fax (17) 229 2306, email britinfo@nsys.by. US: 46 Starovilenskaya Street, 220002, Minsk, tel (17) 210 1283, fax (17) 234 7853, email minskinfo@state.gov.

PEOPLE AND PLACE

Capital Minsk.

Language Belarusian.

Peoples Belarusian, Russian, Polish and Ukrainian.

Religion Russian Orthodox. Roman Catholic, Protestant, Muslim and Jewish minorities.

Size (sq km) 207,595.

Population 9,990,435.

Pop density/km 48.1.

STATE OF THE NATION

Safety Seek local advice.

Life expectancy M 63.03, F 74.69.

BEING THERE

Etiquette Handshaking is the usual greeting. Traditionally hospitality is in their culture, and the people are warm, friendly, and welcoming. Company and business gifts are well received. Smoking is acceptable.

Currency Belarusian *rouble* (BYR).

Finance Major credit cards accepted in the larger hotels, shops and restaurants, traveller's cheques are preferable to cash.

Business hours 0900-1800, Mon-Friday.

GMT +2/3.

Voltage guide 220AC, 50Hz.

Country dialling code 375.

CONSUMING PLEASURES

Food & drink Regional cooking often based on potatoes with mushrooms and berries as favourite side dishes. Belarusian *borshch* and *filet à la Minsk* are

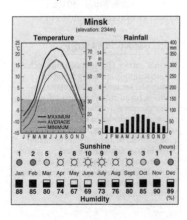

Minsk (elevation: 234m)

	Jan	Feb	Mar	Apr	May	June	July	Aug	Sept	Oct	Nov	Dec
Sunshine (hours)	1	2	5	6	8	10	9	8	6	3	1	1
Humidity (%)	88	85	80	74	67	69	73	76	80	85	90	89

HIGHLIGHTS

MINSK The city has been around since 1067, but little remains from then. A few seventeenth-century buildings remain. Today, the city is symmetrically designed, flanking the Svisloch River. A diverse cultural scene can be found in the city, whether seen in Belarusian Ballet or one of the many museums. Do not leave the city without visiting the Troitskoye Predmestye suburb where colourful ninetenth-century houses line the street, giving an impression of the old Minsk before the war.

OUTSIDE MINSK The picture-postcard village of Raubichi lies not far from the capital and is home to an ethnographic museum. Minsk Lake is situated ten kilometres away. Dense pines surround its countless islets. Forty kilometres from the capital lies the Dudutki Museum of Material Culture, which displays traditional crafts and way of life of the Belarusian people. Logoysk, Krasnoe, and Molodechno, all within 50 kilometres of the capital, have the best examples of those onion-shaped domes of Russian Orthodox churches which dominate the nation's skyline.

BEYOND MINSK Away from the capital travellers will discover wide plains, picturesque villages, ancient castles and monasteries, dense forests, and thousands of lakes. Worth visiting are Zhirovitsa, well known for its beautiful fifteenth-century monastery of the Assumption, and Mir, home to a fifteenth-century castle. Balvezhskaya Pushcha has 500-year-old trees and wild bison roaming free.

recommended. A good selection of international and Russian cuisine available. *Chai* (black tea) is popular, and coffee is available in most places.

SHOPPING & SOUVENIRS Wooden caskets, trinkets, decorative plates, Russian *matreshka* dolls, antiques.

FIND OUT MORE

WEBSITES www.belembassy.org/uk, www.britishembassy.gov.uk/belarus, www.belarusembassy.org, www.belarus.net, http://minsk.usembassy.gov, www.belarus-guide.com/travel1.

LOCAL MEDIA English-language paper *Belarues Today* is published weekly.

TOURIST BOARDS IN UK/US n/a.

> Herbs are widely used in the making of beers: more than one hundred herbs are used to create the distinctive taste of Beloveshskaya Bitters

BELGIUM

WHEN TO GO

WEATHER You're unlikely to encounter extremes in weather during an average Belgian year. April to September is the warmest time, but be prepared for grey skies and soggy streets no matter what time of year you go. Visitors may be forgiven for assuming umbrellas and raincoats are part of the Belgian national dress.

FESTIVALS Brussels' most festive months are July and August. In July there's the historical Ommegang pageant, a huge parade in honour of Emperor Charles and his son. Belgium's colourful National Day is 21 July, which also marks the start of the month-long Brussels Fair.
Throughout the year there are jazz festivals, religious processions, local fairs, film festivals and classical music extravaganzas. Carnival in springtime is a big event. People shake off the winter blues with outrageous celebrations ranging from balls to masked parades.
In Ypres, Armistice Day on 11 November is a particularly important day.
Christmas markets are held throughout the country during the lead up to the festival.

TRANSPORT

INTERNATIONAL AIRPORTS Brussels Zaventum (BRU) 13 km from the city. Antwerp (ANR) 3 km from the city. Ostend (OST) 5 km from the city. Liege (LGG) 8 km.

INTERNAL TRAVEL Good road and rail networks. Good public transport in major towns and cities.

RED TAPE

VISAS REQUIRED (UK/US) None.

VACCINATIONS REQUIRED: See 'Vaccinations required around the world' on page 653.

DRIVING REQUIREMENTS A national driving licence is acceptable. EU nationals with their own cars require a Green Card.

COUNTRY REPS IN UK/US UK: 103-105 Eaton Square, London SW1W 9AB, tel (020) 7470 3700, fax (020) 7470 3795, email belembvisa@ntlworld.com. US: 3330 Garfield Street, NW, Washington, DC 20008, tel (202) 333 6900, fax (202) 333 3079, email washington@diplobel.org.

UK/US REPS IN COUNTRY UK: rue d'Arlon 85 aarlenstraat, B-1040, Brussels, tel (2) 287 6211, fax (2) 287 6360, email brussels.visa.section@fco.gov.uk. US: Regentlaan 27 boulevard du Régent, B-1000 Brussels, tel (2) 508 2111, fax (2) 511 2725.

PEOPLE AND PLACE

CAPITAL Brussels.

LANGUAGE Flemish and French.

PEOPLES Fleming and Walloon. Italian and Moroccan minorities.

RELIGION Roman Catholic (88%), Protestant, Muslim and Jewish minorities.

SIZE (SQ KM) 30,528 km

POPULATION 10,263,414.

POP DENSITY/KM 336.2.

STATE OF THE NATION

SAFETY Safe.

LIFE EXPECTANCY M 75.44, F 81.94.

BEING THERE

ETIQUETTE Belgians will often prefer to answer visitors in English rather than French, even if the visitor's French is good. Dress is similar to other Western nations,

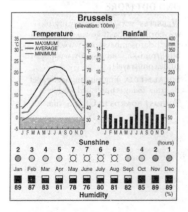

Brussels
(elevation: 100m)

Temperature / Rainfall / Sunshine (hours) / Humidity (%)

	Jan	Feb	Mar	Apr	May	June	July	Aug	Sept	Oct	Nov	Dec
Sunshine (hours)	2	3	4	5	7	7	6	6	5	4	2	1
Humidity (%)	89	87	83	81	78	76	80	81	82	85	89	89

HIGHLIGHTS

BRUSSELS Vibrant city noted for its interesting history, fine beer, tasty chocolates and politicians. The principal centre of the European Union and NATO, Brussels' true focal point is the magnificent Grand Place, fringed by baroque guild halls, a gothic town hall and a plethora of busy pavement cafes and intimate restaurants.

BRUGES Pretty city, easily taken in by a scenic canal boat ride. Home to some of Europe's best preserved medieval buildings and noted for fine art collections. At its core are the two medieval hubs, the Markt and the Burg. The whole historic centre is a Unesco World Heritage site.

THE ARDENNES Tranquil villages, amidst deep river valleys and high forests in Belgium's south-east corner.

MENIN GATE In the town of Ypres, this imposing monument is transcribed with the names of the 55,000 British and Commonwealth troops lost in the trenches of World War I. Each evening, since the end of the conflict, a bugler has played the haunting *Last Post*. Ypres is also a base for tours of other battlefield sites.

GHENT Famous as a centre of lace, Ghent was a medieval powerhouse. Today the friendly town has a large student population. In St Baaf's Cathedral hangs one of the earliest known oil paintings, *De Aanbidding van het Lams God*, by the fifteenth-century artist, Jan Van Eyck.

depending on the formality of the occasion.

CURRENCY Euro (€) =100 *cents.*

FINANCE Major cards, Eurocheques and traveller's cheques widely accepted.

BUSINESS HOURS 0830-1730 Mon-Friday. **GMT** +1/2.

VOLTAGE GUIDE 220 AC, 50 Hz.

COUNTRY DIALLING CODE 32.

CONSUMING PLEASURES

FOOD & DRINK Generally of high quality, style similar to French. Several regional specialities, often rich in butter, cream, wine or beer. Sauces with everything, including *frites* with mayonnaise. Renowned for chocolate - and the local beers: *kriek* cherry beer is a speciality.

SHOPPING & SOUVENIRS Ceramics, hand-beaten copperware, Belgian chocolates, crystals, diamonds, jewellery, lace, woodcarvings and comic books.

FIND OUT MORE

WEBSITES www.diplobel.org/uk, www.belgiumtheplaceto.be, www.visitflan-ders.co.uk, www.britishembassy.gov.uk/belgium, www.diplobel.us, www.visitbelgium.com, http://brussels.usembassy.be, www.expatica.com/belgium.asp, www.belgiumtourism.net.

LOCAL MEDIA International papers are available as is the English-language magazine *The Bulletin.*

TOURIST BOARDS IN UK/US UK: 217 Marsh Wall, London E14 9FJ, tel (0800) 954 5245 or (0906) 302 0245, fax (020) 7531 0391, email info@belgiumtheplaceto.be or Flanders House, 1a Cavendish Square, London W1G 0LD, tel (09063) 020 245, fax (020) 7307 7731, email office@ visitflanders.co.uk. US:220 East 42nd Street, Suite 3402, New York, NY 10017, tel (212) 333 6900, fax (212) 355 7675, email info@visitbelgium.com

Belgium produces over 400 kinds of beer, some of the most famous made by Trappist monks

BELIZE

WHEN TO GO

WEATHER Subtropical, with prevailing winds from the Caribbean sea. Dry and hot from January-April, with rainy season from June-September.

FESTIVALS February sees the traditional annual nationwide Fiesta de Carnaval, and the San Pedro Carnival, a traditional, slap-stick, Mestizo carnival. May's celebrations include the Cashew Festival, a celebration of the harvest season, and the week long Toledo Festival of Arts. A three-day party honouring St Peter is held in June, the Dia de San Pedro. Historical re-enactments are part of the Deer Dance Festival in August. Regattas, billfish tournaments and other celebrations are held throughout the year.

TRANSPORT

INTERNATIONAL AIRPORTS Philip S W Goldson International (BZE), 16 km from Belize City.

INTERNAL TRAVEL Local air services between main towns, also linked by all-weather roads. Good, modern buses.

RED TAPE

VISAS REQUIRED (UK/US) Required.

VACCINATIONS REQUIRED: See 'Vaccinations required around the world' on page 653.

DRIVING REQUIREMENTS A national driving licence is acceptable.

COUNTRY REPS IN UK/US UK: 3rd Floor, 45 Crawford Place, London W1H 4LP, tel (020) 7723 3603, fax (020) 7723 9637, email bzhc-lon@btconnect.com. US: 2535 Massa-chusetts Avenue, NW, Washington, DC 20008, tel (202) 332 9636, fax (202) 332 6888, email ebwreception@aol.com.

UK/US REPS IN COUNTRY UK: PO Box 91, Embassy Square, Belmopan, tel (8) 222 146/7, fax (8) 222 761, email brithicom@btl.net. US: 29 Gabourel Lane, Belize City, tel (22) 77161, fax (22) 35423, email embbelize@state.gov.

PEOPLE AND PLACE

CAPITAL Belmopan.

LANGUAGE English.

PEOPLES Mestizo, Creole, Maya groups, immigrants from Mexico, Guatemala, Asia.

RELIGION Roman Catholic. Smaller groups of Anglicans, Methodists, Mennonites.

SIZE (SQ KM) 22,965.

POPULATION 240,204.

POP DENSITY/KM 10.5.

STATE OF THE NATION

SAFETY Muggings and thefts occur, but not as bad as some parts of Latin America.

LIFE EXPECTANCY M 65.02, F 70.08.

BEING THERE

ETIQUETTE The British influence is still prevalent in most social situations. Flowers and confectionery are good gifts for hosts. Dress is casual but beachwear should not be worn in towns. It is mostly inadvisable to discuss politics, especially if of a partisan nature. Taxi drivers are not tipped.

CURRENCY Belize dollar (Bz$).

FINANCE Credit cards and traveller's cheques accepted.

BUSINESS HOURS 0800-1200, 1300-1700 Mon-Thurs, 0800-1200, 1300-1630 Friday.

GMT -6.

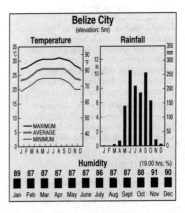

Belize City
(elevation: 5m)

Temperature / Rainfall

MAXIMUM / AVERAGE / MINIMUM

Humidity (19.00 hrs, %)

Jan	Feb	Mar	Apr	May	June	July	Aug	Sept	Oct	Nov	Dec
89	87	87	87	87	87	86	87	87	88	91	90

HIGHLIGHTS

BELMOPAN The new capital is cut out of the tropical jungle, right in the geographic centre of the country, at the foothills of the Maya Mountains.

COROZAL Settled in 1850 by *mestizo* refugees from Mexico, the city is now the centre of a thriving sugar industry. Just outside are the Mayan ruins of Santa Rita and Cerros, a coastal trading centre reachable by a boat trip over Corozal Bay.

THE BELIZE CAYES These islands and mangroves are found between the mainland and the barrier reef perimeters of the offshore atolls. the mangroves are uninhabitable by humans, but ideal for bird and marine life. The island cayes act as a base for watersports. Ambergris Caye has many beaches, and is a paradise for divers, giving access to unspoilt coral reefs.

FIVE BLUES LAKE This National Park is at the foot of the Mayan Mountains, among 4,000 acres of tropical forest. The lake is a collapsed cave system, a blue hole or cenote, that appears in an array of aqua hues, and is surrounded by a wealth of wildlife and fauna.

MAYAN ARCHAEOLOGICAL SITES There are many unspoilt Mayan sites in Belize. Lamanai is one of the largest and is served by an archaeological reserve and museum. Altun Ha contains over 13 temples, has two main plazas, and is looked over by a large jade head of the Sun God Ahau, one of the world's largest jade objects. Canaa Pyramid, the tallest structure in Belize at 43 metres, is found in Caracol - best visited in the dry season.

VOLTAGE GUIDE 110 AC, 60 Hz.
COUNTRY DIALLING CODE 501.

CONSUMING PLEASURES

FOOD & DRINK Generally cheap Latin-American and Creole influenced food. Some international-style and Chinese restaurants. Coconut rum with pineapple juice and the local beer - *Belikin* - are popular drinks.

SHOPPING & SOUVENIRS Handicrafts, woodcarvings, straw products. Coral jewellery and tortoiseshell (not to be imported to US) now under restrictions.

FIND OUT MORE

WEBSITES www.travelbelize.org, www.btia.org, www.bzhc-lon.co.uk, www.caribbean.co.uk, www.britishhighbze.com, www.embassyofbelize.org, www.doitcaribbean.com, http://belize.usembassy.gov.

LOCAL MEDIA *The Belize Times, Government Gazette, The Reporter,* and *Amandala* are the major weeklies, *Belize Today,* the monthly.

TOURIST BOARDS IN UK/US UK: 22 The Quadrant, Richmond, Surrey TW9 1BP, tel (020) 8948 0057, fax (020) 8948 0067, email ctolondon@caribtourism.com. US: 80 Broad Street, 32nd Floor, New York, NY 10004, tel (212) 635 9530, fax (212) 635 9511, email ctony@caribtourism.com.

" If the world had any ends, British Honduras [Belize] would certainly be one of them."
Aldous Huxley, 1934

BENIN

WHEN TO GO

WEATHER The south has an equatorial climate, hot and dry from January-April and during August, and rainy seasons from May-July and September-December. More extreme temperatures in the north, hot and dry from November-June, cool and very wet from July-October.

FESTIVALS The nation celebrates on Martyr's Day on 16 January, to commemorate an attack on Cotonou, Independence Day, 1 August, and Harvest Day, 31 December. Of most interest will be the Voodoo Festival, held on 10 January in Ouidah.

TRANSPORT

INTERNATIONAL AIRPORTS Catonou Cadjehoun (COO), 5 km from the city.

INTERNAL TRAVEL Roads in reasonably good condition but often impassable during the rainy season. A number of local car firms are available in Cotonou for hire. Trains connect main towns.

RED TAPE

VISAS REQUIRED (UK/US) Required.

VACCINATIONS REQUIRED See 'Vaccinations required around the world' on page 653.

DRIVING REQUIREMENTS International Driving Permit.

COUNTRY REPS IN UK/US UK: Dolphin House, 16 The Broadway, Stanmore, Middlesex, HA7 4DW, tel (020) 8954 8800, fax (020) 8954 8844, email l.landau@btinternet.com. US: 2124 Kalorama Road, NW, Washington, DC 20008, tel (202) 232 6656, fax (202) 265 1996, email info@beninembassyus.org.

UK/US REPS IN COUNTRY UK: The British High Commission in Lagos (Nigeria) deals with enquiries relating to Benin. US: 01 BP 2012, Cotonou, tel 300 650, fax 300 670.

PEOPLE AND PLACE

CAPITAL Porto Novo.

LANGUAGE French and indigenous tribal languages.

PEOPLES Fon, Bariba, Yoruba, Fulani.

RELIGION Indigenous and Animist (70%), Christianity and Islam.

SIZE (SQ KM) 112,622.

POPULATION 6,059,000.

POP DENSITY/KM 53.8.

STATE OF THE NATION

SAFETY Armed robbery and muggings increasing. Roads poorly lit at night.

LIFE EXPECTANCY M 50.14, F 50.89.

BEING THERE

ETIQUETTE Religious beliefs are highly prized and should be respected. Voodoo is now prevalent and it carries social and political weight. Only priests can communicate with voodoos and spirits of the dead. Shaking hands is usual practice. Travellers should check itineraries with district and provincial authorities. Casual dress is acceptable in most places.

CURRENCY *Commnauté financiare aficaine franc* (CFA) = 100 *centimes*.

FINANCE Major credit cards and traveller's cheques accepted on a limited basis.

BUSINESS HOURS 0800-1230, 1500-1830 Mon-Fri.

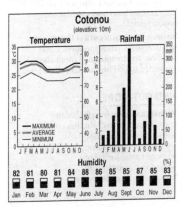

Cotonou (elevation: 10m) — Temperature / Rainfall / Humidity charts

Humidity (%)

Jan	Feb	Mar	Apr	May	June	July	Aug	Sept	Oct	Nov	Dec
82	81	80	81	84	88	86	85	85	87	85	83

HIGHLIGHTS

ABOMEY This town was once a capital of one of the great west African kingdoms in pre-colonial times. Twisted alleyways lead off main roads, lined with *banco* houses and vivid fetish temples. A museum covers the history of the Fon kingdoms, and has a throne made from human skulls. The royal palace in the centre of town is a vast complex of palaces, each descendent built a new extension and would not live in his predecessors quarters.

OUIDAH This voodoo stronghold with a dynamic history is now quieter, the French colonial architecture is cracking, the porches sagging. The Temple of the Sacred Python is found here. The snakes are an authentic part of fetish practice, and now a tourist attraction. Other, local temples may give a truer picture of the religion.

GANVIÉ Africa's largest lake village spreads over the shallow murky waters of Lac Nokoué. Wood and thatch houses, built on stilts, rise out of the water. 15,000 people live here, using *pirogues* as transport over the lake. Most rely on fishing for their income. Women even sell market goods from their canoes.

VOODOO The term signifies a spirit, demigod, or intermediary. Voodoo priests are especially susceptible and able to channel the emotions. A fetish is an object imbued with sacred power. They believe in a supreme God, Mawu, male or female, sometimes a couple, Mawu-Lisa, who created the universe. Lesser divinities have power of certain aspects on earth and possess or help the priests.

GMT +1.

VOLTAGE GUIDE 220AC, 50Hz.

COUNTRY DIALLING CODE 229.

CONSUMING PLEASURES

FOOD & DRINK Restaurants in Cotonou serve French and African specialities, particularly seafood.

SHOPPING & SOUVENIRS Many stalls with handicrafts and souvenirs by the marina in Cotonou. Ritual masks, tapestries, statues and pottery make for the best buys.

FIND OUT MORE

WEBSITES www.ambassade-benin.org, www.beninembassyus.org, http://cotonou.usembassy.gov, www.lonelyplanet.com/worldguide/destinations/africa/benin/

LOCAL MEDIA No English newspapers, all are exclusively in French, *La Nation* is the daily official paper.

TOURIST BOARDS IN UK/US n/a.

Mamissi are female followers of Goddess Mami Wata, a water spirit who appears in dreams and visions as a beautiful mermaid with long dark hair and fair skin. She walks the streets of modern African cities, a gorgeous but elusive woman interested in all things contemporary – sweets, imported perfumes, sunglasses and Coca-Cola

BHUTAN

WHEN TO GO

WEATHER Climate is best between October and November, when skies are clear and high mountain peaks are visible. Spring is also pleasant, between April and mid-June. Nights can be very cold. Monsoon occurs June to August.

FESTIVALS Public holidays include Independence Day on 8 August, the King's birthday on 11 November and National Day of Bhutan on 17 December. Traditional Buddhist holidays are also observed. The largest and most colourful festivals, called *tsechus*, take place at Bhutan's *dzongs* (fortresses) and monasteries once a year, in honour of Guru Rinpoche. They normally take place in spring and autumn. *Tsechus* consist of up to five days of spectacular pageantry, masked dances and religious allegorical plays that have remained unchanged for centuries. As well as being a vital living festival and an important medium of Buddhist teaching, *tsechus* are huge social gatherings. They provide an ideal opportunity to appreciate the essence of Bhutan.

TRANSPORT

INTERNATIONAL AIRPORTS Paro (PBH) - journey into Thimpu takes about 90 mins by bus or taxi.

INTERNAL TRAVEL No internal rail services, good internal road network. Yaks, mules and ponies are the most common transportation, but buses are also run.

RED TAPE

VISAS REQUIRED (UK/US) Required.

VACCINATIONS REQUIRED: See 'Vaccinations required around the world' on page 653.

DRIVING REQUIREMENTS International Driving Permit

COUNTRY REPS IN UK/US UK: n/a. US: 2 United Nations Plaza, 27th Floor, 44th Street, New York NY 10017, tel (212) 826 1919, fax (212) 826 2998, email pmbnewyork@aol.com.

UK/US REPS IN COUNTRY UK: n/a. US: n/a. Tourism Authority of Bhutan, PO Box 126, Thimpu, Bhutan, tel (2) 323 251/2, fax (2) 323 695, email tab@druknet.net.bt. Bhutan Tourist Corporation Ltd (BTCL), PO Box 159 Thimpu, Bhutan, tel (2) 323 517, fax (2) 323 392, email btcl@druknet.net.bt. United Nations Development Programme: United Nations Building, Dremton lam, GPO Box 162, Thimpu, tel (2) 322 424, fax (2) 322 657, email fo.btn@undp.org.

PEOPLE AND PLACE

CAPITAL Thimpu.

LANGUAGE Dzongkha.

PEOPLES Drukpa, Nepalese.

RELIGION Buddhist, Hindu

SIZE (SQ KM) 46,500.

POPULATION 654,269.

POP DENSITY/KM 14.1.

STATE OF THE NATION

SAFETY Safe.

LIFE EXPECTANCY M 54.65, F 54.11.

BEING THERE

ETIQUETTE The strongest influence on social conventions is the country's state religion. Equal rights exist for men and women. Until recently, Bhutan was deliberately isolated. Visitor numbers remain

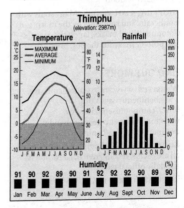

Thimphu
(elevation: 2987m)

Temperature — MAXIMUM, AVERAGE, MINIMUM

Rainfall

Humidity (%)

Jan	Feb	Mar	Apr	May	June	July	Aug	Sept	Oct	Nov	Dec
91	90	92	89	90	91	92	92	92	90	89	90

HIGHLIGHTS

THIMPU The pretty capital of Bhutan, set in a wooded valley on the banks of the Thimpu Chhu (river). It has a medieval feel, thanks to the many brightly painted buildings with beautifully decorated facades. Dominating the horizon is the imposing fortress monastery, Trashi Chhoe Dzong.

BUMTHANG Located in the centre of Bhutan, the country's spiritual centre is home to many precious Buddhist sites, *dzongs*, temples and palaces. Jakar Dzong, founded in 1549, is the largest in Bhutan. The temple of Jampa Lhakhang hosts the spectacular Jampa Khakhang Drup festival, in October.

PARO The heartland of the Drukpa people, with spectacular *dzongs* and a peaceful feel. As in the rest of Bhutan, locals in traditional dress go about their daily business, or play the national sport, archery. The men wear a *gho*, the women a *kira*.

TIGER'S NEST Nestled on a dizzy mountain ledge on the outskirts of Paro is the Taktshang monastery.

THE FLIGHT If you're fortunate enough to fly into Paro from neighbouring Nepal, you'll experience one of the most incredible flights of your life. Soaring up from Kathmandu, the journey passes eight of the world's ten highest peaks, including Everest and Kanchenjunga, before touching down at possibly the most ornate airport in the world. Magical.

SAKTENG WILDLIFE SANCTUARY Wildlife reserve in the east, created to protect the habitat of the yeti, known locally as the *migoi*, or strong man.

limited, but all are welcomed with warm hospitality.

CURRENCY *Ngultrum* (NU) = 100 *chetrum* (Ch).

FINANCE American Express and Diners Club have very limited acceptability. Traveller's cheques accepted in banks and hotels.

BUSINESS HOURS 0900-1700, Mon-Friday.

GMT +6.

VOLTAGE GUIDE 220 AC, 50 Hz.

COUNTRY DIALLING CODE 975.

CONSUMING PLEASURES

FOOD & DRINK Restaurants scarce. Vegetarian based cuisine. Chillies, yaks cheese frequently used, rice ubiquitous. Bhutanese tea (*souza*) most popular drink.

SHOPPING & SOUVENIRS Markets open on weekend. Stock local clothing, jewellery, and foodstuffs. Goldsmiths in Thimpu valley make to order.

FIND OUT MORE

WEBSITES www.kingdomofbhutan.com, www.undp.org.bt, www.farflungplaces.com.

LOCAL MEDIA Very few papers. *Kuensel*, a government news bulletin, is published weekly in English, while *The Bhutan Review* is published monthly. One TV channel and one radio station, both state-owned.

TOURIST BOARDS IN UK/US US: c/o Far Flung Places, 1914 Fell Street, San Francisco, California 94117, tel (212) 826 1919, fax (212) 826 2998, email pmbnewyork@aol.com.

Thimpu is the only world capital without traffic lights. Instead, two white-gloved police officers direct the traffic

BOLIVIA

WHEN TO GO

WEATHER Temperate climate, but wide differences in temperature between day and night. Wettest between the summer months of November to March. Dry in winter between May and October. The capital, La Paz, can be uncomfortable for some visitors because of the very high altitude. In the tropical lowlands, summers can be miserable with mud, steamy heat and downpours.

FESTIVALS Bolivian *fiestas* are invariably of religious or political origin, normally commemorating a Christian or Indian saint or god, or a political event such as a battle or revolution. Festivities typically include lots of folk music, dancing processions, food, alcohol and ritual.

Major *fiestas* include Fiesta de la Virgen de Candelaria, a week-long festival in the virgin's honour, best seen in Copacabana on the shores of Lake Titicaca (early February). Carnaval is a nationwide event but is best seen in Oruro, during the week before Lent. Independence Day is a riotous nationwide party on 6 August.

TRANSPORT

INTERNATIONAL AIRPORTS La Paz (LPB) 14 km from centre. Santa Cruz (VVI), 16 km from centre.

INTERNAL TRAVEL Air travel is the best mode of transport because of the topography and tropical regions. Separate rail networks in the eastern and western parts of the country. Work in progress to improve the condition of major highways. Car hire is possible in La Paz.

RED TAPE

VISAS REQUIRED (UK/US) Not required for tourists.

VACCINATIONS REQUIRED: See 'Vaccinations required around the world' on page 653.

DRIVING REQUIREMENTS International Driving Permit required.

COUNTRY REPS IN UK/US UK: 106 Eaton Square, London SW1W 9AD, tel (020) 7235 4248, fax (020) 7235 1286, email info@ embassyofbolivia.co.uk. US: 3014 Massachusetts Avenue, NW, Washington, DC 20008-3603, tel (202) 483 4410, fax (202) 328 3712, email webmaster@ bolivia-usa.org.

UK/US REPS IN COUNTRY UK: Avenida Arce 2732, Casilla 694, La Paz, tel (2) 243 3424, fax (2) 243 1073, email ppa@ megalink.com. US: Avenida Acre 2780, Casilla 425, La Paz, tel (2) 216 8000, fax (2) 216 8111, email consularlapaz@state.gov.

PEOPLE AND PLACE

CAPITAL La Paz.

LANGUAGE Spanish.

PEOPLES Aymara and Quecha Indians.

RELIGION Roman Catholic.

SIZE (SQ KM) 1,098,581.

POPULATION 8,238,700.

POP DENSITY/KM 7.6.

STATE OF THE NATION

SAFETY One of the safest Latin American countries, but take care in any cocaine-growing areas.

LIFE EXPECTANCY M 62.89, F 68.25.

BEING THERE

ETIQUETTE Refer to rural Bolivians as *campesinos*, rather than Indians to avoid causing offence.

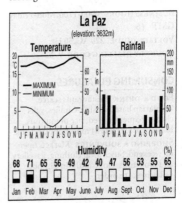

La Paz (elevation: 3632m)

	Jan	Feb	Mar	Apr	May	June	July	Aug	Sept	Oct	Nov	Dec
Humidity (%)	68	71	65	56	49	42	40	47	56	53	55	65

HIGHLIGHTS

LA PAZ Built in a steep crater high in the Andes, Bolivia's capital is a bustling and colourful city. It has many museums and some interesting Spanish and *mestizo* architecture, notably the Iglesia de San Fransisco. Nearby, the beguiling Witches' Market has stalls selling potions, silver jewellery, sweets and dried llama foetuses.

LAKE TITICACA The world's highest navigable lake is an immense body of clear sapphire-blue water, revered by local Indians who live on its shore. The Islas del Sol and Islas de la Luna are the legendary sites of the Inca's creation myths. The towns of Copacabana and Sorata nearby are popular with hikers.

SALAR DE UYUNI Massive flat saltpan at 3,650-metre altitude, dotted with piles of salt and cacti. Best explored from the village of Uyuni in the south-east corner.

COCHABAMBA Known as the garden city, this large market town was founded in 1574 and boasts a long tradition of local culture and folklore. It has a clutch of historical and archaeological attractions, including the Convento de Santa Teresa and the Museo Arqueologico.

RURRENABAQUE One of the loveliest lowland villages, on the Rio Beni 300 km from La Paz. The local rainforest offers great jungle trips to see Amazonian wildlife, including river dolphins and birds.

LAGUNA COLORADA & LAGUNA VERDE Stunning lakes high up in the Andes, amid peaks that resemble chocolate sundaes. Laguna Colorada is home to flamingoes.

CURRENCY *Boliviano* (Bs) = 100 *centavos*.

FINANCE US dollar traveller's cheques best form of currency at the moment. Very limited acceptance of credit cards.

BUSINESS HOURS 0830-1200, 1430-1830 Monday-Friday, 0900-12300 Saturday.

GMT -4.

VOLTAGE GUIDE 110/220 AC in La Paz. 220 AC, 50 Hz in the rest of the country.

COUNTRY DIALLING CODE 591.

CONSUMING PLEASURES

FOOD & DRINK National dishes often based on meat, for instance *lechon al homo* (young roast pig). *Empanada saltena* is a pastry filled with diced meat, chicken, chives, raisins, diced potatoes, pepper and hot sauce). Bolivian beer (especially *paceña*) is reputed to be the best on the continent.

SHOPPING & SOUVENIRS Wood carvings, jewellery, llama and alpaca blankets, Indian handicrafts, costume jewellery.

FIND OUT MORE

WEBSITES www.embassyofbolivia.co.uk, www.britishembassy.gov.uk/bolivia, www.bolivia-usa.org, http://lapaz.usembassy.gov.

LOCAL MEDIA *The Bolivian Times* is the English weekly.

TOURIST BOARDS IN UK/US n/a.

Bolivia has had more *coups d'etats* and revolutions than years since independence from Spain, back in 1825

BOSNIA & HERZEGOVINA

WHEN TO GO

WEATHER Moderate continental conditions, hot summers and very cold winters.

FESTIVALS July sees Sarajevo host the Nights of Bascarsija, different cultural events of all kinds, the Film Festival takes place in August, and International Theatre Festival in October and an International Jazz Festival in November.

TRANSPORT

INTERNATIONAL AIRPORTS Sarajevo (SJJ). Banja Luka(BNX) and Mostar (OMO) receive some international flights.

INTERNAL TRAVEL Rail links have generally been restored. The risk of landmines on major roads has been reduced, but caution should be used outside main cities.Some car hire available at the airport. Rail links restored.

RED TAPE

VISAS REQUIRED (UK/US) Required by Australian travellers.

VACCINATIONS REQUIRED: See 'Vaccinations required around the world' on page 653.

DRIVING REQUIREMENTS International Driving Permit.

COUNTRY REPS IN UK/US UK: 5 - 7 Lexham Gardens, London W8 5JJ, tel (020) 7373 0867, fax (020) 7373 0871. US: 2109 East Street, NW, Washington, DC 20037, tel (202) 337 1500, fax (202) 337 1502, email info@bhembassy.org.

UK/US REPS IN COUNTRY UK: Tina Ujevica 8, 71000 Sarajevo, tel (33) 282 200, fax (33) 666 131, email britemb@bih.net.ba. US: Alipassina 43, Sarajevo, tel (33) 445 700, fax (33) 659 722, email bhopa@state.gov.

PEOPLE AND PLACE

CAPITAL Sarajevo.

LANGUAGE Bosnian, Croat - both Latin alphabet, Croat - Cyrillic alphabet.

PEOPLES Before the war, 44% ethnic Bosnian, 31% Serb, 17% Croat, other minorities.

RELIGION Muslim 40%, Serbian Orthodox 31%, Roman Catholic 15%, small Protestant population.

SIZE (SQ KM) 51,129.

POPULATION 4,126,000.

POP DENSITY/KM 80.7.

STATE OF THE NATION

SAFETY Dangerous. Many landmines and some tensions remain from the wars.

LIFE EXPECTANCY M 70.09, F 75.8.

BEING THERE

ETIQUETTE Characterised by ethnic and religious diversity, travellers need to respect all customs and traditions of the various groups. Drinking alcohol in public places may offend Muslims. Opinions about the war and other sensitive issues should not be expressed.

CURRENCY Bosnia and Herzegovina *Konvertibilna Marka* (KM) = 100 *pfenings*.

FINANCE Generally a cash-only economy, only euros and US dollars practical.

BUSINESS HOURS 0800-1600 Mon-Friday.

GMT +1/2.

VOLTAGE GUIDE 220 AC, 50 Hz.

COUNTRY DIALLING CODE 387.

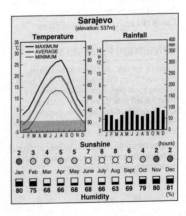

HIGHLIGHTS

SARAJEVO Once, like the rest of the country, a melting pot of cultures, a place of peaceful co-existence of Christians, Muslims, and Jews that showed its unusual background in the wonderful architecture where beautiful churches sat next to splendid mosques. Such towns were devastated in the war. The capital, where half a millennium of Turkish rule was most conspicuous, has largely rebuilt its Turkish Quarter. Colourful bazaars, part of the Ottoman heritage, rattling trams, and countless cafes are bringing the city back to life. A labyrinth of cobbled alleyways form the heart the city, where craftsmen ply their trade. Evidence of past war is always around the corner, though. The Latin Bridge, at the end of Zelenih Beretki, was the spot where the anarchist Gavrilo Princip shot Archduke Ferdinand of Austria, sparking off World War I. Elsewhere 'Sarajevo roses', the indentations of shell impacts, some filled with red cement, line the pavements.

OUTSIDE SARAJEVO Mostar, a tourist attraction before the fighting, has begun to be rebuilt. However, most of the monuments, sixteenth- and seventeenth-century mosques, have been destroyed. Banja Luka, the Republika Srpska capital, still has a sixteenth-century fort and amphitheatre. Spas operate in the region.

ACTIVITIES There is good hiking, rafting, fishing and skiing in the forests and mountains. However, much work needs to be done before the tourist potential can be fully developed.

CONSUMING PLEASURES

FOOD & DRINK Turkish influenced cuisine, including *bosanski lonac* (meat and vegetable stew), Turkish delight, and *Halva*, crushed sesame seeds in honey.

SHOPPING & SOUVENIRS Wood-carvings, brass coffee pots, ceramics, carpets, woollen wear, wine, folk-art, tapestries, embroidery and leather goods.

FIND OUT MORE

WEBSITES www.britishembassy.ba, www.bhembassy.org, www.usembassy.ba, www.lonelyplanet.com/worldguide/destinations/europe/bosnia_herzegovina/

LOCAL MEDIA No English-language newspapers.

TOURIST BOARDS IN UK/US n/a.

In 1981 six teenagers claimed to have seen the Virgin Mary in the poor mountain village of Medugorje. An instant economic boom began. Today the streets are filled with pilgrims, souvenir stands and travel agencies

BOTSWANA

WHEN TO GO

WEATHER Rainy season October to April, and this is the hottest time of year. Drier and cooler weather from May to September, with an average temperature of 25˚C . This is the best time to visit, as the days are generally pleasant and the wildlife never wanders far from water sources.

FESTIVALS Botswanans enjoy public holidays on New Year's Day and the day after, at Easter, Ascension Day (in April or May), and Labor Day (1 May), as well as a two-day sleep-in around President's Day in July. Independence Day is celebrated on 30 September and the day following, and there are three public holidays over Christmas: on 25, 26 and 27 December. Other events include the Maitisong Festival, in April, a performing arts festival in Gaborone with theatre, music and dance.

TRANSPORT

INTERNATIONAL AIRPORTS Gaborone Sir Seretse Khama International (GBE), 15 km from the city, Maun International Airport (MUB).

INTERNAL TRAVEL Major areas linked by air and rail. Some tarmac roads, four-wheel-drives necessary in many areas. Car hire can be arranged in Gaborone, Francistown or Maun. Buses run between major towns, taxis available in major towns.

RED TAPE

VISAS REQUIRED (UK/US) None.

VACCINATIONS REQUIRED: See 'Vaccinations required around the world' on page 653.

DRIVING REQUIREMENTS An International Driving Permit not legally required but recommended for longer stays, otherwise a UK licence must be carried. After 6 months a Botswanan licence is needed and can be given, without test, on the presentation of a UK licence.

COUNTRY REPS IN UK/US
UK: 6 Stratford Place, London W1C 1AY, tel (020) 7499 0031, fax (020) 7495 8595. US: 1531 - 33 New Hampshire Avenue, NW,

Washington, DC 20036, tel (202) 244 4990, fax (202) 244 4164, email mgradikgokong@botswanaembassy.org.

UK/US REPS IN COUNTRY UK: Plot 1079-1084 Main Mall off Queens Road, Gaborone, tel 395 2841, fax 395 6105, email bhc@botsnet.bw. US: PO Box 90 Gaborone, tel 395 3982, fax 395 6947, email ircgaborone@state.gov.

PEOPLE AND PLACE

CAPITAL Gaborone.

LANGUAGE English and Setswana.

PEOPLES Tswana (98%).

RELIGION Majority animist beliefs, 30% Christian.

SIZE (SQ KM) 581,730.

POPULATION 1,680,863.

POP DENSITY/KM 2.9.

STATE OF THE NATION

SAFETY Safe.

LIFE EXPECTANCY M 33.89, F 33.84.

BEING THERE

ETIQUETTE As most people in Botswana follow their traditional pattern of life, visitors should be sensitive to local customs. This is particularly true in rural areas, where people may be unaccustomed to visitors.

CURRENCY *Pula* (P) = 100 *thebe*

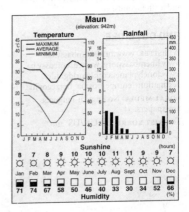

HIGHLIGHTS

OKAVANGO DELTA Described as 'the river that never finds the sea'. Paddle through the maze of waterways and islands in the world's greatest inland delta, teeming with wildlife and as remote as you can get. Travel is by speedboat or dug-out canoe, accommodation is in tents beneath the big African moon.

CHOBE NATIONAL PARK Catch sight of thousands of elephants in perhaps Africa's top park for the pachyderm. A sunset cruise along the Chobe River will bring you up close and personal to crocodile, hippo, gazelle, giraffe and others too.

KALAHARI Marvel at the vastness and greenness of this empty quarter, equivalent to 85 per cent of the country. The Kalahari is home to the last remaining San Bushmen. Today, these traditional hunter gatherers are fighting for their land.

TSODILO HILLS Visit 4,000 rock paintings daubed here by ancestral Bushmen in times gone by, when the land was theirs and these four granite hills were worshipped as the home of the gods. The hills are sacred to the San, in much the same way as Uluru is to Australia's aborigines.

GABORONE Sprawling modern capital city. Its premier attraction is the National Museum & Art Gallery, including historic artefacts and some pieces of San artwork.

FINANCE Limited acceptance of credit cards. Hotels accept traveller's cheques but the surcharge can be high.

BUSINESS HOURS 0800-1700 April-October, 0730-1630 October-April.

GMT +2.

VOLTAGE GUIDE 220-240 AC, 50 Hz.

COUNTRY DIALLING CODE 267.

CONSUMING PLEASURES

FOOD & DRINK Basic outside major hotels. Local dishes include Morama, an underground tuber, Mopane worm, boiled, cooked or fried, and the Kalahari truffle.

SHOPPING & SOUVENIRS Woodcarvings, handcrafted jewellery and basketry.

FIND OUT MORE

WEBSITES www.botswanatourism.org.uk, www.britishhighcommission.gov.uk/botsw ana, www.botswanaembassy.org, http://gaborone.usembassy.gov, www.botswanatourism.org.

LOCAL MEDIA Botswana Daily News is produced daily in Setswana and English, The Botswana Gazette, The Botswana Guardian, Mmegi and The Midweek Sun are weekly English-language papers. Two TV channels, one state-owned, three radio stations, one state-owned.

TOURIST BOARDS IN UK/US UK: c/o Southern Skies Marketing, Old Boundary House, London Road, Sunningdale, Berkshire SL5 0DJ, tel (01344) 298 980, fax (0870) 706 0116, email botswanatourism@ southern-skies.co.uk.

"The miraculous thing about the Kalahari is that it is a desert only in the sense that it contains no permanent surface water. Otherwise its deep fertile sands are covered with grass glistening in the wind like fields of gallant corn."
Laurens Van Der Post, 1958

BRAZIL

WHEN TO GO

WEATHER The Amazon basin has tropical temperatures and high humidity throughout the year. The coastal lands also have a hot tropical climate. The south is more temperate. Rainy seasons occur from January-April in the north, April-July in the north-east, November-March in the Rio/São Paulo area.

FESTIVALS *Carnaval* takes place through-out the country, but it is Rio that can lay claim to having the wildest, largest, and simply the best party in the world. It takes place over four days, from Friday afternoon after Shrove Tuesday, the official start date, until Ash Wednesday. A small, intimate, *fête* is held in Olinda for those wanting to escape Rio at this time. Bahia hosts another Carnival just after Christmas. A three day celebration of dances and medieval tournaments is held in Cavalhadas, locals re-enact Christ's removal from the cross during Easter Week in Goriás Velho. For an unforgettable New Year's Eve party head to Rio's Copacabana beach.

TRANSPORT

INTERNATIONAL AIRPORTS Brasilia International (BSB), 11 km from the city, Rio de Janiero (GIG), Sao Paulo (GRU).

INTERNAL TRAVEL One of the largest internal air networks in the world. Limited rail services to most major cities and towns. Extensive road network. Car hire available in major centres.

RED TAPE

VISAS REQUIRED (UK/US) Required by all apart from UK.

VACCINATIONS REQUIRED: See 'Vaccinations required around the world' on page 653.

DRIVING REQUIREMENTS International Driving Permit.

COUNTRY REPS IN UK/US UK: 32 Green Street, London W1K 7AT, tel (020) 7399 9000, fax (020) 7399 9100, email info@brazil.org.uk. US: 1185 Avenue of the Americas, 21st Floor, New York, NY 10036, tel (917) 777 7777, fax (212) 827 0225, email consulado@brazilny.org.

UK/US REPS IN COUNTRY UK: Praia do Flamengo, 284 (2nd floor), 22210-030 Rio de Janeiro, tel (21) 2555 9600, fax (21) 2555 9672, email consular.rio@fco.gov.uk. US: Avenida das Naçnões, Quadra 801, Lote 3, 70403-900 Brasilia, tel (61) 312 7000, fax (61) 312 7676.

PEOPLE AND PLACE

CAPITAL Brasilia.

LANGUAGE Portuguese.

PEOPLES Highly diverse population including Portuguese and African descendants, more recent Italian and Japanese immigrants and indigenous Indian groups.

RELIGION Mainly Roman Catholic.

SIZE (KM) 8,547,404.

POPULATION 176,876,443.

POP DENSITY/KM 20.7.

STATE OF THE NATION

SAFETY Beware of petty crime (theft, pickpocketing).

LIFE EXPECTANCY M 67.74, F 75.85.

BEING THERE

ETIQUETTE Normal European courtesies observed. Offers of tea and coffee are customary. Casual dress is normal. Night-clubs are smart-casual. Smoking is accepted. The Catholic Church is highly respected.

CURRENCY *Real* (R$) = 100 *centavos*.

FINANCE Most international credit cards and traveller's cheques are accepted.

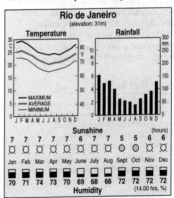

HIGHLIGHTS

RIO DE JANEIRO

The spectacular harbour, dominated by Sugar Loaf Mountain and the statue of Christ the Redeemer on top of the Corcovado peak, leaves you in no doubt the city deserves its tag of *cidade maravilhosa*, 'the marvellous city'. Magnificent views of the city are gained from the Corcovado peak, reachable by cog train. The beaches of Copacabana (home to 24-hour entertainment) and Ipanema (especially popular with young people) are its other famous landmarks, reflecting various lifestyles and fashions. A rich collection of museums give a strong insight to the country, its people and culture.

THE PANTANAL & THE AMAZON

RAINFOREST Many trek to the Amazonian rainforest in an attempt to spot elusive wildlife through the foliage. Better to go to these vast wetlands to appreciate the most dense concentration of fauna in the world, 270 bird species, jaguars, ocelots, capybaras, monkeys - to name just a few. The rainforest itself is home to a 15,000 species, including sloths, armadillos and manatees. Some areas are yet to be explored.

SALVADOR DA BAHIA

Split into upper and lower sections. Cidade Alta is perched atop a 50 metre high cliff, linked to Cidade Baxia by steep streets, a funicular railway and the grand Art-Deco Elevador Lacerdo. Home to many museums, palaces and churches.

IGUAZU FALLS

These spectacular 70-metre high waterfalls see 5,000 cubic metres of water fall per second.

BUSINESS HOURS 0900-1800 Mon-Friday.

GMT from -3 to -5.

VOLTAGE GUIDE 220 AC , 60 Hz (Brasilia). 110AC, 60 Hz for the rest of the country.

COUNTRY DIALLING CODE 55.

CONSUMING PLEASURES

FOOD & DRINK Each region has its own speciality. A Rio de Janeiro favourite is *feijoada* (a thick stew of black beans, beef, pork, sausage, chops, pigs ears and tails). A typical Bahain dish is *vatapá* (shrimps, fish oil, coconut milk, bread and rice). In the northeast dried salted meat and beans are the staple diet. The national drink is *caipirinha*, based on the phenomenally strong whisky liqueur *cachaça*, mixed with sugar, ice and limes.

SHOPPING & SOUVENIRS Precious stones (emeralds), jewellery, antiques, crystal, and pottery available in São Paulo. Belém has jungle items for sale.

FIND OUT MORE

WEBSITES www.brazil.org.uk, www.reinounido.org.br, www.uk.org.br, www.brasilemb.org, www.brazilny.org, www.embaixada-americana.org.br, www.ipanema.com.

LOCAL MEDIA International newspapers and magazines are available, *Rio Visitor* is an English-language publication in Rio de Janeiro, *The Brazil Post* is a global Brazilian news service.

TOURIST BOARDS IN UK/US n/a.

Football is a national passion. The Maracana Stadium in Rio once held a world record crowd of 199,854 fans for an international match with Uruguay. It also witnessed the thousandth goal of football legend Pelé

BRUNEI

WHEN TO GO

WEATHER Very hot, humid tropical climate most of the year. Monsoon season from November to December.

FESTIVALS Most festivals are religious celebrations or mark the anniversaries of important events in the sultanate's history. Ramadan, the Islamic month of fasting, is one of the most important events on Brunei's calendar. Chinese New Year takes place in January/February, and Brunei's National Day is 23 February

TRANSPORT

INTERNATIONAL AIRPORTS Bandar Seri Begawan (BWN)

INTERNAL TRAVEL No air travel. Water taxis. Self-drive or chauffeur-driven cars available for hire.

RED TAPE

VISAS REQUIRED (UK/US) Required by Australians and Canadians if staying more than 14 days.

VACCINATIONS REQUIRED: See 'Vaccinations required around the world' on page 653.

DRIVING REQUIREMENTS International Driving Permit. A temporary licence is available on presentation of a valid driving licence from the visitor's country of origin.

COUNTRY REPS IN UK/US UK: 19 - 20 Belgrave Square, London SW1X 8PG, tel (020) 7581 0521, fax (020) 7235 9717. US: 3520 International Court, NW, Washington DC 20008, tel (202) 237 1838, fax (202) 885 0560, email info@ bruneiembassy.org.

UK/US REPS IN COUNTRY UK: Unit 2.01, 2nd Floor, Block D, Kompleks Yayasan Sultan, Haji Hassanal Bolkiah, Jalan Pretty, Bandar Seri Begawan BS8711, tel (2) 222 231, fax (2) 234 315, email brithc@ brunet.bn. US: 3rd Floor, Teck Guan Plaza, Jalan Sultan, Bandar Seri Begawan BS8811, (2) 220 384, fax (2) 225 293, email amembassybrunei@state.gov.

PEOPLE AND PLACE

CAPITAL Bandar Seri Begawan.

LANGUAGE Malay and English.

PEOPLES Malay, Chinese, indigenous groups.

RELIGION Sunni Muslim, significant Buddhist, Confucian, Daoist, Christian communities.

SIZE (SQ KM) 5,765.

POPULATION 332,844.

POP DENSITY/KM 57.7.

STATE OF THE NATION

SAFETY Safe.

LIFE EXPECTANCY M 72.36, F 77.36.

BEING THERE

ETIQUETTE Shoes should be removed when entering Muslim homes and institutions and visitors should not pass in front of a person at prayer or touch the Koran, the Muslim holy book. There are many honorific titles in Brunei. *Awang*, for example, is equivalent to Ms or Mrs.
If food is served without cutlery, eat using the right hand only. It is also considered impolite to beckon someone with your fingers. Instead, the whole hand should be waved, with the palm facing downwards. Visitors should note that there are severe penalties for all drug offences. Women should ensure that their head, knees and arms are covered.

CURRENCY Brunei dollar (Br$).

FINANCE Major credit cards and traveller's

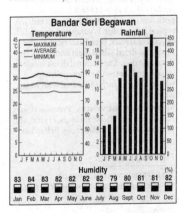

Bandar Seri Begawan

HIGHLIGHTS

BANDAR SERI BEGAWAN A neat, clean and modern capital with wide roads and grand public buildings. The golden domed Omar Ali Saifuddin Mosque stands close to the Brunei River. Its opulent interior features Italian marble walls and an elevator. The city also has some good museums, but nightlife is pretty scarce. Along the river, the Kampung Ayer area is a collection of 28 water villages, built on stilts in the water and home to half the city's population.

JERUDONG The playground of the Sultan, where he indulges in his favourite pastime, polo. The Jerudong complex features a polo stadium, stables, a golf course, trapshooting and croquet facilities. Unfortunately, you can only go if you've been invited. There is also a modern theme park, with a huge range of rides. Behind the park, Jerudong Beach has some impressive cliffs and stalls selling fish.

PULAU RANGGU Home to a large colony of proboscis monkeys. There are also plenty of macaques to be seen. Take a river taxi around sunset to catch a glimpse of them.

BATANG DURI An Iban longhouse on the Temburong River south-east of the capital. A short boat-ride from here is the Kuala Belalong Field Studies Centre, which researches tropical rainforest species. There are pleasant walking trails and a zoo where you can see civets, monkeys, otters and birds.

WASAI KANDAL Lush forest area with waterfalls and pools, popular for picnics and reached by car.

cheques generally accepted.

BUSINESS HOURS 0745-1215, 1330-1630 Mon-Thu, 0900-1200 Sat.

GMT +8.

VOLTAGE GUIDE 220/240 AC, 50 Hz.

COUNTRY DIALLING CODE 673.

CONSUMING PLEASURES

FOOD & DRINK Local food similar to Malay cuisine with fish and rice, often spicy. Malaysian, Chinese, Indian food widely served. European food served in hotel restaurants. Alcohol is prohibited.

SHOPPING & SOUVENIRS Handworked silverware, brass and bronze jugs, trays, gongs, boxes, napkin rings, spoons and bracelets. Sarongs, baskets, mats of *pandan* leaves. Fruit, spices, poultry and vegetables available from the 'Tamu' Night Market in Bandar Seri Begawan.

FIND OUT MORE

WEBSITES www.tourismbrunei.com, www..britishhighcommission.gov.uk/ brunei, www.bruneiembassy.org, www.brunei.gov.bn

LOCAL MEDIA *Borneo Bulletin* is the only English-language newspaper, but the government produces *Daily News Digest* and *Brunei Darussalam* (fortnightly) in English. One TV channel, and one radio station, both state-owned.

TOURIST BOARDS IN UK/US n/a.

Brunei's population enjoy, statistically at least, one of the highest per capita incomes on earth. But most of this tiny, oil-rich state's wealth is in the hands of the Sultan, one of the richest men in the world

BULGARIA

WHEN TO GO

WEATHER Climate varies with altitude. Warm summers with some rain, cold winters with snow. Rain in spring and autumn.

FESTIVALS Varna Summer International Festival is held between May and October The arrival of Baba Marta, Spring, is marked with the exchanging and wearing of red and white tassles, on 1 March. Late march sees men with grotesque masks perform ritualistic processional dances as part of Kukerov Den. The Kazanluk Rose Festival is held in early June. September sees Bulgaria's oldest coastal colony, Sozopol, celebrate the Greek god of music and dance over ten days with jazz, rock, and theatre.

TRANSPORT

INTERNATIONAL AIRPORTS Sofia (SOF) 10 km from city, Varna (VAR) 9 km from city, Bourgas (BOJ)13 km from city.

INTERNAL TRAVEL Comparitively cheap air travel. Regular boat and hydrofoil services along the Danube link many centres. Roads generally of good quality, car hire can be arranged through hotels. Good network of buses, taxis in every town.

RED TAPE

VISAS REQUIRED (UK/US) None.

VACCINATIONS REQUIRED: See 'Vaccinations required around the world' on page 653.

DRIVING REQUIREMENTS International Driving Permit. Green Card is compulsory.

COUNTRY REPS IN UK/US UK: 186-188 Queen's Gate, London SW7 5HL, tel (020) 7584 9400, fax (020) 7584 4948 ,email info@bulgarianembassy.urg.uk. US: 1621 22nd Street, NW, Washington, DC 20008, tel (202) 387 7969, fax (202) 387 7969, email office@bulgaria-embassy.org.

UK/US REPS IN COUNTRY UK: 9 Moskovska Street, Sofia 1000, tel (2) 933 9222, fax (2) 933 9250, email britembinf@mail.orbitel.bg. US: 16 Kozyak Street, Sofia 1407, tel (2) 937 5100, fax (2) 937 5320, email irc@usembassy.bg.

PEOPLE AND PLACE

CAPITAL Sofia.

LANGUAGE Bulgarian.

PEOPLES Bulgarian, Turkish, Macedonian, Romany.

RELIGION Bulgarian Orthodox (85%), Muslim, Roman Catholic and Jewish.

SIZE (SQ KM) 110,994.

POPULATION 7,845,499.

POP DENSITY/KM 70.7.

STATE OF THE NATION

SAFETY Beware of hazardous drivers.

LIFE EXPECTANCY M 68.41, F 75.87.

BEING THERE

ETIQUETTE Dress is conservative but casual. If invited into someone's home a souvenir from your homeland is a good gift. Do not give money. Nodding means 'no', shaking the head means 'yes'.

CURRENCY *Lev* (Lv) = 100 *stotinki*.

FINANCE Credit cards and traveller's cheques accepted in major hotels and restaurants.

BUSINESS HOURS 0900-1730, Mon-Friday.

GMT +2/3.

VOLTAGE GUIDE 220 AC, 50 Hz.

COUNTRY DIALLING CODE 359.

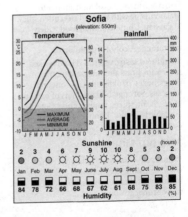

Sofia (elevation: 550m)

HIGHLIGHTS

SOFIA The ancient capital dates back to the fourth century BC. Greek, Roman, Byzantine, Bulgarian, and Turkish architectural styles are found in the city. Attractions include theatres, museums, opera houses, art galleries, open-air markets, and churches. The Alexander Nevsky Memorial Church built to celebrate the liberation from Turks in the Russo-Turkish war is extraordinary.

VITOSHA Just outside the capital sits this mountain range. Chairlifts and cable cars can take you to its 1,80-metre summit. The medieval church of Boyana, a World Heritage Site dating from 1200, with beautiful frescoes, is found here. Ski-runs operate between December and April: two of the runs are suitable for international events. The National Park is home to butterflies, wolves, bears, and wild cats.

TSAREVETS FORTRESS One kilometre from Veliko Târnovo, an unchanged hilly medieval capital, is this mammoth fortress. Thracians, Romans, and Byzantines have all added to it. Today a triangular high-walled fortress with the ruins of 400 houses and 18 churches is all that remains. Veliko Târnovo itself is the best citadel ruin in the region.

SOZOPOL Located on the Black Sea, the two sandy beaches, pretty offshore island and the historic centre on the peninsula make it the number one coastal town. Swimming is safe here, even further out, and any dangerous currents are clearly marked. The Black Sea has half the salt content of the Mediterranean.

CONSUMING PLEASURES

FOOD & DRINK Spicy, hearty dishes, including *kebapcheta* (strongly spiced minced meat rolls) and pastries stuffed with cheese or fruit. Standard west European food widely available. Heavily sweetened coffee is widely popular. Mountain herbs and dried leaves, particularly lime, are used to make drinks. Heavy red wines and potent liquors such as *mastika* and *rakia* also available.

SHOPPING & SOUVENIRS Handicrafts, wines, spirits, and confectionery.

FIND OUT MORE

WEBSITES www.bulgariatravel.org, www.bulgarianembassy.org.uk, www.balkanholidays.co.uk, www.british-embassy.bg, www.bulgaria-embassy.org, www.usembassy.bg.

LOCAL MEDIA *Sofia Echo* and *Pari* are weekly English-language papers.

TOURIST BOARDS IN UK/US UK: Sofia House, 19 Conduit Street, London W1S 2BH, tel (0845) 130 1114, fax (020) 7543 5577, email res@balkanholidays.co.uk.

> "They are a fine people with a passion for freedom: so great that it made them able to remain 500 years under the Turk and come out pure Bulger at the end."
> *Freya Stark, 1939*

BURKINA FASO

WHEN TO GO

WEATHER Travel during the dry season from November to February, following the dusty *harmattan* winds, which arrive from the east between December and February. The months afterwards are dry and cool. Rainy season from June-October.

FESTIVALS In odd-numbered years, Ouagadougou hosts the Pan-African Film Festiva,l showcasing up-and-coming West African film makers. It usually begins on the last Saturday in February. In April, in even-numbered years, the city of Bobo-Dioulasso, hosts La Semaine Nationale de la Culture, a week-long event featuring traditional and contemporary forms of music, dance and theatre.
On Friday mornings, a traditional drama is performed at the Moro-Naba Palace in the capital, called *Nabayius Gou*– 'The Emperor Goes to War'.

TRANSPORT

INTERNATIONAL AIRPORTS Ouagadougou (OUA), 8 km from the city.

INTERNAL TRAVEL Trains are overcrowded. Roads generally impassable during the rainy season. Car hire is a new development and cars may be in poor condition.

RED TAPE

VISAS REQUIRED (UK/US) Required.

VACCINATIONS REQUIRED: See 'Vaccinations required around the world' on page 653.

DRIVING REQUIREMENTS International Driving Permit recommended although a temporary licence available on presentation of a valid national driving licence.

COUNTRY REPS IN UK/US UK: 16 Place Guy d'Arezzo, 1180 Brussels, Belgium, tel (2) 345 9912, fax (2) 345 0612, email ambassade.burkina@skynet.be, since the Honorary Consulate of Burkina Faso in London closed enquiries should be directed here. US: 2340 Massachusetts Avenue, NW, Washington, DC 20008, tel (202) 332 5577, fax (202) 667 1882, email ambawdc@ verizon.com.

UK/US REPS IN COUNTRY UK: Hotel Yibi, 10 BP 13593, Ouagadougou 10, tel 5030 7323, fax 5030 5900, email ypi@cenatrin.bf, provides limited assistance, the embassy in Abidjan (see Cote d'Ivoire) deals with most enquiries. US: 01 BP 35, 602 avenue Raoul Folereau, Ouagadougou 01, tel 5030 6723, fax 5031 2368, email amembouaga@state.gov.

PEOPLE AND PLACE

CAPITAL Ouagadougou.

LANGUAGE French and several indigenous.

PEOPLES Mossi, Fulani, Tuareg, Songhai.

RELIGION Traditional beliefs, Muslim, Roman Catholic.

SIZE (SQ KM) 274,200.

POPULATION 12,624,000.

POP DENSITY/KM 46.

STATE OF THE NATION

SAFETY Towns can be dangerous after dark. Take care in remote rural areas.

LIFE EXPECTANCY M 42.19, F 45.7.

BEING THERE

ETIQUETTE Within the urban areas many French customs prevail. Outside the cities little has changed for centuries and visitors should respect local customs and traditions.

CURRENCY *Communauté Financiaire Africaine Franc* (CFA) = 100 *centimes*.

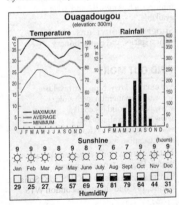

Ouagadougou (elevation: 300m)

HIGHLIGHTS

OUAGADOUGOU
In the middle of this landlocked country, the capital city stands at the crossroads of several ancient trade routes. It's relaxed and friendly - hospitality is one of the city's trademarks. It also has a lively nightclub scene.

BANFORA The town itself is pretty lifeless, but the surrounding countryside is among the best in Burkina Faso. As such, Banfora is a great jumping-off point for hikers and bikers. Karfiguéla waterfalls is one of the most interesting spots on the trail.

RÉSERVA DE NAZINGA South of the capital, near the Ghanaian border, this game park plays a crucial role in protecting native wildlife and has been instrumental in the growth of elephant numbers in the country - Burkina Faso is now estimated to have the largest elephant population in west Africa.

BOBO-DIOULASSO
Home to the Bobo people, this is another laid-back and friendly city, characterised by tree-lined streets and thriving market places, including the Grand Marché. The old Kibidwé district,

full of artisans, is worth a look. Elsewhere, the Museé Provincial du Houët showcases regional African art, batik and sculpture.

MORO-NABA PALACE
Burkina Faso's equivalent of the changing of the guard. Traditional drama performed every friday morning.

GOROM-GOROM A typical Sahelian town, its edges smudged by a sea of sand dunes and wide open spaces. The town's busy and colourful market is a fascinating spot to watch the various Sahelian and Saharan ethnic groups mix.

FINANCE Limited acceptance of major credit cards.

BUSINESS HOURS 0700-1230, 1500-1730 Monday-Friday.

GMT GMT.

VOLTAGE GUIDE 220 AC, 50 Hz.

COUNTRY DIALLING CODE 226.

LOCAL MEDIA French papers only. The main dailies being *L'Express du Faso* and *Le Pays*.

TOURIST BOARDS IN UK/US n/a.

CONSUMING PLEASURES

FOOD & DRINK Staple foods include sorghum, millet, rice, maize, nuts, potatoes and yams. Specialities include *brochettes* (meat cooked on a skewer) and chicken dishes.

SHOPPING & SOUVENIRS Wooden statuettes, bronze, masks, jewellery, fabrics, blankets, leather goods, and craftworks such as chess sets and ashtrays.

FIND OUT MORE

WEBSITES www.burkinaembassy-usa.org, http://ouagadougou.usembassy.gov, www.lonelyplanet.com/worldguide/destinations/africa/burkina-faso/

The name 'Burkina Faso' translates as 'Land of the Honourable'. It comes from two local languages – the Moré word for 'pure' and the Dioula word for 'homeland'

BURUNDI

WHEN TO GO

WEATHER Rainy season from October-May, dry season from June-September. Hot equatorial climate near Lake Tanganyika, the rest of the country is mild.

FESTIVALS Independence Day is celebrated on 1 July, marking the anniversary of sovereignty in 1962. The assasinated Prince Louis Rwagasore is remembered on Murder of the Hero Day, 13 October. Other celebrations follow religious contacts.

TRANSPORT

INTERNATIONAL AIRPORTS Bujumbura International (BJM), 11 km from the city.

INTERNAL TRAVEL Many roads are sealed. Road travel difficult during the rainy season. Car hire may be possible in Bujumbura, through Avis or local garages. Bus services in Bujumbura and main towns. Taxi trucks, or *tanus-tanus*, are available but crowded.

RED TAPE

VISAS REQUIRED (UK/US) Required.

VACCINATIONS REQUIRED: See 'Vaccinations required around the world' on page 653.

DRIVING REQUIREMENTS Driving licences issued by the UK are acceptable.

COUNTRY REPS IN UK/US UK: 46 square Marie-Louise, 1000 Brussels, Belgium, tel (2) 230 4535, fax (2) 230 7883, email ambassade.burundi@skynet.be, London office now closed so enquiries should be directed here. US: Suite 212, 2233 Wisconsin Avenue, NW, Washington, DC 20007, tel (202) 342 2574, fax (202) 342 2578, email burundiembassy@erols.com.

UK/US REPS IN COUNTRY UK: The British Embassy in Kigali (see Rwanda) deals with enquiries relating to Burundi. US: BP 1720, avenue des Etats-Unis, Bujumbura, tel 223 454, fax 222 926.

PEOPLE AND PLACE

CAPITAL Bujumbura.

LANGUAGE French and Kirundi.

PEOPLES Hutu (85%), Tutsi (14%).

RELIGION Mainly Roman Catholic.

SIZE (SQ KM) 27,834.

POPULATION 6,602,000.

POP DENSITY/KM 237.2.

STATE OF THE NATION

SAFETY Extremely dangerous. Guerrilla warfare is widespread, and the rule of law cannot be guaranteed outside the capital.

LIFE EXPECTANCY M 42.91, F 44.12.

BEING THERE

ETIQUETTE Normal social courtesies should be adhered to. Outside of the cities people may not be used to visitors, and so a degree of care and tact should be used, and local customs must be respected. Inhabitants of modern towns live by a more modern way of life. Dress is conservative.

CURRENCY Burundi *Franc* (Bufr) = 100 *centimes*.

FINANCE Limited acceptance of traveller's cheques, MasterCard and Diners Club.

BUSINESS HOURS 0730-1200, 14-1730 Mon-Fri.

GMT +2..

VOLTAGE GUIDE 220 AC, 50 Hz.

COUNTRY DIALLING CODE 257.

CONSUMING PLEASURES

FOOD & DRINK Limited choice, hotel restaurants in Bujumbura serve meals of reasonable quality but at high prices. Good French and Greek restaurants in the capital.

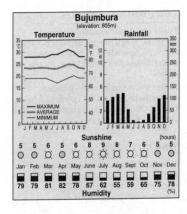

Bujumbura
(elevation: 805m)

HIGHLIGHTS

BUJUMBURA A bustling town with a population of around 300,000 on the shore of Lake Tanganyika. The region was colonised by Germany towards the end of the nineteenth century. The architecture still dates from that period. A good example is the Postmaster's House. There are three museums and an Islamic Cultural Centre. The shore of the lake is lined with cafe's and restaurants, and, in safe times, watersports such as sailing, water-skiing and fishing can be enjoyed here. There is an excellent market.

ELSEWHERE Other visitor attractions in the country include the former royal cities of Muramvya and Gitega, where the Chutes de la Kagera waterfall and a recently renovated National Museum are found. The monument at Rutovu marks Burundi's claim to the source of the Nile.

STANLEY AND LIVINGSTONE David Livingstone was sent by the London Missionary Society to Africa to convert the locals to Christianity. He became better known as an explorer and was the first white man to cross the continent and see Victoria Falls. In the 1860s, while exploring the Lake Tanganyika region, he disappeared. In 1869 the *New York Times* financed a search for him. Their reporter, Henry Stanley, eventually found him four years later, frail and short of supplies. He greeted him with the immortal line, "Dr Livingstone, I presume?" Stanley was the first white man to speak to him in five years. A stone marks this historic meeting place, 10 kilometres south of the capital.

SHOPPING & SOUVENIRS Local crafts, especially the basketwork, are the best buys.

FIND OUT MORE

WEBSITES www.burundiembassy-usa.org, http://bujumbura.usembassy.gov, www.lonelyplanet.com/worldguide/destinations/africa/burundi, www.burundi.nu.

LOCAL MEDIA No English-language newspapers, some in French or local languages but the two main papers are government controlled. One TV station, state-controlled.

TOURIST BOARDS IN UK/US n/a.

The famous meeting of Livingstone and Stanley is commemorated by a stone landmark just outside the capital

CAMBODIA

WHEN TO GO

WEATHER Tropical monsoon climate, with the monsoon season from June to October. The best time to visit is from November to May, during the dry season.

FESTIVALS Chaul Chnam Chen, the Lunar New Year, is celebrated by ethnic Chinese and Vietnamese in late January or early February. The Chaul Chnam, or Khmer New Year, celebrations bring the country to a standstill for three days in April. The Khmer calendar's most important festival is Bon Om Tuk, celebrating the end of the wet season in early November.

TRANSPORT

INTERNATIONAL AIRPORTS Pochentong (PNH), 12 km from Phnom Penh.

INTERNAL TRAVEL Some rail services operate, but many need restoration. Boats and government run ferries frequently used. Driving can be hazardous, due to the poor conditions of the roads and accidents caused by reckless driving are relatively frequent. Reliable information about security should be obtained before considering extensive road journeys. Car hire is generally not recommended and visitors are advised to hire a car with driver for approximately the same cost.

RED TAPE

VISAS REQUIRED (UK/US) Required.

VACCINATIONS REQUIRED: See 'Vaccinations required around the world' on page 653.

DRIVING REQUIREMENTS International Driving Permit not recognised. Visitors advised to hire car with driver.

COUNTRY REPS IN UK/US
UK: Wellington Building, 28-32 Wellington Road, St John's Wood, London NW8 9SP, tel (020) 7483 9063, fax (020) 7483 9061, email cambodianembassy@btconnect.com. US: 4530 16th Street, NW, Washington, DC 20011, tel (202) 726 7742, fax (202) 726 8381, email cambodia@embassy.org.

UK/US REPS IN COUNTRY UK: 27-29 Street 75, Phnom Penh, tel (23) 427 124, fax (23) 427 125, email britemb@online.com.kh. US: 16 Street 228, Phnom Penh, (23) 216 436/8, fax (23) 216 437.

PEOPLE AND PLACE

CAPITAL Phnom Penh.

LANGUAGE Khmer. Chinese and Vietnamese also spoken.

PEOPLES Khmer (94%), Small Chinese and Vietnamese communities.

RELIGION Mainly Buddhist.

SIZE (SQ KM) 181,035.

POPULATION 13,311,000.

POP DENSITY/KM 73.5.

STATE OF THE NATION

SAFETY Politically calm at present. Highest incidence of landmines and unexploded ordnance in the world, so travel off the beaten track is very hazardous. Even local information on landmines is unreliable. Be wary in areas affected by covert activities such as drug-production or illegal logging.

LIFE EXPECTANCY M 55.92, F 61.96.

BEING THERE

ETIQUETTE Sensitivity to politically-related subjects in conversation is advisable. Avoid pointing your foot at a person or touching someone on the head. Women

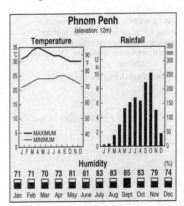

Phnom Penh
(elevation: 12m)

	Jan	Feb	Mar	Apr	May	June	July	Aug	Sept	Oct	Nov	Dec
Humidity (%)	71	71	70	73	81	81	83	83	85	83	79	74

HIGHLIGHTS

ANGKOR WAT The amazing temples near the town of Siem Reap are Cambodia's most famous tourist attraction - and justifiably so. The three most magnificent temples are the Bayon, Ta Prohm and the immense Angkor Wat itself. The whole complex contains some 100 temples and sacred ruins, scattered through the jungle. Together they are the remnants of a once mighty Khmer city, the first urban centre in the world to reach one million inhabitants.

SIHANOUKVILLE The country's only maritime port, this south coast resort has some nice beaches, offering diving for the active, or just chilling out for less frenetic souls.

TONLÉ SAP AND MEKONG RIVER The country's 'Great Lake' and mighty riverway offer the chance for scenic boat trips, passing houseboats and traditional villages. The permanently floating town of Kompong Luong on the Tonlé Sap has houses, restaurants and even karaoke bars, rising and falling with the tide.

PHNOM PENH Vibrant capital city with a scarred and often violent past, yet Phnom Penh retains a distinct French colonial charm and also has some impressive *wats* (temple monasteries). The chilling Toul Sleng Museum of Genocide shows the inhumanity of Pol Pot's regime.

UDONG Historic capital and site of several fine *stupas*. You'll probably have the place to yourself. There is also a memorial here to the victims of Pol Pot, containing the bones of people buried in the many mass graves nearby.

should wear long clothing that covers the body. It is polite to ask permission before photographing Cambodian people, especially monks.

CURRENCY *Riel* (CRI)= 100 *sen.*

FINANCE Very limited acceptance of major credit cards and traveller's cheques. US dollars widely accepted.

BUSINESS HOURS 0700-1130 and 1400-1730 Monday-Friday .

GMT +7.

VOLTAGE GUIDE 220AC, 50 Hz.

COUNTRY DIALLING CODE 855.

CONSUMING PLEASURES

FOOD & DRINK Influenced by Thai and Vietnamese cuisine, but with less spice. Restaurants and food stalls abound in Phnom Penh. Fish, soup, and salad are favourite dishes, incorporating coriander, lemon grass and mint flavours. Nuts, bananas, coconuts, jackfruit, and lychees are often used in sweet dishes.

SHOPPING & SOUVENIRS Antiques, woodcarvings, *papier mâché* masks, brass figures, jewellery, silver, precious stones.

FIND OUT MORE

WEBSITES
www.cambodianembassy.org.uk,
www.britishembassy.gov.uk/cambodia,
www.embassy.org/cambodia,
http://phnompenh.usembassy.gov,
www.cambodia.org.

LOCAL MEDIA *Phnom Penh Post* (fortnightly), *Cambodia Daily, Cambodia Times* (weekly) are all printed in English.

TOURIST BOARDS IN UK/US n/a.

> "It is grander than anything left to us by Greece or Rome."
>
> *Henri Mouhot,*
> *rediscoverer of Angkor, 1864*

CAMEROON

WHEN TO GO

WEATHER The south is hot and dry from November to February, main rainy season is July to October. In the north the rainy season is May to October.

FESTIVALS A 27 km race up and down a 3000 metre high mountain, the Mt Cameroon Race, is held every January. Tabaski is celebrated in February or March, according to the Muslim calendar, with a parade of wise men and fortune tellers. The Cameroon National Festival, non-religious, is held on 20 May, and is best seen in Maroua. During Nso Cultural Week in mid-November, horses race through the streets of Kumbo. Other festivals follow the religious calendars.

TRANSPORT

INTERNATIONAL AIRPORTS Douala (DLA), 10 km from the city, Nsimalen (NSI), 25 km from the city.

INTERNAL TRAVEL Air travel most efficient, slow but cheap rail services. Paved roads between main towns but others poorly maintained and impassable in the rainy season. Limited car hire available.

RED TAPE

VISAS REQUIRED (UK/US) Required.

VACCINATIONS REQUIRED: See 'Vaccinations required around the world' on page 653.

DRIVING REQUIREMENTS International Driving Permit not legally required but recommended. A driving licence must be carried while driving - a Cameroonian licence can be obtained in 24 hours for a small fee.

COUNTRY REPS IN UK/US UK: 84 Holland Park, London W11 3SB, tel (020) 7727 0771, fax (020) 7792 9353. US: 2349 Massachusetts Avenue, NW, Washington, DC 20008, tel (202) 265 8790, fax (202) 387 3826, email cdm@ ambacam-usa.org.

UK/US REPS IN COUNTRY UK: BP 547, Avenue Winston Churchill, Yaoundé, tel 222 0545, fax 222 0148, email bhc.yaounde@ fco.gov.uk. US: BP 817, Rue Nachtigal, Yaoundé, tel 223 4014, fax 223 0753, email consularyaound@state.gov.

PEOPLE AND PLACE

CAPITAL Yaoundé.

LANGUAGE French and English.

PEOPLES 230 ethnic groups, the Bamileke being the largest.

RELIGION Roman Catholic, Muslim, Protestant, traditional beliefs.

SIZE (SQ KM) 475,442.

POPULATION 16,018,000.

POP DENSITY/KM 33.7.

STATE OF THE NATION

SAFETY Relatively safe, but Douala can be dangerous after dark.

LIFE EXPECTANCY M 47.04, F 48.67.

BEING THERE

ETIQUETTE Islamic traditions must be respected, and travellers should be careful not to step inside a Muslim prayer circle of rocks. Use tact in areas of traditional beliefs. Only use cameras with discretion, particularly in rural areas, and always seek permission before photographing people. Official buildings, military sites, and airports should not be photographed.

CURRENCY *Communauté Financiare*

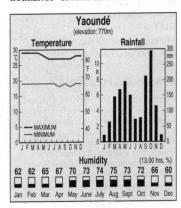

Yaoundé
(elevation: 770m)

Temperature / Rainfall / Humidity (13.00 hrs, %)

	Jan	Feb	Mar	Apr	May	June	July	Aug	Sept	Oct	Nov	Dec
Humidity	62	62	65	67	70	73	74	75	73	72	66	60

HIGHLIGHTS

YAOUNDÉ The capital is built on seven hills. The mountains rise to 1,000 metres, and are covered in lush jungle vegetation. Mont Fébé has been turned into a tourist resort over-looking the city. Its altitude ensures a pleasant climate. A small population of lowland gorillas in-habit Moloundou, an area outside of the city teeming with wildlife.

BUÉA A town full of character on the slopes of Mount Cameroon, west Africa's tallest mountain at 4,095 metres. It is also the highest active volcano in Africa.

WAZA NATIONAL PARK Covering over 400,000 acres, the park contains forest, grassland and wet plains where elephants, giraffes, antelopes, hartebeest, cobs, lions, cheetahs, warthogs, and various bird species may be spotted.

KORUP NATIONAL PARK Africa's oldest and most biologically diverse rainforest. Home to numerous species of primates, birds, trees, and plants. Many new species have been discovered here recently. Travellers to the park need to prepare for 100 per cent humidity and crossing waist-high pools.

DOUALA The economic capital of the country, only 24 kilometres from the sea, lies alongside the Wouri River under the shadow of Mount Cameroon. It holds a number of attractions for the visitor, includ-ing the craft market or Artisanat National, Deido market, the harbour, the museum, and Wouri bridge. The restaurants and live music are some of the best in west Africa.

Africaine Franc (CFAfr) = 100 centimes.

FINANCE Very limited acceptance of major credit cards, limited acceptance of traveller's cheques .

BUSINESS HOURS 0730-1700 Mon-Friday.

GMT +1.

VOLTAGE GUIDE 220 AC, 50 Hz.

COUNTRY DIALLING CODE 237.

CONSUMING PLEASURES

FOOD & DRINK Excellent street food, including spiced brochettes (meat on skew-ers) grilled over charcoal, meat dishes with spicy sauces served with rice or fufu, pâte, or couscous - mashes made from corn, manioc, plantains or bananas. French and Lebanese dishes widely available. The nation has a plentiful supply of avocados, manoic leaves citrus fruits, pineapples and mangoes. Prawns are supplied from the south.

SHOPPING & SOUVENIRS Decorated pots, jugs, bottles, earthenware bowls, delicate pottery, mats and rugs made from grasses, and beadwork.

FIND OUT MORE

WEBSITES www.britcam.org, www.ambacam-usa.org, http://yaounde.usembassy.gov, www.cameroonnews.com.

LOCAL MEDIA The Herald (3 times a week), Cameroon Times (weekly), and the Cameroon Post (weekly) are published in English. The Cameroon Tribune is the main newspaper, published daily in French and English by the government.

TOURIST BOARDS IN UK/US n/a.

Mount Cameroon is the highest active volcano in Africa. Every January, runners from around the world compete in a race to the top

CANADA

WHEN TO GO

WEATHER March-April cool, May-September warm, October-November cool, December-February cold with heavy snow.

MEDICAL CARE Good, but expensive; insurance recommended.

FESTIVALS Toronto takes on Hollywood every September with screenings of hundreds of films from around the world at the Toronto International Film Festival. If you arrive in October, you'll be in time for the largest Bavarian festival in North America, the Kitchener-Waterloo Oktoberfest, which includes a Thanksgiving day parade but is otherwise all beer, music and dancing.

TRANSPORT

INTERNATIONAL AIRPORTS (With distances from the city) Calgary (YYC) 8 km, Edmonton (YEG) 28 km, Gander (YQX) 3 km, Halifax (YHZ) 42 km, Hamilton (YHM) 10 km, Montréal (Dorval) (YUL) 25 km, Montréal (Mirabel) (YMX) 53 km, Ottawa (YOW) 15 km, St John's (YYT) 8 km, Saskatoon (YXE) 7 km, Toronto (YYZ) 27 km, Vancouver (YVR) 15 km, Winnipeg (YWG) 10 km.

INTERNAL TRAVEL Numerous regional airlines, an extensive rail and road network. Car hire is easy to arrange for full licence holders aged over 21.

RED TAPE

VISAS REQUIRED (UK/US) None.

VACCINATIONS REQUIRED: See 'Vaccinations required around the world' on page 653.

DRIVING REQUIREMENTS International Driving Permit recommended, although not legally required. National driving licences will generally suffice for up to 3 months (shorter in some provinces).

COUNTRY REPS IN UK/US UK: Immigration: 38 Grosvenor Street, London W1K 4AA, tel (020) 7258 6600, fax (020) 7258 6533. Cultural: Canada House, 5 Pall Mall East, Trafalgar Square, London, tel (020)

7258 6366, fax (020) 7258 6434, email ldn-ld@international.gc.ca. US: 1251 Avenue of the Americas, New York, NY 10020, tel (212) 596 1628, fax (212) 596 1793, email cngny-td@international.gc.ca.

UK/US REPS IN COUNTRY UK: 80 Elgin Street, Ottawa, Ontario, K1P 5K7, tel (613) 237 1530, fax (613) 237 7980, email generalenquiries@britainincanada.org. US: 490 Sussex Drive, Ottawa, Ontario K1N 1G8, tel (613) 238 5335, fax (613) 688 3080, email ottawareference@state.gov.

PEOPLE AND PLACE

CAPITAL Ottawa.

LANGUAGE French and English.

PEOPLES Of French, English and European origin (89%), Indigenous Indian and Innuit

RELIGION Roman Catholic, Protestant.

SIZE (SQ KM) 9,984,670.

POPULATION 31,629,700.

POP DENSITY/KM 3.5.

STATE OF THE NATION

SAFETY Safe.

LIFE EXPECTANCY M 76.73, F 83.63.

BEING THERE

ETIQUETTE Normal social courtesies apply: handshakes at first meetings, small gifts when visiting homes and dress is often informal and practical for the climate.

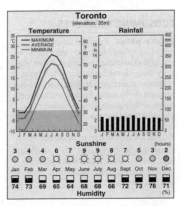

HIGHLIGHTS

VANCOUVER Fun and active city on the west coast. Highlights include joining local joggers, rollerbladers and cyclists in the delightful Stanley Park, in which stands a fine collection of totem poles. The park also has a fascinating aquarium, with beluga whales, killer whales and other aquatic life. In the downtown area, historic Gastown and the thriving Chinatown are other notable city sights. Vancouver has some fun festivals and also offers skiing on Grouse Mountain.

PRINCE EDWARD ISLAND The home of Anne of Green Gables and the birthplace of Canadian Confederation. A very beautiful island, with tranquil farmlands and the lovely Cavendish beach, a long stretch of white sand washed by the warm Gulf Stream and visited by seals and porpoises.

NUNUVUT Vast region in Canada's far north and home to the Inuit people, together with seals, whales and wandering polar bears. Isolated and wild, it includes the Auyuittuq National Park. The pristine wilderness offers great hiking, while climbers enjoy Mount Thor, the world's tallest uninterrupted cliff face.

NIAGARA FALLS Not far from Toronto, this mighty waterfall is shared by neighbouring USA. However, the best view is on the Canadian side in a small boat.

ROCKY MOUNTAINS Sprawling mountain range, barely contained by the gigantic Banff and Jasper national parks. The Rockies offer walking, climbing, camping and much more. From the base of the range stretch the prairies.

CURRENCY Canadian dollar (C$)

FINANCE Most major credit cards and traveller's cheques in Canadian dollars widely accepted.

BUSINESS HOURS 0900-1700 Mon-Friday.

GMT From -3.5 to -8.

VOLTAGE GUIDE 110 AC, 60 Hz.

COUNTRY DIALLING CODE 1.

CONSUMING PLEASURES

FOOD & DRINK As varied as the country. Excellent seafood along the coast, good beef from the central plains. Colonial influence still discernable in cuisine, European menus in all major cities and good French food in Québec.

SHOPPING & SOUVENIRS Woodcarvings, pottery and native artefacts.

FIND OUT MORE

WEBSITES www.canada.org.uk, www.travelcanada.ca, www.britainincanada.org, www.canadianembassy.org, www.ski-guide.com, www.discoveralberta.com, www.ontariotravel.net, www.infoniagara.com, www.bonjour-quebec .com, www.touryukon.com.

LOCAL MEDIA Toronto's *The Globe and Mail* has national distribution as does *The National Post*. Numerous regional dailies in English.

TOURIST BOARDS IN UK/US UK: PO Box 1770, Ashford, Kent, TN24 0ZX, tel (0906) 871 5000, fax (0870) 165 5665, email visitcanada@dial.pipex.com. US: n/a.

> "Such a land is good
> for an energetic man.
> It is also not bad
> for a loafer."
> *Rudyard Kipling, 1908*

CAPE VERDE

WHEN TO GO

WEATHER Generally temperate. The best time to visit is from August to October, when the weather is pleasantly warm. The rest of the year is cooler.

FESTIVALS Cape Verde has one of Africa's most vibrant Carnivals. It's the country's major party, with street parades in February in Praia and also in Mindelo. On São Tiago and Fogo, Tabanka is celebrated in May and June and marked by music and abstinence. Each island also has its own festival, with week-long parties.

TRANSPORT

INTERNATIONAL AIRPORTS Amilcar Cabral (SID) on Sal, 2 km from Espargos.

INTERNAL TRAVEL Ferry service connects Santiago, Fogo and Brava, cargo boats travelling between the islands may also take passengers. About one third of the roads are paved. Car hire is available on the main islands. Driver hire is also available for sightseeing. Buses satisfactory.

RED TAPE

VISAS REQUIRED (UK/US) Required.

VACCINATIONS REQUIRED: See 'Vaccinations required around the world' on page 653.

DRIVING REQUIREMENTS International Driving Permit required.

COUNTRY REPS IN UK/US UK: n/a, nearest: Avenue Jeanne 29, 1050 Brussels, Belgium, tel (2) 643 6270, email emb.caboverde@skynet.be US: 3415 Massachusetts Avenue, NW, Washington, DC 20007, tel (202) 965 6820, fax (202) 965 1207, email ambacvus@verison.net.

UK/US REPS IN COUNTRY UK: c/o Shell Cabo Verde, Sarl, Avenida Amilcar Cabral CP4, São Vincente, tel 232 6625-7, fax 232 6629, email antonio.a.canuto@scv.sims.com. US: CP 201, Rua Abilio, Macedo 6, Praia, Santiago, 261 5616, fax 261 1355, email praiaconsularpraia@state.gov.

PEOPLE AND PLACE

CAPITAL Ciudade de Praia.

LANGUAGE Portuguese.

PEOPLES Mestico, African.

RELIGION Roman Catholic. Protestant minority

SIZE (SQ KM) 4,036.

POPULATION 434,625.

POP DENSITY/KM 112.5.

STATE OF THE NATION

SAFETY Safe.

LIFE EXPECTANCY M 67.13, F 73.86.

BEING THERE

ETIQUETTE The usual European social courtesies should be observed.

CURRENCY Cape Verde *escudo* (CVEsc) = 100 *centavos*..

FINANCE Credit cards rarely used, travellers cheques accepted in main towns.

BUSINESS HOURS 0800-1230, 1430-1800 Monday-Friday.

GMT -1.

VOLTAGE GUIDE 220 AC, 50 Hz.

COUNTRY DIALLING CODE 238.

CONSUMING PLEASURES

FOOD & DRINK Main local speciality is *cachupa,* based on maize and beans. A mix

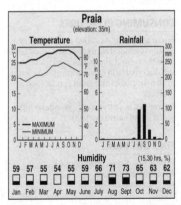

HIGHLIGHTS

SAL Flat desert island, home to the international airport and popular with European package-tourists. It has several good dive schools. Windsurfing is also possible. The settlement at Espargos offers accommodation in a *pensão* and restaurants. Boats run from Sal to Praia around twice a week.

SÃO TIAGO The largest of the country's nine inhabited islands. The principal city is the lively and pleasant capital, Praia, perched on a rocky plateau known as Platõ. Praia has a fun nightlife, while other attractions include the Cidade Velha, the first Portuguese settlement on Cape Verde, and the remains of an old Portuguese fort. At the northern end of the island is the fishing village of Tarrafal, which is known for its fine beaches. Its old colonial prison held dissidents during the rule of the Portuguese dictator, Salazar.

SÃO VICENTE Cape Verde's second most important island and home to its liveliest city, Mindelo, which bustles with the through-flow of ships in the harbour.

BRAVA The smallest of Cape Verde's inhabited islands, it's mountainous and scenic and offers some splendid hiking. The western side of the island also has some good beaches.

SANTO ANTÃO The greenest island in the archipelago. It has a spectacular, hilly and lush interior, offering great hiking. The main trail is up Ribeira Grande Mountain: the walk to the top and back takes most of a day. A ferry connects Santo Antão with Mindelo, but the seas can be rough.

of tuna, onions, tomatoes, pastry, boiled potatoes and corn flour is used to create *pastel com diablo dentro* - pastry with the devil inside. Increasing number of restaurants and cafes. Grogue is a popular alcoholic drink.

SHOPPING & SOUVENIRS Daily markets, selling carved coconut shells, pottery, lacework and basketry.

FIND OUT MORE

WEBSITES www.virtualcapeverde.net, http://capeverde.usembassy.gov.

LOCAL MEDIA No English-language newspapers. One, state-controlled, TV station.

TOURIST BOARDS IN UK/US n/a.

The Cape Verde islands are Africa's most westerly point. First discovered by the Portuguese in the fifteenth century, they have been used ever since as a stop-off point for seafarers and traders between Europe, Africa and Latin America

CENTRAL AFRICAN REPUBLIC

WHEN TO GO

WEATHER Hot all year. The rainy season is from May to October.

FESTIVALS TheCAR celebrates all the Christian festivals, and in the north, all the Muslim ones (dates vary). Tabaski, or Id al Kabir, is the most important celebration in northern central Africa. It also coincides with the end of the pilgrimage to Mecca. Independence Day is celebrated on 13 August.

TRANSPORT

INTERNATIONAL AIRPORTS Bangui M'Poko (BGF), 4 km from the city.

INTERNAL TRAVEL Domestic flying limited to charter planes. Ferries serve towns on the Ubangi River. Good roads connecting main towns, but often impassable during the rainy season. Car hire available.

RED TAPE

VISAS REQUIRED (UK/US) Required.

VACCINATIONS REQUIRED: See 'Vaccinations required around the world' on page 653.

DRIVING REQUIREMENTS International Driving Permit.

COUNTRY REPS IN UK/US UK: n/a, nearest 30 rue des Perchamps, 75016 Paris, France, tel (1) 4224 4256, fax (1) 4251 0021. US: 1618 22nd Street, NW, Washington DC 20008, tel (202) 483 7800, fax (202) 332 9893.

UK/US REPS IN COUNTRY UK: The British Consulate is currently closed. The British High Commission in Yaoundé (see Cameroon) deals with enquiries relating to the Central African Republic. US: BP 924, Avenue David Dacko, Bangui, tel 610 200, fax 614 494, email emb-usa@intnet.cf, not currently open, Yaoundé and N'djamena (see Cameroon and Chad) are dealing with enquiries.

PEOPLE AND PLACE

CAPITAL Bangui.

LANGUAGE French and Sango.

PEOPLES Baya, Banda, Mandija, Sara.

RELIGION Mostly animist. Remainder Christian, and a small Islamic minority.

SIZE (SQ KM) 622,984.

POPULATION 3,819,000.

POP DENSITY/KM 6.1.

STATE OF THE NATION

SAFETY Potentially volatile and subject to occasional *coups d'état*. Banditry on remoter country roads.

LIFE EXPECTANCY M 39.21, F 42.86.

BEING THERE

ETIQUETTE Dress is informal. Care should be taken to dress modestly in Muslim areas, and Muslim customs should be respected and observed. Shorts are also generally frowned upon, and women are expected to dress modestly. Women are strictly segregated, especially in towns. Show caution and discretion when photographing local people and ask for permission.

CURRENCY *Communauté Financiaire Africaine franc* (CFA) = 100 *centimes*.

FINANCE Traveller's cheques and some credit cards accepted.

BUSINESS HOURS 0730-15.30 Mon-Friday.

GMT +1.

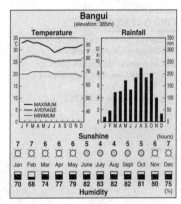

HIGHLIGHTS

BANGUI Located on the banks of the River Ubangi, Bangui has some seedy and dangerous areas, but also a charming administrative district. Shaded by tropical greenery, this capital city has a colourful central market, renowned for malachite necklaces. The Boganda Museum, the Arts and Crafts School, the cathedral and the Saint Paul Mission are other places of interest. The Grande Corniche leads to the banks of the Ubangi and offers a picturesque view of the fishermen's round huts and canoes.

M'BAÏKI A major timber and coffee growing area and also the home of the Lobaye, a forest tribespeople, as well as pygmies. North-east of M'Baïki is a village of *ébonistes*, where you can watch men carving ebony. There is also a lovely waterfall near the town.

BANGASSOU Near the border with the Democratic Republic of the Congo, this large town has a bustling market, selling all kinds of bushmeat, including anteater, buffalo, bush pig, gazelle, monkey and warthog. The town also has the extraordinary Kembe Falls on the River Kotto.

DZANG-SANGHA RESERVE Contains the last remnants of CAR's virgin rainforest and some of the highest densities of lowland gorillas and forest elephants anywhere in Africa, along with many other animal species. Trekking is a popular activity and park entrance fees help to protect the wildlife, assist villagers and pygmies, and preserve the forest.

VOLTAGE GUIDE 220/380 AC, 50 Hz.

COUNTRY DIALLING CODE 236.

CONSUMING PLEASURES

FOOD & DRINK Basic. Street food in towns is simple, burgers and *brochettes* (meat on a skewer). Restaurants serve French and other cuisines but otherwise travellers must call at local villages to barter for provisions. Away from Muslim areas are numerous beer halls, with a high standard product. Two popular drinks are palm wine and banana wine.

SHOPPING & SOUVENIRS Ebony, gold jewellery, butterfly collections, butterfly wing *objets d'art*, handmade goods.

"At Bangui, when I tried to get some films developed, the photographer said: 'It is impossible. The water here is too hot. It would melt your films'."
Negley Farson, 1940

FIND OUT MORE

WEBSITES
www.lonelyplanet.com/worldguide/
destinations/africa/central-african-
republic/

LOCAL MEDIA No English-language newspapers. One, state-owned, TV channel.

TOURIST BOARDS IN UK/US n/a.

CHAD

WHEN TO GO

WEATHER Hot, tropical climate. Rainy season in the south from May-October, in the central region from June-September. Very little rain in the north.

FESTIVALS Celebrations in Chad are confined to religious events, such as Muslim feasts, or ceremonies performed by indigenous tribes. N'Djamena has a modern ritual on Sundays where a bar is booked by a young woman or group of women who hope to profit from alcohol sales to friends and whoever else may join them. It is known as a *pari-match*.

TRANSPORT

INTERNATIONAL AIRPORTS N'Djaména (NDJ) 4 km from the city.

INTERNAL TRAVEL Some internal flights accepting cash payment only. Many roads need urgent repairs. Travelling outside N'Djaména only possible with 4-wheel-drives. Permits are usually needed. Due to security conditions and a lack of food, petrol and vehicle repair facilities, the government has prohibited travel in some parts of the country.

RED TAPE

VISAS REQUIRED (UK/US) Required.

VACCINATIONS REQUIRED: See 'Vaccinations required around the world' on page 653.

DRIVING REQUIREMENTS International Driving Permit and official *autorisation de circuler*.

COUNTRY REPS IN UK/US UK: n/a, nearest 65 rue des Belles Feuilles, 75116 Paris, France, tel (1) 4553 3675, fax (1) 4553 1609. US: 2002 R Street, NW, Washington, DC 20009, tel (202) 462 4009, fax (202) 265 1937, email info@chadembassy.org.

UK/US REPS IN COUNTRY UK: The British High Commission in Yaoundé (see Cameroon) deals with enquiries relating to Chad. US: BP 413, avenue Félix Eboué, N'Djaména, tel 517 009, fax 515 654, email consularndjame@state.gov.

PEOPLE AND PLACE

CAPITAL Ndjaména.

LANGUAGE French, Arabic, 50 indigenous languages.

PEOPLES Sara, Toubou, Peul-Fulani, Tuareg.

RELIGION Muslim, traditional beliefs, Christian.

SIZE (SQ KM) 1,284,000.

POPULATION 8,348,000.

POP DENSITY/KM 6.5.

STATE OF THE NATION

SAFETY Potentially dangerous. Seek latest information at time of visit.

LIFE EXPECTANCY M 46.84, F 49.09.

BEING THERE

ETIQUETTE Relaxed and friendly on the whole, Chadians expect their traditional beliefs and customs to be respected. Though dress is informal it is also conservative in respect of Muslim laws. Do not use the left hand to offer or accept food, or expose the sole of the foot in a Muslim's presence. Always carry identification.

CURRENCY *Communauté Financiaire Africaine franc* (CFA) = 100 *centimes*.

FINANCE Traveller's cheques, Diners Club and MasterCard accepted on a limited basis.

BUSINESS HOURS 0700-1530 Mon-Thurs, 0700-1200 Friday.

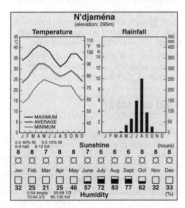

N'djaména
(elevation: 295m)

Temperature — Rainfall — Sunshine — Humidity chart for N'djaména.

HIGHLIGHTS

N'DJAMÉNA Once one of central Africa's liveliest cities, the capital has been rebuilding its reputation since the recent war. Bullet holes in the buildings still remind people of bad times past, but also serve to show that the mood now is more optimistic. A colourful daily market in the historic quarter is a great place for finding vividly coloured rugs and jewellery. The National Museum has collections of similar items dating to the Sarh culture, which lived in the area in the ninth century. Visitors will quickly notice the difference between the quiet Arab section of town, and the southern area, full of lively bars and nightlife.

TIBESTI MOUNTAINS This astonishing landscape of chasms and crags, seldom seen by non-Muslims, and still closed to travellers, is home to the world's best racing camels and the fierce Toubou tribe, distantly related to the Tuareg of the Western Sahara, made famous by Herodotus as 'Troglodytes' or cave dwellers. Their underground homes were sure to be cool in summer and warm in winter.

ABÉCHÉ Surrounded by desert, this town was once the capital of the powerful Ouadaï sultanate. It retains its oriental charms with beautiful mosques, old bazaars, and narrow cobbled streets.

LAKE CHAD Once the centre of Africa's lucrative salt trade, the area is now sparsely populated, and the lake is shrinking. It is best visited between August and December, when hippos and crocodiles can be spotted in the higher water levels.

GMT +1.

VOLTAGE GUIDE 220/380 AC, 50 Hz.

COUNTRY DIALLING CODE 235.

CONSUMING PLEASURES

FOOD & DRINK French and African, grilled meat and fish at stalls, *tiéboudienne* (fish with mixed vegetables and rice). Shortages of some foodstuffs outside the capital. *Gala* is the excellent locally produced beer.

SHOPPING & SOUVENIRS Camel hair carpets, leatherware, embroidery, calabashes, knives, weapons, pottery, brass animal figures.

FIND OUT MORE

WEBSITES www.chadembassy.org, http://ndjamena.usembassy.gov, www.lonelyplanet.com/worldguide/destinations/africa/chad.

LOCAL MEDIA No English-language papers. One, state-owned, TV channel.

TOURIST BOARDS IN UK/US n/a.

One of the world's poorest countries, with a *per capita* income of US$200 a year, Chad has been hampered by civil war, poor infrastructure, few natural resources and natural droughts. Seventy percent of the population are subsistence farmers

CHILE

WHEN TO GO

WEATHER Hot and arid in the north. Very cold in the far south. Central areas have a mild Mediterranean climate with a wet season from May to August. Beyond Montt in the south is one of the stormiest, wettest areas in the world.

FESTIVALS The Easter and Christmas holidays are the most important celebrations. There are also many secular holidays, including Independence Day in September, a day of partying and rodeos.
At the Fiesta de la Virgin del Rosario held each December in Andacollo, pilgrims follow a colourful procession of the Virgin's image to a huge shrine, while vast crowds camped on surrounding hills watch horse races and cock fights.

TRANSPORT

INTERNATIONAL AIRPORTS Santiago (SCL), 21 km from the city.

INTERNAL TRAVEL Frequent air services between main towns. The state railway runs throughout Chile, from Santiago to Puerto Montt in the south. The Pan American Highway runs from the Peruvian border to Puerto Montt. Although most of the roads in Chile are in good condition, it is advisable in remoter areas to carry spare petrol and a spare tyre. Car hire available in major towns.

RED TAPE

VISAS REQUIRED (UK/US) None.

VACCINATIONS REQUIRED: See 'Vaccinations required around the world' on page 653.

DRIVING REQUIREMENTS International or Inter-American Driving Permit.

COUNTRY REPS IN UK/US
UK: 12 Devonshire Street, London W1G 7DS, tel (020) 7580 6392, fax (020) 7436 5204, email embachile@embachile.co.uk. US: Suite 601, 6th Floor, 866 United Nations Plaza, New York, NY 10017, tel (212) 980 3366, fax (212) 888 5288, email recepcion@chileny.com.

UK/US REPS IN COUNTRY UK: Casilla 72D, Avenida el Bosque Norte 0125, Las Condes, Santiago, tel (2) 370 4100, fax (2) 370 4170, email embsan@britemb.cl. US: Avenida Andrés Bello 2800, Las Condes, Santiago, tel (2) 232 2600, fax (2) 330 3710.

PEOPLE AND PLACE

CAPITAL Santiago.

LANGUAGE Spanish.

PEOPLES Mixed Spanish-Indian descent, European, Indian.

RELIGION Roman Catholic.

SIZE (SQ KM) 756,096.

POPULATION 15,589,147.

POP DENSITY/KM 20.

STATE OF THE NATION

SAFETY Safe.

LIFE EXPECTANCY M 73.3, F 80.03.

BEING THERE

ETIQUETTE Most Chileans use a double surname and only the first part should be used in addressing them. Normal courtesies should be observed when visiting local people. Informal, conservative clothes are acceptable in most places, but women should not wear shorts outside resort areas.

CURRENCY Chilean *peso* (*peso*) = 100 centavos.

FINANCE Major credit cards accepted. May

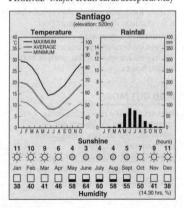

HIGHLIGHTS

TORRES DEL PAINE Explore this beautiful national park in southern Chile, noted for its many lakes, waterfalls, glaciers and rocky peaks, and the centrepiece of which are the majestic 2,000-metre granite pillars that give the park its name. You can also try to spot the Patagonian guanaco in its native habitat.

SANTIAGO Watch the world go by in this bustling cosmopolitan capital, or in winter head out to the *cordillera* ski fields at Valle Nevado and Portillo to tackle some of the highest commercial peaks in the world.

SAN PEDRO DE ATACAMA Explore the bizarre lunar landscapes surrounding this charming town in the heart of the Atacama Desert, one of the driest places on earth.

PUCON Get active in the adventure sports centre of the country, located in the heart of Chile's fabulous Lake District. The scenic region of lush farmland, dense forest, snow-capped volcanoes, waterfalls and clear lakes, offers superb whitewater rafting, fishing, horse riding, mountain biking, and the chance to spot the rare puma.

EASTER ISLAND Stand beneath one of the colossal and mysterious stone *moais* on Rapa Nui, as the world's most remote inhabitable island (3,790 kilometres west of the Chilean mainland) is known: all the while, wondering just how these giant structures got here.

LA SERENA Beachside city with a colonial air, beautiful stretches of beach, a handful of museums and pretty villages and vineyards nearby.

---

be some difficulty changing traveller's cheques outside major towns.

BUSINESS HOURS 0900-1830.

GMT -5..

VOLTAGE GUIDE 220AC, 50Hz.

COUNTRY DIALLING CODE 56.

LOCAL MEDIA No English-language but foreign papers available.

TOURIST BOARDS IN UK/US n/a.

CONSUMING PLEASURES

FOOD & DRINK Typical national dishes include *empanadas* (filled pastries), *humitas* (seasoned corn paste, wrapped in corn husks and boiled), *cazuela de ave* (soup with rice, vegetables, chicken and herbs) Meat and seafood of good quality. Chile is well known for its wine, and for *pisco*, a powerful grape liqueur.

SHOPPING & SOUVENIRS Handwoven ponchos, vicuna rugs, copper work, lapis lazuli, jade, amethyst, agate and onyx.

FIND OUT MORE

WEBSITES www.echileuk.demon.co.uk, www.britemb.cl, www.chile-usa.org, www.chileny.com, www.usembassy.cl.

> "I can see how puzzling a country can be that starts at the frozen South Pole and stretches upwards to salt mines and desert where it hasn't rained for eons."
>
> *Pablo Neruda*

CHINA

WHEN TO GO

WEATHER Great diversity of climates. The north-east has hot, dry summers and bitterly cold winters. The north and central region has almost continuous rainfall, hot summers and cold winters. The south-east has substantial rainfall, semi-tropical summers and cool winters.

FESTIVALS Most festivals follow the Chinese lunar calendar. The Spring Festival is celebrated during the first two weeks of the new lunar year. March sees the celebration of Guanyin's birthday, China's most popular deity. Mid-April is time for the Water Splashing Festival in Yunnan Province. The Dragon-boat Festival, where races are held in memory of Qu Yuan, a poet who drowned himself in 280 BC, takes place in June or July. The Moon Festival is held in September or October, a time for family reunion.

TRANSPORT

INTERNATIONAL AIRPORTS Beijing/Peking (BSJ/PEK), 26 km from the city, Guangzhou/Canton (Baiyun) 7 km from the city, Shanghai (SHA) 12 km from the city.

INTERNAL TRAVEL Most long-distance internal travel is by air. Ferries serve major rivers. Railways are the principal means of transport for people and goods. Eighty per cent of settlements can be reached by road. These are not always of good quality, and vehicles should be reliable as mechanical services are few. Car hire is available.

RED TAPE

VISAS REQUIRED (UK/US) Required.

VACCINATIONS REQUIRED: See 'Vaccinations required around the world' on page 653.

DRIVING REQUIREMENTS Car-hire companies hold on to passports, better to hire car and driver.

COUNTRY REPS IN UK/US UK: 49-51 Portland Place, London W1B 1JL, tel (020) 7299 8426, fax (020) 7436 9178, email press@chinese-embassy.org.uk. US: 2300 Connecticut Avenue, NW, Washington, DC 20008, tel (202) 328 2500, fax (202) 328 2582, email chinaembassy_us@fmprc.gov.cn.

UK/US REPS IN COUNTRY UK: 11 Guang Hua Lu, Jian Guo Men Wai, Beijing 100600, tel (10) 5192 4000, fax (10) 6532 1937/8/9, email commercialmail@beijing.fco.gov.uk. US: 3 Xiu Shui Bei Jie, Beijing 100600, tel (10) 6532 3831, fax (10) 6532 5141, emailbeijingwebmaster@state.gov.

PEOPLE AND PLACE

CAPITAL Beijing.

LANGUAGE Mandarin Chinese.

PEOPLES Han, Hui, Zhaung.

RELIGION Buddhism, Confucianism, Daoism.

SIZE (SQ KM) 9,572,900.

POPULATION 1,284,530,000.

POP DENSITY/KM 134.2.

STATE OF THE NATION

SAFETY Safe.

LIFE EXPECTANCY M 70.65, F 74.09.

BEING THERE

ETIQUETTE Generally reserved in manner, be courteous. If applauded as a welcome, applaud back. Anger should be concealed. Arrive to meetings early. Bring gifts when invited into homes.

CURRENCY *Renminbi yuan* (RMBY)

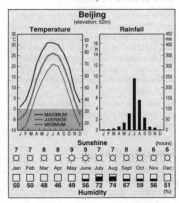

HIGHLIGHTS

THE GREAT WALL OF CHINA Walk along this vast structure which runs from the east coast to the Gobi desert. Most visitors start at Badaling, 70 kilometres from Beijing.

TERRACOTTA WARRIORS Wander among 6,000 life-size statues buried 2,000 years ago .

THE FORBIDDEN CITY Visit the palaces of the ancient emperors in Beijing, off-limits for 500 years but now open to all.

YELLOW MOUNTAINS Enjoy breath-taking views among the craggy, cloud-clad peaks of the sacred Huang Shan region of Anhui province, surrounded by paddy fields and villages.

SHANGHAI Glimpse the future in this frenetic city, whose skyscraper skyline embodies China's drive to modernity.

INNER MONGOLIA Take a tour of the vast 'grass sea' of Inner Mongolia, setting off from Hohhot. Nomads on horseback pursue their age-old lifestyle and visitors can stay in their traditional *yurts*.

HONG KONG Popular with tourists and a major business centre, it has become an eclectic mix of skyscrapers, colonial buildings and traditional temples.

= 10 *chiao/jiao* or 100 *fen*.

FINANCE Major credit cards and traveller's cheques accepted by designated establishments in major provincial cities .

BUSINESS HOURS 0800-1130, 1300-1700, Monday-Friday.

GMT +8.

VOLTAGE GUIDE 220/240 AC, 50 Hz.

COUNTRY DIALLING CODE 86.

CONSUMING PLEASURES

FOOD & DRINK Diverse regional styles. In the north, Mongolian Hotpots are popular, eaten in a communal style with meats and vegetables being cooked, fondue style, in a pot of simmering soup. Beijing is famous for Peking Duck. Southern cuisine is probably the most exotic - markets in Guangzhou are full of the various (sometimes endangered) animals used. The east is noted for rich, sweet cooking, seafood, hot and sour soup, noodles and vegetables. In the west, spicy, peppery food is a speciality.

SHOPPING & SOUVENIRS Jade jewellery, embroidery, calligraphy, paintings and carvings on wood, stone, bamboo. Prices set by government. No bargaining except in outdoor market stalls selling items such as antique ceramics and silk. Keep receipts, may be needed at customs.

FIND OUT MORE

WEBSITES www.chinese-embassy.org.uk, http://manchester.chineseconsulate.org/eng www.cnta.gov.cn, www.uk.cn, www.china-embassy.org, www.discoverchinaforever.com, www.usembassy-china.org.cn, www.chinadaily.com.cn, www.chinaoninternet.com, www.chinatoday.com, www.flashpaper.com/beijing.

LOCAL MEDIA *China Daily* and weekly news magazine *Beijing Review* are published in English.

TOURIST BOARDS IN UK/US UK: 71 Warwick Road, London SW5 9HB, tel (020) 7373 0888, fax (020) 7370 9989, email london@cnta.gov.cn. US: Suite 6413, 350 Fifth Avenue, New York, NY 10118, tel (212) 760 8218, fax (212) 760 8809, email info@cnto.org

" China? There lies a sleeping giant. Let him sleep! For when he wakes he will move the world."

Napoleon Bonaparte

COLOMBIA

WHEN TO GO

WEATHER Very warm and tropical on the coast and in the north, with a rainy season from May-November. Cooler in the uplands and cold in the mountains. Bogotá has cool days and crisp nights.

FESTIVALS Carnaval de Blancos y Negros, held in Pasto in January. Carnival del Diablo is a biennial festival in January in Riosucio, Cartagena stages the Festival Internacional de Música del Caribe in March. Bogotá has a biennial celebration in April for the Festival Iberoamericano de Teatro. August sees Medellín celebrate the Feria de las Flores. Many other festivals are held in this party-loving country.

TRANSPORT

INTERNATIONAL AIRPORTS Bogotá (El Dorado) (BOG) 12 km from the city, Barranquilla (BAQ) 10 km from the city, Cali (CLO) 19 km from the city, Cartagena (CTG) 2 km from the city.

INTERNAL TRAVEL Excellent internal air network. Inter-city passenger rail services virtually non-existent. Good highways and other roads usually passable except during rainy seasons. Car hire available but driving in cities not recommended.

RED TAPE

VISAS REQUIRED (UK/US) None.

VACCINATIONS REQUIRED: See 'Vaccinations required around the world' on page 653.

DRIVING REQUIREMENTS International Driving Permit.

COUNTRY REPS IN UK/US UK: 3rd Floor, 35 Portland Place, London W1B 1AE, tel (020) 7637 9893, fax (020) 7637 5604, email info@colombianconsulate.co.uk. US: 2118 Leroy Place, NW, Washington, DC 20008, tel (202) 387 8338, fax (202) 232 8643, email enwas@colombiaemb.org.

UK/US REPS IN COUNTRY UK: Carrera 9, No 76-49, Piso 8-10, Bogotá, DC, tel (1) 326 8300, fax (1) 326 8302, email bogota.info@fco.gov.uk US: Calle 22D-bis, 47-51, Santa Fe de Bogotá, DC, tel (1) 315 0811, fax (1) 315 2197, email nib@estate.gov.

PEOPLE AND PLACE

CAPITAL Santa Fe de Bogotá.

LANGUAGE Spanish.

PEOPLES Mestizo, European, European-African, Black Amerindian, African.

RELIGION Roman Catholic.

SIZE (SQ KM) 1,141,748.

POPULATION 44,583,577.

POP DENSITY/KM 39.

STATE OF THE NATION

SAFETY Very unsafe, kidnapping and violence are commonplace. Do not accept sweets or drinks from strangers (even Westerners), they may be drugged. Many areas are subject to guerrilla warfare or covert activities (cocaine-growing, emerald-mining) and should be avoided.

LIFE EXPECTANCY M 67.88, F 75.7.

BEING THERE

ETIQUETTE Offer guests *tinto*, well sugared black coffee. Spanish culture is seen in much of the country, but in Bogotá, North American attitudes are prevalent.

CURRENCY Colombian *peso (peso)* = 100 *centavos*.

FINANCE Major credit cards accepted,

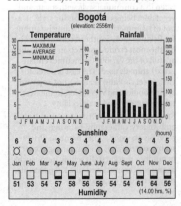

HIGHLIGHTS

Bogotá Blending Colombian tradition, Spanish colonial influence, and a liking for North American attitudes, the capital has a number of historical landmarks to visit. The Capitol Municipal Palace, the monumental neoclassical cathedral on the Plaza Bolivar, and the Gold Museum are all of interest.

Caribbean Coast With a 1,600-kilometre Caribbean coastline, most hotels are found near Santa Marta, one of the first Spanish cities founded in South America. Modern hotels and fashionable white sandy beaches draw the crowds, and provide a base to explore the coast. Beyond the resort is the Tayrona National Park, an area of deep bays, coral reefs, and beautiful beaches shaded by coconut trees.

Cartagena The ancient walled fortress city is deserving of its glorification in books and on canvas over time. The country's most fascinating city, unique to South America, was founded in 1533. Any visit requires several days to savour its beauty.

The Amazon Basin Covering nearly a third of Colombia's land, the dense tropical forest has few roads and is inhabited by Indians. Travellers should explore via Leticia, with well-developed tourist facilities on the banks of the Amazon near Brazil and Peru. Trips into the jungle of Amacayu National Park can easily be made from there.

San Augustin Archaeological Park A place of archaeological wonder, home to numerous relics and enormous stone statues.

Traveller's cheques difficult to change in smaller towns.

Business hours 0800-1200, 1400-1700 Monday-Friday.

GMT -5..

Voltage guide 110/120 AC, 60 Hz.

Country dialling code 57.

CONSUMING PLEASURES

Food & drink Varied, Spanish influenced local cuisine. Specialities include *ajiaco* (chicken stew served with cream, corn on the cob and capers) and *bandeja paisa* (meat dish with cassava, rice, fried plantain and red beans). Notable lobsters and seafood served on the Caribbean coast. Different types of rum are produced, *canelazo*, a rum-based cocktail, is drunk hot or cold.

Shopping & souvenirs Local handicrafts, cotton, wooden goods, leather goods, blankets, travel bags, reproduction ancient Colombian jewellery, emeralds.

FIND OUT MORE

Websites www.colombianembassy.co.uk, www.colombianconsulate.co.uk, www.britain.gov.co, www.colombiaemb.org, http://bogota.usembassy.gov, www.poorbuthappy.com/colombia.

Local media No English-language newspapers. Four TV channels, one state-owned.

Tourist boards in UK/US n/a.

Colombia is home to the wettest place on Earth: Lloro averages 523 inches of rainfall a year – more than 40 feet. That is 10 times more than what we would call wet cities in Britain or the United States

COMOROS

WHEN TO GO

WEATHER Warm and tropical with a hot and rainy season from November to May. This includes a tropical monsoonal wind called *kashkazi*, or cyclone. It is cooler and dryer from June to October.

FESTIVALS Most of the events on Comoros are connected to Islamic holy days, the dates of which differ from year to year. Of central importance is Ramadan, the traditional period of fasting for the Islamic world. Id-ul-Fitr, which marks the new moon, and signals the end of Ramadan, is also a time of celebration. Mayotte celebrates both Muslim holidays and the European holidays of Bastille Day, on 14 July, and Christmas Day, on 25 December.

TRANSPORT

INTERNATIONAL AIRPORTS Moroni International Prince Said Ibrahim (HAH), 25 km from the city.

INTERNAL TRAVEL Air and ferry connections between the islands. All the islands have tarred roads, 4-wheel-drive vehicles advisable for outlying islands and in the interior, particularly during the rainy season. Many roads are narrow and domestic animals roam freely, so drive slowly.

RED TAPE

VISAS REQUIRED (UK/US) Required.

VACCINATIONS REQUIRED: See 'Vaccinations required around the world' on page 653.

DRIVING REQUIREMENTS International Driving Permit required.

COUNTRY REPS IN UK/US UK: n/a, nearest 20 rue Marbeau, 75016 Paris, France, tel (1) 4067 9054. US: 866 United Nations Plaza, Suite 418, New York, NY 10017, tel (212) 750 1637, fax (212) 750 1657, email comoros@un.int.

UK/US REPS IN COUNTRY UK: The British Embassy in Antananarivo (see Madagascar) deals with enquiries relating to Comoros. US: The American Embassy in Port Louis (see Mauritius) deals with enquiries relating to Comoros.

PEOPLE AND PLACE

CAPITAL Moroni.

LANGUAGE French and Arabic.

PEOPLES Mainly mixed race, with Polynesians, Africans, Indonesians, Persians, Arabs, Europeans and Indians.

RELIGION Sunni Muslim (98%).

SIZE (SQ KM) 1,862.

POPULATION 747,000.

POP DENSITY/KM 401.2.

STATE OF THE NATION

SAFETY Safe.

LIFE EXPECTANCY M 59.65, F 64.33.

BEING THERE

ETIQUETTE Religious customs associated with Islam should be respected. Although Comorans are tolerant towards other cultures (for instance, alcohol is not banned and is available in hotels and restaurants), they expect moderate behaviour from non Muslim visitors, such as non consumption of alcohol in public places and modest dress.

CURRENCY Comoros *franc* (Cfr) = 100 *centimes*.

FINANCE Limited acceptance of credit cards and traveller's cheques.

BUSINESS HOURS 0730-1430 Mon-Thurs, 0730-1100 Fri, 0730-1200 Saturday.

GMT +3.

VOLTAGE GUIDE 220 AC, 50 Hz.

COUNTRY DIALLING CODE 269.

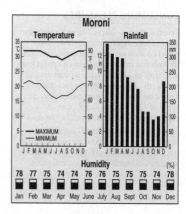

Moroni

Humidity											(%)
78	77	75	74	74	76	76	75	75	75	74	78
Jan	Feb	Mar	Apr	May	June	July	Aug	Sept	Oct	Nov	Dec

HIGHLIGHTS

NGAZIDJA Largest of the islands, characterised by grassy plains, remnants of rainforest and the still-active volcano, Mount Karthala - into the crater of which it is possible to climb. The volcano is claimed to be the largest still active anywhere in the world. Also known as Grande Comore, Ngazidja has some fine beaches of black lava or white sand, as well as coral reefs. The west coast is a buzzy mix of resorts, casinos, bars and French-style restaurants.

NDZUANI Also known as Anjouan, this beautiful island could be an advertisement for tropical island living. Forests, rivers, fields of exotic oils - ylang ylang, jasmine and orange flower, among others. However, soil erosion and deforestation are a threat.

MORONI Peaceful capital, located on Ngazidja, with some broad squares and modern government buildings, together with old, narrow, winding streets and a market place. It also has some fine mosques, including the Vendredi Mosque, which affords a great view of the surrounding landscape.

MAYOTTE French-administered island, close to the Comoros. It is surrounded by coral reef and has good beaches and excellent scuba diving facilities. Another attraction is the lagoon, claimed to be the largest in the world, and best explored by canoe.

MITSOUDJÉ This is a good place in which to pick up locally-made handicrafts, particularly hand-carved items such as candle holders and small plaques.

CONSUMING PLEASURES

FOOD & DRINK Spiced sauces, rice-based dishes, barbecued meat (mostly goat), plentiful seafood and tropical fruits, cassava, plantain, couscous. There may be restrictions on alcohol within Muslim circles.

SHOPPING & SOUVENIRS Gold, pearls, shell jewellery, woven cloth, embroidered skull caps (*koffia*) and slippers, pottery, basketry.

FIND OUT MORE

WEBSITES www.un.int/comoros, www.ksu.edu/sasw/comoros/comoros.html

LOCAL MEDIA No English-language papers. One, state-owned, TV channel, some independent radio stations and one under state control.

TOURIST BOARDS IN UK/US n/a.

Some 65 per cent of the world's perfume essence comes from the Comoros, the principal scents coming from locally harvested ylang ylang, jasmine and orange

CONGO (BRAZZAVILLE)

WHEN TO GO

WEATHER Equatorial climate. Short rains October-December and long rains between mid-January and mid-May. Main dry season from June-September.

FESTIVALS Public holidays are held throughout the year. President's Day is held on 5 February, Congolese Women's Day on 8 March, and Independence day on 15 August.

TRANSPORT

INTERNATIONAL AIRPORTS Brazzaville (BZR) 4 km from the city, Pointe-Noire (PNR) 5.5 km from the city.

INTERNAL TRAVEL Regular air services between Brazzaville and Pointe-Noire. Rivers vital to inland transport and are served by steamers. Rail services can be erratic. Roads are sandy in the dry season and impassable in the wet, only suitable for 4-wheel-drive vehicles. Poorly marked army checkpoints throughout the country. Road travel at night can be dangerous. Several car-hire firms in Brazzaville.

RED TAPE

VISAS REQUIRED (UK/US) Required.

VACCINATIONS REQUIRED: See 'Vaccinations required around the world' on page 653.

DRIVING REQUIREMENTS International Driving Permit.

COUNTRY REPS IN UK/US UK: Arena, 24 |southwark Bridge Road, London SE1 9HF, tel (020) 7922 0695, fax (020) 7401 2566. US: 4891 Colorado Avenue, NW, Washington, DC 20011, tel (202) 726 0825, fax (202) 726 1860.

UK/US REPS IN COUNTRY UK: Et-Lisa Avenue Foch (a cote de DHL), Brazzaville, tel 620 893, fax 838 543, email vorick@congonet.cg, th e British Embassy in Kinshasha (see Congo (Dem Rep)) deals with most enquiries. US: n/a.

PEOPLE AND PLACE

CAPITAL Brazzaville.

LANGUAGE French.

PEOPLES Bakongo, Sangha, Teke, Mbochi.

RELIGION Animist, Roman Catholic.

SIZE (SQ KM) 342,000.

POPULATION 3,633,000.

POP DENSITY/KM 10.6.

STATE OF THE NATION

SAFETY Politically volatile and subject to periodic rebellions. Seek latest information at time of visit.

LIFE EXPECTANCY M 47.94, F 50.04.

BEING THERE

ETIQUETTE Mini-skirts and shorts should not be worn in public places, otherwise dress is casual and informal. Do not photograph public buildings. A knowledge of French is essential, as good translators are hard to find.

CURRENCY *Communauté Financiare Africaine franc* (CFA) = 100 *centimes*.

FINANCE Traveller's cheques. Limited use of Master Card and Diners Club cards.

BUSINESS HOURS 0700-1400 Mon-Friday, 0700-1200 Saturday.

GMT +1.

VOLTAGE GUIDE 220 AC, 50 Hz.

COUNTRY DIALLING CODE 242.

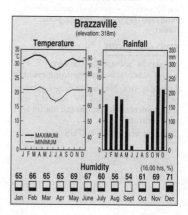

Brazzaville
(elevation: 318m)

Humidity										(16.00 hrs, %)	
65	66	65	65	69	67	60	56	54	61	69	71
Jan	Feb	Mar	Apr	May	June	July	Aug	Sept	Oct	Nov	Dec

HIGHLIGHTS

BRAZZAVILLE The colourful capital lies to the west side of Malebo Pool on the River Congo. A number of attractive sites should be visited by the traveller including the impressive Basilique Sainte Anne, the vivid suburb of Poto Poto, the mystical Temple mosque, the National Museum, and the lush Municipal gardens. Also of note is the house built for Charles de Gaulle during the war years when Brazzaville was the capital of Free France.

SOUTH OF BRAZZAVILLE Situated six kilometres south of the capital are the Congo Rapids, the Loufoulakari Falls and the Trou de Dieu, which has panoramic views of this awesome landscape.

THE COAST A number of good beaches, part of the Côte Sauvage, are located around the town of Pointe-Noire, home to a lively evening market. Along the coast is Loango, the main departure point for the two million slaves transported from here.

GORGES OF DIOSSO Here the sea and wind have combined to form dramatic cliffs, battered by nature.

THE NORTH Travel north from Brazzaville for 150 kilometres and you will arrive in the historic village of M'Bé, once the capital of King Makoko. Lac Bleu, with plenty of good fishing opportunities, is also situated here. Huge swathes of untouched forest bursting with wildlife and a number of indigenous tribes still living the traditional life, are found in the north country.

CONSUMING PLEASURES

FOOD & DRINK African dishes include *Mouamba* chicken in palm oil, palm cabbage salad and cassava leaves, *Saka Saka* (ground cassava leaves cooked with palm oil and peanut paste) and *Maboke* (fresh water fish cooked in large marantacee leaves). Excellent fish, giant oysters and shrimps on the coast. French cuisine in restaurants.

SHOPPING & SOUVENIRS Local paintings, carved wooden masks and figures, pottery.

FIND OUT MORE

WEBSITES www.congoweb.net.
LOCAL MEDIA No English-language papers. One, state-controlled, TV station.
TOURIST BOARDS IN UK/US n/a.

Sixty per cent of Congo's land mass is covered in tropical forest, half of which may be exploited economically. Yet Congo still relies on large amounts of imported foods.

CONGO (DEMOCRATIC REPUBLIC)

WHEN TO GO

WEATHER The dry season in the north is from December to March, in the south from May to October. Warm temperatures and high humidity throughout the year.

FESTIVALS Public holidays take place at various points in the year. They include Liberation Day on 17 May and Independence Day on 30 June.

TRANSPORT

INTERNATIONAL AIRPORTS Kinshasa (FIH) 25 km from the city.

INTERNAL TRAVEL Indefinite restrictions for tourist travel. Overland journeys by local public transport, hitch-hiking, or by foreign vehicle or motorcycle are forbidden. Over 40 internal airports, small planes may be available for charter. River and rail services available. Roads are among the worst in Africa. Hijackings/vehicle thefts at gunpoint do occur. Limited car hire available at the airport.

RED TAPE

VISAS REQUIRED (UK/US) Required.

VACCINATIONS REQUIRED: See 'Vaccinations required around the world' on page 653.

DRIVING REQUIREMENTS International Driving Permit.

COUNTRY REPS IN UK/US UK: 281 Gray's Inn Road, London WC1 X8QF, tel (020) 7278 9825, fax (020) 7833 9967. US: 1726 M Street, Suite 601, NW, Washington, DC 20036, tel (202) 234 7690/1, fax (202) 234 2609.

UK/US REPS IN COUNTRY UK: 83 avenue Roi Baudouin, Kinshasa-Gombe, tel (98) 169 100/111/200, fax (88) 46102, email ambrit@ic.cd. US: 310 Avenue des Aviateurs, Kinshasa-Gombe, tel (81) 225 5872, fax (81) 301 0560, email AEKinshasaConsular@state.gov.

PEOPLE AND PLACE

CAPITAL Kinshasa.

LANGUAGE Officially French, many African languages used.

PEOPLES Bantu, Hamitic, Nilotic.

RELIGION Traditional beliefs, Roman Catholic, Protestant.

SIZE (KM) 2,344,885.

POPULATION 51,201,000.

POP DENSITY/KM 21.8.

STATE OF THE NATION

SAFETY Highly unsafe. Continuing civil war in some areas. Lawlessness widespread.

LIFE EXPECTANCY M 47.29, F 51.47.

BEING THERE

ETIQUETTE There are more than 200 ethnic groups in DRC and recent conflicts have shown that many of these groups are far from friendly with each other. Some 50 percent of the population adhere to animist beliefs. The rest are mostly Christian, while Muslims make up 10 per cent of the population. Photography: a permit is required, but local authorities may still be sensitive.

CURRENCY *Franc Congolais* (FC) = 1000 *centimes.*

FINANCE Very limited use of MasterCard and Visa. Traveller's cheques are generally not recommended.

BUSINESS HOURS 0730-1500 Mon-Friday.

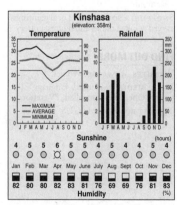

HIGHLIGHTS

KINSHASA There aren't too many sights of historic interest in the DRC's capital, however the prehistoric and ethological museums at Kinshasa University are worth a look. Nearby there is a pretty corner of equatorial forest surrounding a beautiful lake called Ma Vallée, with a tavern on its banks. Other attractions include the fish market in Kinkole and the Gardens of the Presidential Farm of Nsele, which has pools popular with anglers and swimmers.

UPEMBA NATIONAL PARK Straddling the River Lualaba, this lush national park has several lakes, inhabited by crocodiles and aquatic bird species. They live alongside local fishermen, cattle farmers and peasants.

GARAMBA NATIONAL PARK Large reserve in the north of the country. Home to lions, leopards, rhinos and giraffes, if any remain.

BUNIA Small, pretty town with pleasant villas, restaurants and hotels. From here, it's a short hop off to the region's mountains and forests, as well as Lake Albert - which contains more fish than any other lake in Africa.

CONGO RIVER The country's defining geographic feature, this mighty waterway is the real highway of central Africa. Jump aboard a barge in Kinshasa and travel inland to Kisangani to experience the buzz of life on the water.

RUWENZORI RANGE Scenic mountain range, of which Pic Marguerite is the highest peak, at 5,119 metres tall. The region is populated by mountain gorillas and the rare okapi.

GMT From +1 to +2.

VOLTAGE GUIDE 220 AC, 50 Hz.

COUNTRY DIALLING CODE 243.

CONSUMING PLEASURES

FOOD & DRINK National specialities include *moambe* chicken, cooked in palm oil with rice and spinach. Restaurants in Kinshasa and Lubumashi serving French, Belgian and local cuisine can be good but are expensive, catering essentially for business people.

SHOPPING & SOUVENIRS Bracelets, ebony carvings, paintings.

FIND OUT MORE

WEBSITES http://usembassy.state.gov/kinshasa, www.cia.gov/cia/publications/factbook/geos/cg.html

LOCAL MEDIA No English-language papers.

TOURIST BOARDS IN UK/US n/a.

> "Nothing could be more quintessentially the heart of tropical Africa."
> *John Gunther, 1955*

COSTA RICA

WHEN TO GO

WEATHER Temperatures in the Central Valley average at 22C. Much hotter in the coastal areas. Rainy season May-November, dry season December-May.

FESTIVALS March sees one thousand people run from San José to Villa Colón, as part of the Carrera de la Paz. At the same time 500 different species are part of the National Orchid Show in Sabana Sur. Again in March, a Craft Fair on the Plaza de la Cultura sees 150 to 200 artists display their works. 1, 500 people run the Carrera de San Juan to San Juan de Tibás. The Freedom Torch is relayed around the country on 15 September, Independence Day. December is the liveliest time, for Christmas celebrations, and bull fights are also held then.

TRANSPORT

INTERNATIONAL AIRPORTS Juan Santamaria (SJO) 17 km from the city.

INTERNAL TRAVEL Some internal flights - reservations cannot be made outside Costa Rica. Standard of roads generally good. Car hire available in San José.

RED TAPE

VISAS REQUIRED (UK/US) None.

VACCINATIONS REQUIRED: See 'Vaccinations required around the world' on page 653.

DRIVING REQUIREMENTS International Driving Permit or national driving licence.

COUNTRY REPS IN UK/US UK: Flat 1, 14 Lancaster Gate, London W2 3LH, tel (020) 7706 8844, fax (020) 7706 8655, email costarica@btconnect.com. US: 2114 S Street, NW, Washington, DC 20008, tel (202) 234 2945, fax (202) 265 4795, email embassy@costarica.com.

UK/US REPS IN COUNTRY UK: Apartado 815-1007, 11th Floor, Edificio Centro Colón, San José, tel 258 2025, fax 233 9938, email britemb@racsa.co.cr. US: Calle 120 Avenida 0, Pavas, San José, tel 5199 2000, fax 519 2305, email info@usembassy.or.cr.

PEOPLE AND PLACE

CAPITAL San Jose.

LANGUAGE Spanish.

PEOPLES Mestizo, African descent.

RELIGION Mainly Roman Catholic.

SIZE (SQ KM) 51,100.

POPULATION 3,925,331.

POP DENSITY/KM 79.2.

STATE OF THE NATION

SAFETY Safe (apart from strong tides when swimming).

LIFE EXPECTANCY M 74.26, F 79.55.

BEING THERE

ETIQUETTE When addressing people first names are preceded by Don for men, and Doña for women. Beachwear should not be worn away from the beach.

CURRENCY Costa Rican *colón* (c) = 100 *centimes*.

FINANCE Major credit cards and traveller's cheques accepted.

BUSINESS HOURS 0800-1200, 1400-1600, Monday-Friday.

GMT -6.

VOLTAGE GUIDE 110/220 AC, 60 Hz.

COUNTRY DIALLING CODE 506.

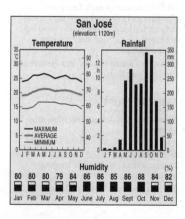

San José
(elevation: 1120m)

Temperature / Rainfall

MAXIMUM
AVERAGE
MINIMUM

J F M A M J J A S O N D

Humidity											(%)
80	80	80	79	84	86	86	85	86	88	84	82
Jan	Feb	Mar	Apr	May	June	July	Aug	Sept	Oct	Nov	Dec

HIGHLIGHTS

SAN JOSÉ Founded in 1737, this capital is now a great mix of traditional and modern Spanish architecture. A number of parks and museums keep the visitor intrigued. Not far from the city is the crater of Irazú. Not only can you see from here to the Caribbean on a clear day, but the scenery surrounding the crater is akin to a lunar landscape, and is thought of as one of Costa Rica's most stirring sights.

SAN LUCAS ISLAND & ISLA DEL COCO Just into the Pacific waters are these two islands. San Lucas is just off the coast from the port of Puntarenas, and home to marvellous beaches. The Isla del Coco is worth exploring: keep in mind its stories of hidden treasure buried by pirates.

POÁS VOLCANO Located within a national park is this smouldering active volcano, with the only dwarf cloudforest in Costa Rica. A boiling sulphurous lake in the crater of the volcano changes colour, from turquoise to green to grey.

SANTA ROSA NATIONAL PARK This park contains at least ten different habitats, including savannah, deciduous and non-deciduous forests. It also has the last major tropical dry forest in Central America.

ARENAL One of eight active volcanoes, this one in the Sierra Volcánica Guanacaste provides one of Costa Rica's most magical sights when red hot lava runs down its slopes. Night-time eruptions are the most spectacular. Mud pools bubble permanently among the foothills.

CONSUMING PLEASURES

FOOD & DRINK Common local dishes include *casado* (rice, beans, beef, plantain, salad and cabbage), *sopa negra* (black beans with a poached egg) and *picadillo* (vegetable and meat stew). Snacks, often sold at street stalls, are very popular, especially *gallos* (filled *tortillas*). Restaurants serve anything from French to Chinese cuisine.

SHOPPING & SOUVENIRS Wood and leather rocking chairs, local crafts.

FIND OUT MORE

WEBSITES www.visitcostarica.com, www.britishembassycr.com, www.costarica-embassy.org, www.usembassy.or.cr, www.infocostarica.com.

LOCAL MEDIA *The Tico Times* is the weekly English-language newspaper.

TOURIST BOARDS IN UK/US n/a.

Costa Rica has a literacy rate of 90 per cent, the best in South America, thanks to its free and compulsory education system

COTE D'IVOIRE

WHEN TO GO

WEATHER Dry from December to April, long rains May to July, short dry season August to September, short rains from October to November. More extreme in the north with rains from May to October and dry from November to April.

FESTIVALS One of the most famous festivals is the Fêtes des Masques, or the Festival of Masks. It takes place in villages in the Man region in February. In April, it's the Fête du Dipri in Gomon, a festival that starts around midnight, when women and children sneak out of their huts and, naked, carry out nocturnal rites to exorcise the village of evil spells. Before sunrise the chief appears, drums pound and villagers go into trances. The frenzy continues until late afternoon of the next day.

TRANSPORT

INTERNATIONAL AIRPORTS Abidjan (ABJ) 16 km from the city, Yamoussoukro (ASK).

INTERNAL TRAVEL Advanced rail service and good road system, with many surfaced roads. Car hire available in main towns.

RED TAPE

VISAS REQUIRED (UK/US) Required.

VACCINATIONS REQUIRED: See 'Vaccinations required around the world' on page 653.

DRIVING REQUIREMENTS Insurance compulsory, national licence plus attestation from the issuing Embassy required.

COUNTRY REPS IN UK/US UK: 2 Upper Belgrave St, London SW1X 8BJ, tel (020) 7201 9601, fax (020) 7462 0087. US: 2424 Massachusetts Avenue, NW, Washington, DC 20008, tel (202) 797 0300, fax (202) 244 3088.

UK/US REPS IN COUNTRY UK: 01 BP 2581, Immeuble 'Bank of Africa', 3rd to 4th Floors, angle Avenue Terrasson de Fougeres et RueGourgas, Abidjan-Plateau, Abidjan, tel 2030 0800, fax 2030 0834, email britemb@aviso.ci. US: 01 BP 1712, 5 rue Jesse Owens, Abidjan 01, tel 2021 0979, fax 2022 3259, email abidjancons@state.gov.

PEOPLE AND PLACE

CAPITAL Yamoussoukro.

LANGUAGE French.

PEOPLES Over 60 ethnic groups including Baoulé, Agri, Senufo, Dioula, Bété, and Dan-Yacouba.

RELIGION Mostly traditional beliefs, Islam, Christianity.

SIZE (SQ KM) 322,462.

POPULATION 16,365,000.

POP DENSITY/KM 50.8.

STATE OF THE NATION

SAFETY Recently fell into a vicious civil war, despite years of stability. Remains volatile.. Usual petty crime after dark.

LIFE EXPECTANCY M 46.05, F 51.27.

BEING THERE

ETIQUETTE French is the official language of schools, cities and government. However, most Ivorians also speak the mother tongue of their native village and adhere to local traditions within their ethnic group. Dress tends to err on conservative - men wearing long trousers and women wearing long skirts, dresses and trousers. Snakes are regarded as sacred by some ethnic groups. The ban on wearing camouflage clothes by

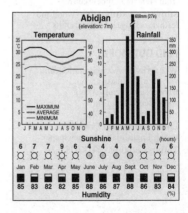

HIGHLIGHTS

YAMOUSSOUKRO
Lively administrative
and political capital,
unlike any other place
in Africa. It's a bizarre
example of wasteful
spending, typified by
deserted eight-lane
highways and the
lavish Basilique de
Notre Dame de la
Paix. Fractionally
smaller than St Peter's
in Rome, this cathe-
dral incorporates a
greater area of stained
glass than all the
stained glass in
France. The city also
has a lively market and
an international
standard golf course.

ABIDJAN Sometimes
called the 'Paris of
West Africa', this
cosmopolitan city
abounds in French
charm, in the wealthy
areas at least. The
largest city in the
country, its streets
bustle with people
going about their
daily lives. The tradi-
tional heart of the city
is Treichville, noted
for many bars, restau-
rants and nightclubs.

MAN Set in a region
of thickly forested
mountains and
plateaux, this attrac-
tive town in the west
of Côte d'Ivoire, is
known for its first rate
market. The area
around Man is home
to the Yacouba stilt
dancers, who perform
at the annual Fête des
Masks. There's also
the impressive La
Cascade waterfall in a
bamboo forest west of
the town and the
nearby peak of Mount
Tonkoui, popular
among climbers.

**PARC NATIONAL DE
LA COMOË** View
wildlife in west
Africa's largest game
park. Tracks along the
Comoë River attract
game during the dry
season, in particular.
Lions, elephants,
green monkeys,
hippos, baboons and
waterbucks can be
spotted, together with
several species of
antelope and wild pig.

civilians is still in effect.

CURRENCY *Communauté Financiaire
Africaine franc* (CFA) = 100 *centimes.*

FINANCE American Express and
MasterCard widely accepted, more limited
acceptance of other cards and traveller's
cheques.

BUSINESS HOURS 0730-1200, 1430-1800
Monday-Friday, 0800-1200 Saturday.

GMT GMT.

VOLTAGE GUIDE 220 AC, 50 Hz.

COUNTRY DIALLING CODE 225.

CONSUMING PLEASURES

FOOD & DRINK Spicy African food.
Traditional dishes include *kedjenou*
(chicken and vegetables sealed in banana
leaves), and *n'voufou* (mashed bananas or
yam mixed with palm oil and served with
aubergine sauce). Restaurants in main
towns serve French, Italian, Lebanese and
Vietnamese food.

SHOPPING & SOUVENIRS Wax prints,
Ghanaian kente cloth, indigo fabric and
woven cloth, wooden statues and masks,
bead necklaces, pottery, and basketware.

FIND OUT MORE

WEBSITES http://abidjan.usembassy.gov,
www.geographia.com/ivory-coast.

LOCAL MEDIA No English-language
papers. One state-owned TV channel.

TOURIST BOARDS IN UK/US n/a.

Côte d'Ivoire lost 42
per cent of its forest and
woodland between 1977
and 1987 – the highest
rate of habitat loss
anywhere in the world

CROATIA

WHEN TO GO

WEATHER Varied climate, with continental conditions in the north, Mediterranean on the Adriatic coast.

FESTIVALS Devoutly Catholic, the country has a number of religious festivals and feasts throughout the year. The Carnival is the biggest, and its climax before Shrove Tuesday sees processions and masked parties throughout Croatia. Split has the most relaxed atmosphere. Youths jump over bonfires as part of St John's Day on 24 June. St Martin's Day, 11 November, is the traditional day to taste the year's wines, and a good excuse for a party. Pig slaughtering, in preparation for the making of sausages and hams is done a the end of November. The International Folklore Festival is held in Zagreb over the last weekend in July, when dances and songs from all over Croatia are performed.

TRANSPORT

INTERNATIONAL AIRPORTS Zagreb (ZAG) 17 km from the city, Dubrovnik (DBV) 18 km from the city.

INTERNAL TRAVEL Some internal air services. Regular ferry services connect Rijeka and Split, services to Dubrovnik operate two or three times a week. Road and rail networks are adequate.

RED TAPE

VISAS REQUIRED (UK/US) None.

VACCINATIONS REQUIRED: See 'Vaccinations required around the world' on page 653.

DRIVING REQUIREMENTS International Driving Permit or national licence. A Green Card should be carried by non-EU visitors taking their own car into Croatia. Passports should be carried at all times.

COUNTRY REPS IN UK/US UK: 21 Conway Street, London W1T 6BN, tel (020) 7387 1144, fax (020) 7387 0310, email consulardept@croatianembassy.co.uk. US: 2343 Massachusetts Ave, NW, Washington, DC 20008, tel (202) 588 5899, fax 202 (588) 8936, email amboffice@croatiaemb.org.

UK/US REPS IN COUNTRY
UK: Ivana Lucica 4, 10000 Zagreb, tel (1) 600 9100, fax (1) 600 9111, email british.embassyzagreb@fco.gov.uk.
US: U Thomasa Jeffersona 2, 10010 Zagreb, tel (1) 661 2200, fax (1) 661 2373, email irc@usembassy.hr.

PEOPLE AND PLACE

CAPITAL Zagreb.

LANGUAGE Croat-Serb and Serb-Croat.

PEOPLES Before the war Croats made up nearly 80% of the population, Serbs 12%.

RELIGION Roman Catholic (76 %), Orthodox (11%), Muslim (1%), others.

SIZE (SQ KM) 56,542 .

POPULATION 4,437,460.

POP DENSITY/KM 78.4.

STATE OF THE NATION

SAFETY Recovering well from recent wars.

LIFE EXPECTANCY M 70.79, F 78.31.

BEING THERE

ETIQUETTE Normal social courtesies apply. There are restrictions on smoking in certain public buildings and on public transport.

CURRENCY *Kuna* (K) = 100 *Lipa*.

FINANCE Most cards and traveller's cheques widely accepted.

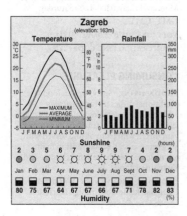

Zagreb
(elevation: 163m)

	Jan	Feb	Mar	Apr	May	June	July	Aug	Sept	Oct	Nov	Dec
Sunshine (hours)	2	3	5	6	7	8	9	9	7	4	2	2
Humidity (%)	80	75	67	64	67	67	66	67	71	78	82	83

HIGHLIGHTS

ZAGREB On the bank of the River Sava sits this historical city, a labyrinth of cobbled streets dating back to the Middle Ages. Dolac, a colourful open air market and the main square below Upper Town provide the hustle and bustle for a city full of fine monuments and buildings. Maksimir park provides the relaxation, and is one of Europe's first planned parks, with lakes, pavilions, and sculptures, from as far back as 1794.

DUBROVNIK Within the thirteenth-century city walls is the jewel in the crown of Croatia. Overlooking the Adriatic Sea, the city of terracotta rooftops is today a World Heritage Site, but was, until 1808, an independent state. Rector's Palace, the Franciscan monastery, and many baroque churches date from this period.

ISTRIA The largest peninsula on the Croatian coast, only a stone's throw from Italy, has become one of the main tourist destinations. The region was settled by the Romans in the fifth century and interesting sites remain, such as the well-preserved Arena, still hosting summer concerts and film festivals.

DALMATIA Many intriguing sights are found within this area. An archipelago of 90 islands spread over 300 square kilometres, it is almost uninhabited. Tourists usually take day trips but some stay in renovated stone cottages. Further south is the second largest city, Split, and Trogir, a tiny city founded by Greeks 2,300 years ago. Today, a World Heritage Site loved for its Venetian Gothic stone buildings.

BUSINESS HOURS 0800-1600 Mon-Friday. **GMT** +1.

VOLTAGE GUIDE 220 AC, 50 Hz.

COUNTRY DIALLING CODE 385.

CONSUMING PLEASURES

FOOD & DRINK Interior specialities include *manistra od bobica* (bean and maize soup). The coast is renowned for seafood dishes such as *brodet* (mixed fish stewed with rice) and good shellfish. Good regional wines, and Italian espresso.

SHOPPING & SOUVENIRS Embroidery, wood carvings, ceramics. Keep all receipts, financial police may fine visitors without proper paperwork.

FIND OUT MORE

WEBSITES http://uk.mvp.hr, www.croatia.hr, www.britishembassy.gov.uk/croatia, www.croatiaemb.org, www.usembassy.hr, www.zagreb-convention.hr, www.hvar.hr

LOCAL MEDIA No English-language papers. Two TV channels, four radio stations.

TOURIST BOARDS IN UK/US UK: 2 The Lanchesters, 162-164 Fulham Palace Road, London W6 9ER, tel (020) 8563 7979, fax (020) 8563 2616, emailinfo@cnto.freeserve.co.uk. US: 350 Fifth Avenue, Suite 4003, New York, NY 10118, tel (212) 279 8672, fax (212) 279 8683, email cntony@earthlink.net.

> Plitvice Lakes National Park, in a densely forested valley, has 16 deep-blue lakes joined by a series of spectacular waterfalls

CUBA

WHEN TO GO

WEATHER Hot, sub-tropical climate all year. Most rain falls May-October. Hurricanes can occur from August-November.

FESTIVALS The Havana Carnival in late July and early August features parades in front of the Capitolio or along the Malecón on Friday, Saturday and Sunday evenings. Santiago de Cuba's famous Fiesta del Fuego is in July, with theatre and dance culminating in vibrant street parades around during the last fortnight of the month. The International Festival of Latin American Film is held in Havana in December of each year.

TRANSPORT

INTERNATIONAL AIRPORTS Havana (HAV) 18 km from the city.

INTERNAL TRAVEL Advance booking essential for internal flights. Adequate rail system. Car hire relatively easy to arrange.

RED TAPE

VISAS REQUIRED (UK/US) Required.

VACCINATIONS REQUIRED: See 'Vaccinations required around the world' on page 653.

DRIVING REQUIREMENTS Valid national driving licence required. Drivers must be over 21.

COUNTRY REPS IN UK/US UK: 167 High Holborn, London WC1V 6PA, tel (020) 7240 2488, fax (020) 7836 2602, email embacuba@cubaldn.com. US: (Cuba Interests Section) 2630 16th Street, NW, Washington DC 20009, tel (202) 797 8518-20, fax (202) 797 8521, email secconscuba@worldnet.att.net.

UK/US REPS IN COUNTRY UK: PO Box 1069, Calle 34 No 702/4, Entre 7 ma Avenida y 17, Miramar, 11300 Havana, tel (7) 204 1771, fax (7) 204 8104, email embrit@ceniai.inf.cu. US: (US Interests Section) Swiss Embassy, Entre Calle L y M, Calle Calzada, Vedado, 10400 Havana, tel (7) 833 3551-9, fax (7) 833 1084.

PEOPLE AND PLACE

CAPITAL Havana.

LANGUAGE Spanish.

PEOPLES Mainly of Spanish descent (70%), African descent, and European-African.

RELIGION Non-religious (49%), Roman Catholic (40%).

SIZE (SQ KM) 110,860.

POPULATION 11,251,000.

POP DENSITY/KM 101.5.

STATE OF THE NATION

SAFETY Safe, apart from bag-snatchers.

LIFE EXPECTANCY M 74.94, F 79.65.

BEING THERE

ETIQUETTE Cubans generally address each other as *compañero*, but visitors should use *señor* or *señora*. Some Cubans have two surnames after their Christian name and the first surname is the correct one to use.

CURRENCY Cuban *peso* = 100 *centavos*.

FINANCE American Express not accepted, limited acceptance of other cards. Traveller's cheques accepted, but US dollar cheques issued by American banks are not acceptable.

BUSINESS HOURS 0830-1230, 1330-1630 Monday-Friday.

GMT -5.

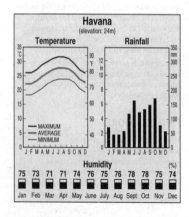

HIGHLIGHTS

HAVANA The vibrant city and centre for all things Cuban; cigars, Castro, Hemingway, rum, sex. Many of the old buildings are being restored, but there's a satisfying air of faded glory that hangs about this glorious Spanish colonial city. Paint peels from the walls of its buildings, while American cars from the 1950s and 1960s cruise the streets. Havana's old town is on UNESCO's World Heritage List.

BAY OF PIGS Site of the famous, yet disastrous US invasion of 1961.

SANTIAGO DE CUBA The island's first capital and a cosmopolitan city. Called the Ciudad Heroe, or Hero City, Santiago was a focal point for revolutionary activity due to its proximity to the majestic Sierra Maestra - Castro's mountainous battleground. It was here that the energetic music called *son* originated and, in July, the city hosts one of Cuba's most amazing carnivals.

ISLA DE LA JUVENTUD One of 350 islands in the Archipiélago de los Canarreos, this swampy place was formerly a hideout for pirates and inspired Robert Louis Stevenson's *Treasure Island*.

BASEBALL Catch a game in the Major League. It's the national game, the locals love it and it's a super atmosphere.

BEACHES Cuba has some fine coastline, with sandy beaches and azure sea. Snorkelling, diving and other watersports are popular among visitors, as well as boat tours out to the reef. After a hard day on the water, grab a *daiquiri* or *mojito*, local rum cocktails, and watch the sunset.

VOLTAGE GUIDE 110/120 AC, 60 Hz.
COUNTRY DIALLING CODE 53.

CONSUMING PLEASURES

FOOD & DRINK Restaurants generally inexpensive although choice can be restricted by shortages. Strong emphasis on seafood, other Cuban favourites include roast suckling pig, thick soups made from chicken and black beans, baked or fried plantains. Food in tourist hotels adequate, not exciting, but does feature a wide variety of exotic tropical fruit. Cuban coffee is strong, beer tasty but weak, rum is plentiful and used in cocktails like *daiquiris* and *mojitos*.

SHOPPING & SOUVENIRS Cigars, rum, coffee, local handicrafts.

FIND OUT MORE

WEBSITES www.cubaldn.com, www.britishembassy.gov.uk/cuba, www.cubanculture.com, www.cubanet.org, www.granma.cu/ingles/index.html, www.cubatravel.cu.

LOCAL MEDIA Both the weekly *Granma International* (website above), and the fortnightly *Prisma* are published in English.

TOURIST BOARDS IN UK/US UK: 154 Shaftesbury Avenue, London WC2H 8JT, tel (020) 7240 6655, fax (020) 7836 9265, email tourism@cubasi.info. US: n/a.

"'I am Cuban,' he said. 'You know the type. We are very wild kind of men. All we are interested in is dames and revolutions – OK?' He wriggled with self-delight."
Laurie Lee, 1969

CYPRUS

WHEN TO GO

WEATHER Warm Mediterranean climate. Hot, dry summers with mild winters during which rainfall is most likely. Summer, June to August, can be very hot. Spring and Autumn are generally the most pleasant times weather-wise.

FESTIVALS The Republic celebrates basically the same festivals as Greece. Easter is the biggest celebration of the year and is characterised by candle-lit processions, fireworks and feasting. Cyprus Independence Day is celebrated on 1 October. The North observes Muslim holidays, the major one being Ramadan, a month of fasting, which ends with a huge feast, Eid al-Fitr. The Proclamation of the Turkish Republic of Northern Cyprus is celebrated on 15 November.

TRANSPORT

INTERNATIONAL AIRPORTS Larnaca (LCA) 5 km from the city, Paphos (PFO) 15 km from the city.

INTERNAL TRAVEL Efficient cheap bus service connects all towns and villages. Car hire widely available, but should be hired well in advance during the summer season.

RED TAPE

VISAS REQUIRED (UK/US) None.

VACCINATIONS REQUIRED: See 'Vaccinations required around the world' on page 653.

DRIVING REQUIREMENTS International Driving Permit or a national driving licence accepted for stays of one year.

COUNTRY REPS IN UK/US UK: 93 Park Street, London, W1K 7ET, tel (020) 7499 8272, fax (020) 7491 0691, email cyphclondon@dial.pipex.com. US: 13 East, 40th Street, New York, NY 10016, tel (212) 686 6016/7, fax (212) 686 3660, email consulgenofcyprus@earthlink.net.

UK/US REPS IN COUNTRY UK: Alexander Pallis Street, PO Box 21978, 1587 Nicosia, tel (2) 286 1100, fax (2) 286 1125, email infobhc@cylink.com.cy. US: Metochiou

and Ploutarchou Streets, Engomi, 2407 Nicosia, tel (2)239 3939, fax (2) 278 0944, email info@americanembassy.org.cy.

PEOPLE AND PLACE

CAPITAL Nicosia.

LANGUAGE Greek.

PEOPLES Greek, Turkish minority.

RELIGION Greek Orthodox, small Muslim community.

SIZE (SQ KM) 9,251.

POPULATION 793,100.

POP DENSITY/KM 119.3.

STATE OF THE NATION

SAFETY Safe.

LIFE EXPECTANCY M 75.29, F 80.13.

BEING THERE

ETIQUETTE Respect should be shown for religious beliefs. It is viewed as impolite to refuse an offer of Greek coffee or a cold drink. For most occasions, casual attire is acceptable. Beachwear should be confined to the beach or poolside. Photography is forbidden near military camps or installations. No flash photography is allowed in churches with murals or icons.

CURRENCY Cyprus pound (C£) = 100 cents

FINANCE Credit cards and traveller's cheques generally accepted.

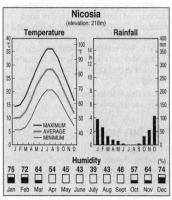

Nicosia
(elevation: 218m)

Humidity											(%)
75	72	64	54	45	43	39	43	48	57	64	74
■	■	□	□	□	□	□	□	□	□	■	■
Jan	Feb	Mar	Apr	May	June	July	Aug	Sept	Oct	Nov	Dec

HIGHLIGHTS

FAMAGUSTA Once the richest city in the world, often mistaken for the setting of Shakespeare's *Othello*. Known as Gazimagusa by the Turks. Has a decaying old town surrounded by a Venetian city wall. The city sits at the base of the desolate Karpas Peninsula. South of the town are some fine sandy beaches.

KYRENIA Pleasant coastal resort, with an atmospheric old town and a modern strip of hotels. Also known as Girne, it has a strong Mediterranean feel, with outdoor cafes and Kyrenia Castle. Originally built in Roman times and overhauled by the Venetians, it houses an interesting museum on shipwrecks.

MOUNT OLYMPUS Highest peak on the island and part of the forested Troodos range. The summit soars 1,952 metres and is invariably snow covered in winter. Skiing on its slopes is a popular activity at that time of year, while it attracts hikers in the summer.

PAFOS Booming tourist town, which manages to retain its identity. Souvenir shops abound, but there's also the remains of Saranta Kolones, a Lusignian fortress struck by an earthquake in the Middle Ages. Nearby is Kato Pafos, an area of tombs carved into the sea-cliff.

AGIA NAPA Has a sixteenth-century monastery and family beaches, but is more famous for its boisterous clubbing scene, attracting party-goers from around the world.

NICOSIA Laid back Greek Cypriot capital, with good restaurants and museums, and a lively art scene.

BUSINESS HOURS 0800-1300, 1600-1930 in summer, in winter 0800-1300, 1430-1800 (shopping hours; business hours n/a)

GMT +2.

VOLTAGE GUIDE 240 AC, 50 Hz.

COUNTRY DIALLING CODE 357.

CONSUMING PLEASURES

FOOD & DRINK Charcoal grilled meat and kebabs popular. Other Cypriot dishes include *dolmas* (vine leaves stuffed with meat and rice) and *tava* (a stew of meat, herbs and onions). Meals often preceded by a selection of snacks (*mezze*). Sweet desserts like the fantastic *baklava* are available. Excellent wine, spirits, and beer locally produced. Greek coffee.

SHOPPING & SOUVENIRS Handmade lace, woven curtains and tablecloths, silk, basketry, pottery, silverware, leather goods, traditional and contemporary jewellery, silver spoons, local wines and brandies.

FIND OUT MORE

WEBSITES www.cyprus.gov.cy, www.visitcyprus.org.cy, www.britain.org.cy, www.cyprusembassy.net, www.americanembassy.org.cy.

LOCAL MEDIA Papers in English are *The Blue Beret*, *Cyprus Financial Mirror*, *Cyprus Mail* (daily), *Cyprus Today* and *Cyprus Weekly*. Most English papers are also available.

TOURIST BOARDS IN UK/US UK: 17 Hanover Street, London W1S 1YP, tel (020) 7569 8800, fax (020) 7499 4935, email informationcto@btconnect.com. US: n/a.

> " History in this island is almost too profuse. It gives one a sort of mental indigestion."
> *Robert Byron, 1937*

CZECH REPUBLIC

WHEN TO GO

WEATHER Cold winters, mild summers.

FESTIVALS The Anniversary of Jam Palach's Death, a student who set himself on fire in Wenceslas Square in 1969 as a protest over the Soviet invasion, is marked on 19 January. Witches' Night, a mix of Halloween and May Day festivals, is held on 30 April. Medieval activity takes over Prague in the first week of May as part of the Karlovy Vary Blessing of the Waters. Renaissance costumes and street parades flood the city in the third week of June for the Slavnost Petiliste Ruze.

TRANSPORT

INTERNATIONAL AIRPORTS Prague (PRG) 17 km from the city.

INTERNAL TRAVEL Extensive domestic air service. Several daily express trains between Prague and main cities and resorts, and the bus network covers areas not accessible by rail. Car hire easy to arrange.

RED TAPE

VISAS REQUIRED (UK/US) Required by Australians.

VACCINATIONS REQUIRED: See 'Vaccinations required around the world' on page 653.

DRIVING REQUIREMENTS Valid national driving licence, if without photo card then International Driving Permit required.

COUNTRY REPS IN UK/US UK: 28 Kensington Palace Gardens, London W8 4QY, tel (020) 7243 1115, fax (020) 7727 9654, email london@embassy.mzv.cz. US: 3900 Spring of Freedom Street, NW, Washington, DC 20008, tel (202) 274 9100, fax (202) 966 8540, email amb_washington@embassy.mzv.cz.

UK/US REPS IN COUNTRY UK: Thunovská 14, 118 00 Prague 1, tel (2) 5740 2111, fax (2) 5740 2296, email info@britain.cz. US: Trziste 15, 118 01 Prague 1, tel (2) 5753 0663, fax (2) 5753 4028, email consprg@state.gov.

PEOPLE AND PLACE

CAPITAL Prague.

LANGUAGE Czech.

PEOPLES Czech (80%), Morovians, Slovak and Romanian minorities.

RELIGION Atheist, Roman Catholic.

SIZE (SQ KM) 78,866.

POPULATION 10,203,269.

POP DENSITY/KM 129.4.

STATE OF THE NATION

SAFETY Safe.

LIFE EXPECTANCY M 72.74, F 79.49.

BEING THERE

ETIQUETTE Normal courtesies apply.

CURRENCY *Koruna* (Kc) or *Crown* = 100 *hellers*.

FINANCE Major cards and traveller's cheques widely accepted.

BUSINESS HOURS 0800-1600 Mon-Friday.

GMT +1.

VOLTAGE GUIDE 220 AC, 50 Hz.

COUNTRY DIALLING CODE 420.

CONSUMING PLEASURES

FOOD & DRINK Often based on Austro-Hungarian dishes such as *Wiener Schnitzel*. Meat dishes are often served with *knedilky* (dumplings) and *zeli* (sauerkraut).

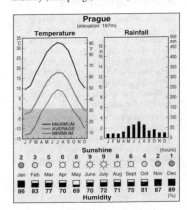

HIGHLIGHTS

PRAGUE On the banks of the Vltava River, Prague is known as the 'Paris of the east'. It's a mix of architectural styles: Gothic, Baroque, Romanesque, Art Nouveau, and Cubism all sit next to one another. Its centre escaped the bombs of World War II, and so the city is much as it always was. Worth visiting are Prague Castle, Vladislav Hall, St Vitus Cathedral, St George Basilica, Charles Bridge, Wenceslas Square, and the Old Town Hall. It's also worth spending some time in Lesser Town, beneath the castle, wandering through its narrow streets, seemingly unchanged since the seventeenth and eighteenth centuries.

BOHEMIA Sandstone is sculpted into mini-canyons and steep bluffs in the thick forest area of Bohemian Switzerland. The Krkonose Mountains National Park is a fantastic setting for winter sports, with great scenery and great facilities. Spas and health resorts in western Bohemia are still a major attraction, and have been since the days of Beethoven, Wagner, and Goethe, past patrons.

MORAVIA A number of intriguing buildings are found here, including the Capuchin Church, home to its very own mummies, the Gothic castles of Spilberk and Pernstejn (a fine example of a medieval castle), and the castle of Bucovice, complete with a mural of hares having revenge on dogs and men.

OUTDOOR PURSUITS Great landscape for skiing, climbing, caving, cycling, and more.

Other specialities include *bramborak* (potato pancakes filled with garlic and herbs). Most popular drinks are beer and specialist brandies, including *Becherovka* (herb), *slivovice* (plum) and *merunkovice* (apricot) Drink Pilsner and Budvar.

SHOPPING & SOUVENIRS Bohemian glass and crystal, pottery, porcelain, wooden folk carvings, hand-embroidered clothing, food, china, geyserstone carvings, semi-precious stones.

FIND OUT MORE

WEBSITES www.czechembassy.org.uk, www.czechtourism.com, www.britain.cz, www.mzv.cz/washington, www.czechtourism.com, www.usembassy.cz, www.czech-tourism.com, www.pragutourist.com.

LOCAL MEDIA *The Prague Post* and the *Prague Wochenblatt* are both weekly English papers.

TOURIST BOARDS IN UK/US Morley House, 320 Regent Street, London W1B 3BG, tel (020) 7631 0427, fax (020) 7631 0419, email info-uk@czechtourism.com. US: 1109 Madison Avenue, New York, NY 10028, tel (212) 288 0830, fax (212) 288 0971, email info-usa@czechtourism.com.

> The Czech Republic has over 3,000 castles, palaces, and monuments, 176 spas, 3 National Parks, 24 Protected Landscape Areas, 113 National Nature Reserves, and 453 Nature Reserves

DENMARK

WHEN TO GO

WEATHER Summer from June-August, winter from December-March and very wet with long periods of frost. February is the coldest month, spring and autumn are mild.

FESTIVALS The Copenhagen Jazz Festival is the capital's biggest event, held over ten days in early July, the Roskilde Festival, Europe's largest music festival, rocks in late June/early July, attracting top acts like U2, Radiohead, the Chemical Brothers and Bob Dylan. A European Medieval Festival is takes place in Horsens each August, with up to 2,500 people in costume.

TRANSPORT

INTERNATIONAL AIRPORTS Copenhagen (CPH) 8 km from the city, Århus (AAR) 44 km from the city, Billund Airport (BLL) 2 km from Legoland.

INTERNAL TRAVEL Frequent ferry services between islands. The main cities on all islands are connected by rail. The road system makes frequent use of ferries.

RED TAPE

VISAS REQUIRED (UK/US) None.

VACCINATIONS REQUIRED: See 'Vaccinations required around the world' on page 653.

DRIVING REQUIREMENTS National driving licence. EU nationals taking their own cars are strongly advised to obtain a Green Card for insurance purposes.

COUNTRY REPS IN UK/US UK: 55 Sloane Street, London SW1X 9SR, tel (020) 7333 0200, fax (020) 7333 0270, email lonamb@um.dk. US: 3200 Whitehaven Street, NW, Washington, DC 20008, tel (202) 234 4300, fax (202) 328 1470, email wasamb@um.dk.

UK/US REPS IN COUNTRY
UK: Kastelsvej 36-40, DK2100 Copenhagen Ø, tel 3544 5200, fax 3544 5293, email info@britishembassy.dk.
US: Dag Hammarskjølds Allé 24, DK-2100 Copenhagen Ø, tel 3341 7100, fax 3543 0223, email info@usembassy.dk.

PEOPLE AND PLACE

CAPITAL Copenhagen.

LANGUAGE Danish.

PEOPLES Danish. Very small Inuit and Faroe population.

RELIGION Evangelical Lutheran (89%).

SIZE (SQ KM) 43,098.

POPULATION 5,383,507.

POP DENSITY/KM 124.9.

STATE OF THE NATION

SAFETY Safe.

LIFE EXPECTANCY M 75.34, F 80.03.

BEING THERE

ETIQUETTE Normal courtesies apply, but be sure to only drink once the host has made a toast your health. Denmark's seaside resorts often allow nude bathing.

CURRENCY Danish *krone* (DKr) = 100 *øre*

FINANCE Credit cards and traveller's cheques widely accepted.

BUSINESS HOURS 0800/0900-1600/1700 Monday-Friday.

GMT +1(+2 in the summer).

VOLTAGE GUIDE 220 AC, 50 Hz.

COUNTRY DIALLING CODE 45.

CONSUMING PLEASURES

FOOD & DRINK Smørrebrød - slices of

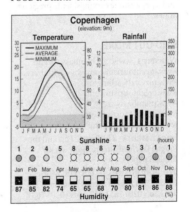

HIGHLIGHTS

COPENHAGEN
Founded in 1167, the largest urban area in Scandinavia has many old buildings and monuments. The greatest single crowd-puller is the Little Mermaid statue by the harbour. A number of museums, castles, and palaces, and even the Carlsberg factory, can be looked around, but for something totally different check out Christiana, a commune set up in 1971 by hippies and anarchists in an abandoned military barracks. Self-declared as immune from Danish law, a vivid mix of psyche-delic houses, vegan restaurants, vibrant music and art make up this home to 1,000 people. It is an in-triguing experiment in alternative living.

ZEALAND
The island on which Copenhagen sits is also home to fine beaches, lakes, forests, and royal palaces. The fortress of Kronbørg in Helsinør may be the setting of Hamlet.

BORNHOLM
A slow-paced self-contained island in the Baltic, 200 kilometres east of the capital. Wheat fields and forests cover the centre, the coast is all powdery white sand and fishing villages. Hammerhaus, the country's largest castle ruin, dating from 1260, is here.

FYN (FUNEN)
Called the 'Garden of Denmark', Fyn contains beautiful and impressive historic castles and manor houses.

JUTLAND
Making up the main part of Den-mark, these gorgeous sandy beaches are unsafe due to chang-ing winds and tides.

bread topped, often smothered, with a variety of fish, cheese, meat and garnishes - is the most popular Danish dish. Seafood plays a large part in the diet and a variety of international dishes are widely available. Fantastic coffee and many famous beers are made here, the national drink though is *akvavit*, or more as its more commonly known *snaps* - ice cold and served with cold food and a beer chaser.

SHOPPING & SOUVENIRS Bing & Grøndal and Royal Copenhagen porcelain, Holmegard glass, Bornholm ceramics, Lego.

FIND OUT MORE

WEBSITES www.denmark.org.uk. www.visitdenmark.com, www.britishembassy.dk, www.denmarkemb.org, www.denmark.org, www.goscandinavia.com, www.usembassy.dk, www.woco.dk, www.cph.dk, www.faroeislands.com,

LOCAL MEDIA English-language papers are available.

TOURIST BOARDS IN UK/US UK: 55 Sloane Street, London SW1X 9SR, tel (020) 7259 5959, fax (020) 7259 5955, email dtb.london@dt.dk. US: PO Box 4649, Grand Central Station, New York, NY 10063, tel (212) 885 9700, fax (212) 885 9710, email info@goscandinavia.com.

Legend has it that the Dannebrog, the national flag, fell from the sky in 1219 into the hands of King Valdemar II, during his crusade against Estonia. He held onto it and won the battle. If true, this would make it the oldest national flag still in use

DJIBOUTI

WHEN TO GO

WEATHER Extremely hot and arid June-August when the dusty *khamsin* wind blows from the desert. Slightly cooler with occasional light rain October-April.

FESTIVALS Friday is a holiday for offices and government institutions. Other important dates are Labour Day on 1 May and Independence Day on 27 June. Djibouti observes all Islamic feasts and holidays, the dates of which vary according to the religious calendar.

TRANSPORT

INTERNATIONAL AIRPORTS Djibouti (JIB) 5 km from the city.

INTERNAL TRAVEL Ferry services to Tadjoura and Obock from Djibouti. The only rail service runs to the Ethiopian border, but travellers are prohibited from using this. Four-wheel-drive vehicles are recommended for the interior. Car hire available in Djibouti.

RED TAPE

VISAS REQUIRED (UK/US) Required.

VACCINATIONS REQUIRED: See 'Vaccinations required around the world' on page 653.

DRIVING REQUIREMENTS International Driving Permit recommended, although not legally required. A temporary licence is available from local authorities on presentation of a valid British or Northern Ireland licence.

COUNTRY REPS IN UK/US UK: n/a, nearest 26 rue Emile Menier, 75116 Paris, France, tel (1) 4727 4922, fax 356 322. US: 1156 15th Street, Suite 515, NW, Washington, DC 20005, tel (202) 331 0270, fax (202) 331 0302, email usdjibouti@aol.com.

UK/US REPS IN COUNTRY UK: BP 169, rue de Djibouti, Djibouti, tel 385 007, email martinet@intnet.dj. US: Plateau du Serpent, boulevard Maréchal Joffre, Djibouti, tel 353 995, fax 353 940.

PEOPLE AND PLACE

CAPITAL Djibouti.

LANGUAGE Arabic and French.

PEOPLES Issa, Afar.

RELIGION Muslim. Roman Catholic, Protestant and Greek Orthodox minorities.

SIZE (SQ KM) 23,200.

POPULATION 693,000

POP DENSITY/KM 29.9.

STATE OF THE NATION

SAFETY Some areas closed to foreigners. Some risk of banditry after dark.

LIFE EXPECTANCY M 41.84, F 44.39.

BEING THERE

ETIQUETTE Djibouti is an Islamic country and certain codes of behaviour should be observed. Ramadan, the month of fasting, is a particularly important time of year.

CURRENCY Djibouti franc (Dfr) = 100 centimes.

FINANCE Credit cards are only accepted by airlines and the larger hotels.

BUSINESS HOURS 0620-1300 Sat-Thurs.

GMT +3.

VOLTAGE GUIDE 220 AC, 50 Hz.

COUNTRY DIALLING CODE 253.

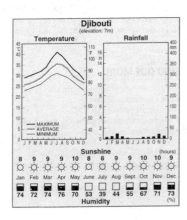

HIGHLIGHTS

DJIBOUTI Young capital city, with a distinctly Arabic feel. It's home to two-thirds of the country's people. Attractions include the small marina, where various fishing vessels, private pleasure boats and traditional dhows are moored. There's also a colourful central market - a bustling place where stallholders sell their assorted wares. These include fresh sprigs of *qat*, a mild stimulant flown in daily from Ethiopia. Other things of note include Djibouti's Tropical Aquarium, in which can be seen a wide range of aquatic life from the Red Sea region, and the Presidential Palace. Djibouti also has some fine beaches nearby, at Dorale and Kor Ambado.

THE LAKES Lac Assal, surrounded by dormant volcanoes and lava fields 100 kilometres south-west of the capital, which lies 150 metres below sea level. Driving there, you'll pass Lac Goubet, a seawater loch known as the 'pit of demons' by local people. Near the border with Ethiopia is a third lake, Lac Abbé, a place populated by thousands of flamingoes and pelicans. You'll need a four-wheel-drive vehicle to reach it.

TADJOURA Town with seven mosques situated across the Gulf of Tadjoura from the capital. It has a scenic setting, sur-rounded by several large mountains. Tadjoura also provides access to some superb Red Sea coral reefs, popular with snorkellers and divers.

ALI SABIEH Try windsurfing on wheels on the salty Petit Bara and Grand Bara desert plains in the south of Djibouti.

CONSUMING PLEASURES

FOOD & DRINK Local food is often spicy. Oven-baked or barbecued fish in the harbour area is popular. Restaurants serve French, Arabic, Vietnamese and Chinese food. Drink can be limited in Muslim areas.

SHOPPING & SOUVENIRS Lively markets stock local crafts and artefacts. Worth a visit.

FIND OUT MORE

WEBSITES www.office-tourisme.dj, www.infohub.com/travelguide/traveller/africa/djibouti.html.

LOCAL MEDIA No English-language papers. One TV station, one radio station, both under state control.

TOURIST BOARDS IN UK/US n/a.

Djibouti lies in a geographical region known as the Afar Triangle – one of the hottest and most desolate places on earth

DOMINICA

WHEN TO GO

WEATHER Hot, subtropical climate, cooler in the mountains. Main rainy season between June and October.

FESTIVALS One of the main events in the calendar is Carnival, celebrated during the traditional Mardi Gras period, in the two weeks prior to Lent, in February/March. Carnival features calypso competitions, a Carnival Queen contest, 'jump-ups' and a costume parade. Another important date is Creole Day, usually held on the Friday before Independence Day (3 November). It's a celebration of the island's Creole language and culture and includes traditional dancing, folklore, local food and music.

TRANSPORT

INTERNATIONAL AIRPORTS Melville Hall (DOM) 64 km from Roseau, Canefield (DCF) 5 km from Roseau.

INTERNAL TRAVEL Well maintained roads, car hire available, good bus service, and efficient taxis.

RED TAPE

VISAS REQUIRED (UK/US) None.

VACCINATIONS REQUIRED: See 'Vaccinations required around the world' on page 653.

DRIVING REQUIREMENTS International Driving Permit recommended. A valid foreign licence can be used to get a Temporary Visitor's Permit.

COUNTRY REPS IN UK/US UK: 1 Collingham Gardens, London SW5 0HW, tel (020) 7370 5194/5, fax (020) 7373 8743, email highcommission@dominica.co.uk. US: 3216 New Mexico Avenue, NW, Washington, DC 20016, tel (202) 364 6781, fax (202) 364 6791, email embdomdc@aol.com.

UK/US REPS IN COUNTRY UK: c/o Courts Dominica Ltd, PO Box 2269, Roseau, tel 255 240, fax 448 7817. US: n/a.

PEOPLE AND PLACE

CAPITAL Roseau.

LANGUAGE English.

PEOPLES Of African descent.

RELIGION Mainly Roman Catholic. Protestant (15%).

SIZE (SQ KM) 751.

POPULATION 71,727.

POP DENSITY/KM 95.5.

STATE OF THE NATION

SAFETY Safe.

LIFE EXPECTANCY M 71.73, F 77.71.

BEING THERE

ETIQUETTE Casual dress is normal, but swimwear is not worn on the streets in town. The Catholic Church is one of the most dominant social influences. Visitors should ask before taking photographs of local people.

CURRENCY East Caribbean dollar (EC$) = 100 cents.

FINANCE Most major credit cards and traveller's cheques accepted.

BUSINESS HOURS 0800-1300, 1400-1700 Mon, 0800-1300, 1400-1600 Tues-Friday.

GMT -4.

VOLTAGE GUIDE 220/240 AC, 50 Hz.

COUNTRY DIALLING CODE 1 767.

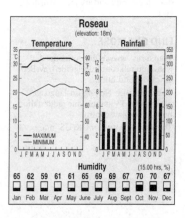

Roseau
(elevation: 18m)

Temperature — Rainfall

Humidity (15.00 hrs, %)

Jan	Feb	Mar	Apr	May	June	July	Aug	Sept	Oct	Nov	Dec
65	62	59	61	61	65	69	69	67	70	70	67

HIGHLIGHTS

Roseau One of the Caribbean's poorest capitals, but in a scenic setting backed by verdant mountains. The main centre for visitors, Roseau has been recently restored after hurricane damage and the city now boasts a new promenade and a cruise ship dock. Strolling through the quieter back streets can feel like stepping back in time. Jeep safaris can be made from here into the hinterland. Canoe trips up the island's rivers can also be organised.

Morne Trois Pitons National Park Impressive rainforest reserve, encompassing much of Dominica's mountainous volcanic interior. The park is characterised by beautiful cloud forest, while it also has a pretty little pool beneath a gentle waterfall, called the Emerald Pool. Another place of interest is the Boiling Lake, the second-largest actively boiling lake in the world.

Cabrits National Park Known as the site of Fort Shirley, a large eighteenth-century British fort that could house 600 soldiers. Scramble through the stone ruins, skirted by jungle. The section which was formerly the officer's quarters affords great views down over Prince Rupert Bay.

Carib territory Home to the only remaining Carib Indians in the region. There are 3,000 on the island, their numbers dwindled dramatically in the seventeenth-century when disease arrived from Europe.

Portsmouth Second city on the banks of Prince Rupert Bay. Columbus sailed into the bay in 1504.

CONSUMING PLEASURES

Food & drink Island cooking includes Creole and American dishes. Creole specialities include *crabbacks* (backs of red and black crabs stuffed with seasoned crab meat), *lambi* (conch) and *tee-ree-ree* (tiny freshly spawned fish). Locally made *Bello Hot Pepper Sauce* served with almost everything. Island fruit juices combined with rum are excellent.

Shopping & souvenirs Hats, bags and rugs all made from vetiver grass and joined with banana strands. Other local crafts.

FIND OUT MORE

Websites www.dominica.co.uk, www.dominica.dm, www.caribbean.co.uk.

Local media All in English. Main papers are *The Chronicle, The Tropical Star, The Independent Newspaper,* the *Official Gazette* and *The Sun.* No terrestrial TV.

Tourist boards in UK/US UK: MKI Ltd, Mitre House, 66 Abbey Road, Bush Hill Park, Enfield, Middlesex EN1 2QE, tel (020) 8350 1004, fax (020) 8350 1011, email dominica@ttg.co.uk, or Caribbean Tourism Organisation, 22 The Quadrant, Richmond, Surrey, TW9 1BP, tel (020) 8948 0057, fax (020) 8948 0067, email ctolondon@caribtourism.com. US: 110-64 Queens Boulevard, Forest Hills, NY 11375, tel (718) 261 9615, fax (718) 261 0702, email dominicanny@msn.com.

> Dominica's national bird, the Sisserou parrot, is the largest of all the Amazon parrots

DOMINICAN REPUBLIC

WHEN TO GO

WEATHER Hot with tropical temperatures all year. Rainy season and the occasional hurricane between June-October.

FESTIVALS Santo Domingo plays host to two Carnivals, the first begins a few days before Independence Day on 27 February and ends a few days after. Fantastic costumes, great floats, and all the rum you can manage. The second coincides with Restoration Day on 15 August. Music and dance takes control of the capital once again as part of the *merengue* festival in late July/early August. A three day Latin music festival comes to Santo Domingo in March. Puerto Plata hosts a Cultural Festival in June, with jazz, blues, *merengue*, and folk concerts. Cabarte Alegria is the dedication of February to fun, with weekend events bringing communities together.

TRANSPORT

INTERNATIONAL AIRPORTS Santo Domingo (SDQ) 30 km from the city, Puerto Plata (POP), Punta Cana (PUJ) 10-30 minutes travel time to Punta Cana and Bávaro resorts.

INTERNAL TRAVEL Planes can be chartered. Reasonable network of roads, but not all roads are all-weather and 4-wheel-drive vehicles are recommended for wet weather.

RED TAPE

VISAS REQUIRED (UK/US) Not required for stays up to 30 days. A tourist card will be issued.

VACCINATION S REQUIRED: See 'Vaccinations required around the world' on page 653.

DRIVING REQUIREMENTS A national or International Driving Permit valid, but only for 90 days.

COUNTRY REPS IN UK/US
UK: 139 Inverness Terrace, Bayswater, London W2 6JF, tel (020) 7727 6285, fax (020) 7727 3693, email info@dominicanembassy.org.uk.
US: 1715 22nd Street, NW, Washington, DC 20008, tel (202) 332 6280, fax (202) 265 8057, email emb.domrepusa@msn.com.

UK/US REPS IN COUNTRY UK: Avenida 27 de Febrero 233, Edifico Corominas Pepin, 7th Floor, Santo Domingo, tel 472 7111, fax 472 7574, email brit.emb.sadom@ codetel.net.do. US: Calle César Nicolás Pensón & Calle Leopoldo Navarro, Santo Domingo, tel 221 2171, fax 686 7437, email infovisas@codetel.net.do.

PEOPLE AND PLACE

CAPITAL Santo Domingo.
LANGUAGE Spanish.
PEOPLES Of Spanish and African descent.
RELIGION Roman Catholic.
SIZE (SQ KM) 48,072.
POPULATION 8,230,722.
POP DENSITY/KM 175.9.

STATE OF THE NATION

SAFETY Safe.
LIFE EXPECTANCY M 65.52, F 69.1.

BEING THERE

ETIQUETTE With more of an American lifestyle than Latin one, Dominicans take short siestas but not long lunches. Beach-wear should not be worn in towns.

CURRENCY Dominican Republic *peso* (peso) = 100 *centavos*.

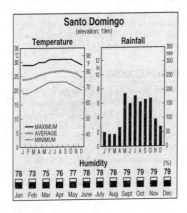

Santo Domingo (elevation: 19m)

	Jan	Feb	Mar	Apr	May	June	July	Aug	Sept	Oct	Nov	Dec
Humidity (%)	78	73	75	76	77	78	78	78	79	79	79	79

HIGHLIGHTS

SANTO DOMINGO

With the restoration of the colonial part complete, the capital is full of its original charm. Check out the Cultural Plaza with the Gallery of Modern Art and the National Theatre. Just out from the city, underground rivers feed a cave complex full of stalactites and stalagmites, and tropical vegetation. The turquoise lagoons sit on three different levels, giving the cave system its name, The Three Eyes of Water.

SAN CRISTÓBAL

Thought to be the most visited city in the country as historical sites used by Trujillo, the dictator between 1930 and 1961, draw large crowds.

CASA DE CAMPO

A 7,000-acre resort elegantly designed by Oscar de la Renta. Within its boundaries is the village of Altos de Chavón which overlooks the Chavón River and Caribbean Sea from its vantage point high up on the edge of a cliff. A 5,000-seat amphitheatre hosts major events.

THE AMBER COAST

The northern coast is the location for some of the world's finest amber, seen in the Amber Museum. Puerto Plata, home of the Cultural Festival, also has some of the best beaches in the Caribbean. Sosúa is one of the more popular of the unspoilt beaches.

WATERSPORTS

Excellent opportunities exist here. Swimming at magnificent beaches, diving among reefs, wrecks, and caverns, sailing, windsurfing, whitewater rafting, tubing, cascading (climbing a gorge and abseiling down the fall)canyoning (jumping not abseiling), and fishing are all offered here.

FINANCE Major credit cards accepted. Traveller's cheques accepted by some banks.

BUSINESS HOURS 0830-1200, 1400-1800 Monday-Friday.

GMT -4.

VOLTAGE GUIDE 110 AC, 60 Hz.

COUNTRY DIALLING CODE 1 809.

CONSUMING PLEASURES

FOOD & DRINK Spanish influences combined with local produce. Typical examples are *chicharonnes de pollo* (small pieces of seasoned, fried chicken), *sopa criolla dominicana* (soup of meat and vegetables), *la bandera* (rice, red beans, stewed meat with salad), *pastelon* (baked vegetable cake). Local rum and beer are very good.

SHOPPING & SOUVENIRS Amber jewellery and decorations. Turquoise and conch shells. Rocking chairs, woodcarvings, pottery, Creole dolls, baskets, carvings.

FIND OUT MORE

WEBSITES www.dr1.com/travel,
www.dominicanembassy.org.uk,
www.dominicanrepublic.com,
www.usemb.gov.do, www.domrep.org.

LOCAL MEDIA English Language paper *Santo Domingo News* (weekly) is published on Wednesdays and can be found in hotels.

TOURIST BOARDS IN UK/US UK: 18-21 Hand court, High Holborn, London WC1V 6JF, tel (020) 7242 7778, fax (020) 7405 4202, email inglaterra@sectur.gov.do. US: 136 East 57th Street, Suite 803, New York, NY 10022, tel (212) 588 1012, fax (212) 588 1015, email newyork@sectur.gov.do.

Baseball is the national sport, played in floodlit stadiums across the country. Top players go on to play in the US major leagues

EAST TIMOR

WHEN TO GO

WEATHER Tropical monsoon climate, hot and dry from July to November, rains from December to March. Cooler and more humid in the mountains.

FESTIVALS Festivals follow the Christian calendar, and other events follow new landmark dates in the new country - the most important being Independence Day on 20 May and Liberation Day on 20 September.

TRANSPORT

INTERNATIONAL AIRPORTS Comoro Airport (DIL), Dili and Baucau Airport, in the province of Baucau.

INTERNAL TRAVEL Roads and driving conditions are very poor, with drivers advised to take extreme caution. Bus links are bad and those that remain following the fighting are overcrowded. Car hire is available, but mountain bikes may be more viable outside of the capital.

RED TAPE

VISAS REQUIRED (UK/US) None.

VACCINATIONS REQUIRED: See 'Vaccinations required around the world' on page 653.

DRIVING REQUIREMENTS National driving licence.

COUNTRY REPS IN UK/US
UK: n/a, nearest Avenue de Cortenbergh, Cortenberghlaan 12, 1040 Brussels, Belgium, tel (2) 280 0096, fax (2) 280 0377. US: 3415 Massachusetts Avenue, NW, Washington, DC 20007, tel (202) 965 1515, fax (202) 965 1517.

UK/US REPS IN COUNTRY UK: n/a. US: Avenida do Portugal, Farol, Dili, tel (3) 324 684, fax (3) 313 206/008. United Nations Development Programme: UN Agency House, Caicoli Street, Dili, tel (3) 312 481, fax (3) 312 408, email registry.tp@undp.org.

PEOPLE AND PLACE

CAPITAL Dili.

LANGUAGE Tetum, Portuguese, English.

PEOPLES Austronesian, Papuan

RELIGION Christian (86% Catholic), Islam, animist beliefs.

SIZE (SQ KM) 14,609.

POPULATION 779,000.

POP DENSITY/KM 50.5.

STATE OF THE NATION

SAFETY Same terrorist threat as the rest of South-East Asia, separate potential trouble in border areas.

LIFE EXPECTANCY M 63.63, F 68.29.

BEING THERE

ETIQUETTE Fairly formal manners. Many conventions similar to Indonesia, despite political and religious differences. Old East Timorese conventions are expected to re-turn and the country rediscovers its identity.

CURRENCY US Dollars (= 100 cents).

FINANCE Take hard cash, Cirrus and Maestro can withdraw US Dollars from ATMs.

BUSINESS HOURS n/a.

GMT +8.

VOLTAGE GUIDE 220 V, 50 Hz.

COUNTRY DIALLING CODE 670.

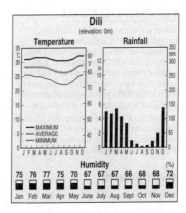

HIGHLIGHTS

HISTORY Under Indonesian occupation since 1975, the country suffered horrific scenes of conflict in 1999. East Timor only became fully independent in May 2002, and is still receiving aid from the UN.

DILI The capital during Portuguese colonialism remains the capital of the new country. The architecture of the colonial period remains, as does the Portuguese castle built in 1627. Only ten per cent of the collection remains in the State Museum, but you can still see religious wood carvings, figures, traditional crafts, musical instruments and paintings. Among the catholic churches in the city is a giant statue of Christ on a hilltop near Cape Fatucama.

BAUCAU The second largest city has plenty of delights, despite its war wounds. The journey from Dili here takes in magnificent coastal views, and the beaches around the city are some of the most beautiful.

OECUSSI PROVINCE Politically East Timorese, geographically in and surrounded by Indonesian West Timor. Cut off from the rest of the country, 95 per cent was destroyed in the fighting, leaving only small hamlets and villages. The capital of the region, Pantemakassar, holds a special significance as the first Portuguese colony. Now a sleepy town nestled between the sea and mountains, it offers good diving amongst the coral reefs nearby, mountain biking opportunities and hiking either in the interior or in the mountains.

CONSUMING PLEASURES

FOOD & DRINK Rice and spices, similar to Indonesian dishes. Limited supply of foodstuffs due to political instability. Western cuisine available in Dili.

SHOPPING & SOUVENIRS Batiks, embroidered fabrics, woodcarvings, silverwork.

FIND OUT MORE

WEBSITES www.undp.east-timor.org, www.lonelyplanet.com/worldguide/destinations/asia/east-timor.

LOCAL MEDIA The *Timor Post* (daily) and *Tais Timor* (fortnightly) are both published in English. One, state-controlled, TV channel.

TOURIST BOARDS IN UK/US n/a.

East Timor is the world's youngest country, having won independence from Indonesia only in 2002

ECUADOR

WHEN TO GO

WEATHER Warm and subtropical all year. Andean regions are cooler. Rainfall is high in coastal and jungle areas.

FESTIVALS Major festivals are based around the Roman Catholic calendar and are celebrated with a combination of great pageantry and elements of traditional Indian *fiestas*. Celebrations in the rural areas have a real party atmosphere. All Soul's Day on 2 November is especially colourful. Other holidays of historical interest are Simón Bolívar's Birthday on 24 July and Columbus Day on 12 October. The pre-Easter Carnival includes water fights, together with fruit and flower festivals. Corpus Christi is a movable feast in June and runs in conjunction with harvest fiestas in many highland towns.

TRANSPORT

INTERNATIONAL AIRPORTS Quito (UIO) 5 km from the city, Guayaquil (GYE) 5 km from the city.

INTERNAL TRAVEL Flying is the usual mode of transport between cities. Very limited passenger services to the Galapagos Islands, but once there it is relatively easy to take boats between the islands. Much of the railway network enjoys spectacular views. Road conditions remain variable as a result of frequent earthquakes and flooding. Car hire available.

RED TAPE

VISAS REQUIRED (UK/US) Required for business only.

VACCINATIONS REQUIRED: See 'Vaccinations required around the world' on page 653.

DRIVING REQUIREMENTS International Driving Permit not required.

COUNTRY REPS IN UK/US UK: Flat 3B, 3 Hans Crescent, London SW1X 0LS, tel (020) 7584 1367, fax (020) 7823 9701, email embajada.ecuador@btclick.com. US: 2535 15th Street, NW, Washington, DC 20009, tel (202) 234 7200, fax (202) 667 3482, email embassy@ecuador.org.

UK/US REPS IN COUNTRY UK: Piso 14, Edificio Citiplaza, Avenida Naciones Unidas y Republica de El Salvador, Quito, tel (2) 297 0800/1, fax (2) 297 0809, email britembq@uio.satnet.net. US: Patria y Avenida 12 Octubre, Quito, tel (2) 256 2890, fax (2) 250 2052.

PEOPLE AND PLACE

CAPITAL Quito.

LANGUAGE Spanish.

PEOPLES Mestizo (Indian-Spanish extraction), indigenous Indians.

RELIGION Roman Catholic.

SIZE (SQ KM) 272,045.

POPULATION 12,810,000.

POP DENSITY/KM 44.7.

STATE OF THE NATION

SAFETY One of the safest countries in Latin America.

LIFE EXPECTANCY M 73.35, F 79.22.

BEING THERE

ETIQUETTE It is best to ask permission before taking a photograph of somebody. They may also ask for a tip for the privilege. Although English may be spoken in business circles in Quito and Guayaquil, any attempts at speaking Spanish will be warmly welcomed.

CURRENCY *Sucre* (Su) = 100 *centavos*.

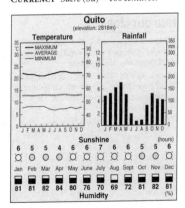

HIGHLIGHTS

QUITO One of South America's most beautiful cities, with a pleasant spring-like climate and set against the stunning backdrop of the snow-capped volcano, Pichincha. Climb to the top of El Panecillo, a hill affording great views of the colonial old town and topped by a giant statue of the Virgin of Quito. Elsewhere, the modern centre bustles with businesses and street cafes.

OTAVALO Small town and handicrafts centre, famous for its colourful Saturday Indian market, which dates back to pre-Inca times. It's a festive affair and the local Otaveleños wear their traditional dress.

BANOS A good base for outdoor pursuits, such as walking, horse riding and mountain biking. Or for just taking advantage of the thermal springs and hot pools from which the town gets its name.

COTOPAXI Mighty cone-shaped peak, at 5,900 metres the world's tallest active volcano, located to the south of the capital in the Parque Nacional de Cotopaxi. Popular with experienced climbers seeking to reach its summit.

GALÁPAGOS ISLANDS Made famous by Charles Darwin's scientific voyage aboard the *Beagle*, this island group 1,000 kilometres west of the mainland, is home to rare and unique animal species. Lizards, iguanas and giant tortoises can all be seen. Half the islands' species are found nowhere else on earth.

JUNGLE *El Oriente* is the local name for Ecuador's Amazon region, inhabited by indigenous tribes.

FINANCE Credit cards and traveller's cheques widely accepted.

BUSINESS HOURS 0900-130, 1500-1900 Monday-Friday, 1000-2000 Saturday (shopping hours; business hours n/a).

GMT -5 (-6 Galapagos Islands).

VOLTAGE GUIDE 110/120 AC, 60 Hz.

COUNTRY DIALLING CODE 593.

CONSUMING PLEASURES

FOOD & DRINK Specialities include *llapingachos* (pancakes mashed potato and cheese), shrimp or lobster *ceviche*, locro (stew of potatoes and cheese), *humitas* (flavoured sweetcorn tamale), and baked guinea pig. *Pilsner* is the most popular beer, *naranjilla* is an unique fruit juice and a Ecuadorian speciality tasting somewhere between peaches and citrus. *Canelazo* is regarded as the best drink - a mix of sugar cane, alcohol, lemon, and cinnamon.

SHOPPING & SOUVENIRS *Ferias* are special market days when a variety of local crafts are sold. Indian crafts, silver, native woodcarvings, Indian tiles, woollen and orlon rugs, blankets, basket, leather goods, indigenous art and *shigras* (shoulder bags).

FIND OUT MORE

WEBSITES www.britembquito.org.ec, www.ecuador.org, www.usembassyy.org.ec, www.ecuadorexplorer.com.

LOCAL MEDIA *Inside Ecuador* and *Q* are published irregularly in English, other international papers and magazines are available at main post offices and some bookshops.

TOURIST BOARDS IN UK/US n/a.

Pizarro reached Ecuador in 1532. Within a year, his handful of desperadoes had destroyed the vast and mighty Inca empire forever

EGYPT

WHEN TO GO

WEATHER Warm all year. Hottest June-September. Negligible rainfall, except on the coast. In April the hot, dusty *Khamsin* wind blows from the Sahara.

FESTIVALS The Islamic calendar is central to Egyptian life. Ramadan, the month of fasting, is an especially significant time.

TRANSPORT

INTERNATIONAL AIRPORTS Cairo International (CAI) 22 km from the city, El Nouzha (ALY) 7 km from Maydan al-Tahir (Alexandria), Luxor (LXR) 5.5 km from the city.

INTERNAL TRAVEL Daily flights between main centres. A steamer service links Hurghada with Sharm el-Sheik in Sinai. Feluccas can be hired for sailing on the Nile and regular Nile cruises operate between Luxor and Aswan and sometimes between Cairo and Aswan. Comprehensive east-west rail network. The Nile Valley and Delta and the Mediterranean and Red Sea coasts are served by paved roads. Motoring in the desert without suitable vehicles and a guide is not recommended. Car hire available.

RED TAPE

VISAS REQUIRED (UK/US) Required.

VACCINATIONS REQUIRED: See 'Vaccinations required around the world' on page 653.

DRIVING REQUIREMENTS Own insurance and an International Driving Permit required. *Carnet de passage* or deposit needed if bringing own vehicle in. All vehicles, including motorbikes, must carry a fire extinguisher and red triangle.

COUNTRY REPS IN UK/US
UK: 2 Lowndes Street, London SW1X 9ET, tel (020) 7235 9777, fax (020) 7235 5684, email info@egyptianconsulate.co.uk.
US: 3521 International Court, NW, Washington, DC 20008, tel (202) 895 5400, fax (202) 244 4319, email embassy@ egyptembc.org.

UK/US REPS IN COUNTRY UK: 7 Ahmad Ragheb, Garden City, Cairo, tel (2) 794 0850-8, fax (2) 795 1235, email webmaster@britishembassy.org.e.g..
US: 5 Latin America Street, Garden City, Cairo, tel (2) 797 3300, fax (2) 797 3200, email consularcairo@state.gov.

PEOPLE AND PLACE

CAPITAL Cairo.

LANGUAGE Arabic.

PEOPLES Eastern Hamitic (90%), Nubian, Armenian, Greek.

RELIGION Sunni Islam, small Coptic Christian minority.

SIZE (SQ KM) 1,002,000.

POPULATION 67,886,000.

POP DENSITY/KM 67.8.

STATE OF THE NATION

SAFETY Same potential terrorist threat as many other Islamic states. Otherwise fairly safe, though women should beware of sexual harassment or worse. Observe Islamic customs carefully.

LIFE EXPECTANCY M 68.5, F 73.62.

BEING THERE

ETIQUETTE As a Muslim country, dress should be conservative. Western style of dress is accepted in modern nightclubs, restaurants and hotels in Cairo, Alexandria and tourist resorts. Visitors to ancient sites

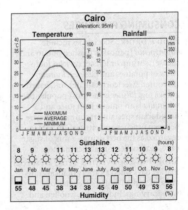

Cairo (elevation: 95m)											
Sunshine (hours)											
8	9	9	11	11	13	13	12	11	10	9	8
Jan	Feb	Mar	Apr	May	June	July	Aug	Sept	Oct	Nov	Dec
55	48	45	38	34	38	45	49	50	49	53	56
Humidity (%)											

HIGHLIGHTS

CAIRO A stir to the senses, this chaotic, noisy and intoxicating city on the River Nile is home to 16 million people. Widely regarded as one of the greatest cities in the Islamic world, its old quarter features one of the world's largest bazaars, Khan-el Khalili, a place crammed with spices, perfume and trinkets. Don't miss the superb museums, and of course the nearby Great Pyramids.

RIVER NILE Travel the way Egypt should be seen, be it on a traditional *felucca* or an ultra-modern cruise boat. Sail through the land of the pharoahs, passing historic sites, spotting birds and watching ancient villages on the river banks.

SINAI & THE RED SEA Busy tourist resorts line the Sinai coast, which has fine beaches and offers some of the world's best scuba diving and snorkelling. Inland it's all vast desert – a fun place to explore by jeep or camel. A highlight is St Catherine's Monastery.

ASWAN Relaxing market city located on ancient caravan routes and steeped in Nubian culture. The Nile here is truly wonderful, as *feluccas* glide down from the High Dam and Lake Nasser.

LUXOR Buzzing tourist hub, built on the site of the ancient city of Thebes. Famous for its magnificent monuments of Luxor, Karnak, Hatshepsut and Ramses III. The Valley of the Kings includes the tombs of Nefertari and the boy-king Tutankhamun.

---

may have to pay fees to take photographs.

CURRENCY Egyptian pound (E£) = 100 *piastres*.

FINANCE Credit cards and traveller's cheques widely accepted.

BUSINESS HOURS 0900-1900 every day except Monday and Thursday (0900 -2000) in winter, 0900-1230, 1600-2000 Saturday-Thursday in summer (shopping hours; business hours n/a).

GMT +2.

VOLTAGE GUIDE 220 AC, 50 Hz most areas, 110-380 AC in some rural areas.

COUNTRY DIALLING CODE 20.

CONSUMING PLEASURES

FOOD & DRINK *Foul* (bean) based dishes, kebabs and seasoned chickpeas are popular. As are stuffed vine leaves, roast pigeon, grilled aubergines and *humus* (chickpeas).

SHOPPING & SOUVENIRS In Cairo go to *Khan-el-Khalili* where reproduction antiques, jewellery, spices, copper items and Coptic cloth can be found.

FIND OUT MORE

WEBSITES www.egyptianconsulate.co.uk, www.egypttreasures.gov.e.g., www.britishembassy.org.e.g., www.egypttourism.org, www.egyptvoyager.com, www.cairotourist.com.

LOCAL MEDIA *Egyptian Gazette* (daily) and the *Middle East Observer* (weekly) are English-language papers.

TOURIST BOARDS IN UK/US UK: Egyptian House, 3rd Floor, 170 Piccadilly, London W1V 9EJ, tel (020) 7493 5283, fax (020) 7408 0295, email info@visitegypt.org.uk. US: 630 Fifth Avenue, Suite 2305, New York, NY 10111, tel (212) 332 2570, fax (212) 956 6439, email info@egypttourism.

Egypt may have more ancient artefacts still buried beneath its sands than have so far been uncovered above them

EL SALVADOR

WHEN TO GO

WEATHER Hot subtropical climate. Coastal areas are particularly hot, with a rainy season between May-October. Upland areas have a more temperate climate.

FESTIVALS Celebrations are held in the week before Easter, known as Samana Santa, across the country and on other religious dates. On 6 August celebrations are had for the patron saint of El Salvador. Celebrations in the capital begin several days early with a fair and large parade. Individual towns have their own festivals to honour their own patron saints.

TRANSPORT

INTERNATIONAL AIRPORTS San Salvador (SAL) 45 km from the city.

INTERNAL TRAVEL Flights between San Salvador and main centres, also linked by a rail network. About a third of the road system allows all-weather use. Car hijackings and burglaries are common. Car hire is available in San Salvador.

RED TAPE

VISAS REQUIRED (UK/US) Not required by UK nationals. US nationals need a tourist card, Australian and Canadian visitors require a visa.

VACCINATIONS REQUIRED: See 'Vaccinations required around the world' on page 653.

DRIVING REQUIREMENTS A national or International Driving Permit required. Vehicle can remain in country for 30 days, another 60 on application to Customs and Transport authorities.

COUNTRY REPS IN UK/US UK: Mayfair House, 39 Great Portland Street, London W1W 7JZ, tel (020) 7436 8282, fax (020) 7436 8181, email embajadalondres@rree.gob.sv. US: 2308 California Street, NW, Washington, DC 20008, tel (202) 265 9671/2, fax (202) 234 3834, email correo@elsalvador.org.

UK/US REPS IN COUNTRY UK: The British Embassy is closed indefinitely, enquiries should be directed to the British Embassy in Guatemala City (see Guatemala). US: Boulevard Santa Elena, Residencia Santa Elena Sur, La Libertad, Antiguo Cuscatlán, San Salvador, tel 900 6011, fax 278 5522.

PEOPLE AND PLACE

CAPITAL San Salvador.
LANGUAGE Spanish.
PEOPLES Mestizo.
RELIGION Roman Catholic, Evangelical.
SIZE (SQ KM) 21,041.
POPULATION 6,517,300.
POP DENSITY/KM 314.6.

STATE OF THE NATION

SAFETY Robbery and murder are not uncommon. Seek latest information at time of visit.
LIFE EXPECTANCY M 67.61, F 75.01.

BEING THERE

ETIQUETTE Do not point your finger or foot at anyone. Only use first names when invited to do so. Conservative casual dress is accepted. Military buildings and other sensitive areas should not be photographed.

CURRENCY El Salvador *colón* ('*peso*') = 100 *centavos*

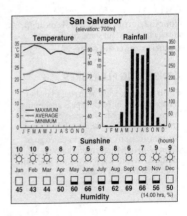

HIGHLIGHTS

SAN SALVADOR The second largest city in Central America was founded in 1525 by Spaniard Pedro De Alvarado at the foot of the San Salvador volcano. A mix of modern architecture, colonial design, wide plazas and monuments give the city its character today.
An amusement park on San Jacinto Mountain, reachable by cable car, gives excellent panoramic views of the city.

MAYA CIVILISATION Ancient archaeological sites dating back to the third century BC can be found in El Salvador. The village of Joya de Cerén was preserved by volcanic ash that buried it 1,400 year ago. The San Andrés area contains an architectural marvel, the acropolis. The best preserved site, however, is at Tazumal, or 'pyramid where the victims were burned', where artefacts were found stretching over a thousand-year period, and show trade links with places as far as Panama and Mexico.

MONTECRISTO CLOUD FOREST At the border with Honduras and Guatemala, 200 centimetres of rain fall every year. The area suffers from 100 per cent humidity. Oak and laurel tress grow to such heights that their leaves form canopies 30 metres high, impenetrable by sunlight. A wealth of flora and fauna thrives on the forest floor. Local wildlife includes spider monkeys, anteaters, pumas, agoutis and toucans.

CERRO VERDE NATIONAL PARK Two hundred years ago a hole blasted black columns of sulphuric smoke into the air. A cone formed and now it is 1,910 metres tall. 'The lighthouse of the Pacific' still steams away today.

FINANCE Major credit cards and traveller's cheques accepted.

BUSINESS HOURS 0800-1230, 1430-1730 Monday-Friday.

GMT -6.

VOLTAGE GUIDE 110 AC, 60 Hz.

COUNTRY DIALLING CODE 503.

LOCAL MEDIA No English-language papers.

TOURIST BOARDS IN UK/US n/a.

CONSUMING PLEASURES

FOOD & DRINK The popular stuffed *tortillas* (*pupusas*) come in several varieties including cheese (*queso*) and pork (*chicharrón*). Small dishes of yucca, avocado or *chorizo*, known as *boca*, are served with a drink before meals.

SHOPPING & SOUVENIRS Various local crafts, towels with Maya designs.

FIND OUT MORE

WEBSITES www.elsalvador.org, http://sansalvador.usembassy.gov, www.elsalvadorturismo.gob.sv.

Twenty-five volcanoes are found within the borders of El Salvador. Only three of them are still thought to be active

EQUATORIAL GUINEA

WHEN TO GO

WEATHER Tropical all year, with heavy rainfall for most of the year, decreasing slightly between December and February.

FESTIVALS The country's main events coincide with Christian or traditional religious ceremonies. Many of these are family or village based. Independence is celebrated on 12 October and this is when you're most likely to see public events in Malabo and Bata. President's Day is celebrated on 5 June. Sorcerers still play an important role in village life and among the most fascinating celebrations is the *abira*, a ceremony that helps cleanse the community of evil.

TRANSPORT

INTERNATIONAL AIRPORTS Malabo (SSG), 7 km from the city, Bata 6 km from the city.

INTERNAL TRAVEL Regular flights between Malabo and Bata, and light aircraft can be chartered. However, it is reported that maintenance procedures on internal flights are not always properly observed. Roads of variable condition - not all are paved.

RED TAPE

VISAS REQUIRED (UK/US) Required.

VACCINATIONS REQUIRED: See 'Vaccinations required around the world' on page 653.

DRIVING REQUIREMENTS n/a.

COUNTRY REPS IN UK/US
UK: n/a, nearest 29 Boulevard de Cour-celles, 75008 Paris, France, tel (1) 5688 5454, fax (1) 5688 1048.
US: 2020 16th Street, NW, Washington, DC 20009, tel (202) 518 5700, fax (202) 518 5252, email e.g._africa@yahoo.com.

UK/US REPS IN COUNTRY UK/US: The British and American Consulates in Yaoundé (see Cameroon) deal with en-quiries relating to Equatorial Guinea.

PEOPLE AND PLACE

CAPITAL Malabo.
LANGUAGE Spanish.
PEOPLES Fang, Bubi and Creole minority.
RELIGION Roman Catholic.
SIZE (SQ KM) 28,051.
POPULATION 481,000.
POP DENSITY/KM 17.1.

STATE OF THE NATION

SAFETY For the adventurer. Seek latest information at time of visit.
LIFE EXPECTANCY M 53.38, F 57.8.

BEING THERE

ETIQUETTE Foreign visitors, particularly Westerners, are a comparative rarity in Equatorial Guinea. You will likely be met with a deal of curiosity and, possibly, suspi-cion. A knowledge of Spanish is useful.

CURRENCY *Communauté Financiaire Africaine franc* (CFAfr) = 100 *centimes*.

FINANCE Very limited acceptance of Diners Club. Traveller's cheques not recommended.

BUSINESS HOURS 0800-1300, 1600-1900 Monday-Saturday (shopping hours; business hours n/a).

GMT +1.

VOLTAGE GUIDE 220/240 AC.

COUNTRY DIALLING CODE 240.

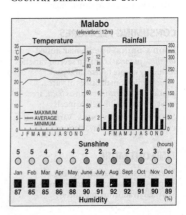

Malabo
(elevation: 12m)

Temperature — Rainfall — Sunshine — Humidity chart

	Jan	Feb	Mar	Apr	May	June	July	Aug	Sept	Oct	Nov	Dec
Sunshine (hours)	5	5	4	4	2	2	2	2	2	3	5
Humidity (%)	87	85	85	86	88	90	91	92	92	91	90	89

HIGHLIGHTS

MALABO Small, vibrant, Spanish influenced capital city located on Bioko Island northwest of the mainland. Has a genuine feel of the African tropics, it's characterised by open plazas, outdoor bars, thriving nightclubs and colourful markets. The city is overlooked by the striking Pico Malabo volcano, which can be climbed after obtaining a special government permit - it's a military area. Little known fact: Frederick Forsyth wrote *The Dogs of War* in Malabo.

LUBA Also situated on Bioko island, Luba is a gateway to some of the islands's natural attractions. These include deserted white sand beaches, such as Arena Blanca. There are also some pretty fishing villages nearby and two hiking trails.

BATA On Equatorial Guinea's mainland and the capital of the Rio Muni province. Larger than Malabo, its a clean and charming town with bustling markets, and plenty of restaurants, bars and hotels. To the north and south of Bata lie some of the most beautiful beaches anywhere in the world, which are great for swimming. The town of Mbini has some of the best.

EBEBIYIN Entry point for travellers arriving from neighbouring Cameroon, with bars on virtually ever corner. Out of town is the interesting Museum of Biyabiyan, featuring traditional Fang sculptures and other examples of native artwork.

MONTE ALEN NATIONAL PARK Hike in search of gorillas, elephants, chimpanzees, crocodiles and other beasties in this lush reserve.

CONSUMING PLEASURES

FOOD & DRINK Most restaurants serve Spanish or continental cuisine. Beer is expensive, but local brew *malamba*, made from sugar cane, is very cheap.

SHOPPING & SOUVENIRS Fang wooden statues, wooden masks.

FIND OUT MORE

WEBSITES www.lonelyplanet.com/worldguide/ destinations/africa/equatorial-guinea/.

LOCAL MEDIA No English language papers. One, state-owned, TV channel.

TOURIST BOARDS IN UK/US n/a.

Equatorial Guinea's Olympic swimmer, Eric 'the Eel' Moussambani, shot to international fame at the Sydney games in 2000 – for completing the 100 metres race so slowly

ERITREA

WHEN TO GO

WEATHER May-June and September-October are the best times to travel. The short rainy season is March-April, long rains from end June to beginning of September. Temperatures can fall as low as freezing between December-February.

FESTIVALS Festivals follow the religious calendar of Orthodox Christianity. Christmas, or Leddet, is celebrated on 7 January.

TRANSPORT

INTERNATIONAL AIRPORTS Asmara (ASM) 6 km from the city.

INTERNAL TRAVEL Internal flights between Asmara and Assab. Roads were badly damaged during the fighting, repairs are underway. Reasonable roads still connect business centres and holiday resorts. Car hire available through the Eritrean Tour Service in Asmara.

RED TAPE

VISAS REQUIRED (UK/US) Required.

VACCINATIONS REQUIRED: See 'Vaccinations required around the world' on page 653.

DRIVING REQUIREMENTS International Driving Permit.

COUNTRY REPS IN UK/US UK: 96 White Lion Street, London N1 9PF, tel (020) 7713 0096, fax (020) 7713 0161, email eriemba@freeuk.com. US: 1708 New Hampshire Avenue, NW, Washington DC 20009, tel (202) 319 1991, fax (202) 319 1304, email sessahaie@embassyeritrea.org.

UK/US REPS IN COUNTRY UK: 66-68 Mariam Ghimbi Street, House 24, Asmara, tel (1) 120 145, fax (1) 120 104, email asmara.enquiries@fco.gov.uk. US: 179 Allah Street, PO Box 211, Asmara, tel (1) 120 004, fax (1) 127 584.

PEOPLE AND PLACE

CAPITAL Asmara.

LANGUAGE Arabic and Tigrinya.

PEOPLES Tigrinya, Tigre, Afar and other indigenous groups.

RELIGION Islam and Christianity.

SIZE (SQ KM) 121,144.

POPULATION 3,991,000.

POP DENSITY/KM 32.9.

STATE OF THE NATION

SAFETY Relatively safe, but avoid borders with Ethiopia and Sudan. Do not travel after dark, and register with embassy on arrival.

LIFE EXPECTANCY M 53.38, F 57.8.

BEING THERE

ETIQUETTE Dress modestly as a tourist, business people should wear suits. Smoking is unpopular with traditional and elderly Eritreans. Shoes must be taken off in churches and mosques.

CURRENCY *Nafka* (Nfka) = 100 *cents*.

FINANCE Credit cards accepted on a limited basis, traveller's cheques are generally accepted.

BUSINESS HOURS 0800-1200, 1400-1700 Monday-Friday, 0800-1200 Sat.

GMT +2 (+3 in summer).

VOLTAGE GUIDE 110/220 AC.

COUNTRY DIALLING CODE 291.

CONSUMING PLEASURES

FOOD & DRINK Staple foods include *kitcha*, a thin bread made from wheat, and *injera*, a spongy pancake. Local specialities are often spicy. Massawa is renown for excellent seafood, particularly lobster and prawns. Italian cuisine dominates in

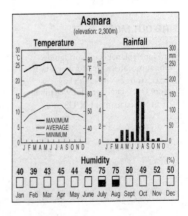

Asmara (elevation: 2,300m)

HIGHLIGHTS

ASMARA Situated on a high plateau, the capital has a pleasant climate, which led the colonising Italians to choose it as their main base. A small collection of villages just over 200 years ago, today it is full of striking Italian architecture and bougainvillaea lines the streets. Carrara marble was used in building its mosque. It is a lavish town, with Italian trimmings.

MASSAWA Coming here from the capital you descend 2,438 metres to sea level, passing breath-taking views of coastal desert. The Turko-Egyptian city has the largest deep water port in the Red Sea. Batsi island connects with the mainland via a series of dams. Sadly damaged during the struggle for independence from Ethiopia, the old town is being rebuilt in keeping with its original style. Some parts remain impressive.

QOHAITO An archaeological site whose beginnings are still being questioned. What is not in doubt is its impressiveness. Of the area excavated, around 20 per cent of the total area, digs have found the Temple of Mariam Wakiro, an early Christian church, temples, and tombs. The largest, most significant find, has been the Saphira Dam - 60 metres long and thought to be 1,000 years old.

DAHLAK ARCHIPELAGO Over 350 islands lie off the coast of Eritrea. Underwater is where their real beauty lies, packed with fish and coral life. Wreck-diving is also possible. Island and Arabian ruins are found on the largest island, home to nine ethnic villages.

restaurants in larger cities. Tea and espresso are drunk without milk, but a lot of sugar, coffee comes with ginger or black pepper and sugar. Exotic fruit juices available.

SHOPPING & SOUVENIRS Gold and silver jewellery, woodcarvings, leather items, spears, drums, carpets, and wicker goods.

FIND OUT MORE

WEBSITES
www.lonelyplanet.com/worldguide/destinations/africa/eritrea/.

LOCAL MEDIA *Eritrea Profile* (weekly) is published in English, *Hadas Eritrea* (three times a week) is printed in English, Arabic and Tigrinya. One TV station, two radio stations, all state-controlled.

TOURIST BOARDS IN UK/US n/a.

"The infamous Danakil Depression is said to be the hottest place on earth: summer temperatures reach heights feared by even the whippet-thin Afar tribesmen."
Michela Wrong

ESTONIA

WHEN TO GO

WEATHER Summer is warm with relatively mild weather in spring and autumn. Rainfall distributed throughout the year, heaviest in August. Winter, from November to mid-March, can be very cold and heavy snowfalls are common.

FESTIVALS Tallinn's July Baltika Folk Festival is a week of music, dance, exhibitions and parades focusing on Baltic and other folk traditions, held every few years. The All-Estonian Song Festival, which climaxes with a choir of up to 30,000 people singing traditional Estonian songs on a vast open-air stage in front of a massive audience is held every five years. The night of 23 June is the eve of Jaanipäev, the climax of midsummer events. Traditionally, Estonians head out into the countryside to dance, sing and make merry around bonfires. Many people take a holiday during the week around Jaanipäev.

TRANSPORT

INTERNATIONAL AIRPORTS Tallinn (TLL) 4 km from the city.

INTERNAL TRAVEL Domestic flights in summer from Tallinn to the islands of Saaremaa and Hiiumaa. Frequent ferry services between the mainland and islands. Underdeveloped rail system but major cities are connected. High density of roads. Car hire available at the airport or in Tallinn.

RED TAPE

VISAS REQUIRED (UK/US) Canadians need a visa for Latvia or Lithuania. Visas not required for UK/US/Australian visitors.

VACCINATIONS REQUIRED: See 'Vaccinations required around the world' on page 653.

DRIVING REQUIREMENTS EU nationals should have an EU or national driving licence and insurance.

COUNTRY REPS IN UK/US UK: 16 Hyde Park Gate, London SW7 5DG, tel (020) 7589 3428, fax (020) 7589 3430, email embassy.london@estonia.gov.uk. US: 600 Third Avenue, 26th Floor, New York, NY 10016, tel (212) 883 0636, fax (212) 883 0648, email nyconsulate@nyc.estemb.org.

UK/US REPS IN COUNTRY UK: Wismari 6, 10136 Tallinn, tel (6) 674 700, fax (6) 674 724/5, email information@britishembassy.ee. US: Kentmanni 20, 15099 Tallinn, tel (6) 688 100, fax (6) 688 134, email tallinn@usemb.ee.

PEOPLE AND PLACE

CAPITAL Tallinn.

LANGUAGE Estonian.

PEOPLES Russian, Estonian.

RELIGION Mainly Protestant (Lutheran).

SIZE (SQ KM) 45,227.

POPULATION 1,356,045.

POP DENSITY/KM 30.

STATE OF THE NATION

SAFETY Safe.

LIFE EXPECTANCY M 66.28, F 77.6.

BEING THERE

ETIQUETTE Normal courtesies should be observed. Estonians are proud of their culture and national heritage, and visitors should take care to respect this sense of national identities.

CURRENCY *Kroon* (Ekr) = 100 *sents.*

FINANCE Credit cards and traveller's cheques widely accepted.

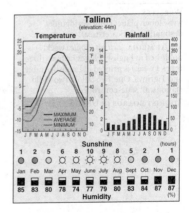

HIGHLIGHTS

TALLINN Charming capital with a medieval old town, the Vanalinn. Its cobbled streets, red-capped towers and pretty spires are surrounded by ancient city walls with imposing gates. Tallinn's Toompea Castle is one of the oldest and grandest architectural monuments. Raekoja Plats, the cobbled market square and general hub, is as old as the city itself. It is dominated by the fifteenth-century Town Hall, on top of which sits Vana Toomas, a sixteenth-century weather vane that is the city's emblem. Alexander Nevsky Cathedral is Tallinn's largest and grandest cathedral. It was built when Estonia was part of the Russian tsarist empire and named after the Prince of Novgorod.

PIRITA Seaside resort, just outside the capital, where pine-forested parks and good beaches are a popular destination for Sunday rides and bathing. Nearby is the viewing platform of Tallinn's 314-metre high TV Tower, offering picturesque views over the city and its surroundings and, on a clear day, the coast of neighbouring Finland.

NATIONAL PARKS Estonia has three national parks - Lahemaa, Soomaa and Vilandsi - with almost totally unspoiled and untouched forest and swamps, picturesque old fishing villages and historic manor houses.

PÜHTITSA CONVENT Stay overnight in this beautiful nineteenth-century Russian Orthodox nunnery, located in the village of Kuremäe in north-eastern Estonia, and which draws thousands of pilgrims every year.

BUSINESS HOURS 0830-1830 Mon-Friday.
GMT +2 (+3 in summer).
VOLTAGE GUIDE 220 AC, 50 Hz.
COUNTRY DIALLING CODE 372.

CONSUMING PLEASURES

FOOD & DRINK Local specialities include *rosolje* (herring with vinagrette and beets), *sült* (jellied veal), *täidetud vasikarind* (roast stuffed shoulder of veal). Roast goose stuffed with apples and plums is another Baltic speciality.

SHOPPING & SOUVENIRS Local folk art, amber.

> "I once told a Russian how much I liked Estonia. 'Ah,' he smiled, 'now I can see you are anti-Soviet.'"
> *Michael Binyon, 1980*

FIND OUT MORE

WEBSITES www.estonia.gov.uk, www.britishembassy.ee, www.estemb.org, www.nyc.estemb.org, www.usemb.ee, www.visitestonia.com, www.tallinn.ee/eng.

LOCAL MEDIA *The Baltic Times* is published in English in Latvia weekly.

TOURIST BOARDS IN UK/US n/a.

ETHIOPIA

WHEN TO GO

WEATHER Most rainfall is from June-September. Hot and humid in the lowlands, warm in the hill country, cool in the uplands.

FESTIVALS The main events are Islamic and Coptic religious festivals. On 19 January Timkat (Epiphany) is widely celebrated when a sacred tablet representing the Biblical Ark of the Covenant is carried from churches and paraded in the streets. 23 July marks the birthday of the late Emperor Haile Selassie. Another big event is the Ethiopian New Year, on September 11.

TRANSPORT

INTERNATIONAL AIRPORTS Addis Ababa (ADD) 8 km from the city.

INTERNAL TRAVEL Internal flights can be infrequent. The only operative rail line runs between Addis Ababa and Djibouti, via Dire Dawa. A good network of all-weather roads exists to most business and tourist centres, otherwise 4-wheel-drive vehicles are recommended. Frequent fuel shortages, and driving after dark outside Addis Ababa can be risky. Car hire available in Addis Ababa.

RED TAPE

VISAS REQUIRED (UK/US) Required.

VACCINATIONS REQUIRED: See 'Vaccinations required around the world' on page 653.

DRIVING REQUIREMENTS British driving licence valid for 1 month, otherwise obtain a temporary Ethiopian driving licence.

COUNTRY REPS IN UK/US UK: 17 Princes Gate, London SW7 1PZ, tel (020) 7589 7212, fax (020) 7584 7054, email info@ethioembassy.org.uk. USA: 3506 International Drive, NW, Washington, NW, Washington, DC 20008, tel (202) 364 1200, fax (202) 587 0195, email info@ethiopianembassy.org.

UK/US REPS IN COUNTRY UK: PO Box 858, Fikre Mariam Abatechan Street, Addis Ababa, tel (1) 612 354, fax (1) 610 588, email BritishEmbassy.AddisAbaba@fco.gov.uk.

US: PO Box 1014, Entoto Street, Addis Ababa, tel (1) 174 000, fax (1) 174 001, email usemaddis@state.gov.

PEOPLE AND PLACE

CAPITAL Addis Ababa.

LANGUAGE Amharic.

PEOPLES Oromo, Amhara, Sidamo, Shankella, Somali.

RELIGION Ethiopian Orthodox, Coptic Church, Islam, traditional beliefs.

SIZE (SQ KM) 1,133,380.

POPULATION 65,370,000.

POP DENSITY/KM 57.7.

STATE OF THE NATION

SAFETY Relatively safe, but avoid borders with Eritrea, Somalia and Sudan. Do not travel after dark, and register with embassy if travelling outside the capital by road.

LIFE EXPECTANCY M 47.67, F 50.03.

BEING THERE

ETIQUETTE Fairly formal and conservative in dress. In small towns locals may expect a payment for being photographed. Do not photograph military buildings.

CURRENCY Ethiopian *birr* = 100 *cents*.

FINANCE Limited acceptance of traveller's cheques, very limited acceptance of Diners Club and MasterCard.

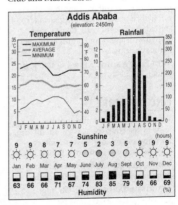

HIGHLIGHTS

AKSUM The ancient royal capital and holiest city in Ethiopia, renowned for multi-storeyed ancient carved granite obelisks and for the church where the Ark of the Covenant is said to rest.

BLUE NILE FALLS Trace the path of the Blue Nile from its source near Lake Tana, famed for its island monasteries, down stream to the wide Blue Falls, a spectacular sight, especially after the rains.

SIMIEN MOUNTAINS NATIONAL PARK Here you can spot a variety of unique wildlife species and scale the 4,620 metre-high Ras Dashen, Africa's fourth-highest peak, in the heart of the Ethiopian Highlands. The Rift Valley Lakes to the south are also great for wildlife, notably flamingos.

GONDAR 'Africa's Camelot', the former capital, and focal point of the country's historical routes, distinguished by its many castles and churches.

LALIBELA Pilgrims flock to the 11 rock-hewn churches, carved straight out of the bedrock. Legend has it that these were made with the help of angels.

ADDIS ABABA A city founded in 1887 and almost abandoned when a lack of fuel hampered the city. Eucalyptus intro-duced to the area solved the problem Now an urban sprawl, its most interesting singular attraction is the Ethnographic Museum, home to Lucy, the 3.5 million year old skeleton.

BUSINESS HOURS 0800-1200, 1300-1700 Monday-Friday.

GMT +3.

VOLTAGE GUIDE 220 AC, 50 Hz.

COUNTRY DIALLING CODE 251.

LOCAL MEDIA *The Ethiopian Herald* is the English daily, weeklies are also available. One, state-owned, TV channel.

TOURIST BOARDS IN UK/US n/a.

CONSUMING PLEASURES

FOOD & DRINK Local food based on *we't* - meat, chicken or vegetables cooked in a hot pepper sauce, served with *injera* (a flat, spongy bread). Other dishes include *shivro* and *misir* (based on chickpeas and lentils) and *tibs* (crispy fried steak). Wide choice of fish available. *Tej* - an alcoholic drink based on fermented honey - is unique to Ethiopia.

SHOPPING & SOUVENIRS Local jewellery, woodcarvings, manuscripts and prayer scrolls, wooden and metal crosses, leather shields, spears, drums and carpets.

> "Never have I seen such strange mountains. They look like peaks in a cartoon film."
> *Dervla Murphy, 1968*

FIND OUT MORE

WEBSITES www.ethioembassy.org.uk, www.flyethiopian.com, www.britishembassy.gov.uk/ethiopia, www.ethiopianembassy.org, www.tourethio.com.

FIJI

WHEN TO GO

WEATHER Tropical climate, with southeast trade winds from May to October bringing dry weather. The rainy season is from December to April.

FESTIVALS New Year's Day is celebrated with gusto in Fiji and the festivities can last a week or more in some villages. In February or March, Hindu Holi, the Festival of Colours, sees people squirt each other with coloured water. Ram Naumi, the Birth of Lord Rama, is a Hindu festival held in March or April and includes a religious festival and party on the shores of Suva Bay. In June, the nation honours Ratu Sir Lala Sukuna, a man considered Fiji's greatest statesman, soldier, high chief and scholar. The Constitution Day holiday falls in July. During October or November Hindus celebrate Diwali, the Festival of Lights.

TRANSPORT

INTERNATIONAL AIRPORTS Nadi (NAN), 8 km from Nadi on Viti Levu island. Suba (SUV) is at Nausori, 21 km from Suva.

INTERNAL TRAVEL Air and sea services between islands. Roads in good condition and usable year round. Car hire is available. Open-top and air-conditioned buses are available.

RED TAPE

VISAS REQUIRED (UK/US) None.

VACCINATIONS REQUIRED: See 'Vaccinations required around the world' on page 653.

DRIVING REQUIREMENTS International Driving Permit.

COUNTRY REPS IN UK/US UK: 34 Hyde Park Gate, London SW7 5DN, tel (020) 7584 3661, fax (020) 7584 2838, email mail@fijihighcommission.org.uk. US: Suite 240, 2233 Wisconsin Avenue, NW, Washington, DC 20007, tel (202) 337 8320, fax (202) 337 1996, email fijiemb@earthlink.net.

UK/US REPS IN COUNTRY UK: PO Box 1355, Victoria House, 47 Gladstone Road, Suva, tel 322 9100, fax 322 9132, email consularsuva@fio.gov.uk. US: PO Box 218, 31 Loftus Street, Suva, tel 331 4466, fax 330 0081, email usembsuva@connect.com.fj.

PEOPLE AND PLACE

CAPITAL Suva.

LANGUAGE Fijian and Hindi.

PEOPLES Fijians, Indo-Fijians.

RELIGION Hindu, Methodist. Muslim and Roman Catholic minorities.

SIZE (SQ KM) 18,376.

POPULATION 819,000.

POP DENSITY/KM 44.6.

STATE OF THE NATION

SAFETY Safe.

LIFE EXPECTANCY M 67.05, F 72.14.

BEING THERE

ETIQUETTE Fijians are a very welcoming, hospitable people and visitors should not be afraid to accept hospitality. It is customary to purchase a bundle of unpounded *yaqona* (*kava*) – the traditional *sevusevu*, or gift, before visiting. One celebrated tradition is the practice of fire-walking which has its origin in legend, although the Indian variant is performed for religious reasons.

CURRENCY Fijian dollar (F$) = 100 cents.

FINANCE Credit cards and traveller's cheques generally accepted.

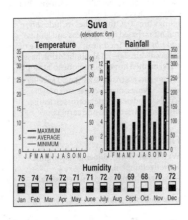

Suva
(elevation: 6m)

Temperature | Rainfall

MAXIMUM
AVERAGE
MINIMUM

Humidity (%)

Jan	Feb	Mar	Apr	May	June	July	Aug	Sept	Oct	Nov	Dec
75	74	74	72	71	71	72	70	69	68	70	72

HIGHLIGHTS

THE MAMANUCAS Group of tiny islands off the western coast of Vitu Levu, easily accessible by boat from the town of Nadi. Take a day trip of alternatively stay awhile in one of the plush resorts. The islands' waters are alive with colourful fish and offer excellent surfing, snorkelling and scuba diving. Or get into 'Fiji time' and lie back on one of the lovely white-sand beaches.

SUVA Fiji's capital is one of the South Pacific's largest and most sophisticated cities. The Fiji Museum, situated in the lush Thurston Gardens, is worth a look and the city also has some fine colonial architecture. Suva's many old shops and markets are a good place to pick up handicrafts.

NAUSORI HIGHLANDS Beautiful landscapes and the village of Navala - one of the most picturesque in Fiji. Its buildings are traditional *bure* huts arranged around avenues with a central promenade leading down to a river. Visitors aren't too commonplace, however, so its customary to ask to see the village chief first.

LAU GROUP Halfway from the main Fijian islands and neighbouring Tonga, this island group is popular with divers. Tongan influences can be seen in names, language, food and architecture.

VANAU LEVU Meaning 'big land' this volcanic outcrop is Fiji's second-largest island and a good place to get a feel for traditional Fijian life. It lacks beaches, but has excellent diving, snorkelling, kayaking and birdwatching. The rugged interior offers good hiking.

BUSINESS HOURS 0830-1700 Mon-Friday. GMT +12.

VOLTAGE GUIDE 240 AC, 50 Hz.

COUNTRY DIALLING CODE 679.

CONSUMING PLEASURES

FOOD & DRINK Fijian/Indian cuisine such as *kakoda* (marinated local fish served in coconut cream and lime). Curries are popular, as are Fijian *lovo* feasts, where meat, fish and vegetables are cooked in covered pits. The root of a pepper plant is used to produce the local hooch *yaqona* or *kava*, originally made by virgins chewing the root into a soft pulpy mass before adding water to make a drink.

SHOPPING & SOUVENIRS Filigree jewellery, woodcarvings (kava bowls), coconut shells, seashells, woven items (mats, coasters), tapa cloth, and pearls.

FIND OUT MORE

WEBSITES www.bulafiji.com, www.fijihighcommission.org.uk, www.britishhighcommission.gv.uk/fiji, www.fijiembassy.org, www.bulafijiislands.com

LOCAL MEDIA *The Fiji Times* (daily) and *Fiji Daily Post* are both in English.

TOURIST BOARDS IN UK/US UK: c/o Hills Balfour, Notcutt House, 36 Southwark Bridge Road, London SE1 9EU, tel (020) 7202 6365, fax (020)7928 0722, email fiji@hillsbalfour.com. US: Suite 220, 5777 West Country Boulevard, Los Angeles, CA 90045, tel (310) 568 1616, fax (310) 670 2318, email infodesk@ bulafiji-americas.com.

The Fiji Times claims to be the first newspaper published in the world each day, since Fiji lies just to the west of the International Date Line

FINLAND

WHEN TO GO

WEATHER Relatively mild in spring and autumn, brief warm summers. Snow cover in the north lasts from October to mid-May.

FESTIVALS Midsummer's Day on 25 June is the largest celebration, when people leave the cities and towns to toast the longest day of the year. Savonlinna Opera Festival, held in the medieval Olavinnlinna Castle, is famous, but it is the Pori Jazz Festival in July that is popular. On Sleepyhead Day on 27 July the laziest persons from Naantali and Hanko are thrown into the sea, Sonkajärvi hosts the wife-carrying championship every July, and the Air Guitar World Championships are held in Oulu in August.

TRANSPORT

INTERNATIONAL AIRPORTS Helsinki (HEL) 20 km from the city, Turku (TKU) 7 km from the city, Tampere (TMP) 15 km from the city, Rovaniemi (RVN) 10 km from the city.

INTERNAL TRAVEL Excellent network of domestic flights. Rail travel is cheap and efficient. Lake steamers and motor vessels ply the inland waterways. Main roads are passable at all times. Car hire available.

RED TAPE

VISAS REQUIRED (UK/US) None.

VACCINATIONS REQUIRED: See 'Vaccinations required around the world' on page 653.

DRIVING REQUIREMENTS National driving licence or International Driving Permit and insurance required.

COUNTRY REPS IN UK/US UK: 38 Chesham Place, London SW1X 8HW, tel (020) 7838 6200, fax (020) 7838 9703, email sanomat.lon@formin.fi. US: 3301 Massachusetts Avenue, NW, Washington, DC 20008, tel (202) 298 5800, fax (202) 298 6030, email info@finland.org.

UK/US REPS IN COUNTRY UK: Itäinen Puistotie 17, 00140 Helsinki, tel (9) 2286 5100, fax (9) 2286 5262, email visa.mail.helsinki@fco.gov.uk. US: Itäinen Puistotie 14, 00140 Helsinki, tel (9) 616 250, fax (9) 6162 5800, email arc@usembassy.fi.

PEOPLE AND PLACE

CAPITAL Helsinki.

LANGUAGE Finnish.

PEOPLES Finnish, small Sami population.

RELIGION Evangelical Lutheran.

SIZE (SQ KM) 338,145.

POPULATION 5,206,295.

POP DENSITY/KM 15.4.

STATE OF THE NATION

SAFETY Safe.

LIFE EXPECTANCY M 74.82, F 82.02.

BEING THERE

ETIQUETTE Normal courtesies apply. Wait to drink until the host toasts your health with a 'kippis' or a 'skol'. Fins may be reserved, so visitors should not worry about a lack of small talk. Shoes should be removed on entering someone's home.

CURRENCY Euro (€) = 100 *cents*.

FINANCE Credit cards and traveller's cheques widely accepted.

BUSINESS HOURS 0800-1615 Mon-Friday.

GMT +2.

VOLTAGE GUIDE 230 AC, 50 Hz.

COUNTRY DIALLING CODE 358.

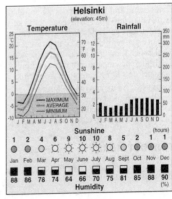

HIGHLIGHTS

HELSINKI The most densely populated area of Finland, its capital, covers 800 sq km. But only half of that is developed, the rest being parks, forests, shoreline and lakes, making it one of the greenest cities anywhere. Historical old manor houses and churches are never far from more modern architectural designs such as Dipoli Hall, part of the Helsinki University of Technology.

LAKELAND Finland has around 180,000 lakes, most of which are found here in this labyrinth of headlands and bays. Lake Saimaa has a shoreline 50,000 km long, and has at least 33,000 islands within it.

FOREST The remoteness of the Finnish forest has meant that it has been unspoilt by man, and the beautiful wilds can now be explored in canoeing and hiking trips.

LAPLAND For those who like to be left alone you can now choose between luxury or the wilds. Covering 100,000 sq kilometres, visitors must eat local food. And the choice is delightful, fresh salmon, reindeer, and golden cloudberry, can all be tried. Winter sports centres are located near the Arctic Circle, and traditional lumberjack competitions are held. The gold-panning town of Tankavaara, and the Sami Museum of Lapp history should both be visited.

WINTER SPORTS Aside from all the variations on skiing, visitors can try dog or reindeer sledging, snowmobile tours and icebreaker cruises. Bear trails, bird and reindeer watching and pony treks are also possible.

CONSUMING PLEASURES

FOOD & DRINK Potatoes, meat, fish, butter and rye bread form the basis of Finnish diet, but the cuisine has been greatly influenced by French, Swedish and Russian cooking. Expect excellent fresh fish, such as pike, perch, trout, whitefish, salmon and Baltic herring. Reindeer is also on menus, often smoked. Drinks include berry liqueurs, such as *mesimarja* (arctic bramble) and *polar* (cranberry), and good beers.

SHOPPING & SOUVENIRS Handicrafts, jewellery, handwoven ryijy rugs, furniture, glassware, porcelain, ceramics, furs.

FIND OUT MORE

WEBSITES www.finemb.org.uk, www.visitfinland.com/uk, www.britishembassy.fi, www.finland.org, www.gofinland.org, goscandinavia.com, www.usembassy.fi, www.mek.fi, http://virtual.finland.fi.

LOCAL MEDIA No English-language homegrown papers, but UK and American newspapers are available.

TOURIST BOARDS IN UK/US UK: PO Box 33213, London W6 8JX, tel (020) 7365 2512, fax (020) 8600 5681, email finlandinfo.lon@mek.fi. US: PO Box 4649, Grand Central Station, New York, NY 10163, tel (212) 885 9700, fax (212) 885 9710, email mek.usa@mek.fi

Finnish Lapland is home to 200,000 reindeer, roaming wild, the property of 5,800 different owners

FRANCE

WHEN TO GO

WEATHER Temperate and continental climate in the north, Mediterranean in the south, mountains are cooler with heavy snows in the winter.

FESTIVALS Main national days off are May Day, on 1 May, and Bastille Day, on 14 July. The world-famous Cannes Film Festival takes place in mid-May. In August, the country goes on holiday and many places will be closed. Saintes-Maries-de-la-Mer in the Camargue is the venue for a colourful gypsy festival in late May, characterised by wild singing and dancing.

TRANSPORT

INTERNATIONAL AIRPORTS (And distances from the nearest city) Paris-Charles de Gaulle (CDG) 23 km, Paris-Orly (ORY) 14 km, Bordeaux (BOD) 12 km, Lille (LIL) 12 km, Lyon (LYS) 25 km, Marseille (MRS) 30 km, Nice (NCE) 6 km, Strasbourg (SXB) 12 km, Toulouse (TLS) 8 km.

INTERNAL TRAVEL All domestic networks (air, rail and road) are efficient.

RED TAPE

VISAS REQUIRED (UK/US) None.

VACCINATIONS REQUIRED: See 'Vaccinations required around the world' on page 653.

DRIVING REQUIREMENTS National driving licence acceptable. EU nationals taking their own car to France are strongly advised to obtain a Green Card.

COUNTRY REPS IN UK/US UK: 58 Knightsbridge, London, SW1X 7JT, tel (020) 7073 1000, fax (020) 7073 1059, email press@ambafrance.org.uk. US: 4101 Reservoir Road, NW, Washington, DC 20007, tel (202) 944 6000, fax (202) 944 6166, email info-washington@diplomatie.gouv.fr.

UK/US REPS IN COUNTRY UK: 35 rue de Faubourg St Honoré, 75383 Paris, tel (1) 4451 3100, fax (1) 4451 3128, email visamailpavis@fco.gov.uk. US: 2 rue St Florentin, 75382 Paris Cedex 08, tel (1) 4312 2222, fax (1) 4266 9783.

PEOPLE AND PLACE

CAPITAL Paris.

LANGUAGE French.

PEOPLES French, North African, German, Breton.

RELIGION Roman Catholic. Protestant, Muslim, Jewish and Buddhist minorities.

SIZE (SQ KM) 543,965.

POPULATION 59,481,919.

POP DENSITY/KM 109.3.

STATE OF THE NATION

SAFETY Safe, apart from some separatist activity in Corsica and the Basque area.

LIFE EXPECTANCY M 75.96, F 83.42.

BEING THERE

ETIQUETTE Kissing both cheeks is the usual form of greeting. The form of personal address is simply *Monsieur* or *Madame*. Mealtimes are often long and leisurely with many courses. Topless sunbathing is tolerated on most beaches but naturism is restricted to certain beaches - check with the local tourist office.

CURRENCY Euro (€) = 100 *cents*.

FINANCE Credit cards, traveller's cheques widely accepted.

BUSINESS HOURS 0900-1200, 1400-1800 Monday-Friday.

GMT +1 (+2 in summer).

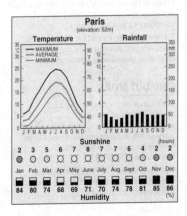

Paris (elevation: 52m)

	Jan	Feb	Mar	Apr	May	June	July	Aug	Sept	Oct	Nov	Dec
Sunshine (hours)	2	3	5	6	7	8	7	7	6	4	2	2
Humidity (%)	84	80	74	68	69	71	70	74	78	81	85	86

HIGHLIGHTS

PARIS Captivating and full of romance, this cultural centre is one of the world's great cities. Lining the banks of the River Seine, cosmopolitan Paris is characterised by breezy boulevards, charming cafes and restaurants selling French gastronomic fare. It is also brimming with world-renowned landmarks, including Notre Dame Cathedral, the Arc de Triomphe and the dizzying Eiffel Tower.

NORMANDY Rolling countryside on the Channel coast. Visit the beaches where the Allied forces landed on D-Day in World War Two, or stroll through the narrow streets of the pretty abbey island of Mont St-Michel. Then there's historic Rouen and the Bayeux Tapestry.

CÔTE D'AZUR Chic seaside resorts dot the Mediterranean coast along the French Riviera. Nice, Monaco, Cannes, St-Tropez have long been playgrounds of the rich and famous: fine beaches, bronzed bodies, warm waters and cultural events such as the Cannes Film Festival.

THE ALPS Fun on the slopes and equally active *après-ski* are the hallmarks of this spectacular mountain area on the border with Italy and Switzerland. In summer, trails through green valleys and soaring peaks make for wonderful hiking. Mont Blanc is the highest peak.

THE LOIRE World Heritage region famous for its many lavish *châteaux*, set in picturesque towns such as Blois, Tours and Amboise. The area is also known for the super-charged atmosphere of the Le Mans 24 Hour Race each summer.

VOLTAGE GUIDE 220 AC, 50 Hz.
COUNTRY DIALLING CODE 33.

CONSUMING PLEASURES

FOOD & DRINK France boasts one of the most varied and developed cuisines in the world. *Haute-cuisine*, bistro-fare and family cooking all rely on quality produce, and each region is proud of its own specialities. The country is famous for producing fine wine and over 365 different types of cheese.

SHOPPING & SOUVENIRS Lace, crystal glass, cheese, coffee, wines, spirits, liqueurs, textiles. Hypermarkets sell everything - food, clothing, bikes, electrical goods, furniture.

FIND OUT MORE

WEBSITES www.ambafrance-uk.org, www.institute-francais.org.uk, www.franceguide.com, www.amb-grandebretagne.fr, www.tourisme.fr, www.aeroport.fr

LOCAL MEDIA International papers widely available. *International Herald Tribune* published from Paris.

TOURIST BOARDS IN UK/US
UK: 178 Piccadilly, London W1J 9AL, tel (09068) 244 123 or (020) 7399 3520, fax (020) 7493 6594, email info.uk@franceguide.com. US: 444 Madison Avenue, 16th Floor, New York, NY 10022, tel (212) 838 7800, fax (212) 838 7855, email info.us@franceguide.com.

The French motorways are justly famous, but they were also the scene of the world's longest-ever traffic jam, when cars queued in February 1980 northwards from Lyons for 176 kilometres

GABON

WHEN TO GO

WEATHER Equatorial climate with high humidity. Dry season from June-August, main rainy season from October-May.

FESTIVALS Independence Day, celebrated from 16-18 August, is the biggest national holiday, with revelries lasting up to three days long.

TRANSPORT

INTERNATIONAL AIRPORTS Libreville (LBV) 12 km from the city.

INTERNAL TRAVEL Some local flights. The Trans-Gabon railway connects Libreville with Ndjole, Booué and franceville. Most of the country consists of impenetrable rainforest and the roads are generally of poor standard. Road travel during the rainy season is inadvisable. Car hire available at main hotels and airports.

RED TAPE

VISAS REQUIRED (UK/US) Required.

VACCINATIONS REQUIRED: See 'Vaccinations required around the world' on page 653.

DRIVING REQUIREMENTS International Driving Permit and international insurance.

COUNTRY REPS IN UK/US UK: 27 Elvaston Place, London SW7 5NL, tel (020) 7823 9986, fax (020) 7584 0047, email armellepambou@hotmail.com. US: 2034 20th Street, NW, Washington, DC 20009, tel (202) 797 1000, fax (202) 332 0668, email info@ambagabonusa.net.

UK/US REPS IN COUNTRY UK: PO Box 486, Libreville, tel 762 200, fax 765 789. US: BP 4000, Boulevard Bord de la Mer, Libreville, tel 762 003/4, fax 745 507.

PEOPLE AND PLACE

CAPITAL Libreville.

LANGUAGE French.

PEOPLES Fang, Eshira and other Bantu.

RELIGION Christian (mainly Roman Catholic), Islam, Animist.

SIZE (SQ KM) 267,667.
POPULATION 1,329,000.
POP DENSITY/KM 5.

STATE OF THE NATION

SAFETY Generally stable.

LIFE EXPECTANCY M 54.21, F 57.34.

BEING THERE

ETIQUETTE Never photograph military installations.

CURRENCY *Communauté Financiaire Africaine france* (CFAfr) = 100 *centimes.*

FINANCE Relatively limited acceptance of credit cards, limited acceptance of traveller's cheques.

BUSINESS HOURS 0730-1200, 1430-1800 Monday-Friday.

GMT +1.

VOLTAGE GUIDE 220 AC, 50 Hz.

COUNTRY DIALLING CODE 241.

CONSUMING PLEASURES

FOOD & DRINK Many restaurants serve Cameroonian, Congolese, French and Senegalese food. Bush meats such as wild boar, antelope, porcupine, monkey and crocodile often form part of Gabonese cuisine. French *baguettes* are one of the Gabonese staples, along with smoked or salted fish, *manioc*, plantain and rice.

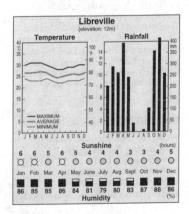

Libreville
(elevation: 12m)

HIGHLIGHTS

LAMBARENE
The famous and still functioning Schweitzer Hospital, founded in 1924by the great missionay doctor Albert Schweitzer, can be visited in the heart of the pretty lakes region. A motorised *pirogue* will take you out into the lakes, where hippos and other wildlife can be sighted.

LIBREVILLE Gabon's bustling modern capital, is characterised by big ocean-view hotels, modern offices and fancy shops – the product of the country's oil boom in the 1970s – and noted for the interesting National Museum and a buzzing nightlife.

LOPE NATIONAL PARK Home to lowland gorillas, mandrills and elephants, alongside other wildlife, in the savannah and rain-forests of this abundant game reserve. White-water rafting is available.

CIRQUE DE LECONI Spectacular red-rock canyons, a favourite area for camping and off-road driving, and noted for their diverse wildlife and beautiful scenery. The red rocks turn a golden colour at sunset.

MAYUMBA One day Mayumba will have become the major beach destination for tourists in Gabon. At the moment though it remains difficult to reach, yet is deserted and enchanting.

PORT GENTIL
This town boomed during the discovery and mining of oil in the 1970s. Modern luxury hotels are located at one end of town, poorer, cheaper quarters, the locals' area, at the other. The town has a community of expatriates and good beaches, and claims to have more evening entertainment by way of bars and restaurants than any other African city.

SHOPPING & SOUVENIRS Stone carvings, masks, figurines, clay pots, traditional musical instruments.

FIND OUT MORE

WEBSITES www.gabontour.ga, http://gabon.embassyhomepage.com, www.africaguide.co/country/gabon. www.lonelyplanet.com/worldguide/destinations/africa/gabon/

LOCAL MEDIA No English-language newspapers.

TOURIST BOARDS IN UK/US n/a.

" I hope that our next journey together may not be over a country that seems to have been laid down as an obstacle race track, and to have fallen into bad repair."
Mary Kingsley, 1897

GAMBIA

WHEN TO GO

WEATHER Pleasantly tropical climate. Coastal areas dry November-May, rainy June-October. Inland very hot March-June.

FESTIVALS A number of religious festivals are held throughout the year, according to the religious calendars. Between June and July the International Roots Festival attempts to re-engage American and European descendants with their history.

TRANSPORT

INTERNATIONAL AIRPORTS Banjul (BJL) 20 km southwest of the city.

INTERNAL TRAVEL Excellent river connections to all parts of the country. About a third of the roads are paved. Unsealed roads become impassable in the rainy season. Some car hire available, check with major companies before travelling.

RED TAPE

VISAS REQUIRED (UK/US) Required by American and Canadian visitors.

VACCINATIONS REQUIRED: See 'Vaccinations required around the world' on page 653.

DRIVING REQUIREMENTS International Driving Permit accepted for 3 months. A temporary licence available from local authorities on presentation of a valid UK licence.

COUNTRY REPS IN UK/US UK: 57 Kensington Court, London W8 5DG, tel (020) 7937 6316, fax (020) 7937 9095, email gambia@gamhighcom.fsnet.co.uk. US: Suite 905, 1156 15th Street, NW, Washington, DC 20005, tel (202) 785 1399, fax (202) 785 1430, email gambiaembassy1@aol.com.

UK/US REPS IN COUNTRY UK: 48 Atlantic Road, Fajara, Banjul, tel 449 5133/4, fax 449 6134, email bhcbanjul@gamtel.gm. US: 92 Kairaba Avenue, Fajara, Banjul, tel 439 2856, fax 439 2475, email consularbanjul@state.gov.

PEOPLE AND PLACE

CAPITAL Banjul.

LANGUAGE English.

PEOPLES Mandingo, Fulani, Wolof, Jola, Serahull.

RELIGION Islam 80%, Christian, Animist.

SIZE (SQ KM) 11,295.

POPULATION 1,364,507.

POP DENSITY/KM 120.8.

STATE OF THE NATION

SAFETY Calm.

LIFE EXPECTANCY M 53.14, F 57.31.

BEING THERE

ETIQUETTE A friendly and welcoming people. Islamic beliefs should be respected. Only use the right hand for giving and receiving food or other items. Do not wear beachwear away from the beach or pool.

CURRENCY Gambian *dalasi* (D) = 100 *bututs*.

FINANCE Limited acceptance of credit cards and traveller's cheques.

BUSINESS HOURS 0800-1600 Mon-Thurs, 0800-1230 Friday

GMT GMT.

VOLTAGE GUIDE 220 AC, 50 Hz.

COUNTRY DIALLING CODE 220.

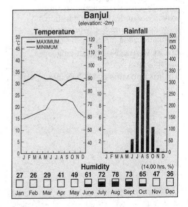

HIGHLIGHTS

BANJUL Located on St Mary's Island at the five-kilometre wide mouth of the River Gambia, with a well protected harbour, sits the country's only large town, the capital. And yet it remains a sleepy town by comparison to most, with an atmosphere to remind you of an older Africa. Colonial architecture surrounds MacCarthy Square, and the bustling market is just around the corner.

ABUKO NATURE RESERVE The River Gambia is the counrtry's main feature. Boat trips up river can take in this area abundant in bird species, and home to crocodiles, monkeys, birds, and antelope.

WASSAU STONE CIRCLES Over 160 kilometres upriver from the capital, archaeologists have identified a series of standing stone circles built as burial sites 1,200 years ago. The stones vary in height from one metre to two and a half. A museum explains possible reasons for them.

BASSE SANTA SU The major trading post of the upper reaches of the River Gambia, far beyond the old colonial trading centre of Georgetown. Fine trading houses ,built in a boom at the start of the twentieth century, line the streets, but the old shops once run by Europeans, Gambians, and Lebanese have been abandoned.

ACTIVITIES Banjul operates a watersports centre, with good water-skiing and winddurfing facilities. Sea and river fising are good all year - try line fishing at the beach. Fajara is home to an 18-hole golf club.

CONSUMING PLEASURES

FOOD & DRINK Typical dishes include 'Jollof Rice' or *benachin* (a mixture of spiced meat and rice with tomato puree and vegetables), *chere* (steamed millet flour balls), *base nyebe* (rich stew of chicken or beef with vegetables), *plasas* (meat and smoked fish cooked in palm oil with green vegetables). A good selection of wines, spirits and beers are available. The local speciality beer is Jul Brew.

SHOPPING & SOUVENIRS The brightly coloured Gambishirt, made of printed and embroidered cotton, woodcarvings, beaded belts, silver and gold jewellery, and handbags. Some items gaudy, others exceedingly attractive.

FIND OUT MORE

WEBSITES www.visitthegambia.gm, www.britishhighcommission.gov.uk/ thegambia, www.usembassybanjul.gm, http://gambiagateway.atspace.com.

LOCAL MEDIA All papers published in English. Main papers are *The Gambia Weekly, The Nation, The Gambia Daily, The Gambian Times.* One, state-owned, TV channel.

TOURIST BOARDS IN UK/US UK: As for Country Reps in UK, tel (020) 7376 0093, fax (020) 7938 3644, email office@ ukgta.fsnet.co.uk.

> "'Gambia' is said to mean clear water, surely a misnomer, it is as muddy as the Mersey."
> *Richard Burton, 1863*

GEORGIA

WHEN TO GO

WEATHER Hot summers (May-September); mild winters.

FESTIVALS Each town celebrates the founding of the settlement. The country representatives in the UK or US can give specific dates for specific towns. Tbilisoba, the largest celebration, held for the capital, comes each year on 30 October.

TRANSPORT

INTERNATIONAL AIRPORTS Tbilisi (TBS) 18 km from the city.

INTERNAL TRAVEL Single-track, slow rail lines. Approximately 20,000 kilometres of asphalt roads. Difficult to buy fuel outside cities without specialised local knowledge. No reliable maps or signposts. Buses are reliable but uncomfortable.

RED TAPE

VISAS REQUIRED (UK/US) Required.

VACCINATIONS REQUIRED: See 'Vaccinations required around the world' on page 653.

DRIVING REQUIREMENTS International Driving Permit.

COUNTRY REPS IN UK/US UK: 4 Russell Gardens, London W14 8EZ, tel (020) 7603 7799, fax (020) 7603 6682, email embassy@geoemb.plus.com US: 1101 15th Street, Suite 602, NW, Washington DC 20005, tel (202) 387 2390, fax (202) 393 4537, email embgeorgiausa@yahoo.com.

UK/US REPS IN COUNTRY UK: 20 Telavi Street, Sheraton Metechi Palace Hotel, 0103 Tbilisi, tel (32) 955 497, fax (32) 001 065, email british.embassy@caucasus.net. US: 25 Atoneli Street, 0105 Tbilisi, tel (32) 989 967, fax (32) 933 759, email consulate-tbilisi@state.gov.

PEOPLE AND PLACE

CAPITAL Tbilisi.

LANGUAGE Georgian, Russian.

PEOPLES Georgian (70%), Armenian, Russian, Azeri, Ossetian.

RELIGION Georgian Orthodox, Eastern Orthodox, Muslim, Jewish.

SIZE (SQ KM) 69,700.

POPULATION 5,177,000.

POP DENSITY/KM 74.3.

STATE OF THE NATION

SAFETY Avoid travelling at night outside the capital.

LIFE EXPECTANCY M 72.59, F 79.67.

BEING THERE

ETIQUETTE A generous people, it is not uncommon for travellers to have drinks bought for them by strangers in restaurants - followed by much toasting. Foreign women may be subject to immense flattery, especially when invited to someone's home. If this is too much, be sure not to give the slightest hint of encouragement. Do not wear shorts, and women should cover heads, when entering churches. Be extremely cautious about travelling in the dark.

CURRENCY *Lari* (GEL) = 100 *tetri*.

FINANCE Limited acceptance of credit cards and traveller's cheques.

BUSINESS HOURS n/a.

GMT +4.

VOLTAGE GUIDE 220 AC, 50 Hz.

COUNTRY DIALLING CODE 995.

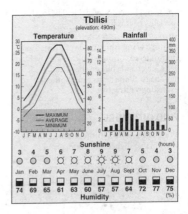

Tbilisi
(elevation: 490m)

HIGHLIGHTS

TBILISI 'Tbili' means 'warm', and the effect of the temperature has not only been felt on the city's name. It has also given the capital a Mediterranean quality, one that survived the Soviet period. Streets wind past stone houses with courtyards at their centre. Travellers should visit the frescoed churches dotted around the city, and the castle. But for a look at Tbilisi as a whole, try walking up Mount Mtatsminda, or go to the Narikala Fortress: originally built in the fourth century and rebuilt in the seventeenth century, it gives good views of the old city.

MTSKHETA The capital until the fifth century, and now a World Heritage site. Famous as the legendary town where Christ's crucifixion robe was dropped on the ground in AD 328, today a cathedral stands on this spot, and claims to have fragments of the cloth inside.

GORI This is the last place where you can see a statue of Stalin in public in the former USSR. His birthplace also has a park and museum dedicated to him. The museum is 'temporarily' closed, and has been for some time.

BATUMI More Turkish, than Georgian, located as it is near the border. But it is not the mosque or the bathhouse that give the town its character but the lush vegetation, a vibrant backdrop of citrus groves and tea plantations.

UPLISTSIKHE The 'Fortress of God' is a system of underground caves, lived in between the sixth and fourteenth century and enclosing shops, public buildings, theatres, dungeons and wine cellars.

CONSUMING PLEASURES

FOOD & DRINK Meals usually start with mixed hot and cold dishes, including grilled liver, *lobio* (bean and walnut salad), marinated aubergines, fresh and pickled vegetables. Walnuts are used extensively - anything including the word *satsivi* will be served in a rich sauce flavoured with herbs, garlic, walnuts and egg. Roast suckling pig is often served. Red and white wines are produced in Georgia. Stalin's favourite tipple was *Kindzmareuli*, a fruity red.

SHOPPING & SOUVENIRS Ceramics, embroidery, and jewellery all distinctive.

Georgia produces the cheapest champagne in the world. But its people take home an annual per capita income of just US$600

FIND OUT MORE

WEBSITES www.goemb.org.uk, www.britishembassy.gov.uk/georgia, www.georgiaemb.org, http://georgia.usembassy.gov, www.opentext.org.ge.

LOCAL MEDIA *Georgian Times* is a weekly English-language paper.

TOURIST BOARDS IN UK/US n/a.

GERMANY

WHEN TO GO

WEATHER Temperate throughout the country with warm summers (May- September) and cold winters (November-March).

FESTIVALS Germany's rich musical heritage is showcased in a number of prominent festivals, such as the Thuringian Bach Festival in March or the Richard Wagner Festival in Bayreuth in July. Jazz festivals in Stuttgart (April) and Berlin (November) are lively and popular. Autumn highlights include the famous Oktoberfest, Munich's annual beer bash. Christmas fairs occur in Munich, Nuremberg, Lübeck, Berlin, Münster and Heidelberg, among other places.

TRANSPORT

INTERNATIONAL AIRPORTS (And distances from nearest city): Berlin-Tergel (TXL) 8 km, Berlin-Schönefeld (SXF) 20 km, Berlin-Tempelhof (THF) 6 km, Cologne (CGN) 14 km, Düsseldorf (DUS) 8 km, Hamburg (HAM) 9 km, Munich (MUC) 28.5 km, Stuttgart (STR) 14 km, amongst others.

INTERNAL TRAVEL Air, river, rail and road networks all well maintained and efficient in the western part, and is being improved in eastern Germany.

RED TAPE

VISAS REQUIRED (UK/US) None.

VACCINATIONS REQUIRED: See 'Vaccinations required around the world' on page 653.

DRIVING REQUIREMENTS International Driving Permit or national licence, car registration papers, insurance legally required, Green Card recommended.

COUNTRY REPS IN UK/US UK: 23 Belgrave Square, London SW1X 8PZ, tel (020) 7824 1300, fax (020) 7824 1449, email info@german-embassy.org.uk. US: 4645 Reservoir Road, NW, Washington, DC 20007, tel (202) 298 4000, fax (202) 298 4249, email ge-embus@ix.netcom.com.

UK/US REPS IN COUNTRY UK: Wilhelmstrasse 70-71, 10117 Berlin, tel (30) 204 570, fax (30) 2045 7579, email info@berlin.mail.fco.gov.uk. US: Neustädtische Kirchstrasse 4, 10117 Berlin, tel (30) 238 5174, fax (30) 238 6290.

PEOPLE AND PLACE

CAPITAL Berlin.

LANGUAGE German.

PEOPLES German (92%), other European and Turkish minorities.

RELIGION Protestant, Roman Catholic.

SIZE (SQ KM) 357,027.

POPULATION 82,536,680.

POP DENSITY/KM 231.2.

STATE OF THE NATION

SAFETY Safe, apart from racist violence against non-white targets.

LIFE EXPECTANCY M 75.66, F 81.81.

BEING THERE

ETIQUETTE When entering a shop, restaurant or similar venue, visitors should say a greeting such as *Guten Tag* (or *Grüss Gott* in Bavaria) before saying what it is that they want. Likewise, to leave without saying *Auf Wiedersehen* can also cause offence. Also, be prepared for an early start to the day - businesses andschools often open at 8 am.

CURRENCY Euro (€) = 100 *cents*

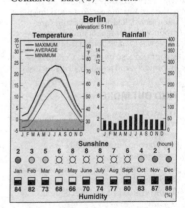

Berlin (elevation: 51m)

HIGHLIGHTS

BAVARIA Culturally unique, with the city of Munich its heart and soul. The world-famous Oktoberfest, sees all the stereotypes fulfilled; beer-quaffing, sausage-eating, men in tight fitting *lederhosen* and oompah bands. But this southern region is also known for its beautiful forests and charming walled towns. The Romantic Road, from Würzberg to Füssen, takes in some of the best bits.

BERLIN Buzzing and fun capital city, full of history, fine museums and urban culture.

The knocking down of the Berlin Wall led to a vast transformation of the city, as East and West reunified.

RIVER RHINE Scenic waterway, noted for breathtaking riverside landscapes, charming towns and wine-growing. Best enjoyed on a pleasure cruise.

NEUSCHWANSTEIN Fairytale-style castle, perched 200-metres above a picturesque wooded valley. Close to the border with Austria, this romantic alpine retreat was created by King Ludwig II, along with nearby Hohenschwangau Castle.

TRIER Germany's oldest city, Trier was historically the capital of the Western Roman Empire, and residence of the Emperor Constantine. It was an important early city of Christianity and preserves some impressive Roman monuments.

BLACK FOREST Home of the cuckoo clock and the chocolate gateaux, this region skirts the borders with France and Switzerland to the east of the Rhine. Named after dark evergreens that line the landscape, it offers great walking, skiing and swimming in lakes.

FINANCE Credit cards and traveller's cheques widely accepted.

BUSINESS HOURS 0800-1600 Mon-Friday.

GMT +1 (+2 in summer).

VOLTAGE GUIDE 230 AC, 50 Hz.

COUNTRY DIALLING CODE 49.

CONSUMING PLEASURES

FOOD & DRINK Meals commonly based on meat, with typical dishes such as *Leberkäs* (pork and beef loaf) often served with dumplings. Sausages, from *Weisswurst* (white sausages), *Rostbratwurst*, to *Frankfurters* are popular. Beer is the national drink, and German wines are good too.

SHOPPING & SOUVENIRS Binoculars and cameras, porcelain, handmade crystal, silver, steelware. Solingen knives, leatherware, sports equipment, musical instruments, wooden carved toys, Meissen china.

FIND OUT MORE

WEBSITES www.germany-tourism.co.uk, www.britischebotschaft.de,
www.germany-info.org, www.germany.info,
www.cometogermany.com, www.bahn.de,
www.berlin.de, www.frankfurt.de,
www.hamburg-highlights.de,
www.stuttgart-tourist.de.

LOCAL MEDIA No homegrown English-language papers, but international press widely available.

TOURIST BOARDS IN UK/US UK: PO Box 2695, London W1A 3TN, tel (020) 7317 0908, fax (020) 7317 0917, email gntolon@d-z-t.com. US: 20th Floor, 122 East 42nd Street, New York, NY 10168, tel (212) 661 7200, fax (212) 661 7174, email gntonyc@d-z-t.com.

Germany produces more than 300 different types of bread and some 1,200 varieties of biscuits

GHANA

WHEN TO GO

WEATHER Tropical, hot and humid. Rainy seasons from March-July, September-October.

FESTIVALS Panafest is held in the summer as a celebration of Ghanaian roots where people come to celebrate their heritage. The Homowo Festival celebrates the harvest with dances that are 'making fun of hunger', (the translation of 'Homowo'). The Aboakyer Festival is celebrated in central Ghana to mark the migration of this group from Western Sudan.

TRANSPORT

INTERNATIONAL AIRPORTS Accra (ACC) 10 km from the city.

INTERNAL TRAVEL Limited domestic air services and rail network - the rail service is a loop serving the coastal strip and towns. Almost 40,000 km of roads. Car hire available but expensive.

RED TAPE

VISAS REQUIRED (UK/US) Required.

VACCINATIONS REQUIRED: See 'Vaccinations required around the world' on page 653.

DRIVING REQUIREMENTS International Driving Permit recommended. British driving licence valid for 90 days.

COUNTRY REPS IN UK/US UK: 13 Belgrave Square, London SW1X 8PN, tel (020) 7201 5919, fax (020) 7245 9552, email enquiries@ghana-com.co.uk. US: 19 East 47th Street, New York, NY 10017, tel (212) 832 1300, fax (212) 751 6743, email ghanaperm@aol.com.

UK/US REPS IN COUNTRY
UK: PO Box 296, 2 Osu Link, off Gamel Abdul Nasser Road, Osu Ara, Accra, tel (21) 701 0650, fax (21) 701 0655, email high.commission.accra@fco.gov.uk.
US: PO Box 194, Ring Road East, Accra, tel (21) 775 348, fax (21) 776 008, email consulateaccra@state.gov.

PEOPLE AND PLACE

CAPITAL Accra.

LANGUAGE English.

PEOPLES Ashanti, Fanti, Mole-Dagbani, Ga-Adangbe, Ewe.

RELIGION Christianity, traditional beliefs, Islam.

SIZE (SQ KM) 238,537.

POPULATION 18,845,265.

POP DENSITY/KM 79.

STATE OF THE NATION

SAFETY Usual petty crime, especially after dark. Otherwise relatively safe.

LIFE EXPECTANCY M 55.04, F 56.99.

BEING THERE

ETIQUETTE Always address people by their formal titles unless requested not to. Do not use the left hand to touch food. Do not photograph military installations.

CURRENCY *Cedi* = 100 *pesewas*.

FINANCE Credit cards and traveller's cheques accepted in main towns.

BUSINESS HOURS 0800-1200, 1400-1700 Monday-Friday, 0830-1200 Saturday.

GMT GMT.

VOLTAGE GUIDE 220 AC, 50 Hz.

COUNTRY DIALLING CODE 233.

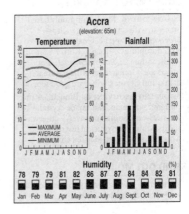

Accra
(elevation: 65m)

Temperature / Rainfall

MAXIMUM
AVERAGE
MINIMUM

J F M A M J J A S O N D

Humidity (%)

78	79	79	81	82	86	87	87	84	84	82	81
Jan	Feb	Mar	Apr	May	June	July	Aug	Sept	Oct	Nov	Dec

HIGHLIGHTS

ACCRA Accra hosts a celebration of Ghanaian art. A large collection is housed in the National Museum, and the Centre for National Culture is an art centre and craft market: you can come here to see the creation and buy the finished product. The Makola Market is another bustling market selling crafts and other goods. The Kwame Nkrumah Mausoleum is a splendidly adorned monument to the first President, and the National Theatre is home to musicals, plays and dance.

CENTRAL REGION On the border with the Gulf of Guinea, this area is home to ancient castles and forts - holding areas, it is thought, for those caught in the ancient slave trade. Cape Coast Castle was built in the 16th century and remained the seat of the British administration in the Gold Coast until the late nineteenth century.

KUMASI The ancient capital of the Ashanti civilisation. Lord Baden-Powell burnt down the Manhyia Palace and the Royal Mausoleum, but their ruins can still be explored for an idea of how the Ashanti lived.

ABURI BOTANICAL GARDENS These gardens were planted by British naturalists in colonial days and have a fine collection of sub-tropical plants, including the 'monkey pot' tree in which poor ancestors were said to be trapped.

KAKUM NATIONAL PARK Conservation area for elephants, antelope, monkeys, 800 species of rare bird, butterflies, amphibians and reptiles. Visitors can walk in the canopy, 333 metres above ground.

CONSUMING PLEASURES

FOOD & DRINK Dishes include traditional soups of palm nut and ground nut, *kontomere* and *okro* (stews) accompanied by *fufu* (pounded cassava).

SHOPPING & SOUVENIRS Luxury items, handmade gold and silver jewellery, modern and old african jewellery, Ashanti stools and brass weights.

FIND OUT MORE

WEBSITES www.ghana-com.co.uk, www.britishhighcommission.gov.uk/ghana, www.ghanaembassy.org, www.ghanaweb.com, www.geographia.com/ghana.

LOCAL MEDIA *The Ghanaian Times, Daily Graphic, The Mirror, Weekly Spectator* are all printed in English.

TOURIST BOARDS IN UK/US n/a.

Ghana is home to Lake Volta, the largest man-made lake on Earth. It stretches for two-thirds of the country's entire length.

GREECE

WHEN TO GO

WEATHER Warm Mediterranean climate with dry hot summers (April-September). Most rain falls between November-March.

FESTIVALS Carnivals are held between February and March, with feasts and dancing. Easter is the most religious of festivals. Mid-June to late September sees the Hellenic Festival host drama and music events in Greece's many ancient theatres. Men stay at home to do the housework, women drink in cafes - but only once a year, as a role reversal on 8 January.

TRANSPORT

INTERNATIONAL AIRPORTS Athens (ATH) 14 km from the city. International airports on most major islands.

INTERNAL TRAVEL Cheap and easy to travel round the islands on frequent ferry and boat services. Good road network on the whole. Train services from Athens to northern Greece and Peloponnissos.

RED TAPE

VISAS REQUIRED (UK/US) None.

VACCINATIONS REQUIRED: See 'Vaccinations required around the world' on page 653.

DRIVING REQUIREMENTS National driving licence acceptable for EU nationals, otherwise an International Driving Permit and contact with ELPA (Automobile & Touring Club of Greece). EU nationals taking their own cars must obtain a Green Card for stays over three months.

COUNTRY REPS IN UK/US UK: 1A Holland Park, London W11 3TP, tel (020) 7229 3850, fax (020) 7229 7221. US: 2221 Massachusetts Avenue, NW, Washington, DC 20008, tel (202) 939 1300, fax (202) 939 1324, email greece@greekembassy.org.

UK/US REPS IN COUNTRY
UK: 1 Ploutarchou Street, 106 75 Athens, tel (210) 727 2600, fax (210) 727 2743, email information.athens@fco.gov.uk.
US: 91 Vassilissis Sophias Avenue, 101 60 Athens, tel (210) 721 2951, fax (210) 364 2986, email usembassy@usembassy.gr.

PEOPLE AND PLACE

CAPITAL Athens.
LANGUAGE Greek.
PEOPLES Greek.
RELIGION Greek Orthodox.
SIZE (SQ KM) 131,957.
POPULATION 11,018,400.
POP DENSITY/KM 83.5.

STATE OF THE NATION

SAFETY Safe.
LIFE EXPECTANCY M 76.59, F 81.76.

BEING THERE

ETIQUETTE With a strong sense of history and culture, customs may vary throughout the country, but the people retain a great sense of unity. The Greek Orthodox Church has a strong influence on rural people's way of life. Throwing the head back is a negative gesture. Smoking is prohibited in public.

CURRENCY Euro (€) = 100 *cents.*

FINANCE Credit cards and traveller's cheques widely accepted.

BUSINESS HOURS 0800-1430 Mon, Wed, Sat. 0800-1400, 1730-2030 Tue, Thu, Fri. (Shopping hours; business hours n/a)

GMT +2 (+3 in summer).

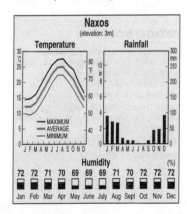

Naxos (elevation: 3m)
Temperature / Rainfall / Humidity

HIGHLIGHTS

ATHENS The capital of Greece, and the birthplace of Western civilisation. The 2,400-year-old Parthenon still dominates the skyline from its position on the Acropolis. The Theatre of Dionysus and Odeon of Herodes Atticus are close by, as are many other ancient sites. The flea market in Plaka, narrow streets winding past tavernas and craft shops, is a good area to feel the bustle of Athens that has continued for so long.

DELPHI Home to the Oracle, who offered guidance to the rulers of ancient Greece, and the huge Temple of Apollo.

IONIAN ISLANDS Ithaca was the setting for *The Odyssey*, Cefalonia beside it for *Captain Corelli's Mandolin*, Corfu to the north for youthful revelry. Sedate and party areas can be found in the Ionian group as each island has its own character.

AEGEAN ISLANDS The Aegean Islands are not as lush as their Ionian counterparts, but can be just as attractive. Lesbos, the largest of the islands, has beautiful beaches, therapeutic springs, vast olive groves, and a propensity for attracting lazing lesbians.

MYKONOS The most expensive and most visited of all the islands. There is much to see in the white-washed cobbled labyrinth of a town, full of beautiful boutiques. A lively nightlife is especially popular among the international gay community. Take the boat trip to Paradise beach, but stay on the boat, and enjoy the captain call, "Next stop, Super Paradise!". It can't get much better.

VOLTAGE GUIDE 220 AC, 50 Hz.
COUNTRY DIALLING CODE 30.

CONSUMING PLEASURES

FOOD & DRINK Charcoal grilled meat and kebabs, *dolmades* (stuffed vine leaves), *moussaka* and *avgolemono* (chicken broth with rice, eggs and lemon juice) are found everywhere. They are often preceded by a selection of *meze* (appetisers). *Retsina* wine is made from pine-needle resin. Spirits include *ouzo*, which is aniseed-based.

SHOPPING & SOUVENIRS Lace, jewellery, metalwork, pottery, knitwear, furs, rugs, leather goods, local wines and spirits.

FIND OUT MORE

WEBSITES www.greekembassy.org.uk, www.gnto.co.uk, www.greekembassy.org, www.greektourism.com, www.hri.org/infoxenios, www.travel0greece.com, www.athensguide.com, www.athens-today.gr, www.crete.tournet.gr, www.ionian-islands.com, www.helios.gr/rhodes.

LOCAL MEDIA *Athens News, Athens Daily Post* are printed in English.

TOURIST BOARDS IN UK/US UK: 4 Conduit Street, London W1S 2DJ, tel (020) 7495 9300, fax (020) 7287 1369, email info@gnto.co.uk. US: Olympic Tower, 645 Fifth Avenue, 9th floor, Suite 903, New York, NY 10022, tel (212) 421 5777, fax (212) 826 6940, email info@greektourism.com.

> The Olympics were first held in ancient Olympia in 776 BC, according to the philosopher Hippias of Elis. The modern Games were reinaugurated in Athens in 1896

GRENADA

WHEN TO GO

WEATHER Tropical climate with a dry season from January to May.

FESTIVALS Like many Caribbean islands, Carnival is one of the biggest festivals in the Grenadan calendar. It takes place in August and includes calypso and steel band competitions and features revellers in bright costumes. Carriacou island holds its Carnival in February, while it also hosts the Carriacou Regatta sailing event in July or August.

TRANSPORT

INTERNATIONAL AIRPORTS Point Salines International Airport (GND), 11 km from St George's.

INTERNAL TRAVEL Large fleet of charter yachts available for round-island trips. Most main roads in good condition. Car hire available in St George's and St Andrew's.

RED TAPE

VISAS REQUIRED (UK/US) None.

VACCINATION S REQUIRED: See 'Vaccinations required around the world' on page 653.

DRIVING REQUIREMENTS Temporary licences available on presentation of a valid driving licence. An international driving licence is recommended, but not required.

COUNTRY REPS IN UK/US UK: 5 Chandos Street, London W1G 9DG, tel (020) 7631 4277, fax (020) 7631 4274, email grenada@high-commission.demon.co.uk. US: 1701 New Hampshire Avenue, NW, Washington, DC 20009, tel (202) 265 2561, fax (202) 265 2468, email grenada@oas.org.

UK/US REPS IN COUNTRY UK: PO Box 56, Netherlands Building, Grand Anse, St George's, tel 440 3222, fax 440 4939, email bhcgrenada@caribsurf.com. US: PO Box 54, Lance aux Epines, St George's, tel 444 1173-6, fax 444 4820, email usemb_gd@caribsurf.com.

PEOPLE AND PLACE

CAPITAL St George's.

LANGUAGE English.

PEOPLES Of African descent. European and indigenous Indian minorities.

RELIGION Roman Catholic, Anglican.

SIZE (SQ KM) 344.5.

POPULATION 100,895.

POP DENSITY/KM 292.9.

STATE OF THE NATION

SAFETY Safe.

LIFE EXPECTANCY M 62.74, F 66.31.

BEING THERE

ETIQUETTE Local culture reflects a colonial past, with British and French customs an influence on modern-day Grenada. Likewise, African culture, imported by the slaves, can be seen through practices such as the Shango dance. Roman Catholicism is a further influence on local life.

CURRENCY East Caribbean dollar (EC$).

FINANCE Traveller's cheques widely accepted, limited acceptance of major credit cards.

BUSINESS HOURS 0800-1330 Mon-Thurs, 0800-1600 Friday.

GMT -4.

VOLTAGE GUIDE 220/240 AC, 50 Hz.

COUNTRY DIALLING CODE 1 473.

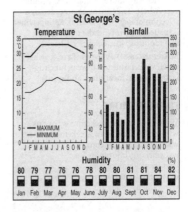

St George's — Temperature / Rainfall / Humidity chart

	Jan	Feb	Mar	Apr	May	June	July	Aug	Sept	Oct	Nov	Dec
Humidity (%)	80	79	77	76	76	78	80	80	81	81	84	82

HIGHLIGHTS

ST GEORGE'S
Picturesque hillside capital, with a deep horseshoe-shaped harbour called the Carenage, lined with eighteenth-century warehouses and restaurants. It has a small museum, two old forts - Fort George and Fort Frederick - a bustling waterfront and a colourful public market. The botanical gardens and zoo are also worth a visit.

CARRIACOU
Laid-back rural island to the northeast of Grenada island, with an unspoiled West Indian character and uncrowded beaches. A yachtsman's paradise, it holds a large regatta in summer. Carriacou also has an impressive museum with a collection of artefacts from the French and British occupation of the islands.

PETIT MARTINIQUE
Small dependency of Grenada, which can be walked around in about an hour. A large mountain dominates the island, from the top of which one can enjoy superb views over the neighbouring Grenadine Islands .

GRAND ANSE BEACH
Grenada's main resort area, a beautiful stretch of turquoise water fringed by fine white sand. Beach vendors sell t-shirts and spice baskets, and offer to braid hair, but generally it's all quite low-key. The beach is good for snorkelling and is also the starting point for diving tours.

GRAND ETANG NATIONAL PARK
Verdant park in the central highlands, set around Grand Etang Lake, a crater that forms the starting point for several walking trails. The park has a wealth of flora and fauna and there are fantastic flower displays at various points in the year.

CONSUMING PLEASURES

FOOD & DRINK Specialities include seafood with vegetables, *calaloo* soup, crabs, conches (*lambi*), avocado ice-cream. The local rum and beer is excellent and is called *Carib*.

SHOPPING & SOUVENIRS Leather crafts, jewellery, spices, straw goods, printed cottons.

FIND OUT MORE

WEBSITES www.grenadagrenadines.com, www.grenadaconsulate.org, www.grenadaembassyusa.org, www.spiceisle.com, www.grenadaexplorer.com, www.geographia.com/grenada.

LOCAL MEDIA All newspapers in English, including *The Grenadian Voice, Grenada Today, The Informer*.

TOURIST BOARDS IN UK/US UK: c/o Representation Plus, 11 Blades Court, 121 Deodar Road, London SW15 2NU, tel (020) 8877 4516, fax (020) 8874 4219, email grenada@representationplus.co.uk. US: PO Box 1668, Lake Worth, FL 33460, (561) 588 8176, fax (561) 588 7267, email cnoel@grenadagrenadines.com.

Wooden houses have been banned in the capital, St George's, since the eighteenth century, when two devastating fires swept through the city

GUATEMALA

WHEN TO GO

WEATHER Climate affected by altitude. Coastal regions and northeast hot all year. Rainy season May to September.

FESTIVALS A number of official public holidays take place throughout the year, including Independence Day on 15 September and the period of Semana Santa, the four days of Holy Week leading up to Easter. Additionally, *fiestas* are a major part of Guatemalan life, with celebrations often connected with local saints' days. They are frenetic and joyous affairs, with processions, beauty contests and *salsa* music. Often participants will don costumes and perform traditional dances. It's all capped off with drink, dance and fireworks. The Easter processions in Antigua, the Day of the Dead Kite festival in Santiago Sacatepéquez in November and the Day of the Dead festival in Todos Santos in December are among the most captivating events.

TRANSPORT

INTERNATIONAL AIRPORTS Guatemala City (GUA) 4 km from the city.

INTERNAL TRAVEL Air transport most efficient mode of internal travel. Extensive road network but less than a third of the roads are all-weather. Car hire available in Guatemala City.

RED TAPE

VISAS REQUIRED (UK/US) None.

VACCINATIONS REQUIRED: See 'Vaccinations required around the world' on page 653.

DRIVING REQUIREMENTS Local licences issued on presentation of national licences.

COUNTRY REPS IN UK/US UK: 13 Fawcett Street, London SW10 9HN, tel (020) 7351 3042, fax (020) 7376 5708, email embaguate.gtm@btconnect.com. US: 2220 R Street, NW, Washington, DC 20008, tel (202) 745 4952, fax (202) 745 1908, email info@guatemala-embassy.org.

UK/US REPS IN COUNTRY UK: Avenida La Reforma 16-00, Zona 10, Edificio Torre Internacional, Nivel 11, Guatemala City, tel 2367 5425-9, fax 2367 5430, email embassy@intelnett.com. US: Avenida La Reforma 7-01, Zona 10, Guatemala City, tel 2326 4000, fax 2334 8477.

PEOPLE AND PLACE

CAPITAL Guatemala City.

LANGUAGE Spanish.

PEOPLES Amerindian, Mestizo.

RELIGION Catholicism. Protestant minority.

SIZE (SQ KM) 108,889.

POPULATION 11,600,000.

POP DENSITY/KM 107.

STATE OF THE NATION

SAFETY Possible low-level guerrilla conflict in some areas. Otherwise safe.

LIFE EXPECTANCY M 64.27, F 66.04.

BEING THERE

ETIQUETTE Spanish influence, but also a strong ethnic culture, as the only Central American republic with a predominantly Indian population.

CURRENCY *Quetzal* (Q) = 100 *centavos*.

FINANCE Visa, American Express accepted more widely than other cards. Limited acceptance of traveller's cheques.

BUSINESS HOURS 0800-1800 Mon-Friday,

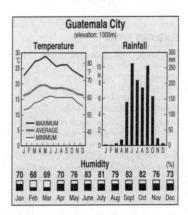

Guatemala City
(elevation: 1300m)

Temperature — Rainfall

— MAXIMUM
— AVERAGE
— MINIMUM

J F M A M J J A S O N D   J F M A M J J A S O N D

Humidity (%)

Jan	Feb	Mar	Apr	May	June	July	Aug	Sept	Oct	Nov	Dec
70	68	69	70	76	83	81	79	83	82	76	73

HIGHLIGHTS

TIKAL Majestic and massive Mayan ruins in the middle of green jungle and located in the heart of Tikal National Park close to the town of Flores. A vast complex of pyramidal temples, ball courts, causeways, plazas and public buildings, it was an inhabited city for 1,000 years before being abandoned. The reserve is home to native wildlife, including howler monkeys, tropical birds, reptiles and deer.

CARIBBEAN COAST Unspoilt coastal villages and a shoreline offering sailing, fishing and scuba-diving. This area retains a strong Afro-Caribbean feel due to the settling of the descendants of slaves, or *garifunas*, around here.

GUATEMALA CITY Polluted, sprawling urban agglomeration. Rickety 'chicken buses' rumble through this chaotic capital, a busy transport hub and administrative centre. Its museums have some superb Mayan artefacts and good modern Guatemalan art.

THE HIGHLANDS Home to the greatest numbers of indigenous Mayan groups, who still retain the language and rituals of their ancestors.

XELA Also known as Quetzaltenango, Xela is a good base for excursions to nearby hot springs and picturesque handicraft-making villages. Set among a group of high mountains and volcanoes, it contains narrow colonial streets, fine public buildings and a pleasant central square. It's also a centre for language schools.

TAJUMULCO VOLCANO You can hike to the top of this dramatic 4,220-metre peak, the highest point in Central America.

0800-1200 Saturday.
GMT -6..
VOLTAGE GUIDE 110 AC, 60 Hz.
COUNTRY DIALLING CODE 502.

CONSUMING PLEASURES

FOOD & DRINK Usual Central American food such as *tortillas* and *tacos*. Specialities include *chiles rellenos* (stuffed chiles) and *pepián* (meat stew with vegetables).

SHOPPING & SOUVENIRS Textiles, handicrafts, jewellery, jade carvings, leather goods, ceramics and basketry.

FIND OUT MORE

WEBSITES www.guatemala-embassy.org, http://guatemala.usembassy.gov, www.guatemalaweb.com.

LOCAL MEDIA English-language newspapers include *The Review, Guatemala Weekly, Central America Report,* and *Siglo News.*

TOURIST BOARDS IN UK/US n/a.

The great Mayan ruins at Tikal are still known by their ancient name, which means 'Place of Voices'

GUINEA

WHEN TO GO

WEATHER Tropical and humid. Wet season from May-October, dry season from November-April.

FESTIVALS Visitors will be most likely to find festivals when travelling between January and March. During the Touré regime (1958 - 1984) regional and non-Islamic festivals were attacked as sectarian and unproductive. This repression over a generation removed the festivals' viability and tradition. Accordingly, the main events these days follow the Islamic calendar. Tabaski, the Feast of Sacrifice, and Ramadan, the month of fasting, are key times.

TRANSPORT

INTERNATIONAL AIRPORTS Conakry (CKY) 13 km from the city.

INTERNAL TRAVEL Rail travel is generally not recommended. Roads are generally in poor condition.

RED TAPE

VISAS REQUIRED (UK/US) Required.

VACCINATIONS REQUIRED: See 'Vaccinations required around the world' on page 653.

DRIVING REQUIREMENTS International Driving Permit.

COUNTRY REPS IN UK/US UK: 83 Victoria Street, London SW1H 0HW, tel (020) 7078 6087, fax (020) 7078 6086, email genevieverippon@guineaconsuluk.freeserve .co.uk. US: 2112 Leroy Place, NW, Washington, DC 20008, tel (202) 986 4300, fax (202) 986 4800.

UK/US REPS IN COUNTRY UK: BP 6729, Conakry, tel 455 807, fax 456 020, email britcon@oury@biasy.net. US: BP 603, Second Boulevard and Ninth Avenue, Conakry, tel 411 520/1/3, fax 411 522.

PEOPLE AND PLACE

CAPITAL Conakry.

LANGUAGE French.

PEOPLES Fila (Fulani), Malinke, Soussou.

RELIGION Islam, Animist and Roman Catholic minorities.

SIZE (SQ KM) 245,857.

POPULATION 8,359,000.

POP DENSITY/KM 34.

STATE OF THE NATION

SAFETY High levels of street crime, do not carry valuables.

LIFE EXPECTANCY M 48.61, F 51.15.

BEING THERE

ETIQUETTE Islamic beliefs should be respected. It is important to go through niceties before beginning a conversation. Use titles when addressing people. Request permission before photographing people, it is inadvisable to photograph military installations or government buildings. If unavoidable, permits can be obtained from the Ministère de l'Intérieur et de la Sécuité.

CURRENCY Guinea *franc* (F.G) = 100 *centimes.*

FINANCE Limited acceptance of credit cards and traveller's cheques.

BUSINESS HOURS 0800-1630 Monday-Thursday, 0800-1300 Friday.

GMT GMT.

VOLTAGE GUIDE 220 AC, 50 Hz.

COUNTRY DIALLING CODE 224.

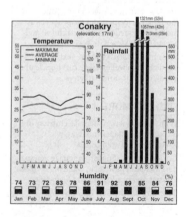

HIGHLIGHTS

CONAKRY Once called the 'Paris of Africa', Guinea's capital is today an unappealing urban sprawl. Sitting on the island of Tumbo, it's connected to the mainland by a 300-metre pier to the Kaloum Peninsula. The centre is a maze of alleys, shaded by mangroves and coconut palms. The city cathedral and museum are worth a browse.

FOUTA DJALON Beautiful highland area, populated by Fula herders and farmers. Known as 'the land of waters, fruit, faith and freedom', it offers dramatic scenery, with hills, valleys and impressive waterfalls. While local roads and tracks are of unpredictable quality, the landscape is ideal for off-the-beaten-track travel by foot or mountain bike.

GUÉCKEEDOU Situated in jungle-tufted hills near the Liberia border, this is part of the Guinée *forestière*, a region of rainforests and old, pre-Islamic tribes. The town is famous for holding one of the biggest weekly markets in West Africa, every Wednesday. The lively occasion sees tradesmen from Guinea exchange wares with merchants from Sierra Leone, Liberia and Ivory Coast, as well as Senegal, Mauritania, Mali and Gambia.

KAKIMBON CAVES In the village of Ratoma in a suburb of Conakry, these caves are the source of interesting local myths and legends and have deep religious significance for local Baga people.

ÎLES DE ROUME On the coast south of the capital, with some of the best beaches for swimming in the country. Currents can be strong, however.

CONSUMING PLEASURES

FOOD & DRINK Local dishes include *jollof rice* (rice with tomato puree, vegetables and spiced meat), stuffed chicken with ground nuts, spicy fish dishes served with rice. Locals are fond of very hot maize soup.

SHOPPING & SOUVENIRS Brightly coloured Guinean clothes, woodcarvings, leather rugs, local music, calabashes, and jewellery.

FIND OUT MORE

WEBSITES http://conakry.usembassy, http://bubl.ac.uk/link/r/republicofguinea.htm.

LOCAL MEDIA No English-language papers. One newspaper, one TV station and one radio station, all state-owned.

TOURIST BOARDS IN UK/US n/a.

> Guinea is the source of three great rivers, the Niger, Senegal and Gambia, all of which – by a quirk of history – have given their names to other countries

GUINEA-BISSAU

WHEN TO GO

WEATHER Tropical climate with a wet season between June and October. It's dry from December to April. There's high humidity exists in the months of July to September.

FESTIVALS The colourful Latin-style Carnival in Bissau in February is one of the most atmospheric events and sees elaborate floats and costumes. Besides this, some of the major festivals are connected with the Islamic calendar, the dates of which vary year-on-year. Tabaski, the feast of Sacrifice, and Ramadan, the holy month of fasting, are among the most significant.

TRANSPORT

INTERNATIONAL AIRPORTS Bissau (OXB) 11 km from the city.

INTERNAL TRAVEL A few internal flights, some serving the outlying islands. Most towns are accessible by ship, riverboats or ferry. A small proportion of the roads are all-weather.

RED TAPE

VISAS REQUIRED (UK/US) Required.

VACCINATIONS REQUIRED: See 'Vaccinations required around the world' on page 653.

DRIVING REQUIREMENTS International Driving Permit recommended. A temporary licence is available on presentation of a valid UK licence.

COUNTRY REPS IN UK/US UK: n/a, nearest 94 Rue St Lazare, 75009 Paris, France, tel (1) 4526 1851, fax (1) 4526 6059. US: 15929 Yukon Lane, Rockville, MD 20855, tel (301) 947 3958.

UK/US REPS IN COUNTRY UK: CP 100, Bissau, tel 201 224, fax 201 265 (the British Consulate, which can only provide limited assistance). The British Embassy in Dakar (see Senegal) usually deals with enquiries relating to Guinea-Bissau. US: The US Embassy in Dakar (see Senegal) deals with enquiries relating to Guinea-Bissau.

PEOPLE AND PLACE

CAPITAL Bissau.

LANGUAGE Portuguese.

PEOPLES Balante, Fulani, Malinke.

RELIGION Indigenous beliefs, Islam.

SIZE (SQ KM) 36,125.

POPULATION 1,449,000.

POP DENSITY/KM 40.1.

STATE OF THE NATION

SAFETY Calm at present, though recently subject of a failed coup by Western mercenaries probably seeking oil concessions.

LIFE EXPECTANCY M 45.09, F 48.92.

BEING THERE

ETIQUETTE Casual wear is widely accepted. Social customs should be respected, especially in Muslim areas. If photographing military or police installations, request permission first.

CURRENCY *Communauté Financiare Africaine franc* (CFA) = 100 *centimes*.

FINANCE Very limited use of credit cards, traveller's cheques rarely accepted.

BUSINESS HOURS 0730-1230, 1430-1830 Monday-Friday.

GMT GMT.

VOLTAGE GUIDE Limited supply on 220 AC, 50 Hz.

COUNTRY DIALLING CODE 245.

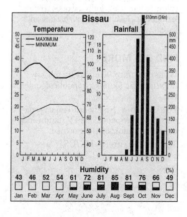

	Jan	Feb	Mar	Apr	May	June	July	Aug	Sept	Oct	Nov	Dec
Humidity (%)	43	46	52	54	61	72	81	85	81	76	66	49

HIGHLIGHTS

BISSAU Relaxed and pleasant capital. Although not abundant with sightseeing opportunities, it has some interesting architecture and a good museum, the Museum of African Artefacts. This houses some interesting exhibits of traditional sculpture, pottery, weaving and basketware. Close by, the colourful central market has a lively ambience.

BIJAGÓS ARCHIPELAGO Group of islands infrequently visited by foreigners, some uninhabited. Of these, the island of Bolama - once the country's capital - has some fine beaches. Bubaque, a former Portuguese favourite accessible by motorised *pirogue*, is another option. Outside of these two islands, be prepared for some discomfort.

JEMBEREM Wildlife spotting in an area of unspoilt tropical rainforest. It's central to a community-based conservation project, the Cantanhez Natural Park, set up to protect birds, monkeys and chimpanzees. This lush and sacred forest is best navigated with a guide. You can arrange such a tour through the local chief.

GABÚ Guinea-Bissau's eastern capital is also the Fula and Muslim capital. It has an animated commercial centre thanks largely to its trade with nearby Guinea and Senegal.

BUBA Transport hub of the south, with some pleasant swimming beaches and waterfalls nearby. The Falls, on the Rio Cirubal, turn to mere rapids in the dry season, but at other times are extremely popular during weekends and school holidays.

CONSUMING PLEASURES

FOOD & DRINK Spicy chicken and fish dishes, *jollof rice* (rice with tomato puree, spiced meat and vegetables), cassava, yams and maize.

SHOPPING & SOUVENIRS Locally made artefacts and carvings.

FIND OUT MORE

WEBSITES www.guineabissau.com, www.lonelyplanet.com/worldguide/destinations/africa/guinea-bissau/.

LOCAL MEDIA No English-language newspapers. One, state-owned TV channel.

TOURIST BOARDS IN UK/US n/a.

Every year in November, after the rains, Bissau is struck by a swarm of flying crickets. They bash into walls and lights, while locals try to clear them away with hoses and brooms

GUYANA

WHEN TO GO

WEATHER Warm and tropical all year, with generally high rainfall and humidity. Rainy seasons November-January and April-August.

FESTIVALS Most public holidays are religious ones, and with such diverse peoples, different celebrations are not far away. Everyone celebrates at each other's festivals, so cultures are shared and the country remains united. The major festivals are Christmas, Easter, Divali, Phagwah, Eid-ul-Azha, and Mashramani. The latter is celebrated on 23 February, and means 'the celebration of a job well done': it marks the birth of the Republic. Steel bands play, people dress in spectacular costumes, and floats parade the dancing streets.

TRANSPORT

INTERNATIONAL AIRPORTS Georgetown (GEO) 40 km from the city.

INTERNAL TRAVEL Air most reliable means of internal transport. Irregular river services. No scheduled passenger rail services. All-weather roads concentrated on eastern strip. Because of Guyana's many rivers, most journeys outside the capital will involve ferries and the attendant delays. Limited car hire in Georgetown.

RED TAPE

VISAS REQUIRED (UK/US) None.

VACCINATIONS REQUIRED: See 'Vaccinations required around the world' on page 653.

DRIVING REQUIREMENTS International Driving Permit or foreign licence.

COUNTRY REPS IN UK/US UK: 3 Palace Court, Bayswater Road, London W2 4LP, tel (020) 7229 7684, fax (020) 7727 9809, email ghc.1@ic24.net. US: 2490 Tracy Place, NW, Washington, DC 20008, tel (202) 265 6900, fax (202) 232 1297, email guyanaembassydc@hotmail.com.

UK/US REPS IN COUNTRY UK: PO Box 10849, 44 Main Street, Georgetown, tel 226 5881-4, fax 225 3555, email

enquiries@britain-in-guyana.org. US: PO Box 10507, 100 Young and Duke Street, Kingston, Georgetown, tel 225 4900-9, fax 225 8497, email visageorge@state.gov.

PEOPLE AND PLACE

CAPITAL Georgetown.

LANGUAGE English.

PEOPLES Afro-Guyanese, Indo-Guyanese.

RELIGION Christian, Hindu. Muslim minority

SIZE (SQ KM) 214,969.

POPULATION 767,000.

POP DENSITY/KM 3.6.

STATE OF THE NATION

SAFETY Violent crime common in the capital

LIFE EXPECTANCY M 62.86, F 68.28.

BEING THERE

ETIQUETTE Men should avoid wearing shorts, otherwise casual dress is acceptable.

CURRENCY Guyanese dollar (G$) = 100 cents.

FINANCE Limited acceptance of credit cards. Traveller's cheques not recommended for those wishing to change money quickly.

BUSINESS HOURS 0800-1130, 1300-1630 Monday-Friday.

GMT -4.

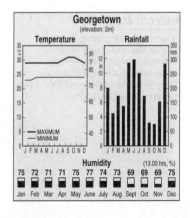

Georgetown
(elevation: 2m)

Temperature — Rainfall — Humidity (13.00 hrs, %)

	Jan	Feb	Mar	Apr	May	June	July	Aug	Sept	Oct	Nov	Dec
Humidity	75	72	71	71	75	77	74	73	69	69	69	75

HIGHLIGHTS

GEORGETOWN Considered to be the 'Garden City of the Caribbean', the capital, at the mouth of the Demerrara River, is furnished with impressive wooden colonial buildings, palm trees, orchids, and lotus lilies. However, its name is rather hopeful as its location is on the Atlantic. More than that, it lies below the Atlantic's high water mark, and has to be protected from flooding by an esplanade on the sea front and a s eries of walls on the river.

RUPUNUNI This vast area of Amazonian forest is not often considered as a destination, since the rainforest draws attention away. But these lands have their own unique peoples and ecosystems. Cattle ranching and gold mining are the major employers here. It is worth investigating the Macuxi and Wapixana Amerindian villages in the area.

IWOKRAMA RAINFOREST This rainforest, in the centre of the country, is lush with lowland tropical forest but dominated by the tall dense canopy 20 to 30 metres above. It has a rich species count, but was once home to many now extinct creatures.

KAIETEUR FALLS Able to rival Iguazu, Niagara, and Victoria for size and awe, these falls are one set of three on the Potaro River, with a straight drop of 250 metres.

BEACHES Beautiful beaches line the coast of the country. Almond Beach, Shell Beach, No 63 Beach, and Saxacalli Beach are perhaps the most impressive. Shell Beach runs for 140 kilometres to the border with Venezuela. Four species of sea turtle nest along the beach.

VOLTAGE GUIDE 110 AC, 60 Hz.

COUNTRY DIALLING CODE 592.

CONSUMING PLEASURES

FOOD & DRINK Mixed influences including Indian curries, African plaintain and coconut cooking, Portuguese stews and Amerindian dishes. Favourites are chicken, pork, steak and shrimp. Demerara Rum is well worth a try.

SHOPPING & SOUVENIRS Straw hats, baskets, clay goblets, jewellery, bows and arrows, hammocks, pottery, salad bowls, magnificent jewellery using gold, silver and precious stones.

FIND OUT MORE

WEBSITES www.carribean.co.uk, www,britain-in-guyana.org, www.guyana.org, www.georgetown. usembassy.gov, www.geographia.com/guyana.

LOCAL MEDIA Local papers in English include, *The Guyana Chronicle, Stabroek News, Kaieteur News, The Mirror,* and *The Sunday Chronicle.*

TOURIST BOARDS IN UK/US UK: Caribbean Tourism Organisation, 22 The Quadrant, Richmond, Surrey, TW9 1BP, tel (020) 8948 0057, fax (020) 7727 9809, email ctolondon@caribtourism.com.

A jungle vine leaf, Nibbee, is used to make a handy fibre from which to craft almost anything, from clothing to furniture: it's real 'jungle twine'

HAITI

WHEN TO GO

WEATHER Tropical, with intermittent rain throughout the year.

FESTIVALS The Carnival is held from a few days before Ash Wednesday in Port-au-Prince over three days. Music, parade floats, singing and dancing fill the streets. All-night parties ensue. The Peasant Carnival continues where the Carnival left off, with celebrations each weekend throughout Lent. A vivid image of voodoo culture is visible during this time, with costumes, rare musical instruments and rituals.

TRANSPORT

INTERNATIONAL AIRPORTS Port-au-Prince (PAP) 8 km from the city.

INTERNAL TRAVEL Cancellations and delays common on scheduled internal flights. Planes may be chartered. All-weather roads from Port-au-Prince to Cap-Haiten and Jacmel. Car hire available in Port-au-Prince.

RED TAPE

VISAS REQUIRED (UK/US) Required by Australians.

VACCINATIONS REQUIRED: See 'Vaccinations required around the world' on page 653.

DRIVING REQUIREMENTS International Driving Permit.

COUNTRY REPS IN UK/US UK: The Embassy in Brussels is accredited to the UK (139 Chaussée de Charleroi, B-1060, Brussels, Belgium, tel (2) 649 7381, fax (2) 640 6080). USA: 271 Madison Avenue, 5th Floor, New York, NY 10016, tel (212) 697 9767, fax (212) 681 6991, email info@haitianconsulate-nyc.org.

UK/US REPS IN COUNTRY UK: PO Box 1302, Apartment 6, Hotel Montana, Rue de F Cardazo, Bourdon, Port-au-Prince, tel 257 3969, fax 257 4048, email britcon@transnethaiti.com. USA: BP 1761, 5 boulevard Harry Truman, Port-au-Prince, tel 222 0200, fax 223 1641.

PEOPLE AND PLACE

CAPITAL Port-au-Prince.

LANGUAGE French and Creole.

PEOPLES Mainly of African descent.

RELIGION Roman Catholic (80%), Protestant and other, including voodoo (often practiced alongside other religions).

SIZE (SQ KM) 27,750.

POPULATION 8,132,000.

POP DENSITY/KM 293.

STATE OF THE NATION

SAFETY Highly unstable, subject to political violence and serious crime.

LIFE EXPECTANCY M 51.58, F 54.31.

BEING THERE

ETIQUETTE Beachwear should not be worn away from the beach, otherwise casual dress is acceptable.

CURRENCY *Gourde* = 100 *centimes.*

FINANCE American Express widely accepted, traveller's cheques generally accepted.

BUSINESS HOURS 0800-1600 Mon-Friday.

GMT -5.

VOLTAGE GUIDE 110 AC, 60 Hz.

COUNTRY DIALLING CODE 509.

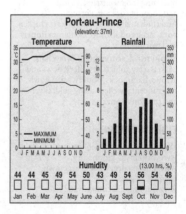

Port-au-Prince
(elevation: 37m)

Temperature   Rainfall

Humidity   (13.00 hrs, %)

Jan	Feb	Mar	Apr	May	June	July	Aug	Sept	Oct	Nov	Dec
44	44	45	49	54	50	43	49	54	56	54	48

HIGHLIGHTS

PORT-AU-PRINCE
The capital, home to a million people, is bursting at the seams. Open sewers flow past dilapidated buildings, the brown dirt floor is in sharp contrast to the bright murals on the walls. The Iron Market is the centre of this chaos - stalls, vendors, and piles of fruit vie for space among the shoppers. A calmer atmosphere can be found in the hillside suburb of Pétionville, where visitors can enjoy some of the best dining. For great views head further up the hill to Boutillier, high in the mountains.

CAP-HAÏTIEN
More laid back, more Latin than the capital. But then, sandwiched between lush green mountains and pleasant beaches, with Spanish-influenced architecture and Cointreau in the air, you might expect it to be. Not far from here, on Christmas Eve 1492, Columbus ran aground on the north coast of Hispaniola. The wreck of his ship the *Saint Maria* remains near by.

CITADELLE This remarkable mountain fortress took 15 years for Henri Christophe to complete. Balanced at the top of the 900-metre Pic la Ferrière, with views of Cap-Haïtien, it was designed to resist French invasions. The ruins of Sans Soucie Palace, modelled on Versailles, lie nearby.

JACMEL A town of Victorian elegance and stuccoed palaces, set among magnificent mountain scenery, serves as a centre for voodoo, with a number of intriguing temples to visit. It draws international crowds at Carnival time.

CONSUMING PLEASURES

FOOD & DRINK Creole specialities combine French and African elements. Dishes include *langouste flambé* (local lobster), *grillot et banane pese* (pork chops and island bananas), *diri et djondjon* (rice and black mushrooms) and Guinea hen with sour orange sauce. Deserts include sweet potato pudding, mango pie, and fresh coconut ice-cream. The local drink is rum, but French wines are available in better restaurants.

SHOPPING & SOUVENIRS Carvings, printed fabrics, leatherwork, paintings, straw hats, seed necklaces, jewellery.

FIND OUT MORE

WEBSITES www.haiti.com, http://usembassy.state.gov/haiti, www.discoverhaiti.com

LOCAL MEDIA No English-language papers.

TOURIST BOARDS IN UK/US n/a.

Haitians are the poorest people in the Western hemisphere. Their average annual income is only US$500, and 85 per cent of the population are thought to live below the absolute poverty line

HONDURAS

WHEN TO GO

WEATHER Tropical climate with cooler weather in the mountains. Dry season from November-April, wet from May-October.

MEDICAL CARE Limited, insurance strongly recommended.

FESTIVALS The Fiesta de San Isidro is held in La Ceiba in May for a week. Lavishly dressed locals parade the streets. The Fiesta of San Antonia, in the banana port of Tela begins with people setting off fire crackers and making sure no one is sleeping, at 4 am. Parades and events follow for a week. Danli goes mad on the last weekend of August for the Corn Festival, where cultural and sporting events give way to an all night street party. Independence from the Spanish is celebrated each year on 15 September.

TRANSPORT

INTERNATIONAL AIRPORTS Tegucigalpa (TGU) 5 km from the city.

INTERNAL TRAVEL Frequent internal flights between Tegucigalpa and major towns. There are only three railways, mainly used for transport between plantations. Some all-weather roads, and car hire is available at the airport.

RED TAPE

VISAS REQUIRED (UK/US) None.

VACCINATIONS REQUIRED: See 'Vaccinations required around the world' on page 653.

DRIVING REQUIREMENTS Both foreign and international driving licences accepted.

COUNTRY REPS IN UK/US UK: 115 Gloucester Place, London W1U 6JT, tel (020) 7486 4880, fax (020) 7486 4550, email hondurasuk@lineone.net. USA: 3007 Tilden Street, NW, Suite 4M, Washington, DC 20008, tel (202) 966 7702, fax (202) 966 9751, email embassy@hondurasemb.org.

UK/US REPS IN COUNTRY UK: The British Embassy in Guatemala deals with enquiries relating to Honduras. USA: Avenida La Paz, Apdo 3453, Tegucigalpa, tel 238 5114, fax 236 9037.

PEOPLE AND PLACE

CAPITAL Tegucigalpa.

LANGUAGE Spanish.

PEOPLES *Mestizo (mixed-race)*. Small community of indigenous Indians.

RELIGION Roman Catholic.

SIZE (SQ KM) 112,492.

POPULATION 6,535,344.

POP DENSITY/KM 58.1.

STATE OF THE NATION

SAFETY Since Hurricane Mitch in 1998, the devastation on this poor island led to a soaring crime rate with incidents of violent crime, sexual assault, and car jacking. Avoid travelling at night.

LIFE EXPECTANCY M 64.66, F 66.59.

BEING THERE

ETIQUETTE A strong Spanish influence runs throughout the country, but the people are *mestizo*, lead an agricultural way of life, and survive on a low standard of living. Courtesies should be paid to those living the traditional lifestyle. If invited to someone's home, do not bring flowers, but send them before or after the event. Do not wear beach clothing away from the beach.

CURRENCY *Lempira (La)* = 100 *centavos*.

FINANCE Credit cards and traveller's cheques accepted.

BUSINESS HOURS 0800-1200, 1400-1700

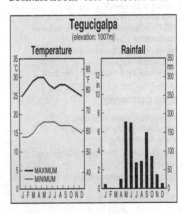

Tegucigalpa (elevation: 1007m)
Temperature / Rainfall

HIGHLIGHTS

TEGUCIGALPA

Untouched by those common Central American disasters - fire and earthquake - the capital has retained its traditional core. However, the city's parks were affected by the hurricane of 1998. A visit to the United Nations Park is worthwhile for the splendid views of the city that it affords, but remain vigilant to a rise in crime in the area.

COPÁN

This ancient city, just over 170 km from the banana and sugar centre of San Pedro Sula, remains the best example of Mayan Indian culture. The ruins include the Great Plaza, a grand amphitheatre, the Court of the Hieroglyphic Stairway, and the Great Acropolis. Sculptures found in excavations are displayed in the museum - a full scale replica of a recently excavated temple is truly awesome.

THE CARIBBEAN COAST

This area was once tied to the banana industry. Now, as Honduras attempts to change its image away from a 'banana republic', the airport's use is turning from bananas to tourists.

The coast has plenty of good hotels and tropical beaches, but you can also take a day to explore the nearby Pico Bonito National Park, a rainforest on steep slopes with countless waterfalls and great views.

THE BAY ISLANDS

This archipelago of three major islands and several smaller ones, hilly and tropical, with a coral reef, great diving, and sandy beaches sounds idyllic. But it is the history that impresses, spanning Mayan civilisation, Spanish exploration, colonial adventuring, and the British Empire.

Mon-Friday, 0800-1100 Saturday.
GMT -6.
VOLTAGE GUIDE 110/120/220 AC, 60 Hz.
COUNTRY DIALLING CODE 504.

CONSUMING PLEASURES

FOOD & DRINK Typical dishes include *curiles* (seafood), tortillas, enchiladas, and *tamales de elote* (corn tamales). Typical tropical fruits.

SHOPPING & SOUVENIRS Excellent inexpensive craftsmanship. Woodcarvings, cigars, leather goods, straw hats and bags, seed necklaces and baskets.

FIND OUT MORE

WEBSITES www.hondurasemb.org, http://honduras.usembassy.gov, www.honduras.com.

LOCAL MEDIA *Honduras This Week* is published in English every week.

TOURIST BOARDS IN UK/US n/a.

The term 'banana republic' was coined for Honduras. The story goes that the US-owned United Fruit Company wanted tax breaks for its banana plantations there: so it brought in armed heavies from New Orleans to install a new president who would do its bidding. The new man duly waived the company's taxes for the next 25 years

HUNGARY

WHEN TO GO

WEATHER Spring and autumn are mild, summers are hot and winters are very cold with snowfall.

FESTIVALS Hungary's largest free summer festival runs from July to August and is known as 'Summer on Chain Bridge'. It's a display of Hungarian culture aimed to tempt foreign and domestic tourism. Likewise, 'Summer in Debrecen' runs during the same period and includes several events, for theatre, wine, flowers, and culture. Elsewhere, a folklore festival takes place in August in Százhalombatta. Opera and ballet are performed in Budapest as part of the Budafest in July and August. Many other festivals run throughout the year.

TRANSPORT

INTERNATIONAL AIRPORTS Budapest Ferihegy (BUD) 16 km from the city.

INTERNAL TRAVEL No scheduled internal air services. Efficient rail service and a good road network. Car hire is available at tourist offices and at the airport.

RED TAPE

VISAS REQUIRED (UK/US) Required by Australians.

VACCINATIONS REQUIRED: See 'Vaccinations required around the world' on page 653.

DRIVING REQUIREMENTS Pink format EU licence accepted but International Driving Permit required if green licence held.

COUNTRY REPS IN UK/US UK: 35 Eaton Place, London SW1X 8BY, tel (020) 7235 5218, fax (020) 7823 1348, email office@huemblon.org.uk. USA: 3910 Shoemaker Street, NW, Washington, DC 20008, tel (202) 362 6730, fax (202) 966 8135, email office@huembwas.org.

UK/US REPS IN COUNTRY UK: Harmincad utca 6, 1051 Budapest, tel (1) 266 2888, fax (1) 266 0907, email info@ britemb.hu. USA: Szabadság tér 12, 1054 Budapest, tel (1) 475 4400, fax (1) 475 4764, email usconsular.budapest@state.gov.

PEOPLE AND PLACE

CAPITAL Budapest.

LANGUAGE Hungarian.

PEOPLES Magyar (90%), small groups of Slovaks, Germans, Romanies.

RELIGION Roman Catholic, Calvinist.

SIZE (SQ KM) 93,030.

POPULATION 10,142,000.

POP DENSITY/KM 109.

STATE OF THE NATION

SAFETY Safe.

LIFE EXPECTANCY M 68.18, F 76.89.

BEING THERE

ETIQUETTE Few people speak English outside of the large hotels, large restaurants and tourist offices, particularly outside of Budapest. A knowledge of German can be useful. In the capital, be wary of unscrupulous taxi drivers. Smoking is prohibited on public transport in towns and in public buildings, but smokers may light-up on long-distance trains.

CURRENCY Hungarian *forint* (Ft) = 100 *fillér*.

FINANCE Credit cards and traveller's cheques widely accepted.

BUSINESS HOURS 0800-1630 Mon-Thurs, 0800-1400 Friday.

GMT +1 (+2 in summer).

VOLTAGE GUIDE 230 AC, 50 Hz.

COUNTRY DIALLING CODE 36.

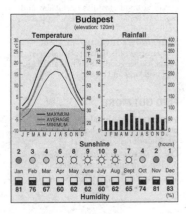

HIGHLIGHTS

BUDAPEST Atmospheric capital city set on the banks of the River Danube. Graceful Buda is characterised by fine old buildings on steep Gellért Hill, while buzzing Pest is the lively modern centre on the opposite bank of the river, with bars, cafes and businesses. Giant Communist statues, which once lined the city's streets, now stand in the fascinating Statue Park, a scrub of land 30 minutes out of town by car. Figures include Lenin, Marx, Engels, as well as workers.

BATHS Budapest is perhaps best known for its numerous and characterful thermal baths. These include the Gellert Baths, housed in a historic hotel on the Buda side and the Széchenyi Baths, a large yellow complex in City Park, with an open-air pool and large communal saunas frequented by old men playing chess.

LAKE BALATON Known as the 'Hungarian Sea', Balaton is a popular holiday spot and the largest freshwater lake in central Europe. It's fringed by sandy beaches and has shallow waters, making it ideal for swimming. The nearby countryside is dotted with pretty villages.

THE DANUBE BEND A good day trip, just 45 kilometres north of the capital. Europe's second-longest river passes the Börzsöny and Pilis hills ranges, the sharp curve is one of the prettiest stretches, winding past picturesque towns. The hills are popular with hikers.

THE GREAT PLAINS Comprising half of the country, the plains are vast areas of vineyards, orchards and farmland. To the east are the Asian steppes.

CONSUMING PLEASURES

FOOD & DRINK Specialities include *halászlé* (fish soups) with pasta, *gulyás* or goulash soup and stuffed vegetables. Sweet pastries and *gundel palacsinta* (pancakes) are popular. Try *Tokaji* a strong dessert wine and Bull's Blood, a strong red wine. Apricot brandy, *barack*, is typical of the region.

SHOPPING & SOUVENIRS Embroideries, porcelain and national dolls.

FIND OUT MORE

WEBSITES www.huemblon.org.uk, www.hungary.org, www.britishembassy.hu, www.huembwas.org, www.gotohungary.com, www.usembassy.hu, www.budapestweek.com.

LOCAL MEDIA *Budapest Week, The Budapest Sun, The Hungarian Observer, The Hungarian Economy* are some of the English-language newspapers.

TOURIST BOARDS IN UK/US UK: 46 Eaton Place, London SW1X 8AL, tel (020) 7823 1032, fax (020) 7823 1459, email htlondon@hungarytourism.hu. US: 150 East 58th street, 33rd Floor, New York, NY 10155, (212) 355 0240, fax (212) 207 4103, email info@gotohungary.com.

The culture of bathing has been an integral part of Hungarian life since Roman times. Budapest alone has more than 100 thermal springs and some 50 swimming pools and medicinal baths.

ICELAND

WHEN TO GO

WEATHER Mild summers (May-August) with nearly 24 hours of daylight. Very cold winters (November-March). The Northern Lights, also known as the Aurora Borealis, appears from the end of August, although is best seen in the winter months. The weather can be very changeable throughout the year.

FESTIVALS Summertime is the busiest for events, often held out-of-doors. Reykjavik hosts the annual Cultural Night in August, which features outdoor concerts, performances, fireworks and fairs going on until the wee hours. Bars, restaurants, shops and galleries also stay open late. Other notable events include the gluttonous Beer Day on 1 March, which marks the end of probation in 1989, and the International Viking Festival, held in Hafnarfjordur in June.

TRANSPORT

INTERNATIONAL AIRPORTS Keflavik (REK) 51 km from Reykjavik.

INTERNAL TRAVEL Sea ferry services to all coastal ports. No rail system. Most roads are gravel. Use of headlights obligatory at all times. Car hire easily available. Efficient buses in summer, limited service in winter.

RED TAPE

VISAS REQUIRED (UK/US) None.

VACCINATIONS REQUIRED: See 'Vaccinations required around the world' on page 653.

DRIVING REQUIREMENTS International Driving Permit recommended. A temporary licence is available on presentation of a valid UK licence. Drivers must be over 20 years.

COUNTRY REPS IN UK/US UK: 2A Hans Street, London SW1X 0JE, tel (020) 7259 3999, fax (020) 7245 9649, email icemb.london@utn.stjr.is. USA: 1156 15th Street, Suite 1200, NW, Washington, DC 20005, tel (202) 265 6653, fax (202) 265 6656, email icemb.wash@utn.stjr.is.

UK/US REPS IN COUNTRY
UK: Laufásvegur 31, 101 Reykjavik, tel 550 5100, fax 550 5105, email britemb@centrum.is. USA: Laufásvegur 21, 101 Reykjavik, tel 562 9100, fax 562 9110, email consularreykja@state.gov.

PEOPLE AND PLACE

CAPITAL Reykjavik.
LANGUAGE Icelandic.
PEOPLES Icelandic.
RELIGION Evangelic Lutheran.
SIZE (SQ KM) 103,000.
POPULATION 288,471.
POP DENSITY/KM 2.8.

STATE OF THE NATION

SAFETY Safe.
LIFE EXPECTANCY M 78.13, F 82.34.

BEING THERE

ETIQUETTE Iceland is a classless society. It also has a strong literary tradition. In terms of people's names, an Icelander is called by his first name, as his surname is comprised of his father's Christian name, plus *son* (e.g. John, son of Magnus, is called John Magnusson). Women add the suffix *dóttir*, meaning daughter.

CURRENCY Icelandic *krona* (Ikr) = 100 *aurar*.

FINANCE Credit cards and traveller's cheques widely accepted.

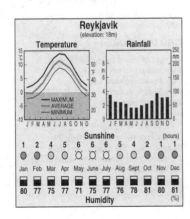

Reykjavik (elevation: 18m)
Temperature / Rainfall

Sunshine (hours)

Jan	Feb	Mar	Apr	May	June	July	Aug	Sept	Oct	Nov	Dec
1	2	4	5	6	6	6	5	4	2	1	1

Humidity (%)

| 80 | 77 | 75 | 77 | 71 | 75 | 77 | 76 | 78 | 81 | 80 | 81 |

HIGHLIGHTS

REYKJAVIK Meaning 'Smoky Bay', this busy and vibrant capital set on a broad bay is in an area of geothermal hot springs - the source of the city's central heating system. Old-fashioned wooden buildings sit side-by-side with modern buildings. In the daytime, hang out at one of the many coffee shops, or browse the interesting art galleries, book-shops and museums. At night, the city comes alive to the sound of its buzzing music scene, especial-ly at weekends.

BLUE LAGOON Steaming, aquamarine pool that is Iceland's most famous attrac-tions. The unique mineral-rich lagoon is set amid a black lava field in the heart of the Icelandic wilder-ness and the water's properties are said to have a beneficial effect on the skin. At 35° C it's like a huge hot tub. Don a silica-mudpack and join the many swimmers floating by.

GULFOSS Waterfalls abound in this spec-tacular landscape. Perhaps the most impressive of these is the so-called Golden Waterfall, a stunning rainbow-tinged double cascade of the Hvitá River.

GEYSIR The place from which the name for all spouting hot springs originates. Strokkur spouts up to 35 metres every six minutes.

FRIDAY NIGHTS IN THE CAPITAL Reykjavik is renowned for its wild weekend *runtur*, when Icelanders go out on the town and get sozzled. Starting with drinks at friends' houses, revellers head to bars and nightclubs from midnight onwards.

BUSINESS HOURS 0800-1600 (summer) and 0900-1700 (winter), Mon-Friday.
GMT +1.
VOLTAGE GUIDE 220 AC, 50 Hz.
COUNTRY DIALLING CODE 354.

CONSUMING PLEASURES

FOOD & DRINK Influenced by Scandinavian and European cuisines, and based heavily on fish and lamb. Salmon served in many forms, most popularly as *gravlax*. Specialities include *hangikjot* (smoked lamb) and *hardfiskur* (dried fish).

SHOPPING & SOUVENIRS Fluffy wool blankets, coats, hats, and jackets, pottery (often with crushed lava inset).

FIND OUT MORE

WEBSITES www.iceland.org/uk, www.britishembassy.is, www.iceland.org/us, www.usa.is, www.icelandtouristboard.com, www.goscandinavia.com, www.icetourist.is, www.randburg.com/is, www.rvk.is.

LOCAL MEDIA International press available.
TOURIST BOARDS IN UK/US US: c/o The Scandinavian Tourist Board, 655 Third Av-enue, New York, NY 10017, tel (212) 885 9700, fax (212) 885 9710, email usa@ icetourist.is.

Reykjavik is the world's northernmost capital city – and also one of the smallest

INDIA

WHEN TO GO

WEATHER Coolest from December-February, with fresh mornings and dry, sunny days. Very hot March-May. Monsoon rains June-September.

FESTIVALS Impossible to mention them all, with a wealth of colourful celebrations taking place throughout the year in this immense and vibrant country. Some are national, others regional, while some festivals are specific to a certain temple. Holi, the Festival of Colours, in March, is a definite highlight. It's all great fun, with people throwing coloured powder and water at each other, although it can get rather rowdy. In autumn, the festival of lights, Diwali, is celebrated with particular enthusiasm in northern Indian, with fireworks being lit, together with candles and oil lamps.

TRANSPORT

INTERNATIONAL AIRPORTS (And distances from nearest city) Mumbai (BOM) 29 km, Calcutta (CCU) 13 km, Delhi (DEL), Chennai (MAA) 14 km.

INTERNAL TRAVEL Domestic air network connects over 70 cities. Second-largest rail system in the world, relatively inexpensive. Cars with drivers available for hire, self-drive cars not generally available.

RED TAPE

VISAS REQUIRED (UK/US) Required.

VACCINATIONS REQUIRED: See 'Vaccinations required around the world' on page 653.

DRIVING REQUIREMENTS International Driving Permit.

COUNTRY REPS IN UK/US UK: India House, Aldwych, London WC2B 4NA, tel (020) 7836 8484, fax (020) 7836 4331, email fc.office@hcilondon.net. USA: 3 East, 64th Street, New York, NY 10021, tel (212) 774 0600, fax (212) 861 3788.

UK/US REPS IN COUNTRY UK: Shanti Path, Chanakyapuri, New Delhi 110 021, tel (11) 2687 2161, fax (11) 2687 0065, email Postmaster.NewDelhi@fco.gov.uk. USA: 1 Shantipath, Chanakyapuri, New Delhi 110 021, tel (11) 2419 8000, fax (11) 2419 0017, email ndcentral@state.gov.

PEOPLE AND PLACE

CAPITAL New Delhi.

LANGUAGE English, Hindi.

PEOPLES Indo-Aryan, Dravidian.

RELIGION Hindu (83%), Muslim, Sikh, Christian and Buddhist minorities.

SIZE (SQ KM) 3,166,414.

POPULATION 1,049,000,000.

POP DENSITY/KM 331.

STATE OF THE NATION

SAFETY Safe, if sensible. Beware petty scams. Certain areas very unsafe (e.g. Kashmir and Bihar).

LIFE EXPECTANCY M 63.57, F 65.16.

BEING THERE

ETIQUETTE The Hindu greeting is to fold the hands, tilt the head forward and say *namaste*. Visitors will be expected to remove footwear when entering temples and other places of religious significance. A fee is often charged for visitors to take photographs of monuments. Many Hindus are vegetarian and many, especially women, do not drink alcohol. Sikhs and Parsees do not smoke. Above all, the various traditions of India's religions should be respected at all times.

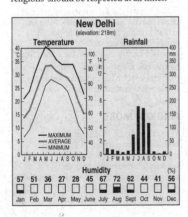

New Delhi (elevation: 218m)

	Jan	Feb	Mar	Apr	May	June	July	Aug	Sept	Oct	Nov	Dec
Humidity (%)	57	51	36	27	28	45	67	72	62	44	41	56

HIGHLIGHTS

RAJASTHAN Dust-dry landscapes in this desert region near Delhi, once home to the great Moghul rulers, who built fabulous cities and lasting monuments. Camels pulling carts, jostle with *tuk-tuks* and other motorised traffic in the so-called 'red city' of Jaipur. The romantic city of Udaipur captivates with fine architecture and scenic lake palace.

VARANASI Burning *ghats* on the banks of the sacred River Ganges. Perhaps India's most holy city.

TAJ MAHAL The chaotic city of Agra is the somewhat unlikely location for one of the world's most beautiful buildings. Its glistening marble facade shines under the moonlight, like 'a tear on the face of eternity'.

KERALA The picturesque town of Cochin, with its traditional Chinese fishing nets, lies at the coastal fringe of this verdant landscape of idyllic backwaters - lush streams, rivers, lagoons and canals.

MUMBAI Bustling port city and commercial centre, formerly called Bombay. It's the home of the colourful B ollywood film industry, not to mention 18 million citizens.

AMRITSAR Friendly city and spiritual home of the Sikh faith, the focal point of which is the peaceful and awe-inspiring Golden Temple.

HIMALAYA Mighty snow-covered peaks, cool hill stations and vast tea plantations.

CURRENCY Rupee (Rs) = 100 paise.

FINANCE Credit cards and traveller's cheques accepted in most cities.

BUSINESS HOURS 0930-1700 Mon-Friday, 0930-1300 Saturday.

GMT +5.30.

VOLTAGE GUIDE 220 AC, 50 Hz. Some areas have a DC supply.

COUNTRY DIALLING CODE 91.

CONSUMING PLEASURES

FOOD & DRINK Huge regional variations. Curries are based on individual *masalas*, each containing a unique blend of freshly ground spices. More meat dishes in the north, generally served with breads - *nan*, *chapatis* or *pooris*, mainly fish and vegetarian in the south, served with rice. *Chai* - tea brewed with milk and sugar - is the most popular drink.

SHOPPING & SOUVENIRS Silks, spices, jewellery, silverware, carpets and antiques.

FIND OUT MORE

WEBSITES www.hcilondon.net, www.incredibleindia.org, www.ukinindia.org, www.indianembassy.org, www.indiacgny.org, www.indiatraveltimes.com.

LOCAL MEDIA Many English-language newspapers, including *The Times of India, Indian Express, The Hindu, Hindustan Times, The Telegraph.*

TOURIST BOARDS IN UK/US UK: 7 Cork Street, London W1S 3LH, (020) 7437 3677, fax (020) 7494 1048, email info@india-touristoffice.org. US: Suite 1808, 1270 Avenue of the Americas, New York, NY 10020, tel (212) 586 4901, fax (212) 582 3274, email ny@itonyc.com.

> "All the convergent influences of the world run through this society. There is not a thought that is being thought in the West or East that is not active in some Indian mind."
> *Edward Thompson*

INDONESIA

WHEN TO GO

WEATHER Tropical climate varies across the huge archipelago. Driest June-September, rainiest December-March.

FESTIVALS Numerous festivals occur, their dates varying with the Islamic, Hindu or Buddhist calendars. The Bali Arts Festival in June-July 2005 is a month of dance and musical performances and craft exhibitions.

TRANSPORT

INTERNATIONAL AIRPORTS Jakarta (CGK) 20 km from city. For Bali, Denpasar (DPS) 13 km is 13 km from city.

INTERNAL TRAVEL Extensive local flight network of Garuda Indonesia (national airline) is good for island-hopping. Sea ferries operate slowly but efficiently. Larger islands have railways and good roads. Local buses good for remoter places.

RED TAPE

VISAS REQUIRED (UK/US) Not required for up to 60 days tourism for Australia, Canada, EU, USA. Required for all journalists and business people.

VACCINATIONS REQUIRED: See 'Vaccinations required around the world' on page 653.

DRIVING REQUIREMENTS International Driving Permit.

COUNTRY REPS IN UK/US UK: 38 Grosvenor Square, London W1K 2HW, tel (020) 7499 7661, fax (020) 7491 4993, email kbri@btconnect.com. USA: 5 East 68th St, New York, NY 10021, tel (212) 879 0600, fax (212) 570 6202, email kjriny@ix.netcom.com.

UK/US REPS IN COUNTRY UK: Deutsche Bank Building, 19th floor, Jalan Iman Bonjol 80, Jakarta 10310, tel (21) 390 7484-7, fax (21) 316 0858. USA: Jalan Medan Merdeka Selatan 4-5, Jakarta 10110, tel (21) 3435 9000, fax (21) 435 9922.

PEOPLE AND PLACE

CAPITAL Jakarta.

LANGUAGE Bahasa Indonesian.

PEOPLES Many island peoples, including Javanese, Sundanese, Malays, Madurese and Chinese.

RELIGION Muslim (87%), Christian, Hindu, Buddhist.

SIZE (SQ KM) 1,922,570.

POPULATION 217,131,000.

POP DENSITY/KM 112.9.

STATE OF THE NATION

SAFETY Seriously volatile. Many islands have experienced rioting and murder due to ethnic/religious conflict and political tensions. Authorities unable to guarantee safety in some areas. Seek latest information at time of visit.

LIFE EXPECTANCY M 67.13, F 72.13.

BEING THERE

ETIQUETTE Social courtesies remain formal - do not touch food until you are invited to by the host, do not use the left hand, do not display affection publicly (especially kissing), but touching members of the same sex in conversation is fine and common. Pointing and patting heads is to be avoided. Locals are polite and generous and courteous to those they like and are respected by. Smile. Remain calm. Observe Muslim dress codes.

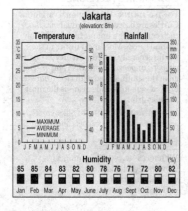

Jakarta (elevation: 8m)

Temperature / Rainfall

Humidity (%)

Jan	Feb	Mar	Apr	May	June	July	Aug	Sept	Oct	Nov	Dec
85	85	84	83	82	80	78	76	71	72	80	82

HIGHLIGHTS

BALI Savour the rich and enchanting cultural heritage of this beautiful and green Hindu island, which has attracted travellers for centuries, seeking its exotic architecture, religious events and sweeping rice-field terraces. Known as the Island of the Gods, it also offers fine sandy beaches, popular among surfers and other watersports enthusiasts. Ubud, in the middle of Bali, is a fascinating centre for art and local handicrafts.

KOMODO DRAGONS Prehistoric-looking , the world's largest lizards can be found on the islands of Komodo and Rinca. The muscular reptiles can grow to over two metres in length.

SHADOW PUPPETS Exquisite theatre shows retelling ancient epics with up to 200 beautifully carved silhouettes, particularly fine on Java.

BOROBUDUR Perched on a hill in central Java, this awesome architectural feat is one of the structural wonders of the world. This is the largest Buddhist temple complex anywhere and comprises some 232 temples - many of which were lost in the jungle until rediscovered by the British in 1815. The walls feature five-kilometres of relief carvings.

ORANGUTANS The russet-furred 'forest men' can be seen in their jungle habitat at the rehabilitation centre on Kalimantan - an island still home to dense jungle and tribal nomads.

SUMATRA Second-largest island in the archipelago, located on the equator. Its fine jungle reserves protect varied wildlife, such as tigers, elephants, tapirs and rhinos.

CURRENCY *Rupiah* = 100 *sen*.

FINANCE Mastercard, Amex and visa accepted in cities; for remote areas take US dollars in small bills.

BUSINESS HOURS Private businesses 0900-1700 Mon-Friday. Government offices 0800-1430 Mon-Thurs, 0800-1200 Friday.

GMT +7.

VOLTAGE GUIDE 220 AC, 50 Hz (rural areas 110 AC, 50 Hz).

COUNTRY DIALLING CODE 62.

CONSUMING PLEASURES

FOOD & DRINK Rice is the staple diet for most Indonesians, and is served in a variety of ways. One of the most popular is the Dutch-influenced *rijstafel*, combinating meat, fish and vegetable curries. *Satay* and seafood are also common. Each island has regional specialities, from *gado-gado* in Java (a salad of raw and cooked vegetables and peanuts) to *babi guling* in Bali (roast pig).

SHOPPING & SOUVENIRS Batiks, woodcarvings, sculpture, silverwork, baskets, hats, bamboo, paintings.

FIND OUT MORE

WEBSITES
www.indonesianembassy.org.uk,
www.britain-in-indonesia.or.id,
www.embassyofindonesia.org,
www.indony.org,
www.indonesia-tourism.com,
www.bali-paradise.com.

LOCAL MEDIA Many, notably *The Indonesian Times*, *Indonesian Observer*, *Jakarta Post*, *Bali Post*.

TOURIST BOARDS IN UK/US n/a.

Indonesia is the largest archipelago in the world and incorporates some 583 separate languages and dialects – many as different as English from Welsh

IRAN

WHEN TO GO

WEATHER Dry and hot April-October, harsh winter December-February.

FESTIVALS Zoroastrian festival Yalda is on 21 December, the longest night of the year, when families get together to feast, as the Good versus Evil battle of day and night reaches a peak. In March Chahar Shanbeh Suri marks the end of the Zoroastrian year. People jump through bonfires to end the old year and welcome the new.

TRANSPORT

INTERNATIONAL AIRPORTS Tehran (THR) 5 km from city.

INTERNAL TRAVEL Good road network between main towns; widespread, cheap buses, if erratic; taxis available. Some trains..

RED TAPE

VISAS REQUIRED (UK/US) Required.

VACCINATIONS REQUIRED: See 'Vaccinations required around the world' on page 653.

DRIVING REQUIREMENTS *Carnet de passage*, International Certificate of Vehicle Ownership, personal insurance. An International Driving Permit may prove useful but is not legally recognised.

COUNTRY REPS IN UK/US
UK: 50 Kensington Court, Kensington High St, London W8 5DB, tel (020) 7937 5225, fax (020) 7938 1615, email consulate@iran-embassy.org.uk. USA: c/o The Embassy of Pakistan, 2209 Wisconsin Avenue, NW, Washington, DC 20007, tel (202) 965 4990, fax (202) 965 1073, email requests@daftar.org.

UK/US REPS IN COUNTRY UK: 198 Ferdowsi Avenue, Tehran 11316--91144, tel (21) 670 5011-7, fax (21) 670 8021, email BritishEmbassyTehran@fco.gov.uk. USA: n/a.

PEOPLE AND PLACE

CAPITAL Tehran

LANGUAGE Farsi.

PEOPLES Persian (50%), Azeri, Lur and Bakhtiari, Kurd, Arab.

RELIGION Shi'a Muslim (95%), Sunni Muslim.

SIZE (SQ KM) 1,648,043.

POPULATION 66,479,838.

POP DENSITY/KM 40.3.

STATE OF THE NATION

SAFETY Generally welcoming and safe. Observe Islamic customs strictly. Note that there is a total ban on video cameras.

LIFE EXPECTANCY M 68.58, F 71.4.

BEING THERE

ETIQUETTE Emotions concerning the UK and US are fragile, so avoid contentious issues. The Westernisation of the country has been halted, Koranic law is much more traditional. Western influences are discouraged. Handshaking should not be done with the opposite sex. Intimate relations between non-Muslim men and Muslim women are illegal and can result in imprisonment. Address hosts by surname or title. Accept offers of tea. Dress is conservative, especially for women - cover heads in public, wear loose clothing, conceal arms and legs. Don't smoke, eat, or drink between sunrise and sunset during Ramadan.

CURRENCY Iranian *rial* (IR) = 100 *dinars*.

FINANCE Traveller's cheques not accepted. Unlimited foreign cash can be imported.

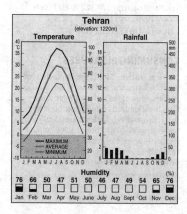

Tehran (elevation: 1220m)

Temperature / Rainfall / Humidity

	Jan	Feb	Mar	Apr	May	June	July	Aug	Sept	Oct	Nov	Dec
Humidity (%)	76	66	50	47	51	50	46	47	49	54	65	76

HIGHLIGHTS

TEHRAN This unattractive modern capital is Iran's trend-setter, whether for fashion, restaurants or politics. For those that can manage, check out the Shahid Motahari Mosque, complete with eight minarets, the maze of vaulted alleys in the north, the opulent Golestan Palace, the spectacular views from the slopes of Park-e Jamshidiyeh, and the cheap skiing in Dizin and Shemshak.

ISFAHAN The jewel of Iran..Take the 'Half the World' walking tour to admire the city's oldest mosque, the bustling bazaar and Qiyam Square's bird market. Wander on past the 48-metre-high minaret of the Mosque of Ali to the sixteenth-century Mausoleum of Harun Vilayet, with its impressive frescoes. Watch the sun go down in Imam Square, flooding the area with golden light as it sets. Later, drive out to Manar Jomban, a fourteenth-century tomb with 'shaking' minarets, then climb the Ateshkadeh-ye Isfahan, or Fire Temple, for a view over the city. Finally, stroll along the Zayandeh river to appreciate its bridges and ponder its healing properties.

THE GOLDEN TRIANGLE The area encircled by the ancient cities of Hamadan, Kermanshah, and Khorramabad, with rich historical links from the time when the Silk Road passed through this area.

BUSINESS HOURS 0800-1600 Sat-Wed, closed Thurs-Friday.

GMT +3.5

VOLTAGE GUIDE 220 AC, 50 Hz.

COUNTRY DIALLING CODE 98.

CONSUMING PLEASURES

FOOD & DRINK Rice based dishes, including *chelo khoresh* (rice topped with vegetables and meat in a nut sauce), *polo sabzi* (pilau rice with fresh herbs) and *adas polo* (rice, lentils and meat). Other popular dishes are *kofte gusht* (meatloaf) and *badinjan* (mutton and aubergine stew). Alcohol is strictly forbidden.

SHOPPING & SOUVENIRS Woodwork, carpets, rugs, silks, leather goods, mats, tablecloths, gold, silver, glass, and ceramics.

FIND OUT MORE

WEBSITES www.iran-embassy.org.uk, www.britishembassy.gov.uk/iran, www.un.int/iran, www.daftar.org.

LOCAL MEDIA *Teheran Times, Keyhan International, Iran News, Iran Daily* are all printed in English.

TOURIST BOARDS IN UK/US n/a.

"I have never encountered splendour of this kind before. Other interiors came into my mind as I stood there, to compare it with: Versailles, or the porcelain room at Shonbrun, or Saint Peter's. All are rich; but none so rich... [I rank] Isfahan among those rarer places which are common refreshment of humanity."
Robert Byron, 1937

IRAQ

WHEN TO GO

WEATHER South has desert climate, hot and dry March-October, mild winters December-February. North has the same summers, but winter is harsh in the mountains.

FESTIVALS Muslim festivals are a major part of Iraqi life, the dates of which vary according to the Islamic calendar. Ramadan, the month of fasting, is a key event.

TRANSPORT

INTERNATIONAL AIRPORTS All air travel into Iraq is currently prohibited by the UN. Nearest permitted international airport is Amman in Jordan, 15 hours by road from Baghdad. If sanctions are lifted, use Baghdad (BGW) airport, 18 km from the city.

INTERNAL TRAVEL No land crossing into Kuwait. No internal flights at present. Good railway and road network.

RED TAPE

VISAS REQUIRED (UK/US) Required. Currently only being issued for business travel, not tourism. No Israeli passports or visa stamps.

VACCINATIONS REQUIRED: See 'Vaccinations required around the world' on page 653.

DRIVING REQUIREMENTS International Driving Permit and third-party insurance.

COUNTRY REPS IN UK/US UK: 169 Knightsbridge, London SW7 1DW, tel (020) 7602 8456, fax (020) 7581 2264, email lonemb@iraqmofa.net. USA: 1801 P Street, NW, Washington, DC 20036, tel (202) 483 7500, fax (202) 462 5066, email amboffice@ iraqiembassy.org.

UK/US REPS IN COUNTRY
UK: Convention Centre opposite Rasheed Hotel, International Zone, Baghdad, tel (0) 790 192 280, email britishconsulbaghdad@ gtnet.gov.uk. USA: APO AE 09316, Baghdad, tel (1) 703 343 7604.

PEOPLE AND PLACE

CAPITAL Baghdad.

LANGUAGE Arabic.

PEOPLES Arab (79%), Kurdish, Persian, Turkoman.

RELIGION Shi'a Muslim (62%), Sunni Muslim (33%), Christian.

SIZE (SQ KM) 438,317.

POPULATION 24,510,000.

POP DENSITY/KM 55.9.

STATE OF THE NATION

SAFETY Highly dangerous, still an active war zone. Likely hostility to Westerners. Seek latest information at time of visit.

LIFE EXPECTANCY M 67.49, F 69.97.

BEING THERE

ETIQUETTE Islam is the official religion and the dominant influence on society. *Sharia* customs play an active role in the day-to-day life of the country. Visitors should be careful to respect this and act accordingly. Conservative and discreet dress should be worn in observance of local Islamic laws. Female visitors might think about wearing a veil across their hair as a sign of respect for the culture. Women should also avoid looking into men's eyes too much, as this could be interpreted as an attempt to seduce.

CURRENCY Iraqi *dinar* (ID) = 20 *dirhams*.

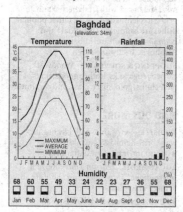

HIGHLIGHTS

At the time we go to press it is very difficult to nominate Iraq highlights as the country is a war zone. However, in future, the following are likely to figure:

BABYLON The legendary Hanging Gardens of Babylon were one of the Seven Wonders of the Ancient World and part of a great city ruled over by the Semitic King Hammirabi. Sadly, in recent times the area has been subsumed into a military base. However, tourism officials have expressed a desire to restore both the city and the ruined Gardens to some of their former glory.

BAGHDAD Straddling the River Tigris, Iraq's capital - like the country as a whole - has had its fair share of difficulties over the past few decades. Shabby back streets contrast with new buildings, while historic places such as the Ike Abbasid Palace have stood firm amid the violent turmoil. The museums of Iraqi Folklore and Modern Art are worth visiting.

KURDISH AUTONOMOUS REGION Winding mountain roads through dramatic scenery, this autonomous region is characterised by pleasant towns, orchards and waterfalls, together with a proud local people.

ANCIENT SITES Iraq has a wealth of heritage sites and is a land steeped in history. Home to the ancient cities of Ur and Nineveh, it is also the land where writing began and where the tales of the *One Thousand and One Nights* were told. Iraq was the home of the mythical Tower of Babel, and Qurnah is reputed to be the site of the biblical Garden of Eden.

FINANCE Credit cards and traveller's cheques not widely used. Unlimited foreign currency can be imported.

BUSINESS HOURS 0800-1400 Sat-Wed, 0800-1300 Thursday, closed Friday.

GMT +3.

VOLTAGE GUIDE 220 AC, 50 Hz.

COUNTRY DIALLING CODE 964.

CONSUMING PLEASURES

FOOD & DRINK Middle Eastern cuisine. Popular dishes include *quozi* (small lamb boiled whole and grilled, stuffed with rice, minced meat and spices), *tikka* (small cubes of charcoal-grilled mutton) and *dolma* (vine leaves, cabbage, lettuce, onions, aubergine, marrow or cucumbers stuffed with rice, meat and spices).

SHOPPING & SOUVENIRS Copperware, silver, spices, carpets, rugs.

FIND OUT MORE

WEBSITES www.fco.gov.uk, www.britishembassy.gov.uk/iraq, www.iraqiembassy.org.

LOCAL MEDIA Main English-language daily is the *As-Sabah*.

TOURIST BOARDS IN UK/US n/a.

"It has become a civil war, fought out with car bombs and shots to the head, while the foreign forces, US and British and the rest, look on, incapable of stopping it. This isn't how things were supposed to turn out here."
John Simpson, 2005

IRELAND

WHEN TO GO

WEATHER Warm summers between June and September, temperatures from October to March are much cooler. Rain falls all year.

FESTIVALS St Patrick's Day on 17 March is the most famous Irish celebration of the year, an occasion observed across the Emerald Isle and, it seems, everywhere else. In summer, 23/24 June marks Midsummer's Day, a Celtic fire festival. Later in the year, Lughnasa, on 29 September, marks the beginning of the harvest with festivities for Lugh, a pre-Christian god; and a three-day Puck's Fair is held in August in Killorhlin, County Kerry, revolving around a livestock show. The Galway International Oyster Festival in September attracts an increasingly international crowd.

TRANSPORT

INTERNATIONAL AIRPORTS Dublin Airport (DUB) 8 km from the city, Shannon (SNN) 26 km from Limerick, Cork (ORK) 8 km from the city.

INTERNAL TRAVEL EU-funded projects have improved roads, particularly around Dublin. Nationwide network of buses, cruising taxis infrequent.

RED TAPE

VISAS REQUIRED (UK/US) None.

VACCINATIONS REQUIRED: See 'Vaccinations required around the world' on page 653.

DRIVING REQUIREMENTS International Driving Permit. For EU nationals: full EU driving licence and motor registration book. A Green Card strongly recommended. Vehicles must have nationality coding stickers.

COUNTRY REPS IN UK/US UK: 17 Grosvenor Place, London SW1X 7HR, tel (020) 7235 2171, fax (020) 7245 6961. USA: 2234 Massachusetts Avenue, NW, Washington, DC 20008, tel (202) 462 3939, fax (202) 232 5993, email embirlus@aol.com.

UK/US REPS IN COUNTRY UK: 29 Merrion Road, Ballsbridge, Dublin 4, tel (1) 205 3700, fax (1) 205 3890, email britishembassy@abtran.com. USA: 42 Elgin Road, Ballsbridge, Dublin 4, tel (1) 668 8777, fax (1) 668 9946.

PEOPLE AND PLACE

CAPITAL Dublin.

LANGUAGE English and Gaelic.

PEOPLES Irish (95%).

RELIGION Roman Catholic.

SIZE (SQ KM) 70,182.

POPULATION 4,048,800.

POP DENSITY/KM 56.7.

STATE OF THE NATION

SAFETY Increasingly safe as the peace process gathers force.

LIFE EXPECTANCY M 74.95, F 80.34.

BEING THERE

ETIQUETTE A gregarious race, the Irish are always famously 'up for the *craic*'. Pubs are often at the centre of local community life and visitors can expect a warm welcome, be they in small villages or the larger towns.

CURRENCY Euro (€) = 100 cents.

FINANCE Credit cards and traveller's cheques widely accepted.

BUSINESS HOURS 0900-17.30 Mon-Friday.

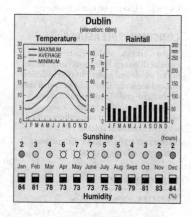

Dublin (elevation: 68m)											
Sunshine (hours)											
Jan	Feb	Mar	Apr	May	June	July	Aug	Sept	Oct	Nov	Dec
2	3	4	6	7	5	5	4	3	2	2
Humidity (%)											
84	81	78	73	73	73	75	78	79	81	83	84

HIGHLIGHTS

DUBLIN Lively, friendly and buzzing capital city set on the banks of the River Liffey. The area of Temple Bar is a throng of pubs and bars, a loud centre for Guinness-fuelled revelry. Stroll through streets of Georgian buildings, or enjoy a bus tour of the city's sights, including Dublin Castle, Trinity College, the zoo.. and the guinness brewery.

ROCK OF CASHEL Visit the Romanesque church, medieval cathedral, castle tower house, eleventh-century round tower, an early example of a high cross and the fifteenth-century Hall of Vicars.

CONNEMARA Hope for good weather and head to a beach. The white sand and clear blue water, with the Twelve Bens and Maam Turks mountain ranges on the horizon, will have you believing in paradise.

BURREN Wrap up warm and head to this huge plateau of limestone and shale in northwest Clare. Watch as the stone white cliffs turn silver and metallic in the rain and ponder the area's beauty and starkness.

KILLARNEY NATIONAL PARK Slip on your hiking boots and head to the 24,700 acre park. Or if you've had enough walking take a tour with a pony trap, or take the bike-on-boat tour through the Gap of Dunloe and over the three lakes.

BANTRY HOUSE Step inside to catch a glimpse of the life led by the Anglo-Irish aristocracy. Full of art treasures, the house contains French Napoleonic furniture, Gobelin tapestries, Aubusson carpets and a landscaped garden overlooking the bay.

GMT GMT.
VOLTAGE GUIDE 220 AC, 50 Hz.
COUNTRY DIALLING CODE 353.

CONSUMING PLEASURES

FOOD & DRINK Ireland is noted for good meat, bacon and dairy produce. Irish Stew, *colcannon* (mashed potatoes and cabbage cooked together), *crubeens* (pigs trotters) and soda bread are national favourites, and Irish oysters are notable, often served with Guinness. Irish whiskey has a unique flavour, having matured for at least seven years in a wooden barrel.

SHOPPING & SOUVENIRS Hand-woven tweed, woollens and cottons, sheepskin goods, gold and silver jewellery, knitwear, linen, pottery, crystal, and basketry.

FIND OUT MORE

WEBSITES www.tourismireland.com, www.britishembassy.ie, www.irelandemb.org, www.countydublin.com.

LOCAL MEDIA Several English-language dailies, including *The Irish Times* and the *Irish Independent*. British papers also available. Access to UK media widespread.

TOURIST BOARDS IN UK/US UK: Nations House, 103 Wigmore Street, London W1U 1QS, tel (0800) 039 7000, fax (020) 7493 9065, email info.gb@tourismireland.com. US: 345 Park Avenue, 17th Floor, New York, NY 10154, tel (212) 418 0800, fax (212) 371 9052, email info@shamrock.org.

"The luck of the Irish
is a wish more than
a characteristic."
Jan Morris, 1976

ISRAEL

WHEN TO GO

WEATHER November-March is wet, but mild. Hot and dry from June-September.

FESTIVALS Religious festivals are of great importance. The key Christian festivals are Christmas and Easter, when there is a special atmosphere in Jerusalem and Bethlehem. There are many Jewish festivals: in March, Purim is celebrated (while around the same time, Jerusalem celebrates Holy Week). Hanukkah, in December, is a festival of lights and freedom. In May, Israelis mark Holocaust Martyrs and Heroes Remembrance Day. Among Islamic festivals, Ramadan, the month of fasting, is particularly significant.

TRANSPORT

INTERNATIONAL AIRPORTS Tel Aviv (TLV) 14 km from the city, Eilat Central Airport (ETH) 8 km from the city.

INTERNAL TRAVEL Excellent roads link all Israeli towns. Railroads are being extended. Ferries run across the Sea of Galilee. Car hire is available in major cities.

RED TAPE

VISAS REQUIRED (UK/US) None.

VACCINATION S REQUIRED: See 'Vaccinations required around the world' on page 653.

DRIVING REQUIREMENTS Full driving licence and insurance. An International Driving Permit is recommended.

COUNTRY REPS IN UK/US UK: 2 Palace Green, London W8 4QB, tel (020) 7957 9500, fax (020) 7957 9577, email cons-sec@london.mfa.gov.il. USA: 3514 International Drive, NW, Washington, DC 20008, tel (202) 364 5500, fax (202) 364 5429, email ask@israelemb.org.

UK/US REPS IN COUNTRY
UK: 192 Hayarkon Street, Tel Aviv 63405, tel (3) 725 1222, fax (3) 527 8574, email webmaster.telaviv@fco.gov.uk.
USA: 71 Hayarkon Street, Tel Aviv 63903, tel (3) 519 7575, fax (3) 519 7619, email ac5@bezegint.net.

PEOPLE AND PLACE

CAPITAL Jerusalem.

LANGUAGE Hebrew and Arabic.

PEOPLES Jewish (82%), Arab.

RELIGION Jewish. Sunni Muslim minority.

SIZE (SQ KM) 22,145.

POPULATION 6,631,000.

POP DENSITY/KM 306.

STATE OF THE NATION

SAFETY Mainly safe, but significant unrest in some areas due to civil conflict. Seek latest information at time of visit.

LIFE EXPECTANCY M 77.21, F 81.55.

BEING THERE

ETIQUETTE The word *shalom*, meaning peace, is used for hello and goodbye. Respect local customs and behaviour: people generally feel strongly about their beliefs. In Christian, Jewish and Muslim holy places, visitors should dress modestly. At some significant places, such as the Wailing Wall, male visitors are given a cardboard *yarmulke* (scull cap) to wear. It is considered a violation of the *shabbat* (Saturday) to smoke in some restaurants and hotels. Discussion of Middle East politics, the legitimacy of the state of Israel and the rights of Palestinians can and does raise the ire of many in Israel and the Occupied Territories.

CURRENCY New *shekel* (IS) = 100 *agorots*.

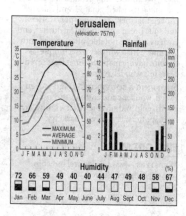

Jerusalem (elevation: 757m)

HIGHLIGHTS

JERUSALEM The narrow streets of the Old City house sites of great historic and religious significance to a third of the world's population. Enchanting at dawn.

BETHLEHEM Typical Palestinian Arab town in appearance, which throbs with pilgrims drawn to Christendom's oldest complete and working church, built over the site of the Nativity in Manger Square.

DEAD SEA The lowest point in the world, at 400-metres below sea level, this lake is known for its high levels of salt which allow swimmers to float on the surface. Supposedly brimming with health-giving minerals, the Dead Sea has spawned a tourism industry based upon the health and beauty potential of the region.

NEGEV DESERT Arid, stone-strewn landscape, which comprises about half of the country's land mass, but contains just seven per cent of the population. Its trails are suitable for travel by four-wheel-drive jeep, or on the back of a lolloping camel.

EILAT Red Sea resort and watersports centre, with glorious coral reefs fringed by fine beaches. A perfect environment for swimming, windsurfing, parasailing and water-skiing.

KIBBUTZ System of communal farms, in which people are granted food, lodging and some pocket money in return for eight hours' work. It makes for an unforgettable experience, as most former *kibbutzniks* will testify.

FINANCE All major credit cards and traveller's cheques accepted.

BUSINESS HOURS 0830-1200, 1600-1800 Sunday-Tuesday &Thursday, 0830-1230 Wednesday, 0830-1200 Friday.

GMT +2 (+3 from March to September).

VOLTAGE GUIDE 220 AC, 50 Hz.

COUNTRY DIALLING CODE 972.

CONSUMING PLEASURES

FOOD & DRINK A combination of Oriental and Western cuisines, as well as diverse dishes reflecting the previous nationalities of many Israelis - Russian *bortsch*, Viennese *schnitzel*, Hungarian *goulash* and Middle Eastern dishes such as *falafel* (chickpea fritters). Traditional Jewish food includes *gefilte* fish, chopped liver and chicken soup. Good choice of local brandies and liqueurs such as *Arak* (anise), *HardNut* (walnut), and the exquisite *Sabra* (chocolate orange).

SHOPPING & SOUVENIRS Jewellery, diamonds and precious stones, ceramics, embroidery, glassware, and wines.

FIND OUT MORE

WEBSITES http://london.mfa.gov.il, www.go-israel.org, www.brittemb.org.il, www.israelemb.org, www.goisrael.com, www.usembassy-israel.org.il, www.visit-palestine.com, www.infotour.co.il.

LOCAL MEDIA *Jerusalem Post International Edition* is published weekly.

TOURIST BOARDS IN UK/US UK: UK House, 180 Oxford Street, London W1D 1NN, tel (020) 7299 1100, fax (020) 7299 1112, email info@igto.co.uk. US: 800 Second Avenue, 16th Floor, New York, NY 10017, tel (212) 499 5660, fax (212) 499 5665, email info@goisrael.com.

> "No other historic city evokes such inflammatory argument to this day."
> *Amos Elon, of Jerusalem, 1989*

ITALY

WHEN TO GO

WEATHER Hot from June-September, especially in the South. April-May, September-October are generally mild. Mountain regions are cooler with heavy snow in winter.

FESTIVALS Italy's has many festivals, some of religious and historic significance, others of music and the arts. Events in the Roman Catholic calendar are of central importance, notably Easter and Christmas. Holy Week is celebrated in the week before Easter across the country, but with particular enthusiasm in Sicily. The Venice Carnevale, which takes place in the period leading up to Ash Wednesday, is a colourful event, featuring the famous masked balls. Elsewhere, Il Palio is an extraordinary horse race, staged in Siena in the summer.

TRANSPORT

INTERNATIONAL AIRPORTS (And distances from nearest city) Rome, Fiumicino (FCO) 26 km, Bologna (BLQ) 6 km, Genoa (GOA) 6km, Milan, Malpensa (MXP) 45 km, Milan, Linate (LIN) 10 km, Naples (NAP) 7 km, Pisa (PSA) 2 km, Palermo (PMO) 30 km, Turin (TRN) 30 km, Venice (VCE) 10 km.

INTERNAL TRAVEL The Italian State Railways run a nationwide network at reasonable fares. Italian roads are often congested. Car hire widely available.

RED TAPE

VISAS REQUIRED (UK/US) None.

VACCINATIONS REQUIRED: See 'Vaccinations required around the world' on page 653.

DRIVING REQUIREMENTS International Green Card or other insurance. UK driving licence or EU pink format licences are valid but green-coloured licences must be accompanied by an International Driving Permit.

COUNTRY REPS IN UK/US UK: 136 Buckingham Palace Road, London SW1W 9SA, tel (020) 7235 9371, fax (020) 7823 1609, email consulato.londra@esteri.it. USA: 690 Park Avenue, New York, NY 10021, tel (212) 439 8600, fax (212) 249 4945, email enitny@italiantourism.com.

UK/US REPS IN COUNTRY UK: Lungarno Corsini 2, 50123, Florence, tel (055) 284 133, fax (055) 219 112, email Consular.Florence@fco.gov.uk. USA: Lungarno Vespucci 38, 50123 Florence, tel (055) 266 951, fax (055) 284 088.

PEOPLE AND PLACE

CAPITAL Rome.

LANGUAGE Italian.

PEOPLES Italian (94%).

RELIGION Roman Catholic.

SIZE (SQ KM) 301,338.

POPULATION 58,145,360.

POP DENSITY/KM 193.

STATE OF THE NATION

SAFETY Safe.

LIFE EXPECTANCY M 76.75, F 82.81.

BEING THERE

ETIQUETTE Slapping your raised arm on the inside of the elbow, and thumbing your nose, are very offensive gestures.. Also avoid raising your hand or fingers, as this is rude. The Roman Catholic church is a major influence and family ties are stronger than in most other countries in Western Europe.

CURRENCY Euro (€) = 100 cents.

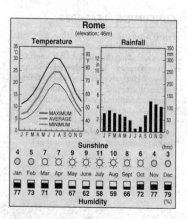

Rome (elevation: 46m) — Temperature, Rainfall, Sunshine, Humidity

HIGHLIGHTS

ROME Endearingly *pazzo* (crazy), this city just oozes history. Whether its Roman remains or Renaissance artistic treasures, the Eternal City will keep you enthralled and entertained for a weekend or a month.

POMPEII Buried for hundreds of years beneath layers of ash and pumice stone f ollowing the eruption of Mount Vesuvius in AD 79, Pompeii and nearby Herculaneum were preserved as a fascinating time-capsule of ancient Roman life.

SIENA Listen to the sound of galloping horses hooves and cheering spectators during Il Palio, a historic horse race staged in the central square of this pretty medieval town in both July and August.

VENICE Gondolas, broad lagoons, narrow canals, breathtaking architecture and unashamed romance make this city on water one of the most enchanting anywhere.

MILAN Glitzy commercial city that is a major centre for the world's fashion industry.

FLORENCE Home to the Medici, Michelangelo, Dante, Machiavelli and many more, this charming city has an almost overwhelming abundance of history, art and culture, and a profusion of tourists to boot.

THE LAKES Beautiful deep blue lakes in the Alps. Lake Maggiore is perhaps the most elegant, Lake Como the most attractive, and Lake Garda the wildest.

FINANCE Credit cards and traveller's cheques widely accepted.

BUSINESS HOURS 0900-1700 Mon-Friday.

GMT +1 (+2 in summer).

VOLTAGE GUIDE 220 AC, 50 Hz.

COUNTRY DIALLING CODE 39 (Do not omit 0 preceding area code).

CONSUMING PLEASURES

FOOD & DRINK Although pasta, pizza, risotto, *minestre* (soups) and meat dishes can be found all over Italy, regions specialise in dishes based on local produce. Risottos are a northern dish, a classic example is *risotto alla milanese* (with saffron and white wine). Liguria is famous for *pesto* sauce made from local basil, Tuscany for bean soups and *bistecca alla fiorentina* (massive T-bone steaks grilled over charcoal), Umbria for truffles, Naples for pizzas. More rice and dairy products are used in the north, the south uses tomato-based sauces and seafood. The many regional wines are of international quality.

SHOPPING & SOUVENIRS World famous for style and quality. Look for Carrara marble, Como silk, Faenza pottery.

Florence, Milan, and Rome are the main fashion centres.

FIND OUT MORE

WEBSITES www.embitaly.org.uk, www.enit.it, www.britain.it, www.italyemb.org, www.italconsulnyc.org, www.italiantourism.com. www.usembassy.it, www.italyguide.com, www.initaly.com, www.romeguide.com, www.informer.it, www.virtualvenice.com.

LOCAL MEDIA No English-language daily papers. International press easily available.

TOURIST BOARDS IN UK/US UK: 1 Princes Street, London W1B 2AY, tel (020) 7408 1254, fax (020) 7399 3567, email italy@italiantouristboard.co.uk. US: 630 fifth Avenue, Suite 1565, New York, NY 10111, tel (212) 245 5618, fax (212) 586 9249, email enitny@italiantourism.com.

"These Romans are crazy!"
Obelix the Gaul, in the Asterix cartoon series

JAMAICA

WHEN TO GO

WEATHER Rainy between May and October, tropical for the rest of the year. Temperate in higher regions.

FESTIVALS July and August sees the two big Jamaican beach festivals, the Reggae Sunsplash and Reggae Sumfest in Ocho Rios and Montego Bay, respectively. Carnival takes place after Easter on the university campus in Kingston. Shake it on down to reggae, calypso, and dance hall soca. Jonkanoo is a Christmas celebration, with a masquerade parade through the streets. Other festivals such as yachting events, cricket matches, a fashion week and a literary festival are held on the island.

TRANSPORT

INTERNATIONAL AIRPORTS Norman Manley International, Kingston (KIN) 17 km from the city, Montego Bay (MBJ) 3 km from the city.

INTERNAL TRAVEL Kingston harbour has been expanded. Main roads encircle the island and car hire is easily available.

RED TAPE

VISAS REQUIRED (UK/US) None.

VACCINATIONS REQUIRED: See 'Vaccinations required around the world' on page 653.

DRIVING REQUIREMENTS Full UK driving licence valid.

COUNTRY REPS IN UK/US UK: 1-2 Prince Consort Road, London SW7 2BZ, tel (020) 7823 9911, fax (020) 7589 5154, email jamhigh@jhcuk.com. USA: 767 Third Avenue, 2nd Floor, New York, NY 10017, tel (212) 935 9000, fax (212) 935 7507, email registry@congenjamaica-ny.org.

UK/US REPS IN COUNTRY UK: PO Box 575, 28 Trafalgar Road, Kingston 10, tel 510 0700, fax 510 0738, email bhckingston@mail.infochan.com. USA: 2 Oxford Road, Kingston 5, tel 935 6053/4, fax 935 6019, email opakgn@state.gov.

PEOPLE AND PLACE

CAPITAL Kingston.

LANGUAGE English.

PEOPLES African descent. Indian, Arab European and Chinese minorities.

RELIGION Mixed Christian (Church of God, Baptist, Anglican) and mixed beliefs, including Rastafarian.

SIZE (SQ KM) 10,991.

POPULATION 2,624,700.

POP DENSITY/KM 238.8.

STATE OF THE NATION

SAFETY High murder rate, but generally safe for tourists.

LIFE EXPECTANCY M 74.23, F 78.45.

BEING THERE

ETIQUETTE A relaxed, welcoming people on the whole. Signs that say 'Jah lives' refer to the name given to the former Emperor of Ethiopia Haile Selassie I by Rastafarians, who revere him as a deity. Beachwear should only be worn on the beach and poolside. Possession of marijuana may lead to imprisonment and deportation.

CURRENCY Jamaican dollar (J$) = 100 cents.

FINANCE Credit cards and traveller's cheques accepted.

BUSINESS HOURS 0830-1630 Mon-Friday. GMT -5.

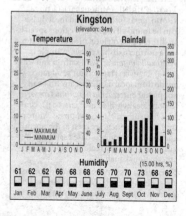

Kingston (elevation: 34m)

Temperature / Rainfall

MAXIMUM / MINIMUM

J F M A M J J A S O N D

Humidity (15.00 hrs, %)

	Jan	Feb	Mar	Apr	May	June	July	Aug	Sept	Oct	Nov	Dec
	61	62	62	66	68	68	65	70	70	73	68	62

HIGHLIGHTS

KINGSTON Not only the capital but also the cultural heart of the country. The seventh largest port in the world has turned the city into an industrial centre. Georgian architecture sits beside modern office blocks, which look out to the urban sprawl on the outskirts. The city centre may be a little stressful so take refuge in the National Art Gallery or Hope Botanical Gardens, made famous by their orchids. Visits should also be made to the Crafts Market and Harbour, where there is a museum to the submerged ancient capital Port Royal, or the 'richest and wickedest city on earth' as it was then called.

MONTEGO BAY The tourism centre of the island. A long reef protects the bay and sizzling beaches. Clear waters lap against the white sand, hotels line the coastline, crowds push through the streets, cars honk horns. You can stay on the beaches, or visit the sugar plantations, Rockland Feeding Station for birds, or the famous Appleton Rum Factory.

OCHO RIOS Known as a garden lover's paradise, this region , named after the roaring river, is home to Dunn's River Falls, a crystal clear waterfall that can be walked up like a staircase.

SPORTS Great facilities for divers exist here. Shipwrecks close to shore, sponge forests, underwater caves, and coral reefs can all be explored. Nurse sharks and vividly coloured fish are there to be spotted. Excellent fishing, (fresh and sea water) and watersport facilities can also be found.

VOLTAGE GUIDE 110 AC, 50 Hz. Some hotel supply 220 AC, 50 Hz.

COUNTRY DIALLING CODE 1 876.

CONSUMING PLEASURES

FOOD & DRINK Fodd is fiery, with pungent spices and peppers. Salt fish (dried cod) with *ackee* (the cooked fruit of the ackee tree), curried goat and rice, 'rice and peas' (rice with kidney beans, coconut milk and spring onions), pepperpot soup (salt pork, salt beef, okra and kale) and patties (pastry filled with spiced ground beef) are all popular dishes. Jamaican rum is world-renowned, especially *Gold Label*. *Red Stripe* beer is excellent, as is *Tia Maria* (a coffee and chocolate liqueur).

SHOPPING & SOUVENIRS Embroidery, woodcarvings, oil paintings, straw items, sandals, rugs, rum.

FIND OUT MORE

WEBSITES www.jhcuk.com, www.visitjamaica.com, www.cogenjamaica-ny.org, www.britishhighcommission.gov.uk/jamaica, www.jamaicatravel.com, www.jamaicans.com.

LOCAL MEDIA *The Jamaica Observer*, *The Daily Star* and *The Daily Gleaner* are all English dailies.

TOURIST BOARDS IN UK/US UK: As for Country reps in UK, tel (020) 7224 0505, fax (020) 7224 0551, email jamaicatravel@btconnect.com. US: 1320 South Dixi Highway, Suite 1101, Coral Gables, FL 33146, tel (305) 665 0557, fax (305) 666 7239, email jamaicatrvl@aol.com.

Nearly a quarter of a million people greeted the Ethiopian emperor Haile Selassie when he visited Jamaica in 1966, convinced that he was a living god

JAPAN

WHEN TO GO

WEATHER Summer is between June and September and ranges from warm to very hot, while spring and autumn are generally mild across the country. Typhoons are likely to occur in September or October but rarely last more than a day.

FESTIVALS Festivals are held across the country throughout the year. For full listings check with the Japan National Tourist Organisation. In March, the country enjoys the delights of the Cherry Blossom Viewing, with people enjoying picnics in parks and gardens bursting with pretty pink tones. Other highlights include the religious Gion Festival in the old imperial city of Kyoto in July. A street parade features finely-dressed participants carrying portable shrines, as well as large floats depicting ancient themes.

TRANSPORT

INTERNATIONAL AIRPORTS New Tokyo (TYO) 65 km from the city, Kansai (KIX) 50 km from Osaka, Fukuoka (FUK) 10 km from the city.

INTERNAL TRAVEL Extensive domestic air network covering Japan and its islands. The efficient rail network is widely used. Driving is complicated for visitors who cannot read the language, and therefore the road signs.

RED TAPE

VISAS REQUIRED (UK/US) None.

VACCINATIONS REQUIRED: See 'Vaccinations required around the world' on page 653.

DRIVING REQUIREMENTS International Driving Permit.

COUNTRY REPS IN UK/US UK: 101-104 Piccadilly, London W1J 7JT, tel (020) 7465 6500, fax (020) 7491 9347, email info@jpembassy.org.uk. USA: 2520 Massachusetts Avenue, NW, Washington, DC 20008, tel (202) 238 6700, fax (202) 328 2187, email eojjicc@erols.com.

UK/US REPS IN COUNTRY UK: No 1 Ichiban-cho, Chiyoda-ku, Tokyo 102-8381, tel (3) 5211 1100, fax (3) 5275 3164. USA: 1-10-5, Akasaka, Minato-ku, Tokyo 107-8420, tel (3) 3224 5000, fax (3) 3505 1862.

PEOPLE AND PLACE

CAPITAL Tokyo.

LANGUAGE Japanese.

PEOPLES Japanese (99%).

RELIGION Shinto and Buddhist.

SIZE (SQ KM) 377,864.

POPULATION 127,450,000.

POP DENSITY/KM 337.3.

STATE OF THE NATION

SAFETY Safe.

LIFE EXPECTANCY M 77.86, F 84.61.

BEING THERE

ETIQUETTE A strict code of behaviour and politeness is recognised and followed by almost all Japanese. They do not expect visitors to be familiar with all their customs but expect them to behave formally and politely. Bowing is the Japanese way of greeting, but it is also used in thanking and apologising. Giving and receiving gifts are part of every day life and it is a good idea to bring an assortment of gifts for your trip so that you can reciprocate. Shoes should be removed before entering most private indoor areas such as Japanese-style restaurants and accommodation, private homes, shrines and

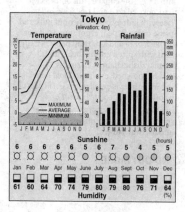

HIGHLIGHTS

MT FUJI This sacred volcano cone is the country's highest mountain at 3,776 metres. The main climbing season is July and August, but the months either side will be less crowded.

KYOTO The historic former capital, Kyoto is blessed with vast numbers of temples, shrines, museums and other historical sites, including the Golden Pavilion and the medieval Nijo Castle.

SUMO You can join enthusiastic crowds at one of the six annual sumo wrestling con- tests, held in the cities of Tokyo, Fukuoka, Nagoya ad Osaka. The tournaments last 15 days and are highly ritualised affairs.

ONSEN Hot springs are an intrinsic part of Japanese life, a way to relax, socialise and get away from the frenetic pace of modern Japan, by sinking deep into a steaming hot pool.

TOKYO The epitome of ultra-modern, technology-savvy Japan, this sprawling and energetic 24-hour city is characterised by futuristic skylines, neon lights and digi- tised vending outlets. It's also a city of contrasts, with many traditional practices still in evidence.

OKINAWA A lush, sub-tropical chain of 161 islands that stretch, like stepping stones, between the southern island of Kyushu and Taiwan. Fine beaches, turquoise seas and warm climate make the islands a Japanese holiday favourite.

HOKKAIDO Home to the indigenous Ainu people, this is an island of busy ski resorts and steamy hot springs - some frequented by snow monkeys.

---

temples. The honorific suffix *san* should be used when addressing people (for instance Mr Yamada would be called Yamada-san).

CURRENCY *Yen.*

FINANCE Major credit cards widely used, traveller's cheques generally accepted.

BUSINESS HOURS 0900-1700 Mon-Friday.

GMT +9.

VOLTAGE GUIDE 100 AC, 60 Hz in the west, 100 AC, 50 Hz in the east and Tokyo.

COUNTRY DIALLING CODE 81.

CONSUMING PLEASURES

FOOD & DRINK Delicate flavours, crisp vegetables, bean curd and rice are the basis of Japanese food. Specialities include *tempura* (vegetables or seafood fried in a light batter), *teriyaki* (marinated chicken, beef or fish seared on a hot plate) and *sushi* - raw seafood served on vinegared rice).

SHOPPING & SOUVENIRS Oriental goods meet Western sales techniques. Look for *kimonos, mingei* (folk toys), *Kyoto* silks, fans, screens, and dolls, Shinto and Buddhist artefacts, lacquerware, electric goods.

FIND OUT MORE

WEBSITES www.uk.emb-japan.go.jp, www.seejapan.co.uk, www.japantravelinfo.com, www.japan- guide.com, www.jnto.go.jp, www.snowjapan.com, http://www.planettokyo.com.

LOCAL MEDIA *The Mainichi Daily News, The Daily Yomiuri, The Japan Times,* and the *Daily Sports* are all printed in English.

TOURIST BOARDS IN UK/US UK: Heath- coat House, 20 Saville Row, London W1S 3PR, tel (020) 7734 9638, fax (020) 7734 4290, email info@jnto.co.uk.

The Japanese are renowned for their longevity. The world's oldest man was Shigechiyo Izumi, who died in 1986 aged 120 years and 237 days

JORDAN

WHEN TO GO

WEATHER May-September is hot and dry. Rain falls between November - March, and December and January can be cold.

FESTIVALS Events in the Islamic calendar are of great importance. Of these, the month of fasting, Ramadan (dates vary), is of particular significance. The end of Ramadan is marked by Eid al-Fitr, a four or five-day holiday. Secular holidays include Independence Day on 25 May and Labour Day on 1 May.

TRANSPORT

INTERNATIONAL AIRPORTS Queen Alia International (AMM) 32 km from Amman.

INTERNAL TRAVEL Adequate roads link main cities. A railroad links Al Aqabah with the Syrian capital, Damascus. Car hire is available from hotels or travel agents.

RED TAPE

VISAS REQUIRED (UK/US) Required.

VACCINATIONS REQUIRED: See 'Vaccinations required around the world' on page 653.

DRIVING REQUIREMENTS National driving licences accepted if issued at least one year before travel. However, an International Driving Permit is also recommended.

COUNTRY REPS IN UK/US UK: 6 Upper Phillimore Gardens, London W8 7HB, tel (020) 7937 3685, fax (020) 7937 8795, email info@jordanembassyuk.org. USA: 3504 International Drive, NW, Washington, DC 20008, tel (202) 966 2664, fax (202) 686 4491, email HKJEmbassyDC@aol.com.

UK/US REPS IN COUNTRY UK: PO Box 87, Amman 11118, tel (6) 592 3100, fax (6) 592 3759, email info@britain.org.jo. USA: PO Box 354, Abdoun, Amman 11118, tel (6) 590 6000, fax (6) 592 0121, email ResponseAmman@state.gov.

PEOPLE AND PLACE

CAPITAL Amman.

LANGUAGE Arabic.

PEOPLES Arab (98%).

RELIGION Islam.

SIZE (SQ KM) 89,342 not including West Bank.

POPULATION 5,329,000.

POP DENSITY/KM 59.6.

STATE OF THE NATION

SAFETY Safe.

LIFE EXPECTANCY M 75.75, F 80.88.

BEING THERE

ETIQUETTE Jordan is a Muslim state and visitors should exercise discretion in dress and behaviour to avoid offending local sensitivities. The working week is from Sunday to Thursday. Jordanians are proud of their Arab culture and hospitality. Visitors are made to feel very welcome and Jordanians are happy to act as hosts and guides, and are keen to inform tourists about their traditions and culture. Arabic coffee will normally be served continuously during social occasions. To signal that no more is wanted, slightly tilt the cup when handing it back, otherwise it will be refilled. It is polite to ask permission to take photographs of people and livestock, and in some places photography is forbidden.

CURRENCY *Dinar* (JD) = 1000 *fils*.

FINANCE American Express and Visa widely accepted, other cards have more limited use. Traveller's cheques accepted.

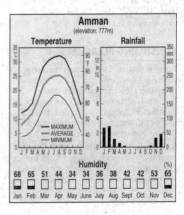

Amman
(elevation: 777m)

Temperature   Rainfall

MAXIMUM
AVERAGE
MINIMUM

J F M A M J J A S O N D   J F M A M J J A S O N D

Humidity (%)

Jan	Feb	Mar	Apr	May	June	July	Aug	Sept	Oct	Nov	Dec
68	65	51	44	34	34	36	38	42	42	53	65

HIGHLIGHTS

PETRA Cultural jewel and one of the great wonders of the Middle-Eastern world, set in a spectacular deep and narrow desert gorge. Founded by the Nabatean Arabs and added to by the Romans, this fascinating complex was lost to the world for 400 years, until being rediscovered in 1812. Enter through the *siq*, a chasm created by a prehistoric quake, at the end of which stands the most famous monument, the Treasury, or Khazneh, a towering facade carved out of the rock. In recent times, it appeared in the final sequence of *Indiana Jones and the Last Crusade*. Beyond the Treasury explore the numerous other rock reliefs, tombs, halls, a monastery and a dramatic 3,000-seat amphitheatre.

WADI RUM Described by T.E Lawrence as "vast, echoing and God-like," this unspoilt desert landscape is popular among climbers and hikers. Less active sorts can take camel rides or sleep under the stars in a Bedouin tent. In springtime the desert blooms with green.

DEAD SEA Float freely in the salt-laden waters of this large lake, or loll in mud, amid this eerie, dry landscape.

AMMAM Often referred to as the 'white city', this modern capital is home to one-third of the country's population. High above the city stands the ancient Citadel, with historic remains from Roman, Greek and Ottoman Turk eras. Ammam also has some charming *suqs* (oriental markets)and coffee shops filled with locals enjoying a friendly game of backgammon.

BUSINESS HOURS 0900-1800 Saturday, Wednesday and Thursday.

GMT +2 (+3 in summer).

VOLTAGE GUIDE 220 AC, 50 Hz.

COUNTRY DIALLING CODE 962.

CONSUMING PLEASURES

FOOD & DRINK Middle Eastern in style, with *meze* to start, followed by kebabs or specialities such as *mensaf* (stewed lamb in a yoghurt sauce) or *musakhan* (chicken in olive oil and onion sauce served on Arab bread). Sweets are popular, and include *baklava* (pastry filled with nuts or honey). Restrictions on alcohol during Ramadan.

SHOPPING & SOUVENIRS Every town has a *souk* (market). Look for Hebron glass, mother-of-pearl boxes, pottery, backgammon sets, embroidered tablecloths, rosaries and worry beads, nativity sets, caftans embroidered with gold and silver thread.

FIND OUT MORE

WEBSITES www.jordanembassyuk.org, www.see-jordan.com, www.britain.org.jo, www.jordanembassyus.org, www.seejordan.org.

LOCAL MEDIA *The Jordan Times* (daily), *The Star* (weekly) and *Arab Daily* are printed in English.

TOURIST BOARDS IN UK/US UK: Kennedy House, 1st Floor, 115 Hammersmith Road, London W14 0QH, tel (020) 7371 6496, fax (020) 7603 2424, email info@jordantourismboard.co.uk. US: 6867 Elm Street, Suite 102, Mclean, VA 22101, tel (703) 243 7404, fax (703) 243 7406, email info@seejordan.org.

> "Nowhere more than in Jordan have I felt a sense that this is where the world began."
> Edward Heath, 1977

KAZAKHSTAN

WHEN TO GO

WEATHER Hot from June to the end of September, cold from October to March.

FESTIVALS Events include the Voice of Asia Festival, an international song contest and folk festival, which draws people from all over the country. It features national music, songs, dance, sports, regional food and people wearing national costumes. Islamic festivals, including Ramadan, the month of fasting, are also important in Kazakh life.

TRANSPORT

INTERNATIONAL AIRPORTS Almaty (ALA) 15 km from the city.

INTERNAL TRAVEL Some domestic flights. Rail links between main centres. Many roads are in need of repair but the network connects most towns and regional centres. Car hire available in Almaty and at the airport.

RED TAPE

VISAS REQUIRED (UK/US) Required.

VACCINATIONS REQUIRED: See 'Vaccinations required around the world' on page 653.

DRIVING REQUIREMENTS International Driving Permit.

COUNTRY REPS IN UK/US UK: 33 Thurloe Square, London SW7 2SD, tel (020) 7581 4646, fax (020) 7584 8481, email london@kazakhstan-embassy.org.uk. USA: 1401 16th Street, NW, Washington, DC 20036, tel (202) 232 5488, fax (202) 232 5845, email kazakh.embusa@verizon.net.

UK/US REPS IN COUNTRY UK: ul Furmanova 174, Almaty 480062, tel (573) 150 2200, fax (573) 150 2212, email british-embassy@nursat.kz. USA: 97 Zholdasbekova, Samal-2, Almaty 480099, tel (3272) 504 802, fax (3272) 504 884, email ConsularAlmaty@state.gov.

PEOPLE AND PLACE

CAPITAL Astana.

LANGUAGE Kazakh.

PEOPLES Kazakh, Russian. Ukrainian, German, Uzbek and Tatar minorities.

RELIGION Islam, Russian Orthodox.

SIZE (SQ KM) 2,717,300.

POPULATION 14,862,700.

POP DENSITY/KM 5.5.

STATE OF THE NATION

SAFETY Some reports of banditry on roads and railways. Seek latest information at time of visit.

LIFE EXPECTANCY M 61.21, F 72.2.

BEING THERE

ETIQUETTE The Cyrillic alphabet is in general use and most people in the cities can speak Russian; people in the countryside tend to only speak Kazakh. English is usually only spoken by those involved in tourism. Kazakhs are generally very hospitable. When greeting a guest the host gives him/her both hands as if showing that he/she is unarmed. At a Kazakh home, the most honoured guest, usually the oldest, is traditionally offered a boiled sheep's head on a beautiful dish as a sign of respect. Inside mosques, women observe their own ritual in a separate room, and must cover their heads and their arms.

CURRENCY *Tenge* (T) = 100 *tiyin*.

FINANCE Larger establishments in cities accept credit cards and traveller's cheques.

BUSINESS HOURS 0900-1700 Monday-

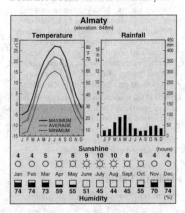

Almaty (elevation: 848m)

	Sunshine										(hours)
4	4	5	7	8	9	10	10	8	6	4	4
Jan	Feb	Mar	Apr	May	June	July	Aug	Sept	Oct	Nov	Dec
74	74	73	59	55	51	45	44	45	55	70	74

Humidity (%)

HIGHLIGHTS

ALMATY Pleasant city in the south-east corner of the country, affording superb views over the surrounding steep mountains and open plains. Panfilov Park features one of the world's tallest wooden buildings, built at the turn of the twentieth century without using a single nail. The park also holds the Arasan Baths, a complex of Eastern, Finnish and Russian saunas. Other sights include New Square, where national ceremonies and parades are sometimes held, and a string of charming museums. Amble through some of the city's bustling markets and you'll likely see Chinese, Uzbek, Russian and Turkish traders exchanging their wares.

SPAS Baths and spas are a big deal in Kazakhstan. Some of the bigger cities have traditional bath houses, while a number of health resorts have also been set up. These include Sari Agach, in the south, and Arasan-Kapal in the Taldikorgan region.

NATURE RESERVES Wild landscapes allow the chance to see rare native species. There are several dotted across the country, including the rugged Almaty Reserve - the habitat of snow leopards and arkhars (big-horned wild sheep). The reserve also has some mighty peaks popular among experienced climbers.

LAKE BALKHASH Half saline, half freshwater, this lake in central Kazakhstan is one of the world's largest.

ASTANA Friendly but rather lifeless city, which replaced Almaty as the capital in 1997 because it was thought less prone to earthquakes.

Saturday.
GMT +4-6 (+1 in summer).
VOLTAGE GUIDE 220 AC, 50Hz.
COUNTRY DIALLING CODE 7.

LOCAL MEDIA No English-language papers.
TOURIST BOARDS IN UK/US n/a.

CONSUMING PLEASURES

FOOD & DRINK Kazakh dishes include *shashlyk* (skewered, grilled mutton), *lepeshka* (round, unleavened bread), *plov* (mutton, rice and yellow turnip) and *laghman* (noodles with a spicy meat sauce). Kazakh *chai* or tea is popular. Beer, vodka, brandy, and wines are available, but the speciality is *kumis* - fermented mare's milk.

SHOPPING & SOUVENIRS A diverse range of items can be bought in Almaty, the town named after apples.

FIND OUT MORE

WEBSITES
www.kazakhstanembassy.org.uk,
www.britishembassy.gov.uk/kazakhstan,
www.kazakhembus.com, www.president.kz.

The world's largest speed-skating ice rink is on the outskirts of Almaty. The Medeu rink has set more than 120 world records in ice skating and ice hockey

KENYA

WHEN TO GO

WEATHER March to May sees the long rains, October to December the short rains. Coastal areas are hot and humid all year, the higher regions are more temperate.

FESTIVALS The Kenyatta International Conference Centre hosts a Cultural Music Festival in August featuring traditional dances, acrobatics, and folk. A food festival, the Uhondo Africa, is held in July, featuring world and Kenyan cuisine. The Dugong festival is held in May in Lamu, to raise money to save the dugong: activities include dhow racing, watersports, dancing, and feasts. Nairobi and Mombasa hold Carnivals in October and November.

TRANSPORT

INTERNATIONAL AIRPORTS Nairobi (NBO) 13 km from the city, Mombasa (MBA) 13 km from the city.

INTERNAL TRAVEL Extensive network of domestic flights, and charter aircraft available from Wilson airport. Major roads are paved, but vary in quality. Roads in the north are poor. Car hire easily available, can be expensive and most agents recommend 4-wheel-drive vehicles.

RED TAPE

VISAS REQUIRED (UK/US) None for tourism, required by all for business.

VACCINATIONS REQUIRED: See 'Vaccinations required around the world' on page 653.

DRIVING REQUIREMENTS Must obtain International Circulation Permit from the licensing officer in Nairobi if bringing own vehicle in. Issued free of charge on production of a permit of customs duty receipt and certificate of insurance. Full British driving licence valid, otherwise an International Driving Permit.

COUNTRY REPS IN UK/US UK: 45 Portland Place, London W1B 1AS, tel (020) 7636 2371/5, (020) 7323 6717, email info@ kenyahighcommission.com. USA: 2249 R Street, NW, Washington, DC 20008, tel (202) 387 6101, fax (202) 462 3829, email info@kenyaembassy.com.

UK/US REPS IN COUNTRY UK: Upper Hill Road, Nairobi, tel (20) 284 4000, fax (20) 284 4088, email bhcinfo@iconnect.co.ke. USA: United Nations Avenue, Village Market 00621, Nairobi, tel (20) 363 6000, fax (20) 363 6410, email consularnairob@ state.gov.

PEOPLE AND PLACE

CAPITAL Nairobi.

LANGUAGE Swahili and English.

PEOPLES About 70 different ethnic groups, with the Kikuyu, Luhya, Luo, Kalenjin and Kamba most prominent. Europeans and Asians form 1% of the population.

RELIGION Christian 60%, traditional beliefs 25%, Islam and other 15%.

SIZE (SQ KM) 580,367.

POPULATION 30,493,792.

POP DENSITY/KM 52.5.

STATE OF THE NATION

SAFETY Not the safe haven it once was. Muggings and carjackings commonplace. Tourists frequently targeted in Nairobi. Do not walk on the beach road, ever.

LIFE EXPECTANCY M 48.87, F 47.09.

BEING THERE

ETIQUETTE Western habits are a hangover of British influence in the country. Friendly people. Casual dress.

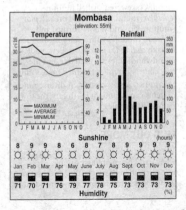

HIGHLIGHTS

AMBOSELI Game park dominated by the imposing snow-capped peak of Mount Kilimanjaro, which forms an impressive backdrop to equally impressive numbers of lion, hippo and cheetah, plus huge herds of buffalo and elephant.

MASAI MARA The most famous of the Kenyan reserves, and with good reason. Home to the Maasai tribe, the Mara also hosts the great wildebeest migration. Gazelle, giraffe and zebra roam across the plains, elephant cool off in the swamps, crocodile and hippo can be seen on the banks of the Mara river; and hot air balloon rides are available for a bird's eye view of it all.

LAKE NAKURU The first and only park in Africa to have been created for the protection of the lesser flamingo: when they gather on the lake in their thousands the entire surface of the water ripples with pink reflections. The park is also home to a herd of black rhino.

TSAVO Explore the flat arid bush of one of Africa's largest parks, divided into east and west sections – the east dotted with baobab trees and especially famous for herds of elephant, the west noted for crystal-clear pools in which hippo wallow and crocodile lurk.

NAIROBI Kenya's capital is a city of tree lined streets and parks. Mainly a business centre, the city affords great shopping opportunities from large malls to small craft stalls. Some places of interest include the National Museum and the indigenous Snake Park. But watch out for muggers.

CURRENCY Kenya shilling (KSh) = 100 cents.

FINANCE Major credit cards and traveller's cheques widely accepted.

BUSINESS HOURS 0800-1300, 1400-1700 Monday-Friday.

GMT +3.

VOLTAGE GUIDE 220/240 AC, 50Hz.

COUNTRY DIALLING CODE 254.

CONSUMING PLEASURES

FOOD & DRINK Strong on meat, including game, some seafood, and tropical fruit. *Nyama choma* (charcoal grilled meat, usually goat) is found in many restaurants and street stalls. *Ugali* (maize meal porridge) is a staple for Kenyans, an acquired taste for most visitors. Curries can be found in most places, and reflect Indian home cooking. *Chai* (tea) and beer (particularly the *Tusker* brand) are popular.

SHOPPING & SOUVENIRS Makonde woodcarvings, bags stained with natural dyes (*kiondos*), *khanga, kitenge,* and *kikoi* cloths, necklaces.

FIND OUT MORE

WEBSITES
www.kenyahighcommission.com,
www.magicalkenya.com,
www.britishhighcommission.gov.uk/kenya,
www.kenyaweb.com, www.visit-kenya.com.

LOCAL MEDIA *Daily Nation, Kenya Times, The People* are the main dailies, in English.

TOURIST BOARDS IN UK/US UK: c/o Hills Balfour, Notcutt House, 36 Southwark Bridge Road, London SE1 9EU, tel (020) 7202 6373, fax (020) 7928 0722, email kenya@hillsbalfour.com. US: n/a.

Ahmed the elephant was a national hero with some of the largest tusks ever recorded. President Kenyatta gave the beast its own 24-hour armed guard

KIRIBATI

WHEN TO GO

WEATHER March-October, when the trade winds temper the equatorial climate of the central islands. The highest rainfall (December to May) is concentrated on the northern islands. November to February is wet and humid.

FESTIVALS Major events are normally those associated with the Christian calendar, or celebrations on public holidays. National Churches Day and Independence Day, both in July, are other annual events.

TRANSPORT

INTERNATIONAL AIRPORTS Tarawa (TRW), Christmas Island (CXI).

INTERNAL TRAVEL Internal flights to outlying islands. All-weather roads are limited to urban Tarawa and Christmas Island, the only places where car hire is available.

RED TAPE

VISAS REQUIRED (UK/US) Required by Australian and American visitors.

VACCINATIONS REQUIRED: See 'Vaccinations required around the world' on page 653.

DRIVING REQUIREMENTS International Driving Permit.

COUNTRY REPS IN UK/US
UK: The Great House, Llanddewi Rhydderch, Monmouthshire NP7 9UY, tel/fax (01873) 840 375, email michael.walsh@sema.co.uk. USA: n/a.

UK/US REPS IN COUNTRY UK: n/a. USA: The US Embassy in Pohnpei (see Micronesia) deals with enquiries relating to Kiribati.

PEOPLE AND PLACE

CAPITAL Bairiki (Tarawa Atoll)

LANGUAGE Kiribati and English.

PEOPLES Gilbertese. Banaban minority.

RELIGION Roman Catholic, Kiribati Protestant Church.

SIZE (SQ KM) 810.5.

POPULATION 87,400.

POP DENSITY/KM 104.2.

STATE OF THE NATION

SAFETY Safe.

LIFE EXPECTANCY M 58.71, F 64.86.

BEING THERE

ETIQUETTE Like other Pacific islanders, the people of Kiribati are very friendly and hospitable and retain much of their traditional culture and lifestyle. European customs still prevail alongside local traditions. Bikinis should not be worn except on the beach. Nudity and overly scant swimming costumes are forbidden by local law.

CURRENCY Australian dollar (A$).

FINANCE Limited acceptance of traveller's cheques, very limited acceptance of cards.

BUSINESS HOURS 0800-1230, 1330-1615 Monday-Friday.

GMT +12-14.

VOLTAGE GUIDE 240 AC, 50 Hz.

COUNTRY DIALLING CODE 686.

CONSUMING PLEASURES

FOOD & DRINK A Kiribati favourite is *palu sami*, coconut cream with sliced onion and curry powder, wrapped in *taro* leaves and

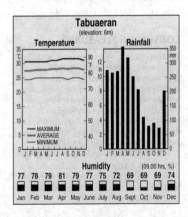

Tabuaeran
(elevation: 6m)

HIGHLIGHTS

BACKGROUND:
Formerly called the Gilbert Islands, the central Pacific nation of Kiribati - pronounced 'Kiribass' - actually comprises three separate island groups. Scattered across a vast area of ocean, the groups are namely Kiribati, the Line Islands and the Phoenix Islands. Between them, they contain 33 individual islands.

CHRISTMAS ISLAND
Try bone-fishing, or perhaps try spotting some of the unique local bird species on the world's largest coral atoll, also known as Kiritimati. Game fishing is especially popular, while the island's lakes and ponds form an ideal habitat for vast colonies of birds. A large bay on the east coast is known as the Bay of Wrecks, due to the numbers of ships that have foundered there. Charmingly, the main towns are London, Paris and - best of all - Banana.

TARAWA One of the most densely-populated areas in the Pacific, this group of islands contains the principal island of Bairiki, the country's capital. It also affords some beautiful views over Tarawa Lagoon. Swimming in the south of the Lagoon is advised against, however, on account of pollution. But then, surely it's far better to save your waterwings for the aquamarine depths off the many white sand beaches spread throughout the islands.

'ISLAND NIGHTS'
Take part in one of these fun and entertaining social occasions featuring traditional Polynesian music and dancing, together with tasty feasts held in *maneabas*, local meeting houses.

---

baked in an earth oven filled with seaweed. It is often served with roast pork or chicken. Local specialities in the southern islands include the boiled fruit of *pandanus* (screwpine), sliced and served with coconut cream.

SHOPPING & SOUVENIRS Baskets, table mats, fans and cups (made from *pandanus* leaves, coconut leaves and shells, and sea shells), sea shell necklaces, shark-tooth swords (shark teeth, sharpened and lashed to the edges of polished coconut wood).

FIND OUT MORE

WEBSITES www.empiremuseum.co.uk, www.tcsp.com.

LOCAL MEDIA *Te Uekera* and *Kiribati Newstar* are both weekly and published in Kiribati and English, *Kiribati Business Link* is in English.

TOURIST BOARDS IN UK/US
UK: Commonwealth Resource Centre, The British Empire and Commonwealth Museum Resource Library, The British Empire and Commonwealth Museum, Clock Tower Yard, Temple Meads, Bristol BS1 6QH, tel (0117) 925 4980, fax (0117) 925 4983, email resources@empiremuseum.co.uk. (Provides information on Kiribati).

By a quirk of geography, the International Date Line used to split the islands of Kiribati down the middle – until 1995, when they decided to have the same day nationwide

KOREA (DEMOCRATIC PEOPLE'S REPUBLIC)

WHEN TO GO

WEATHER Hottest during the rainy season between July and August, coldest from December to January. Spring and autumn are mild but winter in the north can be harsh.

FESTIVALS Events include May Day, on 1 May and Liberation Day, celebrated each August with parades in Pyongyang.

TRANSPORT

INTERNATIONAL AIRPORTS Pyongyang (FNJ) is 24 km from the city.

INTERNAL TRAVEL Good quality roads, many dual carriageways. Security checkpoints requiring identification on routes out of Pyongyang. No buses between cities. Few road signs. Slow rail service, disrupted by country split. Capital has metro and bus service.

RED TAPE

VISAS REQUIRED (UK/US) Required.

VACCINATIONS REQUIRED: See 'Vaccinations required around the world' on page 653.

DRIVING REQUIREMENTS An international driving licence will be of little use, as it is necessary to sit a local driving test and obtain a local licence in order to drive in North Korea.

COUNTRY REPS IN UK/US UK: 73 Gunnersbury Avenue, Ealing, London W5 4LP, teel (020) 8992 4965, fax (020) 8992 2053. US: n/a.

UK/US REPS IN COUNTRY UK: Munsu-dong Diplomatic Compound, Pyongyang, tel (2) 381 7980, fax (2) 381 7985, email postmaster.PYONX@ fco.gov.uk. US: The US Embassy in Beijing (see China) deals with enquiries relating to Korea (Dem Rep).

PEOPLE AND PLACE

CAPITAL Pyongyang.

LANGUAGE Korean.

PEOPLES Korean (100%).

RELIGION Buddhism, Christianity, Chundo Kyo.

SIZE (SQ KM) 122,762.

POPULATION 22,541,000.

POP DENSITY/KM 183.6.

STATE OF THE NATION

SAFETY Safe, but severely restricted internal travel. Visitors should register with the British Embassy.

LIFE EXPECTANCY M 68.65, F 74.22.

BEING THERE

ETIQUETTE North Korea has been described as the most closed society in the world. Discretion and a low political profile are advised. When visiting places of national importance, such as statues of former leaders, it is important to dress smartly, as a sign of respect for North Koreans. Visitors may only take photographs when permitted by a guide or a North Korean official. Taking photographs after having been told not to can have serious implications.

CURRENCY Won (Won) = 100 chon.

FINANCE Mastercard and Visa accepted in Pyongyang, traveller's cheques not, use US Dollars as alternative method of payment.

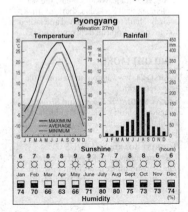

HIGHLIGHTS

PYONGYANG Gape at the larger-than-life monuments of North Korea's Great Leader, Kim Il Jung and his father, the late Kim Il Sung, which line the streets of the capital - the country's attempt at the model Communist capital. Walk, accompanied by minders of course, past a number of other extravagant landmarks, including the 13-lane boulevard connecting the city centre with the suburb of Kwangbok, more than three kilometres away, and two fountains in the middle of the River Taedong, which spout up to a height of 150-metres.

KUMGANGSAN Stunning resort, with spectacular pristine mountain views. Meaning 'diamond mountains' in Korean, it is part of a beautiful landscape that forms the country's largest national park. Peppered with former Buddhist temples, waterfalls and springs, the unspoilt environment is popular with birdwatchers, photographers and botanists. Hiking and mountaineering are, in theory at least, other possibilities.

PANMUNJEOM Just to the north of the Demilitarised Zone (DMZ) which divides North Korea and South Korea lies the fascinating Kijong-dong propaganda village. Like some surreal model town, it stands empty but for some resident soldiers. By the entrance to the villages stands the world's highest flag tower, on which proudly hangs North Korea's national flag. The massive construction can be seen from the South Korean side of the DMZ and loud propaganda music can also be heard across no-man's land.

BUSINESS HOURS 0900 - 1800 Monday - Saturday.

GMT +9.

VOLTAGE GUIDE 110/220 AC. 60 Hz.

COUNTRY DIALLING CODE 850.

LOCAL MEDIA Several English-language monthly magazines, and *The Pyongyang Times* is published weekly in English, French, and Spanish.

TOURIST BOARDS IN UK/US n/a.

CONSUMING PLEASURES

FOOD & DRINK Most cooking is usually based on the staple food of rice. Western or Russian cooking in restaurants is not good so it's better to try Chinese, Japanese or Korean meals. Try the rice wines and *insam-ju*, Korean vodka infused with ginseng roots.

SHOPPING & SOUVENIRS Books and videos on the immortal achievements of Juche and its Great Leaders, stamps depicting socialist solidarity and other scenes, expensive ginseng, acupuncture needles.

> North Korea is the world's last full-blooded Communist dictatorship and the world's most closed society

FIND OUT MORE

WEBSITES www.kimsoft.com/dprk.htm, www.lonelyplanet.com/destinations/north_east_asia/north_korea.

KOREA (REPUBLIC)

WHEN TO GO

WEATHER The hottest part of the year is the rainy season between July and August. December and January are very cold. The rest of the year is mild and mainly dry.

FESTIVALS South Korea celebrates many festivals throughout the year. One of the most significant is Buddha's Birthday, during which the Feast of Lanterns is performed in city streets. Other events include annual village rituals, when mountain spirits, great generals and royalty of the past are remembered and celebrated. Festivities are often characterised by processions, dancing and music, with traditional costumes and masks.

TRANSPORT

INTERNATIONAL AIRPORTS Seoul (SEL) 17 km from the city, Pusan 27 km from the city, Cheju (CJU) on the island of Cheju-do.

INTERNAL TRAVEL Steamers and ferries serve southern coastal ports and islands. Extensive, efficient rail service. The road network is also extensive, but while the motorways are in good condition, minor roads are often bad. Car hire is available.

RED TAPE

VISAS REQUIRED (UK/US) Required by American visitors.

VACCINATIONS REQUIRED: See 'Vaccinations required around the world' on page 653.

DRIVING REQUIREMENTS International Driving Permit. Drivers must also have at least one year of driving experience, hold a valid passport and over 21-years-old.

COUNTRY REPS IN UK/US UK: 60 Buckingham Gate, London SW1E 6AJ, tel (020) 7227 5505, fax (020) 7227 5504, email koreanembuk@mofat.go.kr. USA: 2450 Massachusetts Avenue, NW, Washington, DC 20008, tel (202) 939 5661-3, fax (202) 342 1597, email consular_usa@mofat.go.kr.

UK/US REPS IN COUNTRY UK: Taepyung-ro 40, 4 Chung-dong, Choong-gu, Seoul 100-120, tel (2) 3210

5500, fax (2) 725 1738, email bembassy@britain.or.kr. USA: 32 Sejong-ro, Jongno-gu, Seoul 110-710, tel (2) 397 4114, fax (2) 397 4101, email seoul_acs@state.gov.

PEOPLE AND PLACE

CAPITAL Seoul.

LANGUAGE Korean.

PEOPLES Korean (100%).

RELIGION Mahayana Buddhism, Protestant, Roman Catholic.

SIZE (SQ KM) 99,313.

POPULATION 47,925,318.

POP DENSITY/KM 482.6.

STATE OF THE NATION

SAFETY Safe.

LIFE EXPECTANCY M 72.19, F 79.76.

BEING THERE

ETIQUETTE Bow slightly when meeting someone for the first time. *Annyeong haseyo* is an informal greeting between friends. Shoes should be removed before entering a Korean home. In general, Koreans are a very friendly people and will often go out of their way to make visitors feel at home, or to help lost souls find their way. It is not unusual to be offered food or drinks in restaurants and bars, sometimes by complete strangers. Traditional costume, or *hanbok*, is worn on holidays and other special occasions.

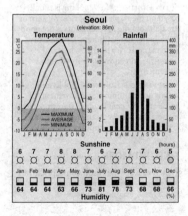

HIGHLIGHTS

SEOUL The country's capital is a mix of modern-day commerce and an interesting past. Several royal residences are UNESCO-listed sites. Among the most enchanting are Changdokkung Palace and Kyongbokkung Palace, the latter also housing the National Folk Museum.

OLYMPIC PARK Stroll through the leafy Olympic Park in the suburbs of Seoul, scene of many of the athletic and other sporting contests during the 1988 Olympic Games.

DEMILITARISED ZONE Look out over the DMZ to North Korea on a fascinating excursion from Seoul. Incredibly, the heavily mined frontier is also home to abundant wildlife, left alone by man for 50 years. It's also possible to enter several vast tunnel networks, which the North dug in secret as part of an invasion plan designed to transport its troops across the border, but which were discovered by the South.

GYONGJU Historical heartland with wonderful temples, tombs, palaces and monuments , remains of the ancient capital of the Silla kingdom.

CHEJU-DO Scenic resort island, with some beaches. The island is also known for *harubang*, small carved stone 'grand father statues'. South Korea's highest peak, Mount Hallasan, dominates the interior of the island.

CURRENCY *Won* (W).

FINANCE Credit cards and traveller's cheques accepted in larger cities.

BUSINESS HOURS 0900-1800 Mon-Friday.

GMT +9.

VOLTAGE GUIDE 110/220 AC, 60 Hz.

COUNTRY DIALLING CODE 82.

CONSUMING PLEASURES

FOOD & DRINK Rice is a staple food, and a typical meal consists of rice, soup, rice water and at least eight side dishes of vegetables, poultry, eggs, bean-curd and sea plants. Korean cuisine is generally quite spicy and has a heavy use of red pepper. Almost all meals will be accompanied by *kimchi*, a spicy pickle of cabbage or radish with turnips, onion, salt, fish, chestnuts and the ubiquitous red pepper. *Bulgogi*, which comprises marinated, charcoal-broiled beef is a speciality. *Ghengis Khan* is another beef dish, accompanied by vegetables boiled at the table. *Jungjong* is an expensive rice wine, while *soju* is a rather harsh tasting vodka-type drink made from potatoes or grain. Notable beer brands are Cass, Hite and OB.

SHOPPING & SOUVENIRS Hand-tailored clothes, silks, brocades, handbags, leather-work, gold jewellery, topaz, amethyst, amber, jade, ginseng, costume dolls, screens.

FIND OUT MORE

WEBSITES www.mofat.go.kr, www.tour2korea.com, www.britishembassy.or.kr, http://english.seoul.go.kr/.

LOCAL MEDIA *The Korea Herald, The Korea Times* and *The Korea Daily News* are all English-language newspapers.

TOURIST BOARDS IN UK/US UK: 3rd Floor, New Zealand House, Haymarket, London SW1Y 4TE, tel (020) 7321 2535, fax (020) 7321 0876, email london@mail.knto.or.kr. US: 1 Executive Drive, Suite 100, Fort Lee, NJ 07024, tel (201) 585 0909, fax (201) 585 9041, email ny@kntoamerica.com.

The world's largest wedding was held in the Olympic stadium in Seoul in 1995, when 35,000 people were wed by the Moonies

KUWAIT

WHEN TO GO

WEATHER April to October is hot and humid with very little rain. November to March is cool with limited rain.

FESTIVALS National Day on 25 February celebrates the birth of Kuwait as a nation in 1961. National dress is worn, people get together, and towns put on firework displays. The next day is Liberation Day, celebrating the liberation from Iraqi occupation in 1991: a day of remembrance as well as a celebration. When spring arrives Kuwaitis hold the Hala February Festival. Cultural events and entertainment for young and old, and for those visiting at this time when the parched sands turn green with blossoming flora. Other festivals follow the Muslim calendar.

TRANSPORT

INTERNATIONAL AIRPORTS Kuwait (KWI) 16 km from Kuwait City.

INTERNAL TRAVEL Good road network between cities. Car hire available. Taxis and buses also available. *Dhows* and other small craft can be chartered for trips to offshore islands.

RED TAPE

VISAS REQUIRED (UK/US) Required.

VACCINATIONS REQUIRED: See 'Vaccinations required around the world' on page 653.

DRIVING REQUIREMENTS International Driving Permit. Temporary licence available on presentation of a valid British or Northern Ireland driving licence to the local authorities. Insurance must be with the Gulf Insurance Company or Kuwait Insurance Company.

COUNTRY REPS IN UK/US UK: 2 Albert Gate, London SW1X 7JU, tel (020) 7590 3400, fax (020) 7823 1712, email kuwait@dircon.co.uk. USA: 2940 Tilden Street, NW, Washington, DC 20008, tel (202) 966 0702, fax (202) 966 0517.

UK/US REPS IN COUNTRY UK: Arabian Gulf Street, Dasman, Kuwait City, tel 240 3335/6, fax 242 6799, email kuwaitinfo/PPA.Kuwait@fco.gov.uk. USA: Area 14, al-Masjad al-Aqsa Street, Bayan, tel 539 5307, fax 538 0282, email PASKuwaitM@state.gov.

PEOPLE AND PLACE

CAPITAL Kuwait City.

LANGUAGE Arabic and English.

PEOPLES Kuwaiti (45%), other Arab, South Asian, Iranian.

RELIGION Sunni Muslim.

SIZE (SQ KM) 17,818.

POPULATION 2,419,900.

POP DENSITY/KM 135.8.

STATE OF THE NATION

SAFETY Safe. But avoid the border with Iraq, and beware unexploded ordnance.

LIFE EXPECTANCY M 76.01, F 78.1.

BEING THERE

ETIQUETTE Locals mostly wear the national dress, long white robes with white headscarves, while many Kuwaiti women wear *yashmaks*. Women visiting should dress modestly and men should not wear shorts, and never go shirtless. Respect all Islamic laws and customs. Learning the language is greatly appreciated, while gifts from home area always welcome.

CURRENCY Kuwait *dinar* (KD) = 1000 *fils*.

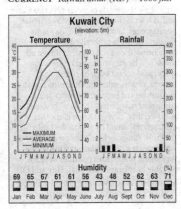

HIGHLIGHTS

KUWAIT CITY The invasion of the country and capital by Iraq in 1990 saw massive, systematic looting by the Iraqis. The rebuild and recovery is estimated to have cost Kuwait a mammoth US$170 billion, raised through the sale of its overseas investment portfolio: this helped safeguard services such as free education and social services. Though a great cost to the country, the recovery has been successful, and the memories of war fade as Kuwait rediscovers its hustle and bustle, and stakes its claim as a relaxed gateway to the Muslim world, where much is open to the visitor. Fifteen years on, the capital is a buzzing metropolis of high-rise offices, luxury hotels, wide boulevards, and tidy green parks and gardens. Visit souks and mosques to search out clues to the old Bedouin days. The Kuwait National Museum has sadly been stripped of most of its collection, but the nearby Sadu House contains Bedouin arts and crafts. The city's remaining and best landmarks are the Kuwait Towers (the tallest standing at 187 metres, dominating the skyline) and Seif Palace. Built in 1896, it still features the original Islamic mosaic tilework.

FAILAKA ISLAND The country's main archaeological site can be reached via ferry. The port is home to many old *dhows*, the sites are full of Bronze Age and Greek artefacts, as well as a Greek temple. Use caution, though, as the island also has many landmines left over after heavy fortification by the Iraqis.

FINANCE Credit cards and traveller's cheques generally accepted.

BUSINESS HOURS 0730-1230, 1600-1900 Saturday-Wednesday.

GMT +3.

VOLTAGE GUIDE 240 AC, 50 Hz.

COUNTRY DIALLING CODE 965.

CONSUMING PLEASURES

FOOD & DRINK Arab cuisine. Spicy meat and poultry dishes, often lamb, served with rice or flat bread. Typical dishes include *hummus, falafel* and *foul*. Alcohol is totally prohibited.

SHOPPING & SOUVENIRS Basic to luxury goods available. The *Souk Sharp Complex* near the capital's waterfront is extensive.

FIND OUT MORE

WEBSITES www.kuwaitinfo.org.uk, www.britishembassy-kuwait.org, http://usembassy.state.gov/kuwait, www.mideasttravelnet.com/mideastsite/kuwait/cs.htm.

LOCAL MEDIA *Arab Times, Kuwait Times* are printed in English. The press remain loyal to the ruling family, but enjoy some freedom.

TOURIST BOARDS IN UK/US UK: Kuwait Information Centre, Hyde Park House, 60/60A Knightsbridge, London SW1X 7JX, tel (020) 7235 1787, fax (020) 7235 6912, email kuwait@dircon.co.uk.

Kuwait holds 10 per cent of the world's known crude oil supply, some 94 billion barrels

KYRGYZSTAN

WHEN TO GO

WEATHER Continental climate with relatively little rainfall and an average of 247 sunny days a year. Temperatures range between 20°C and 30°C from June to August. Heavy snowfalls in winter.

FESTIVALS Special events in Kyrgyzstan usually reflect Muslim holy days. These include Ramadan, the month of fasting, and Eid al-Fitr, the feast which marks the end of Ramadan. In the Spring, the festival of Navrus, or New Days, is also celebrated. Other notable events include 7 January, the Russian Orthodox Christmas, and 31 August, Independence Day.

TRANSPORT

INTERNATIONAL AIRPORTS Bishkek Manas (FRU) 30 km from Bishkek.

INTERNAL TRAVEL Rail travel can be dangerous - numerous robberies have been reported on some routes. Adequate road network although in bad condition in the mountains. Self-drive car hire not available. Cars with drivers may be hired for long distance journeys but petrol shortages make this an expensive option.

RED TAPE

VISAS REQUIRED (UK/US) Required.

VACCINATIONS REQUIRED: See 'Vaccinations required around the world' on page 653.

DRIVING REQUIREMENTS An International Driving Permit and two photos. Anyone planning on staying a long time and buying a car locally, or importing one, is required to obtain a licence from the Protocol Department of the Foreign Ministry.

COUNTRY REPS IN UK/US UK: Ascot House, 119 Crawford Street, London W1U 6BJ, tel (020) 7935 1462, fax (020) 7935 7449, email mail@kyrgyz-embassy.org.uk. USA: 1732 Wisconsin Avenue, NW, Washington, DC 20007, tel (202) 338 5141, fax (202) 338 5139, email embassy@kyrgyzstan.org.

UK/US REPS IN COUNTRY UK: Osoo

Fatboys, 104 Prospekt Chui, Bishkek, tel (312) 680 815, fax (312) 287 360, email fatboys@ekat.kg. USA: Prospekt Mira 171, 720016 Bishkek, tel (312) 551 241, fax (312) 551 264.

PEOPLE AND PLACE

CAPITAL Bishkek.

LANGUAGE Kyrgyz.

PEOPLES Kyrgyz, Russian, Uzbek.

RELIGION Predominantly Sunni Muslim with a Russian Orthodox minority.

SIZE (SQ KM) 199,900.

POPULATION 5,067,000.

POP DENSITY/KM 25.3.

STATE OF THE NATION

SAFETY Generally safe, beware theft.

LIFE EXPECTANCY M 64.16, F 72.38.

BEING THERE

ETIQUETTE Kyrgyzstan is a nation descended from nomadic herds people. Refusing an offer of *koumys*, a mildly alcoholic fermented mares' milk, may cause offence. Tipping is becoming more customary, especially in international hotels.

CURRENCY *Som* (KS) = 100 *tyn*.

Almaty is shown in this chart because it is the nearest place with available and similar data.

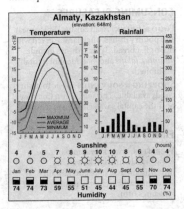

HIGHLIGHTS

BISHKEK Crouched in the fertile Chui river valley at the foot of the Tian Shan mountains, this neat largely-Soviet built city has a spacious atmosphere akin to Almaty in neighbouring Kazakhstan. It has an impressive opera and ballet theatre and several good museums, including the Lenin Museum. The centre is polluted by growing fleets of cars, but the outskirts resemble a Ukranian village, with pretty Slavic houses set in gardens of apricot and apple trees.

SILK ROAD Ancient trading route stretching from China to the Caspian Sea and the Mediterranean Sea, which retains a mysterious allure. It was used by silk merchants for more than a millennium, until its decline in the fourteenth century. The leg here passes the breathtaking Tian Shan mountain ranges and pretty Issyk Kul Lake, the world's second-largest alpine lake and one that never freezes, despite its high altitude. The taxing but thrilling journey from Bishkek to Kahgar in China, via the Torugart Pass, is a major trekking route, served by increasing numbers of adventure tour companies.

ALA ARCHA NATIONAL PARK Enjoy views over high peaks, large glaciers and lush water meadows, in this beautiful alpine nature reserve, home to more than 170 different animal species. Catch a glimpse of eagles, bears, lynx, wild boar, wolves and - if you're lucky - spotted snow leopards. The park is popular among skiers and trekkers.

FINANCE Limited acceptance of credit cards and traveller's cheques.
BUSINESS HOURS 0900-1800 Mon-Friday.
GMT +5.
VOLTAGE GUIDE 220 AC, 50 Hz.
COUNTRY DIALLING CODE 996.

CONSUMING PLEASURES

FOOD & DRINK Cuisine shows some Chinese influences. Mutton is the staple meat, often cubed and grilled (*shashlyk*). *Lipioshka*, an unleavened bread is often sold on street corners. *Laghman*, a noodle soup with mutton and vegetables is also popular. They also eat horse, and are the only Central Asian people to do so. *Koumys*, fermented mares milk, is slightly alcoholic, *dzarma* is fermented barley flour and *boso* is fermented millet.

SHOPPING & SOUVENIRS Purchases include food, handicrafts, paintings and traditional Kyrgyz products like felt hats, called *kalpak*. Carpets and chess sets are other good buys.

FIND OUT MORE

WEBSITES www.kyrgyz-embassy.org.uk, www.kyrgyzstan.org, www.lonelyplanet.com/destinations/central_asia/kyrgyzstan.

LOCAL MEDIA The *Bishkek Observer*, *Kyrgyzstan Chronicle, Times of Central Asia* and *Zaman Kyrgyzstan* are printed weekly in English.

TOURIST BOARDS IN UK/US UK: Regent Holidays Limited, 15 John Street, Bristol BS1 2HR, tel (0117) 921 1711, fax (0117) 925 4866, email regent@regent-holidays.co.uk. US: n/a.

"A wise man isn't he who has lived the longest, but he who has travelled the most."
Kyrgyz saying

LAOS

WHEN TO GO

WEATHER Hot, tropical climate. The rainy season runs from May to October, while it is generally dry from November to April.

FESTIVALS Major festivals are often linked to Buddhist holidays. These include Visakha Bu-saa, in May, which commemorates Buddha's birth, enlightenment and death. Other important events include Têt, the Chinese New Year, enjoyed in January. In April celebrations are held for Pi Mai, the new lunar year, an occasion best experienced in Luang Prabang, where the festivities and processions can keep going for more than a week. In November, the country celebrates Pha That Luang. Best experienced at That Luang in Vientiane, this colourful nationwide event sees processions of monks receiving alms and floral and floral votives. Normally, there will also be fireworks and music.

TRANSPORT

INTERNATIONAL AIRPORTS Vientiane (VTE) 4 km from the city.

INTERNAL TRAVEL Rivers are a vital part of the country's transportation system. Many roads have been paved in recent years, but few are all-weather. Car hire can be made through hotels.

RED TAPE

VISAS REQUIRED (UK/US) Required.

VACCINATIONS REQUIRED: See 'Vaccinations required around the world' on page 653.

DRIVING REQUIREMENTS An international Driving Permit is recommended, although not a legal requirement.

COUNTRY REPS IN UK/US UK: n/a, nearest 74 Avenue Raymond Poincaré, 75116 Paris, France, (1) 4553 0298, fax (1) 4727 5789, email ambalaoparis@wanadoo.fr. USA: 2222 S Street, NW, Washington, DC 20008, tel (202) 332 6416, fax (202) 332 4923, email laoemb@starpower.net.

UK/US REPS IN COUNTRY UK: PO Box 6626, Vientiane, tel (21) 413 606, fax (21) 413 607. USA: BP 114, Rue Bartholonie, That Dam, Vientiane, tel (21) 212 581-9, fax (21) 212 584, email khammanhpx@state.gov.

PEOPLE AND PLACE

CAPITAL Vientiane.

LANGUAGE Laotian.

PEOPLES Lao Loum, Lao Theung, Lao Soung.

RELIGION Buddhist.

SIZE (SQ KM) 236,800.

POPULATION 5,529,000.

POP DENSITY/KM 23.3.

STATE OF THE NATION

SAFETY Safe, but be careful in drug-producing areas.

LIFE EXPECTANCY M 53.07, F 57.17.

BEING THERE

ETIQUETTE Visitors should be warned that extra-marital sexual contact between foreigners and Laotians is prohibited, and is punishable by fines of up to US$5,000 and in some cases imprisonment. Travellers should carry their identity documents at all times, as failure to do so may result in large fines or detention. The country's constitution is religiously tolerant, Buddhism and Animism co-exist peacefully, and in some

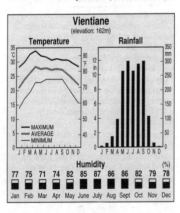

Vientiane (elevation: 162m)

Temperature / Rainfall

MAXIMUM / AVERAGE / MINIMUM

Humidity (%)

	Jan	Feb	Mar	Apr	May	June	July	Aug	Sept	Oct	Nov	Dec
	77	75	71	74	82	85	87	86	86	82	79	78

HIGHLIGHTS

VIENTIANE Take it easy in this relaxed and quiet capital. Nestled on the banks of the Mekong, many of Vientiane's buildings reflect the country's colonial links with France - such as the Arc de Triomphe-esque Victory Monument. However, it is the historic local buildings that most impress, in particular the That Luang stupa, the country's most holy site and a symbol of the Buddhist and Lao union. There are also several beautiful temples, known as *wats*. The city has some good outlets for French and Lao cuisine. After hours, you can listen to live Lao bands in the city's discos.

LUANG PRABANG Historic northern city, a former royal capital with a UNESCO World Heritage status. The city is very much the country's cultural heartland, with 32 dramatic temple complexes. Wat Xieng Thong, decorated with coloured glass and gold, together with Wat May, are particularly notable. It's all set in a pretty upland valley, panoramic views of which can be enjoyed from nearby Mount Phousi.

MEKONG RIVER Take a boat trip along this mighty waterway, a major transport network along which chug slow ferries and speed noisy motor boats. Some of the country's best wildlife can be spotted along its banks, among them primates and birds. Freshwater *irrawaddy* dolphins can be seen swimming near its murky surface.

HILL TRIBES Laos is home to a number of ethnic tribal groups, dotted throughout the country. Hiking trips to villages can be arranged and provide an insight into their lives and customs.

---

cases are blended. Religious beliefs should be respected. It is important to remember that, as Buddhists, Lao people should not be touched on the head.

CURRENCY Lao *kip* (Kip) = 100 *cents*.

FINANCE Limited acceptance of credit cards and traveller's cheques.

BUSINESS HOURS 0800-1200, 1330-1730, Monday to Friday.

GMT +7.

VOLTAGE GUIDE 220 AC, 50 Hz.

COUNTRY DIALLING CODE 856.

CONSUMING PLEASURES

FOOD & DRINK Rice, especially sticky rice, is the staple food and dishes are Indo-Chinese in flavour. Good French restaurants in Vientiane. Rice whisky, known as *lao lao*, is popular. Good beer.

SHOPPING & SOUVENIRS Silk, silver jewellery, handmade shirts.

FIND OUT MORE

WEBSITES www.laoparis.com, www.laoembassy.com, www.visit-laos.com.

LOCAL MEDIA The *Vientiane Times* is published in English.

TOURIST BOARDS IN UK/US n/a.

By the end of the Vietnam War, Laos had the dubious distinction of being the most heavily bombed country in the history of warfare

LATVIA

WHEN TO GO

WEATHER May to August is warm, although August sees the heaviest rainfall. Winter, from November to March can be very cold, with heavy snowfall.

FESTIVALS Latvia has a number of interesting festivals, often marking seasonal change, or simply as an excuse for fun. Singing is central to several large events. Every three years the country holds the Baltika International Folk Festival, with the next one scheduled for 2006. The five-yearly All-Latvian Song & Dance Festival will next be held in 2008. There are also smaller annual Summer Singing Fair's held in market places and town squares. The principle Christian holidays are significant dates in the Latvian calendar. As in much of Eastern Europe, another key time is the summer solstice, when people head out into the countryside and party around bonfires.

TRANSPORT

INTERNATIONAL AIRPORTS Riga (RIX) 7 km from the city.

INTERNAL TRAVEL Reasonable rail network, good road connections from Riga to all parts of the country. Car hire available.

RED TAPE

VISAS REQUIRED (UK/US) Required by Australian and Canadian visitors.

VACCINATIONS REQUIRED: See 'Vaccinations required around the world' on page 653.

DRIVING REQUIREMENTS EU pink format licence or an International Driving Permit.

COUNTRY REPS IN UK/US UK: 45 Nottingham Place, London W1U 5LE, tel (020) 7312 0040, fax (020) 7312 0042, email embassy.uk@mfa.gov.lv. USA: 4325 17th Street, NW, Washington, DC 20011, tel (202) 726 8213, fax (202) 726 6785, email Embassy@Latvia-USA.org.

UK/US REPS IN COUNTRY UK: J. Alunana Street 5, LV-1010 Riga, Latvia, tel 777 4700, fax 777 4707, email british.embassy@ apollo.lv. USA: Raina Blvd. 7, LV-1510 Riga, tel 703 6200, fax 782 0047, email pas@ usembassy.lv.

PEOPLE AND PLACE

CAPITAL Riga.

LANGUAGE Latvian.

PEOPLES Latvian (52%), Russian, Belorussian, Ukrainian.

RELIGION Mainly Lutheran. Roman Catholic and Russian Orthodox minorities.

SIZE (SQ KM) 64,589.

POPULATION 2,311,480.

POP DENSITY/KM 35.8.

STATE OF THE NATION

SAFETY Safe.

LIFE EXPECTANCY M 65.78, F 76.6.

BEING THERE

ETIQUETTE Latvians are rather reserved and formal, however, they are also very hospitable. Like their Baltic neighbours, they are proud of their culture and visitors should take care to respect this sense of national identity. Other than that, normal courtesies should be observed. Costs: taxi fares and restaurant bills usually include a tip, but it is customary to give a little extra for good service.

CURRENCY Latvian *lat* (Ls) = 100 *santims*.

FINANCE Credit cards and traveller's

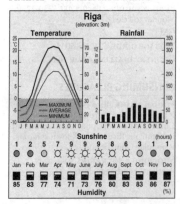

Riga
(elevation: 3m)

	Jan	Feb	Mar	Apr	May	June	July	Aug	Sept	Oct	Nov	Dec
Sunshine (hours)	1	2	5	7	9	9	9	8	6	3	1	1
Humidity (%)	85	83	77	74	71	73	76	80	83	83	86	87

HIGHLIGHTS

RIGA Stroll through the medieval streets of the capital's World Heritage-listed Old Town, dotted with church spires and other fine Gothic, Baroque, Classical and Art Noveau buildings. Afterwards, why not enjoy a few mellow hours in one of the many charming candle-lit bars. There are also more energetic nightspots, something that has led to an influx in stag parties. But if that's not your thing, there's still plenty to enjoy away from the pubs and clubs. Climb up to the 72-metre-high viewing tower of St Peter's church for great city views, try ice-skating in the atmospheric outdoor rink, or do some more ambling - this time through the massive Central Market, or the museums.

JURMALA Relax on this pleasant stretch of white sands, ice-blue seas and sand dunes, dubbed the 'pearl of Latvia'. Lined with pretty pine trees, the resort actually comprises 12 small villages, which extend for 30 km along the Gulf of Riga. It's a popular holiday spot for people of all ages and during the summer swimmers stay in the water until late at night, on account of the midnight sun.

KULDIGA Watch the cascading jet of water descend from the top of the country's highest waterfall, Ventas Rumba, a place where many people go for weekend picnics. It is close to Kuldiga, a town founded by Germanic knights in the thirteenth century.

SIGULDA Castles and caves are the summer highlights of the 'Switzerland of Latvia'. In winter it's a centre for sports and has an Olympic bobsled run.

cheques generally accepted.

BUSINESS HOURS 0830-1730 Mon-Friday.

GMT +2.

VOLTAGE GUIDE 220 AC, 50 Hz.

COUNTRY DIALLING CODE 371.

LOCAL MEDIA *The Baltic Times* is printed weekly in English.

TOURIST BOARDS IN UK/US n/a.

CONSUMING PLEASURES

FOOD & DRINK Local specialities include *kotletes* (meat patties), *skabu kapostu zupa* (cabbage soup), *piragi* (pastries filled with bacon and onions). Potatoes play a large part in the diet. Riga's Black Balsam is a thick black alcoholic liquid, made from ginger, oak bark, bitter orange peel and cognac. Drunk with coffee or vodka.

SHOPPING & SOUVENIRS Amber, folk art, wicker work, earthenware.

FIND OUT MORE

WEBSITES www.london.am.gov.lv, www.britain.lv, www.latvia-usa.org, www.usembassy.lv, www.inyourpocket.com/latvia/en.

Dome Cathedral in Riga is the largest church in the Baltic and boasts the world's fourth-largest organ, with 7,000 pipes

LEBANON

WHEN TO GO

WEATHER Summer (June to September) hot on the coast, cooler in the mountains. December to March is mostly rainy, with snow on the mountains. The rest of the year is warm and pleasant.

FESTIVALS Events are often connected to the major Islamic or Christian public holidays. Other special events include the International Weddings Exhibition in Beirut, held in the spring. A world famous arts festival is held every year in Baalbek, during July.

TRANSPORT

INTERNATIONAL AIRPORTS Beirut (BEY) 16 km from the city.

INTERNAL TRAVEL Ports are served by coastal passenger ferries. Limited public transport. Car hire is available although chauffeur-driven vehicles are recommended.

RED TAPE

VISAS REQUIRED (UK/US) Required.

VACCINATIONS REQUIRED: See 'Vaccinations required around the world' on page 653.

DRIVING REQUIREMENTS International Driving Permit and Green Card.

COUNTRY REPS IN UK/US UK: 21 Palace Garden Mews, London W8 4QM, tel (020) 7229 7265, fax (020) 7243 1699, email emb_leb@btinternet.com. USA: 9 East 76th Street, New York, NY 10021, tel (212) 744 7905, fax (212) 794 1510, email lebconsny@aol.com.

UK/US REPS IN COUNTRY UK: PO Box 11-471, Embassies Complex, Army Street, Zkak Al-Blat, Serail Hill, Beirut Central District, tel (1) 990 400, fax (1) 990 420, email chancery@cyberia.ne.lb. USA: Antelias, PO Box 70-840, Beirut, tel (4) 542 600, fax (4) 544 136, email BeirutNIV@state.gov.

PEOPLE AND PLACE

CAPITAL Beirut.

LANGUAGE Arabic.

PEOPLES Of Arab descent (92%), large Palestinian refugee population.

RELIGION Islam (70%), Christianity.

SIZE (SQ KM) 10,452.

POPULATION 3,700,000.

POP DENSITY/KM 344.

STATE OF THE NATION

SAFETY Currently safe, but be careful near the Israeli border.

LIFE EXPECTANCY M 70.17, F 75.21.

BEING THERE

ETIQUETTE Family is an important part of a traditional Lebanese lifestyle. In the cities in particular, Western influences can also be seen. Nevertheless, dress should remain modest. This is particularly important when visiting mosques and other religious places. Since Lebanon is almost evenly divided between those adhering to the Muslim faith, and those adhering to the Christian faith, visitors should dress according to the custom of the majority in the individual places being visited. Lebanese people are known for their hospitality. Handshaking is the normal form of greeting. It is acceptable to give a small gift, particularly if invited to a person's home for a meal.

CURRENCY Lebanese pound (L£) = 100 *piastres*.

FINANCE Limited acceptance of credit cards and traveller's cheques.

BUSINESS HOURS 0800-1800 Monday-Saturday.

GMT +2 (+3 in the summer).

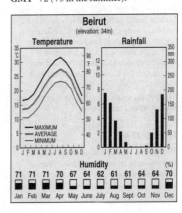

Beirut
(elevation: 34m)

Temperature — Rainfall — Humidity chart.

MAXIMUM
AVERAGE
MINIMUM

Humidity (%)

Jan	Feb	Mar	Apr	May	June	July	Aug	Sept	Oct	Nov	Dec
71	71	71	70	67	64	62	61	61	64	64	70

HIGHLIGHTS

Beirut Potentially one of the most popular tourist and business centres in the Middle East. Jutting out into the Mediterranean and shadowed over by some towering mountains, this vibrant city appears to be recovering from the damage inflicted during Lebanon's 16-year civil war. Many areas have been reconstructed or rebuilt, giving the city a young and modern feel, yet it also retains some charming old *souks* and the Turkish bath at Al-Nouzha gives a glimpse of the old Beirut.

Raouche Enjoy a stroll along the promenade at this lively seaside resort on the outer reaches of Beirut. The imposing Pigeon Rocks are the city's most famous natural attraction - and particularly enchanting at sunset.

Tripoli The feel of Arabia hangs about this captivating second city, overlooking which stands an imposing Crusader castle. The city boasts some splendid Mameluk architecture, fine mosques and medieval markets Nearby the Island of Palm Trees is a nature reserve to green turtles and wild birds.

Baalbek 'What have the Romans ever done for us?' Well for a start they left these amazing Roman ruins near the border with Syria. Take a peek into the Roman world at this temple complex, behind which soar the grand columns of the Temple of Jupiter.

Tyre Historic city, with superb archaeological sites, including one of the largest Roman hippodromes ever found. Close by, nice beaches offer good scuba diving and snorkelling.

Voltage guide 230 AC, 50 Hz.
Country dialling code 961.

CONSUMING PLEASURES

Food & drink Lebanese cuisine has a good reputation, relying on fresh local produce and herbs. The traditional *mezza* may consist of up to 40 small dishes served as a starter, including *kebbeh* (lamb or fish paste with cracked wheat, served raw, baked or fried). Main courses are likely to include the staples of rice, vegetables and mutton, and include *lahm mishwi* (mutton with onions, peppers and tomato).

Shopping & souvenirs Decorative and precious handmade items, traditional pottery, glassware, cutlery, brass and copper goods, silk and wool kaftans, table linen.

FIND OUT MORE

Websites
www.britishembassy.gov.uk/lebanon,
www.lebanonembassyus.org,
www.lebconsny.org,
www.usembassy.gov.lb,
www.lebanon-tourism.gov.lb.

Local media *The Daily Star, Beirut Times* are published in English, together with several weeklies.

Tourist boards in UK/US n/a.

> Lebanon is the site of the Biblical 'land of milk and honey'

LESOTHO

WHEN TO GO

WEATHER Most rainfall occurs from October-April. Snow occurs in the highlands from May-September. The hottest period is from January to February.

FESTIVALS The Christian feasts of Easter and Christmas are major events in the Lesotho year. Other dates worth noting include Moshoeshoe Day, in March, which commemorates and celebrates King Moshoeshoe I, the first king of Lesotho. He is revered as a man who managed to ward off the Zulus and the Afrikaans, keeping Lesotho free from foreign reign. The birthday of the current king is celebrated in July, while 4 October is National Independence Day.

TRANSPORT

INTERNATIONAL AIRPORTS Maseru (MSU) 18 km from the city.

INTERNAL TRAVEL Some main towns are connected by internal flights. The road system is underdeveloped.

RED TAPE

VISAS REQUIRED (UK/US) Required by American visitors.

VACCINATIONS REQUIRED: See 'Vaccinations required around the world' on page 653.

DRIVING REQUIREMENTS International Driving Permit recommended. National driving licences are normally valid, if in English or accompanied by a certified translation. If there's any confusion, it is advisable to check with the appropriate Embassy or High Commission.

COUNTRY REPS IN UK/US
UK: 7 Chesham Place, London SW1 8HN, tel (020) 7235 5686, fax (020) 7235 5023, email lhc@lesotholondon.org.uk. USA: 2511 Massachusetts Avenue, NW, Washington, DC 20008, tel (202) 797 5533, fax (202) 234 6815, email lesothoembassy@verizon.net.

UK/US REPS IN COUNTRY UK: PO Box 521, Maseru 100, tel (22) 313 961, fax (22) 310 120. USA: PO Box 333, 254 Kingsway Road, Maseru 100, tel (22) 312 666, fax (22) 310 116 email infomaseru@state.gov.

PEOPLE AND PLACE

CAPITAL Maseru.

LANGUAGE Sesotho and English.

PEOPLES Basotho (97%), European and Asian.

RELIGION Christian, mainly Anglican, Catholic and Lesotho Evangelical.

SIZE (SQ KM) 30,355.

POPULATION 2,200,000.

POP DENSITY/KM 72.

STATE OF THE NATION

SAFETY Generally safe, but travel with caution.

LIFE EXPECTANCY M 36.86, F 36.49.

BEING THERE

ETIQUETTE If you're planning on spending some time in rural villages, it is polite to inform the Head Chief - who is likely to be very helpful. Dress should be practical and casual but local customs should be respected. Do not take photographs of the palace, police establishments, government offices, the airport or monetary authority buildings.

CURRENCY *Loti* (M) = 100 *lisente*.

FINANCE Limited acceptance of credit

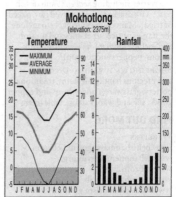

Mokhotlong
(elevation: 2375m)

HIGHLIGHTS

WATERFALLS Get in the saddle and take a pony trek through some of Lesotho's most dramatic landscapes, taking in some truly impressive waterfalls on the way - Ribaneng, Ketane and Maletsunyane, the latter the largest single drop falls in southern Africa. The country is home to the famous Basotho ponies, the result of cross-breeding between short Javanese horses and European full mounts.

MOUNTAINS Situated at the highest point in the Drakensburg range, the country affords some fine views over steep mountains, broad valleys and deep ravines. These imposing peaks contain deposits of minerals including diamonds, while the Caledon, Orange and Tugela rivers all rise in the mountains of Lesotho. With some spectacular and rugged scenery, climbing and walking are increasingly popular activities among visitors.

MASERU The landlocked country's capital and stepping off point for exploring the rest of the region. The King's Palace and the Prime Minister's Residence are worth a look on your way through, as is the historic cemetery. On the edge of Maseru's townships it's possible to spend a night in a traditional Basotho village.

SKIING AND OTHER SPORTS Strange as it sounds, a new resort has opened up in the heart of the Lesotho highlands, less than five hours' drive from Johannesburg in neighbouring South Africa. Horse racing, fishing and football - the national game - are also popular activities.

cards, traveller's cheques widely accepted.

BUSINESS HOURS 0800-1245, 1400-1630 Monday-Friday, 0800-1300 Saturday.

GMT +2.

VOLTAGE GUIDE 220 AC, 50 Hz.

COUNTRY DIALLING CODE 266.

LOCAL MEDIA *Lesotho Today, The Sun,* and *Public Eye* are major English-language papers.

TOURIST BOARDS IN UK/US n/a.

CONSUMING PLEASURES

FOOD & DRINK Street stalls in towns sell good grilled meat. Much food has to be i mported from South Africa, but freshwater fish is in abundant supply and is popular. Hotels and restaurants offer a wide variety of cuisines. Good beer.

SHOPPING & SOUVENIRS Famous conical hats, grass woven items like mats and baskets, pottery, wool and mohair rugs, tapestries, traditional jewellery.

FIND OUT MORE

WEBSITES www.lesotholondon.org.uk, www.lesothoemb-usa.gov.ls, http://maseru.usembassy.gov, www.go2africa.com/lesotho.

Maletsunyane Falls, with a dizzying height of 192-metres, is the highest single drop waterfall in southern Africa

LIBERIA

WHEN TO GO

WEATHER The rainy season is from May to October. Temperatures are consistently high.

FESTIVALS Dates in the Christian calendar are significant. Independence Day, celebrated on 26 July, and National Unification, on 14 May, are other major occasions.

TRANSPORT

INTERNATIONAL AIRPORTS Monrovia (MLW) 60 km from the city.

INTERNAL TRAVEL Most roads unpaved. The railways are primarily used for mining goods and carry little other traffic.

RED TAPE

VISAS REQUIRED (UK/US) Required.

VACCINATIONS REQUIRED: See 'Vaccinations required around the world' on page 653.

DRIVING REQUIREMENTS International Driving Permit recommended. However, a temporary 30-day licence is available on presentation of a valid British, Northern Ireland or US driving licence.

COUNTRY REPS IN UK/US UK: 23 Fitzroy Square, London W1 6EW, tel (020) 7388 5489, fax (020) 7380 1593. USA: 5201 16th Street, NW, Washington, DC 20011, tel (202) 723 0437, fax (202) 723 0436, email info@embassyofliberia.org.

UK/US REPS IN COUNTRY UK: The British Embassy in Freetown (see Sierra Leone) deals with enquiries relating to Liberia. The British Consular Agent at UMARCO, Clara Town, Bush Rod Island, PO Box 1196, Monrovia, tel 226 056, fax 226 061, email chalkleyroy@aol.com provides emergency assistance only. USA: 111 United Nations Drive, Mamba Point, 1000 Monrovia, tel 226 370, fax 226 1490, email mrveduconsular@state.gov.

PEOPLE AND PLACE

CAPITAL Monrovia.

LANGUAGE English.

PEOPLES Indigenous tribes (16 main groups), Americo-Liberians (5%).

RELIGION Officially a Christian state. Animist beliefs practiced widely. Small Muslim community.

SIZE (SQ KM) 97,754.

POPULATION 3,239,000.

POP DENSITY/KM 33.1.

STATE OF THE NATION

SAFETY Highly dangerous. Political violence and periodic *coups* are worsened by spill over from civil wars in neighbouring countries. Travel not recommended.

LIFE EXPECTANCY M 46.75, F 48.65.

BEING THERE

ETIQUETTE Business dress is relatively informal. A shirt and tie is normally sufficient. The language used in business circles is English. Visitors should respect local customs, and Islamic traditions and practices in Muslim areas. It is worth bearing in mind that although there is no need to tip taxi drivers, other tips should normally be around 10 per cent.

CURRENCY Liberian dollar (L$).

FINANCE Very limited acceptance of credit cards, traveller's cheques generally not accepted.

BUSINESS HOURS 0800-1200, 1400-1700 Monday-Friday.

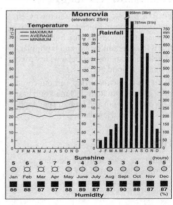

HIGHLIGHTS

MONROVIA Named after the US President, James Monroe, this city was founded in 1822 by the American Cololization Society as a haven for freed slaves from the US and the West Indies. A sprawling hub today, it is known as one of the wettest and most humid capitals in Africa, with 4,500 mm of annual rainfall. However, on the plus side, it has good sandy beaches and dozens of colourful nightclubs, bars and restaurants, centred upon the area around Gurley Street - many of which stay open until the early hours.

SAPO NATIONAL PARK Take a jungle safari through West Africa's largest untouched tract of rainforest (it's never been logged), a major draw for wildlife and nature enthusiasts. This lush reserve is home to rare indigenous wildlife, including elephant, leopard, giant forest hog and pygmy hippo.

RAINFORESTS The Sapo reserve is just part of the country's stunning jungle areas. In all, rainforest covers 40 per cent of the country, and is home to a wealth of wildlife, as well as a number of Liberia's distinct ethnic groups.

BEACHES Swim or sail off Liberia's fine West African coast-line. Fringing the Atlantic Ocean are mile upon mile of white sand beaches. They include Bernard's Beach, Caesar's Beach, Cooper's Beach, Elwa Beach and others.

AN UNUSUAL EXCURSION The Firestone Rubber Plantation offers tours - for your pleasure. It claims to be one of the largest in the world.

GMT GMT.
VOLTAGE GUIDE 110 AC, 60 Hz.
COUNTRY DIALLING CODE 231.

the *Inquirer* and *Monrovia Guardian* are the main papers.
TOURIST BOARDS IN UK/US n/a.

CONSUMING PLEASURES

FOOD & DRINK West African cuisine can be found in 'chop bars' (streetside restaurants) or in 'cookhouses' , where traditional Liberian dishes are served with rice. Only the most basic provisions are available in many towns outside the capital. Own-brand beers are readily available.

SHOPPING & SOUVENIRS Tie-dyed and embroidered cloth, which can be made up into African or European styles, woodcarvings, ritual masks, figurines, soapstone carvings.

FIND OUT MORE

WEBSITES www.embassyofliberia.org, http://monrovia.usembassy.gov, www.infohub.com/travelguide/traveller/africa/liberia.html.

LOCAL MEDIA All newspapers in English,

> Liberia is Africa's oldest republic, founded by American idealists keen to free their slaves. Once there, the former slaves became themselves a slave-owning class, and ruthlessly monopolised Liberia's power and wealth for 150 years

LIBYA

WHEN TO GO

WEATHER Summers (June to September) are very hot and dry, winters are mild with cooler evenings.

FESTIVALS As a Muslim country Libya observes all the main Islamic festivals as holidays. The dates of these events differ from year-to-year. Ramadan, the month of fasting, is a particularly important time for Muslims. Revolution Day, on 23 July, and the annual Date Harvest Festival, in October, are other notable diary dates.

TRANSPORT

INTERNATIONAL AIRPORTS Tripoli (TIP) 35 km from the city, Benghazi (BEN) 19 km from Benghazi, Sebha (SEB) 11 km from the town.

INTERNAL TRAVEL Some internal flights between main centres. The National Coast Road runs from the Tunisian to the Egyptian border. All road signs are in Arabic only.

RED TAPE

VISAS REQUIRED (UK/US) Required.

VACCINATIONS REQUIRED: See 'Vaccinations required around the world' on page 653.

DRIVING REQUIREMENTS National driving licence valid for 3 months, after which a Libyan licence must be obtained.

COUNTRY REPS IN UK/US UK: 61-62 Ennismore Gardens, London SW7 1NH, tel (020) 7589 6120, fax (020) 7589 6087. USA: (Permanent Mission to the UN) 309-315 East 48th Street, New York, NY 10017, tel (212) 752 5775, fax (212) 593 4787, email info@libya-un.org.

UK/US REPS IN COUNTRY UK: PO Box 4206, Tripoli, tel (21) 335 1422, tel (21) 335 1425. USA: c/o Embassy of Belgium, Tower 4, Dhat al-Emad Towers Complex, 5th Floor, Tripoli, tel (21) 335 1633 (room 1050), fax (21) 335 0937, email consulartripoli@yahoo.com.

PEOPLE AND PLACE

CAPITAL Tripoli.

LANGUAGE Arabic.

PEOPLES Arab and Berber.

RELIGION Islam (mainly Sunni Muslim).

SIZE (SQ KM) 1,775,500.

POPULATION 5,678,484.

POP DENSITY/KM 3.2.

STATE OF THE NATION

SAFETY Safe. Observe Islamic customs.

LIFE EXPECTANCY M 74.29, F 78.82.

BEING THERE

ETIQUETTE Life in Libya is regulated fairly strictly along socialist/Islamic principles. The language used in business circles is English. In general, Arab courtesies and s ocial customs prevail and should be respected Travellers should dress modestly, in particular when visiting religious buildings and small towns.

CURRENCY Libyan *dinar* (LD) = 1,000 *dirhams.*

FINANCE Very limited acceptance of Diners Club and Visa, traveller's cheques generally not accepted.

BUSINESS HOURS 0700-1400 Monday-Thursday, Saturday.

GMT +2.

VOLTAGE GUIDE 150/220 AC, 50 Hz.

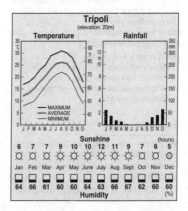

Tripoli (elevation: 20m)

HIGHLIGHTS

TRIPOLI Capital city full of heritage - narrow alleyways, grand mosques, and traditional *khans* (public houses). Tripoli's architecture reflects its past rulers; Turkish, Spanish, Maltese and Italian. A stroll through the bustling *souks* in the Medina (historic city centre)is an fun way to spend a few hours. Above the city stands the Red Castle, or Assai al-Hamra, an imposing fortress, besides which is a museum displaying mosaics, statues and other artefacts.

LEPTIS MAGNA Delve deep into Libya's fascinating history, as you wander through this wonderful archaeological site east of Tripoli, regarded by many as the best Roman site in the Mediterranean. At the mouth of the Wadi Lebda, it's all that is left of a large port city built by the Phoenicians, which then became a major Roman settlement. Beautifully preserved by invading sands, it remains a great splendour to this day. Don't miss the grand Severan Arch, built in honour of Emperor Septimus Severus, or the marble- and granite-lined Hadrianic Baths. There's also an amphitheatre and an impressive forum complex. And while Leptis Magma attracts coach loads of tourists, the site is large enough to absorb most of them.

WAR GRAVES Libya was the scene of much fierce fighting during World War Two. The most famous combatants were the British soldiers garrisoned at Tobruk - the so-called Desert Rats. Today at Tobruk, four cemeteries mark the final resting place for some - a poignant pilgrimage for surviving veterans.

COUNTRY DIALLING CODE 218.

CONSUMING PLEASURES

FOOD & DRINK Based on *couscous*, served with vegetables, chicken, lamb or camel, and macaroni-based dishes influenced by the Italians. Libyan soup, a spicy minestrone with lamb and pasta, is served at most meals. The local fish along the coast is very good. Alcohol is banned.

SHOPPING & SOUVENIRS Spices, metal engravings, jewellery, leather.

FIND OUT MORE

WEBSITES www.britain-in-libya.org, www.dfait-maeci.gc.ca/libya, www.libya-un.org, www.libyaonline.com.

LOCAL MEDIA No newspapers in English.

TOURIST BOARDS IN UK/US n/a.

"The palm tree is a priceless treasure, the lands where it grows will always be settled."
Proverb from the Fezzan region

LIECHTENSTEIN

WHEN TO GO

WEATHER Temperate, alpine climate, with warm wet summers from May-August, and mild winters.

FESTIVALS Masked Balls are held in February. In the summer months Liechtenstein hosts several band music festivals, known as Verbandsmusikfest. They take place in Vaduz, Mauren, Eschen and other locations. Vaduz also hosts an Open-Air Film Festival, usually in June or July. The country's National Day is celebrated on 15 August, with processions and fireworks.

TRANSPORT

INTERNATIONAL AIRPORTS Nearest airport is Zurich, 130 km away.

INTERNAL TRAVEL Single track railroad with few stops, good roads.

RED TAPE

VISAS REQUIRED (UK/US) As for Switzerland.

VACCINATIONS REQUIRED: See 'Vaccinations required around the world' on page 653.

DRIVING REQUIREMENTS National driving licences are valid.

COUNTRY REPS IN UK/US Liechtenstein maintains very few overseas missions and is generally represented by Switzerland (see Switzerland).

UK/US REPS IN COUNTRY UK: 37-39 Rue de Vermont, 6th Floor, CH-1211 Geneva 20, Switzerland, tel (22) 918 2400, fax (22) 918 2322, the British Embassy in Berne (see Switzerland) deals with enquiries relating to Liechtenstein. USA: The American Embassy in Berne (see Switzerland) deals with enquiries relating to Liechtenstein.

PEOPLE AND PLACE

CAPITAL Vaduz.

LANGUAGE German.

PEOPLES Liechtensteiners, Swiss, German.

RELIGION Mainly Roman Catholic, Protestant and other minorities.

SIZE (SQ KM) 160.

POPULATION 34,294.

POP DENSITY/KM 211.6.

STATE OF THE NATION

SAFETY Safe.

LIFE EXPECTANCY M 75.96, F 83.16.

BEING THERE

ETIQUETTE Normal conduct for north-west Europe. As in many European countries, regulations concerning smoking are becoming increasingly strict.

CURRENCY Swiss *franc* (sfr) = 100 *centimes*.

FINANCE Credit cards, traveller's cheques widely accepted.

BUSINESS HOURS 0800-1200, 1330-1700 Monday-Friday.

GMT +1.

VOLTAGE GUIDE 220 AC, 50 Hz.

COUNTRY DIALLING CODE 423 (41 for Switzerland).

CONSUMING PLEASURES

FOOD & DRINK Swiss with Austrian overtones. Specialities include *kaseknopfle*, small dumplings with cheese. Some extremely good wines, including *vaduzer*.

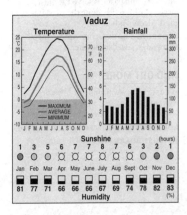

HIGHLIGHTS

VADUZ It may feel more like a small alpine village than a national capital - you can jog end-to-end in five minutes - but Vaduz is still a charming place. The Schloss Vaduz (Vaduz Castle) is not open to the public, but its exterior is well-photographed. The impressive castle sits high above the town, and a short stroll up to its base reveals some magnificent mountain views of the area around Vaduz. A network of marked trails winds along the ridge, making it easy to explore.

BRIEFMARKEN-MUSEUM A haven for philatelists, the Postage Stamp Museum in Vaduz exhibits 300 frames of national stamps issued since 1912. The National Library, National Museum and Ski Museum are also worth a look.

KUNSTMUSEUM Housed in a sleek modern building, the Art Museum exhibits some fine paintings from the Prince's private collection, including works by Rembrandt, Rubens and Van Dyck.

WINTER SPORTS Whizz down the snowy slopes of Liechtenstein's ski resorts. Nestled amid the mountains in the south-east corner of the country, the resort of Malbun has some excellent runs, with good facilities, and is regarded as a good destination for beginners. Close by, the resort at Steg has become popular for cross-country skiing, with its loop offering three separate distances. The track is also open at night.

SCHELLENBERG Little village in the north, with a monument to the night in 1945 when 500 Russian soldiers crossed the border.

SHOPPING & SOUVENIRS Handmade ceramics, pottery, postage stamps.

FIND OUT MORE

WEBSITES http://uk.myswitzerland.com, www.myswitzerland.com, www.travel.org/liechtens.html.

LOCAL MEDIA No newspapers in English. No domestic TV service, one radio station.

TOURIST BOARDS IN UK/US US: 608 Fifth Avenue, New York, NY 10020, tel (212) 7575944, fax (212) 262 6116, email info.usa@myswitzerland.com.

There's no military service in Liechtenstein. The country's small army – of just 80 men – was disbanded in 1868

LITHUANIA

WHEN TO GO

WEATHER Warm summers from May to August. August also sees heavy rainfall. Very cold winters from November to mid-March, heavy snowfalls are common.

FESTIVALS Lithuania hosts a number of events. Some have a cultural or spiritual significance, others are just good fun. Independence Day, on 16 February, and the Restoration of Lithuania's Independence, on 11 March, are both public holidays. Other highlights include the Jazz Festival in Kaunas, a month of jazz events in April, and the classical music-themed Vilnius Festival, throughout June. The capital also holds the colourful Vilnius Carnival in May, an event which first started in 2004.

TRANSPORT

INTERNATIONAL AIRPORTS Vilnius (VNO) 6 km from the city centre.

INTERNAL TRAVEL Few domestic flights. Good rail connections and road network. Car hire available.

RED TAPE

VISAS REQUIRED (UK/US) None.

VACCINATIONS REQUIRED: See 'Vaccinations required around the world' on page 653.

DRIVING REQUIREMENTS EU pink format licences or national driving licences supported by photographic ID.

COUNTRY REPS IN UK/US UK: 84 Gloucester Place, London W1U 6AU, tel (020) 7486 6401, fax (020) 7486 6403, email chancery@lithuanianembassy.co.uk. USA: 2622 16th Street, NW, Washington, DC 20009, tel (202) 234 5860, fax (202) 328 0466, email info@ltembassyus.org.

UK/US REPS IN COUNTRY
UK: 2 Antakalnio Street, 10308 Vilnius, tel (5) 246 2900, fax (5) 246 2901, email be-vilnius@britain.lt. USA: Akmenu 6, 2600 Vilnius, tel (5) 266 5500, fax (5) 266 5510, email WebMailVilnius@state.gov.

PEOPLE AND PLACE

CAPITAL Vilnius.

LANGUAGE Lithuanian.

PEOPLES Lithuanian (80%), Russian, Polish, Belorussian.

RELIGION Roman Catholic. Evangelical Lutheran, Evangelical Reformist, Russian Orthodox, Baptist, Muslim and Jewish minorities.

SIZE (SQ KM) 65,300.

POPULATION 3,462,553.

POP DENSITY/KM 53.

STATE OF THE NATION

SAFETY Safe.

LIFE EXPECTANCY M 68.944, F 79.28.

BEING THERE

ETIQUETTE Normal courtesies for travel in a European country should be observed. The Lithuanians are proud of their culture and their national heritage. Visitors should respect this sense of national identity.

CURRENCY *Litas* (Lt) = 100 *centas*.

FINANCE Credit cards and traveller's cheques accepted in large towns.

BUSINESS HOURS 0900-1300, 1400-1800 Monday to Friday.

GMT +1.

VOLTAGE GUIDE 220 AC, 50 Hz.

COUNTRY DIALLING CODE 370.

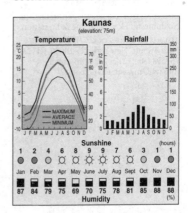

HIGHLIGHTS

VILNIUS Walk along the winding cobbled streets of this picturesque and historic capital city, noted for its fine baroque architecture and a skyline pin-pricked with church spires. Vilnius has the largest Old Town in Europe. At the heart of the city is Gedimas Square, a spacious area that features a lovely Classical-style Cathedral. Elsewhere, the University of Vilnius, among the oldest education institutions in central Europe, has some pleasant old courtyards and arcades, giving the place a distinctly Renaissance feel. Great city views can be had by climbing the tower of Gedimins Castle, built on a hill overlooking the city.

CURONIAN SPIT NATIONAL PARK On a peninsula separating the Baltic Sea from the pretty Curonian Lagoon, this reserve is one of five national parks in Lithuania. The big sand dunes and pine forests are popular with hikers, particularly during the warm summer months. The area is also inhabited by elk, deer and wild boar.

TRAKAI Ancient and dreamy former capital of Lithuania, set on the shore of picturesque Lake Galve. It's a quiet town, in an attractive area of lakes and islands dotted with old wooden cottages. Sailing and windsurfing are some of the activities on offer on the water.

DRUSKININKAI Small riverside spa town, close to which is the Gruto Parkas, a Soviet sculpture park with giant Lenins and Stalins.

KAUNAS Culture, art and excellent bars are the highlights of this historic second city.

CONSUMING PLEASURES

FOOD & DRINK Specialities include smoked eel, *skilandis* (smoked meat), *cepelinai* (made from potatoes and filled with minced meat), *salti barsciai* (cold soup), *vedarai* (potato sausage), *bulviniai blynai* (dumplings). *Midus* is a mild alcoholic spirit made from honey.

SHOPPING & SOUVENIRS Amber, linen goods, local crafts.

FIND OUT MORE

WEBSITES http://amb.urm.lt/jk, www.britain.lt, www.ltembassyus.org, www.usembassy.lt, www.tourism.lt.

LOCAL MEDIA No newspapers in English.

TOURIST BOARDS IN UK/US n/a.

On 11 March 1990 Lithuania was the first of the Soviet republics to declare its independence. This was not formally recognised by Moscow until September 1991

LUXEMBOURG

WHEN TO GO

WEATHER Warm from May to September and snow likely during winter months.

FESTIVALS Fireworks are set off in Luxembourg City on 22 June, as the country celebrates its National Day festivities. Bars and restaurants stay open into the early hours. On 23 June, a torchlight parade wends its way through the city streets. Luxembourg City also hosts a series of outdoors summer concerts and other events, as part of its Summer in the City. One of the highlights of this series of events is the Rock un Knuedler, a one-day rock festival in early July. In August-September, the capital welcomes the Schuerberfouer, one of the largest funfairs in Europe. The town of Echternach is known for its religious dancing procession, which takes place annually on Whit Tuesday, drawing pilgrims from around the world.

TRANSPORT

INTERNATIONAL AIRPORTS Luxembourg (LUX) 8 km from city.

INTERNAL TRAVEL There is an excellent road network although congestion can be a problem. Rail and bus services are integrated.

RED TAPE

VISAS REQUIRED (UK/US) None.

VACCINATIONS REQUIRED: See 'Vaccinations required around the world' on page 653.

DRIVING REQUIREMENTS A valid national driving licence. A green card is strongly recommended.

COUNTRY REPS IN UK/US

UK: 27 Wilton Crescent, London SW1X 8SD, tel (020) 7235 6961, fax (020) 7235 9734, email amb.lux@virgin.net. USA: 2200 Massachusetts Avenue, NW, Washington, DC 20008, tel (202) 265 4171/2, fax (202) 328 8270, email washington.info@mae.etat.lu.

UK/US REPS IN COUNTRY

UK: 14 Boulevard Roosevelt,

L-2450 Luxembourg-Ville, tel 229 864-6, fax 229 867, email jason.lonsdale@fco.gov.uk. USA: 22 Boulevard Emmanuel-Servais, L-2535 Luxembourg-Ville, tel 460 123, fax 461 401, email LuxembourgConsular@state.gov.

PEOPLE AND PLACE

CAPITAL Luxembourg-Ville.

LANGUAGE Lëtzeburgesch, German, French.

PEOPLES Luxembourgers, other western Europeans, mainly Italians and Portuguese.

RELIGION Roman Catholic (97%).

SIZE (SQ KM) 2,586.

POPULATION 448,300.

POP DENSITY/KM 173.4.

STATE OF THE NATION

SAFETY Safe.

LIFE EXPECTANCY M 75.45, F 82.24.

BEING THERE

ETIQUETTE Handshaking is the normal greeting. Normal conduct for a European country is advised. Smart-casual dress is widely acceptable, but some dining rooms, clubs and social functions will expect formal attire. Smoking is prohibited where notified and is becoming increasingly unacceptable. In terms of tipping for service, bills generally include service, but a rounding up

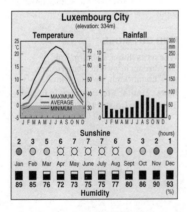

HIGHLIGHTS

LUXEMBOURG-VILLE Capital city of the Grand Duchy, whose skyline is punctuated with turrets and spires, while deep valleys fall to rivers below. The dramatic gorges, which kept invading forces at bay for centuries, also define it as one of the most striking capitals in Europe. For the best views, head up to the Citadelle du St Espirit for stunning panoramic views over Luxembourg City. The country is known as a modern centre of finance, yet it also has some grand old buildings, such as the the Moorish-style Palais Grand Ducal, built in the 1570s during Spanish rule. There are also some fine museums, while in the summer the streets and tree-lined squares are turned into open-air dining areas.

MOSELLE VALLEY Spend a lazy day exploring the wineries of this enchanting valley's Route du Vin, sampling a few glasses of the splendid wine. The River Moselle is a tributary of the Rhine, its wines resemble those of that region and many of the wine cellars are happy to receive visitors.

MÜLLERTHAL Beautiful region known by locals as 'Little Switzerland', which has some popular walking trails and rock climbing routes.

ARDENNES Scenic area which attracts nature and outdoors enthusiasts. It's a quiet region of forested plateaux, wooded hills and lush valleys. The towns of Diekirch and Wiltz are the gateways to the region and also happen to be the site of two of the country's breweries - the perfect reward at the end of a pleasurable day walking or cycling among the trees and trails.

is often given. Taxi drivers will expect 10 per cent of the meter charge.

CURRENCY Euro (€) = 100 *cents*.

FINANCE Credit cards and traveller's cheques widely accepted.

BUSINESS HOURS 0830-1200, 1400-1800 Monday-Friday.

GMT +1.

VOLTAGE GUIDE 220 AC, 50 Hz.

COUNTRY DIALLING CODE 352.

CONSUMING PLEASURES

FOOD & DRINK German and Franco-Belgian influenced cuisine. Specialities include *carré de porc fumé* (smoked pork and broad beans or *sauerkraut*) and *cochon de lait en gelée* (jellied suckling pig). Good pastries and cakes, *kirsch* is liberally used in deserts. Moselle wines resemble those from the Rhine. Beer is another speciality as are local liqueurs such as *eau de vie*.

SHOPPING & SOUVENIRS Porcelain, crystal, earthenware pottery.

FIND OUT MORE

WEBSITES www.luxembourg.co.uk, www.luxembourg-usa.org, www.visitluxembourg.com, www.ont.lu..

LOCAL MEDIA One English-language paper, *The Luxembourg News*, printed weekly.

TOURIST BOARDS IN UK/US UK: 122 Regent Street, London W1B 5SA, tel (020) 7434 2800, fax (020) 7734 1205, email tourism@luxembourg.co.uk. US: 17 Beekman Place, New York, NY 10022, tel (212) 935 8888, fax (212) 935 5896, email info@visitluxembourg.com.

Luxembourg is one of the richest countries in Western Europe. Indeed, in 1998, the World Bank said it had Europe's highest GNP per capita

MACEDONIA

WHEN TO GO

WEATHER Continental climate with hot summers from June to September and very cold winters.

FESTIVALS The annual five-day Balkan Festival of Folk Dances & Songs, is held in Ohrid in early July. It draws folk groups from across the Balkan region, while the Ohrid Summer Festival, offers a variety of music and theatre. Several public holidays take place at various points in the year. Of these, notable events include Orthodox Christmas, on 6-7 January, and Independence Day, celebrated on 8 September.

TRANSPORT

INTERNATIONAL AIRPORTS Skopje (SKP) 25 km from the city.

INTERNAL TRAVEL No regular domestic flights. An east-west road and rail route is being built through Macedonia, linking Tirana and Sofia.

RED TAPE

VISAS REQUIRED (UK/US) Required, except for UK citizens.

VACCINATIONS REQUIRED: See 'Vaccinations required around the world' on page 653.

DRIVING REQUIREMENTS n/a.

COUNTRY REPS IN UK/US UK: Suite 2.1 & 2.2, 2nd Floor, Buckingham Court, Buckingham Gate, London SW1E 6BE, tel (020) 7976 0535, fax (020) 7976 0539, email info@macedonianembassy.org.uk. USA: (Permanent Mission to the UN) 866 UN Plaza, Suite 517, New York, NY 10017, tel (212) 308 8504, fax (212) 308 8724.

UK/US REPS IN COUNTRY UK: 2614 Dimitrija Chupovski, 1000 Skopje, tel (2) 329 9299, fax (2) 311 7555, email britishembassyskopje@fco.gov.uk. USA: Ilinden bb, 1000 Skopje, tel (2) 311 6180, fax (2) 311 7103, email consular skopje@state.gov.

PEOPLE AND PLACE

CAPITAL Skopje.

LANGUAGE Macedonian.

PEOPLES Macedonian (67%), Albanian (23%), Turkish, Serb, Romany.

RELIGION Christianity (Eastern Orthodox Macedonian), Islam.

SIZE (SQ KM) 25,713.

POPULATION 2,022,547.

POP DENSITY/KM 79.7.

STATE OF THE NATION

SAFETY Generally safe.

LIFE EXPECTANCY M 71.28, F 76.37.

BEING THERE

ETIQUETTE Suits and ties are common for men to wear to meetings; skirt, blouse and tights are commonplace for women. Often, English, French or German will be spoken in business circles. It is also worth being prepared for things going very slowly or not at all, owing to the local bureaucracy. Handshaking is the common form of greeting.

CURRENCY Macedonian denar (Den) = 100 deni.

FINANCE Limited acceptance of traveller's cheques, very limited acceptance of credit cards.

BUSINESS HOURS 0700-1500 Mon-Friday.

GMT +1 (+2 in summer).

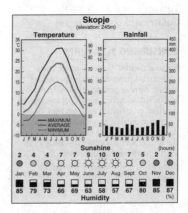

HIGHLIGHTS

LAKE OHRID It may sound rather horrid, but in fact Lake Ohrid is one of the country's most beautiful attractions, a mirror of water at its most enchanting at dusk when swans glide on its surface. The town of Ohrid is arguably the most beautiful in Macedonia, characterised by small cobbled streets, seven gorgeous churches and picturesque pebbly beaches. The former seat of the Macedonian Tsar Samuil, the walls of his fortress survive to this day, and are used as a venue for outdoor concerts during the summer months. Of the churches, the Cathedral of St Sophia is particularly impressive and, like the others, contains some magnificent frescoes.

SKOPJE Urban vibe meets colourful traditional Turkish bazaar. Much of the city is modern in design, rebuilt following an earthquake in 1963 - something that gives the place a contemporary air. This is reflected by the city's up-and-coming music scene. But the earthquake didn't cause everything to be reconstructed, and the Old Town remains Skopje's most agreeable quarter, a charming district of shops, restaurants, historic *caravanserais* and Ottoman-period mosques. There's also a wonderful riverside promenade and the imposing tenth-century Kale fortress is also worth a look.

TRESKAVEC MONASTERY Hike up to this mystical mountain retreat, dramatically positioned atop Mount Zlato, 10 kilometres above the town of Prilep. It houses ancient icons and affords spectacular views of the valleys below.

VOLTAGE GUIDE 220 AC, 50 Hz.
COUNTRY DIALLING CODE 389.

CONSUMING PLEASURES

FOOD & DRINK Similar to Turkish and Greek cuisine - kebabs and moussaka are popular. Local specialities are *gravce na tavce* (beans in a skillet) and Ohrid trout.

SHOPPING & SOUVENIRS Quilts, pottery, jewellery.

FIND OUT MORE

WEBSITES
www.macedonianembassy.org.uk,
www.britishembassy.gov.uk/macedonia,
http://skopje.usembassy.gov,
http://faq.macedonia.org..

LOCAL MEDIA The *Macedonian Times* is published monthly in English and Macedonian.

TOURIST BOARDS IN UK/US n/a.

Home of the all-conquering warrior-king Alexander the Great, Macedonia was also – in more recent times – the birthplace of the peace-loving missionary Mother Theresa, who was born in Skopje in 1910

MADAGASCAR

WHEN TO GO

WEATHER Hot and subtropical. The rainy season is from November to March. Monsoons bring storms and cyclones to the east and north from December to March. The dry season is from April-October.

FESTIVALS There are a wide variety of events, from national celebrations to more localised festivities. These sometimes feature Malagasy singers, known as *mphira gasy*, who sing and dance in theatrical groups. Big occasions include Alahamady Be, the New Year, celebrated in March.

TRANSPORT

INTERNATIONAL AIRPORTS Antananarivo (TNR) 17 km from the city.

INTERNAL TRAVEL Extensive domestic air network. Many roads are impassable during the rains. Car hire only available in main tourist towns. Limited rail network.

RED TAPE

VISAS REQUIRED (UK/US) Required.

VACCINATIONS REQUIRED: See 'Vaccinations required around the world' on page 653.

DRIVING REQUIREMENTS A national driving licence is sufficient.

COUNTRY REPS IN UK/US
UK: 16 Lanark Mansions, Pennard Road, London W12 8DT, tel (020) 8746 0133, fax (020) 8746 0134, email consul@madagascar.org.uk. USA: 2374 Massachusetts Avenue, NW, Washington, DC 20008, tel (202) 265 5525/6, fax (202) 265 3034, email malagasy.embassy@verizon.net.

UK/US REPS IN COUNTRY
UK: Lot II I 164 Ter Alenrobia, Amboniloa, tel (20) 224 9378, fax (20) 224 9381, email ukembant@simicro.mg. USA: BP 620, 14 rue Rainitovo, 101 Antananarivo, tel (2022) 21273, fax (2022) 34539, email Uswebmaster@wanadoo.mg.

PEOPLE AND PLACE

CAPITAL Antananarivo.

LANGUAGE Malagasy and French.

PEOPLES Of Malay-Indonesian, African and Arab descent.

RELIGION Traditional beliefs (52%), Christian (41%), Muslim.

SIZE (SQ KM) 587,041.

POPULATION 15,529,000.

POP DENSITY/KM 26.5.

STATE OF THE NATION

SAFETY Safe.

LIFE EXPECTANCY M 54.57, F 59.4.

BEING THERE

ETIQUETTE Madagascans are extremely hospitable and welcoming. They also have a relaxed attitude to time which can be a touch frustrating. Public forms of transport, for instance, will not generally move until they are full. Bargaining: don't expect to pay as little as the locals, but equally don't be afraid to haggle as the advertised price is often inflated. Respect should be paid to the many local taboos, or *fady*. In some places it remains the practice to invite an ancestor to a village celebration. This involves disinterring the body so that the ancestor may attend physically, then later re-interring the body with new shrouds. This observance, known as *famadihana*, shows the hold of traditional beliefs.

CURRENCY Malagasy *franc* (Mgfr) = 100 *centimes*.

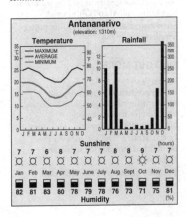

Antananarivo
(elevation: 1310m)

HIGHLIGHTS

WILDLIFE Madagascar is nicknamed the 'eighth continent' because of the diversity of its species. Indeed, as recently as 2005, two new species of lemur were discovered. Like much of the country's wildlife, these endangered primates are found nowhere else on earth. As an indication of this tremendous wealth of flora and fauna, there are 3,000 endemic species of butterfly on the island. There is a similar diversity of reptiles, amphibians and birds.

ANTANANARIVO Interesting capital with a distinctly French feel - road and shops signs are mostly written in French. The city is set among the rugged Hauts Plateaux mountain chain, which runs north to south through Madagascar. It's most striking building is the Queen's Palace, once the residency of the Merina Dynasty and now a national monument. Other sights include the Zuma Market, which claims to be the second largest in the world.

Nearby Lac Itasy and Périnet Reserve, for lemur spotting, are also worth a visit.

NOSY BÉ Luxurious beaches, great diving and a spot popular with whale watchers. An island surrounded by smaller islands, it is the country's most important resort. Exotic scents hang in the air, of lemon grass, patchouli and fragrant ylang-ylang .

AMBOHIMANGA Pretty former capital, surrounded by forests and known variously as the 'blue city', the 'holy city', and the 'forbidden city'.

FINANCE Limited acceptance of credit cards and traveller's cheques.

BUSINESS HOURS 0800-1200, 1400-1800 Monday-Saturday (shopping hours, business hours n/a).

GMT +3.

VOLTAGE GUIDE 220 AC, 50 Hz.

COUNTRY DIALLING CODE 261.

CONSUMING PLEASURES

FOOD & DRINK Rice dishes with sauces, meat, vegetables and seasoning, often served with hot peppers. Some specialities include *vary amid'anana* (rice, leaves or herbs, meat and sometimes shrimps), and *ramazava* (leaves and pieces of beef and pork browned in oil). *Toaka gasy* is distilled from cane sugar and rice, *ranon 'apango* is non-alcoholic and made from burnt rice..

SHOPPING & SOUVENIRS Chessboards, *mahafaly* silver crosses, *vangavanga* bracelets, jewellery made from shells and precious stones, reeds and straw items, *antemore* paper decorated with flowers.

FIND OUT MORE

WEBSITES www.madagascar.org.uk, www.madagascarnews.com.

LOCAL MEDIA No newspapers in English.

TOURIST BOARDS IN UK/US n/a.

> "Madagascar is truly the naturalist's promised land. Here nature seems to have withdrawn into a private sanctuary in order to work on designs which are different from those she has created elsewhere. At every step you are met by the most bizarre and wonderful forms."
>
> *Joseph Philibert Commerson, 1771*

MALAWI

WHEN TO GO

WEATHER Winter, from May-July is dry, and nights can be chilly, particularly in the highlands. The rainy season runs from November to March.

FESTIVALS The Lake of Stars Festival is held in early September and features local bands playing jazz and kwaito as well as international DJ's and bands.

TRANSPORT

INTERNATIONAL AIRPORTS Lilongwe (LLW) 22 km from the city, Blantyre (BLZ) 18 km from the city.

INTERNAL TRAVEL Reasonable air network. Planes are available for charter through local travel bureaux. Trains tend to be slow and crowded but major roads are tarmac and most secondary roads are all-weather. Car hire is available in major towns.

RED TAPE

VISAS REQUIRED (UK/US) None.

VACCINATIONS REQUIRED: See 'Vaccinations required around the world' on page 653.

DRIVING REQUIREMENTS A national driving licence is sufficient.

COUNTRY REPS IN UK/US UK: 33 Grosvenor Street, London W1K 4QT, tel (020) 7491 4172, fax (020) 7491 9916, email tourism@malawi.net. USA: 1156 15th Street, suite 320, NW, Washington, DC 20005, tel (202) 721 0270, fax (202) 721 0270.

UK/US REPS IN COUNTRY UK: PO Box 30042, Lilongwe 3, tel (0) 177 2400, fax (0) 177 2657, email bhclilongwe@fco.gov.uk. USA: PO Box 30016, Area 40, Plot 24, Kenyatta Road, Lilongwe 3, tel (0) 177 3166, fax (0) 177 0471.

PEOPLE AND PLACE

CAPITAL Lilongwe.

LANGUAGE English.

PEOPLES Mostly Bantu, Asian minority.

RELIGION Protestant (55%), Roman Catholic (20%), Muslim (20%), traditional beliefs.

SIZE (SQ KM) 118,484.

POPULATION 11,871,000.

POP DENSITY/KM 100.2.

STATE OF THE NATION

SAFETY Generally safe, but avoid travelling after dark.

LIFE EXPECTANCY M 36.59, F 37.36.

BEING THERE

ETIQUETTE Despite great variation in tribal background, the population is well integrated. An emphasis is placed on hand-shaking on greeting and departing, women and children will sometime curtsey. A modest dress code is conventional, if not casual.

CURRENCY *Kwacha* (K) = 100 *tambala*.

FINANCE Limited acceptance of credit cards and of traveller's cheques.

BUSINESS HOURS 0730-1700 Mon-Friday.

GMT +2.

VOLTAGE GUIDE 220/240 AC, 50 Hz.

COUNTRY DIALLING CODE 265.

CONSUMING PLEASURES

FOOD & DRINK Fresh fish from Lake Malawi is popular, *chambo* (tilapia) being the main lake delicacy. River trout and local beef are also notable. Street stalls in Lilongwe Old Town serve cassava chips and roast meat. Hotel restaurants and many of

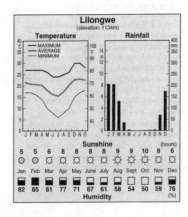

HIGHLIGHTS

LILONGWE The capital is 90 minutes from the lake that dominates this country. An intriguing old town gives way to a modern city, home to funky architecture not seen elsewhere. Beautiful gardens are scattered around. A good base for excursions to the Kasungu National Park.

MZUZU Nestled between the hills of the Viphya Plateau and the lakeshore, the capital of the northern region is the centre from which to explore the amazing plateau, Vwasa March Wildlife Reserve, Manchewe Falls, and the Livingstonia Mission.

LAKE MALAWI This massive lake takes up around half the country, stretching north to south. Sandy beaches, largely free of the parasitic worms of bilharzia, are dotted with thatched huts. The lake appears to be a tideless, salt-free, sea. It contains between 500 and 1,000 species of fish, more than anywhere else on earth, some of which are unique to the lake. Naturally it also supports great bird life as well. Senga Bay is a popular region, and to be recommended. Lizard Island is nearby, home to many lizards and eagles.

LIWONDE NATIONAL PARK The most popular park is found south of the lake. The River Shire flows through, allowing visitors to take boat safaris. Home to a great number of hippos, as well as elephants, rhinos and crocodiles

ZOMBA PLATEAU Sprawling forests and numerous waterfalls provide great walks among striking views. Nearby the mammoth Mulanje Massif has ample opportunity for climbing, walking, or relaxed trout fishing.

those in the cities are of a high standard. Good local beers, well known gin and tonic, wines imported from South Africa.

SHOPPING & SOUVENIRS Woodcarvings, wood and cane furniture, soapstone carvings, colourful textiles, pottery, beadwork, musical instruments.

FIND OUT MORE

WEBSITES www.malawitourism.com, http://usembassy.state.gov/malawi, www.guide2malawi.com.

LOCAL MEDIA *The Daily Times, The Monitor* are English-language dailies. *The Nation* and *The Malawi News* are printed weekly.

TOURIST BOARDS IN UK/US
UK: 4 Christian Fields, London SW16 3JZ, tel (0115) 982 1903, fax (0115) 981 9418, email enquiries@malawitourism.com.
US: n/a.

"The fishes of the lake are almost all of species peculiar."
Dr John Kirk, naturalist with David Livingstone's second expedition, 1858-1864

MALAYSIA

WHEN TO GO

WEATHER Tropical without extremely high temperatures. The main rainy season in the east is between November and February, August is the wettest period on the west coast.

FESTIVALS Malaysian festivals are often colourful occasions with a religious or national significance. Hari Kebangsaan, or National Day, sees a large celebration in Kuala Lumpur on 31 August, with a parade of impressive floats and much partying.

TRANSPORT

INTERNATIONAL AIRPORTS Kuala Lumpur (KUL) 50 km from the city, Penang (PEN) 16 km from Georgetown, Kota Kinabalu (BKI) 6.5 km from the city, Kuching (KCH) 11 km from the city.

INTERNAL TRAVEL Reasonable internal air and rail networks. Most roads in the Peninsular states are paved. Car hire easily available.

RED TAPE

VISAS REQUIRED (UK/US) None.

VACCINATIONS REQUIRED: See 'Vaccinations required around the world' on page 653.

DRIVING REQUIREMENTS An International Driving Permit. UK citizens may use a national licence, which must be endorsed by the Registrar of Motor Vehicles in Malaysia.

COUNTRY REPS IN UK/US UK: 45 Belgrave Square, London SW1X 8QT, tel (020) 7235 8033, email mwlondon@btinternet.com. USA: 3516 International Court, NW, Washington, DC 20008, tel (202) 572 9700, fax (202) 572 9882, email malwash@kln.gov.my.

UK/US REPS IN COUNTRY UK: 185 Jalan Ampang, 50450 Kuala Lumpur, tel (3) 2170 2200, fax (3) 2170 2370, email consular.kualalumpur@fco.gov.uk. USA: 376 Jalan Tun Razak, 50400 Kuala Lumpur, tel (3) 2168 5000, fax (3) 2142 2207, email lrckl@po.jaring.my.

PEOPLE AND PLACE

CAPITAL Kuala Lumpur.

LANGUAGE Bahasa Malaysia.

PEOPLES Malay, Chinese, Indigenous tribes, Indian.

RELIGION Muslim, Buddhist, Chinese faiths, Christian, traditional beliefs.

SIZE (SQ KM) 329,847.

POPULATION 24,530,000.

POP DENSITY/KM 74.4.

STATE OF THE NATION

SAFETY Generally safe.

LIFE EXPECTANCY M 69.56, F 75.11.

BEING THERE

ETIQUETTE Malaysia's population is a mixture of diverse cultures and characters. Malaysia is predominantly Muslim and Islamic religious customs should be respected. Some regions may enforce a stricter Muslim code than others, especially in rural areas. Dress should be modest. Local handshakes may be perceived as weak or limp. However, this is the Malay style, sometimes simply a brushing of fingertips against each other and bringing the hand back to the heart or the lower part of the face or mouth. This signifies that the greeting has been accepted with sincerity.

CURRENCY *Ringgit* (RM) = 100 *sen*.

FINANCE Credit cards and traveller's

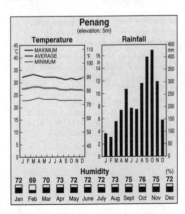

HIGHLIGHTS

KUALA LUMPUR Fascinating mix of old and new. Stroll through the bustling night markets, picking up bargain souvenirs, or take the lift up the the dizzying viewing platform of the Petronas Twin Towers. The world's tallest building, at 452-metres high, it's a vivid demonstration of modern Malaysian energy and engineering, incorporating traditional Islamic symbols in its design. The city also has a buzzing Chinatown and an equally intoxicating Little India.

CAMERON HIGHLANDS Sip a freshly-brewed cup of tea in this cool hill station with a distinctly genteel English feel. The region is home to a number of major tea plantations.

MOUNT KINABALU Scale the craggy and challenging granite peak of this majestic mountain - part of the eastern state of Sabah, in Malaysian Borneo, and the highest point between the Himalaya and New Guinea. Rising early to tackle the final stretch, the view from the top at dawn is worth every ounce of energy exerted in the getting there.

ORANG-UTANS Join the russet-furred 'man of the forest' amid the humid rainforests of Sabah. You can get really close to them on purpose-built wooden walkways at the Sepilok Orang-utan Sanctuary, where the cuddly-looking apes are looked after before being re-introduced into their native habitat. They can also be seen in Sarawak.

PERHENTIAN ISLANDS Snorkle or dive in the aquamarine waters of this beautiful marine park off the northeast coast, which teems with technicolour fish and underwater life.

---

cheques generally accepted.

BUSINESS HOURS 0830-1600/1730 Monday-Friday, 0800-1200 Saturday.

GMT +8.

VOLTAGE GUIDE 220 AC, 50 Hz.

COUNTRY DIALLING CODE 60.

CONSUMING PLEASURES

FOOD & DRINK Every type of South-East Asian cooking. Many dishes are based on a blend of spices, ginger, coconut milk and peanuts. *Sambals* (ground chilli, onion and tamarind based pastes) are often used as side dishes. A national favourite is *satay*, a variety of meats barbecued on small skewers, with a spicy peanut dipping sauce and a salad of cucumber, onion and rice cakes. Alcohol is allowed, top local beer is *Tiger*.

SHOPPING & SOUVENIRS Pewterware, silverware, brassware, batiks, jewellery, pottery, cameras, pens, watches, perfume.

FIND OUT MORE

WEBSITES www.malaysiatrulyasia.com, www.britain.org.my, www.tourismmalaysia.gov.my, www.malaysiamydestination.com, www.borneo-online.com.my.

LOCAL MEDIA Many English-language papers.

TOURIST BOARDS IN UK/US
UK: Malaysia House, 57 Trafalgar Square, London WC2N 5DU, tel (020) 7930 7932, fax (020) 7930 9015, email info@tourism-malaysia.co.uk. US: 120 East 56th Street, Suite 810, New York, NY 10022, tel (212) 754 1113, fax (212) 754 1116, email mtpb@aol.com. Or, 818 West Seventh Street, Suite 970, Los Angeles, CA 90017, tel (213) 689 9702, fax (213) 689 1530, email malaysiainfo@aol.com.

> " The Malay Peninsula [has] the climate of a perpetual Turkish bath."
> *Sir Frank Swettenham, 1906*

MALDIVES

WHEN TO GO

WEATHER Hot and tropical. The best time to visit is between November and April. The south west sees monsoon weather from May to October.

FESTIVALS Major Islamic festivals are observed as public holidays, including Ramadan, the month of fasting. Independence Day is celebrated on 26 July, with processions and brightly decorated floats. Republic Day, on 11 November is another important public holiday, with brass bands and parades in Malé.

TRANSPORT

INTERNATIONAL AIRPORTS Hulule International (MLE) on Hulule Island, 2 km from Malé.

INTERNAL TRAVEL Internal air and ferry services between islands. Individual islands rarely take longer than half an hour to cross on foot.

RED TAPE

VISAS REQUIRED (UK/US) Issued on arrival.

VACCINATIONS REQUIRED: See 'Vaccinations required around the world' on page 653.

DRIVING REQUIREMENTS n/a.

COUNTRY REPS IN UK/US
UK: 22 Nottingham Place, London W1U 5NU, tel (020) 7224 2135, fax (020) 7224 2157 email maldives.high.commission@ virgin.net. USA: (Mission to the UN) 800 Second Avenue, Suite 400E, New York, NY 10017, tel (212) 599 6194/5, fax (212) 661 6405, email maldives@un.int.

UK/US REPS IN COUNTRY UK, USA: Both countries have embassies in Colombo (see Sri Lanka) dealing with enquiries related to the Maldives.

PEOPLE AND PLACE

CAPITAL Malé.

LANGUAGE Dhivehi.

PEOPLES Maldivian, of Arabic descent.

Indian and Sri Lankan minorities.

RELIGION Sunni Muslim (100%).

SIZE (SQ KM) 298.

POPULATION 276,000.

POP DENSITY/KM 926.

STATE OF THE NATION

SAFETY Safe.

LIFE EXPECTANCY M 62.76, F 65.42.

BEING THERE

ETIQUETTE Dress is generally informal, but locals who are Muslim will be offended by nudity or scanty clothing in public places. Likewise, beachwear is not acceptable in the capital, Malé, or on any other inhabited island. The Government rigidly enforces these standards. The indigenous population not involved in the tourist trade lives in isolated island communities maintaining almost total privacy. Religious customs and practices should be respected, particularly during Ramadan, when many locals will be fasting.

CURRENCY Maldivian *rufiya* (Rf) = 100 *laaris*.

FINANCE Most island resorts accept credit cards and traveller's cheques.

BUSINESS HOURS 0730-1430 Sunday - Thursday.

GMT +5.

VOLTAGE GUIDE 220 AC, 50 Hz.

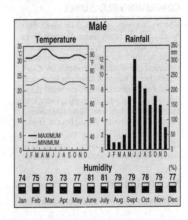

HIGHLIGHTS

BEACH LIFE Well after all, isn't that why most people want to visit the Maldives? Indeed, the country's plethora of tropical, palm tree-lined islands have made it one of the most desired-after destinations in the world and for many it symbolises the very image of island paradise. Soft white beaches, tall coconut trees, warm turquoise waters and uninhabited 'Robinson Crusoe' beaches are the picture-postcard appeal. In recent years, honeymooners have joined the ranks of scuba divers, snorkellers and watersports enthusiasts under its spell.

MALÉ Although most visitors just pass through the Maldives' capital - it's the island on which the airport is located - on the way to their resort island, it also has some interesting character of its own. Good-quality local handicrafts are sold in its shops, while it is also has some bustling fish and vegetable markets. The National Museum houses some impressive artefacts, including Sultanese thrones and palanquins. Malé also has more than 20 mosques, the most beautiful is the golden-domed Hukuru, or Friday Mosque.

THE UNDERWATER WORLD Diving is one of the biggest draws of the islands, with vast numbers of tropical fish scuttering about the reefs. But that's just the start of it - turtles, napoleon wrasse, mantas and morays, whale sharks, nurse sharks, hammerheads and rays. It's like being in your own personal aquarium. Another highlight is the wreck of the *Maldive Victory*, a site alive with coral and fish. The atolls are also beautiful from the air.

COUNTRY DIALLING CODE 960.

CONSUMING PLEASURES

FOOD & DRINK All foodstuffs, other than seafood, are imported and most resorts serve international cuisine. The local seafood is superb, and good curries can be had on most of the islands. A good range of drinks, and some local cocktails, such as *The Maldive Lady*, whose composition varies.

SHOPPING & SOUVENIRS Sea shells, lacquered wooden boxes, reed mats, jewellery with coral, mother-of-pearl, and turtle-shell items.

The Maldives comprise 1,196 coral islands, most of which are uninhabited

FIND OUT MORE

WEBSITES www.visitmaldives.com, www.un.int/maldives.

LOCAL MEDIA *The Maldives News Bulletin* is printed each week in English, other dailies have English sections. One, state-owned, TV channel, two state-run radio stations.

TOURIST BOARDS IN UK/US n/a.

MALI

WHEN TO GO

WEATHER The rainy season runs from June to October. October to February is cool, followed by extremely hot, dry weather until June.

FESTIVALS The principal Islamic festivals are marked with public holidays. These include, Tabaski, the Feast of the Sacrifice, celebrated nationwide early in the year and Ramadan, the month of fasting (dates vary). The Day of Democracy on 26 March is also a public holiday.

TRANSPORT

INTERNATIONAL AIRPORTS Bamako (BKO) 15 km from the city.

INTERNAL TRAVEL Limited air travel. The rail link from Bamako to Kayes is used more than the roads, which range from moderate to very bad, with frequent stops at police checkpoints. Off the main roads, travel in convoy with a set of spare parts. Travel is difficult during the rainy season.

RED TAPE

VISAS REQUIRED (UK/US) Required.

VACCINATIONS REQUIRED: See 'Vaccinations required around the world' on page 653.

DRIVING REQUIREMENTS International Driving Permit recommended, but not legally required. Insurance and a *carnet de passage* are required.

COUNTRY REPS IN UK/US UK: n/a, nearest Avenue Moliere 487, 1050 Brussels, Belgium, tel (2) 345 7432, fax (2) 344 5700. USA: 2130 R Street, NW, Washington, DC 20008, tel (202) 332 2249, fax (202) 332 6603, email infos@maliembassy.us.

UK/US REPS IN COUNTRY UK: Canadian Embassy Compound, Hippodrome, Road of Koulikoro, Bamako, tel 277 4637, fax 221 8377, email belo@afribone.net.ml. USA: 3 rue de Rochester NY et rue Mohamed V, Bamako, tel 222 5470, fax 222 3712, email ConsularBamako@state.gov.

PEOPLE AND PLACE

CAPITAL Bamako.

LANGUAGE French.

PEOPLES Bambara, Malinke, Tuareg.

RELIGION Islam (mainly Sunni Muslim), traditional beliefs.

SIZE (SQ KM) 1,240,192.

POPULATION 12,623,000.

POP DENSITY/KM 10.2.

STATE OF THE NATION

SAFETY Generally safe. Area north of Bamako potentially affected by ethnic tensions: seek latest information at time of visit.

LIFE EXPECTANCY M 44.69, F 45.51.

BEING THERE

ETIQUETTE Mali is a Muslim country and visitors should respect the religious customs and beliefs practised by its people. It is advisable to dress conservatively at all times and obey any restrictions that may be placed on visitors entering places of worship or when taking photographs. Malians are hospitable people and will welcome visitors gracefully into their homes.

CURRENCY *Communauté Financiaire Africaine franc* (CFAfr) = 100 *centimes*.

FINANCE Limited acceptance of credit cards and traveller's cheques.

BUSINESS HOURS 0730-1230, 1430-1600

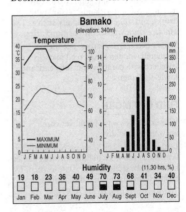

Bamako (elevation: 340m)

HIGHLIGHTS

DJENNE Marvel at the astounding mud-brick buildings of this great commercial town, known as the 'Jewel of the Niger'. One of them stands head-and-shoulders above the rest - the Grand Mosque, the largest mud building in the world. For generations, skilled craftsmen, the Baris, have maintained the architecture of the mosque, as well as the rest of the mud-built town, which tends to melt in the wet season.

NIGER RIVER Most of Mali's population live on or near the banks of this extensive river, one of West Africa's great waterways. Take a boat trip along some of the 1,300-kilometre section navigable in Mali. In doing so you'll be following in the wake of heroic explorers of the past, such as Mungo Park, Gordon Laing, René Caillié and Heinrich Barth -men who longed to find the river's source and the point at which it met the ocean.

DOGON COUNTRY Hike through this wild region, where local people maintain distinct and ancient traditions, largely untouched by Islam.

Their striking masks are a symbol of their culture and are prized collectables.

TIMBUKTU A virtual by-word for remoteness and a mystical trade hub, formerly also a prestigious centre of culture and learning. Camel caravans still make their way here from salt mines in the Sahara. Much of this ancient city is in decay, but some beautiful mosques and tombs survive.

BAMAKO Hunt for bargains at the many pavement market stalls dotted about the dusty, modern capital.

Monday-Thursday, 0730-1230, 1430-1730 Friday.
GMT GMT.
VOLTAGE GUIDE 220 AC, 50 Hz.
COUNTRY DIALLING CODE 223.

CONSUMING PLEASURES

FOOD & DRINK Most towns have small restaurants serving north African and local dishes, including the Malian speciality of *la Capitaine Sangha*, a Nile perch served with hot chilli sauce, whole fried bananas, and rice. Beef *brochettes* and fried plantains are sold at street stalls. Alcohol is available, but most drink the wide range of fruit juices. Tamarind and guava juices are delicious. Malian tea is drunk in three stages, very strong ('as bitter as death'), slightly sweetened ('just like life'), well sugared ('as sweet as love').

SHOPPING & SOUVENIRS Masks, wood-carvings, ebony and bronze designs, woven cloth, mats, pottery. Timbuktu is good for swords and daggers.

FIND OUT MORE

WEBSITES www.maliembassy.us, www.lonelyplanet.com/destinations/africa/mali, www.africaguide.com/country/mali, www.usa.org.ml.
LOCAL MEDIA No newspapers in English.
TOURIST BOARDS IN UK/US n/a.

The Grand Mosque in Djenne is the largest mud building in the world, measuring 100m long and 40m wide

MALTA

WHEN TO GO

WEATHER Warm for most of the year, and rain falls for very short periods. The hottest months are between July and September, but the heat is tempered by cooling sea breezes.

FESTIVALS Important annual events include Carnival, usually celebrated in February, featuring colourful floats, masks and dancing. Between April and September the Maltese enjoy their Festa season, a significant time for families and for village life. During these spectacular feast days each village hosts a range of festivities in commemoration of local saints, with church services, outdoors celebrations and fireworks featuring prominently over the course of five days. Saturday and Sunday are the big nights, with major fireworks displays and brass band parades.

TRANSPORT

INTERNATIONAL AIRPORTS Malta (MLA) 5 km from Valletta.

INTERNAL TRAVEL Helicopter and ferry services between Malta and Gozo. Roads are in good condition. Buses, taxis, and car hire are available.

RED TAPE

VISAS REQUIRED (UK/US) None.

VACCINATIONS REQUIRED: See 'Vaccinations required around the world' on page 653.

DRIVING REQUIREMENTS International driving licence.

COUNTRY REPS IN UK/US UK: Malta House, 36-38 Piccadilly, London W1J 0LE, tel (020) 7292 4800, fax (020) 7734 1831, email maltahighcommission.london@ gov.mt. USA: 2017 Connecticut Avenue, NW, Washington, DC 20008, tel (202) 462 3611, fax (202) 387 5470, email maltaembassy.washington@gov.mt.

UK/US REPS IN COUNTRY UK: Whitehall Mansions, Ta'Xbiex Seafront, Ta'Xbiex, MSD 11, tel 2323 0000, fax 2323 2234, email bhc@vol.net.mt. USA: PO Box 535, 3rd

Floor, Development House, St Anne Street, Floriana, Valletta, tel 2561 4000, fax 2124 3229, email usembmalta@state.gov.

PEOPLE AND PLACE

CAPITAL Valletta.

LANGUAGE Maltese, English.

PEOPLES Of mixed Sicilian, Norman, Spanish, English, Arabic and Italian descent.

RELIGION Roman Catholic (98%).

SIZE (SQ KM) 316.

POPULATION 399,867.

POP DENSITY/KM 1,224.

STATE OF THE NATION

SAFETY Safe.

LIFE EXPECTANCY M 76.7, F 81.15.

BEING THERE

ETIQUETTE The usual European courtesies are expected, but the visitor should also consider the tremendous importance of Roman Catholicism in Maltese life. If visiting a church, for instance, modest dress will be expected. Smoking is prohibited on public transport and in some public buildings, including cinemas.

CURRENCY Maltese *lira* (Lm) = 1,000 *mils*.

FINANCE Credit cards and traveller's cheques generally accepted.

BUSINESS HOURS 0830-1245, 1430-1730

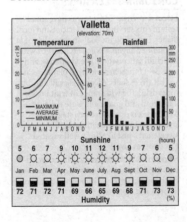

HIGHLIGHTS

VALLETTA Wander through the historic fortified city, built by the Knights of St John in the sixteenth century and commanding an impregnable position over the peninsula. The island's capital, Valletta is home to the Grand Master's Palace and its impressive armoury, as well as the ornate Co-Cathedral of St John, inside of which is housed a painting by Caravaggio and some exquisite marble mosaics on the floor.

MDINA Known as the Citta Notabile, or Noble City, this former Maltese capital exudes an air of elegance and seclusion. It's one of the best surviving examples of a medieval walled city, entered via a stone drawbridge which leads through to a maze of narrow lanes, churches, palaces and pretty piazzas.

GOZO Malta's little sister, a charming island offering fine coastal walking, great swimming in its pretty bays, and plenty to keep history buffs occupied too. Il-Kastel, the citadel of Gozo, is in many ways like Mdina in miniature, complete with cathedral, museums and folklore. Inland - and stepping further back in time - are the Ggantija temples, the oldest freestanding stone structures anywhere on Earth. They pre-date Stonehenge and the Egyptian pyramids by a thousand years.

THE BLUE LAGOON Put your snorkel and flippers on and plunge down into this stunning lagoon. It lies just off the tiny island of Comino, inhabited by just a handful of local farmers. The bay is one of the most beautiful swimming and snorkelling spots in the entire Mediterranean.

Monday-Friday, 0830-1200 Saturday.
GMT +1(+2 in summer).
VOLTAGE GUIDE 240 AC, 50 Hz.
COUNTRY DIALLING CODE 356.

CONSUMING PLEASURES

FOOD & DRINK Local dishes include *fenek* (rabbit cooked in wine), and pork and fish dishes are popular. Good beer, variety of local wines, foreign wines and spirits.

SHOPPING & SOUVENIRS Malta weaving, pottery, blown glass, ceramics, dolls, lace, copper, brass.

FIND OUT MORE

WEBSITES www.gov.mt, www.visitmalta.com, www.britishhighcommission.gov.uk/malta, http://usembassy.state.gov/malta.

LOCAL MEDIA *The Times* and *The Malta Independent* are printed daily in English.

TOURIST BOARDS IN UK/US UK: Unit C, Parkhouse, 14 Northfields, London SW18 1DD, tel (020) 8877 6990, fax (020) 8874 9416, email office.uk@visitmalta.com. US: n/a.

"[Gozo's] coast scenery may be truly called pomskizillious and gromphibberous, being as no words can describe its magnificence."
Edward Lear, 1866

MARSHALL ISLANDS

WHEN TO GO

WEATHER Tropical with frequent rain and cooling sea breezes. Little seasonal variation.

FESTIVALS Events include Fisherman's Day, a public holiday on the first Friday in July, marking the importance of the sea in Marshall Islands life. The Coconut Cup sailing regatta, in early April, and the Outrigger Marshall Islands Cup, a traditional canoe race, are other highlights.

TRANSPORT

INTERNATIONAL AIRPORTS Majuro (MAJ).

INTERNAL TRAVEL Inter-island ships. All main roads are paved. Car hire available. Many cheap taxis.

RED TAPE

VISAS REQUIRED (UK/US) Required.

VACCINATIONS REQUIRED: See 'Vaccinations required around the world' on page 653.

DRIVING REQUIREMENTS National driving licence.

COUNTRY REPS IN UK/US UK: n/a. USA: 2433 Massachusetts Avenue, NW, Washington, DC 20008, tel (202) 234 5414, fax (202) 232 3236 email info@ rmiembassyus.org.

UK/US REPS IN COUNTRY UK:n/a . USA: PO Box 1379, Ocean Site, Nejen Weto, Long Island, Majuro, tel 247 4011, fax 247 4012, email publicmajuro@state.gov.

PEOPLE AND PLACE

CAPITAL Majuro.

LANGUAGE Marshellese, English.

PEOPLES Micronesian.

RELIGION Christian, mostly Roman Catholic.

SIZE (SQ KM) 181.

POPULATION 50,848.

POP DENSITY/KM 280.3.

STATE OF THE NATION

SAFETY Safe.

LIFE EXPECTANCY M 68.05, F 72.06.

BEING THERE

ETIQUETTE Informal dress is usual for both business and social occasions. However, scanty clothing - including topless bathing - is considered offensive. Use of some islands, paths, beaches and so on may require permission; it is best to check locally.

CURRENCY US dollar (US$).

FINANCE Credit cards and traveller's cheques accepted in tourist resorts.

BUSINESS HOURS 0800-1700 Mon-Friday (shopping hours, business hours n/a).

GMT +12.

VOLTAGE GUIDE 110 AC, 50 Hz.

COUNTRY DIALLING CODE 692.

CONSUMING PLEASURES

FOOD & DRINK Coconut crabs, mangrove clams, langusta, octopus, sea cucumber and eels are all regional delicacies. Breadfruit, taro, rice and cassava are staples. Chinese, Marshallese, US and Western specialities are available in restaurants. Alcohol is banned on some islands.

SHOPPING & SOUVENIRS *Kili* handbags, woven by former residents of Bikini, stick charts (used to navigate between islands), floor mats, purses, shell necklaces, baskets.

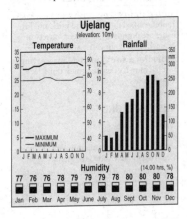

HIGHLIGHTS

MAJURO ATOLL
Kick back on the splendidly chilled-out beaches of Majuro, the principal island and capital of the Marshall Islands. It houses the central government, most of the country's businesses and around half of the population. Yet, while it is the most developed and urban atoll, it also offers a glimpse of what the rest of the country is like. Take a drive out to Laura Village on the western end of the island, go for a picnic to one of the small islands across the lagoon, or take a scuba diving excursion. If you're feeling less active, then just head to the divine beaches, sprinkled with coconut palms and breadfruit trees.

BIKINI ATOLL
A wreck diver's dream. The lagoon teems with fish, circling among the twisted shipwrecks. Now resting on the ocean floor the *USS Saratoga*, a World War II aircraft carrier, is the largest diveable wreck in the region. Bigger even than the famous *Titanic*, this ship is one of several mammoth wrecks including *HIJMS Nagato*, the Japanese flagship that led the attack on Pearl Harbor.

DIVING The Marshalls is home to 250 species of hard and soft coral, together with more than 1,000 species of fish. Divers can experience dramatic steep drop-offs, coral pinnacles and reef points. May to October is the best time to submerge yourself in the bath-like sea, when the waters are calmest.

ARNO ATOLL The most accessible outer island, with three attractive lagoons. Deep-sea fishing is an enjoyable activity, off Longar Point.

FIND OUT MORE

WEBSITES www.visitmarshallislands.com, www.rmiembassyus.org, http://usembassy.state.gov/majuro.

LOCAL MEDIA The *Marshall Islands Journal* is a weekly English/Marshallese paper, the *Marshall Islands Gazette* is monthly.

TOURIST BOARDS IN UK/US n/a.

"So we came to Bikini: a typical Pacific coral atoll, several tiny islands, surrounding a lagoon twenty miles long by ten miles wide. The main island was so precisely the conventional picture of a South Sea Island that it might have been the jacket of a very old novel."
James Cameron, 1967

MAURITANIA

WHEN TO GO

WEATHER Generally hot and dry. The south sees rainfall from July-September.

FESTIVALS Special events celebrated in Mauritania are generally Muslim holy days and feasts, the dates of which vary from year to year. Ramadan, the Islamic month of fasting, and Tabaski, the Feast of Sacrifice, are among the most important festivals. On 28 November the country celebrates Independence Day, a public holiday nationwide.

TRANSPORT

INTERNATIONAL AIRPORTS Nouakchott (NKC) 4 km from the city.

INTERNAL TRAVEL Limited internal flights but possible to charter light aircraft. Only one rail line serving the ore mines, services are free but the journeys are arduous. Main roads are paved and adequate, others are sand tracks requiring 4-wheel-drive vehicles. Car hire available.

RED TAPE

VISAS REQUIRED (UK/US) Required.

VACCINATIONS REQUIRED: See 'Vaccinations required around the world' on page 653.

DRIVING REQUIREMENTS International Driving Permit recommended.

COUNTRY REPS IN UK/US UK: 8 Carlos Place, Mayfair, London W1K 3AS, tel (020) 7478 9323, fax (020) 7478 9339, email ambarim@aol.com. USA: 2129 Leroy Place, NW, Washington, DC 20008, tel (202) 232 5700, fax (202) 319 2623, email info@ mauritaniembassy-usa.org.

UK/US REPS IN COUNTRY UK: The British Embassy in Rabat (see Morocco) deals with enquiries relating to Mauritania. USA: BP 222, 288 rue 41-100 (rue Abdallaye), Nouakchott, tel 525 2660, fax 525 1592, email ConsularNKC@ state.gov.

PEOPLE AND PLACE

CAPITAL Nouakchott.

LANGUAGE Arabic and French.

PEOPLES Maures, Havalin, Senegalese, Tukolor, Peulh and Wolof.

RELIGION Muslim (100%).

SIZE (SQ KM) 1,030,700.

POPULATION 2,807,000.

POP DENSITY/KM 2.7.

STATE OF THE NATION

SAFETY Fairly safe except in disputed border areas with Morocco.

LIFE EXPECTANCY M 50.52, F 55.

BEING THERE

ETIQUETTE Islam has been the major influence on life in this country since the seventh and eighth centuries. Foreigners should respect local laws and dress modestly, particularly if visiting a mosque or other religious site. The bulk of the population is divided into two main Moorish groups, the Bidan (55 per cent) and the Harattin (20 per cent), with the non-Moorish population concentrated in the Senegal River area. Different classes and tribes tend to be contiguous. Visitors should respect local customs.

CURRENCY Mauritanian *ouguiya* (UM) = 5 *khoums*.

FINANCE Credit cards generally not accepted, limited use of traveller's cheques.

BUSINESS HOURS 0800-1500 Saturday-

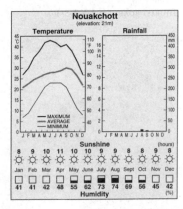

Nouakchott (elevation: 21m)

	Jan	Feb	Mar	Apr	May	June	July	Aug	Sept	Oct	Nov	Dec
Sunshine (hours)	8	9	10	11	10	10	9	9	8	8	9	8
Humidity (%)	41	41	42	48	55	62	73	74	69	56	45	42

HIGHLIGHTS

SAHARA Lollop across the vast arid expanses of dunes and desert, aboard a hardy camel - a beast able to cope with the sweltering Saharan heat. It's harsh, challenging terrain in which to travel, an unforgiving landscape dotted with oases and heat-scorched market towns frequented by salt caravans and nomadic tradesmen.

NOUAKCHOTT Created in the 1960s, Mauritania's capital has grown to become the biggest city in the Sahara region. In fact, whipped by dust storms for nine months of the year, you might well imagine it drowning under a sea of sand. A sprawling urban centre, its 1 million inhabitants comprise almost one-third of the entire population of Mauritania. Its modern buildings reflect the traditional Berber style of architecture, while there are also some rewarding local markets and an impressive stretch of beach on which to laze. If you're after a bit of action then head down to the city's wrestling arena, which stages bouts on Saturday afternoons.

PLAGE DES PÊCHEURS Colourful and atmospheric port on Nouakchott's sandy shoreline, bustling with mostly Senegalese fishermen, hauling in the day's catch. Head down at sunset as the boats come in.

PARC NATIONAL DU BANC D'ARGUIN World Heritage-listed national park located on the Atlantic desert coast between Nouakchott and the northern frontier with Western Sahara. Its islets are a sanctuary for migratory birds, including herons, pelicans and flamingos.

Wednesday, 0800-1300 Thursday.

GMT GMT.

VOLTAGE GUIDE 127/220 AC, 50 Hz.

COUNTRY DIALLING CODE 222.

CONSUMING PLEASURES

FOOD & DRINK Local cuisine is mostly based on lamb, goat and rice. Dishes include *mechoui* (whole roast lamb), dates, spiced fish and rice with vegetables, dried meat with *couscous*. Alcohol may be found in hotel bars. Camel's milk, or *zrig*, is popular.

SHOPPING & SOUVENIRS Dyed leather cushions, engraved silver items, rugs, woodcarvings, silver jewellery, daggers, carpets.

FIND OUT MORE

WEBSITES www.ambarim-dc.org, http://usembassy.state.gov/mauritiana, www.lonelyplanet.com/destinations/africa/mauritiana.

LOCAL MEDIA No newspapers in English.

TOURIST BOARDS IN UK/US n/a.

"Nouakchott was originally the site of a Foreign Legion fort, and it still looks more like a camp than a town. The sand blows across the streets and piles up between the shacks of the metropolis; sweeping it into heaps is about the only source of steady employment that the city can offer."

Patrick Marnham

MAURITIUS

WHEN TO GO

WEATHER Warm coastal climate, particularly from January-April. The cyclone season is from December to March.

FESTIVALS With origins in three separate continents and with three major religions, there is a great diversity of religious and cultural festivals in Mauritius. Public holidays mark the Chinese New Year, in January/February, as well as the major Christian festivals of Easter and Christmas. Holi, the Hindu Festival of Colour, is celebrated around March, with people enthusiastically throwing paint at each other - all in good spirits. Diwali, around November, is another major Hindu celebration. From the Islamic calendar Ramadan, the month of fasting (dates vary), is a particularly significant time. Non-religious public holidays include National Day on 12 March and Labour Day on 1 May.

TRANSPORT

INTERNATIONAL AIRPORTS Mauritius (MRU) 48 km from Port Louis.

INTERNAL TRAVEL Good network of paved roads. Numerous car hire firms. Excellent buses, taxis available.

RED TAPE

VISAS REQUIRED (UK/US) None.

VACCINATIONS REQUIRED: See 'Vaccinations required around the world' on page 653.

DRIVING REQUIREMENTS International Driving Permit recommended, although foreign licences are accepted.

COUNTRY REPS IN UK/US UK: 32-33 Elvaston Place, London SW7 5NW, tel (020) 7581 0294, fax (020) 7823 8437, email londonmhc@ btinternet.com. USA: 4301 Connecticut Avenue, Suite 441, NW, Washington, DC 20008, tel (202) 244 1491, fax (202) 966 0983, email mauritius.embassy@prodigy.net.

UK/US REPS IN COUNTRY UK: PO Box 1063, Les Cascades Building, Edith Cavell Street, Port Louis, tel 202 9400, fax 202 9404, email bhc@intnet.mu. USA: 4th Floor, Rogers House, John Kennedy Avenue, Port Louis, tel 202 4400, fax 208 9534, email usembass@intnet.mu.

PEOPLE AND PLACE

CAPITAL Port Louis.

LANGUAGE English.

PEOPLES Of Indian descent and Creole. Minorities of Chinese and French descent.

RELIGION Hindu, Roman Catholic, Muslim.

SIZE (SQ KM) 2,040.

POPULATION 1,122,811.

POP DENSITY/KM 599.4.

STATE OF THE NATION

SAFETY Safe.

LIFE EXPECTANCY M 68.4, F 76.41.

BEING THERE

ETIQUETTE Handshaking is the customary form of greeting. Travellers should respect the local and religious traditions of their hosts, particularly when visiting a private home. It is appropriate to offer a gift as a token of appreciation if invited for a meal. Dress is normally informal.

CURRENCY Mauritian *rupee* (MRs) = 100 *cents*.

FINANCE Credit cards and traveller's cheques generally accepted.

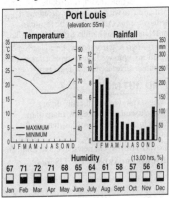

Port Louis (elevation: 55m)

Temperature / Rainfall / Humidity (13.00 hrs, %)

	Jan	Feb	Mar	Apr	May	June	July	Aug	Sept	Oct	Nov	Dec
Humidity	67	71	72	71	68	65	64	61	58	57	56	61

HIGHLIGHTS

PORT LOUIS Main port and the country's capital, which bustles as a commercial centre by day, but which is rather quiet after sundown. Street names are a mixture of English and French, while the city's varied architecture bears testament to the main religious influences and the colonial past. There are some nice mosques in the Muslim area around Muammar El Khadafi Square, some fine French-era buildings such as Government House, and a vibrant Chinatown district, full of the flavours and tasty aromas of the Orient. The Natural History Museum is the place to go to learn about the sad fate of the hapless dodo, Mauritius's most famous bird.

TAMARIN Surf the impressive two-metre waves created by big ocean swells off this coastal spot. Lying in the shadow of the Rivière Noire Mountains, the bathing here is also excellent, mostly besides the lagoon.

PAMPLEMOUSSES GARDENS Known to naturalists the world over, these enchanting gardens house an impressive collection of indigenous and exotic plants. One of them, the *talipot* palm, is said to flower just once every sixty years, and then die. The gardens are also home to tortoises, some over 100-years old.

RODRIGUES ISLAND Tiny, rugged island, 550 km northeast of Mauritius, offering some superb scuba diving. It's considered a relaxing refuge for travellers, many of whom journey here on the *Mauritius Pride*. The volcanic island is covered in coconut palms and pink-flowered bushes called *vielles filles*.

BUSINESS HOURS 0900-1600 Mon-Friday. GMT +4.

VOLTAGE GUIDE 220 AC, 50 Hz.

COUNTRY DIALLING CODE 230.

CONSUMING PLEASURES

FOOD & DRINK French, Creole, Indian and Chinese cuisine, generally of a high standard although restaurants usually depend on imported foodstuff. Specialities include venison in season, *camarans* (freshwater prawns) in hot sauces, creole fish, fresh pineapple with chilli sauce, and rice with curry. Rum and beer are staple beverages.

SHOPPING & SOUVENIRS Jewellery, Chinese and Indian jade, silks, basketry, pottery. Beautifully displayed goods in Port Louis.

FIND OUT MORE

WEBSITES www.mauritiustourism.co.uk, http://ncb.intnet.mu, www.mauritius.net.

LOCAL MEDIA *L'Express* and *Le Mauricien* are published in English.

TOURIST BOARDS IN UK/US UK: 32 Elvaston Place, London SW7 5NW, tel (020) 7584 3666, fax (020) 7225 1135, email mtpa@btinternet.com.

Mauritius is – or rather was – the home of the dodo. The funny, fat, flightless bird was wiped out not long after the island was first settled by the Dutch

MEXICO

WHEN TO GO

WEATHER The plateau and high mountains are warm for much of the year. The Pacific coast has a tropical climate.

FESTIVALS Mexicans celebrate more than 120 festivals every year. Some occasions are of religious significance, others secular, national or local. In nearly all instances, however, they are a time for music, dancing, processions and fireworks. The Day of the Dead is celebrated with enthusiastic fervour throughout the country on 1 November. It is especially dramatic on Lago de Pátzcuaro, where locals converge on the island of Janitizio in canoes, a solitary candle alight in each craft. Other major events include Semana Santa, or Holy Week, in the week before Easter. As in the rest of the Latin world, Carnaval in the week before Lent, is celebrated with costumes, parades, eating and dancing.

TRANSPORT

INTERNATIONAL AIRPORTS (And distances from the nearest city): Mexico City (MEX) 13 km, Guadalajara (GDL) 20 km, Acapulco (ACA) 26 km, Monterrey (MTY) 24 km.

INTERNAL TRAVEL Good domestic air and rail networks. Extensive road network, but less than half is paved. Car hire available.

RED TAPE

VISAS REQUIRED (UK/US) Not required but tourist cards issued.

VACCINATIONS REQUIRED: See 'Vaccinations required around the world' on page 653.

DRIVING REQUIREMENTS International Driving Permit or British driving licence.

COUNTRY REPS IN UK/US UK: 8 Halkin Street, London SW1X 7DW, tel (020) 7235 6393, fax (020) 7235 5480, email info@mexicanconsulate.org.uk. USA: 2827 16th Street, NW, Washington DC 20009, tel (202) 736 1000, fax (202) 234 4498, email consulwas@aol.com.

UK/US REPS IN COUNTRY UK: Rio Lerma 71, Colonia Cuauhtémoc, CP 06500 México DF, tel (55) 5242 8500, fax (55) 5242 8522, email consular.mexico@fco.gov.uk. USA: Paseo de la Reforma 305, 06500 México DF, tel (55) 5080 2000, fax (55) 5511 9980, email ccs@usembassy-mexico.com.

PEOPLE AND PLACE

CAPITAL Mexico City.

LANGUAGE Spanish.

PEOPLES *Mestizo*, indigenous Indian, European.

RELIGION Roman Catholic (95%).

SIZE (SQ KM) 1,959,248.

POPULATION 101,965,000.

POP DENSITY/KM 51.9.

STATE OF THE NATION

SAFETY High levels of crime and violence, often linked to family honour, illegal border-crossing or drug-smuggling.

LIFE EXPECTANCY M 72.42, F 78.1.

BEING THERE

ETIQUETTE English is widely spoken in business circles, but a knowledge of Spanish will go a long way. At beach resorts, dress is very informal. Mexicans regard relationships and friendships as the most important thing in life next to religion.

CURRENCY New *peso* (*peso*) = 100 *centavos*.

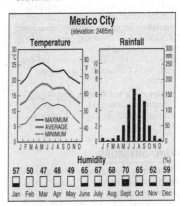

Mexico City (elevation: 2485m)
Temperature / Rainfall
— MAXIMUM — AVERAGE — MINIMUM

	Jan	Feb	Mar	Apr	May	June	July	Aug	Sept	Oct	Nov	Dec
Humidity (%)	57	50	47	48	49	65	67	68	70	65	62	59

HIGHLIGHTS

MAYAN RUINS Stroll among majestic temple complexes, the remains of cities inhabited by the Maya people, fringed by jungle and mostly dotted across the Yucatan peninsula. Chichén Itzá, with its vertiginous temple, *chacmool* figures and dramatic snail-shaped observatory, is the most famous Maya site. But there are plenty more equally noteworthy: hauntingly-beautiful Palenque, strongly linked with lost cities of Guatemala; Tulum, set on a cliff overlooking a stunning stretch of white sandy Caribbean beach and turquoise sea. In parts of the Yucatan, descendants of the Maya retain some of their ancient traditions and lifestyles.

MEXICO CITY Set beneath two snow-capped volcanoes at a dizzying altitude, this heavily-polluted yet fascinating urban sprawl is a throng of people and a centre of art, politics and culture. There's a colonial feel about the place, while everything bustles around the Zócalo, the huge central square, surrounded by the cathedral, Aztec ruins and the Palacio Nacional.

ACAPULCO Watch dare-devil *clavadistas*, professional high divers, as they gracefully swallow-dive from the steep cliffs into the sea far below. Elsewhere, great beaches provide the daytime entertainment, while at night it's the bars and clubs that are the draw. Feel free to go *loco*.

COPPER CANYON RAILWAY Board the train, then settle back for a scenic - and often heart-stopping - 13-hour ride, from the west coast into the Sierra Madre.

FINANCE Credit cards widely accepted, traveller's cheques generally accepted.

BUSINESS HOURS Vary considerably, usually 0900-1400, 1500-1800 Monday-Friday.

GMT -6 to -8.

VOLTAGE GUIDE 110 AC, 60 Hz.

COUNTRY DIALLING CODE 52.

CONSUMING PLEASURES

FOOD & DRINK Each region has its own specialities, but national dishes include *enchilidas* and *tacos* filled with pork, chicken, cheese, chilli or vegetables. *Guacamole*, an avocado salsa, is a popular accompaniment. A national favourite is *turkey mole*. *Moles* are sauces made from several ingredients including chillis, tomatoes, nuts and chocolate *Kahlua*, the coffee liqueur, is world famous, *Hidalgo* is a good white wine, while *Calafia* is an excellent red.

SHOPPING & SOUVENIRS Silverware, ceramics, pottery, wool blankets, silk scarves, charro hats, straw work, blown glass, leather, precious stones, hammocks.

FIND OUT MORE

WEBSITES www.mexicanembassy.co.uk, www.mexicanconsulate.org.uk, www.britishembassy.gov.uk/mexico, www.embassyofmexico.org, www.visitmexico.com, www.mexonline.com, www.gocancun.com, www.ourmexico.com, www.acapulco.com.

LOCAL MEDIA *The News* and *Mexico City Times* are printed in English, the *New York Times* and *USA Today* are also available.

TOURIST BOARDS IN UK/US UK: Wakefield House, 41 Trinity Square, London EC3N 4DJ, tel (020) 7488 9392, fax (020) 7265 0704, email uk@visitmexico.com. US: 375 Park Avenue, Floor 19, Suite 1905, New York, NY 10152, tel (212) 308 2110, fax (212) 308 9060, email newyork@ visitmexico.com.

Mexico City has the world's largest taxi fleet – some 60,000 cars

MICRONESIA

WHEN TO GO

WEATHER Humid and hot all year round with abundant rainfall.

FESTIVALS The four-yearly Micronesian Games are next due to take place in 2006, probably in Yap. The scheduled dates are 23 July to 3 August and sports are likely to include athletics, soccer, basketball, volleyball, outrigger canoeing, baseball, fast-pitch softball, wrestling, weightlifting, tennis, spear fishing and Micronesian All-Around. More regular events include *mitmit*, traditional festivities in Yap. These all-out feasts are accompanied by gift-giving, singing and dancing. One village gives another a *mitmit* to reciprocate for one they received in previous years. The completion of a major village project, such as a new community hall or house, is also a time for revelry in Yap.

TRANSPORT

INTERNATIONAL AIRPORTS Pohnpei (PNI) 5 km from Kolonia.

INTERNAL TRAVEL Ships visit outlying islands. Good roads in major island centres. Car hire available in larger towns. Taxis but no buses.

RED TAPE

VISAS REQUIRED (UK/US) None.

VACCINATIONS REQUIRED: See 'Vaccinations required around the world' on page 653.

DRIVING REQUIREMENTS International Driving Permit or national licence.

COUNTRY REPS IN UK/US UK: n/a. USA: 1725 N Street, NW, Washington, DC 20036, tel (202) 223 4383, fax (202) 223 4391, email fsm@fsmembassy.org.

UK/US REPS IN COUNTRY UK: n/a. USA: PO Box 1286, Kolonia, Pohnpei FSM 96941, tel 320 2187, fax 320 2186, email USEmbassy@mail.fm.

PEOPLE AND PLACE

CAPITAL Palikir (Pohnpei Island).

LANGUAGE English, Trukese, Pohnpeian, Losrean, Mortlockese.

PEOPLES Micronesian, Melanesian.

RELIGION Roman Catholic (50%), Protestant (48%).

SIZE (SQ KM) 700.

POPULATION 107,008.

POP DENSITY/KM 153.

STATE OF THE NATION

SAFETY Safe.

LIFE EXPECTANCY M 67.96, F 71.62.

BEING THERE

ETIQUETTE There are considerable variations of custom and belief. The majority of Kosreans are Congregationalists, for whom Sunday is a rest day. Pre-European influences exist to a greater extent in some of the other island groups. In Yap, for instance, use of paths, beaches and islands may require prior permission. In general, visitors who demonstrate a desire to be courteous should be fine. But it is still best to check beforehand. One thing worth remembering is that the Western understanding of private property is alien to many parts of Micronesia. Personal possessions should be well looked after - out of sight, out of mind.

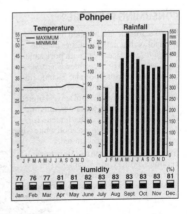

HIGHLIGHTS

DIVING Warm water and stunning underwater scenery attract scuba enthusiasts to this widespread island group. Kosrae alone has more than 50 dive sites to explore, each marked with a buoy to prevent improper anchoring. The coral close to the shore is superb, so diving is possible as a walk-in activity, as well as from boats. The marine life on display is quite amazing; Yap is known for schools of manta rays, while tuna, dolphins and reef fish are also abundant in the waters.

TRUK LAGOON An especially noteworthy dive site is accessible in the state of Chuuk. The Truk Lagoon contains the twisted remains of an entire Japanese fleet, sunk during World War II. Even if you've never passed your PADI, some of the shallower wrecks are also suitable for snorkellers.

PALIKIR Situated on the island of Pohnpei, the Micronesian capital sits on the site of a Japanese World War II airfield. Its building roofs are designed like ancestral Kosrean homes, the beams incorporating Yap and Chuuk styles.

YAP Embrace traditional life in the state of Yap, where some people still wear brightly-coloured loincloths and everyone has a bulge of betel nut in their cheek. The villages are connected via centuries-old stone footpaths and a traditional system of stone money, called *rai*, survives. Yap is also known for its feasts, known as *mitmits*.

SOKEHS MASS GRAVE Marks the spot where, in 1911, 17 native Pohnpeians were executed by firing squad for resisting the German administration.

CURRENCY US dollar (US$).

FINANCE Credit cards and traveller's cheques are accepted on those islands with tourist facilities.

BUSINESS HOURS 0800-1700 Mon-Friday.

GMT +10 to +11.

VOLTAGE GUIDE 110/120 AC, 60 Hz.

COUNTRY DIALLING CODE 691.

CONSUMING PLEASURES

FOOD & DRINK Local specialities include breadfruit, yams, and thin slices of raw fish dipped in peppery sauce. *Sakau* (known as *kava* in the rest of Polynesia) is made from the root of a shrub which yields a mildly narcotic substance when squeezed through hibiscus bark, and served at numerous bars.

SHOPPING & SOUVENIRS Love sticks and war clubs, grass shirts, lava-lavas woven from hibiscus bark, woven baby cradles, betel-nut pouches, stone money, model canoes.

FIND OUT MORE

WEBSITES www.visit-fsm.org.

LOCAL MEDIA *Pacific Daily News* is the main newspaper, *The Island Tribune* is printed twice a week.

TOURIST BOARDS IN UK/US n/a.

Stone money is still used in the Micronesian state of Yap. Known as *rai*, the largest stones are 3 metres wide and 5 tons in weight and – unsurprisingly – are never moved, even when their ownership changes

MOLDOVA

WHEN TO GO

WEATHER Warm summers from May to September. Cold, sometimes snowy winters.

FESTIVALS Winemaking is an important industry in Moldova, with the country producing more than 100 varieties of wine, some of them excellent. This fact is celebrated in autumn, during the two-day National Day of Wine and Wine Festival, on 13-14 October. Other notable events include Independence Day, on 27 August, and Limba Nostra, the country's National Language Day on 31 August. The major events in the Orthodox Christian Church are also celebrated as public holidays. Moldova is famous for its tradition of folk arts and there are many lively musical groups, known as Tarafs, which play a variety of rare folk instruments including the *tsambal* (not unlike a dulcimer) and the *cimpoi* (bagpipe). You may be able to see such groups at folk festivals and other cultural events.

TRANSPORT

INTERNATIONAL AIRPORTS Chisinau (KIV) 14.5 km from the city.

INTERNAL TRAVEL Reasonable rail and road network. Car hire available. Buses run between large towns, taxis are found everywhere.

RED TAPE

VISAS REQUIRED (UK/US) Required.

VACCINATIONS REQUIRED: See 'Vaccinations required around the world' on page 653.

DRIVING REQUIREMENTS International Driving Permit.

COUNTRY REPS IN UK/US
UK: 5 Dolphin Square, Edensor Road, London W4 2ST, tel (020)8995 6818, fax (22) 232 626, email dept@turism.md. USA: 2101 S Street, NW, Washington, DC 20008, tel (202) 667 1130, fax (202) 667 1204, email embassyofmoldova@mcihispeed.net.

UK/US REPS IN COUNTRY
UK: The British Embassy in Bucharest (see Romania) deals with enquiries relating to Moldova. USA: 103 Alexei Mateevici Street, 2009 ChisinauCA, tel (22) 408 300, fax (22) 233 044, email ChisinauCA@state.gov.

PEOPLE AND PLACE

CAPITAL Chisinau.

LANGUAGE Romanian.

PEOPLES Moldovan (65%). Ukranian, Russian, Gagauz.

RELIGION Eastern Orthodox Christian and other Christian denominations. Small Jewish community.

SIZE (SQ KM) 33,800.

POPULATION 3,606,800.

POP DENSITY/KM 106.7.

STATE OF THE NATION

SAFETY Seek latest information at time of visit.

LIFE EXPECTANCY M 43.11, F 37.58.

BEING THERE

ETIQUETTE Few Moldovans speak English, a knowledge of Russian or Romanian is very useful. In general, young Moldovans support developing closer ties with Europe rather than with Russia. Dress should be casual but conservative. For official engagements, men should wear a jacket and tie.

CURRENCY *Leu* (MDL) = 100 *bani.*

FINANCE Very limited acceptance of both

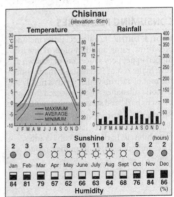

HIGHLIGHTS

CHISINAU Pretty tree-lined avenues, fine museums and a buzzing nightlife are the trademarks of the Moldovan capital. Yet this city on the banks of the river Byk exhibits a stark contrast between poverty and post-Soviet era wealth. Sports cars line up outside posh restaurants, while fashionably-dressed youngsters throng the many boutiques - but it remains one of Europe's poorest states. Even so, the city's *joie de vivre* seems to transcend the poverty line.

LOWER DNIESTR NATIONAL PARK Hike and canoe in this area of wetlands, forest and farmland, dotted with vineyards. and around 40 archaeological sites.

ORHEIUL VECHI Take a trip to this striking thirteenth-century monastery, carved into a remote limestone cliff face. The caves were dug by Orthodox monks.

TRANSDNIESTR Like stepping back in time, this self-styled republic stretching along the east of the country is in many ways a living museum of the Soviet Union. After a bloody civil war was fought in the early 1990s, the region proclaimed its independence, and has subsequently established its own currency, police force, army and borders. The Transdniestrans celebrate their own independence day on 2 September.

CRICOVA Head underground for some serious wine-tasting. In a series of tunnels beneath the village of Cricova, lies a vast winery - a great place to try some of Moldova's well-regarded dry white Sauvignons and sparkling reds.

credit cards and traveller's cheques.

BUSINESS HOURS 0900-1700 Monday to Saturday (shopping hours, business hours n/a).

GMT +2 (+3 in summer).

VOLTAGE GUIDE 220 AC, 50 Hz.

COUNTRY DIALLING CODE 373.

CONSUMING PLEASURES

FOOD & DRINK Specialities include *tocana* (pork stew) served with watermelons and apples, *mititeyi* (grilled sausages with onion and pepper), *mamaliga* (sticky maize pie) served with *brinza* (feta cheese). Over one hundred varieties of local wine which can be excellent. *Nistru* brandy is a good accompaniment with desserts.

SHOPPING & SOUVENIRS Vividly coloured costumes, handmade carpets, local wines and brandies.

FIND OUT MORE

WEBSITES www.usembassy.md, www.allmoldova.com, www.lonelyplanet.com/destinations/europe/moldova.

LOCAL MEDIA No newspapers in English, though some can be found in Chisinau's major hotels sometimes. Western press deliveries are erratic.

TOURIST BOARDS IN UK/US n/a.

Tony Hawks' witty travelogue *Playing the Moldovans at Tennis* was the product of an unlikely bet involving tracking down the entire Moldovan football team

MONACO

WHEN TO GO

WEATHER Mild, with most rain falling during the cool winter months. Hottest months are July and August.

FESTIVALS The most famous and glamourous event must be the Formula 1 Grand Prix each May, but other motorsport events take place here. Firstly the Monte Carlo Rally is held among the snow covered roads each January, and an Historic Car Rally follows in January/February. Other events include The World Music Awards, the Monaco International Showjumping Championship, the Monte Carlo Ballet (January), the Monte Carlo International Circus Festival (January), an International Dog Show (March), a Spring Arts Festival (April), the International Swimming Meeting (June), the Herculis International Athletic Meeting (September), a Summer Exhibition (July to September), and International Antiques Fair (July/August), the Rose Ball and many others.

TRANSPORT

INTERNATIONAL AIRPORTS None, but plenty of helicopter pads. Services run by Héli-Air Monaco (YO) to link with the airport in Nice (NCE).

INTERNAL TRAVEL Good rail and road connections. Taxis available.

RED TAPE

VISAS REQUIRED (UK/US) None.

VACCINATIONS REQUIRED: See 'Vaccinations required around the world' on page 653.

DRIVING REQUIREMENTS National driving licence.

COUNTRY REPS IN UK/US UK: 4 Cromwell Place, London SW7 2JE, tel (020) 7225 2679, fax (020) 7581 8161, email ivanovic_chiara@onetel.com. US: 23rd Floor, 565 Fifth Avenue, New York, NY 10017, tel (212) 286 0500, fax (212) 286 1574, email info@monaco-consulate.com.

UK/US REPS IN COUNTRY
UK: 33 boulevard Princesse Charlotte, 98005 Monaco, Cedex, tel 9350 9954, fax 9770 7200. USA: The American Consulate General in Paris (see France) deals with enquiries relating to Monaco.

PEOPLE AND PLACE

CAPITAL Monaco-Ville.

LANGUAGE French.

PEOPLES French, Italian, American, British, Belgian, native Monégasque.

RELIGION Roman Catholic. Protestant minority.

SIZE (SQ KM) 1.95.

POPULATION 32,020.

POP DENSITY/KM 16,435.

STATE OF THE NATION

SAFETY Safe.

LIFE EXPECTANCY M 75.7, F 83.63.

BEING THERE

ETIQUETTE Casual wear is acceptable in the daytime, more formal dress should be worn in the evening. Familiar greetings are carried out with a kiss to both cheeks.

CURRENCY Euro (€) = 100 *cents*.

FINANCE All major credit cards and traveller's cheques widely accepted.

BUSINESS HOURS 0900-1200, 1400-1700 Monday - Friday.

GMT +1 (+2 in summer).

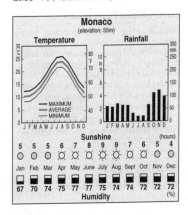

HIGHLIGHTS

MONTE-CARLO

The best known area of Monaco must be the glitz and glamour of Monte-Carlo. Huge motor yachts bob at their moorings in the harbour as their play-boy owners play roulette in the lavish, Charles Garnier-designed Grand Casino, while their wives shop in the most fashionable of boutiques. This is the area that hosts the F1 GP, first raced in 1929 and the tightest track on the calendar due to the Loews hairpin, where drivers have to be inch-perfect to keep their cars from the guardrails. Only twice have cars finished their race in the harbour, Alberto Ascari in 1955 and Paul Hawkins in 1965. Both survived.

MONACO-VILLE

Balanced on the Rock overlooking the harbour and the lights of Monte-Carlo is the Old Town, a medieval labyrinth of private dwellings, palaces, and cobbled streets. At its heart is the Prince's Palace and State Apartments, built in 1215. Take a tour to admire the beautifully adorned marble staircase and the Saint-Martin Gardens, complete with sea view. A number of Monagesque museums are also found here.

FONTEINVILLE

Located beyond Monaco-Ville is this area which houses the Princess Grace Rose Garden, named after Hollywood actress Grace Kelly who married Prince Rainier III in 1956. The garden contains over 150 varieties of rose. The late Prince Rainier's 100-strong car collection is on permanent display nearby. The Naval Museum and Zoological Terraces are worth visiting in this area.

VOLTAGE GUIDE 220 AC, 50 Hz.
COUNTRY DIALLING CODE 377.

CONSUMING PLEASURES

FOOD & DRINK Similar to France. Local specialities include *barbagiuan* (pastry with rice and pumpkin), *socca* (chickpea flour pancakes) and *stocafi* (dried cod with tomatoes). French and international wines available.

SHOPPING & SOUVENIRS Perfume, chocolates, ceramics, clothing, hosiery, shoes, books, jewellery, embroidery, racing car models, postage stamps.

FIND OUT MORE

WEBSITES
www.monacoconsulate.uk.com,
www.monaco-tourisme.com,
www.visitmonaco.com,
www.monaco-consulate.com,
www.monaco.mc, www.monte-carlo.mc.

LOCAL MEDIA No newspapers in English, but international press available. Riviera Reporter, an English-language magazine for residents, is published bimonthly.

TOURIST BOARDS IN UK/US UK: 2nd Floor, 206 Harbour Yard, Chelsea Harbour, London SW10 0XD, tel (020) 7352 9962 or (0500) 006 114, fax (020) 7352 2103, email monaco@monaco.co.uk. US: As for Reps in US, tel (212) 286 3330, fax (212) 286 9890, email info@visitmonaco.com.

In 1997 Monaco celebrated the 700th anniversary of the royal house of Grimaldi

MONGOLIA

WHEN TO GO

WEATHER Winters (October to April) are severe. Summers (June to August) are short and mild.

FESTIVALS The Naadam Festival, held in July, is Mongolia's best-known festival and a major draw for visitors wishing to get a glimpse into traditional Mongolian life. The Ulaanbaatar event is a centuries-old spectacle, at which herdsmen from all over Mongolia congregate to take part in and to watch a range of traditional sports and activities. These large-scale national games include contests of wrestling, horseracing and archery, the three so-called 'manly sports'. The games are also a good opportunity to sample Mongolian food and drink. In January-February, Mongolians celebrate the end of another harsh winter with the festivities of Tsagaan Sar, or White Month. It usually involves lots of food, including hearty mutton dumplings known as *buuz*.

TRANSPORT

INTERNATIONAL AIRPORTS Ulaanbaatar (ULN) 15 km from the city.

INTERNAL TRAVEL Internal flights are recommended for travel to remote regions. Limited rail network. Paved roads are only found in and around major cities. Car hire is available through tourism companies. Some fuel shortages. Camels and horses are often used.

RED TAPE

VISAS REQUIRED (UK/US) Required.

VACCINATIONS REQUIRED: See 'Vaccinations required around the world' on page 653.

DRIVING REQUIREMENTS n/a.

COUNTRY REPS IN UK/US UK: 7-8 Kensington Court, London W8 5DL, tel (020) 7937 0150, fax (020) 7937 1117, email office@embassyof mongolia.co.uk. USA: 2833 M Street, NW, Washington, DC 20007, tel (202) 333 7117, fax (202) 298 9227, email esyam@mongolianembassy.us.

UK/US REPS IN COUNTRY UK: 30 Enkh Taivny Gudamzh, PO Box 703, Ulaanbaatar 13, tel (11) 329 095, fax (11) 320 776, email britemb@mongol.net. USA: PO Box1021, Ulaanbaatar, tel (11) 329 095, fax (11) 320 776, email pao@usembassy.mn.

PEOPLE AND PLACE

CAPITAL Ulaanbaatar.

LANGUAGE Mongolian Khalkha.

PEOPLES Mongol (90%), Kazakh, Chinese and Russian minorities.

RELIGION Buddhist Lamaism.

SIZE (SQ KM) 1,564,116.

POPULATION 2,510,000.

POP DENSITY/KM 1.6.

STATE OF THE NATION

SAFETY Safe.

LIFE EXPECTANCY M 62.3, F 66.86.

BEING THERE

ETIQUETTE Mongolia has a large number of customs and traditions - visitors should respect local customs and also try to familiarise themselves with them as far as possible. Photography is not permitted in temples and monasteries, while in some places fees for photography may be payable. Caution should be exercised when photographing official buildings or borders.

CURRENCY *Tugrik* (Tug) = 100 *mungos*.

FINANCE Limited acceptance of credit

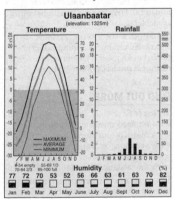

HIGHLIGHTS

THE NAADAM

The biggest event of the year for visitors to Mongolia and locals, this colourful annual event is a fascinating occasion of sporting prowess on the field and excessive drinking off of it. Normally held around 11-13 July, it's all based around the three 'manly' sports of wrestling, horseracing and archery. These disciplines have been central to Mongol life since before the days of Genghis Khan. The main celebration takes place in Ulaanbaatar, but smaller festivities occur in some centres close to the capital, enabling people to attend both local and national events.

ULAANBAATAR The country's political, commercial and cultural centre. Home to a quarter of the country's population, the capital has some atmospheric Buddhist temple museums and the still-functioning Gandan Monastery. The city's museums, especially the Museum of Natural History, with its fine collection of dinosaur skeletons, are well worth a look.

GOBI DESERT Arid expanse, home to rare animals, such as Bactrian wild camels, snow leopards, Prezwalksy horses and Gobi bears. If you're more interested in extinct species than live ones, it's also a great place for finding dinosaur bones.

THE STEPPE Ride horses across the grass plains by day, then sleep overnight in a traditional canvas *yurt* as nomadic Mongols have for centuries.

KARAKORUM Ruins mark the site of the capital of the Great Mongol Empire of the thirteenth century.

---

cards and traveller's cheques.

BUSINESS HOURS 0900-1800 Mon-Friday, 0900-1500 Saturday.

GMT +9 (+8 in summer).

VOLTAGE GUIDE 220 AC, 50 Hz.

COUNTRY DIALLING CODE 976.

CONSUMING PLEASURES

FOOD & DRINK Meat based diet, with plenty of mutton and beef. A notable speciality is *boodog*, a whole carcass of a goat filled with burning stones and roasted from the inside. Mongolian vodka and beer is excellent. Mongolian tea, *suutei tsai* (salty tea, with milk), is very popular.

SHOPPING & SOUVENIRS Pictures, cashmere garments, camel-wool blankets, boots, jewellery, carpets, books, handicrafts.

FIND OUT MORE

WEBSITES
www.embassyofmongolia.co.uk,
www.mongolianembassy.us,
http://us-mongolia.com,
www.visitmongolia.com.

LOCAL MEDIA *The Mongol Messenger* and *The UB Post* are Mongolia's English-language papers.

TOURIST BOARDS IN UK/US n/a.

In 1220 Genghis Khan built the capital of his Mongol empire at Karakorum. Visitors including Marco Polo marvelled at its grandeur, but just 40 years later Kublai Khan moved the Mongol capital to Beijing – which is still a major capital

MOROCCO

WHEN TO GO

WEATHER Warm Mediterranean climate on the coast, inland areas have a hotter, drier climate. Rain falls from November to March in coastal areas. April to August is the most popular time to visit.

FESTIVALS In May, the festival of Sid Mohammed Ma al-Ainin is a chance to see the blue-clad Tuareg nomads of the Sahara, along with other tribes. The National Folklore Festival of Marrakesh is a 10-day event in July attended by dancers, musicians and entertainers. The Tissa Horse Festival is held each year in October where hundreds of riders assemble wearing their finery to present their mounts.

TRANSPORT

INTERNATIONAL AIRPORTS Casablanca (CAS) 30 km from the city, Tangier (TNG) 12 km from the city.

INTERNAL TRAVEL Limited rail network but the services are cheap and regular. Major roads are all-weather, particularly in the north. Road travel in the interior is more difficult. Car hire can be expensive.

RED TAPE

VISAS REQUIRED (UK/US) None.

VACCINATIONS REQUIRED: See 'Vaccinations required around the world' on page 653.

DRIVING REQUIREMENTS International Driving Permit or foreign driving licence.

COUNTRY REPS IN UK/US UK: 49 Queen's Gate Gardens, London SW7 5NE, tel (020) 7581 5001, fax (020) 7225 3862, email mail@sifamaldn.org. USA: 1601 21st Street, NW, Washington, DC 20009, tel (202) 462 7979, fax (202) 462 7643, email embassy@embassyofmorocco.us.

UK/US REPS IN COUNTRY UK: BP 45 RP, 17 boulevard de la Tour Hassan, Rabat, tel (37) 238 600, fax (37) 704 531, email british@mtds.com. USA: BP 120, 2 avenue de Mohamed El Fassi, Rabat, tel (37) 762 265, fax (37) 765 661, email ircrabat@usembassy.ma.

PEOPLE AND PLACE

CAPITAL Rabat.

LANGUAGE Arabic.

PEOPLES Arab and Berber (99%).

RELIGION Muslim (98%).

SIZE (SQ KM) 710,850.

POPULATION 29,631,000.

POP DENSITY/KM 41.7.

STATE OF THE NATION

SAFETY Safe, though women may experience harassment. Beware offers of drugs, which may be a trap.

LIFE EXPECTANCY M 68.35, F 73.07.

BEING THERE

ETIQUETTE A handshake is a customary greeting. Casualwear is widely accepted. Beachwear (swimsuits and shorts) should be for the beach or poolside only. If invited to someone's house, dress smartly. A gift for the hostess is always appreciated, otherwise normal social courtesies should be observed. Many of the manners and social customs emulate French manners, particularly among the middle class. Firmness and patience can pay dividends in some social situations.

CURRENCY Moroccan *dirham* (Dh) = 100 *centimes.*

FINANCE Limited acceptance of credit cards and traveller's cheques.

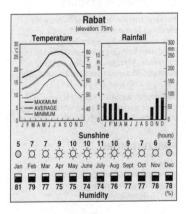

Rabat
(elevation: 75m)

	Jan	Feb	Mar	Apr	May	June	July	Aug	Sept	Oct	Nov	Dec
Sunshine (hours)	5	7	7	9	10	11	10	9	7	6	5
Humidity (%)	81	79	77	75	75	74	74	76	77	77	78	78

HIGHLIGHTS

HIGH ATLAS Trek the steep rocky trails around North Africa's highest peak, Djebel Toubkal, or hike the challenging Todra Gorge. Then sleep overnight at a home-stay to enjoy some warm Berber hospitality.

MARRAKESH Heat, dust and mudbrick ramparts, Marrakesh draws countless travellers under its spell. Watch the wondrous array of storytellers, acrobats, musicians and snake charmers who perform among the open-air food stalls in the city's famous market square, Djemaa El Fna. Tables are piled high with a vast array of exotic foods, including grilled *brochettes*, fresh salads, steaming hot stews and roasted sheeps' heads.

ESSAOUIRA Ride the waves or just relax on the fine beaches of this likeable eighteenth-century coastal town, a haven for surfers. The town also has a maze-like *medina* and a picturesque harbour, frequented by fishing boats unloading the day's catch.

CASABLANCA Join a tour of the imposing Hassan II Mosque, the largest mosque in the world, built recently with sufficient space for 100,000 worshippers and featuring a magnificent 200-metre-high minaret, the tallest structure in the country.

FES Explore enchanting *souks*, *caravanserais*, and *medersas* (Islamic colleges) in the labyrinth streets of this historic walled city, one of the world's largest intact medieval towns.

VOLUBILIS Step back in time at the country's largest Roman ruins, dating largely from the second and third centuries AD.

BUSINESS HOURS 0830-1200, 1430-1830 Monday-Friday.

GMT GMT.

VOLTAGE GUIDE 110/220 AC, 50 Hz.

COUNTRY DIALLING CODE 212.

TOURIST BOARDS IN UK/US UK: 205 Regent Street, 2nd Floor, London W1B 4HB, tel (020) 7437 0073, fax (020) 7734 8172, email info@morocco-tourism.org.uk. US: 20 East 46thStreet, Suite 1302, New York, NY 10017, tel (212) 557 2520, fax (212) 949 8148.

CONSUMING PLEASURES

FOOD & DRINK Specialities include fragrant stews called *tajines*, made from marinated meat and often served with *couscous*. Also popular are *pastilla* (a pigeon-meat pastry), *mchoui* (spit-roasted mutton) and *kab-el-ghzal* (almond pastry). To drink: mint tea, strong coffee.

SHOPPING & SOUVENIRS Tanned and dyed leather from Fes, copperware, silver, silk garments, wool rugs, carpets, blankets.

FIND OUT MORE

WEBSITES www.mincom.gov.ma, www.visitmorocco.com, www.britain.org.ma.

LOCAL MEDIA The main English-language paper is *Morocco Today*.

" The bus to Marrakesh, Morocco,
Traverses landscapes simply socko.
The machine has not replaced the mammal,
And everything is done by camel.
I hope I'll never learn what flesh,
I ate that day in Marrakesh,
But after struggling with a jawful
I thought it tasted humpthing awful."
Ogden Nash, 1964.

MOZAMBIQUE

WHEN TO GO

WEATHER Hottest and wettest from October to March. It is cooler inland, while the coast is warm and dry from April to September.

FESTIVALS Public holidays include National Day (Independence Day) on 25 June and Women's Day on 7 April. Good Friday and Easter Monday are other important holidays, while Maputo has a public holiday on 10 November.

TRANSPORT

INTERNATIONAL AIRPORTS Maputo (MPM) 3 km from the city, Beira (BEW) 13 km from the city.

INTERNAL TRAVEL Air-taxi services are the safest means of transport outside the main cities. Train services are subject to disruption. Some major roads are tarred, but landmines may make travel by road outside the capital risky and up-to-the-minute advice should be sought. Hijackings are possible. Car hire is available - only hard currency is accepted.

RED TAPE

VISAS REQUIRED (UK/US) Required.

VACCINATION S REQUIRED: See 'Vaccinations required around the world' on page 653.

DRIVING REQUIREMENTS International Driving Permit recommended.

COUNTRY REPS IN UK/US UK: 21 Fitzroy Square, London W1T 6EL, tel (020) 7383 3800, fax (020) 7383 3801, email olga@mozambiquehc.co.uk. USA: 1990 M Street, Suite 570, NW, Washington, DC 20036, tel (202) 293 7146, fax (202) 835 0245, email embamoc@aol.com.

UK/US REPS IN COUNTRY UK: CP 55, Avenida Vladimir 1 Lénine 310, Maputo, tel (1) 320 111-2, fax (1) 321 666, email bhc@virconn.com. USA: CP 783, Avenida Kenneth Kaunda 193, Maputo, tel (1) 492 797, fax (1) 490 114.

PEOPLE AND PLACE

CAPITAL Maputo.

LANGUAGE Portuguese.

PEOPLES Makua Lomwe, Thonga, Malawi, Shona, Yao.

RELIGION Traditional beliefs (60%), Christianity (30%), Islam (10%).

SIZE (SQ KM) 799,380.

POPULATION 18,082,523.

POP DENSITY/KM 22.6.

STATE OF THE NATION

SAFETY Generally safe, but many landmines remain.

LIFE EXPECTANCY M 39.9, F 40.75.

BEING THERE

ETIQUETTE Shaking hands is the customary form of greeting. Many of the courtesies and modes of address customary in Portugal and other Latin countries are still observed in Mozambique. Casualwear is acceptable and formal dress is seldom required. Visitors are advised against taking photographs of military personnel, airports, bridges or government/public buildings, since this is illegal. Only photos of beaches and other tourist sites may be taken. It is also courteous to ask permission before taking pictures of locals.

CURRENCY Mozambique *metical* (MT) = 100 *centavos*.

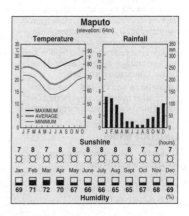

HIGHLIGHTS

Maputo Capital city which has recovered much of its old charm, with bustling markets and relaxed cafes. It also has a lively nightlife, particularly on weekends.

Wildlife While parts of the country remain out of bounds because of unexploded landmines left after the country's destructive 16-year civil war, the country's diverse wildlife is beginning to draw back tourists. The removal of a border fence in neighbouring Kruger National Park has allowed big game to return to ancient migratory routes in the parks near the capital, Maputo. The mighty Limpopo and Zambezi rivers dominate a hinterland that offers great bird-watching.

Indian Ocean coast Watch arab-style *dhows* trawl the seas along this stunning 2,500 km stretch of shoreline, offering superb snorkelling, diving and game fishing. The beaches near the coastal town of Pemba are among the most popular, while the Bazaruto Archipelago offers azure water, pristine reefs and tropical fish in abundance.

Mozambique Island The Palace and the Chapel of Sao Paulo reflect the Portuguese colonial influences that shaped Mozambique in the past, while there are also some interesting mosques worth exploring. Another significant structure is the Church of Senhora Baluarte, reputedly the oldest European building in the southern hemisphere. The northern half of Ilha de Moçambique has been declared a World Heritage Site.

Finance Credit cards rarely used, very limited use of traveller's cheques.

Business hours 0730-1230, 1400-1730 Monday to Friday.

GMT +2.

Voltage guide 240 AC, 50 Hz.

Country dialling code 258.

Local media No newspapers in English.

Tourist boards in UK/US n/a.

CONSUMING PLEASURES

Food & drink Many dishes are Portuguese in origin. Specialities include *piri-piri* (spicy) chicken, Delagoa Bay prawns, and *matapa,* a sauce of ground peanuts and cassava leaves served with rice or maize.

Shopping & souvenirs Basketwork, reed mats, woodcarvings, masks, printed cloth, leather.

FIND OUT MORE

Websites www.mozambiquehc.org.uk, www.embamoc-usa.org, www.lonelyplanet.com/destinations/africa/mozambique.

"The great grey-green, greasy Limpopo River, all set about with fever-trees..."
Rudyard Kipling, from the 'Just So Stories', 1902

MYANMAR (BURMA)

WHEN TO GO

WEATHER Monsoon climate. Myanmar is hottest from February to May. Rainy May to October, dry and cool October to February.

FESTIVALS Myanmar celebrates a number of Buddhist festivals, many of which coincide with the full moon. Other annual events include the Pindaya Cave Festival in March and Thadingyat, the Festival of Light, in October. The Elephant Dance Festival, also in October is a thunderous event in Kyaukse. Theatre, known as *pwe*, and traditional dance are an important part of Burmese culture. They sometimes form a ritual part of religious festivals and can also be witnessed at weddings, sporting events and even funerals.

TRANSPORT

INTERNATIONAL AIRPORTS Yangon (RGN) 19 km from the city.

INTERNAL TRAVEL Air travel is the most efficient and the only permissible means of transport for independent travellers. Rail services are subject to delays caused by climatic, technical and bureaucratic difficulties and tickets must be purchased as part of an organised tour group. Visitors can only use certain public bus services but privately operated buses have been introduced. Roads are being improved.

RED TAPE

VISAS REQUIRED (UK/US) Required.

VACCINATIONS REQUIRED: See 'Vaccinations required around the world' on page 653.

DRIVING REQUIREMENTS An International Driving Permit, which must be endorsed by local police.

COUNTRY REPS IN UK/US UK: 19A Charles Street, Berkeley Square, London W1J 5DX, tel (020) 7499 8841, fax (020) 7629 4169, membloudon@aol.com. USA: 2300 S Street, NW, Washington, DC 20008, tel (202) 332 9044, fax (202) 332 9046, email pyi.thayar@verizon.net.

UK/US REPS IN COUNTRY UK: 80 Strand Road, Box No 638, Yangon, tel (1) 370 863, fax (1) 370 866, email Consular.Rangoon@fco.gov.uk. USA: 581 Merchant Street, Yangon, tel (1) 379 880, fax (1) 538 040, email consularrangoo@state.gov.

PEOPLE AND PLACE

CAPITAL Yangon (Rangoon).

LANGUAGE Burmese.

PEOPLES Burman (Bamah). Shan, Karen and Rakhine minorities.

RELIGION Buddhist (87%). Christian, Muslim, Hindu.

SIZE (SQ KM) 676,552.

POPULATION 48,852,000.

POP DENSITY/KM 72.2.

STATE OF THE NATION

SAFETY Foreigners may be required to keep to officially designated areas. Southern borders affected by low-level guerrilla war. Be aware that this is a military dictatorship.

LIFE EXPECTANCY M 54.31, F 58.24.

BEING THERE

ETIQUETTE Courtesy and respect for tradition and religion is expected, for instance it is customary to remove shoes and socks before entering any religious building or a traditional home. Shorts and miniskirts should not be worn. Penalties for

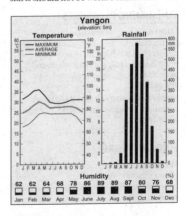

HIGHLIGHTS

BAGAN Witness an awe-inspiring sunrise or sunset over this wondrous site, where thousands of ancient temples rise dramatically out of a vast, treeless plain. The remains of a once-great city, Bagan's golden age spanned the 1040s to the 1280s, during which it was ruled over by eleven great kings before being abandoned. The fine stucco carvings of the Shwegugyi Temple and the Gawdawpalin Temple, are among the most appealing buildings, but many more can be explored.

MANDALAY An old royal city, rich in palaces, stupas, temples and pagodas, it is the main centre of Buddhism and Burmese arts. Wander among the charming craft markets and stone-carving workshops. Don't miss the huge Shweyattaw Buddha, close to Mandalay Hill, whose outstretched finger points to the city. The Great Pagoda, housing the famous Mahumuni image is another major sight.

YANGON Open-air markets, Buddhist temples and some ill-repaired colonial buildings are the hallmarks of this busy capital city.

INLE LAKE Pristine lake on the Shan Plateau, which is famous for its floating villages, water gardens and monasteries.

CHINGLONE Try your hand at the national sport, played in teams of six. The object is to keep the ball in the air for as long as possible using any part of the body - except the hands.

THEATRE Attend a traditional theatre performance, or *pwe*. These shows are colourful occasions and a form of national cultural expressions.

drug-trafficking range are severe: from five years' imprisonment to a death sentence. Homosexuality is illegal.

CURRENCY *Kyat* (Kt) = 100 *pyas*.

FINANCE Limited acceptance of credit cards. Traveller's cheques are accepted.

BUSINESS HOURS 0930-1630 Mon-Friday.

GMT +6.5.

VOLTAGE GUIDE 220/230 AC, 50 Hz.

COUNTRY DIALLING CODE 95.

CONSUMING PLEASURES

FOOD & DRINK Regional food is spicy. Dishes include *lethok son* (vegetarian rice salad), *oh-no khauk swe* (rice noodles, chicken and coconut milk), *mohinga* (fish soup with noodles). Fish, noodles, rice, vegetables, onions, ginger, garlic and chillies are the most common ingredients. Tea is popular (often added spices may make your tongue turn bright red), local soft drinks are poor, coffee is uncommon, and local beers, rums, and whiskies are available.

SHOPPING & SOUVENIRS Handicrafts and jewellery. Mandalay is good for traditional products.

FIND OUT MORE

WEBSITES www.mewashingtondc.com, http://rangoon.usembassy.gov, www.lonelyplanet.com/destinations/southeastasia/myanmar, www.myanmar.com.

LOCAL MEDIA *The New Light of Myanmar* and the *Guardian* are the English-language newspapers.

TOURIST BOARDS IN UK/US n/a.

" On the road to Mandalay
Where the flyin' fishes play,
An' the dawn comes up like thunder
Outer China 'crost the Bay! "
Rudyard Kipling, 1890

NAMIBIA

WHEN TO GO

WEATHER The coast is cool, damp and rain-free for most of the year, although coastal fog is common. Inland, the meagre rain falls from November to April (summer). Winter (June to September) is warm and pleasant, although nights can be cold.

FESTIVALS Not all festivals are open to foreigners. But those that are include Independence Day on 21 March, with celebrations taking place in every town and village, featuring singing, dancing, and speeches, and Maherero Day on 26 August. The Herero people gather in their thousands for a memorial service to their chiefs. This spectacular and fun event takes place in Okahandja, and tours can be arranged from Windhoek. Swakopmund shows its German influences when it hosts the Octoberfest beer festival.

TRANSPORT

INTERNATIONAL AIRPORTS Windhoek (WDH) 40 km from the city.

INTERNAL TRAVEL Flying is the quickest and sometimes most economical way to travel around the country. Planes can also be chartered. Efficient rail service, although limited in extent. Roads are generally well maintained. Car hire available.

RED TAPE

VISAS REQUIRED (UK/US) None.

VACCINATIONS REQUIRED: See 'Vaccinations required around the world' on page 653.

DRIVING REQUIREMENTS International Driving Permit.

COUNTRY REPS IN UK/US
UK: 6 Chandos Street, London W1G 9LU, tel (020) 7636 6244, fax (020) 7637 5694, email namibia-highcomm@btconnect.com. USA: 1605 New Hampshire Avenue, NW, Washington, DC 20009, tel (202) 986 0540, fax (202) 986 0443, email info@ namibianembassyusa.com.

UK/US REPS IN COUNTRY UK: PO Box 22202, 116 Robert Mugabe Avenue, Windhoek, tel (61) 274 800, fax (61) 228 895, email windhoek.general@fco.gov.uk. USA: Private Bag 12029, 14 Lossen Street, Windhoek, tel (61) 221 601, fax (61) 229 792, email HealyKC2@state.gov.

PEOPLE AND PLACE

CAPITAL Windhoek.

LANGUAGE English.

PEOPLES Ovambo (50%), Kavango, Damara, Herero.

RELIGION Christian majority.

SIZE (SQ KM) 824,292.

POPULATION 1,826,854.

POP DENSITY/KM 2.2.

STATE OF THE NATION

SAFETY Safe, except possibly the Caprivi Strip and Angolan border, which have been affected by Angolan civil war.

LIFE EXPECTANCY M 44.71, F 43.13.

BEING THERE

ETIQUETTE Western customs are held in Namibia and normal courtesies apply.

CURRENCY Namibian dollar (NAD).

FINANCE Credit cards and traveller's cheques are generally accepted.

BUSINESS HOURS 0800-1700 Mon-Friday.

GMT +2 (+1 from April-August).

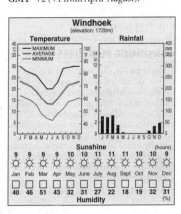

HIGHLIGHTS

DAMARALAND This extremely arid region has much to see: the petrified forest whose trunks turned to stone 200 million years ago, Vingerklip, a pale, 35-metre-high monolith that dominates the skyline, and Twyfelfontein, home to an abundance of ancient rock engravings. A short drive from Grootfontein, on the Hoba farm, is one of the largest meteorites discovered. Mainly iron and weighing 50 tons, it is thought to have hit earth some 80,000 years ago. See amazing red rock formations that make great photos, and sleep under the stars at Spitzkoppe.

NAMIB DESERT Stay at Swakopmund for trips into Sossusvlei, where sand dunes stretch as far as the eye can see. Ride them on ply wood or quad bikes, or simply see the sunrise. Further down the coast visit the multitude of sea lions at Walvis Bay. If you stay at the nearby Luderitz campsite on Shark Island, bear in mind that this was once a concentration camp, holding the Nama and Herero people in 1904-1908. From Luderitz, take a trip to the ghost town of Kolmanskop, once a diamond mining centre, now mostly buried under dunes.

FISH RIVER CANYON A huge, dramatic cleft in the dry landscape and one of the world's largest canyons. Unseen until you are on top of it, it has a vertical drop from the plateau for half a kilometre.

ETOSHA NATIONAL PARK Etosha Pan, a huge, salty hollow was formed 1,000 million years ago, and is one of Africa's greatest wildlife parks, with lion, elephant, zebra and much else.

VOLTAGE GUIDE 220/240 AC.

COUNTRY DIALLING CODE 264.

CONSUMING PLEASURES

FOOD & DRINK Game is a speciality. *Biltong* (air-dried meat) and *rauchfleisch* (smoked meat) are popular. Restaurants and cafes are still under the German influence.

SHOPPING & SOUVENIRS Diamonds, semi-precious stones, *Herero* dolls, woodcarvings, jewellery, *karosse* rugs, liqueur chocolates.

FIND OUT MORE

WEBSITES www.usembassy.namib.com, www.namibiatourism.com.na, www.britishhighcommission.gov.uk/namibia, www.namibianembassyusa.org.

LOCAL MEDIA *The Windhoek Advertiser, The Namibian* are published daily in English, the *Windhoek Advertiser* weekly and the *New Era* twice a week.

TOURIST BOARDS IN UK/US n/a.

> The Skeleton Coast is a strip of sandy wilderness that separates the Atlantic Ocean from the Namib Desert. It took its name from the number of shipwrecks there

NAURU

WHEN TO GO

WEATHER March to October when the equatorial climate is tempered by northeast trade winds. November to February sees the western monsoon.

FESTIVALS Independence Day, on 31 January, is celebrated with an early-morning fishing competition, with prizes for the biggest catch. Other public holidays on Nauru are; Constitution Day on 17 May, Angam Day on 26 October and New Year's Day on 1 January. Angam Day commemorates the day in 1932 when the birth of a baby girl brought the island's population up to 1,500, an event seen as an important landmark for the survival of the Nauruan race, which had previously been decimated by influenza. Today the occasion is a happy day of feasts and gatherings, which often include the traditional Nauruan card game *eporeitid*.

TRANSPORT

INTERNATIONAL AIRPORTS Nauru Island (INU).

INTERNAL TRAVEL 19 km of sealed road circles the island, internal roads in good condition, car hire available.

RED TAPE

VISAS REQUIRED (UK/US) Required.

VACCINATIONS REQUIRED: See 'Vaccinations required around the world' on page 653.

DRIVING REQUIREMENTS National driving licence.

COUNTRY REPS IN UK/US UK: n/a. USA: (Permanent Mission to UN) 800 2nd Avenue, Suite 400D, New York, NY 10017, tel (212) 937 0074, fax (212) 937 0079, email nauru_ny@np1.net.

UK/US REPS IN COUNTRY UK: The British Embassy is Suva (see Fiji) deals with enquiries relating to Nauru. USA: The American Embassy in Suva (see Fiji) deals with enquiries relating to Nauru.

PEOPLE AND PLACE

CAPITAL Yaren District (no official capital).

LANGUAGE Nauruan and English.

PEOPLES Nauruan (62%), other Pacific islanders (25%), Chinese, Vietnamese, European.

RELIGION Christian, mainly Nauruan Protestant Church.

SIZE (SQ KM) 21.3.

POPULATION 11,845.

POP DENSITY/KM 556.

STATE OF THE NATION

SAFETY Safe.

LIFE EXPECTANCY M 59.16, F 66.48.

BEING THERE

ETIQUETTE Nauru has a casual atmosphere in which diplomacy and tact are always preferable to confrontation. European customs continue alongside local traditions.

CURRENCY Australian dollar (A$).

FINANCE Credit cards accepted.

BUSINESS HOURS n/a.

GMT +12.

VOLTAGE GUIDE 110/240 AC, 50 Hz.

COUNTRY DIALLING CODE 674.

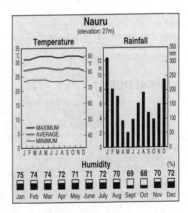

HIGHLIGHTS

THE CENTRAL PLATEAU Nauru was once the rich kid of the Pacific, a wealth that stemmed from large deposits of phosphates found on the island. However, these days the stocks of *guano* have been mined virtually to exhaustion, the result being a scarred interior, a burning wasteland of white rock, bizarre coral pinnacles and ugly pits. Initially dug by shovel, then by modern mining machinery, the surreal moonscape has been created by the workings of the Nauru Phosphate Corporation, the island's largest employer. The company's museum has some good World War II artefacts.

FISHING Either by net or by line, fishing is an essential part of Nauruan life. A fishing contest is also a major part of the Independence Day festivities on 31 January.

WATERSPORTS Swimming is possible at either of two channels cut into the reef that surrounds the island and in the harbour when not in use by boats. The reef itself makes for some good diving, as do the sunken remains of World War II wrecks. Dotted with shady palms, Anibore Bay is the prettiest of the beaches. But beware dangerous currents.

BUADA LAGOON In the centre of the island, most Nauruans live on its shores - as the rest of the island is largely given up for mining. On saturdays the locals play Australian-rules football on a field nearby.

YAREN Houses Nauru's government offices, and also has the remains of Japanese guns, bunkers and pillboxes from World War II.

CONSUMING PLEASURES

FOOD & DRINK Canned cuisine. Almost all foodstuff is imported. Very little fresh food -some fish and a little beef. No local fruit or vegetables. Yet good restaurants offer international cuisine, especially Chinese. International alcohol brands are available.

SHOPPING & SOUVENIRS Menen Hotel boutique stocks gifts and books.

FIND OUT MORE

WEBSITES www.un.int/nauru, www.lonelyplanet.com/destinations/pacific/nauru, www.spto.org.

LOCAL MEDIA The *Nasero Bulletin*, published weekly in English and Nauruan, *Central Star News*, *The NauruChronicle*.

TOURIST BOARDS IN UK/US n/a.

The potato-shaped Pacific island of Nauru is the world's smallest republic, with a land area of just 21 square kilometres

NEPAL

WHEN TO GO

WEATHER Spring (March-May) and autumn (September-November) are the most pleasant seasons.

FESTIVALS Festivals take place in Nepal throughout the year. Many of these are performed in honour of the gods and goddesses. Others mark the seasons or important points in the agricultural cycle. Some are simply family celebrations. The festivals in the Kathmandu Valley are the most spectacular. In late September to November two major festivals occur, Dasain and Tihaar. In August or September, Kathmandu celebrates Indra Jaatra, which sees the city indulge in a wild eight days of festivities to honour the god Indra, with chariot processions and masked dancers.

TRANSPORT

INTERNATIONAL AIRPORTS Kathmandu (KTM) 6.5 km from the city.

INTERNAL TRAVEL The road system is of unpredictable quality. Car hire available in Kathmandu.

RED TAPE

VISAS REQUIRED (UK/US) Required.

VACCINATION S REQUIRED: See 'Vaccinations required around the world' on page 653.

DRIVING REQUIREMENTS International Driving Permit valid for 15 days, thereafter a local licence is required.

COUNTRY REPS IN UK/US UK: 12a Kensington Palace Gardens, London W8 4QU, tel (020) 7229 1594, fax (020) 7792 9861, email rnelondon@btconnect.com. USA: 820 Second Avenue, Suite 17B, 17th Floor, New York, NY 10017, tel (212) 370 3988, fax (212) 953 2038, email nepal@un.int.

UK/US REPS IN COUNTRY UK: PO Box 106, Lainchaur, Kathmandu, tel (1) 441 0583, fax (1) 441 1789, email britemb@wlink.com.np. USA: PO Box 295, Pani Pokhari, Kathmandu, tel (1) 441 1179, fax (1) 441 9963, email consktm@state.gov.

PEOPLE AND PLACE

CAPITAL Kathmandu.

LANGUAGE Nepali.

PEOPLES Nepalese, Sherpas, Newars.

RELIGION Hindu, Buddhist. Small Muslim minority.

SIZE (SQ KM) 147,181.

POPULATION 23,151,423.

POP DENSITY/KM 157.3.

STATE OF THE NATION

SAFETY Although traditionally a safe destination, the last few years have seen an increasingly violent Maoist insurgency in the countryside, and this has now been met by strong reactions from the King, including the suspension of parliamentary government and a crackdown on demonstrations of all kinds. Seek latest information at time of travel.

LIFE EXPECTANCY M 60.09, F 59.5.

BEING THERE

ETIQUETTE Visitors must be careful to respect local customs in order not to cause offence. Nepal is primarily a Hindu country, although ethnic groups in the mountainous region, such as the Sherpas, are Buddhist. Temples and religious sites are found throughout the country. Points for visitors to remember include taking off shoes before entering a place of worship and never entering a Hindu temple wearing leather (shoes, belts etc). Always pass religious sites and prayer flags on the left. Shaking hands is not

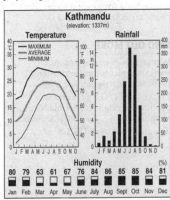

Kathmandu (elevation: 1337m)

	Jan	Feb	Mar	Apr	May	June	July	Aug	Sept	Oct	Nov	Dec
Humidity (%)	80	79	63	61	67	76	84	86	85	85	84	81

HIGHLIGHTS

KATHMANDU

Bustling and magical capital, a truly vibrant city. Fight your way through a chaotic array of bikes, cows, cars, beggars, pilgrims and vendors. In the heart of it all is Durbar Square. Wander through picturesque alleys to this vibrant hub, named after its royal palace (*durbar*) and home to the city's 'living goddess'. Other highlights include the Bagmati *ghats*, a hub of riverside temples and statues amongst the *ghats* that stretch beside the Bagmati River as far as the eye can see.

EVEREST

The big one. If you can't climb to base camp or beyond, then catching a glimpse of it from afar can be equally rewarding. Situated on the border with Tibet, the 8,850-metre peak continues to draw mountaineers from around the globe. The Khumbu region in the mountains' foothills are said to be the home of the yeti.

SWAYAMBHU

Venture out to this magnificent hilltop temple complex, teeming with Tibetan exiles and Buddhist pilgrims spinning thousands of prayer wheels. It is home to countless monkeys and has impressive views of the Kathmandu Valley.

ROYAL CHITWAN NATIONAL PARK

Spot tigers in this forest reserve, where visitors board elephants, then set off into the dense greenery on a lolloping four-legged jungle safari.

TRISULU RIVER

Take to the rapids for some adrenalin-pumping whitewater rafting - a fun and thrilling activity.

---

a common form of greeting, instead it is polite to say *namaste* , while joining the palms together.

CURRENCY Nepalese *rupee* (NRs) = 100 *paisa*.

FINANCE Major credit cards widely accepted, more limited acceptance of traveller's cheques.

BUSINESS HOURS 1000-1600/1700 Sunday-Thursday.

GMT +5.45.

VOLTAGE GUIDE 220 AC, 50 Hz.

COUNTRY DIALLING CODE 977.

CONSUMING PLEASURES

FOOD & DRINK *Dal Baht* - lentils and rice - is eaten most days. *Newar* cuisine includes spiced vegetables, *chapatis* and sweet snacks like *jelabis* (spirals of batter soaked in syrup and fried). Tibetan cooking includes *thukba* (a hearty soup) and *momos* (ravioli). Meat is commonly goat, pork, chicken or buffalo, as beef is forbidden. The national drink is *chiya* (tea with milk, sugar, and spices, and sometimes yak butter). *Chang* (beer made from barley, maize, rye, or millet) is popular in the mountains. *Arak* (potato alcohol) and *raksi* (wheat or rice spirit) are also available.

SHOPPING & SOUVENIRS *Topis* (lopsided caps), knitted mittens and socks, Tibetan dresses, woven shawls, *pashminas*, Tibetan tea bowls, papier maché dance masks.

FIND OUT MORE

WEBSITES www.nepembassy.org.uk, www.britishembassy.gov.uk/nepal, www.nepalembassyusa.org, www.south-asia.com/USA, www.catmando.com/tn, www.welcomenepal.com.

LOCAL MEDIA Many English-language papers, including *The Kathmandu Post*, *The Rising Nepal*, *The Commoner Daily News*, *The Himalayan Times* and *The International Herald Tribune*. *Newsweek* and *Time* also available. Radio and TV may broadcast in English from time to time.

TOURIST BOARDS IN UK/US n/a.

NETHERLANDS

WHEN TO GO

WEATHER Winters can be fairly cold, rainfall is common throughout the year, summers are generally warm, though very hot weather is rare. Mild climate overall.

FESTIVALS The nation hosts many different types of festival from the North Sea Jazz Festival in early July and the salsa festival in Haarlem in October to the Cannabis Cup, akin to a wine tasting event, held in Amsterdam in November, and the Amsterdam Roots Festival, celebrating African heritage, in June. The performing arts festival, or Holland Festival, is held throughout June. A number of film and dance festivals are also held in the country.

TRANSPORT

INTERNATIONAL AIRPORTS (And distances from nearest city): Amsterdam (AMS) 15 km, Rotterdam (RTM) 8 km, Eindhoven (EIN) 8km, Maastricht (MST) 8 km.

INTERNAL TRAVEL Efficient, cheap rail network, excellent road system.

RED TAPE

VISAS REQUIRED (UK/US) None.

VACCINATIONS REQUIRED: See 'Vaccinations required around the world' on page 653.

DRIVING REQUIREMENTS National driving licence, EU pink format licence. Green Card advisable.

COUNTRY REPS IN UK/US UK: 38 Hyde Park Gate, London SW7 5DP, tel (020) 7590 3200, fax (020) 7581 3458, email london@ netherlands-embassy.org.uk.
USA: 1 Rockefeller Plaza, 11th Floor, New York, NY 10020, tel (212) 246 1429, fax (212) 333 3603, email Wanyc@minbuza.nl.

UK/US REPS IN COUNTRY UK: Konigslaan 44, PO Box 75488, 1070 AL Amsterdam, tel (20) 676 4343, fax (20) 676 1069, email visaenquiries.amsterdam@ fco.gov.uk. USA: Museumplein 19, 1071 DJ Amsterdam, tel (20) 575 5309, fax (20) 575 5310.

PEOPLE AND PLACE

CAPITAL Amsterdam.

LANGUAGE Dutch.

PEOPLES Dutch (96%), Moroccan, Turkish.

RELIGION Roman Catholic, Protestant.

SIZE (SQ KM) 41,528.

POPULATION 16,254,933.

POP DENSITY/KM 479.9.

STATE OF THE NATION

SAFETY Safe.

LIFE EXPECTANCY M 76.25, F 81.51.

BEING THERE

ETIQUETTE English is spoken by many as their second language. Otherwise German or French may be spoken. Social conventions largely as for UK or US.

CURRENCY Euro (€) = 100 *cents*.

FINANCE Credit cards and traveller's cheques widely accepted.

BUSINESS HOURS 0830-1700 Mon-Friday.

GMT +1 (+2 in summer).

VOLTAGE GUIDE 220 AC, 50 Hz.

COUNTRY DIALLING CODE 31.

CONSUMING PLEASURES

FOOD & DRINK Filled pancakes and 'green' herring are popular daytime snacks. More

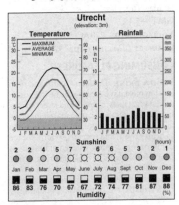

HIGHLIGHTS

AMSTERDAM Take a canal tour through the capital, home to narrow, gabled houses, diamonds, art museums, concert halls and theatres, and a very tolerant people. Of particular note is the Riijksmuseum, home to a large national art collection, including Rembrandt's *Night Watch*. Van Gogh, Cézanne, Monet, and Picasso have work dotted about the city. The city is also home to Anne Frank's House, where the young Jewish girl penned her diary while attempting to evade capture by the Nazi's. The nightlife has equal doses of upmarket and down-market activities. You can spend an evening at the opera, in a bar, in a redlight theatre or in a 'coffee shop', where soft drugs are sold over the counter.

ROTTERDAM Europe's largest port is beginning to compete with Amsterdam as a tourist destination. Largely rebuilt since World War II, very few old buildings remain. Designers and architects have come to the city in their droves. A number of new bars and restaurants have opened recently.

UTRECHT Amsterdam's attractions, but without the crowds: boasts a number of museums and several beautiful churches spanning the Golden Age when the city played an important role in Europe.

ZEELAND The province is home to a number of harbour towns offering excellent seafood. It is here that flood barriers have allowed for the reclamation of land from the sea, and as such most of the province lies below sea level. The town of Flushing was the first place to fly the free Dutch flag in 1572.

substantial dishes include *erwtensoep* (thick pea soup served with smoked sausage, bacon, pig's knuckle and bread), *hutspot* (potatoes, carrots and onions) served with *klapstuk* (stewed lean beef) and *rockworst* (kale and potatoes served with sausage). Dutch beer is excellent, the local spirit is *jenever*, a Dutch gin, taken straight or with cola or vermouth.

SHOPPING & SOUVENIRS Delft blue pottery, costume dolls, silverware, glass and crystal, diamonds.

FIND OUT MORE

WEBSITES www.holland.com/uk, www.britain.nl, www.netherlands-embassy.org, www.cgny.org, www.holland.com, www.usemb.nl, www.visitamsterdam.nl, www.thehague.nl.

LOCAL MEDIA No newspapers in English. International press available.

TOURIST BOARDS IN UK/US UK: PO Box 30783, London WC2B 6DH, tel (020) 7539 7950, fax (020) 7539 7953, email info-uk@holland.com. US: 355 Lexington Avenue, 19th Floor, New York, NY 10017, tel (212) 370 7360, fax (212) 370 9507, email information@goholland.com.

> The Netherlands literally means 'the low lands': almost half of the country lies below sea level, but is saved by a clever system of dykes

NEW ZEALAND

WHEN TO GO

WEATHER All year. Subtropical in the north and temperate in the south.

FESTIVALS Waitangi Day, in February, commemorates the signing of the Treaty of Waitangi on 6 February 1840. It's celebrated with various services and functions around the country, as well as by New Zealanders across the world. ANZAC Day on 25 April remembers the actions of New Zealand troops in major wars, with a particular focus on the Gallipoli campaign of World War I. Public holidays are also held for Christmas, New Year, Easter and the Queen's birthday, in June. Laugh till your sides split at the New Zealand International Comedy Festival, held in Auckland and Wellington in May, or feast on some cinematic treats during the International Film Festival, in Wellington and other big cities each July.

TRANSPORT

INTERNATIONAL AIRPORTS Auckland (AKL) 22.5 km from the city, Christchurch (CHC) 10 km from the city, Wellington (WLG) 8 km from the city.

INTERNAL TRAVEL Reliable rail service, good road networks.

RED TAPE

VISAS REQUIRED (UK/US) None.

VACCINATIONS REQUIRED: See 'Vaccinations required around the world' on page 653.

DRIVING REQUIREMENTS The national driving licences of EU nationals and various other countries are valid.

COUNTRY REPS IN UK/US UK: New Zealand House, 80 Haymarket, London SW1Y 4TQ, tel (020) 7930 8422, fax (020) 7839 4580, email aboutnz@newzealandhc.org.uk. USA: 37 Observatory Circle, NW, Washington, DC 20008, tel (202) 328 4800, fax (202) 667 5227, email nz@nzemb.org.

UK/US REPS IN COUNTRY UK: 44 Hill Street, Thorndon, Wellington, tel (4) 924 2888, fax (4) 473 4982, email PPA.Mailbox@

fco.gov.uk. USA: PO Box 1190, 29 Fitzherbert Terrace, Thorndon, Wellington tel (4) 462 6000, fax (4) 499 0490.

PEOPLE AND PLACE

CAPITAL Wellington.

LANGUAGE English.

PEOPLES European (82%), Maori (9%), Pacific Islanders.

RELIGION Christian denominations.

SIZE (SQ KM) 270,534.

POPULATION 4,009,200.

POP DENSITY/KM 14.8.

STATE OF THE NATION

SAFETY Safe.

LIFE EXPECTANCY M 75.67, F 81.78.

BEING THERE

ETIQUETTE New Zealand lifestyle tends to be relaxed and dress is usually informal, although business dress remains conservative. If invited to a formal Maori occasion, the *hongi* (pressing of noses) is common. It would also be respectful to learn something of Maori history and traditions.

CURRENCY New Zealand dollar (NZ$).

FINANCE Credit cards widely accepted, traveller's cheques generally accepted.

BUSINESS HOURS 0900-1700 Mon-Friday.

GMT +12 (+11 in summer).

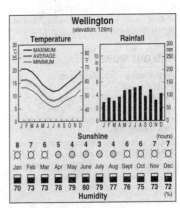

Wellington (elevation: 126m)

HIGHLIGHTS

QUEENSTOWN Strap a giant rubber band to your feet and jump off a bridge into the chilly river below, or get your adrenalin pumping with a jet boat ride on the Shotover River. Now that's just for starters. Fringing the stunning Lake Wakatipu, this buzzing and friendly South Island resort is the country's self-styled outdoor adventure capital. Skiing in the aptly-named Remarkables Mountains is one of the main winter draws, while daredevils from across the globe flock here to throw their sanity (and bodies) to the wind year round.

AUCKLAND Busy commercial centre and home to more than a quarter of the population. A waterfront city and a haven for sailing enthusiasts. Yet while the locals love it, the rest of the country remains somewhat suspicious of big city Auckland.

MILFORD SOUND One of New Zealand's most striking natural wonders. Sheer peaks fall down to scuffed cliffs, over which dramatic waterfalls cascade into icy deep blue fjords below. Take a scenic boat tour, or walk along the famous Milford Track.

ROTORUA Smells of eggs, on account of the countless bubbling mud pools and steam baths throughout the town. It has a strong Maori heritage and is a good place to witness a Maori concert or *hangi* (feast).

ALL BLACKS Not just a world-beating rugby team, but often seemingly at the very heart of what it is to be a New Zealander, these world-beating sports superstars transcend class and race. The pre-match *haka* is something else.

VOLTAGE GUIDE 230/240 AC, 50 Hz.
COUNTRY DIALLING CODE 64.

CONSUMING PLEASURES

FOOD & DRINK New Zealand is a leading producer of meat and dairy products, and cuisine is largely based on these. Venison and game birds are also popular. A wide range of seafood is also available, including snapper, grouper, oysters and crayfish. World-class domestic wines and beers.

SHOPPING & SOUVENIRS Jewellery with New Zealand *greenstone* (jade) and the translucent *paua* shell, Maori arts and crafts such as the carved greenstone *tiki* (charm), carvings, woollen goods, rugs.

FIND OUT MORE

WEBSITES www.nzembassy.com, www.newzealand.com, www.britain.org.nz, www.nzemb.org, http://wellington.usembassy.gov, www.travelplanner.co.nz.

LOCAL MEDIA *New Zealand Herald, The Press, Evening Post, The Dominion, Otago Daily Times* all available in English.

TOURIST BOARDS IN UK/US
UK: Same as Reps in UK, tel (020) 7930 1662, fax (020) 7839 8929, email enquiries@tnz.Government.nz. US: 501 Santa Monica Boulevard, Suite 300, Santa Monica, CA 90401, tel (310) 395 7480, fax (310) 395 5453, email laxinfo@tnz.Government.nz.

"If an English butler and an English nanny sat down to design a country, they would come up with New Zealand."
Anon

NICARAGUA

WHEN TO GO

WEATHER The dry season runs from December to May, the rainy season from June to November. The northern mountains are much cooler.

FESTIVALS The most popular celebration is La Purísima that takes place all over the country as a celebration of the Virgin of the Immaculate Conception. Devotees go from house to house singing special songs. Independence from Spain is marked on 15 September, while 19 July marks the anniversary of the 1979 Revolution. Religious festivals follow the Christian calendar.

TRANSPORT

INTERNATIONAL AIRPORTS Managua (MGA) 12 km from the city.

INTERNAL TRAVEL No passenger rail service at present. Only a fraction of the roads are paved. Car hire available.

RED TAPE

VISAS REQUIRED (UK/US) Required by Australian and Canadian nationals.

VACCINATIONS REQUIRED: See 'Vaccinations required around the world' on page 653.

DRIVING REQUIREMENTS National licence.

COUNTRY REPS IN UK/US
UK: Vicarage House, Suite 31, 58-60 Kensington Church Street, London W8 4DB, tel (020) 7938 2373, fax (020) 7937 0952, email embanic1@yahoo.co.uk. USA: 1627 New Hampshire Avenue, NW, Washington, DC 20009, tel (202) 939 6570, fax (202) 939 6545, email haroldrivas@embanic.org.

UK/US REPS IN COUNTRY UK: The British Embassy in San José (see Costa Rica) deals with enquiries relating to Nicaragua. USA: Apartado 327, Km 4.5 Carretera Sur, Managua, tel 268 0123, fax 266 9943, email EmbassyInfo@state.gov.

PEOPLE AND PLACE

CAPITAL Managua.

LANGUAGE Spanish.

PEOPLES *Mestizo*, indigenous Indian, of European descent, African descent, Zambos.

RELIGION Mainly Roman Catholic.

SIZE (SQ KM) 120,254.

POPULATION 5,482,340.

POP DENSITY/KM 50.3.

STATE OF THE NATION

SAFETY Currently quiet, but stability cannot be entirely guaranteed.

LIFE EXPECTANCY M 68.27, F 72.49 .

BEING THERE

ETIQUETTE Normal social courtesies apply, dress is informal. A knowledge of Spanish is appreciated.

CURRENCY Nicaraguan *gold córdoba* (C$) = 100 *centavos*.

FINANCE Credit cards and traveller's cheques accepted on a limited basis.

BUSINESS HOURS 0800-1700 Mon-Friday.

GMT -6.

VOLTAGE GUIDE 110 AC, 60 Hz.

COUNTRY DIALLING CODE 505.

CONSUMING PLEASURES

FOOD & DRINK Spanish and Latin

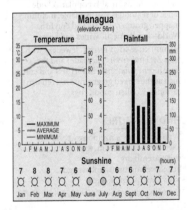

Managua (elevation: 56m)

HIGHLIGHTS

MANAGUA The centre was largely destroyed by an earthquake in 1972 and the civil war in 1978/9. Now being rebuilt, it is the museums that are the greatest draw, and of these it is Las Huellas de Acahualinca that is of real interest. It contains the site where 9,000 year old human footprints were found. Volcanic crater lagoons surround the capital, and boats can be taken out on Lake Managua to visit the smoking Momotombo volcano.

LEÓN The town contains most of the country's intellectual talent, home as it is to a university, religious colleges, the largest Central American cathedral, and several colonial churches.

GRANADA One of the oldest European settlements, once loved by pirates and marauders, it is now a romantic haunt for tourists. At the foot of the Mombacho volcano sit vibrantly painted colonial homes and lush gardens. A number of churches, parks, and squares can be visited.

SAN CARLOS On the banks of Lake Nicaragua lies this old fortress town. Its gritty appearance contrasts heavily with its idyllic surroundings, but there are several historically important military sites for the tourist to visit.

CARIBBEAN COAST The Corn Islands are the best known islands among the deserted coastline and virgin rainforest. Turquoise waters lap against the white beaches, and these undeveloped islands are a reminder of a time before big business altered the Caribbean for ever.

American in style. Dishes include *gallopinto* (rice and pinto beans), *mondongo* (tripe soup). Plantain and tortillas are staples. Cheap local beer. Fresh tropical fruit juice superior to local soft drinks.

SHOPPING & SOUVENIRS Goldwork, embroidery, shoes, paintings.

FIND OUT MORE

WEBSITES www.intur.gob.ni, http://usembassy.state.gov/managua, http://freespace.virgin.net/emb.ofnicaragua

LOCAL MEDIA No newspapers in English.

TOURIST BOARDS IN UK/US n/a.

Many Nicaraguans believe in *duendes* – little people, or demonic elves. Dressed in red, with pointy hats and little beards, they make pacts with the Devil from their hillside homes. They steal unbaptised babies and unwed women, move livestock, and play with the sanity of farmers, laughing their contagious laugh all the while

NIGER

WHEN TO GO

WEATHER During the dry season from October to May. Heavy rains and very high temperatures common in July and August.

FESTIVALS The Cure Salée, between July and September, sees nomads gather their cattle and lead them to the new pastures. Festivities are punctuated with music, dance and camel races. A particular highlight of this period is the Gerewol festival of the Wodaabé tribe. This occasion sees unmarried men adorn and beautify themselves in order to woo women. They put red ochre on their faces, black on their lips, wear jewellery and create elaborate hairpieces. The idea is to accentuate the ideals of male beauty - long slender bodies, bright white teeth and bodies and straight hair. The bachelors then line up, flash their smiles and roll their eyes, while chanting. Elsewhere, in Zinder, you can watch the *durbar* festivals - cavalry charges, clashing costumes and all. The Islamic festivals of Tabaski and the end of Ramadan are also celebrated in style.

TRANSPORT

INTERNATIONAL AIRPORTS Niamey (NIM) 12 km from the city.

INTERNAL TRAVEL Some domestic flights, and charter planes available. Only major roads are all-weather, and others are impassable during heavy rain. Petrol stations are infrequent. Car hire available but chauffeur-driven cars are compulsory outside the capital.

RED TAPE

VISAS REQUIRED (UK/US) Required.

VACCINATIONS REQUIRED: See 'Vaccinations required around the world' on page 653.

DRIVING REQUIREMENTS International Driving Permit, *Carnet de Passage*. Drivers must be at least 23-years-old.

COUNTRY REPS IN UK/US UK: n/a, nearest 154 rue du Longchamp, 75116 Paris, France, tel (1) 4504 8060, fax (1) 733 685. USA: 2204 R Street, NW, Washington, DC 20008, tel (202) 483 4224, fax (202) 483 3169, email ambassadeniger@hotmail.com.

UK/US REPS IN COUNTRY UK: The British Embassy in Abidjan (see Côte d'Ivoire) deals with enquiries relating to Niger. USA: BP 11201, Rue des Ambassades, Niamey, tel 733 169, fax 753 107, email niamy@dfait-maeci.gc.ca.

PEOPLE AND PLACE

CAPITAL Niamey.

LANGUAGE French.

PEOPLES Hausa, Djerma and Songhai, Fulani, Tuareg.

RELIGION Muslim (95%), Christian and Animist minorities.

SIZE (SQ KM) 1,267,000.

POPULATION 11,544,000.

POP DENSITY/KM 9.1.

STATE OF THE NATION

SAFETY Potentially unstable: seek latest information at time of visit.

LIFE EXPECTANCY M 42.46, F 41.8.

BEING THERE

ETIQUETTE Casual wear is widely suitable, but women should avoid wearing revealing clothes. Traditional beliefs, together with Muslim customs, should be respected. Permits are required for photography and filming in Niger, obtainable from police stations.

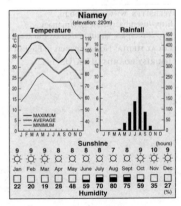

HIGHLIGHTS

THE RIVER NIGER Flowing for over 500 kilometres through the country, this mighty waterway is one of landlocked Niger's few bodies of water and a major transport route.

PARC NATIONAL DU 'W' Part of a reserve that spreads into Burkina Faso and Benin, named after the double U-bend in the River Niger. It may not have the same profusion of animals as parts of southern or eastern Africa, but visitors can still spot a large variety of species and many aquatic birds, particularly between the months of February and May. Keep your eyes peeled for herds of elephant in the Tapoa valley area and buffalo on the wooded savannah. Various species of antelope, baboon, warthog and hippo are common, while lions and leopards are also known to roam the national park.

AGADEZ Beautiful old Tuareg stronghold in the heart of the Nigérian Sahara, and historically a key stop-off on the trans-Saharan trading routes. While some Tuareg tribes continue to work the traditional camel caravan routes to the Bilma salt mines, others have been forced to seek employment in towns. The region's festivals are also a highlight.

NIAMEY Cosmopolitan capital, which draws an intriguing mix of local and regional traders, together with international aid and business workers. It has some pleasant gardens and bustling markets - the Grand Marché is one of the biggest in the Sahel. For a timeless spectacle, catch a *pirogue* and watch the sparkling sunset over the River Niger.

CURRENCY *Communauté Financiaire Africaine franc* (CFAfr) = 100 *centimes*.

FINANCE Credit cards and traveller's cheques accepted on a limited basis.

BUSINESS HOURS 0730-1230, 1500-1800 Monday to Friday, 0730-1230 Saturday.

GMT +3.

VOLTAGE GUIDE 220/380 AC, 50 Hz.

COUNTRY DIALLING CODE 227.

CONSUMING PLEASURES

FOOD & DRINK Local dishes usually based around millet, rice or *niebé*, a type of bean. Beef and mutton supplement these staples. *Brochettes* of meat are commonly sold on street stalls. Alcohol available but restricted.

SHOPPING & SOUVENIRS Multi-coloured blankets, leather goods, engraved calabashes, silver jewellery, swords and knives.

FIND OUT MORE

WEBSITES www.nigerembassyusa.org, http://usembassy.state.gov/niamey, www.lonelyplanet.com/destinations/africa/niger.

LOCAL MEDIA No newspapers in English.

TOURIST BOARDS IN UK/US n/a.

> "The Niger, as has been well observed, is not a lottery in which men may win fortunes, but a field of labour in which they may earn them."
> *Richard Burton, 1863*

NIGERIA

WHEN TO GO

WEATHER November to April. The rainy season is from March to November.

FESTIVALS Official public holidays include the main Christian and Muslim celebrations, together with Independence Day, on 1 October. However, there are more than 250 ethnic groups in Nigeria, each with their own customs, traditions and events. In the predominantly-Muslim north, the most important festival is Sallah, three months after the end of Ramadan. Each family slaughters a ram and festivities follow - with music, dance and horseback processions. Also in the north are Durbars, lines of horsemen led by a band. The horses are fitted with quilted armour, while the riders also dress elaborately and carry ceremonial swords.

TRANSPORT

INTERNATIONAL AIRPORTS Lagos (LOS) 22 km from the city.

INTERNAL TRAVEL Trains are generally slower than buses, but cheaper. A national road system links the main centres. Secondary roads become impassable in the rains. It is advisable to hire cars through hotels, although chauffeur-driven cars are recommended.

RED TAPE

VISAS REQUIRED (UK/US) Required.

VACCINATIONS REQUIRED: See 'Vaccinations required around the world' on page 653.

DRIVING REQUIREMENTS International Driving Permit.

COUNTRY REPS IN UK/US UK: 56-57 Fleet Street, London EC4 1BT, tel (020) 7353 3776, fax (020) 7353 2401, email enquiry@nigeriahighcommissionuk.com. USA: 828 2nd Avenue, 10th Floor, New York, NY 10017, tel (212) 850 2200, fax (212) 687 8768, email info@ nigeria-consulate-ny.org.

UK/US REPS IN COUNTRY UK: Shehu Shangari Way (North), Maitama, Abuja,

tel (9) 413 2010, fax (9) 413 3552, email consular@abuja.mail.fco.gov.uk. USA: 2 Walter Carrington Crescent, Victoria Island, Lagos, tel (1) 261 0050, fax (1) 261 9856, email uslagos@state.gov.

PEOPLE AND PLACE

CAPITAL Abuja.

LANGUAGE English.

PEOPLES Yoruba, Hausa, Ibo, Fulani.

RELIGION Muslim, Christian, traditional beliefs.

SIZE (SQ KM) 923,768.

POPULATION 127,100,000.

POP DENSITY/KM 130.9.

STATE OF THE NATION

SAFETY Very unsafe. High levels of street crime, business fraud and political violence. Avoid the Niger Delta entirely, scene of military operations and local rioting. Do not travel outside cities after dark.

LIFE EXPECTANCY M 46.21, F 47.29.

BEING THERE

ETIQUETTE Africa's most populous nation, with a population of 120 million, Nigeria has more than 250 tribes - the principal ones being the Hausa, the Ibo (or Igbo) and the Yoruba. Generally, Nigerians have a very strong sense of ethnic allegiance. It is unusual to be invited to a Nigerian's home,

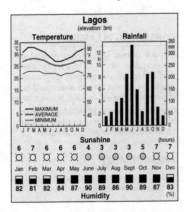

Lagos (elevation: 3m) — Temperature / Rainfall / Sunshine / Humidity climate chart

HIGHLIGHTS

KANO Ancient mud-walled city, the oldest in West Africa and once a strategic stop-off on the trans-Saharan trade routes. A medieval feel still fills the Old City, an area that houses an enormous and vibrant market, selling all manner of souvenirs and local wares. Also located there are the Grand Mosque, the Emir's Palace and age-old dye pits.

YANKARI NATIONAL PARK The country's best wildlife reserve, even though sightings can be a bit hit-and-miss. It is, however, good for birdwatching, while elephants, monkeys and crocodiles do inhabit the park. Other reserves, such as Gashaka Park on the border with Cameroon, provide slim chances to see birds and animals in the wild.

LAGOS Busy and overcrowded *de facto* capital, with the most active night scene in West Africa. The city feels the heartbeat of Nigerian music and you stand a good chance of seeing international music stars such as Femi Kuti, the son of the late Fela Kuti. With more nightclubs than almost anywhere on the continent, night-time energy just oozes from its streets. The city has long since sprawled from its commercial and administrative centre on Lagos Island. Over on the mainland, the infrastructure struggles - unsuccessfully - to keep up.

JOS A popular holiday spot, with a pleasantly cool climate, due to its location 1,200m above sea level. The town has some fine museums, housing pottery and other artefacts from around the country.

as most entertaining, particularly in Lagos, takes place in clubs or restaurants. Women should dress modestly, particularly in the Muslim north, and should avoid trousers.

CURRENCY *Naira* (N) = 100 *kobo*.

FINANCE Credit card fraud is prevalent, and traveller's cheques are generally not recommended.

BUSINESS HOURS 0830-1700 Mon-Friday. GMT +1.

VOLTAGE GUIDE 220/250 AC, 50 Hz.

COUNTRY DIALLING CODE 234.

CONSUMING PLEASURES

FOOD & DRINK Typical West African fare, based on yams, sweet potatoes and plantains. Pepper soup, *kilishi* (spiced dried meat), *egussi soup* (meat, dried fish and melon seed stew) and goat and bush meat are popular. Many locally brewed beers.

SHOPPING & SOUVENIRS *Adire* (patterned, indigo-dyed cloth), batiks, pottery, leatherwork, kaduna cotton, carvings, beadwork, basketry, ceremonial masks.

FIND OUT MORE

WEBSITES www.motherlandnigeria.com www.nigeriahighcommissionuk.com, www.nigeriaembassyusa.org, www.nigeria-consulate-ny.org, http://usembassy.state.gov/nigeria.

LOCAL MEDIA *Daily Times, Guardian, New Nigerian, Daily Sketch, National Concord, Nigerian* are all printed in English.

TOURIST BOARDS IN UK/US n/a.

"Nigeria is one of the most disorderly nations in the world. It is one of the most corrupt, insensitive, inefficient places under the sun."
Chinua Achebe, Nobel Prize-winning Nigerian author

NORWAY

WHEN TO GO

WEATHER Winters (November to March) are very cold. The rest of the year is mild and pleasant.

FESTIVALS The people of Oslo gather at the Royal Palace, in traditional dress, as part on the Constitution Day celebration on 17 May. Skiers come to the city for the Holmenkollen Ski Festival in March. Arts festivals are also held, including the Oslo International Jazz Festival in August, the film festival in October, and the Inferno Metal Festival in April. Bergen hosts its own International Festival over twelve days at the end of May, featuring dance, music, and folklore events.

TRANSPORT

INTERNATIONAL AIRPORTS (And distances from nearest city): Oslo (OSL) 47 km, Stavanger (SVG) 14.5 km, Bergen (BG)) 19 km.

INTERNAL TRAVEL Good domestic air network. Coastal towns and fjords served by ferries. Roads of variable quality, especially under freezing winter conditions in the north. Car hire easily available but costly.

RED TAPE

VISAS REQUIRED (UK/US) None.

VACCINATIONS REQUIRED: See 'Vaccinations required around the world' on page 653.

DRIVING REQUIREMENTS International Driving Permit or national driving licence and log book. Green Card recommended.

COUNTRY REPS IN UK/US UK: 25 Belgrave Square, London SW1X 8QD, tel (020) 7591 5500, fax (020) 7245 6993, email emb.london@mfa.no. USA: 2720 34th Street, NW, Washington, DC 20008, tel (202) 333 6000, fax (202) 337 0870, email info@norway.org.

UK/US REPS IN COUNTRY UK: Thomas Heftyesgate 8, 0244 Oslo, tel 2313 2700, fax 2313 2741, email britemb@online.no USA: Drammensveien 18, 0244 Oslo, tel 2244 8550, fax 2243 0777, email pasoslo@usa.no.

PEOPLE AND PLACE

CAPITAL Oslo.

LANGUAGE Norwegian.

PEOPLES Norwegian (95%), Lapp, other.

RELIGION Evangelical Lutheran.

SIZE (SQ KM) 323,759.

POPULATION 4,552,252.

POP DENSITY/KM 14.9.

STATE OF THE NATION

SAFETY Safe.

LIFE EXPECTANCY M 76.78, F 82.17.

BEING THERE

ETIQUETTE Normal social courtesies apply. Arrive for meetings punctually. Await for the host to make a toast before drinking. Gifts following an invitation to someone's home are much appreciated.

CURRENCY Norwegian *krone* (NOK) = 100 *øre*.

FINANCE Credit cards and traveller's cheques widely accepted.

BUSINESS HOURS 0800-1600 Mon-Friday.

GMT +1.

VOLTAGE GUIDE 220 AC, 50 Hz.

COUNTRY DIALLING CODE 47.

CONSUMING PLEASURES

FOOD & DRINK *Koldtbord* (cold tables)

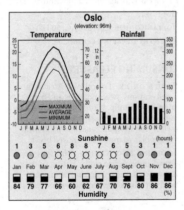

HIGHLIGHTS

OSLO The capital combines the delights of urban living - cafe's, museums, and nightlife - with an easy access to nature. Ski trails surround the city in winter, and double as hiking areas in summer. The Frognerparken should be visited by all travellers in the region. This green space is home to 200 granite and bronze sculptures by Gustav Vigeland. Elsewhere, guided tours can be taken around Det Kongelige Slott, the king's residence. The medieval-cum-Renaissance palace, Akershus Slott, can also be visited.

BERGEN Possibly Norway's most beautiful city, Bergen is set on a peninsula between mountains and sea. Crooked streets climb to give hilltop views over Norway's second largest city. Home to a large university population, the city supports a number of theatres, museums, an orchestra, and a thriving rock music scene. Big for Norway, by most standards, the city still retains a village-like atmosphere.

SOGNEFJORDEN Norway is well known for its deep fjords, and this is the deepest and longest. Running for 204 kilometres, it is 1,308 metres deep at its deepest point. Some areas have sheer vertical walls, rising straight up for more than a kilometre. The cliffs and waterfalls make for spectacular views between Naerøyfjorden and Gudvangen.

TRONDHEIM Founded in 997 AD by a Viking king, Norway's third largest city is bursting with medieval history. Renaissance features were added to the city after a fire destroyed some parts.

consisting of smoked salmon, fresh lobster, shrimp and hot dishes are often found in hotels and restaurants. Open sandwiches topped with fish, cheese, meats and salads are also popular. Main dishes include roast venison, *lutefisk* (hot, highly flavoured cod) and herring prepared in a variety of ways. *Aquavit* (*schnapps*) is popular to drink, otherwise alcohol is limited and expensive, though wines and beers are available.

SHOPPING & SOUVENIRS Silver, pottery, furs, knitwear, woodcarvings, enamel, pewter, glass, porcelain.

FIND OUT MORE

WEBSITES www.norway.org.uk, www.visitnorway.com, www.britain.no, www.norway.org, www.invanor.no/usa, www.usa.no, www.bergen-guide.com, www.osloguide.net.

LOCAL MEDIA No newspapers in English, but British press available next day.

TOURIST BOARDS IN UK/US UK: Charles House, 5 Lower Regent Street, London SW1 4LR, tel (020) 7389 8800, fax (020) 7839 6014, email london@invanor.no. US: 800 Third Avenue, 23rd Floor, New York, NY 10022, tel (212) 421 9210, fax (212) 838 0374, email new.york.trade@invanor.no.

> "'The Norwegians,' one of my Scandinavian friends once put it, 'are like their landscape, rather vertical.'"
> *John Gunther, 1938*

OMAN

WHEN TO GO

WEATHER The months between May and August are particularly hot. The climate is best from September through to April. Rainfall varies according to the region. During the period June to September there is a light monsoon rain in Salalah.

FESTIVALS Events are generally Muslim festivals and feasts. Other notable occasions include the Khareef Festival, held each July and August in the city of Salalah: named after the annual monsoon that transforms and cools the lush south, it is an international event featuring music, cultural programs, arts exhibitions, sport and local crafts. Other attractions include horse races and the even more popular camel races - held on Fridays and public holidays at a variety of locations.

TRANSPORT

INTERNATIONAL AIRPORTS Muscat (MCT) 40 km from the city.

INTERNAL TRAVEL Principal road routes run from north to south. Good roads to neighbouring states. Car hire available.

RED TAPE

VISAS REQUIRED (UK/US) Required.

VACCINATIONS REQUIRED: See 'Vaccinations required around the world' on page 653.

DRIVING REQUIREMENTS A local licence must be obtained from the police by presenting a national driving licence or International Driving Permit.

COUNTRY REPS IN UK/US UK: 167 Queen's Gate, London SW7 5HE, tel (020) 7225 0001, fax (020) 7589 2505. USA: 2535 Belmont Road, NW, Washington, DC 20008, tel (202) 387 1980, fax (202) 745 4933.

UK/US REPS IN COUNTRY UK: PO Box 185, Mina Al Fahal PC 116, Muscat, tel 609 000, fax 609 010, email enquiries.muscat@ fco.gov.uk. USA:Jameat A'Duval Al Arabiya Street, Diplomatic Area of Al Khuwair (Shatti al-Qurum), Muscat, tel 698 989, fax 699 771, email aemctira@omantel.net.om.

PEOPLE AND PLACE

CAPITAL Muscat.

LANGUAGE Arabic and English.

PEOPLES Omani, Baluchi, Jebali.

RELIGION Ibadhi Muslim.

SIZE (SQ KM) 309,500.

POPULATION 2,538,000.

POP DENSITY/KM 8.2.

STATE OF THE NATION

SAFETY Safe.

LIFE EXPECTANCY M 70.92, F 75.46.

BEING THERE

ETIQUETTE Hospitality is fundamental to Omani culture. It is not unusual for an Omani to invite visitors into their home and it would be considered rude to refuse. Islamic ideals provide the conservative foundation of Oman's customs, laws and practices. Foreign visitors are expected to remain sensitive to the Islamic culture and visitors should dress modestly, especially women - long skirts or dresses are appropriate. Beachwear is prohibited anywhere except the beach. Collecting sea shells, abalone, coral, crayfish and turtle eggs is prohibited. Visitors should ask permission before photographing people or property.

CURRENCY Omani *rial* (OR) = 1000 *baiza*.

FINANCE Major cards widely accepted, traveller's cheques easily exchanged.

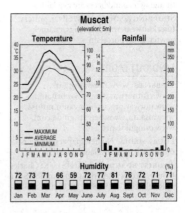

Muscat
(elevation: 5m)

Temperature / Rainfall / Humidity (%)

MAXIMUM / AVERAGE / MINIMUM

	Jan	Feb	Mar	Apr	May	June	July	Aug	Sept	Oct	Nov	Dec
Humidity (%)	72	73	71	66	59	72	77	81	76	72	71	71

HIGHLIGHTS

MUSCAT Haggle for bargains in the enchanting *souks* (Mutrah is the best) and explore the many castles, mosques and towers of Oman's capital, a city full of character ancient and modern. Old Muscat is dominated by the two cliff-side forts of Mirani and Jalali, the al-Alam Palace and the sturdy city walls.

NIZWA Scale the imposing fort that dominates this verdant oasis town and former seat of power, or listen in the evenings as the call of the *muezzin* from the nearby Sultan Qaboos Mosque fills the air. Peaceful, sleepy and safe, Nizwa is popular among tourists looking to amble through its *souk* and fort, before heading out to explore the surrounding region.

WAHIBA SANDS Follow the trails of Bedouin tribes through this isolated desert region, fringed by fortified towns and home to Omani pit-weavers who design elegant textiles from looms dug into the earth.

SUR Snorkel, dive and sunbathe on this enticing stretch of coastline, or wander the quiet and appealing town, said to be the home of Sinbad the Sailor, where traditional *dhows* are still built. A *dhow* trip is another way of exploring the Omani coast. South of Sur lie the breeding grounds of the Green Turtle.

SALALAH Explore the unspoilt beaches and lush landscapes of an area steeped in legend, where frankincense can still be gathered and where migrating birds are drawn by the cool rains of the monsoon. Dolphins sometimes break the surface near the shore.

BUSINESS HOURS 0800-1300, 1600-1900 Saturday to Wednesday, 0800-1300 Thurs.

GMT +4.

VOLTAGE GUIDE 220/240 AC, 50 Hz.

COUNTRY DIALLING CODE 968.

CONSUMING PLEASURES

FOOD & DRINK Arabic, Lebanese and Indian food. *Biryanis*, curries and *felafal* available everywhere. Visitors are only allowed to drink alcohol in licenced hotels and restaurants. Coffee houses are popular.

SHOPPING & SOUVENIRS Silver, gold, jewellery, *khanjars* (Omani daggers), coffeepots, frankincense, carpets, baskets.

FIND OUT MORE

WEBSITES www.usa.gov.om, www.britishembassy.gov.uk/oman, www.destinationoman.com.

LOCAL MEDIA *The Times of Oman, The Oman Daily Observer* are printed in English.

TOURIST BOARDS IN UK/US n/a.

"Muscat was the realisation of a pirate's lair as imagined by any schoolboy: a crescent of white houses huddled in a cove with high cliffs projecting on either side. The place was clearly designed as a centre for piracy and slave-running."
Cedric Belfrage, 1936

PAKISTAN

WHEN TO GO

WEATHER Visit during winter (November to March) when it is warm and dry. April to July is extremely hot and the monsoon occurs from July to September.

FESTIVALS Religious festivals follow the Islamic calendar and are dependent on the sighting of the new crescent moon. National celebrations include Pakistan Day on 23 March, and Independence Day on 14 August.

TRANSPORT

INTERNATIONAL AIRPORTS (And distances from nearest city) Karachi (KHI) 15 km, Lahore (LHE) 18 km, Islamabad (ISB) 15 km, Peshawar (PEW) 4km.

INTERNAL TRAVEL Domestic flights between Lahore and main centres. Extensive rail system. Roads between cities generally well maintained. Car hire available.

RED TAPE

VISAS REQUIRED (UK/US) Required.

VACCINATIONS REQUIRED: See 'Vaccinations required around the world' on page 653.

DRIVING REQUIREMENTS International Driving Permit.

COUNTRY REPS IN UK/US UK: 36 Lowndes Square, London SW1X 9JN, tel (020) 7664 9200, fax (020) 7664 9224, email pareplondon@supanet.com. USA: 12 East, 65th Street, New York, NY 10021, tel (212) 879 5800, fax (212) 517 6987, email nyconsulate@embassyofpakistan.org.

UK/US REPS IN COUNTRY UK: PO Box 1122, Diplomatic Enclave, Ramna 5, Islamabad, tel (51) 282 4728, fax (51) 227 9356, email visqry.islamabad@fco.gov.uk. USA: PO Box 1048, Diplomatic Enclave, Sector G-5, Islamabad, tel (51) 2080 0000, fax (51) 227 6427, email paknivinfo@state.gov.

PEOPLE AND PLACE

CAPITAL Islamabad.

LANGUAGE Urdu and English.

PEOPLES Punjabi, Sindhi, Pashtu, Mohajir, Baluch.

RELIGION Sunni Muslim (77%), Sh'ia Muslim (20%), Hindu and Christian minorities.

SIZE (SQ KM) 896,095.

POPULATION 149,030,000.

POP DENSITY/KM 187.2.

STATE OF THE NATION

SAFETY Politically volatile and tense after the war in neighbouring Afghanistan. Al-Qaida remnants are still being hunted in the western border areas, where tribal areas are largely outside of government control. Many Western and Christian organisations and individuals have been attacked by Islamic militants, including churches.

LIFE EXPECTANCY M 62.04, F 64.01.

BEING THERE

ETIQUETTE Use the right hand for greeting and passing items. Hospitality and courtesy are important at all levels. Respect the Muslim customs and beliefs. Smoking is prohibited in many public places. Informal dress is acceptable at most times. Women should cover arms and legs and wear loose clothing. Society is divided into classes with subtle social grading.

CURRENCY Pakistani *rupee* (PRe/PRs) = 100 *paisa*.

FINANCE American Express is widely

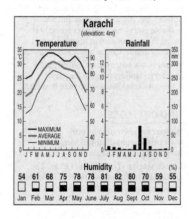

Karachi
(elevation: 4m)

HIGHLIGHTS

KARACHI Once a small fishing village on the shores of the Arabian Sea, the former capital has grown to become a megacity to rival any in the world. Still the centre for commerce, industry, finance, and education, the city has much to explore. Clifton beach and the open air laundry at Dhobi Ghat are great spots for people-watching, and good shopping can be had in the bazaars. The Quaid-e-Azam's Mazar is the city's most impressive building - a mausoleum of the founder of Pakistan, built entirely out of white marble, it features north African arches and Chinese crystal chandeliers.

ISLAMABAD AND RAWALPINDI These twin cities are located beside each other. Islamabad is the modern capital, built in the 1960s to a grid pattern. Rawalpindi is a congested sprawl of winding streets and bazaars, a typically chaotic South Asian city. At some stage they will combine in one urban mass.

THE KARAKORUM HIGHWAY Joining Islamabad and Rawalpindi to Kashgar in the Xinjiang province in China, the highway runs along the ancient silk route, across awesome mountain ranges. Passing through the Himalayas, Hindukush, Karakorum, Kunlun and Pamir, and along the banks of the Indus River to Gilgit and the beautiful Hunza valleys, the route is popular with tourists as well as those travelling to Mecca.

accepted, other cards less so. Travellers' cheques are generally accepted.

BUSINESS HOURS 0800-1500 Monday to Thursday and Saturday, 0800-1230 Friday. GMT +5.

VOLTAGE GUIDE 220 AC, 50 Hz.

COUNTRY DIALLING CODE 92.

www.britishhighcommission.gov.uk/pakistan, www.embassyofpakistan.org, http://islamabad.usembassy.gov.

LOCAL MEDIA *Leader, Pakistan Observer, Pakistan Times, Financial Post, Frontier Post, Dawn, Business Recorder, The Nation, The News.* All are published in English.

TOURIST BOARDS IN UK/US n/a.

CONSUMING PLEASURES

FOOD & DRINK Based on *masala* (spice) sauces with chicken, fish, lamb and vegetables. Typical dishes include *biryanis, brain masala* and *sag gosht* (spinach and lamb curry). Moghul cuisine is found in Lahore. Specialities include tandoori dishes and various kebabs. Alcohol may be bought at major hotels by visitors in possession of a Liquor Permit.

SHOPPING & SOUVENIRS Wooden tables, screens, silvers, pottery, camel-skin lamps, bamboo decorations, brassware, cane items, glass bangles, shawls, rugs and carpets, *saleem shahi* shoes with upturned toes.

FIND OUT MORE

WEBSITES www.pakmission-uk.gov.pk,

> "Since childhood, my greatest passion has been for the northern areas of Pakistan. The magic of being surrounded by some of the highest mountains in the world is unequal to anything else I have ever experienced."
>
> *Imran Khan, former Pakistan cricket captain*

PALAU

WHEN TO GO

WEATHER Warm all year, with the heaviest rainfall between July and October.

FESTIVALS New Year, Easter and Christmas are all celebrated as public holidays in Palau. Youth Day, on 15 March, is marked with sporting events, while Senior Citizens Day, on 5 May, features a parade with floats, dancing contests and art exhibitions. Peleliu and Angaur islands both have a World War II Memorial Day, in commemoration of the day US forces landed on each island. Throughout Palau, Independence Day is celebrated on 1 October.

TRANSPORT

INTERNATIONAL AIRPORTS Koror Badeldaob (ROR), on Babeldaob Island.

INTERNAL TRAVEL Some inter-island boat services. Coral and dirt roads. A 4-wheel drive is recommended to see Babeldoab.

RED TAPE

VISAS REQUIRED (UK/US) Not required for visits of less than 30 days.

VACCINATIONS REQUIRED: See 'Vaccinations required around the world' on page 653.

DRIVING REQUIREMENTS n/a.

COUNTRY REPS IN UK/US UK: n/a. USA: 1800 K Street, NW 714, Washington, DC 20006, tel (202) 452 6814, fax (202) 452 6281, email info@palauembassy.com.

UK/US REPS IN COUNTRY UK: n/a. USA: PO Box 6028, Ngermid Hamlet, Koror, Palau 96940, tel 488 2920, fax 488 2911, email usembassy@palaunet.com.

PEOPLE AND PLACE

CAPITAL Koror.

LANGUAGE English and Palauan.

PEOPLES Micronesian.

RELIGION Roman Catholic, Modekngei.

SIZE (SQ KM) 508.

POPULATION 19,129.

POP DENSITY/KM 37.7.

STATE OF THE NATION

SAFETY Safe.

LIFE EXPECTANCY M 66.98, F 73.48.

BEING THERE

ETIQUETTE While English is the common language of business and government, Palauan is spoken at home and in casual situations. In Palauan, 'hello' is *alii* and 'thanks' is *sulang*. Traditional Palauan society was a complex matriarchal system. Today, Western influences are increasingly strong, not least because many Palauans go overseas for their education. However, a version of traditional religion, called Modekngei, exists alongside the imported Christian beliefs.

CURRENCY US dollar (US$) = 100 cents.

FINANCE Some acceptance of credit cards and traveller's cheques on the main island.

BUSINESS HOURS 0800-2100 Monday-Saturday (shopping hours, business hours n/a).

GMT +9.

VOLTAGE GUIDE 115/230 AC, 60 Hz.

COUNTRY DIALLING CODE 680.

CONSUMING PLEASURES

FOOD & DRINK Fresh local seafood is a highlight. International cuisine available, including Chinese and Japanese food. Exotic local dishes, but pizza is ubiquitous.

SHOPPING & SOUVENIRS The unqiue buys

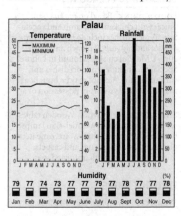

HIGHLIGHTS

THE ROCK ISLANDS

Sail through this twisty maze of some 200 divinely green, mushroom shaped islands: their bases have been undercut by water erosion and grazing fish, hence the unique shape. The Rock Islands offer excellent snorkelling, sea kayaking and fishing. They're also home to crocodiles and fruit bats, and are rich with bird species - including parrots, herons and cockatoos.

BADELDAOB

Palau's largest island, covered with dense foliage and with a landscape that varies from freshwater lakes and steep mountains, to sandy dunes and powerful waterfalls. Visitors can explore the 37 *badrulchau* - stone monoliths that testify to the island's early civilisation. Be sure to keep a respectful distance from a *bai*, a traditional men's meeting house.

KOROR

The capital of Palau, home to two-thirds of the population. Catering for both visitors and locals are some splendid eateries, serving delicious food such as mangrove crab and locally-caught lobster.

The Belau National Museum on Koror has some displays of items such as bead and turtle shell money, as well as local arts and crafts. Climb up Malakal Hill for a good view of the nearby Rock Islands.

DIVING

Zip up your wetsuit and strap on your breathing apparatus, then plunge into Palau's beautiful underwater world. The island of Peleliu - part of the Rock Islands - is the final resting place for a number of ships sunk in World War II. Nestling on the sea floor, the mangled wrecks are a popular dive attraction.

here are storyboards - carvings on lengths of wood depicting stories of around 30 popular legends. You'll also find jewellery, etchings, baskets, purses, hats, mats, figurines.

FIND OUT MORE

WEBSITES www.lonelyplanet.com/destinations/pacific/palau, www.visit-palau.com, www.palauembassy.com.

LOCAL MEDIA *Pacific Daily News.* No terrestrial TV broadcaster.

TOURIST BOARDS IN UK/US n/a.

The early Palauans developed an intricate system of currency. Beads made of clay or glass, called *udoud*, were the most common form, but turtle shell money was also used

PANAMA

WHEN TO GO

WEATHER High temperatures throughout the year. Rainy season from May to November.

FESTIVALS Panamanians dress in costume, and parade through the streets during Carnaval over the four days before Ash Wednesday. Music, dancing, and other festivities are had in Panama City, and on the Península de Azuero re-enactments of religious events are held during Semana Santa, the week before Easter. Famous Corpus Christi celebrations are held in Villa de Los Santos, forty days after Easter, when masked people wear costumes depicting angels, devils, and imps. A number of smaller festivals are held at a local level throughout the country. Different ethnic groups organise their own cultural events.

TRANSPORT

INTERNATIONAL AIRPORTS Panama City (PTY) 27 km from the city.

INTERNAL TRAVEL Some internal flights. Rail system currently only operating freight trains. The Trans-Isthmian Highway links Panama City and Colón. Car hire available.

RED TAPE

VISAS REQUIRED (UK/US) Not required by UK nationals, others issued with a tourist card.

VACCINATION S REQUIRED: See 'Vaccinations required around the world' on page 653.

DRIVING REQUIREMENTS National driving licence.

COUNTRY REPS IN UK/US UK: 40 Hertford Street, London W1J 7SH, tel (020) 7409 2255, fax (020) 7493 4499, email panama@panaconsul.co.uk. USA: Flood Building, 870 Market Street, Suite 551, San Francisco, CA 94102, tel (415) 391 4268, fax (415) 391 4269.

UK/US REPS IN COUNTRY UK: Calle 53, Urbanización Marbella, Swiss Tower, Apartado 889, Zona 1, Panamá City, tel 269 0866, fax 223 0730, email britemb@ cwpanama.net. USA: Building 520, Clayton, Apartado 6959, Panamá 5, tel 207 7000, fax 207 7278, email panama-acs@state.gov.

PEOPLE AND PLACE

CAPITAL Panama City.

LANGUAGE Spanish.

PEOPLES *Mestizo*, of European and African descent, indigenous Indian, Asian.

RELIGION Roman Catholic.

SIZE (SQ KM) 75,517.

POPULATION 3,116,000.

POP DENSITY/KM 41.3.

STATE OF THE NATION

SAFETY Avoid the Colombian border. Beware muggings in tourist areas.

LIFE EXPECTANCY M 69.67, F 74.31.

BEING THERE

ETIQUETTE Largely a mix of American and Spanish lifestyles, the *mestizo* population share characteristics with the *mestizo* culture found throughout Central America. Only three indigenous tribes, having withdrawn into inaccessible areas, have been able to retain traditional lifestyles. Normal social courtesies apply across the country.

CURRENCY *Balboa* (B) = 100 *centésimos*.

FINANCE Credit cards and traveller's cheques generally accepted.

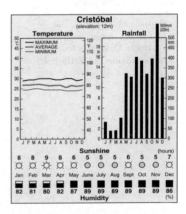

HIGHLIGHTS

PANAMA CITY Like the country as a whole, the capital is a mixture of modern America and old Spain, but with a dash of the East's bazaars. Among the narrow, cobbled streets and colonial architecture of the old town, now a World Heritage site, are the San José and Santo Domingo churches. More impressive, though, is the President's Palace which overlooks the bay.

PANAMA CANAL The main tourist destination in the country is the canal that provides a route through Central America from the Caribbean Sea to the Pacific Ocean. The scenery and engineering are both awe-inspiring. The transit of the canal takes eight hours on average.

CHIRIQUI The province is a place of waterfalls, rivers, mountainous scenery, and volcanic highlands. The resort of Boquete is located near the dormant Baru Volcano and the Baru National Park, famous as a home to Quetzal birds.

THE DARIEN GAP This wilderness is home to two Choco Indian tribes and guerillas, and is extremely hard to navigate. It is the only break on the Pan-American Highway which runs from Argentina to Alaska. It can only be crossed in extreme 4x4 vehicles. The land contains various habitats, from sandy beaches, and rocky coasts, to swamp and rainforest.

AZUERO PENINSULA Characterised by small colonial towns, the area provides a quiet, relaxed contrast to the hectic life of Panama's cities.

BUSINESS HOURS 0800-1200, 1400-1700 Monday-Friday.

GMT -5.

VOLTAGE GUIDE 120 AC, 60 Hz.

COUNTRY DIALLING CODE 507.

www.panamacanalcountry.com, www.panama-guide.com.

LOCAL MEDIA No newspapers in English.

TOURIST BOARDS IN UK/US n/a.

CONSUMING PLEASURES

FOOD & DRINK Native food is hot and spicy. Dishes include *ceviche* (raw fish marinated in lime juice and peppers), *sancocho* (chicken, meat and vegetable stew), *tamales* (pies wrapped in banana leaves) and *empanadas* (pastries filled with cheese, chicken or meat). Many wines and beers to choose from.

SHOPPING & SOUVENIRS Luxury goods available with a saving of a third, in this duty free haven. Local crafts include leather-ware, beaded necklaces, native costumes, carved wood, ceramics, mahogany bowls.

FIND OUT MORE

WEBSITES www.panaconsul.com, www.panamainfo.com,

> " It is the greatest liberty
> Man has ever taken
> with Nature. "
> James Bryce,
> on the Panama
> Canal, 1912

PAPUA NEW GUINEA

WHEN TO GO

WEATHER May to November is the best time. Most rain falls between December and March, although Port Moresby is dry at this time.

FESTIVALS Each of Papua New Guinea's 19 provinces has its own provincial government day - these are often an opportunity to enjoy sing-sings. These are colourful tribal gatherings with dancing, singing and chanting. Some are small, others can involve tens of thousands of people. They are generally local affairs, so keep your ear to the ground to find out about them. Major nationwide events include Independence Day, on 16 September, and the Chinese New Year. Colourful flower festivals and traditional feasts also take place from time to time.

TRANSPORT

INTERNATIONAL AIRPORTS Port Moresby (POM) 11 km from the city.

INTERNAL TRAVEL Cargo/passenger services between some islands. Mountainous and rugged terrain limits roads in the interior. Car hire available in main towns, but driving is not recommended.

RED TAPE

VISAS REQUIRED (UK/US) Required.

VACCINATIONS REQUIRED: See 'Vaccinations required around the world' on page 653.

DRIVING REQUIREMENTS National driving licence.

COUNTRY REPS IN UK/US UK: 14 Waterloo Place, London SW1Y 4AR, tel (020) 7930 0922, fax (020) 7930 0828, email jkekedo@aol.com. USA: 1779 Massachusetts Avenue, Suite 805, NW, Washington, DC 20036, tel(202) 745 3680, fax (202) 745 3679, email info@ pngembassy.org.

UK/US REPS IN COUNTRY UK: Kiroki Street, Port Moresby (Locked Bag 212, Waigani, NCD 131), tel 325 1677, fax 325 3547, email bhcpng@datec.com.pg.

USA: PO Box 1492, Douglas Street, Port Moresby, NCD 121, tel 321 1455, fax 320 0637, email ConsularPortMoresby @state.gov.

PEOPLE AND PLACE

CAPITAL Port Moresby.

LANGUAGE English and Pidgin English.

PEOPLES Mixed race and tribal groups.

RELIGION Indigenous beliefs, Roman Catholic, Protestant, Lutheran, Anglican.

SIZE (SQ KM) 462,840.

POPULATION 5,586,000.

POP DENSITY/KM 12.1.

STATE OF THE NATION

SAFETY Fairly dangerous: Westerners have been kidnapped by tribal protesters for propaganda purposes. High levels of violent crime (including rape), even in cities. Seek latest information at time of visit.

LIFE EXPECTANCY M 62.76, F 67.21.

BEING THERE

ETIQUETTE Business dress is very informal; conventional suits are not necessary. Informality is the order of the day, though while shorts are quite acceptable, beachwear is usually best confined to the beach. Papua New Guinea's culture still includes elements of a tribal lifestyle.

CURRENCY Kina = 100 *toea*.

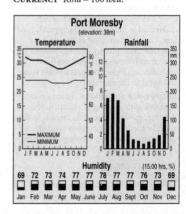

HIGHLIGHTS

SING-SINGS Famed and spectacular shows in the Highlands region. These huge and vibrant occasions can see tens of thousands of people gather, bedecked in *bilas* (finery) - consisting of body paint, striking masks and headdresses of bird-of-paradise feathers. Sing-sings can be held for any number of reasons, but all involve brilliant costumes and lots of singing and dancing.

SEPIK RIVER Take a cruise along this mighty waterway, the longest river in Papua New Guinea and for centuries the principal trade route into the interior. Its waters spill over into oxbow lakes, swamps, lagoons and green backwaters - right up to the point at which it reaches the sea. The villages along its wide banks produce highly-prized examples of primitive art. Many village buildings are ornately carved and built on stilts. Dugout canoe is still the main mode of transport.

MOUNT WILHELM The highest point in Papua New Guinea, at 4,509 metres high. Stand atop the snow-flecked peak on a clear morning and you'll find stunning views towards both the north and south coasts of the world's second-biggest island. Even if you don't make the summit, you'll still enjoy some fine scenery.

WATERSPORTS The reefs teem with underwater life. Snorkel among millions of brightly-coloured fish, or dive in search of giant clams and large marine animals, or among the ghostly remains World War II ship wrecks. Back on the surface, game fishing is popular.

FINANCE American Express is the most widely accepted card. Traveller's cheques are accepted by most shops and hotels.
BUSINESS HOURS 0800-1630 Mon-Friday.
GMT +10.
VOLTAGE GUIDE 240 AC, 50 Hz.
COUNTRY DIALLING CODE 675.

CONSUMING PLEASURES

FOOD & DRINK Traditional dishes are based on root crops such as *taro, kaukau* and yams. A popular dish is *mumu*, a mixture of pork, sweet potatoes, rice and greens. Pigs are baked in earth for feasts. Alcohol available, favourites are Australian and Filipino beers.

SHOPPING & SOUVENIRS Carvings, ceremonial masks and statuettes, *Buka* basketry, bows and arrows, crocodile carvings, pottery.

FIND OUT MORE

WEBSITES www.spto.org, www.tcsp.com, www.pngembassy.org, www.niugini.com, www.britishhighcommission.gov.uk/papuanewguinea, http://portmoresby.usembassy.gov.
LOCAL MEDIA *The National, The Papua New Guinea Post-Courier*, both published in English.
TOURIST BOARDS IN UK/US n/a.

In the Trobriand Islands, yams are more than a staple food: they're a sign of prestige, an indicator of expertise, and a tie between villages and clans. And yes, their size *does* matter

PARAGUAY

WHEN TO GO

WEATHER December to March can be very hot and see the most rainfall. June to September are mild, with few cold days.

FESTIVALS A traditional *fiesta* that includes walking on hot embers, the Verbena de San Juan is held in June. The Expo Feria de la Industria, an arts and crafts folk festival, is held in July. Religious and cultural celebrations are held in August during the Dia de la Virgen de la Asunción. Independence Day falls on 15 May and features parades and dancing.

TRANSPORT

INTERNATIONAL AIRPORTS Asunción (ASU) 16 km from the city.

INTERNAL TRAVEL Some internal flights but often disrupted by weather conditions. Unreliable rail service, with trains running weekly. Roads serving main centres are in good condition, other (unsurfaced) roads may be closed in bad weather. Car hire available.

RED TAPE

VISAS REQUIRED (UK/US) Required by Australian, Canadian and Irish nationals.

VACCINATIONS REQUIRED: See 'Vaccinations required around the world' on page 653.

DRIVING REQUIREMENTS National driving licence or International Driving Permit.

COUNTRY REPS IN UK/US UK: 344 Kensington High Street, 3rd Floor, London W14 8NS, tel (020) 7610 4180, fax (020) 7371 4297, email embapar@btconnect.com. USA: 2400 Massachusetts Avenue, NW, Washington, DC 20008, tel (202) 483 6960, fax (202) 234 4508, email embapar.usa@verizon.net.

UK/US REPS IN COUNTRY UK: n/a. USA: Avenida Mariscal López 1776, Asunción, tel (21) 213 715, fax (21) 213 728, email paraguayusembassy@state.gov.

PEOPLE AND PLACE

CAPITAL Asunción.

LANGUAGE Spanish and Guarani.

PEOPLES Of combined Spanish and native Guarani origin (*Mestizo*), small indigenous Indian minority.

RELIGION Roman Catholic.

SIZE (SQ KM) 406,752.

POPULATION 5,206,101.

POP DENSITY/KM 12.8.

STATE OF THE NATION

SAFETY Volatile.

LIFE EXPECTANCY M 72.35, F 77.55.

BEING THERE

ETIQUETTE Dress is informal. Theatres and cinemas operate a no smoking policy.

CURRENCY *Guarani* (G).

FINANCE Credit cards and traveller's cheques widely accepted.

BUSINESS HOURS 0800-1200, 1500-1730/1900, Monday to Friday.

GMT -4.

VOLTAGE GUIDE 220 AC, 50 Hz.

COUNTRY DIALLING CODE 595.

CONSUMING PLEASURES

FOOD & DRINK Local dishes include *chipas* (maize bread flavoured with egg and cheese), *soo-yosopy* (a soup of cornmeal and ground beef), *albondiga* (meatball soup), *boribori* (diced meat, vegetables and small dumplings mixed with cheese). Good local beef. *Cana*, the national drink, is distilled from sugar cane and honey. *Mosto*, sugar cane juice, is worth a taste, as is the red wine

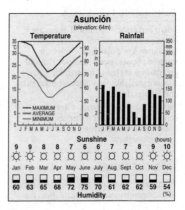

HIGHLIGHTS

ASUNCIÓN The capital lies on an inlet of the Paraguay River, the Bay of Asunción. A variety of architectural styles are found along the waterfront of this colonial Spanish town. With plenty of parks and plazas, a golf course and zoo, there are a number of ways to relax in the city. Tours can be taken from here to the Iguazú Falls, Salto Crystal Falls, the Pilcomayo River, Chaco, and Villeta.

CIUDAD DEL ESTE East of the capital, close to the Brazilian border, is the fastest growing town in the country. This cosmopolitan settlement is a good base for trips to Iguazú Falls and the glorious Monday Falls. A trip can also be taken to the Itaipú Dam, the world's largest hydroelectric complex.

THE CHACO Home to three per cent of the population, these plains and forests cover 61 per cent of Paraguay's landmass. The area contains several national parks, biological reserves and protected forests. The Nacunday forest holds 600 species of bird, 200 different species of mammal, plus numerous reptiles and amphibians. The Chaco is the world's second largest forest, after the Amazonian rainforest.

ACTIVITIES The country has eleven national parks and protected areas for the traveller to visit, abundant in bird and wildlife. Here the Chacoan peccary was recently rediscovered after it had been thought to have become extinct. River trips are a good way to spot flora and fauna, and the journey from Asunción to Concepción on the River Paraguay passes through dramatic landscapes.

and *yerba maté*.

SHOPPING & SOUVENIRS *Nanduti* lace, *aopoi* sports shirts, leather goods, wooden handicrafts, silver *yerba maté* cups, native jewellery.

FIND OUT MORE

WEBSITES www.paraguayembassy.co.uk, http://asuncion.usembassy.gov, www.embassyofparaguay.ca, www.lonelyplanet.com/destinations/south_america/paraguay.

LOCAL MEDIA American newspapers available.

TOURIST BOARDS IN UK/US n/a.

> The Chaco is home to the world's second largest forest, after the Amazon rainforest

PERU

WHEN TO GO

WEATHER Heavy rain in the mountains and jungle from December to April. It never rains in Lima nor on most of the coast.

FESTIVALS Peru celebrates as many as 3,000 festivals each year. Many are held in homage to a patron saint and are part of the Christian calendar, with Easter being a particularly important time. But traditional Inca festivals live on, and the Andean communities still honour Pachamama, the earth goddess, either purely or as a hybrid with their Christian faith. One of the most impressive festivals is Inti Raymi, a spectacular annual ceremony in Cuzco to mark the winter solstice and harvest each June. The central event is acted out on the esplanade below the imposing Inca fortress of Sacsayhuamán on the edge of the city, and the entire city breaks out in festivities lasting for days. Other notable events include Puno Day on 5 November, which features flamboyant costumes and street dancing in the town of Puno, near Lake Titicaca.

TRANSPORT

INTERNATIONAL AIRPORTS Lima (LIM) 16 km from the city, Cuzco (CUZ).

INTERNAL TRAVEL Fairly extensive domestic air network. Peru is home to the highest railroad in the world. Roads are in reasonable condition but affected by landslides in the rainy season.

RED TAPE

VISAS REQUIRED (UK/US) Not required for stays up to 90 days.

VACCINATIONS REQUIRED: See 'Vaccinations required around the world' on page 653.

DRIVING REQUIREMENTS Foreign driving permit or an International Driving Permit.

COUNTRY REPS IN UK/US UK: 52 Sloane Street, London SW1X 9SP, tel (020) 7235 1917, fax (020) 7235 4463, email postmaster@peruembassy-uk.com. USA: 1700 Massachusetts Avenue, NW, Washington, DC 20036, tel (202) 833 9860, fax (202) 659 8124, email webmaster@embassyofperu.us.

UK/US REPS IN COUNTRY UK: Torre Parque Mar, Piso22, Avenida Jose Larco 1301, Miraflores, Lima, tel (1) 617 3000, fax (1) 617 3100, email belima@fco.gov.uk. USA: Avenida La Encalada cuadra 17, Surco, Lima 33, tel (1) 434 3000, fax (1) 618 2397.

PEOPLE AND PLACE

CAPITAL Lima.

LANGUAGE Spanish and Quechua.

PEOPLES Indigenous Indians, *Mestizo*, European.

RELIGION Roman Catholic.

SIZE (SQ KM) 1,285,216.

POPULATION 27,184,101.

POP DENSITY/KM 21.1.

STATE OF THE NATION

SAFETY Relatively safe for travellers. Many reports of petty crime.

LIFE EXPECTANCY M 67.77, F 71.37.

BEING THERE

ETIQUETTE The majority of Peruvians speak Spanish, but many business people also speak English. When leaving Peru, do not take coca leaves or coca tea out of the country, as it is illegal to bring these substances into most countries. Likewise, visitors are not allowed to take any artefacts

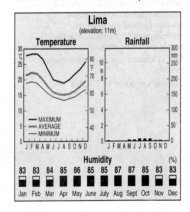

Lima
(elevation: 11m)
Temperature — Rainfall — Humidity (%)

	Jan	Feb	Mar	Apr	May	June	July	Aug	Sept	Oct	Nov	Dec
Humidity	83	83	84	85	86	85	85	87	87	85	83	83

HIGHLIGHTS

MACHU PICCHU
Watch the clouds part for a magical sunrise over a real-life lost city of the Incas, nestled in a crook of the Andes above the sacred river Urubamba. It's the crowning glory of the Inca Trail, a spectacular five-day hike among jagged peaks and Inca ruins, and one of the world's great wonders.

SACSAYHUAMAN
Scale the colossal zigzagging ramparts of this ancient fortress near the former Inca capital, Cuzco. Designed like the teeth of a puma, the site comes alive for the colourful festival of Inti Raymi.

COLCA CANYON
Watch condors float on the early morning thermals, against a backdrop of spectacular scenery in one of the world's steepest and deepest canyons. Sightings are best from the dizzying rocky ledges that rise up more than a kilometre from the river bottom below.

NAZCA LINES Soar high above the arid deserts over Nazca in a light aircraft – the best way to see the mysterious geometric lines, patterns and shapes etched across vast tracts of stony pampa by the ancient inhabitants of the region.

LAKE TITICACA
Sail across the world's highest navigable lake, where indigenous communities still live on islands made from reeds, and the scenery and altitude will leave you totally breathless.

LIMA Charming city, with an old colonial heart. The modern capital, Lima is Peru's commercial and political hub, situated on the coast between the Andean foothills and the Pacific Ocean.

out of the country without the consent of the proper authority

CURRENCY New *sol* (S/.) = 100 *céntimos*.

FINANCE Most credit cards accepted. Changing traveller's cheques can be a slow process outside Lima.

BUSINESS HOURS 0900-1700 Mon-Friday.

GMT -5.

VOLTAGE GUIDE 220 AC, 60 Hz.

COUNTRY DIALLING CODE 51.

CONSUMING PLEASURES

FOOD & DRINK Hot pepper (*aji*) and garlic (*ajo*) flavour most Peruvian food. Typical dishes include *chupe de camarones* (a soup made from shrimps, eggs, cream, potatoes and peppers), *sopa criolla* (spicy soup with beef and noodles) and *anticuchos* (beef or fish marinated in vinegar and spices, then barbecued). A potent brandy-based cocktail, *pisco sour*, is infamous.

SHOPPING & SOUVENIRS Alpaca wool sweaters, alpaca and llama rugs, Indian masks, weaving, jewellery.

FIND OUT MORE

WEBSITES www.peruembassy-uk.com, www.virtualperu.net, www.lonelyplanet.com/destinations/south_america/peru.

LOCAL MEDIA English-language monthly *Lima Times* is available in major hotels and bookstores.

TOURIST BOARDS IN UK/US n/a.

> "Suddenly we found ourselves standing in front of the ruins of two of the finest structures in ancient America. Made of beautiful white granite, the sight held me spellbound."
> *Hiram Bingham, discoverer of Machu Picchu*

PHILIPPINES

WHEN TO GO

WEATHER Rainy from June to September, cool and dry from October to February and hot and mainly dry from March to May.

FESTIVALS Dozens of colourful festivals are celebrated in the Philippines each year. The major Muslim festivals and Catholic feast days in honour of patron saints are particularly important days. Chinese New Year is also a big event. Independence Day, on 12 June, is a national holiday celebrated with military parades. In May, processions take place in honour of the Virgin Mary, with young girls in white dresses decorating the statues of Mary with flowers.

TRANSPORT

INTERNATIONAL AIRPORTS Ninoy Aquino (MNL) 12 km from Manila, Mactan (NOP) on Cebu Island, 45 km from the city.

INTERNAL TRAVEL The local air network and ships connect the islands. Roads on the islands are in variable condition. Car hire available in Manila and major cities.

RED TAPE

VISAS REQUIRED (UK/US) Not required for stays under 21 days.

VACCINATIONS REQUIRED: See 'Vaccinations required around the world' on page 653.

DRIVING REQUIREMENTS International Driving Permit and a national driving licence.

COUNTRY REPS IN UK/US UK: 9a Palace Green, London W8 4QE, tel (020) 7937 1600, fax (020) 7937 2925, email embassy@philemb.org.uk. USA: 1600 Massachusetts Avenue, NW, Washington, DC 20036, tel (202) 467 9300, fax (202) 467 9417, email wdcpe@aol.com.

UK/US REPS IN COUNTRY UK: 15-17 Floors, LV Locsin Building, 6752, Ayala Avenue, Makati 1226, Manila, tel (2) 816 7116, fax (2) 819 7206, email uk@info.com.ph. USA: 1201 Roxas Boulevard, Ermita 1000, Manila, tel (2) 528 6300, fax (2) 522 4361.

PEOPLE AND PLACE

CAPITAL Manila.

LANGUAGE Filipino.

PEOPLES Malay, Indonesian and Polynesian, Chinese, Indian.

RELIGION Roman Catholic (83%), Protestant. Muslim and Buddhist minorities.

SIZE (SQ KM) 300,000.

POPULATION 78,580,000.

POP DENSITY/KM 261.9.

STATE OF THE NATION

SAFETY Highly volatile, due to separatist guerrillas in the south and widespread Christian-Muslim violence. In the recent past tourists have been kidnapped by separatist militias. Seek latest information at time of visit.

LIFE EXPECTANCY M 67.03, F 72.92.

BEING THERE

ETIQUETTE The Philippines are, in many respects, more Westernised than any other Asian country, but there is also a rich stream of Malay culture. In general, casual dress is acceptable in most places, but in Muslim areas the visitor should cover up as an acknowledgement of Islamic custom. Filipino men sometimes wear an embroidered long-sleeved shirt or a plain white *barong tagalog* with black trousers for formal occasions.

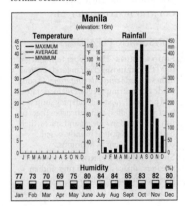

Manila (elevation: 16m) — Temperature / Rainfall / Humidity

	Jan	Feb	Mar	Apr	May	June	July	Aug	Sept	Oct	Nov	Dec
Humidity (%)	77	73	70	69	75	80	84	84	85	83	82	80

HIGHLIGHTS

BORACAY Land by boat on this idyllic white-sand island, for many people a symbol of Pacific island paradise. The beaches are great for snorkelling in the shallows, looking for rare white *puka* shells, or simply lazing around under gently-swaying palms, listening to the soothing crashing of surf on shore.

MANILA Located on the east coast of Luzon, the capital has been a port for hundreds of years. Like many sprawling urban centres, it's a mixture of modern commercial glitz and large slum areas. The oldest part is the Intramuros, or Walled City - some of which remains intact despite fighting here during World War II. Close by are Rizal Park, a popular meeting place, and Chinatown, a throng of stalls and restaurants.

JEEPNEYS Jump on board one of the colourful and iconic Philippine taxis - these days produced locally, but which originally developed from the robust army jeeps left behind by the Americans after World War II. These shining chrome vehicles are brightly decorated with mirrors and figures of horses, and are the most popular method of transport for short journeys - often overflowing with passengers. If you truly fall in love with them, take a tour of the Sarao jeepney factory in Manila.

VIGAN The best preserved Spanish colonial town in the Philippines and birthplace of several national heroes. At dawn, the early morning light makes the city's old buildings especially enchanting.

CURRENCY Philippine *peso* (P) = 100 *centavos*.

FINANCE Credit cards and traveller's cheques accepted in big towns.

BUSINESS HOURS 0800-1200, 1300-1700 Monday-Friday.

GMT +8.

VOLTAGE GUIDE 220 AC, 60 Hz. 110 AC available in most hotels.

COUNTRY DIALLING CODE 63.

CONSUMING PLEASURES

FOOD & DRINK More moderate use of spices than other Asian cooking. Seafood features on most menus, freshly caught and simply served with some lime. *Lechon* (whole roast pig) is served at feasts. *Adobo* (braised pork and chicken in soy sauce, vinegar and garlic) and *relleno* (boned, stuffed chicken or fish) are other specialities. San Miguel is the best-known beer.

SHOPPING & SOUVENIRS *Barong tagalog* (dress shirt in delicate *jusi* material), cigars, Tiffany-style lamps, cloth, brassware, wood-carvings, *papier-maché* horses, silver jewellery, coral trinket boxes, rattan furniture, baskets, antique figurines of saints.

FIND OUT MORE

WEBSITES www.philemb.org.uk, www.wowphilippines.co.uk, www.filipino.com.

LOCAL MEDIA *Manila Times, Manila Bulletin, Philippine Daily Inquirer* and the *Philippine Star* are printed in English.

TOURIST BOARDS IN UK/US UK: 146 Cromwell Road, London SW7 4EF, tel (020) 7835 1100, fax (020) 7835 1926, email info-tourism@wowphilippines.co.uk. US: n/a.

The Philippines is the world's most avid texting-messaging nation. In 2003, the average mobile-phone user sent 2,300 messages

POLAND

WHEN TO GO

WEATHER June to September are warm. Mid-December to April see snow in the south.

FESTIVALS Warsaw hosts a number of music festivals in June and July including the Warsaw Summer Jazz Days, the Mozart Festival, and the 'Warsaw Autumn' Festival of Contemporary Music held in September. Kraków hosts the Summer Jazz Festival in July, and a Corpus Christi Pageant in May or June. Wroclaw stages the Castle Party in July or August as a celebration of dark, independent music.

TRANSPORT

INTERNATIONAL AIRPORTS Warsaw (WAW) 10 km from the city, Kraków (KRK) 14 km from the city, Wroclaw (WRO) 8 km from the city, Katowice (KTW) 34 km from the city.

INTERNAL TRAVEL Cheap, efficient rail network. Roads are in reasonable condition are car hire is available.

RED TAPE

VISAS REQUIRED (UK/US) Required by Australian and Canadian nationals. Not required by UK nationals for stays under 6 months and US nationals for stays under 90 days.

VACCINATIONS REQUIRED: See 'Vaccinations required around the world' on page 653.

DRIVING REQUIREMENTS Visitors with their own cars require their national driving licence and Green Card. An International driving permit is also required.

COUNTRY REPS IN UK/US UK: 73 New Cavendish Street, London W1W 6LS, tel (0870) 774 2800, fax (020) 7323 2320, email polishembassy@polishembassy.org.uk. USA: 2224 Wyoming Avenue, NW, Washington, DC 20008, tel (202) 234 3800, fax (202) 328 2152, email polconsul.dc@ioip.com.

UK/US REPS IN COUNTRY UK: Warsaw Corporate Centre, 2nd Floor, Ul. Emilii Plater 28, 00-688 Warsaw, tel (22) 311 0000, fax (22) 311 0250, email info@britishembassy.pl. USA: Aleje Ujazdowskie 29-31, 00-540 Warsaw, tel (22) 504 2000, fax (22) 504 2688, email publicrw@state.gov.

PEOPLE AND PLACE

CAPITAL Warsaw.

LANGUAGE Polish.

PEOPLES Polish (98%), German, other.

RELIGION Roman Catholic (93%), Eastern Orthodox.

SIZE (SQ KM) 312,685.

POPULATION 38,610,000.

POP DENSITY/KM 122.3.

STATE OF THE NATION

SAFETY Safe.

LIFE EXPECTANCY M 70.3, F 78.76.

BEING THERE

ETIQUETTE The friendly and industrious people are very welcoming of foreigners. Rural peasants maintain their traditional way of life. Respect the Roman Catholic beliefs and customs, as jokes are not appreciated on this subject. Conservative casual dress is the norm. Smoking is restricted.

CURRENCY *Zloty* (Zl) = 100 *groszy*.

FINANCE Credit cards accepted in large establishments, traveller's cheques readily exchanged.

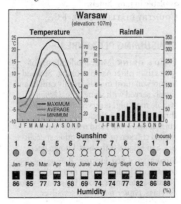

Warsaw (elevation: 107m)											
Sunshine											(hours)
1	2	4	5	6	7	7	7	6	3	1	1
Jan	Feb	Mar	Apr	May	June	July	Aug	Sept	Oct	Nov	Dec
86	85	77	73	68	69	74	74	77	82	86	88
Humidity											(%)

HIGHLIGHTS

WARSAW The capital was largely destroyed by World War II, but following detailed reconstruction the Old Town is again a World Heritage site rebuilt according to original plans. The systematic destruction under Nazi control can be seen in films kept at the Warsaw Historical Museum. The Palace of Culture and Science, an unwanted gift from Josef Stalin, affords spectacular views over the whole city. Lazienki Palace is set in a beautiful park with an open-air Greek theatre and amonument to Frederic Chopin, the Polish composer.

KRAKÓW Largely untouched in World War II, Poland's second largest city has kept its medieval charm. Set in the wooded foothills of the Tatra Mountains, on the southern banks of the River Vistula, it is one of UNESCO's 12 most important historical sites. The largest Market Square in Europe is home to a reconstructed Cloth Hall that houses art and sculpture galleries. Seventy kilometres south of the city is the site of Auschwitz-Birkenau, the Nazi concentration camp where four million people were killed. Today it is a memorial monument.

GDANSK Once known as Danzig, this city has been under constant change. The Order of the Teutonic Knights captured it from the Poles in the fourteenth century, and then lost it to the Prussians. Later occupied by the Germans, it is now recovered and is home to the largest Gothic church in Poland.

BUSINESS HOURS 0800-1600 Mon-Friday.
GMT +1 (+2 in summer).
VOLTAGE GUIDE 220 AC, 50 Hz.
COUNTRY DIALLING CODE 48.

CONSUMING PLEASURES

FOOD & DRINK Dill, marjoram, caraway seeds, wild mushrooms and sour cream are added to many dishes. The national dish is *bigos*, made from *sauerkraut*, fresh cabbage, onions and leftover meat. Pike in aspic, marinated fish in sour cream, and *barszcz* (beetroot soup) are popular starters. Vodka, drunk chilled, is the national drink, and *Wyborowa* is considered to be the best.

SHOPPING & SOUVENIRS Glass and enamelware, handwoven rugs, silverware, handmade jewellery with amber, dolls, woodcarvings.

FIND OUT MORE

WEBSITES www.polishembassy.org.uk, www.polishconsulate.co.uk, www.visit.pl/index.php.
LOCAL MEDIA *The Warsaw Voice* is published weekly in English.

TOURIST BOARDS IN UK/US UK: Level 3, Westec House, West Gate, London W5 1YY, tel (0870) 675 012, fax (0870) 675 011, email info@visitpoland.org. US: 5 Marine View Plaza, Suite 208, Hoboken, New Jersey 07030, tel (201) 420 9910, fax (201) 584 9153, email pntonyc@polandtour.org.

> Poles are proud of their part in the fall of the Soviet Union, when the combination of a Polish Pope and the first recognised trade union in the USSR – Poland's Solidarnosc – created the first cracks in the Communist bloc

PORTUGAL

WHEN TO GO

WEATHER March to October are warm with little rain in the south. The north-west has shorter summers.

FESTIVALS Lisbon hosts most festivals in June for the Santos Populares, on 13, 24, and 29 June. The celebration on 13 June is the largest, and all begin the previous evening. People hit each other over the head in the streets with plastic hammers. City events also run in June as part of the Festas da Lisboa. The Estoril Festival takes place in July and August, and Estoril also hosts a Handicrafts Fair during the same months. A small carnival celebration is held in Lisbon in February or March, while regattas and parades are put on in August as part of the Oceans Festival.

TRANSPORT

INTERNATIONAL AIRPORTS Lisbon (LIS) 7 km from the city, Faro (FAO) 4 km from the city, Oporto (OPO) 11 km from the city.

INTERNAL TRAVEL There is a rail service to every town, and every town and village can be reached by an adequate system of roads. Car hire easily available.

RED TAPE

VISAS REQUIRED (UK/US) Required by Australian nationals.

VACCINATIONS REQUIRED: See 'Vaccinations required around the world' on page 653.

DRIVING REQUIREMENTS International Driving Permit or foreign driving licence, a Green Card must be obtained.

COUNTRY REPS IN UK/US UK: 11 Belgrave Square, London SW1X 8PP, tel (020) 7235 5331, fax (020) 7235 0739, email london@portembassy.co.uk. USA: 2012 Massachussetts Avenue, NW, Washington, DC 20008, tel (202) 328 8610, fax (202) 462 3726, email embportwash@attglobal.net.

UK/US REPS IN COUNTRY UK: 33 Rue de São Bernardo, 1249-082, Lisbon, tel 2139 24000, fax 2139 24185, email ppalisbon@ fco.gov.uk. USA: Avenida das Forças Ar-

madas, Sete Rios 1600-081 Lisbon, tel 2172 73300, fax 2172 69109, email conslisbon@state.gov.

PEOPLE AND PLACE

CAPITAL Lisbon.

LANGUAGE Portuguese.

PEOPLES Portuguese (99%), African.

RELIGION Roman Catholic (97%).

SIZE (SQ KM) 92,345.

POPULATION 10,407,000.

POP DENSITY/KM 112.7.

STATE OF THE NATION

SAFETY Safe.

LIFE EXPECTANCY M 74.25, F 81.03.

BEING THERE

ETIQUETTE A leisurely way of life, coupled with old-fashioned politeness. A unique national character combines with individual traditions for each province. Beachwear is only suitable at the beach. Smoke in restaurants only at the end of a meal.

CURRENCY Euro (€) = 100 *cents*.

FINANCE Credit cards and traveller's cheques widely accepted.

BUSINESS HOURS 0900-1300, 1500-1900 Monday-Friday.

GMT +1 (+2 in summer).

VOLTAGE GUIDE 220 AC, 50 Hz.

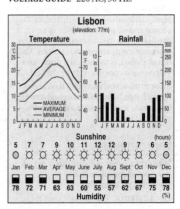

HIGHLIGHTS

LISBON The likeable capital is a relaxed port, overlooked by a ruined castled. Whitewashed, cobbled streets form a labyrinth upon a hill, populated by fantastic architecture, and Art Nouveau shops and cafes. A statue of Christ stands by the river, arms outstretched, surveying the grand suspension bridge and river ferries. Travellers should visit the Mosteiro dos Jerónimos, the Manueline complex that houses the tomb of Vasco da Gama, and the Gulbenkian Museum, home to a superb art collection.

PORTO At the mouth of the Douro River, this atmospheric city of tangled tiers reaching up from the river's north bank has more to offer than simply its port-producing suburb of Vila Nova de Gaia. Spectacular bridges span the wide river, contemporary art is on display at the Fundação de Serralves, and the old town bustles beside its riverbanks.

ESTREMADURA AND RIBATEJO Just north of Lisbon, these regions are home to a number of delights. Surfers should head to the Atlantic rollers at Enceira, those interested in religion should visit Alcobaça's twelfth-century monastery and Fátima's famous shrine, while geologists will want to explore the Grutas de Mira de Aire - a vast and extraordinary cave system.

THE ALGARVE Long sandy beaches have brought mass tourist development to the area. The charms of the area may be overwhelmed, so it's best to skip the high season and the area from Faro to Albufeira.

COUNTRY DIALLING CODE 351.

CONSUMING PLEASURES

FOOD & DRINK Seafood features strongly. Many soups are main dishes, including *sopa de marisco* (shellfish soup cooked and served with wine) and *caldo verde* (green soup with kale leaves). Other specialities are *caldeirada*, a stew with several types of fish, and *carne de porco á Alentejana*, pork covered with clam and tomato sauce. Portuguese wine improved considerably over last decade. Brandies are also good.

SHOPPING & SOUVENIRS Leather goods copper, ceramics, embroidery and tapestry, cork products, porcelain and china, crystal and glassware.

FIND OUT MORE

WEBSITES www.visitportugal.com, www.uk-embassy.pt, www.portugal.org, www.american-embassy.pt, www.portugalvirtual.pt/tourism/algarve, www.drtacores.pt, www.madeiratourism.org.

LOCAL MEDIA *Anglo Porruguese News* (Lisbon) and *The News* (Algarve) are the two English-language newspapers.

TOURIST BOARDS IN UK/US UK: As for Country Reps in UK, tel (0845) 3551 2112, fax (020) 7201 6633, email icep.london@icep.pt. US: 590 Fifth Avenue, 4th Floor, New York, NY 10036, tel (212) 723 0200, fax (212) 764 6137, email tourism@portugal.org.

> Portugal boasts its own version of the blues: *fado*, the bitter-sweet music of Lisbon's old docks, brimful of the sadness of partings and departings

QATAR

WHEN TO GO

WEATHER Summer (June to September) is very hot, spring and autumn are warm and pleasant.

FESTIVALS Qatar observes the five feasts and festivals common all over the Muslim world. Ramadan, the month of fasting, is a particularly significant time. The dates of these events vary according to the Islamic calendar. The country's Independence Day takes place on 3 September.

TRANSPORT

INTERNATIONAL AIRPORTS Doha (DOH) 8 km from the city.

INTERNAL TRAVEL Reasonable road system but conditions deteriorate during wet weather. No buses, but there are taxis.

RED TAPE

VISAS REQUIRED (UK/US) Required.

VACCINATIONS REQUIRED: See 'Vaccinations required around the world' on page 653.

DRIVING REQUIREMENTS International Driving Permit. A temporary licence can be obtained on presentation of a UK licence.

COUNTRY REPS IN UK/US UK: 1 South Audley Street, London W1K 1NB, tel (020) 7493 2200, fax (020) 7493 2661. USA: 4200 Wisconsin Avenue, Suite 200, NW, Washington DC 20016, tel (202) 274 1600, fax (202) 237 0061, email info@qatarembassy.org.

UK/US REPS IN COUNTRY UK: PO Box 3, AKC Building, Al Saad Street, Doha, tel 485 7777, fax 443 8692, email bembcomm@qatar.net.qa. USA: PO Box 2399, Doha, tel 488 4101, fax 488 4298, email consulardoha@state.gov.

PEOPLE AND PLACE

CAPITAL Doha.

LANGUAGE Arabic.

PEOPLES Arab, Indian, Pakistani, Iranian.

RELIGION Sunni Islam.

SIZE (SQ KM) 11,437.

POPULATION 618,000.

POP DENSITY/KM 54.

STATE OF THE NATION

SAFETY Safe.

LIFE EXPECTANCY M 71.15, F 76.32.

BEING THERE

ETIQUETTE While Qatar's official language is Arabic, English is widely understood, due to the country's status as a British protectorate from 1917 until 1971. Islam is the official religion, but is less strictly enforced than in Saudi Arabia. Even so, visitors should respect Muslim religious laws and customs and women should always dress modestly. At business and social functions, traditional Qatari coffee will be served in tiny handleless cups. This is a ritual with strict rules: guests are served in order of seniority – a few drops at first, then, after three or four others have been served, the server returns to fill the first cup. Always hold the cup in the right hand. Two cups are polite, but never take only one or more than three.

CURRENCY Qatari *riyal* (QR) = 100 *dirhams*.

FINANCE Credit cards and traveller's cheques widely accepted.

BUSINESS HOURS 0730-1230, 1430-1800 Saturday to Thursday.

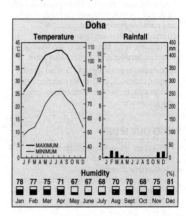

HIGHLIGHTS

CAMEL RACING
While the national sport is football, there are several camel racing tracks, offering a fun four-legged spectacle. The main racetrack is at Shahaniya, about 30 kilometres west of Doha. Rather like an Arabian version of Newmarket or Newbury, the town is given over to the training and breeding of racing camels. The races take place during the cooler months, and spectators follow the camels in 4x4 vehicles, as they canter around the 18-kilometre circuit. Up to 250 camels take part, with big money and prestige at stake. However, travellers should be aware that child jockeys are often badly treated.

DOHA It may not have the glamour and the allure of some of the other big cities in the region, but Doha has a certain innocent charm of its own. The Corniche and the *souks* are the heart of the city, while at night the Downtown area is a throng of people eating, shopping or just hanging out. Daytime activities include strolling around the city's fine museums and lawned gardens. Doha also has several marinas, sub-aqua clubs and some good sailing facilities.

KHOR AL-ADAID
Dubbed the 'inland sea' by tour operators, this tidal lake can only be reached by 4WD. The area is known for its beauty and the surrounding dunes are very Lawrence of Arabia. A tranquil night spent among the sands under the brightly-shining stars is another highlight.

ZUBARAH FORT
Impressive restored fortress, which also houses a museum. The town was the historic stronghold of the al-Khalifa, the ruling family of Bahrain.

GMT +3.

VOLTAGE GUIDE 240/415 AC, 50 Hz

COUNTRY DIALLING CODE 974.

CONSUMING PLEASURES

FOOD & DRINK Curries, *biryanis*, kebabs, *shawarma* (Middle Eastern equivalent of the Turkish doner kebab) and *falafel* are widely available. Alcohol is prohibited and should not be consumed in public. Some international hotels do serve alcohol.

SHOPPING & SOUVENIRS Luxury goods available from malls, *souks* stock local crafts.

FIND OUT MORE

WEBSITES www.experienceqatar.com, www.qatarembassy.net, http://qatar.usembassy.gov, www.qatar-info.com.

LOCAL MEDIA The *Gulf Times* and *The Peninsula* are the main English-language newspapers.

TOURIST BOARDS IN UK/US
UK: Kennedy House, 115 Hammersmith Road, London W14 0QH, tel (020) 7371 1571, fax (020) 7603 2424, email uk@experiencqatar.com. US: n/a.

Weaving is an important art form. Using tools made from wood or gazelle horns, weavers work with sheep, goat and camel wool to create rugs, tents and cushions in traditional styles

ROMANIA

WHEN TO GO

WEATHER May to October. The rest of the year can be bitterly cold, with snow.

FESTIVALS The religious and agricultural calendars play a central part in Romanian life. In the summer, large fairs provide the chance to trade, feast and dance. Sighisoara, or Medieval Days, is a two-week medieval arts, crafts and music festival in August. In the same month the fair at Prislop Pass is a dance festival with local food and drink.

TRANSPORT

INTERNATIONAL AIRPORTS Bucharest (BUH) 16 km from the city.

INTERNAL TRAVEL Efficient and cheap rail network. Road network needs some upgrading.

RED TAPE

VISAS REQUIRED (UK/US) Not required by US nationals for stays of up to 30 days, required by others.

VACCINATIONS REQUIRED: See 'Vaccinations required around the world' on page 653.

DRIVING REQUIREMENTS International Driving Permit or national driving licence an d Green Card insurance.

COUNTRY REPS IN UK/US UK: Arundel House, 4 Palace Green, London W8 4QD, tel (020) 7937 9666, fax (020) 7937 8069, email roemb@copperstream.co.uk. USA: 1607 23rd Street, NW, Washington, DC 20008, tel (202) 332 4747, fax (202) 232 4748, email info@roembus.org.

UK/US REPS IN COUNTRY UK: Strada Jules Michelet 24, Sector 1, 010463 Bucharest, tel (21) 201 7200, fax (21) 201 7317, email Consular.Bucharest@ fco.gov.uk. USA: Strada Tudor Arghezi 7-9, Sector 2, Bucharest 70132, tel (21) 210 4042, fax (21) 210 0395, email infobuch@usia.gov.

PEOPLE AND PLACE

CAPITAL Bucharest.

LANGUAGE Romanian.

PEOPLES Romanian (89%), Magyar, Romany.

RELIGION Romanian Orthodox (89%), other Christian denominations.

SIZE (SQ KM) 238,391.

POPULATION 21,680,974.

POP DENSITY/KM 90.9.

STATE OF THE NATION

SAFETY Bad reputation for petty crime, particularly bogus policemen.

LIFE EXPECTANCY M 67.86, F 75.06.

BEING THERE

ETIQUETTE Handshaking is the most common form of greeting, but it is also customary for men to kiss a woman's hand when being introduced. Visitors should be aware that smoking is prohibited on public transport, in cinemas and theatres. However, many Romanians are smokers and gifts of Western cigarettes are greatly appreciated.

CURRENCY *Leu* = 1,000 *bani*.

FINANCE Limited acceptance of credit cards and traveller's cheques.

BUSINESS HOURS 0800-1600 Mon-Friday.

GMT +2 (+3 in summer).

VOLTAGE GUIDE 220 AC, 50 Hz.

COUNTRY DIALLING CODE 40.

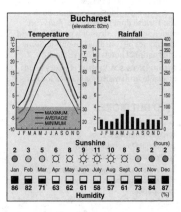

HIGHLIGHTS

DRACULA'S CASTLE Relive the tales of Bram Stoker in the narrow passages and secret stairwells of this mock-Gothic castle in the small town of Bran, with historic links to Vlad the Impaler. Perhaps a bit clichéd, but no trip to Romania would be complete without a passing reference to the blood-sucking count, even if the real-life Dracula is unlikely to have ever lived here.

BUCHAREST One of Eastern Europe's best-kept secrets. Soak up the new optimism in a city once called 'the Paris of the East', now recovering from the effects of earthquakes, World War II bombing and the Ceauses-cus, and dominated by the imposing 3,100-room Palace of Parliament - built by the dictator Ceausescu by bulldozing 7,000 homes and 26 churches, and intended to be the largest building in the world. It is actually the second - beaten by the Pentagon in America.

DANUBE DELTA Unpack your binoculars and head to this protected wetland area of lily-covered lakes and shifting sand dunes, south of the Ukrainian border, a magnet for birds that is best explored in a traditional wooden kayak or a rowing boat, with a local fisherman.

FAGARAS MOUNTAINS Good hiking on the well-marked trails of this wildlife-filled stretch of the Carpathians, a landscape dotted with glacial lakes.

SOUTHERN BUCOVINA Wonderful painted churches near the town of Suceava.

CONSUMING PLEASURES

FOOD & DRINK Hearty and rich. Typical dishes include *ciorba de perisoare* (soup with meatballs), *ciorba tananeasca* (meat with vegetables) and *sarmale* (pork balls in cabbage leaves). Plum brandy, or *tuica*, is served as an entrée. Wines are good.

SHOPPING & SOUVENIRS Embroidery, pottery, porcelain, silverware, carpets, fabrics, wool jumpers, wood carvings, rugs.

FIND OUT MORE

WEBSITES www.roemb.co.uk, www.romaniatourism.com, www.visitromania.com, www.roembus.org.

LOCAL MEDIA *Nine O'Clock, Romanian Economic Daily,* and *Bucharest Business Week* are printed in English.

TOURIST BOARDS IN UK/US UK: 22 New Cavendish Street, London W1M 7LH, tel (020) 7224 3692, fax (020) 7935 6435, email infouk@romaniatourism.com. US: 355 Lexington Avenue, 19th Floor, New York, NY 10017, tel (212) 545 8484, fax (212) 251 0429, email infous@romaniatourism.com.

> " Every known superstition in the world is gathered into the horseshoe of the Carpathians, as if it were the centre of some imaginative whirlpool."
>
> *Bram Stoker, in Dracula, 1897*

RUSSIAN FEDERATION

WHEN TO GO

WEATHER Warm summers (June to August), freezing winters.

FESTIVALS An International Folklore Festival is held in Moscow between August and December. The Russian Winter Festival held over the 12 days of Christmas is hosted in Moscow's Izmailovo Park with folk games, dancing, and sleigh rides. The Malenitsa Festival is held throughout February and March in Moscow to celebrate the coming of spring and advance of Lent. St Petersburg celebrates the founding of the city on 27 May for City Day. The summer solstice there is marked with The White Nights, a period of all-night parties as the sun barely dips below the horizon, leaving a magical grey-white night sky.

TRANSPORT

INTERNATIONAL AIRPORTS Moscow (SVO) 35 km from the city, St Petersburg (LED) 17 km from the city.

INTERNAL TRAVEL Some domestic flights. River transport is popular. The rail network is vital as the road system is poor. Self-drive and chauffeured car hire is available.

RED TAPE

VISAS REQUIRED (UK/US) Required.

VACCINATION S REQUIRED: See 'Vaccinations required around the world' on page 653.

DRIVING REQUIREMENTS International or national driving licence with authorised translation acceptable for car-hire.

COUNTRY REPS IN UK/US UK: 13 Kensington Palace Gardens, London W8 4QX, tel (020) 7229 2666, fax (020) 7229 3215, email info@rusemblon.org. USA: 2650 Wisconsin Avenue, NW, Washington, DC 20007, tel (202) 298 5700, fax (202) 298 5735,email russianembassy@ mindspring.com.

UK/US REPS IN COUNTRY
UK: Smolenskaya Naberezhnaya 10, Moscow 121099, tel (095) 956 7200, fax (095) 956 7201, email moscow@ britishembassy.ru. USA: Novinskiy Bulvar 19/23, 121099 Moscow, tel (095) 728 5000, fax (095) 728 5112, email consulmo@ state.gov.

PEOPLE AND PLACE

CAPITAL Moscow.

LANGUAGE Russian.

PEOPLES Russian (82%), Tatar, Ukrainian, Chuvash.

RELIGION Russian Orthodox (75%).

SIZE (SQ KM) 17,075,400.

POPULATION 144,800,000.

POP DENSITY/KM 8.5.

STATE OF THE NATION

SAFETY Safer than a few years ago, but can be unsafe in city centres. High levels of theft and alcoholism. Strong presence of the so-called 'Russian mafia'. Avoid areas in the Caucasus (e.g. Grozny, Ingushetia) affected by separatist conflicts and kidnapping.

LIFE EXPECTANCY M 60.55, F 74.04.

BEING THERE

ETIQUETTE Dress conservatively, but consider the weather. Avoid displays of wealth and keep expensive items hidden. Gifts are welcomed. Normal social courtesies apply.

CURRENCY *Rouble* (Rbl) = 100 *kopeks*.

FINANCE Credit cards accepted in cities,

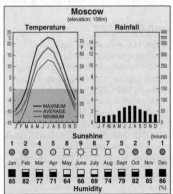

HIGHLIGHTS

MOSCOW The capital's focus is Red Square and the Kremlin. The area still emits a strong Cold War atmosphere. Nostalgic communists should visit Lenin's Mausoleum. Take in a show at the Bolshoi theatre, the location for the premiere of Tchaikovsky's unsuccessful *Swan Lake*, or break into your savings to stay at the spectacular, art nouveau Metropole Hotel.

ST PETERSBURG The exquisite architecture that makes the city one of the most beautiful anywhere on the planet masks the fact that the city was founded on a mosquito-infested swamp. Europe's fourth largest city is one of the most culturally significant too, as the birthplace of Dostoyevsky, Shostakovich, and the Russian Revolution. Head first to Palace Square to wonder at the Winter Palace and browse the Hermitage's fabulous art collection.

THE GOLDEN RING The area north-east of Moscow is famed for its ancient towns, including Suzdal, with great historical, architectural and spiritual significance. Several are on rivers, and river cruises are a great way to see this area.

SIBERIA Covering 12,800,000 sq km, it is a vast stretch of marshy forest and plain. 'Sleeping land', as it translates, contains a million lakes and over 50,000 rivers. Though below freezing in winter, a visit in summer is fascinating.

cash is preferred to traveller's cheques.

BUSINESS HOURS 0900-1800 Mon-Friday.

GMT from +3 to +12.

VOLTAGE GUIDE 220 AC, 50 Hz.

COUNTRY DIALLING CODE 7 (Do not omit 0 in area code).

CONSUMING PLEASURES

FOOD & DRINK Varies from region to region, but national favourites include *borsch* (beetroot soup with sour cream), *blinis* (small buckwheat pancakes) with sour cream and caviar or smoked salmon, and beef stroganoff. *Pirozhky* (filled rolls like ravioli) and *pelmeni*, (dumplings) are popular. Although vodka is the drink to drink, local champagne is cheap and surprisingly good, although a little sweet.

SHOPPING & SOUVENIRS Watches, cameras, furs, ceramics, glass, jewellery, toys, Matryoshka dolls (dolls within dolls), *khokhloma* wooden cups, pottery figurines, Fabergé-style eggs, ex-Soviet paraphernalia.

FIND OUT MORE

WEBSITES www.visitrussia.org.uk, www.rusemblon.org, www.russia.com, www.intouristuk.com, www.spb.ru/eng, www.britemb.msk.ru, www.russia-travel.com, www.usembassy.ru, www.russianembassy.org, www.themoscowtimes.com/travel.

LOCAL MEDIA The *Moscow Times*, and the *St Petersburg Times* are printed in English. There is also *Russia Today*, a daily paper, at www.russiatoday.com.

TOURIST BOARDS IN UK/US UK: 70 Piccadilly, London W1J 8HP, tel (020) 7495 7555, fax (020) 7495 8555, email info@visitrussia.org.uk. US: 130 West 42nd Street, Suite 412, New York, NY 10036, tel (212) 575 3431, fax (212) 575 3434, email info@rnto.org.

The Trans-Siberian Railway is the world's longest continuous railway, crossing an area larger than Western Europe, past arctic waste, tundra, and steppe

RWANDA

WHEN TO GO

WEATHER Warm all year throughout the country, cooler in the mountains. The rainy seasons occur from mid-January to April and mid-October to mid-December.

FESTIVALS Easter, Christmas and New Year are all celebrated as national holidays. Other annual public holidays include Democracy Day, on 28 January; Independence Day, on 1 July; and Republic Day, on 25 September. Genocide Memorial Day, on 7 April, is a particularly emotive occasion, commemorating the savage massacres of 1994, from which the nation is still recovering.

TRANSPORT

INTERNATIONAL AIRPORTS Kigali (KGL) 12 km from the city.

INTERNAL TRAVEL Sparse road network, many roads in bad condition. Driving is not recommended and visitors are advised to exercise caution.

RED TAPE

VISAS REQUIRED (UK/US) Required.

VACCINATIONS REQUIRED: See 'Vaccinations required around the world' on page 653.

DRIVING REQUIREMENTS International Driving Permit.

COUNTRY REPS IN UK/US UK: 120-22 Seymor Place, London W1H 1NR, tel (020) 7224 9832, fax (020) 7724 8642, email uk@ambarwanda.org.uk. USA: 1714 New Hampshire Avenue, NW, Washington, DC 20009, tel (202) 232 2882, fax (202) 232 4544, email rwandemb@rwandemb.org.

UK/US REPS IN COUNTRY UK: Parcelle No 1131, Boulevard de l'Umuganda, Kacyiru-Sud, Kigali, tel 584 098, fax 585 771, email embassy.kigali@fco.gov.uk. USA: 377 Boulevard de la Révolution, Kigali, tel 505 601-3, fax 572 128, email consularkigali@state.gov.

PEOPLE AND PLACE

CAPITAL Kigali.

LANGUAGE Kinyarwanda, French, Kiswahili.

PEOPLES Hutu (90%), Tutsi (8%), Twa.

RELIGION Animist (50%), Christian denominations and an Islamic minority.

SIZE (SQ KM) 26,338.

POPULATION 8,272,000.

POP DENSITY/KM 314.1.

STATE OF THE NATION

SAFETY Many reports that travel is now safe and easy. Potentially volatile in all border areas.

LIFE EXPECTANCY M 45.92, F 48.03.

BEING THERE

ETIQUETTE The traditional way of life is based on agriculture and cattle. Kinyarwanda is the language most widely spoken, while English and French are also spoken. Two-thirds of the population is Christian, however tribal religious beliefs are also widely held. The majority of the population belong to the Hutu tribe. There is a significant Tutsi minority (15 per cent) and a smaller minority of Twa, a pygmy group believed to be the country's first inhabitants. Be aware that anyone aged over 12 will have been affected by the terrible events of 1994, and sensitivities remain.

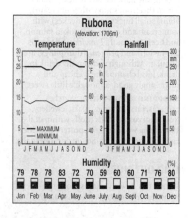

Rubona
(elevation: 1706m)

	Jan	Feb	Mar	Apr	May	June	July	Aug	Sept	Oct	Nov	Dec
Humidity (%)	79	78	78	83	72	70	59	60	60	71	76	80

HIGHLIGHTS

NYUNGWE NATIONAL PARK
Trek through this dense tropical rainforest, one of the oldest in Africa, in search of huge troops of colubus monkeys and other wildlife.

PARC DES VOLCANS
One of the last sanctuaries of the mountain gorilla - there are believed to be no more than 700 left in the world today. The primates live among the forests of this volcanic mountain region, known as the place where American primatologist Dian Fossey undertook her pioneering studies of mountain gorilla behaviour. Her life was recounted in the movie *Gorillas in the Mist*, filmed in the park. The fact that there are any of the gorillas left at all is largely down to Fossey's dedication to curtail poaching, before her brutal and still-unsolved murder, possibly at the hands of poachers. Today, military personnel guard the reserve to keep out poachers and protect visitors. The range's six extinct and three still-active volcanoes are popular with climbers, but the real draw remains the mountain gorillas.

KIGALI Check out the nightlife in Rwanda's capital and commercial centre. It's clean and - these days - peaceful, but doesn't have too many tourist sights. It does, however, make a good base from which to explore the rest of the country.

A'KAGERA NATIONAL PARK
Take a safari in this park devoted to preserving native game. It is home to lions, zebras, antelopes, hippos, buffalo, leopards, giraffes, elephants and various bird species.

CURRENCY Rwanda *franc* = 100 *centimes*.

FINANCE Credit cards and traveller's cheques rarely accepted.

BUSINESS HOURS 0800-1230, 1300-1700 Monday-Friday.

GMT +2.

VOLTAGE GUIDE 220 AC, 50 Hz.

COUNTRY DIALLING CODE 250.

CONSUMING PLEASURES

FOOD & DRINK Maize meal eaten with a sauce of meat gravy or vegetables is a staple. *Brochettes* are available at street stalls and some restaurants serve Franco-Belgian cuisine. Good selection of wines, beers, and spirits.

SHOPPING & SOUVENIRS Woven baskets, clay statuettes, masks, charms. If you see gorilla skulls or hands report the trader to the police.

FIND OUT MORE

WEBSITES www.ambarwanda.org.uk, www.britishembassykigali.org.rw, www.rwandemb.org, www.lonelyplanet.com/destinations/africa/rwanda, http://usembkigali.net, www.africaguide.com/country/rwanda.

LOCAL MEDIA The English-language press is growing.

TOURIST BOARDS IN UK/US n/a.

Rwanda's Nyungwe National Park is home to 13 species of primate, some 25 per cent of the total number in Africa

ST KITTS & NEVIS

WHEN TO GO

WEATHER Driest from January to April, there is increased rainfall from May to October and towards the end of the year. Violent tropical hurricanes are most likely between August and October.

FESTIVALS The week-long Christmas celebration is full of parades, calypso competitions, floats and house parties. It is the most popular event and visitors are more than welcome to join in. Culturama, on 3 August, is Nevis' premier festival and celebrates the emancipation of slaves in the 1830s. It is a seven-day focus on their art and culture. Other events in the year include St Kitts Cricket Festival, St Kitts Football Festival and Oceanfest, in October, which involves music, sunfish racing, dancing, a fishing tournament and lots of food.

TRANSPORT

INTERNATIONAL AIRPORTS St Kitts (SKB) 3.2 km from Basseterre on St Kitts.

INTERNAL TRAVEL Ferries between St Kitts and Nevis, and a good road network on both islands. Cars and mopeds available for hire. Unscheduled, regular, bus service. Taxis on both islands.

RED TAPE

VISAS REQUIRED (UK/US) None.

VACCINATIONS REQUIRED: See 'Vaccinations required around the world' on page 653.

DRIVING REQUIREMENTS Local Temporary Driver's Licence.

COUNTRY REPS IN UK/US UK: 2nd Floor, 10 Kensington Court, London W8 5DL, tel (020) 7460 6500, fax (020) 7460 6505, email sknhighcomm@aol.com. USA: 3216 New Mexico Avenue, NW, Washington, DC 20016, tel (202) 686 2636, fax (202) 686 5740, email info@embskn.com.

UK/US REPS IN COUNTRY UK: PO Box 559, Basseterre, St Kitts, tel 466 8888, fax 466 8889. The British High Commission in St John's (see Antigua) deals with enquiries relating to St Kitts & Nevis also. USA: n/a.

PEOPLE AND PLACE

CAPITAL Basseterre.

LANGUAGE English.

PEOPLES African descent and of mixed-race origin.

RELIGION Christian denominations.

SIZE (SQ KM) 269.

POPULATION 45,841.

POP DENSITY/KM 170.2.

STATE OF THE NATION

SAFETY Safe.

LIFE EXPECTANCY M 69.31, F 75.16.

BEING THERE

ETIQUETTE The islanders' way of life is relatively untouched by the outside world and they maintain the traditions of calypso dancing and music. However, visitors are warmly welcomed. Dress is informal, though beachwear is not appropriate for towns, shops or restaurants. A lightweight suit and tie are recommended for more formal occasions.

CURRENCY Eastern Caribbean dollar (EC$) = 100 cents.

FINANCE Major credit cards and traveller's cheques widely accepted.

BUSINESS HOURS 0800-1200, 1300-1600 Monday to Friday.

GMT -4.

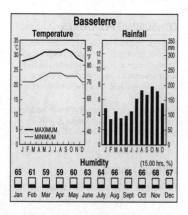

Basseterre

Temperature — Rainfall

	Jan	Feb	Mar	Apr	May	June	July	Aug	Sept	Oct	Nov	Dec
Humidity (15.00 hrs, %)	65	61	59	59	60	63	64	66	66	66	68	67

HIGHLIGHTS

ST KITTS Officially known as St Christopher, the island is made up of three groups of volcanic peaks split by deep ravines. The rolling landscapes and tropical woodland compete with papaya, avocado, mango and banana plantations. The capital, Basseterre, is located on the west coast. Its architecture is a mix of its colonial past. Sadly many buildings were lost in a fire that swept through the city in1867. Frigate Bay, located three miles south of Basseterre, is the island's main beach resort with two beaches, North Frigate Bay and Frigate Bay Beach. Driving north along the Circle Island Road can take just half a day, but it's worth having a stop-over at a plantation inn. Brimstone Hill Fortress is one of the New World's most impressive forts, overlooking the sugar mill plains and the islands of Saba and St Eustatius. The Mount Liamuiga volcanic crater is located in the remote sout-eastern peninsula - here you might spot a vervet monkey or two.

NEVIS The 'Queen of the Caribbean' is dotted with old colonial ruins destroyed by a tidal wave and earthquakes, but is today full of exclusive resorts and spas - a centre for elegance. Charlestown, its capital, is beautifully preserved. Gingerbread houses, weathered in the sea breeze, are covered in beautiful bougainvillaea. Many old plantation houses have been turned into excellent hotels. The silver sand at Pinney's Beach is great for sunbathing, but for views towards St Kitts head for Black Sand Beach or Hurricane Hill.

VOLTAGE GUIDE 230 AC, 60 Hz (110 AC in some hotels).

COUNTRY DIALLING CODE 1 869.

CONSUMING PLEASURES

FOOD & DRINK Local dishes include roast suckling pig, spiny lobster, crab back and curries. Conch, turtle stew, and rice and peas are available in locals' restaurants. *CSR*, a locally produced cane spirit, is excellent.

SHOPPING & SOUVENIRS Carvings, batik, wall hangings, leather art, coconut work.

FIND OUT MORE

WEBSITES www.stkitts-tourism.com, www.doitcaribbean.com, www.stkittsnevis.org, www.geographia.com/stkitts-nevis.

LOCAL MEDIA The *Democrat* (weekly), *The St Kitts and Nevis Observer* (weekly), *The Labour* (twice weekly), all in English.

TOURIST BOARDS IN UK/US UK: As for Country Reps in UK, tel (020) 7376 0881, fax (020) 7973 6742, email uk-europe.office@ stkittstourism.kn. Also Caribbean Tourism Organisation, 22 The Quadrant, Richmond, Surrey, TW9 1BP, tel (020) 8948 0057, fax (020) 8948 0067, email ctolondon@carib-tourism.com. US: 414 East 75th Street, Suite 5, 5th Floor, New York, NY 10021, tel (212) 535 1234, fax (212) 734 6511, email nyoffice@ stkittstourism.kn.

The most commonly seen wild animal is the mongoose. It was introduced by plantation owners to control the rats in their cane fields – but these two creatures rarely meet, because mongooses like to hunt during the day, when rats like to sleep

ST LUCIA

WHEN TO GO

WEATHER Driest from January to April.

FESTIVALS Throughout the year St Lucia is home to many events from calypso celebrations and street parties to the beginning of the cricket season. All are bathed in colour with music, dancing and feasting. The main festivals are the Carnival in February and the Jazz Festival in May, the latter attracting some of the world's finest jazz artists.

TRANSPORT

INTERNATIONAL AIRPORTS George F L Charles (SLU) 3 km from Castries, Hewanorra (UVF) 67 km from Castries.

INTERNAL TRAVEL All major centres served by a reasonably good road network. Car-hire, buses, and taxis available.

RED TAPE

VISAS REQUIRED (UK/US) Not required for Australian nationals, not required by others for stays of up to 42 days.

VACCINATIONS REQUIRED: See 'Vaccinations required around the world' on page 653.

DRIVING REQUIREMENTS A local licence will be issued on presentation of a national driving licence or International Driving Permit.

COUNTRY REPS IN UK/US UK: 1 Collingham Gardens, London SW5 0HW, tel (020) 7370 7123, fax (020) 7370 1905. USA: 3216 New Mexico Avenue, NW, Washington, DC 20016, tel (202) 364 6792, fax (202) 364 6723, email eofsaintlu@aol.com.

UK/US REPS IN COUNTRY UK: PO Box 227, Francis Compton Building, Waterfront, Castries, tel 452 2484, fax 453 1543, email britishhc@candw.lc. USA: The American Embassy in Bridgetown (see Barbados) deals with enquiries relating to St Lucia.

PEOPLE AND PLACE

CAPITAL Castries.

LANGUAGE English.

PEOPLES Mixed race of African, Carib Indian and European descent.

RELIGION Roman Catholic.

SIZE (SQ KM) 616.3.

POPULATION 155,996.

POP DENSITY/KM 253.1.

STATE OF THE NATION

SAFETY Safe.

LIFE EXPECTANCY M 70.05, F 77.42.

BEING THERE

ETIQUETTE The people are very hospitable and encourage visitors to enjoy their lifestyle. It is mainly a West Indian style of life, though some French influences still remain. Casual wear is acceptable, but some restaurants and hotels encourage you to dress for dinner. Beachwear should not be worn in the towns.

CURRENCY Eastern Caribbean dollar (EC$) = 100 cents.

FINANCE Credit cards and traveller's cheques widely accepted.

BUSINESS HOURS 0800-1600 Mon-Friday.

GMT -4.

VOLTAGE GUIDE 220 AC, 50 Hz.

COUNTRY DIALLING CODE 1 758.

CONSUMING PLEASURES

FOOD & DRINK West Indian and Creole

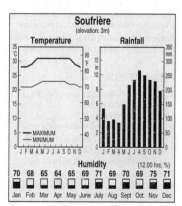

Soufrière
(elevation: 3m)

Temperature   Rainfall

— MAXIMUM
— MINIMUM

Humidity   (12.00 hrs, %)

Jan	Feb	Mar	Apr	May	June	July	Aug	Sept	Oct	Nov	Dec
70	68	65	64	65	69	71	69	70	69	75	71

HIGHLIGHTS

CASTRIES St Lucia's bustling capital is set among a number of hills, and with a wide, safe harbour it is one of the Caribbean's most beautiful towns. Climb Morne Fortune, the 'hill of good luck', for panoramic views across the city.

ST LUCIA FOREST RESERVE As an alternative to the beach, explore this 19,000 acre national park. Achingly beautiful and overcome with flora and fauna.

SOUFRIERE The old capital under French rule boasts one of the most awesome and photographed sites on the island, the volcanic Pitons. The city is encased by hills and these twin peaks are dominant, jutting straight out of the sea like sentinels over the town. Make time to explore the typical West Indian town, as well as the beaches, sulphur springs and mineral baths to the south.

ANSE LA RAYE A colourful and vibrant little fishing village, situated on the west coast, where the locals make fishing boats from gum trees. Every Friday evening there is the Friday Night Fish Fry BBQ for everyone to enjoy.

PIGEON ISLAND NATIONAL PARK One of the island's most popular spots to relax. Just north of Gros Islet, this park offers some excellent hiking, historical sites, beaches and is the venue for the Jazz Festival. The tip is now being developed as a tourist resort.

WATERSPORTS One of the breeziest places on earth, it is an excellent destination for windsurfers and sailors. West coast beaches have safe swimming but the Atlantic coast is rough.

with French influences. Local dishes include *langouste* (native lobster) cooked in a variety of ways, *lambi* (conch) and other fresh seafood. Breadfruit and plantain are popular, and the local spicy dish 'pepper pot' is worth trying. Many imported spirits are available, local favourite is rum in punch and cocktails. Beers and fruit juices also available.

SHOPPING & SOUVENIRS Batiks and silk screens, sports shirts, table mats, bowls, beads, straw hats, sisal rugs, bags, sandals, woodwork.

FIND OUT MORE

WEBSITES www.stlucia.org, www.sluonestop.com, www.stlucia.com.

LOCAL MEDIA English publications include, *The Voice of St Lucia, The Star, The Crusader, The Mirror,* and *Visions Magazine.*

TOURIST BOARDS IN UK/US UK: As for Country Reps in UK, tel (0870) 900 7697, fax (020) 7341 7001, email sltbinfo@ stluciauk.org. US: 9th Floor, 800 Second Avenue, Suite 910, New York, NY 10017, tel (212) 867 2950, fax (212) 867 2795, email stluciatourism@aol.com.

> The official language of St Lucia is English, but the islanders commonly speak a French-based *patois* that incorporates African and English words

ST VINCENT & THE GRENADINES

WHEN TO GO

WEATHER The best months are between January and May, before the rains, which are heaviest from June to November. Hurricanes are likely during this wet period.

FESTIVALS This colourful island hosts many events, often involving music and dancing. Blues Festivals are held in both St Vincent and Mustique, around January and February. The Canouan Regatta celebrates the country's maritime heritage with boat races, calypso competitions and a beauty pageant. The Vincy Carnival in summer is full of street parades and calypso competitions, a mere warm-up to the Dance Festival Month of September.

TRANSPORT

INTERNATIONAL AIRPORTS ET Joshua (SVD) 3 km from Kingstown.

INTERNAL TRAVEL Local and charter air services available. Regular boat and ferry services between islands. Buses, taxis, and car-hire available.

RED TAPE

VISAS REQUIRED (UK/US) None.

VACCINATIONS REQUIRED: See 'Vaccinations required around the world' on page 653.

DRIVING REQUIREMENTS A local licence, available on presentation of a national or international licence.

COUNTRY REPS IN UK/US UK: 10 Kensington Court, London W8 5DL, tel (020) 7565 2874, email highcommission.svg.uk@cwcom.net. USA: 801Second Avenue, 21st Floor, New York, NY 10017, tel (212) 687 4981, fax (212) 949 5946, email svgtony@aol.com.

UK/US REPS IN COUNTRY UK: PO Box 132, Granby Street, Kingstown, tel 457 1701, fax 456 2750, email bhcsvg@caribsurf.com. USA: The American Embassy in Bridgetown (see Barbados) deals with enquiries relating to St Vincent & the Grenadines.

PEOPLE AND PLACE

CAPITAL Kingstown.

LANGUAGE English.

PEOPLES African, European and Carib Indian descent.

RELIGION Christian denominations.

SIZE (SQ KM) 389.

POPULATION 119,000.

POP DENSITY/KM 305.7.

STATE OF THE NATION

SAFETY Safe.

LIFE EXPECTANCY M 71.78, F 75.51.

BEING THERE

ETIQUETTE Life is very informal and relaxed - combining West Indian and English influences. Casual clothing is widely accepted, but do refrain from wearing beachwear or mini-shorts while on the street or shopping. In general, visitors are made to feel very welcome.

CURRENCY Eastern Caribbean Dollar (EC$) = 100 cents.

FINANCE Credit cards and traveller's cheques widely accepted.

BUSINESS HOURS 0800-1600 Mon-Friday.

GMT -4.

VOLTAGE GUIDE 220/240 AC, 50 Hz.

COUNTRY DIALLING CODE 1 784.

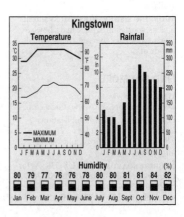

Kingstown — Temperature / Rainfall / Humidity

	Jan	Feb	Mar	Apr	May	June	July	Aug	Sept	Oct	Nov	Dec
Humidity (%)	80	79	77	76	76	78	80	80	81	81	84	82

HIGHLIGHTS

KINGSTOWN This lively port and harbour town sits on the southern coast of St Vincent. The town's energies are focused on the busy dock area, with fishermen hauling in their catch for sale at the fish market. On Saturday mornings, another market sees islanders shopping among stalls of fresh fruit and veg.

TOBAGO CAYS Numerous islets surrounded by a horseshoe-shaped coral reef and noted for beautiful beaches. The area is a designated wildlife reserve and, as such, is only reachable by chartered yacht. However, if you can make it there, the snorkelling and diving are excellent.

LA SOUFRIERE An active volcano, which last erupted in 1979. The mountain has given St Vincent its black beaches of volcanic sand. A five-hour hike to the summit leads through banana plantations, fertile rainforest and along volcanic ridges. The view from the summit is well worth the effort.

BEQUIA The largest of the Grenadine Islands, Bequia still retains its old traditions of boat-building and fishing. Situated on the migration path of the humpback whale, the island was formerly a centre of whaling. These days it attracts yachtsmen from around the world, together with those happy to chill out on its many fine beaches.

MUSTIQUE A privately owned island with verdant hills, glorious white sandy beaches and beautiful turquoise water. Known as a favourite with the British Royal Family, celebrities and other high-rollers.

CONSUMING PLEASURES

FOOD & DRINK Specialities include red snapper, kingfish, *lambi* (conch), *souse* (a sauce made from pigs' trotters) and sea-moss drink. Beer and rum are the local drinks, together with exotic fruit juices.

SHOPPING & SOUVENIRS Sea-island cottons made into clothes, handicrafts, straw items, grass rugs.

FIND OUT MORE

WEBSITES www.svgtourism.com, www.embsvg.com.

LOCAL MEDIA All newspapers in English, including, *The News, Searchlight, The Vincentian,* and *The Herald.*

TOURIST BOARDS IN UK/US
UK: As for Country Reps in UK, tel (020) 7937 6570, fax (020) 7937 3611, email svgtourismeurope@aol.com.
US: 801 Second Avenue, 21st Floor, New York, NY 10017, tel (212) 687 4981, fax (212) 949 5946, email svgtony@aol.com.

The Grenadines comprise 32 islands and cays, but it is St Vincent that dominates, accounting for 90 per cent of the land area and total population

SAMOA

WHEN TO GO

WEATHER Best between May and September, when the tropical climate is tempered by trade winds. Rainfall is heaviest between December and April.

FESTIVALS Events in the Christian calendar are major occasions, with many people taking extended holidays over the Christmas to New Year period, from mid-December until early January. The other big event of the year is the Independence Day celebrations, in June, marked with dancing, feasts, speeches by chiefs, horse races and other sporting events. A particular highlight is the *fautasi* race, with teams of rowers racing in long-boat canoes. The Teuila Tourism Festival in September features events such as church choir competitions, beauty contests and traditional games.

TRANSPORT

INTERNATIONAL AIRPORTS Apia (APW) 34 km from the city.

INTERNAL TRAVEL Inter-island ferries. Roads are in varying condition and drivers should be aware of roving livestock.

RED TAPE

VISAS REQUIRED (UK/US) Not required for visits up to 30 days for tourists.

VACCINATIONS REQUIRED: See 'Vaccinations required around the world' on page 653.

DRIVING REQUIREMENTS International Driving Permit or national driving licence.

COUNTRY REPS IN UK/US UK: n/a. USA: (Permanent Mission to the UN) 800 Second Avenue, Suite 400J, New York, NY 10017, tel (212) 599 6196, fax (212) 599 0797, email samoa@un.int.

UK/US REPS IN COUNTRY UK: c/o Kruse, Enari and Barlow Barristers and Solicitors, 2nd Floor, NPF Building, Beach Road, PO Box 2029, Apia, tel 21895, fax 21407, email barlolaw@keblegal.ws. USA: PO Box 3430, Matafele, Apia, tel 21631, fax 22030, email usembassy@samoa.ws.

PEOPLE AND PLACE

CAPITAL Apia (Upolu Island).

LANGUAGE Samoan, English.

PEOPLES Samoan.

RELIGION Christian denominations.

SIZE (SQ KM) 2,831.

POPULATION 176,848.

POP DENSITY/KM 62.5.

STATE OF THE NATION

SAFETY Safe.

LIFE EXPECTANCY M 67.93, F 73.65.

BEING THERE

ETIQUETTE Samoans adhere to traditional moral and religious codes of behaviour. The *fa'a Samoa*, or Samoan way, continues to flourish. Village life is still regulated by a council of chiefs, who have considerable financial and territorial power. Sunday is a day of peace and quiet: visitors should behave quietly and travel slowly through villages. It is considered impolite to eat while walking through a village, or to talk or eat while standing in a *fale* (family house). Instead, sit down cross-legged on a mat, then talk and eat. Shoes should be removed and left outside. Women are advised to wear a *lavalava* (*sarong*) rather than shorts and pants. Nude or topless bathing is prohibited. Customs may seem complicated, but don't be put off - Samoans are indulgent with foreigners who make an honest blunder.

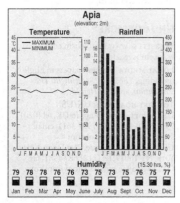

HIGHLIGHTS

APIA Capital city, located on the lush north coast of Upolu. Not far from Apia, at Vailima, is the beautifully restored home of Scottish novelist and poet Robert Louis Stevenson, who spent the last four years of his life in Samoa. Known locally as *Tusitala*, meaning 'teller of tales', he is buried on nearby Mt Vaea, alongside his wife Fanny. On the centenary of his death, in 1994, the house was officially re-opened as the Robert Louis Stevenson Museum and contains a library of his favourite books, together with a fireplace installed to remind him of home.

KIRIKITI Join the locals in a fun - if somewhat baffling - game of *kirikiti*, a Samoan version of cricket and the country's national game. The balls are handmade of rubber, wrapped in *pandanus*, while the three-side bat ensures that nobody has the faintest idea where the ball will end up. Serious competitions go on for days, with the national championships being played during the Teuila Festival, in September.

ALOFA'AGA BLOWHOLES One of the world's largest blowholes.

OLEMOE FALLS Beautiful jungle waterfall, with a deep blue pool which is marvellous for swimming and diving. Grab a snorkel and plunge down in search of freshwater prawns.

PULEMELEI MOUND A 12-metre high pyramid, measuring 50 metres by 60 metres at base level, this is Polynesia's largest and most mysterious ancient monument, not far from Olemoe Falls.

CURRENCY Tala or Samoa dollar (*Tala*) = 100 *sene*.

FINANCE Master Card and traveller's cheques accepted on a limited basis.

BUSINESS HOURS 0800-1200, 1300-1630 Monday-Friday.

GMT -12.

VOLTAGE GUIDE 240 AC, 50 Hz.

COUNTRY DIALLING CODE 685.

www.lonelyplanet.com/destinations/pacific/samoa,
www.samoa.islands-travel.com.

LOCAL MEDIA *The Samoa Observer*, *Savali*, and *Newsline* are printed in English.

TOURIST BOARDS IN UK/US n/a.

CONSUMING PLEASURES

FOOD & DRINK Roast suckling pig cooked in the Samoan earthen oven, the *umu*, is a favourite at feasts. Other popular foods are breadfruit, chicken and seafood. *Kava* is the national drink.

SHOPPING & SOUVENIRS *Siapo* cloth, mats and baskets, *kava* drinking bowls, shell jewellery, Samoan stamps.

FIND OUT MORE

WEBSITES www.visitsamoa.ws, www.samoa.co.uk,

> " [The Samoans] are easy, merry, and leisure-loving... song is almost ceaseless."
> *Robert Louis Stevenson*

SAN MARINO

WHEN TO GO

WEATHER Mediterranean climate moderated by sea breezes and height above sea level. Summer (June to September) is warm, moderate snow in winter.

FESTIVALS The San Marino Etnofestival takes place in mid-July over a number of days, and features ethnic dance and music from various countries and cultures. St Agatha, the patron saint of San Marino, is celebrated on 5 February (she is also the patron saint of nurses, firemen, and jewellers). It is usually late April when the San Marino Grand Prix takes place in near-by Imola, Italy, and it has been confirmed to be on the F1 calendar until at least 2009. The foundation of the Republic is celebrated on 9 September when a Great Crossbow Tournament is staged.

TRANSPORT

INTERNATIONAL AIRPORTS Nearest international airports are in Italy, Bologna (BLQ) 125 km away, and Rimini (RMI) 27 km away.

INTERNAL TRAVEL Good roads, no internal rail system.

RED TAPE

VISAS REQUIRED (UK/US) None.

VACCINATIONS REQUIRED: See 'Vaccinations required around the world' on page 653.

DRIVING REQUIREMENTS As for Italy.

COUNTRY REPS IN UK/US UK: n/a. USA: n/a.

UK/US REPS IN COUNTRY The relevant Consulates in Florence (see Italy) deal with enquiries relating to San Marino.

PEOPLE AND PLACE

CAPITAL San Marino.

LANGUAGE Italian.

PEOPLES Sanmarinesi.

RELIGION Roman Catholic.

SIZE (SQ KM) 61.2.

POPULATION 28,753.

POP DENSITY/KM 469.8.

STATE OF THE NATION

SAFETY Safe.

LIFE EXPECTANCY M 78.13, F 85.43.

BEING THERE

ETIQUETTE Normal social courtesies apply.

CURRENCY Euro (€) = 100 *cents*.

FINANCE Credit cards and traveller's cheques accepted.

BUSINESS HOURS 0830-1300, 1530-1930 Monday to Saturday (shopping hours, business hours n/a).

GMT +1 (+2 in summer).

VOLTAGE GUIDE 220 AC, 50 Hz.

COUNTRY DIALLING CODE 378 (Do not omit 0 in area code).

CONSUMING PLEASURES

FOOD & DRINK Italian food is widely available, with several pasta dishes eaten as starters. Main dishes include roast rabbit with fennel, devilled chicken, Bolognese veal cutlets, Roman veal escalopes. Local wines *muscat, biancale, albana,* and *sangiovese* are all good quality. *Mistra* is the local liqueur.

SHOPPING & SOUVENIRS Ceramics, stamps, coins, local wines, liqueurs, local jewellery, playing cards.

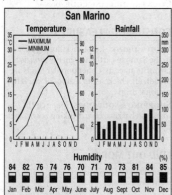

HIGHLIGHTS

SAN MARINO The capital of this tiny country sits on the slopes of Mount Titano. Its medieval heart has been perfectly preserved, and the small winding streets are fun to explore on foot. Which is just as well, as cars are banned. Three walls encircle the city, and have interesting and picturesque features such as gateways, ramparts, and towers. Inside the capital, visitors should look for the Government Palace, the Basilica, the State Museum and Art Gallery, the Exhibition of San Marino Handicrafts, and the ancient churches. The Chiesa di San Francisco is the oldest building in the oldest of republics, and dates to 1361. For those that visit as part of the Grand Prix crowd, a trip should be made to the Maranello Rosso, housing a collection of cars old and new (including 25 Ferraris). If that's not for you, you could try the Museum of Torture, featuring more than 100 instruments of pain and death. Or the Wax Museum depicting various historical scenes from San Marino and international history.

To top off the random museum tour, pop into the Museum of Curiosities.

COUNTRYSIDE Nestled among the pine woods, springs, streams, and lakes that characterise the Republic are eight tiny villages. Travellers should explore Malatesta Castle at Serravalle, the fort at Pennarossa, and the churches of Valdragone and Borgo Maggiore - also home to the stamp and coin museum. Coin collecting is very popular among the Sanmarinese population, as San Marino mints legal tender gold coins, know as *scudi*.

FIND OUT MORE

WEBSITES www.visitsanmarino.com, www.sanmarinosite.com.

LOCAL MEDIA No home-grown newspapers in English, but international press available.

TOURIST BOARDS IN UK/US n/a.

San Marino is the world's oldest republic still in existence. It was founded in 301 AD by a stonemason, St Marinus

SAO TOME & PRINCIPE

WHEN TO GO

WEATHER The main dry season is from early June to late September, a shorter dry season runs from the end of December to the start of February. The rest of the year sees heavy rainfall. High temperatures are experienced throughout the year.

FESTIVALS Alongside the main Christian holidays and New Year's Day, São Tomé and Príncipe also has a number of other public holidays. These include Independence Day, on 12 July, and São Tomé Day, celebrated on 21 December. Theatre has an important place in local life and each island has its own form of traditional dance and mime. The Auto de Floripes (in São Tomé) and the Tchiloli (in Príncipe) date back to the sixteenth century and often relate the Tragedy of the Marquis of Mantua and the Emperor Charlemagne: the lead roles are passed on from father to son.

TRANSPORT

INTERNATIONAL AIRPORTS São Tomé (TMS) 5.5 km from the town.

INTERNAL TRAVEL Limited ferry service between São Tomé and Príncipe. Some roads are asphalt, much of the network is deteriorating. Four-wheel-drive vehicles are recommended for travelling beyond São Tomé.

RED TAPE

VISAS REQUIRED (UK/US) Required.

VACCINATIONS REQUIRED: See 'Vaccinations required around the world' on page 653.

DRIVING REQUIREMENTS International Driving Permit recommended.

COUNTRY REPS IN UK/US UK: n/a nearest Square Montgommery, 175 Avenue de Tervuren, 1150 Brussels, Belgium, tel (2) 734 8966, fax (2) 734 8815, email ambassade.saotome@fi.be. USA: 400 Park Avenue, 7th Floor, New York, NY 10044, tel (212) 317 0533, fax (212) 317 0580, email stp1@attglobal.net.

UK/US REPS IN COUNTRY UK: Residencia

Avenida, Avenida da Independencia, CP257, São Tomé, tel (2) 21026/7, fax (2) 21372. USA: The American Embassy in Libreville (see Gabon) deals with enquiries relating to São Tomé e Principe.

PEOPLE AND PLACE

CAPITAL São Tomé.

LANGUAGE Portuguese.

PEOPLES African descent (90%), Portuguese and Creole (10%).

RELIGION Roman Catholic, other Christian denominations.

SIZE (SQ KM) 1001.

POPULATION 161,000.

POP DENSITY/KM 137.5.

STATE OF THE NATION

SAFETY Safe.

LIFE EXPECTANCY M 65.43, F 68.59.

BEING THERE

ETIQUETTE The colonial Portuguese, who first arrived on the islands in 1471, left a strong cultural legacy. Today, Portuguese is the official language, with a form of Creole also spoken throughout São Tomé and Príncipe. The inhabitants are mainly descendants of slaves brought from mainland Africa. In general, people are friendly and courteous. Normal social courtesies should be observed.

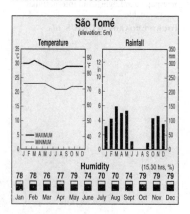

São Tomé
(elevation: 5m)

	Temperature		Rainfall	

Humidity											(15.30 hrs, %)
78	78	76	77	79	74	70	70	74	79	79	79
Jan	Feb	Mar	Apr	May	June	July	Aug	Sept	Oct	Nov	Dec

HIGHLIGHTS

SÃO TOMÉ TOWN Friendly, quiet capital with pretty colonial architecture, scenic side-streets and attractive parks. Established by the Portuguese in 1485, it was a busy slave port in days gone by. The pot-holed streets and faded buildings suggest a town whose heyday has long drifted by, but if you make it down to the markets, or see the fishermen haul in their midday catch of red snapper, wahoo and marlin, it's suddenly a much more energetic place. At night the pace slows down once more, and you could easily amble through the centre and not see a living soul.

COCOA PLANTATIONS São Tomé island has a number of *roças*, or cocao plantations. Agostinho Neto is the largest of them, while at Agua Izé visitors can tour the plantation by train.

ILHÉU DAS ROLAS Tiny islet at the southern tip of São Tomé island, which actually straddles the equator, enabling you to can stand with one leg in each hemisphere. Good diving off the shore and some good beaches.

PRÍNCIPE Go snorkelling in the azure coastal waters, or take an afternoon stroll through the main town of San Antonio, characterised by some distinctive colonial architecture.

OBO NATIONAL PARK Protected area of *capoeiras* (post-agricultural forest), dotted with abandoned plantations, set alongside pristine, ancient tropical forest at higher altitudes. There are some pleasant trails, taking in waterfalls, lakes and fine views.

CURRENCY *Dobra* (Db) = 100 *cêntimos*.

FINANCE Cards generally not accepted, limited acceptance of traveller's cheques.

BUSINESS HOURS n/a.

GMT GMT.

VOLTAGE GUIDE 220 AC.

COUNTRY DIALLING CODE 239.

LOCAL MEDIA Newspapers in Portuguese. One TV station, one radio station, both state owned.

TOURIST BOARDS IN UK/US n/a.

CONSUMING PLEASURES

FOOD & DRINK Most dishes are highly spiced, grilled meats and fish. Avocadoes, pineapples and bananas are popular. A lot of canned food is shipped from Portugal, but bakeries supply fresh bread.

SHOPPING & SOUVENIRS There used to be a trade in sea-turtle shells, happily this has now been legally curtailed.

FIND OUT MORE

WEBSITES www.saotome.org, www.lonelyplanet.com/destinations/africa/sao_tome_and_principe.

The turtle is the most popular and important character in local folk tales – a crafty and clever animal who always wins through in the end

SAUDI ARABIA

WHEN TO GO

WEATHER High temperatures for most of the year and very little rainfall. Winters can be cold, particularly in the northwest.

FESTIVALS Most events in the country follow the Muslim calendar, and most visitors to the country are Muslim pilgrims, usually on a journey to Mecca, Islam's spiritual centre. The Hajj to Mecca occurs in mid to late January. The country also hosts a number of motor shows.

TRANSPORT

INTERNATIONAL AIRPORTS Riyadh (RUH) 35 km from the city, Dhahran (DHA) 13 km from the city, Jeddah (JED) 18 km from the city.

INTERNAL TRAVEL Air travel is the most convenient way of travelling around the country. Adequate rail network, the road network is being improved and extended. Women are not allowed to drive vehicles or ride bicycles on public roads.

RED TAPE

VISAS REQUIRED (UK/US) Required (Business only, no tourist visas issued).

VACCINATIONS REQUIRED: See 'Vaccinations required around the world' on page 653.

DRIVING REQUIREMENTS National driving licence with an officially sanctioned translation into Arabic. International Driving Permit (with translation) recommended.

COUNTRY REPS IN UK/US UK: 30 Charles Street, London W1J 5DZ, tel (020) 7917 3000, fax (020) 7917 3255, email ukemb@mofa.gov.sa. USA: 601 New Hampshire Avenue, NW, Washington, DC 20037, tel (202) 342 3800, fax (202) 7337 4084, email info@saudiembassy.net.

UK/US REPS IN COUNTRY UK: PO Box 94351, Riyadh 11693, tel (1) 488 0077, fax (1) 488 2373, email Visa.Riyadh@ fco.gov.uk. USA: PO Box 94309, Riyadh 11693, tel (1) 488 3800, fax (1) 488 3989, email USEmbRiyadhWebSite@state.gov.

PEOPLE AND PLACE

CAPITAL Riyadh.

LANGUAGE Arabic.

PEOPLES Arab (90%), Afro-asian.

RELIGION Sunni Islam (85%), Shi'a Islam.

SIZE (SQ KM) 2,240,000.

POPULATION 23,370,000.

POP DENSITY/KM 10.4.

STATE OF THE NATION

SAFETY Safe.

LIFE EXPECTANCY M 73.46, F 77.55.

BEING THERE

ETIQUETTE A conservative and fundamentalist Islamic country, women are required by law to dress totally covered in black robes and masks when out of the home. Remote areas stick to the austere Wahhabi tradition, elsewhere life is being modernised. Invitations into private homes are unusual. Eat with the right hand when not using knives and forks. Gifts are welcomed. Women should dress modestly, men should not wear shorts or go shirtless. Public behaviour is extremely conservative. It is illegal to eat or drink in public during Ramadan.

CURRENCY Saudi Arabian *riyal* (SR) = 100 *halalah*.

FINANCE Credit cards and traveller's cheques widely accepted.

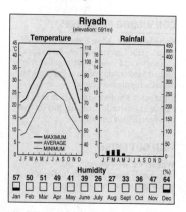

HIGHLIGHTS

RIYADH The royal capital since 1932 has today become a modern city of glass and steel, on the site of the first town captured by Ibn Saud in 1902. The Musmat Fort that he stormed still stands, and there are a number of Najdi palaces close to Deera Square. Though little remains of the old town, travellers will pass through it as it still contains the essentials, such as bus stations. Head to the camel market for a scent of the exotic, and if travelling in April or May take in one of The King's Camel Races.

MECCA The spiritual centre of Islam, the birthplace of Muhammad, and the city that all Muslims must face during their five daily prayers. Every Muslim who can afford and is fit enough to visit, is meant to make a pilgrimage to the city at least once in their life. The significant sites are the Kabbah Enclosure, the Mountain of Light, the Plain of Arafat, and Muhammad's exact birthplace, the House of Abdullah Bin Abdul. Together with Medina, the second holiest city in Islam, visits to the city are forbidden for non-Muslims.

JEDDAH The city has gone through a period of rapid expansion, and continues to grow. However, the ancient city is being carefully preserved. Ottoman architecture is being painstakingly renovated, while leisure facilities and amusement parks spring up simultaneously. Hotels and restaurants have a cosmopolitan feel, and provide a base for sailing, swimming, and snorkelling holidays. Obhir Creek, 50 kilometres further north, is another good area for this.

BUSINESS HOURS 0900-1300, 1630-2000 Saturday to Thursday.

GMT +3.

VOLTAGE GUIDE 125/215 AC, 50/60 Hz.

COUNTRY DIALLING CODE 966.

CONSUMING PLEASURES

FOOD & DRINK *Pitta* bread accompanies every dish. Rice, lentils, chickpeas and cracked wheat (*burghul*) are common. Lamb and chicken are popular and usually served as kebabs, along with soup and vegetables. Most food is spicy. Alcohol is prohibited, even for visitors.

SHOPPING & SOUVENIRS Incense-burners, jewellery, decorated daggers and swords, brass-bonded chests and modern electrical goods.

FIND OUT MORE

WEBSITES www.saudiembassy.org.uk, www.saudinf.com/main/start.htm, www.britishembassy.gov.uk/saudiarabia. www.saudiembassy.net, http://usembassy.state.gov/riyadh.

LOCAL MEDIA *Arab News*, *Saudi Gazette*, and *Riyadh Daily* are the main English dailies.

TOURIST BOARDS IN UK/US
UK: 18 Seymour Street, London W1H 7HU, tel (020) 7486 3470, fax (020) 7486 8211. email sair@saudinf.com. US: n/a.

Saudi Arabia has the world's largest oil reserves, around 20 per cent of all known deposits, and is currently the world's biggest oil producer. Oil and natural gas account for 35 per cent of its GDP

SENEGAL

WHEN TO GO

WEATHER Go during the dry season from December to May, when the trade winds cool the hot coastal area.

FESTIVALS As well as the major Christian and Islamic holidays, Senegal also has public holidays on National Day (4 April), on Labour Day (5 May) and on Independence Day (20 June). Magal, the annual Mouride pilgrimage to Touba (dates vary), is another important time. Elsewhere, the St-Louis International Jazz Festival, in May or June, attracts artists from across the world. *Fanels* (decorated lanterns) parades take place in St-Louis and Gorée in December. Senegalese wrestling events are popular nationwide.

TRANSPORT

INTERNATIONAL AIRPORTS Dakar (DKR) 17 km from the city.

INTERNAL TRAVEL Asphalt roads link major towns. Roads in the interior are rough and may become impassable in the rainy season.

RED TAPE

VISAS REQUIRED (UK/US) Required by Australian nationals. Not required for others for stays up to 90 days.

VACCINATIONS REQUIRED: See 'Vaccinations required around the world' on page 653.

DRIVING REQUIREMENTS French or International Driving Permit and Green Card.

COUNTRY REPS IN UK/US UK: 39 Marloes Road, London W8 6LA, tel (020) 7938 4048, fax (020) 7938 2546, email mail@senegalembassy.co.uk. USA: 2112 Wyoming Avenue, NW, Washington, DC 20008, tel (202) 234 0540, fax (202) 332 6315.

UK/US REPS IN COUNTRY UK: 20 rue du Docteur Guillet, BP 6025, Dakar, tel 823 7392, fax 823 2766, email britemb@sentoo.sn. USA: BP 49, avenue Jean XXIII, angle Rue Kleber, Dakar, tel 823 4296, fax 822 2991, email usadakar@state.gov.

PEOPLE AND PLACE

CAPITAL Dakar.

LANGUAGE French and Wolof.

PEOPLES Wolof, Toucouleur, Malinke, Diola.

RELIGION Muslim (90%), Christian (5%), traditional beliefs.

SIZE (SQ KM) 196,722.

POPULATION 11,000,000.

POP DENSITY/KM 50.1.

STATE OF THE NATION

SAFETY Occasional unrest, seek latest information at time of visit.

LIFE EXPECTANCY M 55.04, F 58.52.

BEING THERE

ETIQUETTE Senegal is the most French-influenced country in West Africa. French remains the common business language, but it would also be courteous to learn at least a few words of Wolof or other local language: 'hello', 'thank you' etc. When visiting a village, it is polite to call upon the village leader or schoolteacher to explain that you want to spend the night there or visit the area. They will often act as interpreter and will be helpful guides to village customs. Return hospitality with a gift of medicines, food or money for the community.

CURRENCY *Communauté Financiaire Africaine franc* (CFAfr) = 100 *centimes*.

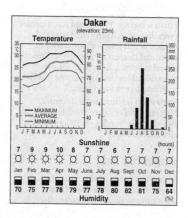

Dakar climate chart (elevation: 23m)

	Jan	Feb	Mar	Apr	May	June	July	Aug	Sept	Oct	Nov	Dec
Sunshine (hours)	7	9	9	10	8	7	7	6	7	7	7	7
Humidity (%)	70	75	77	78	79	77	78	80	82	81	75	64

HIGHLIGHTS

DAKAR Bustling modern capital city and major port at the tip of the Cap Vert peninsula. Nothing symbolises this energy more than the thronging markets of Kermel and Sandaga, where traders and shoppers haggle over clothing, souvenirs, fruit and fabrics. The city also houses the excellent IFAN Museum, with fine collections of masks, statues, musical instruments and other regional artefacts.

PARC NATIONAL DE NIOKOLO-KOBA Drive through this park skirting the south-eastern border with Guinea, looking for hippos, baboons, buffaloes and other native animals. In all, the park is home to 84 species of large mammal, including elephants, panthers, crocodiles and lions - not to mention 300 species of bird.

GORÉE ISLAND Tiny island of about 1,000 inhabitants, just a few kilometres across the bay to the east of Dakar. There are no asphalt roads and no cars on this World Heritage-listed island, formerly a slaving station. The old colonial buildings, some converted into museums, add to its charm. A rocky plateau, Le Castel, affords good views of the island and Dakar.

MUSIC Dakar is a good place to experience *mbalakh* (local modern music), as well as other vibrant West African styles. Elsewhere, the former capital city, St-Louis, has a colourful jazz festival in May-June.

THE PETITE CÔTE Stretching for about 150 km, this palm-fringed section of coast is among Senegal's best beaches, and is popular for swimming.

FINANCE American Express more widely accepted than other cards, which have limited use. Traveller's cheques generally accepted.

BUSINESS HOURS 0800-1230, 1300-1600 Monday to Friday.

GMT GMT.

VOLTAGE GUIDE 220 AC, 50 Hz.

COUNTRY DIALLING CODE 221.

CONSUMING PLEASURES

FOOD & DRINK Dishes include *chicken au yassa* (chicken with lemon, pimento and onions), *tiebou dienne* (rice and fish), *dem á la St Louis* (stuffed mullet). Suckling pig is popular in the Casamance region. The traditional drink is mint tea; the Casamance drink, however, is palm wine.

SHOPPING & SOUVENIRS Woodcarvings game boards, masks and statues, musical instruments, copper pendants, bowls, pottery, clay bead necklaces, costume jewellery.

FIND OUT MORE

WEBSITES www.senegalembassy.co.uk, www.senegal-tourism.com, http://usembassy.gov/dakar, www.senegal-online.com.

LOCAL MEDIA All papers in French, most controlled by political parties.

TOURIST BOARDS IN UK/US UK: n/a. US: 350 Fifth Avenue, Suite 3118, New York, NY 10118, tel (212) 279 1953, fax(212) 279 1958, email sentour@aol.com.

Senegal's capital is the finishing line for the epic Paris-Dakar rally, which crosses the Mediterranean and the Sahara and attracts some 1,500 competitors

SERBIA & MONTENEGRO

WHEN TO GO

WEATHER Cold winters (November-April), warm summers. Montenegro has a Mediterranean climate.

FESTIVALS In Belgrade the FEST film festival is held in February, a Beer festival is held in August, as is a Jazz festival. BITEF international theatre festival is staged in September, while the Classical music festival delights listeners in October. Guca near Cacak hosts a festival of brass band music in August.

TRANSPORT

INTERNATIONAL AIRPORTS Belgrade airport (Surcin) is 20 km from the city. Podgorica (TGD) serves Montenegro.

INTERNAL TRAVEL Railways poor. Road travel affected by fuel shortages, but bus network is efficient.

RED TAPE

VISAS REQUIRED (UK/US) Required.

VACCINATIONS REQUIRED: See 'Vaccinations required around the world' on page 653.

DRIVING REQUIREMENTS National driving licence, car log books, vehicle ownership and registration papers, local valid insurance and Third Party Green Card insurance.

COUNTRY REPS IN UK/US UK: 28 Belgrave Square, London SW1X 8QB, tel (020) 7235 9049, fax (020) 7235 7092, email londre@jugisek. USA: 2134 Kalorama Road, NW, Washington, DC 20008, tel (202) 332 0333, fax (202) 332 3993, email consular@yuembusa.org.

UK/US REPS IN COUNTRY UK: Generala Resavska 46, 11000 Belgrade, tel (11) 264 5055, fax (11) 265 9651, email belgrade.man@fco.gov.uk. USA: Kneza Milosa 50, 11000 Belgrade, tel (11) 361 9344, fax (11) 361 5497.

PEOPLE AND PLACE

CAPITAL Belgrade.

LANGUAGE Serbo-croat.

PEOPLES Serb (62%), Albanian, Montenegrin, Magyar and others.

RELIGION Christian (70%), Muslim.

SIZE (SQ KM) 102,173.

POPULATION 10,664,300.

POP DENSITY/KM 104.4.

STATE OF THE NATION

SAFETY Kosovo region may be volatile.

LIFE EXPECTANCY M 72.15, F 77.51.

BEING THERE

ETIQUETTE Once open and informal, with a secure society, the country has seen an increase in violent crime since the war. Now relatively common in big cities, it was once unheard of. Remain vigilant. Check restrictions on photography before taking pictures.

CURRENCY Serbia: New Yugoslav *dinar* (N Din) = 100 *paras* Montenegro: Euro = 100 *cents*.

FINANCE Credit cards and traveller's cheques widely accepted, but US dollars and euros useful.

BUSINESS HOURS 0800-1500 Mon-Friday.

GMT +1.

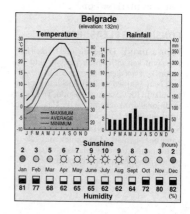

Belgrade
(elevation: 132m)

Temperature / Rainfall / Sunshine (hours) / Humidity (%)

	Jan	Feb	Mar	Apr	May	June	July	Aug	Sept	Oct	Nov	Dec
Sunshine (hours)	2	3	5	6	7	9	10	9	8	3	3	2
Humidity (%)	81	77	68	62	65	65	62	62	64	72	80	82

HIGHLIGHTS

BELGRADE Situated on a hill between the Danube and Sava Rivers, the site was an excellent position for a fortified town. However, that's what enemies also thought, and Belgrade has been destroyed and rebuilt some 40 times in 2,300 years. Parkland now exists where once there were heavy fortifications. A combination of architectural styles have been used in the old town, where visitors will find museums, boutiques, cafes and bars. There are also bars and clubs on boats along the river banks, playing music from Serbian folk to house and techno, making this a new party town.

BUDVA The best seaside resort in the country is made up of a number of lovely beaches between here and Sveti Stefan. Tall, barren coastal mountains provide a stunning backdrop to tanning on the beach. A rebuilt stone wall encircling the city had been destroyed by an earthquake in 1979. So pretty it may seem a little contrived.

KOTOR This walled town, nestled in southern Europe's deepest fjord, has the most beautiful setting in the country. A labyrinth of cobbled alleys connect the squares and churches and once aristocratic mansions. Wander about to soak up the atmosphere before climbing the steep path above the town for awesome views back over it, and over the fjord. Heading toward Cetinje will provide the most spectacular views.

DURMITOR NATIONAL PARK Dramatic mountain scenery, home to 18 lakes and a canyon, this is a place for fine views and winter skiing.

VOLTAGE GUIDE 220 AC, 50 Hz.

COUNTRY DIALLING CODE 381.

CONSUMING PLEASURES

FOOD & DRINK Varies greatly between regions, but national specialities include *pihtije* (jellied pork or duck), *prsut* (smoked ham) and *sarma* or *japrak* (stuffed vine or cabbage leaves). Wine is cheap. Favoured spirits are *slivovica* (a plum brandy) and *loza* (which is made from morello cherries).

SHOPPING & SOUVENIRS Embroidery, lace, leatherwork, *Pec* filigree work, Turkish coffee sets.

FIND OUT MORE

WEBSITES www.yugoslavembassy.org.uk, www.yuembusa.org, http://belgrade.usembassy.gov, www.lonelyplanet.com/destinations/europe/serbia_and_montenegro.

LOCAL MEDIA No newspapers in English.

TOURIST BOARDS IN UK/US n/a.

> "Belgrade is blessed as few cities are with natural beauty, lying high on the confluence of two great rivers, Danube and Save; but it is like a pretty peasant girl with the carriage of a queen and the raiment of a dirty beggar."
>
> *John Gunther, 1938*

SEYCHELLES

WHEN TO GO

WEATHER Hot all year. Humid during monsoon season (November-February).

FESTIVALS Most festivals follow the Roman Catholic calendar, with celebrations for Easter, the Assumption, Corpus Christi, and the Immaculate Conception. The major non-religious festival is the Festival Kreol at the end of October, which celebrates the Creole culture over a week with food, fashion, art, music and dance.

TRANSPORT

INTERNATIONAL AIRPORTS Mahé Island (SEZ) is 10 km from Victoria.

INTERNAL TRAVEL Good air and boat services. Roads are mostly sand-tracks. Regular buses, frequent taxis.

RED TAPE

VISAS REQUIRED (UK/US) Not required.

VACCINATIONS REQUIRED: See 'Vaccinations required around the world' on page 653.

DRIVING REQUIREMENTS National driving licence.

COUNTRY REPS IN UK/US UK: The High Commission for the Seychelles in France deals with UK enquiries: 51 Avenue Mozart, 75016 Paris, tel (1) 4230 5747, fax (1) 4230 5740, email ambsey@aol.com. USA: 800 Second Avenue, 4th Floor, Suite 400C, New York, NY 10017, tel (212) 972 1785, fax (212) 972 1786, email seychelle@un.int.

UK/US REPS IN COUNTRY UK: PO Box 161, Oliaji Trade Centre, Frances Rachel Street, Victoria, Mahé, tel 283 666, fax 283 657, email bhcvictoria@fco.gov.uk. USA: PO Box 251, Oliaji Trade Centre, Suite 23, Victoria, Mahé, tel 225 256, fax 225 189, email usoffice@seychelles.net.

PEOPLE AND PLACE

CAPITAL Victoria.

LANGUAGE Creole, English, French.

PEOPLES Descendants from European, African, Indian and Chinese origins.

RELIGION Roman Catholic (90%).

SIZE (SQ KM) 455.3.

POPULATION 80,800.

POP DENSITY/KM 177.5.

STATE OF THE NATION

SAFETY Safe.

LIFE EXPECTANCY M 66.41, F 77.4.

BEING THERE

ETIQUETTE A simple and unsophisticated way of life is followed on the island, creating an unspoilt charm, and this is carefully protected. The international airport, providing easy access to the islands for the first time, only opened in 1971. The Seychelles had been so remote that a unique culture and language developed. The locals are hospitable people, welcoming of guests and gifts. Imperial and metric weights and measures are used. Casual wear is normal, only churchgoers dress formally, but beach-wear should be kept to the beach.

CURRENCY Seychelles *rupee* (Sre) = 100 *cents*.

FINANCE Amex, Visa and traveller's cheques are widely accepted.

BUSINESS HOURS 0800-1700 Mon-Friday.

GMT +4.

VOLTAGE GUIDE 240 AC, 50 Hz.

COUNTRY DIALLING CODE 248.

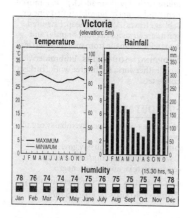

HIGHLIGHTS

MAHÉ The largest of the islands, and home to the airport, port, capital, most of the population and hotels. But it is not spoilt. Protected by coral reefs, and with 70 white, powder-sand beaches, rich, lush vegetation, coconut palm plantations, and forested peaks, it is the stuff of dreams. Victoria is the only town in the country, any other settlement is a village. Glass bottomed boat trips can be taken to nearby islands, some closed, some national parks, and others home to botanical gardens and giant tortoises. A number of museums are found in the capital detailing Seychellois life.

COUSIN Only accessible as part of an organised tour, Cousin is run as a nature reserve by the International Council for Bird Protection. The brush warbler, the Seychelles toc-toc, and the fairy tern are all protected. In April and May, 1.25 million birds come to nest on the island - and it's only two hours from Mahé.

ALDABRA The world's largest atoll is home to 150,000 giant land tortoises, five times as many as their more famous home on the Galapagos Islands. These 13 islands make up one third of the total Seychelles landmass and are a World Heritage Site.

DESROCHES Only recently developed as a resort, the largest of the Amirantes archipelago is surrounded by coral reef, providing calm waters ideal for watersports. Water-skiing, windsurfing, sailing, fishing, scuba diving, and wave runners can all be enjoyed from here. Sea cliffs, tunnels and caves make for interesting diving.

CONSUMING PLEASURES

FOOD & DRINK The Creole cuisine in the Seychelles is influenced by French, Indian and African traditions. Emphasis is placed on the careful blending of fresh spices, and coconut milk and breadfruit are commonly used. Specialities include coconut curries, *salade de palmiste* (palm heart salad) and seafood dishes. Lobster, octopus, pork and chicken feature more often than lamb or beef, which must be imported A wide selection of alcoholic beverages is available. The local lager is *Seybrew*, German in style.

SHOPPING & SOUVENIRS Batiks, baskets, table mats, hats, traditional furniture, pottery, paintings, green snail shell jewellery, tea, vanilla pods, cinnamon.

The world's largest seed is that of the giant palm fan, which looks like two coconuts joined together. This famously naughty-looking nut, known as the *coco de mer*, can weigh up to 20 kilograms and take 10 years to develop

FIND OUT MORE

WEBSITES www.aspureasitgets.com, **LOCAL MEDIA** *The Seychelles Nation* (daily), *The People* (monthly) and *Seychelles Review* (monthly) are all printed in English.

TOURIST BOARDS IN UK/US n/a.

SIERRA LEONE

WHEN TO GO

WEATHER Hot all year. Rainy May-November. Dry *Harmattan* wind blows December-January.

FESTIVALS Festivals follow the usual Muslim and Christian calendars. Independence Day is celebrated on 27 April.

TRANSPORT

INTERNATIONAL AIRPORTS Lungi (FNA) 13 km from the capital.

INTERNAL TRAVEL Roads are appalling. Reasonable flight network.

RED TAPE

VISAS REQUIRED (UK/US) Required.

VACCINATIONS REQUIRED: See 'Vaccinations required around the world' on page 653.

DRIVING REQUIREMENTS International Driving Permit.

COUNTRY REPS IN UK/US UK: Oxford Circus House, 245 Oxford Street, London W1D 2LX, tel (020) 7287 9884, fax (020) 7734 3822, email info@slhc-uk.org.uk. USA: 1701 19th Street, NW, Washington, DC 20009, tel (202) 939 9261, fax (202) 483 1793, email Sierrale@umbc7.umbc.edu.

UK/US REPS IN COUNTRY UK: 6 Spur Road, Wilberforce, Freetown, tel (22) 232 362, fax (22) 232 070. USA: Corner of Walpole and Siaka Stevens Streets, Freetown, tel (22) 226 481, fax (22) 225 471, email taylorJB2@state.gov.

PEOPLE AND PLACE

CAPITAL Freetown.

LANGUAGE English. Also Krio and tribal languages.

PEOPLES Mende (35%), Temne (32%), Limba, other tribal origins.

RELIGION Animist (40%), Muslim (40%), Christian.

SIZE (SQ KM) 71,740.

POPULATION 4,764,000.

POP DENSITY/KM 66.4.

STATE OF THE NATION

SAFETY Dangerous. Recently a war zone subject to particualrly vicious kidnappings, mutilations and rape. Now peaceful, but check latest information at time of travel.

LIFE EXPECTANCY M 40.13, F 44.98.

BEING THERE

ETIQUETTE The population live mainly the traditional agricultural way of life. Ruling chiefs and religions preserve some social stability, together with music, dance, customs and traditions. Small tokens of appreciation are welcomed. Casual wear always suitable, men rarely wear suits or ties.

CURRENCY *Leone* (Le) = 100 cents.

FINANCE Amex and US dollars cash are the only widely accepted means of payment.

BUSINESS HOURS 0800-1200 and 1400-1700 Monday-Friday.

GMT GMT

VOLTAGE GUIDE 220/240 AC, 50 Hz, when available.

COUNTRY DIALLING CODE 232.

CONSUMING PLEASURES

FOOD & DRINK Local dishes include excellent fish, lobster and prawns and a wide array of exotic fruit and vegetables. French, Armenian and Lebanese food is widely available.

SHOPPING & SOUVENIRS Diamonds.

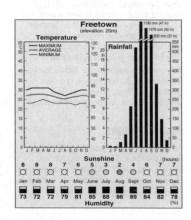

HIGHLIGHTS

FREETOWN The vibrant, historic port is surrounded by heavily vegetated hills. Once a resettlement area for liberated slaves, it is today the most accessible part of the country. Leicester Peak, hovering above the city, affords spectacular views of the sea and mountains, with the city nestled between. Two hundred-year-old Creole villages are not far from here along steep mountainous lanes. A number of museums, churches, and other buildings should be visited here, including the City Hotel, made famous by Graham Greene's novel *The Heart of the Matter*. Other sights include the vibrant, bustling bazaar at the King Jimmy Market, and boat trips up the Rokel River to Bunce Island, one of the first slave-trading stations in West Africa.

GAME PARKS The Outamba-Kilimi National Park has diverse and dramatic scenery and a wide selection of game, theoretically including elephants, chimpanzees, and pygmy hippos. Sakanbiarwa plant reserve is home to a large collection of orchids, best viewed early in the year.

Access to Sierra Leone's game parks is by permit only, obtained through the Ministry of Agriculture and Forestry in Freetown. Guides are provided.

TIWAI ISLAND Sierra Leone's first and only community conservation area covers an area of 12 square kilometres, making it one of the largest inland islands in the country. It claims to have over 135 different bird species and one of the highest concentration and diversity of primates anywhere, but as with all post-conflict zones, such claims may have been overtaken by events.

FIND OUT MORE

WEBSITES www.slhc-uk.org.uk, www.sierra-leone.org, www.visitsierraleone.org, http://freetown.usembassy.gov.

LOCAL MEDIA *The Daily Mail* is published daily in English. One, state-controlled, TV station.

TOURIST BOARDS IN UK/US n/a.

In 2004 Sierra Leone recorded the lowest figure in the UN's Human Development Index – meaning that it is, officially, the worst place in the world to live. Yet it is home to some of the world's most valuable diamonds, a curse that has seen it fought over for years

SINGAPORE

WHEN TO GO

WEATHER Hot and humid all year. Wettest November-January.

FESTIVALS With such diverse cultures over a relatively small area,, travellers are almost certain to encounter a festival or two, as many occur throughout the year. The Chinese community celebrate the Chinese New Year, and operas and dragon dance troupes perform in the streets in January. In February, entranced penitents walk three kilometres in the Hindu festival of Thaipusam. Ramadan occurs in April/May. Vesak Day commemorates the Buddha's birth in May. June/August sees arts festivals, a Dragon Boat festival, and the Festival of the Hungry Ghosts.

TRANSPORT

INTERNATIONAL AIRPORTS Changi (SIN) is 20 km from the city.

INTERNAL TRAVEL Excellent roads, two well-developed, cheap, local bus services. Regular train service. Also ferries around islands. Car-hire is available.

RED TAPE

VISAS REQUIRED (UK/US) Issued on arrival.

VACCINATIONS REQUIRED: See 'Vaccinations required around the world' on page 653.

DRIVING REQUIREMENTS National driving licence (for 1 month stays).

COUNTRY REPS IN UK/US UK: 9 Wilton Crescent, London SW1X 8SP, tel (020) 7235 8315, fax (020) 7245 6583, email info@singaporehc.org.uk. USA: 3501 International Place, NW, Washington, DC 20008, tel (202) 537 3100, fax (202) 537 0876, email singemb.dc@verizon.net.

UK/US REPS IN COUNTRY UK: 100 Tanglin Road, Singapore 247919, tel (65) 6424 4200, fax (65) 6424 4250, email commercial.singapore@fco.gov.uk. USA: 27 Napier Road, Singapore 258508, tel (65) 6476 9100, fax (65) 6476 9232, email singaporecon@state.gov.

PEOPLE AND PLACE

CAPITAL Singapore City.

LANGUAGE Malay, English, Mandarin, Tamil.

PEOPLES Chinese (78%), Malay (14%), European, Tamil.

RELIGION Buddhist, Taoist, Muslim, Christian, Hindu.

SIZE (SQ KM) 659.9.

POPULATION 4,185,200.

POP DENSITY/KM 6,342.2.

STATE OF THE NATION

SAFETY Safe.

LIFE EXPECTANCY M 79.05, F 84.39.

BEING THERE

ETIQUETTE Formal courtesies. Remove shoes before entering a home, temple or mosque. Gifts appreciated. Dress informal. Smart appearance for restaurants and meetings. Each ethnic group has maintained its individual culture and identity, yet is integral to the community. Strict laws cover jaywalking, littering, and chewing gum in urban areas. Smoking is discouraged - smoking illegally or dropping a butt can lead to a S$500 fine.

CURRENCY Singapore dollar (S$) = 100 cents.

FINANCE Credit cards and traveller's cheques widely accepted.

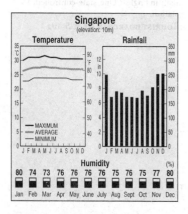

Singapore
(elevation: 10m)

Temperature / Rainfall

— MAXIMUM
— AVERAGE
— MINIMUM

Humidity (%)

	Jan	Feb	Mar	Apr	May	June	July	Aug	Sept	Oct	Nov	Dec
	80	74	73	76	76	76	76	75	76	75	77	80

HIGHLIGHTS

SINGAPORE CITY
Founded in 1819 by Sir Stamford Raffles of the British East India Company, it was he who devised the idea to set aside pockets for different ethnic groups. These areas still exist as Chinatown, Arab Street, Serangoon Road (Indian), and Padang Square (colonial). The different architectural styles and customs of these areas contrast wildly with the lavish but bland luxury shopping in the modern arcades of Orchard Road and Raffles City. Having toured these areas, take a break in the famous Raffles Hotel, for the *de rigueur* Singapore Sling in the Long Bar - though purists find its modern makeover rather dull. Clarke Quay is a complex of warehouses turned into bars, cafes, and clubs: doing the Riverside Walk here gives the best sense of old Singapore.

GREEN SPACE To the west of the city lie 116 acres of Botanic Gardens, home to many animals and plants, including the National Orchid Garden with the world's largest collection. North on the island is the Singapore Zoological Gardens, an open zoo that uses natural barriers and no bars. It's home to 170 animals, including orangutans, Sumatran tigers, Komodo dragons and clouded leopards. Night Safaris can be taken.

SENTOSA The largest off-shore island, close to the mainland, is a multi-million-dollar pleasure island, served by a monorail, with lavish attractions and beaches.

BUSINESS HOURS 0900-1300 and 1400-1700 Mon-Friday, 0900-1300 Saturday.

GMT +8.

VOLTAGE GUIDE 220/240 AC, 50 Hz.

COUNTRY DIALLING CODE 65.

CONSUMING PLEASURES

FOOD & DRINK Over 30 different cooking styles, including local interpretations of Chinese, Indian, Malay, Indonesian, Korean, Japanese, French and Italian cuisine. *Satay*, cubes of skewered, grilled meat served with peanut sauce, is popular, as is *gado gado*, a fruit and vegetable salad in a peanut sauce. Curries such as beef *rendang* are another favourite, and are often based on coconut milk. Bars have no licensing hours.

SHOPPING & SOUVENIRS Antiques, batiks, cameras, carpets, tailored clothing, jewellery, reptile and snake skin items, shoes, briefcases, handbags, wallets, silks, perfumes, wigs.

FIND OUT MORE

WEBSITES www.mfa.gov.sg/london, www.visitsingapore.com, www.britain.org.sg, www.mfa.gov.sg/washington, http://visitsingapore.com, http://singapore.usembassy.gov.

LOCAL MEDIA English-language newspapers include *The Straits Times, The New Paper, The Business Times* and *Streats*.

TOURIST BOARDS IN UK/US UK: 1st floor, Carrinton House, 126-130 Regent Street, London W1B 5JX, tel (020) 7437 0033, fax (020) 7734 2191, email info@stb.org.uk. US: 1156 Avenue of the Americas, Suite 3702, New York, NY 10036, (212) 302 4861, fax (212) 302 4801, email askroc@tourismsingapore.com.

The Suntec City Fountain of Wealth, in Singapore, is the world's largest fountain. It covers 1,683 square metres and cost US$6 million to build in 1997

SLOVAKIA

WHEN TO GO

WEATHER Very cold winters (November-March), warm summers June-August).

FESTIVALS Most towns have folk festivals with dancing, costumes, and food during the summer, leading up to the harvest festivals in September. The largest music festival is the Bazant Pohoda, held each year in July near Trencin, which attracts big international bands. An International Film Festival is held in Bratislava in November.

TRANSPORT

INTERNATIONAL AIRPORTS Bratislava (BTS) is 10 km from city. (Vienna airport is only 50 km across the border from the capital.) Also Kosice (KSC) and Tatry-Poprad (TAT).

INTERNAL TRAVEL Good road and rail links, also a network of navigable rivers and canals.

RED TAPE

VISAS REQUIRED (UK/US) Not required as follows: Canada 90 days, UK 180 days, USA 30 days. Required for Australia.

VACCINATIONS REQUIRED: See 'Vaccinations required around the world' on page 653.

DRIVING REQUIREMENTS International Driving Permit useful.

COUNTRY REPS IN UK/US UK: 25 Kensington Palace Gardens, London W8 4QY, tel (020) 7313 6470, fax (020) 7313 6481, email mail@slovakembassy.co.uk. USA: 3523 International Court, NW, Washington, DC 20008, tel (202) 237 1054, fax (202) 237 6438, email info@slovakembassy-us.org.

UK/US REPS IN COUNTRY UK: Panská 16, 811 01 Bratislava, tel (2) 5998 2000, fax (2) 5998 2269, email bebra@internet.sk. USA: Hviezdoslavovo nám 5, 811 02 Bratislava, tel (2) 5443 3338, fax (2) 5441 8861, email cons@usembassy.sk.

PEOPLE AND PLACE

CAPITAL Bratislava.

LANGUAGE Slovak.

PEOPLES Slovak. Also Hungarian and Czech.

RELIGION Roman Catholic (60%), other Christian denominations, Jewish.

SIZE (SQ KM) 49,033.

POPULATION 5,378,595.

POP DENSITY/KM 109.7.

STATE OF THE NATION

SAFETY Safe.

LIFE EXPECTANCY M 70.52, F 78.68.

BEING THERE

ETIQUETTE Usual courtesies apply. Punctuality much appreciated.

CURRENCY *Slovenská koruna* (Sk) = 100 *halierov*.

FINANCE Credit cards and traveller's cheques accepted, particularly in banks.

BUSINESS HOURS 0800-1600 Mon-Friday.

GMT +2.

VOLTAGE GUIDE 220 AC, 50 Hz.

COUNTRY DIALLING CODE 421.

CONSUMING PLEASURES

FOOD & DRINK Influenced over the ages by Hungarian, Austrian and German cooking.

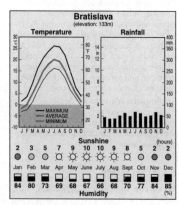

Bratislava
(elevation: 133m)

Temperature — Rainfall

MAXIMUM
AVERAGE
MINIMUM

Sunshine											(hours)
2	3	5	7	9	10	10	9	8	5	2	2
Jan	Feb	Mar	Apr	May	June	July	Aug	Sept	Oct	Nov	Dec
84	80	73	69	68	67	66	68	70	77	84	85

Humidity (%)

HIGHLIGHTS

BRATISLAVA On the banks of the River Danube, at the foot of the Little Carpathian Mountains, lies the nation's capital. The old town is the area to head for, with the Old Town Square, fantastic frescoes in Trinity Church, and icons and jewellery displayed at the museum in the old Corpus Christi Church. The Town Hall is a blend of Gothic, Renaissance, and nineteenth-century architecture, and the Mirbach Palace boasts wonderful stucco decor. Views from the waterfront across the Danube

plain are gasp-inducing, but they get even better from the restaurant atop the single support column of the controversial Bridge of the Slovak Uprising.

HIGH TATRA MOUNTAINS Possibly the greatest tourist attraction in the country, these mountains have a wealth of impressive features. The National Park here has abundant wildlife and 13,000 species of plant. This is thanks to the large variation in altitude, from 900 metres to 2,655 metres. Great Hincovo is the largest of 85 splendid

mountain lakes. Excellent sporting facilities, good accommodation, spas, and hiking trails compete for your time. The best downhill and bobsleigh runs are at Skalnaté Pleso.

THE EAST Home to Spiis Castle, the biggest medieval castle in central Europe; the church of St James, itself housing the world's tallest Gothic altar at 18.6 metres; a pine forest covered in waterfalls; and Europe's oldest ice cave at Dobsiná. Excellent hiking can be had in the area: it is best to begin this from Hrabusice-Podlesok.

Soups, stews, hearty meat dishes with dumplings and a liberal use of dairy products typifies Slavic cuisine. Alcoholic specialities include *borovicka* (strong gin) and *slivovica* (plum brandy).

SHOPPING & SOUVENIRS Pottery, porcelain, woodcarvings, embroidered clothing, glass and crystal, folk ceramics.

FIND OUT MORE

WEBSITES www.slovakembassy.co.uk, www.britishembassy.sk, www.slovakembassy-us.org, www.usembassy.sk, www.slovakia.org, www.heartofeurope.co.uk, www.sacr.sk.

LOCAL MEDIA *The Slovak Spectator* (bi-weekly), *Slovak Foreign Trade* (monthly) are both in English.

TOURIST BOARDS IN UK/US n/a.

The geographical centre of Europe is a hill known as Krahule, near the town of Kremnica, in Slovakia

Priority Membership Enquiry

Membership Services Department

WEXAS

FREEPOST

London

SW3 1BR

HIGHLIGHTS

LJUBLJANA Passing pretty forested peaks and lush blue lakes on the way to Slovenia's capital, you might feel as though you've stepped into a fairytale kingdom - an impression that strengthens when you arrive in this engaging city of cobbled streets and fine Baroque and Hapsburg architecture, overlooked by a hilltop castle. The modern world has been let in too, with pleasant riverside cafes and a fun night scene epitomising the optimism of a young, self-confident nation.

LAKES Like the land of make believe, the fairytale theme continues on Lake Bled, complete with its island church and atmospheric castle. In summer, enjoy a dip in the blue-green waters, or a stroll along the water's edge. In winter, the lake is a popular place for skating and curling. Another splendid alpine lake is Lake Bohinj, less visited but more serene.

JULIAN ALPS Hike through one of Europe's least spoilt ranges, with trails to suit both walking novices and hardened

mountaineers.

WINTER SPORTS Ski, slide and snowboard your way through any of the country's twenty ski resorts. Alpine skiing is Slovenia's number one pursuit.

LIPICA Home to the famous Lippizaner horse, originally bred by the Austro-Hungarian aristocracy for the Spanish Riding School in Vienna. Today, only 3,000 remain in the world, but visitors can tour the stud farm, watch a performance of classical riding, or straddle a horse of their own.

BUSINESS HOURS 0800-1600 Mon-Friday. GMT +1.
VOLTAGE GUIDE 220 AC, 50 Hz.
COUNTRY DIALLING CODE 386.

CONSUMING PLEASURES

FOOD & DRINK Slovenia's cuisine shows Austro-German influences, with *sauerkraut*, grilled sausage and *strudel* often appearing on menus. A national favourite is a wide range of breads made for special occasions. These are often stuffed with sweet or savoury fillings. Western and north-eastern areas are home to outstanding white wines, while the Adriatic coast has red *karstteran* wine.

SHOPPING & SOUVENIRS Lace, crystal glass, speciality wines.

FIND OUT MORE

WEBSITES www.gov.si/mzz/dkp/vlo/eng, www.slovenia-tourism.si, www.british-embassy.si, www.embassy.org/slovenia.

LOCAL MEDIA *Ars Vivendi, Slovenian Business Report, Slovenia Weekly* and *Slovenija* are the English-language dailies.

TOURIST BOARDS IN UK/US UK: The Barns, Woodlands End, Mells, Frome, Somerset BA11 3QD, tel (0870) 225 5305, fax (01373) 813 444, email info@slovenian-tourism.co.uk. US: 2929 East Commercial Boulevard, Suite 201, Fort Lauderdale, FL 33308, tel (954) 491 0112, fax (954) 771 9841, slotouristboard@kompas.net.

Carved out by the Reka River, the 5,800 metre-long Scocjan Caves are said to be the world's largest underground canyon system

SOMALIA

POPULATION 9,480,000.

POP DENSITY/KM 14.9.

WHEN TO GO

WEATHER Hot and dry January-February and August. Rainy March-June and September-December.

FESTIVALS The main festivals in Somalia are those of the Islamic calendar, and are timed according to the various phases of the moon. Ramadan, the month of fasting, is among the most important. In rural areas the Dab-Shid (fire lighting) festival is held with bonfires, stick fights and dances. At other times, feasts may feature ritualistic and recreational dance, music and folk songs.

TRANSPORT

INTERNATIONAL AIRPORTS Mogadishu (MGQ) is 6 km from city.

INTERNAL TRAVEL Poor roads. Reasonable flights. Taxis are available in large towns, which buses run between.

RED TAPE

VISAS REQUIRED (UK/US) Required.

VACCINATIONS REQUIRED: See 'Vaccinations required around the world' on page 653.

DRIVING REQUIREMENTS International Driving Permit.

COUNTRY REPS IN UK/US UK: n/a. USA: n/a.

UK/US REPS IN COUNTRY UK: Somalia enquiries are handled by the embassy in Nairobi (see Kenya), Somaliland enquiries by the High Commission in Addis Ababa (see Ethiopia). USA: Handled by the embassy in Nairobi (see Kenya).

PEOPLE AND PLACE

CAPITAL Mogadishu.

LANGUAGE Somali and Arabic. Also Swahili, Italian, English.

PEOPLES Somali.

RELIGION Sunni Muslim (98%), Christian.

SIZE (SQ KM) 637,657.

STATE OF THE NATION

SAFETY Very unsafe. Subject to random violence and warfare between warlords who control clan-based regions. Somaliland (a splinter state) is marginally calmer. Seek latest information at time of visit.

LIFE EXPECTANCY M 46.36, F 49.87.

BEING THERE

ETIQUETTE Men in Somalia wear basic, casual businesswear on a daily basis. Local customs should be observed and respected. For instance, men should not shake hands with women unless they are close relatives or a family member. The state religion is Islam and the majority of Somalis are Sunni Muslims. Women should wear conservative clothing, mostly skirts or dresses. Other religious practices should be respected. You should only eat with the right hand and it is not acceptable to drink alcohol or eat pork.

CURRENCY Somali shilling (SoSh) = 100 cents.

FINANCE Cash is the only widely accepted means of payment. US dollars are best.

BUSINESS HOURS 0800-1400 Saturday-Thursday.

GMT +3.

VOLTAGE GUIDE 220 AC, 50 Hz.

COUNTRY DIALLING CODE 252.

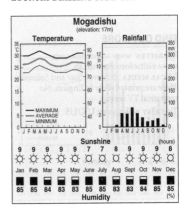

Mogadishu (elevation: 17m)

HIGHLIGHTS

NATIONAL PARKS
Somalia has ten game reserves, including Kismayu National Park. These wildlife areas are home to rare East African species, if any remain.

SOMALILAND
Self-proclaimed re-public, whose capital is Hargeisa, unique for being bombed by the Somali military and subsequently rebuilt by monies provided by the region's overseas citizens. It is considered an area of future growth.

KISIMAYO Located on the coast of the Indian Ocean, Kisimayo is the principal town and port of the Jubbada Hoose region. It's home to several mosques and an elegant palace constructed by the sultan.

BAJUNI ISLANDS
These isolated islands are located off the shore of Kisimayo, at the beginning of the coral reef that stretches from the equator down Africa's east coast. The islands offer good diving.

BERBERA In the north of Somalia on the Gulf of Aden, it served as the winter capital of British Somaliland until 1941 and is home to an old Soviet naval and missile base. Today it's a bustling city port, with little to draw travellers.

MOGADISHU
Former beautiful city, with a recent history of lawlessness and brutality. Since the civil war, the country's dishevelled capital has taken on a *Mad Max* feel, with heavily armed clans protecting their own patch and prowling the ruins in armoured pick-ups.

BEACHES Somalia's Indian Ocean beaches are hugged by coral reefs from Mogadishu to the Kenyan border.

CONSUMING PLEASURES

FOOD & DRINK The staple diet all over Somalia is rice, macaroni or spaghetti with a little sauce, or spiced mutton or kid; and for breakfast, fried liver of goat, sheep or camel with onions and bread. Local seafood is also available.

SHOPPING & SOUVENIRS Gold, silver jewellery, woven cloth, baskets.

FIND OUT MORE

WEBSITES www.somalianews.com, http://allafrica.com/somalia, www.angelfire.com/ar/arawelo/index.html.
LOCAL MEDIA No newspapers in English.
TOURIST BOARDS IN UK/US n/a.

Somalia is one of the few countries in the world with no central government

SOUTH AFRICA

WHEN TO GO

WEATHER Warm all year.

FESTIVALS South Africa stages festivals throughout the year, with something for everyone. Food festivals include the Prickly Pear Festival in February/March in the Eastern Cape, and Lambert's Bay Kreeffees in Cape Town in March. Music festivals include the Origin Festival in the Western Cape, the FNB Dance Umbrella in Johannesburg in February, and Oppikoppi is held in the *bushveld* in the north in August and is South Africa's Glastonbury. The gay Pink Loerie Mardi Gras is held in Knysna in the Western Cape in May.

TRANSPORT

INTERNATIONAL AIRPORTS Cape Town (CPT) is 22 km from city. Johannesburg (JNB) is 24 km from city. Also Durban (DUR), Port Elizabeth (PLZ), Bloemfontein (BFN).

INTERNAL TRAVEL Excellent roads and flights, slightly erratic trains. Several bus companies operate, taxis throughout the country. Car-hire, and chauffeurs are available.

RED TAPE

VISAS REQUIRED (UK/US) Not required.

VACCINATIONS REQUIRED: See 'Vaccinations required around the world' on page 653.

DRIVING REQUIREMENTS International Driving Permit. Minimum age 23 (21 with Amex or Diners Club card). English language licences valid for six months.

COUNTRY REPS IN UK/US UK: 15 Whitehall, London SW1A 2DD, tel (020) 7925 8900, fax (020) 7925 8930, email mailmaster@rsaconsulate.co.uk. USA: 3051 Massachusetts Avenue, NW, Washington, DC 20008, tel (202) 232 4400, fax (202) 265 1607, email info@saembassy.org.

UK/US REPS IN COUNTRY UK: 15th Flr, Southern Life Centre, 8 Riebeeck Street, Cape Town 8001, tel (21) 405 2400, fax (21) 405 2448, email Consular.SectionCT@ fco.gov.uk. USA: 877 Pretorius Street, Pretoria, tel (12) 431 4000, fax (12) 342 2299, email embassypretoria@state.gov.

PEOPLE AND PLACE

CAPITAL Pretoria.

LANGUAGE Afrikaans, English, Ndebele, Pedi, Sotho, Swati, Tsonga, Tswana, Venda, Xhosa, Zulu.

PEOPLES Zulu (23%), Xhosa, Ndebele, European descent (16%), Setswana, Sotho, Venda and other tribal origins.

RELIGION Various Christian denominations, Hindu, Muslim, Jewish.

SIZE (SQ KM) 1,219,090.

POPULATION 45,454,211.

POP DENSITY/KM 36.8.

STATE OF THE NATION

SAFETY Politically stable but experiencing high levels of crime, especially in cities and black townships. Johannesburg is infamous for carjackings and muggings, Cape Town quieter. Rape a serious problem nationwide.

LIFE EXPECTANCY M 43.47, F 43.06.

BEING THERE

ETIQUETTE Normal courtesies apply. Casual dress widely accepted. Evening dress requires a jacket and tie for men, full length

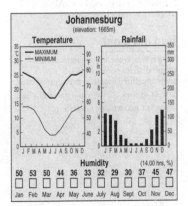

Johannesburg
(elevation: 1665m)

HIGHLIGHTS

CAPE TOWN Lying at the foot of flat-topped Table Mountain is this beautiful seaside city. Views of the city can be had by taking the cable car ride to the top of the mountain, but be sure to do so on a cloud free day. The Victoria And Alfred Waterfront is where it all happens - there's free entertainment, shops, museums, an aquarium, bars and restaurants. Boat trips can be taken from here to Robben Island, the prison where Nelson Mandela was held. Excursions from here can be taken to the wine-tasting country north of the city in towns such as Stellenbosch, while the adventurous should head to the Blaukrans River for a bungee jump: at 216 metres, it is twice the height of the one at Victoria Falls. They can also go shark-cage diving with Great Whites on the Cape.

THE GARDEN ROUTE The route along the south coast takes its name from the days when it was heavily forested. Some hardwood forest remains after development, but the beauty is still there. Excellent beaches, watersports, birdwatching in the wilderness ad nature reserves for dolphins and primates make for a wonderful holiday destination. The Outeniqua Choo-Tjoe steam train runs the route between George and Knysna.

KRUGER NATIONAL PARK A reserve the size of Wales and a great place to spot the Big Five and many other species, with accommodation for all needs from luxury cottages to campsite enclosures. This is one of Africa's top game parks.

---

dress for women. Smoking is prohibited in public places and on public transport.

CURRENCY *Rand* (R).

FINANCE Credit cards and traveller's cheques widely accepted.

BUSINESS HOURS 0830-1630 Mon-Friday.

GMT +2.

VOLTAGE GUIDE 220/230 AC (250 AC in Pretoria), 50 Hz.

COUNTRY DIALLING CODE 27.

CONSUMING PLEASURES

FOOD & DRINK Excellent local produce, including meat, fruit and wine. The long coastline produces fresh, cheap seafood. Typical dishes include *sosaties* (a type of kebab), *bobotie* (a curried mince dish), *bredies* (meat, tomato and vegetable stews). *Poetoepap* or *stywepap*, made with white maize meal, is often served with meat. *Biltong* (dried meat) is a speciality. Excellent red and white wines are produced, as are sherries, brandies and unusual liqueurs.

SHOPPING & SOUVENIRS Upmarket boutiques mix with street traders. Ceramics and crafts from the continent, fur goods, diamond and semi-precious stone jewellery, gold, and local liqueurs.

FIND OUT MORE

WEBSITES www.southafricahouse.com, www.southafrica.net, www.britain.org.za, www.saembassy.org, www.southafrica.com, www.SANParks.org, www.gardenroute.co.za, www.joburg.co.za, www.gocapetown.co.za, www.wine.co.za.

LOCAL MEDIA Published in English and Afrikaans, papers include *Cape Argus, The Citizen, Daily Dispatch, Mercury, The Star* and *Sowetan*.

TOURIST BOARDS IN UK/US UK: 6 Alt Grove, London SW1A 2DD, tel (020) 8971 9364, fax (020) 8944 6705, email info@uk.southafrica.net. US: 500 Fifth Avenue, 20th Floor, Suite 2040, New York, NY 10110, tel (212) 730 2929, fax (212) 764 1980, email newyork@southafrica.net.

SPAIN

WHEN TO GO

WEATHER Hot all year, except the centre and north, which can be very cold in winter (November-April). Searing in summer (July-August).

FESTIVALS Las Fallas Fire Festival, held in Valencia in mid-March is a weird and wonderful spectacle of *papier-maché* statues, some over 30 feet high. which are then set alight on St Joseph's Day (Father's Day). The Tenerife Carnival is the place to be during February and is said to be second only to Rio's festival. Semana Santa (Holy Week) during Easter is one of Spain's most important celebrations. Pamplona's Running of the Bulls takes place in July. La Tomatina, in Buñol, sees the town go mad in an annual tomato fight on the last Wednesday in August.

TRANSPORT

INTERNATIONAL AIRPORTS Madrid (MAD) is 13 km from city. Also Alicante (ALC), Barcelona (BCN), Bilbao (BIO), Malaga (AGP), Santiago de Compostella (SCQ), Seville (SVQ), Valencia (VLC) and island airports.

INTERNAL TRAVEL Excellent road and flight network, railways good.

RED TAPE

VISAS REQUIRED (UK/US) Not required.

VACCINATIONS REQUIRED: See 'Vaccinations required around the world' on page 653.

DRIVING REQUIREMENTS EU pink format licence. Third party insurance. Green Card recommended.

COUNTRY REPS IN UK/US UK: 20 Draycott Place, London SW3 2RZ, tel (020) 7589 8989, fax (020) 7581 7888, email conspalon@mail.mae.es. USA: 2375 Pennsylvania Avenue, NW, Washington, DC 20037, tel (202) 452 0100, fax (202) 833 5670, email embespus@mail.mae.es.

UK/US REPS IN COUNTRY UK: Paseo de Recoletos 7-9, 4th Floor, 28004 Madrid,

tel (91) 524 9700, fax (91) 524 9730, email madridconsulate@ukinspain.com. USA: Serrano 75, 28006 Madrid, tel (91) 587 2200, fax (910 587 2303, email amemb@embusa.es.

PEOPLE AND PLACE

CAPITAL Madrid.

LANGUAGE Spanish, Basque.

PEOPLES Castilian (72%), Catalan (17%), Galician, Basque, Gitano.

RELIGION Roman Catholic (96%).

SIZE (SQ KM) 505,988.

POPULATION 40,280,878.

POP DENSITY/KM 84.4.

STATE OF THE NATION

SAFETY Safe, except for the Basque region, where separatist violence has included political assassinations and car-bombs.

LIFE EXPECTANCY M 76.18, F 83.08.

BEING THERE

ETIQUETTE Spanish life has seen a rapid change recently and much of the old, stricter religious customs are being replaced by more modern views, though many still remain. Conservative casualwear is accepted, beachwear should be confined to the beach or pool. Black tie is normally specified when needed. Evening meals are eaten late, generally after 9pm.

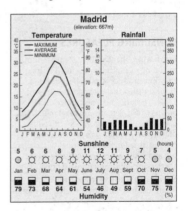

HIGHLIGHTS

MADRID The capital city may be short on monuments, but it is thriving with culture. Visit the Royal Palace before roaming around one its fine art museums, the Prado, Arte Reina Sofia or the Museo Thyssen-Bornemisza. West of the city centre are simpler attractions such as the Casa de Campo exercise village and a large amusement park.

PAMPLONA A quiet charming town with old plazas alongside modern buildings and a vibrant nightlife.

Home to the Fiesta de San Fermin, better know as the Running of the Bulls: the event sees perfectly normal people turn slightly mad as they try to out run hundreds of bulls along tiny, winding streets. The entire town turns out for the event dressed in red and white, and later visits the bull ring to see the *matadors* perform.

BARCELONA The second largest city became the centre of commerce and industry thanks to its large port. Impressive architecture dates back to the fourteenth century. Stroll up the bustling Las Ramblas, from the port, beyond Plaça Real, and up to Plaça de Catalunya passing cafes, street artists and stalls. Gaudi's Parc Güell, La Sagrada Familia cathedral and Casa Batlló are all superb, as is the Picasso museum.

GRANADA The last Moorish city to come under Christian control. It contains the magnificent *Alhambra* palace and gardens, like a setting from the Arabian Nights.

CURRENCY Euro (€) = 100 *cents*.

FINANCE Credit cards and traveller's cheques widely accepted.

BUSINESS HOURS Variable. Generally start 0800 and finish 2000, with a *siesta* of 2-3 hours in the middle.

GMT +1.

VOLTAGE GUIDE 220 AC, 50 Hz.

COUNTRY DIALLING CODE 34.

CONSUMING PLEASURES

FOOD & DRINK The excellent tradition of *tapas* (small portions of olives, cheese, meat and seafood) thrives in bars and restaurants. More substantial dishes include *zarzuelas* (fish stews), rice-based *paellas* and *butifarra* (sausage stewed with beans, partridge with cabbage). *Gazpacho* (a refreshing tomato-based soup), *chorizo* (sausage) and *jamon serrano* (air-dried ham) are well known, as are the excellent Spanish sherries and wines.

SHOPPING & SOUVENIRS Leather goods, especially suede coats and jackets, wooden furniture, toys, shoes, rugs and carpets, sherries, wines.

FIND OUT MORE

WEBSITES www.mae.es, www.spain.info, www.ukinspain.com, www.spainemb.org, www.okspain.org, www.embusa.es.

LOCAL MEDIA *Costa Blanca, Majorca Daily Bulletin,* and English edition of weekly *Sur,* are published in English.

TOURIST BOARDS IN UK/US UK: 2nd Floor, New Cavendish Street, London W1W 6XB, tel (020) 7486 8077, fax (020) 7486 8034, email info.londres@tourspain.es. US: 666 Fifth Avenue, Btwn 52nd and 53rd Street, 35th Floor, New York, NY 10103, tel (212) 265 8822, fax (212) 265 8864, email oetny@tourspain.es.

The modern acoustic guitar is thought to have been invented in Spain – an adaptation of the Arab *oud,* which was brought here by the medieval Moors

SRI LANKA

WHEN TO GO

WEATHER Warm all year, except in the highlands, which are cool and wet. Monsoons occur from May-July and December-January.

FESTIVALS Duruthu Perahera Festival commemorates the visit of Buddha to Sri Lanka. Esala is a season of festivals from July to August - the full moon of Esala signifies its climax. Kandy Esala Perahera is the most magnificent, a medieval pageant for ten nights with Kandyan chieftains, dancers and drummers, all dressed in colourful costumes. The full moon day (Poya) is celebrated each month.

TRANSPORT

INTERNATIONAL AIRPORTS Colombo Bandaranayake (CMB) is 32 km from city.

INTERNAL TRAVEL Good roads and trains. Some flights.

RED TAPE

VISAS REQUIRED (UK/US) Issued on arrival as follows: for 30 days UK, Canada; for 90 days USA, Australia.

VACCINATION s REQUIRED: See 'Vaccinations required around the world' on page 653.

DRIVING REQUIREMENTS International Driving permit. (Temporary local driving licence can be obtained instead, but the red tape is formidable.)

COUNTRY REPS IN UK/US UK: 13 Hyde Park Gardens, London W2 2LU, tel (020) 7262 1841, fax (020) 7262 7970, email mail@slhc.globalnet.co.uk. USA: 2148 Wyoming Avenue, NW, Washington, DC 20008, tel (202) 483 4025, fax (202) 232 7181, email slembasy@slembassyusa.org.

UK/US REPS IN COUNTRY UK: 190 Galle Road, Colombo 3, Kollupitiya, tel (1) 244 8007, fax (1) 243 7345, email bhc@ eureka.lk. USA: 210 Galle Road, Colombo 3, tel (1) 244 8007, fax (1) 243 7345, email consularcolombo@state.gov.

PEOPLE AND PLACE

CAPITAL Colombo.

LANGUAGE Sinhala, Tamil, English.

PEOPLES Sinhalese (74%), Tamil (18%), Arab or European descent.

RELIGION Mainly Buddhist, minority Tamils.

SIZE (SQ KM) 65,525.

POPULATION 19,007,000.

POP DENSITY/KM 286.

STATE OF THE NATION

SAFETY Politically volatile. Separatist guerrilla war by the Tamil Tigers periodically sweeps across the north and east, and sometimes causes attacks in main cities. Seek latest information at time of visit.

LIFE EXPECTANCY M 70.6, F 75.86.

BEING THERE

ETIQUETTE Shaking hands is a normal form of greeting. Punctuality is important and, when visiting, a token of appreciation is always welcomed. It is customary to be offered tea when visiting and it is impolite to refuse. Visitors should be appropriately dressed when visiting a place of worship, where shoes and hats must be removed. Western dress is suitable. For formal functions it is best to wear lightweight suits.

CURRENCY Sri Lanka *rupee* (SLRe) = 100 cents.

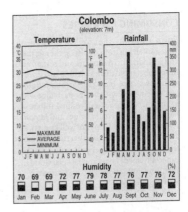

Colombo
(elevation: 7m)

Temperature / Rainfall

MAXIMUM
AVERAGE
MINIMUM

	Jan	Feb	Mar	Apr	May	June	July	Aug	Sept	Oct	Nov	Dec
Humidity (%)	70	69	69	72	77	79	78	77	76	77	76	72

HIGHLIGHTS

COLOMBO The capital blends Western culture with its own traditions and heritage. Fort, so called because it was a military garrison during the Dutch and Portuguese occupation, forms the commercial centre. Pettah is home to a bustling bazaar with much to offer the traveller. Visits to the many Buddhist or Hindu temples are inspiring. Fantastic flowering trees are on display at Vihara Maha Devi Park, and are best seen in spring.

KANDY The capital of the Hill Country was the last stand for the Kandyan Kings who thwarted foreign conquest until 1815. A cultural sanctuary for age-old customs, rituals and way of life, it's a jumble of old shops, and busy markets. A beautiful lake in the centre, fringed by rolling hills, is the setting for important temples. The Hill Country around Kandy has excellent walks, tea factories, colonial bungalows and train rides through beautiful landscapes.

BEACHES

There are 1,000 miles of fine beaches around the island, but be careful to check which are safe for swimming. Surfers head east, hippies south, tourists west: take your pick.

NATIONAL PARKS & RESERVES Blessed with an abundance of flora and fauna, the island's parks are the place to see its unique species. Yala West (Ruhuna) National Park is good for spotting elephant and sambar deer, while Sinharaja Forest Reserve is a magnificent rainforest preserve.

FINANCE Credit cards and traveller's cheques widely accepted.

BUSINESS HOURS 0800-1630 Mon-Friday.

GMT +6.

VOLTAGE GUIDE 230/240 AC, 50 Hz.

COUNTRY DIALLING CODE 94.

CONSUMING PLEASURES

FOOD & DRINK Spicy curries, often made with coconut milk, sliced onion, green chilli, cloves, nutmeg, cinnamon, saffron and aromatic leaves. Local produce is excellent, particularly seafood and fruit. *Toddy* is a popular drink made from the sap of a palm tree. Fermented, it becomes *arrack*, which is available in different strengths.

SHOPPING & SOUVENIRS Handicrafts, silver curios, brass, bone, ceramics, wood, terracotta, cane baskets, straw hats, tea, batiks, lace, masks.

FIND OUT MORE

WEBSITES www.slhclondon.org, www.srilankantourism.org, www.britishhighcommission.gov.uk/srilanka, www.slembassyusa.org, http://usembassy.state.gov/srilanka.

LOCAL MEDIA *Daily News, Evening Observer, The Island, Daily Mirror,* and *Lankadeepa* are published in English.

TOURIST BOARDS IN UK/US
UK: Clareville House, 26-27 Oxendon Street, London SW1Y 4EL, tel (020) 7930 2627, fax (020)7930 9070, email srilankatourism.org. US: n/a.

The world record for balancing on one foot is held by Arulanantham Suresh Joachim, of Sri Lanka. He balanced for 76 hours and 40 minutes at Vihara Maha Devi Park, from 22 to 25 May 1997

SUDAN

WHEN TO GO

WEATHER Very hot all year. Sandstorms April-September.

FESTIVALS Annual events celebrated in Sudan are mainly Muslim holy days, such as Eid-al-Adha, the feast of sacrifice, and Ramadan (dates vary). Local tribes also have their own festivals and customs, often characterised by traditional dancing. Independence Day is celebrated on 1 January, while Revolution Day is on 30 June.

TRANSPORT

INTERNATIONAL AIRPORTS Khartoum (KRT) is 4 km from city.

INTERNAL TRAVEL Bad roads, erratic and slow railway, unsavoury ferries on the Nile. Some good flights.

RED TAPE

VISAS REQUIRED (UK/US) Required.

VACCINATIONS REQUIRED: See 'Vaccinations required around the world' on page 653.

DRIVING REQUIREMENTS *Carnet de passage*, roadworthiness certificate (from embassy), adequate finance. Temporary driving licence obtainable on production of national driving licence.

COUNTRY REPS IN UK/US UK: 3 Cleveland Row, St James', London SW1A 1DD, tel (020) 7839, 8080. fax (020) 7839, 7560, email admin@sudanembassy.co.uk. USA: 2210 Massachusetts Avenue, NW, Washington, DC 20008, tel (202) 338 8565, fax (202) 667 2406, email info@ sudanembassy.org.

UK/US REPS IN COUNTRY UK: PO Box 801, off Sharia Al Baladiya, Khartoum East, tel (183) 777 105, fax (183) 776 457, email Information.Khartoum@fco.gov.uk. USA: Handled by the embassy in Cairo (see Egypt).

PEOPLE AND PLACE

CAPITAL Khartoum.

LANGUAGE Arabic. Also English.

PEOPLES Arabic, Nubian, Nuer, Dinka, other tribal groups.

RELIGION Sunni Muslim (70%), Christian in south (9%), traditional beliefs (20%).

SIZE (SQ KM) 2,505,813.

POPULATION 32,878,000.

POP DENSITY/KM 13.1.

STATE OF THE NATION

SAFETY The long-term separatist war in the south seems to have been settled with a power-sharing deal. But Darfur in the west is seriously unstable. Avoid the Ethiopian or Eritrean borders. Seek latest information at time of visit.

LIFE EXPECTANCY M 57.33, F 59.8.

BEING THERE

ETIQUETTE The culture of the north of Sudan is predominantly Arabic, while the south is dominated by many tribes, each with their own lifestyle and belief. As Sudan is largely Muslim, women should not dress in revealing clothing. In the main cities a curfew is in operation between midnight and 4 am.

CURRENCY Sudanese *dinar* (sD) = 100 *piastres*.

FINANCE Amex is widely accepted. Other

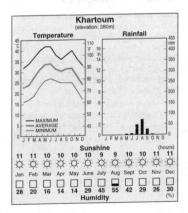

Khartoum (elevation: 380m)

HIGHLIGHTS

KHARTOUM The main attraction of the capital is its location at the confluence of the Blue Nile and White Nile. Venture up on a ferris wheel for commanding views of the two mighty rivers merging into one. Then check out the fun atmosphere of the *souks* - or visit Omdurman's camel market and haggle for the best price.

MEROE The ancient city of Meroe was the centre of the Nubian kingdom around 300 BC. It is now home to many ancient pyramids, built to house the bodies of former Kings and Queens, and has been described as one of the largest archaeological sites in the world.

THE RED SEA The biggest attraction in Sudan, and home to some excellent wreck diving, marine life and coral reefs. You can also visit the ruins of Suakin, a former Red Sea port built of coral houses.

DINDER NATIONAL PARK Large reserve, home to a wide variety of wild animals: including giraffes, lions, leopards, bushbuck and kudu. There are also lots of birds, such as the crown crane, pelican and stork. A good base for entering the park is the village of Dinder. The conditions are difficult, but the friendly nature of the people may well make up for this.

JEBEL MARRA Extinct volcano dominating the western skyline at over 3,000 metres. At its base lies the town of Nyala, surrounded by waterfalls, rolling scenery and orchards. If you venture towards the crater you will be able to rest your limbs in the hot springs.

cards and traveller's cheques not widely used.

BUSINESS HOURS 0800-1430 Saturday-Thursday.

GMT +2.

VOLTAGE GUIDE 240 AC, 50 Hz.

COUNTRY DIALLING CODE 249.

CONSUMING PLEASURES

FOOD & DRINK Local staples are *ful mudamis* (stewed brown beans), *fasooliyya* (stewed white beans), *dura* (cooked maize or millet), often served with *kibda* (liver), *sheya* (charcoal barbecued meat) or *kalawi* (chopped kidney) or *chawarma* (lamb sliced fresh from a roasting spit). Alcohol is banned.

SHOPPING & SOUVENIRS Food, local crafts, spices, jewellery, silver, basketwork, ebony, gold.

FIND OUT MORE

WEBSITES www.sudan-embassy.co.uk, www.britishembassy.gov.uk/sudan, www.sudanembassy.org, www.sudan.net.

LOCAL MEDIA English-language magazines include *Sudanow* and *New Horizons*. *The Sudaan Standard* is the main English-language paper. There is censorship on all publications following the 1989 coup.

TOURIST BOARDS IN UK/US n/a.

The number of pyramids in ancient Nubia (now Sudan) totalled over 200 – twice the number of its more famous neighbour, Egypt

SURINAME

WHEN TO GO

WEATHER Hot and humid all year. Short dry season from February to April, the long dry season from August to October.

FESTIVALS Festivals celebrate the major events in the Christian, Hindu and Muslim calendars, while the colourful End of Surifesta welcomes the new year with dancing and musical performances. Carnival, in February/March, is a riotous time. Independence Day is 25 November.

TRANSPORT

INTERNATIONAL AIRPORTS Johan Adolf Pengel (PBM) is 45 km from Paramaribo.

INTERNAL TRAVEL No railways. Patchy road network. Flights affected by rainy season.

RED TAPE

VISAS REQUIRED (UK/US) Required.

VACCINATIONS REQUIRED: See 'Vaccinations required around the world' on page 653.

DRIVING REQUIREMENTS International Driving Permit.

COUNTRY REPS IN UK/US
UK: n/a, nearest Alexander Gogelweg 2, 2517 JH 3-650844 The Hague, The Netherlands, tel (70) 361 7445.
USA: 4301 Connecticut Avenue, Suite 460, NW, Washington, DC 20008, tel (202) 244 7488, fax (202) 244 5878.

UK/US REPS IN COUNTRY
UK: Honorary Consulate, c/o VSH United Buildings, PO Box 1860, Van't Hogerhuysstraat 9-11, Paramaribo, tel 402 870, fax 403 824, email united@sr.net.
USA: Dr Sophie Redmonstraat 129, Paramaribo, tel 472 900, fax 425 788.

PEOPLE AND PLACE

CAPITAL Paramaribo.

LANGUAGE Dutch.

PEOPLES Creole (34%), Hindustani (34%), Javanese (18%), African or European descent.

RELIGION Christian (45%), Hindu, Muslim.

SIZE (SQ KM) 163,265.

POPULATION 429,000.

POP DENSITY/KM 2.6.

STATE OF THE NATION

SAFETY Safe.

LIFE EXPECTANCY M 66.75, F 71.27.

BEING THERE

ETIQUETTE Informal dress is suitable for most occasions, but beachwear should be kept to the beach or pool. Women are advised to wear long trousers, particularly if travelling to the interior.

CURRENCY Suriname *guilder* (SG) = 100 *cents*.

FINANCE Amex more accepted than other cards. Traveller's cheques only accepted at banks.

BUSINESS HOURS 0700-1500 Mon-Friday, 0700-1430 Saturday.

GMT -3.

VOLTAGE GUIDE 110/220 AC, 60 Hz.

COUNTRY DIALLING CODE 597.

CONSUMING PLEASURES

FOOD & DRINK Varied cuisine reflecting the diversity of the population. Creole, Indian, Chinese and Indonesian dishes all

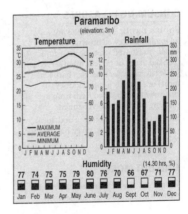

HIGHLIGHTS

PARAMARIBO

A unique blend of European and Asian influences, set on the northern Atlantic coast of South America. There are some lovely Dutch colonial buildings, together with the main Mosque and Roman Catholic Katherdraal. Afterwards, enjoy some of the city's varied dining choices - take your pick of Indian, Creole,Chinese or Javanese cuisine.

FISHING

Suriname is best explored by boat and its 3,000 kilometres of rivers offer some great fishing. Anglers should head for the Palumeu resort, where local Amerindians act as guides and teach visitors their traditional fishing techniques. Catches can include catfish, tarpon and peacock bass.

GALIBI NATURE RESERVE

World famous as a nesting site for endangered sea turtles, with four species coming ashore for mass nesting - namely the green sea turtle, the leatherback, the olive ridley and the hawksbill. The reserve, only accessible by boat, is characterised by its great biological diversity and by Amerindian villages where you can purchase Carib Indian artwork.

KASIKASIMA

Conquer Mount Kasikasima after a five-day trip along the Tapanahoni and Palumeu Rivers, hiking through unspoilt rainforest.

THE RAINFOREST

Suriname comprises 80 per cent rainforest, with numerous species found croaking and cawing high up in the canopy. The forests are also home to indigenous peoples. Enjoy one of the world's most unspoilt habitats, before logging and other human activity destroys it.

---

feature. *Nasi goreng* (Indonesian fried rice) and *bami goreng* (Indonesian fried noodles), Creole dishes like *pom* (ground tayer roots and poultry) and *pastei* (chicken and vegetable pie), and Indian dishes like *roti* (flat bread) with curried chicken are popular. Their drinks include *Dawet* (coconut), *Gemberbier* (Creole ginger drink), and *Pilsener Parbo Bier*.

SHOPPING & SOUVENIRS Maroon tribal woodcarvings, hand-carved and painted trays, Amerindian bows and arrows, cotton hammocks, wicker, ceramics, jewellery, batiks.

FIND OUT MORE

WEBSITES www.surinameembassy.org, http://usembassy.state.gov/paramaribo, www.surinametourism.com.

LOCAL MEDIA Dutch-language papers only.

TOURIST BOARDS IN UK/US n/a.

> Under the 1667 Treaty of Breda, the Dutch colonists retained Suriname and their colonies on the Guyanese coast – in exchange for giving up a small island now known as Manhattan

SWAZILAND

WHEN TO GO

WEATHER Moderate climate, though affected by altitude. Rainy October-March.

FESTIVALS The Ncwala Festival, meaning 'first fruits', is the country's biggest and most colourful occasion. Held each December, Ncwala sees bonfires, singing and dancing, and is attended by warriors and guests dressed in traditional dress. It culminates with the King eating the first fruit of the new season. Other events include Umhlanga Day, or Reed Dance Day, in August and September, a day where the young women pay homage to the Queen Mother. On 6 September Swaziland celebrates its independence, on Somholo Day.

TRANSPORT

INTERNATIONAL AIRPORTS Manzini (MTS) is 5 km from the city.

INTERNAL TRAVEL Extensive road network. Buses and car-hire available.

RED TAPE

VISAS REQUIRED (UK/US) Not required.

VACCINATIONS REQUIRED: See 'Vaccinations required around the world' on page 653.

DRIVING REQUIREMENTS International Driving Permit.

COUNTRY REPS IN UK/US UK: 20 Buckingham Gate, London SW1E 6LB, tel (020) 7630 6611, fax (020) 7630 6564, email swaziland-swaziland@btinternet.com. USA: 1712 New Hampshire Avenue, NW, Washington, DC 20009, tel (202) 234 5002, fax (202) 234 8254, email embassy@swaziland-usa.com.

UK/US REPS IN COUNTRY UK: n/a. USA: PO Box 199, 7th Floor, Central Bank Building, Warner Street, Mbabane, tel (40) 46441/2, fax (40) 45959, email dnmlambo@usembassy.org.sz.

PEOPLE AND PLACE

CAPITAL Mbabane.

LANGUAGE English and Siswati.

PEOPLES Siswati (95%), Zulu, European descent.

RELIGION Christian (60%), traditional beliefs (40%).

SIZE (SQ KM) 17,363.

POPULATION 980,722.

POP DENSITY/KM 56.5.

STATE OF THE NATION

SAFETY Generally stable.

LIFE EXPECTANCY M 37.18, F 34.07.

BEING THERE

ETIQUETTE Traditional ways of life remain strong. Local culture in the form of religious music, dance, poetry and crafts-manship plays an integral part in daily life. If you are planning to camp near villages it is important to first inform the headman - it is courteous and he may also be able to help with customs, or act as an interpreter. It is prohibited to photograph the Royal Palace or royal family, the army, or bank buildings.

CURRENCY *Lilangeni* (E) = 100 cents. Also South African *rands* (notes not coins).

FINANCE Amex, Mastercard and traveller's cheques widely accepted.

BUSINESS HOURS 0800-1300 and 1400-1645 Monday-Friday.

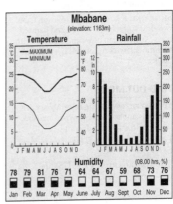

HIGHLIGHTS

MBABANE The Swazi capital is a small, relaxed town situated at the feet of the peaks and dips of the Ezulwini Valley. One of the highlights of the city is the main street, Allister Miller, named after the first European born there.

EZULWINI VALLEY Lobamba, the royal valley known as the 'valley of heaven' by locals, lies at the heart of Ezulwini. It has several museums and monuments, craft stalls and a traditional beehive hut village. For sporting types, there is an 18-hole golf course, together with some top hotels, a casino and a nightclub. Alternatively, take a tour of the lovely Sondzela Nature Reserve, to get up-close-and-personal with the relaxed wildlife and see the daily hippo-feeding.

PARKS Excellent hiking can be had in the Hlane Royal National Park and the Mkhaya Game Reserve, the latter famed for housing black rhino and white rhino. The Milwane Wildlife Sanctuary offers a unique opportunity to see wildlife from the comfort of your own bicycle seat . Throughout Swaziland there are generations-old footpaths, which are the best way to explore the country.

RAFTING The Great Usutu River offers a ride-of-your-life opportunity to tackle its whitewater rapids. The fast-running river also has a dizzying 10-metre waterfall.

GRAND VALLEY Take the road from Manzini to Mahamba, passing through the scenic Grand Valley. The route also takes you past some historic sights of the Swazi royal house.

GMT +2.

VOLTAGE GUIDE 220 AC, 50 Hz.

COUNTRY DIALLING CODE 268.

CONSUMING PLEASURES

FOOD & DRINK The staple Swazi dish is meat stew with maize meal. South African and Indian food is widely available. Good selection of beers, wines, and spirits.

SHOPPING & SOUVENIRS Beading, basketry, grass and sisal mats, copperware, wooden bowls, gemstone jewellery, wooden and soapstone carvings, calabashes, walking sticks, drums, batiks.

FIND OUT MORE

WEBSITES www.mintour.gov.sz, http://usembassy.state.gov/mbabane, www.swazi.com/tourism.

LOCAL MEDIA *The Times of Swaziland* is the English-language paper.

TOURIST BOARDS IN UK/US n/a.

King Sobhuza II, who died in 1982, was an old-fashioned African king. He had 100 wives and an estimated 200 sons. When he died, the nation went into mourning for 75 days

SWEDEN

WHEN TO GO

WEATHER Warm summers (June-August), very cold winters (October-April). Even colder further north. Midnight sun visible May-June.

FESTIVALS Swedish festivals are generally organised around the seasons and are lively occasions as the Swedes like to enjoy themselves. The highlight of the year is the Midsummer Eve/Summer Solstice when the whole country parties into the night. Walpurgis Night is full of hearty celebration with bonfires and songs welcoming spring. Other festivals and events include *Göteborgskalaset*, an annual party open to all-comers as the streets fill with cheering people. The Malmo Festival provides a wide variety of music performances for you to jig the night away.

TRANSPORT

INTERNATIONAL AIRPORTS Stockholm (STO) is 42 km from city. Gothenburg (GOT) is 25 km from city. Malmö (MMA) is 31 km from city.

INTERNAL TRAVEL Excellent road, rail, air and ferry network. Buses, taxis, and car-hire available.

RED TAPE

VISAS REQUIRED (UK/US) Not required.

VACCINATIONS REQUIRED: See 'Vaccinations required around the world' on page 653.

DRIVING REQUIREMENTS National driving licence.

COUNTRY REPS IN UK/US UK: 11 Montagu Place, London W1H 2AL, tel (020) 7917 6400, fax (020) 7917 6475, email ambassaden.london@foreign.ministry.se. USA: 1501 M Street, Suite 900, NW, Washington, DC 20005, tel (202) 467 2600, fax (202) 467 2699, email ambassaden.washington@foreign.ministry.se.

UK/US REPS IN COUNTRY UK: Skarpögaten 6-8, PO Box 27819, 115 93 Stockholm, tel (8) 671 3000, fax (8) 661

9766, email info@britishembassy.se. USA: Dag Hammarskjölds Vag 31, 115 89 Stockholm, tel (8) 783 5300, fax (8) 660 5879, email StockholmWeb@state.gov.

PEOPLE AND PLACE

CAPITAL Stockholm.

LANGUAGE Swedish.

PEOPLES Swedish (91%), Finns, Lapps.

RELIGION Lutheran (89%).

SIZE (SQ KM) 449,964.

POPULATION 8,975,670.

POP DENSITY/KM 19.9.

STATE OF THE NATION

SAFETY Safe.

LIFE EXPECTANCY M 78.19, F 82.74.

BEING THERE

ETIQUETTE Normal European courtesies apply. Casual attire is acceptable for most occasions, though smarter dress is advised for more formal occasions, or when visiting restaurants or clubs. If you're a guest at a meal you should refrain from drinking until the host has made a toast. It is polite to thank your host by saying, *Tack för maten*.

CURRENCY Swedish *krona* (SKr) = 100 *öre*.

FINANCE Credit cards and traveller's cheques widely accepted.

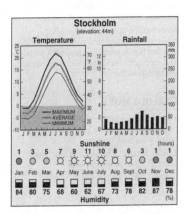

HIGHLIGHTS

AURORA BOREALIS Also known as the Northern Lights, this natural light display is one of the most beautiful and strange sights on earth, filling the night sky with an array of swirling colours that will leave you speechless. As the sky fills with ethereal beams, recall the old rumours surrounding its origins and let yourself drift away. The best time to see this spectacle is in the darker winter months. To see the Lights you will have to travel to the very north of Sweden, near the border with Norway.

THE ICE HOTEL Located near the tiny village of Jukkasjärvi stands the world's largest igloo. Built afresh every year, in various forms, the ice hotel stands firm until it finally melts away in the warmer months. Inside, there are bedrooms for at least 120 guests - the beds are made of ice and covered with reindeer hide. There's also a bar, a chapel and an exhibition hall.

STOCKHOLM Built on a series of islands where the freshwater Lake Mälaren meets the salt water of the Baltic, Stockholm has been labelled 'Beauty on Water'. Visit the national parks and the pretty Old Town area. At weekends, the city fills up with revellers as the locals let their hair down.

HALLAND Situated on the Golden Coast in the south-west, this long, narrow province is lined with sandy beaches, many fringed with pinewoods. Inland, the region is characterised by ridges and valleys that dominate the skyline with forests and moors skirting their ankles.

BUSINESS HOURS Flexible working hours. GMT +1.

VOLTAGE GUIDE 230 3-phase AC, 50 Hz.

COUNTRY DIALLING CODE 46.

CONSUMING PLEASURES

FOOD & DRINK The Scandinavian cold table, *smörgåsbord*, is traditional, and includes pickled herring with boiled potatoes, smoked salmon or anchovies, cold meat, sliced beef, stuffed veal or smoked reindeer, and hot dishes like small meatballs or omelettes. Snapps is usually drunk with the *smörgåsbord*. Beers come in four strengths.

SHOPPING & SOUVENIRS Glassware, crystal, ceramics, stainless steel, silver, *hemslöjd* (cottage industry items).

FIND OUT MORE

WEBSITES www.swedish-embassy.org.uk, www.visit-sweden.com, www.swedenabroad.se, www.swetourism.com, www.usemb.se, www.stockholm.se/english.

LOCAL MEDIA All papers in Swedish.

TOURIST BOARDS IN UK/US UK: Sweden House, 5 Upper Montagu Street, London W1H 2AG, tel (020) 7108 6168, email emelie@swetourism.org.uk. US: Council PO Box 4649, Grand Central Station, New York, NY 10163-4649, tel (212) 885 9700, fax (212) 885 9764, email usa@visit-sweden.com.

On average there are ten collisions on Sweden's roads every day between cars and wild moose

SWITZERLAND

WHEN TO GO

WEATHER Climate affected by altitude. Generally warm April-September, cold November-March.

FESTIVALS There are numerous events in Switzerland, representing the spirit and culture of the country. These include the Prix de Lausanne - a famous dance competition in January-February. From March to May, Bern hosts its International Jazz Festival, while the whole country marks the Swiss National Day on 1 August. In November the town of Samnaun welcomes Father Christmas's from around the world, for the Santa Claus World Championship.

TRANSPORT

INTERNATIONAL AIRPORTS Zurich (ZRH) is 11 km from city. Geneva (GVA) is 5 km from city. Bern (BRN) is 9 km from city. Basel (BSL) is 12 km from city.

INTERNAL TRAVEL Excellent road, rail and air networks.

RED TAPE

VISAS REQUIRED (UK/US) Not required.

VACCINATIONS REQUIRED: See 'Vaccinations required around the world' on page 653.

DRIVING REQUIREMENTS National driving licence.

COUNTRY REPS IN UK/US UK: 16-18 Montagu Place, London W1H 2BQ, tel (020) 7616 6000, fax (020 7724 7001. USA: 2900 Cathedral Avenue, NW, Washington, DC 20008, tel (202) 745 7900, fax (202) 387 2564, email vertretung@was.rep.admin.ch.

UK/US REPS IN COUNTRY UK: 37-39 rue de Vermont, 1211 Geneva 20, tel (22) 918 2400, fax (22) 918 2322. USA: Jubilaumsstrasse 93, 3005 Berne, tel (31) 357 7011, fax (31) 357 7344, email bernniv@state.gov.

PEOPLE AND PLACE

CAPITAL Bern.

LANGUAGE German, French, Italian.

PEOPLES German (65%), French (18%), Italian (10%).

RELIGION Roman Catholic (46%), Protestant (40%).

SIZE (SQ KM) 41,284.

POPULATION 7,261,210.

POP DENSITY/KM 175.9.

STATE OF THE NATION

SAFETY Safe.

LIFE EXPECTANCY M 77.58, F 83.36.

BEING THERE

ETIQUETTE A handshake is a common greeting. Informal clothing is widely accepted, but a jacket and tie may be required for more formal social occasions. When invited for a meal it is customary to give unwrapped flowers to the hostess, avoiding red roses, chrysanthemums or white asters, which are considered funeral flowers.

CURRENCY Swiss *franc* (SFr) = 100 *rappen* or *centimes*.

FINANCE Credit cards, traveller's cheques and Eurocheques widely accepted.

BUSINESS HOURS 0800-1200 and 1400-1700 Monday-Friday.

GMT +1.

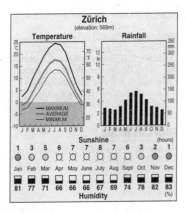

HIGHLIGHTS

LAKE GENEVA The bluest of all the lakes in Switzerland, set in the heart of the wine country, with vineyards sweeping round the lake and up the slopes of the surrounding hills. Quaint villages and castles dot its picturesque shores.

SKIING Switzerland is well known for skiing and other wintersports, with many excellent resorts. You will find it hard to go wrong wherever you decide to enjoy the snow, from the world famous Matterhorn to Saas-Fee. While enjoying the outdoors exertion, be sure not to miss out on the splendid views of high peaks and tranquil lakes - you might find them just as agreeable as the skiing itself.

JUNGFRAU RAILWAYS Of all the Alpine journeys, this section of railway in the Bernese Oberland is one of the most pleasurable. Snaking its way up to Schynige Platte, it takes in some truly unforgettable views, including the triple-peaked ridge of the Jungfrau, Eiger and Mönch.

BERN The country's capital is one of the most charming cities. Squashed against the River Aare, it is a quiet place, with cobbled streets and buildings that look as if they haven't changed for years. It can feel rather like stepping back in time to a quieter and calmer time.

IGLOO BUILDING If snow-trekking and tobogganing are not your cup of tea, why not have a quieter time in the snow building your own igloo? Then spend the night in your icy alfresco home, enjoying the view at dusk with a glass of ever-so-chilled wine.

VOLTAGE GUIDE 220 AC, 50 Hz.
COUNTRY DIALLING CODE 41.

CONSUMING PLEASURES

FOOD & DRINK The best known speciality is fondue (Gruyère and Vacherin cheese melted with white wine, *Kirsch,* and a little garlic), eaten with cubes of bread. Regional dishes include *papet vaudoir* (made from leeks and potatoes), *fondue bourguignonne* (cubed meat with various sauces), *rösti* (shredded, fried potatoes), specialist sausages and salamis, and Geneva's great speciality, *pieds de porc* (pigs' feet).

SHOPPING & SOUVENIRS Embroidery, linen, woodcarving, chocolate, cheese, Swiss army knives, cuckoo clocks, watches.

FIND OUT MORE

WEBSITES www.swissembassy.org.uk, www.myswitzerland.com, www.britain-in-switzerland.ch, www.swissemb.org, http://bern.usembassy.gov.

LOCAL MEDIA International titles available, including *International Herald Tribune* and *USA Today.*

TOURIST BOARDS IN UK/US
UK: 1st Floor, 30 Bedford Street, London WC2E 9ED, tel (00800) 1002 0030, fax (00800) 1002 0031, email sales@stc.ch.
US: 608 Fifth Avenue, Swiss Center, New York, NY 10020, tel (212) 757 5944, fax (212)262 6116, email info.usa@switzerland.com.

" My hat shall ever be ready to be thrown up, and my glove ever ready to be thrown down for Switzerland."

Charles Dickens, 1846

SYRIA

WHEN TO GO

WEATHER Hot dry summers (May-October), cool winters (December-March).

FESTIVALS Many festivals, events and fairs occur throughout the year, these include the Silk Road Festival and the Festival of Folklore and Music, in Bosra, which feature artistic, sports and musical shows from different countries of the Silk Road. There's also the Friendship Festival in Latakia and the International Cotton Festival in Aleppo. There are also many religious events, such as Ramadan and Eid al-Fitr.

TRANSPORT

INTERNATIONAL AIRPORTS Damascus (DAM) is 29 km from city. Also Aleppo (ALP) and Latakia (LTK).

INTERNAL TRAVEL Good roads and cheap flights. Railways erratic.

RED TAPE

VISAS REQUIRED (UK/US) Required for all (Australia can obtain on arrival).

VACCINATIONS REQUIRED: See 'Vaccinations required around the world' on page 653.

DRIVING REQUIREMENTS International Driving Permit, insurance and importation certificates. Green Card not accepted.

COUNTRY REPS IN UK/US
UK: 8 Belgrave Square, London SW1X 8PH, tel (020) 7245 9012, fax (020) 7235 4621, email syrianembassyuk@hotmail.com. USA: 2215 Wyoming Avenue, NW, Washington, DC 20008, tel (202) 232 6313, fax (202) 234 9548, email info@ syrianembassy.us.

UK/US REPS IN COUNTRY
UK: Kotob Building, 11 Rue Mohammad Kurd Ali Street, PO Box 37, Malki, Damascus, tel (11) 373 9241, fax (11) 373 1600, email british.embassy.damascus@ fco.gov.uk. USA: Abou Roumaneh, rue al-Mansour 2, Damascus, tel (11) 333 1342, fax (11) 331 9678, email acsdamascus@ state.gov.

PEOPLE AND PLACE

CAPITAL Damascus.

LANGUAGE Arabic.

PEOPLES Arab (98%), Kurdish (6%).

RELIGION Sunni Muslim (74%), Christian (10%).

SIZE (SQ KM) 185,180.

POPULATION 17,800,000.

POP DENSITY/KM 96.1.

STATE OF THE NATION

SAFETY Generally welcoming and safe.

LIFE EXPECTANCY M 68.75, F 71.38.

BEING THERE

ETIQUETTE Shaking hands on meeting and departure is customary. Visitors will be treated with great courtesy. Syrian hospitality is legendary. A gift or souvenir from the visitor's home will be well received. Conservative casual clothes are suitable, but beachwear or shorts should only be worn at the beach or poolside.

CURRENCY Syrian pound (S£) = 100 *piastres*.

FINANCE Amex widely accepted, others less so. Traveller's cheques not widely accepted.

BUSINESS HOURS 0830-1430 Saturday-Thursday.

GMT +2.

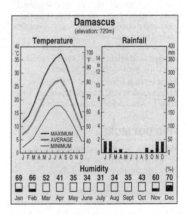

HIGHLIGHTS

DAMASCUS

The world's oldest inhabited city, which stretches majestically into the Jibal Lubnan Ash Sharqiyeh Mountains. It's full of history, fables and culture. The Old City is surrounded by a city wall cordoning off the rest of the city and is home to a number of impressive buildings steeped in history. The National Museum houses Chinese silks dating back to 1BC, while another key landmark is the Ummayyad Mosque, built on the site of a temple to the ancient Aramean god, Haddad.

PALMYRA Described as 'the bride of the desert', it is indeed located in the heart of the Syrian Desert, near the Afqa hot-water spring. Palmyra has magnificent remains from the reign of Queen Zenobia, who fought off the Romans and then conquered Egypt - before poisoning herself when captured by the Romans.

SOUKS An excellent way to immerse yourself into city life is to visit the markets. Soak up the atmosphere and buy some local handicrafts, such as olive wood carvings, leather goods, weaving, embroidery, gold and silver jewellery.

BOSRA A city that grew under the Romans and is most famous for its amphitheatre, later converted into a fortress. The original theatre still remains, with much of it being restored. It seats 15,000 people and is designed so that the audience can hear all the actors' voices without special equipment. Visit the Roman baths, the Mosque of Omar and the Cathedral of Bosra - all built on the original Roman grid pattern.

VOLTAGE GUIDE 220 AC, 50 Hz.

COUNTRY DIALLING CODE 963.

CONSUMING PLEASURES

FOOD & DRINK National dishes include *kubbeh* (minced meat and semolina stuffed with minced meat, onions and nuts), *yabrak* (vine leaves stuffed with rice and minced meat, *ouzi* (pastry with minced meat stuffing), and meat dishes and vegetables cooked with tomatoes and served with rice. Alcohol available except during Ramadan, when it is illegal to drink in public between dawn and dusk.

SHOPPING & SOUVENIRS Mother-of-pearl items, olivewood carvings, weaving and embroidery, leather goods, gold and silver jewellery.

FIND OUT MORE

WEBSITES www.syrianembassy.co.uk, www.syrianembassy.us, http://usembassy.state.gov/damascus, www.syriatourism.org.

LOCAL MEDIA *Syria Times* is published daily in English.

TOURIST BOARDS IN UK/US n/a.

> "What a country this is! I fear I shall spend the rest of my life travelling in it. Race after race, one on top of the other, the whole land strewn with the mighty relics of them."
>
> *Gertrude Bell, 1905*

TAIWAN

WHEN TO GO

WEATHER Typhoon season June-October. South is warm all year, north is cooler January-March.

FESTIVALS The main holidays and festivals can be divided into two categories: festivals associated with the lunar calendar, and official holidays celebrated according to the Western calendar. Major festivals include the Chinese New Year, which begins in mid-December and carries through until the Lantern Festival in mid-January. Other notable events are the Dragon Boat Festival in the fifth lunar month, which drives off evil spirits, the Ghost Festival in the seventh lunar month, and the Double Ninth Day celebrations. Official holidays include Youth Day, Tomb Sweeping Day and Teachers Day.

TRANSPORT

INTERNATIONAL AIRPORTS Chiang-Kai-Shek Taipei (TPE) is 40 km from the city.

INTERNAL TRAVEL Good road and rail network.

RED TAPE

VISAS REQUIRED (UK/US) Not required for 14 days (if no criminal record). For 30 days, available on arrival (need passport-sized photo).

VACCINATIONS REQUIRED: See 'Vaccinations required around the world' on page 653.

DRIVING REQUIREMENTS International Driving Permit.

COUNTRY REPS IN UK/US UK: 50 Grosvenor Gardens, London SW1W 0EB, tel (020) 7881 2650, fax (020) 7730 3139, email request@tro-taiwan.roc.org.uk. USA: 4201 Wisconsin Avenue, NW, Washington, DC 20016, tel (202) 895 1800, fax (202) 363 0999, email tecroinfodc@tecro-info.org.

UK/US REPS IN COUNTRY UK: n/a. USA: 7 Lane 134, Hsin Yi Road, Section 3, Taipei 106, tel (2) 2162 2000, fax (2) 2162 2251, email aitarc@mail.ait.org.tw.

PEOPLE AND PLACE

CAPITAL Taipei.

LANGUAGE Mandarin. Also Taiwanese and some English.

PEOPLES Chinese (98%).

RELIGION Buddhist, Taoist, Confucian.

SIZE (SQ KM) 36,188.

POPULATION 22,560,000.

POP DENSITY/KM 623.6.

STATE OF THE NATION

SAFETY Safe.

LIFE EXPECTANCY M 74.49, F 80.28.

BEING THERE

ETIQUETTE Handshaking is a common form of greeting. Life here is still very Chinese, traditional and adhering to old values where ancient customs, holidays and festivals are celebrated. Casual clothing is accepted. Entertaining is normally done in restaurants, not at home. It is not customary to tip taxi drivers, but a 10 per cent service charge is normally added at hotels and restaurants.

CURRENCY New Taiwan dollar (NT$) = 100 cents.

FINANCE Credit cards and traveller's cheques widely accepted.

BUSINESS HOURS n/a.

GMT +8.

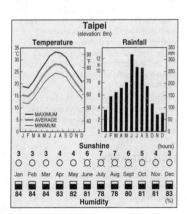

HIGHLIGHTS

TAIPEI A rapidly expanding city, full of hustle and bustle, local and foreign residents. You may either love it or loathe it, but it should not be missed either way. The National Palace Museum is home to a collection of exquisite Chinese artefacts, while the Lungshan (Dragon Mountain) Temple built in 1740 is the island's finest piece of temple architecture. Visit the Fu Hsing Dramatic Arts Academy to watch traditional Chinese Opera and acrobatic stage shows.

TAROKO GORGE Regarded as the premier tourist attraction and the jewel of Taiwan's national parks. A sumptuous park with sheer cliffs of marble and limestone guarding a jade green river. Popular among hikers, who then wind down in its soothing hot springs.

THE COASTAL DRIVE Travelling around Taiwan, it is highly recommended that you hug the coast on your route, particularly the east and northeast stretch. There are spectacular views as you pass through the foothills of the Central Mountain Range, overlooking the Pacific Ocean and the East China Sea.

TAINAN The oldest city in Taiwan with over 200 temples. It is a city bursting with traditional Taiwanese culture and was the island's provincial capital from 1663 to 1885. Take time to discover some of the best temples, hidden by new buildings.

LANYU South of Taiwan lies Lanyu (Orchid Island), an island - despite its name - of volcanic beauty, inhabited by the Yami tribe - some of the world's last hunter-gatherers.

VOLTAGE GUIDE 110 AC, 60 Hz.
COUNTRY DIALLING CODE 886.

CONSUMING PLEASURES

FOOD & DRINK Culinary styles come from all over China, including Canton, Peking, Szechuan and Shanghai. Fried shrimp with cashews, beef with oyster sauce, onion-marinated chicken, eels with pepper sauce, aubergine with garlic sauce, and seafood with thick sauces are all typical examples. Alcohol widely available.

SHOPPING & SOUVENIRS Formosan seagrass mats, hats, handbags, slippers, bamboo items, musical instruments, dolls, silk lanterns, ceramics, teak furniture, coral, jade, decorated chopsticks.

FIND OUT MORE

WEBSITES www.tro-taiwan.roc.org.uk, www.tecro.org, http://taiwan.net.tw, htto://ait.org.tw, www.sinica.edu.tw/tit.
LOCAL MEDIA *Taiwan News* and *China*

Post are published daily in English, *Taipei Journal* weekly and *Tapei Review* monthly.
TOURIST BOARDS IN UK/US n/a.

Once known as Formosa, meaning 'beautiful', recent archaeological tests suggest that the island has been inhabited for at least 10,000 years

TAJIKISTAN

WHEN TO GO

WEATHER Extreme seasonal fluctuations: freezing December-January, searing July-August. Pamir Mountains are near-polar.

FESTIVALS Navruz (Persian New Year) is the biggest annual celebration, occurring in March. The precise date of the celebration depends on the timing of the equinox. There are other national public holidays, such as Constitution Day, on 6 November, and Independence Day, on 9 September. There are also annual Islamic holidays, including Eid-i-Ramazon and Eid-i-Kurbon, the dates of which vary.

TRANSPORT

INTERNATIONAL AIRPORTS Dushanbe (DYU) is 20 minutes from city.

INTERNAL TRAVEL Reasonable road network. Railways are limited and were subject to bomb attack in 1993. Flights are affected by fuel shortages. Bus services between major towns. Car-hire is not available, but taxis are.

RED TAPE

VISAS REQUIRED (UK/US) Required.

VACCINATIONS REQUIRED: See 'Vaccinations required around the world' on page 653.

DRIVING REQUIREMENTS International Driving Permit and insurance documents.

COUNTRY REPS IN UK/US
UK: n/a, nearest Otto-Suhr-Allee 84, 10585 Berlin, Germany, tel (30) 347 9300, fax (30) 3479 3029, email tajemb-germ@ embassy-tajikistan.de. USA: 1005 New Hampshire Avenue, NW, Washington, DC 20037, tel (202) 223 6090, fax (202) 223 6091, email tajikistan@verizon.net.

UK/US REPS IN COUNTRY
UK: 43 Lufti Street, Dushanbe 734017, tel (91) 734 017, fax (91) 901 5079, email dhm@britishembassy-tj.com. USA: 10 Pavlov Street, Dushanbe, (372) 210 348/50, fax (372) 210 362.

PEOPLE AND PLACE

CAPITAL Dushanbe.

LANGUAGE Tajik.

PEOPLES Tajik, Uzbek, Russian.

RELIGION Sunni Muslim (80%).

SIZE (SQ KM) 143,100.

POPULATION 6,245,000.

POP DENSITY/KM 43.6.

STATE OF THE NATION

SAFETY Politically unstable, but travel is possible. Seek local information.

LIFE EXPECTANCY M 61.68, F 67.59.

BEING THERE

ETIQUETTE Removing shoes is customary when entering someone's house. Shorts are rarely seen and if worn by females can attract unwelcome attention. Bread known as *lipioshka* should never be laid upside down.

CURRENCY Tajik *rouble* (TR).

FINANCE Credit cards and traveller's cheques only accepted in some major hotels. US dollars in cash are best.

BUSINESS HOURS 0900-1800 Mon-Friday.

GMT +5.

VOLTAGE GUIDE 220 AC, 50 Hz.

COUNTRY DIALLING CODE 992.

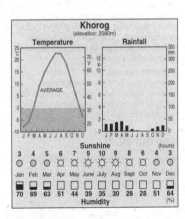

HIGHLIGHTS

KHOJAND The capital of northern Tajikistan, founded by Alexander the Great, and a city that was rich in culture with mosques and palaces before the Mongols destroyed it. The town that emerged from the ashes lies at the gateway to the Fargana Valley.

THE PAMIRS Often described by locales as Bam-i-Dunya (the Roof of the World) this beautiful range of mountains contains three of the four highest mountains in the former Soviet Union. Most of the region is uninhabitable, but if you are very lucky you might see one of the range's hardened inhabitants, the snow leopard. You might also catch a glimpse - if you believe the rumours - of the elusive Yeti. The Pamirs occupy nearly half of Tajikistan and incorporate the Fan Mountains and the Wakhan Corridor- a gorgeous and remote valley with forts and ancient ruins. There's also Lake Kara-Kul, formed by a meteor 10 million years ago.

THE SILK ROAD This ancient trade route was used between the second and fourteenth centuries by merchants trading from China to the Mediterranean or the Caspian Sea. The scenery is stunning, set against the Fan Mountains with clouded peaks, turquoise lakes and luxurious valleys.

CLIMBING One of Tajikistan's biggest attractions, luring climbers from all over the world to test themselves in the country's extensive mountains. The sport is becoming more accessible to the non-climber, but it would be wise to go with an organised tour group.

CONSUMING PLEASURES

FOOD & DRINK Traditional meals start with sweet dishes like *halva* and tea, followed by soups such as *shorpur* (made of meat and vegetables) and then a main dish of *plov*, a Central Asian staple of mutton, shredded yellow turnip and rice. *Shashlyk* (charcoal grilled mutton) served with *lip-ioshka* (unleavened bread) is also common. *Chai* (tea) is most popular, as are alcoholic drinks, including sparkling wine, or *shampanski*.

SHOPPING & SOUVENIRS Handicrafts, paintings by local artists.

FIND OUT MORE

WEBSITES www.britishembassy.gov.uk/tajikistan, www.tjus.org, www.lonelyplanet.com/destinations/central_asia/tajikistan.

LOCAL MEDIA Censored press, no English-language papers.

TOURIST BOARDS IN UK/US n/a.

Tajikistan is the poorest of the five former Soviet Central Asian republics, with many people living below the poverty line. But its vast mineral resources include gold, aluminium and coal – promising a brighter economic future

TANZANIA

WHEN TO GO

WEATHER Rainy season March-June. Coast is hot and humid all year. Interior is hot and dry, northern highlands are cool and temperate.

FESTIVALS On the mainland, festivals follow the Muslim calendar. Independence Day is marked on 9 December. The main annual event is not a festival, but the migration of over two million animals from the Serengeti's southern plains to Kenya's Maasai Mara in April. On Zanzibar, the Swahili Music and Cultural Festival is celebrated on 12-13 February in Stone Town. July sees the largest African film festival take place with the Zanzibar International Film Festival, and in the same month Zanzibaris mark the Shirazi New Year. Muslim holidays and Ramadan are greatly respected.

TRANSPORT

INTERNATIONAL AIRPORTS Dar es Salaam (DAR) is 15 km from city. International flights to Kilimanjaro International Airport (JRO) and Zanzibar (ZNZ).

INTERNAL TRAVEL Good road network, though of variable quality. Ferries on great lakes are erratic. Dar to Zanzibar is well served by ferries. Rail and air links are useful but limited.

RED TAPE

VISAS REQUIRED (UK/US) Required for all (except Australia).

VACCINATIONS REQUIRED: See 'Vaccinations required around the world' on page 653.

DRIVING REQUIREMENTS International Driving Permit is required for hiring cars, must be endorsed by police on arrival. For other situations, a temporary local driving licence should be obtained (available on presentation of national driving licence).

COUNTRY REPS IN UK/US UK: 3 Stratford Street, London WC1 1AS. USA: 2139 R Street, NW, Washington, DC 20008, tel (202) 884 1080, fax (202) 797 7408, email balozi@tanzaniaembassy-us.org.

UK/US REPS IN COUNTRY UK: Umoja House, Garden Avenue, Dar es Salaam, tel (22) 211 0101, fax (22) 211 0102, email bhc.dar@fco.gov.uk. USA: 686 Old Bagamoyo Road, Msasani, Dar es Salaam, tel (22) 266 8001, fax (22) 266 8238, email embassyd@state.gov.

PEOPLE AND PLACE

CAPITAL Dar es Salaam.

LANGUAGE Kiswahili and English.

PEOPLES 99% belong to 120 small tribal groups.

RELIGION Christian (33%), Muslim (33%), traditional beliefs (30%).

SIZE (SQ KM) 945,087.

POPULATION 34,569,232

POP DENSITY/KM 36.6.

STATE OF THE NATION

SAFETY Fairly safe, but be careful after dark. Usual street crime.

LIFE EXPECTANCY M 44.56, F 45.94

BEING THERE

ETIQUETTE Do not use the left hand. Greet and reply to individuals with '*Jambo*'. The more Kiswahili you know, the more delighted locals will be. Dress is smart.

CURRENCY Tanzanian shilling (TSh).

FINANCE Traveller's cheques widely accepted, credit cards less so.

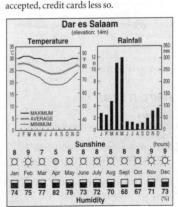

Dar es Salaam (elevation: 14m)

HIGHLIGHTS

THE SERENGETI The greatest game park in the world. At nearly under 15,000 square kilometres, it is home to 35 species of plains-dwelling animal, and it is fairly easy to spot the Big Five. At one time most of East Africa would have been like this. You can even watch it all from the silence of a hot air balloon high above.

NGORONGORO CRATER South of the Serengeti is this crater, formed from a collapsed volcano, with a diameter of 20 kilometres and crater walls 610 metres high. It has protected its inhabitants from outside influences, and also prevented migration. And so it contains nearly all the plain animals, including the endangered black rhino. Very rich in bird species, especially flamingoes.

MT KILIMANJARO Africa's highest mountain at 5,895 metres high. An ascent takes three days, and the peak is cold and requires acclimatisation. Guides are required. The views are magnificent.

ZANZIBAR Meander through the bustling warren of tiny alleyways and streets that is Zanzibar's capital, Stone Town, while marvelling at the town's unique architecture – which draws on Arabic, Indian, European and African styles. Then head to Nungwe at the northern tip to stroll along gorgeous white sandy beaches or feed turtles in the sanctuary. The area also has a vibrant nightlife.

LAKE VICTORIA The largest lake in Africa (a similar size to Ireland) and the source of the River Nile. Take a sunset cruise.

BUSINESS HOURS 0800-1200 and 1400-1630 Monday-Friday, 0800-1300 Saturday.
GMT +3.
VOLTAGE GUIDE 240 AC, 50 Hz.
COUNTRY DIALLING CODE 255.

CONSUMING PLEASURES

FOOD & DRINK Both traditional African food, Afro-Indian and Indian meals are widely available, including roasted meat and maize, cassava, spicy curries and mutton *biryanis*, and chicken and rice. *Safari*, a good lager, is produced locally, as is *Konyagi* gin.

SHOPPING & SOUVENIRS Drums, carved chess sets, jewellery, salad bowls, ebony.

FIND OUT MORE

WEBSITES www.tanzania-web.com, http://usembassy.state.gov/tanzania, www.zanzibar.net.

LOCAL MEDIA Many English-language papers, including *Daily News*, *Business Times*, *The Guardian* and *Sunday News*.

TOURIST BOARDS IN UK/US n/a.

"This is by far the greatest collection of plains-dwelling animals left in the world today. It is a microcosm of what most of East and Central Africa was like little more than half a century ago, a surviving pocket, a remembrance of one of the greatest sights the world has ever known. This is all we have left."
Elspeth Huxley, 1964

THAILAND

WHEN TO GO

WEATHER Best November- February. Hot March-May. Monsoon June-October.

FESTIVALS There are countless festivals in Thailand, some with deep religious significance, others national or local affairs. The Chiang Mai Flower Festival sees the northern city decked in flowers, as floral sculptures are paraded through the streets. Perhaps the most exuberant of the national festivals is Thai New Year, Songkhran, an excuse for a national water fight in April. There are also parades and beauty contests. Kanchanaburi holds the River Kwai Bridge festival in November/December at the bridge made famous by Japanese wartime atrocities. Held over ten nights, dramatic lightshows recount its powerful tale.

TRANSPORT

INTERNATIONAL AIRPORTS Bangkok (BKK) is 22 km from city. Chiang Mai (CNX) is 15 km from town. Phuket (HKT) is 35 km from town.

INTERNAL TRAVEL Excellent road, rail and air networks. Buses, taxis, and car-hire available.

RED TAPE

VISAS REQUIRED (UK/US) Not required.

VACCINATIONS REQUIRED: See 'Vaccinations required around the world' on page 653.

DRIVING REQUIREMENTS International Driving Permit, valid for three months, after which a Thai licence is required.

COUNTRY REPS IN UK/US UK: 29-30 Queen's Gate, London SW7 5JB, tel (020) 7589 2944, fax (020) 7823 7492, email thaiduto@btinternet.com. USA: 1024 Wisconsin Avenue, Suite 401, NW, Washington, DC 20007, tel (202) 944 3600, fax (202) 944 3611, email thai.wsn@thaiembdc.org.

UK/US REPS IN COUNTRY UK: 1031 Wireless Road, Lumpini, Pathumwan, Bangkok 10330, tel (2) 305 8333, fax (2) 255 8619, email visa.bangkok@fco.gov.uk.

USA: 120 Wireless Road, Pathumwan District, Bangkok 10330, tel (2) 205 4000, fax (2) 205 4131, email acsbkk@state.gov.

PEOPLE AND PLACE

CAPITAL Bangkok.

LANGUAGE Thai.

PEOPLES Thai (80%), Chinese, Malay, Khmer.

RELIGION Buddhist (95%).

SIZE (SQ KM) 513,115.

POPULATION 62,193,000.

POP DENSITY/KM 121.2.

STATE OF THE NATION

SAFETY Safe, apart from border with Myanmar.

LIFE EXPECTANCY M 69.39, F 73.88.

BEING THERE

ETIQUETTE Instead of shaking hands, Thais sometimes place their palms together and raise their fingertips level with the chest or face, a form of greeting called the *wai*. The exact position of the hands depends on the status, relationship, and many other factors of the person they are greeting. Visitors don't need to *wai* waitresses, doormen or other people who *wai* you as part of their job. Buddhist culture is an intrinsic part of many Thais' life, while the Thai Royal Family is regarded with an almost religious

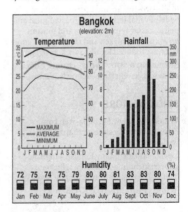

Bangkok (elevation: 2m) — Temperature, Rainfall, Humidity charts

Humidity (%): 72 75 74 75 79 80 80 81 83 83 80 74

Jan Feb Mar Apr May June July Aug Sept Oct Nov Dec

HIGHLIGHTS

BANGKOK Rather like Marmite, you'll either love it or hate it. Hot, humid and energetic, the capital that will hit you from all sides the moment you arrive - from the bustling street stalls catering to backpackers on the Koh San road to the alluring smells of tasty Thai snacks. If the beautiful *wats* (temples) don't leave you amazed, then Bangkok's lively night-time activities of go-go bars and hustling pool halls most probably will. Skirt around the bumper-to-bumper traffic by jumping in a *tuk-tuk* for a street-level tour of this 24-hour city.

KO PHI PHI Divine islands off the west coast that were so beautiful they became the location for the Hollywood movie *The Beach*. Grab a snorkel and fins and while away the hours swimming with tropical fish in a magical setting below limestone peaks.

KO PHA-NGAN Ah yes, the legendary Full Moon party. If you don't wake up in a tree, with half your clothes missing and all your money spent, with *henna* tattoos all over your back... then you've not had a good night. Tread warily.

CHIANG MAI Thailand's hilly and forested northern tip. Set around a large moat, the town itself is a laid-back place, perfect for a few days of relaxation. It's also the gateway to the Golden Triangle, a notorious region tied in with the history of opium. The area offers some great trekking, between the villages of hill tribes such as the Lahu and Karen, as well as elephant safaris and rafting trips.

reverence. Visitors should respect this. Shoes should be removed before entering someone's home or a temple.

CURRENCY *Baht* (Bt).

FINANCE Credit cards and traveller's cheques widely accepted.

BUSINESS HOURS 0900-1700 Mon-Friday.

GMT +7.

VOLTAGE GUIDE 220 AC, 50 Hz.

COUNTRY DIALLING CODE 66.

CONSUMING PLEASURES

FOOD & DRINK Highly spiced and fragrant dishes, including *tom yam* (coconut-milk soup with ginger, lemon grass, prawns or chicken), *gang pet* (hot 'red' curry with shrimp paste, coconut-milk, garlic, chillies and coriander) and *kaeng dhiaw* ('green' curry with baby aubergines, beef or chicken). Curries are served with rice. The popular desert and breakfast dish of mangoes with sticky rice is worth trying. As is the whisky, either *Mekhong*, or *SamSong*.

SHOPPING & SOUVENIRS Thai silks and cottons, batiks, silver, pottery with celadon green glaze, dolls, masks, bamboo artefacts, precious and semi-precious stones.

FIND OUT MORE

WEBSITES
www.thaicomuk.dial.pipex.com,
www.thaismile.co.uk,
www.britishembassy.gov.uk/thailand,
www.thaiembdc.org,
www.tourismthailand.org, www.usa.or.th,
www.bangkok.thailandtoday.com.

LOCAL MEDIA *Bangkok Post, The Nation,* and *Thailand Times* are printed in English.

TOURIST BOARDS IN UK/US UK: 3rd Floor, Brook House, 98-99 Jermyn Street, London SW1Y 6EE, tel (09063) 640 666, fax (020) 7925 2512, email info@thaismile.co.uk. US: 61 Broadway, Suite 2810, New York, NY 10006, tel (212) 432 0433, fax (212)269 2588, email info@tatny.com.

TOGO

WHEN TO GO

WEATHER Dry and hot February-March. Long rains April-July, short rains October-November. *Harmattan* wind December-January.

FESTIVALS Muslim and Christian festivals are celebrated. Many traditional festivals occur such as Evala, an initiation ceremony involving wrestling, which is sometimes shown on national television. Kpessosso is a harvest festival in Aneho with traditional dances such as Gbekon and Adjogbo. Elsewhere, Dispontre is a yam festival in the first week of September. The Agbogbozan is another important festival, on the first Thursday of September, and especially colourful in Notse.

TRANSPORT

INTERNATIONAL AIRPORTS Lomé (LFW) is 4 km from city.

INTERNAL TRAVEL Poor roads, impassable during rains. Some train and ferry services. Horses often used. Minibus services are available, as are taxis in various forms, and car hire.

RED TAPE

VISAS REQUIRED (UK/US) Required.

VACCINATIONS REQUIRED: See 'Vaccinations required around the world' on page 653.

DRIVING REQUIREMENTS International Driving Permit.

COUNTRY REPS IN UK/US UK: n/a, nearest 8 rue Alfred Roll, 75017 Paris, France, tel (1) 4380 1213, fax (1) 4380 0605. USA: 2208 Massachusetts Avenue, NW, Washington, DC 20008, tel (202) 234 4212, fax (202) 232 3190, email embassyoftogo@ hotmail.com.

UK/US REPS IN COUNTRY UK: The British Embassy in Accra (see Ghana) deals with enquiries relating to Togo. USA: BP 852, angle rue Kouenou et rue Béniglato, Lomé, tel (2) 212 994, fax (2) 217 952.

PEOPLE AND PLACE

CAPITAL Lomé.

LANGUAGE French. Also Ewe, Watchi, Kabiyé.

PEOPLES Ewe, Kabye, Gurma.

RELIGION Traditional beliefs (50%), Christian, Muslim.

SIZE (SQ KM) 56,785.

POPULATION 4,801,000.

POP DENSITY/KM 84.5.

STATE OF THE NATION

SAFETY Safe for travellers, although politically troubled. Usual petty crime.

LIFE EXPECTANCY M 50.64, F 54.7.

BEING THERE

ETIQUETTE Practical, casual clothes are best suited here. Wear beachwear at the beach or poolside only. Togo has a varied colonial heritage resulting in various denominations of Christianity and European languages. Be aware that many Togans adhere to voodoo beliefs.

CURRENCY *Communauté Financiaire Africaine franc* (CFA)= 100 *centimes*.

FINANCE Amex widely accepted, traveller's cheques and hard currency best in French francs.

BUSINESS HOURS 0700-1730 Mon-Friday.

GMT GMT.

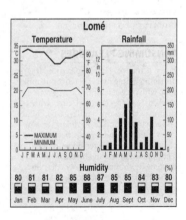

Lomé

Temperature — Rainfall

MAXIMUM / MINIMUM

	Jan	Feb	Mar	Apr	May	June	July	Aug	Sept	Oct	Nov	Dec
Humidity (%)	80	81	81	82	85	88	87	85	85	84	83	80

HIGHLIGHTS

LOME Most of the activity of the capital lies in the bustling market area surrounding the commercial districts, which was laid out by the French and has a pleasant feel. After riots in the 1990s it is only now that Lome is starting to show its spark again. Visit the Grand Marché, which mixes the traditional and modern. Turn to the fetish market with its voodoo charms, lotions and potions on display.

KLOUTO A mountain retreat that offers bush walks and nature tours. The first thing you will see is the spectacular road journey from Kpalime, carved out by the Germans. The trail snakes through cocoa plantations and the dense Missahohe Forest, where tree branches arch over to form a complete tunnel.

AKLOA FALLS A tricky place to find and reach, but well worth the time and effort. Accessing the falls requires a strenuous hike up the mountain and you will have to pay an entrance fee. But don't be put off, because once there a dizzying waterfall of over 30 metres greets you. You can swim in the pool at the bottom, which is believed to be thera-peutic - and is also believed to be sited on a stretch of coveted by voodoo spirits.

ANEHO The former capital, set on a picturesque lagoon, has a certain fading charm. The town is characterised by crumbling buildings - a reminder of long past European occu-pation. The main market sells a bizarre range of goods on its stalls: take your pick from skulls, monkey heads and more.

VOLTAGE GUIDE 220 AC, 50 Hz.
COUNTRY DIALLING CODE 228.

CONSUMING PLEASURES

FOOD & DRINK Soups based on palm nut, groundnut and maize are common, and meat, poultry and seafood is plentiful.
SHOPPING & SOUVENIRS Wax prints, indigo cloth, embroideries, batiks and lace, marble ashtrays, traditional masks, wood sculpture, religious statuettes, voodoo items.

FIND OUT MORE

WEBSITES www.republicoftogo.com, http://usembassy.state.gov/togo, www.lonelyplanet.com/destinations/africa/togo.
LOCAL MEDIA No newspapers in English.
TOURIST BOARDS IN UK/US n/a.

Voodoo is a strong influence in Togo, with many young girls devoting their lives to the religion as assistants to the village voodoo priest. Over half the population is believed to be animist

TONGA

WHEN TO GO

WEATHER Best May-November. Heavy rains December-March.

FESTIVALS The largest festival is the Heilala Festival, incorporating King Taufa'ahau Tuou IV's birthday celebrations. Spread over two weeks in June and July, it is full of local culture with traditional songs, dances, *fêtes*, parades and the Tonga beauty pageant. The Vava'u Festival in May is a week of festivities starting with the Crown Prince's birthday. The capital Nuku'alofa holds the international Miss Galaxy Pageant, in which contestants are all men, or *fakaleiti*, the local version of transvestites.

TRANSPORT

INTERNATIONAL AIRPORTS Fua'Amotu (TBU) is 15 km from the capital.

INTERNAL TRAVEL Good roads, ferries and flights.

RED TAPE

VISAS REQUIRED (UK/US) Issued on arrival. Proof of onward ticket required.

VACCINATIONS REQUIRED: See 'Vaccinations required around the world' on page 653.

DRIVING REQUIREMENTS Local driving licence (available from police headquarters on production of national driving licence).

COUNTRY REPS IN UK/US UK: 36 Molyneux Street, London W1H 5BQ, tel (020) 7724 5828, fax (020) 7723 9074, email vielak@btinternet.com. USA: 360 Post Street, Suite 604, San Francisco, CA 94108, tel (415) 781 0365, fax (415) 781 3964, email tania@sfconsulate.gov.to.

UK/US REPS IN COUNTRY UK: n/a. USA: Enquiries relating to Tonga are handled in Suva (see Fiji).

PEOPLE AND PLACE

CAPITAL Nuku'alofa
LANGUAGE Tongan, English.
PEOPLES Tongan, European descent.

RELIGION Free Wesleyan (64%), Roman Catholic (15%).
SIZE (SQ KM) 748.
POPULATION 100,281.
POP DENSITY/KM 134.1.

STATE OF THE NATION

SAFETY Safe.
LIFE EXPECTANCY M 67.05, F 72.14.

BEING THERE

ETIQUETTE Shaking hands is the common greeting. Tongans are friendly and hospitable, and meals served to visitors will be plentiful. A gift is not expected, but will be greatly appreciated. The International Date Line loops around the island, the so-called Tongan Loop, which causes some confusion on Saturday and Sunday as to when to attend church.

CURRENCY *Pa'anga* (T$) = 100 *seniti*.

FINANCE Traveller's cheques accepted in banks and tourist places, credit cards less so.

BUSINESS HOURS 0830-1630 Mon-Friday.

GMT +13.

VOLTAGE GUIDE 240 AC, 50 Hz.

COUNTRY DIALLING CODE 676.

CONSUMING PLEASURES

FOOD & DRINK Local staples are *'ufi* (white yam) and taro. Other dishes include *lu pullu*

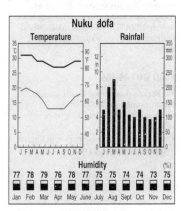

HIGHLIGHTS

HUMPBACK WHALES
These beautiful whales visit Tonga each year from June to November to mate and bear their young. You can take whale-watching trips, where it is possible to snorkel with these huge creatures, an experience that will be remembered for a lifetime. Then put on your scuba gear and head off for some amazing diving in Vava'u and Ha'apai.

EASTERN TONGATAPU The spot where Captain Cook landed on his final Pacific voyage in 1777: he apparently had a rest under one of the banyan trees before visiting his friend Pau in Ma'a, the reigning Tu'i Tonga. There is a memorial near Holonga village in commemoration.

BLOW HOLES One of Tonga's most impressive sights. Along the coastline of Houma, waves come crashing in through holes in the coral reef, causing the water to spurt up to 18 metres in the air. The area is called Mapu'a Vaea (The Chief's Whistle) by locals, because of the whistling sound made by these geyser-like jets.

NIUAFO'OU The most remote of the islands, the 'Tin Can Island', is good for hiking and is made up of barren lava flows that cover more than half the island. An enormous crater contains two spectacular fresh water lakes.

ROYAL TOMBS The Maka'ekula (Royal Tombs) are situated in the southern area of the business district on the Taufa'ahau Road. It's been the burial site for Tongan royalty since 1893.

(meat and onions marinated in coconut milk, baked in taro leaves in an underground oven), *feke* (grilled octopus or squid in coconut sauce) *'ota* (raw fish marinated in lemon juice) and devilled clams. Feasts are an important part of the lifestyle and up to 30 different dishes may be served on a long tray of plaited coconut fronts, including suckling pig, chicken, crayfish, octopus, pork and steamed vegetables.

SHOPPING & SOUVENIRS Tapa cloth, woven floor coverings, woven pandanus baskets, laundry baskets, coconut-shell goblets, tortoiseshell ornaments, jewellery, postage stamps.

FIND OUT MORE

WEBSITES www.tongaconsul.org, www.spto.org, www.tongaholiday.com.

LOCAL MEDIA *The Times of Tonga, Tonga Chronicle* and the *Matangi Tonga* are the English-language newspapers.

TOURIST BOARDS IN UK/US n/a.

In April 1789, off the volcanic Tongan island of Tofua, Captain William Bligh and 18 crewmen of the *Bounty* were set adrift in an open boat by mutineers. They survived after an epic 48-day voyage of 3,600 miles – one of the great feats of navigation and endurance

TRINIDAD & TOBAGO

WHEN TO GO

WEATHER Dry season is November-May. Hottest June-October. Wettest May-July.

FESTIVALS The Trinidad Carnival, held in February just before Lent, is renowned throughout the world. Life grinds to a halt for the duration of the festivities. On neighbouring Tobago, the Tobago Heritage Festival features activities such as traditional weddings, goat races and games. Emancipation Day celebrates the abolition of slavery each year on 1 August. There are many other festivals and events representing the many cultural and religious diversities of the islands.

TRANSPORT

INTERNATIONAL AIRPORTS Port of Spain (POS) is 27 km from city. Crown Point (TAB) is 13 km from Scarborough.

INTERNAL TRAVEL Good air, ferry and road links. Buses, taxis, car and bicycle hire are available.

RED TAPE

VISAS REQUIRED (UK/US) Not required up to 3 months (except Australia).

VACCINATIONS REQUIRED: See 'Vaccinations required around the world' on page 653.

DRIVING REQUIREMENTS National driving licence from Canada, UK, France, Germany, USA, Bahamas. Otherwise International Driving Permit.

COUNTRY REPS IN UK/US UK: 42 Belgrave Square, London SW1X 8NT, tel (020) 7245 9351, fax (020) 7823 1065, email tthc@btconnect.com. USA: 1708 Massachusetts Avenue, NW, Washington, DC 20036, tel (202) 467 6490, fax (202) 785 3130, email embttgo@erols.com.

UK/US REPS IN COUNTRY UK: 19 St Clair Avenue, PO Box 778, St Clair, Port of Spain, tel 622 2748, fax 622 4555, email ppabhc@tstt.net.tt. USA: 15 Queen's Park West, PO Box 752, Port of Spain, tel 622 6371, fax 628 5462, email consularportofspain@state.gov.

PEOPLE AND PLACE

CAPITAL Port of Spain.

LANGUAGE English.

PEOPLES Asian descent (40%), African descent (40%), mixed race.

RELIGION Christian, Hindu and Muslim.

SIZE (SQ KM) 5,128.

POPULATION 1,296,000.

POP DENSITY/KM 252.7.

STATE OF THE NATION

SAFETY Safe.

LIFE EXPECTANCY M 66.62, F 71.3.

BEING THERE

ETIQUETTE Casual attire is accepted for most occasions, but beachwear is not worn in the towns. *Liming*, or talking for the sake of talking, is a popular pastime. Hospitality is an important part of local life.

CURRENCY Trinidad & Tobago dollar (TT$) = 100 cents.

FINANCE Credit cards accepted in many places but may be charged 50% extra. Traveller's cheques better.

BUSINESS HOURS 0800-1600 Mon-Friday.

GMT -4.

VOLTAGE GUIDE 110/220 AC, 60 Hz.

COUNTRY DIALLING CODE 1 868.

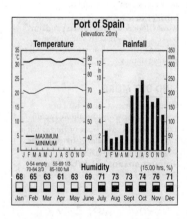

Port of Spain
(elevation: 20m)

Temperature · Rainfall

	Jan	Feb	Mar	Apr	May	June	July	Aug	Sept	Oct	Nov	Dec
Humidity (15.00 hrs, %)	68	65	63	61	63	69	71	73	73	74	76	71

HIGHLIGHTS

CARNIVAL This world-famous event held in Port of Spain is a mass of colour and sound. Weeks are spent preparing for it and the island comes to a halt. Immerse yourself in the vibrancy of steel bands, parades, spectacular costumes and limbo dancing. Join in and let your senses be overwhelmed.

TOBAGO The smaller, quieter, sibling of Trinidad, but appealing in its own right. Tobago is awash with vast stretches of beaches, like Turtle Bay where you can watch pelicans dive for fish as you sunbathe. There are gorgeous, protected rainforests in the volcanic eastern area, as well as botanical gardens and wildlife. The island has drawn foreigners for centuries, in fact nearly every European colonial power has fought to have the island at some stage.

THE BUCCOO GOAT RACE FESTIVAL This highly amusing event is held annually on Easter Tuesday. Jockeys dress in the silk of the goat's owner and betting is taken as the goat and jockey proudly parade in front of the crowd. Races take place on a 100-metre track, with up to ten goats per race. Once the race starts it is the jockey you sympathise with, as the goats tear off up the track, veering off in all directions. The event includes cultural events, plenty of local rum and even crab racing.

CORAL REEF Just a short boat ride away is the lovely Buccoo Reef, where trips can be made in a glass-bottomed boat. Its clear waters make an excellent spot for snorkelling.

CONSUMING PLEASURES

FOOD & DRINK Tobago offers notable seafood specialities, lobster and conch with dumplings amongst them. Both islands serve West Indian, Creole and Indian cuisine, including dishes such as peppery pigeon pea soup with *pilau* rice and *roti* (flat bread stuffed with curried chicken, fish, goat or vegetables). Bean-sized oysters are a Trinidad delicacy. Excellent rums.

SHOPPING & SOUVENIRS Calypso records, steel drums, leather bags, sandals, ceramics, woodcarvings, jewellery, Indian silks and fabrics, rum.

FIND OUT MORE

WEBSITES www.visittnt.com, www.britishhighcommission.gov.uk/ trinidadandtobago, http://usembassy.state.gov/trinidad.

LOCAL MEDIA All papers in English, including, *Newsday, The Trinidad Guardian, Trinidad & Tobago Express* and *Tobago News.*

TOURIST BOARDS IN UK/US UK: c/o MKI, Mitre House, 66 Abbey Road, Bush Hill Park, Enfield, Middlesex EN1 2QE, tel (020) 8350 1009, fax (020) 8350 1011, email mki@ttg.co.uk. US: n/a.

Perhaps the strangest sight on the two islands is Trinidad's Pitch Lake. It is a continually replenishing lake of tar, making it the world's single largest supply of natural bitumen

TUNISIA

WHEN TO GO

WEATHER Warm all year. Very hot inland and June-September.

FESTIVALS There are many religious events based around the lunar year calendar. Other festivals include the International Carthage Festival in July, Festival of the Oases in November - featuring camel racing - and the Sahara Duoz Festival, celebrating desert folklore.

TRANSPORT

INTERNATIONAL AIRPORTS Tunis (TUN) is 8 km from city. Monastir (MIR) is 8 km from city, Djerba (DJE) 8km, Sfax (SFA) 15 km, Tozeur (TOE) 10 km.

INTERNAL TRAVEL Excellent road and air network. Reasonable railway.

RED TAPE

VISAS REQUIRED (UK/US) Not required up to 3 months (except Australia, which can be obtained on arrival).

VACCINATIONS REQUIRED: See 'Vaccinations required around the world' on page 653.

DRIVING REQUIREMENTS National driving licence, vehicle log book, insurance.

COUNTRY REPS IN UK/US
UK: 29 Prince's Gate, London SW7 1QG, tel (020) 7584 8117, fax (020) 7225 2884. USA: 1515 Massachusetts Avenue, NW, Washington, DC 20005, tel (202) 862 1850, fax (202) 862 1858, email atwashington@verizon.net.

UK/US REPS IN COUNTRY UK: Rue du Lac Windermere, Les Berges du Lac, 1053 Tunis, tel (71) 108 700, fax (71) 108 749, email tntolondon@aol.com. USA: Zone Nord-Est des Berges du Lac, Nord de Tunis, 2045, La Goulette, tel (71) 107 000, fax (71) 962 115.

PEOPLE AND PLACE

CAPITAL Tunis.

LANGUAGE Arabic.

PEOPLES Arab and Berber.

RELIGION Muslim.

SIZE (SQ KM) 163,610.

POPULATION 9,889,900.

POP DENSITY/KM 60.4.

STATE OF THE NATION

SAFETY Safe.

LIFE EXPECTANCY M 73.2, F 76.71.

BEING THERE

ETIQUETTE Shaking hands is the usual form of greeting. The country follows Arab culture and traditions, although it is one of the more tolerant and liberal Muslim countries. Dress can be informal, but cover your shoulders and knees when visiting a religious monument. Beachwear should be kept to the tourist resorts. Tunisians are a very hospitable race; a gift would be advised in appreciation of hospitality or as a token of friendship.

CURRENCY Tunisian *dinar* (TD) = 1,000 *millimes*.

FINANCE Credit cards and traveller's cheques widely accepted.

BUSINESS HOURS Winter: 0800-1230 and 1430-1800 Monday-Friday. Summer: 0800-1300 Monday-Saturday.

GMT +1.

VOLTAGE GUIDE 220 AC, 50 Hz.

COUNTRY DIALLING CODE 216.

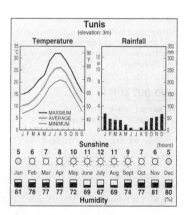

HIGHLIGHTS

TUNIS The capital and heart of modern Tunisia. Visit the Bardo Museum containing pieces from the many cultures and civilizations that have flourished here. Or walk through its busy, meandering streets and admire its architectural beauty.

CARTHAGE The centre of the maritime Punic Empire and later the capital of the Roman Province of Africa, Carthage is rich in history and beauty. The Antonine Baths are one of the best preserved sites. Once the largest baths in Africa, they are positioned between the sea and Avenue Habib Bourguiba. Stroll just south of the baths and you will find the archaeological gardens. A short visit will provide an overview, but a few extra days are needed to fully appreciate this ancient area.

BEACHES Top quality beaches and resorts fill this strip of sun-scorched Mediterranean coast.

SAHARA Sweeping across the southern tip of Tunisia is a gorgeous section of dune-filled desert. If you get a chance it's worth witnessing the grand desolation of it and wandering through the towns on the desert fringe.

TATOUINE Unpack your light sabre and re-enact scenes from one of the most popular film franchises of all time. Locals still inhabit the distinct underground dwellings made famous by the *Stars Wars* films, the landscape formed much of the backdrop for Luke Skywalker's home planet, Tatooine.

TOZEUR Amble through the old quarter of this beautiful oasis town set against the desert dunes.

CONSUMING PLEASURES

FOOD & DRINK Tunisian dishes are often cooked with olive oil, spiced with aniseed, coriander, cumin, caraway, cinnamon or saffron. Lamb or *dorado* (bream) are often served with *couscous*, the *tajines* (stews) are generally excellent. *Brik,* a fried pastry envelope with a savoury filling, is a popular snack. Local wines are excellent.

SHOPPING & SOUVENIRS Copperware, olive-wood items, leather goods, pottery, embroidery, enamelled jewellery.

> " Good reputation is better than wealth."
> *Tunisian proverb*

FIND OUT MORE

WEBSITES www.tourismtunisia.com, www.british-emb.intl.tn, www.tunisiaonline.com, http://tunis.usembassy.gov.

LOCAL MEDIA *Tunisia News* is published weekly in English.

TOURIST BOARDS IN UK/US UK: 77A Wigmore Street, London W1U 1QF, tel (020) 7224 5561, fax (020) 7224 4053, email tntolondon@aol.com. US: n/a.

TURKEY

WHEN TO GO

WEATHER South and west coasts have a Mediterranean climate and are warm and sunny May-September. Inland has cooler winters and the east can be very cold.

FESTIVALS Islamic holidays are of great importance. Among them, Ramadan, the month of fasting, is a particularly significant time. Dates of religious festivals change year-on-year. In the capital, Istanbul, the most prestigious event in the calendar is the International Istanbul Music Festival, in June-July, featuring classical music, dance and ballet in spectacular venues. A highlight is Mozart's opera *Abduction from the Seraglio*, performed in the Topkapi Palace, the exquisite former residence and *seraglio* of the sultans.

TRANSPORT

INTERNATIONAL AIRPORTS Ankara (ESB) is 35 km from the city. Istanbul (IST) is 24 km from the city. Also Izmir, Dalaman, Antalya, Adana.

INTERNAL TRAVEL Excellent roads. Good rail and flight network.

RED TAPE

VISAS REQUIRED (UK/US) Not required up to 3 months.

VACCINATIONS REQUIRED: See 'Vaccinations required around the world' on page 653.

DRIVING REQUIREMENTS An International Driving Permit is required for stays of more than three months. Green Card International Insurance and Turkish third party insurance are also required.

COUNTRY REPS IN UK/US UK: Rutland Lodge, Rutland Gardens, Knightsbridge, London SW7 1BW, tel (020) 7591 6900, fax (020) 7591 6911, email tckons@btclick.com. USA: 2525 Massachusetts Avenue, NW, Washington, DC 20008, tel (202) 612 6700, fax (202) 612 6744, email contact@ turkishembassy.org.

UK/US REPS IN COUNTRY UK: Sehit Ersan Caddesi 46A, Cankaya, Ankara, tel (312) 455 3344, fax (312) 455 3356, email britembinf@tnn.net. USA: Ataturk Bulvar 110, Kavaklidere 06100, Ankara, tel (312) 455 5555, fax (312) 467 0019, email didem@pd.state.gov.

PEOPLE AND PLACE

CAPITAL Ankara.

LANGUAGE Turkish.

PEOPLES Turkish (70%), Kurdish (20%), Arab and others.

RELIGION Muslim, mainly Sunni (99%).

SIZE (SQ KM) 779,452.

POPULATION 69,757,000.

POP DENSITY/KM 89.5.

STATE OF THE NATION

SAFETY Safe, except in Kurdish areas of the south-east, which can be affected by military-guerrilla interactions.

LIFE EXPECTANCY M 69.94, F 74.91

BEING THERE

ETIQUETTE Visitors should always respect Islamic customs. English is widely spoken in business circles, although any effort to speak some Turkish is appreciated. Be aware that a service charge is almost always included in hotel and restaurant bills. Smoking is widely acceptable, but is prohibited in some public places, including cinemas, theatres, city buses and *dolmuses* (collective taxis).

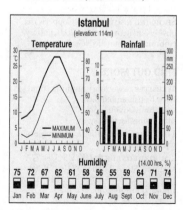

HIGHLIGHTS

ISTANBUL Exotic hub straddling the Bosphorus, where East meets West and modern meets ancient. Formerly Constantinople, it has a wealth of history and culture, exemplified by the spellbinding Aya Sofia - one of the world's architectural wonders. The great cathedral was built by the Romans and converted into a mosque by the conquering Ottomans. Its fabulous central dome, the largest in the world for a millennium, inspired mosque architecture worldwide, and is surrounded by gorgeous Byzantine mosaics in gold. Another major attraction is the Topkapi Palace, the exquisite former palace of the sultans and their harem. Elsewhere, the Grand Bazaar is an intoxicating maze of streets, containing some 4,000 shops, as well as mosques and restaurants. It is said to be the world's oldest shopping mall.

CAPPADOCIA Central region known for its unusual yet spectacular landscape of natural rock formations. Capped pinnacles and jutting ravines include dwellings hewn from the rock, the historic remains of a semi-troglodyte population.

MEDITERRANEAN COAST Drift along the beautiful coastline of southwest Turkey, best sampled on a trip by traditional wooden *gûlet* (sailing boat). Sail to idyllic bays and enchanting secluded coves, dropping anchor to explore historic ruins and snorkel in the clear waters. Pretty harbour towns such as Fethiye dot the coastline, which draws walkers, sailors and those who prefer just to lounge on the beach in the sunshine.

CURRENCY New Turkish *Lira* (YTL) and Turkish *Lira* (TL) in circulation in 2005, only YTL from 1 January 2006.
1 YTL = 1, 000, 000 TL.
1 YTL = 100 New *Kuru* (YKr).

FINANCE Credit cards and traveller's cheques widely accepted.

BUSINESS HOURS 0830-1230 and 1330-1730 Monday-Friday.

GMT +2.

VOLTAGE GUIDE 220 AC, 50 Hz.

COUNTRY DIALLING CODE 90.

CONSUMING PLEASURES

FOOD & DRINK Lamb is featured on most menus, served as *shish* (cubed and grilled on a skewer) or *doner* (carved from a roasting spit) kebabs. Red mullet and swordfish are also popular, as are *dolma* (vine leaves stuffed with nuts and currants) and *karni-yarik* (aubergine stuffed with mince meat). *Ayran* is a yoghurt drink, tea and strong coffee are widely available. *Raki* is an aniseedy liquor, usually taken with *meze*.

SHOPPING & SOUVENIRS Jewellery, carpets, antiques, mother-of-pearl items (such as secretly locking boxes), ceramics (wall plates), shisha pipes, Turkish bath sets, Turkish delight.

FIND OUT MORE

WEBSITES www.tourismturkey.org, http://turkey.embassyhomepage.com, www.turkconsulate-london.com, www.britishembassy.org.tr, www.turkishembassy.org, www.usemb-ankara.org.tr, www.istanbulcityguide.com.

LOCAL MEDIA *Turkish Daily News* is published in English.

TOURIST BOARDS IN UK/US UK: 1st Floor, 170-173 Piccadilly, London W1J 9EJ, tel (020) 7629 7771, fax (020) 7491 0773, email info@gototurkey.co.uk. US: 821 UN Plaza, New York, NY 10017, tel (212) 687 2194, fax (212) 599 7568, emailny@ tourismturkey.org.

TURKMENISTAN

WHEN TO GO

WEATHER Extreme continental climate, with freezing winters (November-April) and searing summers (May-September).

FESTIVALS Festivities in this sparsely populated country include Akilteken Day, a celebration of the Akilteken horse, marked with parades and races. Another important occasion is The Day of the Turkmen Carpet, on 29 May. Eid-ul-Azha, the Feast of the Sacrifice, sees an animal ritually slaughtered and shared with relatives and the poor.

TRANSPORT

INTERNATIONAL AIRPORTS Ashgabat (ASB) is 4 km from city.

INTERNAL TRAVEL Reasonable road network, some internal flights, limited railway lines. Cheap buses, taxis and car hire available.

RED TAPE

VISAS REQUIRED (UK/US) Required.

VACCINATIONS REQUIRED: See 'Vaccinations required around the world' on page 653.

DRIVING REQUIREMENTS International Driving Permit with authorised translation.

COUNTRY REPS IN UK/US
UK: St George's House, 14-17 Wells Street, London W1T 3PD, tel (020) 7255 1071, fax (020) 7323 9184. USA: 2207 Massachusetts Avenue, NW, Washington, DC 20008, tel (202) 588 1500, fax (202) 588 0697, email turkmen@mindspring.com.

UK/US REPS IN COUNTRY UK: PO Box 45, 301-308 Office Building, Four Points Ak Altin Hotel, 744014 Ashgabat, tel (12) 363 462-4, fax (12) 363 465, email beasb@online.tm. USA: 9 1984/Pushkin Street, 744000 Ashgabat, tel (12) 350 045, fax (12) 392 614, email irc-ashabat@iatp.edu.tm.

PEOPLE AND PLACE

CAPITAL Ashgabat.

LANGUAGE Turkmen.

PEOPLES Turkmen, Uzbek, Russian.

RELIGION Sunni Muslim (87%), Eastern Orthodox Christian.

SIZE (SQ KM) 488,100.

POPULATION 4,794,000.

POP DENSITY/KM 9.8.

STATE OF THE NATION

SAFETY Stable, but subject to occasional tensions. Seek latest information at time of visit.

LIFE EXPECTANCY M 58.02, F 64.93.

BEING THERE

ETIQUETTE Dress conservatively, shorts are very rarely seen and might attract undue attention. Hiking boots are frowned upon in polite company. If visiting a house, remove your shoes and leave them pointing inwards. It is traditional, though not compulsory, to take a gift.

CURRENCY *Manat* (TMM) = 100 *tenge*.

FINANCE Credit cards only accepted at a few hotels. Traveller's cheques only accepted from certain banks. US dollars cash is best.

BUSINESS HOURS 0900-1800 Mon-Friday.

GMT +5.

VOLTAGE GUIDE 220 AC, 50 Hz.

COUNTRY DIALLING CODE 993.

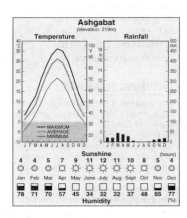

HIGHLIGHTS

ASHGABAT A small city considering it is the capital, Ashgabat is not without its charms. Situated at the southern rim of the KaraKum Desert, it replaced the old city which was destroyed by an earthquake in 1948. The architecture mixes Eastern and Western styles, while new buildings are springing up quickly. Soak in the atmosphere at the Tolkuchka Bazaar, or visit the carpet museum, home to the world's largest handwoven rug.

BAKHARDEN Home to an underground

lake, Kov-Ata. The lake itself is 50-60 metres below the slopes of the Kopet Dag mountains and at the bottom of a 250-metre, damp, dimly-lit stairway. Admire the many clusters of stalactites and listen to the whisper of bats. Once there, bathe in 36 °C waters - that is, if you don't mind the pungent smell.

DARVAZA A small town in central Turkmenistan inhabited by the Teke tribe. These people continue to live a semi-nomadic lifestyle and live in *yurts*, a traditional Turkmen dwelling,

built with a wooden framework then covered in a felt called *koshma*. You can spend a night in a *yurt* and appreciate Turkmen hospitality. Nearby are the Gas Craters, an enormous volcano-like crater at ground level.

REPETEK DESERT RESERVE Air temperatures of more than 50°C have been recorded here, while the surface of the sand has been known to reach as much as 70°C. The desert is inhabited by an array of strange reptiles, lizards, spiders, and scorpions.

CONSUMING PLEASURES

FOOD & DRINK Based on Central Asian staples such as *plov* (mutton, shredded yellow turnip and rice), *shashlyk* (char-grilled mutton kebabs served with flat bread and raw onions), *shorpa* (meat and vegetable soup) and *manty* (like ravioli, with a meat filling). A particular speciality is *ishkiykli* - dough balls filled with meat and cooked in hot sand. Alcoholic drinks widely available. *Kefir*, a thick, drinking yoghurt, is served with breakfast.

SHOPPING & SOUVENIRS Rugs, handicrafts, Turkmen sheepskin hats, costumes.

FIND OUT MORE

WEBSITES www.britishembassy.gov.uk/turkmenistan, www.turkmenistanembassy.org, www.usemb-ashgabat.rpo.at, www.lonelyplanet.com/destinations/central_asia/turkmenistan.

LOCAL MEDIA No newspapers in English.

TOURIST BOARDS IN UK/US

For the nomadic Turkmen, a carpet or two would be the only piece of furniture worth having. Easy to transport, they made good floor coverings, excellent wall linings and effective insulation for the *yurt*. They are still used for these purposes today

TUVALU

WHEN TO GO

WEATHER Humid and hot all year. Rainy November-February.

FESTIVALS There are numerous festivals and celebrations on Tuvalu, involving feasting with traditional entertainments, which visitors are welcome to join. Tuvalu Day on 1-2 October celebrates the country's independence. There are also public holidays throughout the year. If possible, just follow the beat of the drum.

TRANSPORT

INTERNATIONAL AIRPORTS Funafuti (FUN) is 30 minutes outside town.

INTERNAL TRAVEL No air service. Few roads. A single passenger and cargo boat serves all the islands.

RED TAPE

VISAS REQUIRED (UK/US) Not required.

VACCINATIONS REQUIRED: See 'Vaccinations required around the world' on page 653.

DRIVING REQUIREMENTS n/a.

COUNTRY REPS IN UK/US UK: 230 Worple Road, London, SW20 8RH, tel/fax (020) 8879 0985, email tuvaluconsulate@ netscape.net. USA: n/a.

UK/US REPS IN COUNTRY UK: Enquiries are handled by the High Commission in Suva, (see Fiji). USA: Enquiries are handled by the embassy in Suva (see Fiji).

PEOPLE AND PLACE

CAPITAL Funafuti.

LANGUAGE English.

PEOPLES Tuvaluan.

RELIGION Church of Tuvalu (97%).

SIZE (SQ KM) 26.

POPULATION 10,880.

POP DENSITY/KM 418.5.

STATE OF THE NATION

SAFETY Safe.

LIFE EXPECTANCY M 65.79, F 70.33.

BEING THERE

ETIQUETTE The traditional values of the Tuvaluan culture are dominant here. Dress is casual, but it is customary for women to cover their thighs and beachwear should be confined to the beach or poolside. If you are visiting an outer island, take items like tobacco sticks, matches, fish hooks, chewing gum, and volleyballs as gifts for people you may meet, as a form of reciprocation. Remove your shoes before entering a house, church or village meeting house. If invited to a feast, try and find out the local custom and seek advice. Sunday is a day of rest and church-going, and visitors are recommended to undertake activities that do not cause much disturbance.

CURRENCY Tuvaluan dollar (TV$) = 100 cents. Australian dollar (AS$) also used.

FINANCE No credit cards. Traveller's cheques in AS$.

BUSINESS HOURS 0730-1615 Monday-Thursday, 0730-1245 Friday.

GMT +12.

VOLTAGE GUIDE 240 AC, 60 Hz.

COUNTRY DIALLING CODE 688.

Suva is shown in this chart because it is the nearest place with available and similar data.

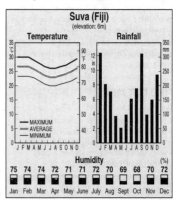

HIGHLIGHTS

FUNAFUTI The capital of these beautiful islands is where most activity is centred. Visit the enormous Funafuti lagoon, a huge pool 14 kilometres wide and 18 kilometres long, which is excellent for swimming and snorkelling. Zip across to the Marine Conservation Park in a private or chartered boat and explore six tiny islets that are home to an abundance of marine life. Join in a game of football at Funafuti's pitch, which also doubles as the airport landing strip.

NANUMEA The northwestern-most island, Nanumea is considered to have the most beautiful lagoon. Swim and relax in this island paradise, visit the US landing craft that lies wrecked on the reef. Climb the church tower for a wonderful view, but ask the pastor's permission first.

FUNAFALA The second most populated island in the atoll is Funafala. You can visit it by taking the Funafuti Island Council's catamaran, which goes three times a week for a two-hour stay. The island is covered with traditional buildings with thatched roofs.

SNORKELLING The numerous lagoons and Funafuti Marine Conservation Area are teeming with marine life, but it can be dangerous to swim in the ocean due to a strong tide.

COMBAT SKILLS Learn to wield the *katipopuki*, a traditional hardwood spear used in an age-old Tuvaluan martial art. This form of personal defence training can be learned on the island of Niutaos. One to impress your friends when you get home.

CONSUMING PLEASURES

FOOD & DRINK Fish and shellfish play a major part in the local diet. Some restaurants serve international dishes. Beer is imported.

SHOPPING & SOUVENIRS Weaving, shell jewellery, wooden boxes.

FIND OUT MORE

WEBSITES www.spto.org, www.timelesstuvalu.com.

LOCAL MEDIA *Tuvalu Echoes* is published in English, fortnightly, by the government. No TV service, one radio station.

TOURIST BOARDS IN UK/US n/a.

The highest point on Tuvalu is just 4.6 metres above sea level. Worried about rising global sea levels, the government has asked New Zealand and Australia to take in Tuvaluans if evacuation should ever be necessary

UGANDA

WHEN TO GO

WEATHER Heavy rains March-May and October-November. Otherwise warm all year, though cooler in hill country.

FESTIVALS NRM Anniversary Day is on the 26 January and 8 March is International Women's Day. During June it's Martyr's and International Heroes Day. Uganda has some colourful local traditions and seemingly spontaneous ceremonies may take place, involving music and dancing.

TRANSPORT

INTERNATIONAL AIRPORTS Entebbe (EBB) is 35 km from city.

INTERNAL TRAVEL Rail network limited and timetables erratic. Fairly extensive roads, though in poor condition. Some internal flights. Ferries on great lakes efficient but not always safe.

RED TAPE

VISAS REQUIRED (UK/US) Required for all.

VACCINATIONS REQUIRED: See 'Vaccinations required around the world' on page 653.

DRIVING REQUIREMENTS International Driving Permit and third-party insurance required. Drivers must carry vehicle log books and pay a temporary road licence.

COUNTRY REPS IN UK/US UK: Uganda House, 58-59 Trafalgar Square, London WC2N 5DX, tel (020) 7839 5783, fax (020) 7839 8925. USA: 5911 16th Street, NW, Washington, DC 20011, tel (202) 726 7100, fax (202) 726 1727, email ugembassy@aol.com.

UK/US REPS IN COUNTRY UK: PO Box 7070, 10-12 Parliament Avenue, Kampala, tel (31) 312 000, fax (41) 257 304, email bhcinfo@starcom.co.ug. USA: PO Box 7007, Plot 1577, Gaba Road, Kampala, tel (41) 259 791, fax (41) 259 794, email KampalaVisa@state.gov.

PEOPLE AND PLACE

CAPITAL Kampala.

LANGUAGE English.

PEOPLES 13 main ethnic groups (principally Luganda, Nkole, Chiga, Lango, Acholi, Teso, Lugbara).

RELIGION Roman Catholic (33%), Protestant (33%), traditional beliefs (13%), Muslim, Hindu.

SIZE (SQ KM) 241,139.

POPULATION 24,748,977.

POP DENSITY/KM 102.6.

STATE OF THE NATION

SAFETY Potentially safe. Be wary in border areas, especially the north-west, haunt of bandits, rebels and religious militias.

LIFE EXPECTANCY M 50.74, F 52.46.

BEING THERE

ETIQUETTE A handshake is a sufficient greeting. Casual dress is appropriate for most occasions. If eating with a family, be sure to wash your hands before and after the meal because most Ugandans eat with their hands. Leaning on your left hand or stretching your legs during the meal is seen as disrespectful. It is customary to tip waiters and taxi drivers 10 per cent.

CURRENCY Uganda shilling (USh).

FINANCE Visa and traveller's cheques widely accepted, other credit cards less so.

BUSINESS HOURS 0800-1245 and 1400-1700 Monday-Friday.

GMT +3.

VOLTAGE GUIDE 240 AC, 50 Hz.

COUNTRY DIALLING CODE 256.

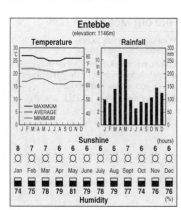

HIGHLIGHTS

KAMPALA Now a bustling capital city, Kampala has come a long way in a short time. Spread across seven hills, the city centre sits on one of them, Nakasero. The top of the hill is a garden city with wide avenues, imposing fences, international embassies and the homes of the rich. The bottom of the hill is full of the hustle and bustle of shops, street markets, Hindu Temples and pavement stalls. Visit the Uganda Museum, featuring a collection of traditional musical instruments, which you can play.

BWINDI NATIONAL PARK Located in the southwest near the border with Congo, it is home to half of the surviving mountain gorillas in the world, approximately 320. Before becoming a national park, the region was known as The Impenetrable Forest and is rich in flora and fauna.

MOUNT ELGON An extinct volcano with excellent wildlife and opportunities for climbing. Elgon hides many caves, which are home to bats, and the walls are decorated with ancient cave paintings. Each night herds of elephants gather at one of the caves, Kitum, to travel deep into the mountain along paths that were made by their ancestors before them: they are looking for salt, which they lick from the scarred rock.

THE SSESE ISLANDS One hour by boat from the shore of Lake Victoria lie these 84 unspoilt, tranquil and virtually uninhabited islands. Home to birds, crocodiles, hippos, chimps, monkeys, and the Basese tribe - with their own language and culture.

CONSUMING PLEASURES

FOOD & DRINK Popular dishes include *matoke* (made from bananas), millet bread, sweet potatoes, cassava, chicken and meat stews and freshwater fish. Banana gin (*waragi*) makes a good cocktail base.

SHOPPING & SOUVENIRS Bangles, necklaces, bracelets, woodcarvings, basketry, tea, coffee, ceramics.

FIND OUT MORE

WEBSITES www.ugandaembassy.com, http://kampala.usembassy.gov, www.visituganda.com.

LOCAL MEDIA *Financial Times, The Monitor, Guide, New Vision* and *The Star* are some of the English-language papers.

TOURIST BOARDS IN UK/US n/a.

"The forests of Uganda, for magnificence, for variety of form and colour, for profusion of brilliant life, for the vast scale and awful fecundity of the natural processes that are beheld at work, eclipsed, and indeed effaced, all previous impressions."
Sir Winston Churchill, 1908

UKRAINE

WHEN TO GO

WEATHER Warm summers (May-September), cold winters (November-March).

FESTIVALS Ukrainian Day on 22 January celebrates the proclamation of the Free Ukrainian Republic in 1918. Ukrainian Independence Day on 24 August marks the declaration of independence in 1991. On the last weekend of May, Kyiv celebrates Kyiv Days with folk festivals, fireworks and a beauty contest. October sees the International Music Festival and International Film Festival come to Kyiv.

TRANSPORT

INTERNATIONAL AIRPORTS Kyiv (IEV)/Borispol (KBP) is 34 km from city.

INTERNAL TRAVEL Flights erratic due to fuel shortages. Railways slow but reliable, though difficult to book. Buses or self-drive not recommended.

RED TAPE

VISAS REQUIRED (UK/US) Required for all.

VACCINATIONS REQUIRED: See 'Vaccinations required around the world' on page 653.

DRIVING REQUIREMENTS International Driving Permits.

COUNTRY REPS IN UK/US
UK: 60 Holland Park, London W11 3SJ, tel (020) 7727 6312, fax (020) 7792 1708, email emb_gb@mfa.gov.ua. USA: 3350 M Street, NW, Washington, DC 20007, tel (202) 333 0606, fax (202) 333 0817, email letters@ukremb.com.

UK/US REPS IN COUNTRY
UK: 9 Desyatinna Street, 01025 Kyiv, tel (44) 490 3660, fax (44) 490 3662, email ukembinf@sovamua.com. USA: 10 Yuria Kotsyubinskiho Street, 10 Kyiv, tel (44) 490 4000, fax (44) 490 4085, email acskiev@state.gov.

PEOPLE AND PLACE

CAPITAL Kyiv (Kiev).

LANGUAGE Ukrainian.

PEOPLES Ukrainian (73%), Russian (22%), Jewish and others.

RELIGION Ukrainian Orthodox.

SIZE (SQ KM) 603,700.

POPULATION 47,622,436.

POP DENSITY/KM 78.9.

STATE OF THE NATION

SAFETY Be wary of carjackings and muggings.

LIFE EXPECTANCY M 61.6, F 72.38.

BEING THERE

ETIQUETTE Ukrainians are generally warm and friendly to visitors. If invited to a family home, it is traditional to bring a gift. Wine, a cake or flowers are fine, though make sure flowers amount to an uneven number - because an even number of flowers is considered bad luck. If there is a child it is appropriate to bring them a gift as well. Avoid ostentatious displays of wealth. Be careful when complimenting a host's belongings, as they may be offered to you.

CURRENCY *Hryvnya* = 100 *kopiyok*.

FINANCE Cash not credit cards.

BUSINESS HOURS 0900-1800 Mon-Friday.

GMT +2.

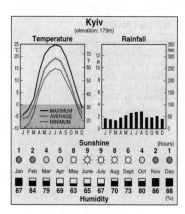

HIGHLIGHTS

KYIV The capital city exudes a cosmopolitan air while maintaining its heritage. Divide your time between the buzz of the modern areas and elegant, quaint historic areas. Be sure to visit the St Sophia complex, home to the city's oldest church, which is registered on UNESCO's World Heritage list. The church is know for its underground labyrinths, lined by eerie mummified monks. Alternatively, saunter down to Andriyivskyuzviz (Andrew's Descent), a colourful market selling a wide variety of local gifts.

LVIV A gem hidden away near the border with Poland, located at the feet of the sweeping Carpathian mountains. It's a city of striking beauty with Gothic, Renaissance and Baroque architecture, as well as pretty cobbled streets. It has often been called 'the open air museum'.

ODESSA A charming port with a distinct local culture, known as The Pearl of the Black Sea. The grand Potemkin Stairs, from Prymorsky Boulevard to the sea, were built between 1837 and 1841 and create an optical illusion through the varying widths of each step. They are a symbol of the city.

THE CRIMEA Located in the south of Ukraine between the Black Sea and the Sea of Azov, this region is steeped in modern history. Churchill, Stalin, and Roosevelt met in the Livada Palace in 1945, and Gorbachev was held in Faros for three days during the coup of 1991. Yalta at the very tip is known as The Pearl of the Crimea.

VOLTAGE GUIDE 220 AC, 50 Hz.
COUNTRY DIALLING CODE 380.

CONSUMING PLEASURES

FOOD & DRINK The cuisine is similar to Russian food, including *borshch* (beetroot soup), *varenniki* (dumplings of cheese, meat or fruit), and *holubtsi* (stuffed cabbage rolls). Crimean wines are excellent, as are the cabernets, and *Artyomov* champagne.

SHOPPING & SOUVENIRS Paintings, ceramics, jewellery.

FIND OUT MORE

WEBSITES www.ukremb.org.uk, www.intouristuk.com, www.ukremb.com, http://kiev.embassy.gov.

LOCAL MEDIA *News From Ukraine* is the English-language paper, Western press also available in Kiev.

TOURIST BOARDS IN UK/US UK: 9 Princedale Road, Holland Park, London W11 4NW, tel (020) 7792 5240, fax (020) 7727 4650, email info@intouristuk.com.

An old legend tells of three brothers, Kiy, Khoriv, and Shchek, and their sister Lybid, who founded Kiev in the fifth century and named it after their elder brother Kyiv

UNITED ARAB EMIRATES

WHEN TO GO

WEATHER Best October-May, very hot June-September.

FESTIVALS There is the Dubai Shopping Festival, in January, which has amused many: and with the International Jewellery Exhibition,also early in the year. Throughout the year there are horse- and camel-race meets. Eid al-Adh, the Festival of Sacrifice, commemorates Abraham's willingness to sacrifice everything for God, and is celebrated in March. The Islamic New Year, Hijra New Year's Day, celebrates the Prophet Mohammed and his followers' move to Medina from Mecca. On 2 December the country celebrates the founding of the UAE; festivities can last to the following week.

TRANSPORT

INTERNATIONAL AIRPORTS Abu Dhani (AUH) is 35 km from city. Dubai (DXB) is 5 km from city. Ras al-Khaimah (RKT) is 15 km from city. Sharjah (SHJ) is 10 km from city.

INTERNAL TRAVEL Good road and flight networks. Limited buses, taxis in town, car hire available.

RED TAPE

VISAS REQUIRED (UK/US) Required for all (except UK up to 30 days).

VACCINATIONS REQUIRED: See 'Vaccinations required around the world' on page 653.

DRIVING REQUIREMENTS A local driving licence can be issued on presentation of a national driving licence and a letter from your sponsor. International Driving Permit useful but not mandatory.

COUNTRY REPS IN UK/US UK: 30 Prince's Gate, London SW7 1PT, tel (020) 7581 1281, fax (020) 7581 9616, email information@uaeembassyuk.net. USA: 3522 International Court, NW, Washington, DC 20008, tel (202) 243 2400, fax (202) 243 2432.

UK/US REPS IN COUNTRY UK: PO Box 248, 22 Khalid bin Al Waleed Street, Abu Dhabi, tel (2) 610 1100, fax (2) 610 1586, email information.abudhabi@fco.gov.uk. USA: Al-Sudan Street, PO Box 4009, Abu Dhabi, tel (2) 414 2200, fax (2) 414 2432, email consularbudha@state.gov.

PEOPLE AND PLACE

CAPITAL Abu Dhabi.

LANGUAGE Arabic.

PEOPLES Arab (42%), other Asian (50%).

RELIGION Sunni Muslim.

SIZE (SQ KM) 77,700.

POPULATION 3,754,000.

POP DENSITY/KM 48.3.

STATE OF THE NATION

SAFETY Safe.

LIFE EXPECTANCY M 72.73, F 77.87.

BEING THERE

ETIQUETTE Muslim religious laws should be taken into consideration. Visitors are expected to observe local standards and should be modestly covered. There are various forms of greeting, so it is advised that you wait for your counterpart to initiate the greeting. Gesture and eat with the right hand, the left hand is for hygiene. Don't point. Gifts are not necessary, and if you give a gift it will be opened in private. Avoid giving alcohol, pork, images of naked or partially clad women, even in art.

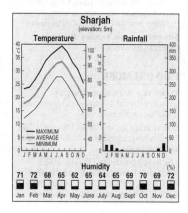

HIGHLIGHTS

DUBAI City of glamour, *sheikhs*, credit cards, outrageous shopping malls, the highest prize in horse racing, beaches, excellent restaurants, strong religious beliefs, a relaxing home for the rich and famous, extravagant hotels and culture. Let yourself be immersed in a city that will woo you with its ebullient lifestyle and charm.

KHOR FAKKAN Picturesque town with an exquisite harbour and spectacular mountains that meet the clean, cool, crisp waters of the Gulf.

Relax on the pristine beaches or tour the mountains above the harbour town.

AL AIN Known as the 'Garden City of the Gulf', Al Ain is an oasis surrounded by sand dunes and built as a garden city. This lush area offers unique displays of landscaping, water, and sculpture. Also home to one of the last remaining camel markets.

ABU DHABI The capital city grew out of pearling and oil to become one of the most modern in the world, while still maintaining parts of

its heritage. It has ancient burial grounds in Um al Nar and nearby building yards where craftsmen demonstrate skills unchanged for centuries. Pretty mosques dot the capital.

HORSE RACING The Dubai World Cup, only started in 1996, has become one of the most prestigious races in the world, attracting thoroughbreds from across the globe. And it's worth winning – the prize money runs into the millions.

CURRENCY UAE *Dirham* (Dh) = 100 *fils*.

FINANCE Credit cards and traveller's cheques widely accepted.

BUSINESS HOURS 0800-1300 and 1600-1930 Sat-Wednesday, 0800-1200 Thursday.

GMT +4.

VOLTAGE GUIDE 220/240 AC, 50 Hz.

COUNTRY DIALLING CODE 971.

CONSUMING PLEASURES

FOOD & DRINK Popular dishes include *tabbouleh* (bulghur wheat with mint and parsley), *hummus* (chickpea and sesame paste), *warak enab* (stuffed vine leaves), *koussa mashi* (stuffed courgettes) and *makbous* (spicy lamb with rice). Consumption of alcohol is permitted for non-Muslims except in Sharjah.

SHOPPING & SOUVENIRS Luxury goods, traditional leather goods and silverware.

FIND OUT MORE

WEBSITES www.uaeembassyuk.net,

www.dubaitourism.ae, www.britain-uae.org, http://usembassy.state.gov/uae, www.uae.org.ae, www.emirates.org, www.dubaitourism.com.

LOCAL MEDIA *The Gulf Today*, *Emirates News*, *Khaleej Times* are some of the English-language newspapers.

TOURIST BOARDS IN UK/US UK: 1st Floor, 125 Pall Mall, London SW1Y 5EA, tel (020) 7839 0580, fax (020) 7839 0582, email dtcm_uk@dubaitourism.ae. US: n/a.

The Burj Al Arab, nine miles south of Dubai, is the tallest hotel in the world, standing 1,052 feet tall. It perches on a man-made island and is shaped like a sail

UNITED KINGDOM

WHEN TO GO

WEATHER Changeable climate, rainy all year. Cold wet winters (November-March).

FESTIVALS Festivals are held throughout the year in England, Scotland, Wales and Northern Ireland. Summer time is known for the music festival circuit, such as Glastonbury. Hogmanay in Edinburgh is considered one of the world's best New Year celebrations. Notting Hill Carnival on the Bank Holiday weekend of August is another big cultural event, while the Edinburgh Fringe Festival showcases new talent for theatre and comedy. Other summer events include Glyndebourne Opera, Henley rowing reggata, Goodwood horse racing, and many more.

TRANSPORT

INTERNATIONAL AIRPORTS Principally Heathrow (LHR) and Gatwick (LGW) which are 1 hour from the capital. Also regional airports.

INTERNAL TRAVEL Good road and rail network. Flights limited but efficient. All cities have bus services, some have underground railways.

RED TAPE

VISAS REQUIRED (UK/US) Not required.

VACCINATIONS REQUIRED: See 'Vaccinations required around the world' on page 653.

DRIVING REQUIREMENTS National driving licence, Third Party insurance and vehicle registration documents.

COUNTRY REPS IN US USA: 3100 Massachusetts Avenue, NW, Washington, DC 20008, tel (202) 588 7800, fax (202) 588 7870.

US REPS IN COUNTRY USA: 24 Grosvenor Square, London W1A 1AE, tel (020) 7499 9000, fax (020) 7495 5012.

PEOPLE AND PLACE

CAPITAL London

LANGUAGE English.

PEOPLES European descent (96%), non-European descent (4%).

RELIGION Protestant and other Christian denominations. Jewish, Hindu and Muslim minorities.

SIZE (SQ KM) 242,514.

POPULATION 59,231,900.

POP DENSITY/KM 244.2.

STATE OF THE NATION

SAFETY Safe. Northern Ireland recently peaceful, with intermittent unrest.

LIFE EXPECTANCY M 75.94, F 80.96.

BEING THERE

ETIQUETTE Handshaking is a customary greeting. Normal courtesies apply when visiting someone's home and it is polite to wait until everyone has been served before eating. Smoking or non-smoking areas will normally be clearly marked. Be prepared to queue and remember to maintain that famous stiff upper lip. Jolly good!

CURRENCY Pounds sterling (£) = 100 pence.

FINANCE Credit cards widely accepted.

BUSINESS HOURS 0930-1730 Mon-Friday

GMT Precisely.

VOLTAGE GUIDE 240 AC, 50 Hz.

COUNTRY DIALLING CODE 44.

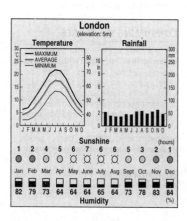

London (elevation: 5m)

HIGHLIGHTS

LONDON The capital and most cosmopolitan of the UK's cities, with a host of iconic landmarks - from Buckingham Palace to Carnaby Street and Westminster Abbey. London is blessed with a multitude of fine galleries, museums, theatres and concert venues. There are also some interesting historic tours. London has a vibrant nightlife, not to mention atmospheric pubs on every corner.

SCOTLAND Renowned for its picturesque scenery of mountains and lochs, this is excellent walking country. Scotland is also home to some beautiful beaches, cities and towns. Edinburgh is divided between the new and old town. Walk along the Royal Mile up to Edinburgh Castle for superb city views.

THE LAKE DISTRICT Located in the northeast of England, this is the largest English National Park. Stay in warm log cabins and enjoy the stunning scenery of villages, lakes, dales and fells. Take long walks and longer lunches in quaint local pubs.

STONEHENGE An emblem of ancient Britain, constructed approximately 5,000 years ago. The mysterious Wiltshire stone circle is a symbol of endurance and power. The origins of this monument remain unknown; it has been called a temple of worship, an astronomical observatory and a sacred burial site for chiefs.

FISH & CHIPS A trip to Britain wouldn't be complete without a visit to a 'chippy'. Though these days British restaurants have undergone a long overdue revolution.

CONSUMING PLEASURES

FOOD & DRINK A range of international cuisines can be found all over the country. There are regional specialities, based on local produce, such as black puddings in Lancashire and Yorkshire, sausages in Lincolnshire. English cheese enjoys a growing reputation. Excellent meat, fish, game and the famous haggis (a sheep's stomach stuffed with oatmeal, spiced liver , onions and offal) can be found in Scotland. Welsh specialities include laver bread, a seaweed and oatmeal cake, and dishes based on local lamb and the national vegetable, leeks. Scotch whisky is in a class of its own.

SHOPPING & SOUVENIRS Tweeds, china and porcelain, antiques, foodstuffs, clothes.

FIND OUT MORE

WEBSITES www.visitscotland.com, www.visitwales.com, www.discovernorthernireland.com, www.gotobelfast.com, www.ukvisas.gov.uk, www.britainusa.com, www.britannia.com, www.visitbritain.com, www.bbc.co.uk, www.nationaltrust.org.uk, www.24hourmuseum.org.uk, www.thisislondon.co.uk.

LOCAL MEDIA Ten major papers, including *The Daily Telegraph, The Financial Times, The Guardian, The Daily Mail* and *The Sun.* There are also daily regionals. International press widely available.

TOURIST BOARDS IN UK/US UK: 1 Regent Street, London SW1Y 4XT, tel (020) 7808 3807, email blvcinfo@visitbritain.org. US: 551 Fifth Avenue, Suite 701, New York, NY 10176, tel (800) 462 2748, fax (212) 986 1188, email travelinfo@visitbritain.org. Or, 625 North Michigan Avenue, Suite 1001, Chicago, IL 60611, tel (312) 787 0464, fax (312) 787 9641.

"Happy is England!
I could be content
To see no other verdure
than its own."
John Keats, 1817

UNITED STATES OF AMERICA

WHEN TO GO

WEATHER Climate varies hugely, check with individual states.

FESTIVALS The USA hosts thousands of different festivals, each with a different feel. Some of the biggest and best are listed here. The Burning Man Festival, held in Black Rock City, Nevada in early September. It has been described as 'the most artistic, survivalist, and utterly surreal spectacle on earth' where ' all the black sheep of the world graze together'. New York's Manhattan Island comes alive over Halloween when two million people form the largest parade in the country, an over-excited, costumed street party. Like the San Francisco Carnival, it has a large gay following who enjoy hamming up the horror. Key West, the most southern island off Florida's coast, hosts the Fantasy Fest in late October. A time of sexuality, nudity, and drinking, this ten-day fancy dress party attracts 70,000 people.

TRANSPORT

INTERNATIONAL AIRPORTS Numerous. Busiest 10 are: Atlanta (ATL), Chicago (ORD), Los Angeles (LAX), Dallas/Fort Worth(DFW), San Francisco (SFO), Denver (DEN), Miami (MIA), Newark (EWR), Phoenix (PHX), Detroit (DTW).

INTERNAL TRAVEL Excellent air, rail and road networks. Buses, taxis, and different types of car-hire available.

RED TAPE

VISAS REQUIRED (UK/US) Not required up to 90 days.

VACCINATIONS REQUIRED: See 'Vaccinations required around the world' on page 653.

DRIVING REQUIREMENTS National driving licence accepted for a year. International Driving Permit recommended, not required.

COUNTRY REPS IN UK USA: 24 Grosvenor Square, London W1A 1AE, tel (020) 7499 9000, fax (020) 7495 5012.

UK REPS IN COUNTRY UK: 3100 Massachusetts Avenue, NW, Washington, DC 20008, tel (202) 588 6500, fax (202) 588 7866, email washi@fco.gov.uk.

PEOPLE AND PLACE

CAPITAL Washington.

LANGUAGE English.

PEOPLES European descent including Hispanic (84%), African descent (12%), Native American (1%), Chinese.

RELIGION Protestant (61%), Roman Catholic (25%), Jewish and other faiths.

SIZE (SQ KM) 9,809,155.

POPULATION 294,800,000.

POP DENSITY/KM 30.5.

STATE OF THE NATION

SAFETY Safe, despite high levels of violent crime and murder.

LIFE EXPECTANCY M 74.89, F 80.67.

BEING THERE

ETIQUETTE Open friendly people of different cultures and origins. Normal courtesies apply. Smoking increasingly unpopular, ask permission first. Dress generally casual.

CURRENCY Dollar ($) = 100 cents.

FINANCE Credit cards widely accepted, cheques less so.

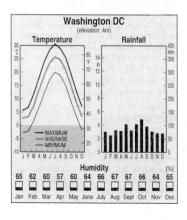

Washington DC (elevation: 4m)

Temperature / Rainfall

Humidity (%)

Jan	Feb	Mar	Apr	May	June	July	Aug	Sept	Oct	Nov	Dec
65	62	60	57	60	64	66	67	67	66	64	65

HIGHLIGHTS

NEW YORK The Big Apple, with that instantly recognisable skyline, and street names from the movies, is a must for trips to America. Visit Staten Island for the best views of Manhatten Island, rollerskate in Central Park, and be sure to have a big, New York breakfast.

GRAND CANYON Visit the South Rim at dawn for a sense of the enormity of nature. Spend a day trekking in the canyon, or get a permit and camp on the canyon floor. Or, for the less energetic, take to the air in a helicopter and watch the ground drop away.

DENALI NATIONAL PARK, ALASKA Admire the tundra and glaciers in Alaska's finest park, home to bears and wolves, with views of North America's highest peak, Mount McKinley.

CALIFORNIA Home to two major but very different US cities, Los Angeles and San Francisco. The former is all gas-guzzling cars stuck in a concrete and glass jungle, home to the rich and vain, with holiday resorts for the many. The latter is eco-friendly, gay-friendly, boho chic, home to great food, an eclectic nightlife and a weird white fog disguising one of America's best views, the Golden Gate Bridge.

NATIONAL PARKS Aside from the Grand Canyon, America has a great geological diversity. Visit the lush parks of Yosemite and Zion for excellent hiking in clean, crisp air. Or enter Badlands, Bryce, or Monument Valley, a world away - dusty, arid and truly spectacular. Or Redwoods, with ancient trees you can drive through, some over 100 metres high.

BUSINESS HOURS 0900-1730 Mon-Friday.
GMT Spans six time zones, from -5 (east coast) to -10 (Hawaii).
VOLTAGE GUIDE 110/120 AC, 60 Hz.
COUNTRY DIALLING CODE 1.

CONSUMING PLEASURES

FOOD & DRINK American breakfasts are legendary. Fast food, from hamburgers to hotdogs, is available everywhere, and international cuisine is available in every city. There are numerous regional specialities, from Spanish flavours in the south-west to Creole or French in the deep south. Many different kinds of bar, with varying 'happy hours'. Californian wines are good.

SHOPPING & SOUVENIRS Clothes, electrical items, traditional artefacts from the different peoples and regions, sports goods.

FIND OUT MORE

WEBSITES www.usembassy.org.uk, www.britainusa.com, www.tia.org, www.usatourism.com, www.areaguides.net, www.us-national-parks.net, www.ski-guide.com.

LOCAL MEDIA Many, including, Los Angeles Times, The New York Times, Wall Street Journal and the Washingon Post. Bulky Sunday papers, especially in The NewYork Times. Many state/regional papers.

TOURIST BOARDS IN UK/US n/a.

> "The United States is a country unique in the world because it was populated not merely by people who live in it by the accident of birth, but by those who willed to come here."
> *John Gunther, 1947*

URUGUAY

WHEN TO GO

WEATHER Mild all year. Best in summer (December-March).

FESTIVALS The big festival for Uruguay is Carnival Week in February. It is only meant to last for the two days leading up to Ash Wednesday, but invariably lasts the week. On 19 April is the Desembarco de los Trienta y Tres (Landing of the 33), celebrating the successful fight for independence by 33 Uruguayans against the Portuguese-Brazilian occupants. Other festivals include La Semana Criolla (Holy Week) in March and All Souls Day on 2 November.

TRANSPORT

INTERNATIONAL AIRPORTS Montevideo (MVD) is 19 km from city.

INTERNAL TRAVEL Internal flights are expensive. Road network is good. Good bus service, car hire from Montevideo.

RED TAPE

VISAS REQUIRED (UK/US) Required for Australia and Canada. Not required for UK and USA up to 3 months.

VACCINATIONS REQUIRED: See 'Vaccinations required around the world' on page 653.

DRIVING REQUIREMENTS Temporary local licence must be obtained from a town hall; valid 90 days. National driving licence may prove useful.

COUNTRY REPS IN UK/US UK: 140 Brompton Road, London SW3 1HY, tel (020) 7589 8835, fax (020) 7581 9585, email emburuguay@emburuguay.org.uk. USA: 1913 I Street, NW, Washington, DC 20006, tel (202) 331 4219, fax (202) 331 8142, email uruwashi@uruwashi.org.

UK/US REPS IN COUNTRY UK: PO Box 16024, Calle Marco bruto 1073, 11300 Montevideo, tel (2) 622 3630, fax (2) 622 7815, email bemonte@internet.com.uy. USA: Lauro Muller 1776, 11200 Montevideo, tel (2) 418 7777, fax (2) 418 8611, email webmastermvd@state.gov.

PEOPLE AND PLACE

CAPITAL Montevideo.

LANGUAGE Spanish.

PEOPLES European descent (90%), mestizo, African descent.

RELIGION Roman Catholic (66%), non-religious (30%), Jewish, Protestant.

SIZE (SQ KM) 176,215.

POPULATION 3,385,000.

POP DENSITY/KM 19.2.

STATE OF THE NATION

SAFETY Generally safe, but seek local information.

LIFE EXPECTANCY M 72.92, F 79.45.

BEING THERE

ETIQUETTE A handshake will suffice for general greetings. Normal courtesies should be observed. Uruguayans are very hospitable and love to entertain.

CURRENCY *Peso Uruguayo* (urug$) = 100 *centécimos*.

FINANCE Credit cards widely used. Traveller's cheques difficult to change unless in US dollars.

BUSINESS HOURS 0830-1200 and 1430-1830 Monday-Friday.

GMT -3.

VOLTAGE GUIDE 220 AC, 50 Hz.

COUNTRY DIALLING CODE 598.

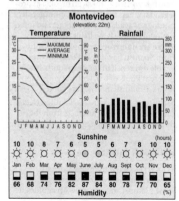

HIGHLIGHTS

MONTEVIDEO The capital city is home to nearly 50 per cent of Uruguay's population. The city is divided between a soaring, buzzing metropolis and the Ciudad Vieja (Old Town), which dates back to colonial times. Here you can stroll through and marvel at eighteenth-century Spanish, Italian and art deco architecture. If you want a more relaxing time, you can laze on the uninterrupted, sandy beach that encases the city.

TACUAREMBO A relaxing, agreeable town situated in the north of Uruguay. Tacuarembo was founded in 1832 and is filled with monuments and busts that commemorate military or literary figures as well as educators and clergy members. For three days in March the town holds the *gaucho* (cowboy) festival, featuring exhibitions, music and riding skills.

THE BEACHES Uruguay is considered a very easy going country and the beautiful beaches here only add to this image as people flock to them in hordes throughout December and January. The two main stretches are The Costa de Oro in the south and Costa del Sol in the east.

TERMAS DEL GUAVIYU An oasis in the middle of the countryside. The hot springs are unspoiled and can be enjoyed under the moonlight. The slowly-running Guaviyu stream is a must for fishing and sailing. Built around the springs are some comfortable hotels and campsites.

CONSUMING PLEASURES

FOOD & DRINK Most restaurants are *parrilladas* (grillrooms) serving the most famous traditional dish, the *asado* (barbecued beef). Other specialities include grilled chicken in wine, *morcilla salada* (salty sausage), *morcilla dulce* (sweet black sausage made from blood, orange peel and walnuts) and *puchero* (beef with vegetables, bacon, beans and sausages). Locally produced wines are good quality, beers very good. Local spirits include *grappa*.

SHOPPING & SOUVENIRS Suede jackets, amethyst jewellery, paintings.

The Uruguayans are meat crazy. This small nation sandwiched between Brazil and Argentina consumes more beef *per capita* than almost any other country

FIND OUT MORE

WEBSITES www.britishembassy.org.uy, www.uruwashi.org, www.lonelyplanet.com/destinations/ south_america/uruguay.

LOCAL MEDIA No English newspapers, all in Spanish.

TOURIST BOARDS IN UK/US n/a.

UZBEKISTAN

WHEN TO GO

WEATHER Extreme continental climate: but generally warmer in south, colder in north. Very cold winters (November-March), hot summers (May-September).

FESTIVALS Uzbekistan holds many festivals and religious holidays throughout the year. The biggest festival is the Navrus (New Days) Festival on 21 March. It consists of renewal celebrations involving tradition-al games, drama, street festivals and fairs. Other festivities include Toi, Uzbek family parties where foreigners are welcome to enjoy the fun. The Uzbeks celebrate their Independence Day on September, by crowding into ex-Lenin Square which becomes a carnival of celebration.

TRANSPORT

INTERNATIONAL AIRPORTS Tashkent (TAS) is 6 km from the city.

INTERNAL TRAVEL Quite good air, road and rail networks, though possessions on trains can be vulnerable to theft. Bus ser-vices connect towns, where taxis are found.

RED TAPE

VISAS REQUIRED (UK/US) Required.

VACCINATIONS REQUIRED: See 'Vaccinations required around the world' on page 653.

DRIVING REQUIREMENTS International Driving Permit.

COUNTRY REPS IN UK/US UK: 41 Holland Park, London W11 2RP, tel (020) 7229 7679, fax (020) 7229 7029, email info@uzbekembassy.org. USA: 1746 Massa-chusetts Avenue, NW, Washington, DC 20036, tel (202) 887 5300, fax (202) 293 6804.

UK/US REPS IN COUNTRY UK: 67 Gulymov Street, Tashkent 700000, tel (71) 120 6288, fax (71) 120 6549, email brit@emb.uz. USA: 82 Chilanzarskaya Street, Tashkent 700115, tel (71) 120 5450, fax (71) 120 5448, email personnel@ usembassy.uz.

PEOPLE AND PLACE

CAPITAL Tashkent.

LANGUAGE Uzbek.

PEOPLES Uzbek (71%), Russian, Tajik, Kazakh.

RELIGION Sunni Muslim (88%), Eastern Orthodox Christian.

SIZE (SQ KM) 447,400.

POPULATION 26,093,000.

POP DENSITY/KM 58.3.

STATE OF THE NATION

SAFETY Avoid travelling at night.

LIFE EXPECTANCY M 60.82, F 67.73.

BEING THERE

ETIQUETTE A heartfelt handshake is a customary greeting. Dress conservatively and abide by local codes. Always remove shoes before entering a house, mosque or sitting on a *chaikhana* bed. A gift from abroad, such as postcards, coins, or a photo from home, will be greatly appreciated as a sign of friendship. Bread is sacred and should be broken up and passed around, and never placed face down (keep the seed-ed side uppermost) or thrown away. Tea is poured three times into *piala* cups and back to the pot before being served.

CURRENCY Uzbek *sum* = 100 *tiyn*.

FINANCE All bills normally settled in cash (US dollars best). Credit cards and

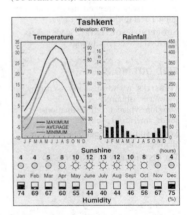

Tashkent (elevation: 479m)

HIGHLIGHTS

TASHKENT Densely populated city which has been rebuilt in large parts due to an earthquake in 1966. Little now remains of the country's 2,000-year history. Wander through the old town and its mud-brick maze, which contrast with imposing squares and tower blocks. Stroll over to the Chorus Bazaar, a huge open market and take in the sights, sounds and aromas, or visit one of the city's many museums. In years gone by, Tashkent saw much of the Silk Road traffic between Central Asia and China.

BUKHARA Believed to be one of the holiest cities in Central Asia. Bukhara has seen many battles, most notoriously being attacked by the Mongols in 1220, by Alexander the Great in 329 BC and most recently coming under the control of Russia. Admire the beautiful architecture, bazaars, old town and mosques and visit the Poi Kalan minaret built in 1127. It stands 47 metres above ground.

CAMEL TREKKING Camel farms are located to the north of Nurata and will supply you with a camel if you want to experience desert life in original Silk Road fashion.

THE FERGHANA VALLEY View its many blossoming parks and gardens. Immerse yourself in its culture and see why it has been called 'The Cradle of Civilisation'.

SAMARKAND A city steeped in history, culture and amazing beauty, Samarkand has been called the 'Centre of the Universe' and is evocative of its position on the ancient Silk Road.

traveller's cheques not widely accepted.
BUSINESS HOURS 0900-1800 Mon-Friday.
GMT +5.
VOLTAGE GUIDE 220 AC, 50 Hz.
COUNTRY DIALLING CODE 998.

LOCAL MEDIA No newspapers in English.
TOURIST BOARDS IN UK/US n/a.

CONSUMING PLEASURES

FOOD & DRINK Central Asian dishes such as *plov* (mutton, yellow turnip and rice) and *shashlyk* (charcoal grilled mutton kebabs) served with raw onions and flat bread are commonly eaten. *Samosas* are sold on street stalls, and a number of restaurants serve European and Korean food. Tea is the staple drink, alcohol widely available.

SHOPPING & SOUVENIRS Carpets, decorated Uzbek knives, silk, wall hangings, embroidered hats.

FIND OUT MORE

WEBSITES www.uzbekembassy.org, www.britain.uz, www.uzbekistan.org, www.lonelyplanet.com/destinations/central_asia/uzbekistan.

"Sweet to ride forth at evening from the wells
When shadows pass gigantic on the sand,
And softly through the silence beat the bells
Along the Golden Road to Samarkand."

James Elroy Flecker, 1913

VANUATU

WHEN TO GO

WEATHER Warm and wet November - April, windy May-October. Cyclones possible December and April.

FESTIVALS Vanuatu's most important annual event is the Independence Day festivities, which take place all around the 83 islands on 30 July. Port Vila hosts activities including sporting events, music, a military parade at Independence Park, canoe races and *kastom* dancing by groups from various islands. There are other festivals throughout the year, such as The Toka in the southern island of Tanna, where clans unite in dance for three days. Aspects of peoples lives are roundly celebrated by extended family, so festivities may seem to ŏccur on a very regular basis.

TRANSPORT

INTERNATIONAL AIRPORTS Port Vila (VLI) is 5 km from town.

INTERNAL TRAVEL Good flight and ferry network between islands. Dirt tracks and compacted coral roads. Buses, mini-buses, taxis, and car-hire all operate on the islands.

RED TAPE

VISAS REQUIRED (UK/US) Not required.

VACCINATIONS REQUIRED: See 'Vaccinations required around the world' on page 653.

DRIVING REQUIREMENTS National driving licence.

COUNTRY REPS IN UK/US UK: n/a. USA: Permanent Mission to UN, 42 Broadway, 12th Floor, Suite 1200-18, New York, NY 10004, tel (212) 425 9600, fax (212) 422 3427, email vanunmis@aol.com.

UK/US REPS IN COUNTRY UK: PO Box 567, La Casa d'Andrea e Luciano, Rue Pierre Lamy, Port Vila, tel 23100, fax 23651, email bhcvila@vanuatu.com.vu.
USA: The embassy in Moresby (see Papua New Guinea) handles enquiries relating to Vanuatu.

PEOPLE AND PLACE

CAPITAL Port Vila.

LANGUAGE Bislama (pidgin), English, French.

PEOPLES Melanesians (ni-Vanuatu) (94%).

RELIGION Various Christian denominations (92%), some traditional beliefs.

SIZE (SQ KM) 12,190.

POPULATION 202,200.

POP DENSITY/KM 15.8.

STATE OF THE NATION

SAFETY Safe.

LIFE EXPECTANCY M 61, F 64.05.

BEING THERE

ETIQUETTE The Vanuatu people are peaceful and gentle and enjoy simple pleasures. Informal dress is normally suitable for most occasions unless specified otherwise. Age-old rituals still occur in many areas of the islands. Vanuatu has quite stringent land ownership regulations, so be careful if you are trekking or exploring areas.

CURRENCY *Vatu* (Vt) = 100 *centimes*.

FINANCE Credit cards and traveller's cheques widely accepted.

BUSINESS HOURS 0730-1130 and 1330-1630 Monday-friday.

GMT +11.

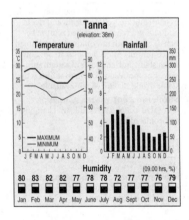

Tanna
(elevation: 38m)

Temperature — Rainfall

	Jan	Feb	Mar	Apr	May	June	July	Aug	Sept	Oct	Nov	Dec
Humidity (09.00 hrs, %)	80	83	82	82	77	78	78	72	77	77	76	79

HIGHLIGHTS

LAND DIVING This quite spectacular event, which occurs on the island of Pentecost throughout April, May and June on Saturdays, is a show of strength and fertility. A tower between 20 and 30 metres high is built among the trees. The men then handpick their very own liana vines as a type of bungee cord, and jump off the top. The goal for each man is for their head or shoulders to touch the ground below, making the earth fertile for the next harvest. This leaves very little room for error. Whilst the men take turns leaping to the floor with their hand-made bungees, villagers dance and stomp on the earth to help bring a bountiful harvest.

NATURE TREKS This may not sound the most appealing activity, but let yourself soak in the beauty of these islands as you traverse volcanoes, walk through coconut plantations and rainforests and meet the locals. You can spend an afternoon wandering, or indulge yourself in a four-day hike.

KAVA This is drunk all over Polynesia and has been cultivated in Vanuatu for 3,000 years, with over 72 varieties. Vanuatu *kava* is considered the strongest around. It's a drink that is narcotic rather than alcoholic, and which looks and tastes like dishwater. Drank from coconut shells, it will leave you relaxed with a clear mind and none of the after-effects that come with alcohol. It's meant to be drank in a big gulp.

SCUBA DIVING There are some beautiful coral reefs and excellent marine life, as well as one of the world's best shipwreck dives, the *SS President Coolidge,* off the island of Santo.

VOLTAGE GUIDE 220/380 AC.
COUNTRY DIALLING CODE 678.

CONSUMING PLEASURES

FOOD & DRINK Seafood features on most menus, and Chinese and French food is widely available. Food is excellent quality and French cheeses, patés, bread, cognac, and wine are available.

SHOPPING & SOUVENIRS Grass skirts, baskets, mats, masks, woodwork, necklaces.

FIND OUT MORE

WEBSITES www.vanuatutourism.com, www.britishhighcommission.gov.uk/vanuatu, www.spto.org.

LOCAL MEDIA *Port Vila Presse, Vanuatu Daily Post,* the *Vanuatu Weekly* and the *Pacific Island Profile* (monthly) all contain English sections.

TOURIST BOARDS IN UK/US n/a.

In Vanuatu, pigs with rounded tusks are a sign of wealth. But riches are measured not by how much you have, but how much you give

VATICAN CITY

WHEN TO GO

WEATHER As for Italy.

FESTIVALS Celebrations of the liturgical year. As the centre of the Roman Catholic Church, the Vatican is an especially spiritual place, in particular at Easter and Christmas when vast crowds gather in St Peter's Square to listen to the Pope. Mass is said daily, and when the Pope is in residence he gives a public audience once a week on Wednesdays, and blesses the crowds from his window every Sunday at noon. He also holds a midnight Mass on Christmas Eve in St Peter's Basilica: the following day at noon he gives his famous Christmas message and blesses the crowd.

TRANSPORT

INTERNATIONAL AIRPORTS Use Rome (FCO) airport.

INTERNAL TRAVEL Walking. There is a mini-railway from Rome into the Vatican City.

RED TAPE

VISAS REQUIRED (UK/US) Not required, but entry is from Italy, so Italian requirements would apply beforehand.

VACCINATIONS REQUIRED: See 'Vaccinations required around the world' on page 653.

DRIVING REQUIREMENTS n/a.

COUNTRY REPS IN UK/US UK: Apostolic Nunciature, 54 Parkside, London SW19 5NE, tel (020) 8944 7189, fax (020) 8947 2494, email nuntius@globalnet.co.uk. USA: Apostolic Nunciature, 3339 Massachusetts Avenue, NW, Washington, DC 20008, tel (202) 333 7121, fax (202) 337 4036.

UK/US REPS IN COUNTRY UK: Via dei Condotti 91, 00187 Rome, tel (06) 6992 3561, fax (06) 6994 0684. USA: Via delle Terme Deciane 26, 00153 Rome, tel (06) 4674 3428, fax (06) 575 8346.

PEOPLE AND PLACE

CAPITAL Vatican.

LANGUAGE Latin and Italian.

PEOPLES n/a.

RELIGION Roman Catholic.

SIZE (SQ KM) 0.44.

POPULATION 900

POP DENSITY/KM 2,045.5

STATE OF THE NATION

SAFETY Safe.

LIFE EXPECTANCY n/a (possibly immortal).

BEING THERE

ETIQUETTE Visitors should be respectful of the Roman Catholic faith. When entering the Sistine Chapel, visitors will be expected to dress modestly - no shorts.

CURRENCY Euro valid, but issues its own Vatican *lire*.

FINANCE Use Italian facilities.

BUSINESS HOURS n/a.

GMT +1.

VOLTAGE GUIDE 220 AC, 50 Hz.

COUNTRY DIALLING CODE 3906 (Italy country code + Rome area code. 0 in area code should not be omitted).

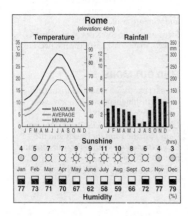

Rome (elevation: 46m)

	Jan	Feb	Mar	Apr	May	June	July	Aug	Sept	Oct	Nov	Dec
Sunshine (hrs)	4	5	7	7	9	9	11	10	8	6	4	3
Humidity (%)	77	73	71	70	67	62	58	59	66	72	77	79

HIGHLIGHTS

ST PETER'S SQUARE
The basilica of St Peter was laid out in 1656-67 by Bernini for Pope Alexander VII and added to by Maderno and Michelangelo in later years. Admire and marvel at its sheer size, ornate decoration and intrinsic mosaics. An Egyptian obelisk stands at the centre, flanked by two fountains and the sculptures of former Popes and Saints in the ellipse. It is all surrounded by a four-pillar-deep colonnade. The centre of the Vatican City, St Peter's is the focal point for many Catholic celebrations.

SISTINE CHAPEL
Located in the Palace of the Vatican, it was built between 1475 - 1483. It houses Michelangelo's famous and exquisite frescoes, painted between 1508-1515, mainly lying on his back. They helped to make the chapel universally famous and can still be seen today. The chapel is rectangular in shape and measures 40.93 metres by 13.41 metres, allegedly the same dimensions as the Temple of Solomon in the Old Testament. The Sistine Chapel held its first Mass in 1483. Inside, you can't help but be astounded by its beauty.

THE VATICAN GARDENS The gardens date back to medieval times and are now divided into two areas by the remains of the medieval walls that used to encircle the Vatican. There are 90 fountains dotted around the garden and Popes have been using the garden as a sanctuary since the ninth century. Enter into the gardens, sit down and savour the moment, enjoy the surroundings and let it soothe your soul.

CONSUMING PLEASURES

FOOD & DRINK   Italian. See Italy.
SHOPPING & SOUVENIRS   Items from the museums' shops.

FIND OUT MORE

WEBSITES   www.vatican.va, http://vatican.usembassy.it
LOCAL MEDIA   As for Italy, plus weekly English edition of *L'Osservatore Romano*.
TOURIST BOARDS IN UK/US   n/a.

Vatican City is the world's smallest independent state and seen by some as the last remnant of the Roman empire

VENEZUELA

WHEN TO GO

WEATHER January-April is best.
Dry season December-April, rainy season
May-December.

FESTIVALS Most celebrations are tied in
with the Church calender. Each town has its
own patron saint and locals will celebrate
their saint's day with feasts. Each region
holds its own festivals throughout the year,
but the biggest festival is Carnaval, which is
celebrated nationwide - but with each
region adding its own touch to their celebrations to reflect part of their heritage.
Festivities can include bull fighting,
parades, dancing and beauty pageants.

TRANSPORT

INTERNATIONAL AIRPORTS Caracas
(CCS) (Simon Bolivar) is 22 km from the
city.

INTERNAL TRAVEL Good air network,
excellent roads, limited railway links. Buses
and taxis operate. Car-hire expensive.

RED TAPE

VISAS REQUIRED (UK/US) Not
required for up to 90 days.

VACCINATIONS REQUIRED: See
'Vaccinations required around the world'
on page 653.

DRIVING REQUIREMENTS National
driving licence or International Driving
Permit.

COUNTRY REPS IN UK/US UK: 56
Grafton Way, London W1T 5DL, tel (020)
7387 6727, fax (020) 7383 3253. USA: 7 East
51st Street, New York, NY 10022, tel (212)
826 1660, fax (212) 644 7471, email
info@consulado-ny-gov.ve.

UK/US REPS IN COUNTRY UK: Torre La
Castellana, Piso 11, Avenida Principal, La
Castellana, Caracas 1060, tel (212) 263 8411,
fax (212) 267 1275, email britishembassy@
internet.ve. USA: Calle F con Calle Suapure,
Urb. Colinas de Valle Arriba, Caracas 1080,
tel (212) 975 6411, fax (212) 975 6710, email
consularcaracas@state.gov.

PEOPLE AND PLACE

CAPITAL Caracas.

LANGUAGE Spanish, Amerindian
languages.

PEOPLES Mestizo (69%), European
or African descent, Amerindian (2%).

RELIGION Roman Catholic (89%),
other Christian or traditional beliefs.

SIZE (SQ KM) 916,445.

POPULATION 25,549,084.

POP DENSITY/KM 27.9.

STATE OF THE NATION

SAFETY Beware violent crime in cities.

LIFE EXPECTANCY M 71.27, F 77.58.

BEING THERE

ETIQUETTE Shake hands while maintaining eye contact and say *Buenos dias* (until
midday) or *Buenos tardes* or *Buenos noches*
(in the afternoon/evening) and wait for a
reply. People on the coast are more relaxed
than in the city. Jackets and ties are generally worn to restaurants and social functions.
A service charge of 10 per cent is included in
the bill at restaurants. If invited for
dinner, send flowers, particularly orchids,
prior to the event. If greeting a group introduce yourself to the eldest person first.

CURRENCY Bolivar (Bs) = 100 céntimos.

FINANCE Credit cards and traveller's
cheques widely accepted.

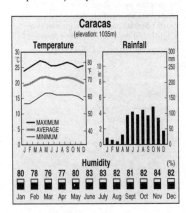

Caracas
(elevation: 1035m)

Temperature | Rainfall

— MAXIMUM
— AVERAGE
— MINIMUM

J F M A M J J A S O N D   J F M A M J J A S O N D

Humidity (%)

Jan	Feb	Mar	Apr	May	June	July	Aug	Sept	Oct	Nov	Dec
80	78	76	77	80	83	83	82	81	82	84	82

HIGHLIGHTS

CARACAS Capital city set 1,000 metres above sea level and nestled in a narrow valley by the emerald slopes of Avila National Park. It's one of the most stunning cities in South America and stretches for 20 kilometres from east to west. Visit the city's historical quarter or, or sit in the charming Plaza Bolivar and soak up the atmosphere while looking at some of the continent's finest architecture.

ANGEL FALLS In the western area of Canaima National Park, it's the world's largest waterfall at 979 metres high. Named after the American aviator, Jimmy Angel, who discovered them in 1935, though local Pemones Indians already called them Churun Meru. There are several ways to view this magnificent *tepuy* (table-top mountain), but the best is from the air, where you can view it from all angles and in all its splendour.

MERIDA The capital of the Merida State, which stands on an alluvial terrace. Merida is surrounded by five of the highest peaks in the Sierra Nevada, known to locals as Las Cinco Aguilas Blancas (The Five White Eagles). There is a very lively, friendly atmosphere as people descend on the town to hike, climb, paraglide and dance. Others come to ride on the world's highest cable car. It is also home to the Universidad de los Andes, helping to add to the town's cultured air.

PARCQUE NACIONAL MOCHIMA Beautiful range of islands and islets surrounded by coral reefs. Offering great scuba diving, snorkelling and swimming off its fine white beaches.

BUSINESS HOURS 0800-1800 Mon-Friday. GMT -4.
VOLTAGE GUIDE 110 AC, 60 Hz.
COUNTRY DIALLING CODE 58.

CONSUMING PLEASURES

FOOD & DRINK Local specialities include *pabellón criollo* (a hash made with shredded meat and served with fried plantains and black beans on rice), *parrilla criolla* (marinated and grilled beef), *hervido* (soup made with beef, chicken or fish and vegetables), *chipi chipi* soup (made from tiny clams) and *empanadas* (meat pastries). Local wine is not good, but foreign wines are bottled locally. Mineral water, beer and gin is good, rum excellent. *Merengada* consists of fruit pulp, ice, milk and sugar, while *batido* has water and no milk: both are recommended.

SHOPPING & SOUVENIRS Gems, jewellery, cacique coins, gold, pearls, pompom slippers, seed necklaces, shoes, handbags, bows and arrows, pipes, baskets, hammocks.

FIND OUT MORE

WEBSITES www.venezlon.co.uk, www.britain.org.ve, www.embavenez-us.org.

LOCAL MEDIA *The Daily Journal* is the English-language newspaper.

TOURIST BOARDS IN UK/US n/a.

Venezuela holds the world record for most Miss World titles, winning the beauty contest five times over. Not content with that, the country has also won the Miss Universe and Miss International pageants four times each

VIETNAM

WHEN TO GO

WEATHER Dry all year, except for the monsoon season (May-October).

FESTIVALS Most regions tend to have their own traditional festivals involving music, dance and opera. Tet Nguyen Dan is the Lunar New Year celebrated nationwide in December with offerings to the ancestors and is a very important calender date welcoming in the new year. The Children's Moon Festival (Tet-Trung-Thu) on the 15th day of the eighth lunar month celebrates and promotes education, culture, music, sports and arts and crafts. Celebrations begin at noon and end at midnight with processions, displays, performances and delicacies on offer.

TRANSPORT

INTERNATIONAL AIRPORTS Noi Bai (HAN) is 45 km from Hanoi. Tan Son Nhat (SGN) is 7 km from Ho Chi Minh City (Saigon).

INTERNAL TRAVEL Good roads and good but limited railway. Buses are overcrowded, tourists can use mini-buses, or hire chauffeur-driven cars.

RED TAPE

VISAS REQUIRED (UK/US) Required.

VACCINATIONS REQUIRED: See 'Vaccinations required around the world' on page 653.

DRIVING REQUIREMENTS International Driving Permit and a test taken in-country.

COUNTRY REPS IN UK/US UK: 12 Victoria Road, London W8 5RD, tel (020) 7937 1912, fax (020) 7937 6108, email consular@vietnamembassy.org.uk. USA: 1233 20th Street, Suite 400, NW, Washington, DC 20036, tel (202) 861 0737, fax (202) 861 0917, email info@vietnamembassy-usa.org.

UK/US REPS IN COUNTRY UK: 4th & 5th Floors, Central Building, 31 Hai Ba Trung Street, Hanoi, tel (4) 936 0500, fax (4) 936 0561, email behanoi@hn.vnn.vn.
USA: 7 Lang Ha Street, Ba Dinh District, Hanoi, tel (4) 772 1500, fax (4) 772 1510.

PEOPLE AND PLACE

CAPITAL Hanoi.

LANGUAGE Vietnamese.

PEOPLES Vietnamese (88%), Chinese, Thai, tribal groups.

RELIGION Buddhist (55%), Christian.

SIZE (SQ KM) 329,247.

POPULATION 78,685,800.

POP DENSITY/KM 239.

STATE OF THE NATION

SAFETY Safe.

LIFE EXPECTANCY M 67.82, F 73.6

BEING THERE

ETIQUETTE A handshake and vocal greeting is normal. Be careful to dress appropriately: only in the larger cities might the dress ethic be relaxed. Avoid shorts if possible, do not wear singlets, short dresses or skirts, or tops with low neck lines, especially if visiting temples or pagodas. Remove your shoes when entering someone's house and always ask permission to take a photograph of someone. Vietnamese people should not be touched on the head.

CURRENCY New *Dong* (D).

FINANCE Traveller's cheques in US dollars widely accepted. Visa and Mastercard becoming accepted.

BUSINESS HOURS 0730-1200 and 1300-1630 Monday-Saturday.

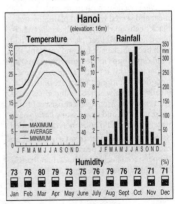

Hanoi
(elevation: 16m)
Temperature | Rainfall

Humidity (%)

Jan	Feb	Mar	Apr	May	June	July	Aug	Sept	Oct	Nov	Dec
73	76	80	79	73	75	76	79	76	72	71	71

HIGHLIGHTS

HANOI Located in the north of Vietnam, the elegant capital city has many highlights including the Temple of Literature and the hectic alleys of the Old Quarter. Another attraction is the Ho Chi Minh Mausoleum, where the former leader's body is displayed in a glass box. Or simply sit at a cafe and soak up the French colonial feel.

HO CHI MINH CITY Known just as well by its former name, Saigon, the old capital of South Vietnam is Vietnam's busiest city. Take a visit to the History Museum to gain a glimpse of the country's 2,000-year history. Or wander down to Cho Lon (Big Market), a vibrant hub selling a vast array of goods where people engage in plenty of friendly bargaining.

THE BEACHES Vietnam is emerging from its old image as a war-torn country and the true beauty of its stunning white beaches - which stretch the entire length of the country - is only just being fully appreciated. Beaches are generally undeveloped, but many offer excellent snorkelling and diving. So take your pick of these beautiful, tranquil spots and enjoy.

THE CU CHI TUNNELS One of the most visited sites in Vietnam, where Viet Cong guerrillas fighting the Americans lived in a series of complex tunnels - originally built during the earlier war with the French - which zigzag from the southern tip of the Ho Chi Minh Trail, near Cambodia, to the Saigon River.

THE MEKONG DELTA Explore the floating markets and gaze at the emerald rice paddies, fruit orchards and coconut palms.

GMT +7.

VOLTAGE GUIDE 220 AC, 50 Hz.

COUNTRY DIALLING CODE 84.

CONSUMING PLEASURES

FOOD & DRINK Based on a mixture of Vietnamese, Chinese and French traditions. Breakfast is generally noodle soup, and noodles or rice provide the basis of most meals. Fish sauce (*nuoc mam*) is an essential accompaniment. Specialities include *nem* (pork mixed with noodles, eggs and mushrooms, wrapped in rice paper and fried) and *banh chung* (glutinous rice, pork and onions). Refreshing green tea is available throughout the country, while coffee is served rich and fresh. Local draught beer, *Bia Hoi,* is additive free, and rice wine is also popular.

SHOPPING & SOUVENIRS Lacquer painting, reed mats, embroidery, mother-of-pearl ornaments, conical hats.

FIND OUT MORE

WEBSITES www.vietnamembassy.org.uk, www.uk-vietnam.org, www.vietnamembassy-usa.org, http://hanoi.usembassy.gov, www.vietnamtourism.com.

LOCAL MEDIA *Saigon Times, Vietnam Economic Times, Vietnam News* and others are published in English.

TOURIST BOARDS IN UK/US n/a.

Nuoc mam is a type of fermented fish sauce – instantly identifiable by its distinctive aroma – without which no Vietnamese meal is complete

YEMEN

WHEN TO GO

WEATHER Generally speaking, April to May and September to October are the best bets wherever you're heading. If you're going to the semi-desert Tihama region, Aden or Hadhramawt, avoid high summer (July). If you're heading for the highlands, winter nights can be very cold. The capital, San'a, has nightly frosts from late November to early January, and in the mountains it's chilly indeed. From October to February most of the country is dry and dusty. In March, April and August the temperature is pleasant but you'll get very wet.

FESTIVALS Festivities are predominantly dictated by the Muslim calendar. Visiting during Ramadan, in particular, can be a trying experience unless you're a frequent traveller in Arab countries.

TRANSPORT

INTERNATIONAL AIRPORTS San'a (SAH) is 13 km from the city. Ta'izz (TAI) is 8 km from the city, Aden (ADE) 11km from the city, Hodeida (HOD) 8 km from the city.

INTERNAL TRAVEL Roads extensive but poor. Flights good. Regular intercity buses, taxis available, and car hire possible in main towns.

RED TAPE

VISAS REQUIRED (UK/US) Required.

VACCINATIONS REQUIRED: See 'Vaccinations required around the world' on page 653.

DRIVING REQUIREMENTS International Driving Permit is required.

COUNTRY REPS IN UK/US UK: 57 Cromwell Road, London SW7 2ED, tel (020) 7584 6607, fax (020) 7589 3350. USA: 2319 Wyoming Avenue, NW, Washington, DC 20008, tel (202) 965 4760, fax (202) 337 2017, email information@ yemenembassy.org.

UK/US REPS IN COUNTRY UK: Abu-al-Hasan-al-Hamadani Street (Hadda Street), Sana'a, tel (1) 264 081, fax (1) 263 059, email visaenquiries.sanaa@fco.gov.uk.

USA: Sa'awan Street, Sheraton Hotel District, Himyar Zone, Sana'a, tel (1) 303 155, fax (1) 303 160.

PEOPLE AND PLACE

CAPITAL San'a.

LANGUAGE Arabic.

PEOPLES Arab (95%).

RELIGION Shi'ite Muslim (55%), Sunni Muslim (42%).

SIZE (SQ KM) 536,869.

POPULATION 19,000,000.

POP DENSITY/KM 36.

STATE OF THE NATION

SAFETY Variable: Westerners have been kidnapped by tribal protesters, with fatal results. Seek latest information at time of visit.

LIFE EXPECTANCY M 59.89, F 63.71.

BEING THERE

ETIQUETTE Yemen is a Muslim country where strong beliefs and customs govern the dress and interaction of members of society and those travelling within it. During Ramadan, the Islamic month of fasting, visitors should refrain from eating, smoking or drinking in public during the daytime.

CURRENCY Yemeny *riyal* (YR) = 100 *fils*.

FINANCE Amex widely accepted, check for other cards or traveller's cheques. Pounds

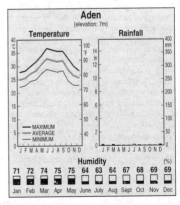

Aden
(elevation: 7m)

Temperature — Rainfall

MAXIMUM / AVERAGE / MINIMUM

J F M A M J J A S O N D

Humidity (%)

Jan	Feb	Mar	Apr	May	June	July	Aug	Sept	Oct	Nov	Dec
71	72	74	75	75	64	63	64	67	68	69	69

HIGHLIGHTS

SAN'A Wander through Yemen's ancient and intoxicating capital, said to have been founded by Noah's son Shem. Long an important citadel on the trade route between Aden and Mecca, the bustling city is centred upon the largest preserved *medina* in the Arab world, where mosque minarets rise above distinct Yemeni tower houses and Ottoman bathhouses.

DAR AL-HAJAR Climb to the top of a large bald rock in the green Wadi Dhar valley, on top of which sits the famous Rock Palace, a former summer residence for kings designed with Yemeni-style *takhrim* windows: this building has become a symbol of the Yemen.

MARIB & BARAQUISH Explore the ancient monuments and ruins of the country's most stunning archaeological sites, which formed the cradle of Yemeni civilisation, in a region now inhabited by Bedouin tribes.

AL-KHAWKHA Watch skilled craftsmen shape wooden boats and rafts using traditional tools in this Red Sea fishing village, the unofficial capital of the wooden boat-building industry. Pelicans and other sea birds can be spotted along the palm-fringed shore.

ADEN Former British colonial town and important sea port. Huge lava mountains by the shore shelter the deep natural port.

SHIHARA Scramble up to one of Yemen's most famous fortified mountain villages, set atop the rocky 2,600-metre Shihara mountain. Its famous stone bridge can be crossed by foot.

---

sterling is most useful currency.

BUSINESS HOURS 0800-1230 and 1600-1900 Mon-Wed, 0800-1100 Thursday.

GMT +3.

VOLTAGE GUIDE 220/230 AC, 50 Hz.

COUNTRY DIALLING CODE 967.

CONSUMING PLEASURES

FOOD & DRINK Indian and Chinese cuisine served in restaurants. Elsewhere the food is typically Arabic. *Haradha* (a mincemeat and pepper dish) is a speciality. Seafood is recommended. Alcohol available in hotels only.

SHOPPING & SOUVENIRS *Foutah* (national costumes), leather goods, jambia (daggers), candlesticks, scarves, amber beads, cushions, ceramics, perfume, incense, sharks' teeth.

FIND OUT MORE

WEBSITES www.yemenembassy.org.uk. www.britishembassy.gov.uk/yemen, www.yemenembassy.org, http://yemen.usembassy.gov, www.al-bab.com/yemen, www.yementimes.com.

LOCAL MEDIA *The Yemen Times* and *Yemen Observer* are published in English.

TOURIST BOARDS IN UK/US n/a.

"You can have no idea of what a sunset is in Aden. The rocks stand up like dolomites, so jagged and old. There is a feeling of gigantic and naked force about it all. One wonders at anything as fragile as man living on these ancient desolations."
Freya Stark, 1953

ZAMBIA

WHEN TO GO

WEATHER Cool and dry May-September, hot and dry October-November, rainy and hot December-April.

FESTIVALS There are many festivals and ceremonies throughout the year. The Kwanga festival in January is a traditional festival full of feasting, dancing and drinking, which lasts for two or three days. Ku-omboka takes place in March, where the Lozi chief and his family are paddled from Leaului to his home during the rainy season. The activities include music, dancing, canoeing and costumes. If you don't fancy any of the festivals on offer, there is the National Fishing Competition held at Lake Tanganyika, or Lusaka's Music Festival, held in October, to keep you entertained.

TRANSPORT

INTERNATIONAL AIRPORTS Lusaka (LUN) is 26 km from the city.

INTERNAL TRAVEL Reasonable road network, though dilapidated in parts. Internal flights quite good. Improved bus service, car hire in main towns.

RED TAPE

VISAS REQUIRED (UK/US) Required for USA. Not required for Australia, Canada. Not required for UK if in an organised tour group for up to 90 days.

VACCINATIONS REQUIRED: See 'Vaccinations required around the world' on page 653.

DRIVING REQUIREMENTS International Driving Permit.

COUNTRY REPS IN UK/US UK: 2 Palace Gate, London W8 5NG, tel (020) 7589 6655, fax (020) 7581 1353, email immzhcl@ btconnect.com. USA: 2419 Massachusetts Avenue, NW, Washington, DC 20008, tel (202) 265 9719, fax (202) 332 0826, email info@zambiainfo.org.

UK/US REPS IN COUNTRY
UK: Independence Avenue 5210, 15101 Ridgeway, Lusaka, tel (1) 251 133, fax (1) 253 798, email BHC-Lusaka@fco.gov.uk.

USA: Corner of Independence and United Nations Avenues, Lusaka, tel (1) 250 955, fax (1) 252 225, email paslib@zamnet.zm.

PEOPLE AND PLACE

CAPITAL Lusaka.

LANGUAGE English.

PEOPLES Bemba, Nyanja, Tonga, Kaonde, Lunda, Luvale, Lozi.

RELIGION Christian (63%), traditional beliefs, some Hindus and Muslims.

SIZE (SQ KM) 752,614.

POPULATION 10,698,000.

POP DENSITY/KM 14.2.

STATE OF THE NATION

SAFETY Relatively safe.

LIFE EXPECTANCY M 39.43, F 39.98.

BEING THERE

ETIQUETTE In the outlying areas travellers should expect to be met with curiosity. Take care to observe local customs and traditions. Shaking hands is the normal mode of greeting, while gifts offered are a sign of honour, friendship or gratitude, and should be accepted with both hands.

CURRENCY *Kwacha* (K) = 100 *ngwee*.

FINANCE Traveller's cheques and Amex are widely accepted, other credit cards less widely.

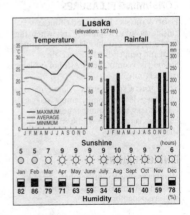

Lusaka (elevation: 1274m)

	Jan	Feb	Mar	Apr	May	June	July	Aug	Sept	Oct	Nov	Dec
Sunshine (hours)	5	5	7	9	9	9	9	10	9	9	7	6
Humidity (%)	82	86	79	71	63	59	34	46	41	40	59	78

HIGHLIGHTS

THE ZAMBEZI RIVER & VICTORIA FALLS

This magnificent river - which also incorporates Zimbabwe and Mozambique on its path - boasts some of the most outstanding terrestrial and riverine wildlife and landscape in Africa. Its many tributaries and wetlands are home to an array of animal and plant species such as buffalo, eland, sable, black rhinoceros, impala and lion, to name a few. There is also the chance for fishing, or whitewater rafting and abseiling for the more adventurous. Victoria Falls, described by the Kololo tribe as 'Mosi-oa-Tunya' - 'the smoke that thunders' - is a sight of phenomenal beauty as up to 546 million cubic metres of water per minute plummet into the gorge below. To fully appreciate the Falls' full magnitude and power, they can be seen from the air by small plane, microlight or helicopter.

KAFUE NATIONAL PARK

Situated in central western Zambia, the park is the size of Wales and is home to more than 400 species of wildlife.

LAKE BANGWEULU

A lake of breathtaking beauty, where the grey-blue waters disappear into the horizon, so that you can't distinguish the sky from the water. Used as a fishing source rather than a tourist trap, it's well worth seeing.

LUSAKA

Capital city with an interesting Cultural Village, pleasant gardens and a zoo.

BUSINESS HOURS 0800-1300 and 1400-1700 Monday-Friday.

GMT +2.

VOLTAGE GUIDE 220/240 AC, 50 Hz.

COUNTRY DIALLING CODE 260.

CONSUMING PLEASURES

FOOD & DRINK Local specialities include bream, Nile perch and other freshwater fish. Imported beers and soft drinks available.

SHOPPING & SOUVENIRS Carvings, pottery, copperware, beadwork, gemstones.

FIND OUT MORE

WEBSITES www.zambiatourism.com, www.britishhighcommission.gov.uk/zambia, www.zambiaembassy.org, http://zambia.usembassy.gov, www.zhcl.org.uk.

LOCAL MEDIA Mostly in English. Main dailies are *Times of Zambia* and *Zambia Daily Mail, The Sportsman,* and *National Mirror.*

TOURIST BOARDS IN UK/US UK: As for Country Reps in UK, email zntb@aol.com. US: n/a.

There are 19 national parks and game reserves in Zambia, taking up nearly 30% of its total land mass

ZIMBABWE

WHEN TO GO

WEATHER Best April-May, August-September. Hot and dry September-October, rainy November-March.

FESTIVALS Independence Day is celebrated on 18 April, while Africa Unity Day takes place in May. The Zimbabwe Agricultural Society Show is hosted in Harare during August, and the capital also hosts the Harare Summer Jazz Festival over August and September.

TRANSPORT

INTERNATIONAL AIRPORTS Harare (HRE) is 12 km from the city. Bulawayo (BUQ) is 24 km from town. Victoria Falls (VFA) is 22 km from town.

INTERNAL TRAVEL Excellent network of roads and flights. Some rail lines, particularly to South Africa. Fuel shortages occur often, so keep a full tank.

RED TAPE

VISAS REQUIRED (UK/US) Not required, though proof of onward travel may be required.

VACCINATIONS REQUIRED: See 'Vaccinations required around the world' on page 653.

DRIVING REQUIREMENTS National driving licence or International Driving Permit.

COUNTRY REPS IN UK/US UK: Zimbabwe House, 429 Strand, London WC2R 0JR, tel (020) 7836 7755, fax (020) 7379 1167, email zimlondon@yahoo.com. USA: 1608 New Hampshire Avenue, NW, Washington, DC 20009, tel (202) 332 7100, fax (202) 483 9326, email zimemb@erols.com.

UK/US REPS IN COUNTRY UK: Corner House, 7th Floor, Samora Machel Avenue/Leopold Takawira Street, Harare, tel (4) 772 990, fax (4) 774 605, email bhcinfo@zol.co.zw. USA: 172 Herbert Chitepo Avenue, Harare, tel (4) 250 593, fax (4) 796 488, email consularharare@state.gov.

PEOPLE AND PLACE

CAPITAL Harare.

LANGUAGE English.

PEOPLES Shona (71%), Ndebele, other tribes and some whites.

RELIGION Christian (75%), traditional beliefs.

SIZE (SQ KM) 390,757.

POPULATION 12,835,000.

POP DENSITY/KM 32.8.

STATE OF THE NATION

SAFETY Usually safe, but in recent years subject to political violence as the political situation has deteriorated and supplies of food and petrol have run short. Possible hostility to white people. Seek latest information at time of visit.

LIFE EXPECTANCY M 37.21, F 36.11.

BEING THERE

ETIQUETTE Urban culture is influenced by Western culture, while in rural areas the traditional customs and values thrive. Casual wear is acceptable in the daytime. Smoking is prohibited on public transport and in some public buildings.

CURRENCY Zimbabwe dollar (Z$) = 100 cents

FINANCE Credit cards and traveller's cheques widely accepted.

BUSINESS HOURS 0800-1630 Mon-Friday.

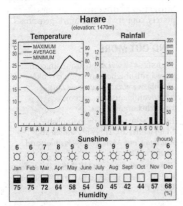

Harare (elevation: 1470m)

HIGHLIGHTS

VICTORIA FALLS & THE ZAMBEZI RIVER

Not the tallest, but certainly the largest waterfall in the world. Visitors are soaked when viewing them by the spray, visible 30 kilometres away. To get a true understanding of the vastness of one of the world's great spectacles, take a light aircraft flight over them, or better still a highly manoeuverable microlight. The falls are a feature of the thundering Zambezi River. The river itself should be thoroughly explored.

Genteel visitors can take a cruise, the more adventurous can raft it. The truly crazy bodysurf the rapids on boogie boards, wake up the next day and bungee jump from the bridge linking Zimbabwe to Zambia.

BULAWAYO

The second largest city after Harare is situated within easy reach of Rhodes Matopos National Park, home to the highest concentration of rhino anywhere, intriguing *kopjes* (strangely shaped boulders), and rock paintings. A number of museums are located here, including the National Museum. The overnight train journey to Victoria Falls conjures up great feelings for a golden age of train travel.

CHIMANIMANI

Striking scenery greets the intrepid traveller who journeys up to this spectacular mountain range, enjoyed by Zimbabweans as a holiday destination as much as foreigners. Totally unspoilt, with peculiar moonscape rock formations, and crystal clear waterfalls and pools.

GMT +2.

VOLTAGE GUIDE 220/240 AC, 50 Hz.

COUNTRY DIALLING CODE 263.

CONSUMING PLEASURES

FOOD & DRINK International cuisine served in restaurants. A staple local dish is *sadza*, stiff maize meal, eaten with meat and/or gravy. Alcohol easily available, including *whawha*, a maize beer.

SHOPPING & SOUVENIRS Copper, wooden and soapstone carvings, leather products, pottery, basketwork, masks, batiks.

FIND OUT MORE

WEBSITES http://harare.state.gov, http://zimbabwe.embassyhomepage.com, www.zimbabwe-embassy.us, www.britishembassy.gov.uk/zimbabwe, www.zimbabwetourism.co.zw.

LOCAL MEDIA Mostly in English. *The Herald*, *The Chronicle* and *The Financial Gazette* are the main dailies.

TOURIST BOARDS IN UK/US UK: As for Country Reps in UK, tel (020) 7240 6169, fax (020) 7240 5465, email zta.london@ btclick.com. US: 128 East 56th Street, New York, NY 10022, tel (212) 486 3444, fax (212) 486 3888.

"We proceeded next morning to see the Victoria Falls. Mosi-oa-tunya is the Makololo name, and means smoke-sounding; Seongo, or Chongwe, meaning the Rainbow or the place of the Rainbow, was the more ancient term they bore."

David Livingstone, 1865

Dependent territories of interest to travellers

American Samoa (USA)

OVERVIEW A group of seven tropical islands in the South Pacific offering some spectacular views and beaches. Highlights: The harbour of Pago Pago formed from the crater of an extinct volcano. Forbidden Bay, one of the most beautiful in the South Pacific.

CAPITAL Pago Pago.

LANGUAGE Samoan and English.

SIZE (SQ KM) 201.

POPULATION 57,291.

WHEN TO GO May-September is best. Heavy rains December-April.

GETTING THERE Airport or harbour at Pago Pago. Airlines: Samoa Aviation, Hawaiian Airlines, Polynesian Airlines.

VISAS Not required for tourist stays up to 30 days.

FIND OUT MORE www.amsamoa.com.

Anguilla (UK)

OVERVIEW Group of Caribbean islands largely dependent on tourism and offshore banking. Coral beaches and secluded hotels. Highlights: Prickly Pear dive site, a beautiful canyon of ledges and caverns. Hidden coves on Anguilla's stretched-out beaches.

CAPITAL The Valley.

LANGUAGE English.

SIZE (SQ KM) 91.

POPULATION 11,430.

WHEN TO GO Hot all year round. July-October is hurricane season.

GETTING THERE Wallblake Airport in The Valley is serviced by many airlines (BA, Delta, KLM, American Airlines, United Airlines, Air Canada etc). Also by sea.

VISAS Not required for America, Australia, Canada, Commonwealth (most but not all), EU, and some others.

FIND OUT MORE www.anguilla-vacation.com.

Aruba (Netherlands)

OVERVIEW Tiny Caribbean island whose beaches vary from white sand to rugged rocks. Mostly US tourists. US government involved in campaigns against drug trafficking and money laundering in late 1990s. Highlights: The Dutch heritage seen in pastel-coloured gabled buildings and a windmill brought piecemeal from Holland.

CAPITAL Oranjestad.

LANGUAGE Officially Dutch, also English and Spanish. Local pidgin is Papiamento.

SIZE (SQ KM) 193.

POPULATION 101,000.

WHEN TO GO Sunny all year round.

GETTING THERE Flights from KLM, Continental, American Airlines. Also by sea.

VISAS Not required by tourists up to 14 days. Not required for up to 3 months for America, Australia, Canada, EU, Japan.

FIND OUT MORE www.aruba.com.

Bermuda (UK)

OVERVIEW Tourist and tax haven in the Caribbean, with one of the world's highest concentrations of golf courses. Actually a chain of 150 islands, it has one of the largest flag-of-convenience shipping fleets. Highlights: The town of St George, Bermuda's old capital, founded in 1612 and today restored so that the narrow winding lanes and historic landmarks are as they were three centuries ago.

CAPITAL Hamilton.

LANGUAGE English.

SIZE (SQ KM) 53.

POPULATION 61,688.

WHEN TO GO May-November is best. Night-time showers occur during November-December and March-April.

GETTING THERE Regular flights from BA, American Airlines, Delta, Air Canada and Continental. Also by sea.

VISAS Not required for up to 6 months for America, Australia, Canada, EU.

FIND OUT MORE www.bermudatourism.co.uk, www.bermudatourism.com.

British Virgin Islands (UK)

OVERVIEW Caribbean archipelago of 40 islands, many uninhabited. Excellent diving and sailing. Thriving offshore finance sector. Highlights: The scenic variation from jagged mountain peaks covered with frangipani to banana and mango groves and palm trees.

CAPITAL Road Town

LANGUAGE English.

SIZE (SQ KM) 153.

POPULATION 21,000.

WHEN TO GO Sub-tropical climate with cooling winds all year round.

GETTING THERE International flights via neighbouring islands (Antigua, Puerto Rico, St Maaretn) and Miami. Airlines: BA, BWIA, Virgin, American Airlines, local airlines. Also by cruise ship or private yacht.

VISAS Not required for up to 30 days for America, Australia, Canada, EU, Japan.

FIND OUT MORE
www.bvitouristboard.com.

Cayman Islands (UK)

OVERVIEW One of the world's largest off-shore finance centres. Big game fishing and diving very popular in its Caribbean waters. Highlights: Hell, a peculiar rock formation evolved from petrified skeletons of shells, some 20 million years old. The Jack Nicklaus-designed 9/18 hole golf course.

CAPITAL George Town.

LANGUAGE English, also Spanish.

SIZE (SQ KM) 262.

POPULATION 40,900.

WHEN TO GO Hot tropical climate all year round. Short rains May-October.

GETTING THERE Regular flights with main British and US airlines, plus Cubana or Cayman Airways. Popular cruise stop.

VISAS Not required for up to 30 days for America, Australia, Canada, Commonwealth (most), EU, Japan.

FIND OUT MORE
www.caymanislands.co.uk.

Channel Islands (UK)

OVERVIEW Small group of autonomous islands close to France. Haven for sailing and offshore finance. Highlights: The cliff tops on Jersey's northwest headlands, offering fine sea views. Guernsey, a quieter charm.

CAPITAL St Helier (Jersey).

LANGUAGE English.

SIZE (SQ KM) 189.2.

POPULATION 149,837.

WHEN TO GO As for UK but milder.

GETTING THERE Well served by ferries and airlines from UK and France.

VISAS As for UK.

FIND OUT MORE www.jersey.com, www.visitguernsey.com.

Cook Islands (New Zealand)

OVERVIEW Twenty-four coral atolls and volcanic islands in the middle of the Pacific, 3,000 kilometres from New Zealand. Economy centred on tourism and banking and trade on giant clams and pearls. Highlights: Whale watching, walking the lagoon's coral fringe, pony treks to Wigmores Waterfall.

CAPITAL Avarua.

LANGUAGE English and Cook Islands Maori.

SIZE (SQ KM) 237.

POPULATION 18,400.

WHEN TO GO Coolest June to August, November to March hottest and wettest.

GETTING THERE Flights from Australia, Europe, North America and elsewhere.

VISAS Not required for stays up to 30 days.

FIND OUT MORE www.cook-islands.com.

Faroe Islands (Denmark)

OVERVIEW These temperate islands lie midway between Scotland and Iceland. Fishing, sheep-farming, and eider-duck and puffin feather export are the main industries. Highlights: Sailing trips around the islands and into the fjords in tall ships, angling, birdwatching.

CAPITAL Tórshavn.

LANGUAGE Faroese, Danish.

SIZE (SQ KM) 1,399.

POPULATION 46,962.

WHEN TO GO Mild winters, cool summers.

GETTING THERE Flights from Denmark, Iceland, Britain and Norway.

VISAS As for Denmark.

FIND OUT MORE www.faroeislands.com.

Falkland Islands (UK)

OVERVIEW Five hundred and sixty miles off the east coast of South America, two main islands are surrounded by hundreds of small outlying islands. Economy driven by fishing licences and sheep-farming, oil being looked for. Highlights: Elephant seals, sea lions, King penguins, and killer whales living in the waters of Sea Lion Island - home to a population of two humans.

CAPITAL Stanley.

LANGUAGE English.

SIZE (SQ KM) 12,173.

POPULATION 2,913.

WHEN TO GO Temperate climate, cooled by the Antarctic Current.

GETTING THERE Fly from RAF Brize Norton, Oxfordshire, or British Airways to Santiago and connect with a LanChile flight.

VISAS Not required for up to 30 days for America, Australia, Canada, Commonwealth (most), EU, Japan.

FIND OUT MORE
www.falklandislands.com,
www.tourism.org.fk.

French Guiana (France)

OVERVIEW The last colony in South America, once home to the infamous Devil's Island penal colony. Luxuriant rainforest has yet to be exploited for eco-tourism. Highlights: Over 400,000 species of bird in the rainforest, more than the whole of Europe. Watching Ariane rockets of the European Space Agency launch from Kourou.

CAPITAL Cayenne.

LANGUAGE French and Creole.

SIZE (SQ KM) 83,534.

POPULATION 156,790.

WHEN TO GO August-December is dry season. Hot all year.

GETTING THERE Air France from Paris to Cayenne airport. Also ships from France.

VISAS Fluctuating: check with French embassy (officially part of France).

FIND OUT MORE
www.tourisme-guyane.com.

French Polynesia (France)

OVERVIEW Huge shoal of Pacific islands centred around Tahiti. Idyllic for tourists, but subject to unrest due to dependence on France and unpopularity of nuclear tests. Highlights: The bustling city of Papeete, visiting the unspoilt and ancient Leeward Islands, watersports around Bora Bora.

CAPITAL Papeete.

LANGUAGE French, Tahitian and various Polynesian languages. Also English.

SIZE (SQ KM) 4,167.

POPULATION 245,516.

WHEN TO GO April-October cool and dry, November- March humid.

GETTING THERE Papeete airport is well served by Air france, Qantas, Air New Zealand, Hawaiian Airlines and others.

VISAS Fluctuating: check with French embassy.

FIND OUT MORE
www.tahiti-tourisme.com, www.spto.org.

Gibraltar (UK)

Overview Drab offshore financial centre with few tourist attractions. Highlights: Cable-car trip to the top of the Rock.

Capital Gibraltar.

Language English.

Size (sq km) 6.5.

Population 28,231.

When to go Hot in summer (May-September), mild in winter.

Getting there Drive from mainland Spain, or fly to Gibraltar airport.

Visas Required for Australia, Canada, USA; not required from EU.

Find out more www.gibraltar.gov.uk.

Greenland (Denmark)

Overview World's second largest island, almost entirely covered in ice. Possible arctic adventures include dog-sledging. Highlights: Visiting Qassiarsuk, the area settled by Viking Eric the Red, to see the surviving ruins a thousand years old. Visiting trading posts.

Capital Nuuk.

Language Inuit (Greenlandic), Danish.

Size (sq km) 2,166,086.

Population 56,676.

When to go Arctic climate, especially in north and interior. Other areas milder in summer (July-September).

Getting there Fly from Iceland or Denmark.

Visas As for Denmark.

Find out more www.greenland.com, www.visitdenmark.com.

Guadeloupe (France)

Overview Caribbean island group with attractive old colonial towns and some good beaches. Some islands quite undeveloped. Highlights: Fascinating underground caves at Fort Fleur d'Épée. The National Park of Guadeloupe offers great natural beauty at the base of a dormant volcano.

Capital Basse-Terre

Language French and Creole.

Size (sq km) 1,705.

Population 444,515.

When to go Warm all year, rainy June-October.

Getting there Air france, Air Canada, American Airlines, and Air Liberté to Pointe-à-Pitre airport.

Visas Fluctuating: check with French embassy (officially part of France).

Find out more www.st-barths.com, www.st-martin.org, www.caribbean.co.uk.

Guam (USA)

Overview Volcanic island in the Pacific, one-third occupied by US military base. Facilities for fishing, diving and golf. Highlights: Visiting the museum that commemorates a Japanese soldier who hid in the interior until 1972 not knowing the Second World War was over.

Capital Hagatna.

Language English and Chamorro.

Size (sq km) 549.

Population 159,547.

When to go Rainy season is July-November, preceded by hot season.

Getting there Virgin Atlantic, Japan Airlines, Northwest Airlines fly to Guam airport. Also by sea.

Visas Not required for US citizens; nor for Australian/EU citizens up to 15 days.

Find out more www.visitguam.org.

Martinique (France)

Overview Beautiful Caribbean island, rugged and volcanic. Highlights: The remains of St Pierre once the 'pearl of the Caribbean', destroyed by a volcanic eruption in 1902. Spearfishing at the coastal resorts.

Capital Fort-de-France.

Language French.

Size (sq km) 1,100.

Population 381,427.

When to go Warm all year, rainy July-November.

Getting there Air France, BWIA and Air Guadeloupe fly to Fort-de-France.

Visas Fluctuating: check with French embassy (officially part of France).

Find out more
www.touristmartinique.com.

Netherlands Antilles (Netherlands)

Overview Two Caribbean island groups off the coast of Venezuela. Watersports heavily promoted. Highlights: Waters teeming with wildlife.

Capital Willemstad.

Language Dutch, Papiamento, English, Spanish.

Size (sq km) 802.

Population 207,175.

When to go Warm all year, islands lie outside hurricane belt.

Getting there Regular flights with Air DCA and KLM.

Visas Not required for tourist stays of up to three months for UK. Required for US.

Find out more www.curacao-tourism.com, www.caribbean.co.uk.

New Caledonia (France)

Overview Island group off northern Australia, subject to serious inter-racial tensions. Origin of much fine tribal art. Beautiful beaches and mountains. Highlights: Spotting humpback whales during mating season between July and September. Visiting the Tjibaou Cultural Centre for concerts, plays, and exhibitions.

Capital Nouméa.

Language French

Size (sq km) 18,575.

Population 220,000.

When to go Warm all year, hot October-May, cooler June-September.

Getting there Air France, Qantas and Air New Zealand, among others, fly to Nouméa. Also by sea.

Visas Fluctuating: check with French embassy (officially part of France).

Find out more www.nctps.com, www.spto.org.

Niue (New Zealand)

Overview World's largest coral island and home to some of the least disturbed forests. Economy dependent on tourism and postage stamps. Excellent fishing, diving and snorkelling, and few tourists. Highlights: Bubble Cave, a shallow system where sea snakes lay their eggs; and Egypt, where divers swim past large columns as if in Egyptian ruins, spotting turtles, parrot-fish, and white-tipped reef sharks.

Capital Alofi.

Language Niuean and English.

Size (sq km) 262.

Population 1,761.

When to go Warm days and cool nights. Rainy February-March.

Getting there Royal Tongan Airlines connects with Niue International airport from Auckland and Sydney.

Visas Not required for tourist stays up to 30 days.

Find out more www.niueisland.com, www.spto.org.

Puerto Rico (USA)

Overview Densely populated and highly developed Caribbean island. Facilities for big-game fishing and other watersports. Highlights: The collection of Pre-Raphaelite paintings in Ponce. The Phosphorescent Bay, where microscopic marine life light up when disturbed by fish, boats, or any movement.

Capital San Juan.

Language English and Spanish.

Size (sq km) 8,959.

Population 3,839,810.

When to go Hot and tropical all year.

Getting there BA, KLM, Northwest Airlines, Canadian Airlines, Iberia and American Airlines, among others, fly to Luis Muñoz Marin airport.

Visas As for USA.

Find out more
www.gotopuertorico.com.

Reunion (France)

OVERVIEW Mountainous island in the India Ocean. Important military base. Highlights: Climbing among the volcanic peaks, trout fishing at the Takamaka Falls.

CAPITAL Saint-Denis.

LANGUAGE French and Creole.

SIZE (SQ KM) 2,507.

POPULATION 753,600.

WHEN TO GO Cyclone season is January-March. Otherwise hot and tropical.

GETTING THERE Air france to St Denis airport. Also by sea.

VISAS Fluctuating: check with French embassy (officially part of France).

FIND OUT MORE
www.la-reunion-tourisme.com,
www.franceguide.com.

Turks & Caicos Islands (UK)

OVERVIEW Coral archipelago in the Caribbean dominated by tourism and off-shore banking. Spectacular beaches, nature reserves and diving, often with few tourists. Highlights: Caicos Cays National Underwater Park, where the reefs of the Caicos bank and the rich variety of coral and brightly coloured fish can be seen.

CAPITAL Cockburn Town.

LANGUAGE English.

SIZE (SQ KM) 430.

POPULATION 19,000.

WHEN TO GO Tropical all year. Some rain October-November.

GETTING THERE Grand Turk airport is served by American Airlines from Miami, Air Jamaica from Jamaica, Bahamasair from Bahamas. Few shipping lines.

VISAS For stays up to 90 days, not required for Australia, Canada, EU, USA.

FIND OUT MORE
www.turksandcaicostourism.com.

Virgin Islands (USA)

OVERVIEW Major stopover for Caribbean cruises, these 50 islands offer good diving and sailing around fine beaches. But they also have the highest density of hotels in the entire Caribbean. Highlights: Spot egrets, herons, and other wildlife on kayak tours through Mangrove Lagoon. Sport-fishing for blue and white marlin, sailfish, and wahoo.

CAPITAL Charlotte Amalie.

LANGUAGE English.

SIZE (SQ KM) 347.

POPULATION 110,000.

WHEN TO GO Hot all year. Wettest August-October.

GETTING THERE St Thomas and St Croix airports are well served by British and American airlines, particularly Britannia, Delta and American Airlines.

VISAS As for USA.

FIND OUT MORE www.usvitourism.vi.

Section 3: **Preparations** ❧

When to go

Rainy seasons worldwide

THIS CHART SHOWS THE AVERAGE RAINFALL in various countries, per month and as an annual total. Full weather charts for each country can be found in Section 2.

KEY TO SYMBOLS R the rainiest months   W wetter than average   D drier than average

	Annual total mm	J	F	M	A	M	J	J	A	S	O	N	D
Afghanistan (Kabul)	34.0	D	W	R	R	D	D	D	D	D	D	D	W
Algeria (Algiers)	76.5	W	W	W	D	D	D	D	D	D	W	R	R
Argentina (Buenos A.)	95.0	D	D	W	W	D	D	D	D	D	W	W	R
Argentina (Tucuman)	97.0	R	W	W	D	D	D	D	D	D	D	W	W
Australia (Cairns)	225.3	W	W	R	W	D	D	D	D	D	D	D	W
Australia (Darwin)	149.1	R	W	W	D	D	D	D	D	D	D	W	W
Australia (Melbourne)	65.3	D	D	W	W	D	D	D	D	W	R	W	W
Australia (Perth)	90.7	D	D	D	D	W	R	R	W	W	W	D	D
Australia (Sydney)	118.1	D	W	W	R	W	W	W	D	D	D	D	D
Benin (Cotonou)	132.6	D	D	W	W	R	R	D	D	D	W	D	D
Bolivia (Concepçion)	114.3	R	W	W	D	D	D	D	D	D	D	R	W
Bolivia (La Paz)	57.4	R	W	W	D	D	D	D	D	D	D	W	W
Brazil (Belem)	243.8	W	R	W	W	W	D	D	D	D	D	D	D
Brazil (Manaus)	181.1	W	W	R	D	D	D	D	D	D	D	W	W
Brazil (Recife)	161.0	D	D	W	W	W	R	W	W	D	D	D	D
Brazil (Rio de Janeiro)	108.2	W	W	W	W	D	D	D	D	D	D	W	R
Brazil (Salvador B.)	190.0	D	D	D	R	R	W	W	D	D	D	D	D
Chile (Santiago)	36.1	D	D	D	D	W	R	W	W	D	D	D	D
Chile (Valdivia)	260.1	D	D	D	W	W	R	W	W	D	D	D	D
China (Beijing)	134.1	D	D	D	D	D	D	W	R	R	W	D	D
China (Guangzhou)	164.3	D	D	D	W	W	R	W	W	D	D	D	D
China (Hong Kong)	216.1	D	D	D	D	W	R	R	R	W	D	D	D
China (Shanghai)	113.5	D	D	D	D	D	R	W	W	W	D	D	D
China (Wuhan)	125.7	D	D	D	W	W	R	W	D	D	D	D	D
Colombia (Bogota)	105.9	D	D	W	W	W	D	D	D	D	R	W	D
Congo (Kananga)	158.2	W	W	W	W	D	D	D	D	D	W	R	R
Congo (Kinshasa)	135.4	W	W	W	W	D	D	D	D	D	W	R	W
Cook Islands (Manih.)	248.2	R	W	D	D	D	D	D	D	D	W	W	W
Costa Rica (San Jose)	179.8	D	D	D	D	W	W	W	W	R	R	D	D
Cuba (Havana)	122.4	D	D	D	D	W	W	W	W	W	R	D	D
Dominican R. (S Dom.)	141.7	D	D	D	D	W	W	W	W	R	W	W	D
Ecuador (Guyaquil)	97.3	R	R	R	W	D	D	D	D	D	D	D	D
Ecuador (Quito)	112.3	W	W	W	R	W	D	D	D	D	D	D	D
Egypt (Cairo)	3.6	W	W	W	D	D	D	D	D	D	D	D	W
Ethiopia (Addis Ababa)	123.7	D	D	D	D	D	W	R	R	W	D	D	D
Ethiopia (Harar)	89.7	D	D	W	W	W	W	W	R	W	D	D	D
Fiji (Suva)	297.4	W	W	R	D	D	D	D	D	D	D	D	W
Fr. Polynesia (Tahiti)	162.8	R	R	W	W	D	D	D	D	D	D	W	R
Gabon (Libreville)	251.0	W	W	W	W	W	D	D	D	D	W	R	W
Ghana (Accra)	72.4	D	D	W	W	W	R	D	D	D	W	D	D

KEY TO SYMBOLS R the rainiest months   W wetter than average   D drier than average

	Annual total mm	J	F	M	A	M	J	J	A	S	O	N	D
Guatemala (G. City)	131.6	D	D	D	D	W	R	W	W	W	W	D	D
Guyana (Georgetown)	225.3	W	D	D	D	W	R	W	D	D	D	D	W
Haiti (Port–au–Prince)	135.4	D	D	D	W	R	D	D	W	W	D	D	D
Hawaii (Honolulu)	64.3	R	W	W	D	D	D	D	D	D	D	W	R
Honduras (Tegucig.)	162.1	D	D	D	D	D	R	W	D	W	W	D	D
Iceland (Reykjavik)	77.2	W	D	D	D	D	D	D	D	W	R	W	W
India (Agra)	68.1	D	D	D	D	D	W	R	R	W	D	D	D
India (Bangalore)	329.2	D	D	D	D	D	R	R	W	D	D	D	D
India (Bombay)	181.4	D	D	D	D	D	R	R	W	W	D	D	D
India (Calcutta)	160.0	D	D	D	D	W	W	R	R	W	D	D	D
India (Delhi)	64.0	D	D	D	D	D	W	R	R	W	D	D	D
India (Hyderabad)	75.2	D	D	D	D	D	W	W	W	R	W	D	D
India (Madras)	127.0	D	D	D	D	D	D	D	W	W	R	R	W
Indonesia (Jakarta)	179.8	R	R	W	D	D	D	D	D	D	D	D	W
Iran (Tehran)	24.6	R	W	R	W	D	D	D	D	D	D	D	W
Iraq (Baghdad)	15.0	W	W	R	W	D	D	D	D	D	D	W	W
Israel (Jerusalem)	53.3	R	R	W	D	D	D	D	D	D	D	W	W
Jamaica (Kingston)	80.0	D	D	D	D	W	W	D	W	W	R	W	D
Japan (Nagasaki)	191.8	D	D	D	W	W	R	W	W	W	D	D	D
Japan (Osaka)	133.6	D	D	D	W	W	R	W	W	W	W	D	D
Japan (Tokyo)	156.5	D	D	D	W	W	W	W	W	R	W	D	D
Jordan (Amman)	27.9	R	R	W	D	D	D	D	D	D	D	W	W
Kenya (Nairobi)	95.8	D	D	W	R	W	D	D	D	D	D	W	W
Kenya (Mombasa)	120.1	D	D	D	W	R	W	D	D	D	D	D	D
Korea (Seoul)	125.0	D	D	D	D	D	W	R	R	W	D	D	D
Kuwait (Kuwait City)	12.7	W	W	R	D	D	D	D	D	D	D	W	R
Lebanon (Beirut)	89.7	R	W	W	D	D	D	D	D	D	D	W	R
Leeward Island (Dom.)	197.9	D	D	D	D	D	W	R	W	W	W	W	D
Liberia (Monrovia)	513.8	D	D	D	D	W	R	R	D	W	W	D	D
Libya (Tripoli)	38.9	W	W	W	W	D	D	D	D	D	W	W	R
Madagascar (Tamatav.)	325.6	W	W	R	W	D	W	W	D	D	D	D	D
Malaysia (K.L.)	244.1	D	D	W	R	W	D	D	D	W	W	W	D
Malaysia (Sandakan)	314.2	R	W	D	D	D	D	D	D	D	D	W	W
Malawi (Lilongwe)	78.7	R	R	W	D	D	D	D	D	D	D	D	W
Mali (Timbuctou)	24.4	D	D	D	D	W	R	R	W	D	D	D	D
Mexico (Acapulco)	154.2	D	D	D	D	D	R	W	W	W	W	D	D
Mexico (Mazatlan)	84.8	D	D	D	D	D	D	W	W	R	D	D	D
Mexico (Merida)	92.7	D	D	D	D	W	R	W	W	W	W	D	D
Mexico (Mexico City)	74.9	D	D	D	D	D	W	R	W	W	D	D	D
Morocco (Marrakesh)	23.9	W	W	R	W	D	D	D	D	D	W	W	W
Morocco (Tangier)	90.2	W	W	W	W	D	D	D	D	D	W	R	W
Mozambique (Maputo)	75.9	R	W	W	D	D	D	D	D	D	D	W	W
Myanmar (Mandalay)	82.8	D	D	D	D	R	R	W	W	W	D	D	D
Myanmar (Yangon)	261.6	D	D	D	D	W	W	R	W	W	D	D	D
Nepal (Kathmandu)	142.7	D	D	D	D	W	W	R	R	W	D	D	D
New Zealand (Auck.)	124.7	D	D	D	D	W	W	R	W	D	D	D	D
New Zealand (Christ.)	63.8	W	D	D	D	W	W	R	D	D	D	D	W
New Zealand (Welltn.)	120.4	D	D	D	D	W	W	R	W	D	W	D	D
Nigeria (Lagos)	183.6	D	D	D	D	W	R	W	D	D	W	D	D
Nigeria (Zungeru)	115.3	D	D	D	D	W	W	W	W	R	D	D	D
Pakistan (Karachi)	18.3	D	D	D	D	D	D	R	W	D	D	D	D

KEY TO SYMBOLS   R the rainiest months   W wetter than average   D drier than average

	Annual total mm	J	F	M	A	M	J	J	A	S	O	N	D
Panama (Balboa H.)	177.0	D	D	D	D	W	W	W	W	W	R	R	D
Papua NG (Port Msby.)	101.1	W	R	W	W	D	D	D	D	D	D	D	W
Paraguay (Asunçion)	131.6	W	W	D	W	W	D	D	D	D	W	W	R
Peru (Lima)	4.8	D	D	D	D	W	W	W	R	R	D	D	D
Philippines (Manila)	208.5	D	D	D	D	D	W	R	R	W	W	D	D
Samoa (Apia)	285.2	R	W	W	W	D	D	D	D	D	D	W	W
Saudi Arabia (Jeddah)	8.1	D	D	D	D	D	D	D	D	D	D	R	R
Saudi Arabia (Riyadh)	9.1	D	W	W	R	W	D	D	D	D	D	D	D
Senegal (Dakar)	155.4	D	D	D	D	D	D	W	R	W	D	D	D
Sierra Leone (Freetwn.)	343.4	D	D	D	D	D	W	R	R	W	W	D	D
Singapore	241.3	R	D	D	D	D	D	D	D	D	W	R	R
Sri Lanka (Colombo)	236.5	D	D	D	W	R	W	D	D	D	R	R	D
Solomon Islands (Tul.)	313.4	W	R	W	W	D	D	D	D	D	D	D	W
South Africa (Jo'burg)	70.9	W	W	W	W	D	D	D	D	D	D	W	R
South Africa (Cape T.)	50.8	D	D	D	W	W	W	R	W	W	D	D	D
Sudan (Khartoum)	17.0	D	D	D	D	D	D	W	R	W	D	D	D
Sudan (Mongalla)	94.5	D	D	D	W	W	W	R	W	W	W	D	D
Syria (Damascus)	22.4	R	RD	D	D	D	D	D	D	D	D	W	W
Taiwan (Taipei)	212.9	D	D	W	D	W	W	W	R	W	D	D	D
Thailand (Bangkok)	139.7	D	D	D	D	W	W	W	W	R	W	D	D
Turkey (Istanbul)	80.5	W	W	W	D	D	D	D	D	D	W	W	R
Uganda (Entebbe)	150.6	D	D	W	R	W	D	D	D	D	D	W	D
Uruguay (Montevideo)	95.0	D	D	R	R	W	W	D	D	D	D	D	D
Venezuela (Caracas)	83.3	D	D	D	D	W	R	R	R	R	R	W	D
Vietnam (Hanoi)	168.1	D	D	D	D	W	W	W	R	W	D	D	D
Yemen (Aden)	4.8	D	W	D	W	D	D	D	W	R	D	D	D
Zambia (Lusaka)	83.3	R	W	W	D	D	D	D	D	D	D	W	W
Zimbabwe (Harare)	82.8	R	W	W	D	D	D	D	D	D	D	W	W

Festivals of the world
by Jeremy Atiyah

CAN'T WAIT FOR CHRISTMAS? WHY NOT GO ABROAD for your festivals instead? There is always something going on somewhere. Visiting festivals is not only a way of crashing other people's parties, it is also a way to see local people at their best and take great photos. If you don't lose your camera in the mêlée, that is.

Humans have been cluttering the calendar with special dates since the dawn of history. Some of these have never stopped, other new ones started up yesterday. Some are a fantastic spectacle; others offer nothing to see. If you are going halfway round the world to see one, make sure you have got the dates right.

Not that you need to go far. Every country in the world, perhaps every city, contains its own festivals, and Britain is no exception. Annual examples here include the explosive Guy Fawke's Night on 5 November, as well as curiosities such as the 300-year-old Shrovetide football match in Ashbourne, Derbyshire, in February.

Worldwide however, the origins of the oldest festivals revolve round agricultural rites, marking seasonal changes like the beginning of spring or the coming of the rains. Such festivals tend to follow the lunar calendar (lunar cycles were easier to count), which means that tourists have to check their calendars carefully. Given common agricultural origins, it is no coincidence that the end of winter is marked almost simultaneously in Europe and China by two of the world's largest festivals.

Carnival, which takes place on the days leading up to Ash Wednesday, 40 days before Easter, is a mad party throughout the Catholic world. Fat Tuesday or Mardi Gras is the climactic finale of these celebrations. In Europe, Mardi Gras is celebrated in all Catholic countries, but perhaps most famously in Venice, where harlequins and incognito strangers in chalk-white masks stalk the streets. Fantastically ostentatious fancy-dress balls are also held in Vienna at this time, while in the German city of Cologne, women run around cutting off men's ties.

Mardi Gras in the Americas is even more outrageous. In New Orleans bizarrely dressed paraders march to the accompaniment of an insane amount of bead-flinging, flambeaux-carrying, chanting and boozing. But even this is nothing compared to what goes down in Rio de Janeiro, probably the single most famous street party in the world, where the emphasis is heavily on transvestism, erotic costumes, scantily clad dancers and alcohol. Finally Sydney's Gay and Lesbian Mardi Gras parade (which actually falls a couple of weeks into Lent) is the latest spin-off from the Carnival scene.

By contrast to which, the end-of-winter festival at the other end of the Eurasian landmass – Chinese New Year – is altogether low key. Instead of street parties, this is a time for families to come together, the main consequence of which is closed restaurants and horribly crowded train stations. From the traveller's point of view, it is a time to avoid China.

Other festivals with ancient roots are to be found all over Asia. No Ruz, the Iranian new year marking the spring equinox, provides travellers with a fascinating glimpse into the ancient heart of Iran; apart from feasting, one age-old custom is for everyone to join in leaping over street bonfires. The symbolism of this comes straight from the pre-Islamic fire-worshipping cult of Zoroastrianism.

Hindu and Buddhist communities, in countries such as India, Nepal, Thailand and the Indonesian island of Bali, retain traces of ancient cults in virtually every town and village, to the extent that travellers need hardly consult their calendars to be sure of running into colourful festivities.

India is the country with the oldest recorded surviving festivals. In the north particularly, the beginning of spring is marked by a major festival, Holi, the Festival of Colour, during which people bombard each other with water and paint. In Bombay, the holiday Ganesh Chaturthi is dedicated to the Hindu god Ganesh, (late August/early September: check dates), and sees huge processions carrying images of the god to immerse in the sea. The whole country in fact gets through a lot of rampant celebrations at the end of the monsoons, ostensibly commemorating events from the great Hindu epic, the Ramayana.

In contrast to these ancient ceremonies, the holidays associated with the world's monotheistic religions represent attempts to modernise ancient festivals, to tie them into an up-to-date framework. It is not, for example, coincidental that Christmas falls at the time of the winter equinox, and Easter at the spring equinox. This probably reflects ancient Mediterranean beliefs in a god who is born at the coming of the winter rains, only to die again at the beginning of the summer heat.

Interesting though the myths may be, for the traveller Christmas is rarely more than a family affair outside Bethlehem and the Vatican in Rome, where huge crowds congregate to hear the Pope lead mass. Easter is a better time to travel: southern Spain, above all, celebrates Semana Santa (Holy Week) in flamboyant style, especially in the Andalucian city of Seville, where colossal processions of hooded, masked figures take place with figures of the Virgin Mary and Jesus being carted around in tow. Greek Easter, which follows some weeks later, is likewise an excellent time to be in Greece. Islamic festivals are widely observed in the religious sense, but are not exactly occasions for tourist gawping. Eid El Fitr (the breaking of the fast after the holy month of Ramadan) and Eid El Adha are big family occasions, though if you happen to be in an Islamic country at this time you may be invited to banquets involving the slaughter of goats.

The biggest Shiite festival is Ashura, commemorating the martyrdom of the Shiite hero Hussein, killed in the battle of Kerbala in 680 AD. This is an occasion for mourning and grief rather than celebration, with young men each competing to flagellate themselves more bloodily than the next. This can be seen in Iran and parts of Iraq and Lebanon, though tourists may not feel very welcome.

Jewish holidays are notable for their extreme frequency, and again, where travellers are concerned, these might not be the best times to actually visit Israel. Several of the holidays, notably Yom Kippur and Sukkoth, involve varying degrees of abstinence and self purification. Purim, on the other hand, (February/March – check dates) is an occasion for outright revelry – and it's the only chance you'll have to get drunk with orthodox Jews.

Moving away from ancient myths and religions, it is perhaps refreshing at the dawn of the twenty-first century to realise that festivals are not exclusively rooted in the remote past. In truth, most of us spend more time celebrating secular festivals than religious ones.

National holidays can be exciting occasions anywhere. Independence Day, the USA's birthday bash on 4 July is a great time to be around, with fireworks, music and large crowds gathering in towns and cities. France's Bastille Day, just ten days later on 14 July, is another patriotic extravaganza.

The secular holiday that comes nearer than any other to being a truly world holiday is 1 January. Huge crowds at places as diverse as the Vatican, Times Square, Trafalgar Square, the Brandenburg Gate and Sydney Harbour (to name but a few) spiritually unite for heavy drinking and singing of *Auld Lang Syne*, Robert Burn's song, which was composed to mark Scotland's own Hogmanay.

But the modern world's real contribution to the festival lies in the great sporting events of the twenty-first century: the football World Cup and, above all, the Olympic Games, two four-yearly events for which virtually the entire world comes to a standstill. Being able to attend either event in person is the equivalent – perhaps – of what a religious pilgrimage would have been in another age. Political occasions – the American elections spring to mind – can also make pretty good jamborees. If you are able to travel, it really can be Christmas every day. ❧

Jeremy Atiyah is Travel Editor of 'The Independent on Sunday' and co-author of the 'Rough Guide to China'.

Researching your trip

In love with travel books
by Joanna Lumley

I AM IN LOVE WITH TRAVELLING AND BOOKS – also with travel books: books to read whilst travelling and books as secret personal journeys. Ever since in childhood I hacked in desperation with my Bowie knife to try to save Injun Joe from his ghastly bat-fed death, or listened to the wind blowing in the fir trees as I lay on my straw bed with Heidi, I have known that I can travel everywhere in the world, skip through centuries, experience glory and terror all in my own head, all through books. Everyone reading this reads books, so there's no need to over-egg the custard; but struggle with me along a sustained metaphor of books as travel. They are at the same time travel agent, courier, packhorse and advisor. First the dust jacket, titled, beckoning you inwards, advertising its wares with alluring design, stark or twiddly lettering, vivid or subtle colouring... come on in! See what I've got inside! Then, upon opening it, you meet the sleeve notes, summarising the contents, a wish-you-were-here to tempt you. Is there a photograph of the writer (your guide and dragoman)? Yes; and look – he/she's got a dog, a pearl necklace, a thick jersey, a wryly humorous expression; this will be a trusty companion. Chapter One! We have lift-off. Now the journey itself has begun.

Turning my face into the sun as the path leads steeply upwards, I take a short walk (Eric Newby) towards precipitous places clinging to the handrails of humour. The view is over vast open plains of Africa or Tartary (Wilfred Thesiger and Peter Fleming), deserts which seem to have no end; through Central Europe and the Baltic States to the lip of Asia (Patrick Leigh Fermor, Fitzroy Maclean), taking the eastern approach between the woods and the water. Now the mountains loom ahead, impossibly high, probably Himalayan, causing us to lean on our sticks, holding our hammering hearts as we survey that undiscovered land from the roof of the world (Eric Shipton and Peter Hopkirk); but below us, in Caribbean heat and rain, the Malayan monsoon gathers and breaks (VS Naipaul and W Somerset Maugham, not travel writers as such, but what the heck), banana leaves and Mr Biswas dripping in the sunset of a rubber plantation. And rattling past in solitary splendour on an ill-lit train comes Colin Thubron, who has learnt the language and can translate for you as you go. They are your friends and you, a complete stranger, are theirs. They wrote their books for you. It doesn't matter if you lose your way and turn back a few pages, because the jeep will still be waiting, with its engine running, for you to drive on or pitch your camp for the night.

What were the earliest travel books I read? The Bible, I suppose, with huge journeys, but not many of the geographical descriptions I crave: the odd mention of a hill or plain, sea or cave. And then Caesar's *Gallic Wars*, a Roman general fighting his way through France – but his main concerns were with army formations and how to storm a castle. Early explorers are the heroes of this genre, their logs and diaries revealing the splendours and hardships of an undiscovered world.

There is no shadow of doubt in my mind that books as cut-price travel are the best value for money in history (apart from a box of matches: when you think of the little box with its cleverly fitting drawer, striking pad, separate matches beautifully laid side by side, a motto, joke or exhortation – well, one totters with gratitude). No traveller is complete without a book, and no journey is so slight or so immense that it cannot provide a decent basis for some delicious observations. One of my most treasured travel books, published in 1876, is *The Indian Alps and How We Crossed Them* by Nina Mazuchelli, an insanely daring and ill-prepared expedition in the eastern Himalayas. On the gold-embossed cover her name doesn't appear, just 'by a Lady Pioneer'. The book is spotted, browned, but not shaved, silked or made-up; slightly rubbed, but the joints are not cracked; not washed or guarded, but not sophisticated: in fact, rather like me. ❧

JOANNA LUMLEY is one of Britain's best-loved actresses. This is an extract from her book 'No Room for Secrets', published by Penguin Books.

Recommended reading

by Sarah Anderson and Alex Stewart

Africa (central and southern)

The Dust Diaries,
Owen Sheers
A poignant journey through contemporary Zimbabwe in an attempt to understand a relation's devotion to the country and the bloody differences that span the years.
Don't Let's Go To The Dogs Tonight
Alexandra Fuller
Fine memoir of growing up in 1970s war-torn Rhodesia, which provides an unsentimental account of the civil war and one family's bond with a continent that shapes and defines them.
Scribbling the Cat,
Alexandra Fuller
Travels through Zambia, Zimbabwe and Mozambique in the bloody footsteps of the Rhodesian war, meeting veterans who survived the conflict and discovering the countries still reeling from the racial strife and violence.
My Gorilla Journey
Helen Attwater
The author and her husband set up an orphanage for baby gorillas in the Congo.
The Rainbird
Jan Brokken
Travelling through the jungles of Gabon, Brokken is haunted by the hosts of his predecessors.

Heart of Darkness
Joseph Conrad
Conrad went to the Belgian Congo in 1890 to captain a river steamer, and it became the setting for this compelling novel.
My Traitor's Heart
Rian Malan
An extraordinarily powerful book about the reality of being brought up in South Africa.
Long Walk to Freedom
Nelson Mandela
Mandela's riveting memoirs recreate the experiences that helped shape his destiny.
The Ukimwi Road
Dervla Murphy
'Ukimwi' of the title is AIDS. Dervla Murphy made a 3,000-mile bicycle journey from Kenya through Uganda, Tanzania, Malawi and Zambia to Zimbabwe.
A Bend in the River
VS Naipaul
Salim travels to the town on a bend in the river and this is the story of his life as a trader in that town, a place which comes vividly alive in Naipaul's prose.
Congo Journey
Redmond O'Hanlon
A gut-wrenching adventure that is also filled with scholarly observations on natural history.
Cry the Beloved Country
Alan Paton
Even today this book remains one of the classics written about racial tension in South Africa.

Africa (east)

Zanzibar Chest
Aidan Hartley
Brave and powerful examination of the underbelly of Africa and the grisly wars in Somalia, Ethiopia, Rwanda and Burundi, experienced

first hand and at no small emotional cost.
Ciao Asmara,
Justin Hill
An account of two years in Eritrea, uncovering a nation rich in history and tradition but struggling with war.
Dark Star Safari,
Paul Theroux
Riveting overland trip from Cairo to Cape Town that explores the legacy of Africa's colonial past.
Out of Africa
Karen Blixen
In 1914 Karen Blixen went to Kenya to run a coffee farm which failed. The friends and animals that she met are vividly portrayed, and we share her sense of loss both for the farm and, in a wider sense, for an era.
White Mischief
James Fox
The 'Happy Valley' clique in Kenya was thrown into confusion when Lord Erroll, founder of the set, was murdered in 1941.
I Dreamed of Africa
Kuki Gallmann
A haunting memoir capturing the magic, beauty and pain of Kenya.
The Weather in Africa
Martha Gellhorn
Three novellas set in East Africa: *On the Mountain,* *By the Sea* and *In the Highlands.*
Warriors
Gerald Hanley
Gerald Hanley spent several years in Somalia, where he got to know the local people very well.
The Flame Trees of Thika
Elspeth Huxley
Elspeth Huxley went with her parents to Thika to become pioneering settlers among the Kikuyu.
North of South
Shiva Naipaul

A brilliant travel narrative about journeying through Kenya, Tanzania and Zambia. Naipaul was extremely observant with a novelist's eye for detail.

Scoop
Evelyn Waugh
Journalist William Boot is sent mistakenly to Ishmaelia by press baron Lord Copper, to cover a war. As Boot blunders along, this becomes an hilarious satire on Fleet Street and war reporting.

Africa (north)

South from Barbary
Justin Marozzi
An epic 1,500-mile journey by camel across the Libyan Sahara, retracing the old slave routes, which captures the poetry and solitude of the desert and the misery of the slave trade.

Travels in Asia and Africa 1325-1354
Ibn Battuta
Ibn Battuta was born in Tangier and as a good Muslim made a pilgrimage to Mecca.

Letter from Egypt
Lucie Duff-Gordon
The author spent seven years in a ruined house in Luxor in the 1860s.

The Pyramids of Egypt
IES Edwards
One of the classic books on Egyptian archaeology.

Hideous Kinky
Esther Freud
Esther Freud was taken by her hippy mother to Morocco during the 1960s, aged five.

Morocco That Was
Walter Harris
Harris arrived in Tangier in 1886 and became the *Times* correspondent there until 1933.

Cairo Trilogy
Naguib Mahfouz
(*Palace Walk*, *Palace of Desire* and *Sugar Sweet*)
One of the most widely read authors and winner of the Nobel prize in 1988.

A Year in Marrakesh
Peter Mayne
Mayne lived in a small house in Marrakesh and wrote this book (originally published as *The Alleys of Marrakesh*) from his observations.

A Cure for Serpents
Duke of Pirajno
Pirajno arrived in North Africa as a doctor and stayed 18 years. His collection of reminiscences and stories makes wonderful reading.

In the Pharoah's Shadow
Anthony Sattin
A look at the ancient customs which survive in today's Egypt.

Old Serpent Nile
Stanley Stewart
A journey from the Nile Delta to the Mountains of the Moon.

Africa (west)

The Innocent Anthropologist
Nigel Barley
The hilarious account of Barley's first field trip to the Dowayo in the Cameroons.

A Good Man in Africa
William Boyd
A very funny novel set in Ghana and Nigeria.

The Viceroy of Ouidah
Bruce Chatwin
A poor Brazilian sailed to Dahomey (now Benin) in the early 1800s, determined to make his fortune and return triumphantly to Brazil.

Difficult and Dangerous Roads
Hugh Clapperton
Clapperton was one of the

first British explorers to enter the central Sahara – this is the account of his travels in the Sahara and Fezzan in 1822-1825.

The Overloaded Ark
Gerald Durrell
Durrell's first book is about an expedition to the Cameroons to collect animals for his zoo.

Journey Without Maps
Graham Greene
This journey across Liberia with his cousin Barbara was Greene's first book.

Mali Blues
Lieve Joris
Four different tales of travelling through Senegal, Mauritania and Mali.

The Famished Road
Ben Okri
A lyrical and compelling book, full of flights of fancy, but also instructive about life in a village.

African islands

Paradise
Abdulrazek Gurnah
Set around Zanzibar in the early years of European involvement. Yusuf, a Muslim boy, is taken into the service of his merchant uncle and, through his eyes, we see the Europeans as colonisers.

Muddling Through in Madagascar
Dervla Murphy
Dervla Murphy travelled through Madagascar with her 14-year-old daughter Rachel.

Lemurs of the Lost World
Jane Wilson
An exploration of the forests and crocodile caves of Madagascar.

America (central and south) and Caribbean

Three Letters From the Andes
Patrick Leigh Fermor
Enthralling , elegantly written letters detailing Fermor's journey into the high Andes of Peru in 1971.

The White Rock
Hugh Thomson
A journey into the Eastern Andes of Peru to explore the mysterious Inca culture, definitively detailing their rise to power, their conquest of a continent and their tragic annihilation by the sixteenth century conquistadors.

Saddled With Darwin
Toby Green
Retraces Charles Darwin's footsteps on an epic horseback trip across 3,730 miles and six countries.

Inca Kola
Matthew Parris
Atmospheric account of travel throughout Peru on a bizarre trip full of incident and adventure.

The Dancer Upstairs
Nicholas Shakespeare
Fictional account of the actual manhunt for the Peruvian guerrilla leader Ezequielw, which explores grand themes and the author's understanding of South America.

The Motorcycle Diaries
Ernesto 'Che' Guevara
Diary of Che's trip through Argentina, Chile, Peru and Venezuela as a young man in search of America, adventure and himself that led to the development of his political consciousness.

The Lost City of the Incas
Hiram Bingham
Historic account of Bingham's search for Machu Picchu and other lost Inca cities in Peru during the early years of the twentieth century.

A Death in Brazil
Peter Robb
Brilliant dissection of modern day Brazil and a compelling look at the past and present of this vibrant but disturbed country through its history, food, art and politics.

The House of the Spirits
Isabel Allende
A family saga spanning four generations in Chile. Full of unforgettable characters, spirits, history and forces of nature.

A Visit to Don Otavio
Sybille Bedford
Sybille Bedford describes the horrors of her train journey to Mexico in graphic detail.

Collected Fictions
Jorge Luis Borges
A collection of subtly ingenious stories.

In Patagonia
Bruce Chatwin
Chatwin never forgot the piece of skin with strands of hair from a Patagonian brontosaurus, which he found in his grandmother's cabinet; it was this that eventually inspired him to go to Patagonia.

Breaking the Maya Code
Michael D Coe
It is only in the last 20 years that the code to Mayan hieroglyphs hasbeen discovered. This is how it was done.

One River
Wade Davis
Science adventure and hallucinations in the Amazon basin.

The Spears of Twilight
Philippe Descola
Life and death in the Amazon jungle: modern anthropology at its best.

Havana Dreams
Wendy Gimbel
Four generations of Cuban women - one of whom is the illegitimate daughter of Fidel Castro.

The Lawless Roads
Graham Greene
Greene was commissioned to go to Mexico in 1938 to find out how people had reacted to the religious persecution and anti-clerical purges of the then President Calles. His trip formed the basis for *The Power and the Glory*.

The Power and the Glory
Graham Greene
The 'whisky' priest of Greene's novel had done everything wrong in the eyes of the Church: taken a 'wife', fathered a daughter, had an addiction to brandy -and yet obstinately remained a priest.

Amazon Frontier
John Hemming
A definitive account, full of original research covering the period from the mid-eighteenth to the early twentieth century.

Personal Narrative of a Journey to the Equinoctial Regions of the New Continent
Alexander von Humboldt
From his youth, von Humboldt had been devoted to the study of nature and 'experienced in my travels, enjoyments which have amply compensated for the privations inseparable from a laborious and often agitated life.'

The Time of the Hero
Mario Vargas Llosa
Set in the Military Academy in Lima, this novel so outraged the Peruvian

authorities that copies were publicly burned.

Under the Volcano
Malcolm Lowry
Set in Cuernavaca, where the alcoholic British consul has a breakdown and dies, this has now become a cult book (although when first published it sold only two copies in two years in Canada).

A House for Mr Biswas
VS Naipaul
Naipaul considers this book to be the one 'that is closest to me' and the one that contains some of his funniest writing.

The Fruit Palace
Charles Nicholl
Charles Nicholl first came into contact with the Colombian drug trade in the early Seventies. Twelve years later he went back to find out about this dangerous world.

The Labyrinth of Solitude
Octavio Paz
A collection of essays analysing Mexico's history and psyche and looking at relations with the USA.

Penguin History of Latin America
ed. Edwin Williamson
Starts with the pre-Columbian Indians and continues through savage colonisations.

Rites
Victor Perera
An autobiography of life in Guatemala City's Jewish community. Perera's father was a first-generation immigrant who worked his way up from being an itinerant pedlar to a leading merchant.

The Final Passage
Caryl Phillips
The story of 19-year-old Leila's struggle to come to terms with life on a small

Caribbean island in the 1950s.

Wide Sargasso Sea
Jean Rhys
This novel set in Dominica and Jamaica describes the lives of Edward Rochester and his mad wife before their introduction as characters into Charlotte Bronte's *Jane Eyre*.

The Vision of Elena Silves
Nicholas Shakespeare
Shakespeare's combination of magical realism with European traditions of fiction make an extremely effectivemixture.

Touching the Void
Joe Simpson
A compulsivly readable book about a climbing accident in the Andes.

The Land of Miracles
Stephen Smith
Smith writes with ironic detachement about this country of paradox.

The Weather Prophet
Lucretia Stewart
A personal account of a single woman's foray into the wider reaches of the Antilles.

The Mosquito Coast
Paul Theroux
Allie Fox takes his family to live in the Honduran jungle and struggles to keep them alive with his inventions.

The Old Patagonian Express
Paul Theroux
Theroux's journey from Boston to Patagonia by train was full of contrast: some were ramshackle and old, others superb and new.

Ninety-Two Days
Evelyn Waugh
Often throughout this book, Waugh philosophises about travel: 'The delight of travel...is a delight just as incommunicable as the love of home.'

Travels in a Thin Country
Sara Wheeler
Sara Wheeler spent six months on her own travelling through Chile.

Time Among the Maya
Ronald Wright
An attempt to discover the ancient roots of the Maya civilization.

America (north)

Snow Geese
William Fiennes
Extraordinarily powerful and moving account of following snow geese on their migration from the Canadian Arctic South to the Gulf of Mexico, which is full of beautiful descriptions and reflections.

Ghost Riders
Richard Grant
Original and clear-eyed book on The USA that provides an excellent introduction to its history and culture through the eyes of itinerants and drifters.

The New York Trilogy
Paul Auster
The trilogy consists of *City of Glass*, *Ghosts* and *The Locked Room* and has been described as 'A shatteringly clever piece of work'.

America Day by Day
Simone de Beauvoir
A fascinating record of de Beauvoir's first impressions of the US.

Midnight in the Garden of Good and Evil
John Berendt
Written as a novel, but based on the true eccentrics of Savannah, Georgia.

A Lady's Life in the Rockie Mountains
Isabella Bird
In 1873 Isabella Bird rode through the Wild West, meeting her 'dear (one-

eyed) desperado', Rocky Mountain Jim, whom she described as 'a man any woman might love, but no sane woman would marry'.

The Penguin History of the United States of America
Hugh Brogan
A complete general history of the States, starting from British colonisation and ending at the fall of Nixon.

New York Days, New York Nights
Stephen Brook
Amusing and energetic observations of New York.

Bury My Heart at Wounded Knee
Dee Brown
The epic bestseller which tells the Indians' side of the Wild West story through the voices of such as Sitting Bull, Cochise, Crazy Horse and Geronimo.

The Lost Continent
Bill Bryson
Born in Des Moines, Bryson left as soon as he could, but after ten years in England he was lured back and drove around small-town America, producing an hilarious acount of his travels.

Notes from a Big Country
Bill Bryson
Having lived in the UK for many years, Bryson at last returns to America with his family.

Almost Heaven
Martin Fletcher
An original look at the weird and wonderful things of small-town America.

Cold Mountain
Charles Frazer
A soldier wounded in the Civil War leaves for the long journey home to Ada, the the woman he had loved.

On the Road
Jack Kerouac
The classic book about

Fifties underground America which has become the epitome of the Beat generation.

Into the Wild
Jon Krakauer
Chris McCandless disappeared in Alaska having reinvented himself andgiven all his possessions to charity. Why?

The Oatmeal Ark
Rory Maclean
The author traces his great-grandfather's voyage from Shetland to Nova Scotia and across Canada.

River Horse
William Least-Heat Moon
Moon's bid to cross America by its interior waterways rivals his previous book *Blue Highways*.

A Turn in the South
VS Naipaul
Naipaul aims to come to terms with themany complexities of the South, with all its paradoxes and contradictions.

Penguin Book of American Short Stories
Includes gems by Washington Irving, John Updike, Ambrose Bierce, Willa Cather, Herman Melville, Mark Twain and many others.

The Shipping News
E Annie Proulx
Pulitzer Prize-winning book about fishing and newspaper life in Newfoundland.

Old Glory
Jonathan Raban
Inspired by memories of reading *Huckleberry Finn* as a child, Jonathan Raban takes a boat up the Mississippi.

Life on the Mississippi
Mark Twain
Nostalgic and humourous mixture of journalism and

autobiography, written in the heyday of steamboating on the Mississippi. Twain's love of the river shines through his prose.

Asia (central)

The Bookseller of Kabul
Asne Seierstad
Colourful portrait of people struggling to survive in Afghanistan at the end of the twentieth century told through the eyes of a bookseller who defied the authorities to sell literature to the people.

An Unexpected Light
Jason Elliot
Award-winning account of travels in Afghanistan, written with deep respect and affection for the country and its people.

The Places In Between
Rory Stewart
An epic trek across Afghanistan in the wake of the recent invasion, dodging hostile nations, warring factions and competing ideologies, redolent of the great age of exploration.

The Lost Heart of Asia
Colin Thubron
Documents the widespread social upheaval across Central Asia in the wake of the break up of the Soviet Union and provides an outstanding guide to the history, people and culture of this region.

The Search for Shangri-La
Charles Allen
An account of four recent journeys into western Tibet.

First Russia Then Tibet
Robert Byron
Byron contrasts post-revolutionary Russia with pre-industrial Tibet, both of which he knew fairly well and describes lucidly.

In Xanadu
William Dalrymple
Dalrymple travelled from
Jerusalem to Xanadu and
Kubla Khan's palace,
crossing Asia by a variety
of transport.
Bayonets to Lhasa
Peter Fleming
An account of the imperial
Younghusband expedition
to Lhasa in 1903/4 which
paved the way for Anglo-
Tibetan friendship.
News from Tartary
Peter Fleming
Fleming made this journey
was to find out what was
happening in Sinkiang
(Chinese Turkestan).
Seven Years in Tibet
Heinrich Harrer
Probably one of the best
known and most widely
read books about Tibet.
*Foreign Devils on the
Silk Road*
Peter Hopkirk
A highly readable account
of the adventures of all the
explorers who have made
archaeological raids on
the Silk Road.
The Great Game
Peter Hopkirk
The secret agents of both
Britain and Russia were
involved in a great
struggle in Central Asia
during the last century;
this became known as
the Great Game.
Setting the East Ablaze
Peter Hopkirk
The story of the Bolsheviks'
attempt to 'set the east
ablaze' with the doctrine of
Marxism between the wars.
*Trespassers on the Roof
of the World*
Peter Hopkirk
The account of how Tibet
was forcibly opened to
foreigners in the nineteenth
and twentieth centuries.
Into Thin Air

Jon Krakauer
A personal account of the
Everest disaster of May
1996.
*Ancient Wisdom, Modern
World*
HH the Dalai Lama
The Dalai Lama's guide to
living today using universal
principles.
A Hero of Our Time
Mikhail Lermontov
Written between 1838 -40,
this was the Russian poet
Lermontov's only
novel; it consists of five
stories set in Russian Asia.
*An English Lady in Chinese
Turkestan*
Lady Macartney
The author was a diplomat's
wife in Kashgar from 1890
until 1918.
Eastern Approaches
Fitzroy Maclean
A tale of high adventure and
politics, superbly told, set in
the Caucasus, Central Asia,
Persia and Yugoslavia.
*A Short Walk in
the Hindu Kush*
Eric Newby
Eric Newby was working
in the rag trade in London
when he set off for the
Hindu Kush; his book has
now become a travel classic.
From Heaven Lake
Vikram Seth
Seth hitch-hiked through
Chinese Central Asia
and Tibet to Nepal. A
delightful book.
Journey to Turkistan
Eric Teichman
In 1935 Teichman left the
British Embassy in China
and travelled through
Mongolia and Chinese
Turkistan to Urumchi by
motor truck and pony.

Asia (south)

Maximum City
Suketu Mehta
Quest to get to the heart

of Bombay and the lives
of the men and women
who live in this hectic,
frenzied megalopolis.
Nanda Devi
Hugh Thomson
Unique visit to the Nanda
Devi Sanctuary, previously
closed to travellers for
political reasons, which
explores the history and
politics that have blighted
this remote landscape.
India In Slow Motion
Mark Tully
Meandering excursion
that attempts to unravel the
mysteries lying at the heart
of India and paint
a portrait of this land
of contrasts.
*The Hall of a Thousand
Columns*
Tim Mackintosh-Smith
Second chapter of
Mackintosh-Smith's
journey in Ibn Battutah's
footsteps, which focuses on
his travel and escapades in
India and reveals a country
far removed from the Taj
and Raj.
Memoirs of a Bengal Civilian
John Beames
Beames was in India from
1858-1893; this lively book
describes his time as a
district officer of the Raj.
An Indian Summer
James Cameron
Cameron captures the
sounds, smells and colours
of India. An invaluable
introduction.
*The Autobiography of
an Unknown Indian*
Nirad C Chaudhuri
Chaudhuri, a distinguished
scholar, was born in East
Bengal in 1897 and did not
finally settle in England
until 1970.
The Age of Kali
William Dalrymple
A series of essays which are
the distillation of ten years

travelling around the sub-continent.

City of Djinns
William Dalrymple
After spending 12 months in Delhi, Dalrymple learned to peel away the successive layers of history.

A Passage to India
E.M. Forster
An incident at the Marabar caves between the Englishwoman Adela Quested and the Indian Dr Aziz formsthe centre of this classic novel: it is one of Forster's masterpieces.

Chasing the Monsoon
Alexander Frater
In 1987 Frater followed the monsoon from Cape Comorin in Southern India to Bangladesh.

Liberty or Death
Patrick French
A controversial reinterpretation of the last years of British rule in India.

Kim
Rudyard Kipling
A book to whet appetites for travel in the great sub-continent.

The Snow Leopard
Peter Matthiessen
Although Matthiessen primarily went in search of the elusive snow leopard in the remote Crystal Mountains of northern Nepal, this book is essentially a spiritual search. Inspiring descriptions of the scenery and wildlife.

Calcutta
Geoffrey Moorhouse
An illuminating book about the city past and present, rich in anecdote and history.

Full Tilt
Dervla Murphy
Dervla Murphy fulfilled a childhood dream when she made a six-month journey riding her bicycle 3,000 miles across Europe, Persia, Afghanistan, Pakistan and into India.

Bachelor of Arts
RK Narayan
One of the Malgudi novels which gets to the heart of Indian life.

Slowly Down the Ganges
Eric Newby
The description of a 1,200- mile journey down the Ganges which Eric Newby made with his wife.

Travels in Nepal
Charlie Pye-Smith
Pye-Smith travelled throughout Nepal from Kathmandu to Namche Bazar, down the Kali Gandaki and south to the Terai along the Indian border.

Sorcerer's Apprentice
Tahir Shah
The gripping story of Shah's apprenticeship into the ways of Indian godmen.

Selected Poems
Rabindranath Tagore
A superb selection from a great poet.

No Full Stops in India
Mark Tully
Mark Tully was born in India and has worked there for the BBC for many years; his knowledge is almost unparalled among foreigners and his sympathy and understanding shine through all of these essays.

Asia (south-east)

Mad About the Mekong
John Keay
History of the first expedition to travel the length of the Mekong in 1866, inspiring an imperial scramble for the region.

The Gate
Francois Bizot
Deeply moving, terrifying first-hand account of the Khmer Rouge take over of Cambodia and the appalling genocide that followed.

Red Lights and Green Lizards
Liz Anderson
A doctor's account of her new job in a brothel in Phnom Penh in the early 1990s.

Freedom from Fear and other writings
Aung San Suu Kyi
A collection of pieces by the Nobel Laureate, written before her house arrest, which reflect her beliefs, hopes and fears for her country and people.

Through the Jungle of Death
Stephen Brookes
Moving account of a boy's escape from war-time Burma.

Three Moons in Vietnam
Maria Coffey
An exploration of the coast from the Mekong Delta in the south to Halong Bay in the north.

The Beach
Alex Garland
A fast-moving adventure story in search of the perfect beach.

The Quiet American
Graham Greene
Set in Saigon in the Fifties, Graham Greene's novel concerns an American on a secret mission.

Playing with Water
James Hamilton-Paterson
An extraordinarily moving and evocative book, which combines fishing for survival on the remote Philippine island of Tiwarik, with a journey of inner exploration.

A Dragon Apparent – Cambodia, Laos and Vietnam
Norman Lewis
Poignant reading now, as the last 40 years have seen

South-East Asia wracked by war. Lewis was writing about countries which no longer exist as they did.
Golden Earth
Norman Lewis
Through sheer pesistence, Lewis managed to travel all over Burma, even though much of the countryside was under the control of insurgent armies then.
Under the Dragon
Rory Maclean
A trip through today's sad and beautiful Burma.
The Trouble with Tigers
Victor Mallet
An account of the turmoil in South-East Asia after the markets collapsed in 1997.
The Lost Tribe
Edward Marriott
When he hearrrd about the 'discovery' of the Liawep tribe of Papua New Guinea Marriott determined to record their stories, hopes and fears.
Into the Heart of Borneo
Redmond O'Hanlon
An extremely funny acount of a journey which O'Hanlon made with poet James Fenton to the mountains of Batu Tiban.
Burmese Days
George Orwell
Set when the British were ruling in Burma. Flory, a white timber merchant, befriends Dr Veraswami, a black enthusiast for Empire who needs help.
A Bright Shining Lie
Neil Sheehan
Written through the eyes of an American Colonel, John Paul Vann, this book encapsulates everything that was most disturbing about the Vietnam War.
A Fortune-Teller Told Me
Tiziano Terzani
Terzani was warned by a Hong-Kong fortune-teller

not to fly for a year – so he travelled by foot, boat, bus, car and train.
The Great Railway Bazaar
Paul Theroux
Theroux takes the Mandalay Express from Rangoon and then the local train to Maymyo and Naung-Peng.
Islands in the Clouds
Isabella Tree
A journey to the remote parts of Papua New Guinea and Irian Jaya.

Australasia and Pacific

In Tasmania
Nicholas Shakespeare
A history of two turbulent centuries in an apparently idyllic place, famous for its dark past and peopled with a cast of unlikely characters.
True History of the Kelly Gang
Peter Carey
Fictional account of the rise and fall of Ned Kelly, Australia's notorious bushranger, bank robber and Robin Hood figure.
Once Were Warriors
Alan Duff
Frank, uncompromising novel that depicts the standing of the Maori in contemporary New Zealand.
Tales From the Torrid Zone
Alexander Frater
A dazzling journey through the 88 nations that comprise the tropics, rooted in Vanuatu but ranging around the globe.
Oscar and Lucinda
Peter Carey
A rich and complex novel which filled Angela Carter 'with a wild, savage envy'.
The Songlines
Bruce Chatwin
A compelling account of

Aboriginal Australia and its meanings: 'I have a vision of the Songlines stretching across the continents and ages.'
Tracks
Robyn Davidson
In 1977 Robyn Davidson set off from Alice Springs by camel to cross 1,700 miles of desert and bush.
The Kon-Tiki Expedition
Thor Heyerdahl
Six men sailed on a primitive raft from Peru to Polynesia to prove that 'the Pacific islands are located well inside the range of prehistoric craft from Peru.'
The Fatal Shore
Robert Hughes
An immensely readable yet scholarly history which traces the fate of those who were transported to Australia from 1787-1868.
The Bone People
Keri Hulme
Set on the South Island beaches of New Zealand, the book combines Maori myth and Christian symbols.
In the Land of Oz
Howard Jacobson
An entertaining and perceptive journey round Australia.
Kangaroo
DH Lawrence
A partly autobiographical novel in which Lawrence examines politics and power.
The Collected Stories of Katherine Mansfield
The 73 short stories and 15 unfinished fragments in this collection are representative of New Zealand-born Katherine Mansfield's writing.
Sydney
Geoffrey Moorhouse
A celebration - through

history and culture - of
this exciting city.
Promised Lands
Jane Rogers
An intertwining of the first
years of the convict-colony
with present-day lives.
In the South Seas
RL Stevenson
The record of Stevenson's
first year in the Marquesas.
The Happy Isles of Oceania
Paul Theroux
Theroux travelled from the
Solomons to Fiji, Tonga,
Tahiti, the Marquesas and
Easter Island.
The Singing Line
Alice Thomson
The story of the man who
strung the telegraph line
across Australia and of the
woman who gave her name
to Alice Springs.
The Tree of Man
Patrick White
The story of a man and
woman who make their
home in the outback; as
their children grow up and
the wilderness begins to
disappear, changes occur.

Europe (central and eastern)

Black Earth
Andrew Meier
Fascinating analysis of
Russia today as it comes to
terms with its grim
communist past and
wrestles with its chaotic
capitalist present.
Black Earth City
Charlotte Hobson
Touching account of
a year spent in deepest
Russia, offering real and
tender insights into the lives
of the locals that she meets.
Imperium
Ryzard Kapuscinski
Captures people's
memories, hopes and fears
at the time of the demise of
the Soviet Socialist

Republics as the empire
collapsed and died in 1989.
Stories I Stole
Wendell Steavenson
Sparkling ode to the
chaotic post-Soviet mess
that is the Caucuses,
gleaned over two years
living in Georgia.
*In the Empire of
Ghengis Khan*
Stanley Stewart
A 1,000-mile adventure on
horseback across the old
Mongol Empire
investigating this beguiling
medieval land marooned in
a modern world.
Danube
Claudio Magris
A wide-ranging and
excitingly original book
about the Danube and the
history, philosophy, people,
war and politics that occur
along its route.
Stalingrad
Antony Beevor
A brilliant and scholarly
new look at the city and its
wartime seige.
The Accursed Mountains
Robert Carver
A journey into wild and
inaccesible Albania.
Utz
Bruce Chatwin
A novel about a compulsive
porcelain collector in the
Jewish quarter of Prague.
The Heart of Europe
Norman Davies
Although this history
begins in 1945, Davies
looks back to the past to
illustrate his theories.
Prague in Black and Gold
Peter Demetz
A love-hate account of
the author's obsession
with Prague.
Stalin
Isaac Deutscher
The classic biography
of one of Russia's more
controversial figures.

*One Hot Summer in
St Petersburg*
Duncan Fallowell
An honest, funny and
passionate book.
The House by the Dvina
Eugenie Fraser
Russia before, during
and after the revolution
is delightfully evoked by
Eugenia Fraser, who
was half-Scottish and
half-Russian.
The Fall of Yugoslavia
Misha Glenny
Causes, effects and dangers
of the latest Balkan crisis.
On Foot to the Golden Horn
Jason Goodwin
A record of Goodwin's
journey through Eastern
Europe to Istanbul.
The Tin Drum
Günter Grass
A scathing dissection of the
years 1925-1955 through
the eyes of a dwarf.
The Good Soldier Svejk
J Hasek
A rambling but classic story
about Svejk, an everyman
figure who creates havoc
in the Czech army during
World War I.
The Castle
Franz Kafka
Modernist allegory about
K the unwanted Land
Surveyor, who is never
admitted to the Castle.
*The Unbearable Lightness
of Being*
M Kundera
A tragic and entertaining
novel which puts a new
perspective on living.
*Between the Woods
and the Water*
Patrick Leigh Fermor
Second part of his trilogy,
describing his journey from
the woods of Transylvania
to the waters of the Danube.
A Time of Gifts
Patrick Leigh Fermor
The first of a trilogy in

which Leigh Fermor walked from London to Istanbul in the 1930s.

The Drowned and the Saved
Primo Levi
Levi committed suicide shortly after completing this book which dispels the myth that he forgave the Nazis for Auschwitz.

Kosovo - A Short History
Noel Malcolm
A brilliantly researched and authoratative book.

The Bronski House
Philip Marsden
Marsden accompanies exiled Polish poet Zofia Ilinska back to her childhood home.

The Crossing Place
Philip Marsden
A journey in search of the Armenians through the Middle East, Eastern Europe and the Caucasus.

The Spirit-Wrestlers
Philip Marsden
A journey into the strange, ambiguous world of the Russia's ancient religions.

The Big Red Train Ride
Eric Newby
Newby went from Moscow to Nakhodka in 1977 with diverse companions and some vodka.

Queen of Romania
Hannah Pakula
Princess Marie of Edinburgh was the grand-daughter of both Queen Victoria and Tsar Alexander II.

Magic Prague
Angelo Maria Ripellino
All the mystery and magnetism of Prague.

Echoes of a Native Land
Serge Schmemann
A lyrical look at two centuries in a Russian village.

And Quiet Flows the Don
M Sholokhov
Set in a Cossack village,

Sholokhov wrote this after returning to his native Don from Moscow.

The Pianist
Wladyslaw Szpilman
A young Jewish pianist survived in Warsaw against all odds.

Among the Russians
Colin Thubron
Thubron drove around Russia by car when this was still extremely difficult.

Pushkin's Button
Serena Vitale
The story of the duel which killed the great poet.

Europe (Mediterranean)

Istanbul
Orhan Pamuk
Portrait of Istanbul and of one man's life growing up amid this teeming, melancholic city that straddles East and West.

The Tomb in Seville
Norman Lewis
The great writer's last book explores southern Spain in 1934 as the country teeters on the brink of civil war.

The Basque History of the World
Mark Kurlansky
Diligently researched, anecdotal and partisan history of one of Europe's oldest, most fascinating peoples.

Roads to Santiago
Cees Nooteboom
A many-tangented pilgrimage through ten centuries of Spain's history, politics, art, literature and people.

Our Lady of the Sewers
Paul Richardson
Illuminating tour of traditional Spain with a glimpse of the surviving eccentricities and ancient ways to be found there.

France in the New Century
John Ardagh
Changes in French society since 1945.

The Italians
Luigi Barzini
Barzini, being an Italian himself, manages to get to the real core of Italy and the Italians by cutting through the familiar clichés.

Captain Corelli's Mandolin
Louis de Bernieres
The young Italian officer Corelli is posted to a Greek island during World War II.

South from Granada
Gerald Brenan
Brenan lived in the village of Yegen in the Sierra Nevada for many years; here he writes about his life there and what Granada was like in the 1920s.

The Golden Honeycomb
Vincent Cronin
Excellent descriptions of Sicily's art, architecture and folklore, written in the form of a quest for the golden honeycomb which Daedalus is said to have offered to Aphrodite in return for his escape from King Minos of Crete.

Bitter Lemons
Lawrence Durrell
Durrell was entranced by Cyprus in 1953, buying a house and becoming a local teacher.

Prospero's Cell
Lawrence Durrell
A guide to the landscape and manners on the island of Corfu.

Reflections on a Marine Venus
Lawrence Durrell
'The marine Venus' is a statue which was found by sailors in their nets at the bottom of Rhodes harbour and which much appealed to Durrell.

The Journal of a Voyage to Lisbon
Henry Fielding
Fielding went to Portugal knowing he was dying.

Istanbul
John Freely
The imperial city of Romans, Byzantine and Ottoman Empires.

Lords of the Horizons
Jason Goodwin
A history of the Ottoman Empire.

For Whom the Bell Tolls
Ernest Hemingway
A novel which takes place during only four days of the Spanish civil war, but which feels as if it encompasses the whole of Spain.

Barcelona
Robert Hughes
Hughes places Barcelona firmly in its Catalan past, realising that there is little point in describing the new without the old.

Backwards out of the Big World
Paul Hyland
Hyland crosses Portugal and meets a cross-section of people.

Between Hopes and Memories
Michael Jacobs
Michael Jacobs travelled through every region of mainland Spain, meeting many prominent Spaniards as well as many lesser known poets, eccentrics and mystics.

Italian Journeys
Jonathan Keates
Over a period of 20 years, Keates wandered around northern Italy visiting off-beat places.

The Olive Grove
Katherine Kizilos
The author returns to her father's village in the heart of the Greek mountains.

The Leopard
Giuseppe di Lampedusa
In 1860 the old order still reigns in Sicily, but there are echoes of a new political movement, with Garibaldi on the mainland.

DH Lawrence and Italy
Lawrence's three books about Italy collected together: *Sea and Sardinia*, *Twilight in Italy* and *Etruscan Places*.

As I Walked Out One Midsummer Morning
Laurie Lee
Lee walked through pre-Civil War Spain from Vigo to Malaga in 1936, busking with his violin.

Mani and *Roumeli*
Patrick Leigh Fermor
Two of the best books on modern Greece, these are full of scholarship and anecdotes about the history and gradual demise of many rural communities in Greece, as well as offering superb descriptions of the countryside.

Christ Stopped at Eboli
Carlo Levi
Set in a remote region of Basilicata where Levi was exiled under the Fascists, a world cut off from history and the state: 'We're not Christians, Christ stopped short of here, at Eboli.'

Naples 44
Norman Lewis
Norman Lewis arrived in Naples as an Intelligence Officer attached to the American Fifth Army and after a year there decided that, given the chance to be born again, he would choose to be an Italian.

Voices of the Old Sea
Norman Lewis
Norman Lewis lived in a remote Catalan fishing village in the 1950s. This record of how life was then offers stark contrasts to the area today.

The Towers of Trebizond
Rose Macaulay
The book opens with a much quoted sentence: ' "Take my camel, dear," said my Aunt Dot, as she climbed down from this animal on her return from High Mass.'

The Stones of Venice and Florence Observed
Mary McCarthy
An interpretation of Florence in the 1950s.

Constantinople
Philip Mansel
Constantinople portrayed as the imperial capital of the Ottomans.

Under the Tuscan Sun
Frances Mayes
Captures the feeling of living in a foreign country.

The Turkish Embassy Letters
Lady Mary Wortley Montagu
Lively letters from travels through Europe to Turkey in 1716.

Venice
Jan Morris
An essential companion to Venice – entertaining, ironical, witty and high-spirited.

Love and War in the Apennines
Eric Newby
The story of Newby's capture in Sicily in 1942; he escaped from the prison camp with help from a local girl, Wanda – who later became his wife.

On the Shores of the Mediterranean
Eric Newby
A Mediterranean journey which took in Italy, the Adriatic, Greece, Turkey, the Levant, North Africa and Spain.

Portrait of a Turkish Family
Irfan Orga
The author was born into a prosperous family under the Sultans, but in World War I the family was ruined and Turkey transformed.

Homage to Catalonia
George Orwell
The heady feelings of the early days of the Spanish Civil War, in Barcelona, are followed by disillusion as the Republicans are split by factional in-fighting.

The Elusive Truffle
Mirabel Osler
A quest for the rapidly disappearing traditional cuisine and culture of France.

Italian Education
Tim Parks
A look at the family in Italy, through the eyes of the author who lives near Verona.

Italian Neigbours
Tim Parks
A very readable account of how an Englishman copes in the Veneto; he learns to accept what the locals take for granted, thereby getting to grips with the real Italy.

History of the Italian People
Giuliano Procacci
Professor Procacci pinpoints 1000 AD as the time when European supremacy began to take root, and traces Italy's progression within its European context, through the communes of the eleventh century to the birth of the European Renaissance and the two world wars.

Midnight in Sicily
Peter Robb
Robb uses history, painting, literature and food in this exploration of Sicily.

The Tuscan Year
Elizabeth Romer
An account of traditional life and cooking in Italy.

Blindness
José Saramago
Blindness becomes contagious and spreads throughout the city.

Citizens
Simon Schama
A marvellous chronicle of the French Revolution.

A Fez of the Heart
Jeremy Seal
Travels through Turkey.

The Volcano Lover
Susan Sontag
Based on the lives of Sir William Hamilton, his wife Emma and Lord Nelson and set against the backdrop of Vesuvius.

Within Tuscany
Matthew Spender
Spender went to live in Tuscany and has written a book about his experiences which is 'by turns informative, ruminative, funny and touching'.

Travels with a Donkey
R.L. Stevenson
The account of Stevenson's trip through the Cevennes with his recalcitrant donkey, Modestine.

Driving Over Lemons
Chris Stewart
A sympathetic account of living in southern Spain, by ex-Genesis drummer Stewart.

The Spanish Civil War
Hugh Thomas
Huge and comprehensive book about the Spanish Civil War which traces in scrupolous detail a complicated story.

Journey into Cyprus
Colin Thubron
Thubron made a 600-mile trek around Cyprus during the last year of its peace.

The South
Colm Toibin
A painter on the run from a broken marriage flits between Spain and rural Ireland.

Memoirs of Hadrian
Marguerite Yourcenar
As Hadrian was dying he wrote a long valedictory letter to Marcus Aurelius explaining his philosophy about ruling the far-flung Roman Empire.

Labels – a Mediterranean Journey
Evelyn Waugh
Waugh's account of a Mediterranean cruise on which he visited Naples, Port Said, Constantinople, Athens and Barcelona.

Europe (northern)

Stasiland
Anna Funder
Spirited attempt to understand the German Democratic Republic through the stories of ordinary men and women whose lives were shaped by the Berlin Wall

Independent People
Halldor Laxness
Funny, sardonic novel full of lyrical prose and Nordic myths.

Neither Here Nor There
Bill Bryson
Bryson's humourous sweep through Europe.

Notes from a Small Island
Bill Bryson
Before leaving Yorkshire for America, Bill Bryson made a last, hilarious trip round Britain.

On the Black Hill
Bruce Chatwin
Rural isolation and its effect on two brothers who lived and farmed a Welsh hill farm all their lives.

Walled Gardens
Annabel Davis-Goff
The author is called home
from America to southern
Ireland on the death of her
father, and finds herself
back in the world of her
Anglo-Irish chilhood –
with haunting memories
of drafty houses, noisy
rooks and faded chintzes.
*Miss Smilla's Feeling
for Snow*
Peter Hoeg
A small boy falls to his death
from a rooftop. Compulsive
reading.
Journey to the Hebrides
Johnson & Boswell
Both Johnson's and
Boswell's books are records
of the same journey in the
eighteenth century, to the
Western isles and
throughout Scotland.
Cider with Rosie
Laurie Lee
Classic account of rural
childhood in the Cotswolds
in the 1920s.
A Place Apart
Dervla Murphy
Northern Ireland from the
inside out.
Round Ireland in Low Gear
Eric Newby
Eric and Wanda Newby
went to Ireland by bicycle in
the autumn of 1985
'to enjoy ourselves'.
Njal's Saga
This, the greatest of
Icelandic sagas, was written
by an unknown author
in the late thirteenth
century but based on the
historical events of 300
years earlier.
The English
Jeremy Paxman
Good and amusing
descriptions of the English
today.
Coasting
Jonathan Raban
Jonathan Raban wanted to

see his island home from
the sea and, in 1982,
set sail round the British
Isles in a 30-foot ketch.
*Berlin - the Biography
of a City*
Anthony Read & David
Fisher
An essential guide to the
past, present and future.
*Stones of Aran: Pilgrimage
and Labyrinth*
Tim Robinson
An encyclopaedic survey
of the Aran Islands.
*The Embarrassment
of Riches*
Simon Schama
The social and cultural
history of Holland in its
golden age - and much
more.
Kingdom by the Sea
Paul Theroux
An account of a three-
month journey round
Britain by foot, bus and
train. An attempt not only
to see Britain but to
describe the British in all
their aspects.
*A Short Residence in Sweden,
Norway & Denmark*
Mary Wollstonecroft
The author travelled alone
through Scandinavia in
1795, in search of
happiness in the remote
backwoods.

Far East

The Good Earth
Pearl Buck
A riveting family saga and
story of female sacrifice set
against the backdrop of
China on the brink of
change.
Red Dust
Ma Jian
Enthralling depiction of the
teeming contradictions of
China, gathered in the
course of three years travel
across the country by a
disenchanted insider.

The Good Women of China
Xinran
Unflinching, revealing
portrayal of what it meant
to be a woman
in modern China.
Tibet, Tibet
Patrick French
A history of Tibet,
recounting its tumultuous
past, complex culture and
complicated relationship
with China, which strips
away the propaganda.
*Tales from the South
China Seas*
Charles Allen
Relates the adventures
of the last generation of
British men and women
who went East in search of
their fortunes.
The Mummies of Urumchi
Elizabeth Wayland Barber
3,500 year-old mummies
were found in north-west
China. Where did they
come from?
Wild Swans
Jung Chang
An extremely moving
account of three
generations of Chinese
women, showing their
harrowing lives and
extraordinary resilience.
Memoirs of a Geisha
Arthur Golden
A novel that totally
transports you to another
time and place.
The Korean War
Max Hastings
The Korean War which
began in 1950 can today
be seen as the prelude to
Vietnam.
The Tyranny of History
W.J.F. Jenner
Jenner argues that China
has been both held together
and held back by its
deference to history.
*Twilight in the
Forbidden City*
Reginald F. Johnston

Johnston was a British colonial official, scholar, writer and poet, who lived in Chinas as tutor to the last Emperor between 1919 and 1924.

The Japanese – Strange but not Strangers
Joe Joseph
The author was Tokyo correspondent for *The Times* and has a particular insight into Japanese institutions and customs.

Forbidden Colours
Yukio Mishima
CP Snow described Mishima as 'A most beautiful writer of prose – clear, eloquent, visual....Mishima's characters are observed with one of the sharpest of eyes and with maximum chill.'

The Silent Cry
Kenzaburo Oe
Awarding the Nobel Prize for Literature, the Committee said: 'His poetic force creates an imagined world, where life and myth condense to form a disconcerting picture of the human predicament.'

East and West
Chris Patten
The experiences of the last governor of Hong Kong.

The China Voyage
Tim Severin
Six men and one woman sailed across the Pacific on a bamboo raft to test the theory that Asian sailors reached America 2,000 years ago.

Frontiers of Heaven
Stanley Stewart
Stewart travelled from Shanghai to the Indus.

Riding the Iron Rooster
Paul Theroux
Theroux spent a year travelling by every kind of train throughout China,

observing his companions in razor-sharp detail.

Behind the Wall
Colin Thubron
Thubron is a perceptive traveller who writes beautiful prose; without being in any way pretentious, he manages to teach us an enormous amount about the country and its people.

A History of Hong Kong
Frank Welsh
A comprehensive, absorbing and up-to-date book about the former colony.

Hand-Grenade Practice in Peking
Frances Wood
A remarkable account of the year Wood spent as a student in China in 1976 .

Slow Boats to China
Gavin Young
A journey to China by every kind of boat.

Middle East

Southern Gates of Arabia
Freya Stark
Traces the old incense roads through Yemen to the coast on a solitary journey, capturing the beauty and atmosphere of the still unspoilt Arabia of the 1930s.

The Travels of Ibn Battutah
ed. Tim Mackintosh-Smith
Abridged version of Ibn Battutah's Travels, as he set out from Morocco to make a pilgrimage to Mecca in 1325, an odyssey that lasted 29 years.

Travels With a Tangerine
Tim Mackintosh-Smith
Travels in the footsteps of Ibn Battutah from Morocco to Mecca.

Lady Hester
Lorna Gibb

Enthralling biography of Lady Hester Stanage, who defied social convention in the early 1800s to become a powerful figure in the Middle East.

Wilder Shores of Love
Lesley Blanch
Biographies of four redoubtable nineteenth-century women travellers: Isabel Burton, Jane Digby, Aimee Dubucq de Rivery and Isabelle Eberhardt.

The Road to Oxiana
Robert Byron
One of the classic travel books about Persia and Afghanistan. Robert Byron made this journey in 1933-4 and vividly describes the people he met and scenes he saw.

From the Holy Mountain
William Dalrymple
Dalrymple followed in the footsteps of the sixth-century Byzantine monk John Moschos on what has already become a classic journey.

The Hittites
OR Gurney
The Hittites created an advanced civilisation in Biblical times; they were politically well organised and their literature was inscribed on clay tablets in cuneiform writing.

The Gates of Damascus
Lieve Joris
An intimate portrait of contemporary Arab society.

Politics in the Middle East
Elie Kedourie
An historical analysis which attempts to explain why ideological politics, such as nationalism and fundamentalism, have triumphed in the Middle East and why democratic governments have not worked in Islamic countries.

Eothen
Alexander Kinglake
One of the classic travel
books, written by the
young Kinglake in 1844.
The account of his travels
to the East is interesting as
much for the descriptions
of what he saw as for the
effect these places had
upon him.
Seven Pillars of Wisdom
TE Lawrence
This book has been
criticised for its historical
inaccuracy, as it is a very
personal account of the
Arab Revolt, but Lawrence's
lively prose ensures that it
will remain a classic.
Yemen
Tim Mackintosh-Smith
Mackintosh-Smith lived in
the Yemen for 15 years and
wrote this quirky, learned
and poetic book.
The Arabs
Peter Mansfield
An introduction to the
modern Arab world
from political and
historical aspects; the
second half of the book
looks at each Arab state
separately.
A Reed Shaken By the Wind
Gavin Maxwell
In 1956 Gavin Maxwell
accompanied Wilfred
Thesiger to the marshlands
of Iraq. He describes the
people he met and his
experiences during these
travels.
Among the Believers
VS Naipaul
This first part of Naipaul's
Islamic journey visits Iran.
Arabia
Jonathan Raban
Raban was living in Earls
Court in the 1970s when it
began to fill up with Arabs;
he decided to go and see for
himself their countries
of origin - and produced

what has been called 'one of
the most delightful travel
books in 30 years'.
*The Oxford History
of the Crusades*
ed. Jonathan Riley-Smith
Written by a team of
scholars, the book covers
material from the First
Crusade in 1095 through
to ideas that we have about
the crusades today.
Arabian Sands
Wilfred Thesiger
Thesiger crossed the Empty
Quarter and says of the
book 'For me this book
remains a memorial to a
vanished past, a tribute to a
once magnificent people.'
The Life of My Choice
Wilfred Thesiger
Thesiger's autobiography
explains how he got the
urge for travel and who
it was that influenced him.
The Marsh Arabs
Wilfred Thesiger
A book about the fast-
disappearing people who
live in the marshes in
Iraq, around the junction
of the Tigris and Euphrates.
Mirror to Damascus
Colin Thubron
The history of Damascus
from Biblical times until
the revolution of 1966.

The Poles

Cherry
Sara Wheeler
Eloquent biography
of Apsley Cherry-Garrard,
one of the youngest
members of Scott's final
expedition to Antarctica.
*The Worst Journey
in the World*
Apsley Cherry-Garrard
A narrative of Scott's last
expedition from when it left
England in 1910
until its return to New
Zealand in 1913.
Ninety Degrees North

Fergus Fleming
Lucid historical account
of the race to the North
Pole and the people
involved in the pursuit
of this polar grail.
Arctic Dreams
Barry Lopez
Magical descriptions of the
Arctic landscape and the
animals and peoples
who live there.
Nunaga
Duncan Pryde
An autobiographical
account of the author's time
spent among the hunters
and traders of the Canadian
Arctic.
I May Be Some Time
Francis Spufford
A cultural history of our
obsession with ice.
Terra Incognita
Sara Wheeler
A wonderful account of the
author's stay on both British
and US bases.

*SARAH ANDERSON
founded The Travel
Bookshop in London,
and now runs Umbrella
Books.*

*ALEX STEWART is the
international book buyer
at Stanfords Book and
Map Shop.*

Choosing guidebooks
by Alex Stewart

U NTIL THE SECOND HALF OF THE TWENTIETH CENTURY, only the very wealthy could afford to go abroad as tourists. The very earliest guidebooks concentrated on instructing their pampered readers how to minimise the discomfort and disturbance of travel and to cope with the idiosyncrasies of the natives they encountered obscuring superlative views or outside historic buildings. In 1836, John Murray wrote and published the first modern guidebook, initiating a wide-ranging and comprehensive series of Handbooks that dispensed accurate information and advice for the sophisticated and affluent traveller. In one of his earliest Handbooks, to Switzerland, the author set out his mission statement: 'In order to travel with advantage in a country previously unknown, something more seems necessary than a mere detail of certain lines of road, and an enumeration of towns, villages, mountains, etc.' Thus his guides contained vivid accounts of abandoned ruins, tortuous journeys along primitive roads and scenic marvels. The volumes also featured summaries of a country's history, geography, demographic, culture and climate, along with maps and town plans. The Murray Handbooks have become much sought after collector's items, and are frequently listed by antiquarian booksellers with a value of up to £750.

Karl Baedeker provided competition for a burgeoning guidebook market. He introduced the practice of awarding stars to places of particular merit, generally improved the quality of the publications, and reduced their price, thereby making them more accessible. In 1918 Macmillan produced the first guide in the Blue Guide series (to London), and shortly after other publishers began to follow suit.

More than a century and a half after John Murray cut a trail across Europe, the guidebook remains an essential accessory. A guide has two main functions: to explain to tourists why they ought to visit a particular place, then to provide them with enough detailed information to render their visit enjoyable, instructive and simple. The range and depth of factual detail often determines the choice of guide. However, publishers are desperate not to be pigeonholed and go to great lengths to stress their broad appeal. Although practical detail is important, the best books should balance it with a welter of information on a country's culture, history, politics and people, in line with the ethos first set down by John Murray, thereby building bridges between visitors and their hosts.

As little as five years ago, most bookshops only featured a small selection of guidebooks, dominated by the publishing heavyweights and mainstays of the industry. These days the sections and the range of publishers are much larger. Although the traditional travel publishers still represent the majority of the market, smaller, more specialist outfits are stealing a march on them. The travel market is as buoyant as ever, despite international terrorism, natural disasters and accidents, and it is constantly evolving. The changes in how we travel, driven by the development of the internet and the establishment of budget airlines, have fuelled people's desires for different guidebooks to new destinations and new types of trip. Consequently, travel publishers are battling to reach as much of this diverse market as possible. As the book buying public evolves, so guidebook publishers are having to re-evaluate who they think their customers are and in turn are rethinking, rewriting and redesigning their products to suit these new types of traveller. Consequently, there are books available for almost each and every individual and it is now possible to select a book tailored to your personal holiday requirements. The result is a dizzying array of titles, and the best book for you may not be immediately obvious.

Detailed below are most of the main guidebook publishers and a guide to the style of book that they produce. They have been divided up in order for the information to be more accessible, but many of the larger publishers now have series that cross the boundaries arbitrarily attributed here.

Independent guides

These guides are ideal for independent-minded travellers of all ages. All of the guides abound with a wealth of practical information regarding where to stay, where to eat, what to see, how to get to places from and around each destination, and so forth. They all also have varying degrees of background information relating to the destination's history, culture and people. However, each publisher has its own identity and whilst each claims to appeal to people across the board, each will have its own strengths and particular points of emphasis.

Lonely Planet has been setting the standard for independent traveller guidebook publishing since its inception in 1973, when Tony and Maureen Wheeler produced the *Yellow Bible, a guide to South-East Asia on the Cheap*, in response to questions about their own travels throughout the region. The brand is now one of the most recognisable in the world and there are over 650 titles in an array of series, covering pretty much every country in the world. Frank and informal in style, with a layout that makes for exceptionally easy use, these guides are comprehensive, clear and informed. Alongside the core titles for countries and regions are continent-wide Shoestring Guides; city guides in various formats; outdoor activity guides; language guides; and food guides. Lonely Planet has also recently started to produce practical guides to travel writing and photography, and has drawn on its vast photo library to create a number of lavishly illustrated pictorial books that capture the essence of and inspire travel.

Lonely Planet's closest rival is the Rough Guides. These highly popular and respected books came about as a result of a trip to Greece by Mark Ellingham and a couple of friends in 1982. When they failed to find a guidebook to their destination that combined practical information and candid opinions about the main sights as well as political and cultural detail, they set about creating their own. Over the years the list has expanded and become increasingly diverse, but at heart remained intelligent and cultured. Perceptive and substantial background chapters complement the extensive practical information on offer, to provide a thoroughly rounded appreciation of the destination in question. Spin-off series include dictionary-phrasebooks, world music CDs and guides, and pocket sized

Directions guides that come with a mini-CD containing an e-book version of the entire text.

Footprint Handbooks have continued to go from strength to strength, drawing on the reputation of their seminal guide to South America, which has been published annually since 1924. Printed on bible-style thin paper and containing a treasure-trove of information, the guide has been the foundation on which the imprint has grown. A host of titles for Latin America followed in the traditional hardback format that set them apart from other publishers. This was unfortunately discarded in favour of a more conventional look, but the list has continued to expand and now covers more than 150 destinations in Africa, Asia, Australasia, Europe and the Middle East in an interesting, impeccably researched fashion. Pocket format guides focusing on short-break European cities were launched in 2003, followed by Activity guides to surfing and a Backpacker series that combines in one book popular destinations people may want to visit on the same trip.

Unlikely destinations are the hallmark of Bradt travel guides. For over thirty years Bradt has been producing timely guides to out-of-the-way destinations just as they become accessible to travellers. For adventurous souls heading to Albania, Gabon, Macedonia, Nigeria, Rwanda or the Sudan there are few guidebooks available, yet Bradt are always on hand. Guides to Kabul and Iraq were thought to be pushing it, but both became successes and cemented the company's reputation for introducing fresh destinations to people in an engaging, personal style that brims with considered opinion and insight. Specialist walking and wildlife guides are also available, as are Eccentric guides that explore the eclectic curiosities of a handful of cities.

Moon Handbooks is an American travel guide publisher, specialising in coverage of the US, for which there are individual guides to each state. Practical data and strategic advice also extend to destinations in South and Central America as well as the Caribbean, Asia and the Pacific.

Let's Go began in 1960, when a group of Harvard University students compiled their experiences and advice in a pamphlet for travellers on charter flights to Europe. The books are still produced by students on shoestring budgets, and retain the founders' adventurous attitude to travel, but now cover over 30 countries around the world and a further dozen cities in Europe and the US. Designed to show you just how far your money will go and inspire you to travel close to the ground, interacting with places and the people you meet, these are the last word in budget travel.

Illustrated/pictorial guides

These guides are highly visual in content, relying on photographs, drawings or diagrams to illustrate the text and capture the essence of a country or city. Although practical information is usually included to some degree, it is not the main focus of the book, which sets out to inspire and encourage travel, often in a cultured and intelligent fashion.

Eyewitness Guides have a very distinctive look that combines pithy text and line drawings, diagrams, cutaways and photographs. The guides to more than 100 destinations worldwide have an enduring appeal, but despite receiving a number of plaudits in 2004 and 2005, the company has chosen to revamp and re-launch itself at the start of 2006. The new guides will include short break features, in line with the Top 10 spin-off series, which aimed to condense information for the reader and highlight the best bits of each destination. They also produce a series of E-guides that link directly to an exclusive website that is regularly updated with information and useful links.

Everyman Guides have a similar look and feel to them as Eyewitness Guides. High-quality illustrations and imaginative visual devices such as cutaways and bird's eye views characterise these intelligent cultural guides, which focus on art and architecture but also detail history and wildlife in depth.

Insight Guides are highly visual, using colour images to illustrate the magazine-style articles that describe elements of the destination and the everyday lives of the people who live there. Designed to appeal to both actual and armchair travellers, they are available in a variety of sizes, and can be used on trips of almost any length, although the smaller sized Pocket and Compact series are weighted in favour of practical information and laid out around a number of potential itineraries. Specialist Museum and Gallery guides and Shopping and Eating guides are also available

Traditional guides

The American publisher Fodor has been busy making changes and alterations to its leading series of Gold Guides. Younger tourists often deride these comprehensive guides as stuffy, but they are knowledgeable and accurate. Detailed reviews and smart tips mean that although these aren't the most exciting guides to read, and there are no photographs either, they do manage to achieve a balance between practical information and the presentation of sights. Alternative series include citypacks and pocket guides as well as the Compass series of historical and cultural guides for America. They also distribute the Karen Brown series of accommodation guides.

Frommer is another long-standing giant of the American publishing scene, which now doubles as a travel agency. The mainstays of its range are the Complete Travel Guides for countries or cities, although it also produces budget, $-a-Day guides, shopping guides, national park guides, driving tour guides, portable guides and titles for people travelling with kids. The books deal predominantly with the US and have a distinct American orientation. Although they claim strict editorial independence, there is nonetheless an emphasis on steering readers to the online Frommer's travel site.

Cultural and historical guides

For those people travelling to explore the history or culture behind a destination, there are a number of excellent guides tailored to this need. Eyewitness and Everyman guides, mentioned above, are good places to start if you are less concerned with practical information or independent travel but want to get something more out of your trip.

Alternatively, Blue Guides emphasise cultural sight-seeing and are justly renowned for their extensive coverage of architecture and the arts. Updated and revised guides are no longer dry academic tomes, but accessible, intelligent commentators. Their reputation as 'serious' guidebooks should not be taken too seriously though, since the information contained within is dynamic and presented in such a way as to make the destinations come alive.

Companion Guides are written to be read, rather than simply consulted, much like the best travel writing. They too form a well-respected, established series, which although small comes highly recommended. Suffused with anecdotes and wry observations, they are informed, stylish and often idiosyncratic guides that effectively communicate the author's knowledge and affection for his subject.

Odyssey Guides are suitable for both the armchair traveller and the actual visitor. They are lavishly produced, well-illustrated and suffused with well-researched texts that explore aspects of each nation's culture. Both popular and less obvious destinations are covered, although they are perhaps best known for books on Afghanistan, Uzbekistan, Iran and individual regions of China.

Touring guides

These are aimed at people who are likely to want to explore a region in more depth. They are based on two formats: an easy-reference format and a series of itineraries that detail the sights, as well as a selection of places to stay and eat.

AA Publications has a vast list of more than 300 guides to destinations all over the world. The emphasis remains on being practical, but each series is focused on individual traveller needs. The relaunched Explorer guides are attractive, picture-filled books that are usually arranged around a tour of a country or city's main sights. Essential guides are condensed, pocket-sized books, as are City Packs, which combine a guidebook and a map in a flexi-pack and are popular with both leisure and business travellers. Key guides are full of facts, photos, points of interest and maps, whilst Spiral guides have a wire-bound spine that makes them easy to open and read.

Michelin is one of the best-known names in the industry. Famous enough to be identified solely by colour, the Red and Green guides make excellent touring companions, once you master the language and key coding. The Red guides are a series of hotel and restaurant guides for the rather more affluent connoisseur. Updated annually, they have an unparalleled reputation for reliability and consistency. All entries are inspected and graded by reviewers, using the famous symbols of recommendation. Green Guides are slimmer, paperback volumes that list the cultural, historical and natural attractions of cities and regions alongside a comprehensive survey of places of interest.

Cadogan has an ever-expanding list of guides that feature a number of successful spin-off series. These are highly readable, literary books that are particularly strong on history and cultural sightseeing, but not at the expense of practical detail. Elegantly written, these self-styled 'grown up independent guides' have an informed, individual voice that gently conveys a sense of contemporary life in each place. Country, regional and city guides sit comfortably alongside Flying Visit guides for European short breaks, Take The Kids guides for families and fact-filled Pick Your Brains guides actually for children. They also have several series of practical advice guides on moving, working and living abroad, and have begun to publish one-off travel literature titles.

Alastair Sawday began producing guidebooks to charming, quirky, elegant inns, B&Bs and hotels in response to the bland accommodation lists he felt were becoming the norm. Celebrating the unusual and full of attitude, these Special Places To Stay guides are beautifully produced, passionate champions of individuality that now cover much of Europe in addition to India and Morocco.

Purple Guides produce surprising guides to regions of Italy. Unlike traditional guides they are full of sumptuous photographs, stories and secrets, anecdotes and facts, which add another dimension to the experience of visiting each destination and help provide insights into the characters and places mentioned.

City guides

If you intend to spend time in a particular city, or even explore its surroundings, you ought to consider a more focused guide to that destination, since it will inevitably contain more information than a country guide is able to cram into the available space. Most of the major publishers produce city guides as part of their publishing programme, and you should be able to find one that suits your style of visiting, be it a standard-format, condensed, or pocket guide.

Time Out produces highly regarded, up-to-date guides that follow the format of the successful magazines. Hip, savvy reviews of restaurants, bars and hotels are detailed and honest, ensuring that you'll be seen in all the right places. Encyclopaedic arts and cultural coverage means that the guides no longer simply sell to younger travellers but have a broader appeal. Walking guides and one-off titles such as *Skiing and Snowboarding in Europe* or *European Breaks* are also available.

Everyman produces a series of City MapGuides in addition to their traditional books. These small-format guides open out to reveal clear large-scale maps of each district that feature a selection of the must-see sights as well as hordes of practical advice and photographs of what to expect.

Hedonists

Hedonism guides are a new series of guides targeting discerning, professional urbanites who like their travel books stylish and well designed. Beautiful photographs illustrate a wealth of information contained in incisive, independent reviews of the most fashionable places in town. The guides are about maximising time away and making the most of the city and all it has to offer. Insider knowledge designed to make you feel like a sophisticated local is now available on a host of happening European cities, but also on longer-haul destinations such as Miami, and perhaps surprisingly, Beirut.

Trekking guides

Whilst general guides will invariably contain some information on trekking in the popular regions of the country in question, specific walking guides will provide much more information and far better mapping to accompany the routes. The additional background detail and explanation of the sights along the trails means that these separate guides are often worth taking in addition to a more general title. Lonely Planet and Bradt both produce specific trekking guides based around day-to-day descriptions of each route in addition to their standard country and regional guides.

Cicerone were founded over thirty years ago and specialise in producing reliable, respected guides for outdoor enthusiasts. They now publish an impressive range of almost 300 books to walking in Europe and around the world, as well as climbing guides, cycling guides, winter activity guides, a World Mountain Ranges series and a Technique series written by experts in that field.

Trailblazer has gone from strength to strength, producing an excellent range of trekking guides for adventurous travellers that are full of valuable background material and unique, detailed hand-drawn maps. Its list now covers much of Europe, the Himalayas, Africa, New Zealand, and individual routes such as the Inca Trail. A series of British Walking Guides deal with the UK's long-distance trails. Trailblazer's By Rail series, centred on the distinguished *Trans-Siberian Handbook*, provides comprehensive information on how to enjoy this form of travel in China, Japan, Siberia, Canada and Australia. Route and planning guides for the Silk Road, Tibet and the Sahara are godsends for those approaching these regions, whilst the *Adventure Motorcycling Handbook* and its companion, the *Adventure Cycling Handbook* provide invaluable advice and anecdotes for the would-be two-wheel adventurer.

Sunflower has been producing the distinctive Landscape series of guides to car tours and walks since 1981. These focus on short excursions and day walks to points of interest or natural beauty, often off the beaten track. Largely restricted to popular walking regions in Europe, they are nonetheless useful companions. A new Walk and Eat range is designed to build up your appetite while trekking.

Living/working/buying abroad

One of the most significant developments in travel publishing has been the explosion in guides devoted to helping people move and live abroad. The property boom is underway in Eastern Europe and the surrounding Mediterranean countries, and these guides are designed to lead you through the pitfalls of upping sticks or investing in a second home.

Cadogan publishes a range of books that combine sensible advice and travel expertise with legal and practical advice from property specialists. If you are set on making a fresh start abroad, be it in Australasia, Europe, the US or Canada, its series on Buying a Property, Working and Living and Starting a Business is essential reading that covers all aspects of a potential move.

Survival Guides and Vacation Work also publish guides to *Buying Abroad* and *Living and Working Abroad* that investigate the nuts and bolts of a move to another country. Survival Guides publishes a guide to *Retiring Abroad*, whilst Vacation Work is also responsible for annual guides to *Summer Jobs Abroad* and *Summer Jobs Britain* for those not looking to actually leave the country permanently.

Literary guides

Literary guides are an optional extra that can reward the decision to carry additional weight with illuminating insights into a place. The background material contained within such guides can prepare you for the culture shock of visiting a new country and provide you with an introduction to each place's unique present-day identity and links with its past. The best in this category include the Cities of the Imagination series published by Signal, which comprises ostensibly cultural and literary histories of various cities; the Traveller's Companion guides from Robinson and the Traveller's History series by Chastleton.

Suggestion guides

A further area that has seen a real upturn in interest is in guides that tantalise readers by showing them what they could be doing whilst on holiday. The most successful series of these books are those published by the BBC. *Unforgettable Places to See Before You Die*, *Unforgettable Things to Do Before You Die* and *Unforgettable Journeys to Take Before You Die* are all lavishly illustrated lists of both accessible and adventurous activities and destinations for all types of travel, which should inspire you to look beyond your surroundings and expand your horizons.

Phrasebooks

A handful of phrases can go a long way and make a real difference to a visit to a foreign country. Just trying to interact in the local language will usually open doors and guarantee you a warm response, or at least generate a giggle from your hosts at your attempt to master their language. Most phrasebooks are handy, pocket-sized books that are usually picked up as additional purchases by curious travellers eager to make a connection. Although general guidebooks usually contain a smattering of the most common, essential phrases, specific language guides contain much more useful information on grammar and pronounciation as well as a larger vocabulary list that is designed not just to kick-start a conversation but to maintain one. Lonely Planet now produces 56 phrasebooks for 120 languages, giving it the most comprehensive language coverage by a travel publisher. Berlitz is well-respected in this field for its user-friendly phrasebooks and more in-depth Travel Packs, which contain a phrasebook and an audio recording designed to help you learn the language, whilst Rough Guide and Eyewitness also have extensive lists of language books full of everyday phrases and useful menu-reader sections.

Inevitably, this list does not include all travel publishers or their available guides. New books are constantly being produced, whilst older ones go out of print or become unavailable. If possible, you should visit a specialist travel bookshop before you make your decision, in order to see the comprehensive range of books on offer, to gain inspiration and to speak to someone with experience either of the guides themselves or of the destination that you intend to visit.

Choosing maps
by Alex Stewart

MOST OF US RELY ON MORE THAN JUST THE SUN, the stars and the help of a few friendly locals to get around when we travel. Whilst guidebooks often contain a limited selection of maps, most of us opt for an actual map. A good map does a lot more than simply prevent you from getting lost; it enables you to see things you might otherwise have missed and to select the quickest, safest or most scenic route to your destination. Lightweight, inexpensive paper maps represent a truly concentrated source of information. Used correctly, they can far surpass the usefulness of a guidebook or even local knowledge in the pursuit of the remote or the unknown. In some circumstances, they may even get you out of trouble.

Often advance planning is the key to a successful trip and maps can form an invaluable part of this preparation. However, the information contained on a map can be difficult to decipher and it only becomes a useful tool if you have chosen the correct map for your purpose and can read it properly. Below are a handful of tips to try and make the process of selecting a scale and an appropriate map easier. Do bear in mind however, that trying to pick up good quality maps locally, particularly in certain parts of the world, can be surprisingly difficult or even nigh impossible, so you should buy what you need before you depart when possible. Because standards of map production are not the same the world over, you may have to settle for what you can get, which may be less detailed than you'd ideally like or older than you'd hoped for.

Try to purchase the most up-to-date map since an area will inevitably continue to develop over time and as it does, so the information shown on older maps will become inaccurate and even obsolete. This is of vital importance in urban or developed areas where rates of change occur very rapidly, but is obviously of less significance if you are buying a map purely for the representation of terrain, since relief is likely to only change very slowly. Most cartographers are sensitive to the relative rates of change and update their maps accordingly, choosing to revise urban maps far more frequently than those for rural or wilderness areas.

The key element when choosing a map is to find a knowledgeable source for your purchase that can offer sensible advice and an appraisal of the options currently available to you.

Map components

A map is essentially a plan of the ground, a bird's eye view of the terrain. The shape of the land is shown by contours at regular intervals. However, a map is selective in what it shows and for this reason you must be aware that it may not be 100% accurate. Most maps contain a plethora of information, not all of which will be relevant to you. Most mapmakers have to find a compromise between the often-conflicting demands of different groups of users and usually choose to display the information required by the most number of readers. This information is represented by cartographer's symbols, a kind of conventional shorthand, since space is limited on a map. Experience will mean that these symbols become recognisable, but if in doubt there will be a key in one of the margins that explains the meaning of the symbol. The symbols representing individual features are not shown to scale since they are purely diagrammatic and designed to draw attention clearly to the feature, thus for example, roads appear wider on maps than they are in reality, simply to highlight their route.

Most maps are either topographic or thematic. Topographic maps show the general nature of the country; physical features, type of terrain, location of waterways, forests, marshes, foreshore features and all communication links including roads, railways and water courses, be they man made or natural. Thematic maps are very different. These are usually either tourist or trekking maps. Tourist maps tend to be more basic and simplify the geographical features in order to show only the main roads, landmarks or established points of interest to tourists. Comprehensive coverage is sacrificed for clarity and ease of viewing, meaning that minor roads, smaller towns and less obvious sights are omitted. Trekking maps tend to be more focussed and to show a greater amount of detail, albeit for a specific purpose. The route of the trek is usually overlaid on a topographic representation of the land, which may have been simplified to only show the main features pertinent to a trekker, such as ridges, rocky outcrops, rivers and settlements. These maps are generally sufficient to prevent you from getting lost, at least on the better known routes, but may still be inadequate for venturing off the beaten track or exploring remoter areas. For this you will need a more detailed survey map showing all of the terrain at a far better scale.

Scale

The scale of a map is an indication of how much detail the map contains. Large-scale maps have the most detail whilst small-scale maps contain less detail but usually cover a larger area, giving a better overview of the land. The scale is always shown as the ratio between a unit of length on the map and the equivalent distance on the ground. The main source of confusion arises because large-scale maps have the smallest number, e.g. 1:25,000, whilst a small-scale map is one that may show a much larger figure, for instance 1:7,500,000.

Most national surveys were originally based on the scale 1:50,000, meaning that 1cm on the map represents 500m on the ground, or to put it at its most literal, 1cm on the map is the equivalent to 50,000cm on the ground. At this scale it is obvious that a number of maps are required to cover a country or even a region, so a grid is overlaid over the area and used to relate map sheets of equal size to the areas that they cover and to each other.

Maps are produced at varying scales for different purposes. Since large-scale maps have the highest amount of detail, but cover the smallest area of ground, they are ideal for walkers and people exploring an area in depth. Orienteering maps or maps of town centres tend to be drawn at around 1:15,000; good quality walking maps at 1:25,000 or 1:50,000; Cycling or touring maps at 1:100,000; Motoring maps at 1:250,000 and maps of the entire UK at around 1:1,000,000.

Maps available for parts of the world

Unfortunately, space does not permit a complete analysis of all the main map producers throughout the world and an examination of their relative merits. A general overview by area can however highlight the main cartographers and explore the products that are available.

Worldwide

Few topographic map series cover the entire world. However, air navigation charts come pretty close. They are available at 1:1,000,000 scale (TPC) and 1:500,000 (ONC), which may not sound that impressive but is in some cases – and for some places – the best scale available. Thus they should be considered if all else fails and no alternative is forthcoming. More detailed survey maps are available from the Russian military, but the supply and delivery of these is increasingly erratic and difficult to organise, meaning that they should not be relied upon. The maps are all in Cyrillic, but cover the world at 1:200,000 and occasionally at 1:100,000 and 1:50,000 scale.

Europe

For general travel and route planning, it is hard to beat the maps produced by Michelin, Geocenter, Freytag and Berndt, Kummerley and Frey, Cartographia, Collins and Reise Know-How, a number of which are published in conjunction with Rough Guides, and carry the Rough Guide branding and logo. These publishers also produce good street mapping of the major towns and cities. Unusual, pocket-sized pop-out maps are available for a range of cities worldwide from Compass Maps. For less well known towns please refer to the country text. For want of a better way of listing the more detailed maps I shall start in the west and work east along the Mediterranean coast to Turkey, then start northwards.

In Portugal the main source of large-scale mapping is the Instituto Geografico e Cadastral, which produce maps at 1:50,000 and 1:100,000; some military maps are also available at 1:25,000. Detailed road and tourist mapping for the Algarve is available from a number of different publishers.

For the popular walking areas of mainland Spain, such as the PICOS DE Europa and the Sierra Nevada, excellent commercial maps are available from Editorial Alpina and Migual Adrados. Contoured walking maps for some of the Canary and Balearic Islands are available from Freytag and Berndt. Tourist maps for the popular coastal regions are readily available – IGN Spain publish a provincial series at 1:200,000 that offer a good combination of topographic and road detail. If you are travelling to Barcelona or the Catalan end of the Pyrenees, Survey Catalunya produces a superb series of 1:50,000 maps for the entire province. For the rest of Spain, military survey maps at 1:100,000, 1:50,000 and occasionally at 1:25,000 are available. Town plans can be sourced from Distimaps Telstar.

France is extremely well catered for by its national survey, IGN France, which produces maps at 1:25,000, 1:100,000 and 1:250,000 (1:50,000 also exists but is not readily commercially available) for the entire country. A number of special sheets are also available at variable scales. The IGN France Top 25 series are great for trekkers. Town plans are available from Blay Foldex, Michelin and IGN France.

Italy has a far less comprehensive map coverage and this can present problems for the map user. The national survey is patchy and many of the sheets remain unpublished. Consequently, commercially produced maps are often the most reliable. Touring Club Italiano (TCI), the equivalent of the British AA, and the Instituto Geografico De Agostini both publish excellent maps of the whole country in series at 1:200,000. Frequently these are the best large-scale maps available. However, publishers including IGC, Tabacco, Edizioni Multigraphic and Kompass cover all of the popular walking destinations at 1:25,000 and 1:50,000. Town plans are available from TCI and FMB.

Freytag and Berndt publish the most detailed maps of the Dalmatian Coast and of regions of Croatia at a scale of 1:100,000. Maps at a similar scale are also available from Geodetski Zavod Slovenije. Coverage for the rest of the Balkans is poor, with the best maps generally being available from Freytag and Berndt at around 1:500,000. A map of Kosovo is available however at 1:250,000 from Gizimap.

Greece used to be very difficult to find large-scale mapping for, but a company called Road Editions now produces a number of maps to popular walking regions at 1:50,000 and the Greek Islands at scales from 1:40,000-1:100,000. The quality of the maps varies, but in general they provide reasonable contour information, trekking routes and up-to-date road information. Toubis also publish a set of good maps for the Greek Islands whilst Harms Verlag has two 1:100,000 contoured maps covering Eastern and Western Crete.

Finding maps of Turkey can be difficult. The largest-scale mapping that is readily available, as a consistent series, is from Ryborsch at 1:500,000, although supply of these can be erratic. The popular coastal areas are also covered by a selection of Turkish and other European publishers, but at smaller scales.

The best maps of Switzerland come from the Swiss national survey. Produced at scales of 1:100,000, 1:50,000 and 1:25,000 the maps are generally considered to be exemplary in terms of accuracy and clarity. Special series highlighting trekking and skiing routes are also available. Kummerley and Frey also publish a series of walking and cycling maps at 1:60,000 in addition to the Official Public Transport Map. A strong series of street maps are available from Orell Fussli.

Austria's national survey is a reliable source of information, but excellent coverage of walking and skiing areas at 1:25,000 and 1:50,000 comes from Kompass, Freytag and Berndt and Alpenvereinskarte. Germany is more complicated as each state has its own mapping department. These usually produce reliable maps though, and the Baden-Wurttemburg survey of the Black Forest is particularly strong. ADFC produces cycling maps at 1:150,000 whilst ADAC are responsible for publishing the most detailed street plans and probably has the most comprehensive list of titles.

Each of the Benelux countries are well covered by their national surveys at 1:25,000 and 1:50,000 and there are also a number of very detailed road atlases available. The Dutch publisher ANWB publishes good cycling maps for the Netherlands at 1:50,000 as well as an excellent series of road maps at 1:100,000.

The Czech and Slovak Republics are well mapped by local outfits and the resulting maps are easily available from specialist map stores. Good walking maps for the Czech republic are available from compass, whilst Freytag and Berndt produce those for Slovakia.

In the far north, the Scandinavian countries all have their own national surveys, which produce high-quality topographical mapping at 1:50,000. In addition, special sheets often cover the most popular areas and are frequently excellent value for money.

North America

Survey mapping is available for the United States and Alaska, although it is not of the highest quality. This is understandable given the huge distances involved. Scales range from 1:24,000 to 1:500,000 and one-off sheets are often available for particularly popular areas. If you are travelling to any of the National Parks, you are better off with one of the excellent NGS/Trails Illustrated maps. Printed on waterproof, tear-resistant paper they are aimed at the outdoor enthusiast. In California, the Tom Harrison maps are good alternatives too. Detailed road atlases for each state are available from De Lorme. Good quality regional, state and city mapping is available from Rand McNally for almost the entire country.

The Canadian survey covers the entire country at scales of 1:50,000 and 1:250,000 and is readily available. Specially prepared sheets that are accompanied with tourist information also cover some of the National parks. Trekking maps are available from Gemtrek at a variety of scales. Motorway coverage and town plans come courtesy of Allmaps, ITMB and Mapart.

Central America, Mexico and the Caribbean

Survey maps or indeed any large-scale mapping for these countries is difficult to obtain, but you should be able to secure reasonable coverage for the more popular destinations. Good general maps are available from ITMB and in some areas Rough Guides. In Mexico, local publisher Guia Roji produces good road maps of each state. The Caribbean is well catered for by IGN France, which publishes a host of excellent maps at scales appropriate for both general use and walking.

South America

Topographic survey maps for a number of South American countries can be ordered from their national survey organisations. You should be aware though that many of these maps are out-of-date and supply is slow and erratic and may take months. Good quality regional maps of Chile are available from JLM Mapas at a variety of scales. Most of South America's popular trekking destinations have good commercial maps covering them. Maps produced by the South American Explorer's Club cover all the mountain ranges of Bolivia and Peru, the Inca Trail in Peru and Aconcagua in Argentina. Zagier & Urruty publish topographic maps for chunks of Patagonia and also produce two excellent maps of Aconcagua. Street mapping of major cities only is available from a number of local sources and these can generally be ordered.

Africa

The African continent presents a number of problems for the traveller looking to buy maps and it is useful to know a little about the colonial history of each country in order to help try and track down survey material. Ex-British colonies were surveyed by the Directorate of Overseas Survey, which has unfortunately ceased to exist. Ex-French colonies are covered by IGN France, although often at scales no better than 1:1,000,000. Some African countries have their own surveys, but these are generally very difficult to come by and supply can take many months. The exception is South Africa, which has an excellent survey organisation that produces high quality maps. Many of the national parks here are mapped by commercial publishers to a very high standard. Availability is often affected by the current political climate and you may consequently have to settle for general road maps or air navigation charts.

Middle East

Survey mapping is frequently restricted in many of the Middle Eastern countries and not available for public sale. At present, the only country selling maps of this calibre to the public is Israel. Geoprojects produce an excellent series of general maps that provide an overview of each country. Once again, air navigation charts often represent the best alternative in terms of large-scale mapping.

Indian Subcontinent

Although this part of the world remains hugely popular with travellers, there is an inverse amount of detailed mapping available to the general public. Consequently, a number of publishers have produced good maps for the walking and trekking regions of Northern India, Pakistan and Nepal. Nepal is particularly well covered, with a survey of its own that covers most of the popular areas and a wonderful series of contoured maps for eastern and central Nepal from Nelles. Two other trekking companies, Mandala and Himalayan Map House, also produce a variety of trekking maps for Nepal. There are also specific sheets to be had for Everest and its national park, the most striking of which is from the National Geographic Society at 1:50,000. Outside of Nepal, Leomann produce a series of sketched trekking maps for nearly all of the accessible parts of the Indian Himalaya and the Karakoram. Regional relief mapping for the whole of India and Pakistan is available from Nelles at 1:500,000, whilst a basic series of state and city maps for India can be had from TTK. Finally, reprints of some of the AMS/U502 series at 1:250,000 are available from Stanfords Map and Travel Bookshop, although these are now quite old and the coverage is incomplete.

China, Japan and Korea and South-East Asia

Excellent survey mapping is available for Japan, but the text is in Japanese and it can be time consuming and costly to secure. Survey mapping for China and Korea is not available, and the Russian military version is now increasingly difficult to obtain. Nelles produce a number of good regional maps of China at 1:1,500,000, whilst Reise Know-How have less detailed maps of Eastern and Western China. Individual province or city maps can be obtained but often only with Chinese or Korean script. Basic topographic maps for Hong Kong are however available.

The vast areas of South-East Asia, Indonesia, Malaysia, Papua New Guinea, the Philippines and the Pacific Islands again poses many problems to the traveller who wishes to obtain accurate, detailed mapping. Nelles and a company called Periplus produce the best general maps, which often feature inset maps at a larger-scale of the most popular regions.

Australia and New Zealand

Excellent survey mapping exists for Australia and New Zealand, as does a wide range of good quality commercial mapping. Australian publisher UBD produces a comprehensive range of state and regional maps, as does Hema, whilst a range of town plans and road atlases can be had from UBD, Hema and Gregory's. New Zealand survey maps are produced under the brand name Infomap and these range from walking scale up to route-planning scale maps of the entire country. An excellent general road atlas for both islands is available from New Zealand Mini Maps, as are maps of each island individually. Hema also produce good quality maps for each island. Detailed walking scale maps for many of the National Parks and popular tracks are available from the New Zealand Department of Conservation.

Inevitably no one map supplier can hold all of these maps in stock, so allow plenty of time when ordering or trying to source unusual maps. As with guidebooks, the most solid piece of advice is to consult a specialist retailer who can then talk you through the various options open to you and best advise you on what to take and how to get hold of it. ❧

ALEX STEWART *is Senior Buyer at Stanfords, the map and travel book retailer. He is also a freelance travel writer and has written several guidebooks, including 'New Zealand's Great Walks' and 'Kilimanjaro – A Complete Trekker's Guide'.*

Book and map sources

Publishers

AA PUBLISHING
UK tel: 0990 448866
www.theAA.com
Britain's largest travel
publisher.

A & C BLACK
UK tel: 020 7758 0200
www.acblack.com

BBC WORLDWIDE
UK tel: 020 8433 2000
www.bbcworldwide.com
Mainly publishes books
related to TV and radio
series also language
learning books and
materials.

BFP BOOKS
UK tel: 020 8882 3315
www.thebfp.com
Publishes *The Freelance
Photographer's Market
Handbook.*

BRADT TRAVEL GUIDES
UK tel: 01753 893 444
www.bradt-travelguides.
com
Publishers of travel guides.

**THE BRITISH
CARTOGRAPHIC SOCIETY**
UK tel: 02380 792 477
www.cartography.org.uk
Association dedicated to
developing the world of
maps.

CADOGAN GUIDES
UK tel: 020 7611 4660
www.cadoganguides.com
Series of specialist guides
for travellers.

CHATTO & WINDUS LTD
UK tel: 020 7840 8522
www.randomhouse.co.uk
Travel books.

CHRYSALIS BOOKS GROUP
UK tel: 020 7314 1400

www.chrysalisbooks.co.uk
Compendium of books on
all subjects.

CICERONE
UK tel: 01539 562069
www.cicerone.co.uk
Outdoor guide books.

CROWOOD PRESS
UK tel: 01672 520280
www.crowoodexpress.
co.uk
Mountaineering and
walking books.

COLLINS BARTHOLOMEW
UK tel: 0141 306 3752
www.bartholomewmaps.
com
Publishers of maps in all
forms, topographic, guides
and atlases to name a few.

**COLUMBUS TRAVEL
PUBLISHING**
UK tel: 01322 616 344
www.
columbustarvelguides.
com
Publishes *The World Travel
Guide,* the travel agents'
bible, plus many more
titles.

DG&G GAZETTEERS PLUS
UK tel: 0800 731 0163
www.dggtravelinfo.co.uk

DICK PHILLIPS
UK tel: 01434 381440
www.cycleweb.co.uk
Through cycle tours has a
specialist mapping
knowledge of Iceland.

FODORS
UK tel: 020 7840 8400
www.fodors.com
Guidebook publisher.

**FOOTPRINT TRAVEL
GUIDES**
UK tel: 01225 469141
www.footprintguides.com
Travel guides for the
independent traveller.

FROMMERS
www.frommers.com

Publishes many travel
books and website features
specialist travel section.

GLOBE PEQUOT PRESS
USA tel: (203) 458 4500
www.globepequot.com
Travel publisher, mainly
on USA and Canada.

**HARPER COLLINS WORLD
ATLAS RANGE**
UK tel: 020 8741 7070
www.collins.co.uk
Up-to-date atlases for
every kind of desire.

HODDER HEADLINE
UK tel: 020 7873 6000
www.hodderheadline.
co.uk
Travel guides to
mountaineering sites.

HYDROGRAPHIC DEPT, UK
UK tel: 01823 723 364
www.nahste.ac.uk
Admiralty Charts and
publications used by
British Navy.

INSIGHT GUIDES
UK tel: 01476 541 080
www.insightguides.com
Publishers of visual
guidebooks and maps.

**INSTITUT GEOGRAPHIQUE
NATIONAL**
France tel: 01 43 98 80 00
www.ign.fr
Publishes and sells maps
of France with
recommendations for
activities.

KUMMERLY + FREY
www.swissmaps.ch
Publishes charts and
political, topographic,
road and other maps.

**LONELY PLANET
PUBLICATIONS**
UK tel: 020 7841 9098
USA tel: 510 893 8556
www.lonelyplanet.com
Huge guidebook
publisher, books on most
countries and cities.

MAP MARKETING
UK tel: 08705 862 013
www.mapmarketing.com
Laminated maps framed
or unframed of the world.

MICHELIN ROUTE PLANNER
www.viamichelin.co.uk
Route planner, maps and
driving directions.

MOON TRAVEL GUIDE BOOKS
UK tel: 0208 804 0400
USA tel: 800/285 4078
www.moon.com

NATIONAL GEOGRAPHIC SOCIETY
UK tel: +1 813 979 6845
USA tel: 800 647 5463
www.nationalgeographic.com
Publishes maps, atlases,
books to accompany
National Geographic
magazine.

NATIONAL OCEAN & ATMOSPHERIC ADMINISTRATION (NOAA)
USA tel: 202 482 6090
www.noaa.gov
Provides geographical
weather maps.

NPA SATELLITE MAPPING
UK tel: 01732 865023
www.npagroup.com
Offers detailed satellite
mapping.

OAG
UK tel: 01582 695 050
USA tel: 800 DIALOAG
www.oag.com
Has a comprehensive
range of guides for the
professional travel planner.

NPA SATELLITE MAPPING
UK tel: 01732 865023
www.npagroup.com
Offers detailed satellite
mapping.

ORDNANCE SURVEY
UK tel: 08456 05 05 05
www.ordnancesurvey.

co.uk
Official UK agency with
the latest digital mapping,
including international
mapping.

RAND MCNALLY
USA tel: 800 777 6277
www.randmcnally.com
Publishers of maps, atlases
and offer advise on trip
planning.

RANDOM HOUSE
UK tel: 020 7840 8400
www.randomhouse.co.uk
Publishers of travel and
holiday titles.

ROUGH GUIDES TRAVEL
UK tel: 020 7010 3701
USA tel: 212 414 3635
www.roughguides.com
Travel guide series for
independent travellers,
also accessible on their
website.

ROYAL GEOGRAPHIC SOCIETY
UK tel: 020 7591 3000
www.rgs.org
Publishes the Royal
Geographic Society
Illustrated featuring
images from all over the
world plus academic books
and Geographical.

THAMES AND HUDSON
UK tel: 020 7845 5000
www.thamesandhudson.co.uk
Publisher of high-quality
illustrated books on world
cultures.
Time Out
UK tel: 020 7813 3000
USA tel: 646 432 3000
www.timeout.com
Growing number of
international city guides.

ULYSSES TRAVEL GUIDES
UK tel: 01 4338 8950
USA tel: 514 843 9447
www.ulyssesguides.com
Guide books for travellers.

US GEOLOGICAL SURVEY (USGS)
USA tel: 1 888 275 8747
www.usgs.gov
Information and
distribution of maps
relating to the USA.

VACATION WORK PUBLICATIONS
UK tel: 01865 241 978
www.vacationwork.co.uk
Books and guides for the
budget traveller.

WILDERNESS PRESS
USA tel: (510) 558 1666 /
(800) 443 7227
www.wildernesspress.com
Outdoor books and maps
of North America.

W W NORTON & COMPANY
USA tel: 212 354 5500
www.wwnorton.com
Publishers of the Blue
Guides.

Bookstores and shops

BLACKWELL'S
UK tel: (1865) 261 381
www.blackwell.co.uk
Excellent selection of
books and staff to guide
you through them.

THE BOOKSELLERS ASSOCIATION
UK tel: 020 7802 0802
www.booksellers.org.uk
Directory of members and
information on bookshops
worldwide.

BORDERS AND BOOKS ETC
UK tel: 734 477 1100
www.bordersgroupinc.com
Chain of stores with a
good travel section.

DAUNT BOOKS
UK tel: 020 7224 2295
www.allinlondon.co.uk/directory/
Bookshop with a

comprehensive travel section, guides, fictional and non-fiction.

THE GOOD BOOK GUIDE
UK tel: 01626 831122
www.thegoodbookguide.com

FOYLES
UK tel: 020 7437 5660
www.foyles.co.uk
Famous English bookshop with a good travel department.

HATCHARDS
UK tel: 020 7439 9921
www.hatchards.co.uk
Classic English bookshop in London's Piccadilly.

HIPPOCRENE BOOKS
USA tel: 718 454 2366
www.hippocrenebooks.com
Can order, online, travel guides and literature, plus language guides.

LATITUDE MAPS & GLOBES
UK tel: 01707 663090
www.latitudemapsandglobes.co.uk
Map and globe specialists.

MAPS WORLDWIDE LTD
UK tel: 01225 707 004
www.mapsworldwide.com
Map retailer plus a worldwide store guide.

NATIONAL MAP CENTRE
UK tel: 020 7222 2466
www.mapstore.co.uk

STANFORDS
www.stanfords
The world's largest map and travel bookshop stocks 40,000 maps, atlases, globes, travel guides, travel literature, charts, marine and diving books, maps on CD-ROM and GPS receivers. Recent additions include travel accessories, children's books and fiction. Branches in London, Bristol and Manchester.

TRAILFINDERS TRAVEL CENTRE
UK tel: 020 7292 1888
www.trailfinders.com
Stocks maps and guides alongside travel equipment.

THE TRAVEL BOOKSHOP
UK tel: 020 7229 5260
www.thetravelbookshop.co.uk
Provides the traveller with a complete package, regional guides, cookery, relevant fiction, history and much more.

WATERSTONES
UK tel: 020 7851 2400
www.waterstones.co.uk
Branches throughout the UK with an excellent travel section.

Web-only booksellers and sites

www.amazon.com

www.barnesandnoble.com

www.booksonline.co.uk

www.mapblast.com
Worldwide maps and driving directions.

Top travel periodicals

African Affairs
Journals Subscription Department
Oxford University Press
Great Clarendon Street
Oxford, OX2 6DP, UK
http://afraf.oxfordjournals.org
Published on behalf of The Royal African Society by Oxford University Press the journal features political, economic and social developments.

Australian Gourmet Traveller
ACP Magazines Ltd
54-58 Park Street
Sydney, NSW 2000
Australia
Tel: (02) 9282 8000
http://gourmet.ninemsn.com.au
Consumer publication for travellers who enjoy food.

BBC Wildlife Magazine
Origin Publishing Ltd
14th Floor Tower House
Fairfax Street, Bristol
BS1 3BN, UK
Tel: 0117 927 9009
www.bbcwildlifemagazine.com
Monthly magazine on wildlife, conservation and environmental issues.

BBC On Air Magazine
BBC World Service
Bush House
Strand, London
WC2B 4PH, UK
Tel: 020 7557 2211
www.bbc.co.uk/worldservice/onair

Business Traveller
68-69 St Martin's Lane
London WC2N 4JS, UK
Tel:020 7845 6510

Travel magazines at a glance

There are now quite a few magazines devoted solely to travel, and most mainstream magazines also include travel articles of one kind or another. Many such publications are included in the list below, alongside specific travel titles. Of the dedicated travel magazines, the best known are:

Traveller Heavyweight and high-quality, offering adventurous and authentic coverage of cutting edge travel. Grandaddy of the genre at 35 years old.

Wanderlust Has established itself as the best practical magazine for independent travellers. Lively and useful.

Condé Nast Traveller The glamour-seeker's bible. Originally claimed to offer 'luxury on a budget', but is now such stuff as dreams are made on.

Sunday Times Travel Newest on this shortlist, but highly successful as a guide to where and how to take your holidays.

National Geographic Still the best in the world, though sometimes accused of blandness. Explores the world in stunning photographs and highly accessible text.

For information on travel sections within national magazines and newspapers, check the Writers' & Artists' Yearbook, which also lists the editors. If you are considering submitting your own work for publication, you might find The Writer's Handbook useful. If you want training as a travel journalist or photographer, the UK field leaders are Travellers' Tales, a training agency offering courses for beginners (see www.travellerstales.org).

www.businesstraveller.com
Information for the business traveller on health, security, dining, airline and hotel information on a monthly basis.

Canadian Geographic
39 McArthur Avenue
Ottawa, ON
K1L 8L7 Canada
Tel: (613) 745 4629
www.canadiangeographic.ca

Camping and Caravanning Club
Greenfields House
Westwood Way
Coventry
CV4 8JH, UK
Tel: 024 7669 4995

www.campingandcaravanningclub.co.uk
Journal for camping enthusiasts.

Comet Newsletter
Lonely Planet Publications
72-82 Roseberry Avenue
Clerkenwell
London
EC1R 4RW, UK
Tel: 020 7841 9000
also at:
150 Linden Street
Oakland, CA
94607, USA
Tel: 510 893 8555
www.lonelyplanet.com/comet/

Conde Nast Traveller
Vogue House
Hanover Square
London

W1S 1JU, UK
Tel: 020 7499 9080
www.cntraveller.com

Escape
www.escapetotheedge.co.uk
Online magazine dedicated to the Highlands and Islands of north and west Scotland.

Essentially America
Phoenix International Publishing
PO Box 615
Horsham
West Sussex
RH13 5WF, UK
www.essentiallyamerica.com
Dedicated to travel and lifestyle within the USA and Canada, quarterly.

Explore
54 St. Patrick Street
Toronto, Ontario
M5T 1V1, Canada
Tel: (416) 599 2000
www.explore-mag.com
Canada's outdoor
adventure magazine

The Explorers Journal
The Explorers Club
46 East 70th Street
New York
NY, 10021, USA
Tel: 212 628 8383
www.explorers.org/
publications/journal/
Published quarterly and
written by Club Members
around the globe,
highlighting areas of
exploration.

Flight International
www.flightinternational.
com
Aviation interest.

Food and Travel
12 King Street
Richmond
Surrey
TW9 1ND, UK
Tel: 0208 332 9090
www.foodandtravel.com
Monthly glossy featuring
articles on food and travel
worldwide.

Geographical Magazine
Winchester House
259-269 Old Marylebone
Road, London
NW1 5RA, UK
Tel: 020 7170 4360
www.geographical.co.uk
Magazine of The Royal
Geographic Society with
high quality articles on
travel, environment and
wildlife.

Globe
The Globe Trotters Club
BCM/Roving
London

WC1N 3XX, UK
www.globetrotters.co.
uk/globe/
Club members share their
travelogues, information
and experiences for the
independent traveller.

tgo (The Great Outdoors)
Newsquest Magazines
200 Renfield Street
Glasgow
G2 3QB, UK
Tel: 0141 302 7718
www.tgomagazine.co.uk
Monthly magazine for
hill-walkers, backpackers,
trekkers and scramblers.

Holiday Which?
Castlemead
Gascoyn Way, Hertford
SG14 1LH, UK
Tel: 01903 828557
www.
holidaywhichfreetrial.
co.uk
Consumer issues magazine
on what to look out for,
published by the
Consumers' Association.

Islands
460 North Orlando
Avenue, Suite 200,
Winter Park, FL
32789, USA
Tel: 407 628 4802
www.islands.com
Guide to island travel,
small and large.

International Travel News
2120 28th Street
Sacramento, CA
95818 USA
Tel: 916 457 3643
www.intltravelnews.com
Subscribers write into this
monthly publication with
practical travel
information.

Mountain Biking UK
30 Monmouth Street
Bath, BA1 2BW, UK

Tel: 01225 442244
www.mbuk.com
Monthly publication for
mountain bikers.

National Geographic
National Geographic
Society
1145 17th Street NW
Washington, DC
20036-4688, USA
Tel: 800 647 5463
www.nationalgeographic.
com

*National Geographic
Traveller*
711 Fifth Avenue, 17th
floor
New York, NY
10022, USA
Tel: +1 212 610 5535
www.nationalgeographic.
com/traveler/

*New York Times Travel
website*
www.nytimes.com/pages
/travel/
Readers' reviews, advice
for practical and cultural
travel: excellent website.

*Nomad Adventure
Newsletter*
www.noadadventure.com/
content/home/newsletter
For rock climbing,
kayaking and other
outdoor activities.

*Official Airlines Guide
(OAG)*
Church Street
Dunstable
Bedfordshire
LU5 4HB, UK
UK Tel: 01582 695 050
USA Tel: 800 DIALOAG
www.oag.com
Airline database with
details of over 1000 airlines
and 3000 airports.

Outside Magazine
400 Market Street

Santa Fe
New Mexico,
87501, USA
www.outside.away.com
Lifestyle magazine with
adventure travel, gear
reviews and archive issues.

Salon website
41 East 11th Street, 11th
floor
New York, NY
10003, USA
Tel: 212 905 6120
www.salon.com./travel/
Articles on travel and food.

South American Explorers
Calle Piura 135
Miraflores, Lima
Peru
Tel:51 1 445 3306
USA Tel: 607 277 0488
www.saemexplo.org/
Source of information for
South American travel
with four club houses
around the continent.

Sunday Times Travel
1 Virginia Street
London
E98 1XY, UK
Tel: 020 7782 6000
www.timesonline.co.uk

Travel and Leisure
1120 Avenue of the
Americas, 10th floor
New York, NY
10036, USA
Tel: 212 382 5856
www.amexpub.com
Glossy title for American
Express members.

Travel Trade Gazette
CMP Information
7th Floor Ludgate House
245 Blackfriars Road
London, SE1 9UY, UK
Tel: 020 7921 8029
www.ttglive.com/
Weekly travel industry
paper.

Traveller
WEXAS
45-49 Brompton Street
Knightsbridge
London, SW3 1DE, UK
Tel: 020 7581 4130
www.traveller.org.uk

Travel Smart
PO Box 397
Dobbs Ferry,
NY, 10522, USA
Tel: 800 327 3633
www.travelsmart.com
Monthly newsletter for
affluent travellers.

Traveltips
PO Box 580188
Flushing, New York
NY, 11358, USA
Tel: 800 872 8584
www.travltips.com
First hand accounts of
freighter trips and other
voyages.

Wanderlust
PO Box 1832
Windsor, Berkshire
SL4 1YT, UK
Tel: 01753 620 426
www.wanderlust.co.uk

World factsites

www.wexas.com
Website of Wexas, the
traveller's club, with online
version of *The Traveller's
Handbook*, links and trip-
planning facilities.

Travellers' tips

www.travellerslounge.
co.uk
Information by and for the
international traveller.

www.virtualtourist.com
Real travellers join to share
experiences.

http://geocities.yahoo.com
Network of people around

the world willing to share
their experiences or
answer questions about
their area.

www.webfoot.com/travel/
tips/tips.top.html
Advise for the traveller,
from learning about where
you are going to what to
pack.

www.travelling-tips.com
Tips covering all areas,
from airlines to
preparation.

Destination data

www.traveldex.co.uk
Efficient site checking
destination details.

www.travel-guides.com
Click on your destination
for a full briefing.

www.tourist-offices.org.uk
www.towd.com
Details of tourist offices
worldwide and where they
are, plus links to country
and destination sites.

www.officialtravelinfo.
com
Information and
destination details and
overviews.

www.kropla.com
Helping travellers
worldwide with guides to
everything electrical:
dialling codes, mobile
phone guide, electricity
guides.

www.worldtimeserver.com
Find out the time
anywhere in the world.

www.officialtravelguide.
com
Quick and efficient guide
to your travelling needs.
www.bugbog.com

Comprehensive information guide, plus pictures and maps of destinations.

www.cities.com
Database containing information on cities around the globe.

www.fco.gov/
knowbeforeyougo
Foreign Office travel advice on all areas.
It is also worth looking at Section 2 for individual country websites.

News overseas

www.thepaperboy.com.au
www.onlinenewspapers.
com
www.newsdirectory.com
www.worldpress.org
Websites containing links to the world's newspapers.

www.bbc.co.uk/
worlservice
www.cnn.com
www.reuters.com
World news coverage from global networks.

Internet cafes

www.world66.com/
netcafeguide

www.cybercaptive.com

www.netcafes.com

Finance

www.xe.net/ucc/
www.oanda.com
www.x-rates.com
These show currency rates and conversion guides.

www.travlex.co.uk
Buy foreign currency online and collect it at the airport.
www.americanexpress.
com

Information on travellers' cheques, flight and travel insurance and links to currency converters.

www.thomascook.com/
currency/
Guide to buying foreign currency online, travellers' cheques and currency guides.

www.globalrefund.com
Where and how to get VAT refunds and a credit card that allows you to pay in your own currency at point of sale.

www.news.ft.com/
yourmoney/
http://visa.via.infonow.net
/locator/global/jsp/Search
Page
www.mastercard.com/
atmlocator/index
ATM locators worldwide.

Emergencies

http://travel.state.gov/law/
info/judicial/judicial_702.
html
Legal help abroad, country-by-country.

www.ofj.admin.ch/
themen/rechtshilfe/
index-rh-e.html
Site offering international legal assistance in criminal matters.

It is also worth looking at Section 2 for emergency contacts in each country and embassy contacts.

Travel industry

www.airmiles.co.uk
Check your air-miles balance and shop for special offers.
http://flyaow.com
Information and links to most airlines.

www.travelsource.com
Links to travel deals and travel related business worldwide.

www.lastminute.com
Late travel bargains, going out advise and offers.
www.ThisIsTravel.co.uk
Website offering travel guides and cheap deals.

www.hometravelagency
.com/dictionary/
Helping you decipher travel jargon.

Official representation

www.projectvisa.com
Visa and embassy information worldwide.

www.fco.gov.uk
Links to foreign and commonwealth offices.

It is also worth looking at Section 2 for countries' embassy contacts.

General interest

www.mumsnet.com
Advice for family travellers.

www.bugpacific.com
Backpackers travel guide.

www.artoftravel.com
World backpacking guide.

www.sleepinginairports.
net
The budget travellers guide to sleeping in airports.

www.travel-library.com
Online guide covering all areas of travelling.

www.charitychallenge.
com
Travel while raising funds for charities.

www.bikersadvice.co.uk
Travelling tips for motor
cyclists.

And finally...

http://goeurope.about.
com/cs/blogs/a/travel_
blogs.htm
Advice on creating your
own web log for your
travels.

Language learning services

BBC WORLDWIDE SERVICE
Woodlands 80 Wood Lane
London, W12 OTT, UK
or PO Box 1922, Glasgow,
G2 3WT, UK
Tel: 08700 100 222
www.bbc.co.uk/languages/
Good range of learning
materials including books,
CDs, videos, courses for all
levels and advice.

THE BRITISH INSTITUTE OF FLORENCE
Palazzo Strozzino
Piazza Strozzi 2
50123 Firenze, Italia
Tel: +39 055 2677 8200
www.britishinstitute.it

CENTRE FOR INFORMATION ON LANGUAGE TEACHING (CILT)
20 Bedfordbury, London
WC2N 4LB, UK
Tel: 020 7379 5101
www.cilt.org.uk/
Government sponsored
centre for languages
providing information,
research and teaching for
business or recreation.

COMMERCIAL TRAINING LANGUAGE LTD
Ameycroft House 91
Greenaway Lane
Hackney Matlock
Derbyshire
DE4 2QA, UK
Tel: 01629 732653
www.languagetraining.
com

LINGUAPHONE GROUP LTD
Liongate Enterprise Park
80 Morden Road
Mitcham, Surrey
CR4 4PH, UK
Tel: 020 8687 6000
www.linguaphone.com
Centres based all around
the world, Linguaphone
offers an all round
comprehensive service in
many languages.

INSTITUT FRANCAIS
14 Cromwell Place
London SW7 2LA, UK
Tel: 020 7581 2701
Offers an array of courses
ranging from learning
about French culture to
business French for all
levels of students.

GOETHE INSTITUTE
50 Princes Gate
Exhibition Road
London SW7 2PH, UK
Tel: 020 7596 4000
www.goethe.de
German cultural centre.

INSTITUTE OF LINGUISTS
Saxon House 48
Southwark Street
London SE1 1UN, UK
Tel: 020 7940 3100
www.iol.org.uk/
Offers translators, linguists
and language tutors.

KEY LANGUAGES
16/18 Douglas Street
London SW1P 4PB, UK
Tel: 020 7630 6113
www.keylanguages.com
Language and cultural
awareness training.

THE OPEN UNIVERSITY
The Faculty of Education
and Language Studies
Walton Hall
Milton Keynes
MK7 6AA, UK
Tel: 01908 652896
www.open.ac.uk/
education-and-languages

RICHARD LEWIS COMMUNICATIONS
Riversdown House
Warnford, Southampton
Hampshire
SO32 3LH, UK
Tel: 01962 77 11 11
www.crossculture.com
Tailor-made courses for
the corporate market in
UK and abroad.

TRAINING ACCESS POINTS (TAPS)
Up-to-date information
on training and education
all over the country
promoted by the UK
government. Look in the
Yellow Pages or
alternatively ask any local
Civic Library or Chamber
of Commerce for your
local TAPS centre.

Related websites

www.travelang.com

www.freetranslation.com

www.maps2anywhere.com

www.ethnologue.com

Culture shock

Culture shock
by Adrian Furnham

NEARLY EVERY TRAVELLER MUST HAVE EXPERIENCED culture shock at some time or other. Like jet lag, it is an aspect of travel that is both negative and difficult to define. But what precisely is it? When and why does it occur? And, more importantly, how can we prevent it – or at least cope with it?

Although the experience of culture shock has no doubt been around for centuries, it was only 25 years ago that an anthropologist called Oberg coined the term. Others have attempted to improve upon and extend the concept and have come up with alternative jargon, such as 'culture fatigue', 'role shock' and 'pervasive ambiguity'.

Strain

From the writings of travellers and interviews with tourists, foreign students, migrants and refugees, psychologists have attempted to specify the exact nature of this unpleasant experience. It seems that the syndrome has six facets. Firstly, there is strain caused by the effort of making necessary psychological adaptations – speaking another language, coping with the currency, driving on the other side of the road, etc. Secondly, there is often a sense of loss and a feeling of deprivation with regard to friends, possessions and status. If you are in a place where nobody knows, loves, respects and confides in you, you may feel anonymous and deprived of your status and role in society, as well as bereft of familiar and useful objects. Thirdly, there is often a feeling of rejection – your rejection of the natives and their rejection of you. Travellers stand out by virtue of their skin, clothes and language. Depending on the experience of the natives, they may be seen as unwanted intruders, an easy rip-off or friends.

A fourth symptom of culture shock is confusion. Travellers can become unsure about their roles, their values, their feelings and sometimes about who they are. When a people lives by a different moral and social code from your own, interaction for even a comparatively short period can be very confusing. Once one becomes more aware of cultural differences, typical reactions of surprise, anxiety, even disgust and indignation occur. The way foreigners treat their animals, eat food, worship their god or perform their *toilettes* often cause amazement and horror to naive travellers. Finally, culture shock often involves feelings of impotence, due to an inability to cope with the new environment.

Little England

Observers of sojourners and long-term travellers have noted that there are usually two extreme reactions to culture shock: those who act as if they 'never left home' and those who immediately 'go native'. The former chauvinists create 'little Englands' in foreign fields, refusing to compromise their diet or dress and, like the proverbial mad dogs, insisting on going out in the midday sun. The latter reject all aspects of their own culture and enthusiastically do in Rome as the Romans do.

Most travellers, however, experience less dramatic but equally uncomfortable reactions to culture shock. These may include excessive concern over drinking water, food, dishes and bedding; fits of anger over delays and other minor frustrations; excessive fear of being cheated, robbed or injured; great concern over minor pains and interruptions; and a longing to be back at the idealised home, "where you can get a good cup of tea and talk to sensible people."

But, as any seasoned traveller will know, often one begins to get used to, and even learns to like, the new culture. In fact writers have suggested that people go through a number of phases when living in a new culture. Oberg, in his original writings, listed five stages. First, the 'honeymoon', which is characterised by enchantment, fascination, enthusiasm and admiration for the new culture, as well as the formation of cordial (but superficial) relationships. In this stage, people are generally intrigued and euphoric. Many tourists never stay long enough to move out of the honeymoon period. The second phase heralds crisis and disintegration. It is now that the traveller feels loss, isolation, loneliness and inadequacy, and tends to become depressed and withdrawn. This happens most often after two to six months of living in the new culture.

The third phase is the most problematic and involves reintegration. At this point people tend to reject the host culture, becoming opinionated and negative, partly as a means of showing their self-assertion and growing self-esteem. The fourth stage of 'autonomy' finds the traveller assured, relaxed, warm and empathic because he or she is socially and linguistically capable of negotiating most new and different social situations in the culture.

And finally the 'independent' phase is achieved, characterised by trust, humour and the acceptance and enjoyment of social, psychological and cultural differences.

U-curve

For obvious reasons, this independent phase is called the 'u-curve' hypothesis. If you plot satisfaction and adaptation (x axis) over time (y axis), you see a high point at the beginning, followed by a steep decline, a period at the bottom, but then a steady climb back up. More interestingly, some researchers have shown evidence not of a u-curve but a w-curve, i.e. once travellers return to their home country, they often undergo a similar re-acculturation, again in the shape of a u. Hence a double-u- or w-curve.

Other research has shown similar intriguing findings. Imagine, for instance, that you are going to Morocco for the first time. You are asked to describe or rate both the average Briton and the average Moroccan in terms of their humour, wealth, trustworthiness, etc., both before you go and after you return. Frequently, it has been found that people change their opinions of their own countrymen and women more than that of the foreigners. In other words, travel makes you look much more critically at yourself and your culture than most people think. And this self-criticism may itself be rather unhelpful.

The trouble with these stage theories is that not everyone goes through the stages. Not everyone feels like Nancy Mitford did when she wrote: 'I loathe abroad, nothing would induce me to live there... and, as for foreigners, they are all the same and make me sick.' But I suspect that Robert Morley was not far from the truth when he remarked: "The British tourist is always happy abroad, so long as the natives are waiters."

Then there is also the shock of being visited. Anyone who lives in a popular tourist town soon becomes aware that it is not only the tourist but also the native who experiences culture shock. Of course, the amount and type of shock that tourists can impart to local people is an indication of a number of things, such as the relative proportion of tourists to natives, the duration of their stay, the comparative wealth and development of the two groups and the racial and ethnic prejudices of both.

Of course not everybody will experience culture shock. Older, better-educated, confident and skilful adults (particularly those who speak the language) tend to adapt best. Yet there is considerable evidence that sojourners, such as foreign students, voluntary workers, businessmen, diplomats and even military people, become so confused and depressed that they have to be sent home at great expense. That is why many organisations attempt to lessen culture shock by a number of training techniques. The Foreign Office, the British Council and many multinational companies do this for good reason, having learned from bitter experience.

Training

For a number of reasons, information and advice in the form of lectures and pamphlets, etc., is very popular but not always very useful. The 'facts' that are given are often too general to have any clear, specific application in particular circumstances. Facts emphasise the exotic and ignore the mundane (how to hail a taxi, for example). This technique also gives the impression that the culture can be easily understood; and even if facts are retained, they do not necessarily lead to accommodating behaviour.

A second technique is 'isomorphic training'. This is based on the theory that a major cause of cross-cultural communication problems comes from the fact that most people tend to offer different explanations for each other's behaviour. This technique introduces various episodes that end in embarrassment, misunderstanding or hostility between people from two different cultures. The trainee is then presented with four or five alternative explanations of what went wrong, all of which correspond to different attributions of the observed behaviour. Only one is correct from the perspective of the culture being learned. This is an interesting and useful technique, but depends for much of its success on the relevance of the various episodes chosen.

Perhaps the most successful method is 'skills training'. It has been pointed out that socially inadequate or inept individuals have not mastered the social conventions of their own society. Either they are unaware of the rules and processes of everyday behaviour or, if aware of the rules, they are unable or unwilling to abide by them. They are therefore like strangers in their own land. People newly arrived in an alien culture will be in a similar position and may benefit from simple skills training.

This involves analysing everyday encounters such as buying and selling, introductions and refusal of requests. You will also observe successful culture models engaging in these acts and will practice yourself, helped in the learning process by a video tape of your efforts. This may all sound very clinical, but can be great fun and very informative.

Practical advice

Many travellers, unless on business and with considerable company resources behind them, do not have the time or money to go on courses that prevent or minimise culture shock. They have to leap in at the deep end and hope that they can swim. But there are some simple things they can do that may well prevent the shock and improve communications.

Before departure it is important to learn as much as possible about the society you are visiting. Areas of great importance include:

LANGUAGE: Not only vocabulary but polite usage, when to use higher and lower forms, and particularly how to say "yes" and "no".

NON-VERBAL CUES: Gestures, body contact and eye gaze patterns differ significantly from one country to another and carry very important meanings. Cues of this sort for greeting, parting and eating are most important, and are relatively easily learnt.

SOCIAL RULES: Every society develops rules that regulate behaviour so that social goals can be attained and needs satisfied. Some of the most important rules concern gifts, buying and selling, eating and drinking, timekeeping and bribery and nepotism.

SOCIAL RELATIONSHIPS: Family relationships, classes and castes, and working relationships often differ from culture to culture. The different social roles of the two sexes is perhaps the most dramatic difference between societies, and travellers should pay special attention to this.

MOTIVATION: Being assertive, extrovert and achievement oriented may be desirable in America and Western Europe but this is not necessarily the case elsewhere. How to present oneself, maintain face, etc., is well worth knowing.

Once you have arrived, there are a few simple steps that you can take to help reduce perplexity and understand the natives:

CHOOSE LOCALS FOR FRIENDS: Avoid mixing only with your compatriots or other foreigners. Get to know the natives, who can introduce you to the subtleties and nuances of the culture.

PRACTICAL SOCIAL ACTIVITIES: Do not be put off more complex social encounters but ask for information on appropriate etiquette. People are frequently happy to help and teach genuinely interested and courteous foreigners.

AVOID 'GOOD/BAD' OR 'US/THEM' COMPARISONS: Try to establish how and why people perceive and explain the same act differently, have different expectations, etc. Social behaviour has resulted from different historical and economic conditions and may be looked at from various perspectives.

ATTEMPT MEDIATION: Rather than reject your or their cultural tradition, attempt to select, combine and synthesise the appropriate features of different social systems, whether it is in dress, food or behaviour.

When you return home, the benefits of foreign travel and the prevention of the w-curve may be helped by the following:

BECOME MORE SELF-OBSERVANT: Returning home makes one realise the comparative and normative nature of one's own behaviour, which was previously taken for granted. This in turn may alert one to behaviour that is culturally at odds (and, perhaps, why) – in itself helpful for all future travel.

HELPING THE FOREIGNER: There is no better teaching aid than personal experience. That is why many foreign language schools send their teachers abroad not only to improve their language but to experience the difficulties their students have. Remembering this, we should perhaps be in a better position to help the hapless traveller who comes to our country. Travel does broaden the mind (and frequently the behind), but requires some effort. Preparation, it is said, prevents a pretty poor performance, and travelling in different social environments is no exception. But this preparation may require social, as well as geographic, maps. ❧

ADRIAN FURNHAM is a lecturer in psychology at London University. He is the co-author of 'Culture Shock: Psychological Consequences of Geographic Movement'.

Keeping a sense of humour
by Mark McCrum

MUCH AS I LOVE TRAVELLING, I also find it intensely irritating. The American 'mom' next to you on the Eurostar sharing a crackling sack of candy with her fat-faced kid while her equally plump older sister, the child's *ant*, tells him that he's got a bit of French in him, in fact he's got a bit of German in him, in fact he's got a bit of everything in him, in fact he's *whad ya call a mutt*. This wasn't what you went to Paris for, was it?

So look at it another way. It's funny! And contemporary! And a darn sight more real than a train full of claret-sipping onion-sellers in berets would ever be! So stop trying to read your boring book and just enjoy. And when the ant asks the French guard how long it is before the train goes into the channel tunnel, and the French guard goes "Pff," turns his back and walks off – that's hilarious.

Keeping your sense of humour not only leavens the traveller's way, it brings relief from the inevitable frustrations of travel. At Malaga airport I was once on the verge of strangling the representative of a charter flight operator who had shamelessly diverted our plane to service a football match in Dublin. Then, suddenly, watching a woman from Newcastle asking the glowering Spanish barman repeatedly, and ever more loudly, for "a small cock", my anger melted into laughter. In the end, she got her Coke (with ice, in a glass, no less) and we got our flight. What's a few hours of your life compared to the profits of a dodgy bucket shop anyway?

For the serious, long-term traveller, being able to see the funny side of things can be a lifesaver, not just when it comes to external problems, but also when pitted against the internal bogeymen: the exhaustion, loneliness and depression that can ambush you in even the most gorgeous of places.

Towards the end of a seven-month trip around Australia I found myself driving for three days along the coast road from Adelaide to Melbourne. I'd started out cheerfully in the lovely Adelaide hills, felt exhilarated as I sped across the vast-skied, dazzling salt flats of the Coorong. But by the time I reached the wild-flowered hedgerows of Victoria and, finally, the spectacular rollercoaster they call the Great Ocean Road, I was drained and nervy. At seven pm I finally had to admit to myself that I wasn't going to make my jolly Saturday night rendezvous in the Two Dogs Bar, St Kilda. It was going to be another grim hotel room in another resort where I knew nobody. But even that wasn't available. Typically, I'd picked one of the busiest weekends of the year and there wasn't a bed to be had on the coast. Just as I was in danger of driving off the cliff in a stupor of tiredness, I finally saw a gleaming pink vacancies sign. The only free room the place had cost $140 a night, the lisping Greek receptionist told me, but it had a "luck-thurry double thpa". For some reason, that *thpa* did it. My self-pity alchemised into careless extravagance. I threw my budget to the Southern Ocean winds and lay alone in the huge, heart-shaped pool of bubbles laughing, profoundly grateful that a single word had delivered me from certain death.

Can humour actually protect you from physical danger? In Belfast I went exploring with an English friend down the infamous Falls Road, through the bleak estates where pro-IRA slogans are scrawled on every dirty grey concrete wall to a pub known as The Fort, whose windows were entirely covered with thick steel mesh. We ordered pints of the black stuff and sat down, sharing a booth with a pair of white-haired gents who seemed genial enough, yarning away to each other as Irishmen do. But on hearing our English accents their mood changed. The older of the two leant forward to warn me that I should be very careful, an Englishman walking into a republican pub in an area like this. "Ten years ago, five years ago," he told me, "if you'd walked in here with that accent they'd have had you out the back." In the toilet, he elaborated fiercely, with a gun to my head, finding out exactly who I was. Maybe I was writing a book, but there were plenty of undercover Brits who'd come up with stories like that.

I was as open as I could be with him. I wasn't anti-republican, I said, if I could get to interview Gerry Adams I would. The other man laughed loudly. "Well, you've got the right feller here," he said. "This is Gerry Adams's brother-in-law." He was, too. The laughter broke the ice and half an hour later the brother-in-law paid us the compliment of telling us that the *craic* had been good. We wrote our names on a piece of paper and left feeling considerably safer.

There are numerous instances where a shared sense of the ridiculous can break down even the most vexed of cultural barriers. Visiting South African townships in the last days of apartheid, it was always laughter that bonded. "You know what that stands for," one township host told me, pointing thoughtfully to the label of his bottle of lager. "Let Africans Get Equal Rights." I was in another cramped dwelling with a few guys when there was a knock at the door and a pair of po-faced white American missionaries stood before us. Everyone was very polite to them, even when they asked, in deeply patronising tones, what we all "did". Geoffrey, whose house it was, went round with formal and elaborate career descriptions for each of our group in turn, ending, "and Mr McCrum tells us he is a writer. Indeed we were just saying how unusual it was for us to have a white person among us and now I'm beginning to feel like this is my lucky day." The missionaries nodded seriously, and suddenly I felt that the colour barrier was much less important than the humour barrier.

Being actively prepared to have the mickey taken out of you is in general a wise move. In Kalgoorlie, Western Australia, I stumbled one evening into a bar full of miners, yelling their heads off as they let off steam from their long day in the gold pits. Trying to buy a drink I was harangued by a huge bearded bloke with shaved head and elaborate tattoos who was intrigued by my unusual accent. "We've got a bloody Pom here!" he was soon bellowing, hand clamped on my arm, half turned in his seat towards the gallery of mates behind. Then to the bargirls, who were wearing – this being one of WA's famous "skimpy" bars – nothing more than bra and panties. "Mark's a Pom. The Pom wants to see your tits, Donna – I didn't say that, the Pom said it. Ha ha ha!" Not a situation I'd choose to be in again, but non-directional loud laughter did the trick and Rob ended up showing me the town.

While keeping your sense of humour, don't go thinking that it is the answer to everything. It's at the point where you're getting a joke that others aren't, that you have to be most careful. Especially if they're carrying a machine gun or have the capacity to lock you up. On those occasions the ability to keep a straight face is even more important. Even the twitch of a smirk could be your undoing. ❧

MARK McCRUM has published three travel books – 'Happy Sad Land' (about South Africa), 'No Worries' (about Australia) and 'The Craic' (about Ireland). He has also had seven one-man shows of his landscape watercolours, in galleries from London to Botswana.

Breaking the barriers
by Jon Gardey

B ARRIERS TO COMMUNICATION OFF THE BEATEN TRACK exist just because of who you are: a visitor from another civilisation. It is necessary to show the local people that underneath the surface impression of strange clothes and foreign manners exists a fellow human being.

The first step is to approach local inhabitants as if you are their guest. You are. It is their country, their village, their hut, their lifestyle. You are a welcome, or perhaps unwelcome, intruder into their familiar daily routine. Always be aware that they may see very few faces other than those of their family or the other families in the village. Their initial impression of you is likely to be one of unease and wariness. Be reassuring. Move slowly.

If possible, learn a few words of local greeting and repeat them to everyone you meet in the village. It is very important to keep smiling; carry an open face, even if you feel exactly the opposite. Hold your body in a relaxed, non-aggressive manner.

In your first encounter, try to avoid anything that might anger them or make them shy with their initial approaches to you. If they offer a hand, take it firmly, even if it is encrusted with what you might consider filth. Don't hold back or be distant, either in attitude or voice. On the other hand, coming on strong in an effort to get something from a local person will only build unnecessary barriers to communication.

Words and pictures

Begin with words. If you are asking for directions, repeat the name of the place several times, but do not point in the direction you think it is, or suggest possible directions by voice. Usually the local person, in an effort to please his visitor, will nod helpfully in the direction in which you are pointing, or agree with you that, yes, Namdrung is that way, "if you say so". It may be in the opposite direction.

Merely say "Namdrung" and throw up your hands in a gesture that indicates a total lack of knowledge. Most local people are delighted to help someone who is genuinely in need, and, after a conference with their friends, will come up with a solution to your problem. When they point, repeat the name of the place several times more (varying the pronunciation) to check if it is the same place you want to go. It is also a good idea to repeat this whole procedure with someone else in another part of the village (and frequently along the route) to check for consistency.

In most areas it is highly likely that none of the local people will speak any language you are familiar with. Communicating with them then becomes a problem in demonstration: you must show them what you want or perform your message.

If you are asking for information that is more difficult to express than simple directions, use your hands to build a picture of what you need. Pictures, in the air, on the sand, on a piece of paper, are sometimes your only means of communication and, frequently, the clearest. Use these symbols when you receive blank stares in answer to your questions. Use sound or objects that you have in your possession that are similar, or of which you would like more.

Giving and getting

Not all of your contact with local people will be about getting something from them. Don't forget that you have a unique opportunity to bring them something from your own culture – try to make it something that will enrich theirs. Show them what it looks like with the help of postcards and magazines. Let them experience its tools. If you have a camera, let the local people, especially the children, look through the viewfinder. Put on a telephoto lens so they can get a new look at their own countryside. If you have a Polaroid camera, photograph them and give them the print (a very popular offering, but be careful, you might end up being asked to photograph all the villagers). And, most important of all, become involved. Carry aspirin to cure headaches – real or imagined. If someone in the village seems to need help, say in lifting a log, offer a hand. Contribute yourself as an expression of your culture.

If you want to take photographs, be patient. Don't bring out your camera until you have established a sufficient rapport, and be as unobtrusive as possible. If anyone objects, stop. A bribe for a photograph or payment for information is justified only if the situation is unusual. A simple request for directions is no reason for a gift. If the local people do something out of the ordinary for you, reward them as you would a friend at home.

The best gift you can give them is your friendship and openness. They are not performers doing an act, but ordinary people living out their lives in circumstances that seem strange to us.

I have found myself using gifts as a means of avoiding contact with remote people – especially children – as a way of pacifying them. I think it is better to enter and leave their lives with as much warmth as I can give, and now I leave the sweets at home. If you are camped near a village, invite some of the local people over to share your food, and try to have them sit among your party.

On some of the more travelled routes, such as Morocco or the main trekking trails of Nepal, the local children, being used to being given sweets by passing trekkers, will swarm around for more. I suggest that you smile (always) and refuse them. Show them pictures or your favourite juggling act, then give them something creative, such as pencils.

If a local event is in progress, stand back, try to get into a shadow, and watch from a distance. You will be seen and noticed, no matter what you do, but it helps to minimise your presence. If you want to get closer, edge forward slowly, observing the participants, especially the older people, for signs that you are not wanted. If they frown, retire. Respect their attempts to keep their culture and its customs as free as possible from outside influence.

Many people in remote places are still in an age before machines, and live their lives close to the earth in a comfortable routine. Where you and I come from is sophisticated, hard and alien to them. We must come into their lives as gently as possible, and when we go, leave no trace.

Officialdom

In less remote areas where the local people have had more experience of travellers, you must still observe the rule of patience, open-mindedness and respect for the lifestyle of others. But you will encounter people with more preconceived notions about foreigners – and most of those notions will be unfavourable.

In these circumstances – and indeed anywhere your safety or comfort may depend on your approach – avoid seeming to put any local person, especially a minor official, in the wrong. Appeal to his emotions, enlist his magnanimous aid, save his face at all costs. Your own calmness can calm others. If you are delayed or detained, try 'giving up', reading a book, smiling. Should you be accused of some minor misdemeanour, such as 'jumping' a control point, far better to admit your 'mistake' than to be accused of spying – though even this is fairly standard practice in the Third World and shouldn't flap you unduly.

Wherever you go in the Third World, tones and pitches of voice will vary; 'personal distance' between people conversing may be less than you are used to, attitudes and priorities will differ from your own. Accept people as they are and you can hope that, with time and a gentle approach, they will accept you also.

Language

When you have the opportunity of learning or using a smattering of the local language, try to make things easier for yourself by asking questions that limit answers to what you understand and prompt responses which will add helpfully and manageably to your vocabulary. Make it clear to your listeners that your command of the language is limited. Note down what you learn and try constantly to build on what you know.

Always familiarise yourself with the cultural limitations that may restrict topics of conversation or choice of conversation partner.

Keep your hands to yourself

Gestures can be a danger area. The British thumbs-up sign is an obscenity in some countries, such as Sardinia and parts of the Middle East, where it means roughly 'sit on this' or 'up yours'. In such places (and anywhere, if in doubt) hitch a ride by waving limply with a flattened hand.

The ring sign made with thumb and forefinger is also obscene in Turkey and other places. And in France it can mean 'zero', i.e. worthless – the exact opposite of the meaning 'OK' or 'excellent' for which the British and Americans use it.

By contrast, our own obscene insult gesture, the two-finger sign, is used interchangeably in Italy with the Churchillian V-sign. Which way round you hold your fingers makes no difference – it's still understood as a friendly gesture meaning 'victory' or 'peace'.

In Greece, as the anthropologist Desmond Morris tells us, there is another problem to do with the gesture called the *moutza*. In this, the hand is raised flat, 'palm towards the victim and pushed towards him as if about to thrust an invisible custard pie in his face'. To us it means simply to 'go back', but to a Greek it is a hideous insult. It dates from Byzantine times, when chained prisoners were paraded through the streets and abused by having handfuls of filth from the gutter picked up by onlookers and thrust into their faces. Though naturally the brutal practice has long since ceased, the meaning of *moutza* has not been forgotten.

JON GARDEY is a writer, traveller and film-maker.

Westerners abroad
by Rob Penn

D O NOT GIVE TO BEGGARS. Leave no trace in the wilderness. Dress sensitively. Don't photograph women. Stay in community-owned lodges. The myriad dos and don'ts of travelling in Third World countries are more complicated than ever, ironically at a time when it has never been so easy or swift to get to the remotest corners of the planet.

In this sense, the history of travel is back to front. The Victorians voyaged by ship, train and foot. They had months on the road to shift sensibilities and culturally acclimatise. Yet, save for the errant few who went 'native', they reached the furthest corners of the planet and behaved just as they would have done at home. Conversely, we tend to jet directly into the Third World from our harried lives and expect to hit the ground with our global ethics and cultural receptivity – not to mention our stomachs – all up to speed. So, how do we tackle this paradox?

The travel writer Sebastian Hope once said: "Preparation is a key and there is enough information – in the media, on the web and in the plethora of guidebooks – that you can brief yourself with a full intelligence report on anywhere from Togo to Tajikistan before you go." In this aim, many travel companies now hand out pre-departure packs that contain bibliographies, along with such information as taking photographs, road conditions and tipping.

Forewarned is forearmed, up to a point. Travellers, like spies, need to be adaptable, quick to read situations, able to grasp conversations in foreign languages and ready to make friends in unlikely situations. While some people inherit such skills, most of us acquire them by spending time on the road. Without a thought, experienced travellers always seem to know when they are being deceived, what to wear and how not to cause offence. If you are not a veteran traveller, go with one.

Often the most difficult aspect of travelling in the Third World is the economic disparity. Despite the massive growth in tourism, only a few local people have a stake in the industry; wandering around with the aggregate annual income of an entire African village in your wallet can make everyone uneasy. We have become better at dealing with this (revealing the cost of a loaf of bread in London usually breaks the ice) and more calculated in our generosity. In recent years, however, it is religious and cultural differences that have become more pronounced.

How Westerners can and should behave abroad was changed dramatically by the events of 11 September 2001. Many speculated then that the window of opportunity to travel freely, which began with the Jet Age, closed with the attacks that day. Many countries – Indonesia, Kenya, Morocco, Saudi Arabia, Eritrea, Malaysia, Jordan and Pakistan to name a few – suddenly seemed off-limits. The way we travel was thought to have been altered forever.

And, in a sense, it has. The Japanese and Americans, notoriously nervous travellers at the best of times, have become even more so. The British, however, have returned to normal remarkably quickly. We tend to be resilient and self-assured, relying on our own means of information as much as the hard-line advice of such institutions as the Foreign Office. We are able to recognise that many isolated incidents are unconnected to global events. Crucially, we appreciate that terrorist attacks against tourists are rare – although it may not always appear so.

That said, the ramifications of the 'War on Terror' haunt us everywhere now. Where we come from has even become an issue. Travelling through the Serbia on a bicycle shortly after the Balkan War had ended in 1996, rather than be associated with the much-resented British military intervention, I told people that I was Irish. Today, such disingenuousness is commonplace and a rucksack with a maple leaf stitched on the pocket might be carried by a wary American rather than a real Canadian. As a traveller one is often exposed and in places that are simmering with anger, it is best to 'temper discretion with deceit,' as Evelyn Waugh put it.

The piecemeal advice security experts hand out – book late, fly on wide-bodied planes, avoid buildings full of glass – is useful in itself. But the emphasis is on us to be better travellers: more aware, more sensitive to the culture, more knowledgeable about the religion and better-prepared to debate our differences, whatever they are. The time when a packet of sweets and some postcards of home secured a safe and enjoyable passage around the globe is gone.

This new climate should not put people off travelling, though. In fact, the pleasures of travel are magnified by a new appreciation of our freedom to experience them. And the fact is that British tourists are far more likely to injure themselves skiing in the Alps or in a traffic accident on the African continent than be involved in a terrorist attack. That the British still travel freely, and in Muslim countries, is a positive thing. In my own experience, Muslim countries are the most welcoming and easy to travel in, something that has been too quickly forgotten. That they may be more so now is unspoken.

When I first went to Iran in the mid-1990s, my friends and family fretted. Yet I met a gracious and engaging people who fell over themselves to make me feel welcome. Hospitality to strangers is fundamental to the Muslim faith, and I will never forget leaving a simple household on the road from Esfehan to Shiraz: the man of the house thanked me extravagantly for staying whilst his wife wailed with grief that I could not stop longer. As the Moorish proverb goes, 'He who does not travel does not know the value of men.' ❧

ROB PENN photographs and writes about travel and the environment. His first book is 'The Sky Is Falling On Our Heads', about a journey through the Celtic Fringe.

Respecting Hinduism
by Justine Hardy

H E LOOKED AT ME WITH SLIGHTLY GLAZED EYES through the pulse of bodies on the banks of the Ganges.

"Hinduism is as big as your mind or as small as your mind," said the smiling sadhu, stroking a belly that was as swollen and smooth as a spacehopper. Well, that seemed to wrap it all up really, one of those great throwaway lines that the wandering holy men of India, the *sadhus*, know the foreigners want to hear and will cogitate over for hours in the shimmering heat of the subcontinent. But beneath the glaze-eyed guru gimmick was the nut of Hinduism.

It is a huge religion, the oldest in the world, with a confusion of thousands in the Hindu pantheon of gods. And even if you were to crack the caste of thousands, each one of them has a vehicle, an animal of some description, that flies or trundles them around the heavens on their otherworldly missions. It is this hugeness that is daunting, but Hinduism is an onion religion that is heavy with the ritual paraphernalia attached to it by the Indian nature and culture. As you peel away the layers you'll find the simple moral codes of human behaviour that are at the root of Hinduism. If you dig down through the extraordinary scriptures to one of the main works, the *Upanishads* (400-200 BC), you'll find a text that incorporates the central theme of the majority of the world's main religions: 'The Great God is One, and the learned call him by different names.'

Hinduism's thousands of gods lead to the big three – Brahma the creator, Vishnu the preserver and Shiva the destroyer (sometimes also seen as a creator) – three in one, and also to the physical representations of the unseen omnipotent God, Parabrahma.

When the glaze-eyed *sadhu* with the spacehopper belly said that it was "as big as your mind", he was referring to the ability of Hinduism to embrace so many forms of worship; every family has a favourite god or goddess to whom they turn for guidance, support and comfort. But from out of all the layers of belief comes one core creed: the acceptance of *Samsara, Moksha, Karma* and *Dharma; Samsara*, the cycle of rebirth through many lives on the way to attaining perfection; *Moksha*, spiritual salvation and release from the cycle of reincarnation; *Karma*, the law of cause and effect, whatever you do, good or bad, there will be a consequence and crimes and good deeds that are not recognised in the current life may be punished or rewarded in the next; and *Dharma*, the natural balance of the universe, the law of the caste system and the moral code that each person should follow.

For the visitor to India and Asia, whether travelling through Hindu societies or living in them, a basic understanding of the caste system is important. The control of the caste system has been profoundly challenged for centuries, most dramatically in 1947 when Jawaharlal Nehru became the first prime minister of independent India and called for secular government. Nehru's hope, to form a government free of religious undertone, was an idealistic cry for a newly independent nation that has always ebbed and flowed on the tides of religious passion. The caste system is deeply ingrained in the Indian psyche and, even though it no longer officially exists as a class structure, the four main castes still affect daily life at every level. It has become largely diluted in the cities but it remains the rule of thumb in most rural areas. To ignore it is to bypass a great chunk of India at its pulse.

There are two things about Hinduism that were historically set in stone: you were either born a Hindu with a caste or you were not, and you could not truly convert to Hinduism. This may well be one of the reasons that foreigners have found Hinduism so fascinating, because ultimately we could find out as much about it as we liked, we could read the *Mahabharata*, the *Bhagavad Gita*, the *Ramayana*, the *Vedas*, the *Upanishads* and the *Puranas*, we could go to *puja* prayer rituals, we could pray with Hindus, sing their mantras, accept the blessing of their priests, but we could not claim a caste and convert, in spite of the openness that the religion offered to non-Hindus. Aspects of that are changing as times change and, increasingly, people marry across religions. Within its own fluidity, Hinduism has become more relaxed about conversions beyond the caste system.

So from the big stuff of gods and systems to the smaller but equally important stuff. Hinduism is a living religion in that it is a part of the daily round and there are some things that need to be understood.

Some people think that the Indians are prudish, that they cover up and hide everything. By Western standards they do, but there is a very beautiful sensuality in that very covering. When I work in India with men fresh out of England, when they catch their first sight of sari-clad bathers in a river or beside a village tank, the material wrapped and clinging to their curves, their response has always been to be awed by the feminine beauty. Hindus find it difficult to deal with the Western idea of stripping down to as little as possible in a hot country. If you have ever lived through a hot season in India you become only too aware of the fact that loose, flowing, light cotton clothes are the coolest and most practical. You just get burnt and bitten in shorts and T-shirts.

I had one of my closest shaves with the early edges of middle age when I was taking a young American student out to a primary school project located in a Delhi slum. She was gorgeous, blonde and curvy, and she turned up wearing a sleeveless shirt that showed a fantastic display of cleavage and a flippy skirt. She challenged my disapproval with a tone of voice that made me feel 30 going on 90. She had picked up the skirt in a local market without realising that it was actually a sari petticoat. She was unintentionally breaking every code of decent dressing in Hindu eyes. She was wearing underwear, for a start, and she was also displaying her upper arms and cleavage. All that is fine and acceptable in the nightclubs and bars of Delhi and Mumbai, but it is just not fair outside of these cities, particularly in rural areas. It is confusing for the people and unfortunately helps to reiterate the belief held by many rural and village Indians that all white women are basically asking for it.

When it comes to going into a temple or attending a family prayer puja, both men and women should cover their heads, arms and legs. No naked flesh is the easiest rule to follow. You will almost always be asked to take your shoes off before going into a temple by an official shoe-minder. It is worth checking that you are handing your precious shoes over to the official minder rather than a likely lad who is going to skip off down the road with his booty, leaving you hopping around on boiling roads where rats and broken glass loiter. The official minder should be tipped a few rupees for his labours.

Weddings have a dress code all of their own. My pet theory is that it is wise for foreigners is to stick to Western dress, but keep it simple and elegant, and again no exposed flesh. Hindu weddings are all about glitter and show and there is just no point in trying to match the efforts of the native population. I don't know why but it always make me a bit sad seeing Western girls struggling with saris at weddings or parties. Indian women were born to it and carry this exquisite garment with grace. Most Westerners just get it a bit wrong and would look much more elegant and have more fun if they stuck to their own clothes. I've lost count of the number of Western girls and women that I have seen in glitzy hotel loos tacking saris up with safety pins, and looking totally miserable about their failure to float within the folds of silk, while their sinuous Indian counterparts waft on by.

While on the female take, historically and culturally Hindus have great respect for women – one of their favourite deities is the gorgeous Lakshmi, goddess of wealth and prosperity and consort of Vishnu, the preserver in the big three. But if a woman does not carry herself within the cultural boundaries of Hindu sensibilities men will understandably regard it as OK to leer and provoke to their hearts' content. If you give them something to stare at, they will stare and go on staring.

Hindus do not eat beef. The cow is sacred to them, hence the vast numbers of cows, decorated with gaily painted horns, wandering around the streets, half-chewed plastic bag in mouth, looking not unlike fag-ash Lil on jaunty hat day. Many people are vegetarians, but just as many eat meat – mutton and chicken being the most popular.

The eating implement of India, and most of Asia, is the right hand. If you are eating with locals and joining in with your hands, too, don't use the left, it is reserved for the washing of the bum. To use it for eating is both offensive and embarrassing for your hosts or fellow eaters.

One further warning about partying with Hindus, or more generally Indians: theoretically most of them do not drink as it is against some aspect of their religion, but at flash weddings or parties the booze flows freely and for a long time. And the drinking goes on until about midnight. Then, when most people are very blurred around the edges, a great dinner is produced. Everyone eats hugely and then rolls off home repeating the Indian late-night chorus of indigestion. If you get hungry early, eat before you go and nibble politely at the midnight binge.

Hinduism is a bright, brilliant culture and religion that, like its partying, can seem indigestible if taken on too quickly but, when absorbed slowly, is as deep and voluptuous as the Ganges – or your mind, as the man with the spacehopper belly said. ❧

JUSTINE HARDY is a globe-trotting journalist whose first novel, 'The Wonder House', is set in Kashmir.

Respecting Islam
by Barnaby Rogerson

EACH DAY, AS THE DAWN LIGHT RIPPLES AROUND THE WORLD, it awakens a chant of morning prayer from the thirteen hundred million Muslim believers spread over the globe. For the last 1,400 years there has not been so much as a minute when this community has not offered up praise to the divinity. The public call to prayer that echoes from the minarets of all the great mosques of Islam is like a circular beacon that wraps up the world in ribbons of faith.

It would be unwise, however, to imagine that worldwide Islam – which includes the Brazilians of West African descent, the Uighurs of Chinese Central Asia, Malay villagers, the highlanders of the Yemen, the Moors of Ceylon, the Asian Muslim community within South Africa, the citizens of Turkey's secular republic, the well-heeled Persian expatriate community in California and the converted followers of a Sufi sheikh in Britain – could ever be viewed as members of a single culture.

What these Muslims share is much more important than any common material culture, language or social customs: it is the animating glow of faith. Islam is a matter of trust, a complete submission to the infinite power and knowledge of a God who is known to be ever merciful and compassionate, and who loathes injustice and oppression of the weak.

This knowledge of an all-powerful but intimately present God ('closer to you than your jugular vein,' according to the Koran) was preached to humankind by hundreds, if not thousands, of prophets before it was articulated by the Prophet Muhammad in sixth-century Arabia. Muhammad was proud to be numbered in the long line of prophets stretching back through the Jewish, Christian and Arab traditions to include Issa (Jesus), Yahya (John the Baptist), Sulaiman (King Solomon), Daoud (King David), Musa (Moses) and Harun (Aaron), as well as Yunus (Jonah), Noah, Abraham, Abraham's son Ishmael and our first parents Adam and Eve. The testaments of all these prophets of God, most noticeably the Hebrew Bible and the Gospels, are honoured by true Muslims, although they also believe that the Koran (also spelled Qoran or Qur'an) is the definitive revelation that supersedes all others. I recently saw this belief illustrated by the shelving labels of a Muslim bookshop in London, which stocked 'The Old Testament', 'The New Testament' and 'The Living Testament'. In his own life, the Prophet Muhammad's tolerance of the different patterns of belief amongst the Jews and Christians of Arabia was revealed when he answered some theological quibble thus: 'Will you dispute with us about God? When he is our Lord and your Lord! We have our words and you have your words, but we are sincerely his.' This must still remain the answer to any interfaith dialogue, not with the triumph of one belief or some well-worded compromise, but the lifelong struggle of believers to understand fully their own faith tradition.

There are six basic principles that define a Muslim. The first and most important is the belief in the absolute oneness of God, the unitary nature of the divinity that allows for no pantheon of saints, demigods or divine consorts and children. Second is the understanding that Muhammad, though just a mortal like any one of us, is the messenger of God. He is the seal of the prophets, the last to be granted a divine revelation before the end of the world. The third principle is that the Koran is the word of God dictated to Muhammad through the archangel Gabriel. The 114 different chapters (*sura*) and 6,236 component verses of the Koran were delivered over a 22-year period. The first revelation came upon Muhammad as a 40-year-old merchant of Mecca (and father of four daughters) in 610 AD; the last was delivered in the final year of his life, in Medina, in 632 AD. The fourth principle is the belief in angelic presences on earth and that Satan (Shaitan or Iblis) and his demons who tempt us to sin are fallen angels. The fifth principle is an acceptance that sin exists and that mortals can actively choose between doing good or evil. The sixth principle is the existence of a final judgement and the division of mankind between heaven and hell.

Souls are believed to remain in the grave until the great day of judgement, when a person's own limbs will be free to testify against them and an assessment made of their sins and good deeds. Even the most virtuous, though, will have to rely on God's mercy while crossing over the mouth of hell (*jahannam*) on a fiery bridge as narrow as the edge of a sword. The hell beneath this bridge is visualised as a vast fiery pit made up of seven ever-deeper terraces of progressive damnation, each guarded by gates. There are verses that seem to promise ultimate redemption, however, when even Satan will be forgiven by the overflowing mercy of God. Heaven is imagined as a reverse of hell: a pyramid of shaded garden terraces filled with rivers of sweet water, milk, wine and honey, though elsewhere the Prophet declared: 'What is paradise? It is what eye hath not seen, nor the ear heard, nor ever flashed across the mind of Man.'

The essential duties of a Muslim are set out in the five pillars of Islam. The initial profession of faith: 'There is no divinity but God, and Muhammad is his Prophet' (*Ila ilaha ill'Allah, Muhammad rasul Allah*) is known as the *shahada* ('the testimony'). It is made at the time of one's entry to Islam and henceforth repeated at the end of each of the daily prayers. The second pillar is the practice of daily prayer. In the lifetime of the Prophet, public prayers seem to have occurred at dusk (the start of the Muslim day), just before dawn and at noon, times of the day which believers could calculate for themselves without the intervention of any priesthood. Later, this practice was extended to five times a day, so Maghreb is held four minutes after sunset, Esha when it is quite dark, Sobh Fejr at dawn, Duhe at noon and Asr at the end of the siesta hour, halfway between noon and sunset. The third pillar, that of almsgiving, ensured that the less fortunate in society, including the sick, the old, orphans and travellers, have food, gifts and shelter. This pillar was later codified in an annual tax, a tithe of the harvest or a fortieth of one's portable wealth, which allowed for centralised care on behalf of the whole community. The fourth pillar is the annual fast during the ninth lunar month of the Muslim year at Ramadan, when the entire Muslim community abstains from food, drink, sex and smoking during the daylight hours. It allows the community, whatever its wealth, to share deprivation and taste absolute poverty. It is also a time of all-night prayer sessions and public readings of the Koran mixed up with a carnival-like atmosphere at dusk when the daily fast ends. The fifth pillar is the pilgrimage (*hajj*) to Mecca for all those who are strong and wealthy enough to perform it. The *hajj* can only be made in the twelfth lunar month of the Muslim year, the Dhu al-Hijjah. It consists of five days of prescribed duties, including the Day of Standing (*wukuf*) beside the Hill of Arafat and the stoning of Satan. It culminates in the Day of Sacrifice (commemorating Abraham's willingness to offer up his son Ishmael to God), which is celebrated by the worldwide community of Islam. The meat is shared, and most of it is given to the poor.

True Muslims can always be recognised by their relationship to poverty. Not only do sincere believers help the disadvantaged in society, but they also recognise that material poverty is a gift from God that can allow a true believer a clearer vision away from the corrupting distractions of this world. The Prophet Muhammad loathed the pride of the rich and the powerful and said: 'What is pride? Holding another man in contempt.' On other occasions he declared: 'poverty is my pride' and prayed to God: 'O Lord keep me alive a poor man, and let me die poor; and raise me amongst the poor.' ❧

BARNABY ROGERSON is the managing director of Eland Publishing, which specialises in publishing classic travel books.

Respecting Buddhism
by Denise Heywood

L YING IN A FRAGRANT STEAM BATH, I was having my limbs manipulated by a talented masseur. But the reason I was in a sweat was that he was in a saffron robe and I was in a monastery. Yet we were both improving our *karma*.

In Asia, Buddhism is more than a religion, it is a way of life. Thus, in Laos, a steam bath attended by a monk in the compound of a pagoda fulfills the religious centre's role as the heart of a community, providing physical as well as spiritual needs. Not only can you meditate and pray, but you can eat, sleep and even reside there for a while, in an environment supported by donations. In Buddhism, the spiritual and temporal are inseparably linked, forming a seamless whole, from birth to death, incorporating the rhythms of rural life, its seasons and festivals, education and, most significantly, a system of ethico-philosophical beliefs.

It started in India in 563 BC with Prince Siddharta Gautama, the original Buddha, meaning 'the enlightened one'. He abandoned his palace and became an ascetic, reaching enlightenment when meditating under a *bodhi* tree. He founded a community of monks and preached that there were four noble truths: all life is suffering; suffering is caused by desire; the cessation of desire will bring peace; and, the end of suffering is achieved by following the eightfold path. The Wheel of the Law symbolised his doctrine, including theories about *samsara*, the unavoidable cycle of death and rebirth. Buddhism increased in influence as it spread eastwards, splitting into strands, adapting and harmonising within different cultures. Theravada Buddhism, 'the path of the elders', took root in south-east Asia. Meanwhile, Mahayana Buddhism, the 'greater path', evolved in east Asia.

Like Christianity, Buddhism has inspired some of the most dazzling religious edifices on earth, such as the temple of Borobodur in Java and the Bayon at Angkor in Cambodia. We cross the world to marvel at these awesome sites and the rich legacy of sculpture, painting, textiles, manuscripts and objects created for sacred use. And in travelling, we experience Buddhism palpably, on a daily basis.

It starts at dawn when the monks leave their pagodas to beg for alms, a procession of orange figures moving silently through the twilit streets. Local people wait and place food in their bowls, offered with a bow, in exchange for blessings. Their gestures earn merit for their *karma*, the cause and effect of moral acts in present and future lives. So simple a ritual is infused with all the ideals of Buddhism, especially *dana*, the act of giving.

On entering a temple, visitors must remove their shoes and be modestly dressed. Asian women don't wear revealing clothes. Monks take vows of celibacy, and even in the steam, I was enveloped in a sarong. Inside a temple, when seated or kneeling, never point the feet towards the altar, as they are the lowest part of the body, physically and spiritually. Resist the temptation to be photographed leaning against a Buddha image or a *stupa*. This is taboo.

The pagoda is also the centre of festivals. These are raucous affairs during which loudspeakers ensure that noise levels soar. In countries such as Cambodia there always seems to be a festival in progress. Weddings and funerals last at least three days, as does the Day of the Dead. Then there's the harvest festival, the water festival, the full moon festival, the Buddha's birthday, the King's birthday, the Queen's birthday, the day of independence from the French, the day of liberation from the Khmer Rouge, the Buddhist new year, the Chinese new year, the Gregorian new year and - increasingly popular - Christmas, when tinsel and plastic reindeer are strung up among the palm trees. If no-one's celebrating anything, then the monks still hoist up the loudspeakers and chant anyway.

In Pursat, in north-western Cambodia, I was walking along a street where a colourful wedding reception was in full swing, music blaring. Down a street on the right, a funeral cortège advanced in a miasma of noise. As it reached the corner, the procession of mourners, dressed in white, with the bier on a wooden cart, turned into the street of the wedding. They were creating such a cacophany that they didn't even notice the nuptials until they found themselves colliding with the festivities, almost knocking over the bride and groom with their coffin. Dance music vied with incantations and threnodies, while guests intermingled in an ear-splitting celebration of life and death.

Offerings of rice and incense at shrines are made daily by everyone. Even lavish five star hotels have a spirit house outside where bananas and fragrant jasmine are placed each morning. In Buddhist countries, all boys spend a few months in a pagoda studying the scriptures, rather like national service, except that the end result is peace, not war. At a temple in Luang Prabang I was delighted by the teenage novices with their shaved heads and bright smiles who, eager to speak English, were as keen to discuss football as the Pali canon. They also learn meditation, the core of Buddhism, practised across Asia. Acceptance of life's vicissitudes and inner calm are among the attributes this produces – qualities coveted by Westerners, and especially advantageous during festivals.

Never raising the voice or showing anger are among the rules of etiquette. These originate in the Buddhist principles of peace and tolerance and are considered 'loss of face'. A mark of respect is the traditional greeting, the *wai*, where both hands are brought together near the chin as if in prayer, with the head bowed. This gesture, filled with subtle signals depending on how deep the bow, is another practice with religious resonance. Alas, the Western handshake is rapidly replacing this graceful custom.

By nightfall, when thinking of food, remember that many Buddhists are vegetarian, as the taking of any life is forbidden. Once, when I asked my hotel to spray insecticide for the mosquitos buzzing round my room, they gently declined as it was Buddhist Lent, and suggested I do it myself. After that aromatic steam bath in the temple, I had become irresistible to those tiny carnivores, so I sprayed mercilessly. So much for my *karma*. 🙦

DENISE HEYWOOD is a journalist, lecturer and photographer and has worked in Cambodia for three years. She has just completed a book on the Buddhist temples of Laos, 'Ancient Luang Prabang', and is writing another on Cambodian dance.

Keeping in touch while abroad
by Charlotte Hindle

TECHNOLOGY HAS REVOLUTIONISED the way that travellers keep in touch. The internet, digital cameras and mobile phones have made overseas communication fast, easy and, if you shop around, inexpensive.

One of the most exciting ways to communicate while you are away is to keep an online travel diary. Discard your fountain pen and leather-bound travel journal to embrace the new world of interactive maps, online journal entries, digital photo albums and a personal message board. To do so costs less than £3 a month and is just like creating your own travel website, only much easier. Best of all, your friends and family can log in, catch up with your news and send you messages.

Numerous companies offer online travel diaries with different features and functions. A number of them are accessible by anyone. Others allow you to keep sections of your diary completely or partially private. Most have maps and some track your progress across them. Some automatically inform your family and friends, by email, when you have updated your journal.

Further information

www.cybercafes.com
(lists 4,000 internet cafés)

www.hotspot-locations.com
(lists 26,000 hotspots worldwide.)

Online travel diaries/blogs

www.mytripjournal.com

www.offexploring.com

www.roughguidesintouch.com

www.offtravelling.com

www.prnewsnow.com

www.travelblog.org

Free web-based email accounts

www.hotmail.com

www.yahoo.co.uk

www.mail.google.com

Email

www.hotmail.com

www.bt.openworld.com

http://mail.lycos.com

www.email2me.com

http://idnnow.com

www.mail.com

Phone Cards

kropla.com (worldwide electrical
and telephone data)

www.ekit.com: global SIM
(card provider and integrated
communication packages)

www.0044.co.uk: SIM
(cards for a wide range of countries)

www. 1st-phonecards.co.uk

http://cloncom.com

www.phonecardsavers.com

www.1st4phoneards.com

www.justphonecards.com

Mobile phones

ww.ukstudentlife.com/Life/
Telephone/International.htm

www.virginmobile.com/mobile/
services/abroad/

Alternatively contact the company
you are already contracted with, to
see if they offer deals.

Whatever type you choose, check what happens to your diary at the end of your trip – don't get caught out by the sites offering only online storage. An online diary may be an innovative communication tool, but it is also a great souvenir of your trip. You want to make sure that you can download it to your PC or have it burnt onto CD when you arrive home.

If this sounds a little too fancy or you are only travelling for a short time, then online communication is still the way to go. Sign up for a free web-based email account, such as those offered by Hotmail or Yahoo – or Gmail (from Google) which is pretty good for storage and easier to organise than many other web-based accounts. This way, you can send and receive emails at internet cafés around the world. Like backpacks or suitcases, what you are looking for in a 'freemail' account is lots of storage space. Currently, Yahoo offers more space than Hotmail, though frequent 'storage wars' mean that this may change before you travel.

An increasing number of travellers are choosing to go away with their own laptops. There is a growing number of Hotspots in all corners of the world where your laptop can use Wi-Fi technology (wireless connection to the internet). These are usually found in airports, hotels and coffee houses.

Email is often the cheapest method of keeping in touch – internet cafés usually charge in blocks of 15 minutes or by the hour. However, don't forget the humble telephone. The cost of international phone calls is dropping by the minute and prepaid phonecards are excellent value for money. For between £5 and £10 you can buy a piece of plastic with a freephone access number and a code on it. This allows you to make calls for much less than it costs to use a hotel phone or an official phonecard from the local telecom provider. In most countries, prepaid phonecards can be bought at newsagents.

The big question is what to do with your mobile phone. If you decide to take it with you, ask your provider to activate 'international roaming' so that it can receive and transmit abroad. If you own a standard dual-band phone, it will work in Europe, Asia or Africa. But, for round-the-world, you will need a tri-band handset.

However, using your mobile phone overseas can be prohibitively expensive – between £1 and £3 per minute – even if you are just texting. If you are staying in one country, the simplest solution is to buy a local, prepaid SIM card. Calls will be a lot cheaper this way since you are accessing the local network, instead of your home network. Alternatively, the communication service provider Ekit sells a global SIM card, which is advertised as saving you up to 70 per cent off traditional roaming costs. Some mobile phones are 'simlocked', so you will have to ask your UK service provider to 'unlock' your phone before you can swap SIM cards.

Despite the technology, there is nothing stopping you and your friends and family from corresponding by good, old-fashioned snail mail. It may take longer, it might be less sophisticated but, these days, there's something very special about a hand-written letter. On the road, letters can be addressed to you c/o poste restantes at post offices in major cities. Or, if you are an American Express cardholder or carry its traveller's cheques, at American Express offices worldwide. ❧

CHARLOTTE HINDLE is a freelance travel journalist and co-author of 'The Lonely Planet Guide To Travel Writing'.

Healthy travel

Health planning and precautions before you go
by Alastair Miller, Nick Beeching and Lisa Ford

IT IS AMAZING HOW MUCH TIME AND MONEY travellers will put into planning their itinerary, and how little many are prepared to invest in simple precautionary measures to protect their health while abroad. A simple diarrhoeal illness can ruin an expensive holiday, but might be avoided with basic precautions. It is not in the commercial interests of travel agents to highlight the health risks of travel, and often their advice is limited and woefully inaccurate. A few years ago a reputable company advised clients on a trip to India to have vaccination against malaria (no such vaccine exists), yellow fever (there is no yellow fever in Asia) and cholera (the risk to travellers is negligible and the old vaccine was relatively ineffective).

Pre-travel consultation

Traditionally, the pre-travel consultation is regarded as a time to have one's 'jabs' before departure. However, the number of vaccine-preventable infections encountered overseas is relatively limited and there should be far more to the well-structured travel clinic visit. The golden rule is to seek advice at an early stage so that if vaccines are required they can be given in time to become fully effective, and a complex schedule of vaccination can be constructed if necessary. There is sometimes difficulty in actually acquiring the vaccines (e.g. there has been a recent problem with supply of yellow fever vaccine) and this may cause delay.

At least three months before departure you should consult your family doctor and, if necessary, a more specialised travel clinic in order to:
- Obtain information about specific health problems at your destinations.
- Consider current health and medications.
- Obtain adequate health insurance (and form e111 if travelling to an EU country).
- Plan and obtain necessary immunisations and malaria prophylaxis.
- Plan and obtain any medications, first aid items and documentation.
- Consider the need for a first-aid training course.

Do not neglect your dental health – one look at the street dentists in Marrakech will ensure that you will not wish to avail yourself of the local facilities! Dental treatment overseas may also prove expensive, so adequate insurance is important and you should have a good dental check before departure.

The depth of preparation required before travel clearly depends on the general health of the individual and on his or her destination(s). In the last few years, accessible information on health for travellers has improved considerably. The sections in this chapter are intended to provide a brief outline of the steps to be considered. Although minor infections (particularly of the gut, leading to traveller's diarrhoea) are common, major life-threatening infection is rare and the greatest risk of death for travellers stems from road traffic accidents, as those who have negotiated Delhi's Connaught Circus in a rickshaw will well appreciate.

Vaccinations

Boosters of standard childhood vaccines such as tetanus and polio should be up to date in order to avoid the need for a booster to be given in an overseas casualty department should an injury occur. When travelling to most developing countries, it is advisable to be vaccinated against hepatitis A and sometimes against typhoid (these two vaccines can be given in a combined preparation). Yellow fever is only a problem in Africa and tropical South and Central America, so is not required for travel to the Middle East or Asia. This is the only vaccine for which an international certificate of vaccination still exists and this may be demanded if one enters Asia from a yellow fever-infected area. Travellers to Saudi Arabia, particularly during the Haj pilgrimage, will be expected to provide a certificate of vaccination against meningococcal meningitis strains ACWY. Hepatitis B is a viral infection spread from mother to child, or between others by sexual contact and contact with blood and body fluids; in much of the world more than 5-10 per cent of all adults carry the infection. If the traveller is likely to have such an exposure, vaccination should be obtained before travel. It should be considered by all travellers going to endemic countries, which includes most of Eastern Europe as well as much of the tropics, for more one monthis also usually advised for all travellers going to endemic areas for more than 6 months.

In some circumstances, other vaccines may be recommended. These include rabies (particularly for long-term expatriates or travellers to remote areas), Japanese encephalitis, especially for travellers to rural Asia during the rainy season, and tick-borne encephalitis (for visitors to parts of Central and Eastern Europe). Specific vaccine recommendations for a given destination change frequently, but a country-by-country summary can be found in Section 3.

Antimalarials

Malaria is a potentially life-threatening infection caused by parasites in the blood that are transmitted between people by the bite of mosquitoes. It is very common in many parts of the tropics, causing over two million childhood deaths per year, especially in Africa. About ten people die unnecessarily in the UK each year from malaria that they have acquired overseas. Prevention depends on a combination of measures to avoid mosquito bites and taking antimalarial drugs. The different drug combinations used are complex and will not be discussed in detail here. Some need to be taken for several weeks before departure, partly in order to detect possible side effects, and partly to get enough drug into the system before travelling, so it is important to consult your doctor and/or travel clinic well in advance of travel to discuss what is most appropriate for you. Most drugs need to be taken for up to four weeks after leaving a malarial area, and this is just as important as taking the medication while overseas. While antimalarials are reasonably effective if taken as advised, they do not provide complete protection and it is also essential to follow the advice on how to avoid being bitten in the 'Flies' section of this chapter. The species of mosquitoes that transmit malaria are especially likely to bite around dusk or soon after, and it is particularly important to cover or protect limbs and other exposed skin when outdoors at this time of day.

Main sources of infection

The main routes by which travellers are exposed to risks of infection can be described by the three 'Fs' of 'food, flies and flirtation'. Risks can be minimised by being careful with food and water, avoiding insect bites and limiting casual sexual encounters (or at least using barrier protection).

Food (and water)

It is said that 'Travel broadens the mind and loosens the bowels.' Travellers' diarrhoea (see below) is one of the commonest afflictions to ruin an overseas holiday and, while some cases are unavoidable, the risks can be minimised. Unfortunately, in the very climates where a good fluid intake is required to avoid heat exhaustion and dehydration, a ready supply of infection-free fluid may not be easy to obtain.

A huge variety of micro-organisms cause diarrhoeal illness, with or without vomiting, and these are usually ingested with food or water. Food may carry other health hazards – unpasteurised milk and milk products transmit brucellosis in the Middle East and parts of Africa, and raw fish and crabs harbour a number of unpleasant worm and fluke infections. Even polar explorers face hazards: the liver of carnivores, such as polar bears and huskies, causes human illness due to Vitamin A poisoning.

Some basic rules

Although it is impossible to avoid infection entirely, the risk can be reduced by following some simple rules. The apparent prestige and expense of a hotel is no guide to the degree of hygiene employed in its kitchens, and the following guidelines apply equally to luxury travellers and those travelling rough.

Assurances from the local population (including long-term expatriates) that food is safe should not be taken too literally. They are likely to have developed immunity to organisms commonly present in their water supply. Sometimes it is impossible to refuse locally prepared food without causing severe offence, and invitations to village feasts will need to be dealt with diplomatically.

The major sources of external contamination of food are unclean water, dirty hands, and flies. Pay scrupulous attention to personal hygiene (medicated 'wipes' are useful), and only eat food with your fingers (including breads or fruit) if they are clean. Avoid food handled by others who you suspect have not been so careful with their hands – and remember that in many countries toilet paper is not used.

Water

The mains water supply in many countries is contaminated with sewage, while streams, rivers, lakes and reservoirs are freely used as toilets and for personal bathing and washing clothes. The same water may be used for washing food (especially salads and fruit) and may also be frozen to make ice cubes for drinks. Water should always be boiled or treated before drinking or used in the preparation of uncooked food (detailed advice is given in the chapter on Water Purification).

Hot tea or coffee are usually safe, as are beer and wine. Bottled water and carbonated drinks or fruit juice are not always safe, although the risk of adulteration or contamination is reduced if you keep to internationally recognised brands. Insist on seeing the bottle (or can) before it is opened, thus confirming that the seal is tight and the drink has not been tampered with.

If you have any doubts about the cleanliness of plates and cutlery, they can be rinsed in a sterile solution such as tea or coffee, or wiped with an injection swab. If this is not feasible, leave the bottom layer of food on the plate, especially if it is served on a bed of rice. If drinking utensils appear to be contaminated, it may be preferable to drink straight from the bottle.

Several strategies can be used to purify water. Boiling at 100°C will kill all significant organisms. The water needs to be fully on the boil for two minutes and it needs to be boiled for an extra minute for each 300 metres that you are above sea level. Water can be purified chemically by the addition of silver, chlorine or iodine. Silver is very slow acting and ineffective against cysts of amoebae and giardia, so is of less practical use to the traveller. Chlorine and iodine are both active against cysts, but need enough time and concentration to take effect.

There are now several filters available commercially that can be used to pump water from contaminated sources and purify it very effectively. They are expensive to buy but are usually very lightweight and effective.

The most effective way to provide safe drinking water for personal use is to purchase a portable water filter pump. These employ a filter on the end of a rubber tube that is inserted into the contaminated water and will remove all visible debris and larger microbiological contamination. The water is then pumped through a ceramic filter, which will remove particles larger than 0.2 microns, and will therefore eliminate all pathogenic bacteria and parasites (but will not destroy viruses). The pump is light and reasonably quick to operate (mine takes about 2 minutes to produce a litre of fresh water from some disgustingly contaminated streams and stagnant pools). The filters will last for several years – or several thousand litres of water – but the initial cost can be quite substantial (between £50 and £150).

In order to eliminate all viruses, you would need to use an additional purifying device (either chemical or electrostatic): but provided that you are immune to hepatitis A (by vaccination or previous exposure), and you are not very close to human habitation, this is generally not necessary.

Food

Food that has been freshly cooked is the safest, but must be served really hot.

Beware of food that has been pre-cooked and kept warm for several hours, or desserts (especially those containing cream) that have been inadequately refrigerated after cooking. This includes many hotel buffets. Unpasteurised milk or cheese should be avoided, as should ice cream. Food that has been visited by flies is certain to have been contaminated by excrement and should not be eaten.

Salads and peeled fruit prepared by others may have been washed with contaminated water. In some parts of the tropics, salads may be highly contaminated by human excrement, used as fertiliser. Salads and fruits are best avoided, unless you can soak them in water that you know is clean. Unpeeled fruit is safe, provided that you peel it yourself without contaminating the contents. "Wash it, peel it, boil it or forget it" remains excellent advice.

Shellfish and prawns are particularly high-risk foods because they act as filters, concentrating infecting organisms (they often thrive near sewage outfalls). They should only be eaten if thoroughly cooked, but still remain a risk. Shellfish and prawns also concentrate biological toxins at certain times of the year, causing a different form of food poisoning. Raw fish, crustaceans and meat should always be avoided. Hot spices and chillies do not sterilise foods, and chutneys and sauces that are left open on the table may have been visited by flies. Be cautious with chillies: they contain capsaicin, which is highly irritable to the bowel lining, with resulting diarrhoea and painful bottom ("tasting the chillies twice"). Beware of trying to impress your hosts by matching their consumption of hot foods.

Alcohol

The temptation to over-indulge starts on the aeroplane, but in-flight alcohol should be taken sparingly as it increases the dehydration associated with air travel and worsens jet lag. Intoxicated airline passengers are a menace to everybody, and most airlines have a zero-tolerance policy towards them. Drinking will also impair your ability to cope on arrival.

In hot countries, beware of dehydrating yourself with large volumes of alcoholic drink. Alcohol promotes the production of urine and can actually make you more dehydrated. Excessive alcohol consumption promotes diarrhoea, and prolonged abuse reduces the body's defences against infection. Alcohol use is an important factor in promoting unprotected casual sexual encounters.

Flies

Many infections overseas are transmitted by insects, and we have already referred above to their role in contaminating food. Blood-sucking insects, such as mosquitoes, ticks and mites, can also transmit many infections, such as malaria, dengue fever, Japanese encephalitis (insects do not transmit HIV). It therefore makes good sense to minimise exposure to this form of risk by taking sensible precautions to avoid insect bites.

Personal insect repellents will be needed by most travellers and usually contain DEET (diethyltoluamide). Liquid formulations are the cheapest but are less convenient to carry. Lotions and cream are available and sprays are the easiest to apply but are bulky to carry. Sticks of repellent are easier to carry and last the longest. All these should be applied to the skin and to clothing adjacent to exposed areas of skin, but should not be applied around the eyes, nose and mouth (take care with children).

DEET dissolves plastics, including contact lenses, watch straps, carrier bags, etc, so beware. An alternative to DEET-containing repellents is Mosiguard Natural. Marketed by MASTA, this is made from a blend of eucalyptus oils and is as effective as repellents based on 20-30 per cent DEET. It is more suitable for people who are sensitive to DEET and may be more acceptable for children.

When abroad, try to reduce the amount of skin available to biting insects by wearing long sleeves and long trousers or skirts. If a mosquito net is provided with your bed, use it. Permethrin-impregnated mosquito nets are effective and can be purchased before travel to malarial areas. 'Knock-down' insecticide sprays may be needed, and mosquito coils are easy to carry. Electric buzzers (imitating male mosquito noises) are useless and candles or repellent strips (containing citronella) are not very effective.

Flirtation and fixes

Despite the huge publicity about HIV and other infections, the risks taken by many travellers constantly amaze healthcare workers in sexual health. In many countries, HIV rates in adults in towns exceed 20 per cent, and old-fashioned sexually transmitted infections such as syphilis and antibiotic-resistant gonorrhoea are rampant. Many surveys confirm that travellers often have sexual encounters with fellow travellers as well as with local people at their destination. Some places are notorious as sex holiday destinations, including those within the UK. A survey of 1,000 young people visiting Torquay showed that over 600 had unprotected sex with a casual partner during a short stay. Loneliness and alcohol (and perhaps other drugs), as well as freedom from domestic constraints and opportunities in new surroundings all contribute to promote casual sex.

All unprotected sexual encounters while travelling carry high risks of infection with various sexually transmitted diseases, in addition to HIV and hepatitis B. Some protection will be provided by condoms, which should always be carried and used. If you have sex while away, a post-travel check up is strongly advised, even if you have no symptoms. Your local hospital will advise about the nearest clinic – variously called genito-urinary medicine (GUM) clinics, sexually transmitted disease clinics, sexual health clinics, VD clinics or 'special' clinics. Absolute anonymity is guaranteed, and no referral is needed from your general practitioner.

Drug misuse also carries infection risks from practices such as the sharing of syringes. etc, as well as heavy legal penalties in many countries. Blood products and shared syringes can transmit HIV, syphilis, hepatitis B and C, and various tropical infections, including malaria, trypanosomiasis and leishmaniasis. Never share syringes, needles or any other injecting paraphernalia with others.

Pre-travel health status

If in any doubt about possible hazards of travel because of a pre-existing medical condition, consult your family doctor. On a commercial flight the cabin pressure is equivalent to being about 2,000 metres above sea level, so the reduced atmospheric pressure may have an adverse effect on those with heart, lung and circulatory problems. There may also be risks for those with epilepsy, psychiatric disorders and chronic sinus or ear problems. Late pregnancy is a contraindication to flying, diabetics taking medication will need special advice, and the disabled will have specific requirements for airline and airport authorities may need notification. People with chronic health problems or women who are obviously pregnant should ask their doctor to complete a standard airline form certifying their 'fitness to fly'. This form should be obtained from the airline concerned.

Adequate supplies of all routinely prescribed medications, including oral contraceptives, should also be obtained before departure. For short trips within Europe, these can be provided as NHS prescriptions. Those planning longer stays abroad should determine the availability of their medication overseas or take adequate supplies (you may need to pay for these on private prescription). It is also strongly recommended that you obtain a certificate from your doctor detailing the drugs prescribed, including the correct pharmacological name, as well as the trade name. This will be necessary to satisfy customs officials and you may need to obtain certified translations into appropriate languages. Some drugs readily obtainable in UK are viewed with great suspicion elsewhere (codeine, for example, is considered a controlled drug in many countries, and tranquillisers such as diazepam can cause problems). Women working in Saudi Arabia should take adequate supplies of oral contraceptives and will need a certified Arabic translation of the certificate stating that the contraceptives have been prescribed for their personal use.

Those with recurring medical problems should also obtain a letter from their family doctor detailing the condition(s) – the letter can then be shown to doctors abroad if emergency treatment becomes necessary. People with surgically implanted devices are also advised to carry a doctor's certificate to show security officials. Artificial hip replacements frequently set off metal detection security alarms at airports, as do in-dwelling intravenous (e.g. Portacath) central venous lines. People with cardiac pacemakers are unlikely to run into problems due to electrical interference from British or North American airport metal detectors, but should try to avoid going through them and arrange instead for a personal body check by security officials.

Spare spectacles, contact lenses and contact lens solutions should also be obtained before travelling. If you are planning a vigorous holiday or expedition (e.g. skiing, hill-walking, etc) it is a good idea to begin an appropriate fitness regime before you leave. Expatriates taking up a contract abroad will often have to submit to a detailed medical examination as a condition of employment.

Individuals with specific chronic health problems, such as epilepsy, diabetes or long-term steroid treatment, should obtain a 'Medic-alert' bracelet or similar, which is more easily located in a medical emergency than a card in your pocket.

The pregnant traveller

Pregnancy can complicate travel for several reasons. Prior to travel, it alters advice about vaccination and malaria prevention. Live viral vaccines are not advised during pregnancy. These include oral polio vaccine (which is being phased out for everyone now), the measles, mumps and rubella vaccine (MMR), BCG, oral typhoid, varicella and yellow fever vaccines. If the requirement for yellow fever vaccine is bureaucratic rather than because of a real risk, a letter can be supplied to say that the pregnant traveller does not need the vaccine. If the risk of catching yellow fever is significant, the traveller may have to postpone travel or weigh up the relative risks of the vaccine against the risks of contracting yellow fever. Clearly, specialist consultation will be essential.

Drug-resistant malaria poses a problem for the pregnant traveller because malaria tends to be more severe in pregnancy and some of the more effective drugs for malaria prevention may not be safe. Therefore the pregnant traveller is advised not to visit areas where resistant malaria is highly endemic. Of the three preparations that are advised in areas where resistant malaria exists, doxycycline is completely contraindicated, mefloquine is advised against by the manufacturer, although studies have revealed little direct evidence of harm, and Malarone is not recommended unless there is no alternative. Options are therefore limited, and mosquito avoidance should be maximised.

Airlines will not allow women to fly in late pregnancy due to the risks and difficulty of premature delivery while in the air, and the cost of diverting for an unplanned landing. Check with the airline for specific limitations, and remember this applies to the return leg of travel too. Pregnancy is an additional risk factor for deep venous thrombosis (DVT), which is discussed elsewhere in this section. The precautions discussed later should be followed assiduously. Pregnant women are generally advised to limit long-haul flights because of increased radiation exposure. The radiation on a transatlantic flight would be roughly equivalent to one chest X-ray, and risk of harm to the foetus is likely to be very low.

Tropical disease may cause high fever and dehydration, which may put the foetus at risk, and premature delivery and/or miscarriage may require gynaecological/obstetric/neonatal intervention in a facility where standards of hygiene and medicine are not as they are in the West. There may be particular risks of blood-borne viruses to mother or the new-born.

The diabetic traveller

It is important that you carry details of your medical history and current medications with you in case of having to consult a doctor overseas. It would be advisable to have some form of letter specifically detailing your diabetes, otherwise airport security guards and immigration authorities/customs may take exception to carriage of syringes and needles. Ensure also that you carry adequate and appropriate medical insurance as well as a full supply of all essential medications. Although your insulin needs to be kept reasonably cool, a vacuum flask or cool box is adequate for most situations. Other specific areas of concern include:

- Time zones. It may be necessary to adjust your insulin regimen by taking an additional dose of short acting insulin on a westbound ('time lengthening') flight and reducing your dose on an eastbound flight.

- Avoid dehydration secondary to heat and/or gastrointestinal infection leading to diarrhoea and/or vomiting.
- Be careful with foot care (especially if you have any nerve damage secondary to your diabetes).

Diabetes UK is a valuable source of advice for the diabetic traveller (http://www.diabetes.org.uk/faq/trav.htm).

HIV-positive travellers

Many countries insist on a negative HIV antibody test before allowing foreigners to work. Some will not allow any known HIV-positive individual to enter the country (http://travel.state.gov/hivtestingreqs.html) despite advice from the World Health Organisation (WHO) that such regulations are ineffective as a means of controlling the spread of HIV infection. HIV-positive travellers should consult their medical specialists and local support groups about specific travel insurance problems and the advisability of travel. Vaccination advice for HIV-positive travellers is a specialised area, as live vaccines are contraindicated and some extra vaccinations may be indicated. Provision of extra 'standby treatment', e.g. for diarrhoeal illness while overseas, may be specifically indicated. Antiretroviral drug availability varies overseas, and some drugs need to be kept cool or refrigerated, so there are additional logistical constraints, and the side effects of some drugs are much worse in a very hot climate. ❧

Dr Nick Beeching is a senior lecturer at the Liverpool School of Tropical Medicine and clinical director of the Infectious Disease Unit at University Hospital Aintree. Dr Lisa Ford is a clinical lecturer in travel medicine at the Liverpool School of Tropical Medicine.

Essential medical kit for the traveller

CLEARLY REQUIREMENTS WILL VARY according to the destination, duration of stay, proposed activity and pre existing health of the traveller. Large medical kits are not required for most travel and the subject of expedition medical kits is not covered here.

PAINKILLERS: We always carry soluble aspirin (in foil-sealed packs), which is an excellent painkiller and reduces inflammation associated with sunburn (just be careful about the water you dissolve it in). Aspirin should not be given to children aged less than twelve, so take paracetamol or ibuprofen syrup for young children. Both paracetamol and aspirin reduce fever associated with infections. Adults who cannot tolerate aspirin because of ulcer problems, gastritis or asthma should instead take paracetamol (not paracetamol/codeine preparations). To avoid potential embarrassment with customs officials, stronger painkillers should only be carried with evidence that they have been prescribed.

CUTS AND GRAZES: A small supply of waterproof dressings (e.g. Band-Aids) is useful and a tube of antiseptic cream such as Savlon.

SUNBURN: British travellers frequently underestimate the dangers of sunburn and should take particular care that children do not get burnt. Protect exposed areas from the sun, not forgetting the back of the neck. If exposure to the sun is to increased, it should be done gradually, and remember to use adequate sunblock creams (waterproof if swimming), particularly at high altitude, where UV light exposure is higher. Sunburn should be treated with rest, plenty of non-alcoholic drinks and paracetamol or aspirin. Those who burn easily may wish to take a tube of hydrocortisone cream for excessively burnt areas.

MOTION SICKNESS: If liable to travel sickness, try to sleep through as much of the journey as possible and avoid reading. Avoid watching the horizon through the window and, if travelling by boat, remain on deck as much as possible. Several types of medication give potential relief from motion sickness when taken before the start of a journey, and sufferers should experiment to find out which suits them best. Antihistamines (e.g. Phenergan) are popular, especially for children, but should not be taken with alcohol. Adults should not drive until all sedative effects of antihistamines have worn off. Other remedies include Kwells (hyoscine tablets), Dramamine (dimenhydrinate) and Stugeron (cinnarazine). Scopoderm patches, only available on prescription, release hyoscine through the skin for up to three days. Hyoscine taken by mouth or by skin patch causes a dry mouth and can cause sedation.

CONSTIPATION: The immobility of prolonged travel, body clock disruption, dehydration during heat acclimatisation and reluctance to use toilets of dubious cleanliness all contribute to constipation. Drink plenty of fluids and try to eat a high-fibre diet. Those who are already prone to constipation may wish to take additional laxatives or fibre substitutes (e.g. Fybogel).

DIARRHOEA: This is a common problem. It may be worth taking a small supply of an antibiotic called ciprofloxacin and taking one 500mg tablet twice a day for one or two days if diarrhoea is severe, especially if it is accompanied by fever and/or passage of blood. The important thing is to maintain hydration. If you are not too unwell but the frequency of bowel movement itself is very inconvenient (e.g. when embarking on a long bus journey), it may be helpful to use an anti-motility agent such as loperamide. Diarrhoea reduces absorption of the contraceptive pill and women may wish to carry supplies of alternative contraceptives.

FEMALE PROBLEMS: Women who suffer from recurrent cystitis or vaginal thrush should consult their doctor to obtain appropriate antibiotics to take with them. Tampons are often difficult to buy in many countries and should be bought before travelling. Periods are often irregular or may cease altogether during travel but this does not mean that you cannot become pregnant.

INSECT BITES. If bitten by insects, try to avoid scratching, which can introduce infection, particularly in the tropics. Eurax cream or calamine lotion can relieve local irritation, and antihistamine tablets may help those who have been bitten extensively.

Antihistamine creams should be used with caution, since they can cause local reactions, and we prefer to use weak hydrocortisone cream on bites that are very irritating. Hydrocortisone cream should only be used if the skin is not obviously broken or infected. Increasing pain, redness, swelling or obvious pus suggest infection, and medical attention should be sought.

HIV PREVENTION: Most HIV infections are acquired sexually. All adults should consider taking a supply of condoms. Travellers to countries with limited medical facilities should consider taking a supply of sterile needles and syringes so that injections required abroad are not given with re-usable needles of doubtful sterility. Personal supplies of syringes and needles can make airlines and customs officials very suspicious, and condoms are not acceptable in some countries – particularly the Middle East.

To avoid problems at the border, it is worth buying these items as part of a small HIV/AIDS prevention pack, which is available from most of the medical equipment suppliers listed in the directory. Larger HIV prevention packs, which include blood product substitutes, are rarely worth carrying.

Health on the flight
by Alastair Miller and Nick Beeching

Deep Venous Thrombosis (DVT)

Deep venous thrombosis (DVT) occurs when the circulation in the deep veins of the legs and pelvis is disturbed in some way. There are three basic causes for DVT: one is because the blood has become more coaguable ('sticky, thickened') e.g. as a result of cancer or other medical problems. The second is that the walls of the deep veins have been damaged (e.g. by previous DVT or surgery) and, finally, the blood flow through the deep veins may be impaired by immobilisation. DVT may occur after surgical operations or after prolonged hospitalisation and it is increasingly recognised that it can occur after flights of any duration, but the longer the flight the more likely the clot. DVT is sometimes been known as 'economy class syndrome', although travellers in first and business class have a similar risk. DVT also occurs after other forms of travel with prolonged immobility, e.g. long, cramped coach or bus journeys.

The DVT itself can cause considerable pain, swelling and inflammation of the affected limb and may be followed by permanent swelling and discomfort. Portions of clot may become detached from the wall of the vessel and enter the circulation. These clots may then travel back to the heart in the veins, pass through the heart and end up in the lungs. This is a condition called pulmonary embolus (PE). (A clot in situ is often called a thrombus whereas a clot or other foreign body moving through the circulation is an embolus.) PE usually causes chest pain and breathlessness and, if large enough, will completely obstruct the circulation leading to collapse and death. Provided the diagnosis is made quickly there are effective treatments for DVT and PE. They involve the use of a drug called heparin that has to be given daily by injection for about a week, followed by a period during which oral anti-coagulant drugs such as warfarin (which is also used to poison rats) must be taken.

Airlines are well aware of the risks of DVT/PE and promote sensible techniques to reduce the risk. General precautions should include:

- Try to walk around the cabin as often as possible.
- Carry out the recommended exercises while sitting to promote blood flow.
- Drink plenty of (non-alcoholic) fluid.
- Wear loose fitting clothing and avoid tight ankle socks, although support stockings may be appropriate if there is a high risk of DVT.
- The use of a single low-dose (50-75mg) aspirin tablet before a flight is controversial. Although aspirin will reduce blood 'stickiness', there is no direct evidence of its benefit in this situation and it can certainly cause adverse reactions, such as indigestion and occasionally stomach bleeds. If you are at high risk for DVT, you should discuss the problem with your doctor.
- If you are in a high-risk group for DVT, your doctor may advise a small injection of heparin shortly before you travel (and before the return flight).

Jet lag

Crossing several time zones from east to west or west to east can disrupt natural body rhythms and lead to jet lag. The main features are general fatigue, disturbed sleep patterns, disturbed eating and bowel habits and impaired mental and physical performance. It may take several days to adjust to the new time zone.

There is no panacea for jet lag but several coping strategies can be employed:

- A westbound flight will lengthen your day, so try to stay awake during the flight and, on reaching your destination, go to bed based on the local time rather than your 'biological time'.
- On an eastbound overnight flight, try and sleep for the maximum duration and consider using a mild sleeping tablet (but see below for dangers).
- Limit caffeine and alcohol intake during the flight as they may disturb sleep.
- 'Get into' the new time zone as quickly as possible by setting your watch to the new time zone in which you find yourself and eating, going to bed and rising at appropriate local times.
- Be aware that your intellectual and physical performance will be impaired for the first day or so after arrival.

There is anecdotal support for the use of melatonin, but this is difficult to obtain in the UK. It does not appear to have any serious adverse effects. Sleeping pills may be of use on overnight eastbound flights (see above) and for the first few days after arrival to help in getting to sleep at an unaccustomed time. Ensure you use a short-acting preparation, such as Zopiclone or Zolpidem. However, taking sleeping tablets during the flight is not advised by most doctors because they promote prolonged immobility and hence DVTs.

Children

Children may find prolonged periods of flying particularly tedious, although many airlines now have individual game and TV consoles by each seat, which provide extra diversions. It is normal for babies to cry during the air pressure changes associated with take off and landing, and this helps to equalise pressures in their ears. Feeding infants during this time promotes swallowing (which has the same effect) and may be less noisy. It is wise to carry appropriate painkillers, e.g. paracetamol syrup, on the flight, together with adequate supplies of favourite snacks and drinks. Some parents have used antihistamines to sedate children during flights, but we do not recommend this.

Fear of flying

Many people have anxieties about flying for a variety of reasons, despite the excellent statistical safety records. In some people it may amount to a genuine phobia. It may be helpful to discuss fears with your doctor who may be able to give a short-term sedative or a beta-blocker to reduce the panic. Some airlines run fearful flyer programmes to help reduce anxiety levels.

Day-to-day health abroad
by Nick Beeching, Alastair Miller and Lisa Ford

Finding a doctor

Travellers should always seek qualified medical attention if any illness they are suffering from gets worse despite their own remedies. Large hotels usually have access to doctors, typically a local family doctor or private clinic. In remote areas, the nearest qualified help will be a rural dispensary or pharmacist, but seek advice from local expat groups, your consulate or embassy for details of local doctors.

Mission hospitals usually offer excellent care and they often have English-speaking doctors. In large towns, university-affiliated hospitals should be used in preference to other hospitals. The International Association for Medical Assistance to Travellers produces useful lists of English-speaking doctors overseas. If you feel that your medical condition is deteriorating despite (or because of) local medical attention, consider travelling home or to a city or country with more advanced medical expertise sooner rather than later.

Medication

Medicines sold in tropical pharmacies may be sub-standard. Always check the expiry date and that medications which should have been refrigerated are not being sold on open shelves. There is a growing market in counterfeit drugs, and locally prepared substitutes are often of low potency. Stick to brand names made by large international companies, even if these cost more. Insist on buying bottles that have unbroken seals and, wherever possible, purchase tablets or capsules that are individually sealed in foil or plastic wrappers. It is difficult to adulterate or substitute the contents of such packaging.

It is usually wise to avoid medications that include several active pharmacological ingredients, most of which will be ineffective and will push up the cost. Medication that is not clearly labelled with the pharmacological name as well as the brand name of ingredients is suspect (e.g. Nivaquine contains chloroquine, and this should be stated on the packaging).

Fever

Fever may herald a number of exotic infections, especially when accompanied by a rash. Fever in a malarial area should be investigated by blood tests, even if you are taking antimalarials. A raised temperature is more commonly due to virus infections such as influenza or localised bacterial infections that have obvious localising features such as middle ear infections or sinusitis (local pain), urinary tract infections (pain or blood passing water), skin infections (obvious) or chest infections including pneumonia (cough, chest pain or shortness of breath).

It may be worth taking a small supply of the antibiotic ciprofloxacin with you. This is active against most common bacteria that cause food poisoning, although there is increasing antibiotic resistance throughout Africa and Asia. It is usually possible to buy antibiotics overseas but there quality cannot be assured. Another useful antibiotic to take would be coamoxiclav (Augmentin). This is a penicillin-based compound, so is unsuitable for people who are allergic to penicillin. It is active against most common bacteria that cause ear/sinus infection, chest infections (such as pneumonia), urinary infection and skin/wound infections. An antibiotic commonly available overseas is cotrimoxazole (Septrin/Bactrim). This is active against some gut infections and most of the other common bacteria described above and is cheap. However, it can cause very unpleasant skin reactions.

If you are going to be travelling in very remote, highly malarial areas it may be worth carrying so-called 'standby' treatment for malaria. This is a treatment anti-malarial drug, to be taken if you get a major fever that could herald malaria despite taking your malaria prevention tablets. Seek urgent medical help swiftly thereafter.

Local infections

ATHLETE'S FOOT: Can become very florid in the tropics so treat this problem before departure. The newer antifungal creams and sprays, e.g. Canesten, are very effective and supersede the older antifungal dusting powders, but do not eliminate the need for sensible foot hygiene. In very moist conditions, e.g. in rainforests, on cave explorations or in small boats, lacerated feet can become a real and incapacitating problem. An adequate supply of silicon-based barrier cream is essential under these conditions.

BLISTERS: Burst with a sterile blade or needle (boiled for three minutes or hold in a flame until red hot). Remove dead skin. Cover the raw area with zinc oxide plaster and leave in place for several days to allow new skin to form.

EARS: Keep dry with a light plug of cotton wool, but don't poke matches in. If there is discharge and pain, take an antibiotic.

EYES: If the eyes are pink and feel gritty, wear dark glasses and put in chloromycetin ointment or drops. Seek medical attention if relief is not rapid.

FEET: Feet take a hammering so boots must fit and be comfortable. Climbing boots are rarely necessary on the approach march to a mountain, trainers are useful. At the first sign of rubbing, put on a plaster.

SINUSITIS: Gives a headache (feels worse on stooping), 'toothache' in the upper jaw and often a thick, snotty discharge from the nose. Inhale steam or sniff tea with a towel over your head to help drainage. Decongestant drops may clear the nose if it is mildly bunged up, but true sinusitis needs an antibiotic, so seek advice.

Skin infections

In muddy or wet conditions, many travellers will get some skin sepsis or infections in small wounds. Without sensible hygiene these can be disabling, especially in jungle conditions. Cuts and grazes should be washed thoroughly with soap and water or an antiseptic solution. Large abrasions should be covered with a Vaseline gauze, e.g. Jelonet or Sofratulle, then a dry gauze, and kept covered until a dry scab forms, after which they can be left exposed. Anchor dressings are useful for awkward places, e.g. fingers or heels. If a cut is clean and gaping, bring the edges together with Steristrips in place of stitches.

Teeth

When it is difficult to brush your teeth, chew gum. If a filling comes out, a plug of cotton wool soaked in oil of cloves eases the pain; gutta-percha, softened in boiling water, is easily plastered into the hole as a temporary filling. Hot salt mouthwashes encourage pus to discharge from a dental abscess, but an antibiotic will be needed.

Throat

Cold dry air irritates the throat and makes it sore. Gargle with a couple of aspirins or table salt dissolved in warm water, or suck antiseptic lozenges.

Unconsciousness

The causes range from drowning to head injury, diabetes to epilepsy. Untrained laymen should merely attempt to place the victim in the coma position – lying on their side (preferably the left side) with the head lower than the chest to allow secretions, blood or vomit to drain away from the lungs. Hold the chin forward to prevent the tongue falling back and obstructing the airway. Don't try any fancy manoeuvres unless you are practised, as you may do more harm than good. All unconscious patients, from any cause, but particularly after trauma, should be placed in the coma position until they recover. This takes priority over any other first aid manoeuvre.

In cases of fainting, lay the unconscious person down and raise the legs to return extra blood to the brain.

Injury

Nature is a wonderful healer if given adequate encouragement.

Burns: Superficial burns are simply skin wounds. Leave open to the air to form a dry crust under which healing goes on. If this is not possible, cover with Melolin dressings. Burn creams offer no magic. Deep burns must be kept scrupulously clean and treated urgently by a doctor. Give drinks freely to replace lost fluids.

Sprains: A sprained ankle ligament, usually on the outside of the joint, is a common and likely injury. With broad Elastoplast 'stirrup strapping' walking may still be possible. Put two or three long lengths downwards from mid-calf on the non-injured side, attach along the calf on the injured side. Follow this with circular strapping from toes to mid-calf overlapping by half on each turn. First aid treatment of sprains and bruises involves immobilisation (i), cold, e.g. cold compresses (c), and elevation (e); remember 'ice'. If painful movement and swelling persist, suspect a fracture.

Fractures: Immobilise the affected part by splinting to a rigid structure: the arm can be strapped to the chest, both legs can be tied together. Temporary splints can be made from a rolled newspaper, an ice-axe or a branch. Pain may be agonising and is due to movement of broken bone ends on each other, in such circumstances full doses of strong pain killers are needed.

The aim of splinting fractures is to reduce pain and bleeding at the fracture site, and thereby reduce shock. Comfort is the best criterion by which to judge the efficiency of a splint, but remember that to immobilise a fracture when the victim is being carried, splints may need to be tighter than seems necessary for comfort when at rest, particularly over rough ground.

Wounds at a fracture site or visible bones must be covered immediately with sterile material or the cleanest material available. Under such circumstances, start antibiotic treatment at once. Pneumatic splints provide excellent support but may be inadequate when a victim with a broken leg has a difficult stretcher ride across rough ground. They are of no value for fractured femurs (thigh bones). If you decide to take them, get the Athletic Long Splint, which fits over a climbing boot where the Standard Long Leg splint does not.

WOUNDS (DEEP WOUNDS): Firm pressure on a wound dressing will stop most bleeding. If blood seeps through, put more dressings on top, secured with absorbent crêpe bandages and keep up the pressure. You should elevate the injured part if possible.

On expeditions to remote spots, at least one member of the party should learn to put in simple sutures. This is not difficult – a friendly doctor or casualty sister can teach the essentials in ten minutes. People have practised on a piece of raw meat and on several occasions this has been put to good use. Pulling the wound edges together is all that is necessary, and a neat cosmetic result is usually not important.

Swimming

SAFE SWIMMING: Try to swim in pairs: a friend nearby in the water is more likely to distinguish between waving and drowning.

WHEN TO SWIM: Drowning seems too obvious a risk to mention, but it is the most common and the most serious risk of any water sport, and in many cases alcohol is involved. Don't swim when drunk. Some authorities still maintain that swimming after meals runs a risk of stomach cramps, although this is now a minority view.

WHERE TO SWIM: Safe swimmers find local advice before taking to the water. Deserted beaches are often deserted for a reason, whether it be sharks, invisible jellyfish or vicious rip tides. Beware of polluted water, as it is almost impossible to avoid swallowing some. Never dive into water of unknown depth. Broken necks caused by careless diving are a far greater hazard to travellers than crocodiles.

FRESHWATER SWIMMING: Is not advisable when crocodiles or hippopotamuses are in the vicinity. Lakes, ponds, reservoirs, dams, slow streams and irrigation ditches may harbour bilharzia (schistosomiasis). This is a widespread infection in Africa, the Middle East and parts of the Far East and South America, and is a genuine hazard for swimmers.

STRONG CURRENTS: In the sea and rivers, watch out for tides and rips: even a current of one knot is usually enough to exhaust most swimmers quickly. Swimming directly against a strong current is especially exhausting, and, if possible, it is best to swim across the flow, and so gradually make your way to the shore.

SNORKELLING: Snorkelling is a great way to see the seabed, provided that a proper mask is used, one that encloses the nose. Eye-goggles can cause bruising and eye damage from the pressure of water. A more serious risk is the practice of hyperventilating (taking several deep breaths) before diving in the hope of extending a dive. This can kill. Normally, the lungs tell the body to surface for air when the carbon dioxide level is too high. Hyperventilation disrupts this mechanism, so the body can run out of oxygen before the lungs send out their danger signals. This can lead to underwater blackouts, and drowning.

SCUBA DIVING: Scuba divers should be sure that local instruction and equipment is adequate and should always dive with a partner. The length of time between flying and diving is dependent on a number of factors, such as duration, depths and number of recent dives. It usually wise to wait 12-24 hours after diving before flying. Travellers who anticipate scuba diving in their travels are strongly advised to have proper training before setting out.

Diarrhoea

The worldwide distribution of traveller's diarrhoea is reflected in its many geographical synonyms, such as Delhi belly, the Aztec two-step, Turista, Malta dog, Rangoon runs, to name but a few. Typically, the illness starts a few days after arrival at your destination and consists of diarrhoea without blood, nausea with some vomiting and perhaps a mild fever. The mainstay of treatment is adequate rehydration and rest, and the illness is usually self-limiting within a few days. Antibiotics to treat or prevent this common problem are not usually prescribed in anticipation of an infection. Exceptions to this rule are business travellers or others embarking on short trips (less than two to three weeks) for whom even a short period of illness would be disastrous, e.g. athletes attending international meetings (see below for further details).

The most important aspect of the treatment of diarrhoea is the replacement of fluids and salts that have been lost from the body. For most adults, non-carbonated, non-alcoholic drinks that do not contain large amounts of sugar are quite adequate. For adults with prolonged diarrhoea and for children, it is more important to use balanced weak salt solutions that contain a small amount of sugar, which promotes absorption of the salts. These can be obtained in pre-packaged sachets of powder (e.g. Dioralyte, Rehidrat) that are convenient to carry and are dissolved in a fixed amount of sterile water. Dioralyte can also be bought in the UK as effervescent tablets, or as Dioralyte Relief sachets, which contain pre-cooked rice powder. This has the advantage of returning the watery stools to normal more rapidly, as well as replacing the salts that have been lost in the diarrhoea. If pre-packaged mixtures are not available, a simple rehydration solution can be prepared by adding eight level teaspoonfuls of sugar or honey and half a teaspoon of salt to one litre of water (with flavouring to tempt small children).

Nausea, which frequently accompanies diarrhoea, can usually be overcome by taking small amounts of fluid as often as possible. It may be necessary to give small children spoonfuls of fluid every few minutes for prolonged periods. If you or your child have severe vomiting that prevents any fluids being taken, medical attention must be sought immediately.

Anti-diarrhoeal drugs are not usually recommended and should rarely be given to children. Kaopectate is safe for children aged over two years, but not very effective (kaolin and morphine should not be carried). For adults, codeine phosphate, loperamide (Imodium or Arret) or diphenoxylate (Lomotil) are sometimes useful. These drugs should never be given to children and should not be used for bloody or prolonged diarrhoea as they can also prevent your body from eliminating the diarrhoea-causing organisms and toxins. They are best reserved for occasional use to prevent accidents while travelling – for example before a prolonged rural bus trip. Prolonged use of these medications may lead to troublesome constipation.

Preparations containing clioquinol are still widely available outside the UK, where it was previously sold under the trade name Enterovioform. These preparations are useless and should not be taken (they have been linked with severe side effects in some parts of the world). Other than rehydration solutions or the medications discussed in this article, we do not recommend purchasing medicines for diarrhoea from pharmacies or chemists.

Prevention

Travellers who wish to prevent diarrhoea should consult their medical adviser about preventative medication (a controversial issue within the profession) before travel. Liquid bismuth preparations (not an antibiotic) are effective, but huge volumes need to be carried in luggage (very messy if broken), and bismuth tablets are difficult to obtain in the UK. Various groups of antibiotics have been used in the past, including tetracyclines (e.g. doxycycline), sulphur-containing antibiotics (e.g. Steptrotriad or cotrimoxazole, Septrin or Bactrim) and quinolone agents (e.g. ciprofloxacin, norfloxacin, ofloxacin). In most parts of the world, the bacteria are now resistant to most of these agents and the quinolone class is the usual best choice.

Prophylactic antibiotics are not recommended for the majority of travellers, because of the limited duration of effectiveness and the possibility of side effects, including, paradoxically, diarrhoea. However, ciprofloxacin or similar may be used for short periods by those at special risk. A new non-absorbed antibiotic called rifaximin is showing promise, and is likely to become more widely available. The new oral cholera vaccine also offers protection against some of the bacteria causing traveller's diarrhoea, but is not licensed for this purpose in most countries (and is not needed for cholera protection by most travellers). Other vaccines are being developed.

Self-treatment with antibiotics for mild diarrhoeal illness is usually inappropriate, but a single dose or two doses of a drug such as ciproloxacin often stops troublesome traveller's diarrhoea. Travellers to remote areas may wish to carry a course of antibiotics for this and for more serious diarrhoeal illness, as discussed above. Bloody diarrhoea with abdominal pain and fever may be due to bacillary dysentery (shigella organisms) or a variety of other organisms such as campylobacter or salmonella. The most appropriate antibiotic would again be a quinolone such as ciprofloxacin. Prolonged bloody diarrhoea with mucus (jelly), especially without much fever, may be due to amoebic dysentery, which is treated with metronidazole (Flagyl) or tinidazole (Fasigyn). Prolonged, explosive diarrhoea with pale creamy motions may be due to giardia, a common hazard for overlanders travelling through the Indian subcontinent. This responds to metronidazole or tinidazole. These two antibiotics should not be taken at the same time as alcohol because of severe reactions between them.

If you have to treat yourself, obtain qualified medical investigation and help at the earliest opportunity. This is essential if symptoms do not settle after medication. Diarrhoea may be caused by other, more severe illnesses, including typhoid and malaria, and these would need specific treatment

Travellers who anticipate the need for self-treatment should take Richard Dawood's book *Travellers Health: How to Stay Healthy Abroad* (OUP).

Heat problems

Many travellers still leave temperate climates in search of the sun and, although warmth and sunshine make us feel good, they can also cause health risks and problems.

Dehydration

In a hot (and especially a humid) climate you will lose a large amount of body fluid through sweat, and therefore run the risk of dehydration. You are more at risk if you are overweight and unfit. It is important therefore to increase your normal fluid intake and this is especially important if you are exerting yourself with trekking or some other physical activity. Early symptoms of dehydration will be headache, lethargy and irritability. You may notice that you are not passing urine as frequently as usual and when you do, it may look very dark and concentrated. Paradoxically you may not actually feel very thirsty and it is therefore imperative that you make yourself drink at regular intervals. Caffeinated beverages and alcohol will promote urine flow and potentially worsen dehydration. If you are taking diuretics (water tablets) for high blood pressure or heart failure they too may exacerbate the situation. As discussed above, diarrhoea will lead to dehydration if fluid intake is not augmented to compensate for increased fluid loss. You should try and drink enough to ensure that your urine remains pale in colour. If you are drinking large amounts it may be sensible to increase your salt intake by adding extra salt to your food or taking salty snacks.

In heat stroke there is a failure of the body temperature-control mechanism. Sweating diminishes and body temperature rises. It is essential to try and cool the victim with cold baths or whatever mechanisms are available. They may require hospital admission for intravenous fluids, more aggressive cooling measures and exclusion of other underlying illness, such as malaria or meningitis.

Prickly heat

This is the irritating rash with tiny blisters on the sweatier parts of the body. It is usually a combination of sunburn and blockage of sweat pores. Some people seem to have a particular predisposition. The risk can be reduced by keeping the skin as clean and dry as possible. Calamine lotion may provide relief of symptoms.

Sunburn

The risks of skin damage from the sun are being increasingly recognised, both in terms of the ageing effect and the enhanced risks of skin cancer (especially malignant melanoma). In many countries it is no longer considered fashionable to be sporting a 'healthy' tan. Fair people are at particular risk and should take special care. Certain prescribed medication (e.g. doxycycline for malaria prevention or for acne, or amiodarone for heart disease) can cause photosensitivity – i.e. an increased risk of sunburn. The principle for prevention is to expose the minimum amount of skin for the minimum amount of time and use appropriate proprietary sunscreens.

Cold problems

Travellers are now beginning to visit the polar regions and many visit mountainous area where cold can be a major problem. Even in the desert the temperatures may drop precipitously at night. Cold problems can be divided into localised damage, such as frostbite or non-freezing cold injury, and the generalised problem of hypothermia (often known as 'exposure'). These conditions are covered elswhere in this section.

Altitude problems

One of the main problems of mountain travel is the effect of altitude. The percentage of oxygen in the atmosphere is the same at the top of Mount Everest as it is at sea level (21 per cent) but as the atmospheric pressure at the top of Everest is about one-third of that at sea level, the pressure of oxygen (known as the partial pressure) in the lungs is reduced and therefore a lower amount of oxygen gets into the bloodstream. Low oxygen in the lungs is called hypoxaemia and it leads to low oxygen concentrations in the tissues of the body – a condition called hypoxia. When you ascend to altitude and become hypoxic your body initially compensates by increasing the depth and frequency of your breathing and during the day it is usually very obvious that you are breathing more deeply both at rest and when exerting yourself.

At night your breathing tends to become shallower, so that your blood oxygen drops and you become hypoxic. Hypoxia stimulates your breathing and you breathe more deeply. As you breathe more deeply you blow off more carbon dioxide from your lungs. This reduces the amount of carbon dioxide in your lungs. As carbonic acid (a product of carbon dioxide) is the main cause of blood acidity your blood becomes less acidic (i.e. more alkaline) as you blow off carbon dioxide. Alkalinity of the blood (known as alkalosis) will inhibit your breathing centre and you then stop breathing until hypoxia then becomes a problem again and kick starts your breathing. This alternate deep breathing followed by cessation of breathing (apnoea) is called periodic or Cheyne Stokes respiration and can regularly be heard if you spend a night in the communal dormitory of a mountain hut. Various scientific studies have shown that as a result of Cheyne Stokes breathing people can become profoundly hypoxic at night when they go to altitude and it may be this hypoxia (or the associated lack of carbon dioxide) that precipitates the features of mountain sickness.

A drug called acetazolamide (Diamox) is often taken to reduce the risks of mountain sickness. This was originally developed for the treatment of an eye condition called glaucoma. It is a carbonic anhydrase inhibitor that works in the kidney to increase the loss of bicarbonate (the major alkali in the blood) and therefore make the blood more acidic. This so called metabolic acidosis will counterbalance the respiratory alkalosis caused by blowing off excessive carbon dioxide. It therefore smoothes out the respiration overnight and reduces overnight hypoxia.

Acute mountain sickness (AMS)

AMS will usually develop within 24-48 hours of arriving at altitude (above 3,000 metres above sea level). The precise mechanism is poorly understood, but nocturnal hypoxia is certainly a contributory factor (see above). The major risk is in going too high too fast. Being physically fit before ascending does not seem to offer major protection, but those with chronic chest conditions may be at additional risk. Having an infection or exerting yourself on arrival at latitude are also precipitants of AMS. Given time, the body will adapt itself to altitude (acclimatisation) but you must ascend slowly. The maxim is to 'climb high, sleep low' if at all possible. Above 3,000 metres you should try and limit the daily increase in your sleeping altitude to 300 metres if at all possible. On arrival at altitude, do not go for a run, an energetic swim (or a vigorous mountain bike ride as one of my travelling companions did). Keep well hydrated as dehydration may upset your kidney physiology and increase the chances of AMS.

Many of the features of AMS resemble a bad hangover or the early stages of seasickness. They include lethargy, fatigue, lassitude, nausea, loss of appetite, headache and depressed mood. In severe cases the sufferer may actually vomit and be unsteady on their feet. These early features of an altitude problem are sometimes known as 'benign AMS', as distinct from the more serious, potentially fatal complications.

Most people who have AMS will recover over 24-48 hours and can then safely ascend further. However, in some cases AMS may develop into its more extreme complications of high-altitude pulmonary oedema (HAPO) or high-altitude cerebral oedema (HACO). Oedema means fluid that has passed through blood vessel walls into the surrounding tissue, so HACO means fluid swelling of the brain. It is quite likely that so called benign AMS represents early cerebral oedema and, as the swelling worsens, the symptoms deteriorate to produce full-blown HACO, which may progress to coma and death. In HACO the headache and unsteadiness worsen and the individual may become drowsy and have blurred or double vision. HACO may appear out of the blue as the first indication of a problem or it may manifest itself as a worsening of benign AMS. HAPO similarly may develop out of the blue or following AMS. Its main features are inappropriate breathlessness or breathlessness at rest. There may be a cough, which is initially dry, as it worsens may be accompanied by production of pink, frothy sputum and cyanosis (a blue discolouration of the lips). HAPO and HACO may co-exist. It may be difficult to distinguish HAPO from pneumonia and, again, these conditions may co-exist.

Management of AMS and HAPO/HACO

If the symptoms of mild/benign AMS are present then the individual should not ascend further but should take plenty of oral fluid and drugs, such as paracetamol for the headache and various tablets for vomiting, to relieve symptoms. Some doctors may choose to give a powerful steroid called dexamethasone for early AMS. If symptoms settle over 24-48 hours then it may be reasonable for the sufferer to carry on climbing slowly, but if there is any doubt that symptoms are not fully resolved they should descend. Any features suggesting HAPO/HACO should precipitate urgent descent and dexamethasone treatment.

Larger expeditions may choose to carry a portable decompression chamber (known as a Gamov bag), which can be inflated with a foot pump. It may buy time, as may the administration of supplementary oxygen, but neither is a substitute for rapid descent. We can recount, from personal experience, that a descent of only 500 metres can make you feel like a new man,

Prevention of AMS

As previously described, the main way to avoid AMS is to ascend slowly and climb high, sleep low. Acetazolamide may aid acclimatisation by stimulating overnight breathing and ameliorating hypoxia. Various studies have demonstrated its efficacy, although there is still controversy over its use and it is certainly no substitute for slow ascent. Our advice is to take 500 mg at about 4 pm on the afternoon that you are first going to sleep at above 3,000 metres. Remember that it is a diuretic (water pill) but, hopefully, most of the diuretic effect will be over by the time you get into your sleeping bag. The advice from NaTHNaC is: "A dose of 125mg twice daily is likely to be effective and to be associated with fewer adverse events than higher doses. However, this dose has not been extensively studied in comparison with higher doses". This area remains controversial and many people find the frequent side effects of the drug to be unacceptable. ☙

Health on your return
by Alastair Miller, Nick Beeching and Lisa Ford

O N YOUR RETURN FROM A LONG TRIP it is not unusual to feel a mixture of euphoria, relief and anti-climax. Often the thought of returning to a seemingly mundane existence can be disturbing. It is fairly unusual to experience serious illness as a result of infections acquired overseas, but any untoward symptoms must be taken seriously and investigated appropriately. The main symptoms seen in returning travellers are fever, diarrhoea, skin rashes/lesions and jaundice. It is essential that not only do you consult your GP or get seen in a hospital emergency department, but that you specifically inform them of your recent travel. All doctors are trained to enquire about recent travel but they do not always remember. Some infections have a long incubation period, for example malaria may not appear until several months after travel, so you should alert your doctor to any travel within the last year.

Tell your physician where you have travelled (in detail), including brief stopovers. It may be that you are carrying some illness outside the spectrum normally considered. Sadly this has been known to cause mistaken diagnosis so that malaria, for example, has been labelled as influenza, with occasionally fatal consequences.

Some companies provide routine tropical disease check ups for their employees during or after postings abroad. They are not generally required by other travellers, particularly who have not been ill while abroad or after their return. Travellers who feel that they might have acquired an exotic infection or who have received treatment for infection abroad, should ask their doctor about referral to a unit with an interest in tropical diseases. Most health regions have a suitable unit. All travellers who have had freshwater exposure of their skin (e.g. when swimming, canoeing or wind-surfing) in a bilharzia (schistosomiasis) area should be screened at least three months after the last freshwater contact, or sooner if symptoms develop. Risk areas include many countries in Africa, the Middle East and parts of Asia, South and Central America and a few Caribbean islands. Symptoms may include wheezing, with fever and rashes or headache, or blood in urine, stool, or occasionally in semen, and may commence weeks to months after freshwater exposure.

After leaving malarial areas, many will feel less motivated to continue their anti-malarial drugs. It is strongly recommended that they be taken for the whole recommended period (which may be at least 28 days, depending on the drugs used) after leaving the affected area. Failure to do this has caused many travellers to develop malaria some weeks after they thought they were totally safe. This is more than a nuisance: it has occasionally been fatal.

Fortunately, the majority of travellers return home with nothing other than pleasant memories of an enjoyable interlude in their lives. ❧

ALASTAIR MILLER is a consultant physician in the Tropical & Infectious Disease Unit at the Royal Liverpool University Hospital. He has climbed on Everest and led treks and expeditions in the Himalayas, East Africa and Borneo.

Vaccinations required around the world

THIS TABLE SHOWS IMMUNISATIONS AND MALARIA RECOMMENDATIONS for each country. These can change at short notice, so it is essential that you seek current advice. Updated advice is available online at www.fitfortravel.scot.nhs.uk, www.nathnac.org. www.cdc.gov and www.who.int/ith/.

General observations

- All travellers should be up to date with their tetanus vaccination.
- Vaccines to consider in special circumstances (eg long-stay, rural or adventurous travel) include the following: BCG, diphtheria, typhoid, hepatitis B, japanese encephalitis (if travelling in Asia), rabies, tick-borne encephalitis (TBE) (in European forests).
- Hepatitis B and rabies vaccinations are commonly advised for long-term travel (ie more than 6 months): they are not shown on this chart, so seek specific advice on these.
- Hepatitis A is a common food- and water-borne infection. Vaccination provides protection for at least 10 years.
- Polio is still a problem in many areas, as indicated.
- Typhoid vaccine is important if travelling in parts of Asia. It may be less important for short stays in tourist or business hotels in other areas.

Special cases

YELLOW FEVER In some countries, yellow fever vaccination is a legal entry requirement. This is noted below with a superscript [1]. In other countries, it is an essential entry requirement only if the traveller has come from an infected area. This is noted with a superscript [2]. In either case, the immigration authorities will require documentary proof, such as a vaccination certificate, before allowing the traveller to enter their country. The superscript [3] indicates countries where we recommend yellow fever vaccination for all travellers for their personal protection, although officials require a certificate only for travellers from infected areas.

CHOLERA At some borders, officials may request a cholera certificate. However, this is an outdated requirement. The oral cholera vaccine is usually reserved for travellers visiting areas where cholera epidemics are occurring and there is limited access to medical care, or for relief and disaster aid workers.

MENINGITIS This refers to the meningitis ACWY vaccine, usually recommended for long- or local-stay travellers or during epidemics, unless otherwise stated.

MALARIA In many of these countries, malaria may only be present in certain localities. You should ask your travel clinic for the latest advice before you leave, as malaria recommednations may change at short notice. In addition, some countries are only partly endemic for yellow fever, and yellow fever vaccine recommendations may vary depending on your itinerary within a country.

Afghanistan	*Hep. A, Polio, Typhoid, Malaria, Y. Fever[2]*
Albania	*Hep. A, Polio, Typhoid, Y. Fever[2]*
Algeria	*Hep. A, Polio, Typhoid, Malaria, Y. Fever[2]*
American Samoa	*Hep. A, Y. Fever[2]*
Angola	*Hep. A, Polio, Typhoid, Malaria, Y. Fever[1]*
Antigua & Barbuda	*Hep. A, Typhoid, Y. Fever[2]*
Argentina	*Hep. A, Typhoid, Malaria, Y. Fever[4] (Iguacu only)*
Armenia	*Hep. A, Polio, Typhoid, Malaria*

Australia	Y. Fever[2]
Azerbaijan	Hep. A, Polio, Typhoid, Malaria, Diphtheria
Bahamas	Hep. A, Typhoid, Y. Fever[2]
Bahrain	Hep. A, Polio, Typhoid
Bangladesh	Hep. A, Polio, Typhoid, Malaria, Y. Fever[2]
Barbados	Hep. A, Typhoid, Y. Fever[2]
Belarus	Hep. A, Polio, Typhoid, Diphtheria
Belize	Hep. A, Typhoid, Malaria, Y. Fever[2]
Benin	Hep. A, Polio, Typhoid, Malaria, Y. Fever[1], Meningitis
Bermuda	Hep. A (if long stay)
Bhutan	Hep. A, Polio, Typhoid, Malaria, Y. Fever[2], Meningitis
Bolivia	Hep. A, Typhoid, Malaria, Y. Fever[3]
Borneo (see Malaysia or Indonesia)	
Bosnia Herzegovina	Hep. A, Polio, Diphtheria
Botswana	Hep. A, Polio, Typhoid, Malaria, Y. Fever[2]
Brazil	Hep. A, Typhoid, Malaria, Y. Fever[3]
British Virgin Islands	Hep. A, Typhoid
Brunei	Hep. A, Polio, Typhoid, Y. Fever[2]
Bulgaria	Hep. A, Polio, Typhoid
Burkina Faso	Hep. A, Polio, Typhoid, Malaria, Y. Fever[1], Meningitis
Burundi	Hep. A, Polio, Typhoid, Malaria, Y. Fever[1], Meningitis
Cambodia	Hep. A, Polio, Typhoid, Malaria, Y. Fever[2]
Cameroon	Hep. A, Polio, Typhoid, Malaria, Y. Fever[1], Meningitis
Cape Verde	Hep. A, Polio, Typhoid, Malaria, Y. Fever[2]
Cayman Islands	Hep. A, Typhoid
Central African Rep.	Hep. A, Polio, Typhoid, Malaria, Y. Fever[1], Meningitis
Chad	Hep. A, Polio, Typhoid, Malaria, Y. Fever, Meningitis
Chile	Hep. A, Typhoid
China	Hep. A, Polio, Typhoid, Malaria, Y. Fever[2]
China (Hong Kong)	Hep. A, Polio, Typhoid
China (Macau)	Hep. A, Polio, Typhoid
Colombia	Hep. A, Typhoid, Malaria, Y. Fever
Comoros	Hep. A, Polio, Typhoid, Malaria
Congo (Brazzaville)	Hep. A, Polio, Typhoid, Malaria, Meningitis, Y. Fever[1]
Congo (DRC)	Hep. A, Polio, Typhoid, Malaria, Y. Fever[1]
Cook Islands	Hep. A, Polio, Typhoid
Costa Rica	Hep. A, Typhoid, Malaria
Côte d'Ivoire	Hep. A, Polio, Typhoid, Malaria, Y. Fever[1], Meningitis
Croatia	Hep. A, Polio, Typhoid
Cuba	Hep. A, Typhoid
Czech Republic	Hep. A, Polio, Typhoid
Djibouti	Hep. A, Polio, Typhoid, Malaria, Y. Fever[2], Meningitis
Dominica	Hep. A, Typhoid, Y. Fever[2]
Dominican Republic	Hep. A, Typhoid, Malaria

East Timor	Hep. A, Polio, Typhoid, Malaria
Ecuador	Hep. A, Typhoid, Malaria, Y. Fever[1]
Egypt	Hep. A, Polio, Typhoid, Malaria , Y. Fever[2]
El Salvador	Hep. A, Typhoid, Malaria, Y. Fever[2]
Equatorial Guinea	Hep. A, Polio, Typhoid, Malaria, Y. Fever[3], Meningitis
Eritrea	Hep. A, Polio, Typhoid, Malaria, Y. Fever[2], Meningitis
Estonia	Hep. A, Polio, Typhoid, Diphtheria
Ethiopia	Hep. A, Polio, Typhoid, Malaria, Y. Fever[3], Meningitis
Fiji	Hep. A, Polio, Typhoid, Y. Fever[2]
French Guiana	Hep. A, Typhoid, Malaria, Y. Fever[1]
French Polynesia	Hep. A, Polio, Typhoid, Y. Fever
Gabon	Hep. A, Polio, Typhoid, Malaria, Y. Fever[1]
The Gambia	Hep. A, Polio, Typhoid, Malaria, Y. Fever[3], Meningitis
Georgia	Hep. A, Polio, Typhoid, Diphtheria, Malaria
Ghana	Hep. A, Polio, Typhoid, Malaria, Y. Fever[1], Meningitis
Greece	Y. Fever[2]
Grenada	Hep. A, Typhoid, Y. Fever[2]
Guadeloupe	Hep. A, Typhoid, Y. Fever[2]
Guam	Hep. A, Typhoid
Guatemala	Hep. A, Polio, Typhoid, Malaria, Y. Fever[2]
Guinea Republic	Hep. A, Polio, Typhoid, Malaria, Y. Fever[3], Meningitis
Guinea-Bissau	Hep. A, Polio, Typhoid, Malaria, Y. Fever[3], Meningitis
Guyana	Hep. A, Typhoid, Malaria, Y. Fever[3]
Haiti	Hep. A, Typhoid, Malaria, Y. Fever[2]
Honduras	Hep. A, Typhoid, Malaria, Y. Fever[2]
India	Hep. A, Polio, Typhoid, Malaria, Y. Fever[2], Meningitis
Indonesia	Hep. A, Polio, Typhoid, Malaria, Y. Fever[2]
Iran	Hep. A, Polio, Typhoid, Malaria
Iraq	Hep. A, Polio, Typhoid, Malaria, Y. Fever[2]
Israel	Hep. A, Polio, Typhoid
Jamaica	Hep. A, Typhoid, Y. Fever[2]
Japan	Polio, Typhoid
Jordan	Hep. A, Polio, Typhoid, Y. Fever[2]
Kazakhstan	Hep. A, Polio, Typhoid, Y. Fever[2], Diphtheria
Kenya	Hep. A, Polio, Typhoid, Malaria, Y. Fever[3], Meningitis
Kiribati	Hep. A, Polio, Typhoid, Y. Fever[2]
Korea (North)	Hep. A, Polio, Typhoid, Malaria
Korea (South)	Hep. A, Polio, Typhoid
Kuwait	Hep. A, Polio, Typhoid
Kyrgyzstan	Hep. A, Polio, Typhoid, Diphtheria
Laos	Hep. A, Polio, Typhoid, Malaria, Y. Fever[2]
Latvia	Hep. A, Polio, Typhoid, Diphtheria
Lebanon	Hep. A, Polio, Typhoid, Y. Fever[2]
Lesotho	Hep. A, Polio, Typhoid, Y. Fever[2]

Liberia	*Hep. A, Polio, Typhoid, Malaria, Y. Fever[1], Meningitis*
Libya	*Hep. A, Polio, Typhoid, Y. Fever[2], Malaria*
Lithuania	*Hep. A, Polio, Typhoid, Diptheria*
Macedonia	*Hep. A, Polio, Typhoid*
Madagascar	*Hep. A, Polio, Typhoid, Malaria, Y. Fever[2]*
Madeira	*Y. Fever[2]*
Malawi	*Hep. A, Polio, Typhoid, Malaria, Y. Fever[2], Meningitis*
Malaysia	*Hep. A, Polio, Typhoid, Malaria, Y. Fever[2]*
Maldives	*Hep. A, Polio, Typhoid, Y. Fever[2]*
Mali	*Hep. A, Polio, Typhoid, Malaria, Y. Fever[1], Meningitis*
Malta	*Y. Fever[2]*
Marshall Islands	*Hep. A, Typhoid*
Martinique	*Hep. A, Typhoid*
Mauritania	*Hep. A, Polio, Typhoid, Malaria, Y. Fever[1]*
Mauritius	*Hep. A, Polio, Typhoid, Malaria, Y. Fever[2]*
Mayotte	*Hep. A, Polio, Typhoid, Malaria*
Mexico	*Hep. A, Typhoid, Malaria, Y. Fever[2]*
Micronesia	*Hep. A, Typhoid, Malaria*
Moldova	*Hep. A, Polio, Typhoid, Diphtheria*
Mongolia	*Hep. A, Polio, Typhoid*
Monserrat	*Hep. A, Polio, Typhoid*
Morocco	*Hep. A, Polio, Typhoid, Malaria*
Mozambique	*Hep. A, Polio, Typhoid, Malaria, Y. Fever[2], Meningitis*
Myanmar (Burma)	*Hep. A, Polio, Typhoid, Malaria, Y. Fever[2]*
Namibia	*Hep. A, Polio, Typhoid, Malaria, Y. Fever[2]*
Nauru	*Hep. A, Polio, Typhoid, Y. Fever[2]*
Nepal	*Hep. A, Polio, Typhoid, Malaria, Y. Fever[2], Meningitis*
Netherlands Antilles	*Hep. A, Typhoid, Y. Fever[2]*
New Caledonia	*Hep. A, Polio, Typhoid, Y. Fever[2]*
Nicaragua	*Hep. A, Typhoid, Malaria, Y. Fever[2]*
Niger	*Hep. A, Polio, Typhoid, Malaria, Y. Fever[1], Meningitis*
Nigeria	*Hep. A, Polio, Typhoid, Malaria, Y. Fever[1], Meningitis*
Niue	*Hep. A, Polio, Typhoid, Y. Fever[2]*
Oman	*Hep. A, Polio, Typhoid, Malaria, Y. Fever[2]*
Pakistan	*Hep. A, Polio, Typhoid, Malaria, Y. Fever[2]*
Palau	*Hep. A, Typhoid*
Panama	*Hep. A, Polio, Typhoid, Malaria, Y. Fever[3]*
Papua New Guinea	*Hep. A, Polio, Typhoid, Malaria, Y. Fever[2]*
Paraguay	*Hep. A, Typhoid, Malaria, Y. Fever[2]*
Peru	*Hep. A, Typhoid, Malaria, Y. Fever[3]*
Philippines	*Hep. A, Polio, Typhoid, Malaria, Y. Fever[2]*
Pitcairn Island	*Hep. A, Polio, Typhoid, Y. Fever[2]*
Portugal	*Y. Fever[2]*
Puerto Rico	*Hep. A, Typhoid*

Qatar	*Hep. A, Polio, Typhoid*
Réunion	*Hep. A, Polio, Typhoid, Y. Fever[2]*
Romania	*Hep. A, Polio, Typhoid*
Russian Federation	*Hep. A, Polio, Typhoid, Diphtheria*
Rwanda	*Hep. A, Polio, Typhoid, Malaria, Y. Fever[1], Meningitis*
St. Helena	*Hep. A, Polio, Typhoid, Y. Fever[2]*
St Kitts & Nevis	*Hep. A, Typhoid, Y. Fever[2]*
St. Lucia	*Hep. A, Typhoid, Y. Fever[2]*
St. Maarten	*Hep. A, Polio, Typhoid, Y. Fever[2]*
St.Vincent & Grenada	*Hep. A, Typhoid, Y. Fever[2]*
Samoa (American)	*Hep. A, Polio, Typhoid, Yellow Fever[2]*
Samoa (Western)	*Hep. A, Polio, Typhoid, Y. Fever[2]*
São Tomé & Principe	*Hep. A, Polio, Typhoid, Malaria, Y. Fever[1]*
Saudi Arabia	*Hep. A, Polio, Typhoid, Malaria, Meningitis, Y. Fever[2] ([1] for pilgrims)*
Senegal	*Hep. A, Polio, Typhoid, Malaria, Y. Fever[3], Meningitis*
Seychelles	*Hep. A, Polio, Typhoid, Y. Fever[2]*
Sierra Leone	*Hep. A, Polio, Typhoid, Malaria, Y. Fever[3], Meningitis*
Singapore	*Hep. A, Polio, Typhoid, Y. Fever[2]*
Slovak Republic	*Hep. A, Polio, Typhoid*
Slovenia	*Hep. A, Polio, Typhoid*
Solomon Islands	*Hep. A, Polio, Typhoid, Malaria, Y. Fever[2]*
Somalia	*Hep. A, Polio, Typhoid, Malaria, Y. Fever[3], Meningitis*
South Africa	*Hep. A, Polio, Typhoid, Malaria, Y. Fever[2]*
Sri Lanka	*Hep. A, Polio, Typhoid, Malaria, Y. Fever[2]*
Sudan	*Hep. A, Polio, Typhoid, Malaria, Y. Fever[3], Meningitis*
Surinam	*Hep. A, Polio, Typhoid, Malaria, Y. Fever[3]*
Swaziland	*Hep. A, Polio, Typhoid, Malaria, Y. Fever[2]*
Syria	*Hep. A, Polio, Typhoid, Malaria, Y. Fever[2]*
Taiwan	*Hep. A, Polio, Typhoid, Y. Fever[2]*
Tajikistan	*Hep. A, Polio, Typhoid, Malaria, Diphtheria*
Tanzania	*Hep. A, Polio, Typhoid, Malaria, Y. Fever[3], Meningitis*
Thailand	*Hep. A, Polio, Typhoid, Malaria, Y. Fever[2]*
Togo	*Hep. A, Polio, Typhoid, Malaria, Y. Fever[1], Meningitis*
Tokelau	*Hep. A*
Tonga	*Hep. A, Polio, Typhoid, Y. Fever[2]*
Trinidad & Tobago	*Hep. A, Typhoid, Y. Fever[2]*
Tunisia	*Hep. A, Polio, Typhoid, Y. Fever[2]*
Turkey	*Hep. A, Polio, Typhoid, Malaria*
Turkmenistan	*Hep. A, Polio, Typhoid, Malaria, Diphtheria*
Turks & Caicos I.	*Hep. A*
Tuvalu	*Hep. A, Polio, Typhoid*
Uganda	*Hep. A, Polio, Typhoid, Malaria, Y. Fever[3], Meningitis*
Ukraine	*Hep. A, Polio, Typhoid, Diphtheria*
United Arab Emirates	*Hep. A, Polio, Typhoid, Malaria*

Uruguay	*Hep. A, Typhoid*
Uzbekistan	*Hep. A, Polio, Typhoid, Diphtheria*
Vanuatu	*Hep. A, Polio, Typhoid, Malaria*
Venezuela	*Hep. A, Typhoid, Malaria, Y. Fever*
Vietnam	*Hep. A, Polio, Typhoid, Malaria, Y. Fever[2]*
Virgin Islands	*Hep. A, Typhoid*
Wallis & Futuna I.	*Hep. A, Typhoid*
Yemen	*Hep. A, Polio, Typhoid, Malaria, Y. Fever[2]*
Yugoslavia	*Hep. A, Polio, Typhoid*
Zambia	*Hep. A, Polio, Typhoid, Malaria, Y. Fever*
Zimbabwe	*Hep. A, Polio, Typhoid, Malaria, Y. Fever[2]*

Travel health websites

US Centres for Disease Control and Prevention
www.cdc.gov/travel

UK Department of Health
www.dh.gov.uk/PolicyAndGuidance/HealthAdviceForTravellers/

Epilepsy Action
www.epilepsy.org.uk

UK Foreign Office, Know Before You Go Campaign
www.fco.gov.uk
Official health and safety awareness campaign

www.fitfortravel.scot.nhs.uk
Regularly updated website by the Travel Medicine Division at Health Protection Scotland (HPS).

www.flyana.com
Air travel health news

www.ifrc.org
International Federation of Red Cross and Red Crescent Societies.

www.tmb.ie/
Tropical medical bureau

www.tropicalscreening.com
Offers full check-ups for travellers about to leave or returning

www.who.int
www.who.int/topics/en/
World Health Organization, and its health topics page

www.thirdworldtraveler.com/Travel/TravelHealth.html
Information provided on disease risks and precautions

www.tmvc.com.au
The Travel Doctor, fact sheets, travel health advisory report and health alerts

www.bbc.co.uk/health/healthy_living/travel_health
BBC website for travel health

www.malariahotspots.co.uk
Website dedicated to the dangers of malaria and where it is prevalent

www.interhealth.org.uk
International medical aid agency

Travel health organisations

**BRITISH AIRWAYS
TRAVEL CLINICS**
213 Piccadilly
London
W1J 9HQ, UK
Walk-in service
also
101 Cheapside
London
EC2V 6DT, UK
Tel: 0845 600 2236

**CENTRAL PUBLIC HEALTH
LABORATORY**
61 Colindale Avenue
London
NW9 5HT, UK
Tel: 020 8200 4400
Fax: 020 8200 8264
www.hpa.org.uk
Independent advisory
board to doctors and other
medical professionals.

**DEPARTMENT OF
INFECTIOUS AND TROPICAL
DISEASES**
London School of Hygiene
& Tropical Medicine
Keppel Street
London
WC1E 7HT, UK
Tel: 020 7636 8636
www.lshtm.ac.uk/itd/

**TRAVEL MEDICINE
DIVISION OF SCOTTISH
CENTRE FOR INFECTION
AND ENVIRONMENTAL
HEALTH (SCIEH)**
Clifton House
Clifton Place
Glasgow G3 7LN, UK
Tel: 0141 300 1130

**INTERNATIONAL
ASSOCIATION FOR
MEDICAL ASSISTANCE TO
TRAVELLERS (IAMAT)**
www.iamat.org
Non-profit membership
organisation dedicated to
informing travellers of
health risks involved on

any trip. IAMAT has
offices located worldwide.
Call the number above for
enquiries. The addresses
for some offices are:
Canada
40 Regal Road
Guelph, Ontario
N1K 1B5, Canada
Tel: 519 836 0102
Fax: 519 836 3412
USA
IAMAT
1623 Military Rd #279
Niagara Falls,
NY 14304-1745, USA
Tel: 716 754 4883
New Zealand
PO Box 5049
Christchurch 5, NZ
Switzerland
57 Chemin des Voirets
1212 Grand-Lancy
Geneva, Switzerland

HEALTH CONTROL UNIT
Terminal 3 Arrivals
Heathrow Airport
Hounslow, Mdsx
TW6 1NB, UK
Tel: 020 8745 7209
Up-to-date information
on immunisations.

MASTA
0113-238-7575 Moorfield
Road, Yeadon, Leeds, UK
LS19 7BN
Tel: 0906-550-1402
www.masta.org

**THE HOSPITAL FOR
TROPICAL DISEASES**
Mortimer Market Bldng,
Capper Street,
Tottenham Court Road,
London WC1E 6AU, UK
Travellers healthline
tel: 09061 33 77 33
Appointments
tel: 0207 388 9600
Reference centre for travel
medicine with large range
of medical products

**US DEPARTMENT OF
HEALTH AND HUMAN
SERVICES**

Centers for Disease
Control
1600 Clifton Road,
NE Atlanta, GA
30333, USA
Tel: (404) 639-3534 / (800)
311-3435
www.cdc.gov

Medical kit suppliers

BCB
UK tel: 0808 100 2867
www.bcb.ltd.uk
Email sales@bcb.ltd.uk

HOMEWAY
UK tel: 0870 748 9562
Fax: 0870 748 9564
Email admin@
travelwithcare.com
www.travelwithcare

JOHN BELL & CROYDEN
UK tel: 020 7935 5555
fax: 020 7935 9605
email: jbc@
johnbellcroyden.co.uk
Professional medical
advice on travel and
expedition supplies.

**MEDICAL ADVISORY
SERVICE FOR TRAVELLERS
(MASTA)**
Travellers Health Line tel
0906 8224 100
Travel Clinic Location Line
tel 01276 685040
www.masta.org
Medical advice tailored to
your journey.

**NOMAD TRAVEL STORE AND
MEDICAL HEALTH INFOLINE**
UK tel: 09068 633414
www.nomadtravel.co.uk

THE TRAVEL DOCTOR
www.traveldoctor.co.uk
Email: info@
traveldoctor.co.uk
Customised medicine lists
to meet your needs.
E-MED TRAVEL CLINIC
Private medical services
www.e-med.co.uk

Safe travel

Everyday safety hazards
by safety consultants at Red24

A TRAVELLER'S BEST FRIEND IS EXPERIENCE, and it can take dozens of trips to build this the hard way. Most problems encountered by travellers could have been avoided with careful planning and proper precautionary measures. Information about your destination is readily available from various sources, including the relevant red24 country pages, travel publications, journals, magazines, tour operators, the internet, and recently returned travellers. It is important to be aware of the current situation in the country of your destination prior to travel, and of factors such as crime levels, and political and civil stability. The following tips are intended to offer assistance to potential travellers.

Travel health tips

Travellers should consult a travel medicine clinic or doctor 4–6 weeks before departing on a journey to another country. The consultation will determine the need for any vaccinations and/or anti-malarial medication, as well as any other medical items that the traveller may require. It is also worth enquiring whether it is necessary or advisable to get a dental check-up. This is particularly important for people with chronic or recurrent dental problems. It is also important to obtain comprehensive medical insurance prior to travel. Medical emergencies and evacuations can be costly.

In general, it is best to avoid tap water and ice when travelling; rather stick to bottled or boiled water. Food from street vendors should generally be avoided; and ensure that food is thoroughly cooked before eating. Problems can be further reduced by taking your own utensils with you.

Airport problems

Prior to travel ensure that you obtain correct travel documentation to ensure easy entry. Book flights well in advance; check visa requirements and expiry dates of passports. Have official photocopies available of all your official documentation. Some countries insist on a passport validity of at least six months. The traveller should also find out in advance whether he or she will be required to pay an airport tax on departure, and if so how much. This is normally only a token sum, and almost always payable in local currency. Occasionally an equivalent sum in US dollars will be accepted.

Always pack your own bag and do not offer to carry any parcels if you are unsure as to what is inside. On luggage tags rather give an office address, without the name of the company; do not include personal details. When passing through airport security keep an eye on any items that go through the luggage scanners; try to go through security points as the items pass through the scanner. To ensure a smooth passage through customs, find out beforehand what items are prohibited in the country, and do not carry these. If you need to take prescribed medicines while travelling, keep the medicines in the original containers, and also carry a doctor's letter explaining the prescriptions.

Taking public transport

When catching taxis or shuttles try to use established and registered companies or ask airport information and hotel reception for reputable taxi drivers and shuttles; carry around the number of the company for future reference. Ensure that you have small change or a few low-denomination banknotes in your pocket for paying transport fares. Two good tips for dealing with the drivers of unmetered taxis are:

- Know a little of the local language – at least enough to be able so say 'Hello', 'Please take me to ...', 'How much?' and 'Thank you'. After all, the driver's aim is only to try and make some extra money. He doesn't want to get involved in a major row at the risk of being reported to the authorities.
- Try and have the correct amount ready to hand over. This prevents the driver pleading that he has not got sufficient change – a ruse that often succeeds, particularly when the passenger is in a hurry. It also avoids 'misunderstandings', and prevents the driver from charging an amount higher than what was agreed upon.

Be especially vigilant at transport hubs, such as bus and train stations, and keep an eye on your belongings as these locations are often frequented by pickpockets.

Travel security

One of the most important things to keep in mind when travelling is the safety of your possessions.

To minimise the chances of theft try to separate your funds, dividing them between your luggage and your person, so as to frustrate thieves and reduce losses. Try to carry only one credit card; photocopies of important documents; and only as much money as you think you'll need for that day. Before you leave home make arrangements with a reliable person whom you can contact for help in an emergency. Generally, American Express issue the most reliable and easily negotiable travellers' cheques, have the most refund points in the world, and usually have the speediest reimbursements.

It is often extremely difficult to separate the con man from a genuinely friendly person when travelling; however, beware of the 'smiling stranger' when abroad. A favourite ploy of the con artist is for him to offer his services as a guide. This advice also applies to some extent to street traders: the kind who wander about with their arms full of bracelets or wooden carvings. They may give the souvenir hunter a good deal, but prices on the stands or in the shops should be checked first, as items may sometimes be cheaper here.

Many thefts will be carried out (without your noticing) from your hotel room, or by pickpockets in a crowded street. Never use a handbag without a zip, and keep your hand over the fastener at all times. Never carry anything valuable in the back pocket of your trousers or the outside pocket of a jacket. A money-belt is the most secure method of carrying valuables, although even this is not foolproof. While on the move, never let your luggage out of your sight. Wrap the straps of your bag round your leg while sitting down (a good reason for a longer shoulder strap) so you can feel it if not see it. Lock or padlock everything to lessen the chance of casual pilfering. It should be noted that a slightly tatty case is far less inviting than brand new leather Gucci luggage. In many poorer countries it is advisable not to wear or hold anything that is too obviously expensive, especially at night. You should be particularly wary in Africa and South America.

In urban areas, the best advice is to stay in the city centre at night. If it is imperative to move away from the lights, go by taxi and try not to go alone. And don't forget to press down the door locks when you get in. If by some mischance you do find yourself walking along a remote, unlit road at night, at least walk in the middle of it. This will lessen the chances of being surprised by someone concealed in the shadows.

Backpacks are good to travel with, but in crowded trains or buses beware of those pouches and zippers that can be opened by someone standing close behind you. Make sure you carry your most important documentation in a place that cannot be accessed from a pouch you cannot see.

Muggings

If you come face-to-face with your robbers, use all the communication skills you have picked up on your travels. Try humour. At least try to elicit their sympathy, and always ask them to leave items which will be of no immediate value to them but are inconvenient for you to replace. Robbers are usually after cash, and valuables that are easily converted into cash. Violence is usually committed with a view to robbery; to avoid this it is important to offer no resistance. The idea that a pistol under the car seat or your belt offers protection is usually nonsense; protecting yourself from attack by carrying a firearm is not recommended. Use a dummy wallet that can carry out of date credit cards and a small amount of cash that can be given to a mugger in such an instance.

If mugged, consider what action you can take if you find yourself penniless in a foreign land. Report thefts to the police and obtain the necessary forms for insurance purposes. You may have to insist on this and even sit down and fill the form in for them to sign. Whatever it takes, you mustn't leave without it. It may be essential to you for onward travel.

If there is an embassy or consulate, report to them for help. In a remote spot you are more likely to get help from the latter. In cases of proven hardship, they will pay your fare home in exchange for your passport and the issue of travel papers. If you are having money sent to you by your family or your bank, have the money sent either to the embassy via the Foreign Office or to the bank's local representative, with a letter or cable sent to you under separate cover. This will give you proof that the money has been sent when you turn up at the bank. Some countries do not always use our order of filing: for example letters for Mr John Smith could be filed under 'M' or 'J'. Have your communications addressed to your family name followed by initials (and titles if you feel the need).

An effective way of getting home in such a situation is to phone your contact at home and ask him or her to telex or fax air tickets for a flight out. This has the advantage of circumventing currency regulations that various countries impose. In desperate situations, help can be obtained from people locally, ranging from well-off and well-connected expatriates to religious communities. Do not abuse assistance and repay it when you can.

Women travellers

To avoid the dangers of sexual assault and rape, women travellers should be especially aware of their surroundings and the people around them. Stay away from remote or deserted areas, keep to well-lit and well-travelled areas, and avoid short cuts; never hitch hike. In general, conservative clothing (skirt below the knees, demure neckline, covered arms) is less likely to attract unwanted male attention and harassment.

Female travellers should also be cautious when travelling to Islamic countries and should expect more conservative norms than previously experienced. As each Muslim country differs in its degree of Sharia law, it is advisable to find out beforehand what types of dress and behaviours are considered acceptable.

It is also advisable to carry a wooden wedge with you to secure your room door.

Cultural considerations

One of the biggest minefields for the unsuspecting traveller is local courtesies and customs, and it is useful to find out what cultural practices should be observed in a particular country. For example, it is worth knowing that you should not insult a Brazilian by talking to him in Spanish (the Brazilians are proud of the fact that they are the only nation in South America to speak Portuguese). It's also important to understand that the Chinese, Japanese and Koreans believe in formalities before friendship – and that they adore business cards.

It is important to research the countries you intend to visit; talk to people who have lived in or visited them and find out what problems you are likely to encounter. If you go prepared and adopt a sympathetic, understanding frame of mind you should be able to manage without trouble. Respect is always crucial when facing local customs, and civility, politeness, warmth and straight dealing transcend most linguistic or cultural barriers. Be aware of cultural differences. Actions that might seem acceptable in your country could lead to an incident or even detention in another.

Hotel security

Theft is rife in hotels all over the world, from bag-snatching and pickpocketing in the lobby to full-scale theft. The following points should be considered when choosing a hotel:

● Do the room doors open on to a hallway, or directly to the outside (the safer option)?

● What sort of keys system does the hotel use? The electronic card keys and metal keys with a magnetic strip now used in most business hotels provide greater security than traditional locks, as they can be changed after each visitor.

● What sort of locks do the doors have on the inside? Ideally the door should be self-locking, with a deadbolt, peephole and security chain or bar. Also check the door frames to make sure they are sturdy.

● Is the front desk staffed on a 24-hour basis?

● Never leave your room key exposed in a public place, such as on a bar table.

● Never leave valuables of any description in your hotel room. Buy a good insurance policy and leave valuables in the hotel safe.

Budget travellers may find there are no locks on the doors at all, in which case the best strategy is probably to take no valuables and carry the essentials with you at all times. As with everything, prevention is better than cure. Never leave valuables in a hotel room, even out of sight; put valuables in the hotel safe and make sure you get a proper receipt.

Fire

When choosing a hotel it is important to select one with adequate safety precautions, such as a smoke detection system, fire exits, protected escape routes, and fire doors. After a long and gruelling journey, searching out the nearest hotel fire exits is probably not going to be your number one priority, but it should be. Ultimately, responsibility for your safety lies in your own hands. Although fire regulations in the United Kingdom are tight and generally strictly enforced, it is important to remember that this is not the case in all countries. If fire does break out, remember that it is the smoke, rather than the fire itself, that is the major killer. The following precautions will maximise your chances of survival in case of fire:

● On arrival, check the ground floor layout and identify escape routes.

● If there are no alternative stairways or exits from the ground floor, and if dining rooms, bars and discos seem cramped or inadequate, you might want to consider staying somewhere else.

● Read the fire emergency instructions in your room and find the fire exit, making sure that it is free of obstruction (if it is not, complain).

● Walk to the nearest escape route, counting the doors from your room to the exit. This will help should the lighting fail or smoke obscure visibility.

● Note the location of fire alarm call points in the vicinity of your room, and familiarise yourself with the layout of your room and the way to the door.

● Find out what (if anything) lies outside and beneath the window and keep your valuables next to the bed for easy access.

● Don't smoke in bed, and never ignore a fire alarm. ❧

RED24 *is a global security and risk assessment consultancy. See www.red24.info.*

The executive target
by safety consultants at Red24

How POTENTIAL SECURITY THREATS ARE TACKLED, and the steps that can be taken to eradicate them, depends on the location of the business interest and the broad socio-political situation of the country. Security advice can vary from urging employees to avoid certain areas and locking up their belongings, to recommending more serious measures to take when facing a terrorist attack. Naturally, before security advice is sought, an organisation needs to assess what is required in each environment. Staff must also be prepared for the fear and shock of working in a potential high-risk environment. Below are some general issues that can be discussed and developed to ensure the safety of all employees.

Political kidnappings are on the rise, and they are not quite as random as one would think. The victim's nationality or supposed nationality, as well as their position in the company, is often the sole reason for him or her being attacked. Being a foreigner, especially in some areas of the Middle East and Central America, can increase your risk of harm dramatically, regardless of your stature or wealth. Instead, political and religious fanatics often regard ordinary citizens as legitimate targets, and this view will become more prevalent as prominent people take ever more effective steps to protect themselves. One only needs to look at the recent horrific kidnappings and beheadings in Iraq.

Colombia has just recently been overtaken by Mexico as the world's kidnapping capital. The more people with the means protect themselves, the more will the average traveller be targeted. No-one travelling to certain parts of the world can sensibly afford to ignore the danger.

Do your homework

Awareness is vital, and it is surprisingly easy for any intelligent person to do the sort of homework that can save your life. Terrorist violence is rarely, if ever, carried out as randomly as it sometimes appears. Particularly in the case of kidnapping, the victim will first be observed for days before a move is made. Taking a few simple precautions often means that the would-be perpetrators will just as simply look elsewhere. The majority of terrorist abductions are facilitated by the victim developing a regular pattern of behaviour, or being ignorant of the dangers in a strange country. Testing the political climate should be on top of your homework list, just like researching the quality of the drinking water or the availability of banks. Make a clear threat assessment before you go, and get the best advice available. An intelligent interest in available media is a fundamental requirement for making such an assessment of your safety. Sensible analysis of media reports will answer many questions about known trouble spots and help predict others. If you are still unsure, speak to someone, ask red24, or check out the website www.red24.info to receive a detailed country report.

It is crucial to get a balanced idea of the official attitude in the country to be visited. The host government's status and its relationship with the visitor's country are always critical factors. A basically hostile or unstable government will always increase the danger to individual travellers in a number of ways. It is just as well to know as much as possible about feelings amongst the local populace, which are by no means guaranteed to be the same as those of the authorities. National identity, and even religion, is often viewed quite differently on the street, although the bias is just as likely to be favourable as not.

Before you go you need to have a good idea of how well you or your organisation is known there. Is your visit being reported in the press? Are you expected by the general populace?

Here is what executives need to know before they travel:
- Avoid wearing clothing with a corporate logo.
- Refrain from wearing expensive jewellery and watches or carrying expensive luggage.
- Never place your business card on your luggage tag.
- Avoid carrying too many credit cards, as this may attract kidnappers who may take you from bank to bank to withdraw cash – commonly called 'express kidnapping'
- Understand that the most simple of questions can lead to danger if answered truthfully. For example, the innocent question 'What do you do for a living?' may have dire consequences.

The traveller will need to know how his company is perceived by various local factions. Previous threats or attacks on company employees should be studied with great care, as should incidents involving similar organisations. In the absence of any actual events, examine the company's standing in the community, especially where a conflict of interest exists between government and opposition groups. Once you have the answers to these questions, you will be much better prepared to make an educated and intelligent decision on future action. In many cases, even if a danger does exist, you need to go; this is especially true for business travellers where the decision to cancel is not always an option.

What to do when there

Terrorists generally have a need for soft targets. They seem to have a reluctance to proceed beyond basic research to find targets, and this can be used to your advantage. Sensible precautions, such as varying times of arrival and departure, parking in different places, watching for and reporting suspicious activity before leaving home, and entering and leaving by different doors, are simple precautions that really do work. If a target is perceived to be cautious and vigilant, there is not much to tempt the would-be attacker to continue surveillance.

All travellers to high-risk areas should follow certain basic rules:
- Where possible have your host set up transportation and hotel accommodation. In some countries it is advisable to engage the services of a driver/bodyguard after checking their credentials.
- Inform your local embassy or consulate of the details of your stay, such as its duration and places you will be staying at. If the situation deteriorates, contact

Security information websites

UK Government travel warnings: www.fco.gov.uk/travel

UK Government travel warnings: www.travel.state.gov/travel/warnings.html

CIA world factbook: www.odci.gov/cia/publications/factbook

Troublespots: www.csoonline.com

the local embassy or consulate, particularly if you need to be evacuated.

- Establish whether any demonstrations that could lead to unrest could be occurring during your stay (e.g. if elections are planned). If such an incident occurs, stay indoors for its duration.
- Keep friends and colleagues informed of your whereabouts and stay in company as much as possible.
- Dress down and leave expensive accessories at home.
- Don't book hotels in the company's name.
- In all, practise being nondescript in public.

Concerning residential areas, security advisors should undertake investigations into suitable residential areas, outlining areas which are considered safe and those thought to be dangerous. Foreign staff should be housed in a safe area which, if possible, should be located close to the company premises and within easy access. The residence should be adequately protected and secure, and important security factors to consider include outer walls; fencing; secure access points; the number of security personnel required, such as trained or armed guards at entrance and exit points and guard patrols; surveillance cameras; and also protection of doors and windows, emergency buttons and central alarm systems. Executives should even have an evacuation plan in place.

Transport is a big issue when abroad, and offers the offender plenty of opportunity. Transportation methods may vary. Employees may use private vehicles, or the situation may require the use of a trained security driver. High-profile foreign staff may need additional security such as armed bodyguards and bullet-proof vehicles. Private vehicles should be adequately safe and secure in terms of accident prevention and standard vehicle safety. Make a habit of changing places in the car if you have a driver, or use a taxi now and then instead. The chances of being attacked on the move are extremely remote. It follows that road junctions, traffic signals, etc., are always more dangerous than, say, stretches of dual carriageway. A prospective attacker will study his victim's route carefully and identify vulnerable spots.

- Be aware of these danger areas and stay on the alert when negotiating them.
- If driving yourself, keep the car in gear and ready for a quick getaway at temporary halts.
- Keep sufficient space between yourself and any leading vehicles to avoid being boxed in.
- Routinely lock all doors and keep the windows wound up.

- Use inconspicuous means of transport, but avoid public transport in favour of taxis. If in doubt, wait for the second cab in the rank.
- Never take a taxi if the driver is not alone.
- Only tell the taxi driver where you want to go once you are in the taxi with the door closed instead of on the street

Make sure you come home safely

Try not to think of these rules as an inconvenience but as a natural consequence of your stay in a strange country. It is better to extend precautions than to limit them. You stand more chance of being an accident casualty than a victim of terrorism. Far from being dangerous, a little knowledge can stack the odds even higher in your favour. ❧

How to survive a war zone
by safety consultants at Red24

IT IS A GOOD IDEA BEFORE TRAVELLING to a foreign country to do a little research and establish the current political climate or crime situation there. If, for example, there have been recent incidents of rioting or anti-government protests, the likelihood of encountering further such incidents is likely and you should plan accordingly. Watch local media reports to help you decide which areas may be safe for you to travel in. For example, say you were backpacking through Mauritania on 3 August 2004 and the coup took place just as you settled in your hotel. You were probably aware, if you had done your homework, that Mauritania was having a few problems and you should have thought of that before you went, but, surprises do happen. In such a case, what do you do?

You are stuck in a conflict zone where the threat of bodily harm is very real. Communications with the outside world cease, public utilities go wrong and airports close. This is the guaranteed scenario. What do you do after the street blocks, cordons, summary arrests and general paralysis, as order is imposed on a troubled area? That presents the visitor with new problems.

Precautions

First off, you need to make an assessment of your situation. Once you are out of immediate harm's way, take a look at what you have with you. The first and best rule is worth observing before you leave home for a troubled land – never pack more than you can run with. Always include a smaller, lighter bag such as an airline bag, because if things get really nasty you need something handy with a shoulder strap to pick up and clear out with in a hurry. If you are in a situation in which something is likely to happen, it is worth keeping this bag packed with essentials. Do not run about with suitcases, they will be to heavy and you will leave it behind before too long.

Because these situations happen without warning and you will most likely be unprepared, it is probable that your hotel will also be unable or even unwilling to help you, and you will need to get creative if you are going to survive or at least do so with some level of comfort. As the water supply will either shut down completely or turn a threatening colour, it is just as well to have a means of making water sterile. It is a good idea to fill the bath. You can keep filling it if supplies continue, but you cannot get water at all if they really stop. Not only do you then have a means of keeping a working toilet, but you can also wash yourself and stave off thirst (boil or sterilise the water). It is also a good idea to take a torch with fresh batteries. If the water is being turned off, the electricity can't be that far behind.

Although red24 would advise that you stay put in the event of an emergency, if you do decide to leave your hotel room, take note that stealing and looting will increase dramatically. It would be a good idea not to leave your things in your hotel room, or better still take everything with you that is essential in case you can't get back to your room.

It is also likely that in such a situation you will have to bribe officials. If you are going to a conflict zone, knowingly bring some duty-free allowances; cigarettes, alcohol and perfume are the stuff of which bribes and rewards for favours are made. And as banks close or the money exchange goes berserk, they may end up as your only bargaining resource. However, if you do have enough cash on you, do not carry large wads together. Rather keep smaller denominations in various pockets to create the impression that this is all you have.

You are much more likely to be holed up in your hotel, however. If things are exploding under fire, get any movable glass down on the floor, draw curtains and blinds against window glass and drape mirrors you can't take down with blankets and towels. Glass is the biggest danger you face. Locate the fire escape, and if it's remote get yourself somewhere else to stay either in the same hotel or elsewhere.

While ordinary communications often stop altogether, it is a good idea to tell your family or company to keep on telephoning you from the outside. In such times of emergency it is often the case that incoming calls can still come in while it is impossible to get calls out.

Approaching checkpoints

Eventually, assuming everything goes well, you will be able to leave the hotel. When you do, one thing there will certainly be is checkpoints. In developing countries or countries which are governed by military regimes, vehicle checkpoints or manned roadblocks are commonplace; it is not unusual to travel through an area in conflict and encounter checkpoints manned by opposing factions along the same road. In areas where conflict is taking, or has taken place, the purpose is to check the movement of civilians and opposition military personnel. Should you be cautious of walking with too many papers/information, red24 advises that when travelling you make copies of your documents and scan them, or send yourself an email with your travel details/important document numbers written down so you can access them via email.

When approaching a checkpoint, begin to slow down some distance away and drive up slowly and try to assess if it is a genuine checkpoint or an illegal one. If you determine that it is an illegal checkpoint you will have to decide whether you are going to carry on and approach it or reverse and turn around. In adopting the latter course of action you will have to ensure that it is safe to do so. If you decide to continue towards the checkpoint, approach it slowly.

Regardless of where you are and who has stopped you, it is important that you be polite and cooperate with the personnel manning the checkpoint and do as they tell you. Failure to comply with their instructions will only invite trouble, and if they are particularly ill-disciplined or just inexperienced, they may over-react. In some circumstances you will have to pay the officials in order to be let through – a decision to do so should not be taken lightly.

It may be difficult to see a roadblock at night, but if you are signalled to stop by military personnel or a police patrol you should obey their instructions. Do not attempt to reverse or turn around or attempt to leave the checkpoint zone. The accepted protocol at night is to slow down and turn on the vehicle's interior lights so that all passengers are clearly visible. Dim the headlights when stopping for inspection. It is customary to keep your engine running unless directed otherwise. When you stop your car, place both hands in a position where they will be visible.

Only present documentation when requested to do so. It is recommended that if asked to produce documents that you hand over copies. If it can be avoided, do not hand over your passport or original documents. It is not uncommon for a corrupt official to demand money for the return of your documents once he has possession of them, but do not argue if the original is insisted on by the checkpoint personnel.

Should you be asked to open the boot of your vehicle for inspection, it is advisable to stop the engine, take your keys out of the ignition and move slowly around the vehicle to watch the guards as they check the boot to ensure that nothing is removed, but more importantly, that nothing untoward is placed in the boot. There have been cases of rounds of ammunition or other contraband being secreted in the boot by unscrupulous guards for their colleagues at a later checkpoint to find. You would have extreme difficulty talking your way out of this situation.

Stuck in a crowd

Dangerous instances of civil unrest occur with frightening frequency in many foreign countries, and in certain countries, especially those undergoing fierce political change, it can happen for a variety of reasons. Civil unrest can range from small organised rallies to large-scale demonstrations and rioting. Demonstrations all too easily turn into civil disorder, and an orderly crowd can take on a sinister and frightening dynamic when stimulated by agitators or security forces. Protestors can cross the line from heated resistance to violence with little or no warning and the resulting aggression is rarely focused.

Despite this, it is rare for travellers or expatriates to be directly targeted during civil unrest, and in most cases should they be harmed, it is a matter of being in the wrong place at the wrong time. There are a number of things you can do, but essentially keep to the edge and take the first escape possible. When leaving the fringe of the demonstration just walk away – don't run, as this will draw attention to you. If you are arrested by the police or military, do not resist. Go along peacefully and if necessary contact a security agency like red24 or your embassy to help resolve your predicament. If shooting breaks out, drop to the ground and try to roll to the outskirts.

If you are in a car:

- Never drive through a crowd.
- If you find yourself in the path of a crowd, turn down the nearest side road, reverse or turn around and drive away calmly.
- If you cannot drive away, park the car, lock it and leave it, taking shelter in a side street or doorway.
- If you don't have time for this, stop and turn the engine off. Lock the doors and remain calm. Be sure not to show hostility or anger.

Make friends where you can

One trick is to make friends where you can. Many reporters and seasoned travellers speak very highly of taxi drivers in their time of need. This involves picking a driver you think you can trust and then using him all the time. Take an interest in him and his family, and you will find a friend. A taxi driver not only knows where everything is and what is going on, but can also act as interpreter and spare hand. Explain what you are trying to do and they soon enter into the spirit of things. In such a dire situation you will need all the friends you can get. ❧

In trouble with the law
by Christina Georgiou

YOU GET ARRESTED ABROAD... the nightmare begins. You are locked up in a dirty cell awaiting questioning... the nightmare continues. Police officials are interrogating you in a language you don't understand... the nightmare worsens.

Getting arrested abroad, whether you are guilty or innocent, can be a terrifying experience. Local cultures can be very different, and what may be legal or culturally acceptable in the UK may be illegal in other countries and carry with it a harsh sentence. Most of all, the fear invoked by not understanding what is happening or not knowing what the implications are of being locked up abroad could make this experience your worst nightmare.

Taking on board some of the advice and information outlined in this section could help you survive a potential nightmare.

Committing the crime

People can get arrested abroad for a multitude of reasons. Travellers can be vulnerable either wittingly or unwittingly to arrest. Offences can include expired visas, photographing military buildings and breaking local laws such as purchasing alcohol without a licence or drinking alcohol in a public place. The list of potential offences is vast. However, many travellers who get arrested and subsequently receive a prison sentence do so because of drugs. No matter how trivial or serious the drug offence, of which there are many, sentences are likely to be severe, and in some countries could even mean the death penalty.

Police officials will not normally care whether you claim to be innocent or not; just being in a room or vehicle where there is a stash of drugs or someone who is carrying drugs can land you in prison. Even if you did not know about the drugs, you could find yourself arrested and detained. Also, be aware of the consequences of transporting drugs across country borders, whether knowingly or unknowingly. Be wary of the person who befriends you and gives you a sob story about their sick uncle, who was unable to make it to their wedding. Coincidentally, your next stop just happens to be where the uncle lives – would it be too much to ask you to take a copy of the wedding video across the border with you? They don't want to post it in case it gets lost or damaged. Be warned, you could be carrying a cassette filled with heroin not videotape.

Don't be coerced into transporting drugs across borders in return for money; the financial gain may appear to be huge but you could be caught and left with nothing but 40 other cellmates sharing a room built for ten. In particular, young female travellers are targets for drug trafficking; they often fall victim, all too easily, for the charming, rich drug dealer who promises them the earth in return for transporting a package. However, the young woman is nothing more to the dealer than a decoy who is intended to be caught at the airport in order to allow a much bigger package to go through unnoticed.

Sentences for trafficking offences are among the harshest, especially in Asia, South America and the West Indies.

Upon arrest

On your arrest, despite the serious and frightening situation, try to keep as calm as possible. You will probably be feeling panic stricken and scared, this is natural, but try to keep your cool and avoid showing anger and aggressive behaviour towards the police; they are in a more powerful position than you and will want to maintain their power and not lose face in front of colleagues. Don't resist arrest through violence and, unless demanded on your arrest, keep hold of your passport.

There may be language differences: if so, communication will be extremely difficult. This in itself can cause problems due to misunderstandings. Ask for an interpreter or someone who is familiar with the language to be with you before you answer any police questions or sign a document that you do not fully understand.

Ask that the British consul be notified of your arrest. He or she will be able to offer you advice and support, and will contact your family for you.

Conditions of police cells and prisons will vary from country to country. You may be held in conditions that you find totally unacceptable – but this is the harsh reality and you must deal with it. Conditions in South America and South-East Asia are particularly grim, with overcrowding, poor sanitation and little food.

Make sure family and friends back home know what has happened to you. You will probably be feeling lonely and scared and will need their support. Your family will also feel extremely anxious, but this is better than the worry and uncertainty they would feel if they had not heard from you at all. They may also be in a position to help you as they will have access to telephones, faxes and computers, etc, and will be able to find out what is going on, in a way that you will not be able to.

Help is at hand

As previously mentioned, insist that the British consul for that area be notified. This is your right. British consuls are there to protect the interests of Britons abroad; this includes helping Britons who have got into trouble. They cannot get you out of prison, but will offer advice and support. The consul will visit you as soon as possible.

You should also contact Prisoners Abroad, details below. You can do this directly, or through the British consul or your family and friends. Prisoners Abroad is the only charity that provides practical support and campaigns for the welfare of Britons imprisoned abroad. It is a non-judgemental, humanitarian organisation with a team of caseworkers who have detailed knowledge of specific countries and will be able to provide you and your family with support and advice by explaining criminal justice systems, prisoners' rights and prison conditions; by contacting other agencies, including the Foreign and Commonwealth Office and foreign Ministries of Justice; and by providing families with advice on how to send money abroad and helping to arrange visits.

Unofficial help can come in the form of the friends you have been travelling with and locals, especially expatriates. Being locked up, far away from family and friends, can be extremely isolating. Local people, especially those who speak the same language, can keep you in touch with the outside world, bring you things you need such as extra food or clothing, and get messages to consuls, family and friends.

Doing the time

After the initial arrest and questioning phase it is unlikely that you will get bail due to being a foreigner. This means that you will be held in prison on remand until the trial date. The length of time you will be held on remand varies, but it is not unheard of for this to last for two years and more.

Being held far away from home, probably isolated from others by language and culture, it will be important to try to keep your spirits up. Prisoners Abroad can help you keep in touch with the outside world and can provide a service to ensure that your specific needs are met. This includes providing advice about lawyers; translating documents, letters and court papers; supporting any application for parole, remission, pardon and appeal; negotiating with prison authorities; providing essentials such as medicine, food and clothing; linking prisoners with pen pals; sending out magazines and books, particularly to non-English-speaking countries with limited library materials.

False accusations

It has been known for travellers to find themselves falsely accused of committing a crime. If it is simply a case of mistaken identity, stay calm. Do not panic and aggressively protest your innocence, this may only aggravate your captors.

You could find yourself in the situation where you feel officials could have set you up and are demanding a pay-off. Officials, particularly in Asia, are often earning low wages and may supplement their income by demanding pay-offs from travellers. You will need to use your judgement to decide whether, if you have the funds, to give money to such officials. There is no guarantee that it will stop at one payment and that, afterwards, they will leave you alone. However, if you decide to do so, you could be making a number of expensive pay-offs to each police official involved. If you find yourself falsely accused, immediately inform the consul and tell them exactly what has happened.

Buying yourself out

Once you are being held in custody, there are some countries where you may be offered freedom in exchange for unofficial payments or bribes to certain officials. You or your family may be tempted to try this, but it is extremely dangerous and you may lose a lot of money with nothing to show for it – there is no guarantee that the officials will uphold their part of the bargain. You may also find yourself in the difficult position of being charged with bribery.

If you are actually being held on remand in prison it is important to know that bribery and corruption are rife in many prisons around the world and are a way of life. You may find that you have to pay for a space in a cell, your bedding, food and indeed anything else you may need.

Holiday hotspots

- In Thailand, if you are caught trafficking any amount, no matter how small, of drugs such as heroin or ecstasy, if convicted you will automatically receive the death penalty. The death penalty is sometimes commuted to life imprisonment which in Thailand means 50 years. Simple possession of 100 grammes of narcotics such as cocaine will also get you a life sentence.
- In Japan, if you are caught in possession of 800 grammes of hashish you could receive a four-year jail sentence.
- In Spain, if are caught in possession of cannabis, the minimum sentence is three years. For possession of cocaine, you could be looking at anything between nine and 14 years. If you are arrested, it is highly unlikely that bail will be granted being a foreigner and this could mean spending anything up to a year on remand while the investigation takes place.
- In South America, conditions are extremely harsh and prisoners often have to buy basic items such as mattresses, beds and bedding as well as food and

water. Foreigners are at a disadvantage as they do not have a local family network to supply them with these basic necessities.

● In France, possession of even a very small amount of drugs can result in a sentence of six months to one year. Foreigners are unlikely to be granted bail and in addition to your prison sentence, you will be fined the street value of the drugs in your possession, which, even for small amounts, will be a substantial amount of money. Therefore, even if you serve your full sentence, you will not be released until the fine is settled.

● In Venezuela possessing just 2 grammes of cocaine will attract an automatic 10 year sentence.

Prevention is better than cure

Prevention is always better than a cure. There are a number of factors travellers should take into consideration to ensure that they avoid getting into trouble:

● Check your passport and visa and make copies of them. Make sure you keep them safe, that the information contained in them is correct and that they are valid.

● Make sure you have adequate insurance cover. Some insurance companies will pay legal costs: check that, to make sure they provide this cover before you buy the policy.

● Find out about and respect local laws and regulations.

● Watch your luggage at all times at airports, as well as on trains and buses when crossing borders.

● Be wary of taking lifts across borders; the one between France and Spain is particularly notorious as it is a well-known drug route into Europe from North Africa (but this is only one example).

● Do not agree to carry a suitcase or package for a friend or acquaintance, especially if you are offered large sums of money.

● Do not get drunk and into fights.

● Carry a list of British consular offices for the countries you plan to visit: see www.fco.gov.uk.

● Let your family and friends back home know your movements and any changes you make to your route.

● Make sure you prepare yourself and know the consequences of your actions; saying you didn't realise that something was illegal is no excuse. This advice may seem obvious, but it is surprising how many people say "If only…."

For more information, contact Prisoners Abroad, 89-93 Fonthill Road, London N4 3JH, UK, tel +44 (0)20 7561 6820, fax +44 (0)20 7561 6821, email info@prisonersabroad.org.uk.

CHRISTINA GEORGIOU is a volunteer for Prisoners Abroad.

How to survive a kidnap
by safety consultants at Red 24

KIDNAPPINGS CAN BE FOR POLITICAL REASONS OR FOR FINANCIAL REASONS, but they are always very tense and chaotic. The kidnappers are under intense pressure to succeed and the kidnapped are terrified. Kidnapping for political gain (such as the kidnap and subsequent murder of Kenneth Bigley in Iraq, to try and force the withdrawal of American troops from that country) do occur, but kidnappings for financial gain are far more common. Wealthy individuals and their families are the most common targets, as are businessmen. Kidnap and ransom is a phenomenon on the rise, even though it is estimated that only 10–15 per cent of kidnappings are reported.

At present, Colombia, Mexico and Brazil have the highest rate of kidnappings, although the Russian Federation, Nigeria, India, Philippines, Pakistan and some other Latin American countries also have a high incidence of this crime. Experts believe that at least three quarters of all kidnappings take place in Latin America.

A kidnapping situation is extremely nerve-wracking, especially when the kidnapping has not been planned but is spontaneous. Often the person being abducted does not realise what is going on until they have been forced into the car. The aim of the kidnapper is to intimidate his hostage, in order to make the hostage immediately follow his instructions. Therefore he will yell and make threats.

How to avoid being kidnapped

Most countries have some form of internal strife, or some group that would like to replace the government. That means, unfortunately, that there is a chance of being kidnapped in many countries, although in some more than others. If you plan to stay on the beaten track, follow the advice given by the Foreign and Common-wealth Office and red24; your chances of being kidnapped will be much reduced.

However, for those people who leave the safety of the track, there are precautions that can be taken to avoid being kidnapped:

- Keep a low profile and dress down. Don't wear expensive or flashy jewellery.
- Do not publicise your itinerary and always vary your routine. If possible, do not travel alone but with someone you trust.
- Carry a cellular or satellite telephone, and ensure that it is adequately charged.
- Keep all car doors and windows locked, especially when you leave the car, and do not pick up hitch-hikers.
- Be aware of any unusual or suspicious activity taking place around you.
- Be wary of strangers approaching you.
- Be aware of any publicity that may have preceded your arrival in the country.

Conduct during an incident

Being kidnapped is extremely stressful, and it is important to remain calm. The most important thing for the victim is to concentrate on staying alive, until they can be rescued or set free. If you react violently towards the kidnappers, it is likely that they will react violently towards you. Getting injured at this stage will hamper any possible attempts to escape. Be as cooperative as possible, since most kidnappers want to trade you for money and it is not to their advantage to kill you. Note as many details as possible about your captors and your surroundings. Noises and smells can also help to give you an idea of where you are. You may need to identify your kidnappers later, so try to memorise their faces and any identifying features. Keeping your mind active will also help you stay calm and focused. Try to communicate with the kidnappers, explain that you will cooperate as you want to stay alive. However, do not provoke them or fight against them.

Hostage survival

Many hostage situations are resolved within days and the victims released. However, some (as Daniel Start found when his conservation expedition was kidnapped in Irian Jaya by the Free Papua Movement in 1996) can last for months. During this time, negotiations may be taking place to secure the release of the hostages.

It is easy, in this situation, to believe everything that the kidnappers tell you. However, much of their information may be false and could be used to break a hostage's spirit. Unfortunately, although you would like to believe that you are a special case, the authorities will not be likely to give in to the kidnappers' demands. Try to keep your mind busy and not think about what could happen – play games with your fellow hostages, remember details and even talk to your kidnappers. It will help if they see you as human beings rather than just objects to be traded.

However, avoid political discussions or ideological confrontations. Be careful not to get too involved in their way of thinking, or it could lead to the 'Stockholm Syndrome', by which the hostages start to identify with the kidnappers. Always remember that these kidnappers see you as a means to an end or as a source of finance, rather than a person.

Food and clean water may not always be available to you, so make sure you eat whatever you can get and expect some diarrhoea and even food poisoning. You may be deep in the jungle or other vast natural area, so keep an eye out for snakes and spiders.

Frustration and boredom will probably be your greatest enemies. Your fellow hostages may well become your major support in this situation, and you will have to be strong and independent and look after each other. Use memories, prayer and even fantasy worlds as a place of solace that you can retreat into. Ask your kidnappers for things that you want – this will help you create a conversation with them, which will allow them to humanise you.

If you need any form of medication, it is particularly important to ask the kidnappers to get it for you. Remember that you are valuable to them.

Escape

If you see an opportunity for escape you should take it, if you have thought it through. There are many things to be considered when escaping: what is your location and what is the terrain like? Are you in a jungle or the street? If you are in a jungle, it may be harder to survive on your own than staying with the kidnappers. If you attempt an escape and are caught, expect to be beaten and treated badly. Only attempt an escape if you are almost certain you will make it.

Coming home

Returning home after such an experience will be harder than you expect. More than likely you will be afraid to leave the house and to do what were once everyday activities. People and newspapers will want to speak to you and there will be many questions. Go somewhere that you feel comfortable and surround yourself with people you know. It may be necessary to have counselling to readjust and work through any horrors that you may have witnessed.

Stay safe

Although kidnappings take place all over the world and every day, this does not mean that you will be unlucky enough to be kidnapped. By taking adequate precautions, you will return home tanned, safe and with good memories. ❧

Living through a kidnap
by Daniel Start

IRIAN JAYA – INDONESIAN NEW GUINEA – is a vast tropical wilderness of glacier-capped mountains, pristine rain forest and lowland swamps, sparsely populated by tribal peoples living much as they have done for thousands of years. It might seem an unlikely place to be taken 'hostage' by 'terrorists', both words being so modern in their connotations, but this is what happened to our group of 12 biologists in January 1996. It goes to show that no corner of the world is so remote and untouched that it can be assumed immune from such threats.

Every country has some form of internal strife, some group that is fighting the state. Even if there is no history of kidnapping, there is no guarantee that one of these groups might not decide to take hostages as part of some crazy new strategy. However, if you are an independent traveller who stays on the beaten track and follows FCO or State Department advice closely, the chances of ending up in shackles are negligible. But those people whose work, study or inquisitive nature takes them to more unusual places must do extra research.

Our group spent two years in preparation. We knew about the existence of the OPM Papuan independence movement and knew that the Indonesian military had committed atrocities in Irian Jaya. The missionaries, mining companies, governments and many other organisations that we consulted suggested there was no risk. It seemed a sensible conclusion. The atrocities were too far in the past, the current trouble spots were too far away from us and the OPM had too few supporters. We were all wrong. Resentment among a people lingers and spreads. The OPM had wide support and although they could not read or write and had only bows and arrows they were still very dangerous. It is essential to understand the history of an area: don't ever underestimate the risks and don't always believe the experts' advice, however much you want to.

When we first arrived by light aircraft at our remote village in the mountains everything seemed peaceful and trouble-free. The village head men greeted us and smiled happily and for two months everything went very well. It is easy to be lulled into a false sense of security, and important to be aware that there may be other factions who see your arrival differently. In our case they numbered 200, were from the next valley and they ambushed us on 8 January 1996. We knew some of them already. Almost all of them were young men about our own age living normal Papuan lives. These are the type of people who make up most guerrilla outfits.

The ambush was a very frightening experience. The crowd had worked themselves into a frenzy and sported painted bodies, head-dresses and machetes. We thought we would be killed, but much of the aggression was theatre and no harm was done to us. When it started to rain the mood seemed to pass, they introduced themselves as OPM rebels and we all went inside and ate lunch together.

At first we were worried that they would abuse the women (men in large phallic penis gourds tend to look quite threatening) but none of the five women was seriously molested. One of the hostages was pregnant, and was greatly respected because they believed pregnant women could cast powerful curses. We made it clear that each woman was married to at least one of the men. We were also very concerned for the Indonesians – the obvious enemies of the Papuans. Thankfully the OPM had accepted that we were all there with good intentions, so we were treated with respect; more like guests than prisoners.

In fact our group was seen as a gift from the Lord. White people are almost revered by the Papuans because of the work of the missionaries. In our case it was naïvely believed that we were so important and powerful that we could be traded for independence – a 'free country'. The unborn child of the pregnant hostage was even perceived as the new Messiah who would lead the Papuans to victory. These interpretations helped to seal our fate. Be aware that other cultures may see things in radically different ways from us. To minimise the effects of this, keep visits short. It takes time for rumour and superstition to spread and even longer for people to act on it.

The first night in the village seemed quite exciting, but it was so bizarre I found it difficult to take seriously. The next morning, however, our captors announced that they were taking us into the forest to hide us, and I suddenly became very frightened. We packed up everything; about half a tonne of the stuff. Much of the useless equipment made good presents for people – even cameras and Walkmans were valued for their shiny components. As we were marched into the jungle I remembered the old army adage that 'the longer you wait the harder it becomes to escape', and began to make many daredevil plans. Thankfully I didn't attempt any, but from then on I always kept a knife, compass, matches and iodine in my pocket – just in case.

At first we were sure it would all be over within days, but we quickly realised the situation was very serious. For a start, they declared that the baby – the new Messiah – had to be born on Papuan soil, and it wasn't due for another six months. Our main fear, though, was that the Indonesian military would come in and bomb the whole place and declare we had been murdered by the rebels. The OPM were as frightened of them as we were. Almost immediately we found we had common ground. The first priority was to get news of our kidnapping to the outside world, so that our embassies could prevent the military from wiping everyone out. As only one or two of the OPM men could read or write, we prepared all the letters for them. They were sent out by runner to the nearest town (about a week away), but finally our short band radio was found and used to negotiate with the missionaries. Thankfully in those first days we were able to communicate a lot of information about our situation. We also became very involved with the negotiations on the OPM's behalf and got quite carried away with our demands, thinking that we could organise both sides into compromising a little. It is tempting to imagine that your situation is a special case: always remember, however, that no respectable authority will openly make concessions to terrorists.

This alliance with our captors ensured they treated us well. Many were very nervous at first and hid this with a false bravado which was fairly easy to break through. I made a concerted effort to joke and laugh with the men, believing they would be less likely to kill me if they liked me. In fact we soon realised that all the OPM actively wanted to be our friends, because it gave them status. We used this to our advantage by giving presents only to those who treated us well or seemed to think we should be released. This created competition and jealousy among the OPM and gave us more power.

While we also wanted the OPM to like us, we had to be careful not to be too compliant. The odd refusal or confrontation made them think twice about asking us to do stupid things. As time went by we made a point of showing our frustration and unhappiness, so that they would not forget that they had taken innocent people prisoners.

Over the four months of our captivity, conditions in the mountainous jungle were harsh. We were moved 28 times; sometimes staying in villages but more often being hidden in remote forest. Although we were never tied up and were able to wander around reasonably freely, there was little chance of escape. Our captors knew we were almost totally dependent on them for food, shelter and direction.

Many of us suffered from malaria, dysentery, tropical ulcers and infections, but we had just enough basic medicines to treat ourselves. Thankfully we suffered no serious accidents and no run-ins with snakes or poisonous spiders. For me, boredom and hunger were the worst things, especially when they were combined. You can only make conversation with your companions for so long. After that it is a matter of reliving old journeys, daydreaming, making plans or playing games – if you can find the material to make dice or a pack of cards. The OPM worked hard to find us what food they could (mainly sweet potatoes), but we soon learned to appreciate anything that moved: frogs, rats, bats, tree kangaroos, weevils. More than once we got food poisoning from meat that was too old.

Food was so limited and we were so hungry that initially this became the cause of all major arguments. After a while we realised that if we could rise above our animal instincts, giving a little extra rather than taking a little extra, the world became a much more pleasant place to be. Despite these conflicts, the entire group became very loyal to one another, like a family. But it was a lonely time. You can't expect to find a soul mate in everyone. In a way this was good because we learned to be strong, independent and self-supporting. This made us better able to take care of each other in a crisis. Images of family and home were very important in battling with depression and despair. Some found solace in fantasy worlds, others in prayer or meditation. Certainly we all rekindled the remnants of any faith we had once had.

The OPM promised many times to release us, but not one promise was kept. There was so much conflicting news that it was tempting to attach too much significance to rumours of release. The disappointments were bitter and it took us several months to realise that the most painless way to get through was to let go of our hopes of release. Once I had resigned myself to being there forever I began to appreciate the present more, taking pleasure in the small things in life such as a beautiful sunrise or a moment of shared laughter. I also gained comfort and enjoyment from simple habits and routines, such as going to wash, collecting water or preparing food. The moment I stopped counting the hours the days seem to pass more quickly. Most important for me was understanding that this captivity wasn't wasted time, but an experience that would make me stronger and become an important part of who I was.

After about two months, the Red Cross made contact. From then on we were able to receive and write letters to our families about once a fortnight. There were also medicines, books and food, but soon the OPM came to enjoy the free presents so much that the Red Cross had to stop bringing in anything. This made the OPM angry but also focused their minds on the negotiations. Finally they agreed to hold a pig feast and release us on 8 May 1996, but at the last minute they refused. Perhaps they thought they should hold out for more. Maybe it was an act of angry defiance. Whatever, the next day we heard helicopters, gunfire and then a series of huge explosions (possibly blanks, but certainly powerful enough to blow down trees and start landslides).

This was the military operation we had dreaded. After an initial period of intense fear and panic we managed to think rationally. We had been told by the Red Cross that if things got nasty we should just lie down. But this was not an option, as we had to get away from the house in case the military bombed it or the hard-line OPM came to get us. We heard about four helicopters circling, trying to find us, but the canopy was too thick. Then we heard a high-pitched whine which I now know was the sound of troopers being winched down into the forest. In hindsight, we should probably have split up and hidden in the forest close by until the military found the house. Instead, we made for a clearing from which we could signal but were intercepted by a group of OPM before we got there. We were taken into the mountains, and for five days the military tracked us with sniffer dogs, a heat-imaging camera mounted on a pilotless drone and trackers who followed our footprints (the Papuans do not wear shoes). On the sixth day, quite unexpectedly and very calmly, our captors attacked us and killed the two Indonesian men. The rest of us were able to get away. We ran down to a river, where we found a small military patrol camped on the bank. The OPM had seen the patrol, realised everything was over and killed the Indonesians to show that they would not be beaten.

We were flown out by helicopter and looked after incredibly well by the Indonesian government and British Embassy, but it was difficult to celebrate with the horror hanging over us. The press followed us everywhere and were such a problem that we decided to do an exclusive for one newspaper so that the others would leave us alone. Although we would have liked to address the political and human rights issues in a broadsheet interview, we were so confused and angry that we felt happier telling our story to a tabloid who would leave these things well alone. We chose the *Mail on Sunday*, which did one big feature, treated us exceptionally well, reported very accurately and paid us enough to provide some security in the coming months of readjustment.

For a few weeks I found I was very nervous and frightened of simple things such as going outside alone. It was exhausting speaking to friends on the telephone, so everybody wrote instead. We were offered counselling by the Foreign Office, but we needed to arrange it through our GPs and in the end it all seemed too much hassle and none of us bothered. I decided the best therapy was time with my family in Cornwall. Within three weeks I plucked up the courage to go and see friends in Cambridge, and I was amazed at how quickly I was back in the swing of going to pubs and parties. I felt very detached from my experiences in Irian Jaya, perhaps because they seemed so surreal. It might have been easy to pretend the whole thing never happened, but I could feel the experience had changed me and I was not happy having all these subconscious emotions inside me. I decided to write a book, not only for cathartic reasons but also because I felt it was a story that needed to be told.

Writing the book was a gruelling experience which felt a little like a penance, but those six months helped me to come to terms with my anger and guilt. Once the book was finished I found I had little idea of what I wanted to do. But perhaps that is no bad thing. Being taken hostage teaches you that you never know what's around the corner.... ❧

DANIEL START was kidnapped in Irian Jaya while on a conservation expedition in 1995. He was released after being held hostage for four months by the Free Papua Movement. He described these experiences in 'The Open Cage'.

How to survive an aircraft hijacking
by safety consultants at Red 24

Although incidents of aircraft hijackings have increased over the years, they are still rare. However, such an occurrence is always a possibility, and you may find yourself in the wrong place at the wrong time. There are three main types of hijacking:

● The hijackers have taken control of the plane and are demanding to be flown to a particular destination. These hijackers are likely to be escaping refugees or criminals or possibly asylum seekers. (For example, in 1996, three Ethiopians hijacked a Ethiopian Airlines plane and demanded to be taken to Australia as they wished to escape the poverty of Ethiopia.)

● The second reason for hijackings is extortion and the hijackers will make demands for money or political concessions. They will use the threat of harm against the passengers to back up their demands. (This was the case in Karachi, Pakistan, in 1986: the hijackers sought the release of Palestinian prisoners being held in Cyprus.)

● Since 9/11, there has been a third type of hijacker, the kind that will embark on a suicide mission and use the aircraft as a bomb. There are usually heavy casualties in this situation, and high-profile targets are targeted.

If you are ever caught up in a hijack situation, remember that the captain is in charge and should s/he be indisposed, then you should take instructions from the flight attendants. The flight crew will have all received training on what to do in this situation.

All hijackings will be different – some may take place on the ground, such as the storming of the Pan Am 747 aircraft in Karachi, and some may take place in the air, such as the 9/11 hijackings. Any hijacking situation, however, will occur extremely quickly and passengers will have little chance of doing anything to stop it. If you do have an opportunity to escape when the hijack attempt begins, make sure that it is a clear opportunity, because the hijackers will be very tense and likely to shoot if they see that people are trying to escape. However, trying to escape is only advisable if the plane is still on the ground.

If your plane is hijacked, it is important to remain calm. The situation around you will be chaotic and tense and you need to remain as inconspicuous as possible. Do not make eye contact and do not volunteer for anything. Do not make any hostile movements or statements that will allow the attackers to single you out.

Once the hijackers have the situation under control, you could be in for a long wait. You need to make yourself as comfortable as possible, without too much movement. Accept that you may not get much food and water over the next few hours, and that you will not be moving around. Spend the time memorising the faces of the hijackers and other little details that may help investigators later. Although you might want to gather as much information about the attackers and their weapons as possible, do not take any risks or play the hero.

Although it is important to get comfortable, always remember that a rescue mission could be sent in at any moment and/or you might have to move quickly. Thus it is not advised that you take your shoes off, in case you need to move over broken glass or uneven terrain. People who had taken their shoes off and then jumped out of the Boeing 747 in Karachi were more seriously injured than those with shoes.

It is more than likely that the hijackers will take your passport; they might also divide passengers up by nationality. If you have anything that the terrorist might consider 'incriminating', you should discard it immediately. Whatever you are told to do, be obliging and do it as quickly and calmly as possible. Stay calm and do not act confrontationally towards the hijackers.

Rescue missions can be as chaotic as the actual hijack. If a rescue is attempted, you should remain as low as possible and not do anything that may make the rescuers mistake you for a terrorist. The situation will again be noisy and confusing, and it is best to stay out of the way.

It is possible that when the rescue mission is over everyone will be handcuffed and taken off the plane – do not be alarmed by this, as hijackers sometimes try and hide among the hostages in order to escape. You will be released as soon as your identity has been verified.

Since the attacks of 9/11, airport security has been increased and it is now even more difficult for terrorists to get weapons onto a plane. If your flight originated in a European or American airport, there is less chance of the aircraft being hijacked. However, this does not mean there will be no more attacks. The potential for hijackings remains, so always remain aware to the possibility. In short, keep your wits about you. 🙠

Surviving a skiing accident
by Arnie Wilson

SKIING INJURIES CAN AND DO HAPPEN when you least expect them, let alone when you are taking risks: there are documented cases of skiers breaking a leg as they climb down the aircraft steps before even setting foot in a ski resort. And some years, ago a producer working on a television commercial – in which the hero clutching a box of chocolates had to out-ski an avalanche – fell over and broke her leg while standing on a mountainside watching.

Not so long ago, I met a ski holiday rep who had damaged his cruciate ligament while skiing without even falling over – he hit a bump awkwardly and tore it. Konrad Bartelski, Britain's most successful world cup skier ever, once damaged his cruciate ligament during a race without even realising until he crossed the finishing line. Ligaments, cartilages and tendons are the things that get hurt these days.

Thanks to modern equipment, including more and more sophisticated bindings, broken legs are much rarer than they used to be. But something's got to give, and if it's not your leg, it's likely to be your cruciate.

Although advanced skiers travel at speed and are vulnerable to spinal and head injuries, surprisingly it is the beginners who frequently prove to be most at risk. They tend to ski slowly, and more often than not it is the slow, sickening, twisting fall that causes the damage – not the high-speed fall that catapults the skier out of his bindings – unless of course the fall hurls the unfortunate victim against a rock. Which leads us to head injuries, and protective helmets. Are they really necessary? In Scandinavian resorts they are virtually compulsory for young children, and many people believe that adult skiers should also be required to wear them. Yet statistics show that remarkably few skiing accident cause head injuries. They also show that a frightening number of accidents on the slopes are drink-related.

Drink is freely available – and its consumption encouraged – in a host of mountain restaurants. Marco Grass, a member of the Saas Ski School in Klosters, Switzerland, warns: "Drinking when you are skiing is just as dangerous as when you are driving a car. You think you are in control but in reality your reactions are slow and ill-judged. Statistics relating to injuries in this major ski area of Klosters/Davos show that more and more are drink-related. And we have no reason to think this trend is only happening here."

In North America, reckless skiers can have their lift ticket confiscated and even be put under arrest. In practice – unless they actually injure another skier – they often get away with it. Having monitored American skiing in almost 100 resorts right across the continent, the closest I have come to seeing an errant skier being punished was in Snowshoe, Virginia, when a member of the ski patrol leapt onto a chair to catch the culprit but lost him on the mountain.

Colin Allum, whose Fogg (as in Phileas) Travel Insurance Services specialises in skiing insurance, observes: "Skiing is a high-risk sport. About one person in 50 who goes skiing is liable to receive some form of medical treatment during the course of a normal winter-sports holiday. This can range from a twisted ankle or bruised shoulder to the extreme cases of serious back or head injury, or – fortunately very rarely – to death."

If you happen to be first on the scene after an accident, it is important to cross two skis in the snow about ten metres up the slope from the injured skier. Don't try to move the victim, and if there is a leg injury, don't try to remove the boot, as it can act as a splint. Keep the injured person warm, and do not give him or her any alcohol. Knees are the most prone to injury, but almost no part of the human body is immune from one sort of skiing injury or another.

A fracture or damaged cruciate ligament are among the worst things than can happen to your legs: but it is not always the big injuries that cause the most pain and curtail skiing. Some skiers – myself included –endure endless agonies because of ill-fitting boots. Like many other skiers, I am the unfortunate owner of feet that are fundamentally the wrong shape for most boots (one expert boot-fitter in Aspen described them as 'brick-shaped').

I remember cracking, or at least bruising, a rib or two when I was learning to ski

Prevention is better than cure

Gliding over crisp snow in sparkling air – probably the most fun you can have without sprouting a pair of wings and taking flight. However, taking to the slopes also equates to repeated muscle stress and exertion at high altitude – a combination that can result in injury. That risk is considerably lower if you're fit to begin with and know the basics about equipment and safety.

Before you go:

■ Increase your aerobic fitness by running, cycling, going to an aerobics class or dancing for at least 20 minutes, three times a week. This is worth a few extra hours on piste.

■ Strengthen those muscles. Skiing or snowboarding puts pressure on thighs, hamstrings, calves, hips and groins, so some advance exercise targetting these muscles should reduce the chance of jelly legs on the slopes. Many fitness clubs offer special ski-preparation classes before the season starts

On the slopes:

■ Make sure your equipment works. Bindings must release properly during falls, boots should fit securely enough to protect the ankle from moving inside the boot, but not so tightly that you lose all sensation.

■ Stretch – without bouncing – before and after exercising. Hold each stretch for thirty seconds. A hot tub at the end of the day always helps – or a massage.

■ If you are a beginner: before hitting the slopes and playing desperate catch-up as your expert friends zoom off, you should take a few lessons from a qualified instructor to learn proper techniques.

■ Whatever your level, stop and have a rest if you're tired. Many injuries occur when you are tired. Always stay within your own limitations, even if you're in a group.

in Verbier, Switzerland, and a friend of mine is always damaging hers. You can't do much with cracked ribs except perhaps strap them up, but she always continues to ski regardless. As with many skiing injuries, it is often less painful to carry on skiing than to walk around or even lie down in bed. The same goes for shoulders.

In California, I fell heavily on my left shoulder twice in two days and the pain affected me for months. Skiing was not a problem (except the worry of falling on it again), but lying in bed could be agony. Usually an anti-inflammatory cream and resting it will do wonders in such cases. Wearing a sling can help.

Shoulders are always a problem. They have such a sophisticated collection of moving parts, any one of which may be damaged in an accident without the others being affected. You may find you can ski yourself silly without so much as a twinge, but looking at your watch almost kills you. Still – at least I haven't torn my dreaded cruciate ligament yet (though no doubt it is only a matter of time).

Says Allum: "The advent of quick-release bindings has dramatically reduced the number of fractures – but dramatically increased the number of ligament injuries. In the days when bindings simply did not release, it was almost inevitable that a leg would be broken. Nowadays, 50 per cent of what may be regarded as 'serious' injuries – those which in due course will require some operative treatment – are knee ligament injuries.

"Many accidents are caused by people skiing across the tops of protruding rocks which are seen too late. This type of accident tends to produce head injuries, because the skier is released from the bindings and propelled forward, rather on the lines of a swimmer at the start of the 100-metres Olympic swimming trials.

"Skis themselves can cause accidents if they are the wrong ski for the skier concerned. It is always important that skiers ski within their limitations, and ski a length of ski to which they are suited rather than one decided by bravado. It is much more sensible to have a happy and successful holiday skiing a 195 centimetre ski than to finish up in hospital skiing a 210."

So much for the skis. But what about the skier? "There are those of us who may readily admit to being beginners even after 20 years of skiing. And there are others who will only admit to being advanced after 20 minutes," says Allum.

One good way to try to prevent injury on the slopes is to get fit before you go. Enter the Cybex machine, used by better fitness clinics. It sounds like something out of *Dr Who*, but what it actually does is check the strength of your hamstrings, quads abductors and adductors, and then targets any of these for strengthening with a customised programme of weight-training and exercises.

Weather and altitude can also play their part in making a skier's life a pain. Some people get serious altitude sickness in America, where skiing in the Rockies can mean altitudes of 11,000 or 12,000 feet or more. At such heights it is not unusual to feel some effects, including headaches, nausea, breathlessness etc. These should wear off after two or three days (a good reason not to go skiing in the USA for just a week, as your holiday may well be half over before you're ready to face it), but if they persist you should see a doctor. Drinking plenty of water – much more than you think you need – helps to alleviate the problem. But serious altitude sickness can only be dealt with by getting the patient to a lower altitude as quickly as possible. Your doctor can prescribe tablets to lessen the impact of altitude.

As for weather: watch out for frostbite. I got my first taste of it in Colorado, skiing Breckenridge's peak 7. The trouble is, you don't know you've been affected unless someone tells you. My nose went white, but I had no idea. As a damage limitation exercise, it is important to cover any frostbitten extremity and keep it warm. Experts argue over whether it is better just to cover it or knead it slightly to restore the blood supply. Those against kneading claim it could damage the cells while they are frozen. The consensus is just keep it warm.

Strong sunlight can be a major problem too. Always wear good protective creams, even when it may seem that the sun is not coming out that day. As the saying goes, you may not be able to see the sun, but the sun can see you. Even a couple of hours' skiing in high altitude without protection, especially during the later months of March, April and May, can cause serious sunburn and even sunstroke because of the strong ultra-violet rays.

Much has been said and written of the dangers of skiing off-piste, and it is true that skiers leaving marked trails without a guide may cause avalanches or be caught up in them, or even fall into a crevasse. However, skiing in a resort on a marked run is arguably just as dangerous. When you compare the numbers of people on piste with those who ski off them, the chances of a collision in a resort must surely be just as high as those of falling foul of nature outside a resort.

Almost ten per cent of skiers who end up in Davos hospital have been involved in collisions. And collisions nearly always cause injuries, sometimes serious ones. I found this out in a very tragic way when my girlfriend Lucy Dicker was killed in La Grave, following our successful mission to ski every day in 1994. Even skiing off-piste with a guide is no guarantee that no harm will come to you. Or to the guide for that matter. There is a cynical saying that all the avalanche experts are dead.

According to the rescue service sos which operates in the Parsenn area of Davos – one of the most extensive ski areas in Europe, which also prides itself on its avalanche research centre – "Avalanches are a natural phenomenon and therefore no absolute safety from them can be guaranteed. We must emphasise that even after the most experienced judgement and safety measures have been taken, an avalanche can still break loose and run over an open and marked piste."

Always obey avalanche warning signs and stay out of high-risk areas unless a qualified high mountain guide is skiing with you. He or she will have specialist knowledge and will certainly not take you off-piste if there is a serious risk.

Just as experts argue over the best way of dealing with frostbite, so they have different views about how to try to survive an avalanche. There is no way of guaranteeing that you will not die. There are all sorts of avalanche patterns, from powder avalanches which drown you to slab avalanches which can break every bone in your body, or at least batter you senseless. You might start it yourself, or you might be engulfed in one started by another skier. Most likely it will start spontaneously and trap you in its path.

Avalanches can move frighteningly fast. You may have only a second or two to react. One possible reaction is to ski diagonally out of the avalanche's path. Another is to take your skis off and try to 'swim' on the surface of the snow. If you are sucked under the surface, try to keep a pocket of air in front of you by cupping your mouth and nose with your hand. When skiing off-piste wear an avalanche transceiver, never ski alone and if possible always take a guide.

Ueli Frei, President of the Mountain Guides Association in Grindelwald, who specialises in helicopter skiing and regularly rescues climbers stranded on the much-feared north face of the Eiger, remarks: "You have to respect the mountain. But for me there is more risk in crossing a busy street in London." But he admits that two of his most experienced colleagues have recently died in avalanches.

In general though, skiing statistics are encouraging. While the risk of minor injury – sprains, bruises, cuts – is high; major injuries – broken bones or torn ligaments – are much rarer, occurring once in every 200 days worth of skiing. For most recreational skiers, that is the equivalent of 20 years.

Incidentally, three per cent of injured skiers each year suffer from broken thumbs. But you can break a thumb even before you go skiing. Many people who practice on dry ski slopes sprain or break thumbs when they fall on the unforgiving plastic surface and sandwich a thumb between the slope and their body. But don't let that encourage you to give skiing the thumbs down. It's far too much fun. Just take it easy. And take care. ❧

ARNIE WILSON is the skiing correspondent of 'The Financial Times', and the author of 'Tears in the Snow', an account of spending a record-breaking 365 consecutive days on skis in 1994.

Surviving wild animals
by Nigel Marven

EVEN WITH A WETSUIT ON I WAS COLD. The waters south of Cape Town in South Africa are closer to Antarctica than they are to the tropics. The creature ahead of me was chilling, too: its girth was so huge I couldn't have circled its body with my arms. And its environment was alien to me. In the sea, I was comparatively clumsy, coping with the twin problems of staying afloat and breathing with a snorkel. Unless underwater technology changes radically, we'll always be half blind and deaf in the ocean – but that doesn't mean that what I could see wasn't magnificent. Sunlight splashed onto the shark's eye and the dead black hole transformed itself into a shining blue-black, coming alive in the process. On the side of the creature's head, five gill slats flared open. I imagined I could see the vortices of oxygen-stripped water spiralling away from the clefts, which looked like knife cuts in blotting paper. The five-metre-long animal seemed curious and circled slowly. Its great head was tapered to a point, which is why Australians call the most feared of all sharks the white pointer.

The image of its mouth is forever burned into my consciousness – it was smiling with a clownish grin. This rictus smile was fixed, so the teeth were always on show. The great white shark was thrilling, more like a jet fighter than a fish. If it wanted to it could have given me a devastating, perhaps lethal, bite. I wasn't in a cage and a wetsuit was my only protection (my companion André Hartman had a spear gun, but it didn't work). I didn't want this encounter to end, but after a while the great white became a little too curious and André gave it a sharp rap on the nose with his heavy camera housing and sent it on its way.

This sequence was the finale to a film I produced about the world's largest sharks. My purpose was to show that great whites are not malicious monsters with a taste for human flesh. But then they're not harmless herbivores either – there is no doubt they have the potential to eat us, and that's what makes them so exciting, one of the last predators of humanity.

I would never have dared do what I did if I hadn't spent ten days observing the behaviour of great whites – and nearly the same amount of time reading every single thing I could about them. I also had a companion who'd swum with great whites hundreds of times before. I'd seen that the great fish are careful about what they bite; white marks, as if a child had scribbled with chalk on their snouts, bore testament to injuries caused by the teeth or claws of fur seals, their main prey. Great whites are cautious before they bite – their eyes are vulnerable. I also knew that they aren't particularly fond of humans as food: we don't have enough blubber to be energy-rich, fur seals are power bars compared to us. Andre had also waited until the visibility was good. In dirty water the sharks couldn't see us clearly and we wouldn't be able to see them.

Most attacks by great whites (there have been 245 since 1846, and of these only 60 were fatal) have been cases of mistaken identity. The hungry shark has seen movement at the surface of the water and has launched a vertical lunge before discovering that it has bitten a human rather than a seal. The predator doesn't even bother delivering the *coup de grace* to our scrawny bodies, which is why many human victims survive shark attacks.

But even with all this knowledge and my direct experience, I still wouldn't recommend that other travellers swim freely with great whites. By all means, view them from a cage, but even then, without expert help and perfect conditions you could be taking a risk.

Most divers feel elated if they catch a glimpse of a shark. Tales of waters infested with them, just like those of deserts teeming with scorpions or rainforests writhing with venomous snakes, are usually just that, travellers' tales. As a wildlife filmmaker, it didn't take me long to find this out. It takes weeks, possibly months, of meticulous planning to ensure that you are in the right place at the right time to get the pictures used in documentaries. If we just turned up on the off chance, with a vague hope of seeing animals, hazardous or otherwise, it's unlikely that any wildlife film would ever be completed. But we do have more opportunities than most other travellers to meet potentially dangerous creatures – and, most importantly, to do so safely.

If you follow a couple of simple rules, shark watching shouldn't be any more hazardous than badger watching. I've dived with tiger sharks, hammerheads and reef sharks without any problems at all. Spear fishing when sharks are around is, of course, a no-no: the blood in the water and the death throes of the punctured fish excite sharks too much so they tend to come too close for comfort. Don't touch or approach sharks too closely, just watch and marvel. If a shark is going to attack, it usually displays warning signs, arching its back, raising its head and lowering its pectoral fins (the big wing-like ones at the front).

If a shark does look likely to attack (this really is a million to one chance), the worst thing you can do is panic and try to flee – the shark is far swifter in the water than you are, and may confuse your flailing behaviour with that of an ailing fish. Instead, stand your ground and remember that the eyes and heads of sharks are vulnerable. If one comes at you, be prepared to give it a punch or even gouge its eyes with your fingernails. If possible, seek a retreat on the reef or rock wall, making sure you keep your back against something solid.

As well as sharks, there are other potentially hazardous animals in the sea.

Animals made of jelly, the sea gooseberries, salps, sea butterflies and jellyfish, are some of my favourites – then there's the glories of the plankton, some of which have brightly coloured tentacles or delicate air-filled floats. Others have rows of cilia that flash with iridescent colours when they catch the light. Sea butterflies live up to their name, flapping languidly through the water with transparent wings. Many of these animals, particularly jellyfish, have a battery of stinging cells for catching prey – but they can also lash unwary swimmers.

Most cause nothing worse than a mild prickling or tingling sensation, perhaps with some swelling and reddening of the skin, but stings from the infamous Portuguese man o' war can be excruciating, and those from the box jellyfish lethal. To avoid the former watch out for dead man o' wars washed up on the shore (this creature is usually quite big, with tentacles up to nine metres long that hang from a gas-filled flotation bladder that is tinted with blue, purple and pink). If a few of these are beached, the waters could be infested, so avoid swimming there. If you can't resist a dip, wear long pants and a long-sleeved shirt, as these will give protection from the stinging cells.

The box jellyfish is a different proposition. Travellers need to seek local advice about its presence or watch out for warning signs. It's prevalent in some regions of the Pacific and Indian oceans, particularly in the tropical waters of Australia. This jellyfish has been responsible for the deaths of 90 people to date, and about 70 of these fatalities were in Australian waters. This cube of jelly has four groups of trailing tentacles – blunder into these and they discharge into your skin, causing savage and excruciating pain. There's acute inflammation and a florid flare on the skin where the tentacles have made contact. Venom is absorbed into the bloodstream, attacking the victim's nervous system. I've seen the warning signs about stinger season in northern Australia, and I'd be petrified about swimming at that time without a stinger suit (a thin wetsuit) for protection. If anyone is unlucky enough to get stung, the injured region should be doused with vinegar for a minimum of 30 seconds (there are vinegar supplies on many of the beaches). This inhibits any of the other stinging cells from firing off; prompt medical attention must then be sought. If the victim loses consciousness, resuscitation techniques should be used. Unless the unfired stings have been deactivated with vinegar, no attempt should be made to rub or wipe off adhering tentacles.

There are other hazards that lie in wait for anyone getting to or from a swim. If you happen to be on a coral reef, beware of intricately patterned shells in the shape of a perfect cone. In 1935 in Queensland, Australia, a 27-year-old man handled such a cone shell. He felt an immediate mild stinging sensation in the palm of his hand, within ten minutes his lips felt numb, after four hours he was in a deep coma and dead an hour after that. Cone shells harpoon their prey, usually small fish, with poisonous darts; if we handle these molluscs with bare hands they can sting us, too.

Anywhere along the Australian coast, you may find miniature octopuses stranded in rock pools. When they get excited or annoyed circles of iridescent blue develop on their tentacles and bodies, but beware of picking them up, however much they may look like colourful toys. A bite from a blue-ringed octopus causes nausea, vomiting then paralysis. This can happen within minutes and a victim may soon experience difficulties with breathing. In such cases, first aid to maintain breathing is crucial until the patient can be got to an artificial ventilator.

Stingrays can be concealed on the muddy or sandy bottom of bays. At the base of their tails they have a venomous bony sting with short barbs along its length, which tear through flesh as it is withdrawn. If you've been told they're in the area, avoid stepping on them by shuffling your feet to disturb them as you're wading (the stings are long enough and tough enough to pierce plastic sandals). A stingray victim should put the affected area into a bath of hot water (as hot as they can bear) for 30 to 90 minutes, which denatures the proteins in the venom.

Stingrays are not restricted to salt water, either. I had to use the foot shuffling technique in the Llanos, a swampy region in Venezuela. I'd taken my shoes off for tactile sensitivity because I was feeling for anacondas with my toes. I certainly didn't want my snake hunt to be disrupted by a stingray sting.

I've always been a fan of snakes and whenever I get the chance I actively search them out. There are over 2,700 species, and only a small proportion of these are dangerous to us.

Given the chance, nearly all snakes will disappear into cover when they sense the vibrations from a human footfall. So stamp your feet when moving through snake country. Personally, I walk carefully and slowly so I can see them.

The big constrictors, species that suffocate their prey, rarely attack us; most fatalities are from people molesting them or accidents with captive snakes. Pythons or anacondas that hunt people are figments of the imaginations of Hollywood scriptwriters – our shoulders are just too broad for all but world-record-sized snakes (over eight metres) to work their jaws over to allow them to swallow us.

Venomous snakes can be hazardous to travellers. Boots and thick socks should be worn where they abound. I actively turn over rocks and logs looking for reptiles (I always gently replace them back in the position that I found them in when I'm doing this). I'm always careful not to put my hand underneath or into dark cracks and crevices. While most travellers won't be turning things over, the same rule applies when climbing or scrambling through snake country: don't plunge your hands into chinks in rocks or into hollow logs.

But I've had a close shave myself because of a failure to take common-sense precautions. Camping in Turkmenistan on the Iranian border I had to relieve myself at night. I didn't put on shoes or take a flashlight. When I shone one around the next night I found that there were rodent burrows with saw-scaled vipers lying outside in the sand, next to one of them there was a footprint I'd made the night before. That was a close shave. If I'd trodden on one of these snakes (they are highly venomous and can be irascible) in this remote region, far from medical help, I'd have put my life at great risk.

If I had been bitten, I would have put a compression bandage (this can be made from strips of towel or clothing) just above the puncture wound. This shouldn't block arterial flow and should be loose enough to get a finger between the constriction band and the affected area. The bandage will stop the venom spreading through the superficial veins and lymph vessels. I'd then try to keep calm and rest on the journey as I travelled towards the nearest medical care. In most parts of the world this is usually only a short distance away.

For most travellers the chances of being bitten by a snake are rare. Venom is a complex mix of organic chemicals, usually proteins, which are 'expensive' for the snake to make. Its main use is for immobilising prey and as a method of preliminary digestion. Venom is used in self-defence, but only as a last resort; that's why snakes have developed ingenious warning devices such as a cobra's hood, a rattlesnake's rattle or the bright warning colours of the coral snake. No snake will go after a human being (with one exception, a king cobra guarding its nest, but that would be a rare find indeed), so if you're lucky enough to come across one of these reptiles just stand back and watch. If you're patient, the snake will eventually move. I always marvel at the streamlined design and effortless flowing movement of a snake. If it's close enough or you have binoculars, you can make out its pattern and colour scheme – these can be dazzling. When the snake has disappeared into cover, as it will invariably do, just think for a while about a snake's elegant solution to life without limbs. Snakes will only bite us in self defence, so they should be treated with caution and admiration, not fear and hatred.

Furred predators rarely get as much of a bad press as snakes, sharks or creepy-crawlies, probably because, as mammals ourselves, we feel an affinity with them. Big cats are a potential danger in the tropics (there are some tigers in Siberia, but their numbers have declined so much it would be an honour to be attacked by one), as are bears in temperate or Arctic climates. While it's very unusual for people to be on their menus, there have been cases of rogue lions, tigers or bears that, because of injury or old age, are forced to treat us as food – but these individuals are so rare you've more chance of the plane that's taking you to your destination dropping out of the sky than you have of meeting one of them.

Usually big predators will run when a human approaches them on foot. Accidents tend to happen when they're surprised or when food brings them into close proximity with us. Most travellers will be escorted and/or in vehicles when viewing lions and tigers; but in North America and Russia bears can turn up in many areas – even outside protected parks. I spent two weeks in Alaska's Katmai National Park working on a film about brown bears. I'd never seen these magnificent creatures before, but on encountering them it soon became apparent that they were more interested in the succulent sedge grass and salmon than in us. We always remembered we were visitors to their home, so as we walked along their trails we talked and clapped so as not to surprise them – and, of course, they always had right of way. If they approached us, we'd talk to them calmly, "Hi, bear. Hullo, bear, we're still here," so that they didn't forget we were there; but if they came to within ten metres or so of us, we slowly retreated.

Campers in bear country shouldn't put temptation in a bear's way. Food should be kept in sealed containers and away from the sleeping areas. Surprising as it may seem, recent research has shown that bears seem to be excited by the odours of menstruation or love-making; so, if possible, a trip should be planned to avoid these from happening when under canvas with bears prowling around outside. The same basic rules apply for polar bears. They can be seen around the town of

Churchill in Manitoba, Canada, between July and November, and on the Norwegian island of Spitzbergen in spring.

It's clear that, in most habitats, animals aren't usually a threat to us – but there's just one case where they are – and this is somewhere I'd never venture. The habitat in question is the tropical freshwaters inhabited by saltwater crocodiles (northern Australia and some parts of South-East Asia) or Nile crocodiles (Africa). (If the river or pool was in Africa, hippos could mean a double whammy of danger. There's every chance they'd kill human swimmers, particularly when defending young.) Crocodiles aren't as fussy as sharks about what they attack: anything swimming in their territory is potential food. If I go for a dip in croc country I always check with the locals whether the water I'm entering is really clear of the animals. I don't want to experience becoming prey for an animal that can be up to ten times my size.

So, in conclusion, I think you can probably tell by now that I'd love it if the world were teeming with exciting and potentially dangerous animals, but this really isn't the case. While modern travellers can get anywhere and do anything with relative ease – we hike, camp or snorkel in areas that used to be exclusive territory for animals – when compared with the chances of being harmed by another human being, the danger posed by other creatures is negligible.

The Smithsonian Institute and us Navy have calculated that, right around the world, there are 50 shark attacks each year. During the same period, people in the United States suffer six million dog bites – our best friend causes ten deaths per year. However, there will be under 200 attacks by bears, sharks, crocodiles and alligators, with fewer than ten deaths. Snakes bite 3,000 people in Australia every year, but 90 per cent of these bites are from non-venomous species. Medical care and anti-venom treatment are so efficient nowadays that, even among the 300 or so people who are actually envenomated, deaths are extremely rare.

In most situations, all that's required to avoid a bite or attack is an awareness of the presence of animals that could be a threat. No creatures show malice aforethought, we just need to be careful and not blunder into a curtain of jellyfish tentacles or tread on a camouflaged viper. If we keep our eyes skinned and senses alert, an encounter with a predator can be one of the most thrilling and memorable experiences of our lives. ❧

NIGEL MARVEN has presented numerous wildlife documentary films for BBC and ITV. He spends about five months each year seeking wild animals to film.

Survival at sea
by Sir Robin Knox-Johnston

A VERY SENSIBLE LIST OF SAFETY EQUIPMENT to be carried on board a boat was published by the Offshore Racing Council (ORC) in its *1994/5 Special Regulations Governing Offshore Racing*. The list is extensive, but because it is comprehensive, it is given opposite.

Medical

The health of the crew is the skipper's responsibility and he or she should see that the food is nourishing and sufficient, that the boat is kept clean and that the crew practise basic hygiene. A good medical kit must be carried.

There is an excellent book (published by HMSO for the British Merchant Navy) called *The Ship Captain's Medical Guide*. It is written for a ship that does not carry a doctor and includes a recommended list of medical supplies. Most doctors will supply prescriptions for antibiotics when the purpose has been explained. Two other books to recommend are *The International Medical for Ships*, published by the World Health Organisation, and *First Aid at Sea*, by Douglas Justins and Colin Berry (Adlard Coles Nautical, London).

Safety on deck

Prevention is always better than cure. Everyone on board should know their way about the deck, and know what everything is for. A good way of training is to take the boat out night sailing so that the crew get to know instinctively where everything is and what to avoid. Train the crew to squat whenever the boat lurches – it lowers the centre of gravity and makes toppling overside less likely.

In rough weather, make sure that all the crew wear their life-jackets and safety harnesses when on deck, and that they clip their harness to a strong point. A good attitude on board is that crew should wear their lifejackets at night, when told to and when they want to. If the crew have to go out from the cockpit, they should clip the harness to a wire jackstay that runs all the way from right forward to the cockpit for this purpose.

Man overboard

If someone falls overside, immediately throw a life-buoy into the water and summon the whole crew on deck. The aim is to get back and pick them up as quickly as possible, so post a look-out to keep an eye on the casualty, and the rest of the crew should assist with turning the boat around. It is worthwhile putting the boat straight into the wind, as this stops you close to the casualty, then start the engine and motor back. On one occasion in the Southern Ocean, we lost a man overside, and we ran on more than a mile before we could get the spinnaker down. Because of the large swell, the only way we could locate him when we turned round was by heading for the sea birds that were circling him. We got him back, after about 20

Safety equipment

- Two fire extinguishers, easily accessible and kept in different places.

- Two manually operated bilge pumps.

- Two buckets, of strong construction, fitted with lanyards.

- Two anchors and cables (chain for cruising is sensible).

- Two flashlights: water resistant and capable of being used for signalling, with spare bulbs and batteries.

- Foghorn.

- Radar reflector.

- Set of international code flags and a code book.

- Set of emergency navigation lights.

- Storm trysail.

- Storm jib.

- Emergency tiller.

- Tool kit.

- Marine radio transmitter/receiver.

- Radio, capable of receiving weather forecasts.

- Life-jackets: sufficient for the whole crew.

- Buoyant heaving line at least 16m long.

- Life-buoys or rings.

- Set of distress signals.

- Twelve red parachute flares.

- Four red hand flares.

- Four white hand flares.

- Two orange smoke day signals.

- A hand-held VHF radio.

- A life-raft of a capacity to take the whole crew, which has: a valid annual test certificate, two separate buoyancy compartments, a canopy to cover the occupants, a sea anchor and drogue, bellows or pump to maintain pressure, a signalling light, three hand flares, a baler repair kit, two paddles, a knife, emergency water and rations, a first aid kit and manual.

- In addition, it is worth carrying a portable, waterproof VHF radio and an emergency distress transmitter (EPIRB).

minutes, by which time he was unable to assist himself because of the cold.

In the upper latitudes, there is a real danger of hypothermia, so it is vital to warm the person as quickly as possible. Strip off their wet clothing and towel them dry, then put them in a warm sleeping bag. The heat is retained better if the sleeping bag can be put into a large plastic bag. If the person is very cold, it may be necessary for someone else to strip and climb into the bag with the casualty and warm them with their own body.

If the casualty is conscious, feed them hot soup or tea. Remember that it can be a nerve-shattering experience and that they may need time to get over the shock. Do not give them alcohol.

Abandoning the boat

When, as a last resort, it becomes necessary to leave the boat, set off the EPIRB, and, if possible, send out a digital selective distress call on the appropriate frequency or by satellite communications. Inflate the life-raft and pull it alongside. Put one or two of the crew on board, and, if there is time, pass over as much food, water and clothing as possible, plus the EPIRB and SART. If the boat's dinghy is available, tie it to the life-raft, to give extra space and help create a larger target for rescuers. Only leave the boat if there is absolutely no alternative. Life-rafts are small and not particularly robust, and it is always preferable to keep the boat afloat if possible.

The usual reason for abandoning a boat is that it has been holed. One method of improving its survivability is to fit it with water-tight bulkheads so that its volume is roughly divided into three. The Marine and Coastguard Agency insists on water-tight sub-division on yachts that take paying crew, which means that if the boat is holed the chances are that it will lose only a proportion of its buoyancy and there will still be dry, safe shelter for the crew. From the comparative safety of one of the 'safe' parts of the boat, a plan can probably be made to fix the leak.

When it is necessary to abandon the boat, having got as much food and useful equipment aboard the life-raft as possible, cut the painter and get clear. Then take stock of what you have, and post a look-out.

Ration supplies from the start. The best way to do this is to avoid food for the first day, as the stomach shrinks and the body's demand for food falls. Ration water to about a quarter of a litre a day and issue it in sips. On no account should sea water be drunk, but it can be used for washing and cooling in hot weather. Humans can last for amazingly long periods without food, but they do need water. Any rain should be trapped and saved. The canopy of the life-raft can be used for this purpose, as could the dinghy, if it has been taken along. Do not eat raw fish unless there is a plentiful water supply, as they are very rich in protein and ruin the liver unless the surplus can be washed out of the system. As a general rule, one volume of protein will require two volumes of water. Where water is plentiful, fish should be hunted. Most pelagic fish are edible, and quite often they will swim around a boat or dinghy out of curiosity. Inedible fish are found close to land or on reefs.

Keep movement to a minimum to conserve energy and, in cold weather, hold on to urine as long as possible to retain its heat. In hot, sunny weather, try to keep everyone in the shade. Find some mental stimulus in order to maintain morale, and remember that the crew will be looking to the skipper to set an example, so remain positive. Humans have survived for well over three months on a life-raft, but only because they had a strong will to live and were able to improvise. My book, *Seamanship* (Hodder and Stoughton), may prove useful further reading. ❧

Sir Robin Knox-Johnston, cbe, was the first man to sail around the world single-handedly and without stopping. He also set a global record for sailing around the world in a catamaran. He is the author of numerous books on sailing.

Survival in the desert
by Jack Jackson

T HE MOST IMPORTANT THING ABOUT DESERT SURVIVAL is to avoid the need for it in the first place! Be aware your vehicle's capabilities and do not overload it, and know how to maintain and repair it. Carry adequate spares and tools. Be fit yourselves and get sufficient sleep. Start your journey with 25 per cent more fuel and water than you calculated would be needed to cover extra problems, such as bad terrain, leaking containers and extra time spent over repairs or sitting out a bad sandstorm.

Know accurately where your next supplies of fuel and water are. Carry plastic sheets to make desert stills and take space blankets with you. Pack more than one compass and know how to navigate properly. When using magnetic compasses, keep them well away from vehicles and cameras. Do not rely exclusively on electronic Global Positioning Systems (GPS) or the batteries that power them, and do not leave the piste unless you really do know what you are doing. Travel only during the local winter months. Know how correct your odometer is in relation to the wheels and tyres fitted to the vehicle. Make notes of distances, compass bearings and obvious landmarks as you go along so that you can retrace your route easily if you have to.

Observe correct check-in and out procedures with local authorities. If possible, travel in a convoy with other vehicles. When lost, do not continue. Stop, think and, if necessary, retrace your route.

Back-up plans

If you are travelling in a large party, you should arrange a search and rescue plan before you start out. This would include the use and recognition of radio beacons or flares for aircraft search. Many countries do not allow you to use radio communications, but if you can use them, carry modern portable satellite communications systems.

Should the worst happen, remember that, for most people, an air search is highly unlikely and high-flying commercial passenger aircraft passing overhead are unlikely to notice you, whatever you do. A search, if it does come, will be along the piste or markers. Most often this will consist of other vehicles travelling through the area, whose drivers have been asked by the local authorities to look out for you because you have failed to check in at a pre-appointed time and place.

Local drivers will not understand or appreciate coloured flares, so your best signal for local outside help is fire. If you hear a vehicle at night, cardboard boxes or wood are quickly and easily lit, but during the day you need lots of thick black smoke. The best fuel for this is a tyre. Bury most of a tyre in the sand to control the speed at which it burns (keep it well away from and downwind of the vehicles and fuel) and start the exposed part burning with a rag soaked in either petrol or diesel fuel. As the exposed part of the tyre burns away, you can uncover more from the sand to keep it going, or cover all of it with sand if you wish to put out the fire. You should always avoid inhaling the sulphurous fumes. While the battery still carries a charge, headlights switched on and off at night can also be used to draw attention to your plight.

Should you be lucky enough to see low-flying aircraft overhead, remember that the international ground/air code for a request to be picked up by such a plane is to stand up with your arms held aloft in an obvious 'v' shape.

A need to survive

Once you are in a 'need-to-survive' situation, the important things are morale and water. Concentrate on getting your vehicles moving again. This will keep you occupied and help to keep up morale. To minimise water loss, avoid manual work during the day and, instead, work at night or in the early morning. Build shade and stay under it as much as possible, keeping well covered with loose cotton clothing. 'Space blankets', with the reflective side facing out, make the coolest shade. Keep warm and out of the wind at night. In really hot climates, replacing lost potassium with Slow K can make a big difference to your general alertness.

Unless you are well off the piste with no chance of a search, you should stay with your vehicle. If someone must walk out, pick one or two of the strongest and most determined people to go. They must carry with them a compass and a GPS receiver, if available; a torch; salt; anti-diarrhoea medicine; loose, all-enveloping clothes; tough footwear; good sunglasses and as much water as they can sensibly carry. In soft sand, a jerrycan of water can easily be hauled along on a rope tied to the waist. On mixed ground, tie the jerrycan to a sand ladder, one end of which is padded and tied to the waist.

Those who walk out should follow the desert nomad pattern of walking in the evening until about 11pm, sleeping until 4 am, walking again until 10 am, then digging a shallow hollow in the sand and lying in it under a space blanket, reflective side out, until the sun has lost its heat. If it's a full moon they can walk all night. In this way, fit men would make 60–70 km on ten litres of water – less in soft sand.

Water

In a 'sit-it-out-and-survive' situation, with all manual labour kept to a minimum, food is unimportant and dehydration staves off hunger, but water is vital. The average consumption of water in a hot, dry climate should be eight litres per person per day. This can be lowered to four litres a day in a real emergency. Diarrhoea increases dehydration, so should be controlled by medicine where necessary. Salt intake should be kept up – in the worst scenario, licking your bare arms will replace some lost salt.

Water supply should be improved by making as many desert stills as possible. To make one, dig a hole about one-third of a metre deep and one metre in circumference, place a clean saucepan or billycan in the centre of the hole, and cover it with a two-metre-square plastic sheet weighted down at the edges with stones, jerrycans or tools. Put a stone or another heavy object in the centre to weigh it down directly over the billy. Overnight, water vapour from the sand will evaporate and then condense on the underside of the plastic sheet. In the morning, running a finger down from the edge of the sheet to the centre will cause the condensation to run down and drip into the pan. All urine should be conserved and put into shallow containers around the central billycan. The water so collected should be boiled or sterilised before drinking.

If you have antifreeze in your radiator, don't try to drink it as it is highly poisonous. Even if you have not put antifreeze in the radiator yourselves, there is still likely to be some left in it from previous use or from the factory at the time that the vehicle was first manufactured. Radiator water should be put into the desert still in the same way as the urine and the resulting condensate should be boiled or sterilised before drinking. Water from bad or brackish wells can be made drinkable in the same way. Note, however, that solar stills can take a lot of energy to create and will yield little water in return. Until the situation is really desperate, they are probably not worth considering as a viable means of collecting water.

The minimum amount of water per day required to maintain the body's water balance at rest in the shade is as follows: if the mean daily temperature is 35°c, you will need 5.3 litres per 24 hours. If it is 30°c, then 2.4 litres; if 25°c you need 1.2 litres; and at temperatures of 20°c and below, one litre will suffice. It must be stressed that this is the bare minimum necessary for survival. If such an intake is prolonged, there will be a gradual kidney malfunction and possibly urinary tract infection, with women more at risk than men.

The will to live is essential. Once you give up, you will be finished. If you find people in such a situation and do not have a doctor to handle them, feed them water to which rehydration salts have been added, a teaspoonful at a time, every few minutes for a couple of hours. If you do not have sachets of rehydration salts, you can make your own by adding one level teaspoon of salt and two tablespoons of sugar per litre of water. If the person is unconscious, the dissolved rehydration salts can be administered anally. It is essential to try to stabilise someone in this way before trying to take them on a long, tough drive to hospital. ❧

JACK JACKSON is an expedition leader, mountaineer and diver. He is the author of 'The Four Wheel Drive Book' and co-author of 'The Asian Highway'.

Survival in the jungle
by Robin Hanbury-Tenison

THE KEY TO SURVIVAL IN THE TROPICS IS COMFORT. If your boots fit, your clothes don't itch, your wounds don't fester, you have enough to eat and you have the comforting presence of a local who is at home in the environment, then you are not likely to go far wrong.

Of course, jungle warfare is something else. The British, Americans and, for all I know, several other armies, have produced detailed manuals on how to survive under the most arduous conditions imaginable and with the minimum of resources. But most of us are extremely unlikely ever to find ourselves in such a situation. Even if you are unlucky enough to be caught in a guerrilla war or survive an air crash in the jungle, I believe that the following advice will be as useful as trying to remember sophisticated techniques that probably require equipment you do not have to hand anyway.

A positive will to survive is essential. The knowledge that others have travelled long distances and lived for days and even months without help or special knowledge gives confidence, while a calm appraisal of the circumstances can make them seem far less intimidating. The jungle need not be an uncomfortable place, although unfamiliarity may make it seem so. Morale is as important as ever, and comfort, both physical and mental, a vital ingredient.

Clothing and footwear

To start with, it is usually warm, but when you are wet, especially at night, you can become very cold very quickly. It is therefore important to be prepared and always try to keep a sleeping bag and a change of clothes dry. Excellent strong, lightweight plastic bags are now available in which these items should always be packed with the top folded over and tied. These can then be placed inside your rucksack or bag so that if dropped in a river or soaked by a sudden tropical downpour – and the effect is much the same – they, at least, will be dry. I usually have three such bags, one with dry clothes, one with camera equipment, notebooks, etc., and one with food.

Wet clothes should be worn. This is unpleasant for the first ten minutes in the morning, but they will soon be soaking wet with sweat and dripping in any case, and wearing them means you need carry only one change for the evening and sleeping in. It is well worth taking the time to rinse them out whenever you are in sunshine by a river so that you can dry them on hot rocks in half an hour or so. They can also be hung over the fire at night, which makes them more pleasant to put on in the morning, but also tends to make them stink of wood smoke.

Always wear loose clothes in the tropics. They may not be very becoming but constant wetting and drying will tend to shrink them and rubbing makes itches and scratches far worse. Cotton is excellent but should be of good quality so that the clothes do not rot and tear too easily.

There are now many excellent specialist manufacturers of tropical clothing. Some are expensive, but it is worth investing in good quality for comfort and durability. One of the best suppliers is Nomad Camping at 3 Turnpike Lane, London N8 (tel 020 8889 7014).

For footwear, baseball boots or plimsolls are usually adequate, but for long distances good leather boots will protect your feet much better from bruising and blisters. In leech country, a shapeless cotton stocking worn between sock and shoe tied with a drawstring below the knee, outside long trousers, gives virtually complete protection. As far as I know, no one manufactures these yet, so they have to be made up specially, but they are well worth it.

Upsets and dangers

Hygiene is important in the tropics. Small cuts can turn nasty very quickly and sometimes will not heal for a long time. The best protection is to make an effort to wash all over at least once a day if possible, at the same time looking out for any sore places, cleaning and treating them at once. On the other hand, where food and drink are concerned, it is usually not practical or polite to attempt to maintain perfectionist standards. Almost no traveller in the tropics can avoid receiving hospitality and few would wish to do so. It is often best therefore to accept that a mild stomach upset is likely – and be prepared. There is an excellent medical section in this book with the best up-to-date advice on prevention and cure of all the illnesses to which travellers in the tropics are likely to be exposed and they should read it carefully. However, constant use of prophylactics and antibiotics can produce side-effects. Many of us now use homeopathic remedies, including malaria pills, while carrying conventional cures as well.

In real life-and-death conditions, there are only two essentials for survival, a knife or machete and a compass (provided you are not injured, when, if possible, the best thing to do is to crawl to water and wait for help). Other important items I would put in order of priority as follows:

1. A map.
2. A waterproof cover, cape or large bag.
3. Means to make fire: lifeboat matches, lighter with spare flints, gas or petrol.
4. A billycan.
5. Tea or coffee, sugar and dried milk.

There are few tropical terrains that cannot be crossed with these, given time and determination. Man can survive a long time without food, so try to keep your food supplies simple, basic and light. Water is less of a problem in the jungle, except in limestone mountains, but a metal or lightweight plastic water container should be carried and filled whenever possible. Rivers, streams and even puddles are unlikely to be dangerously contaminated, while rattans and lianas often contain water, as do some other plants whose leaves may form catchments, such as pitcher plants. It is easy to drink from these, though best to filter the liquid through cloth and avoid the 'gunge' at the bottom.

Hunting and trapping are unlikely to be worth the effort to the inexperienced, although it is surprising how much can be found in streams and caught with hands. Prawns, turtles, frogs and even fish can be captured with patience and almost all are edible – and even tasty if you're hungry enough. Fruits, even those that are ripe and being eaten by other animals, are less safe, while some edible-looking plants and fungi can be very poisonous and should be avoided. Don't try for the honey of wild bees unless you know what you are doing as stings can be dangerous and those of hornets even fatal.

As regards shelter, there is a clear distinction between South America and the rest of the tropical world. In the South American interior, almost everyone uses a hammock. Excellent waterproof hammocks are supplied to the Brazilian and US armies and are obtainable commercially. Otherwise, a waterproof sheet may be stretched across a line tied between the same two trees from which the hammock is slung. Elsewhere, however, hammocks are rarely used and will tend to be a nuisance under normal conditions. Lightweight canvas stretchers through which poles may be inserted before being tied apart on a raised platform make excellent beds and, once again, a waterproof sheet provides shelter. Plenty of nylon cord is always useful.

Fight it or like it

The jungle can be a frightening place at first. Loud noises, quantities of unfamiliar creepy-crawlies, flying biting things and the sometimes oppressive heat can all conspire to get you down. But it can also be a very pleasant place if you decide to like it rather than fight it – and it is very seldom dangerous. Snakebite, for example is extremely rare. During the 15 months of the Royal Geographical Society's Mulu expedition, in Borneo, no one was bitten, although we saw and avoided or caught and photographed many snakes and even ate some! Most things, such as thorns, ants and sandflies, are more irritating than painful (taking care to treat rather than scratch usually prevents trouble).

Above all, the jungle is a fascinating place – the richest environment on earth. The best help for morale is to be interested in what is going on around you and the best guide is usually a local resident who is as at home there as most of us are in cities. Fortunately, in most parts of the world where jungles survive, there are still such people. By accepting their advice, recognising their expertise and asking them to travel with you, you may help to reinforce their self-respect in the face of often overwhelming forces that try to make them adopt a so-called 'modern' way of life. At the same time, you will appreciate the jungle far more yourself – and have a far better chance of surviving in it. ❧

ROBIN HANBURY-TENISON is a distinguished explorer and champion of tribal peoples, and one of the founders of Survival International.

Surviving the cold: 1 Take it seriously
by Dr Mike Stroud

THE WIND WAS BLOWING BRISKLY AS I STEPPED OUT OF THE TENT, but the sun was shining and it didn't feel too bad. When I had been out earlier, briefly, answering nature's call, the air had been still, and despite it being –40°C it had seemed quite warm in the sunshine. I had decided to wear only a cotton windproof over underwear and fleece salopettes. It was amazing how little one needed to keep warm as long as you kept on working hard.

Ran and I took down the tent and packed up our sledges. The south pole was only 30 km away and, with luck, we would reach it within two days. It helped to have it so close. We had been going 12 hours a day for more than two months, and the effort had taken a terrible toll. It had been both mental and physical hell. It was not long after we set off that I realised my mistake. As well as only putting on a single jacket, I was wearing only thin contact gloves inside outer mitts and, after an hour, with the wind rising even more, my hands were suffering badly and not warming up despite moving. They became so bad that Ran had to help me put on the extra mittens from my sledge, my fingers were too useless to get them on. When we set off again, I was getting generally chilled. After the long stop fighting with the gloves, I found that I could barely pull the sledge with my cold muscles. I was in trouble, and I realised I would have to stop and put my fleece jacket on as well, but to do this meant removing my outer jacket completely and once again my fingers were useless and I was unable to do up the zips. Ran was there to help again, but I had entered a vicious circle. My thinking was beginning to fade, and although I kept walking for another half-hour or so, I was never with-it. It is only through Ran's description that I know what happened next.

I had apparently begun to move very slowly and to wander from side to side. When Ran asked if I was OK, I had been unintelligible, and he had realised immediately that I must be hypothermic. He then tried to get me to help with the tent, but I just stood around doing nothing. So he put it up alone and pushed me inside. Eventually he got me in my sleeping bag and forced me to take some hot drinks. After an hour or so I recovered, but it had been another close call. Obviously we were getting vulnerable and we discussed pulling out at the pole....

The above is an excerpt from my book, *Shadows on the Wasteland*, about my crossing of Antarctica with Sir Ranulph Fiennes. Under the circumstances, it was perhaps not surprising that I became hypothermic, for cold easily creates casualties and can even kill. Yet, with the correct preparation, man can operate successfully even in the harshest of climates. The secret is to match the body's heat production – chiefly dictated by activity – with its heat losses – chiefly governed by clothing and shelter. You should aim to neither overheat nor cool down. Both can have unwelcome consequences.

An inactive adult produces about a light bulb's-worth of heat (100 watts), which is not really much to keep the whole body warm in the face of the cold, wind and rain. It is, therefore, generally wise to keep moving for the most of the time in cold conditions, until you have either reached or created proper shelter. However, many reasons, such as getting lost or injured, may force you to halt or lie up under adverse circumstances, and you are then going to need to reduce your heat losses to less than the 100 watts that you will be producing. This may be an impossibility if ill equipped or conditions are really harsh. If you can't reduce heat losses enough, your body will cool and you will start to shiver. This can increase your resting heat production to as much as 500 watts, but even this may be inadequate and the shivering itself is uncomfortable and tiring for the muscles. If cooling still continues, you will become hypothermic and can be in great danger. It is definitely best to carry enough protection to deal with getting stuck out in the worst possible conditions you may meet.

When you are active, things are quite different. Working hard leads the body to produce as much as a good room heater – 2,000 watts or even more. It is therefore more common to get too hot rather than too cold, even in the worst conditions. Initially, getting too hot may not be important, but it does lead to sweating, which can ruin the insulation of your clothing by wetting it from the inside and later, when you have decreased your activity or the conditions have worsened, this wet clothing will have lost its ability to protect you properly. Sweating may also lead to dehydration, which in turn will make you vulnerable to fatigue, and it is with the onset of tiredness and the ensuing slow-down in activity that heat production will start to fall and you will cool rapidly to become at risk from the 'exhaustion/hypothermia' syndrome. Even the most experienced of people have become victims under such circumstances.

In order to match heat losses to heat production, clothing must have the flexibility to be both cool and warm. It must also be able to provide windproofing and waterproofing. Such flexibility can only be achieved by the use of layers, which must be easy to put on and take off and comfortable to wear together. In all but the very coldest regions – where rain or melting snow won't occur – I would favour the use of modern synthetics in the insulation layers as they tend not to degrade much when wetted by sweat or the environment, and they also dry spectacularly quickly. If affordable, waterproofs/windproofs should be moisture vapour permeable (MVP) since these will limit the accumulation of sweat and condensation in inner garments and will allow the evaporation of some sweat, which will help to keep you cool if overheating. However, it needs to be remembered that even MVP garments are only partially vapour permeable (especially in the cold, when water vapour will condense or even freeze on the inner surface of the garment and will then be trapped by its waterproof qualities), and so it is always better to remove the waterproof if it is not actually raining and activity is making you too hot.

Additional flexibility when trying to maintain a comfortable body temperature can be granted by changing your head covering. In the cold, when wearing good clothing, as much as 90 per cent of your heat losses can come from your head, so by putting on or taking off a warm hat or balaclava and by adjusting a windproof hood, you can make enormous changes to your heat losses much more easily than by adjusting other garments. It is often said that if you get cold hands you should put on a hat.

Eating is also an important factor in keeping warm. Even at rest a meal will rev up your metabolism and make that 100-watt bulb glow brighter, while during exercise it will considerably increase your heat output for any given level of activity. More importantly, food also helps to sustain the supply of fuels to the muscles, and this will allow you to continue working, or for that matter shivering, for longer. In addition, it will make it much less likely that you will develop a low blood sugar – a factor now thought to be important in the onset of some cases of exposure/exhaustion. Almost any food will help, but it is probably best for it to contain a fair amount of carbohydrate. Grain-based snack bars are as good as anything, but snacks based on chocolate are also excellent, even if there is a greater fat content.

When hypothermia does begin to occur in an individual, a number of changes are seen that make the diagnosis pretty easy as long as the possibility is carefully considered. Unfortunately, the person suffering from the cold is often unable to consider things properly, since he or she may not realise what is happening and often, after feeling cold, shivery and miserable initially, they may feel quite happy and even warm. It therefore goes without saying that a problem may only become evident when things have already become quite bad, and that if a victim is alone or everybody in a party becomes hypothermic simultaneously, things are very serious. The signs to watch out for are quite similar to those seen when a person becomes increasingly drunk. At first the victim may slur speech and begin to be unnaturally happy with the situation. This normally corresponds to a core temperature of around 35°C, compared to the normal 37°C, although the actual temperature varies from individual to individual and some people feel quite unwell at 36°C. Then, as cooling continues, the victim may begin to stumble or stagger and may go on to become aggressive or confused. This often correlates with a core temperature of around 33°–34°C. Eventually, at a core temperature of around 32°C, they will collapse and become unconscious, and they can go on cooling to stop breathing at around 27°C. However, their heart may not stop until core temperature is as low as 22°C, and so it is vital to remember that, however bad things seem, attempting rewarming and resuscitation may still work.

When someone first starts getting cold, act quickly by increasing their clothing insulation, increasing activity or seeking shelter. However, if choosing to shelter, remember that it may entail lying up in bad conditions and the loss of activity will cut heat production right down. This may have devastating results, and so the decision to go on or to seek emergency protection requires great judgement. Generally, I would recommend that if the victim is only just beginning to cool, push on if proper warm conditions are likely to be reached reasonably quickly. Hot drinks and food are also of great value, but will only be helpful while the victim is conscious and cooperative. Once again, however, remember that sitting around preparing them may have adverse effects.

If the victim is worse and is actually showing signs of staggering or confusion, the situation is becoming dangerous. Obviously additional clothing, hot drinks or seeking a course out of the wind remain of paramount importance, but the question of carrying on becomes more difficult since now it is probably better to stop if reasonable shelter is available. When going out in cold environments, you should always plan to carry some sort of windproof and waterproof bivouac protection – noting that, although tempting weight-wise, lightweight silvered survival blankets have been shown to be no more effective than a plastic sheet and definitely worse than a plastic or more rugged waterproof bag.

You may, of course, be planning on camping anyway, in which case you need only ensure that your tent is adequate and that you have practised pitching it when the wind is up. It is no good finding out that it cannot be done with your model when you need it in emergency. Ideally, you should also be carrying a sleeping bag, even if you had no plans to get trapped outside, for there is no doubt that putting a victim in a good bag, and if necessary getting in it with them, is the best course of action if you are forced to stop.

Obviously, shelter can be sought as well as carried. In an emergency, it is a nice warm building that is best, but this is not normally an option. The priority then becomes getting out of the wind and wet, and any natural feature that you can get under or into the lee of is of great value. Also remember that effective shelter may often be found close in on the windward side of an object, particularly if it has a vertical side that will generate back pressure and a 'dead spot' immediately in front of it. Much to many people's surprise, the shelter there may even be better than to leeward since swirling vortices of snow do not come curling round and drifting over you.

In conditions with decent snow cover, compacted snow or ice can be used to create a whole range of possible shelters, ranging from simple snowholes to multiple-roomed camps, but really you need to have been taught how to make them and be carrying a suitable snow shovel. Reading about building such shelters cannot replace experience, and before going out in really severe conditions one should have practised in safe conditions. Ideally, you should have attended a proper course on winter survival such as those run by the British Mountaineering Council in Scotland or North Wales.

If a victim has cooled so much that they are unconscious, they need medical attention urgently. However, while this is sought or awaited, every measure mentioned above should be made to protect them from further cooling. As a general rule, never give up trying to protect and warm them, even if they appear to be dead. People have been successfully resuscitated many hours after they have apparently stopped breathing, and you cannot rely upon being able to feel a pulse or hear their heart. It is said that hypothermia victims are 'not dead until they are warm and dead' and so, generally speaking, it is impossible to be sure while you are still out in the field.

I would reiterate that, with the correct preparation, you can operate safely and relatively comfortably in terrible conditions, but doing so is an art. That art needs to be learned and it is a mixture of education, preparation and forethought. Remember that hypothermia could happen to you or one or your party even in a temperate climate and indeed, it is more likely to happen in milder, wetter conditions than in the truly cold regions of the Earth.

I will finish with another extract that illustrates just how easy it is to be caught out, and how simple it is to remedy the situation.

'As he approached, I wondered what was wrong. He was moving slowly and seemed to be fiddling with his clothing, trying to undo the zip on the front of his sodden jacket. He was smiling and certainly looked happier than he had done 15 minutes back but I noticed that he stumbled a couple of times despite it being pretty flat. He drew up beside me where I stood with my back to the gale.

"Jusht a moment," he said, and then after quite a pause, "I've jusht got to get thish jacket off."

His voice was slurred and I looked at him more closely. Although he smiled, there was a strange, wild expression on his face and his eyes were slightly glazed. He wasn't shivering any more but his skin was as white as marble and I noticed that he had taken his gloves off and they were nowhere to be seen. He was also swaying as he began to almost rip at his clothing, frustrated by his fruitless attempts to pull down the zip with cold fingers.

"Are you OK?" I asked, but I got no reply, only an inane black grin as he continued with his attempts to undress. The truth began to dawn on me.

"Come on," I said, grasping him by the arm and pulling him towards the edge of the ridge. "We'll go down here and drop out of the wind."

The effect was quite spectacular. As we entered the lee of the Cwm, the noise and buffeting that we had endured all day ceased and the world became an almost silent place. It seemed so much warmer that as I hurried downward, I began to sweat, but for my companion, who I almost dragged along beside me, the move into shelter brought a different experience. Although he, too, began to warm, it only brought him back towards the normal and, with it, he began to shiver and feel miserably cold.

I could scarcely believe what I had just witnessed. It was only September on Snowdon, yet my father had been to the edge of disaster….'

Remember, always treat the cold with respect and never underestimate what even the UK weather can produce. ❧

DR MIKE STROUD set a polar record with Sir Ranulph Fiennes by completing the longest unsupported journey in the Antarctic. He specialises in the effect of physical extremes on the body.

Surviving the cold: 2 Some guidelines
by Dr Richard Dawood

COLONEL JIM ADAM, THE MILITARY PHYSIOLOGIST who was, until recently, responsible for maintaining 'combat-effectiveness' of British troops under all conditions, advises observing the following steps in the event of hypothermia:

1. Stop all activity.
2. Protect those at risk by rigging a makeshift shelter from the wind, rain and snow; lay the victim on the ground, on a ground sheet or space blanket.
3. Remove wet clothing, and insulate the victim in a sleeping bag.
4. Rewarm the victim with hot drinks, then hot food or high-energy snacks; unconscious victims should be rewarmed by a companion's body warmth.
5. Observe the victim for the cessation of breathing or pulse, and start mouth-to-mouth resuscitation or cardiac massage if necessary.
6. Send for help.
7. Insist on treating the victim as a stretcher case.

Acute hypothermia

This is a medical emergency, and is almost always the result of falling into water

Some guidelines

- Don't drink. Alcohol causes peripheral vasodilation – it increases blood flow through the skin – which can dramatically increase heat loss in extreme temperatures.

- Don't smoke. Nicotine can cause vasoconstriction – reduction in blood flow to hands, fingers and toes – increasing the likelihood of frostbite.

- Carry high-energy carbohydrate snacks, such as glucose sweets or Mars bars.

- Carry extra layers of clothing.

- Carry chemical hand-warming sachets to put inside gloves and shoes.

- If you are on an expedition, or are looking after a large group, carry a special low-reading thermometer to measure body temperature: normal clinical thermometers are not adequate for detecting hypothermia. You may also be well advised to carry instruments for measuring high wind speed and estimating wind chill.

- Anything that reduces activity, such as being stranded on a chair lift or being injured, can result in a rapid fall in body temperature; if this happens to you, try to maintain some muscular activity to generate warmth.

- Children are at special risk. In particular, they need extra head protection (mechanical as well as against heat loss). Frost nip and frostbite can affect later growth.

- In cold conditions it is easy to underestimate the need to protect skin and eyes against excessive sunlight. Take extra care.

colder than 5°C. The victim shivers violently, inhales water, panics, may have respiratory or cardiac arrest, and is dead from drowning in about five to 15 minutes. Survival is more likely if the victim is wearing a life-jacket that keeps the face out of the water and is able to keep perfectly still. Careful first aid is essential. Following rescue from the water, do not allow the victim to move or make any physical effort. Keep the victim horizontal or slightly head-down, protect against further heat loss and arrange transportation immediately to a hospital so that rapid rewarming may begin. The most effective way of rewarming is a bath – at 42°C or as hot as the bare elbow can tolerate. Until normal body temperature is restored, the victim is at high risk from sudden death, partly because rewarming may actually trigger an initial further drop in body temperature; many victims of accidents at sea die after they have been removed from the water – sometimes even in hospital.

Frostbite

Localised injuries from the cold can affect limbs with exposed skin even when core body temperature is entirely normal. This happens when insulation is not adequate or on account of other factors, such as a restricted blood supply due to clothing that is too tight. Injuries of this kind range from frostbite following freezing of the tissues of the nose, checks, chin, ears, fingers and feet, to more common problems such as frost nips and chapping of the skin, especially of the lips, nose and hands, and often compounded by sunburn.

The best way to deal with frostbite is to take careful steps to prevent it. Ensure, particularly, that gloves, socks and footwear are suitable for the conditions and the task in hand, and do not choose extreme conditions to wear any of these items for the first time. Carry a face mask to protect yourself from high wind and driving snow and carry chemical hand-warmers that can be used when needed.

Impending frostbite is usually signalled by intense pain in the part at risk, this should not be ignored and prompt rewarming is necessary. For example, hands and fingers should be slipped under the clothes and warmed in the opposite armpit. If the pain is ignored it eventually disappears, the part then becomes numb, white and hard to touch – it is frozen.

Established frostbite is a serious problem that may need lengthy hospital treatment. Once thawing has taken place, tissue is liable to much more extensive damage from even slight chilling. During evacuation, keep the affected part clean and dry and give painkillers and antibiotics (if available) to prevent infection. Never rub frostbite with snow or anything else, because the tissues are extremely fragile and will suffer more damage. ❧

Red tape and organisation

Organising your finances, before and during a trip
by Charlotte Hindle

ACCORDING TO LIZA MINNELLI in the musical *Cabaret*, money makes the world go round. But, more important to travellers, is how to get your money around the world. The problem is – there is no single or easy answer to this conundrum.

Your best bet remains to take a mixture of debit and credit cards, traveller's cheques and old-fashioned notes and coins. There are pros and cons to all four, although the combination should ensure you are rarely caught short, wherever you are in the world.

Debit and credit cards

The easiest way to get hold of your money abroad is to use your plastic in an Automatic Teller Machine (ATM). To check the density of these in the countries that you are visiting, log onto www.mastercard.com/atmlocator/index.jsp for MasterCard or http://visa.via.infonow.net/locator/global for Visa.

It is wise to travel with more than one brand of card as ATMs can be unpredictable; a perfectly servicable card with the right logo on it might be declined where another one is immediately accepted.

Other things to consider when travelling with an armoury of plastic include:

● Communication. Tell your credit card company that you are going abroad because your user pattern will change. If the company thinks that your card has been stolen, it will be blocked.

● Demagnetisation. If the magnetic strip on the back of a card is damaged, it might not work. The only way you can be sure that none of your strips is scratched is to replace all cards you intend to travel with prior to departure. (This chore will become obsolete when new 'contactless' cards are introduced.)

● Expiration. Don't let your cards run out on you when you are abroad. Check their use-by dates before you travel, particularly if you are planning a big trip.

If you are withdrawing cash from ATMs abroad, you will get a reasonable rate of exchange. However, this is often offset by expensive transaction charges, which can mount up during a long trip. One answer to this is to obtain a Nationwide FlexAccount Visa debit card since Nationwide will not charge you for taking your money out abroad. In addition, you get to keep your hard-earned savings in a relatively high interest-bearing account. However, there is a major disadvantage with this card: it cannot be replaced abroad if it is lost or stolen.

If you are travelling for more than a month, you will need to organise how to pay your credit card bills. There are a number of options, but the simplest one is to set up a direct debit for the full or minimum amount each month.

Traveller's cheques

Some travellers don't have a good word to say about traveller's cheques: you often pay commission when you buy them; you are sometimes charged to convert them; and they sometimes attract a lousy rate of exchange. Nevertheless, it is a good idea to carry a few when you travel.

The main advantage of traveller's cheques is that they are fully refundable when lost or stolen – as long as you have recorded their serial numbers and they haven't been cashed before you report the loss. Another reason to carry them is that you can often change them out of office hours at big hotels (although you will pay heavily for the privilege).

Shop around when you are buying and exchanging. For instance, you can purchase American Express traveller's cheques for free from UK post offices, as long as you don't want them in sterling. This should not present a problem as the best currency for your travellers cheque's is still US dollars. You won't always want to change significant amounts of money, so ensure that they comprise of both high and low denominations. American Express traveller's cheques can be exchanged commission-free at most American Express offices worldwide.

Cash

For obvious reasons, don't travel with a huge wadge of cash. Still, the odd US$100 or £100 in small denominations can be useful in many parts of the world. In addition, if you are travelling to one country only, small change in the correct currency can be handy for the airport bus or taxi. It will buy you time to make yourself familiar with the fairest rate of exchange.

Safe not sorry

There are a few basic rules to managing your money back home while accessing it abroad:

- Keep a record of all your debit and credit card numbers, the serial numbers of your traveller's cheques and of the emergency phone numbers of all financial organisations. The safest way of doing this is to keep all this information in an online travel vault, such as those provided by Ekit (www.ekit.com).
- Some countries still insist that you are able to account for your spending; those with thriving black markets for currency are particularly sensitive. Don't forget to keep receipts for currency exchange, accommodation and other transactions.
- Many travellers use internet banking on the road. But you must take extra precautions when accessing your accounts online at internet cafes, to ensure no one else accesses them as well.
- It is not uncommon for travellers to get mugged on the day that they have exchanged or withdrawn money by villains who track them from the bank. Be particularly vigilant and discreet when you change money. ❧

Passports, visas and official permits
by David Orkin

WHILE YOU CAN ARRANGE AND BUY TICKETS for a round-the-world itinerary in a matter of minutes, obtaining the necessary documentation for your travels tends to be a far less smooth and speedy process.

With very few exceptions, a citizen of a nation must hold a valid passport to visit another country – and to be allowed back to into their home country. Unless you pay a premium for an 'express' service, getting a British passport will take at least a couple of weeks.

All countries, including the UK, regulate those wishing to visit or pass through their territory and such regulations are constantly under review.

If you already hold a passport, note that many countries will only let you in if your passport is valid for at least six months after your departure date from that country.

Many countries insist on a visitor obtaining a visa before their entry is allowed. In some cases these are issued on arrival, but in many cases they must be arranged in advance.

While regulations vary widely from country to country, different rules may also apply depending on the visitor's nationality and on such factors as the purpose of the visit. For instance, a business visitor may require a visa whereas a tourist one may not.

If you book through a travel agent, they should be able to advise you about visa requirements for the countries included on your itinerary.

An Israeli exit or entry stamp in your passport can cause problems should you wish to visit certain countries. Despite the expense, if such a country is on your list, it may well make sense to get a new passport.

Before applying for a visa, ensure that your passport is signed and that there are at least two empty pages: a blank page for each visa required, plus sufficient space for entry and exit stamps.

Passports no longer state occupations. Where 'profession' is asked for on visa forms, should you be a journalist, photographer, or member of the armed forces, consider giving yourself a fictional new job – unless, of course, you are travelling in your official capacity and you do not anticipate that this will cause problems. Note that those travelling on business may require a letter from a sponsor before a visa will be issued.

Although some countries issue visas that are valid for 12 months and allow multiple entries with no restrictions, most visas are only valid from the date of issue and expire after a set time. This is usually three months. So, if you are travelling for a number of months, visiting different countries, you may have to obtain some visas en route. This will avoid the problem of the visa expiring before you reach the relevant destination.

You will also need to budget in visa costs. Some visas are free and the majority cost under £25. However, others cost considerably more. Going through a visa company will save trips to embassies and a lot of queuing time. But it will add to your financial outgoings. The exception is where countries don't have representation in the UK. In these cases, such services may be cheaper than a trip to, say, Brussels or Paris to arrange the visa yourself.

Do your research regarding visas early in your travel planning process, because – according to where you are going, your reasons for visiting a country and your nationality – the issuing time can vary from a matter of hours to weeks.

Even if you have your visas on arrival, immigration officials have the power to deny you entry. In this respect it is always sensible to have an onward or return ticket with you, along with proof of sufficient funds to support yourself.

Once you have satisfied immigration requirements and have been granted entry, there may be special procedures to follow, such as registering with the local police within a certain number of days.

Some countries, particularly those with flourishing black markets, require visitors to complete a currency declaration on entry. This details all monies, jewellery, cameras, tape recorders and so on, and is checked on departure against bank receipts for any money changed.

Other documents that may occasionally be required are up-to-date vaccination certificates. And, if you carry a camera, some countries require that you obtain a photography permit. This is often only available in the capital and can therefore be awkward for overland travellers.

Sometimes efforts are made to prevent travellers from visiting certain 'sensitive' areas, either for the traveller's own safety (for example, remote desert areas or regions of political instability) or because of the presence of military bases. Some areas may be strictly 'no-go', for others you may need to obtain a permit in advance.

Losing or having your passport stolen on your travels can be a nightmare, especially if you are a long way from one of your country's embassies. So, before you leave home, it is advisable to make photocopies of your birth certificate and the information pages of your passport. Keep these separately from your passport.

Be prepared for delays, harassment and palms held out hopefully. However unreasonable and frustrating any officials you come across may be, be firm but keep your cool. Hassles that you can recount to fellow voyagers and large doses of the unexpected are parts of the magic of travel. ✒

DAVID ORKIN is a travel writer. Before that he spent eight years working for Trailfinders and another eight working for Quest Worldwide Travel. During that time and since he has traveled extensively.

Passport offices and visa agencies

Passport offices in UK

UK PASSPORTS
www.ukpa.gov.uk/
The government's online passport agency

PASSPORT ADVICE LINE
0870 521 0410
Available 24 hours a day, 7 days a week
Application form request line 0901 4700 110

Visa agencies in UK

CORPORATE VISA SERVICES
LG-5 James House
22-24 Corsham Street
London N1 6DR
0207 336 0101
www.visa4travel.com/ContactUs.html

THAMES CONSULAR SERVICES
Unit 4, The Courtyard
Swan Centre
Fishers Lane
London W4 1RX
Tel: +44 (0) 20 8995 2492
www.thamesconsular.com

THE VISA SERVICE
Ground Floor
4-8 Rodney Street
London N1 9JH
Phone: 08708 900 185
www.visaservice.co.uk

ROSS CONSULAR SERVICES
Beech Court
29 Summers Road
Burnham
Bucks SL1 7EP
Tel: 01628 666001
www.rcsluk.co.uk

VISA WORLD
Online visa agency
www.visaworld.co.uk

DJB PASSPORTS AND VISAS
24 Kingsland Road
London E2 8DD
Tel: 020 76846242
http://djbvisas.com/

TRAVCOUR (UK) LTD
Tempo House
15 Falcon Road
Battersea
London SW11 2PJ
Tel: 020 7223 5295
www.travcour.com

Visa agencies in USA

VISAS INTERNATIONAL
6525 W Sunset Blvd Ste G7
Los Angeles, CA 90028-7212
(323) 462-3636

INTERCONTINENTAL VISA SERVICE
Los Angeles World Trade Center
350 South Figueroa Street
Suite 185
Los Angeles CA 90071
Phone: (213) 625-7175
www.ivisaservice.com

AMERICAN PASSPORT EXPRESS
National Call Center located at 10 Vaughan Place
Portsmouth NH 03801
1-800-841-6778
or 1-800-455-5166
www.americanpassport.com

Passing through customs
by officers of the British Revenue & Customs department

CONTRARY TO POPULAR BELIEF, CUSTOMS OFFICERS do accept that most travellers are ordinary citizens going about their legitimate business and are not smugglers. So why is it that most travellers claim to feel nervous whenever they approach Customs, and actually feel guilty when negotiating a Green Channel?

It may be uncertainty about the extent of allowances and precisely what is and is not permissible. It may also be apprehension about the possibility of being singled out for checking – having bags emptied and even being personally searched. The modern Customs service recognises these pressures and considerable effort is made to make checks highly selective and well targeted at areas of highest risk so that the vast majority of travellers are not inconvenienced.

Today, Customs face a dramatically changing scenario, as trade barriers are dismantled, fiscal and physical frontiers are removed, journey times are reduced and ever-increasing traffic flows demand fast and efficient customs clearance.

A balance must be struck between the often conflicting demands of the free movement of travellers while at the same time protecting society. But from what? Serious threats are posed by the considerable number of prohibited and restricted items that may be either unwittingly carried by the uninformed traveller, or smuggled by and on behalf of the unscrupulous. Customs, consulates and ministries can give advice, often in the form of leaflets, about what can and cannot be imported. Examples which may be encountered by travellers include the following:

PLANT AND ANIMAL HEALTH RISKS: Commercial importations are carefully controlled to prevent the spread of pests and disease, but thoughtless importation could quickly introduce an epidemic. Rabies is the most publicised threat but there are many more, including bugs and grubs which could devastate crops in a new environment. A health certificate, licence and/or quarantine is necessary for many plants and animals, and all live birds.

ENDANGERED SPECIES: Few people bring home a wild animal from their travels. But many buy articles made from them (a skin handbag and shoes, an ivory ornament) without knowing that the species is in danger of extinction. Even trade in tourist souvenirs can threaten the most endangered species. In many countries it is illegal to cut or pick wild plants and flowers for the same reasons. They may be freely available and on sale in the country you are visiting but if you do not get a permit before you import them they are likely to be seized.

OBSCENE AND INDECENT MATERIAL: Changing social and cultural attitudes make this a sensitive area so check first and you will not be embarrassed.

FIREARMS, WEAPONS, EXPLOSIVES, GAS CANISTERS: Travellers face stringent security checks before the start of their journey in an effort to separate them from even the most legitimate of these such as the sporting gun or the fisherman's knife. But on arrival at the destination their importation is likely to require a licence, and may be prohibited. Check first, or be sure to tell Customs on arrival.

DRUGS: Personally-prescribed drugs and medicaments are best carried in labelled containers and, if for regular use, carry a letter from your doctor. Illicit drugs are a major and increasing concern for all Customs services and are often the principal reason for checks on travellers. Whilst the possession of very small quantities may be permissible in a few countries, their carriage across frontiers is invariably prohibited. Penalties are severe, and often carry a risk of imprisonment.

Countries with long land frontiers may choose to exercise some controls inland but travellers through ports and airports provide a concentrated flow which enables an efficient screening and checking by Customs. Particularly in the prevention of drug trafficking, the search at the frontier enables Customs to identify and seize large commercial shipments, before they are distributed inland for sale in small, usable quantities. In addition, Customs and police will often cooperate to monitor the delivery of a consignment to its inland destination in order to identify principals in smuggling organisations.

Many people think that drugs are found from tip-offs, and that routine checks are not necessary. That is not so. Valuable intelligence does come from co-operation between Customs and police services around the world. But detections made in the day-to-day work of ports and airports depend on the Customs Officer's initiative and experience in assessing risks and choosing the right passenger. The overall Customs effort against drug trafficking is a mix of intelligence, information, judgement and intuition. Officers are carefully trained to observe, select, question and examine. 'Profiles' are built up from instances where patterns have emerged, but they are but one tool in a large bag, and need to be constantly updated and refined as methods and types of courier change. Checks may need to be done to test out Customs' perception of risk, and that is where the innocent traveller may come under examination. Co-operation will help allay suspicion of the innocent, and full searches – including a body search – are only undertaken under strict supervision and where there are strong grounds for suspecting an offence.

Checking travellers

An officer who stops a passenger needs information before making a decision (whether or not a full examination is needed) and so questions must be asked. The officer is looking for tell-tale signs that something is not right. The smuggler cannot be completely honest about themselves and must tell lies to stand any chance of success. It is that deceit that a Customs officer is trying to see through. Travel documents, identification documents, questions about the purpose of the journey – all give a picture which the officer can test for credibility against what he sees and hears and, ultimately, feels. He may not get it right every time, but intelligent, intuitive assessments do result in the discovery of people attempting to smuggle.

The traveller who objects to the way he or she is dealt with at Customs should complain to a Senior Customs official at the time of the incident. In that way most complaints can be dealt with to everyone's satisfaction, and while events are fresh in everyone's mind. By all means follow up with a letter if you feel you have not got satisfaction. But a written complaint made for the first time several days after an incident is more difficult to investigate.

In addition to their role in protecting society, the Customs service has a duty to collect import taxes (which can still be substantial on luxury goods, despite moves to harmonise more tax rates and remove barriers to trade). The expensive watch, silk carpet, video camera or item of jewellery can still result in a hefty tax bill on arrival home. Goods in excess of allowances must be declared to Customs, or you risk having them confiscated, and criminal proceedings taken for smuggling. Many offences of this nature are settled between Customs and the traveller by the payment of a fine and few cases go to court. However, if you also have to buy your confiscated goods back, the overall penalty can amount to a large sum. In addition, the amount of time and effort spent by Customs dealing with such irregularities increases the opportunity for the drugs courier to get through undetected.

The business traveller can usually be relied on to know what personal allowances can be carried into each country, but a misunderstanding can occur when business goods are carried. Lap-top computers, replacement parts for equipment, parts for repair and sample prototypes can all find their way into a business traveller's baggage. Sometimes he will act only as a 'courier' for another part of his company. Such items are invariably liable to some form of control as frontiers are crossed and a declaration to Customs on each occasion is the safest way – unless you have personally checked with a reliable authority and you are confident you know what you are doing.

As a general rule, do not carry packages for anyone if you are unsure what they contain. Whether it is personal or business, your freedom or even your life could be at stake if something goes wrong.

In 1993 the Single European Act heralded the free movement of goods and people within the European Community (EC). For visitors, controls on goods and the collection of taxes generally take place at the first point of entry into the Community, and subsequent travel involves only checks for prohibited and restricted goods. Travellers within the EU do not have to pay tax or duty in the UK on foreign goods if tax was paid in the EU country where they were bought. 'Own use' includes goods for your own consumption and gifts, but remember that you may be breaking the law if you sell goods that you have bought; and that if you are caught selling the goods they will be taken off you and you could get up to seven years imprisonment. Any vehicle you use to transport the goods could also be confiscated.

The EU sets out guidelines for the amount of alcohol and tobacco a person can bring into the UK from an EU country. These are intended as indicative levels for 'own use' consumption. If you bring in more than this, you must be able to satisfy customs officers if you are asked that the goods are for your own use. If you can't the goods may be taken off you. For your information the indicative levels are:

SMOKING

- Cigarettes: 3,200
- Cigarillos: 400
- Cigars: 200
- Smoking tobacco: 3 kilogram

ALCOHOL

- Spirits: 10 litres
- Beer: 110 litres
- Fortified wine (such as port or sherry): 20 litres
- Wine: 90 litres (of which no more than 60 litres sparkling).

Since the advent of the single market, Customs' controls on EC passengers at airports and ferry ports have been improved to provide a faster and more efficient service which targets the high-risk traveller, but permits the majority to move unimpeded through customs.

Make sure you are properly informed when you travel. A confident traveller will project his or her innocence and help Customs to concentrate on their own priorities, for all our good. &

Travel insurance
by Ian Irvine

THE WORLD IS MY OYSTER could not these days be a more appropriate way of describing the incredible number of holiday destinations for the adventurous traveller. Never before have so many countries opened their frontiers to tourists, who can now travel to virtually every corner of our planet. Exciting times, and if all goes well an experience not to be missed; but what happens if, whilst travelling, problems arise?

The excitement of travel often lulls individuals into a false sense of security without, adequate thought being given to pitfalls that sometimes arise. Foreign Office warnings, acts of terrorism, sudden illness or accident, and the collapse of airlines or travel companies are all palpable risks, but ones that, unfortunately, many travellers disregard until it is too late. What action can you take to minimise the likelihood of your travels being spoilt by an unexpected incident?

First, consider where you want to go. The Foreign Office has set up a website (www.fco.gov.uk) to assist travellers and, using its slogan 'Know Before You Go', invites you to check the stability of the country to which you wish to travel. If a country has a history of instability, and even though it may be possible to travel there, would you still want to do so? The choice is yours, but if you travel and instability develops, do not blame your travel company if your holiday was not as you would have liked.

A must for holidays is travel insurance, and no sensible individual should travel without it. The unexpected is always around the corner, and you never know whether you may be the unfortunate individual to whom something very serious happens. Ask the 52-year-old man who went to America with his wife and two children, within three days suffered a brain haemorrhage, spent three months in hospital (most of it in intensive care), and ended up with a bill totalling £420,000. Was he glad he had travel insurance? Most certainly, but he is typical of the majority of travellers who always think 'it will never happen to me'.

Compared to the cost of a holiday, travel insurance is inexpensive, but you must make sure the policy is suitable for your particular purposes. The duration of travel and geographical location determine the level of premium, but look out for pitfalls. Older travellers are more prone to accident and sickness, both before and after departure, and extra premiums are invariably charged. These can start at as low as 60 years of age. The activities in which you intend to participate need to be insured, and you must make certain your travel policy covers them. Adventurous activities are increasingly popular for all ages, but many are excluded from the standard travel policy. For example, sub-aqua diving is increasingly popular yet many policies either exclude it or impose depth limits. Check before you dive!

If you are not a UK resident, you would want to be repatriated to your country of residence in the event of serious accident or illness. Does your policy simply repatriate you to the UK, or further afield? Does it cover acts of terrorism? That's not something about which we had to be concerned a few years ago, but now it is on everyone's mind.

There is no substitute for a comprehensive travel insurance policy, but you do need to make sure the product you are purchasing will meet your needs. It should at least cover the following principal risks.

Medical expenses

These are without doubt the most essential part of travel insurance. Worldwide advances in medical treatment and the greater availability of medical attention constantly increase costs, necessitating an absolute minimum cover of £2 million. Repatriation costs are an essential part of medical insurance, and there should be no limit in the policy. Such costs can be high for repatriation from remote areas, and if air ambulances are subsequently used to bring seriously ill travellers back to their country of residence, the costs can run into many thousands of pounds.

Travel policies must provide a 24-hour emergency service so that immediate assistance can be requested. This service will coordinate essential air evacuation anywhere in the world, but this does not normally include 'search and rescue' expenses if someone is missing. Additional insurance for this can be arranged at an extra premium, dependent on location, duration and type of travel.

Whilst many travellers have private medical insurance, which sometimes applies on a worldwide basis, it does not normally include repatriation cover and the benefits are often more restrictive than that of a travel policy. Private medical insurance is not, therefore, a substitute for travel insurance.

Pre-existing medical conditions

Most travel policies exclude cover if an insured person is suffering from a pre-existing medical condition or, if anyone upon whom travel depends, such as a close relative, is suffering from a pre-existing medical condition. The interpretation of pre-existing medical conditions varies between insurance companies, but they all provide a medical helpline.

It is most important that if you have any doubts about a pre-existing medical condition you should speak to your travel insurer's helpline to ascertain whether or not it can be insured. There is no point in taking a chance, finding that the condition becomes prevalent whilst you are travelling and then, to your dismay, discovering that your insurers will not deal with a claim. In the event of an emergency this could have dire consequences.

Personal accident

This insurance pays a lump sum benefit if a traveller is unfortunate enough to have an accident that results in death, permanent disability or the loss of an eye or limb. Some travellers may already have life assurance that applies on a worldwide basis and which, in the event of death, would also pay a lump sum. For this reason the death benefit under travel insurance is often less than other benefits. Additional insurance can easily be arranged if a traveller feels increased benefits are required.

Cancellation or curtailment

When travel has to be unavoidably cancelled or curtailed the traveller will lose any money not refunded by the travel company. This can be recovered under a travel insurance policy, but it is important to make sure that the sum insured is sufficient to cover the total cost of travel. This may include car hire, accommodation, excursions and tours, as well as air fares and other transportation. If the sum insured under the travel insurance is not adequate, it is normally possible to arrange for this to be increased.

Personal liability

If a traveller injures another party or damages their property they could be liable to pay compensation. Personal liability cover protects you against claims being made by other parties, and should provide protection of at least £1 million. Remember, however, that this insurance does not cover claims arising from the use of cars or motorcycles, which must be insured independently.

Personal effects, money and tickets

Travellers normally take no more clothing and personal effects than is necessary, and with the increased use of credit cards and traveller's cheques, cash is usually kept to a minimum. Travel insurance limits are not normally very high, and it is essential to make sure that the value of your property and money is adequately insured. Many travellers have household policies which also cover personal effects and money on a worldwide basis, particularly for those more affluent individuals who often take more belongings with them when travelling.

All travel policies limit cover for valuables (defined as jewellery, gold and silver articles, watches, photographic equipment, binoculars, telescopes and hand-held electronic equipment) and normally impose conditions regarding their security. The normal limit for any one valuable article is £250, and for all such articles, £350. If valuables are worth more than this they cannot normally be covered under a travel policy and should be insured under a household policy on an all-risks-worldwide basis.

Security limitations for valuables mean they either have to be kept in hotel safes or locked hotel bedrooms, or carried on the traveller's person. Valuables are not insured if left in checked-in luggage.

Insurance for tickets these days normally includes any type of ticket, not just airline tickets, but it is important to remember that if an airline ticket is lost you must contact your travel insurers immediately rather than simply purchase a replacement. Travel insurers are normally able to come to an arrangement with the airline regarding lost tickets.

Travel by vehicle outside Europe

Many UK motor insurance policies these days automatically grant cover for travel in Europe or can be extended to do so by the issue of a Green Card. Outside Europe, particularly in Third World countries, vehicle insurance is difficult to arrange and there is no such thing as a comprehensive policy.

Vehicle insurance can be arranged in two ways: the first granting third-party cover to protect against claims by other parties, and the second to insure the vehicle for accidental damage, fire and theft. Third-party cover can normally only be purchased at the borders of countries being entered, although some countries are indifferent. It is not possible to arrange this third-party insurance from the UK. The traveller's own vehicle can be insured for accidental damage, fire and theft risks on a worldwide basis, but specialist advice needs to be taken from an insurance broker.

A word of warning: vehicle insurance in North America differs from state to state, but generally speaking has very low third-party limits. Compared with UK limits they are inadequate, and it is essential to purchase top-up liability insurance when hiring a vehicle in North America.

Carnet indemnity insurance

Travel by vehicle outside Europe necessitates the payment of import duty on the vehicle every time you enter a country. This is impractical and the problem is resolved by obtaining a Carnet de Passage before leaving the UK. This is a multi-page document that is stamped when entering a country and stamped again when leaving the country to show that the vehicle has both been imported and exported and as such, no duty is payable.

Carnet indemnity insurance is arranged with the Royal Automobile Club, which spares travellers from having to provide a bank guarantee or tying up funds. The RAC will require a financial guarantee equivalent to the highest duty of the various countries through which travel is to take place. This can be as high as four times the value of the vehicle in the UK. Applications for Carnet indemnity insurance should be made directly to the RAC.

How to make a claim when travelling

Whatever type of insurance you have and whatever necessitates making a claim, it is important that you obtain as much information as possible for your insurers. For serious claims, contact must immediately be made with the appropriate emergency service, details of which will be provided in your insurance documentation.

Of greatest concern are medical claims necessitating immediate medical assistance and possibly repatriation, and all travel policies have a 24-hour emergency service available for this purpose.

For more routine claims, whilst these can be dealt with whilst the traveller is abroad it is often very much easier to deal with them once you return to your country of residence. All insurance companies operate a routine claims service and will send a claim form on request.

It is worth remembering that if you wish to claim for any expenditure you incur, the insurers will require invoices or confirmation of payment, and if property is lost or stolen an independent report is required. Whilst ideally this should be from the police, it is normally acceptable if provided by airport or security personnel or even holiday representatives or tour leaders.

Finally, do remember that most insurance policies are subject to an excess for any claim, which is always clearly shown on policy documents, and travellers are well advised to check these before travelling. ໃ

IAN IRVINE is Chairman of Campbell Irvine Ltd, specialist insurance brokers to the travel industry. He has over 35 years experience arranging travel insurance schemes for travel companies, particularly those involved in long-distance travel or sporting and adventurous activities.

Protecting your trip
by David Richardson and Edwina Townsend

The travel industry has an enviable record in protecting customers' money, but when the system breaks down there are inevitably heartbreak stories in the media and the image of the travel industry suffers. This was common 20 years ago, before financial safeguards were put in place, but it can still happen today. The vast majority of travellers either continue their arrangements or get their money back if their travel organiser goes bust, but this is of little comfort if you are one of the unlucky ones.

Package holidays

The package holiday customer enjoys the highest level of financial protection, and it is well worth choosing a package rather than making your own arrangements if you are in the least worried about losing your money. And don't forget, a package holiday doesn't have to mean a chartered flight followed by a week on the beach in Benidorm. Tour operators are increasingly targeting the independent traveller, and many people who go trekking in the Himalayas or scuba diving on the Great Barrier Reef are also on a package.

When Air Europe collapsed in 1991, travellers who had simply booked their own scheduled flight almost certainly lost their money. But those booked on the same flight as part of a package holiday were fully protected through arrangements made by tour operators, who have been regulated and licensed since the early 1970s. New regulations implemented in 1993 as a result of European Community (now European Union) legislation have widened the gap still further between the cosseted package customer and the independent traveller.

The situation with package holidays by air is straightforward, and the same is true for charter flight passengers buying a seat-only deal rather than a package. All tour operators must have an Air Travel Organiser's Licence (ATOL) issued by the Civil Aviation Authority (CAA), and to get one they must satisfy the CAA that they are financially secure, providing a bond that will be used to reimburse or repatriate customers if they collapse. If the bond proves insufficient, the CAA draws on the Air Travel Trust Fund, financed by a levy on package holidays since the 1970s.

The ATOL system is virtually fail-safe as regards package holidays by air departing from the UK, and now has been extended to cover packages using scheduled as well as charter flights. This includes most discounted scheduled air seats sold as 'seat-onlys' or as part of tailor-made itineraries for independent travellers. Some companies advertise themselves as 'agents for ATOL holders', and it is worth checking this out with the CAA. In such cases, the ATOL holder must take responsibility for travellers if the agent fails.

The situation regarding package holidays by surface transport is much more complex. Until recently, tour operators using coach or rail transport, cruises or ferries were not obliged to offer financial protection. Many opted to do so through various trade associations, but this was purely voluntary. But in January 1993, the British Government adopted the EC directive on package travel, which introduced a wide range of consumer protection measures including the requirement for all package organisers to protect money. This was no great innovation in the UK, because of the ATOL system and the large number of tour operators providing bonds through trade associations. In some other EU countries, however, public protection lagged far behind the UK. But what might have seemed a good idea to the Eurocrats and MEPs gathered together in Brussels can in practice cause UK travellers a lot of confusion and give them a false sense of security.

The regulations affect all package travel arrangements sold in the UK, not just for travel to EU countries (including within the UK) but worldwide. It is generally believed that the EU's concern was to protect the traditional package holiday customer, but in fact the legislation goes much further. Many areas are poorly defined and the British Government has not made things any clearer.

First of all, what is a package? According to the regulations, it is a combination of any two of three elements – transport; accommodation; and/or other tourist services making up a significant element of a package. The latter is open to interpretation, but could include theatre tickets, riding lessons, or golf, for example. Even a country hotel in England that includes a fishing licence in its weekend rates could be deemed to be selling a package, with the consequent requirement to protect any money paid in advance.

This goes a long way beyond the idea of a traditional holiday package. When the regulations were debated in Parliament, the British Government admitted to having no idea how many package organisers there might be in the UK. Its 'educated guess' was between 10, 000 and 20, 000, when the total number of tour operators belonging to trade associations is less than 1, 000. Many of the organisers are coach operators, who are considered to be package travel organisers even if all they do is a one-night trip to Blackpool. Others include social clubs, societies and even individuals, such as the local vicar leading an annual pilgrimage to the Holy Land. 'Occasional' organisers of package travel are exempt from the regulations, but the meaning of 'occasional' remains to be defined if and when a case comes to court.

This situation has been unresolved for some years. However, ABTA (The Association of British Travel Agents) and the CAA, in conjunction with the British Government, are actively discussing how to better protect British travellers by renegotiating the current legislation or by introducing new measures.

If you ask a travel agent to put together a flight and hotel, it could well be that they will have to provide protection as a package organiser, even if the arrangements are not sold at an inclusive price. But business travel packages may not be affected, as most business travellers are on credit and do not pay until their return.

Not surprisingly, the regulations are causing grief not only in the travel industry but also among many other organisations and individuals who had no idea that they could be considered package travel organisers. But what is causing even more heartache among established tour operators is that there is no effective way of policing the regulations. A gaping consumer protection loophole is still there.

Organisers of packages using air travel must have an ATOL – that much is straightforward. But there is not a parallel licensing authority for surface travel operators. These are required to provide evidence to travellers that their money is protected in one of three ways: they can provide a bond, possibly to a trade association which has reserve funds in place; they can insure against the risk of financial failure; or they can place customers' money in a trust account and not touch it until travel has been completed.

Travellers taking a package by surface transport should look for some evidence that their money is protected – but the only policing authority is local trading standards officers, who by their own admission lack the resources and expertise to do the job properly. It is now a criminal offence to operate packages without protecting customers' money, but although the maximum fine is £5, 000 the first case to come to court resulted in a fine of only £250. The unlucky traveller caught up in a collapse could try to sue the directors – but if the company has gone bust, the kitty will probably be empty.

Trade associations

The weakness of the new legislation means that trade associations continue to play a strong part in protecting travellers' money – especially ABTA, the only one with a strong public profile. Surveys show that members of the public identify strongly with ABTA because their money is safe, and this is true despite its changing role.

Your money is still 100 per cent safe if you book with an ABTA tour operator, as ABTA has never reneged on its promise to repay customers who have booked a package holiday with a failed member. This is because ABTA requires all its 600 tour operators to be bonded, either with the CAA through an ATOL, or through ABTA itself in the case of surface travel operators. In both cases, back-up funds are in place if bonds prove insufficient.

ABTA will not accept insurance against possible failure, or trust funds, as a substitute for bonding – as allowed by the Government for non-ABTA members. It points out that insurance against failure is of no help to travellers stranded abroad after a collapse, while trust accounts are open to abuse.

ABTA is going through major changes, but its consumer promise remains intact. Before the new regulations it acted as a quasi-licensing authority, and tour operators had to join up if they wanted to sell through ABTA's 7, 000 travel agents. But it is no longer a closed shop, and tour operators and agents can leave ABTA if they wish. When dealing with a non-ABTA company, the onus is on the traveller to ensure his or her money is safe –if in doubt, contact your local authority trading standards officers for advice.

ABTA will also protect your money if a member travel agent goes bust, whatever kind of travel arrangement you have bought. If you already have your tickets then normally you will be able to continue; if not, ABTA will reimburse you. This applies to independent travel as well as to packages, but only when the agent (rather than the travel provider) is the one who goes bust.

Other trade associations also bond their members to protect public money, although it is CAA member organisations such as AITO (the Association of Independent Tour Operators) who license all air packages. Other members include the Bus and Coach Council's Bonded Coach Holidays scheme, the Passenger Shipping Association (Cruises) and the Federation of Tour Operators, formerly known as Tour Operators Study Group. But remember, protection applies only to packages, not to simple ferry crossings or express coach tickets, for example.

The independent traveller

If you book independently rather than buying a package (depending on the definition of a package, which may one day become clear), your money is theoretically much more at risk. But in reality there are few occasions when a failure will leave you out of pocket. The main area of risk is scheduled airlines, bringing us back to the Air Europe collapse of 1991. Despite the outcry that followed, neither the British government nor the eu in Brussels has yet made any moves to protect scheduled airline passengers' money, much to the outrage of tour operators and travel agents, who were bonded to the hilt. Another British airline, Dan Air, came within a whisker of going bust in 1992 before British Airways picked up the pieces.

The risks are definitely increasing as airlines all over the world go private, free of government control but also of government support. Several us airlines are technically bankrupt, but continue to operate under us bankruptcy laws. New private airlines are starting all the time, while new state airlines in the former Soviet Union look particularly unstable. The British government has failed to act on a CAA proposal for a levy, partly because it would involve only British airlines' passengers, and British Airways objected. As little as £1 added to ticket costs for even a short period would soon build up a substantial protection fund, but there seems no likelihood of this happening in the short term.

But the risk of a scheduled airline collapsing is small enough for most travellers to accept, and the same is true for ferries and scheduled coach companies, who will often help out passengers if a rival collapses. Car rental companies pose a slightly greater risk, while the position of a private railway company that collapses holding customers' money is unknown – a point to consider in the wake of the privatisation of British Rail. And although hotels go into liquidation all the time, they nearly always stay open in order to keep some money coming in.

The sale of discounted scheduled air tickets was a grey area for a long time, but the CAA has now cracked down, requiring agents offering them to be covered by ATOLs unless they hand over tickets on the spot, immediately on receipt of payment. More recently, it has acted to make agents accept responsibility when an airline goes bust, which has led to many agents offering passengers AFFP (Airline Financial Failure Protection) insurance to cover scheduled airline tickets should the airline go bust. This is likely to cost upwards of £1.50 per passenger.

It gives them three options. They can offer insurance against the possibility of a scheduled airline failure – either free or by charging a premium on top of the fare. They may sign a formal guarantee that they will accept responsibility for customers if an airline goes under, re-booking them on alternative flights. Or they can opt to do neither. But if they do opt out, they must warn customers in all their paperwork and promotional material – and in suitably large print – that they part with money at their own risk. Independent travel arrangements are further safe-guarded if you book through an ATOL-bonded agent.

Another way of safeguarding your money is to pay by credit card. This is in-creasingly popular, and is much more convenient when booking direct with travel suppliers in foreign countries, who may not even be subject to package travel regu-lations. Credit card companies are to some extent required by the Consumer Credit Act to ensure that the service paid for is provided. But like all legislation this is open to interpretation. The waters are further muddied by the fact that there are now about 40 organisations in the UK issuing credit cards, and their attitude towards refunds varies. If in doubt ask your bank, building society or whatever, especially when an expensive travel purchase is at stake.

Some banks see this as an opportunity to boost card usage: since 1992, for instance, Barclays which has guaranteed to protect anyone buying a flight or holi-day in the UK with Barclaycard, for transactions of over £100 with a ceiling of £30,000. However, Barclays accepts no legal liability, and looks to the travel industry to take primary responsibility. Credit card companies tell customers to seek refunds from the CAA or ABTA in the first instance, but for non-packaged arrangements there are no bonds in place.

There are probably enough scenarios in this chapter to make even the most resolute traveller wonder if his or her money is safe, but in general the travel in-dustry's record is good. If you pay in advance for a carpet, a cooker or almost any other consumer goods and the company goes bust, there is no equivalent to the CAA or ABTA to turn to. ❧

Insurance specialists

In the UK

THE AA TRAVEL INSURANCE
Tel: 0800 085 7240
www.theaa.com/services/
insuranceandfinance/
travel

ASSOCIATION OF BRITISH INSURERS
Tel: 020 7600 3333
www.abi.org.uk

BRITISH INSURERS AND INVESTMENT BROKERS ASSOCIATION
Tel: 020 7623 9043

CAMPBELL IRVINE INSURANCE BROKERS
Head office 020 7937 6981
Travel scheme &
administration centre
01737 248336
www.campbellirvine.com

FOREIGN & COMMONWEALTH OFFICE, TRAVEL INSURANCE
www.fco.gov.uk
Advice centre for travel
insurance.

GILES INSURANCE BROKERS LIMITED
Head office 01294 274629
www.thebroker.co.uk/

HANOVER PARK INSURANCE BROKERS
Tel: 0845 345 0815
www.hanover-park.co.uk

MEDI TRAVELCOVER LTD
Tel: 01252 782392
www.meditravelcover.com

OPTIONS TRAVEL INSURANCE
Tel: 0870 876 7878
www.
optionstravelinsurance.
co.uk

R. L. DAVISON & CO LTD

Tel: 020 7816 9876
www.rldavison.co.uk

WEXAS
Tel: 020 7589 3315
www.wexas.com

In the USA

ATLAS DIRECT
Tel: 800-335-0611
www.atlasdirect.net/us

KEMPER GROUP
Tel: 1-877-KEMPER-6
www.kemperinsurance.
com

ASSIST-CARD
Tel: 1 800 874 2223
www.assist-card.com

GLOBAL HEALTH INSURERS
Tel: 1.417.882.1413
www.eglobalhealth.com

Consumer advice and complaints

ASSOCIATION OF BRITISH TRAVEL AGENTS LTD (ABTA)
UK tel: 020 7637 2444
www.abta.com
Pre-departure tel: 020
7637 2444
On return tel: 020 7307
1907
The UK travel industry's
professional body with a
responsibility to protect
travellers.

CONSUMER AFFAIRS USA
USA tel: 213 291-8086
www.consumeraffairs.
com/

AIR TRANSPORT USERS COUNCIL
UK tel: 020 7240 6061
www.caa.co.uk

Consumer advice line,
9.30am-2.30pm.
Funded by the Civil
Aviation Group to
independently investigate
complaints.

CIVIL AVIATION AUTHORITY
UK tel: 020 7379 7311
www.caa.co.uk
Regulator of the airline
industry in the UK.

howtocomplain.com
www.howtocomplain.com
Provides information
about the regulatory
bodies and how they
should conduct themselves
and advises the best course
of action.

holidaycomplaint.com

www.independenttraveler.
com

http://europa.eu.int/
comm/transport/air/rights

www.ifg-inc.com/
Consumer_Reports/
FlyRights.shtml

Freighting your kit by air, sea or road
by Paul Melly

FEW PEOPLE BOTHER TO THINK ABOUT BAGGAGE. Until, that is, they become that annoying person at the front of the airport check-in queue, searching for a credit card to pay the extortionate bill for bringing home an extra suitcase on the same plane.

The alternative – shipping separately – is often disregarded, or looked upon as the sort of thing that people did in the days when Britain had an empire. Shipping luggage seems to conjure up images of capacious Victorian trunks or battered tea chests creaking home from the Far East in the hold of a mail steamer. But it is actually worth investigating. With just a little planning, you can save a fair sum of money for relatively little delay by sending your surplus bags as freight.

The alternative is to pay the full whack for excess baggage while making a handsome contribution to airline profits. This is such a good earner that it has a separate entry in the multi-million dollar revenue graph of one airline's annual report.

Costly limits

The reason excess baggage charges are so high is the strict limit on how much weight an airliner can carry. There is a premium on the limited reserve space. So if you significantly exceed your individual quota as a passenger and want to take that extra bag on the same flight, you must pay dearly for the privilege. Of course, it then comes up on the luggage carousel with everything else at the end of your journey, which is convenient. But it is also very much more expensive than sending it unaccompanied by air, sea, road or rail. Advance planning can ensure that your baggage will be waiting for you on arrival.

For those caught unawares, one UK operator, the Excess Baggage Company (tel 020 7247 4297) is conveniently located by Victoria Station, the London check-in terminal for several airlines flying out of Gatwick.

Your local *Yellow Pages* will give details of all the various specialist companies under 'Freight Forwarding and Shipping and Forwarding Agents', while the British International Freight Association (Redfern House, Browells Lane, Feltham, Middlesex TW13 7EP, tel 020 8844 2266, www.bifa.org) publishes the *Year Book*, listing all BIFA members with their freight specialities.

Of course freight services are not only useful for those who have too much travel baggage. If you are going to work abroad, take an extended holiday, or embark on a specialist expedition or even a long business trip, you may well have equipment or samples to take. And if you have just finished or are about to start a course of academic or vocational study, there could be a hefty pile of books for which your normal baggage allowance is totally inadequate.

The more you send...

Although one, two, three or even half a dozen cases may seem a lot to you, for a specialist freight forwarder, airline or shipping company it is peanuts. Generally in the cargo business, the more you send (by weight above a basic minimum), the cheaper the price. Naturally, you can send less than the minimum weight, but you still have to pay that standard bottom rate as most freight companies are in business to cater for the needs of industry, not individuals.

When industry does not come up with the traffic, however, they can be glad to get whatever private business is around. The depressed oil market in 1986, for example, led to an economic slowdown in the Gulf and a consequent slump in export cargo to the region, but airline freight bookings out of Bahrain, Abu Dhabi and Dubai were bolstered by expatriate workers sending home their goods and chattels after their contracts expired and were not renewed.

Specialist outfits do nevertheless exist to cater for private individuals, using their bulk buying power to obtain cheap rates which are then passed on to their customers. They can also help with technical problems, such as how to pack, what you cannot send, insurance and so on.

Sending by sea

Sea freight is little used these days except for shipments between Europe and Australia or New Zealand, where the great distances involved make it a lot cheaper than air. The time difference between air and sea freight is from seven weeks by sea as opposed to seven to ten days by air. Air takes longer than one might expect because of red tape, the time needed for goods to clear customs and the wait until the freight company has a bulk shipment going out.

The London Baggage Company reports that nearly all its sea freight bookings are for Australasia, with most of the remainder bound for New York or California. On these routes, there is enough business for freighting firms to arrange regular shipments of personal cargo, but when it comes to developing countries the traffic is more limited so the price is higher. In such cases it is often just as cheap – and more secure – to use the air. Sea freight is charged by volume rather than weight, and is therefore particularly suitable for books or heavy household items. The goods can be held in the UK and then shipped out to coincide with your expected date of arrival in, say, Melbourne or Auckland.

If you want to send stuff straight away, you should remember it will wait an average of seven days before actually leaving: freight forwarders book a whole container and send it only when there is enough cargo to fill it. Shipping on some routes is regarded as high risk, so insurance premiums increase – thus further reducing any price differential with air freight.

Road and rail

Within Europe, rail is a useful option, especially for Italy. While there is only limited and relatively expensive air freight capacity from London to Milan and Rome, a rail shipment to Naples from the UK may take just six to eight days. Rail has the added advantage that most stations are in city centres, so you can avoid the tiresome trek out to an airport cargo centre to collect your bags. Of course, it may well be cheaper to travel by train yourself and pay porters at each end to help you carry the cases, than to spend hundreds of pounds having items sent separately while you fly. There is normally no official limit on what baggage you are allowed to take free with you on a train.

Trucking is also an option for continental travellers. There is a huge range of haulage services and some carriers do take baggage. But prices are often comparable to air freight and journey times are probably a day or two slower. European air freight is a highly competitive business and can actually be cheaper than trucking if you measure size and weight carefully. There are direct routes to most destinations and delivery can normally be guaranteed the next day.

However, the short distances involved mean that rail and road operators can often compete on timing: although most flights last only a couple of hours (or less) many more hours can be used up waiting for a consolidation – bulk air shipment – or for customs clearance on arrival.

Express services, operated by the airlines themselves or specialist companies, are growing rapidly, but are expensive and only worthwhile for items of high monetary or commercial value, such as scientific equipment, computer disks, spare parts or industrial samples. Normally these will offer a guarantee of transit time.

Whatever your method of shipment, there are some practical problems to be wary of. For example, Spanish and Portuguese customs can be finicky if items are sent by truck, and you may find yourself paying duty on some goods on which you were originally told there would be no charge.

Into remoter regions

More surprising is the ease with which you can send stuff to quite remote, long-haul destinations. The key question is: how far is your final delivery point from the nearest international airport? Normally you, or someone representing you, will need to collect the bags at the place where they clear customs, and it is often impossible to arrange local onward shipment, at least under the umbrella of the baggage service in your home country. Delivery can sometimes be arranged within the city catchment area of the airport, but this rarely extends for more than 20 or 30 kilometres. If you are based in Europe, it is also often difficult to get detailed information about onward transport services in the developing world.

One option is to go to a specialist freight forwarder who has detailed knowledge of a particular region of the world and is competent to arrange for local distribution. However, as a personal customer providing a relatively small amount of business, you may not be able to obtain an attractive price, and it could prove cheaper in the end to collect the bags from the airport yourself. There do not have to be direct flights from London, as long as your cargo can be routed to arrive in a country at the right city and pass customs there.

You can take the bags into a country yourself across the land border but you may face more complications taking five suitcases alone through a small rural frontier post than if they arrive at the main airport under the aegis of an established freight company. Customs regulations are complex, and it is vital to that the status of research equipment or commercial samples is checked with customs on arrival by the freight group's local agent.

There is no firm rule as to which places are most difficult to reach, but perhaps the complications are greatest when you want to ship to a remote corner of a large country in the developing world. In these circumstances, you may well find the only reliable option is to collect the bags from the capital city yourself. Shipping to small island destinations, such as Fiji or the Maldives, can be fairly routine, but there are also good services to some places with particularly tough reputations.

Pricing

Prices in general include two elements: a standard service charge which covers documentation, handling and administration by the shipping agent, and a freight charge per kilo which varies according to the airline, destination and particular bulk shipment deal the agent has been able to negotiate. Storage can be arranged, as can collection within the company's catchment area – sometimes free of charge. Outside this radius you will probably have to use a domestic rail or road parcel service rather than asking the agent to arrange a special collection, although a few larger companies do have regional offices.

Dos and don'ts

There are a number of important practical tips to bear in mind. A highly individual distinguishing mark on a case or carton will make it easier for you to pick out when you go to collect it from a busy warehouse or office. It is also important to mark it with your address and telephone number in the destination country, so that the receiving agent can let you know when it has arrived.

If you must send really fragile items, pack them in the middle of the case and tell the freighting office. Many have full packaging facilities and will let you know if they think a bag should be more securely wrapped: for some destinations they cover boxes with adhesive banding tape so that anyone can see if it has been tampered with. Do not overload a case and do watch out for flimsy wheels or handles that can easily be broken off. The agent's packers can provide proper crates if necessary. Proper packing is vital, especially if you plan to send the luggage by road. In many countries the wet season turns cart tracks into swamps. Expedition or development aid teams often have to ship into remote areas with poor roads.

If you are moving abroad, do try and differentiate between household items and personal effects such as clothing or toiletries. The latter are covered by a quite strict legal definition for official purposes. You may find it best to send heavy household items separately by sea.

If you have something awkwardly shaped to send, such as a bicycle, remember that the agent will almost certainly be more experienced in packing such items safely than you are. They will also know what the airline rules are: some carriers will not accept goods unless they are 'properly' packed, which sometimes means banding with sticky tape.

Insurance is essential. You may find you are covered by your own travel or company policy, but agents can also provide cover specially designed for unaccompanied personal freight. Without insurance you are protected only against provable failure on the part of the freighting company with which you booked the shipment, and only in accordance with the limits of their terms and conditions.

As with normal airline baggage, there are certain items you cannot put in the hold of a plane. This extraordinarily eclectic list features a wide range of items including: matches, camping gas cylinders, magnetised material, most aerosols, poisonous weed killer, car batteries, flammable liquids, glue or paint stripper.

Shipments by sea or land are also governed by strict restrictions on dangerous goods, which must be packed specially. ❧

PAUL MELLY is a freelance journalist specialising in foreign news, business and travel.

UK freight forwarders

ARGONAUT FREIGHT FORWARDING LTD
Based in Sheffield's Don Valley, UK
Tel: +44 114 261 8212
www.argonautfreight.co.uk/
Email: admin@argonautfreight.co.uk

ATLASAIR
Atlas House Central Way
Feltham, Middlesex
TW14 0UU, UK
Tel: (020 8890 3644)

BRITISH INTERNATIONAL FREIGHT ASSOCIATION (BIFA)
Redfern House
Browells Lane
Feltham, Middlesex
TW13 7EP, UK
Tel: 020 8844 2266
www.bifa.org
bifa@bifa.org

EXCESS BAGGAGE COMPANY
Units 1-17 Abbey Road
Industrial Park
Commercial Way
London, UK
Tel: +44 (0)181 965 3344

FASTLANE GLOBAL LOGISTICS
Fairview Industrial Estate
Marsh Way
Rainham, London
RM13 8UH, UK
also at
2 Granby Avenue,
Garrets Green Lane,
Birmingham B33 0SG
also at
Unit 9, Clarence Avenue
Westpoint Industrial Park
Trafford Park
Manchester M17 1QS
www.fastlanefwd.co.uk
fastlane@btinternet.com
Tel: 07947 257085

GLOBAL FREIGHT SERVICES LIMITED
Unit D3 Halesfield 23
Telford Shropshire
TF7 4NY, UK
Tel: 01952 270699
www.global-freight.co.uk
01952 270699

INTERCARGO SERVICES LTD
Unit 2 Airside Business Park
Dyce Drive
Dyce, Aberdeen
AB21 0GT, UK
Tel: +44 (0)1224 772120
www.intercargoservices.com

JEPPESEN HEATON
17 Church Street
Epsom, Surrey
KT17 4PF, UK
01372 745678
www.jeppesen.freeserve.co.uk/

WALSH FREIGHT SERVICES LTD
Unit 7
McKay Trading Estate
Blackthorne Road
Colnbrook
Berkshire
SL3 0AH, UK
Tel: 01753 688188
www.walshfreight.com

What to take

Specialist clothing
by Clive Tully

THE WHOLE POINT OF TRAVEL CLOTHING is that it is not 'run of the mill'. When choosing what to pack for a big trip, therefore, comfort, robustness and ease of care should be the prime considerations. The way it all fits into your luggage should be a high priority, too, avoiding garments that are heavy or bulky.

Ease of care is also important. Naturally, the simplest way to travel lighter is to take fewer items of clothing, which means that what is taken should be as washable in a hotel hand basin as it is in a mountain stream. In most cases, synthetic fibres not only wash more easily, they dry more quickly, too. Personally, I have been a fan of the lightweight travel clothing (pioneered by Rohan) since it became available some 25 years ago. It has the benefits of being both light and durable, and while cheap alternatives tend not to have reinforcing bar tacks stitched into the ends of the zippers or securing the belt loops and zipped security pockets (impossible to pick), I still recommend this style. You might not care to try it, but yes, a pair of Rohan's best-selling Bags trousers really does fit into a Coke can.

Local sensibilities

There are plenty of reasons why one should not want to draw undue attention to oneself while travelling. Inappropriate dress can cause unwanted attention when it is often preferable to blend in with the scenery – crossing borders, checking into hotels, even minding your own business waiting at railway stations. Yet often, when it comes down to it, being thin, tall and pale, I know I am going to stick out anyway. My advice is not to go over the top. Nobody expects me to wear a kilt when I go to Scotland (except perhaps for Burns Night), so dressing up in any kind of ethnic kit is likely to leave me looking pretty ridiculous.

Some years ago, DPM (Disruptive Pattern Material) clothing was all the rage in outdoors circles, with everything from clothing to rucksacks sporting camouflage patterns in commando styles. And since the Gulf War, we've also seen a fashion in desert camouflage combat trousers. Great for a night out in Manchester, perhaps, but pretty stupid in Africa. I've even heard reports of DPM-clad backpackers in the Pyrenees being shot at by the local bandits.

Of course, you may have to consider the way you are dressed in certain situations to avoid offending local sensibilities, or in order not to make yourself a target for muggers. There are times when common sense should also prevail. This generally means not exposing too much bare skin when it really is inappropriate (see Sun protection, below), which will generally apply to women much more than men. Having said that, western style is prevalent all over the world, and there are few big towns and cities where you will not see the likes of Coca-Cola t-shirts and baseball caps. Out in the provinces, the situation may well be different. The best advice is simply to be guided by what you see around you.

The practical side of clothing

If we work on a system of layered clothing, you will find you can cater for just about every kind of climate from temperate to downright cold, with only a few adjustments needed for hotter or more humid conditions.

Base layers

What you wear next to the skin is of paramount importance. How comfortable you feel, and how efficiently the layers worn on top work all comes down to wearing the right base layer. In short, the kiss of death is anything made of 100 per cent cotton. The problem with cotton is that it absorbs moisture and it takes forever to dry out. More preferable is the 'wicking effect', where moisture passes through the base-layer fabric so the skin stays as dry as possible, rather like a high-tech nappy. This effect is important in cold conditions, where you have layers on top, because keeping the moisture moving away from you will prevent the chills when you stop moving. And it is particularly important if your outer shell is a breathable waterproof because if cotton is worn next to the skin, you might just as well wear a bin liner rather than a £200 or £300 Gore-Tex jacket.

In warmer conditions, where the base layer may be all you are wearing on top, it helps keep you cool by wicking the moisture to the surface of the garment where it can evaporate most readily and therefore cool you down. Helly Hansen started the ball rolling years ago with polypropylene base layers, but technology has moved on considerably since then. Polypropylene tends to get smelly very quickly, while the latest polyester fabrics have anti-microbial treatments that will keep them working and smelling sweet, even in the most arduous laundry-free conditions.

Mid layers

The traditional garment here is the woolly sweater, and devotees say that not only does wool absorb moisture, but it even generates a certain amount of heat when it does so. But once again, if you are wearing a high-tech breathable waterproof on top, it is not allowed it to do its job by encouraging moisture to hang about inside your little microclimate. The modern alternative is fleece, made from knitted polyester, napped and sheared in a wide variety of different velour finishes, depending on the performance and look required by the manufacturer. As with the polyester used in base layers, it absorbs a mere one per cent of its own weight in water, and the sophisticated techniques used in its construction ensure excellent insulation for the weight of the fabric. Fleece comes in different weights, and the most widely available weight – the best for a broad range of temperatures – is the 200 gsm fabric typified by Polartec 200, which these days also comes with an anti-bacterial finish. The heavier weights are better for very cold conditions or inactivity in less extreme temperatures, while the lighter ones are useful for warding off the chills of a summer evening, or as an extra 'thermal' layer.

On its own, fleece is not windproof. In many situations with high activity – cross-country skiing, for example – a certain amount of air permeability can be an advantage. If wind-proofing is needed then you can either wear your waterproof on top, or a lightweight windproof layer made from poly/cotton or synthetic microfibre. Windproof fleeces made with a laminate sandwiched by two thin layers of fleece fabric are available, and while they do an excellent job, it is inevitably at the expense of flexibility in an overall layered clothing system.

The legs

Cotton canvas jeans have been around for over 100 years, but while they are robust, they have little else to offer. Unless you buy the stretch variety, jeans are unyielding and take forever to dry when washed. In my opinion, they make appalling travel clothing. Get them wet in cold, windy conditions and they become downright dangerous. Water conducts heat away from the body 26 times as efficiently as air, so cotton trousers that absorb gallons of the stuff are not good news for the legs unless you are a fan of hypothermia.

Polyester/cotton or polyester microfibre fabrics fare much better in unexpected extremes of climate because they dry off much quicker. Besides, most travel trousers made from these kinds of fabric look smarter, too.

Waterproofs

The buzzword these days is 'breathability'. Most will have heard of Gore-Tex, the best-known microporous laminate, but there are also microporous polyurethane coatings, and there are, in addition, coatings and laminates that are hydrophilic – Sympatex, for example, the biggest-selling breathable waterproof laminate in Europe. They work by different mechanisms, but the effect is the same. Moisture vapour on the inside gets transmitted through the membrane or coating to the outside. They work best when there is the greatest difference in both temperature and humidity between the microclimate inside your clothing, and the air outside. In other words, cold and dry conditions will see the best performance.

While there are differences in performance between fabrics, and even many different versions of the same fabric, what is probably more useful is to concentrate on the design of the jacket. If the most robust waterproof is needed, you should aim for one of the laminated fabrics in a three-layer configuration. They are good performers, but not necessarily the best for looks if you are seeking something a little more general purpose. Here the two-layer laminate with a separate lining comes into its own, in fact all but budget jackets made from polyurethane-coated nylon or polyester will come with a drop lining as well. The advantage is that they feel softer and look smarter and more sophisticated.

The main zip needs protection to stop water getting through. This should be a double storm flap – either Velcro or press stud fastened – with the inner flap slightly oversized to form a gutter so that any drips managing to infiltrate that far can run down to the bottom hem. Many manufacturers offer lightweight models using very fine denier facing fabrics. Improvements in the manufacture of water resistant zip closures also mean that the extra weight of flaps over zips can be dispensed with, although possibly at the expense of the overall look. Such models are certainly a good deal lighter, and pack smaller when you want to pack them away in your rucksack, but there is an inevitable trade-off in terms of durability.

A good hood is essential. A walking jacket may have a fixed hood, but more are now coming with rollaway hoods that stow in the collar – simply because people want the jackets to be multifunctional. The drawcord adjuster should bring the hood snug around your face without too much fabric bunching up, and it should allow you to turn your head from side to side without your face suddenly disappearing inside the hood.

Something that started out as a feature on mountaineering jackets but is becoming widely available on general models is the volume adjuster. Usually an elasticated drawcord or webbing strap and buckle at the back of the hood, it allows you to take up excess volume in the hood, giving a better fit.

Also useful is a decent peak or visor to keep drips from running down your face. Visors made for typical hill walking or mountaineering will tend to come with some form of stiffening – either a thin plastic strip or malleable wire. In recent years, however, the trend has been towards soft visors, which make stowing the hood in the collar easier, but it is at the expense of functionality when it really counts. In high winds, a floppy peak will simply collapse over your eyes. Old-fashioned designs do give a rather closed-in feel – the more up-to-date ones have cutaways at the side of the face so no peripheral vision is lost – important when you are picking your way across uncertain terrain. If you really want to batten down the hatches in bad weather, look for elasticated drawcords at both waist and bottom hem as well as the hood, while cuffs need to have a good range of adjustment to allow for sealing around gloves.

Pockets are really down to one's own preference and needs. Certainly if you are navigating yourself through wild terrain, a map pocket in the proper place can save you some grief. Decent map pockets will be situated at chest height with the zipped opening beneath the main zip storm flaps, but outside the main zip itself, affording access to your map without opening up the main body of the jacket.

Insulated clothing

If you are heading for really cold climes, or maybe you just need something warm to wear around camp if the temperature plunges to freezing or below, you might consider an insulated jacket, something filled either with polyester wadding or down. As with sleeping bags, the two forms of insulation have their pluses and minuses. Duck or goose down provides the best insulation for the weight – it is also more compressible, and it regains its loft better after compression. The big minus is that it loses its insulation value if it gets damp. Even an insulated jacket with a breathable waterproof shell can suffer from a build-up of moisture that will affect its performance. The first line of attack is to make sure it doesn't get wet. You can also impregnate the whole garment with a waterproofing agent, which will enable the down to loft even in damp conditions.

Synthetic waddings tend to be cheaper than natural fillings and, in general, are bulkier and have a shorter lifespan, though with the huge advances being made in the technology over the last few years, this is not always the case. Their big winning point is the fact that damp does not affect their performance.

Intelligent clothing?

It is now possible to make garments from fabrics incorporating phase change technology, promising superior temperature regulation. The idea is that if, say, you were exerting yourself while wearing a jacket made of the material, it would prevent you from overheating by changing phase and absorbing the excess heat. Then, once you stopped moving and began to cool down, the phase change material would revert to its former state, releasing heat in the process. The technology itself is brilliant – the drawback is that in order to get it working really well, you would end up with prohibitively expensive garments. Those that are currently on the market contain so little phase change material that the benefits are negligible.

Head and hands

The head radiates more heat per square centimetre of skin than any other part of the body (up to 70 per cent of the total heat loss from the body). The moment you start feeling cold it is advisable to put a hat on. A woolly hat is fine, although if you find wool next to the skin a bit irritating, there is a huge range made from polyester fleece. For maintaining any dexterity, in order to operate a camera, for example, you are better off using thin liner gloves with heavier gloves or mittens on top.

Sun protection

The rate of increase in new cases of skin cancer is alarming, and the age of onset is getting lower. We now know there is no such thing as a healthy tan, but also that we can improve our protection against the sun by wearing the right kind of clothes. Most people are unaware that while parts of the body covered by light clothing do not get tanned or burned in strong sunshine, the skin is still being damaged. UVA rays cause tanning and burning, but UVB rays go deeper, causing more long-term damage, and they can penetrate many types of light clothing.

The average cotton t-shirt has a SPF (Sun Protection Factor) of between six and nine. That drops to less than half if the t-shirt is wet. Some travel clothing companies – Rohan and Craghoppers in particular – now quote SPF ratings for their products.

In bright conditions, darker colours absorb more UV and therefore provide better skin protection. The best fabrics for sun protection can still be lightweight, but are close-weave.

As with base layers, synthetic or synthetic/natural fabrics are best. First of all, synthetic fibres can be made much finer than cotton, and are therefore capable of being closer woven. Secondly, their quick-drying ability means enhanced cooling in conditions where you are likely to be sweating. A hat makes good sense, too. The head and neck are prime targets, with one-third of all skin cancers occurring on the nose. A mesh-topped baseball hat or open-weave straw hat might feel good, but they do not offer sufficient protection. A hat with a 10 cm all-round brim is much more effective.

Footwear

What one wears on the feet can make or break any trip. So whether your preferred footwear is trainers, loafers, deck shoes, brogues, walking boots, sandals or wellies, you can do yourself a big favour by making sure they fit properly, and not leaving it until just before you head off into the blue yonder to buy a new pair.

Boots

Walking boots used to be heavy, unbending lumps of leather that were designed to inflict major injuries on feet until they had stomped at least 100 miles in them. Nowadays, while boots may need a little period of 'acclimatisation', they are designed to fit and to be comfortable, straight out of the box. For non-demanding walking and trekking, lightweight boots, such as the mega-selling Brasher Boot, will be just the job, and they don't look too bad for wandering around markets.

The main choice is between all-leather and fabric/leather boots, and within those distinctions there are models built to cater for very wide levels of usage, from general ambling on undemanding terrain to four-season mountaineering, with top of the range models in each category incorporating breathable waterproof liners such as Gore-Tex. Much of what dictates your choice comes down to the stiffness of the sole unit, but even a boot designed for footpath walking – with a reasonable amount of flex in the sole – should still not be able to twist too much. If it does, it will offer little support on rougher terrain, and the feet are likely to tire.

The key to ensuring a decent fit lies in making sure you have the socks you intend to wear with you when you are shopping for boots. Remember that you should leave space in front of your toes to allow for feet expansion, and the easiest way to gauge just how much is to slide your foot forward as far as it will go in the unlaced boot. You should then be able to slip your index finger into the space between the heel and the back of the boot. If you can move the finger about, the next size down is needed, if it is very tight – then the next size up. Any outdoors shop worth its salt will have the means not just to measure feet accurately, but to perform minor modifications such as selective stretching of part of the upper to allow for a wearer's particular foot shape.

Insoles

Since it is likely you will spend lots of time on your feet, it can be worth investing in a pair of specialised insoles to provide superior support. Those that are provided as standard in many walking boots and trainers are generally made from soft closed-cell foam. They help cushion the feet and prevent blisters, but aren't as supportive as they could be. The best insoles you can get for boots, shoes or trainers are the American-made Superfeet, and French-made Conform'able.

Sandals

When the first sandals that took over from flip-flops came into being (mainly for rafting in the USA), they were fairly basic – nothing more than a sole with Velcro-fastened nylon webbing straps. Now sports sandals are extremely sophisticated, employing all the technologies used in high-tech footwear to provide comfort and support. The soles are generally supportive, many with good gripping outsoles, with shaped footbeds to add to the feeling of support and comfort. The straps may be made from nylon webbing, leather or synthetic leather, and most will have soft padding or linings on the underside.

There are versions made for use where immersion in water is likely, but equally there are versions that are suitable for hard walking. Indeed, there are many hikers in the States who prefer to use sandals in hot conditions, even when backpacking heavy loads. Since it is likely that you will be wearing sandals in hot, sunny conditions, do be mindful of the fact that the skin on your feet is very sensitive, so either use sunblock or wear a pair of socks. And yes, as performance socks are available for every conceivable use, it is possible to buy dedicated sandal socks.

Happy feet

Decent socks are as much a key to foot comfort as the shoe or boot itself. Look for socks without bulky protruding seams over the toe or round the heel, and check that the elastication at the top is not too tight. Modern performance socks can also be expected to incorporate moisture transmission fibres such as Coolmax, and have anti-bacterial properties. For walking and general travelling, loopstitch socks provide greater cushioning underneath the heel and ball of the foot, and you do not have to burden feet with the extra insulation of a full loopstitch sock. Socks with the loop pile just in the strategic areas are now available, indeed, manufacturers such as Bridgedale, Thorlo and X-Socks produce numerous varieties aimed at different types of use, with different mixes of fibres and densities of pile areas.

Remember that the layer principle gives the greatest means to mix 'n' match, both in terms of performance and looks. The good backpacker keeps his load light by using items of clothing and equipment, which, where possible, serve more than one purpose. So as one begins to select clothing to put into that rucksack, travel bag or suitcase, think versatility and don't take more than you really need. ≈

Clive Tully is an expert and writer on outdoor clothing and equipment.

Choosing your rucksack (and other luggage)
by Hilary Bradt and Mark McGettigan

THE ORIGINAL MEANING OF 'LUGGAGE' is 'what has to be lugged about'. Lightweight materials and wheels have made lugging obsolete for sensible travellers these days, but a bewildering choice of containers for your possessions is available.

What you buy for luggage and what you put in it will depend on how and where you are travelling. If your journey is in one conveyance and you are staying put when you arrive, you can be as eccentric as the Durrell family, who travelled to Corfu with: 'two trunks of books and a briefcase containing his clothes' (Lawrence), and: 'four books on natural history, a butterfly net, a dog and a jam jar full of caterpillars, all in imminent danger of turning into chrysalids' (Gerald, who described this vast logistical exercise in *My Family and Other Animals*). If, however, you will be constantly on the move and will rarely spend more than a night in any place, your luggage must be easy to pack, transport and carry.

What to take

There are two important considerations to bear in mind when choosing luggage. First, weight is less of a problem than bulk. Travel light if you can, but if you can't, travel small. Second, bring whatever you need to keep you happy. If you can travel, like Laurie Lee, with a tent, a change of clothes, a blanket and a violin or, like some modern travellers, with only a daypack, you will indeed be free. It's perhaps significant that these supremely lightweight travellers usual go solo; you stop noticing your own pong after a few months. Most people, however, are dependent on their customary possessions and must pack accordingly.

Suitcase or backpack?

Your choice of luggage is of the utmost importance and will probably involve making a purchase. Making do with Granny's old suitcase or Uncle John's scouting rucksack may spoil your trip.

Anyone who's had to stand in a crowded Third World bus or the London Underground wearing a backpack will know what an antisocial item of luggage this is. You take up three times more room than normal and every time you turn round you knock someone over. It is no wonder backpackers have a bad name. The trouble is that most modern backpacks are designed for hill walking rather than travelling. The ergonomic design is superb for distributing weight evenly on your shoulders and hips and the fabric keeps out the rain. Fine for hikers, but if you are a backpacker – in the sense of using public transport and being willing to walk a couple of miles to the bus station – you would do better to go for a combination bag and backpack.

Basically, this is a sturdy bag with padded shoulder straps that can be hidden in a special zip compartment when approaching a sensitive border (where backpackers may be given a hard time) or when travelling by plane. New Zealand's favourite outdoor brand, Macpac, produce some superb travel backpacks that offer a range of storage options and different carrying straps for maximum versatility and comfort. The large zip openings allow easy access to all your kit, while they often include a detachable daypack for any quick sightseeing trips. Osprey also produce great all-round travel packs, where the design onus is on function. The large main compartment and shoulder harness ensure that it can easily carry all your kit from airport to hostel and back again.

If you are on an organised group, or do not expect to carry your own luggage, you will find a duffel bag the most practical solution. Or two duffel bags since you have two hands. These soft zipped bags are strong and light and can fit into awkward spaces that preclude rigid suitcases. They fit snugly into the bottom of a canoe or the back of a bus and are easily carried by porters or pack animals. When selecting a duffel bag, choose one made from a strong material with a stout zip that can be padlocked to the side or otherwise secured against thieves. The North Face's Base Camp range provides extremely durable duffel bags in a variety of sizes from 70 litres to 140 litres to match every trip from weekend tour to full-on expedition. The large opening makes accessing everything easy, and the solid shoulder strap is comfortable enough for sustained carrying.

Suppose you are a regular air traveller, what will be the best type of luggage for you? Probably the conventional suitcase and, in that case, you will be well advised – as with most travel purchases – to get the best you can afford, unless you want to replace your 'bargain' luggage after virtually every flight. Cheap materials do not stand up to the airline handling, which usually involves throwing luggage 20 feet onto a hard surface, then allowing it to stand on the tarmac in the rain. For sheer toughness, the traditional hard cases do best. Choose ones made from a strong material such as nylon. These can go up to 1,000 denier. Leather looks smart but is quite heavy. As with all items of luggage, check the zip, which should be strong, and the stitching, which should be even and secure with no gaps or loose threads. Airport carousels can leave black smears on light-coloured items – darker colours stand up to this treatment more happily but are harder to spot among a medley or similar cases. Tie a distinctive ribbon or tag onto the handle for identification.

Few people these days would buy a suitcase that doesn't have wheels. These increase your independence (and save your back). Some wheeled suitcases are far easier to control than others, so check potential purchases out properly in the shop before handing over your money. More and more companies are producing cross-over style luggage, which is constructed from durable ripstop nylon and features extremely tough, rollerblade wheels, ensuring that even the roughest baggage handlers and most potholed car parks will not affect it. They open in half, like traditional suitcases for easy access and straightforward packing, with the added benefit of being soft for safer transportation. DaKine's Split Roller is a prime example of this style of bag, although Snow & Rock produce a very competitively priced version, the Double Deck Wheelie.

Before checking in a backpack or suitcase at the airport, take time to remove all unnecessary appendages (straps, hangers, clips, etc.) and make sure your name and address is both on the label attached to the outside and inside the case as well.

Luggage experts and even those in the airline business often recommend sticking to a carry-on bag if possible. It ensures a speedy exit from the airport and avoids possible damage or loss. In any case, use a carry-on bag for your valuables and anything you can't do without for a few days. To fit under an aeroplane seat, a carry-on bag must measure no more than 45 x 35 x 15 cm.

As well as a carry-on bag, you are allowed the following free items: a handbag (women only: as this is in addition to the carry-on luggage, take as big a handbag as possible to make the most of your luck), an overcoat, an umbrella or walking stick, a small camera, a pair of binoculars, infant's food for the flight, a carrying basket, an invalid's fully collapsible wheelchair, a pair of crutches, reading material

Rucksack recommendations

Top rucksacks

1. Arc'teryx Classic Bora, £200. Premium Brand with the best Hip belt / harness around, Great to carry on longer trips but quality comes at a price.

2. Osprey Crescent, £200. Another top-end product, with a heat-mouldable waist belt.

3. Macpac Glissade, £180. A Classic backpacking style, uncomplicated and very well built with a floating hip belt.

4. Lowe Alpine Frontier, £120. Mid-price pack with excellent fit adjustment and all the right features.

Top travel bags

1. Macpac Utopia, £280. An excellent travel bag with a great harness, removable daypack, hydration system and more, Very durable and great quality.

2. Osprey Waypoint 80, £140. A good mid price bag with a good harness and one of the best removable daypacks.

3. Macpac Orient Express, £135. Durable materials and superior build quality makes this bag a great choice at this price point.

Recommended by Chris Nichols, buyer for the outdoor gear specialists Snow & Rock.

in reasonable quantities and any duty free goods you have acquired since check-in.

Some thought should be given to accessory bags. Everyone ends up with more luggage than they started with, because of presents, local crafts, maps, etc., collected on the way, and a light, foldable nylon bag is very useful. I'm devoted to plastic bags myself and always carry a good supply to separate dirty clothes from clean ones, as well as for those extras.

Security

Choose your luggage with security in mind. Your possessions are at risk in two ways: your bag may be opened and some items removed, or the whole bag may be stolen. Most travellers have been robbed at some time or other, the most frequent occurrence being that small items simply disappear from their luggage. Make sure that your luggage can be locked. With duffel bags, this is no problem – a small padlock will secure the zip to the ring at the base of the handle. Adapt the bag yourself if necessary. Combination locks are more effective than standard padlocks as they are harder to pick. It is harder to lock a backpack, so use your ingenuity.

One effective method is to make a strong pack cover with metal rings round the edges, through which can be passed a cable lock to secure the cover round the pack. Luggage may also be slashed, but this treatment is usually reserved for handbags. Apart from buying reinforced steel cases there is little you can do about it. A strong leather strap around a suitcase may help to keep your luggage safe and will be a life saver should the clasps break.

During my travels, I've been robbed of five small bags. I finally learned never to carry something that is easy to run off with unless it is firmly secured to my person. If you keep your most valuable possessions in the centre of a locked, heavy pack or bag they are pretty safe. If you can barely carry your luggage, a thief will have the same problem.

Weight allowances for air travel

On international flights, the iata tourist and economy class allowance is normally 20 kg, for first class it is 30 kg. For transatlantic flights and some others (e.g. USA to South America), however, you can take far more luggage since the only restriction is to two pieces of luggage no larger than 170 cm. Before you fly, always ask the airline about luggage allowances and ask if the same applies to the home journey. For instance, if you fly Ecuatoriana from Miami to Quito, you will fly down on the two piece system, but will be restricted to 20 kg for your return – a nasty shock for the present-laden tourist.

Packing

Before I go on a long trip I put a large cardboard box into my bedroom and throw in stuff I may need on the trip as I come across it. That, plus a list that is added to as I remember things, makes the build-up to departure relatively unstressful.

Bear in mind that the variable air pressure inside the luggage hold will cause leakage. Shampoos, lotions and other fluids should be in screw-topped tubes or containers. Give the top an extra turn before you pack it. Potentially leaky things such as fountain pens should be carried in your hand luggage. Remember that your Swiss army knife may be classified as an offensive weapon and confiscated.

When packing, put irregular-shaped and heavy items such as shoes at the bottom, remembering where 'bottom' will be when the case is being carried. Clothes crease less if rolled up, or folded round a magazine. Let no space go to waste – fill up shoes with soft or small items such as underwear or jewellery. Top the lot with something large, such as a dressing gown or shawl. Some travellers like to keep their toilet items in different groups, which makes sense when you consider that you do not wash your hair with the same frequency as you wash your face or go out in strong sun. Medicines should be kept in an easily recognised plastic bag. Keep aspirins, etc., in your sponge bag so they can easily be found.

Do not over-pack: if you have to force the lid of your suitcase, you may bend the frame or break the hinges, not to mention what you do to the contents. Better to have plenty of space for those extra purchases. Pad the gaps out with bubble wrap. Then, when everything goes wrong on your holiday, you can relieve the tension by popping the bubbles one by one. ❧

HILARY BRADT is the Managing Director of the Bradt travel guide series and winner of the 'Sunday Times' Small Publisher of the Year Award in 1997.
MARK MCGETTIGAN is a catalogue writer for the outdoor gear specialists Snow & Rock.

Specialist equipment suppliers

in the UK

AGFA UK
27 Great West Road
Brentford, Middlesex
TW8 9AX, UK
Tel: 020 8231 4983
www.agfa.com
Specialist photographic
suppliers.

ARMY & NAVY STORES
297-299 London Road
Westcliff-on-Sea, Essex
SS0 7BX, UK
Tel: 01702 344 181
www.armynavystores.
co.uk

BERGHAUS
12 Colima Avenue
Sunderland Enterprise
Park
Sunderland
Tyne and Wear
SR5 3XB, UK
Tel: 0191 516 5700
www.berghaus.com

BLACKS OUTDOOR GROUP
Mansard Close
Westgate
Northampton
NN5 5DL, UK
Tel: 0800 214 890
www.blacks.co.uk
Equipment for the
novice and the
specialist, from
lightweight mountain
tents to camp
furniture, kitchen kits,
clothing and specialist
sleeping bags.

BRASHER BOOT COMPANY
12 Colima Avenue
Suderland Enterprise
Park
Sunderland
SR5 3XB, UK
0191 516 5770
www.brasher.co.uk

CALUMET
Holborn Studios
49 Eagle Wharf Road
London N1 7ED, UK
Tel: 020 7253 5174
www.calumetphoto.
com
Buying and renting
photo equipment and
accessories with stores
nationwide.

CAMERA CARE SYSTEMS
Fotolynx Limited
Unit 6B, Park Lane
Industrial Estate
Park Lane
Corsham, Wiltshire
SN13 9LG, UK
Tel: 01249 715333
www.ccsystems.co.uk

COLAB
Herald Way
Coventry
CV3 1BB, UK
Tel: 024 7644 0404
www.colab.com
Multi-discipline
imaging company for
professional and
amateur
photographers.

COTSWOLD OUTDOOR LTD
Unit 11 Kemble
Business Park
Crudwell, Malmesbury
Wiltshire
SN16 9SH, UK
Tel: 0870 442 7755
www.cotswoldoutdoor.
com
Comprehensive range
of all your outdoor
equipment.

**ELLIS BRIGHAM
MOUNTAIN SPORT**
211, Deansgate
Manchester
M3 3NW, UK
www.ellis-brigham.
com
Mountain and
snowsports equipment.

FIELD AND TREK
Langdale House
Sable Way
Laindon, Essex, UK
Tel: 0870 777 1071
www.fieldandtrek.com
Outdoor clothing and
equipment with stores
nationwide.

**KARRIMOR
INTERNATIONAL**
Petre Road
Clayton le Moors,
Accrington
Lancashire
BB5 5JZ, UK
Tel: 01254 893000
www.karrimor.com
Manufacturers of
rucksacks, boots and
other outdoor
equipment.

**MAGELLAN'S TRAVEL
CATALOGUE**
106 Avro House
Havelock Terrace
London SW8 4AS, UK
Tel: 0870 600 1601

www.magellans.co.uk
Translators and converters to safety and security items.

MILLETS
Mansard Close
Westgate
 Northampton
NN5 5DL, UK
Tel: 01293 852853
www.millets.co.uk
High street supplier of outdoor goods.

NEVISPORT
20a, Ben Nevis Estate
Fort William
PH33 6PR, UK
Tel: 01397 701 701
www.nevisport.com
UK based outdoor clothing and equipment specialist.

PENRITH SURVIVAL EQUIPMENT
Sandale, Coupland Beck
Appleby, Cumbria
CA16 6LN, UK
Tel: 017683 51666
www.edirectory.co.uk/penrith_survival/pages/
Suppliers of all survival aids and equipment.

ROHAN
9/10 Henrietta Street
Covent Garden
London
WC2E 8PS, UK
Tel: 0870 601 2244
www.rohan.co.uk
Specialist makers of clothing for travelling.

SAFARIQUIP

The Stones
Castleton, Hope Valley
Derbyshire
S33 8WX, UK
Tel: 0870 330 0113
www.safariquip.co.uk
Handpicked equipment specifically tailored for your needs.

SCARPA – THE MOUNTAIN BOOT COMPANY
Unit 5 New York Way
New York Industrial Estate
Newcastle-Upon-Tyne
NE27 0QF, UK
www.scarpa.co.uk
Specialists in footwear specific to every type of requirement - hill walking to skiing. Stockists nationwide.

SNOW+ROCK
The Rock, 2 Thornberry Way
Guildford, Surrey
GU1 1QB, UK
Tel: 01483 445 335
www.snowandrock.com
Outdoor specialists.

TARPAULIN AND TENT MANUFACTURING COMPANY
101-103 Brixton Hill
London
SW2 1AA, UK
Tel: 020 8674 0121
www.applegate.co.uk/company/

TRAVELLING LIGHT
The Old Mill
Morland, Penrith
Cumbria
CA10 3AZ, UK

Tel: 0845 330 3777
www.travellinglight.com
Manufacturer of hot weather travel clothing and accessories.

VIKING OPTICAL CENTRES
Blyth Road
Halesworth
Saxmundham, Suffolk
IP19 8EN, UK
Tel: 01986 875315
www.vikingoptical.co.uk
Specialist supplier for binoculars, digiscoping, tripods and other precision instruments.

Related websites

www.adventuresports.com

www.fellandmountain.co.uk

www.footsloggers.com

http://gorp.away.com

www.mountain-equipment.co.uk

In the USA

LL BEAN
Freeport, ME
04033-0001, USA
Tel: 800 441 5713
www.llbean.com
Leading supplier for outdoor apparel.

MAGELLAN'S TRAVEL CATALOGUE
110, W.Sola Street
Santa Barbara
CA 93101, USA
Tel: 800 962 4943
www.magellans.com

THE NORTH FACE
2013 Farallon Drive
San Leandro, CA
94577, USA
Tel: (800) 447 2333
www.thenorthface.com
Suppliers of equipment
worldwide.

PATAGONIA
34, E. Andrews Drive
Atlanta, GA 30305
USA
Tel: 1 800 638 6464
www.patagonia.com
Supplier of every kind
of outdoor equipment
coupled with advice.
Stores nationwide.

REI (RECREATIONAL EQUIPMENT INC.)
Sumner
WA 98352-0001, USA
Tel: 1 800 426 4840
www.rei.com
Top quality outdoor
equipment and
clothing sold
throughout 78 stores
across the USA.

STEARNS INC
1100 Stearns Drive
Sauk Rapids
Minnesota 56379
USA
Tel: (320) 252 1642
www.stearnsinc.com
Manufacturers for
watersports, outdoor
and safety products.

TAMRAC
9240 Jordan Avenue
Chatsworth, CA
91311, USA
Tel: (800) 662 0717
www.tamrac.com
Suppliers of tough,
waterproof, easy to
carry camera bags for
the outdoor enthusiast.

TENDER CORPORATION
PO Box 290
Littleton, NH 03561
USA
Tel: 1 800 258 4696
www.tendercorp.com
Adventure medical kits,
after bite, insect
repellent, after burn
etc…

THINSULATE – 3M
3M Centre
St. Paul, MN
55144-1000, USA
Tel: 1 888 364 3577
http://3m.com
Insulation materials.

WYETH LABORATORIES
5, Giralda Farms
Madison, NJ 07940
USA
www.wyeth.com
Manufacturers of
anti-venoms against
poisonous snakes,
sold in a freeze-dried
condition suitable
for travelling or
expeditions.

Related websites

www.gearpro.com

www.outdoordirectory.org

www.rivers.com.au

A place to stay

Hotels for business travellers
by Sue McAlinden and Suzanne Nuttall

SECURING TRAVEL ARRANGEMENTS is fast becoming recognised as one of the most stress inducing areas of business life. In many cases companies are reluctant to employ the services of a travel professional, even though the complexities of booking a successful trip are no less time consuming or important than many other more highly regarded areas of a thriving business. In past years business travel has often been a combination of IATA fares and hotel rack rates. Although this booking method often allows the most flexibility, it is by far the least cost effective method of travel.

This article by no means guarantees unbeatable prices at five star hotels, but will point you in the right direction and possibly get you additional benefits.

By choosing to turn up at hotel without pre-booking, you are more than likely going to be offered a room at rack rate (the full nightly rate). One common alternative for business travellers whose company frequently uses the same property/hotel chain, is to set up a corporate account, allowing access to the hotel's corporate rates, these may be specifically negotiated for a particular company (by request). Alternatively, a property may also supply general corporate rates available to all business travellers, based on the meeting of certain criteria.

Travel agencies, clubs and associations are able to offer corporate and negotiated rates, which they will have negotiated on behalf of all their clients. Corporate rates will normally offer a discount of between 10 and 15 percent off the published rack rate. Discount levels will vary depending on the volume of room nights an agency is able to supply over a yearly period. Greater discounts of between 30 and 40 percent off the published rack rate may be offered to agents who are able to secure a higher yearly turnover, these are known as preferred corporate rates. Preferred corporate rates often come accompanied with additional benefits as well as great savings. Some examples are complimentary room upgrades (subject to availability), late check out, free breakfast, etc.

For the above reason, as well as many others, it is advantageous for smaller companies or individual business travellers to become members of associations such as WEXAS. Specialised travel companies and organisations can often secure hotel rates with a much higher discount and greater benefits than they will be able to secure themselves.

With this in mind, booking trends have changed somewhat over the past few years, with the increased value of the 'package rate'. Many corporate travellers are now not only pre-booking their accommodation, they will also pre-pay hotel bookings, travelling on voucher printed accommodation, in order to secure a 'packaged rate', as these often allow for the greatest savings.

Another way of securing lower rates is to travel in off-season. Rates outside of the school holidays and during low booking periods can often be available at up to 50% off the published rack rate. Promotional low season rates can often come accompanied with added benefits and late check out. Great examples of such schemes include the 'Great Affordable' program offered by Leading Hotels of the World and the 'Seasonal Choices' program offered by Mandarin Oriental.

In addition to promotional rates, some chains offer year round benefits to guests who book their non-discounted room rates. At first this may seem the expensive option however, the additional benefits offered definitely make up for the higher nightly rate. A great example of this is Shangri la Hotels and Resorts in the Far East, who offer all guests booking a non-discounted rates additional benefits including complimentary breakfast daily, free airport limousine transfers on arrival and departure (city hotels only), free laundry and dry cleaning services, free broadband access (city hotels only), free local, fax and IDD calls, as well as late check out to 6pm. At their resorts, in place of airport transfers and broadband access guests are offered free buffet dinner or the equivalent credit on room service and free use of non-motorised water sports.

All major hotel chains have web sites, which provide valuable, up to date information on their properties. In the past few years, special 'internet only' rates have appeared as hotels and agents started exploring what used to be seen as a 'new distribution channel'. In reality 'internet only' rates are simply promotional rates under a different name, sometimes without any additional frills; they are no guarantee of getting the best rate for your needs. Like any promotional rates they are often not available at short notice or in busy periods and may not allow any flexibility. Also, take care when comparing rates between websites as not all rates and offers may be displayed over their site.

Whilst the internet empowers travellers to research hotels and rates, it is widely acknowledged that using the web can waste precious time during the working day, and there is still no guarantee of getting the best rate. As such, there is a trend for corporate travellers to go back to entrusting this work to their travel agency or club who will be able to do a full search on your behalf, including negotiated 'package rates' and other rates that you cannot otherwise access.

Which hotel?

One of the greatest deciding influences when choosing a hotel whilst away on business is it inevitably going to be its 'location'. Being near a city's financial/business district is often a staple requirement of most corporate travellers. For this very reason city hotels often pamper to the needs of the business traveller, as majority of the business they will accrue comes from the corporate market and not the budget conscious traveller.

More and more frequent travellers are forming the opinion that 'small is beautiful' and within the corporate travel market it is most definitely the case. Small hotels have a reputation for producing a higher level of service and a more detailed outlay.

Following on from location, another important factor when choosing a business hotel is no doubt it's facilities. Often companies are likely to pay more for their staff to stay in a property that is able to supply a wide range of facilities, easing the stress of employees whilst abroad, in the hope of ensuring a more successful and profitable trip.

For some years now the business executive's choice of hotel may well come down to his choice of loyalty awards program. Frequent flyer schemes were launched in the States by the major U.S airlines in the early 1980s and the hotel industry followed suit. Today virtually every major hotel group has its own reward programme for frequent guests and the majority of hotel loyalty programmes have travel industry partners. For example Hyatt Hotel's loyalty programme is called Gold Passport and is linked to almost all major U.S airline carriers, as well as, Avis and Sixt car rental companies. These loyalty clubs are a huge success, giving the member rewards and the hotels a database of guest information.

Most hotel chains do not charge for joining their frequent guest programme, basing the level of your membership (and subsequently the level of benefits) on the number of stays per calendar year. Rates are not normally affected by the hotel loyalty cards, however members of the schemes often receive priority booking, free upgrades subject to availability and early or late check outs, all of which enhance the business traveller's stay and, in turn, can save money. In addition, points can be collected and redeemed for travel packages, specially selected merchandise, room upgrades, free weekend stays and even free flights.

Airline frequent flyer schemes also attract travel partners in the shape of hotel chains. Executives who predominantly use one airline will tend to use associated hotel chains to boost their air miles.

It goes without saying that airport hotels are just that: good for a day stopover or an early morning departure. In general they are places to be avoided if you plan on visiting a city for any significant length of time. Airport hotels are geared to short stays, odd arrival/departure times or a quick convenient point for a fly-through business meeting.

What's in a room?

Hotel rooms today are looking more and more like a mini home away from home. Long gone are the days where a room is merely a bed, television and coffee maker. The expectations and requirements of guests have risen greatly over the past few years and business travellers especially have become accustomed to expecting much more than simply a place to catch 40 winks at the end of a long day. In addition to the basics, quality toiletries such as Molton Brown or Bvlgari are becoming part and parcel of the hotel experience. In addition, a pillow menu has been added to many hotel rooms in an attempt to yet again raise the level of personal comfort.

Today's rooms not only offer a bed and bathroom, in most cases they are also a self-contained office, with fully laid out desk and broadband access.

Although, many hotels still have a business centre located within the hotel, individual rooms are fast becoming self-sufficient work areas with multiple phone lines and personalised voice mail.

Executive Floors – A business hotel favourite! Usually located on the upper floors of a hotel, giving guests amazing views over the city centre, executive floors are a great selling point to any hotel. They are designed to offer premium paying guests exclusive benefits and first-class service. Benefits aside from a deluxe accommodation may include, express check in, late check out, meet and greet services, complimentary use of health facilities, as well as, express laundry and dry cleaning services.

The biggest selling point to an Executive floor is often it's club or lounge, which offers guests an exclusive area to both work and relax. In addition, most lounges also offer guests complimentary breakfast and evening cocktails/beverages within this exclusive area.

It is becoming clear that in today's travel market, hoteliers are focusing more and more on the requirements and desires of guests in order to seal repeat custom. In the fast changing world of hotels, the knowledge and abilities of your local travel agency or clubs is an extremely valuable asset in securing any successful business venture.

Hotels for leisure travellers

The variance between business and leisure travel is rapidly narrowing. More and more business travellers are tacking a few additional nights of leisure to the end of a work trip. In the same way, work trips taken over school holiday periods are now frequently being extended into family breaks.

In line with the current airline set up, it is often most advantageous for leisure travellers to book their trips under a 'packaged rate'. Packaged rates require travellers to pre-book and pre-pay for their trip, travelling on vouchers and pre-made reservations.

There are two different package types, both of which offer the same desired saving. The first being the 'tailored package', tailored packages allow you to choose your own flights and accommodation, which is then combined to give you one total cost.

The other is a 'set package' booked through a third party such as Cox and Kings or Caribtours. These companies bulk sell pre-packaged accommodation and flights, details as seen in their brochure.

Packages generally hold strict cancellation conditions and are often non refundable within a certain period prior to travel.

If your travel dates are flexible and you are available to travel outside of school holidays and high tourist seasons, hotels often supply additional benefits, aimed at enticing guests to visit. These could be a number of things from daily breakfast to free night offers.

Another popular hotel enticer is the 'early-bird offer'. Early bird offers normally give added value to a guest booking made prior to a certain date (eg. September accommodation, confirmed prior to 31st March). Early Bird offers generally run for around 3-6 months, enticing new bookings for the forthcoming contract year.

Leisure travel rates are more and more favouring pre-paid booking methods, all of which hold quite strict cancellation charges.

Those wanting more flexibility for last minute cancellations, pre-booked locally paid reservations are a good alternative. There are hundreds of different hotel offers available through the GDS via your agency or club and many offer free cancellation up to the day of arrival.

As a general rule most major hotel websites offer the guaranteed lowest rates if booked direct from their official website. Although this is correct for nightly rates, they do not guarantee to beat the 'packaged rate' offered by an agency or club.

In an industry that is continually changing one thing tends to remain the same, the most cost effective hotel bookings, business or leisure, come from pre-booked reservations. ❧

Major hotel chain offices in the UK/USA etc

ACCOR HOTELS
2 rue de la Mare Neuve
91 021 Evry Cedex
France
Tel: +33 (0)1 69 36 8080
(Own Novotel, Ibis, Atria, Etap, Parthenon, Sofitel)
www.accor.com

BEST WESTERN INTERNATIONAL
6201 N. 24th Parkway
Phoenix, AZ 85016
USA
UK UK tel: 0800 393 130
USA tel: (602) 957 4200
www.bestwestern.com

CENDANT
9 West 57th Street
New York NY
10019, USA
Tel: (973) 428 9700
(Own Tavelodge, Ramada Inn, Days Inn, Super 8)
www.cendant.com

CHOICE HOTELS INTERNATIONAL
Premier House
112-114 Station Road
Edgeware, Middlesex
HA8 7BJ, UK
UK tel: 44 208 233 2001
USA tel: 1 877 424 6423
(Own Comfort Inn, Sleep Inn, Quality, Clarion)
www.choicehotels.com

CONCORDE HOTEL AND RESORTS
Marketing Department
31, avenue Jean Moulin
77 200 Torcy, France
UK tel: 0800 0289 880
USA tel: 1800 888 4747
www.concorde-hotels.com

FAIRMONT HOTELS AND RESORTS
Canadian Pacific Tower
100 Wellington Street West
TD Centre PO Box 40
Toronto, Ontario
M5K 1B7, Canada
UK tel: 020 7025 1625
USA tel: (415) 772 7800
www.fairmont.com

FOUR SEASONS
Hamilton Place

Park Lane London
W1A 1AZ, UK
UK tel: 020 7499 0888
USA tel: 1 800 819 5053
(Own Four Season and Regent Hotels)
www.fourseasons.com

HILTON
4 Cadogan Square
Cadogan Street
Glasgow
G2 7PH, UK
Tel: 00 800 888 44
(Own Hilton National/International, Conrad, Hampton Inn, Embassy Suite Hotels)
www.hilton.com

HYATT HOTELS
Tolworth Tower
Ewell Road, Surbiton
Surrey
KT6 7EL, UK
UK tel: 0845 758 1666
USA tel: 1 888 591 1234
www.hyatt.com

INTERCONTINENTAL HOTELS GROUP
67 Alma Road
Windsor
Berkshire

SL4 3HD, UK
Tel: 01753 410100
(Own Crowne Plaza,
Holiday Inn, Candlewood
Suites)
www.ihgplc.com

JOLLY HOTELS
Madison Avenue, 38th
Street, New York,
NY 10016, USA
UK tel: 0800 7310470
USA tel: 800 221 2626
www.jollyhotels.com

KEMPINSKI HOTELS
19-21 Great Marlborough
Street, London
W1F 7HL, UK
Tel: 00 800 426 313 55
www.kempinski.com

**THE LEADING HOTELS OF
THE WORLD**
Avenfield House
118-127 Park Lane
London
W1Y 4LH, UK
Tel: 0207 290 1000
www.lhw.com

LE MERIDIEN HOTELS
CityPoint
1 Ropemaker Street
London, EC2Y 9HT, UK
Tel: 020 7150 7700
www.lemeridien.com

**MANDARIN ORIENTAL
HOTEL GROUPS**
66, Knightsbridge
London
SW1X 7LA, UK
Tel: 020 7235 2000
www.
mandarin-oriental.com

**MARCO POLO HOTEL
GROUP**
The Marco Polo Hong
Kong Hotel
Harbour City, Kowloon
Hong Kong
Tel: +852 2113 0088
www.marcopolohotels.
com

MARITIM HOTELS
1, Burgess Mews

Wycliffe Mews
London
SW19 1UF, UK
Tel: 020 8545 6910
www.maritim.de

**MARRIOTT
INTERNATIONAL**
Global Sales Office
Barnard's Inn
86 Fetter Lane
London EC4A 1EN
UK
Tel: 020 7012 7000
www.marriott.com

**MILLENNIUM COPTHORNE
HOTELS**
Corporate Headquarters
Scarsdale Place Kensington
London
W8 5SR, UK
Tel: 020 7872 2408
www2.millenniumhotels.
com

**MOVENPICK HOTELS &
RESORTS**
Management AG
Zurichstrasse 106
CH-8134 Adliswil
Switzerland
Tel: 020 7690 0609
www.
moevenpick-hotels.com

NH HOTELES GROUP
St Katherine's Way
East London
E1W 1LD, UK
UK tel: 0207 702 3890
USA tel: 888 726 0528
www.nh-hoteles.com

OBEROI
New Delhi 1100033
India
UK tel: 00800 1234 01 01
USA tel: 1 800 562 3764
www.oberoihotels.com

ORIENT EXPRESS HOTELS
Hudavendigar Caddesi
No. 34 Sirkecki 34410
Istanbul, Turkey
Tel: +90 (212) 520 71 61
www.orientexpresshotel.
com

PAN PACIFIC
5th floor 295, Regent Street
London
W1B 2HL, UK
UK tel: 020 7323 2133
USA tel: 1800 538 4040
www.panpacific.com

PENINSULA HOTELS
Weltech Centre
Ridgeway
Welwyn Garden City
Hertfordshire AL7 2AA
UK
UK tel: 01707 871 522 /
00 800 2828 3888
USA tel: 1 866 382 8388
www.peninsula.com

**PREFERRED HOTELS &
RESORTS WORLDWIDE**
311, South Wacker Drive
Suite 1900 Chicago IL
60606-6620, USA
UK tel: 0208 232 5670
USA tel: +1 312 913 0400
www.preferredhotels.com

RADDISON
5th Floor Block 6
Belfield Office Park
Clonskeagh Dublin 14
Ireland
UK tel: 0800 374 411
US tel: 1 800 333 3333
www.radisson.com

RAFFLES HOTELS
2, Stamford Road #06-01
Raffles City Convention
Centre
Singapore 178882
UK tel: 0207 300 1838
USA tel: 212 756 3884
www.raffles.com

RELAIS & CHATEAUX
UK tel: 00 800 2000 00 02
USA tel: (1) 800 735 2478
www.relaischateaux.com

ROCCO FORTE HOTELS
Sir Rocco Forte & Family
(Hotel Management) Ltd
Savannah House
11 Charles II Street
London
SW1Y 4QU, UK
USA tel: 212 515 5776

UK tel: 020 7321 2626
www.roccofortehotels.com

**SHANGRI-LA HOTELS AND
RESORTS**
5 The Courtyard
Swan Centre, Fishers Lane
Chiswick, London
W4 1RX, UK
UK tel: 0800 028 8484
USA tel: 1 866 565 5050
www.shangri-la.com

**SMALL LUXURY HOTELS OF
THE WORLD**
James House, Bridge Street
Leatherhead, Surrey
KT22 7EP, UK
UK tel: 01372 361873
USA tel: +1 212 953 2064
www.slh.com

**SOL MELIA HOTELS AND
RESORTS**
Melia White House
Albany Street
Regents Park, London
NWI 3UP, UK
UK tel: 0800 96 2720
USA tel: 1888 95 MELIA
www.solmelia.com

**STARWOOD HOTELS INC.
THE LUXURY COLLECTION**
111 Westchester Avenue
White Plains, NY
10604, USA
UK tel: ++800325 55555
USA tel: (914) 640 8100
(Own Sheraton, Westin, St
Regis)
www.starwoodhotels.com

STERLING HOTELS
2 Thameside Centre
Kew Bridge Road
London, TW8 0HF, UK
UK tel: 0208 232 5660
USA tel: 1 312 542 9385
www.sterlinghotels.com

**SUMMIT HOTELS &
RESORTS**
2 Thameside Centre
Kew Bridge Road
London, TW8 0HF, UK
UK tel: 020 8232 5650
USA tel: +1 212 541 7222
www.summithotels.com

SUN INTERNATIONAL S.A.
27 Fredman Drive
Sandton, Gauteng
Private Bag 700
Sandton
2146 South Africa
Tel: +27 (11) 780 7800
www.
sun-international.com

SUPRANATIONAL HOTELS
36 Shad Thames
Butlers Wharf
London SE1 2YE, UK
UK tel: 020 7357 0770
USA tel: 1 800 843 3311
www.supranational.co.uk

**SWISSOTEL HOTELS AND
RESORTS**
Temple Place
London
WC2R 2PR, UK
Tel: 0207 836 3555
www.swissotel.com

TAJ HOTELS
51 Buckingham Gate
London SW1E 6AF, UK
Tel: 020 7779 7766
www.tajhotels.com

UTELL
Turtle Creek Blvd.
Suite 1100 Driving
Directions
Dallas, Texas 75219, USA
UK tel: 0208 995 7881
USA tel: 1 (214) 528
5656 3811
www.utell.com

WORLDHOTELS
1st Floor
23-24 Henrietta Street
Covent Garden, London
WC2E 8ND, UK
UK tel: 0207 379 6793 / 00
800 7779 6753
USA tel: 1 800 223 5652
www.worldhotels.com

Related websites

www.accomodata.co.uk
Information and links to
accommodation
worldwide.

www.all-hotels.com
Links to on-line hotel sites.

http://cyberrentals.com
Private homes for rent.

www.ghotw.com
Great Hotels of the World
website.

www.holiday-rentals.co.uk
Private hire homes
worldwide.

www.hotelbook.com

www.hotelguide.com

www.hotelstravel.com
Links to hotels worldwide.

www.innsiye.com
Directory to bed-and-
breakfast and inn
accommodation around
the world.

www.laterooms.com
Late availability and
discounts.

www.milesfaster.co.uk
Guide to hotels in the UK.

www.placestostay.com

www.quikbook.com
Reservations and
availability for hotels in the
USA.

www.spa-collection.info
Site to luxurious spa
holidays.

Budget accommodation
by David Orkin

AFTER TRANSPORT, ACCOMMODATION IS LIKELY TO TAKE THE BIGGEST BITE out of a traveller's budget, but the good news is that – depending on where you are prepared to lay your head – economies can still be made.

The cheapest accommodation is of course that which is free or virtually free. Not surprisingly, such opportunities are few and far between. There are still a few parts of the world where you can sleep on beaches (but you're likely to have to do without facilities): those with a tent may find locals prepared to let them pitch it on their land, but such arrangements tend to depend on negotiating skills. Some temples also offer free accommodation but donations will always be appreciated. Don't expect luxury and as always be sensitive to your hosts' beliefs.

Travellers – particularly those who hitch or use public transport – may find themselves invited to stay with people they meet on the way. This can be the perfect way to find out about a place, but in developing countries may mean staying in houses without running water or toilets, and where conventions, particularly concerning women, may be very different from those at home. Try to read up on local customs in advance: in some countries anything a guest admires must be given to them; in others refusing food can cause offence. Clearly women must be especially careful about accepting offers of hospitality, particularly in Islamic countries where such offers will often come from men.

Long-distance train travellers can avoid accommodation costs by choosing overnight services, but unless you are able to sleep sitting up and drop off again after each interruption (ticket inspectors work at night, too) you might not want to do this too often. On some European trains, couchettes (folding shelf-beds) are cheaper (though less comfortable) than true sleeping berths.

The lowest rung on the ladder of paid-for accommodation is organised camping, but campgrounds are rarely in (or even near) city centres, so unless you have a vehicle you'll have to lug your camping equipment not only between destinations but (quite possibly) from the station out into the suburbs. It's hard to beat sleeping in a tent for experiencing nature and national parks, but if you're thinking of doing a lot of urban camping you may find that by the time you have added the transport costs and time required, it may well be cheaper to stay in something with brick – rather than nylon – walls.

The next step up is a bed in a hostel dormitory. The longest-established and best-known 'chain' of hostels comprises those that come under the auspices of the International Youth Hostel Federation: in the UK contact the YHA (tel. 0870 770 8868; www.yha.org.uk). At time of writing, annual membership is £15.50 (£10 for those under 26). The network includes over 4,000 hostels in over 80 countries and despite the name, in most countries Youth Hostels are open to those of all ages. If you haven't stayed in a Youth Hostel for years you're likely to be pleasantly surprised: huge dormitories, 'lock-outs' during the day and curfews at night now tend to be exceptions rather than the rule, and in general hostels now have much better facilities than they used to.

Part of the reason for the improvements is competition in recent years in the form of a huge boom in independent hostels, often labelled 'backpacker' hostels. There are areas (such as Europe) where there is a high concentration of Youth Hostels and where in many places you won't need to stay anywhere else. But if, for example, you plan to travel across Canada, you may find Youth Hostels in only a couple of cities. Here, and in countries such as Australia and New Zealand, back-packer hostels provide good alternatives.

In the past, rather than sharing a multi-bed dormitory with strangers, if you wanted your own room you would probably have to seek a hotel: however, many hostels now offer private rooms, sometimes with ensuite facilities. These are very popular so try to book in advance where possible. It's worth pointing out that hostel standards and facilities offered vary greatly. If you have the time, don't just flop into the first hostel you come to. For no (or very little) extra cost, a nearby competitor might offer free bike hire or internet use. In addition, some hostels even have well-equipped kitchens for self-catering, cafeterias, bars, swimming pools, cheap or free luggage storage, useful notice boards, and desks where tours can be booked at a discount. In some countries, the cheapest hotels may actually cost less than the price you'd pay in a hostel. The main advantage of hostels over hotels is that the former offer far better opportunities to meet, talk to and swap information with other travellers.

However recently your guide book was published, it's likely that some of the information it contains will already be several months out of date. Getting the lowdown on where to stay at your next destination from someone who was there just a day or two before is hard to beat. But if hostels are full or if you'd prefer to stay in a hotel, guide books do offer somewhere to start looking. Failing that, the best hunting ground for very cheap hotels is likely to be near bus and railway stations (but you might not get a quiet night).

In some European and Mediterranean countries you can rent a room in a private house. Tourist information offices (and sometimes the local police) often have lists of such private rooms, or you will be greeted by touts at points of arrival (such as bus or train stations or ferry terminals).

In the USA (and to a lesser degree, Canada) motels often provide good value budget accommodation, but motels are geared to drivers and are concentrated in the outskirts of cities, often virtually unreachable by public transport.

Always take a look at what you're being offered before accepting a very cheap room. Look at the door locks; the state of mosquito netting where appropriate; check that there are no peep-holes in partition walls; that the walls reach right to the ceiling; and that there are no tell-tale signs of bed bugs, ants or other insects. Don't forget to check the state of the washrooms and toilets.

Sometimes (often in developing countries) the price gap between the most basic, run-down establishment and somewhere quite up-market can be small. Consider treating yourself to an occasional night's 'luxury'. Although pairing up with someone you've just met (to reduce costs by sharing a room) can make financial sense, be as sure as possible that your new 'friend' – who will have the easiest of access to all your valuable possessions – is trustworthy.

It makes sense to book the first couple of nights' accommodation in advance: agencies that specialize in worldwide travel (such as WEXAS) offer excellent rates at safe, reliable hotels. Once you're rested and settled in you'll have more energy to look round. ❧

DAVID ORKIN is a travel writer. Before that he spent 16 years working for Trailfinders and Quest Worldwide Travel. During that time and since he has travelled extensively.

Hostelling associations

International

www.hihostels.com

www.hostels.com

www.hostelworld.com

In UK and Ireland

YOUTH HOSTEL ASSOCIATION (ENGLAND & WALES)
www.yha.org.uk

SCOTTISH YOUTH HOSTELS
www.syha.org.u

HOSTELLING INTERNATIONAL NORTHERN IRELAND
www.hini.org.uk/

USA and Canada

REAL ADVENTURES, CANADA
www.realadventures.com

www.hostelcanada.com

HOSTELLING INTERNATIONAL USA
www.hiusa.org/

Related websites

www.budgettravel.com

www.travel-ys.com

www.backpackers.com/

www.backpackingeurope.com/

www.independenthostelguide.co.uk

Camping associations

Europe

www.campingfellowship.org

www.motorhoming.com

www.excite.co.uk/travel/guides/europe

www.karmabum.com/

www.eurocampindependent.co.uk

http://goeurope.about.com

www.eurocamp.co.uk

www.canvas.co.uk

www.caravanclub.co.uk

USA

www.usacampsites.com/

www.reserveamerica.com

www.suite101.com

www.campingconnection.com/usa/

www.koakampgrounds.com

www.westernwanderer.com

www.gocampingamerica.com

www.trekamerica.co.uk/

South America

www.saexplorers.org/

www.trekamerica.co.uk/

www.latintrails.co

www.southwindadventures.com

www.andeantravel.com

www.south-america.com.au/trekking.htm

www.outdoorguides.com

Australia and New Zealand

www.camping.com.au/

www.exploroz.com

www.letstrekaustralia.com

www.australianoutdoors.com

www.holidayparks.co.nz

www.tourism.net.nz/accommodation/campsites-and-holiday-parks

www.nzs.com/travel/accommodation/camp-sites

www.travelplanner.co.nz

Home exchange and timeshare associations

GREEN THEME INTERNATIONAL
94 Fore Street
Bodmin Cornwall
PL31 2HR UK
www.gti-home-exchange.com

HOME BASE HOLIDAYS
7 Park Avenue
London N13 5PG UK
Tel: 020 8886 8752
www.homebase-hols.com

HOMELINK INTERNATIONAL
www.homelink.org
The website will connect you to all of their offices around the world in USA, Great Britain, England, Ireland, Canada, France, Denmark, Norway, Sweden, Germany, Italy, France, Australia, New Zealand, Netherlands, Holland, Belgium, Mexico, Caribbean, Portugal, Spain, New Zealand and South Africa.

HOME EXCHANGE INC.
Post Office Box 787
Hermosa Beach CA
90254 USA
Tel: 310 798 3864
www.homeexchange.com

INTERHOME
383, Richmond Road
Twickenham, TW1 2EF, UK
Tel: 0208 891 1294
www.interhome.co.uk

INTERVAC HOME EXCHANGE
24 The Causeway
Chippenham Wiltshire
SN15 3DB, UK
Tel: 01249 461 101
www.intervac.co.uk

IVHE NETWORK
163, Mortlake Road, Kew
Richmond, Surrey
TW9 4AW, UK
Tel: 020 8878 3559
www.ivhe.com

RCI
Kettering Parkway
Kettering,
Northamptonshire
NN15 6EY, UK
UK tel: 0870 6090141
USA tel: 317 805 9000
www.rci.com

TIMELINX S.A.
Partido de la Morena
Vega del Canadon
Nave 10
29649 Mijas Costa
Malaga, Spain
Tel: 34 952 665 279
www.timelinx.com

TRADING PLACES INTERNATIONAL
23807 Aliso Creek Road
Suite 100 Laguna Niguel
California USA
Tel: 949 448 5150
www.tradingplaces.com

THE VACATION EXCHANGE NETWORK
PO Box 277
Whippany

New Jersey USA
Tel: 973 386 9208
www.thevacationexchange.com

WORLDWIDE TIMESHARE HYPERMARKET
Bournemouth
Dorset UK
Buyers tel: 0845 330 2830
Sellers tel: 0845 330 2831
Outside UK tel: 0044 870 443 1466
www.timeshare-hypermarket.com

Related websites

www.heig.com

www.holi-swaps.com

www.homelink.com.au

www.home-swap.com

www.profvac.com

www.timeshare.org.uk/
Timeshare consumers association.

www.timesharedirect.com
To rent, sell or exchange.

www.timesharer.com

www.timesharebeat.com

www.timeshare-options.com

www.tug2.net
Unbiased opinions

Home exchanges
by Heather Anderson

LOOKING FOR AN ALTERNATIVE HOLIDAY? Had enough of package tours that herd you into tower-block hotels with rooms the size of your wardrobe at home? If you are looking for a more comfortable base for your holiday which allows you to see a country and its culture in a more natural setting, then a home exchange could be the right holiday for you. Imagine what it would be like to have a five-star holiday anywhere in the world, with all home comforts, and nothing to pay except travelling expenses? Around 50,000 people do just that by swapping their homes for a holiday.

Home exchange holidays started more than 40 years ago, and there are now a number of companies which help make it all possible. The oldest and largest, HomeLink International, has over 132,500 members in 50 countries. Others include Intervac, Home Base and Green Theme, with between 2,000 and 69,000 members each. The procedure is relatively simple. Each member is listed in a directory with a detailed description and a photograph of the home, and contact details. Members give preferred holiday destinations and dates, although many are fairly flexible about both. It is then up to members to contact other members with whom they wish to exchange. Membership fees range from around £640 for the smaller internet-only companies to £95 for the largest, full-service organisation.

The appeal of the home exchange concept is based on the mutual trust and bond of friendship that is built up between members as they correspond and get to know each other in the weeks before their exchange holiday. Ideally a swap should be with a like-minded family or group of a similar size, so both will feel at home, and will look after the property well. Devotees claim that once you have experienced a holiday in the luxury of someone else's home, it is very hard going back to those cut-price hotels and self-catering apartments with their minimalist furnishing and mini fridge.

Others have had more sobering experiences, finding themselves in unsuitable accommodation or returning to find their home looking decidedly scruffy. It depends on how you organise your exchange. Anyone wishing to exchange properties can advertise in a suitable publication, and there are numerous companies around. Whichever method is used, make sure that every eventuality has been covered and agreed in writing. If using a company, it does pay to pick carefully. Those that 'vet' clients thoroughly are obviously safer to exchange through. If you are unsure about anything, check and check again with the company. Bona fide organisations will take time to answer all your queries. In general you're safer with a long-established company that has built up a reputation.

The internet has had a big impact on the way home exchange companies operate, and made swapping disasters less likely as some companies, including Home-Link, will give you access to their on-line listings database (minus members' personal details), so that you can see what's on offer before you join. This will help

Seven easy steps to a successful home exchange

1. Describe your home honestly in your listing and in all correspondence.

2. Leave your home clean. Standards of cleanliness vary, so make sure that floors are cleaned and rooms dusted, refrigerator emptied, oven grease-free, and with special attention to bathrooms and kitchen. No need to repaint the house! Leave space on shelves and in wardrobes and drawers so that your guests can empty their suitcases.

3. Compile a 'Guide to Your Home and Surroundings' which should include local tourist information and household notices about the use of electrical appliances, pet and plant care, etc. Phone numbers of a recommended doctor, dentist, babysitter, good restaurants, and helpful friends are always welcome too.

4. Use your Exchange Agreement form to avoid misunderstandings. If necessary, clarify who pays what in terms of telephone, gas and/or electric bills, and staple foods such as flour, sugar, oil, etc.

5. If arrangements are such that you cannot meet, arrange for a family member, neighbour or friend to call in and welcome your exchange partners when they arrive.

6. It has become a tradition amongst exchangers to leave a small gift of welcome: a bottle of wine or champagne, a local speciality. Always a pleasant surprise.

7. Close the door, turn the key, and go off on your holiday knowing that your home is in the good hands of another member just like you.

you to determine whether the type and number of homes available and the range of destinations appeals to you. HomeLink also provides a facility for members to amend their on-line listing whenever they want, and they provide hot lists of new and last minute exchange offers.

The key point when looking for a suitable organisation is the number of members you can contact or who can contact you, as this factor will largely dictate how successful you will be in finding an exchange for the dates you want and in your choice of country.

When HomeLink member Elsie Butler listed her average three-bedroom house, she was surprised by the response. The directories are published in December and by March she had received over 60 offers – letters, faxes, emails from all over the world. Elsie and her family took the offer of spending Christmas in Sydney followed by two weeks in France during the summer.

Once you have taken the plunge and got your listing into a directory, you will be provided with comprehensive advice on how to set up an exchange.

So is home exchanging the right type of holiday for you?

Yes: If you find hotels or self-catering too impersonal or restricting. If you're outgoing and enjoy experiencing other lifestyles. If you're a good organiser.

No: If you can't be flexible about dates and destination. If if you would be too embarrassed even to let a cleaner into your home. ❧

HEATHER ANDERSON was Managing Director of Homelink International.

Taking a timeshare
by Kim Winter, Michael Furnell and Diana Hanks

THE MAJORITY OF PEOPLE BELIEVE that timesharing is something new which has only developed over the last fifteen years or so, but in fact it is not really a new concept: as far back as the eighteenth century, villagers were timesharing water in Cyprus where there was no piped supply.

Property timesharing is believed to have started in the 1960s, when certain French developers of ski apartments experienced difficulties in selling their leisure accommodation outright, and decided instead to offer for sale the ownership of weekly or fortnightly segments at the same time each year for ever.

The idea spread to other parts of Europe, including Spain. On the Costa Blanca, a British company that was building apartments in Calpe offered co-ownership of two-bedroomed flats in the main shopping street near the sea. Prices were as little as £250 per week's usage in the summer in perpetuity. Winter periods were even cheaper, at £180 for a month, and easy terms were available on the payment of a £50 deposit, with the balance payable at £4.50 per month over three years.

The Americans soon recognised this form of holiday home ownership, and in the early stages converted condominiums, motels and hotels – non-viable in their original form – into time-share units. Often these had rather basic facilities, and it is only in recent years that developers in Florida and elsewhere have realised that top-quality homes with luxury facilities are the key to successful multi-ownership.

It was not until 1976 that timesharing was launched in Britain. The first site was in a beautiful loch-side location in the Highlands of Scotland. This was a luxury development with excellent sporting facilities and prices were set from about £5,000 per week.

How it works

The aim of timesharing is to provide luxury accommodation in return for a once-only capital sum is paid at current prices. Future holidays are secure without the need to pay hotel bills or holiday rents – though buyers still need to pay an annual sum to cover maintenance expenses and local taxes, as well as buying flights and food. Timeshares are sold by a variety of methods, and prices vary according to season and the quality of accommodation.

When a freehold is purchased, as in Scotland, the period of time that you buy is yours to use forever, and you may let, sell, assign or leave the property to your heirs. In England and Wales, the law permits ownership only for a maximum of 80 years, but in many parts of the world ownership in perpetuity is possible.

An alternative is membership of a club which grants the right to a club member to use specified accommodation in a specified property for either specified weeks in the timeshare calendar or for 'floating time' in the high/medium/low season time band (selecting your weeks annually for a stated number of years is an alternative scheme). Under this arrangement, the assets of the property (i.e. buildings, lands and facilities) are conveyed (or leased) to custodian trustees (often a bank or other institution), which holds the property for the benefit of the club members. The rights of all owners collectively are regulated by the club constitution. This legal structure works well both in the UK uk and, with modifications, overseas.

A third alternative is to buy 'points' in a timeshare club, which allows considerable flexibility for taking two short breaks of less than a week's duration, for example, rather than owning a specified week or weeks in a specified timeshare resort.

The formation of a public limited company, with the issue of ordinary shares varying in price according to the season and apartment size, is another form of holiday ownership, although not strictly a timeshare arrangement. Each share provides one week's occupancy for a set period, usually 20 or 25 years. The properties are sold on the open market and the proceeds divided among shareholders.

One company uses capital contributed by participants to purchase land and build holiday homes in various parts of Europe. Each member is entitled to holiday points, to be used for a vacation of a week or more in a chosen development at any time of year.

Another provides for the sums paid by participants to be converted into a single-premium insurance policy. Part of that premium is invested in fixed-interest securities and another portion is used to acquire properties (over 400 in about 20 locations). 'Bondholders' pay a user charge to cover the maintenance cost of the property for each week's holiday taken, on a 'points per week' basis depending on the accommodation's size, location and season chosen. Investors are permitted to cash their bonds (the price of which is quoted daily in the financial press) at any time after two years. A capital sum is repaid on the death of the bondholder, the amount being determined by the age at which the holder took out the insurance policy. Such bond schemes are subject to legal regulations which do not apply to timeshare arrangements.

Over the past few years, various schemes have sprung up that are not covered by timeshare legislation. These include 'trial packs', which are intended to allow the potential customer to experience the product before committing to the final purchase and act like a conventional timeshare but for a period of only 35 months, or others, ; holiday clubs, where buyers pay for holidays up to ten years in advance and apply to the promoter for the accommodation they are interested in (usually timeshare resorts). Or; and holiday or travel packs, where buyers join a club, paying around £3,000 for access to low-cost travel and accommodation (again, usually in timeshare resorts, but also in hotels or other type of accomodation). Check out these offers very carefully: some promoters have been found to have no links with the resorts they are offering, and there is no legislation, unlike in timeshare, that guarantees the delivery of the product offered, so it may be very difficult for them to book you the accommodation you want, and if the promoter goes bust a few months after you have paid your money up-front, your chances of receiving a refund are pretty slim. These schemes should not be confused with timeshare

Golden rules

The rules to remember when buying a timeshare home are:

- Do some research. Read up about the timeshare concept and the resorts available in Europe. Compare resorts to find the most suitable.
- Buy from a well-established developer or selling agent who has a reputation for fair dealing and offering really successful schemes. Developers who are members of the Organisation for Timeshare in Europe (OTE) must comply with a strict code of ethics. Second-hand timeshares bought from a reputable resale agency might be sometimes cheaper are usually considerably cheaper than those bought from a developer.
- The location of the property is vital, so be sure to select a well-situated development with adequate facilities and a quality atmosphere. Be sure that it appeals to the whole family, so that you are all able to enjoy regular visits. If you are likely to want to resell or exchange in the future, the location will prove even more important to your choice.
- Remember that the UK Timeshare Act 1992 and the Timeshare Regulations of 29 April 1997 provide for a 14-day cooling-off period for those who are in the the UKuk when they sign a purchase agreement (the actual location of the timeshare resort is irrelevant). The regulations also ban the company concerned from taking any deposit from you within those 14 days. However, the EUeu Directive on timeshare, which came into force in the member states on 29 April 1997, provides for a minimum ten-day cooling-off period rather than 14 days, and legislation in some member states is more specific stating that the ban on deposits applies only to the vendorallow deposits to , which could be interpreted as allowing deposits to be be taken by third parties (for example a trustee/escrow account). Check what cooling-off period is allowed before signing any contract.
- Get the contract checked, preferably before you sign it. A solicitor can check the wording of agreements relatively easily, but it will be a considerably greater task – and thus more expensive – to consider the occupation rights granted, the nature of the developer's title, details of any mortgages or encumbrances on the timeshare property, the granting of correct local planning permission, the legal structure of the scheme in the context of that country's property laws, the effects of jurisdiction, the safeguards for monies paid for an unbuilt or incomplete property and the arrangements at the termination of the period of lease. Your solicitor should also scrutinise the documentation and perform independent checks regarding payments held in trust pending the issue of title documents, club membership certificates and a licence to use. Is the trustee reputable?
- If all the amenities promised by sales staff are not already in existence, obtain a written commitment from the vendors that they will be completed, and by when.
- Check carefully the annual maintenance costs and be sure you know what they cover. Part of the yearly charges should be accumulated in a sinking fund by the management company to cover replacements, new furnishings and regular major redecorations. Be careful of extra levies to cover refurbishments.
- Ascertain the rights of owners if the builder or management company gets

Further information

Organisation for Timeshare Europe, 15/19 Great Titchfield Street, London w1p 7fb, tel 020 7291 0901. This is the European trade association for timeshare, representing the interests of developers, exchange organisations, resale companies, marketing organisations and finance companies. It has a code of ethics for members and offers an advisory and conciliation service to people dealing with its members.

Timeshare Consumers Association, Hodsock, Worksop, Nottinghamshire s81 0tf, tel 01909 591100, email

info@timeshare.org.uk, website www.timeshare.org. uk. Produces useful fact sheets offering advice on various aspects of timeshare.

The Department of Trade and Industry publishes The Timeshare Guide, available free from its Consumer Publications order line on 0870 1502500 (quote reference urn 97/643). The text is available at www.dti.gov.uk/access/timeshare. ß

RCI, Landmark House, Hammersmith Bridge Road, London, W6 9EJ. For customer equiries tel 0870 6090141, website www.rci.com.

into financial difficulties, and ascertain if it is possible for the owners to appoint a new management company if they are not satisfied with the service of the original one. Show the constitution and management agreement to a specialist lawyer to determine that the title is safeguarded and occupation rights protected. Talk to other owners to find out their views on the relationship between the owners and the management company.

• If you wish to have the flexibility to swap world-wide, the timeshare resort should be affiliated to an exchange organisation, such as Resort Condominiums International (RCI) or Interval International. Check any claim to affiliation.

Investment

Timesharing is not a conventional money-making investment in property, although some owners who purchased time in the earliest schemes have enjoyed substantial capital appreciation over the past ten years. Essentially, you are investing in leisure and pleasure, but you cannot expect inflation-proof holidays. What you are buying is vacation accommodation at current prices. Expenditure on travel, food and entertainment is likely to rise in future years according to the rise of inflation. Owners who sell their timeshare a few years after buying are likely to get back considerably less than they paid for it. The number of owners wanting to sell their timeshare significantly exceeds the number of people wanting to buy; so if you only want to hold a timeshare for a few years it would be worth comparing the cost of alternatives.

Exchange facilities

It became clear a while ago that after a few years many timeshare owners may want a change of scene for annual holidays; as a result, organisations grew up to arrange exchange facilities for timesharing owners. There are exciting possibilities for owners wanting to swap their seaside apartment in, say, England's West Country, for a contemporary-style bungalow in Florida or an Andalucian pueblo in Spain. Today there are two major exchange organisations operating in the UK, the largest being RCI with over 3 million members and 3,700 resorts worldwideworld and Interval International.

There is normally an annual membership fee payable by each family wishing to join the exchange system. The developer usually pays this for each family for the first two or three years as a purchase inducement. An additional fee is due when an exchange is successfully organised.

New markets and trends

Already established in North America, the concept of luxury, shared accommodation, including fractional interests, private residence clubs and condo-hotels, is rapidly becoming established in Europe and the Middle East. Fractional resorts are traditionally luxury establishments sold in one-quarter to one-twelfth shares and appeal to cash-rich, time-poor consumers who want to enjoy luxurious and spacious accommodation without the worry and expense of owning and maintaining a second home. Private residence or destination clubs are run on various different business models but the general premise remains the same. Members pay an annual membership fee to belong to an exclusive club and are able to stay in deluxe properties around the world with the added benefit of concierge and travel services. Condo hotels –offer the possibility of owning a luxury vacation accommodation in the form of a beautifully furnished suite in some of the best hotels and resorts around the world. This concept offers a financial return with owners receiving rental income whenever they don't use it. The fractional market is the fastest growing segment of the North American hospitality industry and is currently worth $515 million. Europe and the Middle East represent huge growth markets for this luxury industry as consumers more and more demand financially savvy solutions when planning their leisure time. ❧

Working abroad

Business travel
by Gillian Upton

THE JURY'S OUT AS TO WHETHER THE BUSINESS TRAVELLER is to be sympathised with or envied. On the one hand they roam the world for free, seeing places and experiencing vastly different cultures, travelling with a degree of comfort few other people enjoy. Once their business is finished, they are able to put their brief-cases away and tack a local side-trip on to their excursion at prices mere mortals will never be offered.

On the other hand, they work long, anti-social hours and spend extended periods away from home and their families, often in alien cultures or high-risk desti-nations; they suffer from higher stress levels than their non-travelling colleagues, are connected to their offices virtually 24 hours a day, and pay higher airfares and hotel and car hire rates than leisure travellers because of their pressing need for flexibility.

Surveys that attempt to determine which of these snapshots is a more accurate representation of the life of the business traveller abound – but their results are in-consistent and so it is difficult to conclude whether the business traveller doth protest too much. Either way, business travellers are a growing and demanding group of executives. What turns them on and off is becoming clearer – and gender plays a big role in the results.

Female business travellers tend to worry about the cost of travel, while men are more concerned by check-in queues. Men choose their hotel by cost, but women choose them by location, which is a reflection of their greater concern over securi-ty. In a recent survey, twice as many women as men (52 per cent against 21 per cent) said that they were concerned about security issues in the UK, although men became more security-conscious when travelling overseas (up to 43 per cent).

Across the board, though, the biggest turn-offs are – not surprisingly – late flights, road congestion, the high airfares to many destinations, long check-in queues, the lack of sleep that business travel entails, and the risk of potential downgrades to economy class. All these concerns give an accurate picture of the current sorry state of the business travel market. Corporate down-sizing and cost-cutting are the order of the day, and more business travellers are having to squeeze themselves into economy-class seats and budget hotels these days than ever before.

And airline punctuality is just getting worse. Sympathise with any traveller who flies regularly into airports such as Milan, Geneva or Munich, as these regularly top the lists of European airports most affected by delays. Generally, over a quarter of intra-Europe departures are delayed by more than 15 minutes, according to figures released regularly by the Association of European Airlines (AEA).

Flight delays exacerbate what is already a stressful and tight business schedule. Reduced budgets and the availability of flights to business destinations at either end of a working day has forced many business travellers to forgo an overnight stay – and the inherent cost – and squeeze all their appointments into one long day. And because more business travellers are flying from airports such as Luton and Stansted, where the 'no-frills airlines' such as Ryanair are based (Ryanair, for example, claims that 40 per cent of its passengers are business travellers), the businessperson often has a longer than usual trip home once the flight finally lands.

Meanwhile, it's a travesty that the UK, home to so many low-cost carriers, stings business travellers. The European Corporate Travel Index, published by American Express, revealed that British companies pay 76 per cent more than the European average for business-class fares to New York, for example. The cost of a business-class seat to New York has increased by 50 per cent since 1994.

But all travellers across the world are having to dig deeper into their pockets for airfares. Airlines are stinging from the huge increases in fuel prices – it's doubled to US$60 a barrel over the last few years. The impact of this is simple. American Airlines, for example, paid US$1.1billion more for fuel in 2004 than it did in 2003.

Stretching budgets for long-haul travel has meant that companies now send their executives via hub airports. In the same American Express survey, it was pointed out that British companies can save almost 30 per cent by sending executives bound for Los Angeles via Paris, for example.

But it's not all doom and gloom for the business traveller. Business-class cabins have never been so comfortable. These days they're fitted with seats that incorporate personal video screens, laptop power points, telephones, head rests, lumbar support – all operated electronically by the touch of a button. Some, notably cabins on the major airlines' long-haul flights, are now fitted with seats that recline fully to become a flat bed. This is the sort of comfort that travellers used to get only in first class.

While first-class cabins are half the size they used to be in the 1980s, there are still business travellers who are able to pay double the price of a business class fare for the comfort offered in first-class. These tend to be the chairmen of large companies or city institutions, bankers, insurers, consultants and lawyers, all of whom can charge the enormous fare back to a client.

For them the status of flying in first class, being first off the aircraft, enjoying a la carte service and the privacy of sitting with probably only half-a-dozen others, is in direct contrast to the experience of those travelling in the business-class cabin, where there are upwards of 50 other passengers. There is also the advantage of superior food and drink and the much higher staff-to-passenger ratio, which translates to virtually one-on-one service. Compare one member of airline staff for every ten passengers in business class, to three crew members for every 14 passengers in first class. And bear in mind the fact that the first-class cabins are generally half full. It's the nearest you get to personal service in the air. And, once on the

Buying smart for business

Air

• Fly via an intermediate hub on long-haul routes (via Amsterdam or Paris to get to New York, for instance) and save up to £1,000.

• The purchase of an air pass if you're flying to several points within a region will give you significant savings.

• The only way to save money on short-haul flights is to downgrade to a 'no-frills' airline, or squeeze all your appointments into one day to avoid the cost of an overnight stay.

• Consider buying consolidated airline tickets to save up to 70 per cent, but be aware of the restrictions attached to such fares. Participating airlines are generally of good reputation.

• Back-to-back airline tickets can save hundreds of pounds on long-haul economy class airfares, as long as you spend a Saturday night at your destination.

Rail

• If your company spends over £500,000 a year on rail travel, you can negotiate volume discounts from the rail operators.

• When travelling less than 500 km within Europe, forget flying and opt for rail travel, as the European train system is infinitely superior.

• It pays to book in advance if journey dates and times are fixed, as you will benefit from heavily discounted tickets.

• If you travel off-peak and, in many European countries, purchase an annual travel card, you will gain a discount of up to 50 per cent on the cost of your fares.

Hotels

• Don't accept the first rate a hotel offers – always ask for better deals.

• Getting a rate from the hotel direct can be cheaper than ringing that hotel chain's central reservation number.

• Consolidate and place your hotel bookings with fewer hotels, giving each of them a higher number of bed nights, to score a heavier discount.

• Specialist hotel-booking agencies are worth looking at as an alternative to booking through a general travel agent/management company.

• Think about booking a room on the executive floor. Yes, it costs about 20 per cent more, but the sum total of all the free benefits – from free meeting space to free food and drinks – and services may make it worthwhile.

• Stay just outside your destination, where hotel rates can be significantly lower.

• Check out airline stopover packages; their hotel rates can be amazingly cheap.

• Look out for cheaper rates at new hotels or hotels re-opening after refurbishment and those trying to win your loyalty.

• Don't stay in a hotel at all if your stay extends over one week. Opt instead for an apartment, save money and enjoy far more home-from-home comforts.

ground, the pampering doesn't stop, whether for first- or business-class travellers. Some airlines, such as Virgin Atlantic and Emirates, treat them to chauffeur-driven cars to and from the airport.

Check-in options nowadays have increased enormously, so they can avoid the long queues at the counter. They can check in by fax or phone, from their car on the way to the airport, or at major train stations. And the comforts of business travel don't stop there. On arrival back in Britain, there are arrivals lounges that enable business travellers to shower, eat breakfast and go straight into the office after a 'red-eye' flight.

And when it comes to staying in hotels, downgrading to a three- or four-star property is not the depressing experience that it was some years ago. Budget accommodation has improved in leaps and bounds; the hotels are usually modern, well-maintained and up to the minute in terms of hi-tech gadgetry such as dataports, idd phones, decent-size desks and ergonomic seating in the rooms. Greater hotel choice has helped the process. Express by Holiday Inn is in the vanguard of this trend.

Business travellers are, naturally, féted by the airlines and hotels. It is these customers that account for the highest profits, so they need to be looked after and recognised as such. It is for this reason that frequent flyer programmes and hotel loyalty schemes have proliferated. Business travellers can earn miles or points while travelling on business, then use them at their leisure. One of the most useful benefits of being a member of such a scheme is the access it gives to airline lounges, upgrades and priority wait-listing on over-booked flights. Finding the time to redeem thousands of air miles is often a problem, though, and billions of them go unused each year.

Technology, of course, is playing an increasing role in alleviating the hassles of travelling on business, with the internet increasingly pivotal in all developments. Business travellers can already surf the net to check the lowest prices for flights and accommodation, then book online. However, some corporations have grave doubts over productivity issues if their staff are booking for themselves. Why should their high-paying executive 'waste' time doing that when a travel agent, who is paid far less, could do it instead?

Some companies, such as baked beans giant Heinz, have taken technology a step farther and bulk buy their travel like any other commodity, using e-auctions, and claim to save significant sums on their travel budget.

Early concerns by corporate travel managers of direct booking tools have been largely satisfied now. The difficulty in consolidating accounting practices, the tracking of travel policy compliance, their lack of experience and skills when it comes to booking complicated itineraries, and the concern that suppliers may not offer their best prices to the direct booker, have largely been eradicated. Having said that, the new generation of online booking tools still favour simple, point-to-point itineraries rather than anything more complicated.

Electronic ticketing has improved the life of a business traveller enormously, because of its speed. The system removes the queuing at tickets desks and generates less paperwork than before. The process of organising refunds on e-tickets is straightforward but time consuming – and some companies are concerned that millions of pounds' worth of unused e-tickets are going uncollected.

One technological advance that has never caught on is video-conferencing. Industry observers claimed it as a huge cost saving tool, but it seems business travellers' egos are at stake here as they like bragging to their colleagues that they have to travel to head office for a meeting.

Unstoppable, on the other hand, is the increasing use of the humble mobile phone. Already a pocket-sized computer terminal, with instant web access, it means that the phone becomes an airline ticket and a check-in and loyalty mechanism. En route to the airport, it will know the status and location of your flight and, once you have arrived, it will guide you to the right terminal and car park.

Such advances in telephony also mean that the airline will know exactly when the last passenger will board the plane, which one day could easily translate into fewer delays.

When all's said and done, business travellers don't have a bad life after all. And it's going to get a lot better. ❧

GILLIAN UPTON is a freelance journalist specialising in business travel.

Business travel contacts

WEXAS
UK tel: 020 7589 3315
www.wexas.com
Long-established customised and corporate travel management

AMERICAN EXPRESS BUSINESS TRAVEL
www.americanexpress.com /businesstravel

AYSCOUGH TRAVEL
UK tel: 0207 357 9220
www.ayscough.co.uk

CARLSON WAGONLIT TRAVEL
UK tel: 01707 667788
www.carlsonwagonlit.com

FCM TRAVEL SOLUTIONS
UK tel: 0208 336 4000
www.fcmtravel.com

GRAY DAWES TRAVEL
UK tel: 0845 6000250
www.gray-dawes.co.uk

GUILD OF EUROPEAN BUSINESS TRAVEL AGENTS

www.gebta.org
Official body representing business travellers

GUILD OF TRAVEL MANAGEMENT COMPANIES (GTMC)
UK tel: 020 7637 1091
www.gtmc.org
Expertise and professional qualifications – the 'Certificate in Business Travel' (CBT).

HOGG ROBINSON – CORPORATE TRAVEL SERVICES
UK tel: 01252 370777
www.hoggrobinson.co.uk

PORTMAN TRAVEL
UK tel: 020 7255 6555
www.portmantravel.co.uk

THE TRAVEL COMPANY
UK tel: 020 7262 5040
www.thetravelcompany. co.uk

Related websites

www.abt-travel.com
Association of Business Travellers website

www.bradmans.com
Business guide books and meeting places worldwide

ww.btbtravel.com
Information, news and resources for the business traveller

www.btnmag.com
Business traveller news

www.businesstraveller. co.uk
Business Traveller magazine

www.red24.com
www.crg.com
Two companies offering travel security consultancy

www.gonative.co.uk
Accommodation solutions

www.iht.com
The International Herald Tribune site, with the business travel column 'The Frequent Traveller'.

www.LaptopTravel.com
Services and kit to ensure accessibility abroad

The expatriate traveller
by Nicki Grihault

SOME TRAVELLERS DON'T JUST STOP FOR TWO DAYS, but stay for two years. This breed, called expatriates, is found in most corners of the world. To 'expatriate' means to move away from one's native country and adopt a new residence abroad. Although financial incentives top the list of reasons for becoming an expatriate traveller, fast-tracking a career or conversely 'downsizing' are other common reasons, as are enjoying a more satisfying or balanced lifestyle or finding a safer or healthier place to bring up children. Expatriate experiences are diverse – it's hard to compare an accompanied lecture post involving living by the beach in Sydney with going to remote Kazakhstan as an unaccompanied construction engineer. What they do have in common is an expatriate contract which offers a competitive and sometimes tax-free salary, and range of other benefits.

You may be contemplating a post in the lucrative telecommunications industry in Finland, setting up a cider press in the Dordogne or taking a law job in far-flung Mauritius as an excuse to go diving. However, the first step is to think about the practical and psychological implications of your dream, before making the move.

To be or not to be

Expatriate postings generally last for two years, with a minimum of period of six months. The consequences of relocating your life need to be carefully considered and/or dealt with before you go. Practical aspects can range from the financial to health and security issues to language considerations. Psychological concerns vary by circumstance.

If you're single, relocation is more simple, but potentially more isolating than if you have a spouse or family. In the days of the dual career, taking an expatriate posting requires a little more thought and discussion between partners. An unhappy spouse is the most frequently cited reason for breaking a contract, and many companies now realise that the spouse and family need as much support as the employee. Some even offer an accompanying spouse allowance. It's important to give your partnership a realistic appraisal before putting it under the strain of relocation, and to deal with any potential partnership or family issues likely to be affected by the move. Going abroad will not patch up a bad marriage if it is not the best move for both of you; instead the cracks are more likely to show.

An unaccompanied posting may be an option if dual-career, dull or danger-zone reasons apply. This may work if it is a weekly commute, but its effects on a marriage need to be considered carefully. Net Expat (www.netexpat.com) assists dual-career couples, but as many countries won't issue work permits to 'trailing spouses' (a growing percentage of whom are now men), accompanying partners would do well to check out www.career-in-your-suitcase.com (run by mobile career specialist Jo Parfitt) for great ideas. Or read *A Moveable Marriage: Relocate Your Relationship Without Breaking It* (Expatriate Press, 2003).

Up and away

Once you've made the decision to go, there is a plethora of publications and websites devoted to living and working abroad. *Living Abroad Magazine* (www.livingabroadmagazine.com) profiles those who have taken the plunge; and useful books include *Live and Work Abroad: A Guide for Modern Nomads* (Vacation Work) and *The Expert Expatriate: Your Guide to Successful Relocation Abroad* (Intercultural Press; www.interculturalpress.com). *The Weekly Telegraph* (www.expat.telegraph.co.uk/global) deals with practical aspects of a move as well as offering online expat mentors around the world. Membership of Expat Network Ltd (www.expatnetwork.com) offers jobs as well as country guides, links and advice from old hands.

Culture shock

Getting married and moving house top the stress list, but expatriates have to deal with the stress of relocating a whole life. This particular stress is known as culture shock. Every expatriate will feel it to a greater or lesser degree, and the symptoms can last up to a year. Culture shock can include debilitating symptoms such as depression, headaches and sleeplessness – not to mention wanting to go straight home again.

Researching the destination and preparing for it will lessen its impact. Country-specific guides exist for living and working in tried and tested places: Western Europe, Australia or New Zealand, America or Canada. Check out the lists at Vacation Work (www.vacationwork.co.uk), Survival Books (www.survivalbooks.net) and How to Books (www.howtobooks.co.uk). Websites www.euroexpats.com, www.expatica.com and www.justlanded.com all cater to expatriates in Europe. Whilst there are no less than three magazines dealing with all things Spanish (and a plethora of websites), your move to Russia may be less clearly signposted, and you'll find even less on the shelves for Borneo. But Culture Shock! Guides (www.cultureshockguides.com) publish over 100 country guides written by and aimed at expatriates as well as a Parent's and a Wife's guide to living abroad.

Taking the time to introduce young children to the idea of moving, through books available from www.expatbooks.com, pays dividends.

Luckily, where the books and sites run out, organisations offering country briefings come into their own. The membership organisation Employment Conditions Abroad (www.eca-international.com) offers in-depth country briefing notes online or on CD-ROM. Richard Lewis Communications (www.crossculture.com) also offers online learning. Face-to-face briefings are offered by the well-established Farnham Castle (www.farnhamcastle.com) and Culture Shock Consulting (www.cultureshockconsulting.com). Larger companies will send employees, and the better ones, the whole family. If they don't, it may prove a good investment.

Education

Depending on the age of children, education will be a central concern. Options largely divide into state schools (perhaps preferable on a long-term posting), private schools and fee-paying international schools, which often have a British curriculum and good academic results. Search on www.international-schools.com to find if there is an international school in the location you're considering, and www.cobisec.org for British International Schools. UK boarding schools can be found on www.schoolsearch.org.uk. If you're really in the sticks, a British curriculum correspondence course is available from World-wide Education Service at www.weshome.demon.co.uk.

Finance

An expatriate job package needs to be analysed bearing in mind the cost of living in the destination. For example, you'd expect a better salary going to Tokyo, where the cost of living is high, than to Buenos Aires. In addition to a competitive and perhaps tax-free salary, paid in UK currency, you'd look for perks such as free housing, schooling for children and medical insurance, superannuation or pensions contributions, removal costs, language classes, trips home, end-of-contract gratuity and repatriation costs, and so on. Hardship postings, like that engineering one in Kazakhstan, are compensated with hard cash and more home leave.

Make sure you have some financial support with you in case your salary is delayed, and keep up your National Insurance payments back home. HSBC Bank International has a range of tools on their website (www.offshore.hsbc.com) including an expenses calculator, and Barclays (www.barclays.co.uk/expats) has a guide to managing your money. E-guides giving tax advice to expatriates can be found at www.taxcafe.co.uk, and at Life Abroad (www.lifeabroad.co.uk), a consortium of companies including solicitors, tax, property and offshore financial experts holds seminars in the UK. A list of financial advisors can be found at www.expats.org.uk.

Health and security

Many companies include provision for health care as part of a package, but if you need insurance, Medibroker (www.medibroker.com), an established and reliable independent health insurance broker, will help you find the appropriate insurer for your circumstances.

Make sure you take prescription drugs with you, and add emergency repatriation to your policy if serious illness isn't catered for at your destination.

Security is a key issue in today's expatriate world. The Foreign Office (www.fco.gov.uk) gives the official line on how safe countries or regions are, informed by embassies based in the location.

Shipping stuff

Don't take it unless you need to. In some countries, such as Singapore and Taiwan, electrical goods are almost the price of an adapter, so why cart the DVD player over? A whole host of international movers exists to cater to your needs, many advertised on the web, such as www.shipmystuff.com, who will also transport vehicles. However, expat tales abound of lousy packing and breakages. My advice is get a personal recommendation, at least from your company. Supervise the packing or do it yourself. Large personal effects will have to be sent by sea, so make provision for delay by taking essential items with you.

Housing

Days to weeks may be spent in a hotel before suitable accommodation can be found. Housing then varies by employer and location, from a serviced compound to an allowance to get your own place which may range from an apartment bang in the city centre to a spacious house in the country. Some expatriate housing is purpose-built, but if you are renting a local place check what to expect – amenities, hidden charges, etc. Word-of-mouth or expatriate noticeboards or newspapers are often useful, especially for obtaining furniture. Accommodation is usually secured through ads in the paper or agencies, similar to back home.

Help in-country

Air travel, telephones and television transformed expatriate life in the twentieth century. In the twenty-first, the internet has revolutionised the expatriate experience. Now, not only can you order job lots of Marmite from www.britishexpatsupplies.co.uk, even if in Outer Mongolia, you can read the *Yorkshire Post* or your local paper online at www.wrx.zen.co.uk. Perhaps more importantly, you can e-chat to people in your prospective location and find a club, nursery or furniture shop. You can keep up with news and sports back home at www.britishexpat.com; join online support communities www.newcomersnetwork.com, www.expatriates. com, www.expatfocus.com or www.escapeartist.com; and stay in touch via email.

Directories of services in English exist in larger expatriate communities, such as the Anglo Phonebook in Nice and Hamburg in Your Pocket in Germany. Local newspapers where you can find anything from a club to a counsellor can be found online at www.refdesk.com or The Internet Public Library (www.ipl.org).

Starting a family can seem a good idea for the non-working woman, and websites like www.expatmum.com and www.expatwoman.com, based in the UAE, can help. Tara, a new mother in Paris, found networking organisation Message Mother Support Group (http://messageparis.org) a godsend and was able to set up a vintage clothing business with the aid of a cheap international telephone service.

In Botswana's capital Gaborone, however, where relatively few expatriates live, support, entertainment and work opportunities may be limited. But domestic help, inexpensive in many developing countries and welcomed as a source of employment there, makes the practicalities of having a baby easier, and smaller expatriate communities tend to be tight-knit.

Single expatriates risk isolation, and find that it helps to get involved and take up new hobbies instead of becoming a permanent fixture at the bar. One single man found getting a dog made him go home as well as exercise. For single women, cultural constraints seem to be the biggest issue.

Taking the kids

Finding appropriate things to do can be a problem for mothers with young

Expatriate services

Employment Conditions Abroad
www.eca@eca-international.com

How To Books
www.howtobooks.co.uk

The Fry Group
www.thefrygroup.co.uk

World-wide Education Service
www.weshome.demon.co.uk

Related websites

www.criterionworld.com

www.escapeartist.com/

www.expatexpert.com/

www.expatfocus.com/

www.expatnetwork.com/

www.expat-reloc.com

www.expattax.co.uk/

www.expatworld.net

www.outpostexpat.nl

children in some countries – for instance, in Taiwan, leisure activities for children are few as all of them attend after-school classes. And while in Cyprus you can head to the beach and the waterpark, in Russia ballet and music lessons are more readily available.

Flexibility and the ability to adapt are key qualities for expatriate families to cultivate – along with a sense of humour. The Hash House Harriers (www.gthhh.com), 'the drinking club with a running problem', is a fun expat club that caters for everyone.

No limits

With a little forward planning, the expatriate traveller can make a move that will benefit their career, their pocket and their lifestyle. For the open-minded and adventurous expatriate traveller, living and working in a place gives a depth of understanding that can't be achieved when passing through: it's a meal versus a snack.

That, coupled with challenging and exciting work and often a lifestyle with more time for friends, family and interests, can make it addictive. Being uprooted from the constraints of normal life and your own culture is liberating, and time freed up often leads to the development of new creative or sporting interests, as well as enjoying what's on offer in a new part of the world.

Barrister Tom, for instance, qualified as a dive instructor in a year in Mauritius; and a BBC journalist in Sri Lanka became an advanced waterskier in two. For some, it is time to write the novel. Adults may broaden their perspectives when living abroad, but their children will become a blend of cultures.

These are referred to as Third Culture or Trans-Culture Kids – TCKs – by TCK World (www.tckworld.com), the largest organisation dedicated to studying and supporting them. If handled correctly, children can be enriched by the experience of living abroad, growing up to be independent, confident, open-minded citizens of the world who often take up international careers themselves. Many expatriate travellers find it hard to come home, and go on to become serial expatriates or uprooters, working their way around the world. ❧

NICKI GRIHAULT grew up in Kenya, Malawi and Mauritius, and has since lived in Australia, Italy and India. She is the author of 'Working in Asia' and 'Culture Smart India', and a contributing editor to 'Trip' magazine.

Working your way around the world
by Susan Griffith

SHORT OF EMIGRATING OR MARRYING A NATIVE, working abroad is an excellent way to experience a foreign culture from the inside. The plucky Briton who spends a few months on a Queensland cattle station will have a different tale to tell about Australia from the one who serves behind the bar in a Sydney pub. Yet both will experience the exhilaration of doing something completely unfamiliar in an alien setting.

Working abroad is one of the means by which it is possible to stay overseas for an extended period, to have a chance to get below the surface of a foreign culture, to meet foreign people on their own terms and to gain a better perspective on your own culture and habits. The kind of job you find will determine the stratum of society in which you will mix and therefore the content of the experience. The traveller who spends a few weeks picking olives for a Cretan farmer will get a very different insight into the life and times of modern Greece from the traveller who looks after the children of a wealthy Athenian shipping magnate. And both will probably have more culturally worthwhile experiences than the traveller who settles for working at a beach café frequented only by his or her partying compatriots.

Anyone with a taste for adventure and a modicum of nerve has the potential for exploring far-flung corners of the globe on very little money. In an ideal world, it would be possible to register with an international employment agency and wait to be assigned to a glamorous job as an underwater photography model in the Caribbean, history co-ordinator for a European tour company or ski tow operator in New Zealand. But jobs abroad, like jobs at home, must be ferreted out. The internet has had an enormous impact and those prepared to spend some time can make their way through the deluge of information to specific job listings overseas.

Exchange organisations and agencies

At the risk of oversimplifying the range of choices, the aspiring working traveller either fixes up a definite job before leaving home or takes a gamble on finding something on the spot. There is a lot to recommend prior planning, especially to travelling novices – students taking a gap year for instance – who have never travelled abroad and who feel some trepidation at the prospect.

A range of mediating organisations and agencies (whether public or private, charitable or commercial, student or general) exists to assist those who wish to fix up a job before leaving home. Some accept a tiny handful of individuals who satisfy stringent requirements, others accept almost anyone who can pay the required fee. For example, various agencies arrange for large numbers of young people to spend the summer working at children's summer camps in the USA, as English teachers in the Far East (mostly for university graduates) and as volunteers on Israeli kibbutzim.

Students occupy a privileged position since a number of schemes are open only to them. Student exchange organisations can help with the nitty-gritty of arranging work abroad (see factbox): for example BUNAC (British Universities North America Club) has a choice of programmes – not all confined to students – in the US, Canada, Australia, New Zealand, South Africa, Ghana and, most recently, Costa Rica and Peru. IST Plus acting on behalf of the Council on International Educational Exchanges offers working opportunities and/or internships in the US, Canada, China, Thailand, Australia and New Zealand, including some for people pursuing specific careers. Lesser-known organisations can arrange short term jobs on Polish or Andalusian summer camps, Norwegian or Swiss farms, French or Israeli archaeological digs, in Maltese youth hostels and Nepalese villages.

It would be wrong, of course, to assume that the love (or shortage) of money is at the root of all decisions to work abroad. Paid work in developing nations is rarely available outside mainstream aid agencies (such as VSO), which require specific training and skills and (in most cases) a two-year commitment. Yet many world travellers arrange to live for next to nothing while doing something positive for a local community. For example, enterprising working travellers have participated in interesting projects that range from helping a local native settlement to build a community centre in Arctic Canada to working at Mother Teresa's charity in Calcutta. Almost without exception, volunteers must be self-funding. For anyone with a green conscience, numerous conservation organisations throughout the world welcome volunteers for short or long periods who want to plant trees, count endangered birds and carry out research on coral reefs; again, volunteers must be prepared to pay for the privilege of helping.

Seasonal work

Most itinerant job-seekers will have to depend on the two industries that survive on seasonal labour: tourism and agriculture. Campsite operators, hoteliers and catering managers from Cannes to Cape Town depend on a temporary workforce. Anyone with some hometown restaurant experience and possibly an acquaintance with a second language is well placed to fix up a job ahead of time by sending a mass of speculative applications to winter and summer tour operators or to the hotels and campsites listed in tourist guides or on websites.

Farmers throughout the developed world are unable to bring in their harvests without assistance from outside their local community and often reward their itinerant labour force well. Finding out where harvesting jobs can be found is a matter of asking around and being in the right place at the right time. Specialist websites can also be useful such as www.pickingjobs.com and for New Zealand only www.seasonalwork.co.nz.

The organic farming movement is a useful source of agricultural contacts especially the organisation WWOOF (World Wide Opportunities on Organic Farms). National WWOOF co-ordinators compile a list of their member farmers willing to provide free room and board to volunteers who help out and who are genuinely interested in furthering the aims of the organic movement. Anyone can obtain these lists for a modest joining fee. WWOOF has affiliates in such countries as Turkey, Togo and Korea as well as Europe, North America and the Antipodes.

Other temporary options

The other major fields of temporary overseas employment are English teaching (see separate chapter) and au pairing. Since 2003 au pair agencies in the UK have not been allowed to charge the applicant a fee which means that the majority of British agencies now concentrate on placing foreign au pairs with paying client families in the UK rather than sending British au pairs abroad. Au pair placement was something that was always done by telephone and correspondence rather than requiring a face-to-face interview, so it is an activity that is very well suited to the web. Internet databases such as au-pair-box.com, aupairsearch.com, aupairconnect.com, au-pair.net and aupair-agency.com enable families and applicants to engage in DIY arrangements. Prospective au pairs are invited to upload their details onto a website (normally free of charge) which can then be accessed by registered families. If relying on the internet it is essential to ascertain exactly the nature of the situation and the expectations of your new employer, and to have a fallback plan if it doesn't work out. If the online agency is simply a database provider, they will not be able to offer back-up.

The casual-cum-seasonal job is always easier to secure on the spot. Advice will be freely given by expats and fellow travellers if sought. If looking for casual work on farms or trying to fix up a passage on a transatlantic yacht, for example, a visit to a village pub frequented by farmers, yachties or the local expatriate community is usually worth dozens of speculative applications from home.

Less structured possibilities abound. Enterprising travellers have managed to earn money by doing a bizarre range of odd jobs, from selling home-made peanut butter to American tourists or busking on the bagpipes, to doing Tarot readings on a Mediterranean ferry or becoming film extras in Cairo or Bombay.

Red tape

Every country in the world has immigration policies that are job protection schemes for their own nationals. The European Union is meant to have done away with all that, though red tape snags persist for those who want to work for more than three months. Note that full mobility of labour with the ten countries that joined the Union in 2004 will not be in place for up to seven years. Outside the EU, work authorisations become decidedly tricky, unless you participate in a government-sponsored scheme such as the Japan Exchange & Teaching/JET programme (www.jet-uk.org) or the Swiss Hotels Association's summer placement scheme for

Useful Addresses

Agriventure, International Agricultural Exchange Association (IAEA), Speedwell Farm Bungalow, Nettle Bank, Wisbech, Cambridgeshire PE14 0SA, tel/fax 01945 450999, www.agriventure.com. Places candidates aged 18-30 on farms in the USA, Canada, Australia, New Zealand and Japan.

Archaeology Abroad, 31-34 Gordon Square, London WC1H 0PY, tel 020-8537 0849, www.britarch.ac.uk/archabroad. Provides information about unpaid archaeological fieldwork outside the UK in its publication Archaeology Abroad published on CD-ROM in spring and autumn volumes each year; annual subscription costs £20.

BUNAC (British Universities North America Club), 16 Bowling Green Lane, London EC1R 0QH, tel 020 7251 3472, fax 020 7251 0215, www.bunac.org.

Camp America, 37a Queen's Gate, London SW7 5HR, tel 020 7581 7333, www.campamerica.co.uk.

Global Choices, Barkat House, 116-118 Finchley Road, London NW3 5HT, tel 020 7433 2501, www.globalchoices.co.uk. Voluntary work, internships, practical training and work experience in Argentina, Australia, Austria, Brazil, Ghana, Ireland, Nepal, Portugal, South Africa, Spain, UK and USA.

Holidaybreak, Overseas Recruitment Department, tel 01606 787525, www.holidaybreakjobs.com. Recruits up to 2000 campsite couriers and children's couriers for the self-drive camping brands Eurocamp and Keycamp. Contracts are between April and September. The courier's job is to clean tents and caravans between visitors, greet clients and deal with difficulties.

IST Plus Ltd, Rosedale House, Rosedale Road, Richmond, Surrey TW9 2SZ, tel 020 8939 9057, www.istplus.com. Partner agency in UK delivering programmes on behalf of CIEE (Council on International Educational Exchange).

Jobs in the Alps, www.jobs-in-the-alps.com. Agency arranges summer and winter jobs in French and Swiss hotels and restaurants in alpine resorts, for students with suitable language skills.

Kibbutz Representatives, 16 Accommodation Road, London NW11 8EP (020-8458 9235/ fax 020-8455 7930, www.kibbutz.org.il.

Natives.co.uk, 39-40 Putney High St, London SW15 1FP, tel 08700 463355/ fax 08700 62636, www.natives.co.uk. For finding jobs in ski and summer resorts.

WWOOF (World Wide Opportunities on Organic Farms), PO Box 2675, Lewes, E Sussex BN7 1RB, tel 01273 476286, www.wwoof.com.

EU students (www.hoteljob.ch), or unless you qualify for special schemes, like the recently expanded New Zealand working holiday visa for travellers aged 18 to 30.

Apart from these specific programmes, the job-seeker from overseas must find an employer willing to apply to the immigration authorities on his or her behalf well in advance of the job's starting date, while they are still in their home country. This is easier for high-ranking nuclear physicists and pop stars than for mere mortals, though there are exceptions, especially in the field of English teaching. Bureaucratic difficulties do make participation in an organised exchange programme appealing, as the red tape is taken care of by the sponsoring organisation.

Planning in advance

Anyone contemplating a stint of serious travelling funded by jobs en route can take some practical steps in the months before departure to prepare for such a trip. In addition to the obvious ones, such as working overtime to save money and investigating visa regulations, you can enhance your employability by collecting together potentially useful documents (character or job references, copies of a short CV, first aid certificate, diplomas in sailing, cooking, computing) or even by doing a course (language, TEFL). One tip is to scan these and email them to yourself so that you can access them from any internet terminal worldwide. And don't forget to pack a smart outfit for interviews.

As in any job hunt, contacts are often the key to success. It is always worth broadcasting your intentions to third cousins and pen friends left over from when you were 12 in case they divulge the details of potentially useful contacts.

Some travellers have their future career prospects in view when they go abroad, for example to teach English as a foreign language, to work on an English language newspaper or for a marketing company. This is easier for people with acknowledged qualifications who can seek information from the professional body or journals in their field of expertise. The internet is a particularly good tool in this case. Try for example www.seasonworkers.com, for summer jobs, outdoor sports jobs, gap year projects and ski resort jobs, the non-commercial free Jobs Abroad Bulletin (www.jobsabroadbulletin.co.uk) and www.anyworkanywhere.com.

Whether you set off to work abroad with the help of a mediating organisation or with the intention of living by your wits, you are bound to experience the usual rewards of travelling, encountering interesting characters and lifestyles, collecting a wealth of anecdotes, increasing your self-reliance, feeling that you have achieved something. Setbacks are inevitable, but it is amazing how often a setback leads to a success once you are on the track.

True 'working holidays' are rare, though they do exist. For example, travellers have exchanged their labour for a free trip with an outback Australian camping tour operator or have earned a free stay in a holiday village in Spain (called Englishtown) by exchanging English conversation with language learners. But in most cases, the expression 'working holiday' is an oxymoron in the same way as 'cruel kindness'. Jobs are jobs wherever you do them. There is seldom scope for swanning around art galleries, cafés and clubs if you are picking grapes seven days a week or teaching English on a Saudi oil base. Sometimes the most distasteful jobs of all are the ones that allow you to save quickly to finance the next leg of your journey.

Those who have shed their unrealistic expectations are normally exhilarated by the novelty and challenge of working abroad. Any individual with guts and gusto, whether a student or a grandmother, has the potential for funding him or herself to various corners of the globe. Persistence, optimism and resilience are the only ingredients essential for such a venture. ✑

Susan Griffith is a travel writer and editor based in Cambridge, who writes books and articles for adventurous working travellers, including the classic 'Work Your Way Around the World' and 'Teaching English Abroad', and also 'Taking a Gap Year' and 'Gap Years for Grown-ups'.

Teaching English abroad
by Susan Griffith

EVERY MORNING AND EVENING THE STREETS of Bogotá, Bratislava, Beijing and a thousand other cities are thronged with people rushing to their English lessons. The demand for instruction or just conversation practice with people who speak English as their mother tongue is enormous, and will continue to increase for the foreseeable future.

The most recent impetus to learn English has come from the explosion in use of the internet, as the vast majority of its sites employ the English language. Even in countries where English has been kept at a distance, people are flocking to English classes so that they won't be left behind.

However the time for assuming that a charming manner and a neat haircut are enough to land you a job is over in all but a handful of places, such as Bangkok and Mexico City. Standards are creeping up, partly because of a dramatic increase in the number of people gaining a qualification in TEFL (Teaching English as a Foreign Language). The number of both public and private institutes in the UK, North America, Australia and New Zealand turning out certified TEFL teachers has greatly increased in the past five to seven years, creating a glut of teachers, especially in the major cities of Europe.

Having sounded that warning note, there are still areas of the world, from Ecuador to Slovenia, Lithuania to Cambodia, where the boom in English language learning seems to know no bounds. In cowboy schools and back-street agencies, being a native speaker and adopting a professional manner are sometimes sufficient qualifications to get a job. But for more stable teaching jobs in recognised language schools, you will have to sign a contract (minimum three months, usually nine) and have some kind of qualification, which ranges from a university degree to a certificate in education with a specialisation in ELT (English Language Teaching is now the preferred label).

TEFL training

The only way to outdo the competition and make the job hunt (not to mention the job itself) easier is to do a TEFL training course. The two standard recognised qualifications that will improve your range of job options by an order of magnitude are the Cambridge Certificate in English Language Teaching to Adults (CELTA) and the certificate in TESOL (Teaching English to Speakers of Other Languages) offered by Trinity College London.

A list of centres, both in the UK and abroad, is available from these two accrediting bodies: Cambridge ESOL (based at 1 Hills Road, Cambridge CB1 2EU, tel 01223 553355, www.CambridgeESOL.org/teaching) and Trinity College London (based at 89 Albert Embankment, London SE1 7TP, tel 020 7820 6100, www.trinitycollege.co.uk).

Certificate courses involve at least 100 hours of rigorous training with a practical emphasis. They are offered full time for four weeks or part time over several months, and the cost averages at between £850 and £950. Although there are no fixed prerequisites, apart from a suitable level of language awareness, not everyone who applies is accepted.

Short introductory courses in TEFL are also available, and these vary enormously in quality and price. Although they are mainly intended to act as preparatory programmes for more serious courses, many people who have completed a brief training course go on to teach. Many (but not all) training centres have good contacts with language schools worldwide and can assist with the job hunt.

Finding a job

Teaching jobs are either fixed up from home or sought out on location. Obviously it is less nerve-racking to have everything sorted out before departure, but this option is usually available only to the highly qualified or to paying volunteers. It also has the disadvantage that you don't know what you're letting yourself in for. One of the possible advantages of fixing up a job well in advance is that you then have a chance of obtaining the appropriate work permit.

English teaching is one area of employment in which governments are relatively generous, since locals are not being deprived of jobs. Yet few nations will process visas unless applications are lodged outside the country. Employers of TEFL teachers in many countries (for example Korea, Taiwan, Turkey and Morocco) can usually sort out visas or at least set the wheels in motion before their employees' arrival.

To fix up a job in advance, make use of the internet – increasingly the preferred recruitment tool – and check adverts in the education section of the Guardian every Tuesday. The best time of year is between Easter and July. In a few cases, particularly for work at summer language camps on the continent, a carefully crafted CV and an enthusiastic personality are as important as ELT training and experience. Well-qualified ELT teachers will already be aware of possibilities at the prestigious end of the market, for example with major providers such as the British Council.

Substantial numbers of teachers are employed by the major language school chains such as International House (www.ihworld.com), Language Link (www.languagelink.co.uk), English First (www.englishfirst.com) and Inlingua (www.inlingua.com). Increasingly online recruitment is replacing the old-style commercial recruitment agencies that matched teachers' CVs with suitable vacancies in client schools.

ELT opportunities are available through a host of voluntary organisations such as VSO and educational charities. There is also increasing scope for untrained but eager volunteers willing to pay an agency such as i-to-i (ww.i-to-i.com), Teaching & Projects Abroad (www.teaching-abroad.co.uk) and Travellers Worldwide (www.travellersworldwide.com) to place them in a language teaching situation abroad.

The alternative to pre-arranging a job is to present yourself in person to language school directors. Jobs in any field are difficult to get without an interview, and English teaching is no exception. Language institutes cannot, under normal operating circumstances, hire someone sight unseen merely on the basis of a CV and photo. Moreover, when the need for a teacher arises, that vacancy must usually be filled immediately. Therefore it is often more effective to base yourself in your preferred destination, introduce yourself to the directors of language schools and relevant companies and be prepared to wait for a vacancy to arise.

It is still possible for people who are well spoken and well dressed and have a confident manner to charm their way into a classroom. A university degree often cuts more ice than a TEFL qualification, particularly in the Far East, where a degree is a prerequisite to getting a visa. If you are job hunting in a capital city, the British Council may be able to provide a list of language schools or advise (informally) on the availability of teaching jobs: much depends on the goodwill of the staff. To gather together a list of addresses where you can ask for work, consult the Yellow Pages (often accessible online), read the adverts in the English-language papers, visit centres where foreigners study the local-language or English-language bookshops to check the notice boards and ask the staff for leads. Business schools and vocational training institutes often need teachers of commercial English.

Several factors will affect the length of time it will take to find an opening. Timing can be crucial; aim to conduct your job hunt in the month before term begins (usually late August/September or around Christmas; summers are usually hopeless). Of course, a knowledge of the vernacular language is an advantage (especially in the Spanish-speaking world), as is the ability to look convincing while carrying a briefcase. If you have no luck in the major cities, consider trying provincial cities less frequented by foreigners (Plzen rather than Prague, Eskisehir not Istanbul, Chongqing rather than Beijing).

An alternative to working for a language school is to set yourself up as a freelance private tutor. While undercutting the fees charged by the commercial institutes, you can still earn more than you would as a contract teacher. Normally you will have to be fairly well established in a place before you can attempt to support yourself by private teaching, preferably with some decent premises in which to give your lessons (either singly or in a group), and with an aggressive marketing strategy of some sort.

You should bear in mind the disadvantages of working for yourself, such as frequent last-minute cancellations by clients, unpaid travelling time (if you teach in clients' homes or offices), no social security and an absence of professional support and teaching materials.

If you are less interested in making money than in integrating with a culture, exchanging English conversation for board and lodging may be an appealing possibility, which usually relies on having contacts or going through a fee-charging agency.

The job itself

Native-speaker teachers are nearly always employed to stimulate conversation rather than to teach grammar. Yet a basic knowledge of English grammar is a great asset, especially when more advanced pupils ask awkward questions.

At least some of the thousands of young people who blithely set off to market their tongue abroad should pause to picture in detail the range of likely scenarios they may encounter. The classroom might be an alcove in a Chinese teacher training college where there are no desks and insufficient light but 25 eager learners. It might be a 'conversation lounge' in a Japanese city, which has an atmosphere more akin to a dating agency than a classroom. You could be faced with a room full of exuberant Taiwanese seven-year-olds who expect you to sing songs and draw pictures. Or you might find yourself standing in front of a class of bored and disaffected Greek teenagers, forced by their ambitious parents to attend lessons after school to improve their chances of passing crucial exams for university entrance. Your 'class' may consist of a lone Peruvian businessman who, despite knowing very little English, expects to be able to swing a big deal with an American company after a few lessons from you. How far does your 'native-speakerhood' get you in these circumstances? Even a minimum of training and/or experience in teaching English is a tremendous advantage.

The wages paid to English teachers are usually reasonable, and in developing countries are quite often well in excess of the average local wage. In return you will be asked to teach some fairly unsociable hours, since most private English classes take place after working hours, and so schedules split between early morning and evening are commonplace.

Teaching of any kind is a demanding job and those who are doing it merely as a means of supporting their travelling habit may find it a disillusioning experience. At the same time, it offers opportunities for creativity, learning about other cultures and attitudes, making friends and, of course, travelling. ❧

Teaching English abroad

BÉNÉDICT SCHOOLS
PO Box 270
1000 Lausanne 9
Switzerland
Tel: 21 323 66 55
www.benedict-
international.com
Over 70 business and
language schools in
Europe (mostly in
Germany), Morocco and
Ecuador.

BERLITZ (UK) LTD
2nd Floor
Lincoln House
296-302 High Holborn
London
WC1V 7JH, UK
www.berlitz.com
450+ centres in 60
countries.

BRITISH COUNCIL
Education & Training
Group, Assistants
Programme
10 Spring Gardens
London SW1A 2BN, UK
Tel: 020 7389 4596
www.languageassistant.
co.uk
Language assistants aged
20-30 spend an academic
year helping local teachers
of English in many
countries of the world
from France to Venezuela.

CACTUS LANGUAGE
4 Clarence House
30-31 North St
Brighton BN1 1EB, UK
Tel: 0845 130 4775
www.cactustefl.com
Free advice service for
prospective teachers on
TEFL training courses.
Assistance with job hunt
for qualified teachers
including CV posting.

**CAMBRIDGE ASSESSMENT
(FORMERLY UNIVERSITY OF
CAMBRIDGE LOCAL
EXAMINATIONS
SYNDICATE)**
1 Hills Road
Cambridge CB1 2EU, UK
www.CambridgeESOL.org
Graduates of the 4-week
Certificate in English
Language Teaching to
Adults (CELTA) course
may be able to access job
placement service if
provided by course centre.

CfBT
The Centre for British
Teachers
60 Queens Road
Reading RG1 4BS, UK
Tel: 0118 902 1000/1621
www.cfbt.com
TEFL qualified
recruitment for CfBT
projects in Brunei,
Malaysia and Oman.

CG ASSOCIATES
83 Clarence Mews
London SE16 5DG, UK
Tel: 07802 211543
www.cgaweb.net
Education recruitment
consultancy, welcomes
applications from
graduates with a
recognised EFL/ESOL/ESL
qualification for vacancies
in Italy and worldwide.

**EF ENGLISH FIRST
TEACHER RECRUITMENT
& TRAINING**
Arthur House
Chorlton Street
Manchester M1 3EJ, UK
Tel: 0161 236 5521
www.englishfirst.com
Recruitment of teachers
for 200 EF schools in 16
countries including
Ecuador, Chile, Mexico,
Lithuania, Poland, Russia,
China, Indonesia.

**ELS LANGUAGE
CENTERS/BERLITZ**
International Division
400 Alexander Park
Princeton, NJ 08540, USA
Tel: 609 750 3512
www.els.edu
TEFL-qualified teachers
recruited for 45 franchised
schools worldwide,
primarily in the Middle
and Far East.

ERC RECRUITMENT
New Tyning
Stone Allerton
Axbridge
Somerset BS26 2NJ, UK
Tel 01934 713892
www.
erc-recruitment.co.uk
Recruitment agency for
vacancies in Germany,
Italy, Spain, Czech
Republic, Poland,
Hungary and Mexico, for
TEFL-qualified teachers.

**INLINGUA TEACHER
TRAINING**
Rodney Lodge
Rodney Road
Cheltenham
Glos GL50 1HX, UK
Tel: 01242 253171
www. inlingua-
cheltenham. co.uk
Offers Trinity TESOL
certificate courses and help
with job-finding in
Inlingua (or other) schools
worldwide.

INTERNATIONAL HOUSE
106 Piccadilly
London W1J 7 NL, UK
Tel: 020 7518 6970
www.ihworld.co.uk
Largest independent
British-based organisation
for teaching English, with
130 schools in 40+
countries.

**INTERNATIONAL TEFL
CERTIFICATE**
Kaprova 12
110 00 Prague 1

Czech Republic
Tel: 420 2-2481 4791
www.itc-training.com.
4-week certificate course
followed by worldwide job
guidance.

IST PLUS
Rosedale House
Rosedale Road
Richmond
Surrey TW9 2SZ, UK
Tel: 020-8939 9057
www.istplus.com
Partner agency in UK of
CIEE (Council on
International Educational
Exchange), organises
Teach in China and Teach
in Thailand programmes
for university graduates.

I-TO-I
Woodside House
261 Low Lane
Horsforth
Leeds LS18 5NY, UK
Tel: 0870 333 2332
www.i-to-i.com
Independent TEFL
training and volunteer
travel organisation which
places volunteer teachers
in many countries
worldwide.

LANGUAGE LINK
21 Harrington Road
London SW7 3EU, UK
Tel: 020 7225 1065
www. languagelink.co.uk
TEFL training and
recruitment agency which
places 200 qualified
(including newly
qualified) teachers in its
network of affiliated
schools in Slovakia, Russia,
Vietnam and China.

**LINGUARAMA
INTERNATIONAL**
Group Personnel Dept
Oceanic House
89 High St, Alton
Hampshire GU34 1LG, UK
Tel: 01420 80899
www.linguarama.com

Specialist in language
training for business.
Recruits qualified teachers
for over 20 centres in
Germany, France, Spain,
Italy and the Netherlands.

**SAXONCOURT & ENGLISH
WORLDWIDE**
59 South Molton St
London W1K 5SN, UK
Tel: 020 7491 1911
www.saxoncourt.com
Specialist educational
recruitment agency places
600+ qualified EFL
teachers in posts in Japan,
Taiwan, Poland, China,
Italy, Spain, Russia,
Thailand, Vietnam, Peru,
Brazil, etc.

**TEACHING & PROJECTS
ABROAD**
Aldsworth Parade
Goring, W Sussex
BN12 4TX, UK
Tel: 01903 708300
www.teaching-abroad.
co.uk
Large volunteer teaching
programmes in Romania,
Russia, India, Sri Lanka,
Ghana, Bolivia, Mexico,
Chile, China, etc. No TEFL
background required.

**VSO (VOLUNTARY SERVICE
OVERSEAS)**
317 Putney Bridge Road
London SW15 2PN, UK
Tel: 0208 780 7500
www.vso.org.uk
Development charity
sending large numbers of
English-language teachers
around the world.

**WALL STREET INSTITUTE
INTERNATIONAL**
Baltimore, Maryland, USA
www.wallstreetinstitute.
com
Chain of about 300
commercial language
institutes for adults,
employing hundreds of
full-time EFL teachers in

Europe, Turkey and Latin
America.

Further Reading

*Teaching English Abroad
by Susan Griffith*
Published every other year
by Vacation Work
Publications, 9 Park End
St, Oxford OX1 1HJ, UK
(www. vacationwork.
co.uk)

*EL Gazette Guide to English
Language Teaching Around
the World*
Published by the trade
newspaper *EL Gazette*. A
guide to TEFL courses
worldwide and an
introduction to the field.

TEFL recruitment
websites

www.eslcafe.com

www.TEFL.com

www.tefljobs.co.uk

www.englishjobmaze.com

www.jobs.edufind.com

www.eflweb.com

www.eslworldwide.com

www.jobsunlimited.co.uk
http://education.guardian.
co.uk/tefl

Other websites are
country specific, such as
www.ohayosensei.com
for jobs in Japan, or
www.ajarn.com for
teaching in Thailand.

Being a tour leader
by John Warburton-Lee

How many times have you been in some exotic part of the world and, caught up in the euphoria of the moment, looked at a guide leading a group on the sort of adventure that you enjoy and thought, 'I would love to do that job'? By comparison to their apparently carefree, action-packed, outdoor existence, your office job appears mundane, depressingly unadventurous and lacking any form of excitement. At that moment, the thought of waking up on the banks of the Zambesi or in a remote camp on the Annapurna circuit, and of spending your days battling your raft-full of excited clients down raging rapids or trekking in the shadow of the Himalayas appears far more romantic than the concept of leaving your home to fight with the commuter crush on the way to a desk full of flickering computer screens and ringing telephones. But before you fire off a letter of resignation to your managing director and shower an unsuspecting adventure tourism industry with your newly rewritten cv, it may be worth considering some of the practicalities.

To begin with, you should ask yourself what it is about foreign travel and adventure holidays that you enjoy so much. Apart from the more obvious pleasures, do you associate travelling with being free from all responsibilities, away from the pressures of deadlines and demanding clients? Is it about being able to take every day as it comes, moving on at whim, without a care in the world, not needing to answer to others? Is it about pushing yourself on challenges that take you towards your physical limits? Is travelling in the comforting knowledge that your secure job will ensure that your mortgage and all other bills are paid a subliminal part of your enjoyment? If any of these scenarios strike a chord, you have some hard truths to confront before putting the stamp on that resignation letter.

First of all, you may as well recognise that no one ever got rich from guiding. It is a lifestyle choice that has little, if anything, to do with paying mortgages or saving a nest egg for your retirement. Rates of pay are low, in many cases amounting to your keep plus a small amount of pocket money. Many companies get enough staff purely by giving them a free trip, and in some cases companies expect staff not only to work for them but also to pay a contribution towards their expenses for the privilege of doing so.

Secondly, working as a guide or tour leader requires an extremely high level of commitment. You are on call 24 hours per day and take on considerable responsibility for the safety of your clients, as well as their wellbeing and enjoyment. In addition to any specialist technical skills, such as mountain leadership or kayaking experience, guides often need to be able to act as group motivator, administrator, cook, driver, mechanic, equipment repairer, camp manager, medic, social worker and agony aunt. Every problem, from the most serious to the most trivial, will find its way straight to your tent door.

One company with a regular requirement for tour leaders is Dragoman

Overland, which employs around 70 overseas crew at any one time. Some leaders work alone, others with one or two other crew, driving groups of up to 24 clients of mixed nationality on itineraries lasting between two and 32 weeks through Africa, Asia and Latin America. Leaders may be deployed for up to 18 months at a time. They are on the road for about 11 months of a year, most of that time leading groups but with some breaks for rest and recuperation and vehicle maintenance.

"It is taken as read that our staff need to be very good drivers with an aptitude for mechanics, but the overriding requirement is excellent people skills," says Mike Sykes, Dragoman Overland's Managing Director. "We demand absolute honesty, guts, stamina and an unbelievably cheerful disposition. The leaders have to do much more than drive and maintain their vehicles. They must be able to manage all of the bureaucracy en route, handle the paperwork and formalities at border crossings and deal with any corruption. They must always be thinking ahead, picking up local route information and remaining alert for security threats. Within the group they need to be motivators with limitless stamina, be constantly aware of group dynamics and be ready to mediate if problems begin brewing between group members."

Sykes reckons that he can normally spot the qualities that he is looking for in a leader within five minutes of meeting someone. "We receive about 1, 000 applications per year. We interview roughly 250 people of whom half go forward to a two-week assessment at our base in Suffolk. Roughly 50 of the original 1, 000 will go forward to our three-month training programme and around 30 will finally make it out on the road."

Dragoman Overland's three-month training programme focuses on learning to drive, repair and maintain the company's vehicles (potential leaders must obtain their passenger carrying vehicle driving licence at their own expense). The programme also covers first aid; operations procedures; group dynamics; how to handle trip meetings; prevention of accidents and illnesses; accounts; the sales process; office work experience; and studying the areas to be visited. On completion of the training a leader/driver spends up to four months on the road apprenticed to an experienced leader before leading their own trips.

Dragoman Overland's leaders work for the company for an average of four years. "If new leaders are going to have problems," says Sykes, "it will normally be difficulty in handling the groups or simply not having the stamina to cope with living in close proximity to 24 people for whom they are responsible, operating on an average of five hours sleep per night."

The emphasis on people skills for group leaders is reiterated by Mark Hannaford, managing director of Across the Divide, a company specialising in mounting treks and cycle rides in remote parts of the world. "Our staff need to have a high level of experience in outdoor education and skills, but the job is mainly about being able to fit into the team and work well with clients. The core values that we look for in our staff are maturity, loyalty, integrity, dependability, good communication skills with people of all ages and backgrounds and the ability to remain calm in a crisis and manage a situation effectively until other help arrives. We tend to have people who are well travelled and have a broad view of the world.

It is important that everyone is fit and able to carry heavy loads – and a good sense of humour is essential."

Across the Divide mounts expeditions of between 30 and 100 clients, and operates in the field for a week to ten days, deploying staff in teams under the guidance of an expedition leader. Group leaders are responsible for up to 20 clients on a daily basis, working together with a local guide. Expedition doctors provide routine and emergency care for up to 50 people, normally with the support of a nurse or paramedic. Doctors are required to have recent accident and emergency department experience and need to be able to operate in field conditions without the level of back-up to which those used to working in hospitals will be accustomed.

Managing large groups in remote areas requires special skills and operating procedures. Across the Divide uses radios and satellite telephones to keep groups in close contact with each other and to facilitate overall control by the expedition leader.

"The ethos of the company is that of a small, close-knit family," says Hannaford. "We mainly recruit new staff through personal recommendations or through other members of staff, although occasionally we meet people whose personality and skills fit our way of doing things. We have a very small permanent staff and maintain a cadre of roughly 30 group leaders and doctors who take part in expeditions as required. In many ways our staff are the company. We have developed the company culture together, both on expeditions and through our twice-yearly staff training camps. The proof of the success of this formula has been evident when there have been serious incidents to manage and everyone has known exactly what their role is and how each other will react and the expedition leader has been able to work to each member of staff's particular strengths."

Each company in the adventure travel field has its own individual style of operating. Some guides enjoy the autonomy of working on their own, whilst others prefer the camaraderie and support of working in a close-knit team. It is extremely important to identify exactly how you will be expected to operate – only work in situations that you feel comfortable with. Dealing with exercise casualties on training courses is excellent practice, but it is a very different matter when you are leading a group on your own and you become faced with a real situation involving a traumatic injury and a group of novices who are frightened by what they have seen when help is a long way away.

Although many companies stress the importance of people skills, that does not in any way diminish the need for technical skills and qualifications. Companies looking for trekking, mountaineering, canoeing or diving guides, for example, will normally specify minimum standards of qualifications from the appropriate British authority such as the Mountain Leader Training Board or the British Sub Aqua Club. In addition, first aid qualifications or validated training will not only make you much more attractive to an employer but give you a great deal of confidence on the ground.

I am constantly amazed by the number of clients who come on arduous adventure trips to remote areas of the world with serious medical conditions that they fail to mention until they find themselves in difficulty. Diabetics, on the whole, are perfectly capable of maintaining their insulin levels, but it is worthwhile to know what to do just in case. Of more concern are those who turn out to have a history of epilepsy, heart conditions, psychiatric problems or, as in one recent instance, a difficult pregnancy. Expedition medicine can involve much more than treating blisters, strapping sore knees and issuing the odd sachet of Imodium, and all of this comes on top of the many other claims on a guide's time.

The life of a tour leader is often far from the glamorous, carefree existence that it may appear at first glance. Working in remote areas of Third World countries often means that the kinds of support systems that we take for granted at home, from garages and hospitals to something as elementary as restaurants where the food is safe to eat, are no longer there. Clients can be unreasonably demanding, utterly frustrating and have a habit of doing the worst possible thing at the most inconvenient moment. As a tour leader you must guide well within your own technical and physical capabilities so that you always have reserves of expertise, strength and stamina to give your clients when they need assistance. By definition, this means that the trips that you lead for commercial organisations may well be fulfilling in a leadership sense, but they are unlikely to satisfy any personal cravings for a physical challenge that will stretch you.

The rewards, however, justify all of the hassle. I never cease to get a thrill from working in areas of great natural beauty. There is a special satisfaction derived from enabling people to realise their dreams or aspirations, whether that involves showing them a part of the world they have never seen before or helping them to complete a physical challenge. For many clients an expedition is truly the experience of a lifetime, one that leaves them profoundly moved. At the end of a trek across the Namib Desert recently, one of my group, a young 18-stone cockney pipe-lagger, burst into tears. "John," he sobbed, "you cannot begin to understand what this means to me. Where I come from in the East End of London, the Namib Desert is unimaginable. It might as well be on Mars – and I have walked the whole way across it." The fact that he had been the joker of the party throughout the trek made his reaction all the more poignant.

If you do decide to post that letter of resignation and look for a job as a tour leader, it is worth looking at the classified section of the various outdoors and adventure travel magazines for companies advertising for staff. The Expedition Advisory Centre at the Royal Geographical Society maintains a register of personnel available for expeditions, with cvs for each person, and also publishes a bulletin of expeditions looking for people with particular skills. Some commercial companies do access the register of personnel when looking for staff, but it is more likely to produce positions on private adventures or scientific expeditions.

Finally, it is beholden to all tour leaders to remember that they bear a responsibility not only to their clients and the organisations that they work for, but to the peoples and places that they visit. Part of doing so is to ensure that you are in a position, through a combination of experience and research, to pass on as much information about the country that you are visiting as you can to assist your clients' ability to enjoy and understand the environment that they are in. It is up to a tour leader to set a standard for group behaviour and attitudes. Groups sometimes need to be educated to respect local cultures, to act in a way that is mindful of the sensitivities of the people whom they meet, and at all times to minimise their impact on the environment through good camp-craft and trail discipline. ⁊

JOHN WARBURTON-LEE is a travel writer and expedition leader. He has led expeditions in Africa and Latin America, which were described in 'Roof of Africa' and 'Roof of the Americas', and is a council member of the Scientific Exploration Society.

Crewing boats
by Alison Muir Bennett

IMAGINE A VOYAGE LIKE THIS... sailing out of Cape Town with Table Mountain and the great continent of Africa behind you, it takes a few days to get away from the influence of coastal currents before picking up the ocean breeze that will take you to the lonely island of Saint Helena, caught in a time warp. As you voyage you will be accompanied by sea birds and schools of dolphins that come to investigate the boat, and maybe the sighting of a whale. Then you have the chance of heading for the laid-back Caribbean or sailing into the spectacular Bay of Guanabara, where Rio de Janeiro and a whole new continent is waiting to be explored.

If the demands, pleasures, and challenges of ocean voyaging are your dream, it's easy enough to make your dream come true.

If you are considering the possibilities of sailing on a private yacht as a crew member, the best way to proceed is by registering your name for a small fee with organisations such as the Cruising Association (tel 020 7537 2828, website www.cruising.org.uk) or Crewseekers (tel 01489 578319, website www.crewseekers.co.uk). They hold lists of members or contributors requiring crew. Consult the personal advertisements in yachting magazines such as *Yachting* or *Yachting World*. Check out your local yacht club – ask the secretary what the procedure is. If you place an advertisement of your own, it should include the following information: name, nationality, sex, age, crewing experience, skills, date available and proposed duration of trip, desired destination, financial arrangements (contributory basis/ proposed payment) and a place/address where you can be contacted. It helps if you date the advertisement and add a photo.

It is very important to meet the skipper and see their yacht, as you will need to make assessments about their ability and the vessel's seaworthiness. Does it have the necessary equipment on board for all weather conditions: sails, navigation lights, navigation sextant and satellite, communications, life-raft, emergency tracking system and dinghy? Is the galley properly set up, are the heads adequate, what are the sleeping arrangements? Are the vessel's documents and the skipper's sailing certificates in order?

In return, they will want to know about your skills. You will be expected to have basic sailing skills at least, but more important than being an expert sailor is a willingness to do anything that may be required. Desirable skills include cooking, computer literacy, an aptitude for diesel mechanics, diving, electronics expertise, an inventive engineering ability, languages, medical knowledge, musical talent, navigation, sewing, experience as a teacher or nanny, and radio/communications experience. You will need to be organised to carry out your duties; for instance, if you've signed on as a cook, do you have recipes and adequate equipment on board? Mechanics should brush up on marine engines, check that manuals and tools are on board. If that's going to be your responsibility, you may want to take overalls. For sewing, do you have sail-repairing needles, 'palms' and other material on board?

Your own gear must be kept to a minimum and packed in a foldaway synthetic holdall. Keep your clothes in plastic bags. Your equipment should include: foul-weather gear, scarf, life-vest, safety harness, deck shoes, gloves, peaked hat, sun screen, sea-sickness remedy, personal medication, sunglasses and spare prescription glasses or lenses.

Keeping in touch needs to be organised. Before you leave, make sure that there is one person at home with whom you can co-ordinate your activities – that way you don't have several people to advise of your schedule. Your nominee can also collect your correspondence and forward it on to you. Make sure people understand that timings will be extremely flexible to save them anxiety when you don't call from, say, Cape Town, on a predetermined date.

Make sure people only use your surname with initials on correspondence, then it won't be accidentally filed under your christian name at your *poste restante*. International telephone calls are often a major exercise in those areas with limited facilities and major time differences. Email has made life easier, so you could consider using a service such as info@nautimail.com, website www.nautimail.com.

Skippers will ask you to contribute to general running costs, including food, mooring and immigration fees. The rate varies according to the situation, but it is usually around US$20-25 a day. It is not usual to contribute financially to yacht maintenance, although your elbow grease will be required. Apart from the 'onboard' living costs you agree, you will have to have a return ticket/MCO or the equivalent amount in travellers' cheques. Be prepared to 'bond' these with the skipper as he will be responsible to immigration and port authorities for crew members' repatriation. Keep all your documents in sealed plastic bags: passport, inoculation certificates, letters of reference, skill certificates, cash, cheques, tickets and insurance documents.

If you are looking for a paid job as skipper, deckhand or cook you will need references from previous skippers and certificates of competence. Information about certificates for all levels of competence is available from the Royal Yachting Association (tel 0845 345 0400, website www.rya.org.uk). Wages are minimal as living is 'all found' on board. Work is usually seasonal with charter and flotilla holiday companies or yacht deliveries. There are training establishments for skills associated with marine leisure activities and agencies which specialise in marine placement. Try the Hamble School of Yachting & Professional Training (tel 02380 452668, email tuition@hamble.co.uk) or Leisure Management International (tel 01983 280641, www.hamble.co.uk). Consult the small ads in the yachting magazines.

Having agreed on finances, duties, and intended destination, the last but most important factor of all is compatibility. In the end it does not matter whether the vessel is state of the art or just adequate or the weather is foul or fair, if you do not get on well together the voyage could be disastrous. This is the hardest thing to get right, since there is no real way of knowing before you are on the high seas. A weekend 'shake-down' cruise is recommended to give everyone the chance to assess each other and the situation, but you could still be in for some surprises if you are considering a long voyage – even if you are sailing with someone you already know well! Personality problems are greatly emphasised in the limited environment of a yacht at sea, the boat has a greater chance of surviving than the crew, and the skipper has the last word on everything, so you must be prepared to obey – like it or lump it!

There are pros and cons for leaving from your country of origin. Skippers usually have family and friends to sail with at the beginning of their voyage, so finding a place can be harder even if you are on home ground. It is when these friends have to return home that the skipper will need to find crew *en route*, and at certain seasonal bottlenecks itinerant crew can be much in demand. Some of the major ones include the Solent in May, Las Palmas and Saint Thomas in November, Grenada and Durban in December, Cape Town in January and Tahiti in April and September. So sometimes it is worth flying out to the area you wish to sail in and putting up a notice in the local yacht club, meeting place, *poste restante* or launderette. Groups of yachts travelling together often operate a 'net' on ham radio or VHF, where crew requirements can be announced. These opportunities for finding a crew position come easier with experience. If you are sailing from the UK, the beginning of May to the end of August is the optimum time; in the Mediterranean it is between the end of March and the end of September. The Caribbean season runs from the end of November until March, but if you are sailing from Europe you should be leaving to cross the Atlantic between the end of September and early November. The Pacific season is from April to September, so yachts should be transiting the Panama Canal during March. The season for the Indian Ocean, via the southerly islands, is July to October. The growing popularity of rallies provides added opportunities to crew for yachts that enter them, find out when the major ones take place from the Cruising Association, details as before or the World Cruising Club (tel 01983 296060, website www.worldcruising.com).

You should remember that sailing is an archaic form of transport. When you travel by yacht you are reliant on the elements to get you from A to B, not a timetable. You play a major role in achieving this, living by a 24-hour watch, sleeping, cooking, eating, cleaning, sail changing and taking the helm to fit in with that routine. Life at sea has to be learnt; the motion of the boat and sea conditions must be accommodated while you fulfil all your roles. Your normal routine: sleeping, washing, eating, all must to be adapted to life on board ship.

The golden rule is: one hand for you, one for the boat. Everything has to have its place, and must be returned there after use and be stowed away properly. Doors, hatches, portholes, cupboards and drawers all have safety latches that must be used or the vessel will become unsafe and unmanageable. You cannot have an untidy boat at sea. The practice of conserving (in as much as it is possible) fresh water (usually for drinking purposes only), fuel, battery power and light is extremely important. You must learn how to use all the pumps properly, from the galley to the bilges – and particularly the heads – if you don't you could sink the vessel.

Life at sea is completely different to life on land. You are always exposed to the elements: sun, wind, rain squalls, and you are absolutely reliant on yourself and your crew mates on the high seas. There will be great challenges and periods of calm, there will be both companionship and solitude, and, above all, there will be the freedom of the oceans and the excitement of landfall and new places to see. ❧

ALISON MUIR BENNETT sailed her own yacht and crewed for others for ten years before writing 'The Hitch-hiker's Guide to the Oceans'. She spent three years on a voyage from from the Far East to South Africa, and has also sailed the coast of Brazil.

The aid worker
by Lucy Markby

TRAVELLING ABROAD AS AN AID WORKER is increasingly popular, because it offers in-depth experience of a country plus the challenges and satisfactions of helping some of the world's neediest people. But it's not a game for amateurs.

The myths

"So what do you do?"—"I work for a humanitarian relief organisation…. Actually I've just come back from Afghanistan."—"Oh."

This is usually followed by one of the following stock responses:
- a) "How fascinating, did you have a nice time? You haven't got much of a tan, though."
- b) "How wonderful. I do think you people are doing a brilliant job out there."
- c) "Don't you think it's immoral to support communities of such extremists?"
- d) "What a bunch of cowboys!"

There are many stereotyped images of aid workers, even within the sector itself. Mercenary, missionary or misfit? Or, in one of their latest manifestations – Land Cruising, Caterpillar boot-wearing, Marlboro-smoking, bullet-dodging, hairy-legged war hero – *'le macho'*. As a French survey in 1995 revealed, there is a certain thrill associated with aid workers: the ideal French lover, apparently, would be a doctor working for Médicins sans Frontières and offering an irresistible combination of intelligence, confidence, professionalism, adventurous spirit and sex appeal – oh, and a little altruism as well.

The truths

The views of aid workers are as varied as the people who choose to do this kind of work. All but a few would agree, however, that it is an experience that challenges your perspectives on life, work and social ethics. In my experience as an aid worker, this kind of work allows you to meet the most remarkable people and develop the strongest of relationships with colleagues from many countries.

The work itself can involve a level of responsibility that would be beyond most people's dreams (or nightmares) at home. This is matched by an intense degree of emotional and physical energy, combined with an equal measure of frustration in the face of antiquated and bureaucratic procedures overseas, for instance, or the laborious paperwork required to clear customs and satisfy donor reporting requirements.

The working environment tends to involve hard work in hot, sticky, mosquito-ridden and remote locations with unreliable water and electricity supplies. But many new aid workers are surprised by the level of technology available to support them, including high-tech satellite communications equipment and well-maintained four-wheel drive vehicles. They may also receive considerable support from domestic staff, employed to maintain the cars, clean the house, cook and even do the laundry, so that aid workers are free to do aid work.

But many organisations avoid this type of conspicuous consumption and find some kind of middle ground. In my experience as a volunteer in Gaza, home was a shared three-bedroom villa surrounded by orange and lemon groves, and transport was a half-share in a dilapidated Renault 4, whose rattling shell gave year-round ventilation but limited protection from stone-throwing youths.

The diversity of staff living standards, as well as general terms and conditions, will depend largely on the resources of the agency you choose. Some overseas staff find themselves posted to a far-flung corner of a country by themselves, while others may be living with a team of twenty- to thirty-somethings and attending NGO (non-governmental organisation) parties in villas in the sun.

On a serious note, any prospective field worker should be aware that aid work is almost inherently a risky business. Staff are vulnerable to disease, to theft, and to being stopped at tense checkpoints by Kalashnikov-toting boys. At worst, aid workers have been a specific target for kidnap or violence. Not all aid work is carried out in conflict areas, but much is conflict-related. It is essential to consider such issues in decisions about where, when and which organisation to choose.

Security management while overseas takes many forms, from armed guards to simple strategies such as adopting appropriate dress codes. When I was in Gaza, a 35-minute drive from Gaza City to the nearby town of Rafah would require a few quick changes: first there was some nifty work with a headscarf to create the impression of a modest, respectful, culturally sensitive woman showing solidarity with the Palestinian refugees; then at the Israeli military checkpoints the scarf disappeared as I metamorphosed into a hair-tossing young Western thing.

Professional considerations

More and more professionals are taking time out from work, or making a deliber-ate move away from the mainstream. Their motivation may be a desire to do something in response to the world's disasters that they see unfolding in the news, to teach their professional skills to others who desperately need them, or to learn new professional skills and experience in a fresh geographical and cultural envi-ronment – or a combination of all three.

The development of the 'global village' means that companies are now looking for global managers. So if you are to hoping to transfer your skills to something more meaningful that satisfies an aspect of your social conscience, or to develop your skills in a truly international context, this may be the path for you.

Aid workers as amateur enthusiasts are a dying breed. Increasingly they are being replaced by highly competent professionals, who work to agreed sector-wide standards and are monitored by donors who demand high levels of accountability and cost-efficiency.

Experienced aid workers, particularly those in senior management positions, can expect to command competitive salaries and benefits packages. The levels of responsibility commensurate with these posts should not be underestimated, however. Operational budgets frequently run to millions of dollars, and are imple-mented by large numbers of staff.

In less senior posts, remuneration for aid workers varies enormously. The min-imum you can expect is to have all expenses covered for the period of work, plus a monthly allowance to cover any ongoing costs you might have at home, such as your mortgage.

What kind of people become aid workers?

Most aid agencies do their best to avoid recruiting people who fall into the stereotypes mentioned at the beginning of this article. It should be noted that war-hungry adrenaline junkies are almost universally unwelcome in the field.

In reality, a broad range of skills and professional backgrounds is potentially in demand from developing countries. VSO, for example, requires experienced professionals from many sectors, including industry, business, media, education, agriculture and more. Even organisations that have a specialist focus, such as the British medical agency Merlin, will want not only medical staff but also all manner of other personnel able to provide the programme with vital support services, such as mechanics and accountants. What unites almost all aid workers is the capacity to be functionally and intellectually flexible, with a skills tool kit that includes some heavyweight common sense.

Other personal requirements include a certain sensitivity and concern for the welfare of other people. But this must be focused by keen pragmatism and a strong determination to make a professional rather than emotional contribution. Even in disaster relief, field workers have to remember that their aim is often to transfer knowledge appropriately into another community.

All this is neatly summed up in S. George's description (albeit satirical) of the ideal aid worker: 'First they must take graduate degrees in social anthropology, geography, economics, a dozen or so difficult and unrelated languages, medicine and business administration. Second, at a slightly more practical level, they must demonstrate competence in agronomy, hydrology, practical nursing, accounting, psychology, automotive mechanics and civil engineering. In addition, they must learn to give a credible imitation of saintliness and it would be well if they could learn sleight of hand as well, since they will often be called upon to perform feats of magic.'

This vision found echoes in an article in *People Management*, which likened the level and diversity of competencies required of field staff to that of the most senior executives in most companies. And as if this were not enough, there are still more requirements. The prerequisite skills and experience must be complemented by an ability to live and work in close proximity with a very mixed team of people, often in a harsh or demanding physical environment.

A survey of aid workers in 1995 revealed that health professionals form the single largest functional/professional group sent overseas. Support staff, including managers, administrators and logisticians, made up the second largest functional group (28 per cent of the 3,000 appointments), followed by teachers and trainers (12 per cent). Other highly sought-after specialists are those who can offer skills in engineering, agriculture, construction, business development, social work and mine clearance. The survey indicates a general lack of opportunities for unskilled volunteers to work overseas. This is a trend that is set to continue, as many agencies are increasingly concerned with providing appropriate training for host country nationals, enabling them to take on the responsibilities that were once the domain of expatriate aid workers.

How to get into aid work

Make a few calls to big charities and you'll find the story is the same. You need at least two years' field experience before they will take a look at your CV. But don't get disillusioned and don't be put off – you are not going for the easy life, after all.

There are some 116 international NGOs in Britain alone, so there is something out there for everyone. But it may take you a while to achieve the right match between what you are looking for, what the agencies are looking for, and what positions happen to be available at the time. NGOs are inundated with people genuinely wanting to help, but to get a look-in you need the right personal qualities as well as the technical/professional skills and experience.

Whatever your profession or work history, all the agencies will want to see you demonstrate some pretty sound skills and an ability to apply them in a relief or development context. Increasingly they like to see an aptitude for transferring your knowledge to your overseas colleagues, both national and international.

There are times, of course, when you just happen be in the right place at the right time, and that is likely to be in the field itself. My strategy for entering the sector led me down the quick and well-trodden path of training as a qualified teacher of English as a foreign language (EFL). On condition that I passed the course, indeed, I was promised a job even before I had started. A major plus of being an EFL teacher is that you can find work anywhere, and the nature of the work takes you right into the heart of a community – giving you a intriguing insights into people's culture, lifestyles, interests and preoccupations. This was how I came to be among the Palestinians in Gaza.

Before you make that first step towards meeting a new challenge, do give your personal circumstances some serious thought. Consider, for example, the impact that working overseas might have on your partner, your children, your friends and family; what financial commitments you are obliged to maintain; what training courses, work opportunities, births, deaths or marriages you may miss while you are overseas.

And if you can't get in

- Find out which skills are the most useful and realistically attainable.
- Join a training course specific to the aid sector, such as those run by Merlin, RedR and International Health Exchange.
- Make applications to organisations with an educational or experiential element, such as Operation Raleigh International.
- Volunteer some time in the UK-based office of an aid agency – but be sure that both you and they know what you are volunteering for.
- Finally, learn a language. French, Spanish and Portuguese speakers are in hottest demand. But bear in mind that a language alone is usually not enough.

The agencies

Aid agencies, like people, come in all shapes and sizes. There are fat cats, rebels with a cause (as well as those without), cowboys and 'happy-clappies'. An agency might be a community-backed band of two people with a truck and a map of Eastern Europe, or conversely it might be part of the United Nations family with an international task force and the bureaucracy to go with it.

The NGO jungle can at first glance be daunting, but once you cut through the thickets of marketing, the interior reflects a high degree of biodiversity. There is a huge variety of technical, professional and geographical specialisations, ages and sizes, levels of bureaucracy, and operational focus.

The most widely known UK sending agencies fall into two main categories: development work and emergency relief. The majority focus primarily on long-term development objectives. During the Nineties, however, many agencies chose to diversify into emergency relief, in response to demand on the ground. Only nine agencies of the 116 surveyed by IHE and People in Aid specialise in relief.

All agencies will have their own selection criteria, requirements, terms and conditions, which you need to consider when choosing which to approach. A summary of the main agencies and contacts can be found in the fact boxes below. It should be stressed, however, that this is only a tiny sample of the better-known agencies, selected from many others that are looking to recruit the right staff. ❧

LUCY MARKBY worked in the overseas aid sector, as a field worker and for Merlin (Medical Emergency Relief International), and is now a human resources specialist.

Volunteering overseas with VSO
by Abigail Fulbrook

Do you want to see the world but give something back? Perhaps you want to experience living in the developing world? Or even to change your life? Then volunteering overseas could be the way to do all of this. Increasingly popular for gap years, volunteering can give you ways to really understand the highs and lows of life in the developing world. It can also provide a sense of achievement, a new outlook and an insight into how other people live. It can help you gain new skills and confidence. And will make real a difference to the community you volunteer in.

One of the best known volunteering agencies, and now one of the biggest in the world, Voluntary Service Overseas (VSO) is often considered to be the ultimate volunteering experience. Every year over 700 people begin a VSO placement. Founded in 1958, VSO has sent more than 30,000 people to work overseas. Originally for graduates and school-leavers, VSO has, in response to requests from overseas partners, developed its placements into focused assignments for people with more professional experience.

What does VSO do?

VSO works by receiving requests from its partners overseas. These are government bodies, local charities and non-governmental organisations (NGOs). VSO works in six specific areas: education; health and social well-being; HIV and AIDS; participation and governance; secure livelihoods; and, disability. In each of the 34 countries that VSO operates in, the programme is focused on two or three of these goals. These are decided by VSO's field staff in conjunction with local organisations. This is ensures that volunteers have the deepest impact. VSO volunteers work closely with colleagues to share their skills. When they leave that impact is sustained.

VSO volunteers are skilled professionals and most placements require a relevant qualification, plus at least two years experience. Skills in demand include, among others, education managers, special education needs teachers, primary teachers, experienced maths, science and English language teachers, doctors, midwives, nutritionists and speech therapists. (Visit the VSO website for the full list; www.vso.org.uk).

VSO placements are usually one or two years long. But, after the organisation's merger with a similar volunteering charity, BESO, from April 2006 VSO will be offering short-term placements. These start from one just month.

There is, of course, a financial implication to volunteering overseas. Pensions, mortgages and loans, plus other commitments, must all be taken into consideration. VSO's financial help to volunteers has been heralded as the Rolls Royce of packages. The charity provides financial advice to volunteers along with a comprehensive financial support, which includes National Insurance and pension contributions, return flights, grants and visas. Student loans can be deferred while on a VSO placement too, as the Student Loan Company recognises VSO as valid voluntary work. While overseas, volunteers receive a monthly allowance that is comparable to local colleagues' wages and accommodation.

What to expect?

The process of applying to VSO is comprehensive. There's a written application form to fill in before you are invited to an assessment day. This involves team exercises and an interview. Once you have been accepted for a placement, you will be assigned an advisor, who will help you find the best placement for you. There is also training to undertake before leaving. This is designed to prepare you for living overseas, give you the background into the developing world and also covers health and safety. That done and you are off. But you won't get abandoned at the airport. On arrival, depending on the country and length of your placement, you will receive a period of training, including language learning, cookery lessons and orientation.

There is no denying it, VSO is hard work. When you start your placement in the developing world you will find that it can be frustrating and that things do move slowly than you are perhaps use to. Your colleagues may not take your suggestions on board straight away and there can be a lot of bureaucracy to deal with. Volunteers don't get paid as much as other ex-pats, so you may find that you can't afford to do everything that you had hope to do. Although volunteers receive a guaranteed three weeks holiday each year, this does not leave much time for travel during your placement.

But, alongside the hard graft, there will be plenty of satisfying professional development opportunities. These might include anything from developing policy with governments to writing strategic plans to training colleagues. What's more there will be festivals and weddings to attend, new shopping experiences in the markets, languages to learn and life-long friends to be made.

18 to 25?

VSO has two schemes for people aged between 18 and 25. These are the World Youth & Global Xchange (WY & GX) and Youth for Development (YfD).

The WY & GX is a six-month exchange programme. Nine young people from the UK are teamed up with nine people from a developing country. They work together for three months in the UK and then go to the developing country for a further three months. No qualifications or experience are necessary, just enthusiasm and a willingness to learning about other cultures in your own country and overseas. Participants work in community projects such as refugee mentoring, children's play schemes, disability projects and environmental regeneration.

The YfD programme is aimed a young people with one year's experience of voluntary or community work. It constitutes a one year placement overseas, which aims to provide VSO partners overseas with willing volunteers. The volunteer gains a worthwhile and meaningful experience while working towards one of VSO's specific goals.

Case study 1

Matt Innes, 38, is working in Kampot, southern Cambodia, as a primary and secondary education advisor.

"I had wanted to do VSO for a few years. I reached a time in my career where I became very interested in teacher training, and I had always been interested in development work. I sweated blood over the decision before I came out, because I would be giving up a settled career, friends and family for a couple of years. You tend to think before you come out of all the things you are giving up and the things you are going to miss. Actually, when you arrive, you find an awful lot of things that you didn't expect to gain. I have already made friends here I will want to come back and visit several years down the line. You can't predict those things; you really can't predict how wonderful it's going to be.

"I work closely with the Ministry of Education, which has prioritised giving all children access to basic education. I've been using a teachers' text book – written by the previous volunteer here – to train teachers in five days with the content and activities to teach English effectively. It was designed for pupils to be able to learn without textbooks, because many schools here can't afford them. I organise training in primary schools in Kampot and I also do follow-up visits to help teachers apply what they have learnt. I am loving it. I wouldn't be anywhere else, although I have to say it is more tiring than you can predict. But you get a feeling of satisfaction, and you learn something every day – you can't ask for more than that really.

"If you are the kind of person who is always wanting to learn, who is fascinated by other people, who just loves other cultures, do VSO. If you don't mind getting dusty and dirty and sweaty and feeling like a fool half the time, you will be alright."

Case study 2

Sheila Lawrence, 60, worked as a physiotherapist in Mzuzu Hospital, Malawi.

"As a single parent I had worked part-time as a physio in a rehabilitation centre while my four daughters were growing up. When the last one left for university I wanted a new challenge and a bit of adventure. I had learnt a lot through training and working for the NHS and felt it was now time to share my skills with people who were less privileged. At first my family didn't believe it, but once I was accepted by VSO they kept telling me how proud they were of me. I was a bit concerned about leaving my mother, who was 88 at the time, but she was delighted for me and encouraged me every step of the way.

"The hospital I worked at was one of only three government referral hospitals in Malawi. There is no training school for physiotherapy in Malawi and, when I was working there, only eight Malawian therapists in government hospitals. I worked with a Malawian therapist to train three assistants in physiotherapy. I enjoyed seeing patients regain their independence, and was able to feel a great satisfaction, knowing that I had a large part to play in the lives of people who, without my help, would still be bedridden.

"But there were also the heartbreaking days when I met patients, especially children, who were so disabled that I was unable to offer any help. I experienced more highs and lows working in Malawi than at home, as I saw people in more extreme need, but I was always amazed at how the people coped with such adversity. Their ingenuity was incredible. They still have such hope even though so much is against them – something that I don't think we in the West really appreciate.

"You are never too old to do something different, I enjoyed the challenge and made some really good friends. Yes, it was scary in the beginning, but I am glad I was able to have such an enriching experience." ❧

For more information telephone VSO on 020 8780 7500, visit www.vso.org.uk or email enquiry@vso.org.uk. You can also write to VSO at 317 Putney Bridge Road, London, SW15 2PN.

Volunteer organisations

ACTION D'URGENCE INTERNATIONALE
France tel: 33 4 67 27 06 09
www.aui-ong.org/
Training courses for people interested in helping communities affected by natural disasters.

BESO
UK tel: 020 8780 7500
www.vso.org.uk/beso
British Executive Service Overseas: has merged with VSO, but still maintains a Response Unit that offers short-term volunteering opportunities.

BTCV
UK tel: 01302 572 244
www.btcv.org
Conservation work, training, leadership courses and special projects around the UK.

CATHOLIC INSTITUTE FOR INTERNATIONAL RELATIONS (CIIR)
UK tel: 020 7354 0883
www.ciir.org
An international development charity with three main aims: civil society , combating HIV and Aids, and creating a sustainable environment.

CORD (CHRISTIAN OUTREACH)
UK tel: 01926 315301
International tel: 00 44 1926 315301
www.cord.org.uk

CHRISTIAN VOCATIONS
UK tel: 0870 745 4825
www.christianvocations.org
Voluntary opportunities from missionary work to engineering and farming.

COMMUNITY SERVICE VOLUNTEERS (CSV)
UK tel: 020 7278 6601
www.csv.org.uk
Volunteering opportunities for between 4-12 months, working with veterans and people with disabilities.

CONCORDIA (YOUTH SERVICE VOLUNTEERS)
UK tel: 01273 422293
www.concordia-iye.org.uk
International volunteer programmes for ages 18-30.

CHURCHES TOGETHER IN BRITAIN AND IRELAND (CTBI)
UK tel: 020 7654 7254
www.ctbi.org.uk
Various denominations uniting for projects.

EARTHWATCH INSTITUTE
Europe tel: 01865 318 838
USA tel: 1 800 776 0188
www.earthwatch.org
Environment and conservation projects.

ECOVOLUNTEER WEBSITE
www.ecovolunteer.org

GLOBAL VOLUNTEERS
USA tel: 800 487 1074
www.globalvolunteers.org/

HEALTH UNLIMITED
UK tel: 020 7840 3777
www.healthunlimited.org
Recruits qualified health professionals for war zones.

INSTITUTE FOR INTERNATIONAL COOPERATION AND DEVELOPMENT (IICD)
www.iicd-volunteer.org/
Up to a years' work in Brazil, South Africa and Mozambique including training and preparation.

INTERNATIONAL HEALTH EXCHANGE (IHE)
UK tel: 0207 233 1100
www.ihe.org.uk/
Provides details of job vacancies and training for health workers overseas.

INVOLVEMENT VOLUNTEERS
www.volunteering.org.au
Volunteering opportunities all over the world.

KIBBUTZ REPRESENTATIVES
UK tel: 0044 181 458 9235
USA tel: 001 212 318 6130
www.kibbutz.org.il
Working holidays on *kibbutzim* in Israel.

MERLIN (MEDICAL EMERGENCY RELIEF INTERNATIONAL)
UK tel: 020 7065 0800
www.merlin.org.uk
Placing qualified medical and support staff in disaster areas.

PEOPLE & PLANET
UK tel: 01865 245678
www.peopleandplanet.org
Student-led conservation society and campaign against global poverty.

PROJECT 67
UK tel: 0207 831 7626
Kibbutz and *moshav* voluntary work in Israel.

PROJECT TRUST
UK tel: 01879 230444
www.projecttrust.org.uk
Gap year opportunities for people aged 17-19 to work in developing countries for a year.

RALEIGH INTERNATIONAL
UK tel: 020 7371 8585
www.raleighinternational.org
Community or conservation projects for 17-25 year olds.

SKILL SHARE INTERNATIONAL
UK tel: 0116 254 1862
www.skillshare.org
Recruits qualified and experienced people to work in Africa and Asia.

TEARFUND
UK tel: 0845 355 8355
www.tearfund.org
A Christian organisation dedicated to helping the poor around the world.

UNITED NATIONS VOLUNTEERS (UNV)
www.unv.org
The volunteer arm of the United Nations, needing experienced workers to help with relief work.

UNIVERSITIES' EDUCATIONAL FUND FOR PALESTINIAN REFUGEES (UNIPAL)
UK tel: 0191 3867124
Educational fund teaching English to Palestinians.

UNIVERSITY RESEARCH EXPEDITIONS PROGRAMME
USA tel: 530 752 8811
www.extension.ucdavis.edu/urep/
Volunteer with University of California research teams abroad.

US PEACE CORPS
USA tel: 800 424 8580
www.peacecorps.gov
Volunteers of all ages working all over the world on various projects.

VACATION WORK PUBLICATIONS
UK tel: 01865 241 978
www.vacationwork.co.uk
Online bookshop with regularly updated publications on travel abroad.

VOLUNTEERS FOR PEACE
www.vfp.org
Publishes an international work camp directory.

VOLUNTARY SERVICE OVERSEAS UK (VSO)
UK tel: 020 8780 7200
www.vso.org.uk
Sends volunteers into Third World countries to help the impoverished.

WORLD COUNCIL OF CHURCHES
www.wcc-coe.org/
Opportunities for volunteers aged 18-30 to work in international camps helping local development.

Further reading

International Directory of Voluntary Work

Directory of Work and Study in Developing Countries

Work Your Way Around The World

All published by Vacation Work

Travel writing for beginners
by Jonathan Lorie

'Dear Editor, You probably won't bother to read this letter, but if you do I can assure you that my article is much better than the ones you have been printing recently. Please consider it for publication.'

'Dear Sir/Madam, This is the first of a stream of letters which you will receive from me over the next two months, keeping you up to date with every day of my round-the-world adventures.'

'Dear Tim, I know that your magazine does not publish articles on package tourism, but I am sure you will be interested in my autobiographical manuscript 'Memoirs of a Tour Rep'. I enclose the first 50 pages.'

I DIDN'T MAKE UP THOSE LETTERS. I COULDN'T. They are real examples which I have received from people who would like to become travel writers. And who wouldn't? But there are ways and ways, and the aim of this article is to help you get a lot further than the people above did.

As the editor of *Traveller* magazine, I receive proposals for articles from travel writers of all kinds – Fleet Street journalists, published authors, commercial publicists, compulsive travellers and enthusiastic beginners. And it's clear that there are just as many versions of what travel writing is: the factual report on a popular destination, the sensitive literary impression of a distant culture, the free 'plug', the backpacker's tale of glory, the raw talent that needs a little technical guidance. Which is where you come in. So let's start at the beginning. What kind of writer do you want to be – and why?

Let me be Devil's Advocate here and put the case against becoming a travel writer. Contrary to popular belief, it won't pay your way around the world. A handful of newspaper and magazine journalists make a regular living and take a lot of trips, but the rest don't. The rest are either travelling anyway, or do something else for a living. And even the successful journalists tend to get short trips that include a lot of factual research (best hotels, cheapest fares, etc.). If you want to spend time savouring a foreign culture, it will usually be at your own expense.

Also contrary to popular belief, the reading public is not waiting breathlessly to hear your – or anyone else's – personal views on the world and all that is in it. Readers want information that is useful or interesting in itself: they don't want deeply personal musings on experiences they are unlikely ever to share.

On the other hand, travel writing might just make you famous. In the wake of Bill Bryson's global success, the market for travel books seems to expand inexhaustibly. Since there's almost nowhere on the planet that's not been written about already, book-publishers are hungry for new angles on old journeys. Hence some current titles that are weird but popular – travelling round Ireland carrying a fridge, for example, or travelling round the globe touching only deserts. And

Travel writing organisations

Association of Authors' Agents
020 7251 0125
www.agentsassoc.co.uk

Book Trust
020 8516 2977
www.booktrust.org.uk

British Guild Of Travel Writers
020 8749 1128

www.bgtw.metronet.co.uk

Foreign Press Association
020 7925 0469
www.foreign-press.org.uk

National Union Of Journalists
020 7278 7916
www.nuj.org.uk

Society Of Authors
020 7373 6642
www.societyofauthors.net

Society Of Women Writers And Journalists
www.swwj.co.uk

Travellers' Tales writing training
www.travellerstales.org

The Writers' Guild Of Great Britain
020 7833 4777
http://cgiwritersguild.force9.co.uk

remember that Bryson's bestsellers are actually based on places most of us can visit (Europe, Australia, America), but described in his own inimitable style.

Other would-be travel writers do it not for the fame or the money, sensibly enough. They do it because they genuinely love to write, or because they have been somewhere that fires them up. In my experience, these are the ones worth watching. A writer who combines talent and passion can go a long way, eventually.

So how do you get your writing published? If you're a total beginner, then the classic route is to slowly build up a reputation through journalistic articles (see below). Having a portfolio of articles in print can help even if you're aiming at book-publishing, because it gives you credibility and something solid to show publishers. It gets your name out there, and establishes your area of expertise.

If your ultimate goal is books rather than articles, you should know that many book-publishers rely largely on literary agents for new talent, so you might do best to approach the agents. There are lists of them in the *Writers' and Artists' Yearbook*, or you may have personal contacts who can help. The classic approach is to send in a brief summary of your book idea, giving the overall theme and a breakdown of the chapters, plus a sample chapter in full – perhaps the opening chapter, so they can see whether you can grab the audience. You should anticipate quite a long haul as you do the round of the agents.

Whichever strategy you're following, it may do no harm to get some professional training. For potential or recent graduates, this may mean a full-time course in journalism at a university: these range from one to three terms, or more, and some are now accredited as BAs or Postgraduate Diplomas. The better institutions include City University and the London College of Communications, both in London, Cardiff University, Falmouth University and Lancaster University. Many other universities also have journalism modules or departments. And many local adult education institutes offer evening classes in, say, general feature writing. Few, however, specialise in travel journalism: so what you get would be a rather wider grounding in general journalistic disciplines.

If you're keen on a travel specialism, or if you're not in a position to devote so much time to training, you might enrol on a short beginners' course in travel writing with Travellers' Tales, a media training agency dedicated to travel writing, both books and articles. They offer week-long or weekend courses, with experienced writers like William Dalrymple and Colin Thubron as tutors. For details, see www.travellerstales.org.

But at some stage, for most aspiring travel writers, comes the process of trying to sell your work to newspaper or magazine editors.

The rules for this are simple but exacting:

1. KNOW THE MARKET. Research who is publishing what, and make sure you send them what they want. There is absolutely no point in submitting articles which are unsuitable because of style, subject matter or length. No matter how good they are, they just won't get published. Equally, find out who takes unsolicited material, and don't waste your time on those who don't.

2. CHOOSE YOUR ANGLE. You can place the same story with several publications, if you find a different angle for each. The crucial trick is to find the angle that will make your material relevant to that particular publication. For example, a woman writer just back from a safari could find distinct angles for the women's, environmental and tourism sections of the press.

3. MAKE A CRISP PRESENTATION. Send in your ideas on one side of A4, keep them short and sharp, don't send too many. You might include back-up material, such as photos or clippings, or perhaps the whole article, but there should be a cover letter that allows a busy editor to assess your proposals quickly and easily.

4. DON'T WASTE THEIR TIME. Journalism is a high-pressure business and editors are often ridiculously busy. Don't expect to reach them in person by phone – but if you do, keep the conversation brief and to the point. Don't hassle them for decisions they haven't made yet. But do keep gently reminding them or their staff about your proposal: polite persistence does pay off.

5. BE RELIABLE. Always meet your deadlines, check your facts, write to length. If you fail on any of these, you're leaving the editor in a real pickle. And it won't be forgotten, either. On the other hand, you'd be surprised at how many journalistic careers are based on being reliable rather than being brilliant.

If you compare these rules of thumb with the letters quoted at the start of this article, you can see where they went wrong. The first letter – apart from its off-putting rudeness – doesn't convey the proposal at all (rule 3). The second letter doesn't suggest an angle (rule 2) and would have most editors scared of a deluge of material. The third letter does have a strong angle but, as the author says, it is unsuitable (rule 1). Interestingly, all three letters break rule 4 in their own delightful ways. Unfortunately, none of them got far enough to test rule 5.

Much better than these is a straightforward letter like this, which just arrived:

'Dear Mr Lorie, I have spent the last 25 years chasing and photographing the world's last remaining steam trains. This might interest your readers, perhaps in your 'Eyewitness' section. I enclose the article written to your length, 25 original photographs of trains in India, and a stamped addressed envelope for their return. This material has not been published in the UK before.'

Doesn't it sound intriguing? Wouldn't you want to know more? The writer has got lots of things right here – for starters, the name of the editor. He's told us the angle, the location, and his own credentials for writing about this. It's clear that he's looked at the magazine and tailored his material to fit one of the sections. He's also made it easy for the busy editor, by enclosing the pictures and a reply envelope. Crucially, he's explained that this article would be a UK 'first': editors love to publish something before their rivals. And all of that is conveyed in 66 words.

Now we've got a grip on how not to sell a story, let's consider what not to submit to an editor. He or she won't want unedited chunks of your travel diaries, since they won't suit the publication's style. Nor postcard-style reminiscences of happy holidays, which are too personal to interest the general reader. Nor thinly disguised 'plugs' for hotels/tour agents/resorts/airlines or anyone else who's obviously done the author some favour or other. Nor, sadly, reminiscences of the travels of ten, 20 or even 30 years ago: no matter how much they mean to the author, they won't be topical enough for the editor.

What the editor does want to receive is material that suits the publication, is entertainingly written, and tells the reader something worth knowing. It must be up-to-date and accurate. It should be written in 'house style'. It could be topical. And it helps if the story can be easily illustrated with photographs. Getting of all that right will get you in print.

So, having passed the test and got your proposal or article accepted, what happens next? My best advice is to regard the publication of your article as a beginning rather than an end. Regard that magazine or newspaper as your prime target, on the assumption that if they liked your material once, they will do again. Try to work out why that particular article got published, and offer them the same 'formula' a second or third time. Try to build some contacts there: perhaps get known for some area of expertise on which they might call you. Crucially, start a contact book in which to note any useful names and addresses, and keep careful track of your submissions and conversations.

With this combination of professionalism and patience, you might find that first article in print is a door opening into your future. ❧

JONATHAN LORIE *is Editor of 'The Traveller's Handbook' and 'Traveller' magazine, and Director of the Travellers' Tales training agency.*

Travel photography for beginners
by Michael Busselle

TRAVEL CAN BE A VERY EXCITING AND STIMULATING EXPERIENCE, and one that generates the sort of memories that can last a lifetime. For many people, photography is a way of helping to preserve those memories as well as a means of expressing the feelings which travel evokes. But the value of photographs taken while travelling is in direct proportion to their effectiveness as images; an indifferent picture can seem devoid of meaning after the event. Taking good photographs requires a degree of skill that can be acquired by anyone who is   motivated to do so. The process of developing this skill can make the experience of travel more vivid and the traveller more observant and perceptive.

The basic skills

There are three key steps involved in taking good photographs. The first is developing the ability to see like a camera. There can be an enormous difference between what is seen by a casual observer and what the camera records. It's important to understand that a beautiful scene will not necessarily translate into a striking photograph. An awareness of this difference is necessary in order to produce images that make a strong visual impact.

A subject that has a well-defined and interesting shape is likely to create an eye-catching image, and the presence of bold lines, patterns and textures can also have a powerful effect. An awareness of the colour content of a scene is vital, as is the effect of light. It's important to know exactly which colours are present in a scene and where they are, and also to notice where shadows are cast and whether they are dense and hard-edged or soft and weak.

Once you have identified the key elements of a subject, the next step is to find the most effective viewpoint. Often a change in camera position of only a metre or two can make a big difference to the relationship between the objects and details within a scene. These possibilities must be explored before you can decide how best to frame the image.

Many photographers use the camera's viewfinder simply to aim the camera. Often they are not fully aware of everything contained within it, and distracting and unwanted details can be inadvertently included as a result. You can avoid this problem by studying the edges of the image in the viewfinder first and then scanning the remainder within it so that everything in the photo is clearly seen.

The photographer needs to identify a focus of interest within the area being photographed in order to decide how best to place the frame. This focus could be something very obvious, like a building in an otherwise empty landscape, or something quite subtle, such a bright highlight, a splash of colour or a nicely shaped cloud. Once this focus has been identified, the camera angle and field of view can be altered until all the key objects and details within the viewfinder create a pleasing balance.

Technical quality

No matter how striking the subject or how well composed the image, a photograph must be sharp and correctly exposed in order for it to be successful and marketable. A sharp picture is dependent upon four factors: a good quality lens which has been focused accurately; a camera held steady enough to prevent camera shake; a shutter speed fast enough to freeze any subject movement; and adequate depth of field. Even inexpensive modern camera lenses are capable of producing sharp, clear images, and auto-focusing mechanisms used with a little care tend to be more reliable than eye and manual adjustment.

When a tripod is not being used, the prospect of camera shake becomes a serious concern, as even a very slight degree of blur can take the crucial edge from a sharply focused image. The risk of camera shake is much greater when a long-focus lens is used. It is best to use a tripod whenever possible, as the risk is then completely removed, and the use of slower shutter speeds, smaller apertures and greater depth of field becomes possible.

Depth of field is the area of acceptably sharp focus behind and in front of the point on which the lens is focused. The use of a small aperture and/or a wide-angle lens increases it, and it is decreased when a long-focus lens is used and/or a wide aperture is set. Maximum depth of field is needed when shooting subjects like landscapes in which close foreground details are included as well as distant objects. Minimum depth of field is effective when shooting subjects such as portraits and animals, as distracting background details can be thrown out of focus.

Modern exposure systems make getting the exposure right much less of an issue than it once was, and normal subjects of average contrast will produce an acceptable image every time. Abnormal subjects are those that contain excessively large areas of very dark or very light tones, or include light sources, such as a sunset or a street scene at night. In the former case less exposure is needed, while in the latter it is necessary to use the camera's exposure compensation setting to give more exposure than indicated. In these instances it is often possible to take a spot or close-up exposure reading from a detail of average tone with the subject.

The equipment

Choice of camera is a very personal matter and, from a quality point of view, similarly priced models from the leading manufacturers will not differ significantly. The main decision to make when deciding upon a film camera is between Medium Format and 35 mm, and Viewfinder or Single Lens Reflex (SLR). For travel photography, in particular, the most popular choice by far is the 35 mm SLR. This is because of its great flexibility and the enormous range of lenses and accessories available for these models, which allow them to cope with subjects ranging from architecture and macro photography to reportage and wildlife.

There are also specialist film cameras, such as the Hasselblad XPan panoramic, which has a format of 65 x 24 mm and uses 35 mm film, or medium format panoramic cameras like the Fuji, which uses 120 film and has a picture size of 6 x 17 cm. Underwater cameras like the 35 mm Nikonos are also widely used, not only

Photography organisations

British Association Of Picture Libraries And Agencies (BAPLA)
020 7713 1211
www.bapla.org.uk

British Institute Of Professional Photography
01920 464011
www.bipp.com

Bureau Of Freelance Photographers
020 8882 3315
www.thebfp.com

Master Photographers Association
01325 356555
www.thempa.com

Photo Marketing Association International
0121 212 0299
www.pmai.org

The Royal Photographic Society
01225 462841
www.rps.org

Travel Photographers Network
www.travelphotographers.net

Travellers' Tales photography training
www.travellerstales.org

for sub aqua photography, but also for subjects like water sports, where an ordinary camera could be seriously damaged.

It must be recognised, though, that film is rapidly becoming sidelined and, certainly in the amateur world, sales of digital cameras greatly exceed those of film cameras. As I write this, a leading retailer has just announced that it will not be renewing its current stocks of film cameras, so the end is nigh. But for the professional or semi-professional photographer that needs high resolution images capable of big enlargement, cost is a serious consideration. At present a film camera does produce superb quality photographs at a significantly lower cost than a similarly specified digital camera. This fact alone will doubtless keep film alive for some time yet, although the resolution of digital camera rises almost on a monthly basis while the price reduces and, of course, for the prolific photographer the saving in film and processing costs is substantial over a period of time.

Those about to invest in a camera should bear in mind that colour transparencies are no longer accepted in many of the markets for travel photography. They must be scanned before being submitted, which involves the cost of buying a film scanner as well as the time and effort required in making digital files from film images. It's also quite likely that in the relatively near future stocks of film will become harder to find, and it will become increasingly difficult to have colour transparency film processed as the demand decreases. Modern travel also makes it difficult to transport film from country to country; it is subjected to security X-rays, with the risk of fogging, and the weight and space allowed for luggage is becoming more and more restricted.

When buying a digital camera, it is necessary to consider the camera's intended usage. The professional or semi-pro photographer shooting on assignment or for stock images is still likely to prefer the SLR because of its flexibility in handling a wide range of subjects and situations, as well as its ability to produce high resolution images. But there is now a good selection of highly specified viewfinder or compact models capable of producing images that will enlarge to A3 or bigger. Fitted with a high-quality zoom lens, they are able to cope with a very high percentage of the shots likely to be taken on a travel assignment, and have the advantage of being much lighter, smaller and cheaper than an SLR.

Other advantages of digital cameras include the ability to check exposures immediately after making them and being able to review a day's work each evening if required. There's also the reassuring knowledge that it is immediately obvious if anything goes wrong or there is a camera malfunction. The ability to review images as soon as they are recorded, combined with the lack of costs involved with film photography, tends to encourage a more adventurous and experimental approach to photography. Another benefit is the facility to change the sensor sensitivity (the digital equivalent of film speed) frame by frame, whereas with film one must carry rolls of varying speeds and either shoot a complete roll in each situation or carry one or more extra bodies loaded with different films.

While the travel photographer who has switched to a digital camera will be overjoyed at not having to carry a big bag of film on each trip, there is a down side. Digital images are stored in the camera on removable memory cards which can accommodate up to several gigabytes of information. But when shooting high resolution images it's possible to fill several high capacity memory cards in the course of a busy day. During a trip lasting a couple of weeks or more, it becomes necessary to download these images periodically onto a portable hard drive or a laptop computer, which, together with their batteries and chargers, creates extra weight and bulk to carry.

Lenses

The standard lens for both 35 mm film and digital cameras is now considered to be the mid-range zoom, which has a variable focal length from about 28 mm to 85 mm, or the equivalent with a digital compact. This provides a field of view ranging from about 60 degrees to 30 degrees and will cover the needs of the vast majority of shots taken on a travel assignment.

There are many situations, though, in which extra lenses are needed, and this is where the SLR has such a big advantage. The range of focal lengths on most mid-range zoom lenses is fairly limited, and many photographers will feel the need for a 24 mm or 20 mm and a 150 mm or 200 mm on occasions. An ultra wide-angle lens with a focal length of 16 mm or 18 mm can be very useful for subjects like architecture, landscapes and reportage, while a very long- focus lens such as a 600 mm is virtually essential for serious wildlife photography. A wide-angle shift lens which allows the optical axis of the lens to be raised or lowered is invaluable for shooting buildings, as it eliminates the need to tilt the camera upwards and avoids the converging verticals this creates. A macro lens makes shooting close-ups of subjects like botanical specimens much easier, and although many standard zoom lenses have a close focusing facility, most will not provide a life-size image.

Alternatives are extension tubes or a bellows unit, which fits between the camera body and the lens to allow it to focus at closer distances.

Accessories

Many photographers would regard a tripod as their most important accessory, as it ensures absolute image sharpness and allows the use of slow shutter speeds and small apertures for maximum depth of field. It will also make it possible to shoot in very low light levels such as at dusk, dawn and after dark, which is when some of the most interesting and striking effects can be created. It's very tempting for the backpacking traveller to consider a tripod an unnecessary addition to the burden, but modern carbon fibre tripods combine light weight with great rigidity and will invariably repay the effort of carrying one many times over.

A monopod is lighter and easier to carry than a tripod and will certainly aid stability when shooting at slower shutter speeds, but will not enable the use of shutter speeds longer than about half a second, which rules out time exposures in very low lighting conditions.

Although many cameras these days have an integral flash, a separate flash gun will provide much more power and faster recycling and will not create a drain on the camera's power supply. The ability to vary the direction and quality of light is also possible with a separate flash gun. This can be achieved by reflecting the flight from the flash via a wall or ceiling, by diffusing it with a translucent screen or by using a long synchronising lead to fire it from an off-camera angle.

For those using film cameras, a set of filters is also essential to control the colour quality of the transparencies. Warm-up filters in the 81A to 81EF range are needed to counter the blue cast created when shooting on overcast days and in open shade under a blue sky, and the blue-tinted filters in the 82A to 82C range are designed to neutralise the reddish hue created when the sun is close to the horizon. When shooting landscapes, neutral graduated filters are useful for making the sky a darker tone without affecting the foreground.

The polarising filter is perhaps the most useful of all, as it eliminates or reduces the light being reflected from non-metallic surfaces such as foliage and water. This will result in a significant increase in colour saturation, making blue skies a deeper, richer blue, for example. Colour balancing and graduated filters are not necessary when shooting with a digital camera, as their effects can be achieved much more accurately and efficiently with image editing software like Photoshop, but the quality created by a polarising filter is not readily replicated in this way.

Although not strictly camera accessories, the travelling photographer should also carry items such as a pocket torch, a small screwdriver, marking pens and perhaps a mini-tape recorder for making notes to aid captioning. Sealable plastic bags are also useful for storing film and pieces of equipment when travelling in dusty or damp environments. Lens cleaning fluid, a blower brush and micro-fibre cleaning cloths are vital for keeping optics free from smears and dust. A blower without a brush is needed for cleaning the digital sensors of SLR cameras, which are prone to collecting dust. A compass is very useful for estimating the best time of day for the angle of the sun when shooting a particular scene or building.

Camera bags

There is a wide variety of camera cases available from a number of specialist manufacturers, and it's worth spending some time to ensure that the best choice is made for your own particular needs and comfort. The backpack design is a popular choice for those who rely upon hiking or climbing to seek their pictures, as are the small, individual cases that can be clipped onto a belt.

A soft shoulder bag is ideal for street photography, as it is quickly and easily accessible for lens changing and can be rather more discreet for candid shots. When choosing a bag it's best to allow a bit more space than you think you need, as a bag designed to take a specific number of items and no more can become awkward to find space in when shooting under pressure.

It's worth considering a hard case for use on flights, as these can be loaded into the hold safely. The size and weight restriction for hand luggage can easily be exceeded when a number of cameras and lenses are being carried, and they can be transferred to a soft, fabric bag for day to day use on arrival.

Logistics

One of the most important things to consider when travelling with camera equipment is the need for adequate insurance cover. If you have more than a single camera and lens it is best not to rely upon the personal possessions element of travel or home insurance, but instead to insure with a company that specialises in photographic equipment cover. It also helps to have a list of all the items you are carrying, together with their serial numbers. As well as being invaluable in the event of loss or theft when reporting it to the police, a list can also be helpful in the event of difficulties with customs officials.

Security controls are much more stringent these days, particularly with air travel, and it is not safe to place film in luggage that will be placed in the aircraft's hold, as this can be randomly scanned by equipment that will cause fogging. The X-ray scanners used for hand luggage are safe for normal films, but there is an element of risk when very fast films are passed through and when the same batch of film is subjected to a sequence of scans. It is possible to request that a carry-on bag be searched by hand, but officials are often reluctant to do this; they are more likely to oblige you if you arrive early and wait until there is a less busy moment at the security gate.

It's worth checking for any regulations or potential problems at a particular destination, as there are sometimes local quirks. In India, for example, it is not uncommon for officials to remove batteries from equipment and not return them.

Planning and research

The anticipation of a forthcoming trip can be a large part of the pleasure of travelling, and the time spent planning it and researching a destination can not only add to the enjoyment, but can also benefit the photography. A good map of the region you are visiting is an invaluable starting point, as is a guidebook or two. National or regional tourist offices often have an abundance of useful information, and the internet provides a uniquely powerful means of discovering details of even the most obscure locations. Search engines such as Google can be especially useful for photographers, as they enable you to get a preliminary view of the places you are planning to visit via on-line images. A good photo library web site will provide the same facility. In addition to places of interest, tourist sites and notable buildings as well as details of festivals, markets and regional crafts can also be identified in order to add local colour to the coverage of a destination.

The travel subjects

Landscape

Good landscape photography is an essential part of travel work, and it often provides the key image for articles and book spreads. Successful landscape pictures are the result of finding a good viewpoint and shooting at a time when the light is sympathetic to the scene. Use periods when the light is poor to look for viewpoints, marking them on a map, and try to estimate the time of day when it will be best to shoot them. With well known views and tourist sites it is very helpful to study postcards and images in travel guides and books, as these are likely to have been shot under ideal conditions and can give you some pointers to the best time of day. They can also suggest viewpoints you may not have discovered yourself.

Sunlight in the early morning and late afternoon is particularly valuable for landscape photography, because the low angle can reveal rich textures and make the contours of the landscape stand out in strong relief. The warm, mellow quality of the light at this time of day can also help to create atmospheric images. The weather and light is seldom ideal for photography for more than a relatively small proportion of a trip and, consequently, it is essential to make the most of such conditions when they do exist by having researched your viewpoints beforehand.

While a wide-angle, sweeping view of a scene can be stunning to look at, it can be disappointing as a photograph unless the lighting conditions are perfect and the atmosphere is extremely clear. Such pictures are often more striking if some close foreground details are included, as they help to create a sense of depth and distance. A common mistake with all photography, but with landscapes, in particular, is to try to include too much in a picture. Often a more tightly cropped image using a longer focal length lens will be more effective.

The sky can be an important element in landscape photography, and it needs to be considered carefully. A featureless grey or white sky can have a distinctly negative effect on an image; it is best either cropped out altogether or restricted to a very small area. A plain blue sky can also have a weakening effect on a picture if a large area is included. A polarising filter will often improve a blue sky with clouds by making the colour richer and the clouds stand out in stronger relief.

Architecture

Finding the right viewpoint is also an important aspect of photographing buildings, and it can often be difficult when shooting in the confined space of towns and cities. A wide-angle shift lens is invaluable for shooting tall buildings when the viewpoint is restricted, as it allows the top to be included without having to tilt the camera upwards. This causes converging verticals, which can be corrected afterwards with image editing software such as Photoshop.

On occasion, though, it can be effective to tilt the camera to create converging verticals in an exaggerated way using a very wide-angle lens. Photographing a building in its entirety is not always the best way of approaching architectural photography, and using a long-focus lens to focus attention on details and textures can often create more striking images.

People

Some photographers find that photographing people can be somewhat daunting, but much depends upon the approach taken. It is best to be open and relaxed rather than tentative or furtive. Candid shots of people who are unaware of being photographed can be an excellent way of capturing spontaneous images with a very natural quality, but unless it is done discreetly and with sensitivity, the subjects may be offended if they catch you. In these cases it is vital to consider the privacy, dignity and religious concerns of people you want to photograph.

When shooting pictures of this type in an alien environment, it is best to allow enough time to let your presence be noted and accepted before attempting to take photographs. It is also a good idea to be as discreet as possible about displaying your camera. Avoid having an ostentatious camera bag, and keep your camera out of sight until immediately before shooting; change lenses in a quiet corner screened from view.

An alternative approach to the candid shot is the informal portrait, where your subject is photographed in a situation with his or her consent and cooperation. This has the advantage of being able to have some control over elements like the lighting and background, and has the benefit of eye contact, which can add considerable impact to an image.

It's best to decide how you want to shoot the picture before approaching your intended subject. Select a spot where the light is good and where there is a suitable background. As a general rule, a soft, diffused light is preferable: the light from an overcast sky or open shade on a sunny day is ideal. Backgrounds need to be uncluttered so that they do not distract from the subject, and should be of a tone or colour with enough contrast to create good separation.

Using a long-focus lens will allow you to shoot close-up portraits from a distant viewpoint. This can be less intimidating for the subject, and it also avoids the exaggerated perspective and distorted features that a very close viewpoint can create. A long-focus lens used with a wide aperture can also be an effective way of throwing distracting background details out of focus.

Nature and wildlife

The fauna and flora of a region can be an important aspect of a travel feature and will provide both variety and interest to a portfolio of images. Some knowledge is an invaluable aid to subjects of this type, especially with wildlife photography, and it can be very helpful to call upon local guides for help and advice.

Taking pictures on safari is something that most photographers will want to do when travelling in countries like Africa and India, and it requires a different approach to most other types of photography. This is partly because, in many cases, you are not allowed to leave the vehicle you're travelling in, and you must shoot from widows and roof hatches. This makes it necessary to take special care over the avoidance of camera shake. You need to be certain there is no movement within the vehicle at the moment of exposure. This can cause blurred images, especially when using very long-focus lenses.

It's usually impractical to use a tripod in these circumstances, but a monopod can be helpful. An effective way to support the camera is to cushion it on the window frame or roof hatch with a beanbag. It's also possible to buy window frame clamps to which you can attach a ball and socket head.

Finding a good viewpoint is dependent upon the driver's ability to place the vehicle in the best position with your guidance. This needs some skill and patience. Your choice of viewpoint depends upon three factors: proximity to the animal, a place with an area of unobtrusive background behind it and an angle where the lighting is most effective.

As a general rule, a soft diffused light is preferable for photographs of animals and birds, as the harsh light of the midday sun creates dense shadows and bright highlights, which can easily conceal the subtle details of fur and feather. Shooting in the early morning and late afternoon can provide a very pleasing and atmospheric light; it is also a time when the animals tend to be more active.

The picture story

The majority of photographs are intended to stand alone as single images. There are times, though, when a sequence of pictures that creates a visual narrative can be more effective, such as a record of a trip or expedition or pictures of a specific subject for a magazine article.

In a picture story the main concern is to capture key moments and events and to ensure there are strong images of the most important places. But it's also essential to make sure that it has a good flow and sustains the viewer's interest. This can be achieved by creating variety in the images with a mixture of wide, scenic views and tightly framed details, for example. Include shots taken in bright midday sunlight and pictures taken at sunrise or dusk. Ensure there is a good variety of subject matter, such as portraits, close-ups, landscapes and architecture.

A sense of place

One of the most important objectives of travel photography is that the images identify the location and evoke something of the experience of being there. Travel features in magazines which only use one or two photographs often achieve this by selecting very obvious images, such as the Eiffel Tower for an article about Paris or Monument Valley for a feature on the USA.

A less obvious approach is to shoot pictures that reflect something of a country or region's culture and lifestyle. Traditional buildings can readily identify a location, for example. The presence of a timbered Normandy cottage, a Tuscan farmhouse, a Scottish croft or a Mexican hacienda in a photograph will go a long way towards establishing where it was taken. Other features that can help to create a sense of place include markets and shops, street food, modes of transport and dress, churches and religious monuments, advertising signs and agriculture.

Marketing your images

Travel photography is one of the most appealing fields to those who would like to become professional photographers and, in a way, it is one of the most accessible. There are numerous and varied markets for travel photography, ranging from holiday brochures to guide books to prestigious magazines like National Geographic. There are two ways to enter this area of the photographic profession: seeking commissions or the stock image route, which involves selling the images you have already taken, either by your own efforts or through the services of a photo library.

You will receive a daily fee for commissioned work as well as expenses, which greatly reduces the financial risk. But obtaining commissions to shoot travel pictures is not easy and tends to be limited to either low-budget publications or glossy magazines, which employ only the very best in the field. Companies producing holiday brochures do commission photographers on a regular basis, but the work is focused heavily on photographing hotels and self-catering properties, which is probably not the type of thing that appeals to most travel photographers.

If you intend to sell your own images, it's important to first identify your potential markets, making a list of magazines and other publications that use the type of photographs you have taken. Before making a submission, it is best to phone or e-mail the editor or picture editor to establish whether there is any interest in the images you have. You might consider sending some low resolution images attached to an e-mail as a sample.

It's best not to set your sights too high to begin with, as the big-selling magazines tend to have well-established sources for their images. There are numerous smaller publications that contain a travel section, such as the free supplements issued by many local newspapers, in addition to those based on travel, such as in-flight publications, 'country' magazines like *Spain* and specialist interest journals such as *Walking* and *Cycling*.

If you are able and willing to write an accompanying article to a set of photographs it can improve your chances of acceptance, as a complete package of words and pictures tends to be an attractive proposition, especially for the smaller publications with limited staff and facilities. It will widen your potential market if you can provide a feature on a specific theme, such as the gardens of Madeira, the vineyards of Burgundy or the street food of Delhi.

But selling your own images is very time consuming and leaves less time for travelling and taking photographs, which makes having your pictures marketed by a photo library an attractive and practical proposition. There are now numerous on-line photo libraries that are actively seeking new images, in addition to the big international agencies that sell through a global network. Photo libraries take care of all the marketing and the costs involved and in return take a commission of the fee paid by their client. This can be anything from 40 or 50 per cent to as much as

70 or 80 per cent where multiple agencies are involved. But it's well worth it: a big international library can sell the same image simultaneously in several countries to different publications, and it has ready access to the very lucrative advertising market, where fees can be many thousands of euros for the single use of an image.

Most on-line libraries' web sites have a page with guidelines for making a submission. Few these days will accept anything other than digital files on a CD or DVD, either from a digital camera or from scanned transparencies. You will be expected to supply informative captions and, in some cases, key words to aid picture searches. Your images will probably, but not necessarily, be selected according to the library's current needs and also by technical criteria, which include clean images free from dust and marks, maximum definition and a full range of tones within the acceptable brightness range.

Before you submit images to your chosen library it's a good idea to take a look at the images they already have on file in the areas you have covered and to make a realistic assessment of yours in comparison.

What sells best? There's no easy answer to this; sometimes stunning images will not attract any interest while seemingly quite ordinary ones will sell and sell. It is something of a lottery. Only time will tell if you have any best- selling pictures among your submissions. ❧

MICHAEL BUSSELLE *is the author of over 50 books on photography, and regular camera columnist on 'Traveller' magazine.*

Underwater photography
by Maria Munn

DO YOU THINK THAT GREAT UNDERWATER PICTURES are only affordable for the professionals? Do you dream of capturing those memories of beautiful fan corals and wondrous encounters underwater to show to friends and family? Well, you will be pleased to know that, thanks to the digital revolution, novices now have a greater chance of creating award winning photographs underwater. And you don't have to lug around bulky plastic housings to achieve such results either.

So where do you start? First of all, this depends on whether or not you already have a consumer type digital camera, such as those made by Olympus, Nikon, Sony, Canon and Fuji. These are the main types of cameras for which underwater housings are made. You may be surprised to learn that underwater housings were originally designed with the traveller in mind – not divers or keen snorkellers, but for people who enjoyed adventure sports or avid whale watchers, who sometimes got too close to a breaching 400-ton whale in the middle of ocean. Housings are now becoming more affordable and can be cheaper than the cost of the digital camera itself. Some can even be taken down to depths of 120 feet.

Further information

Cameras Underwater (01404 812 277, www.camerasunderwater.co.uk) Underwater camera specialist offering sales and advice.

Martin Edge Underwater Photography (www.edgeunderwaterphotography.com) One of the world's leading underwater photographers, Martin Edge. Based in the UK, he runs underwater photography workshops.

Ocean Optics (020 7240 8193, www.oceanoptics.co.uk) Wide range of brands on sale, plus information on different aspects of underwater photography.

Wetpixel (www.wetpixel.com) Information on digital underwater photography and imaging, plus a useful advice forum.

If you haven't yet bought a camera, but are planning to, Olympus makes the most versatile systems and the widest range of accessories to add onto the camera. These include lenses, filters and a hood. The hood is not affected by strong sunlight and allows you to see the screen clearly underwater. Olympus also design housings for more of its models than its competitors.

There are a wide range of add-on accessories available. Macro and wide angle lenses can be put on and taken off underwater to suit the conditions. A macro lens is useful for those wishing to get close-up shots of critters in rocks. However, you need to bear in mind that the camera does come with a built-in macro mode set into the camera to get great close up shots. This works very well for close up shots of corals as well as small fish. A wide angle lens is really for those looking to shoot large fish. Neither of these are big or bulky, and if you are hoping to bump into a whale shark or a manta ray on your travels, a wide angle add on lens is a must to fit these giants into your photo album.

Do you need flash guns to take great shots? Not necessarily: getting close to your subject will help enormously, as will the addition of a red filter – a UR Pro Filter is recommended. This fantastic add on will stop your underwater photographs looking washed out with too much blue. Red is the first colour lost when you are more than ten feet underwater, and these filters are amazing in saving otherwise lost shots. They can be attached to all Olympus and Canon housings.

Sony provides its own filters which push-fit onto its housings. Plus each Sony camera comes with a built-in flash, which can be used underwater as long as you get close enough to your subject so that the particles in the water don't illuminate (a technical term called 'Backscatter').

So now you have the equipment – lenses, filters and a flash – what do else do you need to do in order take those award-winning shots? Firstly, make sure that you put your underwater housing in a bucket of water without the camera inside, as a test before diving. This is as important for your camera as for your sanity – there is nothing worse than using your camera for the first time and it floods.

Technique is key to taking great photographs. Overcoming the wobbles underwater is the hardest thing, whether you are on scuba or simply snorkelling at the surface. Keep away from the bottom, unless you are kneeling. Otherwise you will churn up huge amounts of sand, which is not good for your photography and is unpleasant for the rest of the group. Control your buoyancy, stay as still and as level as possible, look at the LCD screen to frame your shot and look up. The latter allows you to take advantage of the natural light source, which you will find within the first ten feet of the surface. (Some of the most beautiful photographic opportunities lie in the reflections that you can see on a sunny day.) Getting close to your subject is vital: water magnifies marine life, so fish that appear to be close enough for a great photo are usually further away than you think.

When underwater, be careful of the reefs, as coral does not recover from being kicked by fins. And don't hold onto the coral to take your shots either. You will hurt the reef and there is the risk of being stung.

Make sure that you care for your equipment. This is a relatively simple task. Each housing usually comes with either one or two O-rings. These look like elastic rubber bands, but they are the most important piece in your housing as they stop leaks. Take out the O-ring from your housing, check that it has no sand or dirt on it and gently give it a light coating of grease every week. This will protect your camera equipment from flooding depending on how much diving you will be doing. For occasional use, the O-ring should be replaced once a year. Always check the O-ring before you leave dry land for the day ahead.

You must also shelter your housing from the direct sunlight on the boat – if possible keep it covered with a cool towel or place it in a bucket of water, which is normally available on most dive boats. This helps to stop the housing from fogging up when you enter the water.

Finally, make sure that you give your housing a good soak after every encounter with salt water, if possible with dish soap. A soft toothbrush will get rid of the salt crystals, which can quickly build up around the buttons and controls and cause the worst damage. Silicone bags are a must to stop your housing 'fogging up' in hot and humid conditions ashore.

The benefits of underwater digital photography are phenomenal compared to film. You can view your shots straight away, even underwater, ensuring that you have the shot you want. There is also the bonus of being able to download your photos immediately after a dive, discarding the images that you don't like and touching up those you do with software such as Photoshop. This can save you huge amounts of money on developing and printing costs, and also enables you to share your underwater adventures with friends and family via email. This reason alone makes it worthwhile to take digital pictures underwater.

However, for those still using a film camera, the rules for achieving great shots and equipment care are the same. Underwater disposable cameras can still pack a punch too, just so long as you get close to your subject.

Last year, while travelling, I started taking underwater photographs with a housing. I have never looked back. It is, without a doubt, the best way to make your diving memories last a lifetime. ❧

Transport 1: on four wheels

Hiring and trading cars abroad
by Jack Barker

OVER THE LAST FEW YEARS the complexity and the cost of car hire has fallen enormously, thanks, in large part, to the internet. Throughout the developed world car hire companies have sophisticated online booking facilities. And, even in the most remote countries, email now provides a simple and clear way of communicating that survives occasional power cuts, crosses time differences and even hurdles the failures of individual computers.

In this flurry of e-commerce it is even more worthwhile to book ahead. Car hire companies often offer much more tempting rates to potential customers surfing the net than they do to passengers who arrive at their desk, blearily blinking away the effects of a long flight.

In the competitive rush the car hire companies sometimes try to bump up their profits at the expense of the renter. The most infamous method is through mileage charges, gradually going out of fashion but still able to sting the unwary. Limited mileage rentals allow you to travel a certain distance in the rental car but then charge extra for each mile or kilometre after that. Even if each mile costs just a few pence, this can quickly mount up. Unless you know the exact distance you will be driving, opt for unlimited mileage rentals.

At the rental desk, insurance frequently bumps up your costs. The USA has set the lead here, with cars in many states being rented with little or no insurance included. In the case of an accident this would leave you liable to any damage to your rental car, plus the cost of repairing any other vehicle you might hit – and, significantly, in a country where personal injury litigation is practically a national sport. In the face of this, you will need third party insurance at the very least.

In most countries, comprehensive insurance is included in your rental. However, you agree to pay the first part of any claim, which is known as the excess. Usually this is reasonable, requiring the driver to pay the first £250 to £500 of any damage to your vehicle or any other. Be careful, though. At one Kenyan car hire operation I came across, the excess was fixed at US$20,000.

The excess can be avoided by purchasing Collision Damage Waiver (CDW), which is a daily premium anxiously sold as an extra on many car hire desks and usually (check the small print) means that you can crash as much as you like without paying a penny. This can provide peace of mind if you are driving in difficult conditions – in Jakarta, Teheran or Naples for instance. Or, if you will be using the car where theft is likely – Johannesburg or Lagos spring to mind. In general, however, CDW is a bet loaded against the consumer. Over several rentals most drivers are better off saving the money and driving with care.

Another insurance policy often sold with car hire is Personal Accident Insurance (PAI). This covers any costs that you might incur in hospital treatment. Most standard travel insurance schemes will already cover you for this more cheaply. Still, it might be worth considering PAI if you are travelling, uninsured, through a high-cost healthcare country such as The USA or Canada, where a serious car crash might cost millions in hospital fees.

So how do you choose your car hire company? It is usually safer to choose a major brand, as there will be more people to complain to should things go wrong. Their terms and conditions are also likely to be standardised. The most important factors are simple logistics. Will the company be able to provide the car where you want it and at the right time? Does it have offices at the airport or will you have to add the costs of a taxi to your rental? And do you fit their rental criteria? Many companies won't accept drivers with certain endorsements on their licence or below a certain age. The cost of the rental obviously has its place in your decision. But there comes a point where it is absurd to chase a marginal saving. Some of the budget airlines have struck seemingly attractive deals with local car hire companies. But, on the ground, a single car hire desk may be deluged by an entire planeload of pre-booked clients, which take several hours to process. Meanwhile, other companies, just as cheap and efficient, stand idly by on every side.

Although some car hire companies accept traveller's cheques to cover the deposit, these days it is more usual for them to insist on taking an imprint from a credit card. This can easily be the same card used to make the booking online; it is a good idea to reserve a single card for such transactions as it will be quicker and easier to monitor this account for any fraudulent withdrawals. You will also need to show your passport and driving licence (in the case of the new photo-licence, with its paper counterpart as well).

Outside the European Union you will need an international licence, accompanied by your photo and a few soothing words in the local script, which is usually available from the AA, RAC or other motoring organisation.

Even if a queue builds impatiently behind you, don't rush. If you intend to drive across an international border this is your last chance to double check that you are permitted to do this and that your insurance will remain valid. Carefully check the emergency telephone numbers and procedures for breakdown or accident.

More checks follow when you get out to the car. Your rental form should clearly show any dents on the car: you ensure all are marked. The spare tyre should be full of air, wheel brace and jack in position, snow-chains provided if needed (they are legally required in many mountainous regions in winter) and, in Europe, that there is a breakdown warning triangle.

Finally, check the fuel. Sometimes the rental company marks the actual fuel level on your rental form, but more usually it supplies the car full. Even if you are running late at the end of the rental it is worth filling the car to the brim as there is always a surcharge if the rental company has to top up the tank. On the road, avoid

Car hire

Alamo
www.alamo.co.uk

Avis Rent a Car
www.avis.co.uk

Britz Campervan
www.britz.com

Budget
www.budget.com

Europcar
www.europcar.co.uk

Every Car Hire
www.everycarhire.com

Global Car Hire
www.4globalcarhire.com

Hertz Rent-A-Car
www.hertz.co.uk

Related websites

www.auto-europe.co.uk

www.bugbog.com/directory/car_rental.html

www.carrentals.com

www.car4rental.com

www.dotukdirectory.co.uk

parking fines and speed cameras. Most countries are well able to track you down through the rental companies.

The rental vehicle that causes the most problems with travellers abroad isn't even a car: it's the scooter. In many holiday destinations – the Greek Islands, Bali, and Thailand, to name but a few – people who have never ridden a scooter before rent a step-through 100cc model and set off into unfamiliar traffic systems and dressed for the sun rather than gravel rash. These machines can travel more than 50 miles per hour, often on atrocious roads. Fall off dressed in t-shirt and flip-flops and your feet will be first to be shredded. Hit something or someone and you will then realise there is no insurance either. Renting a scooter abroad is a good idea only if you know how to ride one responsibly.

The rules of car rental melt somewhat in the developing world. Here it is more important than ever to look the car over carefully. Brakes, tyres and mechanics all need checking, and the first few miles should be treated as a test drive. Some small operators have no cover in place for breakdown – you will have to arrange repair and recovery yourself. These are usually just the places where there are predatory mechanics who are just longing to get under your bonnet so they can charge a fortune to fix things. In such countries it is only sensible to sacrifice your independence and rent a car with driver. Used to local conditions and taking care of their own vehicles, they are a much safer option. Even if the initial cost is higher, you are likely to save in the long run.

An alternative to rental is to buy your own car and sell it at the end of your travels. This can be practical and even profitable, with overland trade routes in old cars running from Europe to West Africa, South to East Africa and the USA down to Central America. But all of these entail a significant amount of paperwork and some hidden costs. If you are buying a vehicle to travel around Europe, be it a car, campervan or light commercial vehicle, it is best to buy a lefthand drive. Costs of such vehicles are lowest in the Netherlands, Brussels and Germany, but you will need a translator to h elp decipher classified advertisements or auction patter. You will also need a postal address to register the vehicle and arrange insurance. It works out cheaper, usually, to buy the vehicle from home.

Outside Europe a web of differing regulations makes buying vehicles a complex business. To buy Royal Enfield motorcycles in India, for example, you need to be a resident. This means that you will need a local to help you out and fiddle around with fraudulent documents that will cause problems (hopefully only minor) at every step of the journey back to the UK.

When buying any vehicle abroad, bear in mind that a cash-rich tourist is a dream client for anyone trying to offload a shady car, whether clocked, unreliable, crash damaged or stolen. Buying from noticeboards in backpacker hostels can be a good way to sidestep local criminals but may find their globetrotting equivalents.

Once you have bought your car it will put up your travel costs. In many countries you will want to find secure parking, which restricts you to more expensive hotels. In some places you will need to pay for an overnight guard. And then there are fuel costs.

At borders corrupt officials may assume that you are rich and traffic policemen often search out tourists in the hope of a bribe or to use up half-written tickets. I have received a large fine driving a car through Bulgaria, but later translation of the ticket proved it was for overloading a lorry.

Should a sea or ocean interrupt your progress, shipping your vehicle often ends up more expensive than expected with harbour and handling charges providing most of the cost. The only advantage – and it is slight – is that you can show a healthy disregard for most parking regulations. Until, that is, you meet a policeman or your car is impounded.

Selling a vehicle is also fraught with regulations and risk. Most countries charge duty on imported cars and if you bring a vehicle in you will be expected to take the same one out, even if it is a burnt-out wreck after a serious accident. In Italy, it is illegal to dump a car and their computerised records will soon be able to track your details. This means that breakdown cover can be a good investment, especially for older vehicles: within Europe, try the AA or RAC.

To take a car further afield you will either need a Carnet De Passage or resort to a range of forms (in Africa *laissez-passers* or *passavants*) to avoid having your vehicle details entered on your passport, linking you irrevocably with the car. To negotiate customs regulations local advice is vital, but bear in mind that not all of it will be reliable or even honest. The best source of information is the embassy of that country. But be circumspect: there may be ways around the letter of the law.

If you do sell your car, get written confirmation of the sale. This will be useful if the vehicle is later used to commit a motoring offence or crime. And, if you do find yourself in trouble with customs, it will help to establish how much you were paid and therefore how much tax is due: in Nigeria it is 400 per cent, before any penalties. It is also wise to ensure that you are paid in a convertible currency – most cars are worth an awful lot of handicrafts – and check unfamiliar notes for forgeries.

Don't be put off, though. To a true petrol-head the possession of a vehicle, like having children or keeping pets, is worth any sacrifice. ❧

JACK BARKER is a freelance travel journalist and guidebook writer.

Overlanding by truck, van or 4x4
by Jack Jackson

TRAVELLING OVERLAND IN YOUR OWN VEHICLE gives you the independence and freedom to go where you like, in a way that no other form of travel can ever hope to match. It also provides you with a familiar bolt-hole that can take you away from the milling crowds and the alienation one tends to feel in a different culture. The vehicle may seem expensive to start with, and can involve you in mountains of bureaucratic paperwork, but considering the cost of transport and accommodation, it becomes a realistic way to travel, particularly when you can escape the bedbugs and dirt that often accompany cheaper accommodation.

Which vehicle?

The choice of vehicle will be a compromise between what can be afforded, what can best handle the terrain to be encountered, and whether spares, fuel, food and water have to be carried or are readily available en route.

Short-wheelbase Land Rovers or Toyota Land Cruisers, Range Rovers and Land Rover Discoverys are ideal in the Ténéré sand sea, but it is impossible to sleep full-length in one of these without the tailgate being open and all the fuel, stores and water removed. Moreover, they are heavy on fuel. After a while, one may long for the convenience and comfort of a Volkswagen Kombi or another, similar-sized panel van!

For a protracted transcontinental or round-the-world journey, you need to consider what sacrifices have to be made to balance the benefits of the more cramped vehicles, including the length of time you expect to be on the road and the degree of home comforts you will want along the way.

Where tracks are narrow, overhung and subject to landslides, as in outlying mountainous regions such as the Karakoram, the only usable vehicles are the smallest, lightweight four-wheel drives, for instance, the soft-topped short-wheelbase Land Rovers or Land Cruisers and the smaller Jeeps. These vehicles also give the best performance when traversing soft sand and steep dunes, but their small payload and fuel-carrying capacity restrict them to short journeys.

If you do not plan to encounter soft sand, mud or snow and your payload consists mainly of people, who, when necessary, can get out and push, you really only need a two-wheel drive vehicle, provided that it has enough strength and ground clearance.

Avoid large American-style conversions. They have lots of room and such home comforts as showers, toilets, microwave ovens and storage space; but their large size, heavy fuel consumption, high weight, low ground clearance, poor traction and terrible approach and departure angles make them unsuitable for any journey off the asphalt road. They also often have engines with electronic control systems, which are not repairable if they go wrong in the Third World.

If cost presents no problem and all spares are to be carried, the ideal vehicle would be an all-wheel drive with a payload of one tonne, evenly distributed between all wheels. Look for a short wheelbase, forward control, high ground clearance, large wheels and tyres, good power-to-weight ratio and reasonable fuel consumption. The vehicles best fitting this specification are the Mercedes Unimog, the Pinzgauer and the Land Rover Military 101 'one tonne'. These are specialist vehicles designed for best cross-country performance and are often soft topped to keep the centre of gravity low. However, the costs involved in buying, running and shipping such vehicles would deter all but the very wealthy.

Considering price, availability of spares and working life, the most commonly used vehicles are the long-wheelbase Land Rovers, the smaller Mercedes Unimogs and the Bedford M-type trucks. The VW Kombi and the smaller Mercedes panel vans are the most popular two-wheel drive vehicles. These are big enough to live in and carry food, water, spares, cooking stoves, beds, clothes, extra fuel and sand ladders. They also remain economical to run, small enough to negotiate narrow bush tracks and light enough to make digging out less frequent and easier.

These vehicles will carry two people in comfort, more if camping or using other accommodation overnight.

A high-roofed vehicle is convenient to stand up in and provides extra storage, but is more expensive on ferries. It also offers increased wind resistance, thus pushing up fuel consumption and making the engine work harder and run hotter. This shortens engine life and increases the risk of mechanical failure.

Trucks

Where heavier payloads are envisaged, such as in Africa, where you will often have to carry large quantities of fuel, the most popular four-wheel drive vehicles are the Bedford M-type trucks and Mercedes Unimogs. Bedford trucks are cheap, simple and, in some ways, crude. They have good cross-country performance when handled sensibly and slowly, but are too heavy in soft sand. They go wrong and bits fall off, but repairs can usually be improvised, and used spares are readily available.

Bedford M-type trucks are best bought ex-UK military, as are their spare parts.

Ex-NATO Mercedes Unimogs are near to perfect for heavy overland or expedition work. Their cross-country performance is exceptional, and their portal axles give them extra ground clearance, though this also makes them easier to turn over. It is almost impossible to get them stuck in sand, though they will stick in mud. They usually have relatively small petrol engines, so you need to use the gearbox well, but fuel consumption is good. The standard six-speed, one-range gearbox can be converted to a four-speed, two-range gearbox, which is useful in sand. Four-wheel drive can be engaged at any speed without declutching. Differential locks are standard. The chassis is arranged to give good weight distribution over all four wheels at almost any angle, but this causes a bad ride on corrugations.

Mechanically, the Unimog is over-complicated. It doesn't go wrong often, but when it does it is difficult to work on and often requires special tools. Later models have the clutch set to one side of the transmission, instead of in line with it, making it much easier to change. Unimogs are best bought from NATO forces in Germany. Spares must be carried with you. Diesel Unimogs are usually ex-agricultural or building contractor, and are therefore less well maintained than military vehicles and may have rust problems.

Land Rovers

Despite some weaknesses, Land Rovers are the most durable four-wheel drive small vehicles on the market. Their spartan comforts are also their main attributes! Most of their recent challengers are too softly sprung and have too many car-type comforts to be reliable in difficult cross-country terrain. Spare parts are readily available worldwide and they are easy to work on with most parts bolted on. The older Series III leaf-sprung models, are more durable than the newer 'Defender' models, and leaf springs are easier to get repaired in the Third World. The aluminium alloy body does not rust, so bent body panels can be hammered back into rough shape and then forgotten. You don't have to be Hercules to change a wheel.

The short-wheelbase Land Rover is usually avoided because of its small load-carrying capacity; but in off-road use, particularly on sand dunes, it has a distinct advantage over the long-wheelbase models. Hard-top models are best for protection against thieves and safer when rolled, unless you have had a roll cage fitted.

When considering long-wheelbase models, it is best to avoid the six-cylinder petrol engine models. All cost more to buy, give more than the normal amount of trouble, are harder to find spares for and recoup less on resale.

The six-cylinder petrol engine uses more fuel and more engine oil than the four-cylinder petrol engine and the carburettor does not like dust or dirty fuel, which means that it often requires stripping and cleaning twice a day in very dusty areas. The electrical fuel pump gives trouble. The forward control turns over easily and, as with the Series IIa Land Rovers, rear half-shafts break if the driver is at all heavy footed.

The four-cylinder models are underpowered, but the increased power of the six cylinder does not compensate for its disadvantages.

The 109" V8 Land Rover has permanent four-wheel drive, with a lockable central differential. It is an excellent vehicle, but very costly on fuel.

The Land Rover 90 and 110, now renamed 'Defender', are designed for speed, economy and comfort on the newer, improved roads in Africa and Asia. Built on a strengthened Range Rover-type chassis and suspension, with permanent four-wheel drive and centre differential lock, stronger gearbox, disc brakes on the front and better doors all round, the vehicle is a vast improvement on earlier models. It is ideal for lightweight safari or personnel carrier use, but for heavy expeditions the coil springs should be upgraded or fitted with airbag-type helper springs.

In European Union countries, outside of the UK, 12-seat Land Rovers should be fitted with a tachometer and come under bus regulations.

Range Rovers and Land Rover Discoverys are not spacious enough for long journeys, nor do they have the load-carrying capacity.

Any hard-top or station wagon Land Rover is suitable for a long trip. If you buy a new Land Rover in a wet climate, run it for a few months before setting off on a trip. This allows the wet weather to get at the many nuts and bolts that keep the body together. If these bolts corrode a bit, it will save you a lot of time later. If you take a brand-new Land Rover into a hot climate, you will regularly have to tighten loose nuts and bolts, particularly those around the roof and windscreen.

Early Land Rover diesel engines were not renowned for their reliability. The newer five-bearing crankshaft diesel engines are better, but still underpowered. Land Rover Ltd still refuses to believe that the Third World requires a large, trouble-free diesel engine, and it is sometimes sensible to fit another engine, such as the Isuzu 3.9 litre or the Perkins 4,154.

With the new TDI turbo diesel engines, Land Rover appears to have fixed the problems of its earlier turbo diesel, and owners rave about their good fuel economy. The GRP camshaft timing belt is now 50 per cent wider, but still causes problems in hot, dusty climates, though, to be fair to Land Rover, many modern vehicles have engines fitted with this type of belt and suffer the same problems.

The latest Defenders and Discoverys have five-cylinder diesel engines with a chain drive to the camshaft, so they not only give more power but eliminate the problems of unreliable cam-belts. They are also available with electronic traction control, among other electronic gizmos, although this system is not suitable for Third World use as it is not user-repairable if it goes wrong.

Stretched 127/130 versions of Land Rovers are available, including crew cab versions, but they are underpowered when fitted with four-cylinder diesel engines. Modern Land Rovers do not have double-skinned roofs, so a loaded or covered roof rack is useful to keep the vehicle cooler in sunny climates.

Other 4x4s

The Land Rover Defender's superb axle articulation and lightweight body gives it a distinct advantage in mud, snow and soft sand. If these conditions are not likely to be encountered, then the leaf-sprung Toyota Land Cruisers are comfortable and reliable, though heavier on fuel. Many Toyota models have large overhanging front bumpers, rear steps and running boards, which negate off-road performance. Coil-sprung Toyota Land Cruisers are less reliable, and the latest models with independent front suspension are best avoided. Nissan Patrols lack off-road agility and, as with American four-wheel drives, their large engines are heavy on fuel.

Despite its Paris/Dakar successes, the Mitsubishi Shogun (called Montero in the USA and Pajero elsewhere) has not proved reliable in continuous Third World use. The Isuzu Trooper is not well designed for true off-road work. Suzukis are just too small. Spares for Japanese vehicles can be a problem to get hold of in some parts of the world.

As with Range Rovers, Mercedes Geländewagons have poor load-carrying capacity and their high costs limit their appeal. Several of the latest four-wheel drive vehicles are of monocoque construction, which leaves them without a strong chassis; together with the Suzuki Vitara, Toyota RAV4 and the new Land Rover Freelander, they are not suitable for overland or expedition use.

Four-wheel drive versions are available of most popular pick-up trucks. Those most common in Africa are based on the Peugeot 504 and the Toyota Hilux. The Synchro version of the Volkswagen Kombi has an advanced fluid-coupling four-wheel drive system but poor ground clearance.

Two-wheel drives

The Volkswagen Kombi is in use in almost every country outside the Soviet bloc and China. Anyone who has travelled overland through Africa, Asia, the Americas or around Australia will notice that the vw Kombi is still a popular independent traveller's overland vehicle. Its ability to survive misuse (up to a point) and carry heavy loads over rough terrain economically, while providing the privacy of a mobile home, are some of the factors that make it so popular.

The Kombi has a one-tonne payload and far more living space than a long-wheelbase Land Rover or Land Cruiser. It lacks the four-wheel drive capability, but partly makes up for this with robust independent suspension, good ground clearance and engine weight over the driven wheels. With experience and astute driving, a Kombi can be taken to places that will amaze some four-wheel drive vehicle buffs. The notorious 25 km 'sea of sand' between In Guezzam and Assamaka in the Sahara has ensnared many a poorly driven 4x4, while a Kombi has stormed through unscathed! With the use of lengths of chicken wire fencing, as sand ladders, plus some helpful pushing, a Kombi can get through quite soft sand.

The second most popular two-wheel drive vehicle for overlanders is the smaller diesel-engined Mercedes panel van, which is very reliable. All the stronger rear-wheel drive panel vans are suitable for overland use and most are available with a four-wheel drive conversion. Avoid vehicles that have only front-wheel drive; when loaded at the rear, they often lose traction, even on wet grass in a campsite.

Petrol versus diesel
Weight for weight, petrol engines have more power than diesel engines, but they have several disadvantages when it comes to hard usage in Third World areas. In hot countries there is a considerable risk of fire and the constant problem of vapour lock, which is at its worst on steep climbs, or on long climbs at altitude. Dust, which often contains iron, gets into and shorts out the distributor. High-tension leads break down, and if much river crossing has to be done, water in the electrics causes more trouble. A further problem is that high-octane fuel is not usually available and low-octane fuel will soon damage a sophisticated engine. However, petrol engines are more easily repaired by less experienced mechanics.

Avoid engines with electronic engine management systems. These are not normally repairable if faulty and a flat battery can cause problems with some of these.

Diesel fuel is messy, smelly and attacks many forms of rubber, but it does not have the fire risk of petrol and, outside Europe, is usually one-third of the price of petrol. It also tends to be more available, as it is used by trucks and tractors.

Diesel engines are heavier and more expensive to buy, but are generally more reliable and require less maintenance. An advantage is that extra torque is available at low engine revolutions. This allows a higher gear in the rough, which improves fuel consumption. This means that less weight of fuel needs to be carried for a section without fuel supplies – improving fuel consumption still further. There is also no electrical ignition to malfunction where there is a lot of dust or water. Against this is the fact that diesel engines are noisier and lack the acceleration of petrol engines, which can be tiring on a long journey.

A second filter in the fuel line is essential to protect the injection pump from bad fuel, and a water sedimentor is useful, but it needs to be well protected from stones and knocks.

Some Japanese diesel vehicles have 24-volt electrical systems.

Tyres

Long-distance travellers have to cover several different types of terrain, which makes it difficult to choose just one set of tyres for the whole route. Unless you expect to spend most of your time in mud or snow, avoid the aggressive-tread, so-called cross-country or all-terrain tyres. These have large, open-cleated treads that are excellent in mud or snow, but on sand they tear away the firmer surface crust, putting the vehicle into the softer sand underneath. Open treads tear up quickly on mixed ground with sharp stones and rocks.

If you expect to spend a lot of time in soft sand, you will require high-flotation tyres with little tread pattern. These compress the sand, causing the least disturbance to the firmer surface crust. Today's standard for such work is the Michelin xs, which has just enough tread pattern to be usable on dry roads but can slide about on wet roads or ice. The xs is a soft, flexible radial tyre, ideal for low-pressure use but easily cut up on sharp stones.

As most travellers cover mixed ground, they require a general truck-type tyre. These have a closed tread, with enough tyre width and lugs on the outside of the tread to be good mixed-country tyres, although obviously not as good in mud or soft sand. Such tyres, when fitted with snow chains, are better than any all-terrain tyre for snow or mud use and, if of radial construction, can be run soft to improve their flotation on sand. The best tyres in this category are the Michelin xzy series.

Radial or cross-ply, tubed or tubeless

Radial tyres are more flexible and have less heat build-up when run soft than cross-ply tyres. They have less rolling resistance, thus improving fuel consumption. For heavy expedition work, Michelin steel-braced radials last longer. You must use the correct inner tubes with radial tyres, preferably the ones produced by the same manufacturer. Radial and cross-ply tyres should never be mixed.

Radial tyres 'set' in use, so when changed around to even out tyre wear they should, preferably, be kept on the same side of the vehicle. A further advantage of radials is that they are easier to remove from the wheel rim with tyre levers when you get a puncture away from help.

Most radial tyres have soft side walls that are easily torn on sharp stones, so if you have to drive over such stones try to use the centre of the tyre, where the tread is thickest. For soft sand use, radial tyres can be run at 40 per cent pressure at speeds below 25 km per hour and 75 per cent pressure for mixed terrain below 50 km per hour. Remember to reinflate to full pressure when you return to firm ground. Tubeless tyres are totally impractical for off-road work, so always use tubed tyres and carry several spare inner tubes.

A vehicle travelling alone in difficult terrain should carry at least one extra spare tyre, as well as the one on the spare wheel. Several vehicles travelling together can get by with only the tyres on the spare wheels, so long as they all have the same size and type of tyres for full interchangeability.

Wide tyres

There is a tendency for 'posers' to fit wide tyres. Such tyres are useful in soft sand and deep snow, but in other situations they negate performance. Worse still, on asphalt roads, hard-top pistes or ice they lower the weight per unit area (and hence the grip) of the tyre on the road, leading to slipping and skidding. Wheels and tyres that are larger than the vehicle manufacturers recommend can damage wheel bearings and cause problems with steering and braking

Never mix tyres of different sizes on four-wheel drive vehicles.

Roof racks

These need to be strong to be of any use. Many of those on the market are flimsy and will soon break up on badly corrugated pistes. Weight for weight, tubular section is stronger than box section, and it should be heavily galvanised.

To extend a roof rack in order to put jerrycans of water or fuel over or even beyond the windscreen is lunacy. The long-wheelbase Land Rover, for instance, is designed so that most of the weight is carried over the rear wheels. The maximum extra weight allowed for the front axle is the spare wheel and a winch. It does not take much more than this to break the front springs or distort the axle. Forward visibility is restricted when going downhill with extended roof racks. Full-length roof racks can be fitted safely, but must be carefully loaded; remember that Land Rover recommends a total roof weight of not more than 90 kg. A good full-length roof rack will weigh almost that on its own.

Expect damage to the bodywork and reinforce likely points of stress, in particular the corners of the windscreen. Good roof rack designs will have their supports positioned in line with the vehicle's main body supports, and will have fittings along the back of the vehicle to prevent the roof racks from juddering forward on corrugations. Without these fittings, holes will be worn in the roof. Modern Land Rovers have aluminium roof channels, so roof racks fitted to these vehicles require additional supports to the bulkhead at the front and the lower body at the rear.

Nylon or Terylene rope is best for tying down baggage. Hemp rope deteriorates quickly in the sun and holds grit, which is hard on your hands. Rubber roof rack straps are useful, but those sold in Europe soon crack up in the sun. You can use circular strips cut from old inner tubes and add metal hooks to make your own straps. These will stand up to the constant sunlight without breaking. Ratchet straps should not be over-tightened.

In deserts, if one doesn't have a motor caravan, sleeping on the roof rack can be a pleasant way of avoiding spiders and scorpions. Fitting a full-length roof rack with plywood makes it more comfortable, as well as keeping the vehicle cool in the sun. Special folding tents for roof racks are available, at a price.

Conversions

An elevating roof or fibreglass 'pop-top' motor caravan conversion has advantages over a fixed roof van. It is lower on the move, can sleep extra people up top, provide extra headroom while camped and insulates well in tropical heat. Some of the better-designed fibreglass pop-tops do not collect condensation, even when you cook inside them. Some of the disadvantages are that they can be easier to break into, they look more conspicuous and more inviting to thieves than a plain top and they have to be retracted before a driver, disturbed in the night, can depart in a hurry.

In some vans, the hole cut in the roof to fit the pop-top weakens the structure of the vehicle. Driving on very bad tracks can cause cracks and structural failures in the body and chassis; failures that would not normally occur if the vehicle spent its life in Europe. Vans should have roof-mounted support plates added along the elevating roof to give torsional support.

A demountable caravan fitted to four-wheel drive pick-up trucks such as the Land Rover, Land Cruiser or Toyota Hi-Lux could provide a lot more room and comfort, but demountables are not generally robust enough to stand up to the off-road conditions of an overland journey. They also add considerably to the height and width of the vehicle and are more expensive than a proper conversion. Moreover, you cannot walk through from the cab to the living compartment.

Furnishing and fittings

Camper conversions should have fittings made of marine plywood rather than hardboard; it is stronger, more durable and not prone to disintegration when hot or wet. If your vehicle is finally destined for the us, it must satisfy us Department of Transport and state regulations for the basic vehicle and the conversion. The same applies to motor caravans destined permanently for Australia, where equally strict Australian design rules apply to both the vehicle and the conversion.

Most water filtration systems, Katadyn, for instance, are portable and many wall-mounted models can be fitted to a vehicle. On many motor caravans, the water tank and even gas cylinders are mounted beneath the floor, where they are most vulnerable off-road.

Front-opening vents or window quarterlights in the front doors are appreciated in warm climates, as are a pair of fans built in for extra ventilation. However, window quarterlights are attractive to thieves. Fresh air is essential when sleeping inside a vehicle in tropical climates and a roof vent is not enough to create an adequate draught. Equip open windows with mosquito netting and strong wire mesh.

On a long transcontinental journey, one will normally have to do without a refrigerator. (It is often preferable to use the space and weight for more fundamental items such as jerrycans or spare parts.) However, if you are carrying large quantities of film or medicines, you might consider using a lightweight dry-operating, thermoelectric 'Peltier-effect' refrigerator from Koolatron Industries, but fit an alternator and spare battery with a larger capacity and a split-charge system.

Stone-guards for lights are very useful, but you need a design that allows you to clean the mud off the lights without removing them (water hoses do not usually exist off the beaten track) and they should not be fitted with self-tapping screws. Such designs are difficult to find.

Air horns should be located away from mud, e.g. on the roof or within the bodywork, where they can be operated by a floor-mounted switch. An isolator may be located on the dashboard to prevent accidental operation of the horn.

For sunny countries, paint chrome windscreen wipers, wing mirrors and any wing steps matt black to stop dangerous reflections from the sun, and have fresh windscreen wiper rubber blades at the ready for when you return to wet climates.

A good, powerful spotlight fitted on the rear of the roof rack will be invaluable when reversing and will also provide enough light for pitching tents. Normal reversing lights will be of no use. Bull bars, also known as nudge bars, are usually more trouble than they are worth, may invalidate your insurance and damage the body or chassis if struck with any force. The EU wishes to ban them.

Paperwork

As well as the obvious requirement for passports, visas and personal insurance, you will require: vehicle insurance for the whole journey, the vehicle registration document, a letter of permission to drive the vehicle if you are not the owner, each of the two types of international driving licences (these vary in the languages of translation) and a *carnet de passage* for the vehicle. Have photocopies of all of these documents and spare passport-sized photographs. Some countries will insist that you also buy local insurance, but this will only give you the bare minimum of third party cover.

The *carnet de passage* acts as a passport for the vehicle and is intended to stop you selling it; it will be your largest single expense and is obtainable through the AA or RAC by depositing a bond or taking out insurance. A few countries will note the vehicle in your passport instead of requiring a carnet de passage.

All-important paperwork is best kept in a strongbox that is fixed directly to the vehicle chassis.

Finally, whatever type of vehicle you take and however you equip it, you should aim to be as self-sufficient as possible. You should have food to last for weeks, not days, as well as the tools, spare parts and personal ability to maintain your vehicle and keep it going. Without these, and in spite of the occasional genuinely kind person, you will be conned and exploited to the extent that the journey will become a major ordeal. With adequate care and preparation, however, your overland journey will be an experience of a lifetime. ❧

Overland travel organisations

AAT KINGS TOURS
www.aatkings.com
Coach tour operator plus
four-wheel-drive safaris in
the Australian outback.

**ACACIA AFRICAN
ADVENTURES**
UK tel: 0207 706 4700
www.acacia-africa.com
African safaris.

ADVENTURE CENTRE
www.adventure-centre.
com
Worldwide overland
expeditions.

AFRICA TRAVEL CENTRE
UK tel: 0845 450 1520
www.africatravel.co.uk
Consultancy service for
overland travel.

AMERICAN ADVENTURES
USA tel: 1 800 221 0596
UK tel: 01295 256777
www.americanadventures.
com

BRIDGE THE WORLD
UK tel: 0207 209 9418
www.allinlondon.co.uk/
directory/
Travel agency with
overland brochures.

CC AFRICA
UK tel: 01883 349899
www.ccafrica.com
Overland tours in one of
the 37 safari camps.

**DRAGOMAN/ENCOUNTER
OVERLAND**
UK tel: 0870 499 4475
www.dragoman.co.uk
Overland travel in Asia,
Africa, North and South
America.

EXODUS EXPEDITIONS
UK tel: 0870 240 5550
USA tel: 1 800 228 8747
www.exodustravels.co.uk

EXPLORE WORLDWIDE
UK tel: 0870 333 4001
USA tel: 800 227 8747
www.explore.co.uk
Leading tour operator to
over 100 countries.

**THE GLOBETROTTERS
CLUB**
www.globetrotters.co.uk
An association of travellers
worldwide share their
views, advice, knowledge
and experiences of
travelling.

**GUERBA ADVENTURE &
DISCOVERY HOLIDAYS**
UK tel: 01373 826611
www.guerba.co.uk
Leading operator in
overland travel and safaris.

JOURNEY LATIN AMERICA
UK tel: 020 8747 3108 /
0161 832 1441
www.journeylatinamerica.
co.uk
Guided tours using local
transport.

MOUNTAIN TRAVEL SOBEK
UK tel: 01494 448901
USA tel: 1 888 687 6235
www.mtsobek.com
Overland travel plus
wildlife and walking
safaris.

OASIS OVERLAND
UK tel: 01963 363 400
www.oasisoverland.co.uk
Overland travel to Africa,
the Middle East and South
America.

SUNDOWNERS TRAVEL
www.sundownerstravel.
com
Travel on the Mongolian,
Manchurian and Siberian
Railways.

TAUCK WORLD DISCOVERY
UK tel: 0800 961 834
www.tauck.com
Luxury coach tour
operator.

TRAILFINDERS
UK tel: 0845 058 5858
www.trailfinders.com
Independent travel
company that can organise
trips with overland
companies.

TREKAMERICA
UK tel: 0870 444 8735
USA tel: 1 800 221 0596
www.trekamerica.com
Camping and trekking in
North America.

WEXAS
UK tel: 020 7589 3315
www.wexas.com
Travel club for
independent travellers
that can advise and book
overland trips for its
members.

Off-road drivers' checklist
by Jack Jackson

If you are an experienced off-road motorist and vehicle camper, you are, without doubt, the best person to decide exactly what you need to do and take for your trip. Even so, extensive experience doesn't guarantee perfect recall and everyone might find it useful to jog their memories by consulting other people's lists.

The lists that follow do assume some experience – without some mechanical expertise, for example, an immaculately stocked tool-box is of limited use. It is also assumed that the motorist in question will spend at least some time driving off-road, most probably in a four-wheel-drive vehicle.

Vehicle spares and tools

PETROL ENGINES
3 fan belts (plus power steering pump belts and air conditioning pump belts if fitted)
1 complete set of gaskets
4 oil filters (change every 5000 km)
2 tubes of Silicone RTV gasket compound
1 complete set of radiator hoses
2 metres of spare heater hose
2 metres of spare fuel pipe hose

0.5 metres of spare distributor vacuum pipe hose
2 exhaust valves
1 inlet valve
1 complete valve spring
Fine and coarse valve grinding paste and valve grinding tool
1 valve spring compressor
1 fuel pump repair kit (if electric type, take a complete spare pump)
1 water pump repair kit
1 carburettor overhaul kit where fitted
2 sets of sparking plugs
1 timing light or 12 volt bulb and holder with leads
3 sets of contact breaker points (preferably with hard fibre cam follower, because plastic types wear down quickly and close up the gap in the heat)
2 distributor rotor arms
1 distributor condenser
1 distributor cap
1 sparking plug spanner
1 set of high tension leads (older, wire type)
1 ignition coil
Slip ring and brushes for alternator or a complete spare alternator
2 cans of spray type ignition sealant, for dusty and wet conditions
2 spare air intake filters, if you do not have the oil–bath type

EXTRAS FOR DIESEL ENGINES
Delete sparking plugs, contact breaker points, distributor, vacuum pipe hose, rotor arms, distributor cap and condenser, high tension leads, coil, and carburettor overhaul from the above list and substitute:
1 spare set of injectors, plus cleaning kit
1 complete set of high

pressure injector pipes
1 set injector copper sealing washers plus steel sealing washers where these are used
1 set injector return pipe washers
1 metre of plastic fuel pipe, plus spare nuts and ferrules
A second in–line fuel filter
4 fuel filter elements
3 spare heater plugs, if fitted

BRAKES AND CLUTCH
2 wheel cylinder kits (one right and one left)
1 flexible brake hose
1 brake bleeding kit
1 brake, master cylinder seals kit
1 clutch, master cylinder seals kit
1 clutch, slave cylinder kit (or a complete unit for Land Rover series III or 110) (It is important to keep all these kits away from heat)
1 clutch centre plate
If you have an automatic gearbox, make sure you have plenty of the special fluid for this, a spare starter motor and a spare battery, kept charged
If you have power steering, carry the correct fluid and spare hoses
Some Land Rovers have automatic gearbox fluid in a manual gearbox

GENERAL SPARES
2 warning triangles (compulsory in most countries)
1 good workshop manual (not the car handbook)
1 good torch and a fluorescent light with leads to work it from vehicle battery, plus spare bulbs and tubes
1 extra tyre in addition to that on the spare wheel

(Only one spare wheel and tyre will be necessary if two identical vehicles are travelling together)

3 extra inner tubes (6 in areas of Acacia thorns)

1 large inner tube repair kit

1 set of tyre levers and 1 kg sledge hammer for tyres

5 spare inner tube valve cores and 5 valve core tools

4 inner tube valve dust caps (metal type)

1 tyre pump, which fits into the sparking plug socket threads: or a 12 volt electric compressor, which is the only system available if you have a diesel engine

Plenty of good quality engine oil

2 litres of distilled water or 1 bottle of water de–ionizing crystals

12-volt soldering iron and solder

Hand drill and drills

16 metres of nylon or Terylene rope, strong enough to upright an overturned vehicle

1 good jack and wheel brace (if hydraulic, carry spare fluid)

1 (at least) metal fuel can, eg a jerry can

1 grease gun and a tin of multi–purpose grease

5 litres of correct differential and gearbox oil

1 large fire extinguisher suitable for petrol and electrical fires

1 reel of self–vulcanizing rubber tape, for leaking hoses

1 pair heavy-duty electric jump leads at least 3 metres long

10 push fit electrical connectors (of type to suit vehicle)

2 universal joints for prop shafts

0.5 litre can of brake and clutch fluid

1 small can of general light oil for hinges, etc

1 large can of WD40

1 starting handle, if available

2 complete sets of keys, kept in different places

1 small Isopon or fibre glass kit for repairing fuel tank and body holes

2 kits of general adhesive eg Bostik or Araldite Rapid

1 tin of hand cleaner (washing up liquid will do in an emergency)

Spare fuses and bulbs for all lights, including those on the dash panel, the red charging light bulb is often part of the charging circuit

1 radiator cap

Antifreeze —if route passes through cold areas

Spare windscreen wipers for use on return journey (keep away from heat)

Inner and outer-wheel bearings

A good tool kit

Wire brush to clean threads

Socket set

Torque wrench

Ring and open-ended spanners

Hacksaw and spare blades

Large and small flat and round files

Selection of spare nuts, bolts and washers, of type and thread/s to fit vehicle

30cm Stillson pipe wrench

1 box spanner for large wheel-bearing lock nuts

Hammer

Large and small cold chisels, for large and stubborn nuts

Self–grip wrench, e.g. Mole type

Broad and thin nosed pliers

Circlip pliers

Insulating tape

3 metres electrical wire

(vehicle type, not mains)

1 set of feeler gauges

Small adjustable wrench

Tube of gasket cement, eg Red Hermetite

Tube of Loctite thread sealant

Large and small slot head and Phillips head screwdrivers

Accurate tyre pressure gauge

Hardwood or steel plate, to support the jack on soft ground

Extras for off-road use

2 sand ladders per vehicle (4 if the vehicle travels alone)

3 wheel bearing hub oil seals

1 rear gearbox oil seal

1 rear differential oil seal

1 rear spring main leaf, complete with bushes if the vehicle is leaf sprung

1 front spring main leaf, complete with bushes if the vehicle is leaf sprung

4 spare spring bushes

4 spring centre bolts

1 set (4) of spring shackle plates

1 set (4) of spring shackle pins

2 rear axle 'U' bolts

1 front axle 'U' bolt

If instead of leaf springs you have coil springs, carry one spare each for front and back axles plus 2 mountings and 4 bushes

1 set of shock absorber mounting rubbers

2 spare engine mounting rubbers

1 spare gearbox mounting rubber

2 door hinge pins

1 screw jack (to use it on its side when changing springs and/or bushes)

2 metres of strong chain plus bolts to fix it, for

splinting broken chassis axle or spring parts
Snow chains if you expect a lot of mud or snow
5cm paint brush, to dust off the engine, so that you can work on it
Large groundsheet for lying on when working under the vehicle or repairing tyres, so as to prevent sand from getting between the inner tube and the tyre
1 high lift jack
2 long-handled shovels for digging out
2 steering ball joints
2 spare padlocks
Radiator stop leak compound (dry porridge or raw egg will do in an emergency)

SPECIFIC TO SERIES IIA LAND ROVERS
1 set rear axle half shafts (heavy duty)

SPECIFIC TO SERIES III LAND ROVERS
1 complete gear change lever, if you have welded bush type (or replace with groove and rubber ring type)
4 nylon bonnet hinge inserts (or 2 home–made aluminium ones)
2 windscreen outer hinge bolts (no 346984)
2 windscreen inner tie bolts
2 rear differential drain plugs
1 set big end nuts
1 rear axle drive plate (Salisbury)

SPECIFIC TO LAND ROVER TURBO DIESEL AND TDI ENGINES
2 spare glass fibre main timing belts, stored flat and in a cool place
3 pushrods
3 brass cam followers

2 air filter paper elements

Maintenance check before departure

1. Change oil and renew all oil and fuel filters
2. Clean air filter and change oil bath or air filter element
3. Lubricate drive shafts, winch and the speedometer cable
4. Lubricate all locks with dry graphite
5. Adjust and lubricate all door hinges
6. Inspect undercarriage for fluid leaks, loose bolts, etc
7. Rotate all tyres, inspecting for cuts and wear
8. Check and adjust brakes
9. Check adjustment of carburettor or injection pump
10. Check fan belts and accessory belts
11. Check sparking plugs. Clean and re–gap if necessary (replace as necessary). If diesel, clean or replace injectors
12. Check ignition timing
13. Check and top up: front and rear differentials, swivel–pin housings, transmission, transfer case, overdrive, power steering pump, and air conditioning pump (if applicable), steering box, battery, brake and clutch fluid and the cooling system
14. Check that there are no rattles
15. Inspect radiator and heater hoses
16. Check breather vents on both axles, gearbox and fuel filler cap
17. Check all lights and direction indicators

18. Check wheel balance and steering alignment (always do this with new wheels and/or tyres)
19. Check battery clamps and all electrical wiring for faulty insulation

Running repairs
by Jack Jackson

BEFORE YOU DEPART ON AN OVERLAND JOURNEY, use your vehicle for several months, to run in any new parts properly. This will enable you to find any weaknesses and become acquainted with its handling and maintenance.

Give it a thorough overhaul before leaving. If you fit any extras, make sure that they are as strong as the original vehicle. For precise navigation, you should know how accurate your odometer is, for the tyres fitted: larger tyres, e.g. sand tyres, will have a longer rolling circumference. Fit a battery isolation switch: it could save your vehicle in a fire and is an excellent anti-theft device. (New models of these will allow enough power through, to run any necessary clocks and memory systems, when disconnected.)

Loading

Overloading is the largest single cause of broken-down vehicles and the easiest to avoid. Calculate your payload against the manufacturer's recommendation for the vehicle. Water is 1 kg per litre, fuel roughly 0.8 kg per litre, plus the weight of the container. Concentrate on the essentials and cut back on the luxuries. It could make all the difference between success and failure.

By using several identical vehicles travelling in convoy, you can minimise the weight of spares and tyres to be carried. The idea of using one large vehicle to carry fuel etc., accompanying several smaller, more agile vehicles, does not work out well in practice. The larger vehicle will often be heavily bogged down and the smaller vehicles will have difficulty towing it out, often damaging their drive train in the process. Also, the vast difference in general journey speed and the extra spares needed cause many problems, unless you are to have a static base camp.

For rough terrain, trailers are not advisable. They get stuck in sand, slip into ditches and overturn on bad tracks. Powered trailers have been known to overturn the prime vehicle. On corrugated tracks, trailer contents soon become so battered as to be unrecognisable. Trailers are impossible to manhandle in sand or mud, and make life difficult if you have to turn around in an awkward situation. They also reduce the efficiency of the front wheels' driving and put strain on the rear axle.

If you must take a trailer, make sure that it has the same wheels and tyres as the towing vehicle, that the hitch is the strong NATO type, and that the wiring loom is fixed above the chassis, where it will be protected.

Regular checks

Once in the field, check the chassis, springs, spring shackles and bushes, steering, bodywork, exhaust and tyres, every evening when you stop for the day. Every morning, when it is cool, check engine oil, battery electrolyte, tyre pressures and cooling water, and fill the fuel tank. Check transmission oils and hydraulic fluids at least every third day. In dusty areas, keep breather vents clear, on the axles, gearbox, and the fuel tank filler cap. Keep an eye on electrical cables for worn insulation, which could lead to shorting, thus causing a fire. Make sure that you carry and use the correct oils and fluids in all systems. Deionising water crystals are easier to carry than distilled water, for batteries. Remember to lubricate door hinges, door locks, padlocks etc., and remember that in many deserts you need anti-freeze in the engine for night temperatures.

Brush all parts clear of sand or dust before working on them. When working under a vehicle, have a groundsheet to lie on and keep things clean, wear goggles to protect your eyes. A small vice fitted to a strong part of the vehicle will aid repairs. In scrub or insect country you'll need to brush down the radiator mesh regularly.

Punctures

Punctures are the most common problem in off-road travel. Rear wheel punctures often destroy the inner tube, so several spare inner tubes should be carried. Wherever possible, I prefer to repair punctures with a known good tube and get the punctured tube vulcanised properly, when I next visit a larger town. However, you should always carry a repair kit, in case you use all your inner tubes. Hot patch repair kits do not work well enough on the truck type inner tubes that are used in four-wheel drive vehicle tyres.

Michelin radial tyres have the advantage that their beads almost fall off the wheel rim when flat. If you cannot break a bead, try driving over it or using a jack and the weight of the vehicle. If the wheel has the rim on one side wider than the other, remove the tyre over the narrowest side, starting with both beads in the well of the wheel. Narrow tyre levers are more efficient than wide ones. Sweep out sand and grit, file off any sharp burrs on the wheel and put everything back together on a groundsheet, to stop any sand or grit getting in to cause further punctures.

When refitting the tyre, use liquid soap and water or bead lubricant and a Schrader valve tool to hold the inner tube valve in place. Start and finish refitting the tyre, by the valve. Pump the tyre up enough to refit the bead on the rim, then let it down again to release any twists in the inner tube. Then pump the tyre up again to rear tyre pressure. If the wheel has to be fitted on the front later, it is easy to let out some air.

Foot pumps have a short life in sand and are hard work. If your vehicle does not already have a compressor, then use a sparking plug socket fitting pump if you have a petrol engine, or a 12 volt electric compressor which can be used with either petrol or diesel engines. Keep all pumps clear of sand. When using electric compressors, keep the engine running at charging speed.

Damaged steel-braced radial tyres often have a sharp end of wire internally, causing further punctures. These should be cut down as short as is possible and the tyre then gaitered, using thicker truck inner tubes. The edges of the gaiter should be bevelled and the tyre must be at full pressure to stop the gaiter moving about. On paved roads, gaitered tyres behave like a buckled wheel, so they are dangerous. Most truck tyres (including Michelin XZY) can be re-cut when worn and these re-cuts are useful in areas of sharp stones or acacia thorns, where tyres damage easily. (These re-cuts are not legal on light vehicles in the UK.)

Wheel braces get overworked in off-road use, so also have a good socket or ring spanner available, to fit the wheel nuts. With a hot wheel after a puncture, you may need an extension tube on the wheel brace, to undo the wheel nuts; but do not retighten them this way or you will cause damage.

In soft sand, use a strong one-foot-square metal or wooden plate under the jack, when jacking up the vehicle. Two jacks, preferably including a high-lift jack, are often necessary in off-road conditions.

If your vehicle spare wheel is stored under the chassis, it can be difficult to get out, when you have a puncture off-road. Store it inside the vehicle or on the roof.

Fuel problems

Bad fuel is common; extra fuel filters are useful, and essential for diesel engines. The main problems are water and sediment. When things get bad, it is quicker long-term to drain the fuel tank, decant the fuel and clean it out. Always keep the wire mesh filter in the fuel filler in place. Do not let the fuel tank level fall too low, as this will produce water and sediment in the fuel lines. With a diesel engine, you may then have to bleed the system. If fuelling up from 40-gallon drums, give them time to settle and leave the bottom inch, which will often be water and grit.

If you have petrol in jerry cans in a hot, dry climate, always earth them to discharge any static electricity before opening, and earth the vehicle before touching jerry cans to the fuel filler pipe. Fuel starvation is often caused by dust blocking the breather hole in the fuel tank filler cap.

Electric fuel pumps are unreliable; carry a complete spare. For mechanical fuel pumps, carry a reconditioning kit. In hot countries or in low gear at altitude, mechanical fuel pumps on petrol engines often get hot and cause vapour lock. Wrap the pump in bandages and pour water onto it to cool it. If this is a constant problem, fit a plastic pipe from the windscreen washer system to the bandaged fuel pump and squirt it regularly.

Low-pressure fuel pipes can be repaired using epoxy resin adhesives, bound by self-vulcanising rubber tape. High-pressure injector pipes must be brazed or completely replaced. Carry spares of these and spare injectors.

Diesel engine problems are usually fuel or water, you should know how to bleed the system correctly. If this fails to correct the problem, check all fuel pipes and joints, fuel pump and filter seals, for leaks. Hairline cracks in the high-pressure injector pipes are hardest to find. Fuel tank leaks repair best with glass reinforced plastic kits.

Electrical problems

These are a constant problem with petrol engines. Carry a spare distributor cap, rotor arm, sparking plugs, points, condenser and coil where fitted; all tend to break up or short out in hot countries. Replace modern high-tension leads with the older copper-wire type and carry spares. Keep a constant check on sparking plugs and contact breaker points. If you are losing power, first check the gap and wear on the points. Spray all ignition components with silicone sealant to keep out dust and water.

Keep battery connections tight, clean and greased. Replace battery slip-on connections with clamp-on types. Keep battery plates covered with electrolyte, top up only with distilled water or deionised water. Batteries are best checked with a battery hydrometer. There are special instruments for checking the modern sealed-for-life batteries.

Alternators and batteries should be disconnected before performing any electrical arc welding on the vehicle. Never run the engine with the alternator or battery disconnected. Alternators are not as reliable as they should be. If the diodes are separate, carry spares; if not, carry a complete spare alternator. On some vehicles, the red charging warning light on the dashboard is part of the circuit, so carry spare bulbs for all lights. Make sure you carry spare fuses and fan belts.

Regularly check that batteries are well clamped down and that electrical wires are not frayed or passing over sharp edges. The risk of electrical fire due to shorting is very high on rough tracks.

Overturned vehicles

Given the nature of the terrain they cover, overturned vehicles are not unusual on expeditions. Normally it happens at such a slow speed that no one is injured, nor even windows broken. If this happens, your first action should be to make sure the engine has stopped and the battery is disconnected. Check for human injury, then completely unload the vehicle.

Once unloaded, vehicles can usually be righted easily using manpower, though a second vehicle or winch can make things easier, in the right conditions. Once the vehicle is righted, check for damage, sort out all oil levels and spilt battery acid, and any oil that may be in the intercooler (if fitted). Then turn the engine over several times with the sparking plugs or injectors removed, to clear the bores of oil above the pistons.

Caution: Stand well clear of the side of the engine that houses the sparking plug sockets or injector ports, and of any point in line with injector high pressure pipe outlets. Fluids will eject from these at pressure that is high enough to penetrate your skin or blind you. Replace the sparking plugs or injectors and run the engine as normal.

Short-wheelbase vehicles have a habit of breaking away or spinning on bends and corrugations, often turning over. So drive these vehicles with extra care.

Drowned vehicles

Make sure that the occupants are safe, rescue them first, then recover the vehicle to safe ground, where it will not obstruct other traffic. Empty the vehicle and allow it and all electrical components to drain and dry out. Check for water and silt in drum brakes, all oils and fluids, the air filter and the air inlet system, clear and clean as necessary. Water is heavier than oil, it sinks to the lowest point and can be drained at the drain plugs. If oil looks milky, it will have been emulsified by moving parts: wait several hours, drain off any free water and replace with new oils as soon as is possible.

Drowned engines

Note the 'caution' in 'Overturned vehicles' above.

With diesel engines, change the fuel filter and clean the sedimentor if fitted. Remove the sparking plugs or injectors and turn the engine over in short bursts with the starter motor. Continue until there is no sign of water in the cylinders. If there is sediment, strip the engine down. Refit all components and run the engine till warm; check for problems, especially for shorting out of electrical components – these could cause a fire. Stop the engine and recheck fuel filters for water, and drain or clean as necessary.

When you reach civilisation, have the vehicle hosed out with fresh water and replace all oils and fluids with new ones. With diesel engines, fully service the injector pump and injectors. If the vehicle drowned in sea water, have the complete wiring loom replaced and all electrical connections cleaned, or you will be plagued by minor electrical problems for evermore.

Extreme cold

Arctic temperatures are a very specialist situation. Vehicles are stored overnight in heated hangars. When in the field, engines are either left running or else have an electric engine heater, which is plugged into a mains power supply. Oils are either specialist or diluted to the maker's recommendations.

Petrol is the preferred fuel for lighter vehicles but, for heavier uses, diesel vehicles have heaters built into the fuel system and the fuel is diluted with petrol. All fuel is scrupulously inspected for water before being used. Batteries must be in tip-top condition, as they lose efficiency when cold.

General tips and improvisations

Steering locks are best removed; if not, leave the key in them permanently in dusty areas. A spare set of keys should be hidden safely, somewhere under the body or chassis.

When replacing wheel hub bearing oil seals, also replace the metal mating piece.

Wire hose clips are best replaced with flat metal Jubilee type clips. Carry spare hoses, although these can be repaired in an emergency with self-vulcanising rubber tape. Heater hoses can be sealed off with a sparking plug.

Bad radiator leaks can be sealed with epoxy resin or glass reinforced plastic. For small leaks, add some Radweld, porridge, or raw egg, to the radiator water.

Always use a torque wrench on aluminium cylinder heads or other aluminium components.

In hot countries do not leave spanners in direct sunlight, as they can be too hot to use when next picked up.

In sand, always work on a groundsheet and don't put parts down in the sand. In sandstorms, make a protected working area around the vehicle, using groundsheets. If possible, park the vehicle rear on to the wind and cover all windows to prevent them being etched by the sand.

If you get wheel shimmy on returning to paved roads, first check for mud, buckled wheels, gaitered tyres and loose wheel bearings. If it is none of these, check the swivel pins, which can usually be dampened by removing shims.

Carry any spare parts containing rubber well away from heat, including the sun's heat on the bodywork.

If you cannot get into gear, first check for stones caught up in the linkage.

If you use jerry cans, carry spare rubber seals. Always carry water in light-proof polypropylene cans, to stop the growth of algae. (Available ex-military in the UK.)

Lengths of strong chain with long bolts, plus wood or tyre levers, can be used as splints on broken chassis parts, axles or leaf springs. If you do not have a differential lock and need one in an emergency, you can lock the spinning wheel if it has a drum brake, by tightening up the brake adjuster cam, but only use this system for a few metres at a time.

For emergency fuel tanks, use a jerry can on the roof, with a hose connected to the fuel lift pump. Drive slowly and never let the can get lower than half full.

If one vehicle in convoy has a defunct charging system, swap that vehicle's battery every 100 kilometres.

For repair work at night, or camp illumination, small fluorescent lights have the least drain on the battery.

If the engine is overheating, it will cool down quickest going downhill in gear, using the running engine as a brake. If you stop with a hot engine, then unless it is showing signs of seizure, keep the engine ticking over fast; this will cool it down quicker and more evenly than if you stop it. If you switch off an overheating engine, you are likely to get a warped cylinder head.

Make sure that there are no pin holes in the rubber connecting hose, between the air filter and the engine inlet manifold.

If you have a partially seized six-cylinder engine, remove the piston and connecting rod involved, disconnect the sparking plug and high tension lead (or the injector if diesel). Close the valves by removing the push rods, or rocker arms if overhead cam. If diesel, feed the fuel from the disconnected fuel injector pipe to a safe place away from the heat of the engine, and drive slowly. If you have a hole in the block, seal it with any sheet metal plus glass reinforced plastic and self-tapping screws to keep out dust or sand.

In an emergency, you can run a diesel engine on kerosene (paraffin) or domestic heating oil, by adding one part of engine oil to 100 parts of the fuel, to lubricate the injector pump. In hot climates, diesel engine crankcase oils are good for use in petrol engines; but do not use petrol engine crankcase oils in diesel engines.

Bent track rods should be hammered back as straight as possible, to minimise tyre scrubbing and the possibility of a roll.

With four-wheel drive vehicles, if you break a rear half-shaft, you can continue in two-wheel drive, by removing both rear half-shafts and putting the vehicle into four-wheel drive. If the front or rear differential is broken, remove both of the half-shafts on that axle and the propeller shaft concerned and engage four-wheel drive. If a permanent four-wheel drive jams in the centre differential lock position, remove the front propeller shaft and drive on slowly.

Temporary drain or filler plugs can be whittled from wood and sealed in with epoxy resin.

Silicone RTV compound can be used for most gaskets, other than cylinder head gaskets. Silicone RTV compound or PTFE tape is useful when putting together leaking fuel line connections.

Paper gaskets can be reused if smeared with grease.

If you develop a hydraulic brake fluid leak and do not have enough spare fluid, travel on slowly, using the engine as a brake. If the leak is really bad, you can disconnect a metal pipe upstream of the leak, bend it over and hammer the end flat, or fit an old pipe to which this has already been done. Rubber hoses can be clamped, using a round bar to minimise damage. If you have a dual system, then the brakes will still work as normal, but if not, you will have uneven braking on only three wheels. If you lose your clutch, you can still change gear, by adjusting the engine speed, as with double-declutching. It is best to start the engine with the gearbox already in second gear.

Four-wheel drive vehicles are high off the ground and it is often easier to work on the engine if you put the spare wheel on the ground and stand on it. If your bonnet can be hinged right back, tie it back so that the wind does not drop it onto your head.

Steering relays that do not have a filler hole can be topped up by removing two opposite top cover bolts and filling through one of the holes until oil comes out of the other.

If you burst an oil gauge pressure pipe, remove the 'T' piece, remove the electric pressure sender from it, and screw this back into the block. You will then still have the electric low pressure warning light. ❧

The art of motorcycle maintenance
by Chris Scott

SETTING OFF BY MOTORBIKE IS A BOLD but easy decision to make. However, be under no illusions as to the sacrifices needed for two-wheeled life on the road. Chief amongst these is a bike's limited ability to carry little more than essentials. Documentation for bikes is identical to that needed for cars, and one should always carry copies. The cost of a carnet de passage is one good reason not to take an expensive machine, the fact that a long journey will annihilate its resale value is another. Inexpensive bikes, well prepared, are the best way to go.

Before you go

Taking the UK as a departure point, the three classic Big Trips are: across Africa to Cape Town; across Europe and Asia, taking either the 'low road' to India and beyond, or the 'high road' via Central Asia to Mongolia and Far Eastern Russia. Lastly, the trans Americas, from Alaska to Cape Horn, is another great trip, most spectacular in the High Andes around Peru, Ecuador and Bolivia. Africa, with its unavoidable desert, jungles and tedious border crossings is the toughest, while the southern Asia route offers the best value for its cultural and scenic rewards.

Before undertaking these trips, you should consider taking an exploratory run, to Morocco, for example, to see how your bike will perform. Much can be learned on a test run, above all from the shock of finding out how your bike actually handles when fully loaded on dirt roads. Allow at least a year for preparation before starting your trip – and also time enough to acquire your funding. A good place to start researching routes on the internet is www.adventure-motorcycling.com, which features over 800 trip reports from all around the world. As for budgets: trans-Africa will cost about £4, 000, plus the cost of your bike; India and back about £3, 000 and round the world up to £12, 000, depending on your trip duration, route and resistance to temptations.

When it comes to getting your bike to your starting point, remember that while shipping is cheap, it is also slow and unnecessarily complicated; in most cases air freight is much more efficient and reliable. Leave some money at home with a reliable friend, or a credit card number with a friendly bike shop, that way vital items can be quickly despatched with just one call.

Choosing a bike

A four-stroke, single-cylinder trail bike of around 650 cc is best for Africa. For the main overland route to India or the Pan-American Highway any road bike will do and, in this case, a big, comfortable, shaft-driven tourer makes a lot of sense. Road bikes will limit your ability to explore off the highway and are exhausting when you have to detour off-road, but they are a better option for passengers. Whatever bike you choose, consider these factors along with the total weight once loaded:

- Lightness
- Economy
- Comfort
- Mechanical simplicity
- Agility
- Reliability
- Robustness

BMWs are famously popular, both the F650 singles and the much heavier 1150GS twin. Both these models are fuel injected – a growing trend among motorcycles but not one that should put you off. KTM's 640 cc Adventure is an ideal bike for hard off-roading, but at the cost of an uncomfortable seat, high maintenance intervals and sub-Japanese reliability – Honda's 750 cc Africa Twin being a good example. Women or short-legged men might find lower-seated BMW 650s or Suzuki DR400s easier to manage.

Bike modifications and tyres

If you're buying a bike, go for one with a big tank (i.e. at least 20 litres): this will solve a lot of logistical problems. Jerry cans are awkward to carry, but may be essential for a desert crossing. Water-cooled engines are common but choose a model where the radiators are not prone to damage in the event of a fall. Oil coolers can be a useful addition in hot climates. Other tips are to get hold of a bigger footplate for your sidestand to support the bike on soft ground and to fit handlebar lever protectors and security bolts (rim locks) on wheel rims. Use only top-quality o-ring chains, for example DID or Regina. Paper element in-line fuel filters are another wise modification, and if you don't trust foreign motor oil, change it every 2, 000 km or so. Replace cosmetic, plastic sump guards with proper alloy bash plates. Carry a tool for every fitting on your bike, plus duct tape, wire and glue. Modern bikes (especially the ones recommended) are incredibly reliable, and so spares are up to you, but at least carry heavy-duty inner tubes, control levers and anything else that is likely to wear out or break before you can replace it.

Tyre choice is always a quandary. To cross Africa, run down to the Sahara on any old tyre and then fit Michelin Deserts, extremely tough desert racing knobblies that will last well beyond the mudbath of the Congo basin with barely a puncture. Less expensive, though not quite as tough are Pirelli MT21s or Continental TKC80s; both excellent road/dirt compromises. They will wear faster, but in sand or mud knobbly tyres make the difference between constant slithering or sure-footed fun.

If you're heading across Asia or round the world on roads, fit the longest-wearing rubber you can buy. Tubeless radial tyres are relatively new to overlanding, but wear very well and can be easily repaired on the wheel with plugs and glue, plus a pump or carbon dioxide cartridges. Even then, you must be completely at ease with tyre removal and repairs, the most common cause of breakdown – unless you choose to buy an Enfield Bullet in India. If this is the case, go for the 350 cc model and expect to befriend many roadside mechanics. One overlander described her Bullet as being "always sick but never terminal".

Luggage and clothing

Overloading is the single most common mistake, but something to be avoided. Every biking overlander ends up giving stuff away or sending it home. Aluminium boxes have become very popular, the main advantage being security and neatness. Soft throw-over panniers in either tough woven nylon, ex-army canvas bags or rucksacks are lighter, cheaper, crashable, repairable and are less likely to inflict painful injuries in a crash – for hard, off-road routes they are a better choice. They will not be water, dust or theft-proof, but if you keep your baggage nice and dirty no one will want to go near it. Small tank bags are also very handy for valuables. Bear in mind that widely loaded bikes use more fuel and, in all cases, pack heavy weights low and towards the centre of the bike. Bulky, light items such as sleeping bags can be carried high, even over the headlight, but tools are best stored low in an old ammo box or pouch attached to the bash plate. Carry extra fuel in steel jerry cans, which also make useful bike props and stools and are resellable anywhere. Above all, think light and remember that where there are people there is stuff: water, fuel, food, lodgings and welders.

Your choice of clothing is limited only by its usefulness and durability. You will only wear one jacket, so make sure it can protect you from the rain, wind, stones and crashes. Natural fibres are light and comfy, leather can be heavy and hot and takes ages to dry. Top-quality touring jackets, such as those produced in the US by Aerostich, are expensive, but are also light, robust and functional. The merits of breathable fabrics such as Gore-Tex are dubious on a bike, but lots of big, secure pockets are useful; use your jacket like a wallet or safe and never lose sight of it.

Helmet choice is personal, but remember that an open-faced model makes you appear more human to strangers. Always wear goggles or use a visor. Stout footwear will protect your vulnerable legs; proper motocross boots are best for off-road trips, otherwise ex-army boots will last.

Life on the road

Pull over from the roadside and camp out of sight of passing vehicles. Never ride at night (especially in developing countries) or miss a chance to fill up with fuel and water. Be aware of you and your bike's limitations when driving off-road, especially in the early days when you have yet to learn the benefits of less baggage. Even if you're a loner, you will find yourself reassured to team up with other overlanders when faced with remote or dangerous sections of your trip, such as when crossing the Sahara, the DRC, Baluchistan or Colombia. The longer you travel, the lighter and more refined your equipment will become.

Resist the temptation to ride and ride and ride. Whatever your stated goal, it's the people you will meet on the road that will provide the longest memories, both good and, sometimes, if they are in uniform, bad.

Traditionally capricious, border guards are generally easy on bikers, recognising that two-wheel overlanding is no picnic. Nevertheless, approach a border as if you were going to be there for days. Bribes are less common than you think and are usually small and clearly prompted, unless you are in trouble. If there is one common piece of advice most overlanding motorbikers come back with it is this: plan well but trust your ingenuity. Everything works out all right in the end. ❧

Chris Scott is a film maker, tour guide and author of several books, including Adventure Motorcycling Handbook and Sahara Overland.

Vehicle documentation for overlanders
by Chris Scott

FOR MOST OVERLAND TRIPS, AS THE DRIVER OF YOUR OWN VEHICLE you will need to carry the following documentation:

1. Driving licence
2. International Driving Permit (IDP)
3. Vehicle Registration Certificate (ownership documents)
4. Motor insurance and/or Green Card
5. International Registration Distinguishing Sign ('GB' etc)
6. Carnet de Passages en Douanes (CDP)
7. Letter of authority to use borrowed, hired or leased vehicles
8. Motoring organisation membership card

Once you get past Europe, your Vehicle Registration Certificate ('V5', formerly known as a 'logbook' in the UK) is by far the most important document. It is effectively the 'passport' for your vehicle and you will show it, along with your passport and possibly your Carnet at most borders.

Driving licence and IDP

Most countries will allow you to drive for up to six months on your national driving licence, although, unless renting, in practice a driving license is very rarely asked for in developing countries. Where it is, an International Driving Permit is much more useful, particularly in Asia and especially in China.

An IDP is a booklet featuring your photo and all your license details inside the back cover. The order and meaning of these details can be cross-referenced to multi-lingual translations printed on each page of the booklet so that a non-English-reading individual can find their language and distinguish your name from your address, etc. The permit is issued on request by motoring organisations for a small fee and is valid for 12 months.

Note that there are two IDPs, which cover all countries of the world; if you're planning a long trip best get both.

The vehicle registration certificate

As stated above, ownership documents for your vehicle showing the correct information are vital. Ideally, all your personal details should match the document as well as those of your vehicle. In particular make sure your vehicle's VIN (Vehicle Identification Number) and/or engine and chassis numbers match the document exactly. For example, it is not uncommon for older Landrovers to have gone through several components in their service life, and at some point a new engine may have been fitted.

Countries like Egypt, and some in western Asia, are notorious for holding up overlanders when discrepancies are found on the Vehicle Registration Certificate Check now; you have been warned.

Motor insurance certificate and 'Green Card'

When travelling in countries outside the scope of the 'Green Card' – generally outside Europe – third party motor insurance should be bought at the first opportunity – very often this will be the border post or the first town. The further you go, however, the less easy this document can be to obtain and, as in some Central American countries, the less real value it has (apart from a means of extracting a bribe). This is something hard for us to understand, coming from a country where travelling without motor insurance is, at the very least, illegal. Get used to it and don't fret if insurance cannot be bought despite your best efforts. If necessary, use your ingenuity by presenting other official-looking documents (like an IDP) and of course, always drive as if you are effectively uninsured.

Whilst the Green Card is technically no longer necessary in European Union countries, it's worth having as it remains readily acceptable as evidence of insurance to enable a driver to benefit from international claim-handling facilities. In any case, a Green Card is required in all European countries outside the EU and is valid in Morocco and Tunisia (though frontier insurance is available). It is obtained from the company that is currently insuring your vehicle.

International registration distinguishing sign ('GB' etc)

Though some prefer to keep people guessing, this sign is mandatory and should be of the country in which your vehicle is registered, thus identifying your registration plates.

Carnet de Passages en Douanes (CDP)

This is an internationally recognised customs document administered by the Alliance Internationale de Tourisme (www.aitgva.ch). Printed in English and French, it entitles the holder to temporarily import a vehicle into a given country without the need to deposit the appropriate customs duties and taxes. CDPs are needed for transcontinental journeys in Asia, sub-Saharan Africa and Australia, but are not valid in North or Latin America (including Ecuador, as of September 2004). Most countries in these places issue their own inexpensive importation permits. (Note that in practice the full list of CDP countries found on the AIT website is not strictly correct.)

The national issuing authority of the Carnet (RAC, AA, etc) is directly responsible for the payment of customs duties and taxes if the Carnet is not discharged correctly, i.e. if the owner sells the vehicle locally and does not pay the duties. Consequently, the Carnet holder is liable for these charges under the terms of the agreement.

Motoring organisations are national issuing authorities, and will issue documents upon receipt of a bank guarantee, cash deposit or an insurance indemnity from an agreed firm of brokers to cover any liability. The sum required is determined by the motoring organisation, taking into consideration the countries to be visited and the value of your vehicle. This amount is related to the maximum import duty required in the countries on your itinerary; in some Asian countries it will be 400 per cent of the UK value of the vehicle – a figure which can seriously effect your choice of vehicle! In the case of a bank guarantee, you need to have collateral with the issuing bank or funds sufficient to cover the amount required. These funds cannot be withdrawn until the bank's guarantee is surrendered by the motoring organisation when the Carnet is returned and correctly discharged.

Each page contains an entry voucher (*volet d'entrée*), exit voucher (*volet de sortie*) and a counterfoil (*souche*). At a border post the entry voucher, counterfoil and exit voucher are filled out and stamped by the customs and the entry voucher is retained. When the vehicle leaves the country, the exit and the counterfoils are again stamped and this time the exit voucher is removed, leaving you with a counterfoil with dated entry and exit stamps. It is in your own interest to make sure this is done correctly at each border – mistakes could invalidate the document and hinder its eventual discharge.

The vehicle must usually be registered in the country where the Carnet is issued. In some cases (at the discretion of the issuing club or association), being a citizen of the country where the Carnet is issued is an alternative – even though the car has been registered elsewhere. In all cases, membership of the issuing club is a requirement.

To be without a Carnet where it is required usually means being turned back if you have insufficient funds to cover the customs deposit for entry.

A CDP is valid for 12 months from the date of issue, although this date may be extended by either applying to the motoring organisation in the country you are visiting at the point of expiry or returning it to the issuing authority. The name of the motoring organisation is shown in the front cover of the Carnet. An extension should be noted on every page and not just inside the cover, in order to avoid difficulties at borders.

Letter of authority to use borrowed, hired or leased vehicles

This is required when the driver of a vehicle is not the owner as stated on the ownership papers, and it should bear the signature of the owner. A covering letter in all the languages you expect to encounter is not a bad idea either. The owner's Vehicle Registration Certificate should also be taken – something not always so easily agreed to in the case of rented vehicles.

Motoring organisation membership card

Most countries have a motoring organisation which is a member of the AIT (see above) or the Federation Internationale de l'Automobile (FIA) and provides reciprocal membership privileges to members of other motoring organisations.

Additional documents

Among others you may need your birth certificate, extra passport photos and proof of yellow fever immunisation. Although originals are usually required, as a precaution against theft or loss it is wise to carry copies or duplicates of these and other pertinent documents in a secure place, as well as on a CD-ROM or even on a web page available for downloading and printing. ❧

International vehicle licence plates

In some cases, countries have changed their plates, and we have noted these below.

A	Austria
AFG	Afghanistan
AG	Antigua and Barbuda
AL	Albania
AND	Andorra
ANG	Angola
ARM	Armenia
AUS	Australia
AZ	Azerbaijan
B	Belgium
BD	Bangladesh
BDS	Barbados
BF	Burkina Faso
BG	Bulgaria
BH	Belize
BHT	Bhutan
BIH	Bosnia-Herzegovina
BOL	Bolivia
BR	Brazil
BRN	Bahrain
BRU	Brunei
BS	Bahamas
BU	Burundi
BVI	British Virgin Islands
BW	Botswana (after 2003)
BY	Belarus
BZ	Belize
C	Cuba
CAM	Cameroon
CD	Congo (DRC)
CDN	Canada
CH	Switzerland
CI	Côte d'Ivoire
CL	Sri Lanka
CO	Colombia
COM	Comoros
CR	Costa Rica
CS	Czechoslovakia (before 1992)
CV	Cape Verde

CY	Cyprus
CYM	Wales
CZ	Czech Republic
D	Germany
DARS	Western Sahara (Democratic Arab Republic of Sahara)
DJI	Djibouti
DK	Denmark
DOM	Dominican Republic
DVRK	North Korea
DY	Benin
DZ	Algeria
E	Spain
EAK	Kenya
EAT	Tanzania
EAU	Uganda
EC	Ecuador
ER	Eritrea
ES	El Salvador
EST	Estonia
ET	Egypt
ETH	Ethiopia
F	France
FIN	Finland (formerly: SF)
FJI	Fiji
FL	Liechtenstein
FR	Faroes
FSM	Federated States of Micronesia
G	Gabon
GB	United Kingdom
GBA	Alderney
GBG	Guernsey
GBJ	Jersey
GBM	Isle of Man
GBZ	Gibraltar
GCA	Guatemala
GE	Georgia
GH	Ghana
GQ	Equatorial Guinea
GR	Greece
GUY	Guyana
H	Hungary
HK	Hong Kong
HN	Honduras
HR	Croatia
I	Italy
IL	Israel
IND	India
IR	Iran
IRL	Republic of Ireland

IRQ	Iraq
IS	Iceland
J	Japan
JA	Jamaica
JOR	Jordan
K	Cambodia
KIR	Kiribati
KN	Greenland
KS	Kyrgyzstan
KSA	Saudi-Arabia
KWT	Kuwait
KZ	Kazakhstan
L	Luxembourg
LAO	Laos
LAR	Libya
LB	Liberia
LS	Lesotho
LT	Lithuania
LV	Latvia
M	Malta
MA	Morocco
MAL	Malaysia
MC	Monaco
MD	Moldavia
MEX	Mexico
MGL	Mongolia
MH	Marshall Islands
MK	Macedonia
MOC	Mozambique
MS	Mauritius
MV	Maldives
MW	Malawi
MYA	Myanmar
N	Norway
NA	Netherlands Antilles
NAM	Namibia
NAU	Nauru
NEP	Nepal
NIC	Nicaragua
NL	Netherlands
NZ	New Zealand
OM	Oman
P	Portugal
PA	Panama
PAL	Palau
PE	Peru
PK	Pakistan
PL	Poland
PNG	Papua New Guinea
PS	Occupied Palestinian territories
PY	Paraguay
Q	Qatar

RA	Argentina	TO	Tonga
RB	Botswana (before 2003)	TR	Turkey
		TT	Trinidad and Tobago
RC	China (Republic of China)	TUV	Tuvalu
RCA	Central African Republic	UA	Ukraine
		UAE	United Arab Emirates
RCB	Congo (Brazz.)	USA	United States
RCH	Chile	UZ	Uzbekistan
RE	Réunion	V	Vatican City
RG	Guinea	VN	Vietnam
RH	Haiti	VU	Vanuatu
RI	Indonesia	WAG	The Gambia
RIM	Mauritania	WAL	Sierra Leone
RL	Lebanon	WAN	Nigeria
RM	Madagascar	WD	Dominica
RMM	Mali	WG	Grenada
RN	Niger	WL	Saint Lucia
RO	Romania	WS	Samoa
ROK	Korea	WV	Saint Vincent and the Grenadines
ROU	Uruguay	YAR	Yemen
RP	Philippines	YU	originally for Yugoslavia, then for Serbia and Montenegro (latter now SCG)
RSM	San Marino		
RT	Togo		
RUS	Russia		
RWA	Rwanda		
S	Sweden		
SCG	Serbia and Montenegro (formerly: YU)	YV	Venezuela
		Z	Zambia
SCN	Saint Kitts and Nevis	ZA	South Africa
		ZW	Zimbabwe
SD	Swaziland		
SF	formerly Finland (now: FIN)		
SGP	Singapore		
SK	Slovakia		
SLO	Slovenia		
SME	Suriname		
SN	Senegal		
SOL	Solomon Islands		
SP	Somalia		
STP	São Tomé and Príncipe		
SU	Soviet Union (former)		
SUD	Sudan		
SY	Seychelles		
SYR	Syria		
TCH	Chad		
THA	Thailand		
TJ	Tajikistan		
TL	Timor-Leste (East Timor)		
TM	Turkmenistan		
TN	Tunisia		

Transport 2: by air

Air deals and discounts
by David Warne

Essentially the price you pay for a seat on an aircraft is determined by the age-old principle of supply and demand. Most seasoned travellers know that there are low and high seasons, but what is less well-known is that airlines use sophisticated computer programmes to determine how many seats to sell at any given price for every flight. Add in geo-political factors, discounting and clever marketing, and it is no wonder that it is hard to understand why air fares vary so widely. So how do you ensure you get a good deal on your flight? The bad news is that there is no absolute guarantee of getting the cheapest fare, but following these hints can put you on the right track:

- Book early: airlines are increasingly encouraging passengers to pay early with lower 'early booking' fares, as they can earn interest on passengers' money. Last-minute offers are less common than a few years ago and tend to apply only on routes where supply hugely exceeds demand during off-peak seasons. For more unusual destinations and peak travel periods – such as Christmas, Easter, school holidays and bank holidays – the later you book the more the fare is likely to cost.

- Avoid weekends: workers often want to maximise their time away whilst minimising time out of the office. Friday night and Saturday flights outbound and Sunday flights inbound have fewer cheap seats, and these sell out quickly.

- Indirect flights: for long-haul destinations you can often save money by taking a flight with a change of plane en route (for example, Amsterdam and Dubai are popular transit airports from the UK) but this will increase your travelling time.

- Flexibility comes at a price: the more flexibility you need the higher the fare will be. So, if you can fix your travel dates and dispense with any thoughts of changing your plans later you can qualify for the cheapest fare types, which generally don't allow any changes or refunds (remember to take out travel insurance at the time to cover unplanned cancellation).

- Book your hotel, tour or car hire arrangements at the same time: this enables agents such as WEXAS to offer you specially negotiated 'inclusive tour' fares as part of an individually tailored package. Agents are not allowed to advertise these fare levels, but they can work out significantly cheaper than the 'flight only' levels, particularly in the premium cabins.

AIRLINE PASSES

Most airline passes have to be booked before departure. They require a minimum number of flights within a certain region or continent. Air passes can be packaged for round the world trips and are best done through your travel agent.

Due to the ever-changing climate of airline passes it is recommended that you contact the airline directly to see if they can offer a deal with 'coupons' or 'points', which normally require a minimum number of flights. Or contact your travel agent who can negotiate on your behalf and advise you on the best deal for your trip.

Usually you can change the dates of travel (and in some cases the route) at little or no cost, permitting a degree of flexibility, but passes do have a limited shelf life and can expire, even if you haven't used up all your flights.

Now airlines are offering multiple stopovers as part of the main ticket and these are constantly changing.

So it is good to shop around airlines and travel agents to find the best deal for your journey.

Related websites

www.toorista.com/en/transportation/airlines/air_passes/

www.worldtravellers.net/airtravel/airpass.html

www.allairpass.com

- Internet fares: there is a widespread belief that the best fares are available online. Whilst this may be true for some simple flight itineraries, the technology of even the most advanced online bookings systems has limitations. In general, the more complex the trip or the more unusual the destination, the greater the chance that you will find a better fare by speaking to an experienced travel consultant.

There is no magic formula, but planning as far ahead as possible will certainly increase your chances of getting a good deal.

DAVID WARNE works in the travel industry.

Making claims against an airline
by David Warne

YOU HAVE ONLY TO READ THE CORRESPONDENCE COLUMNS in the specialist business travel magazines each month to see what a fashionable occupation it is to complain about airline services. Some people seem to enjoy writing letters of complaint so much that they make a profession of it. They complain at the least hiccup and write long letters detailing every flaw, claiming huge sums in compensation and threatening legal action if it is not forthcoming by return.

But the fact is that no matter how much their inefficiency costs you in time, trouble, missed meetings, lost deals and overnight hotel bills, the airlines, in many cases, are only obliged to pay out limited sums and then only under certain circumstances. In some cases are not obliged to pay you anything. Airlines are covered for most eventualities by their conditions of carriage, which are printed on the inside cover of the ticket or provided separately with an e-ticket. Indeed they are not even obliged to guarantee you seat on the flight, which gives rise to 'overbooking', which is covered later. However, this is not to say that, in an increasingly competitive environment, the more enlightened airlines do not take their customers' attitudes seriously. Some airline chief executives take a personal interest in passenger complaints and have frequent 'purges', when they insist on seeing every letter of complaint that comes in on a particular day.

Recent European Union (EU) legislation has tightened up the rules for passenger handling and payment of compensation in the event of disruption but this only applies to journeys that the EU has legal control over. Some of the main provisions are covered at the end of this chapter.

If you have a complaint against an airline that you cannot resolve satisfactorily, it is worth contacting the Air Transport Users' Council (AUC), CAA House, 45-59 Kingsway, London wc2b 6te (tel 020 7240 6061, fax 020 7240 7071). The council is funded and appointed by the Civil Aviation Authority, but operates completely independently and, indeed, has frequently been known to criticise some of the authority's decisions. It has only a small secretariat and is not really geared up to handle a large volume of complaints, but it has had some success in securing ex gratia payments for passengers who have been inconvenienced in some way.

All the same, the council likes to receive passenger complaints because it is a useful way of bringing to light some serious problems, which can lead in turn to high-level pressure being brought to bear on the airline or airlines involved. Some of the subjects dealt with by the council in 1990 included European and domestic airfares, passenger safety, the pressure on airport and airspace capacity, overbooking and baggage problems.

Procedure

Here are some tips which may make complaining to an airline more effective:

- The first person to write to is the customer relations manager at the airline. You can write to the chairman if it makes you feel better, but it makes little difference – unless that happens to be the day that the chairman decides to have his purge. If you've made your booking through a travel agency, send the agency a copy of the letter and, if it does a fair amount of business with that carrier (especially if it is a foreign airline), it is a good idea to ask the agency to take up the complaint for you.
- Keep your letter brief, simple, calm and to the point. Remember also to give the date, flight number, location and route where the incident took place. All

this may seem obvious, but it's amazing how many people omit these details.

● Keep all ticket stubs, baggage claims and anything else you may have from the flight involved. You may have to produce them if the airline requires substantiation of your complaint.

● If you have no success after all this, write to the Air Transport Users' Council. Send the council copies of all the correspondence you've had with the airline and let it take the matter from there.

Injury or death

Airline liability for death or injury to passengers was originally laid down by the Warsaw Convention, which was signed in 1929. The basic principal was that the infant airline industry could have been crippled if it had been forced by the courts to pay massive amounts of compensation to passengers or their relatives for death or injury in the event of an accident. The trade-off was that the airlines undertook to pay compensation up to a set ceiling irrespective of whether negligence on their part was proved. Some provisions of the Warsaw Convention were recently updated when the Montreal Convention was adopted. Today, the Warsaw/Montreal Conventions specify a limit to airlines' liability for death or injury, which varies between $10,000 and $150,000 per passenger. Additional protection is available by purchasing insurance from a private company.

Lost luggage

Most frequent travellers will, at some time, have experienced that sinking feeling when the carousel stops going round and there is still no sign of their baggage. The first thing to do if your luggage does not appear is to check with an airline official in the baggage claim area. It could be that your baggage is of a non-standard shape – a heavy rucksack, for example – which cannot be handled easily on the conveyor belt. If this is the case, it will be brought to the claim area by hand. But if your baggage really has not arrived on the same flight as you, you will have to complete a property irregularity report (PIR), which will give a description of the baggage, a list of its contents and the address to which it should be forwarded. Ask for a copy for yourself as you will need this – together with the baggage receipt – if you later want to claim compensation from the airline or from your travel insurance.

It is sometimes worth hanging around at the airport for an hour or two because there is always the chance that your baggage may arrive on the next flight. This sometimes happens if you have had to make a tight flight connection – you just squeak on to the flight but your baggage doesn't quite make it – although the current strict security requirements mean that normally a passenger and his or her baggage must travel on the same flight. But if there is only one flight a day there is no point in waiting and the airline will forward the baggage to you at its expense. In this case, ask the airline for an allowance for you to buy the basic necessities for an overnight stay if necessary – nightwear, toiletries and underwear, for example.

If your baggage never arrives at all, you should make a claim against the airline within 21 days. The airlines' liability for lost luggage is limited by international agreement and the level of compensation is based on the weight of your baggage, which explains why it is filled in on your ticket at check-in. The maximum rate of compensation at present is US$20 per kilo for checked baggage and US$400 per passenger for unchecked baggage, unless a higher value is declared in advance and additional charges are paid.

The same procedure applies to baggage that you find to be damaged when you claim it. The damage should be reported immediately to an airline official and, again, you will have to fill in a pir form, which you should follow up with a formal claim against the airline.

Overbooking

Losing one's baggage may be the ultimate nightmare in air travel, but the phenomenon of 'bumping' must run it a close second. Bumping occurs when you arrive at the airport with a confirmed ticket, only to be told that there is no seat for you because the flight is overbooked. Most airlines overbook their flights deliberately because they know that there will always be a few passengers who make a booking and then don't turn up ('no shows' in airline jargon). On some busy routes, such as Brussels to London on a Friday evening, some business travellers book themselves on more than one different flights, so that there is a horrendous no-show problem and the airlines can, perhaps, be forgiven for overbooking.

Similarly many airlines are prepared to overbook their premium cabins. Where too many travellers turn up there could be a need to 'downgrade' passengers to the cabin below, e.g. from business class to economy. This is relatively rare: airlines are more likely to upgrade premium cabin passengers (where there is a higher cabin with available seats) as enforced downgrading can cause immense frustration, particularly to business travellers who are hoping to sleep or work on a flight. Refunds are, naturally, given but this will usually take place after the event and the calculation of the refund amount is not always clear to the traveller. Compensation is also payable for those journeys covered by the EU legislation.

The use of computers has enabled airlines to work out their overbooking factors quite scientifically, but just occasionally things don't quite work out and a few confirmed passengers have to be 'bumped'.

If you are unlucky enough to be bumped, or 'denied boarding', to adopt the airline jargon, you will probably be entitled to compensation. For flights to or from and within the EU recent legislation now obliges airlines to pay fixed sums for specific incidences of disruption.

Compensation for delays

Whatever the conditions of carriage may say, airlines usually take a sympathetic view if flight delays cause passengers to miss connections, particularly if the delay results in having to obtain overnight hotel accommodation. Traditionally the better-known airlines would rebook passengers on to other airline flights to allow disrupted passengers to complete their journeys with the minimum of delay but recent experience suggests that this is no longer to be taken for granted, especially for travellers who have bought cheaper, less flexible tickets.

One increasingly grey area is where a passenger has purchased two separate tickets from different airlines for a 'through' journey (often bought this way to reduce the cost). For example, buying a Manchester-London ticket with one airline and a separate London-New York ticket with another airline with the intention of treating them as 'connecting' flights; if cancellation or delay or the first flight results in a passenger missing the second flight then, technically, two entirely separate contracts for two different journeys have been made and the second carrier may be within their rights to treat this as a 'no show' and/or apply an additional charge to carry you on a later flight.

EU legislation for passenger disruption

Recent European Union legislation obliges all airlines based in the EU – or non-EU airlines departing from the EU – to pay fixed amounts of compensation and/or refreshments and overnight accommodation for clearly defined incidences of disruption. Compensation levels are linked, in some cases, to the degree of disruption (i.e. length of delay, for example) but are fixed and common to all airlines covered by the legislation.

The main disruptions covered are cancellation, delay or denied boarding but payment is only triggered where the situation is not beyond the control of the airline. For example, delay caused by bad weather would not normally trigger compensation payments. The legislation applies equally to scheduled, 'no frills' and charter airlines. All EU based airlines must comply for all flights within and to and from the EU but airlines based outside the EU (e.g. a US carrier) are not legally obliged to offer these levels of compensation if the flight originates from outside of the EU (any compensation payable by them will be determined by legislation in the departure country – where any exists!).

Compensation payments vary according to the length of delay and the distance from the destination involved. Payments for outright cancellation are:

- Euros 250 for flights of 1, 500 km or less
- Euros 400 for flights between 1, 500 km and 3, 500 km
- Euros 600 for flights greater than 3, 500 km

Similar payment levels are triggered in the event that a flight delay exceeds certain set limits. At this point the airline is also responsible for providing refreshments and meals 'in reasonable relation to the waiting time' (often meal and/or drink vouchers are provided for use in airport catering outlets) and covering the cost of two phone calls, telex or emails. The compensation payments for delay are:

- Euros 250 for flights of 1, 500 km or less where flight is delayed by more than 2 hours
- Euros 400 for flights between 1, 500 km and 3, 500 km where flight is delayed by more than 3 hours
- Euros 600 for flights greater than 3, 500 km where the flight is delayed by more than 4 hours
- When delay exceeds 5 hours you may decide not to travel and claim a refund for any parts of the journey that have not been made
- Where the delay is 'overnight' the airline is obliged to provide overnight accommodation and transport to / from the accommodation

Airlines are obliged to provide passengers with written notification of their rights, although in many cases this will happen only when the delay or other event causes compensation to be triggered: if you are delayed by less than two hours no compensation is payable, for example. You may request that an airline provides you with a written copy of your rights at any time but in many cases a summary is available from airlines' websites. The full text of the legislation is available online at http://europa.eu.int/comm/transport/air/rights/index_en.htm.

Claims should be sent direct to the airlines concerned, rather than via your travel agent, but in some instances compensation may be made at the airport (e.g. when being 'bumped'). ଐ

This is based on an earlier article by Alex McWhirter, Annie Redmile and Rajinder Ghatahorde.

Reading an airline ticket
by David Warne

AN AIRLINE TICKET IS REALLY A LEGAL CONTRACT, which specifies and restricts the services that passengers may expect and when they may expect them. Whether it is a scheduled or a charter flight, the duties and liabilities of both passenger and airline are clearly defined. Each passenger must be in possession of a ticket for the journey to be undertaken. The Warsaw and Montreal Conventions limit the liability of most airlines in cases of injury or death involving passengers, and also of baggage loss or damage.

The traditional 'paper' airline ticket, which has a coupon for each flight, is fast disappearing and is being replaced with 'e-tickets'. Some airlines refer to 'ticketless' travel, but in both cases the flight ticket has been superseded with an electronic record of the passenger and travel details.

The main advantage of e-tickets is that there is no physical document to lose; anyone who has ever lost an airline ticket will know how much hassle it used to be to get a replacement or a refund. Airlines and agents who issue e-tickets are supposed to provide an itinerary and an 'e-ticket receipt' (often the same document). This confirms the travel details, the e-ticket number, baggage allowance and various other details. It has no monetary value, but can be reprinted as many times as required and is used as proof of onward or return travel for immigration officials.

The contract between passenger and airline is unchanged when an e-ticket is issued and a copy of the IATA conditions of contract should still be provided. ଐ

Aviation safety
by David Learmount

IT IS EASY TO SAY THAT FLYING IS SAFE: but safe compared with what? Fear of flying is only partly rational, which makes it difficult to persuade the afflicted by using the unfeeling logic of statistics. Even when nervous fliers are provided with a comparison that brings the truth of flight safety into easy perspective, the ultimate hurdle is man's fear of falling from heights, and a sense of disbelief that something as insubstantial as air can support a huge object like an aeroplane full of people. This fear has never been reduced – let alone eliminated – by providing figures to prove that an air traveller is incredibly unlikely to come to grief.

Flying with the world's great airlines has never been risky, but occasionally even the mighty have been known to fall. Today, however, the prospect of a major airline flying the very latest generation of aeroplanes having a serious accident is multiples lower than it was for the same carrier even ten years ago, let alone back in the early 1980s. Flying has, according to the statistics, become steadily safer ever since the Wright Brothers achieved the first powered flight a century ago. By the end of the 1970s, the airline industry was beginning to believe that safety could not get much better. That belief was based on 'the law of diminishing returns': that is, when serious airline accidents had been reduced to very few per year on a global basis, mathematically there seemed to be little room for improvement.

The airlines were wrong. The world's aviation watchdog – the International Civil Aviation Organisation (ICAO) – an offshoot agency of the United Nations – has figures that prove international flying is six times safer now than it was in 1979, and the steadiness of the trend in that direction proves that this is no freakish piece of luck: it is the new status quo, and it will probably get even better. Despite having pointed out that statistics don't make anyone less nervous, here are those unfeeling statistics from ICAO: in 1979 the world average airline accident rate was three fatal accidents per million flights. Today the likelihood of a fatal accident has been reduced to less than half of one fatal accident per million flights or, to put it more sensibly, one fatal accident in every two million flights.

If that still sounds bad, consider that the definition of a fatal accident is an event in which one person or more gets killed. It does not have to be a 'crash'. An event in which a single person in a jumbo jet was killed by being hit by a cabin cinema screen that detached from the bulkhead in turbulence was included in those figures. And those figures are the world average. The world's great airlines are far safer than that.

In the average fatal accident, more than two thirds of the people on board survive, and this average is increasing because the latest generation of airliners – like cars – are required to be designed for better survivability. It has also been shown that frequent air travellers have a better chance of surviving accidents than occasional travellers: this is assumed to be because they know the aeroplane better, panic less easily, and thus get out faster. Since you will want to be one of those who survives any accident that your flight has, take the emergency procedures briefing seriously. This is not paranoid, it's pure sense.

Look at where all the exits are relative to you and imagine finding your way to them in the dark. Count the seat rows to them. Read the emergency cards carefully, study the brace position, have your seat belt firmly (really firmly) fastened at take-off and landing, and slacken it in flight but always have it fastened while you are seated or sleeping. Look with particular care at the diagram showing how to open the exit doors, and imagine opening them yourself in the dark. Having done all this, sit back and enjoy your flight.

Believe it or not, the same procedure is worth applying to your hotel room – no-one ever takes any notice of the fire instructions located in every room, or makes a mental note of which way to turn to the emergency exits nearest their room. But the night the alarm goes off and you emerge into the corridor to find it full of smoke turns out to be an unnerving experience unless you have done just that. It has happened to this traveller.

Airlines specialise in delivering travellers over long distances fast and safely. Risk does not increase with distance on an airline flight, whereas it increases almost directly in proportion to the distance travelled in a car. According to statistics there is no country in the world where the average car driver could expect to survive 2 million journeys if each trip was more than 1, 000 km, which is the safety level offered to airline passengers.

Multiple car journeys of 1, 000 km may sound irrelevant, but the statistics could mean something to the traveller who is considering driving from, say, London to the Côte d'Azur in southern France by car: if the purpose is to enjoy the countryside and the local cuisine en route, then drive; if it is to avoid flying for perceived safety reasons, your mathematics are flawed; if you are driving because of an irrational fear of flying that you cannot conquer, then enjoy the route and good luck – in relative terms you will need it.

The world airline safety average, however, is a very rough guide indeed because of enormous regional variations. Actual safety depends heavily on what nationality the airline is, whether the flight is domestic or international, where the flight is taking place, whether the aircraft is jet- or propeller-powered, and what the prevailing weather is like at take-off and landing.

The world's most statistically safe flight would be with an Australian airline, on an international flight to an American destination in summer (American summer), using a jet aircraft. Conversely, the least safe would be a domestic flight in a country with a 'Third-World' economy in a propeller-driven aeroplane (particularly if the propeller is driven by a piston engine rather than a turbine), in bad weather.

Air travellers at the planning stage sometimes ask whether there is an airline safety league table. Surely, they say, the safe airlines will publicise their achievement, proudly laying claim to their place in the league? In fact, even the safest carriers do not want to. Airline fatal accidents are so statistically rare that even a single fatal disaster could make the top-of-the-league carrier disappear from the top 50 – and what might that do to the clientele's loyalty? Beside which, the airlines know that high places in league tables do not eliminate the basic fear of flying anyway. All a league table would do is to imply that air travel is dangerous. Do travellers require a league table of railway operators? Of coach companies? Of taxi drivers? And where does the league table put a brand-new airline? It is unproven, inexperienced, but has not had an accident yet, so it could be at the top of the league.

Airlines can be crudely graded for air safety by the continent in which they are based: North American airlines, as a whole, are the most consistently safe, and western European airlines are in the same league; Asia, the Indian subcontinent and South-East Asia has a mixture of adequate and poor, with patches of good; Central America is poor, but South America is making an apparently successful attempt to recover from a bad record in the 1980s and earlier; and finally African airlines score lowest for safety, with a couple of exceptionally good airlines among the bad records. Much of the African infrastructure – airports and air traffic control – is really bad. But again, there are exceptions. South Africa is one of them, Ghana is fair, and in the north Egypt and Morocco are adequate.

The disparity is enormous: an average African airline is more than ten times as likely to have an accident involving fatalities than a North American or European one. As for where the accident is most likely to happen, the continents are ranged in a similar order, but the disparity widens still further, with Africa topping the league by far. Finally the majority of accidents happen to domestic airlines – international carriers have a better record on average.

As for the exceptional nations, Australia is the safest, along with the United States, then come the best of the Western Europe and the Middle Eastern nations, and competing for bottom marks are Nigeria, Angola, Namibia, Taiwan (though there are signs that it is hauling itself out of the pit), Indonesia and Korea.

The safest airline in the world is Australia's Qantas, which has not harmed a soul since the days of wood-and-fabric biplanes in 1937, when it was known by its original name, Queensland and Northern Territories Air Services.

The biggest safety improvement in aviation's history came with the introduction of jets and turbo-prop engines because the turbines that form the core of both engine types are far more reliable than piston engines. So safety climbed steadily during the late 1950s and in the 1960s as piston-power gradually left the scene. There was another upward hike from the 1970s to the 1980s, with technology and operating techniques maturing, and in the early 1980s a new generation of jet airliners appearing on the scene. These consisted of the Airbus A310, and Boeing's 757 and 767. What distinguished them from their predecessors was that digital, rather than electro-mechanical instruments, were becoming common in the cockpits, bringing to the pilots greater accuracy of information, greater reliability, and even categories of information they did not have access to before. Instruments began to be replaced by television-like displays, giving rise to the generic term 'glass cockpits' for the new pilots' 'offices'. Navigation displays, for example, were becoming more intuitive – map-like plans of where the aircraft is in real time, with computer-predictions of where it would go next according to what the pilots asked the flight management computer to provide. This all gives pilots a higher level of what is now called 'situational awareness', heightened by providing them with computer monitoring of their aircraft systems so they can more easily monitor the health of the whole aircraft.

After the introduction of the early 'glass cockpits', things moved on a generation further. In 1988 Airbus put into airline service the world's very first digitally computer controlled airliner, the A320, commonly known – rather misleadingly – as having 'fly-by-wire' controls. Actually, wire cables were the physical connections between the pilot's controls and the 'control surfaces' on the wings and tail of the Wright Flyer. But what digital fly-by-wire actually does is to put a computer between the pilot's controls and the aeroplane's external control surfaces. If the pilot asks the aeroplane to do something that it can do safely, the computer passes on the signals without altering them. If the pilot makes a mistake and demands more of the aircraft than it can safely provide, the computer modifies the signal to demand the maximum the aircraft can give without going out of control or causing structural damage.

In the very early days of the A320, it suffered some fatal accidents that were all to do with the pilots not understanding the new system, rather than the system itself performing wrongly. It was as if the pilots thought that, in this new generation of airliner, they could get away with carelessness, and that was not true even of the new machines.

Since that time, just as those who struggled with their first personal computers in the 1980s now feel at home with them, so the pilots of digitally controlled airliners now feel completely at home with them too. Meanwhile, the software and cockpit equipment has become more capable and more intuitive, like today's PCs compared with those of the 1980s. Since the single-aisle A320 first arrived on the scene, Airbus has produced the widebody A330 and A340, and the mega-jumbo A380. Across the Atlantic Boeing created the 777. They are all digitally controlled. Now the A330's replacement – the A350 – is on the way, and Boeing is replacing its conventionally controlled 767 series with the 787 'Dreamliner'.

Never again will a jet airliner be built that is not fly-by-wire. It is, in the end, a better system, as time has proven. None of the latest generation of airliners, starting with the A340 in 1994, has harmed a soul. In 2005 an A340 overran a runway at Toronto's international airport in a thunderstorm, but two things were proven by this event: first, the time-honoured truth that pilots and their new machines still have to respect the power of nature; and second, despite the fact that the aircraft caught fire after falling into a ravine at the end of the runway and was ultimately destroyed, everybody on board evacuated safely – a testimony to the crash-survivability of the latest aircraft types.

Meanwhile, during the 1990s, an unprecedented campaign to improve safety further was mounted by the airline industry, harnessing the increasing power of computer databases to store and analyse incident and accident data from all over the world. Together with the ICAO, the world has identified the areas of greatest risk even in this industry where risks were already very low, and has found both technological and human methodology for reducing them further. The ICAO itself has been given additional powers to audit countries for safety standards, so although the proportion of accidents in Africa compared with America remains as uneven as it used to be, the number of accidents to international airlines in Africa is reducing as well as those elsewhere.

Finally, with the increasing liberalisation of the world airline industry has arrived greater consumer choice. Where there is a choice between airlines, no traveller will choose an airline perceived to be the least safe, so this commercial imperative is probably the greatest motivation of all for airlines that used to be relatively careless.

Once a traveller has arrived in the country of destination and needs to travel within it, even if the local domestic airline does not have a brilliant safety record by international standards, the alternative surface transport should be approached critically, too. In a country where a cash-strapped economy and a laissez-faire culture allows an airline's standards to drop, the same may be true of the infrastructure and watchdog systems supporting road and rail safety. The air transport system, while it does not compare well with American or European airline safety standards, may still be a relatively safe form of transport compared with the surface alternative.

Finally, airline and airport security has become very much a part of air travel worldwide. In some parts of the world, security is a token effort, but that is often because the perceived risk is low. Lockerbie jolted the airline world into a realisation that the subject of airborne terrorism was a serious one, and the uniquely awful attacks on America using its own airlines on 11 September 2001 confirmed that security is an issue the world cannot afford to ignore. The only workable advice to passengers afraid of the terrorist hijack threat is to decide which airlines are the targets of active terrorist groups, and then to travel with airlines which are less likely to be. However, apart from possibly making the wrong choice in second-guessing terrorist motives, the passengers who make that decision should bear in mind that if they cause the 'threatened' airlines' business visibly to suffer, they have handed the terrorist a partial victory, encouraging further terrorism in the future. ❧

DAVID LEARMOUNT has worked at 'Flight International' magazine for 26 years and is a specialist in aviation safety.

Airline head offices worldwide

ADRIA AIRWAYS
Tel: 386 (0) 3691 000
www.adria-airways.com

AEGEAN AIRLINES S.A.
Tel: 30 210 62 61 700
www.aegeanair.com

AERO ASIA INTERNATIONAL (PRIVATE)
Tel: 021 4544 951-4
www.aeroasia.com

AERO CALIFORNIA
Tel: 52 555 207 1392
www.aerocalifornia.de

AERO ZAMBIA
Tel: 260 226 111
www.mbendi.co.za/orgs/ccr5.htm

AEROFLOT RUSSIAN

AIRLINES
Tel: 155 5045 926 6278
www.aeroflot.org/

AER LINGUS
Tel: 0818 365 000
www.aerlingus.com

AEROLINEAS ARGENTINAS
Tel: 64 09 256 8051
www.aerolineas.com.ar

AEROMEXICO
Tel: 5133 4010
www.aeromexico.com

AIR ALGERIE
Tel: 213 021 65 33 40
www.airalgerie.dz/

AIR AUSTRAL
Tel: 011 268 0508
www.air-austral.com

AIR BALTIC CORPORATION
Tel: 371 722 4282
www.airbaltic.lv

AIR BERLIN GMBH & CO.
Tel: 44 0870 7388 880
www.airberlin.com

AIR BOSNA
Tel: 387 33 466 338
www.airbosna.ba/

**AIR BOTSWANA
CORPORATION**
Tel: 267 395 1921
www.airbotswana.com

**AIR CALEDONIE
INTERNATIONAL**
Tel: 25 23 39
www.air-caledonie.nc

AIR CANADA
Tel: 514 422 5000
www.aircanada.com

AIR CHINA LIMITED
Tel: 66 013 336
www.airchina.com

**AIR EUROPA LINEAS
AEREAS**
Tel: 902 401 501
www.air-europa.com

AIR FRANCE
Tel: 0870 142 4343
www.airfrance.com

AIR GABON
Tel: 06 487 1403
www.orariovoli.com

AIR JAMAICA
Tel: 305 670 3222
www.airjamaica.com

AIR LUXOR
Tel: 351 210 062 200
www.airluxor.com

AIR MACAU
Tel: 853 396 6888
http://api.airmacau.com.
mo

AIR MADAGASCAR
Tel: 261 2022 219-74
www.air-mad.com

AIR MALAWI
Tel: 01620 811
www.airmalawi.net/

AIR MALTA
Tel: 356 2169 0890
www.airmalta.com/

AIR MAURITIUS
Tel: 230 207 7070
www.airmauritius.com

AIR MOLDOVA
Tel: 373 22 52 55 02
www.airmoldova.md/

AIR NAMIBIA
Tel: 264 61 299 6000
www.namibweb.com/
airlines.html

AIR NEW ZEALAND
Tel: 6409 255 8758
www.airnewzealand.com/
gateway.jsp

AIR PACIFIC
Tel: 679 6737 421
www.airpacific.com

AIR SENEGAL
Tel: 221 842 41 00
www.air-senegal-
international.com

AIR SEYCHELLES
Tel: 248 38 1000
www.airseychelles.com

AIR TAHITI
Tel: 689 46 0202
www.airtahitinui.com

AIR TANZANIA
Tel: 255 22 2117 959
www.coastal.cc /
www.precisionairtz.com

AIR ZIMBABWE
Tel: 2639 697 37
www.airzim.co.zw/

ALASKA AIRLINES
Tel: 206 392 6580
www.alaskaair.com

ALBANIAN AIRLINES
Tel: 355 4 235 162
www.flyalbanian.com

ALITALIA
36 06656 26513
www.alitalia.com

ALL NIPPON AIRWAYS
Tel: 0120 029 003
www.ana.co.jp/eng/

ALOHA AIRLINES
Tel: 800 367 5250
www.alohaairlines.com

AMERICAN AIRLINES
Tel: 800 321 2121
www.aa.com

AMERICAN WEST AIRLINES
Tel: 800 235 9292
www.americawest.com

ARIANA AFGHAN AIRLINES
Tel: 93 20 2100 351
www.flyariana.com/
worldwide.htm

ARKIA - ISRAELI AIRLINES
Tel: 972 9 8633 480
www.arkia.co.il

ARMENIAN AIRLINES
Tel: 374 1 52 00 51
www.armenianairlines.
com

ASIANA AIRLINES INC
Tel: 603 8024 0279
www.flyasiana.com

ATLAS AIR
Tel: 914 701 8000
www.atlasair.com

AUSTRALIAN AIR EXPRESS
Tel: 03 9297 3100
www.aae.com.au/

AUSTRIAN AIRLINES
Tel: 800 843 0002
www.aua.com

AVIANCA
Tel: 01800 0123 434
www.aviance.com

AVIATECA
Tel: 502 2470 TACA (8222)
www.aviataca.aero/

AZERBAIJAN AIRLINES
Tel: 994 12 493 40 04
http://nac-azal.com

BALKAN BULGARIAN AIRLINES
Tel: 359 2 88 06 63
www.balkan.com

BANGKOK AIRWAYS
Tel: 66 02 265 5678
www.bangkokair.com

BELAVIA
Tel: 375 17 209 73 12
www.belavia.by/

BIMAN - BANGLADESH AIRLINES
Tel: 880 2 897 400 29
www.bangladeshonline.com/biman/

BRAATHENS SAFE AIR TRANSPORT
Tel: 47 915 05400
www.braathens.no

BRITISH AIRWAYS
Tel: 0870 850 9850
www.britishairways.com

BRITISH MIDLAND (BMI)
Tel: 01332 854 000
www.flybmi.com

BWIA WEST INDIES AIRWAYS LTD
Tel: 800 538 2942
www.bwee.com/

CAMEROON AIRLINES
Tel: 237 42 01 11
www.cameroon-airlines.com

CANADIAN AIRLINES
Tel: 800 426 7000
www.cdnair.ca

CARPATAIR - ROMANIAN AIRWAY
Tel: 0040 256 306933
www.carpatair.com

CATHAY PACIFIC
Tel: 852 2747 1888
www.cathaypacific.com

CAYMAN AIRWAYS
Tel: 345 949 8200
www.caymanairways.com

CHINA AIRLINES
Tel: 02 2715 2233
www.china-airlines.com

CHINA EASTERN AIRLINES
Tel: 86 21 5298 0078
www.chinaeastern.co.uk

CHINA SOUTHERN AIRLINES
Tel: 010 6567 2208
www.cs-air.nl/

CIRRUS AIRLINES
Tel: 49 068 9380 0440
www.cirrus-world.de

CITYJET
Tel: 353 18700 100
www.cityjet.com

COMPANIA MEXICANA DE AVIACION
Tel: 01 554 48 09 90
www.mexicana.com

CONGO AIRLINES
Tel: 00 243 46947
www.congonline.com/Tourisme/Conairlines.htm

CONTINENTAL AIRLINES
Tel: 713 324 5152
www.continental.com

CONTINENTAL MICRONESIA
Tel: 691 330 2424
www.continental.com/micronesia

CORSAIR
Tel: 33 1 49 79 49 59
www.corsair.fr/

CROATIA AIRLINES
Tel: 385 1481 96 33
www.croatiaairlines.hr

CUBANA
Tel: 537 2040288
www.cubana.cu

CYPRUS AIRWAYS
Tel: 357 22 663054
www.cyprusairways.com

CZECH AIRLINES
Tel: 420 239 007 007
www.csa.cz

DAALLO AIRLINES
Tel: 971 4 273 3808
www.daallo.com

DELTA AIRLINES
Tel: 800 221 1212

www.delta.com

DENIM AIRWAYS
Tel: 31 040 235 2100
www.denimairways.com

DEUTSCHE LUFTHANSA
Tel: 49 69 696 0
http://biz.yahoo.com/ic/41/41803.html

EASYJET
Tel: 0871 244 2366
www.easyjet.com

EGYPT AIR
Tel: 635 0260
www.egyptair.com

EL AL ISRAEL AIRLINES
Tel: 03 971 6111
www.elal.co.il

EMIRATES
Tel: 00971 4 214 4444
www.emirates.com

ESTONIAN AIR
Tel: 372 6313 302
www.etonian-air.ee

ETHIOPIAN AIRLINES
Tel: 251 161 61 61
www.flyethiopian.com

EUROWINGS AG
Tel: 49 0231 92 45 0
www.eurowings.de

EVA AIRWAYS
Tel: 886 2 2501 9599
www.evaair.com

FINNAIR
Tel: 0600 140140
www.finnair.com

FLYBE AIRLINE
Tel: 01392 366 669
www4.flybe.com

GARUDA INDONESIA
Tel: 021 2351 9999
www.garudaindonesia.co.uk

GULF AIR
Tel: 973 17 339 339
www.gulfair.com

HELIOS AIRWAYS
Tel: 357 24 815 700
www.flyhelios.com

HEMUS AIR
Tel: 359 2 9420 202
www.hemusair.bg

HONG KONG DRAGON AIRLINES
Tel: 852 3193 3193
www.dragonair.com

IBERIA
Tel: 902 400 500
www.iberia.com

ICELAND AIR
Tel: 354 505 0500
www.icelandair.net

INDIAN AIRLINES
Tel: 33 11 225
www.indian-airlines.nic.in

IRAN AIR
Tel: 98 21 911 6591
www.iranair.com

ISLES OF SCILLY SKYBUS
Tel: 0845 710 5555
www.isleofscilly-travel.co.uk

JAPAN AIRLINES
Tel: 0120 25 5931
www.jal.co.jp

JET AIRWAYS (INDIA)
Tel: 022 2850 1313
www.jetairways.com

KENYA AIRWAYS
Tel: 254 20 642 2000
www.kenya-airways.com

KLM ROYAL DUTCH AIRLINES
Tel: 0044 178 4 888 222
www.klm.com

KOREAN AIR LINES
Tel: 82 2 2656 2001
www.koreanair.eu.com/

KUWAIT AIRWAYS
Tel: 434 5555
www.kuwait-airways.com

LAN
Tel: 562 526 2000
www.lan.com

LAUDA AIR
Tel: 43 0820 320 321
www.laudaair.com

LIBYAN ARAB AIRLINES
Tel: 218 21 602093
www.aaco.org/airlines_libyan.asp

LITHUANIAN AIRLINES
Tel: 370 5 275 2585
www.lal.lt/en/index.php

LLOYD AERO BOLIVIANO (LAB)
Tel: 591 4 425 0750
www.labairlines.com

LOT - POLISH AIRLINES
Tel: 0801 703 703
www3.lot.com

LTU INTERNATIONAL AIRWAYS
Tel: 0211 9418 8 88
www.ltu.com/

LUFTHANSA
Tel: 0870 837 7747
http://portal.lufthansa.com

LUXAIR
Tel: 352 2456 1
www.luxair.lu/

MACEDONIAN AIRLINES
Tel: 389 2 329 23 33
www.mat.com.mk/index.htm

MAERSK AIR
Tel: 45 3363 3363
www.maersk-air.com

MALAYSIA AIRLINES
Tel: 603 7846 3000
http://uk.malaysiaairlines.com

MALEV HUNGARIAN AIRLINES
Tel: 36 1 235 3535
www.malev.hu

MANDARIN AIRLINES
Tel: 886 2 2717 1230
www.mandarin-airlines.com

MERIDIANA
Tel: 0845 355 5588
www.meridiana.it

MEXICANA
Tel: 01 554 48 09 90

www.mexicana.com/main/

MIAT - MONGOLIAN AIRLINES
Tel: 976 11 379935
www.miat.com

MIDDLE EAST AIRLINES
Tel: 961 1 818 929
www.mea.com.lb

MONTENEGRO AIRLINES
Tel: 381 11 2621 122
www.montenegro-airlines.cg.yu/

MUSTIQUE AIRWAYS
Tel: 1 784 458 4380
www.mustique.com/

NATIONWIDE AIRLINES
Tel: 0861 777 777
www.flynationwide.co.za/

NORTHWEST AIRLINES
Tel: 1800 447 4747
www.nwa.com

OMAN AVIATION
Tel: 968 2451 9953
www.oman-air.com

PAKISTAN INTERNATIONAL AIRLINES
Tel: 92 21 457 2011
www.piac.com.pk/

PALESTINIAN AIRLINES
Tel: 970 8 284 8884
www.palairlines.com

PHILIPPINE AIRLINES
Tel: 632 817 8000
www.phillipineairlines.com

PHUKET AIRLINES
Tel: 662 67 8999
www.phuketairlines.com

PLUNA LINEAS AEREAS URUGUAYAS
Tel: 598 2 604 2244
www.pluna.com.uy/

POLYNESIAN AIRLINES
Tel: 685 22172 / 21261
www.polynesianairlines.com

QANTAS AIRWAYS
Tel: 61 2 9691 3636

www.qantas.com.au

QATAR AIRWAYS
Tel: 974 4496 000
www.qatarairways.com

ROYAL AIR MAROC
Tel: 044 42 55 00
www.royalairmaroc.com

ROYAL BRUNEI AIRLINES
Tel: 673 221 2222
www.bruneiair.com

ROYAL JORDANIAN
Tel: 800 223 0470
www.rja.com

RWANDAIR EXPRESS
Tel: 250 575757
www.rwandair.com

RYANAIR
Tel: 1530 787 787
www.ryanair.com

SAHARA AIRLINES
Tel: 0522 233 7777
www.airsahara.net/

SAS - SCANDINAVIAN AIRLINES
Tel: 46 8 797 0000
www.scandinavian.net/

SAUDI ARABIAN AIRLINES
Tel: 9200 22222
www.saudiairlines.com

SHANGHAI AIRLINES
Tel: 86 21 6255 8888
www.shanghai-air.com

SIBERIA AIRLINES
Tel: 7 095 777 9999
www.s7.ru

SIERRA NATIONAL AIRLINES
Tel: 01293 433767
www.sirrenationalair.com/

SILK AIR
Tel: 65 6223 8888
www.silkair.com

SINGAPORE AIRLINES
Tel: 65 6223 8888
www.singaporair.com

SOLOMAN AIRLINES
Tel: 677 20031

www.solomonairlines.com.au/

SOUTH AFRICAN AIRWAYS (SAA)
Tel: 011 961 1700
www.flysaa.com

SPANAIR
Tel: 971 74 50 20
www.spanair.com/

SRI LANKAN AIRLINES
Tel: 94 19733 5555
www.srilankan.aero/

SUDAN AIRWAYS
Tel: 962 06 566 7100/1/2
www.sudanair.com/

SURINAME AIRWAYS
Tel: 0900 8050
www.slm.firm.sr/

SWISS INTERNATIONAL AIRLINES
Tel: 0848 85 2000
www.yourcountry.swiss.com

SYRIAN ARAB AIRLINES
Tel: 167 245 0098/97
www.syriaair.com

TACA INTERNATIONAL AIRLINES
Tel: 503 2267 8222
www.taca.com

TAM
Tel: 1 888 2 359 826
www.tamairlines.com

TAP - AIR PORTUGAL
Tel: 702 205 700
www.tap-airportugal.pt

TAROM (ROMANIAN AIR TRANSPORT)
Tel: 4021 204 1355
www.tarom.ro

THAI AIRWAYS INTERNATIONAL
Tel: 66 2 545 3690 92
www.thaiair.com/

TNT AIRWAYS
Tel: 32 4 239 3000
www.tnt.com

TRANSASIA AIRWAYS
Tel: 02 2972 4599

www.tna.com

TRANSMEDITERRANEAN AIRWAYS
Tel: 961 1 629 210
www.tma.com

TUNISAIR
Tel: 261 071 845 346
www.tunisair.com.tn

TURKISH AIRLINES
Tel: 90 212 663 63 00
www.turkishairlines.com

UKRAINE INTERNATIONAL
Tel: 380 44 230 8866
www.ukraine-international.com

UNITED AIRLINES
Tel: 1 877 228 1327
www.unitedairlines.com

US AIRWAYS
Tel: 703 872 7000
www.usairways.com

UZBEKISTAN AIRWAYS
Tel: 99 8172 56 38 37
www.uzbekistan-airways.com

VARIG - BRAZILIAN AIRLINES
Tel: 4003 7000
www.varig.com

VIETNAM AIRLINES
Tel: 84 4 832 0320
www.vietnamairlines.com

VIRGIN ATLANTIC AIRWAYS
Tel: 01293 562345
www.virgin-atlantic.com

VIRGIN EXPRESS
Tel: 32 2 752 05 11
www.virgin-express.com/

VOLARE AIRLINES
Tel: 39 070 460 3397
www.volareweb.com

XIAMEN AIRLINES
Tel: 86 592 573 9888
www.xiamenair.com.cn

YANGON AIRWAYS
Tel: 951 383 100
www.yangonair.com

Yemenia - Yemen Airways
Tel: 9671 201822
www.yemenia.com/

Zambian Airways
Tel: 260 1 271230
www.zambianairways.com

Airline head offices in the UK

Aer Lingus
Tel: 0845 084 4444
www.aerlingus.com

Aeroflot
Tel: 020 7355 2233
www.aeroflot.co.uk

Aerolineas Argentinas
Tel: 020 7494 1001
www.aerolineas.com.ar

Air Canada
Tel: 08705 247226
www.aircanada.com/

Air China
Tel: 020 7630 7678
www.air-china.co.uk/

Air France
Tel: 0870 142 4343
www.airfrance.com/uk

Air India
Tel: 020 8560 9996
www.airindia.com

Air Malta
Tel: 020 8785 3199
www.airmalta.com

Air Mauritius
Tel: 0207 434 4375
www.airmauritius.com

Air Namibia
Tel: 020 7960 6016
www.airnamibia.com.na/

Air New Zealand
Tel: 020 8600 7600
www.airnz.co.uk

Air Seychelles
Tel: 01293 596 656
www.airseychelles.net

Air Zimbabwe
Tel: 0207 963 4050
www.airzim.co.zw

Alitalia UK
Tel: 0870 225 5044
www.alitalia.co.uk

All Nippon Airways
Tel: 020 7224 8866
www.allnipponairways.com

American Airlines
Tel: 0845 7789 789
www.americanairlines.co.uk

Austrian Airlines
Tel: 020 7766 0300
www.aua.com

Biman Bangladesh Airlines
London Tel: 0171 629 0161
Manchester Tel: 0161 228 2636
www.bangladeshonline.com

BMI Baby
Tel: 0870 264 2229
www.bmibaby.com

British Airways
Tel: 0870 850 9850
www.britishairways.com

British Midland
Tel: 01332 854 000
www.flybmi.com

BWIA International
Tel: 0870 499 2942
www.bwee.com/

Cathay Pacific
Tel: 020 8834 8888
www.cathaypacific.com/uk

China Airlines
Tel: 020 7436 9001
www.china-airlines.com

Continental Airlines
Tel: 0845 607 6760
www.continental.com/uk/

Croatia Airlines
Tel: 020 8563 0022
www.croatiaairlines.hr

Cyprus Airways
Tel: 020 8897 2190
www.cyprusairways.com

Czech Airlines (CSA)
Tel: 0870 4443 747
www.csa.cz/en/czechia/cz_home.htm

Delta Airlines
Tel: 020 8601 6000
www.delta.com

Eastern Airways
Tel: 08703 669 100
www.easternairways.com

EasyJet
Tel: 0870 6 000 000
www.easyjet.com

Egypt Air
Birmingham Tel: 0121 643 1249
London Tel: 0207 580 5477
Manchester Tel: 0161 834 2552
www.egyptair.com

El Al Israel Airlines
London Tel: 020 7957 4100
Manchester Tel: 0161 834 6553
www.elal.co.il

Emirates
Tel: 020 7808 0033
www.emirates.com/uk/

Finnair
Tel: 0870 241 4411
www.finnair.com

FlyBe Airline
Tel: 01392 366669
www4.flybe.com

Globespan Airline
www.globespan.com/

Gulf Air
Tel: 0870 777 1717
www.gulfairco.com

Iberia Airlines
Tel: 0870 609 0500
www.iberia.com

ICELAND AIR
Tel: 0870 787 4020
www.icelandair.co.uk/

IRAN AIR
Tel: 020 7603 1246
www.iranair.co.uk

JAPAN AIRLINES
Tel: 0845 7 747 777
www.japanair.com

JAT AIRWAYS
Tel: 0207 629 2007
www.jat.com

JET2 AIRLINE
Tel: 0871 226 1737
www.jet2.com

KLM ROYAL DUTCH AIRLINES
Tel: 08705 074 074
www.klm.com/uk_en/

KOREAN AIR
Tel: 0800 0656 2001
www.koreanair.eu.com/

KUWAIT AIRWAYS
Tel: 020 7412 0006
www.kuwait-airways.com

LOT POLISH AIRLINES
Tel: 845 859 300
www3.lot.com

LUFTHANSA
Tel: 020 8750 3500
http://portal.lufthansa
.com

LUX AIR
Tel: 0800 38 99 443
www.luxair.lu/

MAERSK AIR
Tel: 020 7333 0066
www.maersk-air.com/en/

MALAYSIAN AIRLINES
Tel: 020 7341 2000
www.malaysiaairlines.com

MALEV HUNGARIAN
Tel: 0870 909 0577
www.malev.hu/bp/eng/

MERIDIANA
Tel: 0845 355 5588
www.meridiana.it/en/

MEXICANA
Tel: 020 8492 0000
www.mexicana.com

MIDDLE EAST AIRLINES
Tel: 0207 7758 9000
www.mea.com.lb/MEA/
English/

OLYMPIC AIRWAYS
London Tel: 0870 6060 460
Manchester Tel: 0161 4895
458
www.olympicairlines.com

PAKISTAN INTERNATIONAL AIRLINES
Tel: 0800 587 1023
www.piac.com

QANTAS AIRWAYS
Tel: 0845 7747 767
www.qantas.com.au

QATAR AIRWAYS
Manchester Tel: 0161 435
6056
London Tel: 0207 896 3636
www.qatarairways.com

ROYAL BRUNEI AIRLINES
Tel: 020 7584 6360
www.bruneiair.com

ROYAL JORDANIAN
Tel: 020 787 6333
www.rja.com.jo

SAS - SCANDINAVIAN AIRLINES
Tel: 020 8990 7060
www.scandinavian.net/

SAUDI ARABIAN AIRLINES
Tel: 0207 798 9898
www.saudiairlines.com

SCOT AIRWAYS
Tel: 0870 60 60 707
www.scotairways.co.uk

SINGAPORE AIRLINES
Tel: 0870 608 8886
www.singaporeair.com

SKY EUROPE AIRLINES
Tel: 020 7365 0365
www.skyeurope.com

SOUTH AFRICAN AIRWAYS (SAA)
Tel: 020 7312 5000

www.flysaa.com

SRI LANKAN AIRLINES
Tel: 0208 538 2001
www.srilankan.lk/

SWISS INTERNATIONAL AIRLINES
Tel: 0845 601 0956
www.swiss.com

SYRIAN AIRLINES
Tel: 020 7631 3511
www.syrianairlines.co.uk

TAP - AIR PORTUGAL
Tel: 0845 601 0932
www.tap.pt

THAI AIRWAYS INTERNATIONAL
Tel: 020 7491 7953 / 0870
606 0911
www.thaiairways.co.uk/

THOMSON FLY
Tel: 0870 1900 737
www.thomsonfly.com

TURKISH AIRLINES
London Tel: 0207 766 9300
Manchester Tel: 0161 489
5290
www.turkishairlines.com/
en/

UNITED AIRLINES
Tel: 0845 8444 777
www.unitedairlines.co.uk

VARIG BRAZIL
Tel: 0208 321 7170
www.varig.co.uk

VIRGIN ATLANTIC
Tel: 01293 562 345
www.virgin-atlantic.com

YEMEN AIRWAYS
Tel: 020 7323 3213
www.yemenairways.co.uk

Transport 3: by train

Riding the iron rails
by Keith Strickland

I HAVE SELDOM HEARD A TRAIN GO BY and not wished I was on it: so wrote PaulTheroux at the start of *The Great Railway Bazaar*, his account of a train journey from London to Tokyo. Commuters on the London Underground or the New York Subway might not share this sentiment, but for those of us with a more relaxed attitude to time, there's nothing quite like the anticipation of boarding a train, settling into a window seat, and letting the pleasure of travel take over. For trains are more than just a means of getting from A to B.

At one extreme, they give the traveller an insight into the everyday life of the countries they serve. To see and experience India away from the main tourist attractions, there is no better way than to take the train. Railway stations themselves are a microcosm of Indian life. The homeless and beggars may spend their whole time cooking, drinking, washing, and sleeping on platforms. Then there are the tradesmen – *chai wallahs*, booksellers, stallholders – and, of course, the crowds.

At the other end of the spectrum, South Africa's *Blue Train* from Cape Town to Johannesburg has gold-tinted windows, *haute cuisine* and *en-suite* accommodation, and is generally reckoned to be the world's most luxurious train.

You can take a train for a one-off trip, or you can spend your whole holiday on one. Sometimes there is no alternative form of transport – unless you are a mountain climber, the only way of ascending the Jungfrau in Switzerland is by rail.

Planning the journey

Wherever you want to go, planning is essential. In some parts of the world, trains run much less frequently than in the UK. There's a line in Patagonia whose regular train plies only once a week. Miss it and you have to wait seven days for the next.

The most comprehensive guides are Thomas Cook's *European Timetable* and *Overseas Timetable*. Both concentrate on major routes. For minor lines, one must consult local timetables. The best known is Newman's *Indian Bradshaw*, which contains every passenger train on India's rail network. Sometimes there is no way of getting advance information. In parts of South America, the timetable consists of nothing more sophisticated than a blackboard at the local station.

Tickets

1. No railway administration likes ticketless travellers. You might just get away

without paying in places such as India, especially if you enjoy riding on the carriage roof, but in many countries fines are stiff for passengers without valid tickets. The same goes for riding first class with a second-class ticket.

2. Train travel can be incredibly cheap, particularly in developing countries. If you want relative comfort and space, use first-class accommodation (if it's available) – you won't have to raise a mortgage.

3. There is now a proliferation of discounted tickets. Age, time and day of the week, advance purchase, duration of journey – all may have a bearing on the price you pay. Rover tickets offering unlimited travel within a country or geographical area are real value for money. Finding out about the best buys is, however, not always easy. High-street travel agents are not the best informed when it comes to rail travel. Try to find one who specialises in railways, such as Ffestiniog Travel. As a general rule, it pays to book as much of your overseas journey as you are able to in the UK before you set out. This will save you money, as well as possible hassle later on. A lot of patience is sometimes required if you try to book locally. The sale of tickets is not always the relatively speedy process it is in the UK.

Luggage

Travel light. It's amazing, when looking at pictures of Victorian travellers, to see the massive trunks they took with them. What did they pack?

The station porter may be a rare species in Britain but flourishes elsewhere – at a price. Even so, a mass of luggage is an encumbrance on a train. Pack essentials only. Choose according to the length of the journey and the climate of the country.

A word about security. Petty theft is a fact of life almost everywhere. Unattended luggage is easy game. Remember that in many developing countries the value of a camera may equate to several months' average wage. Keep money and other valuables on you. If you have to leave baggage, make sure it is locked and try to chain it to some immovable object such as the luggage rack. Above all, make sure you have adequate insurance.

Food

On long train journeys, find out in advance if food and drink are likely to be available. On-board catering should be indicated in the timetable, though standards and prices vary enormously. South African dining cars offer superb food and wine at modest prices. France is disappointing – food on the high-speed TGV is no better than average aircraft-style meals. Catering on the *Trans-Siberian Express* is, by most people's accounts, hardly bearable.

Don't overlook the possibilities of station restaurants, though Western stomachs should be wary of platform vendors, especially in Asia. Their wares look colourful but can have devastating effects. Similarly, treat local drinks with caution. Peru has its own version of Coke – green Inca Cola – as nauseating to look at as to drink. *Chai* (sweet, milky tea) is the safest drink at an Indian railway station..

Health

The first item in my personal medical kit is a bottle of eye drops – essential for countries where trains are still pulled by steam engines. Sooner, rather than later, the inevitable smuts will be acquired.

Other than this, there are no special health hazards associated with trains, assuming you won't be riding on the roof or hanging onto the sides. But a long journey is not the best way to pass the time if you are unlucky enough to be ill, and on-board 'bathroom' facilities are pretty primitive in many places. So it's important to take the health precautions necessary for the country you are visiting.

Sleeping

There's no experience quite like sleeping on a train. Again, if you intend to do this, plan ahead. Find out from the timetable whether sleeping facilities are available, and if so, what they are. There may be a sleeping compartment with fresh sheets, its own loo, and an attendant. Couchettes are popular in some countries – beware, the sexes are not always segregated.

In India and Pakistan, sleeping accommodation means a bed-roll spread out on an ordinary compartment seat, if you're lucky; and it's worth remembering that the more important stations on the subcontinent have retiring rooms where a bed can be rented for the night.

Whatever the facilities, a supplementary fee and advance reservation are almost always essential, though greasing the palm of the conductor often works wonders in places where such dealings are a way of life.

How to travel

First or second class? Express or slow train? By day or by night? The answers depend on the money and time at your disposal, and on the aims of your journey. Do you want to be cosseted from the outside world and pampered with luxury? Do you prefer to mix with local people? It's entirely up to you. The choice is enormous. Remember one golden rule: the more comfort you want, the more you will have to pay; and the greater will be the likelihood of having to make reservations in advance. Conversely, second-class travel is cheaper, usually does not need to be booked ahead, but will inevitably be more crowded.

Incidentally, some countries have more than two classes. India has a plethora, though you won't necessarily find them all on the same train.

Suggested routes

Starting at the top of the market, the *Blue Train* has already been mentioned. In the same league is the *Orient Express*. Can there be a more romantic way to arrive in Venice than by this train of restored elegant carriages? So successful has this up-market concept been that sister trains now operate in Malaysia/Thailand and in Australia. Other trains designed specifically for the tourist trade include India's *Palace on Wheels* and Spain's *Andalucian Express*. Though the daily train that took passengers from Montreal to Vancouver and vice versa ceased running a few years ago, it is still possible for tourists to cross the Rockies by luxury train.

Canada aside, the long-distance train does survive in everyday use in many parts of the world. The *Trans-Siberian* (or *Rossiya* to use its local name) runs daily from Moscow eastwards to the Pacific coast. One can still cross the USA by rail, though not as one continuous journey. Trains travel vast distances in India, and in China where a new 'first-class' train links Beijing and Hong Kong. The *Indian Pacific* traverses the complete width of Australia from Sydney to Perth, whilst the *Trans-Alpine* crosses the mountains of New Zealand's South Island.

There are not many railway-less countries, and the possibilities for train travel are limitless. Don't just stick to the well-known routes. Branch out and see what you discover. The most memorable journey is often the least expected. Tucked away in a remote mountainous part of Peru are the towns of Huancayo and Huancavelica. The train takes all day to go from one to the other, stops everywhere and is full of people going to market with their produce and livestock. There are tunnels, steep gradients and river gorges and, all the while, the Andes form a stunning backdrop. A humble line; an extraordinary and exhilarating experience.

Better known and in almost equally breathtaking scenery is the narrow-gauge railway linking the hill station of Darjeeling to the plains 1,800 m below. In just over 80 km, the diminutive engines of the Darjeeling Himalayan Railway climb by way of zigzags and spiral loops into the foothills with stunning views – on a clear day – of Kangchenjunga, at 8,500 m the world's third-highest mountain. Parts of the track are often washed away in the annual monsoons, and it's a wonder the line has survived, especially as the journey by road can be done in half the time it takes by rail. But if the trains are running, it's a journey not to be missed. Such is the unique character of the line that it has just been declared a World Heritage Site by UNESCO.

Special interests

To many, railways are a hobby; some would say an addiction. Every aspect of railway history and operation has been studied in great detail, but it is the steam locomotive that commands the most devotion. Steam has an atmosphere all of its own. One can see it, hear it, smell it, feel it and taste it. Steam buffs travel the world to experience its thrill.

China is the enthusiast's Mecca. With cheap labour and plentiful coal supplies, China was still building steam engines in the late 1980s, and there are hundreds at work on the country's railways. In contrast is Cuba, where ancient engines are brought out of retirement for the annual *zafra* (sugar harvest) to pull cane from the fields to the mills. In this steam paradise, it's possible to combine a beach holiday with the joys of watching trains.

Elsewhere, the number of countries where steam is in everyday use is dwindling. Poland and the eastern part of Germany are the only European ones. Further afield, steam lingers – just – in Zimbabwe, Indonesia, Burma and Argentina. Sadly India, long regarded as a bastion of steam, has finished with steam on all but a couple of branch lines. There is a compensating increase in museum and preserved railways, but to the purist these are a poor substitute for the real thing.

Specialist travel operators for the serious enthusiast include Steam & Safaris, Travel Bureau Railtours, and Dorridge Travel Service. Many tours include general-interest elements to cater for non-railway partners.

Weighed down with cameras and all the accoutrements of photography, steam buffs are instantly distinguished from their fellow travellers. Do not despise them! Their motives for the journey may not be the same as yours, but they're the experts to turn to when the unexpected occurs.

Remember that trains run late the world over – sometimes very late. Occasionally they are cancelled. Connections are missed. Landslides block the line. In these circumstances, your timetable may not be much help. It's a fair bet the enthusiasts will know the solution to the problem – you hope.

Reading material

Trains are places for meeting people. You will rarely be on your own. It's only in England that strangers never converse. Nevertheless, make sure you put a good book in your luggage. Every journey has a dull moment.

Books about railways are legion. Thomas Cook has a series of handbooks for 'rail touring'; and Bradt has books on rail travel in specific countries such as India and Russia. Paul Theroux's *The Great Railway Bazaar* remains the most readable account of one person's journey. Start and you won't be able to put it down.

To appreciate the atmosphere generated by the steam locomotive, browse the transport section of any large bookshop. For a sample, your contributor immodestly suggests his own books *Steam Railways Around the World* and *Steam Through Five Continents*.

Above all, buy a timetable. It is a mine of information. My Pakistan Railways timetable tells me the cost of a bed in the retiring room at Karachi. Breakfast consists of 'choice of two eggs, two toasts with butter and jam, pot of tea'. If I want to take a rickshaw with me as part of my luggage, it will be deemed to weigh 150 kg and charged accordingly. On another page comes the solemn warning: 'Passengers are requested in their own interest not to light or allow any other passenger to light any oil stove or any other type of fire in the passenger carriages as this practice is not only fraught with dangerous consequences but is a penal offence under the Railways Act.' Fascinating! This timetable could keep me occupied for hours.

Finally, turn the pages of the timetable and look at the names of the trains. Whose imagination fails to be stirred by the *Frontier Mail, Himalayan Queen* or *Shalimar Express*?

Trains are not some sort of time capsule. They seem natural – almost a part of the landscape. They certainly reflect the characteristics and atmosphere of the countries and communities through which they run in a way air travel, cruise ships or air-conditioned road coaches can never do. Flanders and Swann put it rather differently in one of their songs: 'If God had meant us to fly, He would never have given us railways.' ❧

KEITH STRICKLAND has travelled the world for 25 years to indulge his passion for trains. He has photographed trains in 40 countries and published three books on the subject.

Rail passes

The list below shows a selection of rail passes that are available to independent travellers and generally not for sale to natives of the country. Prices may vary or change, but they are valid at the time of the handbook going to print. For the most up-to-date idea of prices check the websites, provided below, for details.

Europe

Eurail

www.eurail.com

Eurail offer four variations on their rail passes, varying in time committed and number of countries you would like to travel to.

EurailPass is the most extensive pass on offer by Eurail, with travel between 17 European countries available for periods between 15 days to three months. All prices vary for length you would like to travel for.

Eurailpass 1st Class prices are from $588-$1,654

Eurailpass Saver 1st Class prices are from $498-$1408

Eurailpass Youth 2nd Class prices are from $382-$1075

EurailPass Flexi allows travel between 17 countries by rail and some shipping routes for periods between 10 days to two months on non-consecutive days.

Eurailpass Flexi 1st Class prices are from $694-$914

Eurailpass Saver 1st Class prices are from $592-$778

Eurailpass Youth 2nd Class prices are from $451-$594

Eurail Selectpasses are tailor-made passes between 3,4 or 5 bordering countries (up to 22 countries), between 5 to 10 days travel, within a two month period. Prices depend on length of travel and how many countries you choose to visit.

Eurail Selectpass 1st Class prices are from $370 - $826

Eurail Selectpass Saver 1st Class prices are from $316-$702

Eurail Selectpass Youth 2nd Class prices are from $241-$537

Eurail Regional Passes allow unlimited travel within one of nine available countries, between 4 to 10 days throughout 2 months.

Inter-Rail

www.interrail.net

Rail travel through 8 'zones' covering Europe from Norway to Morocco, available to European citizens for up to a months travel on Europe's railways.

Eurodomino Pass

Three to eight days extensive travel through 28 countries from Europe to North Africa. Prices vary between 1st class and standard, there is also a youth class and children between the ages of 4–11 pay half adult fares.

Australia

Rail Australia

www.railaustralia.com

The Rail Australia Pass offers travel throughout this vast country using the three major rail networks, Great Southern Railway, Queensland Rail and Countrylink. All passes are valid for six months from

Inter-rail price structure

Age group	25 and under	over 25
For 1 zone (16 days)	195 euros	289 euros
For 2 zones (22 days)	275 euros	396 euros
Global (ie all zones)	385 euros	546 euros

when you first start your journey.

General conditions for the pass may vary between rail networks and services.

Austrail Flexipass is available for adult between 15-22 days, costing £400- £561.

Backpacker Railpass is available for up t 90 days, costing between £101-£127.

East Coast Discovery Pass, prices vary from location to location.

Great Southern Railway Pass – for adults £274 and backpackers/students/chil d £209. Prices are economy class and last for 6 months.

Canada and USA

Amtrak Passes

www.amtrak.com

Amtrak offers a list of passes covering America and Canada.

The National Pass covers all areas, though there are more specific passes for the Northeast from Virginia to Montreal.

The Eastern Pass stretches from Chicago all the way to New Orleans.

The Far West Pass lets you travel from Denver to El Paso.

Coastal Passes are the most flexible allowing you freedom in either direction for up to 30 days. Prices vary depending on

when you travel during peak (June-September) and off peak seasons.

Only available to international visitors.

VIA Rail Passes

www.viarail.ca

Canrail Pass covers the whole VIA Rail system for 12 days rail travel during a 30 day period once you have started your journey and allows as many stops throughout.

Peak rail prices (June–October) adults $778 students/children/seniors $700

Off peak prices adults $486 students/children/seniors $437

Extensions for up to 3 days can be obtained on your journey, which you pay extra, prices above are for economy class.

India

Indrail Pass

www.indianrail.gov.in

The indrail pass covers the entire Indian Railways System from half-day to 90 passes.

Passes available inside or outside India, can only be bought with US dollars or Pound Sterling within India.

Prices vary according to period of validity and which class you choose – AC class, First class or

Second class. Children travel for half the price of an adult ticket.

Malaysia

KTM Rail Pass

www.ktmb.co.my

Unlimited travel within Malaysia and into Singapore for up to 15 days, valid only to foreign travellers. Valid from date of first journey.

5 day pass : adult $35, child $18

10 day pass: adult $55, child $28

15 day pass : adult $70, child $35

New Zealand

Scenic Rail Pass

www.tranzscenic.co.nz

Travel passes for 7 days or a month. Or alternatively decide as you go. Jump on and off wherever and whenever you like as you tour New Zealand. Prices include ferry journeys between the north and south islands.

Adult Pass: 7 day $299 monthly $499

Child Pass 7 day $179 monthly $299

Related websites

www.bahn.co.uk Germany's official rail website.

www.raileurope.com
Links to US and UK
website.

www.railpass.com

www.europeonrail.com

www.europeanrail.com
Independent agency
selling European rail
tickets by phone and
website.

www.
international-rail.com

www.railchoice.co.uk
Links to rail passes for the
Balkans, Italy, Switzerland
and more.

Railway companies and tour operators

UK rail services

ARRIVA TRAINS WALES
Tel: 0845 6061 660
www.arrivatrainswales.
co.uk

C2C RAILWAY COMPANY
Tel: 0845 301 4873
www.c2c-online.co.uk

CENTRAL TRAINS
Tel: 0121 634 2040
www.centraltrains.co.uk/

CHILTERN RAILWAYS
Tel: 08456 005 165
www.chilternrailways.
co.uk/

DOCKLANDS LIGHT RAILWAY
Tel: 020 7363 9700
www.tfl.gov.uk/dlr/

ENGLISH, WELSH AND SCOTTISH RAILWAYS
Tel: 01302 766801
www.ews-railway.co.uk/

EUROSTAR
Tel: 08705 186 186
www.eurostar.com

FIRST GREAT WESTERN
Tel: 08457 48 49 50
www.firstgreatwestern.
co.uk

FIRST SCOTRAIL
Tel: 0845 601 5929
www.firstgroup.com/
scotrail/

FIRST TRANS PENNINE EXPRESS
Tel: 0845 600 1671
www.tpexpress.co.uk/

FREIGHTLINER
Tel: 01394 612823
www.freightliner.co.uk/

GATWICK EXPRESS
Tel: 0845 850 15 30
www.gatwickexpress.co.uk

GREAT NORTH EASTERN RAILWAY
Tel: 08457 225 333
www.gner.co.uk/GNER

HEATHROW EXPRESS
Tel: 0845 600 1515
www.heathrowexpress.
com/

HULL TRAINS
Tel: 01482 60 63 88
www.hulltrains.co.uk

ISLAND LINE
Tel: 01983 812591
www.island-line.co.uk

LONDON UNDERGROUND
Tel: 020 7941 4500
www.tfl.gov.uk/tube

MERSEY RAIL
Tel: 0151 702 2071
www.merseyrail.org

MIDLAND MAINLINE
Tel: 08457 125 678
www.midlandmainline.
com

NORTHERN RAIL
Tel: 0845 600 1159
www.northernrail.org/

NI RAILWAYS
Tel: 028 90 66 66 30
www.nirailways.co.uk

ONE RAIL
Tel: 0845 600 7245
www.onerailway.com

STANSTED EXPRESS
Tel: 0845 600 7245
www.stanstedexpress.com

SOUTH EASTERN TRAINS
Tel: 0845 000 2222
www.setrains.co.uk

SOUTH WEST TRAINS
Tel: 0845 6000 650
www.southwesttrains.
co.uk

THAMES LINK
Tel: 0845 330 3660
www.thameslink.co.uk

VIRGIN TRAINS
Tel: 0870 789 1234
www.virgintrains.co.uk

WEST ANGLIA GREAT NORTHERN RAILWAY
Tel: 0870 850 88 22
www.wagn.co.uk

WESSEX TRAINS
Tel: 0845 6000 880
www.wessextrains.co.uk

General enquiries

NATIONAL RAIL ENQUIRIES
UK tel: 08457 48 49 50
www.nationalrail.co.uk

OFFICE OF RAIL REGULATION
UK tel: 020 7282 2000
www.rail-reg.gov.uk

RAIL PASSENGERS COUNCIL
UK tel: 08453 022 022
www.railpassengers.org.uk

Foreign railway offices in the UK

AUSTRALIA - GREAT SOUTHERN RAILWAY
Tel: 0870 6064 012
www.gsr.com.au

AUSTRALIA - QUEENSLAND RAIL
Tel: 0870 751 5000
www.railaustralia.com.au

BELGIAN RAILWAYS SNCB/NMBS
Tel: 0207 922 20 13
www.b-rail.be/corp/e/

DANISH STATE RAILWAYS
Tel: 020 7259 5959 (tourist board)
www.dsb.dk/english

FINNISH STATE RAILWAYS
Tel: 0870 744 7315
(Nortours travel agency)
www.nortours.co.uk

GERMAN RAIL – DEUTSCHE BAHN
Tel: 0870 243 53 63
www.deutsche-bahn.co.uk

INDIAN RAILWAYS
Tel: 020 8903 3411
www.indiarail.co.uk

IRELAND – IARNROD EIREANN
www.iarnrodeireann.ie

LUXEMBOURG NATIONAL RAILWAYS
Tel: 020 7434 2800
www.luxembourg.co.uk/pubtrans.html

NATIONAL RAILWAY OF FRANCE (SNCF)
Tel: 08702 41 42 43
www.sncf.co.uk

RAIL EUROPE
Tel: 08708 371 371
www.raileurope.co.uk

SOUTH AFRICA – SPOORNET
www.spoornet.co.za

TRANS SIBERIA RAIL
Tel: 0207 937 7207
(Russian Tourist Office)
www.trans-siberia.com

USA – AMTRAK
Tel: 1 800 872 7245
www.amtrak.com

Specialist rail tour operators

ABERCROMBIE & KENT
UK tel: 0845 0700610
www.abercrombiekent.co.uk

COX & KINGS TRAVEL
UK tel: 020 7873 5014
www.coxandkings.co.uk
Tours include the Palace on Wheels through India and Rajasthan.

GLOBESPAN
UK tel: 0141 332 3233
www.globespan.com
Rail trips through Alberta and British Columbia in Canada.

THE LUXURY TRAINS
UK tel: 0800 032 7748
www.theluxurytrains.com

THE QUEEN OF SCOTS LUXURY TOURING TRAIN
UK tel: 01773 828666
www.queenofscots.co.uk
Luxurious and exclusive travel around Britain.

TEFS RAILWAY TOURS
UK tel: 01509 262745
www.holidaynet.com/combined/operator.asp
Steam train tours around Europe.

TRAINS UNLIMITED
UK tel: 01565 754 540
USA tel: 1 800 359 4870
www.trainsunlimitedtours.com
Operates rail tours through Asia, the Americas and the former USSR.

VENICE SIMPLON ORIENT EXPRESS
UK tel: 0845 077 2222
www.orient-express.com

Related websites

www.alleuroperail.com

www.amtrak.com
Route maps, timetables, bookings and advise for train travel in America.

www.bluetrain.co.za
South Africa's premier train.

www.bookorbuy.com/rovos
Train travel through Africa.

www.eurorailways.com
Timetables, information about passes, overnight rail etc… for rail trips in Europe.

www.eurostar.co.uk

www.interrailer.net
Inter-railing around Europe.

www.networkrail.co.uk
Information regarding engineering works and redevelopment on UK tracks.

www.orient-express.com

www.railserve.com
Links to international rail timetables.

www.trainweb.org/indiarail/
Indian railways homepage – unofficial.

www.travelnotes.org/Travel/byrail.htm

Transport 4: by boat

Just cruising
by Sue Bryant

CRUISING IS UNDERGOING ENORMOUS CHANGES as it shakes off its stuffy, old-fashioned image and begins to appeal to the young, the hip and the more adventurous. It's ironic that this revolution has received a huge boost recently from Europe's first real 'budget' vessel, EasyCruise, which has made younger travellers wonder if there is after all a kind of cachet to holidays at sea. The irony is that EasyCruise is far from what purists would call a 'real' cruise ship, on which all food and entertainment are included and part of the pleasure of the holiday is derived from the ship itself. But it has nonetheless played its part in waking up the travelling public to the joys of life on the ocean waves.

And not before time. What other kind of holiday takes you deep into the Amazon, or through the Panama Canal, or along the wild, rugged coastline of Alaska, where you can see bears foraging on the stony beaches and whales breaching alongside the ship? On a cruise, you can reach some of the Earth's remotest spots: the isolated Atlantic islands of St Helena and the Falklands; the amazing Galapagos; the mountains and reefs of Tahiti; snowy Spitsbergen in the far north of Norway, where the Northern Lights illuminate the sky; and perhaps the ultimate prize, the ice shelf of Antarctica.

What has really changed about cruising is that there are now so many different styles of ship. Technically, only one can be called a 'liner', and that is Cunard's Queen Mary 2, which is the only vessel to operate an actual 'line voyage' – a regular scheduled service, in this case the six-day Atlantic crossing between Southampton and New York. Some ships roam the world, like those of P&O Cruises, Orient Line, Swan Hellenic, Crystal Cruises and Holland America Line. Others operate regular itineraries from their 'home port' – for example, Royal Caribbean's many variations on the seven-night Caribbean cruise from Miami and other US ports, or the many ships based in Palma, Venice and Barcelona in summer, which repeat a series of one-week loops around the Mediterranean from April to November.

One thing is for sure: ships are getting bigger, as the cruise industry looks for economies of scale. More and more ships nowadays are floating resorts, with cruise lines competing to offer the most lavish and unusual facilities. Royal Caribbean is streets ahead here. It was the first (and is still the only) cruise line to have an ice rink on board; the first to install a climbing wall up the smoke stack; and the first to launch the new generation of 'mega-ships', carrying over 3,000 passengers. Its newest vessel, Freedom of the Seas, is even larger (3,600 passengers) and has a water theme park on board, and jacuzzis cantilevered out over the sides of the vessel, 112 feet above the ocean.

Not to be outdone, Cunard has put the world's first planetarium at sea on board Queen Mary 2. Princess Cruises has installed giant movie screens on the decks of its ships for movies under the stars from the comfort of a deckchair. Radisson Seven Seas Cruises has the only two ships on which every cabin is a luxury suite with a balcony, while Norwegian Cruise Line has successfully broken the mould of formal cruise ship dining, with a choice of 12 restaurants on its newest ships, serving anything from tapas to teppanyaki.

Those cruise lines operating small ships try to divorce themselves from these images as far as possible. Star Clippers operates three beautiful square-riggers, where the only entertainment is climbing the mast, sunbathing in the bowsprit nets and chatting to the resident parrot in the open-air bar. SeaDream Yacht Club's two 100-passenger ships are more like romantic, private mega-yachts. Nobody wears a tie, dining is al fresco wherever possible, the champagne flows, there are MP3 players and jetskis to play with, and guests can sleep under the stars on sexy double sunloungers if they please. Hebridean Island Cruises, a tiny and very exclusive Scottish line, operates wonderful voyages pottering around the Scottish Highlands, and exploratory itineraries on its second ship, the 80-passenger Hebridean Spirit, in the Mediterranean and off South Africa. The guest list reads like Who's Who, and the atmosphere on board is that of a very good private house party.

But small ships like this simply aren't built nowadays, and if this 'boutique' sector becomes as popular as small, designer hotels have done, owners are more likely to acquire existing vessels and convert them than to start from scratch.

There is enormous variation between big ships too, and it would be a mistake to assume they were all the same. P&O, Royal Caribbean, Princess, Norwegian Cruise Line and Carnival, for example, are great for families, with creative and exciting children's clubs, usually from age two to teenagers. P&O also has two ships, Artemis and Arcadia, for adults only. Fred Olsen's four ships are a very British experience favoured by an older market, while Holland America Line's modern fleet appeals mainly to Americans, also of a certain age. Carnival Cruises' ships, on the other hand, are bold, bright and brash, with huge casinos and younger passengers. On Ocean Village, a British-run offshoot of P&O, you can go to dinner in a T-shirt; but on a Crystal Cruises voyage, which costs many, many times more, the serious diamonds come out for the captain's dinner.

Where this armada travels in the world depends on both fashion and politics. After 9/11, no-fly cruises from American ports became enormously popular for the US market. Destinations perceived as 'safe', like the Baltic, the Norwegian fjords and Alaska, also did extremely well. Yet almost perversely, several years on from the atrocities but still in highly unstable times, the ports of the Levant are suddenly enjoying a renaissance as cruise passengers (admittedly on the more cerebral type of voyage) flock to Syria, the Lebanon and even Libya. Those who have 'done' the Caribbean are now choosing cruises that explore the antiquities of Mexico and Guatemala, and the cloud forests and reefs of Costa Rica and Belize.

Cruise operators

Carnival Cruise Lines
Tel: 1 888 2276 4825
www.carnival.com

Celebrity Cruises
UK Tel: 0800 018
2525, USA Tel: 1 800
760 0654
www.celebrity.com

Costa Cruises
Tel: 800 462 6782
www.costacruise.com

Crystal Cruises
UK Tel: 020 7287
9060, USA Tel: 1 800
804 1500
www.crystalcruises.
com

Cunard
Tel: 661 753 1000 /
800 7 CUNNARD
www.cunard.com

Disney Cruise Line
USA Tel: 1 800 951
3532, UK Tel: 01270
758 847
http://disneycruise.
disney.go.com

Fred Olsen Cruise Lines
Tel: 01473 292 200
www.fredolsen.co.uk

Hebridean Island Cruises
Tel: 01756 704 704
www.hebridean.co.uk

Holland America Cruise Lines
UK Tel: 020 7940
4477, USA Tel: 1 206
281 3535
www.hollandamerica.
com

Hurtigruten Norwegian Cruises
Tel: 47 810 30 000
www.hurtigruten.com

Norwegian Coastal Voyage
Tel: 020 8846 2600
www.coastalvoyage.
com

Norwegian Cruise Line
Tel: 0845 658 8010
www.ncl.com

Odysseus Cruising
UK Tel: 07768
508350, USA Tel: 646
623 5533
www.
odysseuscruising.com

Orient Lines
Tel: 1 800 333 7300
www.orientlines.com

Passenger Shipping Association
Tel: 0207 436 2449
www.psa-psara.org

Peter Dielmann Cruises
Tel: 1 800 348 8287
www.deilmann-
cruises.com

P & O Cruises
Tel: 0845 3 555 333

www.pocruises.com

Princess Cruises
Tel: 1 800 PRINCESS
www.princess.com

Radisson Seven Seas Cruises
Tel: 023 80 680 2280
www.rssc.com

Royal Caribbean International
Tel: 1 0800 018 2020
www.royalcaribbean.
com

Silversea Cruises
UK Tel: 0870 333
7030, USA Tel: 877
760 9052
www.silverseacruises.
com

Star Clippers
UK Tel: 377 97 97 84
00, USA Tel: 305 442
0550
www.starclippers.com

Star Cruises
Tel: 020 7591 8225
www.starcruises.com

Swan Hellenic Discovery Cruising
UK Tel: 0845 3 555
111, USA Tel: 877 800
SWAN
www.swanhellenic.
com

Wayne Frieslander
Tel: 0161 491 6677
www.
cruisesandvoyages.
com

When the US dollar is weak, the British (the second-biggest market after the US) make the most of shopping in the Caribbean, while Americans, on the other hand, avoid the Mediterranean.

The real change in cruising is not so much in where ships go – after all, if trouble flares, you can simply move a cruise ship, unlike an hotel – but in what is offered on board. Simply lying on deck contemplating the open sea is no longer enough. Large cruise ships now are packed with self-improvement opportunities, from language and drama lessons to art appreciation classes, web-design seminars and cookery demonstrations. There are gay cruises, naturist cruises, gambling cruises and kosher cruises. Shore excursions have moved on, too, the humble coach tour giving way to sea kayaking, ice climbing in Alaska and even, if you're extremely rich and so desire, flying in a Russia MiG fighter as a little side trip from St Petersburg. When it comes to cruising, the only limitation, wallet aside, is your imagination. ❧

SUE BRYANT is the founder and editor of 'Cruise Traveller' magazine.

By cargo ship
by Hugo Verlomme

WHY, IN THIS AGE OF JET-PLANE COMMUTING, would one travel by freighter? Surely it must be a boring, wet, lonely, and above all terribly slow way to go?

In fact this is exactly why travel by cargo ship is such a pleasure. If you want to go on holiday then a cruise liner, which is a floating luxury hotel that rarely 'goes' anywhere, is for you. If you want to really travel the seas then freighters are the genuine experience. Etymologically, to travel means 'to follow a path', and not simply 'to arrive'. Robert Louis Stevenson understood the nature of leisurely travel when he wrote: 'To travel hopefully is a better thing than to arrive.'

I have indeed noticed that some of my most vivid memories have been related to unexpected events that have happened on my travels. It could be the tail of a typhoon in the China Sea, whales in the St Lawrence river or, most important of all, encounters with people – officers, crew or fellow travellers of different nationalities – of whom some have become friends.

Being on the move for days and days on the rolling hills of the ocean has been described as 'the royal way'. As we walk, drive, fly or travel overland, we tend to forget that 71 per cent of our blue planet is composed of oceans. Why limit our travelling to 29 per cent of the globe?

"But isn't the sea always the same?" is a question I have been asked many times. Anyone who hasn't seen the changing colours of the oceans – the British Channel's ochres, the Atlantic's ultramarine, the Mediterranean's lapis lazuli, the Caribbean's turquoise or the deep Pacific's indigo – might be forgiven for thinking so. The sea

Distance and duration

Distances in Nautical Miles

From Felixstowe to:

New York	3200
Sydney (via Suez)	11590
Hong Kong	9715
Rio de Janeiro	5200
Cape Town	6150

From Los Angeles to:

London	7677
Sydney	6511
Singapore	7867
Cape Town (via Panama Canal)	9421
Le Havre	7557

Duration of Voyage

Approximate journey times at an average speed of 15 knots (equivalent to 15 nautical miles per hour):

500 miles – 1 day 9 hrs
1000 miles – 2 days 19 hrs
2000 miles – 5 days 3 hrs
3000 miles – 8 days 8 hrs
5000 miles – 13 days 21 hrs
10000 miles – 27 days 18 hrs

1 Nautical mile = 1.852km = 1.15 miles

is an incredible, changing prospect full of surprises for those who keep their eyes open: islands, storms, calms, squalls, dolphins and whales, fish and birds, icebergs and atolls. Freighters are privileged platforms from which to observe seas and skies, human activity and marine life.

Not so long ago, liners were the standard way to reach any destination 'overseas'. These were glorious times when microcosms of society crossed the oceans, mixing together families and loners, travellers and businessmen, migrants and adventurers. Today's liners are exclusively dedicated to the holiday cruising industry, which is booming. I remember with nostalgia enchanting Atlantic crossings aboard a Polish liner, one of the last 'Transatlantics', the *Stefan Batory*, who made her last crossing in 1988.

Nowadays, freighters are the only way remaining to travel by sea. Many people believe that embarking on a cargo ship means sleeping in a small cheap cabin, and maybe giving a hand on deck or in the kitchen to pay the fare. The good old times when famous writers such as Joseph Conrad, Blaise Cendrars, Malcolm Lowry or Jack Kerouac travelled (and worked) on freighters are gone forever. The romantic old beaten tramp patched with rust, as in Alvaro Mutis' novels, has been replaced with armadas of modern container ships, some of them so wide they can no longer navigate the Panama Canal.

Tramps, ro-ros, reefers...

To grasp the array of possibilities in today's merchant navy, just try to guess the percentage of world trade that is transported by ship. The answer is no less than 98 per cent, leaving a meagre two per cent for trucks, trains and planes.

Cargo and freighter travel

Andrew Weir Ship Management
Tel: 0207 575 6000
www.aws.co.uk/awsm/
Itineraries include round–the-world via the Pacific Islands.

CMA CGM
Tel: 33 4 88 91 90 00
www.cma-cgm.com
Offers transport solutions all around the world.

Cunrow Shipping – RMS St Helena
Tel: 020 7575 6480
www.rms-st-helena.com
Britain to the Canary Islands, St. Helena, Ascension Island and South Africa.

Frachtschiff-Touristik
Tel: 0 4642 9655 0
www.frachtschiffreise.de
Created by an ex-sea captain, offers many routes.

Freighter World Cruises
Tel: 800 531 7774
www.freighterworld.com

Grimaldi Group
Tel: 39 081 496111
www.grimaldi.napoli.it/
Specialists in roll on/roll off method of shipment and travel.

Mer et Voyages
Tel: 0149 2693 33
www.meretvoyages.com

NSB
Tel: 47 815 00 888
www.nsb.no

Oldendorff Carriers
Tel: 49 451 1500-0
www.oldendorff.com
Integrated shipowner/operator moving bulk and cargoes worldwide.

Polish Ocean Lines
Tel: 45 58 627 8222
www.pol.com.pl
Interesting routes at interesting prices.

P&O Ned Lloyd
Tel: 020 7441 1000
www.ponl.com

TravLtips
Tel: 800 872 8584
www.travltips.com
Unique travel throughout the world.

The sheer amount of cargo that can be piled aboard a ship is such that maritime routes remain the major axes of the world economy. Among the 40,000 or more freighters plying the seas, only a few carry passengers, and even then the available space rarely accommodates more than 12 people. Sometimes there might be only one passenger on board.

Many different kinds of freighters welcome passengers, from luxurious vessels to their more modest, weathered counterparts. Containers have radically changed the picture. These boxes can hold anything from objects large and small to liquids, perishable goods or dangerous chemicals, and because they are standard the world over they can be loaded with machinery direct from trucks or trains. The process is so fast that container ships often do not even spend a whole day in their ports of call, to the great disappointment of passengers wishing to go ashore.

For longer stops choose bulk carriers, which take longer to load and remain in harbour for several days. I once received a postcard from a friend who was delighted because his ship – a Polish bulk carrier on her way to Chile – was delayed for days in the Belgian harbour of Antwerp, as heavy rain prevented the loading of sacks of grain that had to stay dry. My friend took the opportunity to visit the city and its surroundings, using the ship as a floating hotel moored in the harbour.

Container ships, bulk carriers, good old ocean tramps (which take no definite route and may change their port of call mid-route if there is a better cargo to pick up somewhere else), ro-ros (from 'roll on/roll off') loaded with cars – each ship is a different experience. Real fans of cargo-ship travel are particularly fond of tramps, because of the unpredictability and hence added adventure of the route.

If you board one of the refrigerated container ships that carry fruit between the Caribbean and Europe, you will find yourself on the most luxurious of all freighters. Painted white, these so-called 'reefers' are the modern equivalent of 'banana boats': fast, top-of-the-range vessels. A steward will take care of you, and in your cabin you will find your own fridge, coffee machine and VCR, while meals and services are of a high standard. If you embark on a cargo-liner, such as the ship that sails from Great Britain to South Africa via the Canary Islands and St Helena, you will find a warm atmosphere and a happy but all-too-rare marriage between a freighter and a liner, carrying over a hundred passengers as well as cargo and even mail (the island of St Helena has no airport).

On board

Modern technology, computers and satellite communication systems have greatly reduced crews and incidentally allowed space for spare cabins. The number of officers does not exceed four on small ships, with the rest of the crew (usually from poorer countries, especially the Philippine Islands) carrying out work on deck, in the engine room, and general maintenance.

Cabins offered to passengers are usually officers' cabins, which means spacious accommodation (much more than on cruise liners), wide portholes, private bathroom and shower and the best location on the ship's higher decks. Meals are taken in the same room and on the same schedules as officers. Food varies greatly according to the standard of the ship, its nationality and the cook's own country of origin. Travelling on a Chinese cargo-liner between Singapore and Hong Kong, I was introduced to jellyfish soup for breakfast. Later, boarding a French banana boat from Guadeloupe, I was served meals by a *maître d'hôtel* who proposed wine bottled by the shipping company itself. Most of the time, however, passengers are served Western food, unless they want to try spicy, exotic food prepared by a Kenyan or Filipino cook.

It should be remembered that freighters are first of all places of work, and that passengers should not infringe on the ship's life. I was told by a German captain of an indelicate passenger who almost triggered a mutiny by telling the crew that their wages were much too low.

On board freighters, passengers are expected to be self-sufficient as far as entertainment is concerned. Before you leave on an ocean voyage, make sure you take your own 'food for thought'. Time and quietness are among the principal luxuries on board. This is the perfect time to do things you have always wanted to do but never had the leisure for. Books are ideal companions. Some travellers take advantage of lengthy voyages to finally get to grips with the complete works of Proust or Dostoevsky. Others take along drawing or painting materials or music recordings. Some artists, painters, writers and poets travel by cargo ship in order to practise their art without any intrusion from the outside world.

Those who travel by sea range from the retired (in many cases) to young adventurers wishing to savour every mile of their journey. Facilities are shared with officers. It is not rare to find a swimming pool (filled with ocean water), sauna, small gymnasium, table tennis table, bar or video lounge aboard freighters. Since VCRS have become very common on merchant ships, video cassettes are popular among sailors and make good gifts.

So how much does all this cost? First, try to resist the temptation to compare sea-fares with air-fares, as you spend days and weeks aboard these comfortable sailing hotels, with room, board and facilities included, in addition to getting to faraway and exotic destinations. The average fare is around US$120 per day, which – when you consider what you get for your money – is moderate. Naturally prices vary from one ship to another, as well as according to the time of year.

Cargo travelling revival

Back in 1992, I wrote a guide to travelling by cargo ship as so many people were asking me how to go about it. While doing research for this guide – the first of its kind – I encountered scepticism (from merchant navy professionals among others): "You'll find hardly any freighters accepting passengers; not enough to fill a book. Those times are over," I was told many times. But the opposite proved to be true. *Travel by Cargo Ship* has since been published in French, English, German and Italian. It is now possible to sail to most major harbours throughout the world. Travel agencies specialising in freighters are growing and flourishing on all continents, and every day more and more people are discovering the joys of ocean crossings. There are fans who travel at least once a year by freighter, for the sheer pleasure of being on a ship, no matter where it is bound. The trend is clearly established. In Paris, a 'Cargo Club' meets on the first Wednesday of every month in a bookshop on the Ile Saint-Louis, attracting old salts returning from distant oceans, and dreamers eager to hear stories and gather tips before their departure.

But do not travel by freighter if you are likely to have a problem with not departing or arriving on schedule: at sea as in harbour, all kinds of delays can occur, caused by everything from weather to red-tape; some consider this sprinkling of the unexpected an added charm. Sometimes, even the port of call is changed at the last moment (particularly on tramp ships).

Shipping companies themselves are also subject to change: ships change hands, names and flags, and new routes are opened while others are closed. If you are looking for a particular itinerary and are told that no ship is going there, my advice is not to take no for an answer. Faxes and telephones can work miracles. Remember too that public demand does shape the future.

Travelling by cargo ship is here to stay, and we can hope to see more and more space for passengers, not only on freighters, big and small, but also on liners and even scientific ships fully equipped with labs, drilling equipment and helicopters, designed to accommodate (wealthy) passengers wishing to sail in southern Antarctic seas.

If you have never tried sea travel, you could do a trial run of a few days with several ports of call, perhaps in the Baltic Sea or the Mediterranean. If you are seeking the ultimate freighter experience, you could embark on a round-the-world voyage through the Pacific islands, lasting almost three months. And who knows, perhaps the future will see silent, wind-propelled cargo-liners sailing the seas, carrying freight and a happy bunch of passengers? ❧

Hugo Verlomme is the author of 'Travel by Cargo Ship' and has written several other books, fiction and non-fiction, on nautical themes.

By river boat
by John and Julie Batchelor

WHEREVER YOU WANT TO GO IN THE WORLD, the chances are that you can get there by river. Indeed, the more remote your destination, the more likely it will be that the only way of getting there, without taking to the air, will be by river. This is particularly true of tropical regions where, throughout the history of exploration, rivers have been the key that has opened the door to the interior. It is still the case that, for those who really want to penetrate deep into a country, to learn about a place and its peoples through direct contact, the best way to do so is by water. River travel splits neatly into three categories: public transport, private hire and your own transport.

Wherever there is a large navigable river, whether it be in Africa, South America, Asia or even Europe, you will find some form of river transport. This can range from a luxury floating hotel on the Nile to a dugout canoe in the forests of Africa and South America. And between these extremes, all over the world there can be found the basic work-a-day ferries that ply between villages and towns carrying every conceivable type of commodity and quite often an unbelievably large number of people.

Let's start by examining travel on an everyday ferry. First you must buy your ticket. The usual method is to turn up at the waterfront, find out which boat is going in your direction and then locate the agent's office. With luck, this will be a simple matter, but on occasion even finding out where to purchase your ticket can be an endless problem.

Don't be put off. Just turn up at your boat, go on board and find someone, preferably someone in authority, to take your money. You'll have no difficulty doing this, so long as you do not embarrass people by asking for receipts.

Board the boat as early as possible

It is probable that it will be extremely crowded, so if you are a deck passenger you will need to stake out your corner of the deck and defend it against all comers. Make sure of your sleeping arrangements immediately. In South America this will mean getting your hammock in place, in Africa and the Far East making sure you have enough space to spread out your sleeping mat.

Take care about your positioning. If you are on a trip lasting a number of days do not place yourself near the one and only toilet on board. By the end of the journey the location of this facility will be obvious to anyone with a sense of smell. Keep away from the air outlet from the engine room unless you have a particular liking for being asphyxiated by diesel fumes.

If rain is expected, make sure you are under cover. On most boats a tarpaulin shelter is rigged up over the central area. Try to get a spot near the middle as those at the edges tend to get wet. Even if rain is unlikely it is still a good idea to find shade from the sun. For those unused to it, sitting in the tropical sun all day can be unpleasant and dangerous.

Go equipped

There may be some facilities for food and drink on board, but in practice this will probably only mean warm beer and unidentified local specialities which you might prefer not to have to live on. Assume there will be nothing.

Take everything you need for the whole journey, plus enough for a couple of extra days just in case. On the Zaire River, for instance, it is quite common for boats to get stuck on sandbanks for days on end. And don't forget the insects. The lights of the boat are sure to attract an interesting collection of wildlife during the tropical night, so take a mosquito net.

Occasionally, for those with money, there may be cabins, but don't expect too much of these. If there is supposed to be water, it will be only intermittent at best, and there certainly won't be a plug. The facilities will be very basic and you are almost certain to have the company of hordes of cockroaches who will take particular delight in sampling your food and exploring your belongings. Occupying a cabin on a multi-class boat also marks you out as 'rich' and thus subject to attention from the less desirable of your fellow passengers. Lock your cabin door and do not leave your window open at night. In order to do this you will also have to go equipped with a length of chain and padlock. On most boats the advantages of a cabin are minimal.

Longer journeys, especially on African rivers, tend to be one long party. Huge quantities of beer are drunk and very loud music plays through the night. It is quite likely that you will be looked on as a guest and expected to take an active part in the festivities. It's a good way of making friends, but don't expect a restful time.

Given these few common-sense precautions, you will have a rewarding trip. By the time you have reached your destination you will have many new friends and will have learned a few essential words of the local language, all of which make your stay more pleasant and your journey easier.

Private hire

In order to progress further up the river from the section navigable by larger boats, you will have to look around for transport to hire. This may be a small motor boat, but is more likely to be a dugout canoe with an outboard motor. When negotiating for this sort of transport, local knowledge is everything: who's trustworthy and who owns a reliable boat or canoe. With luck, your new-found friends from the first stage of your journey will advise you and take care of the negotiations over price. This is by far the best option. Failing that, it is a question of your own judgement. What you are looking for is a well-equipped boat and a teetotal crew. In all probability such an ideal combination doesn't exist – at least we have never found it. So we are back to common sense.

Look at the boat before coming to any agreement. If possible try to have a test run just to make sure the motor works. Try to establish that the boatman knows the area you want to go to. If he already smells of drink at ten in the morning, he may not be the most reliable man around. This last point could be important. If you are returning the same way, you will need to arrange for your boatman to pick you up again at a particular time and place. The chances of this happening if he is likely to disappear on an extended drunken binge once he has your money are remote in the extreme. Take your time over the return arrangements. Make sure that everyone knows and understands the place, the day and the time that they are required to meet you. Don't forget that not everyone can read or tell the time. If you have friends in the place, get them to check that the boatman leaves when planned. Agree on the price to be paid before you go and do not pay anything until you arrive at the destination. If the part of the deal is that you provide the fuel, buy it yourself and hand it over only when everyone and everything is ready for departure. Establish clearly what the food and drink arrangements are as you may be expected to feed the crew.

Once you are on your way, it is a question again of common sense. Take ready-prepared food. Protect yourself from the sun and your equipment from rain and spray. If you are travelling by dugout canoe, it will be a long uncomfortable trip with little opportunity for stretching your legs. Make sure you have something to sit on, preferably something soft, but don't forget that the bottom of the canoe will soon be full of water.

Once you have arrived at your destination, make sure that you are in the right place before letting the boat go. If the boatman is coming back for you, go over all the arrangements one more time. Do not pay in advance for the return if you can possibly avoid it. If the boatman has the money, there is little incentive for him to keep his side of the bargain. If absolutely necessary, give just enough to cover the cost of the fuel.

Own transport

After exhausting the possibilities of public transport and hire, you must make your own way to the remote headwaters of your river. You may have brought your own equipment, which will probably be an inflatable with outboard motor or a canoe. If you have got this far, we can assume that you know all about the requirements of your own equipment. Both inflatables and rigid kayaks are bulky items to transport over thousands of miles, so you might consider a collapsible canoe, which you can assemble once you have reached this part of the trip. We have not used them ourselves but have heard very good reports of them in use under very rigorous conditions.

Your chances of finding fuel for the outboard motor on the isolated headwaters of almost any river in the world are negligible. Take all you need with you. Your chances of finding food and hospitality will depend on the part of the world you are exploring. In South America, you are unlikely to find any villages and the only people you may meet are nomadic Indians who could be hostile. You will have to be totally self-sufficient. In Africa the situation is quite different. Virtually anywhere that you can reach with your boat will have a village or fishing encampment of some description. The villagers will show you hospitality and in all probability you will be able to buy fresh vegetables, fruit and fish from the people. Take basic supplies and enough for emergencies but expect to be able to supplement this with local produce.

Another alternative could be to buy a local canoe, although this option is fraught with dangers. If you don't know anything about mechanics, buying a second-hand canoe is as tricky as buying a second-hand car. You can easily be fobbed off with a dud. We know of a number of people who have paddled off proudly in their new canoe only to sink steadily below the surface as water seeped in through cracks and patches. This is usually a fairly slow process so that by the time you realise your error you are too far away from the village to do anything about it. A word or two about dugout canoes: these are simply hollowed-out tree trunks and come in all sizes. The stability of the canoe depends on the expertise of the man who made it. They are usually heavy, difficult to propel in a straight line, prone to capsize, uncomfortable and extremely hard work. The larger ones can weigh over a ton, which makes it almost impossible for a small group to take one out of the water for repairs. Paddling dugouts is best left to the experts. Only if you are desperate – and going downstream – should you entertain the idea.

Travel etiquette

When travelling in remote areas anywhere in the world, it should always be remembered that you are the guest. You are the one who must adjust to local circumstances and take great pains not to offend the customs and traditions of the people you are visiting. To refuse hospitality will almost always cause offence. Remember that you are the odd one out and that it is natural for your hosts to be inquisitive and fascinated by everything you do. However tired or irritable you may be, you have chosen to put yourself in this position and it is your job to accept close examination with good grace. Before travelling, take the trouble to research the area you intend to visit and its people. Try to have some idea of what is expected of you before you go to a village. If you are offered food and accommodation, accept it. Do not be squeamish about eating what is offered. After all, the local people have survived on whatever it is, so it is unlikely to do you much damage.

No two trips are ever the same, thank goodness! The advice we have tried to give is nothing more than common sense. If you apply this to whatever you are doing, you will not go far wrong. Just remember that what may be impossible today can be achieved tomorrow… or the next day. Don't be in a hurry. There is so much to be enjoyed. Take your time… and good luck! 🕭

John and Julie Batchelor have travelled widely in Africa and have co-written several books, including 'The Congo'.

Under full sail
by Sir Robin Knox-Johnston

S AILING BENEATH A FULL MOON ACROSS A CALM TROPICAL SEA towards some romantic destination is a wonderful dream, but to make it become a reality requires careful preparation, or the dream can turn into a nightmare.

The boat you choose should be a solid, robust cruiser. There is no point in buying a modern racing yacht as it will have been designed to be sailed by a large crew of specialists and will need weekly maintenance. The ideal boat for a good cruise should be simple, with a large carrying capacity, and easy to maintain. Bear in mind that it is not always easy to find good mechanics or materials abroad, and most repairs and maintenance will probably be done by the crew.

It is important to get to know the boat well before sailing so that you will know how she will respond in various sea states and weather conditions. Try changing her trim by moving weights fore and aft to see the response. Experiment with the sails to obtain the best balance. Remember that a well-balanced boat needs less rudder and will travel faster. Make a proper check-list for the stores and spares that will need to be carried. For example, there is no point in taking a spare engine, but the right fuel, oil and air filters, spare fan belts and perhaps a spare alternator, are advisable. Standardise things as much as possible. If the same size of rope can be used for a number of purposes, then a spare coil of that rope might well cover nearly all your renewal requirements.

Electronics

There is a huge array of modern equipment available and these 'goodies' can be tempting. It pays to keep the requirement to a minimum to reduce expense and complexity. Small boat radars are now quite cheap and can be used for navigation as well as keeping a lookout in fog. The Global Positioning System (GPS), with its worldwide coverage and position updates every few seconds, has proved a boon to the busy yachtsman, but anyone contemplating a long voyage should master astro navigation to fall back upon if the instrument fails or the batteries give up.

Radio communications are now everywhere and are important for the boat's safety. Short range, Very High Frequency (VHF) radio is in use worldwide for port operations and for communications between ships at sea. It is best to buy a good, multi-channel set and make sure that the aerial is at the top of the mast as the range is not much greater than the line of sight, so the higher the aerial, the better. For long-range communications, use Single Side Band in the medium- and high-frequency bands, but the shore stations that used to service these bands are fast disappearing.

The new Global Maritime Distress and Safety System (GMDSS) is already coming into force for commercial traffic for larger ships. By 2005 it will be universal. All vessels will be required to have digital selective calling on their VHF sets, and, if they are going beyond the range of shore VHF stations, MF, and beyond 450 km, HF as well. Satellite communications are also becoming common. The least expensive piece of equipment to handle it is Satcon-C which can handle telex and email. It is inexpensive, but brings instant distress, urgency, safety and general communications to the smallest yacht. All yachtsmen should take a GMDSS course to understand the new safety procedures.

There is a worldwide network of amateur radio operators or 'hams', which can provide a regular link for those who take the relevant licence.

Meteorology plays an important part in any voyage, and the rudiments of weather systems, and how they are going to affect the weather on the chosen route are essential knowledge for anyone making any voyage. Weather forecasts are broadcast by most nations, but it is possible to buy a weatherfax machine, which prints out the weather picture for a selected area and costs about the same as an SSB radio set. Alternatively, these weather faxes may be received with the normal SSB and displayed on a computer.

Charts are now computerised and, when interfaced with the GPS, will show the position of the yacht on the chart in use. There are some small anomalies due to the change in the data and you should, in any case, take the paper charts of the area you will be sailing through.

The crew

The choice of crew will ultimately decide the success or otherwise of the venture. Its members must be congenial, enthusiastic and good work-sharers. Nothing destroys morale on board a boat more quickly than one person who moans or shirks their share of shipboard duties. Ideally, the crew should have previous sailing experience so that they know what to expect, and it is well worthwhile going for a short shakedown sail with the intended crew to see if they can cope and get on well. Never take too many people, it cramps the living quarters and usually means there is not enough work to keep everyone busy. A small but busy crew usually creates a happy, purposeful team.

Beware of picking up crew who ask for passage somewhere at the last minute. For a start, you will not know their background and will only find out how good or bad they are once you get to sea, which is too late. In many countries, the skipper of the boat is responsible for the crew, and you can find that when you reach your destination, immigration will not allow the marine 'hitchhiker' ashore unless they

Sailing associations and agencies

Association of Sea Training Organisations (ASTO)
Tel: 02392 503222
www.asto.org.uk
Links with training associations worldwide.

British Marine Federation
Tel: 01784 473377
www.britishmarine.co.uk
The British boating industry's trade association.

British Universities Sailing Association
www.busa.co.uk
The governing body for university sailing, affiliated with RYA.

Canadian Yachting Association
Tel: 613 545 3044
www.sailing.ca

International Sailing Federation
Tel: 02380 635111
www.sailing.org
The world governing body for sailing.

National Federation Of Sea Schools
Tel: 023 8029 3822
www.nfss.co.uk
Comprehensive list and guide to sailing schools nationwide.

Ocean Youth Trust
England tel:
south 0870 241 2252
north-west 0151 666 1664
east 0115 9399825
north-east 0870 241 6789
Scotland tel:
0141 221 1200
Ireland tel:
028 9023 1881
www.oyc.org.uk/
Personal sail training nationwide for 12-25 age group.

Royal Yachting Association (RYA)
Tel: 0845 345 0400
www.rya.org.uk

The Short Handed Sailing Association of New Zealand
Tel: 021 904 000
www.ssanz.co.uk

US Sailing
Tel: 1 800 USSAIL 1
www.ussailing.org
Maintains the national standards for sailing instructions and develops training programmes.

Yacht Charter Association (YCA)
Tel: 023 8040 7075
www.yca.co.uk

Yachting Australia
Tel: 02 8424 7400
www.yacting.org.au

Related websites
www.intotheblue.co.uk
Training for beginners.

www.saltyseas.com
Global sailing guides.

www.uksail.com
Guide to all national sailing organisations.

www.yacht-charter-world.com
List of yacht charters around the world.

have the onward fare or ticket out of the country. If you do take people on like this, make sure that they have money or a ticket, and I recommend that you take the money as security until they have landed. I once got caught out in Durban with a hitchhiker who told me I would have to give him the airfare back to the US. However, he 'accidentally' fell into the harbour, and when he put his pile of dollars out to dry, we took the amount required for his fare. Never hesitate to send crew home if they do not fit in with the rest of the team. The cost is small when measured against a miserable voyage.

Provisions

Always stock up for the longest possible time the voyage might take, plus ten per cent extra. The system that I use for calculating the food requirement is to work out a week's worth of daily menus for one person. I then multiply this figure by the number of weeks the voyage should take plus the extra, and multiply that figure by the number of crew on board.

Always take as much fresh food as you can. Root vegetables will last a couple of months, greens last about a week, Citrus fruit will last a month, if kept well aired and dry. Eggs, if sealed with wax or Vaseline, will last a couple of months. Meat and fish should not be trusted beyond a day or two unless smoked, depending on the temperature. Dry stores will last a long time if kept in a dry, sealed container.

The rest of the provisions will have to be freeze dried or canned. Such food-stuffs are of good quality in Europe, the USA, South Africa, Australia and New Zealand, but not so reliable elsewhere. The USA does not produce canned stewing steak or minced steak, so if you are going to have to stock up there make sure you have plenty of ways of cooking corned beef, Spam or ham. Code all the cans with paint, then tear off the labels and cover the whole tin with varnish as protection against salt water corrosion and stow securely in a dry place.

When taking water on board, first check that it is fresh and pure. If in doubt, add chloride or lime to the water tanks in the recommended proportions. Very good fresh water can be obtained from rain showers. The most effective method is to top up the main boom, so that the sail 'bags' and the water will flow down to the boom and along the gooseneck, where it can be caught in a bucket. There are a number of desalination plants on the market. If the budget allows, they can be worthwhile in case the water tanks go foul and rain water is hard to come by.

Safety

The safety equipment should be up to the Offshore Racing Council's minimum standards. Ensure that the life raft has been serviced before sailing, and that everyone on board knows how to use their life-jackets and safety harnesses. A number of direction-finding and recovery systems have been developed recently for picking up anyone who falls overside, and this drill should be practised before the start of the voyage. A 406 Mhz EPIRB distress beacon is essential – make sure it is properly registered with its relevant authority. Take a search and rescue transponder (SART). These provide a short-range signal to radar sets and can be invaluable for rescuers looking for a life raft.

Paperwork and officialdom

Before setting out on a long voyage, make sure that someone at home, such as a member of the family or your solicitor, knows your crew list, their addresses and your intended programme – and keep them updated from each port. Make sure your bank knows what you are planning, and that there are enough funds in your account for emergencies. It is better to arrange to draw money at banks *en route* rather than carry large sums on board.

The boat should be registered. This is your proof of ownership and the boat's nationality, and it also means that your boat comes under the umbrella of certain international maritime agreements.

A certificate of competence as a yachtmaster is advisable. Some countries (Germany, for instance) are starting to insist on them. The crew must have their passports with them, plus any visas required for such countries as the USA, Australia and India. More countries are demanding visas these days, and you should check with the embassies or consulates of the countries you intend to visit for details. You should also check the health requirements and make sure that the crew have the various up-to-date inoculation or vaccination certificates. It is always advisable to have tetanus jabs before starting a voyage but most doctors' surgeries can provide list of recommended inoculations.

Before setting out, obtain a clearance certificate from customs. You may not need it at your destination but it will be helpful if you run into difficult officials.

On arrival at your destination, always fly your national flag and hoist the flag of the country you have reached on the starboard rigging, on the yard if possible, and the quarantine flag (Q). If officials from the customs and immigration department do not visit the boat on arrival, only the skipper need go ashore to find them and report, taking the registration certificate, port clearance, crew passports and any other relevant papers.

Smuggling and piracy

Smuggling is a serious offence and the boat may be confiscated if smuggled items are found on board, even if the skipper knows nothing about the offending items.

There are certain areas where smuggling and piracy have become common and, of course, it is largely in the same areas that law enforcement is poor. The worst areas are the Western Caribbean, the north coast of South America, the Red Sea and the Far East, particularly near the Malacca Straits. There have also been a number of attacks on yachts off the Brazilian coast.

The best protection is a crew of fairly tough-looking individuals, but a firearm is a good persuader. Never allow other boats to come alongside at sea unless you know the people on board and, if a suspicious boat approaches, let them see that you have a large crew and a gun. Call on VHF, or send an alert on the Satcom if you feel threatened. If the approaching vessel is official, they are probably listening to VHF channels. When in a strange port, it is a good rule never to allow anyone on board unless you know them or they have an official identity card. If you do carry a firearm, make sure you obtain a licence for it. Murphy's law says that if you carry a rifle, you will never have to use it. ❧

SIR ROBIN KNOX-JOHNSTON, CBE, was the first man to sail around the world single-handedly and without stopping. He also set a global record for sailing around the world in a catamaran. He is the author of numerous books on sailing.

Special interest travel

Adventure and sports tourism

See also 'Transport: on four wheels' for overland travel, and below for 'Expedition organisers'

ADIRONDACK MOUNTAIN CLUB (ADK)
USA tel: 518 668 4447
www.adk.org
Promotes responsible recreational use and protection of the New York State Forest Preserve.

ADRIFT
UK tel: 01488 71152
www.adrift.co.uk
Whitewater rafting holidays around the globe.

AIRTRACK SERVICES LTD
UK tel: 01895 254088
www.airtrack.co.uk
Organises motor sport and football holidays.

ATG OXFORD
UK tel: 01865 315 679
www.atg-oxford.co.uk
Walking, trekking and cycling specialists around Europe, Africa and Asia.

THE AMERICAN HIKING SOCIETY
USA tel: 301 565 6704
www.americanhiking.org

APPALACHIAN TRAIL CONSERVANCY
USA tel: 304 535 6331
www.appalachiantrail.org
Hike parts of the 2,175 mile trail.

ARCTURUS EXPEDITIONS
UK tel: 01389 830 204
www.arcturusexpeditions.co.uk
Specialist trips to the poles, including dogsledging, kayaking and natural history.

BIKERS' ADVICE BUREAU
UK tel: 0161 835 3681
www.bikersadvice.co.uk
Offers 'biker friendly' holidays and a database of vetted biker friendly areas, pubs, B&Bs etc.

BRITISH ACTIVITY HOLIDAY ASSOCIATION
UK tel: 020 8842 1292
www.baha.org.uk
A consumer guide to activity holidays in the UK.

BRITISH CANOE UNION
UK tel: 0115 9821 100
www.bcu.org.uk
Advice, links and information for canoeing around the UK.

BRITISH GLIDING ASSOCIATION
UK tel: 0116 253 1051
www.gliding.co.uk

BRITISH MOUNTAINEERING COUNCIL
UK tel: 0870 010 4878
www.thebmc.org

BRITISH ORIENTEERING FEDERATION
UK tel: 01629 734042
www.britishorienteering.org.uk

BRITISH PARACHUTE ASSOCIATION
UK tel: 0116 278 5271
www.bpa.org.uk

BRITISH SUB-AQUA CLUB
UK tel: 0151 350 6200
www.bsac.com
Information on regional and international schools and advice on diving abroad.

CANADIAN WILDERNESS TRIPS
Canada tel: 416 960 2298
www.canadianwildernesstrips.com
Guided sea kayaking and canoe trips in the Canadian wilderness.

CONTINENTAL DIVIDE TRAIL SOCIETY
www.cdtsociety.org/
Treks along the Rocky Mountains from Canada to Mexico.

CORAL CAY CONSERVATION EXPEDITIONS
UK tel: 0870 750 0668
www.coralcay.org
Divers needed to help with the conversation and building of marine parks.

ENCOUNTER OVERLAND
UK tel: 0870 499 4478
www.encounter-overland.com
Overland adventure travel group with trips to Asia, Africa and South America.

ERNA LOW
UK tel: 0870 750 6820
www.ernalow.co.uk
Specialists for skiing trips.

**EVOLUTION 2 -
PROFESSIONNELS DE
L'AVENTURE**
France tel: 450 55 9022
www.evolution2.com
Mountaineering and snow
sports holidays with
centres around France.

EXODUS
UK tel: 0870 240 5550
www.exodus.co.uk
Adventure holidays on all
seven continents.

EXPLORE WORLDWIDE
UK tel: 0870 333 4001
USA tel: 227 8747
www.exploreworldwide.
com
Adventure travel organiser
with offices worldwide to
cater to your needs.

**THE GRAND TOURING
CLUB**
UK tel: 0870 609 1176
www.grandtouringclub.
co.uk
Classic car tours and rallies
to classic sites and routes.

**GUERBA ADVENTURE &
DISCOVERY HOLIDAYS**
UK tel: 01373 828303
www.guerba.co.uk
Overland travel and
wildlife safari specialists.

HEADWATER HOLIDAYS
UK tel: 01606 720099
www.headwater.com
Adventure sports holidays
from Scandinavia to Latin
America.

JOURNEY LATIN AMERICA
UK tel: 020 8747 3108
www.journeylatinamerica.
co.uk
Trips exclusively to Latin
America.

KE ADVENTURE TRAVEL
UK tel: 017687 73966
www.keadventure.com
Climbing, mountain
biking and trekking
holidays.

OUTWARD BOUND TRUST
UK tel: 0870 513 4227
www.
outwardbound-uk.org
Adventure holidays in
Cumbria, Aberdovey and
Loch Eil.

PACIFIC CREST TRAIL
USA tel: 916 349 2109
www.pcta.org
Planning and advice for all
types of trips on the trail.

PAGE & MOY
UK tel: 0870 833 4012
www.page-moy.co.uk
Specialists offering motor
racing holidays as well as
golfing, music and
archaeological tours.

RAMBLERS ASSOCIATION
UK tel: 020 7339 8550
www.ramblers.org.uk
Membership association
for walks, treks and hikes.

RAMBLERS HOLIDAYS
UK tel: 01707 331133
www.ramblersholidays.
co.uk
Rambling around the
world from the Great Wall
of China to Barbados.

SAFARI DRIVE
UK tel: 01488 71140
www.safaridrive.com/
Self drive safaris through
Africa, also camel trekking
and fly camping.

SCOTT DUNN
UK tel:020 8682 5010
www.scottdunn.com
Specifically tailored
holidays to destinations
around the world.

SHEARWATER ADVENTURES
www.
shearwateradventures.
com/
Zimbabwe-based
all-adventure company,
including whitewater
rafting the Zambezi and
helicopter flights over
Victoria Falls.

THE SIERRA CLUB
USA Tel: 415 977 5500
www.sieraclub.org/
Every kind of adventure
holiday.

**SKI CLUB OF GREAT
BRITAIN**
UK tel: 020 8410 2001
www.skiclub.co.uk
Membership benefits inc.
fact sheets, weather
reports, unbiased advice
on resorts and equipment.

TANA DELTA CAMP
www.eco-resorts.com/
TanaDelta.php
From beachcombing
expeditions to photo-
stalking buffalo, in the
Kenyan wilderness.

WORLD EXPEDITIONS
UK tel: 020 8870 2600
USA tel: 415 989 2212
www.worldexpeditions.
co.uk

**WORLDWIDE FISHING
SAFARIS**
UK tel: 01733 271 123
www.
worldwidefishingsafarisco.
uk

Related websites

www.adventuretravel.com

www.atb.away.com
Specialist website for
books and maps on travel.

www.gapadventures.com

www.gorptravel.away.com
Comprehensive online
website packed with
information, links and
listings.

www.intrepidtravel.com

www.serioussports.com
Online guide providing
advice on outfitters,
schools, guides and
sporting holidays.

www.travel-library.com

www.wherewillwego.com
Website for travel and
culture.

www.
worldtourismdirectory.
com

www.4real.co.uk
Online adventure travel
company.

Ski and snowboard websites

www.ski1.com
Holiday, accommodation
and flight information.

http://complete.skier.com

www.powderbyrne.com
Luxury individual skiing
holidays.

www.skiclub.co.uk/skiclub
Ski Club of Great Britain
website.

www.snow-line.co.uk

Diving websites

www.aquanaut.com
Online magazine for
recreational and technical
diving community.
www.bsac.com
British Sub-Aqua Club

online directory.

www.naui.org
Up-to-date information
on courses, dive centres,
medicine, travel insurance
and product catalogue.

www.padi.com
International diving
society with schools all
over the world.

www.scubatravel.co.uk

www.ukdiving.co.uk/
Packed full of information
on UK diving for the
beginner or seasoned
diver.

Cultural tourism

ACE STUDY TOURS
UK tel: 01223 835055
www.study-tours.org
Cultural holidays to
educate and entertain,
from houses and gardens
to theatre and literature
appreciation to
architecture and
archaeology.

ASSOCIATION OF INDEPENDENT TRAVELLERS (AITO)
UK tel: 020 8744 9280
www.aito.co.uk
Cultural holidays
incorporating Holy Land
tours, architecture,
heritage tours using expert
speakers and guides.

THE BRITISH INSTITUTE OF FLORENCE
Italy tel: 39 055 2677 8270
www.britishinstitute.it
Founded to develop
cultural understanding

between the UK and Italy
offering opportunities to
study in Florence and
various short excursions to
cultural sites.

THE BRITISH MUSEUM COMPANY
UK tel: 020 7323 8000
www.
britishmuseumtraveller.
co.uk

CRICKETER HOLIDAYS
UK tel: 01892 66242
Cultural tours
incorporating painting
and drawing.

FESTIVAL TOURS INTERNATIONAL
USA tel: 310 454 4080
www.gumbopages.com
Offices in Los Angeles
and London providing
music lovers with trips
to festivals.

GALINA BATTLEFIELD TOURS
UK tel: 01244 340777
www.wartours.com/
Tours of European
battlefields.

HOLTS TOURS
UK tel: 01293 455 345
www.holts.co.uk
Tours of battlefields from
the Franco-Prussian War
to the Boar War.

HOSKING TOURS
UK tel: 01728 861113
www.hosking-tours.co.uk
Wildlife photography
holidays.

IMAGINATIVE TRAVELLER
UK tel: 0800 316 2717
www.
imaginative-traveller.com
Tours through Turkey and
beyond.

MARTIN RANDALL TRAVEL
UK tel: 020 8742 3355
www.martinrandall.com
Art history and
archaeological tours.

McCabe Pilgrimages
UK tel: 020 8675 6828
www.mccabe-travel.co.uk
A wide range of tours to
the Bible Lands.

Page & Moy
UK tel: 0870 833 4012
www.page-moy.co.uk
History, music and
archaeology tours as well
as motor racing holidays.

Prospect Music & Arts Tours
UK tel: 020 7486 5704
www.prospecttours.com
A vast array of music and
arts tours.

Silk Road Travellers Club
UK tel: 01491 410 510
www.silkroadtravel.co.uk
Adventure and cultural
trips along the Silk Road
countries.

Skylark Battlefield Tours
UK tel: 01354 696779
www.skylark-uk.com
School and college tours of
Belgium and France.

Special Tours
UK tel: 020 7730 2297
www.specialtours.co.uk
Small-group tours of
cultural sites, including
archaeology, painting,
wine tasting and ballet.

Specialised Travel Ltd
UK tel: 020 8799 8300
www.stlon.com/
Music tours with 'Travel
for the Arts' to some of the
great opera houses of the
world.

Steamond Travel
UK tel: 0207 730 8646 /
3024
www.steamondtravel.com
Birdwatching holidays.

Swan Hellenic
UK tel: 0845 3 555 111
USA tel: +1 877 800 SWAN
www.swanhellenic.com
Guided archaeological and
art cruises with guest
speakers.

Related websites

www.arca.uk.net
Residential courses
covering subjects from
wine appreciation to
natural history.

www.culturaltravels.com

www.eventsworldwide.com

www.farhorizon.com/

www.festivalfinder.com

www.transitionsabroad.com
Cultural and special
interests.

www.museums.co.uk

www.whatsonwhen.co.uk

www.wherewillwego.com

www.worldculturaltours.com

Cycling

Apex Cycling
UK tel: 020 7622 1334
www.apexcycles.co.uk
Nationwide UK bike
retailer.

Backroads Bicycling USA
USA tel: 510 527 1555
www.backroads.com

Bents Bicycling Tours
UK tel: 01568 780800
www.bentstours.com

Bicycle Africa
USA tel: 981081919
www.ibike.org

Bicycle Australia
www.woa.com

British Cycling Federation
UK tel: 0870 871 2000
www.bcf.uk.com
UK's governing body
for cycle sport.

Canadian Cycling Association
Canada tel: 613 248 1353
www.canadian-cycling.com

Cycling New Zealand Federation
www.cyclingnz.com

Cycle Rides UK
UK tel: 01225 428 452
www.cyclerides.co.uk

Cyclists' Touring Club
UK tel: 0870 873 0060
www.ctc.org.uk
The UK's oldest cycling
group providing
information, insurance,
and organised cycling
trips.

Evans Cycles
UK tel: 020 8877 1878
Bike retailer with shops all
over London, providing
advice and custom fit
services.

League Of American Bicyclists'
USA tel: 202 822 1333
www.bikeleague.org

London To Paris Bike Ride
www.parentsforinclusion.org/londonparis4.htm
A 300-mile cycle through
the countryside.

Roberts Cycles

UK tel: 020 8684 3370
www.robertscycles.com
UK specialist for
custom-made frames.

SUSIE MADRON'S CYCLING FOR SOFTIES
UK tel: 0161 248 8282
www.cycling-for-softies.co.uk
Cycle at your own pace
on a tailor-made route
through rural France with
everything catered for.

USA CYCLING
USA tel: 719 578 4581
www.usacycling.org/

Related websites

www.GFonline.org/
BikeAccess/
A useful guide to planning
a cycling trip with cyclists
previous experiences there
to help.

www.rough-tracks.co.uk
Specialist biking tours for
all cyclists.

www.cycleactive.co.uk
Offer detailed cycling
holidays all over the world.

www.travel-quest.co.uk
Directory to cycling
holidays on the web.

www.redspokes.co.uk
Adventure cycling trips
around the world.

Disability services

ABLE TO GO
UK tel: 01924 364634
www.abletogocom

ACCESS TRAVEL
UK tel: 01942 888844
www.access-travel.co.uk
Advice and information
on accommodation that
has been personally
checked by their team.

ACCESSIBLE KIWI TOURS
NZ tel: 64 7 315 6988
www.toursnz.com

ACCESSIBLE TRAVEL & LEISURE
UK tel: 01452 729 739
www.accessibletravel.co.uk

ACROSS TRUST
UK tel: 020 8783 1355
www.holidaywizard.
co.uk/companies/
The-Across-Trust/
Uses converted buses
known as 'jumbalences'
taking groups on holidays
and pilgrimages.

ASSOCIATION OF BRITISH INSURERS
UK tel: 020 7600 3333
www.abi.org.uk
Travel insurance
information for the
disabled.

AUSTRALIAN COUNCIL FOR THE REHABILITATION OF THE DISABLED (ACROD)
Aus tel: 61 62 824 333
www.acrod.org.au
Australia's national
organisation for disability,
offering information for
disabled travellers.

BARRIER-FREE TRAVEL
www.demosmedpub.com/
book171.html
Magazine with detailed
information about the
logistics of planning

accessible travel by plane,
train, bus and ship.

BREAK
UK tel: 01263 822161
www.break-charity.org
Holidays for the physically
and mentally handicapped
along the Norfolk coast.

BRITISH RED CROSS
UK tel: 0870 170 7000
www.redcross.org.uk

BRITISH ASSOCIATION OF ADVISORS AND LECTURES IN PHYSICAL EDUCATION
UK tel: 01905 855584
www.baalpe.org

MOBILITY INFORMATION SERVICE (MIS)
UK tel: 01743 340269
www.mis.org.uk
UK's resource for
physically disabled people
who drive or want to drive.

CAMPING FOR THE DISABLED
c/o Mobility Information
Service
UK tel: 01743 463 072
www.mis.org.uk
Practical help and
information for those who
want to go camping.

CANADIAN REHABILITATION COUNCIL FOR THE DISABLED
Canada tel: 506 458 8739
www.sjfn.nb.ca/
community_hall/C/
CANA8739.html
Publishers of
Handi-Travel, a book with
advice for the disabled
traveller.

CAREFREE HOLIDAYS
UK tel: 01493 732176
www.carefree-
holidays.co.uk

CCS NEW ZEALAND
NZ tel: 0800 227 200
www.ccs.org.nz
Provides support and
services.

DIAL UK (DISABILITY INFORMATION AND ADVICE LINE)
UK tel: 01302 310 123
www.dialuk.info

DISABILITY PERSONS TRANSPORT ADVISORY COMMITTEE (DPTAC)
UK tel: 020 7944 8011
www.dptac.gov.uk

THE DISABLED DRIVERS' ASSOCIATION
UK tel: 0870 770 3333
www.dda.org.uk

DISABLED LIVING FOUNDATION
UK tel: 020 7289 6111
www.dlf.org.uk

DISABLED PERSON ASSEMBLY NEW ZEALAND
NZ tel: 64 6 801 910
www.dpa.org.nz

DISAWAY TRUST
UK tel: 020 8390 2576
www.disaway.co.uk
Organises group holidays in the UK and overseas.

DR YACHTING
www.disabledsailingholidays.com
Greek organisation with sailing holidays for the disabled and visually impaired.

3H FUND (HELP THE HANDICAPPED FUND)
www.3hfund.org.uk
Provides holidays for the disabled and helps low-income families with disabled dependents.

GOOD ACCESS GUIDE
UK tel: 01452 741585
www.goodaccessguide.co.uk

HOLIDAY CARE
UK tel: 0845 124 9971
www.holidaycare.org.uk
Holiday and travel information service.

JOHN GROOMS CHARITY GROOM HOLIDAYS
UK tel: 020 7452 2000
www.groomsholidays.org.uk
Provider of services for people with disabilities.

JUBILEE SAILING TRUST
UK tel: 0870 443 5781
www.jst.org.uk
Work as a crew member on a tall ship.

MOBILITY ADVISE & VEHICLE INFORMATION SERVICE (MAVIS)
UK tel: 01344 661000
www.dft.gov.uk/access/mavis

MOBILITY INTERNATIONAL USA
USA tel: 541 343 1284
www.miusa.org
USA organisation offering travel and international exchanges.

PHAB (PHYSICALLY HANDICAPPED AND ABLE BODIED)
UK tel: 020 8667 9443
www.phabengland.org.uk
Annual summer programme at purpose built centres for disabled and non disabled children.

RADAR
UK tel: 020 7250 3222
www.radar.org.uk
RADAR can find accommodation and facilities for the disabled and publishes a wealth of reference literature.

REHABILITATION INTERNATIONAL
www.rehab-international.org
US-based global network providing information for the disabled traveller.

SOCIETY FOR ACCESSIBLE TRAVEL & HOSPITALITY
USA tel: 212 447 7284
www.sath.org
Non-profit US organisation raising awareness and expanding travel opportunities for the disabled.

TRIPSCOPE
UK tel: 08457 58 56 41
www.tripscope.org.uk
Provide travel advice and information for local or international journeys.

UPHILL SKI CLUB OF GREAT BRITAIN
UK tel: 01479 861272
www.uphillskiclub.co.uk
Winter sports holidays for disabled people, from Rossendale to Canada.

VITALISE (FORMERLY WINGED FELLOWSHIP TRUST)
UK tel: 0845 345 1972
www.vitalise.org.uk
Holidays for disabled people and their careers.

THE WHEEL RESORT
Aus tel: (066) 856 139
www.deh.gov.ay/coasts/publications/coastal-tourism/thewheel.html
Luxury cabins in Australia designed for people with disabilities.

Related websites

www.abilities.fsnet.co.uk

www.access-able.com
Information and database on access, accommodation and holidays.

www.adviceguide.org.uk/em/index/yourworld/travel/transportoptionsfordisabledpeople
Advice and options for disabled travellers.

www.blvd.com
Online guide for the
disabled by the disabled.

www.canbedone.co.uk
Holidays for disabled
people.

www.disabilityworld.com
News, reports, travel tips
and ideas.

www.independentliving.
org
Self-help organisation for
disabled people with a
travel and recreation
section.

www.internationaldisabilit
yalliance.org

www.newmobility.com
Online magazine with
travel tips and real-life
stories.

Ecotourism and responsible travel

**ACTION D'URGENCE
INTERNATIONALE (A.U.I)**
France tel: 04 67 27 06 09
www.aui-ong.org
French-based training
courses to help with rescue
operations at times of
natural disasters.

ARCTURUS EXPEDITIONS
UK tel: 01389 830204
www.arcturusexpeditions.
co.uk
Polar travel linking
tourism with conservation
in the Arctic.

BELLERIVE FOUNDATION
http://geneva.intl.ch/index
.htm
Dedicated to protecting all
life, from environmental
protection and
conservation to human
and animal rights.

BORN FREE FOUNDATION
UK tel: 01403 240170
www.bornfree.org.uk
Wildlife charity protecting
threatened species.

**CENTRE FOR THE
ADVANCEMENT OF
RESPONSIVE TRAVEL**
70, Dry Hill Park Road
Tunbridge, Kent
TIN 3BX, UK
Publishers of credible and
alternative tourism to
understand environmental
and cultural sensitivity.

CORAL CAY CONSERVATION
UK tel: 0870 750 0668
www.coralcay.org
Marine conservation.

DISCOVER THE WORLD
UK tel: 01737 218800
www.arctic-discover.co.uk
Specialist travel
programmes committed to
responsible tourism.

DISCOVERY INITIATIVES
UK tel: 01285 643333
www.discoveryinitiatives.
co.uk

EARTHWATCH INSTITUTE
UK tel: 01865 318838
USA tel: 1 800 776 0188
www.earthwatch.org
Research projects
worldwide.

ENGLISH NATURE
UK tel: 01733 455000
www.englishnature.org.uk
Protecting and enhancing
landscapes and wildlife
and raising public
awareness.

**ENVIRONMENTAL
INVESTIGATION AGENCY**
UK tel: 020 7354 7960
USA tel: 202 483 6621
www.eia-international.org

EUROPA NOSTRA
Lange Voorhout 35
NL-2514 EC The Hague
Holland
Neth tel: 31 70 302 4050
www.europanostra.org
Netherlands-based forum
representing 200 NGOs on
Europe's cultural heritage.

**FAUNA & FLORA
INTERNATIONAL**
UK tel: 01223 571 000
www.fauna-flora.org
Conservation body that
provides support to
organisations concerning
all forms of plant and
animal.

FIELD STUDIES COUNCIL
UK tel: 01743 852100
www.
field-studies-council.org
Pioneers in environmental
education with 17
education centres.

**FRIENDS OF
CONSERVATION**
UK tel: 020 7603 5024
www.foc-uk.com

FRIENDS OF THE EARTH
UK tel: 020 7490 1555
www.foe.co.uk
UK-based conservation
charity for protecting the
natural environment.

**GREEN TOURISM
ASSOCIATION**
Canada tel: 416 392 1288
www.greentourism.ca

GREENPEACE
UK tel: 020 7865 8100
www.greenpeace.org
International
environmental pressure
group.

INSTITUTE OF TRAVEL AND TOURISM
UK tel: 0870 770 7960
www.itt.co.uk

INTERNATIONAL ECOTOURISM SOCIETY
US tel: 202 347 9203
www.ecotourism.org

THE LAND IS OURS
www.tlio.org.uk
UK lands right charity.

MARINE CONSERVATION SOCIETY
UK tel: 01989 566017
www.mcsuk.org

MEDITERRANEAN ACTION PLAN (MAP)
c/o United Nations
Environment Programme
in Athens, Greece
Greece tel: 30 210 727 3100
www.unepmap.gr
Concerned with the
protection of the region's
marine and coastal
environment.

NATIONAL TRUST VOLUNTEERING
UK tel: 0870 458 4000
www.nationaltrust.org.uk
For UK heritage and
wilderness charity.

NATURETREK
UK tel: 01962 733051
www.naturetrek.co.uk
UK company offering
bird-watching and wildlife
tours worldwide.

NORTH SOUTH TRAVEL
UK tel: 01245 608291
www.northsouthtravel.
co.uk
Travel agency that devotes
its profits to third world
projects.

REEF AND RAINFOREST TOURS
UK tel: 01803 866965
www.reefandrainforest.
co.uk

ROYAL SOCIETY FOR THE PROTECTION OF BIRDS (RSPB)
UK tel: 01767 680551
www.rspb.org.uk

SAVE THE RHINO
UK tel: 020 7357 7474
www.savetherhino.com
Safari expeditions to see
desert rhinos, proceeds
fund their protection.

SURVIVAL INTERNATIONAL
UK tel: 020 7687 8700
www.
survival-international.org
UK-based charity
protecting the human
rights of the world's tribal
peoples.

SYMBIOSIS EXPEDITION PLANNING
UK tel: 0845 123 2844
www.
symbiosis-travel.com
Tailor-made holidays for
the ecologically and
culturally sensitive
traveller.

TOURISM CONCERN
UK tel: 020 7133 3331
www.tourismconcern.
org.uk
Responsible travel charity,
with directory listing tour
companies benefiting local
communities.

UNEP WORLD CONSERVATION MONITORING CENTRE
UK tel: 01223 277314
www.unep-wcmc.org
Provides information for
policy and action for
conservation.

WHALE AND DOLPHIN CONSERVATION SOCIETY
UK tel: 0870 870 0027
www.wdcs.org

WORLD CONSERVATION UNION (IUCN)
Switzerland tel:
41 22 999 0000

www.iucn.org
World's largest
conservation network,
encouraging and assisting
charitites.

WORLD WILD FUND FOR NATURE (WWF)
UK tel: 01483 426444
USA tel: 202 293 4800
www.wwf.org
International conservation
society.

Related websites

www.angel-ecotours.com

www.btcv.org
British Trust for
conservation volunteers.

www.coralcay.org
Marine conservation
protecting tropical forests
and coral reefs.

www.ecosourcenetwork.
com
Links to other
conservation websites.

www.ecotour.org
Conservation
International service,
benefiting environment
and local communities.

Expedition organisers

ALPINE CLUB
UK tel: 020 7613 0755
www.alpine-club.org.uk
Has a comprehensive collection of mountaineering literature, journals and guidebooks by some of the UK's most prominent mountaineers.

ARCHAEOLOGY ABROAD
UK tel: 020 8537 0849
www.britarch.ac.uk
Based at University College London's Institute of Archaeology, they provide fieldwork opportunities outside the UK.

ARCTURUS EXPEDITIONS
UK tel: 01389 830204
www.arcturusexpeditions.co.uk
A small company specialising in polar expeditions off the unbeaten track with dog-sledging, kayaking and cruises.

BRATHAY EXPLORATION GROUP
UK tel: 015394 33942
www.brathayexploration.org.uk
Expedition and training opportunities.

BSES EXPEDITIONS
UK tel: 020 7591 3141
www.bses.org.uk
A youth development charity organising adventurous expeditions, incorporating leadership, communication and teamwork skills.

EARTHWATCH INSTITUE
UK tel: 01865 318816
www.earthwatch.org
Environmental institute for scientific field research and education to promote environmental understanding.

EXPEDITIONARY ADVISORY CENTRE
UK tel: 020 7591 3030
www.rgs.org
UK's national centre for information, training and planning for expeditions.

EXPLORATION LOGISTICS
UK tel: 44 1594 545100
www.exlogs.com
Offers safety advice, equipment purchase, survival and driver training for all forms of expeditions.

THE EXPLORERS CLUB
USA tel: 212 628 83 83
www.explorers.org
Finances expeditions all over the world and offers expertise, technology and experience.

HIGH & WILD
UK tel: 01749 671 777
www.highandwild.co.uk
Expedition organisers promoting conservation and responsible travel.

NATIONAL GEOGRAPHIC SOCIETY
www.nationalgeographicsociety.com
Promoting research and exploration by the pursuit and promulgation of geographical knowledge.

RALEIGH INTERNATIONAL
UK tel: 020 7371 8585
www.raleigh.org.uk
Runs environmental and community projects/expeditions overseas for young volunteers.

ROYAL GEOGRAPHIC SOCIETY (RGS)
UK tel: 020 7591 3000
www.rgs.org
UK's national centre for explorers and geographers. Finances and organises its own scientific expeditions as well as supporting others. They have the largest map collection in Europe and a library of books and periodicals.

ROYAL SCOTTISH GEOGRAPHIC SOCIETY
UK tel: 0141 552 3330
www.geo.ed.ac.uk
Scottish affiliate of RGS.

SCIENTIFIC EXPLORATION SOCIETY
UK tel: 01747 853353
www.ses-explore.org
Initiates expedition groups and offers non-financial support to others.

SCOTT POLAR RESEARCH INSTITUTE
UK tel: 01223 336540
www.spri.cam.ac.uk
Academic specialists working alongside many other affiliates in polar research.

SOUTH AMERICAN EXPLORERS CLUB
www.samexplo.org
Provides clubhouses around South America providing information, guide maps, travel logs, advice and promoting safe exploration.

SYMBIOSIS EXPEDITION PLANNING
UK tel: 0845 123 2844
www.symbiosis-travel.co.uk
Expedition planning in South-East Asia.

TREKFORCE EEXPEDITIONS
UK tel: 020 7828 2275
www.trekforce.org.uk
Experts in rainforest expeditions offering year-long projects.

UNIVERSITY RESEARCH EXPEDITIONS PROGRAM
US tel: 510 752 0681
www.lalc.k12.ca.us/
catalog/providers/
196.html
Organises exhibitions in
all areas of research from
social to environmental.

WORLD CHALLENGE EXPEDITIONS
UK tel: 01298 767900
www.worldchallenge.co.uk
Offers four different
project expeditions for the
12-24 age group,
emphasizing youth
development.

THE YOUNG EXPLORERS TRUST
www.theyet.org
UK-based trust providing
advice and information for
youth expeditions so that
they can be run in a safe
and responsible manner.

Related websites

www.british-explorers.org

www.explorers.org

www.wexclub.com

www.thepoles.com

Gay travel

DAMRON
USA tel: 415 255 0404
www.damron.com

FRIENDS OF DOROTHY TRAVEL
USA tel: 415 864 1600
www.
freindsofdorothytravel.
com
Cruises, tours and gay
adventures.

GAY JOURNEY
www.gayjourney.com

GAY TRAVEL LINKS
www.gaytravellinks.com

GAY TRAVEL NET
USA tel: 64 4 917 9175
www.gaytravel.net.nz

HIV TRAVEL INSURANCE
UK tel: 0845 222 2226
www.hivtravelinsurance.
com

INTERNATIONAL GAY AND LESBIAN TRAVEL ASSOCIATION
USA tel: 1 954 776 2626 / 1
800 448 8550
www.iglta.com

MAN AROUND
UK tel: 020 8902 7177
www.manaround.com
One of Europe's largest
travel agencies, dealing
with the gay and lesbian
community.

OLIVIA CRUISES & RESORTS
US tel: 800 631 6277
www.olivia.com
Lesbian tour operator.

ORBITZ
UK tel: 1 312 416 0018
USA tel: 1 888 656 4546
www.orbitz.com

RESPECT HOLIDAYS
UK tel: 0870 770 0169
www.
respect-holidays.co.uk

RSVP VACATIONS
USA tel: 800 328 7787
www.rsvpvacations.com
Cruises and land tours.

SENSATIONS HOLIDAYS
UK tel: 020 8902 7177
www.sensationsholidays.
com

SOUTH AMERICA GAY TRAVEL
UK tel: 0800 011 2540
www.southamericagaytrav
el-uk.com

Related websites

www.gaydartravel.com

www.gayhometrade.com

www.gaymart.com

www.gaytravelnews.com

www.igogay.com

www.ourworldmagazine.
com

www.outandabout.com

www.outtraveler.com

www.passportmagazine.
net

www.pupleroofs.com

www.rainbowtourism.
com

Gourmet travel

ATG OXFORD
UK tel: 01865 315 678
www.atg-oxford.co.uk
Organises wine tours in
France and Italy.

ARBLASTER & CLARKE WINE TOURS WORLDWIDE
UK tel: 01730 893 344
www.arblasterandclarke.
com
Champagne weekends and
wine tours from Chile to
New Zealand.

CATACURIAN – THE PRIORAT EXPERIENCE
UK tel: +34 93 511 0738
USA tel: 1 800 945 8606
www.catacurian.com
Food and wine holidays set
in the village of El Masroig.

GOURMET TRAVEL EXPERIENCE
USA tel: 403 762 8175
www.gourmet-experience.com
Travel to destinations
worldwide tasting fine
foods and wine.

INDIA ON THE MENU
UK tel: 020 7371 1113
www.indiaonthemenu.com
Culinary holidays in Goa.

THE INTERNATIONAL KITCHEN
USA tel: 312 726 4525
Toll Free: 800 945 8606
www.theinternationalkitchen.com
Cooking vacations to
France, Italy and Spain.

KAO HOM THAI COOKING SCHOOL
Thailand tel: 66 5386 2967
www.kaohom.com
Day courses in Chiang
Mai.

LA MAISON ARABE
Morocco tel:
212 44 3870 10
www.lamaisonarabe.com/en/
Cooking workshops for
novice and professional
alike who want to discover
Moroccan cuisine in
Marrakech.

SYMBIOSIS EXPEDITION PLANNING
UK tel: 0845 123 2844
www.symbiosis-travel.com
Gastronomic and cultural
tours in South-East Asia.

SUSHI-MAKING SCHOOL
Japan tel: 00 813 5722 5055
www.theyummyco.com
Morning, afternoon or
evening courses at the
Tokyo school.

A TASTE OF PROVENCE
USA tel: 415 383 9439
www.tasteofprovence.com
Weeklong trips to an 18th
century farmhouse for
'cooking, eating, relaxing
and enjoying life'.

TASTING PLACES
UK tel: 020 8964 5333
USA tel: 1877 695 2469
www.tastingplaces.com
Exquisite food and wine
tours in romantic
destinations.

THE VILLA SAN MICHELE SCHOOL OF COOKERY
Italy tel: 39 055 567 8200
www.villasanmichele.com
Discover the secrets of
Italian cuisine with a
veritable smorgasbord of
famous chefs and courses.

VILLA VALENTINA COOKERY SCHOOL
UK tel: 020 8651 2997
www.villavalentina.com
Hands on gastronomic
excursions in Tuscany.
Culinary tours to South
Africa are also available.

Related websites

www.patanegra.net
Comprehensive directory
of culinary programmes.

www.globalgourmet.com/destinations/
Choose a country and
check out the cuisine.

www.restaurantrow.com

www.tudocs.com
Directory of cooking sites
worldwide.

www.mygourmetguide.com
Worldwide restaurant
guide and listings.

Honeymoon specialists

ABECROMBIE & KENT
UK tel: 0845 0700 610
www.abercrombiekent.co.uk
Direct line to a
'honeymoon specialist'

AUDLEY TRAVEL
UK tel: 01869 276200
www.audleytravel.com

BEACHCOMBER
www.beachcomber.co.zav
Honeymoon specialists to
the Seychelles and
Mauritius.

BEST OF MOROCCO
UK tel: 01380 828533
www.morocco-travel.com

BRIDGE THE WORLD
UK tel: 0870 814 4400
www.bridgetheworld.com

BRITISH AIRWAYS
UK tel: 0870 850 9850
www.britishairways.com

CARIBBEAN CONNECTIONS
UK tel: 0870 751 9300
Email: reservations@itc-uk.com

CARIBTOURS
UK tel: 020 7751 0660
www.caribtours.co.uk

COX & KINGS
UK tel: 020 7873 5000
www.coxandkings.co.uk

CV TRAVEL
www.cvtravel.co.uk

ELEGANT RESORTS
UK tel: 01244 897 000
www.elegantresorts.co.uk

HAYES & JARVIS
UK tel: 0870 366 1636
www.hayesandjarvis.co.uk

JOURNEY LATIN AMERICA
London tel: 020 8747 3108
Manchester tel: 0161 832
1441
www.journeylatinamerica.
co.uk

KUONI
UK tel: 01306 747000
www.kuoni.co.uk

MAGIC TRAVEL GROUP
UK tel: 0800 980 3378
www.magictravelgroup.
co.uk

MONTROSE TRAVEL
USA tel: 818 553 3387
www.montrosetravel.com

SANDALS RESORTS
UK tel: 0207 581 9895
www.sandals.co.uk

STEPPES TRAVEL
UK tel: 01285 880980
www.artoftravel.co.uk

SUNSET TRAVEL
UK tel: 020 7622 5466
www.sunsettravel.co.uk

TANZANIA ODYSSEY
UK tel: 020 7471 8780
www.tanzaniaodyssey.com

**THOMAS COOK
HONEYMOONS**
UK tel: 0870 750 5711
www.
honeymoonsdirect2u.com

**WORLDWIDE JOURNEYS
AND EXPEDITIONS**
UK tel: 020 7386 4646
www.worldwidejourneys.
co.uk

Related websites

www.cloud9celebrations.
co.uk

www.confetti.co.uk/travel/
weddings_abroad

www.tigermountain.com

www.travel-quest.co.uk/
tqwedding.htm

www.weddingsabroad.
com

www.
weddings-abroad.com

www.wellingtontravel.
co.uk

Horse-riding organisations

AGRITURISMO MALVARINA
Italy tel: 39 075 806 4280
www.malvarina.it

ARCTIC EXPERIENCE
UK tel: 01737 214214
www.
arctic-experience.co.uk

CABALGATAS LA SIERRA
Mexico tel: 52 726 26
20636
www.mexicohorsevacation
.com

**THE EQUESTRIAN
FEDERATION OF
AUSTRALIA**
Australia tel: 61 28762
7777
www.efanational.com

EQUINE CANADA
Canada tel: 613 248 3433
www.equinecanada.ca

EQUUS HORSE SAFARIS
South Africa tel: 27 14 721
0063
www.equus.co.za

EXPLORE WORLDWIDE
UK tel: 0870 333 4002
www.explore.co.uk

**FEDERATION EQUESTRE
INTERNATIONAL**
Switzerland tel: 41 21 310
47 47
www.horsesport.org

HOLIDAYS ON HORSEBACK
Canada tel: 1 403 762 4551
www.horseback.com

HORSE HOLIDAY FARM
UK tel: 00 353 71 9166152
USA tel: 011 353 71
9166152
www.
horse-holiday-farm.com

INNTRAVEL LTD
UK tel:01653 617788
www.inntravel.co.uk

MOUNTAIN TRAVEL SOBEK
www.mtsobek.com

**KARAKORUM EXPEDITIONS
MONGOLIA**
Mongolia tel: 976 11
315655
www.gomongolia.com

**THE NEW ZEALAND
EQUESTRIAN FEDERATION**
New Zealand tel: 04 499
8994
www.nzequestrian.org.nz

OFFBEAT HORSE SAFARIS
Kenya tel: 254 720 461300
www.offbeatsafaris.com

**PEREGRINE HOLIDAYS
EQUITOR**
UK tel: 01865 511642
www.traveleshop.com

RIDE WORLD WIDE
UK tel: 01837 82544
www.rideworldwide.co.uk

RIDING HOLIDAYS
USA tel: 215 659 3281
www.ridingholidays.com

**RIDING HOLIDAYS IN
TRANSYLVANIA**
Romania tel: 263 378470
www.riding-holidays.ro

STEAMOND TRAVEL
UK tel: 0207 730 8646
www.steamondtravel.co

UNICORN TRAILS
UK tel: 01767 600606
www.unicorntrails.com

THE UNITED STATES EQUESTRIAN FEDERATION
USA tel: 859 258 2472
www.usef.org

WORLD HORSE RIDING
Sweden tel: 4646 145225
Italy tel: 39 0363 301434
www.worldhorseriding.com

Related websites

www.apachestables.com
Grand Canyon riding trips.

www.equestrianvacations.com

www.equineadventures.co.uk

www.free-rein.co.uk
Riding through the Cambrian Mountains and Randor Hills of Wales.

www.gorptravel.away.com
Stay in a great Western dude ranch.

www.inthesaddle.co.uk
Riding holiday specialists.

www.ranchoferrer.com
Horse riding holidays in Spain.

www.ranchweb.com

www.ridingtours.com

www.hiddentrails.com

www.equitour.co.uk

www.equitrek.com.au
Australia by horseback.

www.cmfortravel.co.uk
Arranges horse riding holidays on the Puszta, Hungary.

Luxury travel

ABERCROMBIE & KENT
UK tel: 0845 0700610
www.abercrombiekent.co.uk
USA tel: 00 1 630 954 2944

ATLANTIS TRAVEL
UK tel:020 8501 0917
www.atlantistravel.co.uk

CARIBTOURS
UK tel: 020 7751 0660
www.caribtours.co.uk

COX & KINGS TRAVEL LIMITED
UK tel: 020 7873 5006
www.coxandkings.co.uk

CROWN LUXURY TRAVEL
USA tel: 800 628 8929
www.crownluxurytravel.com

CUNARD SEABOURN
UK tel: 023-8071-6500
www.cunardline.com

CV TRAVEL
UK tel: 0207 384 5850
www.cvtravel.net/

ELEGANT RESORTS
UK tel: 01244 897 000
www.elegantresorts.co.uk

EXSUS TRAVEL
UK tel: 020 7292 5060
www.exsus.com

LLOYD AND TOWNSEND-ROSE
UK tel: 01573 229797
www.ltr.co.uk

NOMADIC THOUGHTS
UK tel: 020 7604 4408
www.nomadicthoughts.com

SILVERSEA CRUISES
UK tel: 0870 333 7030
www.silversea.com

TUSCANY NOW
UK tel: 020 7684 88 84

VENICE SIMPLON-ORIENT-EXPRESS
UK tel: 0845 077 2222
www.orient-express.com

VIRTUOSO
USA tel: 866 401 7974
or 817 870 0300
(international customers)
www.virtuoso.com

WESTERN & ORIENTAL GROUP
UK tel: 020 7821 4000
www.wo-group.co.uk

WEXAS
UK tel: 020 7589 3315
www.wexas.com

WORLDS APART TRAVEL
Cheltenham UK
UK tel: 01242 226578
www.worldsaparttravel.co.uk

Related websites

FIRST CLASS TRAVEL

www.bluetrain.co.za/
South Africa's premier train

www.flightfantasy.com

www.rovos.co.za

www.bombardier.com
The leading learjet family

www.luxurytravelsource.com/

FIRST CLASS HOLIDAYS

www.islandhideaways.com

www.itcclassics.co.uk

www.onlyexclusivetravel.com
Exclusive offers for luxuries locations around the world.

www.tailor-made.co.uk
Customised itineraries to suit you.

www.tcs-expeditions.com
Private planes and trains make sure you keep up with the schedule around the world.

www.turtlefiji.com
Turtle Island stay, all inclusive.

www.unchartedoutposts.com
Custom designed trips for a unique intimacy across the globe.

LUXURY ACCOMMODATION

www.caribtours.co.uk

www.dreamvillarentals.com

http://www.lhw.com/
Guide to the world's leading hotels.

www.quality-villas.co.uk/
Unique and hand picked accommodation.

www.slh.com/index.shtml
Small Luxury Hotels of the World.

www.tuscanynow.com
Italian villa rental specialist.

www.villa-rentals.com
Exclusive villas around the world.

www.villasofdistinction.com
Luxury villa rentals.

www.worldexecutive.com/
Directory to some of the best hotels in the world.

www.worldhotels.com/

Mountaineering associations

THE ALPINE CLUB
UK tel: 020 7613 0755
www.alpine-club.org.uk

THE BRITISH MOUNTAINEERING COUNCIL
UK tel: 0870 010 4878
www.thebmc.co.uk

MOUNT EVEREST FOUNDATION
UK tel: 01761 472998
www.mef.org.uk

UIAA INTERNATIONAL MOUNTAINEERING AND CLIMBING FEDERATION
www.uiaa.ch

USA CLIMBING
Colorado USA
www.usaclimbing.org

Related websites

www.expeditionmedicine.co.uk

www.thecrag.com

www.alpineclub.org.nz

www.highplaces.co.uk/

www.americanalpineclub.org

Older travellers

ACE STUDY TOURS
UK tel: 01223 835055
www.study-tours.org
Providing cultural tours and holidays across the globe.

AGE CONCERN
UK tel: 020 8765 7200
www.ageconcern.org.uk
Advice, books and fact sheets.

GOLDEN GAP TEARS
UK tel: 0113 266 0880
www.goldengapyears.com
From a gap year as a volunteer to retiring abroad, this site is full of choice for the older traveller.

HELP THE AGED
UK tel: 020 7278 1114
www.helptheaged.org.uk

SAGA HOLIDAYS
UK tel: 0800 414 525
www.saga.co.uk
A wide variety of holiday choices for the over 60s.

TRIPSCOPE
UK tel: 08457 58 56 41
www.tripscope.org.uk
Travel and transport information for disabled or elderly people.

WALLACE ARNOLD WORLDCHOICE
UK tel: 0800 092 0102
www.waworldchoice.info
Coach holidays throughout the UK and Europe.

WORLD EXPEDITIONS
UK tel: 020 8870 2600
www.worldexpeditions.co.uk
Australian based expedition company offering adventure holidays for the over 50's.

Related websites

www.eldertreks.com

www.expat.ca/links_retirement.htm

www.laterlife.com

www.poshnosh.com
Travel for older women.

www.seniorhomeexchange
.com

www.thisistravel.co

Further reading

Retiring Abroad
(Survival Books)

The Good Non-Retirement Guide
(Kogan Page)

Polar travel

ABERCROMBIE & KENT
UK tel: 0845 0700610
USA tel: 00 1 630 954 2944
www.abercrombiekent.
co.uk
Cruises to Antarctica on the Explorer II.

ARCTIC EXPERIENCE
UK tel: 01737 214214
www
.arctic-experience.co.uk
Tours around the arctic specified to the season.

ARCTURUS EXPEDITIONS
UK tel: 01389 830204
www.arcturusexpeditions.
co.uk
Polar tours including dog-sledging, kayaking and cruises.

AURORA EXPEDITIONS
Australia tel: 61 2 9252 1033
www.aururaexpeditions.
com
Founded by the first Australian to climb Everest and K2, Aurora tours to the Antarctic and Arctic aboard the Polar Pioneer and Academic Shokalskiy.

GAP ADVENTURES
UK tel: 0870 080 1756
www.gapadventures.com

GLOBAL EXPEDITION ADVENTURES
USA tel: 1 800 770 5961
International tel: 1 850 217 9974
www.north-pole-
expeditions.com
Founded by the first Americans to hot-air balloon over both poles, GEA offers a wide variety of activities.

GMMS POLAR JOURNEYS
Australia tel: 61 2 264 3366

THE POLAR TRAVEL COMPANY
UK tel: 01364 631 470
www.polartravel.co.uk
A variety of expeditions from Polar Bear Odyssey to the Heart of Antarctica and Polar Flight.

SPITSBERGEN TRAVEL
Norway tel: 47 79 02 61 00
www.spitsbergentravel.
no/eng/

TRAVEL DYNAMICS INTERNATIONAL
USA tel: 800 257 5767
www.traveldynamicsinter
national.com
Trips to Antarctica offering insight into the continent's culture, history and nature on small ships.

WILDWINGS
UK tel: 0117 9658 333
www.wildwings.co.uk
Wildlife and birdwatching holidays to both poles.

Related websites

www.polar-circle.com

www.polar-travel.com

Student travel

TRAVEL AWARDS, GRANTS AND SCHOLARSHIPS

BP CONSERVATION PROGRAMME
UK tel: 01223 277 318
http://conservation.
bp.com/
Supports conservation projects prioritising, social, biological and economic research and works in collaboration with BirdLife International, Wildlife Conservation Society, Conservation International and Fauna & Flora International.

FEDERAL GRANTS
www.federalgrantswire.
com
Listings of grant departments for USA.

MOUNT EVEREST FOUNDATION
UK tel: 01761 472 998
www.mef.org.uk
Works with the Alpine Club and the Royal Geographical Society to support mountain exploration and science. Primarily supports British and New Zealand expeditions.

ROYAL GEOGRAPHIC SOCIETY
UK tel: 020 7591 3000
www.rgs.org
Grants awarded in various fields of research from students (post/under graduates) to established researches all pursuing geographic research and education. Plus details of other grant giving organisations.

THE EXPLORERS CLUB
USA tel: 212 628 8383
www.explorers.org
Grants are awarded to scientists, writer, photographers and are judged on their scientific and practical methods.

UCL
www.ucl.ac.uk/
expeditions
Awards grants to students undertaking expeditions challenging expeditions.

WEXAS
Expedition grants administered by The Royal Geographic Society on behalf of Wexas. Contact Grants Secretary at RGS.

THE WINSTON CHURCHILL MEMORIAL TRUST
UK tel: 020 7584 9315
www.wcmt.org.uk
The Council of the Trust select annual categories to offer grants in many fields to acquire knowledge and experience abroad. All British citizens can apply.

GAP-YEAR PROJECTS

BLUE VENTURES
UK tel: 020 8341 9819
www.blueventures.org
Expeditions to their marine conservation site at Andavadoaka in Madagascar, to help with research and maintenance. Dive training can be provided.

CHANGING WORLDS
UK tel: 01892 770 000
www.changingworlds.
co.uk
Volunteers for teaching, orphanage and rural work in five continents.

CORAL CAY CONSERVATION
UK tel: 0870 750 0668
www.coralcay.org
Volunteers and divers needed for coral reef and rainforest conservation, with training provided.

FRONTIER WILDLIFE CONSERVATION EXPEDITIONS
UK tel: 020 7613 2422
www.frontierprojects.
ac.uk/
Environmental surveys, scientific research, re-building impoverished communities in Nicargua, Tanzania, Cambodia to name a few.

I TO I INTERNATIONAL PROJECTS
UK tel: 0870 333 2332
www.i-to-i.com
Teaching English abroad, gap year students, conservation volunteers and sports coaches in developing countries.

QUEST OVERSEAS
UK tel: 01444 47474
www.questoverseas.com
Gap years, summer volunteering expeditions in Africa, even take you football team on a tour of Brazil.

RALEIGH INTERNATIONAL
UK tel: 020 7371 8585
www.raleighinternational.
org
Leading organisation for sending volunteers on projects worldwide.

TEACHING & PROJECTS ABROAD
UK tel: 01903 708300
www.
teaching-abroad.co.uk
Volunteers and gap year students can arrange to teach English in schools or companies abroad.

TRAVELLERS WORLDWIDE
UK tel: 01903 502595
www.travellersworldwide.
com
Work placements overseas for volunteers and gap year students.

TREKFORCE EXPEDITIONS
UK tel: 01444 474 123
www.trekforce.org.uk
Jungle expeditions ranging from one to five months.

TWO WORLDS UNITED EDUCATIONAL FOUNDATION
USA tel: 888 696 8808
www.twoworldsunited.
com
Various exchange programmes in over 45 countries.

VENTURE CO
UK tel: 01926 411122
www.ventureco-
worldwide.com/
Your time can be split into three phases, expeditions, volunteer work and language courses from Africa to the Andes.

TRAVEL PROVIDERS

BUNAC
www.bunac.org.uk/
Programmes lasting from eight weeks to 18 months.

COUNCIL ON INTERNATIONAL EDUCATION EXCHANGE
USA tel: 1 800 40 STUDY
www.ciee.org

EN FAMILLE OVERSEAS
UK tel: 0468 914990
www.enfamilleoverseas.
co.uk
Immerse yourself in family life in Italy, Spain, Germany and France from one week to one year.

INTERNATIONAL ASSOCIATION FOR THE EXCHANGE OF STUDENTS FOR TECHNICAL EXPERIENCE
UK tel: 020 7389 4771
www.iaeste.org/
Opportunities for students

to gain technical knowledge and experience in their field worldwide.

INTERNATIONAL AGRICULTURAL EXCHANGE ASSOCIATION
UK tel: 01203 696578
USA tel: 406 727 1999
http://members.ozemail.com.au
Offers the chance to stay with a host family and help with their horticultural and agricultural work.

ISTC
www.istcstudytravel.com
Combining travel with work placements and studies.

SOCRATES ERASMUS COUNCIL
UK tel: 01227 762 712
www.erasmus.ac.uk
European exchange programme enabling students to study for part of their degree abroad.

STA TRAVEL
UK tel: 0780 1 600 599
www.statravel.co.uk
Student travel agents.

STUDENT FLIGHTS
www.studentflights.co.uk
Discounts for students for air, rail and car.

YOUTH FOR UNDERSTANDING
USA tel: 1866 4 YFU-USA
UK tel: 0141 812 5561
www.yfu.org/
Promoting international understanding and world peace through school student exchange courses.

Tailor-made travel

ABERCROMBIE & KENT
www.abercrombiekent.co.uk
Specialising in Africa, but offers trips around the world.

THE ASSOCIATION OF INDEPENDENT TOUR OPERATORS (AITO)
www.aito.com
Forum for UK tour operators.

BRIDGE THE WORLD
www.bridgetheworld.com
Provides on-line route planner for complex itineraries.

COLLINEIGE CHAMONIX
www.collineige.com
Specialists for every kind of holiday in Chamonix.

COX AND KINGS
www.coxandkings.co.uk
Europe, India, Africa, Latin America, Middle East and Far East.

CV TRAVEL
www.cvtravel.com

EXSUS TRAVEL
www.exsus.com
Luxurious tailor-made travel.

GULLIVERS SPORTS TRAVEL
www.gulliversports.co.uk
Follow your favourite sports around the world.

HEADWATER HOLIDAYS
www.headwater.com
Multitude of travel choices.

INTERNATIONAL EXPEDITIONS
www.ietravel.com
Nature travel throughout the world.

JOURNEY LATIN AMERICA
www.journeylatinamerica.co.uk
Latin America specialists.

JOURNEYS ELITE
www.journeyselite.com
Holidaying in Cuba, Morocco and Russia.

LATIN AMERICAN TRAVEL ASSOCIATION (LATA)
www.lata.org
Information for all countries in Latin America and useful links.

NOMADIC THOUGHTS
www.nomadicthoughts.com
Individually tailored travel worldwide.

SILVERBIRD
www.silverbird.co.uk
Specialists in the Far East.

TAILOR MADE TRAVEL
www.tailor-made.co.uk
Canada, Africa, Australia, New Zealand and South Pacific.

TRANSINDUS
www.transindus.co.uk
India and South-East Asia.

TRAVELBAG
www.travelbag.co.uk
Itineraries for travel around the globe.

TRIPS WORLDWIDE
www.tripsworldwide.co.uk
Specialists in Latin American trips.

WESTERN & ORIENTAL TRAVEL
www.westernoriental.com
Worldwide itineraries.

WEXAS
www.wexas.com
Worldwide itineraries.

Walking associations

RAMBLERS ASSOCIATION
England tel: 020 7339 8500
Wales tel: 029 2064 4308
Scotland tel: 01577 861222
www.ramblers.org

THE LONG DISTANCE WALKERS ASSOCIATION
www.ldwa.org.uk

Related websites

www.countrywalkers.com
Worldwide expeditions on foot.

http://countrywalks.defra.gov.uk

www.fs.fed.us/
Info on all routes, walking, hiking, biking in the US by the Forest Service.

www.nps.gov/trails
National Park Service trekking routes.

www.travelsource.com/trekking
Walking and trekking worldwide.

www.explore.co.uk
Guide to exploring the world on foot.

Women's organisations

ADVENTURES IN GOOD COMPANY
USA tel: 410 435 1965
www.adventuresingoodcompany.com
Guided adventure holidays throughout the world.

ADVENTURE WOMEN TRAVEL
USA tel: 406 587 3883
www.adventurewomen.com
Adventure travel trips for women aged 35-65.

ARCTIC LADIES
USA tel: 1 877 0783 1954
www.arcticladies.com
Trips around the world and Alaska, including cross-country skiing, horseback riding and dog-sledging.

CORONA WORLDWIDE, WOMAN'S CORONA SOCIETY
UK tel: 020 7793 4020
Offers support and advice to female expatriates.

LUNA TOURS
USA tel: 406 222 9631
www.lunatours.com
Bicycle tours around USA, Iceland and New Zealand.

SILVERMOON WOMEN'S BOOKSHOP
UK tel: 020 7440 1562
www.silvermoonbookshop.co.uk

WOMANSHIP
USA tel: 1 800 342 9295
www.womanship.com
Sailing cruises for women.

WOMEN WELCOME WOMEN WORLD WIDE
UK tel: 01494 465441
www.womenwelcomewomen.org.uk
Promotes international friendship by helping female travellers with accommodation through their network of members.

WOODSWOMEN
USA tel: 800 279 0555
Adventure trips for women.

Related websites

www.adventurouswench.com

www.christinecolumbus.com
Website catalogue specifically for female travellers.

www.goingplacestours.com
Walking tours for women.

www.journeywoman.com
On-line magazine with travel tips and newsletters.

www.northshorestories.com
Advice and stories, plus links to other websites.

www.seniorwomen.com

www.thelmandlouise.com
Helps women find someone like-minded as a travel companion.

www.womenstravelclub.com

www.womensquest.com
Trips to fulfil your spiritual and physical needs.

http://www.roadandtravel.com/clubsandorgs/travel.htm
Website indexing women's travel sites. Also advice, security and destinations.

Section 4: **Considerations** ❧

Moral dilemmas of travel
by George Monbiot

IN 1999, THE OWNERS OF A TOURIST ATTRACTION in north-west Thailand appeared in court on charges of running a 'human zoo'. Twelve adults and twenty-one children of the Padaung tribe had been discovered by a British journalist and a Thai human rights campaigner in a compound near the Burmese border. They had been tricked into leaving a refugee camp, then displayed to tourists who came to see their famously elongated necks. They were forced to dance, sing and sell artefacts to the visitors, and those who tried to escape were beaten up. By the time the slaves were discovered, one woman had died, due, her husband said, to a 'broken heart'.

These were the lucky ones. Their human zoo was closed down when exposure forced the reluctant authorities to start an investigation. But in many parts of South-East Asia, slavery is either ignored or promoted by the state. As both tourists and Thai men demand HIV-free prostitutes in Bangkok, brokers and bawds scour the Thai hills for girls to trick or kidnap. Across the border in Burma, the entire tourist industry has been built on slave labour, as hundreds of thousands of men and women have been forced, on pain of death, to construct the roads, airstrips, hotels and golf courses demanded by an industry that neither sees nor cares. Thousands have died of beatings, malnutrition and exhaustion. Yet still the vampire tourists come, purchasing a pound of human flesh with every kyat they spend.

Of course, it's not the tourists who are imprisoning people, forcing them to work and beating or killing them if they refuse. Our ignorance is exploited, our perception of where we should and shouldn't tread is complicated by the knowledge that some tourism can do more good than harm. But we are the ones who buy these slaves: ours, as William Wilberforce first pointed out nearly two centuries ago, is therefore the primary responsibility. It is up to us to discover whether or not our money will ruin or enhance people's lives. Today, you don't have to be evil to be a slave-driver, only unthinking.

Tourism has often been presented as a force for global salvation, bringing people closer together and providing alternative livelihoods for the victims of exploitation. It has also, however, become one of the world's principal sources of oppression and destruction.

Clearances are a common component of national tourist industries. All over South-East Asia, farms, forests, villages, even suburbs, have been destroyed to make way for golf courses. Slums are razed for fear of offending visitors. In many parts of Africa, conservation is used to justify the creation of new parks and reserves for tourism. Their inhabitants are excluded from the lands they have possessed for centuries, and if they dare to re-enter them they do so (in Kenya) on pain of death.

Wherever it occurs, tourism is an extractive industry. It extracts the differences between our land and culture and those of the nations we visit, until they scarcely exist. Remote and romantic beaches become mundane resorts. Remote and remarkable people tailor their culture to suit those who pay for it, until, in the words of a Maasai man, "We have ceased to be what we are; we are becoming what we seem." The exotic, of course, is illusory: as we approach it, it disappears. Tourism will never be sated, therefore, even when it has penetrated the remotest parts of the world.

While organised tours may be most directly responsible for the muffling of diversity, it is the backpackers who blaze the trail others follow. An independent travellers' destination becomes a mainstream resort within a few years. Indeed as travel becomes easier and tourists more adventurous, the distinction between the two groups is breaking down: hundreds of tour companies organise journeys that mimic those of independent travellers. Independent travel itself has had an enormous impact on places such as Goa, the South African coast and several Thai resorts, which have become increasingly unwilling hosts of the European dance scene. Neither category – if they can still be categorised – is blameless.

Whatever happens when you get there, travelling itself has begun to ruin the lives of millions of people. By 2016, for example, the number of passengers using London's airports is expected to double to 160 million, an average of nearly three flights per year for every man, woman and child in the United Kingdom. This, of course, means ever noisier skies. Sedative use increases by eight per cent (over the average) in areas affected by aircraft noise, while people living within ten kilometres of an airport consume 14 per cent more anti-asthma drugs. Around Los Angeles airport, mortality rates are five per cent higher than in quieter places: suicide accounts for much of the difference. One study shows that the reading ability of 12- to 14-year-olds whose schools lie under flight paths is impaired by 23 per cent, while children of all ages are more likely to develop anxiety disorders when routinely exposed to aircraft noise.

The impact on the environment is even graver. The transport specialist Dr Meyer Hillman has shown that every passenger on a return flight to Florida is single-handedly responsible for generating 1.8 tonnes of carbon dioxide. Climate scientists estimate that, if the worst effects of climate change are to be avoided, total emissions per person *per year* should be little more than half this amount.

Now several companies are vying to become the first to propel tourists into space. It is hard to think of a project better designed for maximum environmental destruction. If the industry takes off as some of its boosters would like us to believe, it will rapidly become the world's primary source of carbon dioxide emissions. In our quest to populate the barren interplanetary wastes, we threaten to lay waste to the only life-sustaining planet astronomers have been able to detect.

None of the ethical questions raised by tourism have easy answers. Tour organisers have justified their work to me on the grounds that it is a form of 'cultural exchange'. Yet what I have seen of their activities suggests that this is not how the transaction actually works. While the visitors get culture, the hosts – if they are lucky – get money. As identity is rooted in place, the tourists have little to offer.

Other people claim that tourism breaks down the barriers between our lives and those of the people we visit. Yet in most cases tourists remain firmly behind barriers, be they the windows of a coach, the walls of a hotel or the lens of a camera. In many parts of the world, tourism has served to compound misunderstanding and hostility, as local people's sensitivities are trampled.

Tourism, we are told, brings wealth to local people. My experience suggests that the opposite is more likely to be true: in most places, tourism makes a few people extremely rich while impoverishing the majority, who lose their land, their resources and their sense of self, gaining in return (if anything) a tiny amount of money.

Even the oldest maxim of all, that travel broadens the mind, is questionable. Tourists are the aristocracy of the New World Order. They are pampered and protected wherever they go; they are treated with deference and never corrected. Indeed, tour companies do their best to provide what the tourists expect, rather than educating the tourists to expect what the country can reasonably provide. For most tourists, the only surprises will be unpleasant ones, when the reality of the countries they visit pricks the bubble in which they travel. At this point the shock of discovery tends to compound fears rather than assuaging them, and thus many people return home more convinced than they were when they left that foreigners are dirty, deceitful and dangerous.

And yet it is also true that some people – those who manage to engage with the place they visit on its own terms – come back from their travels better than they were before, able to see both themselves and the rest of the world in a new light, able to grasp, perhaps for the first time, that theirs is not the only valid way to live. Visiting other countries can help us to understand the impacts that our lives exert on other people's.

Like almost everything else, travelling is much harder to do the right way than the wrong way. We must collectively reduce the number of flights we take, but as flights become cheaper and other forms of travel more expensive, this becomes increasingly difficult. Perhaps we should try to reverse the trends of the past few years, and either travel closer to home or take longer, less frequent breaks, which would enable us both to fly less and to engage more effectively with the people we visit. We should read as much as we can before we go and try to learn the rudiments of the local language, so that when we get there we can discover things for ourselves, rather than allowing intermediaries to tell us only what they want us to hear.

Travelling, like all other forms of consumption, is not a neutral activity. Everything we do affects other people, everything we own is taken from someone else. If you can't travel carefully, don't travel at all. ❧

GEORGE MONBIOT is a columnist for the 'Guardian' newspaper and author of 'Poisoned Arrows: an Investigative Journey through Indonesia', 'Amazon Watershed' and 'No Man's Land: an Investigative Journey through Kenya and Tanzania'. He helped to found The Land Is Ours campaign.

The ethical traveller
by David Bellamy

NOMADS TRAVEL IN ORDER TO MAKE A LIVING from harsh landscapes, conquerors and business people to search for power and resources, holidaymakers to escape the monotony of the workplace. Adventurers, backpackers and Grand-Tourers travel because they have to. Theirs is the quest for knowledge, a quest to be worldly-wise.

It is somewhat awe-inspiring to realise that many areas which were marked as *terra incognita* on the maps of my youth are now stop-overs on regular tour itineraries. So much so that the two-edged sword of tourism now hangs heavily over every aspect of the heritage of this world.

If it had not been for the spotlight which has been turned onto these special regions by Grand-Tourers, past and present, the threat, to coin a phrase, of 'Costa-Brava-isation' would not be there. Yet it is equally true to say that without those spotlights of interest and concern, much of their heritage could have been lost through apathy and ignorance.

Whatever regrets we weavers of travellers' tales may have, I believe the die is now cast. Tourism is the world's fastest growing industry and the only hope for much of our heritage, both natural and people-made, lies within the wise use of its tourist potential.

A row of toilets at Everest base camp, or the importation of food to service tourists in Bali, don't make for confidence in the sustainability of the industry, unless either the tourist industry grows up and shoulders all its responsibilities, or the expectation of all travellers sinks to the current norm of home entertainment: a diet of soaps and game shows.

Fortunately, there are some bright lights at the end of the tunnel. At one end are well-appointed and -run establishments like South Africa's Sun City. There, a fun oasis has been created out of what was degraded veldt. Many thousands of local jobs have been created and an adjacent area has been restocked with game both big and small. It packs the tourists in, corralling them where they can do little harm to local culture. The only really negative effect is the use of fossil fuel and too much water but, living up to its name, it could become solar-powered and water-wise. At the other end of the spectrum of caring holidays are groups like Earthwatch and Coral Cay Conservation, where customers pay to be trained and then work hard on scientific research. Furthermore, a recent study of caravan parks, not usually renowned for their eco-friendliness, revealed that some had already taken up the eco-challenge and were putting their houses into green order, caring not only for their customers but for the local community, wildlife and wider environment.

Unfortunately there is also much bad news, but that is where *you* all come in, for there is an immense amount of work to be done. Attitudes are changing, but is it fast enough with 1.3 billion Chinese about to be industrialised? If only ten per cent of them had the funds to travel, that would make an extra 130 million tourists.

If all of them decided that they must visit the English Lakes in their travelling lifetime, that would mean an extra 2.6 million visitors a year in Cumbria. Could they be accommodated? The answer from the industry is "yes". But at what cost to Wordsworth's 'open air university'?

One thing the whole industry must do, and fast, is realise that its success depends on other people's resources, landscapes and lifestyles, so they must help pay for their upkeep. They must help create local jobs, pay for local infrastructure, give more than they get. If they don't, the resource will eventually collapse.

As you lap up the challenges of pushing back the bounds of your personally unknown lands, and discovering these pearls of heritage for yourselves, remember they are only there thanks to the natural living systems on which we all depend.

You are the ambassadors of everything that the concerned traveller should be. Set the golden example. Respect local customs and buy only local craft goods made from sustainable resources, and always put as much as you can into the local economy. Be careful where you put your tripod and your feet. Flowers have power, you know. Leave only ripples of good will – and if you see an operator disobeying national or local rules, refuse his services. Thank you for caring. ❧

PROFESSOR DAVID BELLAMY is one of the world's leading environmentalists. He has championed the cause through television appearances, books, campaigns, and his own charity, The Conservation Foundation.

The world impact of tourism
by Sir Crispin Tickell

THE BIG PROBLEM ABOUT TOURISM IS THE OTHER TOURISTS. We see yet another boatload in motorised canoes in the wide waters of the Amazon; yet more louts demanding lager and chips in Mediterranean villages; yet another tourist procession between endangered species in the Galapagos Islands; yet more feet along the ever-widening trails that expose the mountain rocks; yet another cruise liner pouring people like an ant army on to white Caribbean beaches or even whiter Antarctica; yet more Land Rover tracks across the African savannah. We love tourism and we hate it.

The problem is relatively new. As with the industrial revolution some 250 years ago, it was the British who started it. In the early days travel abroad was the preserve of the rich, who did it to enlarge their education and enjoy exotic pleasures. With the new wealth generated by business and industry, it moved rapidly down the social scale. While the Duke of Wellington was against railways because they gave the lower orders ideas above their station,

Thomas Cook organised the first rail excursion from Leicester to Loughborough, for a shilling. But it was only in the lifetime of present generations that tourism became the world's biggest industry, with the impacts and consequences of industrial development: the generation of wealth and employment, the opening of minds to new horizons, the pleasures of new ways of life, the impact on the environment, consumption of natural resources, production of wastes and pollutants, and not least effects on the cultural attitudes of all in contact with it.

It is worth looking at some of the figures. Tourism accounts for over six per cent of world gross national product. Employing 200 million people, it accounts for eight per cent of the world's work force. In 2002 there were 715 million tourists, and this figure could exceed 1 billion by 2010. Some countries have become dependent on tourism for the good health of their economies: they range from Egypt, Spain, Jamaica and Kenya to the islands of the Caribbean and the Pacific. Some of the environment in such countries has been radically changed as a result.

There has been a substantial diversion of resources to tourist use. This is particularly important in countries short of water. Some figures produced by the United Nations Food and Agriculture Organisation illustrate the problem. Fifteen thousand cubic metres of water can irrigate one hectare of high-yielding modern rice; support 100 nomads and 450 cattle for three years; maintain 100 rural families for three years and 100 urban families for two years; or meet the needs of 100 guests in a tourist hotel for 55 days. The cost of meeting tourist needs, whether in terms of clearing land for golf courses, building major works of infrastructure, producing specialised foods, disposing of wastes and pollution and the rest, are immeasurably large. The cultural impact is also beyond measurement. I remember my shock when, wearing academic dress at Oxford, I was the subject of tourist curiosity with flashbulbs. For once I was at one with the Matabele guide or the Amazonian Indian (who reasonably charge for having their photographs taken). Like seeing television or hearing radio programmes from another world, tourists generate unrealisable expectations and consequent frustration in others.

Yet the right to travel has become an icon of liberty, especially for those under oppressive regimes. So it should be. But rights carry obligations, and if tourism is not to be like the Indian goddess Kali, the creator of wealth and at the same time the destroyer of what generated it, we need to see how tourism can be brought into balance, particularly in relation to its impact on the environment.

What can we do? I believe that the first requirement in this, as in so many other environmental matters, is to establish true costs, and make sure that they are met. It has been well said that markets are marvellous at fixing prices but incapable of recognising costs. Some time ago a brave attempt was made to establish the true costs of natural services, ranging from the fertility of the soil to its ability to absorb wastes within the natural ecosystem of which humans are a tiny part. Although the results were approximate, they are very interesting: the average works out at about $33 trillion a year, while the world's gross national product is less than $30 trillion a year. A good example is the price of coal. In no country does it include the cost of the effects of burning it, whether on human health, on buildings or on the chemistry of the atmosphere. The same goes for transport.

It is not easy to establish environmental costs. There is no generally accepted methodology. Energy prices are everywhere distorted by subsidies, tax breaks and the rest. A particular perversion is the lack of any tax on aviation fuel. It has become cheaper to convey people as well as materials by air than to use other means of transport, with effects throughout the economy. Air traffic contributes carbon to the atmosphere, and is changing the character of the skies. Much air travel is now tourist related, particularly in the low cost airlines.

Another perversion is that little of the wealth generated by tourism goes to the people who live on the spot. This means that many local communities resent tourism, and in sensitive environmental areas have little incentive to protect and conserve their surroundings. If local people are to identify themselves with the good health of their own environment, then they must see most of the return from it. Individual tourists could make a big difference by spending their foreign currency on goods and services bought directly from the local communities.

At present most fees charged for admission to National Parks or other areas of conservation are derisory. They scarcely cover the most elementary requirements of conservation. In a way tourists rent other people's environments for brief periods, and should be ready to pay a fair price for them. This in turn requires stronger local control. Nothing is more important than control of numbers. This can be done relatively easily in such isolated places as the Galapagos Islands, Machu Picchu in Peru, or Bhutan in the Himalayas, but control elsewhere, notably in our own Lake District or the Scottish highlands, has been ineffective. Many feel that the natural environment or ecosystem should come for free, without realising that nothing is for free. The human threat to the natural world continues to increase almost everywhere. The recent Millennium Ecosystem Assessment concluded that 60 per cent of the ecosystem services evaluated were either being degraded or being used unsustainably.

I am sure that the tourist industry is already aware of these problems. But so far there are few signs that they are being taken as seriously as they deserve. So long as the philosophy is primarily commercial, with the usual stuff about competitive markets, economic growth and promotion of mass movements of people, things are not likely to change, whatever the gloss put on them. True environmental costing has to enter in at all points. As a committed traveller and tourist, I am ready to pay for what I enjoy, and others should be ready to do so too.

Just as the industrial revolution did much good, but created multiple problems for the good health of our planet, so its product, tourism, risks doing likewise. Indeed it is already doing so, and things could get worse before they get better. There is a simple principle we should always bear in mind. Do not kill the goose that lays the golden eggs. ❧

SIR CRISPIN TICKELL is one of the founders of the environmental movement. His seminal work was 'Climate Change and World Affairs'. He is Director of the Green College Centre for Environmental Policy and Understanding at Oxford, and Chancellor of the University of Kent. He was formerly British Ambassador to the United Nations, and Warden of Green College, Oxford.

Can tourism save the planet?
by Kevin Fitzgerald

TOURISM IS LIKE FIRE: YOU CAN COOK YOUR DINNER ON IT, but if you are not careful it will burn your house down. That's not the most profound of statements, but it serves as a reminder of the contradictions which surround global tourism. Climate change, pollution, multi-national corporate greed and many other issues might lead us to cancel all future travel, but we should consider the devastating impact of aborted tourist trips on the local populations of post-tsunami Sri Lanka and post-bombing Bali, for example, to bring matters back into focus. Perhaps awareness of some of the economic, environmental and cultural facts, coupled with a quiet determination to influence where we can, will offer some hope.

Economic reasons in favour of tourism begin with employment. The World Travel and Tourism Council estimates that some 200 million people around the world are employed in the industry, a figure generally predicted to double by the year 2020. Ten per cent of global domestic product is estimated to come from the industry, and it provides the main source of foreign exchange for one third of developing nations. Providing income and infrastructure to local populations in many of the world's poorest places, as these figures demonstrate is possible, are firm and positive reasons for us to consider that tourism can be a force for good in the world.

The bulk of the tourism industry is represented currently by global travel agencies and tour operators. These are focused on maximising their profits, which they achieve through 'vertical integration', where all elements of the holiday package are owned or controlled by the same company. This mantra of the last ten years or so has led to bookings being made in a travel agency, which reserves seats on a plane, going to, typically, a Spanish hotel, on an all-inclusive package, with tour-op reps waiting to take further money for day-trips, ensuring that all profits remain with the originating travel company.

Clearly, this type of tourism does not have much of a positive impact on the local economy or population. Such an extreme example of poor practice is already being challenged, in our free economy, by the 'dis-intermediation' (self-packaging, or dynamic packaging) stimulated by use of the internet. Even some of the Spanish tourist authorities realise that their model is not sustainable in the long term, as tourists are becoming more discerning and local communities and environments have been destroyed. They are beginning to re-create their tourist model to be more attractive to tourists for the long term.

Organisations such as Tourism Concern (www.tourismconcern.org.uk) have long campaigned for tour operators to take greater consideration of the needs of local communities when managing their operations. They have even produced a list of ten points for us to reflect on, entitled 'Avoid Guilt Trips'.

We have to be realistic and realise that most tourists only take a two-week annual holiday, with their family, and their priority is to ensure that their children have a good time. So, although the Tourism Concern list is helpful, I would suggest that a list of ten questions to put to our travel agents and tour operators each time we book, might exert a more direct sort of pressure. These questions will need to focus on 'community tourism' and ensure that local businesses are given the maximum opportunity to benefit from incoming tourists, rather than tour operators imprisoning them in the golden handcuffs of the all-inclusive package.

The environmental impact of the tourist industry ranges from fuel consumption to sewage. There's no escaping the fact that every flight we take emits carbon dioxide, water vapour and oxides of nitrogen and sulphur, contributing heavily to the problem of global warming. Even if one were to believe in a conspiracy of Exxon and the Bush administration to defeat the Kyoto protocols, the recent Gleneagles G8 summit gives us some ray of hope, as the US president finally admitted that human activity has a role in climate change.

Radical changes in fuel for our air transport are some way off, but in the meantime, we should consider making up for the impact with 'CO2 sinks'. It is possible to calculate the number of air miles flown, and how many trees should be planted to compensate for this. A number of organisations offer this service, and www.carbonneutral.com has a very interesting calculation table. To give just one example, a return flight to Sydney will take 12 trees 30 years to absorb the incremental CO2, which will cost about £25 to plant. Maybe we should consider encouraging airlines to offer this 'upgrade' facility.

Unlike aviation technology, more immediately tangible advances have been made in the production of wind and solar electricity, water recyling and sewage filtration. But just because an establishment labels itself as 'eco' does not mean that it is not allowing its sewage waste to filter 'naturally' into local marshlands. A particularly interesting development has just been installed at Expo 2005 in Aichi, Japan, which takes the high-volume sewage of that site and through the services of micro-organisms, the bio-toilets render wastewater reusable.

My personal ideal, to bring real benefits to local communities, is to emulate some of the lodges springing up in the Masai lands of East Africa. Some of these lodges are built entirely out of sustainable local materials, by local people, all waste products are naturally re-cycled, the management and staff are drawn from the local population and the profits are paid entirely into the local community.

Whilst accepting that this nirvana is not going to be globally rolled out tomorrow, creating a list of issues which are important to us, and challenging each aspect of our travel plans with their compliance, would be a few moments of time well spent.

Cultural interaction is, perhaps, the most important way in which tourism can save the planet. After 9/11, the Oxford academic and evolutionary biologist Richard Dawkins declared that 'the most dangerous weapon in history is a mind brainwashed by the prospect of eternal bliss'. And this comment is just as applicable to the Inquisition of medieval times as it is to today's Muslim (or Christian) fundamentalism. The sustainable way to combat religious extremists is to promote respect and understanding for the hugely varied cultures of the world.

At a personal level this means making more effort to seek out 'homestays' when we travel, and to actively engage with locals rather than treating them as quaint photo opportunities. To offer a recent personal example, when travelling recently in Kerala, rather than stay in a package hotel, with the 'inclusive' rice boat tour, we made an extra effort to select a homestay. This meant staying in the family's guest room, eating in their dining room and benefiting from their enhanced local knowledge; we were the only foreigners in the local snake-temple, and because we were alone, rather than accompanied by a guide, a local man made the effort to explain the ceremonies and traditions.

The real benefit of this arrangement was not our 'authentic' tourist experience, nor even the money we paid to the local family, but in the conversations we had with our host family and the others we met, where we enquired, discussed and challenged each other's beliefs and cultures. And all parties left with a smile and nod of understanding. We cannot all resolve the Palestinian issue (and thereby bring about world peace!), but we can make a difference at grass roots level.

I conclude that a combination of respect and pressure will help the tourism industry to save the planet. Proponents of eco- or community tourism have urged, when we travel, that we should leave nothing more than a footprint and take nothing more than a photograph. I would suggest that we should leave an impression of respect and take home a new friendship. Realistically, we are not all going to join pressure groups, but we can all write a list of 'pressure questions' which we can use when talking to airlines and travel agents – the message will get through. My personal choice would be 'Can I upgrade to the carbon offset fare please?' ❧

KEVIN FITZGERALD is the Managing Director of Rough Guides.

The future of the travel industry
by Steve Allen

WE ALL LOVE TO TRAVEL, TO EXPLORE NEW PLACES and enjoy new experiences. And we'd all love to do much more, time and money permitting. It's no wonder that the tourism industry is the largest employer in the world today. In the UK our appetite for travel remains as healthy as ever, boosted by attractive prices and ease of access.

The travel industry is changing fast, in terms of driving change as well as responding to it. We live in the 'instant era', with information available at the touch of a button, and travel companies are responding in a number of ways.

Looking back

It wasn't that long ago that some of us booked most of our travel with our local high street travel agent who in turn organised the necessities with a tour operator.

While this is still a popular way to arrange a holiday, there's no doubt that it accounts for a much smaller proportion of our travel today. The Eighties and Nineties saw the emergence of large travel agency chains such as Lunn Poly, Pickfords and Thomas Cook, owned by increasingly dominant tour operators who also owned charter airlines.

These 'vertically integrated' companies, as they were known, benefited from economies of scale with each part of the holiday run as a profit centre. The four main companies, Thomson, Airtours (now known as MyTravel), First Choice and Thomas Cook also embarked on a number of acquisitions of smaller, specialist tour operators – companies that focused on particular types of holiday and destination. They recognised that increasingly consumers were looking for something more than the standard beach holiday fare that they had developed into the staple diet of millions. They knew too that they did not have the brand reputation or skills to easily migrate into these new growth areas.

As the new millennium dawned, the UK had over 1,000 tour operators and some 7,000 travel agents. The internet was taking off, with many new kids on the block as well as the established companies hopping online. As the larger companies sought greater control of their sales, they directed more business through their in-house travel agencies, directionally selling in many cases. Clear polarisation developed – the big boys selling through their agencies, and other channels, with the rest selling through increasingly specialist, independent agencies as well as direct to the consumer.

Meanwhile, customers were growing in confidence. Travel abroad had become the norm for the majority, familiarity with overseas destinations had grown, and with the proliferation of media coverage, we were all becoming experts on travel worldwide. The rapid expansion of the no-frills carriers selling direct to consumers meant that our options for travel grew, and our buying behaviour changed. Throw in the internet, and the associated information explosion, and suddenly we could in theory do it all ourselves. And many did.

Looking around today

As with most areas of business, innovative and entrepreneurial people create and build companies around their ideas and products. Travel has been no exception. There are still well over 1,000 tour operators in the UK offering pretty much everything under the sun. We now have no-frills carriers flying from virtually every UK airport and competing against revitalised scheduled airlines, albeit that a large number have failed over the last few years. The number of travel agencies has fallen to nearer 6,000 and in the case of the big four they have been renamed. You can now buy a Thomson holiday from a Thomson shop and fly there on a Thomson aeroplane.

It's a marketer's dream in terms of 'brand recognition', and one that also brings a smile to the accountants' faces with the reduced costs of communication flowing through to the bottom line. But it is certainly not to everyone's taste or needs. The internet plays a very important role in providing information whenever and wherever we are. We have the tools to make bookings online if we want, and this business is growing fast. Travel companies have embraced the web, as it provides a relatively low cost of distribution or sale. In some cases, notably in the no-frills airline sector, virtually all bookings are made online, and with the rapid growth of this form of travel we have been encouraged to use the web, thereby shaping our buying behaviour for other forms of travel.

The industry has matured, from a business perspective, and, arguably, not before time. Today the big four are either public companies in their own right, or owned by larger corporations. Profit is now king, and with low margins, scale is being sought through geographical expansion. German companies now own both Thomson and Thomas Cook, each with a significant pan-European travel reach. MyTravel emerged in 2005 from a significant financial restructuring, while First Choice has spent the last five years acquiring many businesses here in the UK, in Europe and in North America. Success is measured by increasing shareholder value, and size is key.

At the same time, more and more of us want greater flexibility and independence in our travel arrangements. We are also looking to get more from our time off, whether in terms of new activities and sports that we can learn or watch, or experiences that enrich the moment. Time is precious and never more so. And while technology can do many things for us, there is no substitute for good personal service to ensure we get the right solution.

What are the key trends that will shape the industry of tomorrow? Of course there are many, and these affect the travel industry at different levels. At the macro level, the economic environment determines how much we might spend on our holidays. The prevailing view is that the rate of UK economic growth will slow in the second half of this decade. We will also be influenced by concerns for our well-being, both from a healthy living perspective as well as from a risk-averse standpoint. How safe our travel might be, and the threat of terrorism, affects our choice of destinations, and will be an ever-present consideration in our planning.

Also at a macro level, we will increasingly consider environmental and human factors such as pollution, quality of infrastructure, the well-being of the indigenous population and the impact our travelling makes on our fragile world. More and more of our children are taking time out to travel, often in association with a charity or an environmental project as part of a gap year. Their experiences, often in less well-known parts of the world, will influence their thinking about where and how they will travel in the future.

Meanwhile, with a growing recognition that humankind's behaviour does need to adjust, given the climate changes we are now witnessing as well as predicting, it is possible that taxation will be used to try to contain the amount of travel we undertake. Of course there will be great variability worldwide in terms of the likely effectiveness of such measures, given the variation in economic prosperity and the desire of the less well-off countries to emulate those nations that appear to have so much more. We will continue to want to travel, to explore places we have never visited and to do things we have not done before. And with more of us living longer and with more wealth available than in previous generations, our appetite for travel will surely grow.

The number of second_homes abroad continues to increase as our horizons expand. Our 'living space' has changed so much in the last 25 years, and is set to expand further as more of us recognise that we should try to work to live rather than the other way around. A related trend will be the gradual increase in the number of career breaks offered, designed to retain good staff while fulfilling the individual's desire to see more of the world, to do something different and in many cases a combination of the two. This will gradually become an established employee benefit, particularly in larger organisations.

More of us today are travelling further afield. Europe continues to be the most popular region, although the rate of growth is slowing. The Americas is a growth region, and the Caribbean is now firmly established as a key sunshine destination, while both Central and South America are emerging as rapidly growing areas. Expect Canada to grow in popularity too. Africa, the Indian subcontinent, Asia and Australasia are all expanding at differing rates, and Australia and New Zealand continue to be the aspirational destinations that most of us want to visit. Even though air travel is no faster, we are travelling further.

How will the travel industry respond? The big will get bigger and less personal whilst the small will prosper and thrive. To continue to satisfy shareholders, the large travel companies need to grow and to reduce their costs of operation. This means going global whilst harnessing the cheapest means of production and distribution possible. We will see the likes of Expedia and Cendant, two large American corporations, increasing their presence worldwide. There will be further consolidation of companies within Europe, helped too by the emergence of new source markets as the eastern European countries prosper. Expect to see airline mergers as regulations are relaxed and pressures grow to achieve improved returns for shareholders.

Meanwhile, the smaller companies will thrive, based on their in-depth knowledge of the destinations and types of travel, and by developing a real affinity with their customers. The larger predators may snap some up, but it is certain that others will rise to take their place.

The traditional definitions of tour operator, travel agent, scheduled, charter and no-frills airlines will be less valid as blurring takes place. In their place, just think airlines and travel companies.

The internet will be an increasingly important tool for all types of travel company, especially the larger commodity-style businesses, although for the smaller enterprises personal and attentive service offline will set them apart. While we all want to be efficient and buy our travel well, there is no doubt that 'web fatigue' will affect many of us where time is short and certainty needed. Policing the web will become a major issue, as will financial protection.

Too many people buy travel today in the belief that their money is protected should the company fail or not deliver. Unfortunately, this is not always the case, and the degree of protection is much less now than just ten years ago. New legislation and effective policing are needed to protect us and our hard earned cash.

Airline manufacturers will add a further dimension of polarity, as the first super jumbos emerge for longhaul flying (such as the Airbus A380) and smaller, ultra-efficient aircraft such as the new Boeing 'Dreamliner' are built. And at the luxury end, more people will use private jets for business and leisure travel.

There is no replacement for Concorde yet, although I would be very surprised if a super-fast alternative is not planned in the medium term. Fuel costs will be relatively more significant than in recent years and will influence the design of future aircraft. By 2010, some 130 million passengers are forecast to fly on UK airlines, up 13 per cent compared to 2005. The no-frills carriers will consolidate as growth slows as a result of over-capacity and competition from the traditional carriers. At the same time, the channel tunnel will see train traffic grow, although the cross-channel ferries will continue to decline.

More of us will be taking cruises, trying out new adventures and making journeys by train, especially on established scenic routes in key destinations, thereby avoiding the hurly-burly of congested roads and busy airports.

And what is the future for my own company, WEXAS? Not for us the numbers game. The company will maintain its focus on providing a quality, personal service from travel experts who really know the destinations and who ensure that members get great value. Put simply, WEXAS is a specialist travel company that creates individual solutions for its members. If you're already a member, you've made the right choice. If not, WEXAS would relish the opportunity to look after your travel needs in the years ahead, wherever in the world you choose to go. ❧

STEVE ALLEN is the Managing Director of WEXAS, the traveller's club.

Afterword: From our archive

THE TRAVELLER'S HANDBOOK has been in print for three decades. In that time, the world of travel has changed enormously. But some things stay the same, and we reprint below some of the *Handbook*'s past articles that have stood the test of time – either because they are timeless, or because they are so deliciously of their own era.

Travel by camel
by René Dee

In this mechanised and industrial epoch, the camel does not seem to be an obvious choice of travelling companion when sophisticated cross-country vehicles exist for the toughest of terrains. Add to this the stockpile of derisory and mocking myths, truths and sayings about the camel and one is forced to ask the question: why use camels at all? Purely as a means of getting from A to B when time is the most important factor, the camel should not even be considered. As a means of transport for scientific groups who wish to carry out useful research in the field, the camel is limiting. It can be awkward and risky transporting delicate equipment and specimens. However, for the individual, small group and expedition wishing to see the desert as it should be seen, the camel is an unrivalled means of transport.

Go safely in the desert

From my own personal point of view, the primary reason must be that, unlike any motorised vehicle, camels allow you to integrate completely with the desert and the people within it – something it is impossible to do at 80 kmph enclosed in a 'tin can'. A vehicle in the desert can be like a prison cell, and the constant noise of the engine tends to blur all sense of the solitude, vastness and deafening quiet that is so intrinsic to the experience.

Travel by camel allows the entire pace of life to slow down from a racy 80 kmph to a steady 6.5 kmph, enabling you to unwind, take in and visually appreciate the overall magnificence and individual details of your surroundings. Secondly, camels do, of course, have the ability to reach certain areas that are inaccessible to vehicles, especially through rocky and narrow mountain passes, although camels are not always happy on this terrain and extreme care has to be taken to ensure they do not slip or twist a leg. They are as sensitive as they appear insensitive.

Thirdly, in practical terms, they cause far fewer problems where maintenance, breakdown and repairs are concerned. No bulky spares or expensive mechanical equipment are needed for repairs. Camels do not need a great deal of fuel and can exist adequately (given that they are not excessively burdened) for five to ten days without water. Camels go on and on and on and on until they die; and then one has the option of eating them, altogether far better tasting than a Michelin tyre.

Lastly, camels must be far more cost effective if you compare them directly with vehicles, although this depends on whether your intended expedition/journey already includes a motorised section. If you fly direct to your departure point, or as near as possible to it, you will incur none of the heavy costs related to transporting a vehicle, not to mention the cost of buying it. If the camel trek is to be an integral portion of a motorised journey, then the cost saving will not apply as, of course, hire fees for camels and guides will be additional.

In many ways, combining these two forms of travel is ideal and a very good way of highlighting my primary point in favour of transport by camel. If you do decide on this combination, make sure you schedule the camel journey for the very end of your expedition and that the return leg by vehicle is either minimal or purely functional for I can guarantee that after a period of ten days or more travelling slowly and gently through the desert by camel, your vehicle will take on the characteristics of a rocket ship and all sense of freedom, enquiry and interest will be dulled to the extreme. An overwhelming sense of disillusion and disinterest will prevail. Previously exciting sights, desert towns and Arab civilisation, will pall after such intense involvement with the desert, its people and its lifestyle.

First steps

For the individual or group organiser wanting to get off the beaten track by camel, the first problem is to find them and to gather every bit of information possible about who owns the camels. Are they for hire, for how much, what equipment/ stores/provisions are included (if any) and, lastly, what are the guides/owners capable of and are they willing to accompany you? It is not much good arriving at Tamanrasset, Timbouctou or Tindoug without knowing some, if not all, of the answers to these questions. Good pre-departure research is vital, but the problem is that 90 per cent of the information won't be found from any tourist office, embassy, library or travel agent. Particularly if you're considering a major journey exclusively by camel, you'll probably have to undertake a preliminary fact-finding recce to your proposed departure point to establish contacts among camel owners and guides. It may well be that camels and/or reliable guides do not exist in the area where you wish to carry out your expedition.

I would suggest, therefore, that you start first with a reliable source of information, such as the Royal Geographical Society, which has expedition reports and advice that can be used as a primary source of reference, including names and addresses to write to for up-to-date information about the area that interests you. Up-to-date information is, without doubt, the key to it all. Very often this can be gleaned from the commercial overland companies whose drivers are passing through your area of interest regularly and who may even have had personal experience of the journey you intend to make.

In all the best Red Indian stories, the guide is the all-knowing, all-seeing person in whom total faith is put. However, as various people have discovered to their cost, this is not always such a good idea. Many so-called guides know very little of the desert and its ways. How then to find someone who really does know the route/area, has a sense of desert lore and who preferably owns his best camel? I can only reiterate that the best way to do this is through personal recommendation.

Having found him, put your faith in him, let him choose your camels and make sure that your relationship remains as amicable as possible. You will be living together for many days in conditions that are familiar to him but alien to you, and you need his support. Arrogance does not fit into desert travel, especially from a *nasrani*. Mutual respect and a good rapport are essential.

Pack up your troubles

Once you've managed to establish all this and you're actually out there, what are the dos, don'ts and logistics of travel by camel? Most individuals and expeditions (scientifically orientated or not) will want, I imagine, to incorporate a camel trek within an existing vehicle-led expedition, so I am really talking only of short-range treks of around ten to 15 days' duration, and with a range of up to 400 km. If this is so, you will need relatively little equipment and stores, and it is essential that this is kept to a minimum. Remember that the more equipment you take, the more camels you will need, which will require more guides, which means more cost, more pasture and water, longer delays in loading, unloading, cooking and setting up camp and a longer wait in the morning while the camels are being rounded up after a night of pasturing.

Be prepared also for a very swift deterioration of equipment. In a vehicle you can at least keep possessions clean and safe to a degree, but packing kit onto a camel denies any form of protection, especially since it is not unknown for camels to stumble and fall or to roll you over suddenly and ignominiously if something is not to their liking, such as a slipped load or uncomfortable saddle. My advice is to pack all your belongings in a seaman's kit-bag that can be roped onto the camel's side easily, is pliable, hard-wearing and, because it is soft and not angular, doesn't threaten to rub a hole in the camel's side or backbone. (I have seen a badly placed baggage saddle wear a hole the size of a man's fist into an animal's back.)

If rectangular aluminium boxes containing cameras or other delicate equipment are being carried, make sure that they are well roped on the top of the camel and that there is sufficient padding underneath so as not to cause friction. Moreover, you'll always have to take your shoes off while riding because over a period of hours, let alone days, you could wear out the protective hair on the camel's neck and eventually cause open sores.

Water should be carried around in goat-skin *guerbas* and 20-litre round metal *bidons* which can, again, be roped up easily and hung either side of the baggage camel under protective covers. Take plenty of rope for tying on equipment, saddles etc., and keep one length of 15 metres intact for using at wells where there may be no facilities for hauling up water. Don't take any sophisticated tents either; they will probably be ruined within days and anyway are just not necessary.

I have always used a piece of cotton cloth approximately six metres square, which, with two poles for support front and rear and with sand or boulders at the sides and corner, makes a very good overnight shelter for half a dozen people. Night in the desert can be extremely cold, particularly in the winter, but the makeshift 'tent' has a more important role during the day when it provides shelter for the essential two-hour lunch stop and rest.

The day's schedule

Your daily itinerary and schedule should be geared to the practical implications of travelling by camel. That is to say that each night's stop will, where possible, be in an area where pasture is to be found for the camels to graze. Although one can take along grain and dried dates for camels to eat, normal grazing is also vital. The camels are unloaded and hobbled (two front legs are tied closely together), but you will find they can wander as much as three or four kilometres overnight and there is only one way to fetch them: on foot. Binoculars are extremely useful as spotting camels over such a distance can be a nightmare. They may be hidden behind dunes and not come into view for some time.

Other useful equipment includes goggles for protection in sandstorms, prescription sunglasses and, of course, sun cream. Above all, take comfortable and hard-wearing footwear, for it is almost certain that you will walk at least half the way once you have become fully acclimatised. I would suggest that you take Spanish felt boots or something similar, which are cheap, very light, give ankle support over uneven terrain and are durable and very comfortable.

The one disadvantage of boots by day is that your feet will get very hot, but it's a far better choice than battered, blistered and lacerated feet when one has to keep up with the camel's steady 6.5 kmph. Nomads wear sandals, but if you take a close look at a nomad's foot you will see that it is not dissimilar to the sandal itself, i.e. as hard and tough as leather. Yours resembles a baby's bottom by comparison, so it is essential that you get some heavy walking practice in beforehand with the boots/shoes you intend to wear. If your journey will be a long one, then you could possibly try sandals, as there will be time for the inevitable wearing-in process with blisters, as well as stubbed toes and feet spiked by the lethal acacia thorn.

For clothing, I personally wear a local, free-flowing robe such as the *gandoura*, local pantaloons and *cheche*, a three-metre length of cotton cloth, which can be tied round the head and/or face and neck for protection against the sun. You can also use it as a rope, fly whisk and face protector in sandstorms. In the bitterly cold nights and early mornings of winter desert travel, go to bed with it wrapped around your neck, face and head to keep warm.

If local clothing embarrasses and inhibits you, stick to loose cotton shirts and trousers. Forget your tight jeans and bring loose-fitting cotton underwear. Anything nylon and tight fitting next to the skin will result in chafing and sores. Do, however, also take some warm clothing and blankets, including socks and jumpers. As soon as the sun sets in the desert, the temperature drops dramatically. Catching cold in the desert is unbearable. Colds are extremely common and spread like wildfire. Take a good down sleeping bag and a groundsheet.

Your sleeping bag and blankets can also serve as padding for certain types of camel saddle. In the Western Sahara you will find the Mauritanian butterfly variety, which envelops you on four sides. You're liable to slide back and forth uncomfortably and get blisters unless you pad the saddle. The Tuareg saddle is commonly used in the Algerian Sahara. This is a more traditional saddle, with a fierce-looking forward pommel that threatens man's very manhood should you be thrown forward against it. In Saudi Arabia, female camels are ridden, and seating positions are taken up behind the dromedary's single hump rather than on or forward of it.

Culture shock

Never travel alone in the desert, without even a guide. The ideal group size would be seven group members, one group leader, three guides, 11 riding camels and three baggage camels. The individual traveller should take at least one guide with him and three or four camels.

Be prepared for a mind-blowing sequence of mental experiences, especially if you are not accustomed to the alien environment, company and pace, which can lead to introspection, uncertainty and even paranoia. Travel by camel with nomad guides is the reversal of our normal lifestyle. Therefore it is as important to be mentally prepared for this culture shock as it is to be physically prepared. Make no mistake, travel by camel is hard, physically uncompromising and mentally torturing at times. But a *meharee* satisfactorily accomplished will alter your concept of life and its overall values, and the desert's hold over you will never loosen. ❧

RENÉ DEE *has travelled overland to India and Nepal and led a series of trips to Morocco, specialising in treks by camel and mule.*

Travel by pack animal
by Roger Chapman

THE DONKEY IS THE MOST DESIRABLE BEAST OF BURDEN for the novice and remains the favourite of the more experienced camper – if only because the donkey carries all the traveller's equipment, leaving him free to enjoy the countryside unburdened. Although small and gentle, the donkey is strong and dependable; no pack animal excels him for sure-footedness or matches his character. He makes the ideal companion for children old enough to travel into the mountains or hills, and for the adult who prefers to travel at a pace slow enough to appreciate the scenery, wildlife and wilderness that no vehicle can reach.

The rock climber, hunter, fisherman, scientist or artist who has too much gear to carry into the mountains may prefer to take the larger and faster mule, but if they are sensible, they will practice first on the smaller and more patient donkey. The principles of pack animal management are the same, but the mule is stronger, more likely to kick or bite if provoked, and requires firmer handling than the donkey. The advantage of a mule is obvious. Whereas a donkey can only carry about 50 kg, the mule, if expertly packed, can carry a payload of 100 kg. Although both are good for 24 km a day on reasonable trails, the donkeys will have to be led on foot; whereas mules, which can travel at a good speed, require everyone to be mounted, unless their handlers are fast hikers.

Planning

To determine the number of donkeys needed before a trip, the approximate pack load must be calculated. The stock requirement for a ten-day trip can be calculated by dividing the number of people by two, but taking the higher whole number if the split does not work evenly. Thus, a family of five would take three donkeys. It is difficult to control more than ten donkeys on the trail, so don't use them with a party of 20 or more unless certain individuals are prepared to carry large packs to reduce the number of animals. Mules are usually led by a single hiker or are tied in groups of not more than five animals led by a man on horseback. This is the 'string' of mules often mentioned in Westerns; each lead rope passes through the left-hand breech ring of the preceding animal's harness and is then tied around the animal's neck with a bowline. One or more horses are usually sent out with the pack mules because mules respect and stick close to these 'chaperones'.

Whichever method you decide to use, don't prepare a detailed itinerary before your journey; wait and see how you get on during the first few days, when you should attempt no more than 12–16 km a day. Later you will be able to average 20–24 km, but you should not count on doing more than 24 km a day although it is possible, with early starts and a lighter load, if you really have to.

Campers who use pack animals seldom restrict themselves to the equipment list of a backpacker. There is no need to do so, but before preparing elaborate menus and extensive wardrobes, you would do well to consider the price of hiring a pack animal. The more elaborate and heavy your equipment, the more donkeys or mules there are to hire, load, unload, groom and find pasture for. In selecting your personal equipment you have more freedom – a 'Karrimat', or a larger tent instead of the small 'Basha' – but it should not exceed 12 kg and should be packed into several of those small cylindrical soft bags or a seaman's kit-bag. You can take your sleeping bag as a separate bundle and take a small knapsack for those personal items such as spare sweaters, camera, first aid kit and snacks required during the day. But there are some special items you will require if you are not hiring an efficient guide and handler: repair kit for broken pack saddles and extra straps for mending harnesses. An essential item is a 45 kg spring scale for balancing the sacks or panniers before you load them on the pack animals in the morning. Remember, too, that each donkey/mule will be hired out with a halter, lead rope, tow 'sacks', a pack cover, and a nine-metre pack rope. In addition, there will be pickets and shackle straps, curry combs, frog picks, canvas buckets, tools and possibly ointment or powders to heal saddle sores.

Animal handling

The art of handling pack animals is not a difficult one, but unfortunately you cannot learn it entirely from a book. With surprisingly little experience in this field, the novice soon becomes an expert packer, confident that he can handle any situation that may arise on the trail and, above all, that he has learnt the uncertain science of getting the pack animal to do what he wants it to do. The donkey is more responsive than the mule and is quick to return friendship, especially if he knows he is being well packed, well fed and well rested. The mule tends to be more truculent, angry and resentful until he knows who is in charge. Therefore, an attitude of firmness and consideration towards the animal is paramount.

Perhaps the easiest way to learn the techniques of handling pack animals is to look at a typical day and consider the problems as they arise.

Collecting in the morning: Pack animals can either be let loose, hobbled or picketed during the night. The latter is preferable as even a mule that has its front legs hobbled can wander for miles during the night searching for suitable grass. If the animal is picketed, unloosen the strap around the fetlock that is attached to the picket rope and lead him back to the campsite by the halter. If the animals are loose, you may have to allow a good half hour or so to catch them. Collect the gentle ones first, returning later for the recalcitrant animals. Approach each animal cautiously, talking to him and offering a palmful of oats before grabbing the halter.

Tying up and grooming: Even the gentlest pack animal will need to be tied up to a tree or post before packing. The rope should be tied with a clove hitch at about waist height. Keep the rope short, otherwise the animal will walk round and round the tree as you follow with the saddle. It also prevents him from stepping on or tripping over the rope. It is advisable to keep the animals well apart, but not too far from your pile of packed sacks or panniers.

Often, donkeys in particular, will have a roll during the night, so they require a good work-over with the brush or curry comb to remove dust or caked mud. Most animals enjoy this, but you mustn't forget that one end can bite and the other end can give a mighty kick. Personally, I spend some time stroking the animal around the head and ears, talking to him before I attempt to groom him. Ears are very good indicators of mood. If the ears are upright he is alert and apprehensive, so a few words and strokes will give him confidence; soon the ears will relax and lie back. If the ears turn and stretch right back along his neck, then there is a good chance you are in for trouble. The first time he nips, thump him in the ribs and swear at him. He will soon learn that you do not appreciate this kind of gesture.

Your main reason for grooming is to remove caked dirt, which may cause sores once the animal is loaded. Remove this dirt with a brush and clean rag and, if there is an open wound, apply an antiseptic ointment or sprinkle on boric acid powder, which will help dry it up. Finally, check each hoof quickly to see that no stone or twig has lodged in the soft pad. Lean against the animal, then warn him by tapping the leg all the way down the flank, past the knee to the fetlock before lifting the hoof; otherwise you will never succeed. If there is a stone lodged between the shoe and the hoof, prise it out with a frog pick.

Saddling and loading

Animals are used to being loaded from the left or near side. First you fold the saddle blanket, place it far forward then slide it back into position along the animal's back so that the hair lies smooth. Check that it hangs evenly on both sides, sufficient to protect the flanks from the loaded sacks. Stand behind the mule or donkey – but not too close – and check it before you proceed further. Pick up the pack saddle (two moulded pieces of wood jointed by two cross-trees) and place it on the saddle blanket so it fits in the hollows behind the withers. Tie up the breast strap and rear strap before tying the girth tight. Two people will be required to load the equipment in the soft canvas sacks onto the saddle pack, but it is essential to weigh the sacks before you place them on the cross-trees; they should be within two kg of each other. If the saddle is straight, but one sack is lower than the other, correct the length of the ear loops.

On the trail

Morning is the best time to travel, so you must hit the trail early, preferably before 7 am. At a steady two km an hour, you will be able to cover the majority of the day's journey by the time the sun is at its hottest. This will allow you to spend a good three hours' rest at midday before setting off once more for a final couple of hours ride and the search for a camp-site. Avoid late camps, so start looking by 4 pm.

During the first few days you may have some trouble getting your donkeys or mules to move close together and at a steady pace. One man should walk behind each animal if they are being led and if there are any hold ups, he can apply a few swipes of a willow switch to the hindquarters. It is a waste of time to shout at the animals or threaten them constantly, as it only makes them distrustful and skittish. The notorious stubbornness of the mule or donkey is usually the result of bad handling in the past. Sometimes it is a result of fear or fatigue, but occasionally it is sheer cussedness or an attempt to see how much he can get away with. The only occasion when I could not get a mule moving was travelling across some snow patches in the mountains of Kashmir. Eventually, after losing my temper and lashing him with a switch, I persuaded him to move slowly across the icy surface, where he disappeared into a snow hole. It took us three hours to unload him, pull him out and calm him down before we could re-pack. I learned a good lesson from my lack of awareness of the innate intelligence of the mule.

Understanding

There is no problem with unpacking, which can be done quickly and efficiently. Just remember to place all the equipment neatly together so it is not mixed up. Keep individual saddles, sacks and harnesses close enough together to cover with the waterproof cover in case of rain. Once unloaded, the donkeys can be groomed, watered and led off to the pasture area where they are to be picketed for the night.

Not long ago, I took my wife and two young daughters on a 195 km journey across the Cevennes mountains in south-east France. We followed Robert Louis Stevenson's routes, which he described in his charming little book *Travels With a Donkey*. We took three donkeys – two as pack animals and one for the children to take turns in riding – on a trail which had not changed much over the past hundred years. It made an ideal holiday, and we returned tanned, fitter, enchanted by the French countryside and aware that it was the character of our brave little donkeys that had made our enjoyment complete.

The speed with which the children mastered the technique of pack animal management was encouraging because it allowed us to complete our task with enough time to explore the wilder parts of the mountains and enjoy the countryside at the leisurely pace of our four-footed companions. We also took a hundred flies from one side of the Cevennes to the other, but that is another story. 🙠

ROGER CHAPMAN, MBE,has been involved in many expeditions – down the Blue Nile and Zaire rivers, to Central and South America, to East Greenland with the British Schools Exploration Society, and to Papua New Guinea with Operation Drake.

Espionage and interrogation
by Christopher Portway

B EING SOMETHING OF AN INQUISITIVE JOURNALIST with a penchant for visiting those countries which normal people don't, I have, over the years, developed a new hobby. Some of us collect stamps, cigarette cards or matchboxes. I collect interrogations. And the preliminary to interrogation is, of course, arrest and detention, which makes me, perhaps, a suitable person to dwell a few moments on some of the activities that can land the innocent traveller in prison, as well as the best way of handling matters arising thereof.

In some countries, there are no set rules governing what is and is not a crime. Different regimes have different ways of playing the game, and it's not just cut-and-dried crimes such as robbing a bank or even dealing on the black market that can put you behind bars. Perhaps a brief resumé of some of my own experiences will give you the idea and suggest means of extracting yourself from the clutches of a warped authority.

That nasty word 'espionage' has become a stock accusation, beloved by perverted authority worldwide. Spying covers a multitude of sins and is a most conveniently vague charge to lay against anyone who sees more than is good for him (or her). It is often in dictatorial countries that you have to be most careful, but some other states have picked up on the idea, too. Spying, of a sort, can also be directed against you. In my time, I have been followed by the minions of the secret police forces in Prague and Vladivostok for hours on end. Personally, I quite enjoyed the experience and led them a merry dance through a series of department stores in a vain effort to shake them off. If nothing else, I gave them blisters.

During World War II, to go back a bit, I escaped from a POW camp in Poland through the unwitting courtesy of the German State Railway. The journey came to an abrupt end at Gestapo HQ in Krakow. In post-war years, the then Orient Express carried me, visa-less, into the Stalin-controlled former Czechoslovakia. That journey put me inside as a compulsory guest of the STB, the former Czech secret police. I have met minor inconveniences of a similar nature in countries such as Russia, Albania and Yugoslavia, as well as several Middle Eastern nations, but it was only in the 1970s that I bumped into real trouble again – in Idi Amin's Uganda. Interrogations *à la* James Bond....

The venues of all my interrogations have been depressingly similar. In Kampala, for instance, it consisted of a bare, concrete-walled office containing a cheap desk, a hard-backed chair or two, a filing cabinet, a telephone and an askew photograph of Idi Amin. This consistently describes Krakow, Prague and Kishinev, except that in Nazi days nobody would have dreamt of an askew Fuhrer. Prague boasted an anglepoise lamp, but then communist methods of extracting information always did border on the cinematic.

Methods of arrest or apprehension obviously vary with the circumstances. For the record, in World War II, I was handed over to the Gestapo by a bunch of Bavarian squaddies who could find no excuse for my lobbing a brick through the window of a bakery after curfew. In Czechoslovakia I was caught crossing a railway bridge in a frontier zone and, with five guns aligned to one's navel, heroics are hard to come by. In the Soviet Union it was simply a case of my being caught with my trousers down in a 'soft-class' toilet while in possession of an out-of-date visa valid only for a place where I was not. And in Uganda there was no reason at all, beyond an edict from Idi that stipulated a policy of "Let's be beastly to the British".

But in Uganda, the line of questioning was different. It wasn't so much why had I come, but why had I come for so brief a period? The other sticking point was the presence of the young Ugandan law student arrested with me. Being in close confinement in a railway carriage for 24 hours, we had become travelling companions, which, coupled with my suspiciously brief stay, spelled 'dirty work at the crossroads' to the Ugandan authorities.

Upon rummaging about in our wallets and pockets, they found bits of paper on which we had scribbled our exchanged addresses. It had been the student's idea and a pretty harmless one but, abruptly, I was made aware how small inconsistencies can be blown up into a balloon of deepest suspicion. All along I maintained I hardly knew the guy. (Which reminds me that the Gestapo, too, had an irksome habit of looking for a scapegoat among the local populace.) Then we came to the next hurdle. "How is it your passport indicates you are a company director but this card shows you are a journalist?" To explain that I was once a company director and had retained the title in my passport in preference to the sometimes provocative 'journalist' would only have complicated matters. So I offered the white lie that I was still a company director and only a journalist in my spare time.

In another of Kampala's Police HQ interrogation rooms, all my proffered answers had to be repeated at dictation speed. It was partly a ruse, of course, to see if the second set matched the first – and I was going to be damn sure it did.

And, you know, there comes a moment when you actually begin to believe that you are a spy or whatever it is they are trying to suggest. It creeps up in some harmless answer to a question. In Kampala I felt the symptoms and resolved to keep my answers simple – and remember them for the second time round.

For instance: "What school did you attend?" I named the one I was at the longest. There was no need to mention the other two.

My regimental association membership card came up for scrutiny. "What rank were you?" I was asked. —"Corporal," I replied, giving the lowest rank I had held. Pride alone prevented me from saying "Private". —"Which army?" came the further enquiry. I had to admit that it was British.

Every now and again, I would put in a bleat about having a train to catch – more as a cornerstone of normality than a hope of catching it. And finally, in most interrogations, there does come a point when there is a lull in proceedings during which you can mount a counter-attack. The "Why-the-hell-am-I-here? What-crime-am-I-supposed-to-have-committed?" sort of thing, which at least raises your morale if not the roof.

Of course, in Nazi Germany such outbursts helped little, because in a declared wartime one's rights are minimal, and the Gestapo had such disgusting methods of upholding theirs. But in the grey world of undeclared wars, the borderline of bloody-mindedness is less well defined. At Kishinev, the KGB had the impertinence to charge me a fiver a day for my incarceration in a filthy room in a frontier unit's barracks. I voiced my indignation loud and clear and eventually won a refund.

In Czechoslovakia, my outburst had a different effect. The interrogator was so bewildered that he raised his eyes to the ceiling long enough for me to pinch one of his pencils. And in the cell that became my home for months, a pencil was a real treasure.

I should add that, in general, the one demand you have a right to make is to be put in touch with your own embassy or consulate. I once wasn't – and it caused an international incident.

I suppose one lesson I ought to have learnt from all this is to take no incriminating evidence, such as press cards, association membership cards, other travellers' addresses and the like. But a few red herrings do so add to the entertainment. ✎

CHRISTOPHER PORTWAY has been a freelance travel writer for over 20 years.

Guide or porter?
by Richard Snailham

THERE IS SOMETHING TIMELESS ABOUT THE PROBLEMS of travel with guides and porters. Stories in Henry Morton Stanley's late-Victorian bestsellers find their echoes today, and it was instructive to learn that a recent Cambridge University Expedition to Sangay in Ecuador had the same problems that I had had on an ill-fated expedition to Sangay ten years before: the local Indians had either refused to take their mules to the agreed objective or simply defected.

Nevertheless, a local guide is often useful, sometimes indispensable. Small boys hover outside the souk in Marrakech and we once spurned them only to become comprehensively lost in the myriad covered alleyways. Rather less useful is the young boy who tags along on the streets of a Third World city with which you might be quite well acquainted. He will get into a conversation with you and then offer to show you the principal sights. Before your tour is finished you may find you are sponsoring him through school.

Sometimes a guide is obligatory, as at a French château – and generally provides good value. Where they are not, a judgement has to be made. In wild, sparsely populated, ill-mapped country, I would say that a guide was essential, especially where you do not speak the prevailing language and the local people do not speak yours. In Samburu country recently, with a map that was far too large in scale, I needed our camel handlers to steer us to the objective.

How to get the best

Fix your price. If a journey is involved and you require any form of transport for any great length of time, it is best to find out the cost in advance – if only to minimise the shock of the often inordinate sum asked. Guides have no meters and rarely are they governed by any regulations. The price agreed at the outset, especially if there are other guides in the offing (and thus a choice), is often substantially less than that demanded at the end. Even in Nairobi I recently fell into the trap of failing to establish the price before taking a taxi to the outer suburbs (and was still mightily stung, even after an unedifying argument at the journey's end). Before you clinch the deal, bargaining is generally possible and is often expected.

Pick the right man. Your selection of the right guide is very important. Unfortunately this often involves a snap judgement based on appearances. Women often seem to have better intuitive judgement than men, I find, and a few quick questions on the spot before departure are valuable in ensuring you have a good man. For how things can go wrong, read Geoffrey Moorhouse's *The Fearful Void*. Some unscrupulous guides lead their charges into remote regions and then refuse to conduct them back without a big bonus.

Never entirely trust a guide's navigational ability. He will not usually admit to being lost, but can often become so. Try to keep a check on distance covered, note all prominent landmarks and take their bearings from identifiable points on your route and the time that you took them. Avoid questions like "Is it far?" or "Will we get there tonight?" Guides often have more inclination to please their employers than to tell the sometimes painful truth, and the answers to these two questions will invariably be "no" and "yes".

Problems with porters

The days of mammoth expeditions, undertaken with armies of porters, are probably over. I was once manager and paymaster of a constantly changing team of about 130 porters in Nepal, but smaller, faster-moving assaults are now the order of the day and they normally require less manpower. The problems are otherwise the same, however, and most have been hinted at above.

Here are a few further suggestions:

- Be totally familiar with the local currency and its exchange rate before you embark on any negotiation.
- Try and secure the services of a local 'minder' to help firm up the local *bundobust* (a useful Hindi word, meaning 'logistical arrangements'). On a recent camel safari I took a young NCO from the Kenya General Service Unit who was excellent in his dealings with porters and headmen. Policemen, soldiers, students have all served me well in this role.
- Remember that guides and porters have to have food and shelter. Who is providing this, you or they? You may have to offer advance payment and provide for their journeys home.
- This goes for their animals, too. Camels often have to carry their own forage across deserts and yaks carry theirs up the last stages of the climb to the Everest base camp. Remember that they always travel home faster than they travel out.
- A head porter or *sirdar* is often a good idea if you have a large number in your party. He will be worth his extra pay.
- Only pay a portion of the agreed fee at the outset. Keep the balance in your money belt until you get there.
- Guides should, of course, lead, but porters should take up position in the middle of your party. This prevents 'disappearances' and enables you to react if a porter becomes ill or tired.

The brighter side

Finally, if in doubt, take a guide or porter rather than try to struggle on without them. They add colour to the whole enterprise, are generally honest and good hearted and could well end up firm friends. It is worth while taking a few presents with you as a mark of gratitude. Some of your own kit will be much appreciated. Otherwise, penknives, folding scissors and cigarettes go down well. British commemorative coins, postcards of the Queen, empty screw-top tobacco tins – even my old shirts – have proved acceptable gifts. 🐾

RICHARD SNAILHAM is a veteran expeditionary and a co-founder of the Scientific Exploration Society.

The television traveller
by Clive Anderson

MAKING TELEVISION DOCUMENTARIES is a great way to travel. Since I have managed occasionally to creep out of the studio and onto the road (and rail and aeroplane), for the purposes of making television programmes, I have been despatched to Hong Kong, China, Mongolia, Hawaii, Cuba, Dominica, Goa,

Calcutta, Kenya, Nigeria, Beirut and a variety of bits of the United States. Not to mention Montreal and Edinburgh to cover comedy festivals, and Bayeux to film a tapestry. Join the BBC, it turns out, and see the world.

Overall, I have enjoyed myself hugely – and I hope some of the programmes have turned out all right as well. But there are some disadvantages. Documentary-making is not one long holiday, nor even one long *Holiday Programme*, whatever viewers might suspect. Or indeed whatever I secretly hoped before I started. Sad to say, even though you might spend two weeks on location making a 40-minute film, there is precious little time to lounge around on the beach, or to spend 'researching' local night clubs. Rather disappointingly, even relatively straightforward films seem to take endless amounts of time to shoot. And films never seem that straightforward when you are on location trying to film them. Also, budgets being what they are, filming has to start virtually from the moment the presenter arrives and continue until the minute he leaves. Even rare days timetabled as days off turn all too regularly into days catching up.

There are, of course, plenty of meals and drinks to be had with the crew, but this is a vital part of bonding together as a group and should not be seen as a pure pleasure. And if you meet up with local people as well, this must be regarded as a vital process of learning about other cultures, and not just partying for the hell of it.

Time to acclimatise never seems to be allowed at all. Take Hawaii. I landed late at night on the other side of the world. Had we crossed the international date line? I literally did not know what day of the week it was. But I soon discovered I had to be up at the crack of dawn the next morning to row in a Hawaiian canoe. Several gorgeous, sun-tanned twentysomething oarsmen teamed with me: pale of skin, lacking of sleep, slight of frame and spread of middle age. All to produce a few frames of *Hawaii 5-0* parody for the end credits. However, as the director pointed out, it could have been so much more if I had had the sense to fall in and start drowning on camera.

Then there is the travelling itself. As I know to my cost, the modern child requires a vast amount of baggage in order to get from A to B. Cuddly toys, back-packs and buggies, snack foods and nappies, plus an array of items constructed entirely from garish coloured plastic are *de rigeur*. This, however, is not a patch on a film crew. Even the most solitary-looking TV journey is made by a small army of voyagers: a cameraman, a soundman, a camera assistant, a director and/or a producer, and perhaps a researcher, translator or local fixer. With them come their equipment. Metal boxes full of film or video tape, metal boxes full of lights, reflectors, batteries, cameras, tripods, metal boxes full of tape recorders, tape and microphones. Metal boxes, for all I know, full of spare metal boxes.

All of these have to be dragged around airports, checked onto planes, and loaded into vans, boats and trains. On the first leg of the great railway journey across China, we were worried about getting our equipment stolen, so we locked it in a 'soft-class' sleeper, while we mere humans struggled onto 'hard-class' bunks at the cheaper end of the train. Who else would give up their seats, and their beds, to their luggage? On a later leg of the same journey, all the equipment travelled on to

Beijing with just our Chinese-speaking translator for company, while the rest of us stayed the wrong side of the barrier at Jinan station getting arrested. On a later film, the whole lot flew to the wrong island because some idiot (me, since you ask) said the wrong thing at an airport check-in. Still, in these days of high security awareness, it is nice to know that 50 or so metal boxes can still fly unaccompanied on a small passenger plane without let or hindrance!

In Lagos, we managed to get arrested twice in two weeks. Firstly for filming for several days with the full knowledge of the Ministry of Information but without the express permission of the secret police, and secondly for filming a roadside food stall without the permission of the local police station. It is remarkable the effect that cameras have on insecure members of the security forces the world over.

Cameras do bring out the more adventurous side of some people, though. The most stressful part of my normal travelling life is attempting to hail a taxi in Oxford Street. But in my documentary existence I am forever leaping onto tiny aeroplanes, dodgy helicopters, over-laden Land Rovers, unstable fishing boats, unconventional ferries and unpredictable horses. Needless to say, each owner, pilot, guide or driver, inspired by the presence of a camera, races, shows off and generally pushes his or her vehicle to its limit. It is as though they want them and me to die on camera, or at any rate come close to it.

I know how they feel. I was fortunate enough to be given the chance to take over the controls of a small aeroplane flying over the sea between Cuba and Florida. You pull the joystick one way to go up, the other way to go down, left to go left, right to go right, in, out, in, out, shake it all about... I was ordered to stop by the director getting seasick and squeezed in the back. "For God's sake Clive," he said, "let the real pilot take over again and let's go back to base as soon as...." (Sound track then obscured by retching sound.)

Ah, illness. All travellers risk upset, infection and disease, but the TV presenter risks his particular bout of Delhi belly, sleeping sickness or raging fever being caught on camera for the delight of the watching millions. Indeed, when I turned to Michael Palin for advice on this point, he assured me that being ill on screen is vital to maintain viewers' interest. But when you feel your insides are about to become outsides, it is no fun being Our Man In A Pale Suit trying to conduct an interview in a steaming location miles away from your old friend Armitage Shanks.

This brings me to another danger. It is important that the film-maker does not wind up filming someone else's film crew. With Michael Palin circling round the world in every possible direction, with every holiday destination covered by the *Holiday Programme*, or *Wish You Were Here*, with every war zone attracting crews from all over the world, with every Amazon Indian tribe apparently attached to its own resident camera crew, with every part of the natural world negotiating a series with David Attenborough, with every exotic railway journey the subject of a TV travelogue, this becomes ever more difficult.

I was once filming on the beautiful but little-known island of Dominica in the Windward Islands. At exactly the same time, Tony Robinson was on the same island making another film for the BBC. Now what are the chances of that?

But it has to be said, documentary-making abroad is much less dangerous than fighting a war, less demanding than relief work, better paid than VSO, less exhausting than grape-picking, more fun than a sales conference, and less uncomfortable than travelling on the Northern Line. In fact my only real complaint is that I am at home writing this, rather than away on another trip. Maybe next year. ❧

CLIVE ANDERSON *has presented numerous travel documentaries on British television, including the series 'Our Man In...'. As a chat show host, he has developed a reputation for fearless and funny interviewing.*

Travels with my camera
by Benedict Allen

IT IS AN EXCITING PROSPECT TO HAVE YOUR TRAVELS shown on television to a potentially huge and enthusiastic audience. Thanks to the advent of comparatively cheap and light broadcast-quality video cameras, as well as the proliferation of television channels, this is now a real possibility. However, it is still a highly specialised field, and one that is strewn with ghastly difficulties.

Getting your idea commissioned

Let's face it, you are not going to be granted a 'TV spectacular' about your forthcoming round-the-world gypsy caravan odyssey. Why not? Because it all comes down to cost. A standard-length (say 50-minute) travel programme would be budgeted at about £150,000 – this is for a three-week shoot. Surprisingly, the cost of a Video Diary (a format made without a film crew) isn't exactly chicken feed either – here the expense lies in the editing.

This means that your film proposal has to be a very bankable proposition in order to even be considered – you are expected to be notable in your field and to be undertaking a journey that is unique as well as fascinating. And, as if that weren't enough, unlike a writer or a photographer you must be able to communicate your own feelings, even when under pressure – the pressure of, say, working under the constant attention of four bored, moronic members of a film crew – and you must be authoritative, articulate and 'personable'. In short, climbing Everest – even climbing it solo, without oxygen, up the southwest face – nowadays simply isn't good enough.

Still not put off?

An independent production company would consider itself lucky if one in 25 of its programme proposals were to be commissioned by a TV channel – this ratio might be as high as one in ten for the first rank of 'independents'. The process is this: whether through independents or directly, your proposal is submitted on paper (one or two sides of A4, maximum) to a TV channel, and its merits assessed, along with hundreds of other, through the long (up to nine months) selection process. Your proposal might find a slot in a magazine programme – it might become a five-minute item on *Blue Peter* by a teenager questing after hairy-footed gerbils in the Kalahari. Alternatively, it might end up as a full programme on one of the occasional 'strands' so beloved of TV programmers – examples include Channel 4's *Travels with My Camera* or the BBC's *Great River Journeys*.

Of these two options, the magazines are most likely to offer the commissions – they have more slots because they are always looking for 5- or 10-minute items and will probably accept Hi-8 video quality. Although the emergence of digital Hi-8 technology will bring down the cost of foreign filming and open other avenues, at present the only other option is to ask a channel for a whole TV series – and there's fat chance of getting one of those beauties unless you already have a proven track record on telly.

Although the BBC has its own production base, and so can be approached directly with an idea, most channels – including the other two major travel programme outlets, Channel Four in the UK and The Discovery Channel in the US – commission from independents. One way or another, unless you are an experienced operator, with a nose for a marketable storyline, the general rule is that you need a commission, or at least a definite expression of interest, before you set off. The obvious exceptions are regional news programmes, which might welcome a 'local explorer' item, especially if you have potential headline material – which, sadly, means that you'll need to be involved in some kind of disaster story yourself or become a witness to someone else's misery as they succumb to massacre, coup or mudslide.

Behind the camera

Before undertaking this tedious commissioning process, it is as well to consider whether dragging about camera equipment or – horror of horrors – a camera crew is quite your cup of tea in the first place. For many travellers, it suffices simply to have a visual record of the journey – on your return you might want to give a presentation to the worthy businessmen who supported your venture, or wish to use a film clip as an educational tool for the local primary school.

Similarly, footage brought back on a recce trip might raise sponsorship prior to you setting out in earnest, or act as valuable briefing material for the main body of the expedition team. For such purposes it's enough to pack into your rucksack a Hi-8 camcorder, tripod and a stash of batteries.

For those who are prepared to 'go the whole way', and try for that TV commission, there are obvious financial advantages. The income you are likely to accrue from the programme probably will not do more than cover the cost of a modest expedition, but television coverage can have a pleasing effect on those to whom you are indebted. This can mean commercial sponsors – though rules on product placement are now very strict – or even political ones.

A few years ago I applied to the Namibian government to walk up the Namib Desert, something a TV crew had never previously been permitted – not least because diamonds lie scattered in the sands. Armed with a commission, I was in a position to offer the Namibian government worldwide coverage of an exquisitely beautiful portion of the country, which I suggested would be a fillip to its tourist industry; but the master stroke turned out to be that I had also persuaded the BBC to offer free broadcast of the programme on Namibian television, which would allow Namibians to make the journey themselves by watching my rather painful progress across the sand dunes on TV.

So, for the first time, total access was granted by the government to this very special place, while chunks of the delicate desert were still protected from the impact of tourists. However, there was a proviso: I would be filming my progress alone, without a camera crew. And this is where the real problems with telly begin.

The dreadful film crew

There's no escaping the fact that travelling with a film crew is not travelling at all. In bringing a crew, you bring a part of your world with you, and that part happens to be a circus. However hard you try, travelling becomes an act. Forget the lone caver, inching forward through slime on his belly. As likely as not the cameraman, lighting man, soundman and director have got there first.

It's the same for every market scene and every mountain-top soliloquy. In Kenya and Uganda, filming a BBC *Great Railway Journey*, I found myself lumbered with a crew that was ten-strong, including the official government minder, two local 'fixers' and two minibus drivers, who served as roadies, ferrying everyone else around along with their kit.

And here we come to the main point: keeping this show on the road costs a fortune, so before you even leave home, an hour-by-hour itinerary has to be worked out – worked out according to the needs of a film crew, not a traveller. 'Chance encounters' are arranged, tribal dances ordered up. Effectively, the film-maker is re-assembling the components of a journey for the enjoyment of others. He or she is not actually making a real journey at all. There may be many justifications for this – for me, watching the film crew scrambling aboard a crowded Kampala train was in itself good for a comedy sequence. But if you say you are doing your trek along the Great Wall of China for your own sake, and it just happens to be filmed, then you are deceiving yourself. The answer is that, like the very best circus act, it's little more than a stunt.

Video – the one-man band

There is another option. Modern technology now enables expeditions to be filmed on video with the help of a small, or no, additional film crew. In addition to the possibilities offered by the somewhat cumbersome Beta video camera, the Hi-8 camcorder, now with digital technology, brings the small camera well up to broadcast standard. While glossy shots and a first-grade soundtrack are still best captured by a crew, these cameras and the tape they use are cheap and robust. For the first time ever, expeditions can now be recorded comprehensively as they unfold. Thus for my three-and-a-half-month Namib trek, I simply strapped solar panels either side of the hump of Nelson (my lead camel) and used them to recharge the batteries for my little Hitachi VM-80. I was totally self-sufficient with the aid of the

Hi-8 and tripod, recording whatever befell me (and camel companions) as we plodded hopefully through the dunes.

In the Peruvian Amazon, a camcorder (Sony TR805) again enabled me to record a journey over an extended period. The use of video also helped me in recording the everyday life of my guides. Instead of feeling like a predatory outsider, as I'd always felt before when taking photographs of indigenous people, I was now able to involve them in the process, in this case getting the local Matses Indians to film themselves. The hundred or so hours of tape from the expedition proved to be an invaluable record of life in the jungle – there was footage of drug dealers, and even of an ocelot-type cat, which, rightly or wrongly, the Matses believe often exhibits aggressive behaviour to humans.

A further note of warning. Just when you are congratulating yourself on having survived the film crew, the tangles of the battery charger units, the frogmarch to jail, it's time to begin battling at home in the cutting room. Your producer knows what makes 'good TV' – and that usually means giving your precious journey a 'comic twist'. That said, TV at its best gives the traveller something unique – the chance to pass on to others direct experience of different worlds. This is far more than simple gratification. Travellers must nowadays be able to justify the act of imposing themselves on foreign turf. Sharing their journey with millions back home who are not privileged to have made it themselves is one way of doing that. ❧

BENEDICT ALLEN is an explorer, author and broadcaster. His television series have documented arduous journeys across the Gobi desert, along Namibia's Skeleton Coast, and in search of the world's last remaining shamen.

On diplomatic service
by Sir David Hannay

THE DIPLOMAT TRAVELS NOT JUST BECAUSE HE ENJOYS TRAVEL, although it is as well that he should do so since he is fated to spend much of his professional life on the road, but because it is an essential part of his job. He travels to and from his posts abroad, he travels around the countries to which he is posted and, even when he is based in London, he tends to be caught up in the constant round of international meetings of which the web of modern diplomacy is composed. It all sounds pretty glamorous but, like so many other forms of modern business travel, it can easily become exceedingly humdrum if you let it. Similar airports, with similar flight delays, similar hotel rooms in impersonal international chains, and similar meeting rooms are not the stuff of which romantic travel experiences are made. The modern diplomat who wants to enjoy and benefit from his travel is going to have to work at it, not just sit back and have it ordered up by the travel section in the Foreign Office or his embassy.

Diplomatic travel begins with the journey to your posting, which can be extremely banal if you are heading for a western European capital or merely crossing the Atlantic, or potentially a bit more interesting if you are going further afield. Of course it will still be a far cry from the journey described so delightfully by Lady Macartney in *An English Lady in Chinese Turkestan*, when she set off in the nineteenth century with her husband, the British Consul General in Kashgar: they travelled on the newly completed Russian railway system to Tashkent and then covered the final leg of their journey by riding hundreds of miles over the Pamirs to reach their destination.

One personal rule I did try to stick to was always to travel to your post overland. This made for some very interesting experiences, particularly driving out to Tehran in 1960 – which involved some circuitous avoidance of East European Communist countries, then out of bounds to mere travellers – and through Eastern Turkey and Western Iran where a hard-top road was a rarity.

My system finally broke down after 25 years, when I was sent first to Washington and then New York, but I did manage a kind of revenge by returning on retirement from the latter via a long land journey through China and Central Asia. The object of going by land to your post is not mere whimsy, it is to try and arrive for the first time with some idea of what the country and its people look like and live like, and it is something you are unlikely to achieve on the road between the airport and the embassy.

Once you are in your posting, the opportunities for travel are greater, but again they need to be carefully planned. It is all too easy to get trapped into the bureaucratic grind of modern diplomacy – a far greater pitfall than the fabled cocktail party circuit, now largely a thing of the past – producing paper for the slave-drivers at home and missing the opportunities to get to know the complexities and attractions of the country you are in, not just its government. Once again it is a good deal less easy than it used to be to take off for a few weeks or even months into the wild blue yonder, as Sir Fitzroy Maclean chronicled in *Eastern Approaches*, a record of his travels in the Soviet Union in the 1930s, or as Hugh Carless did when he accompanied Eric Newby on *A Short Walk in the Hindu Kush* in the 1950s. Nor are there many opportunities such as I had in Afghanistan between 1961 and 1963 when I was grandly titled the 'Oriental Secretary' and managed to persuade my ambassador that I was more use to him on the road than in the office. It seems odd to think that we used to camp in the Panjshir Valley or catch trout at Bamyan in the shadow of the 50-metre-high statues of Buddha, where now the various factions of Afghanistan's eternal civil war are slugging it out.

It is almost equally odd to think that, as a Persian language student, I was encouraged, i.e. paid, to travel around southern Iran, on the condition that I went by public transport, which meant bus if I was lucky and the back of a lorry if I was not. It brings home the reality of the fact that war and instability are as often rapidly closing off places to which the diplomat may travel, just as technological advances are opening them up. But political developments are not always obstacles, as is demonstrated by the scope now for travel in China where not so long ago it was hard to get permission to go outside Beijing.

It would be nice if the diplomat only had to plan his own travel, but it is not so. One of his more demanding and thankless tasks is to act on occasion as a cross between a travel agent and a courier. A spell as a private secretary comes the way of many, and that is when qualities such as improvisation and endurance are put to the test. It is not just a question of getting your boss to the right place at the right time, it is a matter of getting there in the right frame of mind, often a good deal less easy. I worked for four years for Christopher Soames when he was a European Commissioner, during which we travelled pretty widely. One of his main characteristics was not simply to insist on absolute punctuality, reasonable enough when catching aeroplanes or calling on Prime Ministers, but also to avoid ever arriving anywhere more than 30 seconds ahead of the appointed time. The second part of the equation caused his private secretaries a good deal of anxiety, particularly when travelling in Asia and Latin America, or trying to calculate in advance the density of traffic between the airport in, say, Paris or Rome and the Foreign ministry. His other principal characteristic as a traveller was to insist that, if he was to go sightseeing – and he was not averse to that – then there had to be a three-star restaurant handy in which to recuperate. Travel as a private secretary is not, on the whole, life-enhancing, though it can provide a good deal of amusement, particularly in retrospect.

The most daunting challenge for the diplomat as traveller is to make something of those one-day stands which involve rushing from airport to meeting room, endless tours of the table, which have nothing to do with travel, and then a rush back to the airport – which is now the general form of modern diplomatic life. It is not easy to do. The frequency of airline flights makes it hard to convince one's employers that one simply had to travel the night before. The tendency of all international meetings to conform to a Parkinsonian law, which ensures that they last slightly longer than the time available for them to complete their work, is another complication. Nevertheless the really determined diplomatic traveller, whether his tastes be cultural, artistic or merely gastronomic, can usually manage to squeeze in the odd visit to a cathedral, an exhibition or a restaurant if he is sufficiently ruthless. Just occasionally the country caters for the travelling propensities of their guests by arranging the meetings in surroundings of beauty and interest; more often, unfortunately, they calculate that you will get more work out of people if you prevent their surroundings from being too attractive. Certainly, of the many meetings of the European Council I attended while I was dealing with the European Union, a great deal more fell into the latter rather than the former category. It took a hardy spirit, when Mrs Thatcher was leading the British delegation, to slip away, say, to that fascinating modern museum in Stuttgart.

But of course the diplomatic traveller is not limited to professional travel, important a part of his life though that may be. If he is really bitten by the bug and if he can persuade his long-suffering family to share his passion, a lifetime of diplomacy provides some ideal jumping-off points for wider travel. Brussels may not be exciting in itself, but it is a remarkably good base from which to travel the European continent. New York is quite exciting for a traveller, but so is the possibility of using it as a base for visiting the furthest corners of Latin America. There are few better ways to spend a tedious afternoon in one of those subterranean meeting rooms at the United Nations than in planning how to get from Machu Picchu across Lake Titicaca to Bolivia (the answer: take the train from Cusco to the lake and hydrofoil across it).

So do 35 years or so of diplomacy dull the taste for travel? In my own case apparently not. The list of places still to be visited and 'vaut le detour', in Michelin's inimitable phrase, seems if anything to grow longer. A willingness to rough it has certainly diminished, but so, fortunately, has the need to do so. The real challenge is to resist successfully what one could call the homogenisation of travel, the tendency to sell travel as McDonald's sells hamburgers. The diplomatic travellers should be in the vanguard of consumer resistance to any such tendency. ❧

Sir David Hannay was a British diplomat for 36 years, latterly as Britain's Ambassador to the European Union and the United Nations. He has also served in Tehran, Kabul, Brussels, Washington and New York.

The editors wish to thank...

SPECIAL THANKS
Steve Allen, Sarah Anderson, Mick Kidd, Sue McAlinden, Joseph Legate, Susanne Nuttall, Edwina Townsend, David Warne, Matthew Whitehead, Ian Wilson.

SOURCES
World Travel Guide, published by Columbus Travel Guides, World Desk Reference, published by Dorling Kindersley, Fielding's The World's Most Dangerous Places, published by Fielding Worldwide.

ACKNOWLEDGEMENTS
The extract from 'A Writer's World: Travels 1950-2000', by Jan Morris, published by Faber and Faber, is reproduced with kind permission from AP Watt. The extract from 'By Behind The Wall', by Colin Thubron, published by William Heinemann/Vintage, is reproduced with kind permission from The Random House Group Ltd.

Selected quotes from Earl MacRauch, Miriam Beard, Jon Carroll, Bettina Selby, Lin Yutang, Ken Welsh, Louis L'Amour, John Steinbeck, Douglas Adams, Paul Theroux, Orson Welles, Willie Nelson, Hunter S.Thomson, Tom Clancy and Larry McMurtry are reprinted with permission from The Quotable Traveler, A Running Press® Miniature Edition™, copyright © 1994 by Running Press Book Publishers, Philadelphia and London. We would also like to acknowledge the Trustees of the Joseph Conrad Estate, The Society of Authors, on behalf of the Bernard Shaw estate, The Society of Authors as the literary representative of the estate of Norman Douglas, Peters Fraser & Dunlop Group for permission to quote from Hilaire Belloc (Complete Verse published by Random House UK Ltd). Quotes from My African Journey by Sir Winston Churchill reproduced with permission of Curtis Brown Ltd, London, on behalf of the estate of Sir Winston Churchill. Copyright Winston S. Churchill 1908. While every effort has been made to credit copyright holders and to acknowledge source material, the publishers would be happy to rectify any omissions in a future edition.

WEXAS membership offer

WEXAS
THE TRAVELLER'S CLUB

Free trial travel club membership

WEXAS IS THE TRAVEL CLUB FOR INDEPENDENT TRAVELLERS. Our 35,000 members enjoy the unbeatable combination of value-for-money prices, travel ideas and information, and outstanding service.

As a reader of *The Traveller's Handbook* you can take out a month's FREE TRIAL membership.

Take a look at the benefits you'll receive and see how you'll save your subscription many times over.

- Savings on airfares, hotels and car hire worldwide
- Annual travel insurance from just £48 per year
- FREE subscription to *Traveller*, the highly acclaimed travel magazine
- Expert personal service from experienced travel consultants, and access to our members-only phone numbers
- Privileged access to airport VIP lounges – free at 18 UK airports, if you're flying long-haul and have at least 2 nights' accommodation booked through WEXAS

- Currency and travellers' cheques available by post, commission-free
- Special rates for airport parking
- Discounts at British Airways travel clinics
- Free international emergency assistance 24 hours a day
- Additional benefits for business travellers
- www.wexas.com – for members only
- Customised round-the-world itineraries
- Quarterly *Vista* newsletter with special offers and discounts exclusive to WEXAS members

- -

COMPLETE THIS FORM AND POST IT TODAY FOR FULL DETAILS OF **WEXAS** MEMBERSHIP AND THE FREE TRIAL OFFER.

You can post this form to us at WEXAS, FREEPOST (no stamp required), London, SW3 1BR, UK.

Alternatively you can fax it to us on (0)20 7589 8418, or email mship@wexas.com for details, or simply go to www.wexas.com and join online.

Name (Mr/Mrs/Miss/Ms)

Address

Postcode

Telephone

Email

5HBK1

Index